KOSSEK/BLOCK: *Managing Human Resources in the 21ˢᵗ Century*
ISBN 0-324-00753-1

Unparalleled Flexibility: Develop Your Perfect Course…

The "**Modular Approach**" of *Managing Human Resources in the 21ˢᵗ Century* offers you the **FLEXIBILITY** to teach the subject matter in the order which best suits your classroom needs!

Over two dozen modules are written by leading experts in the human resource field, including both academicians and practitioners. The modules are approximately 30 pages in length, and are grouped by themes. Each student module comes with an instructor's module as support found online at http://kossek.swcollege.com.

HOW DO I ORDER MY OWN CUSTOMIZED VERSION OF *Managing Human Resources in the 21ˢᵗ Century*?

- Determine your topics or "modules" that create your perfect HRM course.
- Consider adding your own material.
- Select the sequence required for your course.
- Fill out the form attached on the opposite page and fax or e-mail this information to our Custom Publishing Representatives.
- Visit our Custom Publishing Web site for more information http://www.swcollege.com or call our **ITP Custom Publishing Center at (800) 355-9983** for more details.

I LIKE THE ENTIRE TEXT!
HOW DO I ORDER THIS COMPREHENSIVE EDITION?

- If you would like to use all the modules found in Managing Human Resources in the 21ˢᵗ Century, you may choose to order the whole text. There is no special ordering procedure for the whole text. Orders go through **ITP Customer Service (800) 487-5510**. You will want to order the comprehensive edition with **ISBN 0-324-00753-1**.

For Instructors:
Bookstore Ordering Information

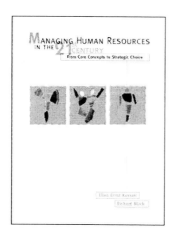

Product Information

Please contact your Local South-Western College/ITP Representative or our Academic Resource Center at (800) 423-0563 to learn more about this product and the selected modules option.

Bookstore Ordering Information

Comprehensive Text: (0-324-00753-1)
ITP Customer Service
Phone: (800) 487-5510   Fax: (800) 487-8488

Selected Modules:
ITP Custom Publishing Center
Phone: (800) 355-9983   Fax: (800) 451-3661

If you would like to fax your order to Custom Publishing please complete the following. Custom Publishing will then telephone you with an ISBN for your customized modules:

Account Number _____

Purchase Order _____

Order Quantity _____

Need By Date _____

Phone Number _____

Contact Name _____

South-Western College Publishing

Visit http://www.swcollege.com

Selected Modules Ordering Checklist

PART 1: OVERARCHING EMPLOYER PRINCIPLES FOR MANAGING HUMAN RESOURCES.
- [ ] 1: New Employment Relations: Challenges and Basic Assumptions [0-324-01800-2]
- [ ] 2: Human Resource Strategy: From Transactions to Transformation [0-324-01801-0]
- [ ] 3: Leadership by Human Resources: Organizational Roles and Choices [0-324-01804-5]
- [ ] 4: Managing Change: Scenario Planning and Other Tools [0-324-01803-7]
- [ ] 5: Mergers and Human Resources [0-324-01802-9]
- [ ] 6: Collective Bargaining, Industrial Relations, and Human Resource Systems: Managing in Environments [0-324-01805-3]
- [ ] 7: Human Resource Information Systems [0-324-01806-1]

PART 2: BUILDING THE HUMAN RESOURCE BASE: RECRUITMENT AND SELECTION STRATEGIES AND LEGAL CONCERNS IN CONSTRUCTING THE WORKFORCE.
- [ ] 8: EEO in the Workplace: Employment Law Challenges [0-324-01807-X]
- [ ] 9: Managing Diversity: Human Resource Issues [0-324-01808-8]
- [ ] 10: Administering the Family and Medical Leave Act [0-324-01809-6]
- [ ] 11: Support of Work/Life Integration: Cultural Issues Facing the Employer [0-324-01810-X]
- [ ] 12: Workforce Planning for Flexibility: Staffing with Temporary Employees [0-324-01811-8]
- [ ] 13: Recruitment and Selections: Hiring for the Job or the Organization? [0-324-01812-6]
- [ ] 14: Selecting Employees Today: What Managers Need to Know [0-324-01813-4]

PART 3: SOCIALIZING, MOTIVATING, AND DEVELOPING EMPLOYEES TO COMPETE.
- [ ] 15: Moving from Performance Appraisal to Performance Management [0-324-01814-2]
- [ ] 16: Compensation Fundamentals and Linkages to Organizational Performance [0-324-01815-0]
- [ ] 17: Pay and Incentive Systems: Transitional, Transformational, and Nontraditional [0-324-01816-9]
- [ ] 18: Benefits: Current Challenges in Providing Cost-Effective Employee Supports [0-324-01817-7]
- [ ] 19: Training and Employee Development [0-324-01818-5]
- [ ] 20: Using the Internet for Training and Development [0-324-01819-3]

PART 4: CONTINUOUS IMPROVEMENT OF ORGANIZATIONAL PROCESSES AND WORK RELATIONSHIPS.
- [ ] 21: Systems Approaches to Human Resource Management: New Assumptions [0-324-01820-7]
- [ ] 22: Organizational Development and Change: The Role of Human Resources [0-324-01821-5]
- [ ] 23: Employee Safety and Health [0-324-01823-1]
- [ ] 24: Managing Careers [0-324-01824-X]

PART 5: GROWING HUMAN RESOURCE CHALLENGES FOR THE MILLENNIUM AND BEYOND.
- [ ] 25: Globally Managing Human Resources [0-324-01826-6]
- [ ] 26: Comparative Industrial Relations [0-324-01827-4]
- [ ] 27: Ethical Perspectives in Employment Relations and Human Resources [0-324-01830-4]

MANAGING HUMAN RESOURCES
IN THE 21st CENTURY

From Core Concepts to Strategic Choice

Ellen Ernst Kossek

School of Labor and Industrial Relations
Michigan State University

Richard N. Block

School of Labor and Industrial Relations
Michigan State University

South-Western College Publishing
Thomson Learning™

Australia • Canada • Denmark • Japan • Mexico • New Zealand • Philippines
Puerto Rico • Singapore • South Africa • Spain • United Kingdom • United States

Sophie

Managing Human Resources in the 21st Century: From Core Concepts to Strategic Choice,
by Kossek and Block

Publisher: Dave Shaut
Executive Editor: John Szilagyi
Developmental Editor: Bryant Editorial Development
Marketing Manager: Joseph A. Sabatino
Production Editor: Tamborah E. Moore
Manufacturing Coordinator: Dana Began Schwartz
Cover Design: Tin Box Studio
Cover Photographs: Copyright Shoji Sato/Photonica
Production House: The Left Coast Group, Inc.
Printer: West Group

Printed in the United States of America
1 2 3 4 5 02 01 00 99

For more information contact South-Western College Publishing, 5101 Madison Road, Cincinnati, Ohio, 45227 or find us on the Internet at *http://www.swcollege.com*
For permission to use material from this text or product, contact us by
- telephone: 1-800-730-2214
- fax: 1-800-730-2215
- web: *http://www.thomsonrights.com*

ISBN: 0–324–00753–1

Library of Congress Cataloging-in-Publication Data
Kossek, Ellen Ernst.
      Managing human resources in the 21st century : from core concepts
to strategic choice / Ellen Ernst Kossek, Richard N. Block.
          p.   cm
      Includes bibliographical references and index.
      ISBN 0–324–00753–1
      1. Personnel management.   I. Block, Richard N.   II. Title.
HF5549.K663 1999   99–33395
658.3—dc21   CIP

This book is printed on acid-free paper.

Contents

OVERVIEW AND PREFACE **xvii**
Origins of This Book **xvii** ▪ Features of This Book **xviii** ▪ Overview of Modules and Contributors **xxi** ▪ About the Editors **xxx** ▪ Acknowledgments **xxxi** Dedication **xxxi**

PART 1 OVERARCHING EMPLOYER PRINCIPLES FOR MANAGING HUMAN RESOURCES

1 New Employment Relations: Challenges and Basic Assumptions **1.1**
Ellen Ernst Kossek ▪ *Richard N. Block*

MODULE OVERVIEW **1.4**
Pressure on Human Resources to Demonstrate Value Added **1.4** ▪ Variation in Employment Strategies **1.5**

OBJECTIVES **1.6**

A FRAMEWORK FOR UNDERSTANDING HUMAN RESOURCE MANAGEMENT DECISION MAKING AND CAPABILITIES: STRATEGIC ROLES AND CHOICES **1.6**
HR Roles: The Four "Ts" **1.8** ▪ Roles Delivered by Many Sources and Reflected in All Policy Domains **1.9** ▪ Managerial Discretion in HR Decision Making **1.10** ▪ Using the Framework as a Managerial Diagnostic Tool **1.11**

CORE CONCEPTS IN NEW EMPLOYMENT RELATIONS **1.13**
Historical Roots of Organizational Approaches to Managing Employment Relationship **1.14** ▪ Current Variation in Employment Relations **1.16** Workforce Commitment Employment Model **1.17** ▪ Labor Transactional Employment Model **1.20** ▪ Mixed Approach: Core-Noncore Workforce Model **1.22** ▪ Summary of Contrasting Approaches to Employment **1.23**

STRATEGIC ISSUES IN NEW EMPLOYMENT RELATIONS **1.24**
Determining a Firm's Place on the Transactional Continuum **1.24** Alignment Between Business and Human Resource Strategy **1.25**

APPLICATION **1.25**
Chainsaw Al Dunlap at Scott Paper **1.25** ▪ High Commitment at Starbucks Coffee **1.26**

IN CONCLUSION **1.27**
Debrief **1.27** ▪ Suggested Readings **1.27** ▪ Relevant Web Sites **1.28** Critical Thinking Questions **1.28** ▪ Expanded Exercise **1.28** ▪ Exercise **1.30** References **1.31**

INDEX **1.34**

2 Human Resource Strategy: From Transactions to Transformation **2.1**
Ellen Ernst Kossek

MODULE OVERVIEW **2.4**

OBJECTIVES **2.5**

RELATION TO THE FRAME **2.5**

CORE CONCEPTS IN HUMAN RESOURCE NEW EMPLOYMENT RELATIONS **2.7**
Organizational Strategy **2.7** ■ Human Resource Strategy **2.15** ■ Allocated
Resources and Develop Processes and Systems to Support HR Delivery **2.27**
Organizational Adaptation and Performance Outcomes **2.27** ■ Alternative
Strategic HR Perspectives **2.28**

STRATEGIC ISSUES IN CREATING COMPETITIVE ADVANTAGE
THROUGH PEOPLE **2.31**

APPLICATION **2.31**
Daehan Corporation **2.31** ■ Company Background **2.37** ■ The Staff Meeting **2.40**

IN CONCLUSION **2.42**
Debrief **2.42** ■ Suggested Readings **2.42** ■ Relevant Web Sites **2.42**
Critical Thinking Questions **2.43** ■ Exercises: Strategic HRM Vignettes **2.43**
References **2.48** ■ Index **2.52**

3   Leadership by Human Resources: Organizational Roles and Choices   3.1

Ellen Ernst Kossek ■ *Karen S. Markel*

MODULE OVERVIEW **3.5**

INTRODUCTION **3.6**

OBJECTIVES **3.7**

RELATION TO THE FRAME **3.8**

CORE CONCEPTS IN HR LEADERSHIP ROLES AND CHOICES **3.9**
What Is HRM? Responsibilities and Objectives **3.10**

HUMAN RESOURCE ROLES: THE FOUR "TS" **3.18**
The Transaction Role **3.18** ■ The Translation Role **3.19** ■ The Transition
Role **3.20** ■ The Transformation Role **3.21** ■ Roles Occur in All HR Policy
Domains **3.21**

MANAGEMENT DECISION-MAKING CONSTRAINTS AND CHOICES **3.22**
Unilateral **3.22** ■ Negotiated **3.23** ■ Imposed **3.23**

DELIVERY OF HUMAN RESOURCE ROLES **3.24**
Basic Organizational Criteria for Effective Role Delivery **3.24** ■ Integrated Line-
Staff Role Delivery **3.26** ■ Reengineering the Mix and Structure of HR **3.26**
Centralizing HR Role Delivery: Shared Services **3.28** ■ Outsourcing **3.28**

HUMAN RESOURCE EFFECTIVENESS: CONTRASTING APPROACHES **3.28**
People Poll: How Do You Measure HR's Impact on the Bottom Line? **3.28**
Stakeholder/Multiple Constituency **3.29** ■ Business Consulting **3.29** ■ Utility
Approaches: Assessing Quantitative Value Added **3.30**

STRATEGIC ISSUES IN HUMAN RESOURCE LEADERSHIP ROLES
AND CHOICES **3.30**
Strategic Challenges Across HR Policy Clusters **3.30** ■ HR Roles: Strategic
Issues **3.31** ■ HR Outsourcing and Role Delivery **3.31**

APPLICATION: AT&T CASE **3.32**
Case Study Exercises **3.33**

IN CONCLUSION **3.34**
Debrief **3.34** ■ Required Readings **3.34** ■ Relevant Web Sites **3.34**
Critical Thinking Questions **3.35** ■ Exercises **3.35** ■ References **3.40**

INDEX **3.44**

4 Managing Change: Scenario Planning and Other Tools **4.1**
Steve S. Fitzgerald

MODULE OVERVIEW **4.4**

RELATION TO THE FRAME **4.4**

CORE CONCEPTS IN MANAGING CHANGE **4.5**
The Pace and Impact of Rapid Change **4.6** ■ Building the Change-Ready Culture **4.8** ■ HR's Emerging Role in the Formulation and Execution of Strategy **4.12** ■ Scenario Planning **4.17**

IN CONCLUSION **4.26**
Debrief **4.26** ■ Suggested Readings **4.26** ■ Relevant Web Sites and Other Resources **4.27** ■ Critical Thinking Questions **4.27** ■ Student Class Assignment **4.28** ■ Consumer Lifestyle Worksheet **4.29** ■ References **4.31**

APPENDIX **4.32**
Developing Scenarios for HR **4.32** ■ How the Scenarios Were Created **4.32**
The "Just Do It" World in 2020 **4.34**

INDEX **4.39**

5 Mergers and Human Resources **5.1**
Susan K. Graaff ■ *William N. Case*

MODULE OVERVIEW **5.4**

OBJECTIVES **5.4**

RELATION TO THE FRAME **5.4**

CORE CONCEPTS IN MERGERS AND ACQUISITIONS **5.5**
Key Distinctions between Mergers and Acquisitions **5.5** ■ Mergers and Acquisitions: A Brief History **5.6** ■ Relevant Legislation **5.7** ■ General Categories of Mergers and Acquisitions **5.7** ■ Characteristics of Merger and Acquisition Types **5.8** ■ After the Financial and Legal Hurdles: The Integration of Multiple Organizations **5.9** ■ The Role of the Human Resource Professional **5.10** Critical Tasks in Integrating Organizations **5.11**

STRATEGIC ISSUES IN MERGERS AND ACQUISITIONS **5.12**
The Process of Integration **5.12** ■ Predictable Dynamics of Mergers and Acquisitions **5.12**

APPLICATION **5.13**
Failure Case Study: Great Southern Railroad **5.14** ■ Task Force Integration Examples **5.15** ■ Success Case Study: Star-Excel Building Corporation **5.17**

IN CONCLUSION **5.18**
Debrief **5.18** ■ Suggested Readings **5.19** ■ Critical Thinking Questions **5.19**
Exercises **5.19**

APPENDIX **5.20**
Task Force Integration Application Case Forms **5.20**

INDEX **5.24**

6 Collective Bargaining, Industrial Relations, and Human Resource Systems: Managing in Environments **6.1**

Richard N. Block

MODULE OVERVIEW **6.4**

OBJECTIVES **6.4**

RELATION TO THE FRAME **6.4**

CORE CONCEPTS IN COLLECTIVE BARGAINING **6.5**
Workplace Rules **6.5** ■ Collective Bargaining **6.6** ■ Labor Unions **6.7**
Multiple Perspectives on the Employment Relationship **6.9**

STRATEGIC ISSUES IN COLLECTIVE BARGAINING **6.9**
Institutionalized Adversarialism Through the 1970s **6.9** ■ Collective Bargaining
Since the 1970s **6.11**

FIRM CHOICES IN LABOR RELATIONS **6.12**
Deunionization **6.12** ■ Cooperation **6.13** ■ Traditional Adversarialism **6.14**

APPLICATION 1 **6.14**
Deunionization Strategy in Labor Relations: The Case of Phelps Dodge and the
United Steelworkers of America **6.14** ■ Other Examples of Conflict **6.15**
Deunionization in the Rubber Tire Industry **6.16**

APPLICATION 2 **6.16**
Traditional Adversarialism in Labor Relations: The Case of United Parcel Service
and the International Brotherhood of Teamsters **6.16**

APPLICATION 3 **6.18**
Cooperation in Collective Bargaining: Ford and the UAW **6.18**

IN CONCLUSION **6.19**
Debrief **6.19** ■ Suggested Readings **6.19** ■ Critical Thinking Questions **6.19**
Exercise **6.20** ■ Reference **6.20**

INDEX **6.22**

7 Human Resource Information Systems **7.1**

Brian T. Pentland

MODULE OVERVIEW **7.4**

OBJECTIVES **7.4**

RELATION TO THE FRAME **7.4**

CORE CONCEPTS IN HUMAN RESOURCE INFORMATION SYSTEMS **7.5**
Kinds of Systems in the HR Function **7.6** ■ Storing and Retrieving Information:
Relational Database Technology **7.10** ■ Distributing Information: Network
Technology **7.14** ■ Implementing and Maintaining Systems: The Software Life
Cycle **7.16** ■ Requirements **7.16**

STRATEGIC ISSUES IN HUMAN RESOURCE INFORMATION SYSTEMS **7.18**
Organizational Design and System Design **7.19**

APPLICATION: WEB-BASED RECRUITING **7.19**

IN CONCLUSION **7.23**
Debrief **7.23** ■ Suggested Readings **7.23** ■ Relevant Web Sites **7.24**
Critical Thinking Questions **7.24** ■ Exercises **7.24** ■ Endnote **7.25**

INDEX **7.26**

PART 2 **BUILDING THE HUMAN RESOURCE BASE: RECRUITMENT AND SELECTION STRATEGIES AND LEGAL CONCERNS IN CONSTRUCTING THE WORKFORCE**

8 EEO in the Workplace: Employment Law Challenges **8.1**
Ben Wolkinson

MODULE OVERVIEW **8.4**

OBJECTIVES **8.4**

RELATION TO THE FRAME **8.4**

CORE CONCEPTS IN EQUAL EMPLOYMENT OPPORTUNITY **8.5**
Who Is Covered Under Title VII **8.5** ■ Prohibited Acts of Discrimination **8.6**
Administration and Enforcement of Title VII **8.6** ■ Remedies **8.7** ■ Evidence and
Proof in Equal Employment Opportunity Cases **8.8** ■ Affirmative Action **8.13**
Religious Discrimination **8.13** ■ Sex Discrimination **8.15** ■ Sexual
Harassment **8.16** ■ National Origin Discrimination **8.18**

APPLICATION **8.19**

IN CONCLUSION **8.20**
Debrief **8.20** ■ Suggested Readings **8.20** ■ Critical Thinking Questions **8.20**
Exercises **8.21** ■ References **8.21**

INDEX **8.24**

9 Managing Diversity: Human Resource Issues **9.1**
Stella M. Nkomo ■ *Ellen Ernst Kossek*

MODULE OVERVIEW **9.4**

RELATION TO THE FRAME **9.4**
External Environmental Forces Contributing to a Diverse Workplace **9.5**
Why Employers Seek to Manage Diversity **9.7**

CORE CONCEPTS IN MANAGING DIVERSITY **9.7**
Primary and Secondary Dimensions of Diversity **9.7** ■ Identity **9.8**
How Managing Diversity Differs from AA/EEO **9.9** ■ Multiculturalism **9.10**
Managing Diversity Paradigms **9.10** ■ Diversity Processes **9.12**

STRATEGIC ISSUES IN MANAGING DIVERSITY **9.13**

APPLICATION **9.14**

IN CONCLUSION **9.15**
Debrief **9.15** ■ Suggested Readings **9.15** ■ Relevant Web Sites **9.16** ■ Critical
Thinking Questions **9.16** ■ Exercises **9.16** ■ References **9.19**

INDEX **9.21**

10 Administering the Family Medical Leave Act **10.1**
Tina M. Riley

MODULE OVERVIEW **10.4**

OBJECTIVES **10.4**

RELATION TO THE FRAME **10.4**

CORE CONCEPTS IN ADMINISTERING THE FAMILY AND MEDICAL LEAVE ACT **10.5**
Enforcement **10.5** ■ Covered Employers **10.5** ■ Joint Employment **10.6**
Eligible Employees **10.6** ■ Continuation of Benefits **10.6** ■ Job Restoration **10.6**
Leave Entitlement **10.7** ■ Determining the Amount of Leave Used **10.7**
Limitations and Exceptions **10.7** ■ Serious Health Condition **10.7** ■ Intermittent
or Reduced Schedule Leave **10.8** ■ Obligations and Policy Issues **10.8**
Defining the "12-Month Period" **10.10** ■ Substitution of Paid Leave **10.12**
Coordination with Other Statutes **10.12**

STRATEGIC ISSUES IN ADMINISTERING THE FAMILY AND
MEDICAL LEAVE ACT **10.12**

APPLICATION **10.13**

IN CONCLUSION **10.14**
Debrief **10.14** ■ Suggested Readings **10.14** ■ Critical Thinking Questions **10.14**
Exercises **10.14** ■ References **10.15**

INDEX **10.16**

11 Support of Work/Life Integration: Cultural Issues Facing the Employer **11.1**
Ellen Ernst Kossek

MODULE OVERVIEW **11.4**

OBJECTIVES **11.5**

RELATION TO THE FRAME **11.6**

CORE CONCEPTS IN MANAGING CULTURAL SUPPORT OF
WORK/LIFE POLICIES **11.7**
Traditional U.S. Business Cultural Assumptions Regarding the Integration of Work
and the Family **11.7** ■ Common U.S. Cultural Assumptions Regarding Work
and Family **11.8** ■ Stages in the Organizational Development of Work/Life
Programs **11.9** ■ Cultural Assumptions Regarding Work and Family Integration
Outside of the United States **11.10** ■ Alternative Organizational Approaches for
Managing Employer Involvement in Employees' Personal Lives: Competing
Values **11.10** ■ Importance of Encouraging Employee Self-Reflection on
Work/Life Integration Preferences **11.14**

STRATEGIC ISSUES IN MANAGING CULTURAL SUPPORT OF
WORK/LIFE POLICIES **11.15**
Work/Life Responsiveness Is a Critical Management Challenge **11.15**
Employer-Concern for Personal Needs On and Off the Job: A Strategic Investment
in Human and Social Capital and High-Performance Work Systems? **11.15**

APPLICATION **11.16**

IN CONCLUSION **11.17**
Debrief **11.17** ■ Suggested Readings **11.17** ■ Critical Thinking Questions **11.18**
Exercises **11.18** ■ References **11.19**

INDEX **11.21**

12 Workforce Planning for Flexibility: Staffing with Temporary Employees **12.1**

Karen Roberts ■ *Sandra E. Gleason*

MODULE OVERVIEW **12.4**

OBJECTIVES **12.4**

RELATION TO THE FRAME **12.4**

CORE CONCEPTS IN WORFORCE PLANNING **12.5**
What Is Contingent Work? Types of Alternative Employment Arrangements **12.5** Who Are Contingent Workers? Characteristics of the Workforce in Alternative Employment Arrangements **12.6** ■ How to Use Alternative Work Arrangements to Advance Organizational Strategic Goals **12.10**

STRATEGIC ISSUES IN WORKFORCE PLANNING **12.11**
Contingent Workers as Strategic Response **12.12**

APPLICATION **12.13**
Step 1: Calculate the Costs of Using Core (Core Cost) and Temporary (Contingent) Workers (Temp Cost) **12.16** ■ Step 2: Calculate Per-Unit-of-Time Productivity for Core Workers (Core Productivity) **12.16** ■ Step 3: Calculate the Productivity Needed from Contingent Workers **12.17** ■ Step 4: Calculate the Cost of Training Contingent Workers **12.19** ■ Step 5: Calculate How Long It Will Take to Recover Training Costs **12.19**

IN CONCLUSION **12.20**
Debrief **12.20** ■ Suggested Readings **12.21** ■ Relevant Web Sites **12.21** Critical Thinking Questions **12.22**

INDEX **12.23**

13 Recruitment and Selections: Hiring for the Job or the Organization? **13.1**

Mark L. Lengnick-Hall

MODULE OVERVIEW **13.4**

OBJECTIVES **13.4**

RELATION TO THE FRAME **13.4**

CORE CONCEPTS IN RECRUITMENT AND SELECTION **13.5**
Staffing Matches Individual and Organizational Needs **13.5** ■ Recruitment and Selection Are Processes **13.7** ■ Organization and Job Analyses Are Prerequisites to the Recruitment and Selection Process **13.9** ■ Hiring for the Job Requires Person-Job Fit **13.12** ■ Hiring for the Organization Requires Person-Organization Fit **13.13** ■ Recruiting Involves Identifying and Attracting Applicants **13.17** Selecting Involves Assessing and Evaluating Applicants **13.20** ■ The Legal Environment Constrains Recruitment and Selection **13.24**

STRATEGIC ISSUES IN RECRUITMENT AND SELECTION **13.25**
The Strategic Impact of Human Resources **13.25** ■ Traditional Approaches **13.25** Staffing as Strategy Implementation **13.25** ■ Staffing as Strategy Formation **13.26** Melding the Three Strategic Approaches **13.27** ■ Make vs. Buy Human Resources **13.27** ■ Summary **13.29**

APPLICATION **13.29**
Preparing for Class Discussion **13.29**

IN CONCLUSION **13.30**
Debrief **13.30** ■ Suggested Readings **13.31** ■ Critical Thinking Questions **13.31**
Exercises **13.32** ■ References **13.33**

14 Selecting Employees Today: What Managers Need to Know **14.1**
Sandra L. Fisher ■ *Michael E. Wasserman*

MODULE OVERVIEW **14.4**

OBJECTIVES **14.4**

RELATION TO THE FRAME **14.4**

CORE CONCEPTS IN SELECTION SYSTEMS **14.5**
Traditional Core Concepts **14.6** ■ Emerging Core Concepts **14.12**

STRATEGIC ISSUES IN SELECTION SYSTEMS **14.15**
Selection for Competitive Advantage: Developing Organizational
Capabilities **14.15**

APPLICATION **14.16**
Selecting for Information Technology Jobs **14.16** ■ Developing "Internal"
Selection Systems **14.17** ■ Adaptability in the Army **14.17**

IN CONCLUSION **14.18**
Debrief **14.18** ■ Suggested Readings **14.18** ■ Critical Thinking Questions **14.21**
Exercises **14.21**

INDEX **14.23**

PART 3 SOCIALIZNG, MOTIVATING, AND DEVELOPING EMPLOYEES TO COMPETE

15 Moving from Performance Appraisal to Performance Management **15.1**
Theodore H. Curry II

MODULE OVERVIEW **15.4**

OBJECTIVES **15.4**

RELATION TO THE FRAME **15.4**

CORE CONCEPTS IN MOVING FROM PERFORMANCE APPRAISAL
TO PERFORMANCE MANAGEMENT **15.5**
Performance Appraisal and Performance Management Defined **15.5** ■ Principal
Goals of Performance Management **15.5** ■ Legal Issues in Performance
Management **15.7** ■ The Performance Management Cycle **15.8**
New Developments in Employee Performance Management **15.14**

STRATEGIC ISSUES IN MOVING FROM PERFORMANCE APPRAISAL TO
PERFORMANCE MANAGEMENT **15.16**
Involvement of Users in Development **15.16** ■ Alternative Implementation
Models **15.17**

IN CONCLUSION **15.19**

Debrief **15.19** ■ Suggested Readings **15.19** ■ Critical Thinking Questions **15.19**
Exercises **15.20** ■ References **15.20**

INDEX **15.21**

16 Compensation Fundamentals and Linkage to Organizational Performance **16.1**

Michael L. Moore

MODULE OVERVIEW **16.4**

OBJECTIVES **16.4**

RELATION TO THE FRAME **16.4**

MODELS OF BEST PRACTICES IN PAY SYSTEM DESIGN **16.6**

CORE CONCEPTS IN COMPENSATING EMPLOYEES **16.8**

Types of Pay **16.8** ■ Direct Pay Components: Basic Elements of the Work-Reward Exchange **16.8** ■ Indirect Pay Elements **16.9**

STRATEGIC ISSUES OF JOB-BASED PAY COMPARED TO SKILL/ COMPETENCY-BASED PAY **16.10**

Internal Equity Tools **16.11** ■ Job Evaluation Methods for Internal Equity **16.12** Person-Based Pay Methods for Internal Equity **16.16** ■ External Equity Issues **16.16** ■ Individual Equity **16.18** ■ Disadvantages of Each System **16.19** Balance of Pay Elements Over the Organization's Life Cycle **16.19** Tangibles and Intangibles **16.20**

IN CONCLUSION **16.20**

Debrief **16.20** ■ Suggested Readings **16.20** ■ Relevant Web Sites **16.20** Critical Thinking Questions **16.21** ■ Exercises **16.21** ■ Application Exercises **16.21** ■ References **16.21**

INDEX **16.23**

17 Pay and Incentive Systems: Transitional, Transformational, and Nontraditional **17.1**

Edilberto F. Montemayor

MODULE OVERVIEW **17.4**

OBJECTIVES **17.4**

RELATION TO THE FRAME **17.4**

CORE CONCEPTS BEHIND THE USE OF GROUP INCENTIVES **17.5**

The Nature of Group Incentives **17.5** ■ A Taxonomy for Group Incentive Plans **17.7**

STRATEGIC ISSUES IN DEPLOYING GROUP INCENTIVES **17.9**

Need for Alignment with Business Strategy **17.10** ■ Group Incentives as an Organizational Change/Development Intervention **17.10**

IN CONCLUSION **17.21**

Debrief **17.21** ■ Suggested Readings **17.21** ■ Critical Thinking Questions **17.21** Exercises **17.22** ■ References **17.22**

INDEX **17.24**

18 **Benefits: Current Challenges in Providing Cost-Effective Employee Supports 18.1**

MaryAnne M. Hyland

MODULE OVERVIEW **18.4**

RELATION TO THE FRAME **18.4**

CORE CONCEPTS IN EMPLOYEE BENEFITS **18.5**

Benefit Basics **18.5** ■ The Regulatory Environment **18.7** ■ Social Insurance Programs **18.9** ■ Retirement Benefits **18.11** ■ Health and Welfare Benefits **18.13** Work/Life and Miscellaneous Benefits **18.17** ■ Design **18.18** ■ Funding **18.19** Administration **18.20**

STRATEGIC ISSUES IN EMPLOYEE BENEFITS **18.21**

APPLICATION **18.22**

IN CONCLUSION **18.22**

Debrief **18.22** ■ Suggested Readings **18.23** ■ Critical Thinking Questions **18.23** Exercise **18.23** ■ References **18.23** ■ Endnotes **18.24**

INDEX **18.25**

19 **Training and Employee Development 19.1**

Laura L. Bierema

MODULE OVERVIEW **19.4**

OBJECTIVES **19.4**

RELATION TO THE FRAME **19.5**

SETTING THE CONTEXT FOR ORGANIZATIONAL LEARNING IN A NEW MILLENNIUM **19.6**

CORE CONCEPTS IN TRAINING AND EMPLOYEE DEVELOPMENT **19.7**

Making the Decision to Train **19.8** ■ Models of Training Planning and Design **19.9** ■ The Role of Adult Learning in Training and Employee Development **19.14** ■ Adult Learning: Establishing Goals for Learning and Respecting Diverse Learning Styles **19.15** ■ The Nuts and Bolts of Delivering Training **19.17** ■ Effective Training Facilitation Strategies **19.20** ■ Facilitating Training Transfer **19.23** ■ Evaluating Training **19.24**

STRATEGIC ISSUES IN TRAINING AND EMPLOYEE DEVELOPMENT **19.26**

Linking Training to Organizational Strategy **19.26** ■ The Shift from Training to Learning **19.26** ■ The Learning Organization **19.26** ■ Action Learning: Real Learning in Real Time **19.27** ■ The Emergence of the "Learning Executive" **19.27** ■ On-the-Job Training **19.28** ■ Responding to a Rapidly Changing Environment **19.28** ■ Deciding When to Hire a Consultant **19.28** Adopting a Customer Focus **19.28** ■ Ethical Issues in Employee Training and Development **19.29**

APPLICATION **19.29**

IN CONCLUSION **19.29**

Debrief **19.29** ■ Suggested Readings **19.30** ■ Relevant Web Sites **19.30** Critical Thinking Questions **19.30** ■ Exercises **19.31** ■ References **19.31**

INDEX **19.33**

20   Using the Internet for Training and Development   **20.1**
Linda A. Jackson

MODULE OVERVIEW **20.4**

OBJECTIVES **20.4**

RELATION TO THE FRAME **20.4**

CORE CONCEPTS IN INTERNET TRAINING **20.5**
What Is the Internet? **20.5** ■ What Is Internet-Based Training? **20.7**
Components of Internet-Based Training **20.7** ■ Theories of Learning and
Internet-Based Training **20.12** ■ "Good" Internet-Based Training:
Key Elements **20.14** ■ Implementing Internet-Based Training **20.15**

STRATEGIC ISSUES IN INTERNET-BASED TRAINING   **20.17**
Why Choose Internet-Based Training? **20.17** ■ Why Not Choose Internet-Based
Training? **20.17** ■ What Type of Internet-Based Training? **20.18** ■ Critical Issues
for the Future of Internet-Based Training **20.19**

APPLICATION **20.20**

IN CONCLUSION **20.21**
Debrief **20.21** ■ Suggested Readings **20.23** ■ Critical Thinking Questions **20.26**
Exercises **20.26** ■ References **20.27**

INDEX **20.30**

PART 4   **CONTINUOUS IMPROVEMENT OF
ORGANIZATIONAL PROCESSES AND
WORK RELATIONSHIPS**

21   Systems Approaches to Human Resource Management: New
Assumptions **21.1**
Mary Jenkins ■ *Tom Coens*

MODULE OVERVIEW **21.4**

OBJECTIVES **21.4**

RELATION TO THE FRAME **21.5**

CORE CONCEPTS IN HUMAN RESOURCES SYSTEMS, POLICIES,
AND PRACTICES **21.7**
Systems **21.7** ■ Assumptions **21.9** ■ Building HR Systems Based on a New Set
of Assumptions **21.10** ■ Management Is Prediction **21.12**

STRATEGIC ISSUES IN REDESIGNING HR SYSTEMS **21.14**
Stage 1: Inquiry and Reflection **21.14** ■ Stage 2: Critical Questions **21.14**
Stage 3: Unearthing Assumptions **21.15** ■ Stage 4: Applying Change Theory **21.15**

APPLICATION OF THE DESIGN METHOD **21.15**
GM-Powertrain **21.15** ■ Placon Corporation **21.18** ■ Falk Corporation **21.20**

IN CONCLUSION **21.21**
Debrief **21.21** ■ Suggested Readings **21.21** ■ Critical Thinking Questions **21.22**
Exercises **21.22** ■ References **21.22**

INDEX **21.24**

22 Organizational Development and Change: The Role of Human Resources **22.1**

Ben B. Benson ■ *Angela Endres*

MODULE OVERVIEW **22.4**

RELATION TO THE FRAME **22.4**

CORE CONCEPTS IN HUMAN RESOURCES' ROLE IN ORGANIZATIONAL DEVELOPMENT AND CHANGE **22.5**
The State of Human Resources **22.5** ■ Toward a New HR Framework **22.6**
HR Membership and Guerrilla Warfare **22.6**

STRATEGIC ISSUES IN HUMAN RESOURCES' ROLE IN ORGANIZATIONAL DEVELOPMENT AND CHANGE **22.7**
Restructure to Adequately Assess Needs **22.7** ■ Radical Reengineering to Operate as a Team Member **22.8** ■ Clear Deliverables, Not Paradigms and Models **22.9**
Mitigating Common Errors of Winging It, Antagonizing, and Dropping the Ball **22.9** ■ Responses Using Best Practices, Key Performance Indicators, and Value Analysis **22.11** ■ HR and Change Management: The Chrysler Finance Example **22.12** ■ A Clear Change Model **22.13** ■ The Modified HR Organization **22.16** ■ Change Management and Human Resources **22.17**
The HRD Landscape **22.18**

APPLICATION 1 **22.19**
Ford Motor Manufacturing Education, Training, and Development Case Study **22.19**

APPLICATION 2 **22.20**

IN CONCLUSION **22.22**
Debrief **22.22** ■ Suggested Readings and Resources **22.22** ■ Critical Thinking Questions **22.22**

INDEX **22.23**

23 Employee Safety and Health **23.1**

Scott H. Tobey

MODULE OVERVIEW **23.4**

OBJECTIVES **23.4**

RELATION TO THE FRAME **23.4**

CORE CONCEPTS IN EMPLOYEE SAFETY AND HEALTH **23.5**
The Extent of Occupational Injuries and Illnesses **23.5** ■ Accident Causation **23.7**
The Regulatory Framework for Employee Safety and Health **23.9**

STRATEGIC ISSUES IN EMPLOYEE SAFETY AND HEALTH **23.11**
Building Organizational Effectiveness Related to Safety and Health **23.11**
Implementing Safety and Health Controls **23.13** ■ Utilizing a Joint Employee/Employer Approach **23.15** ■ Devising Training Strategies **23.15**

APPLICATION **23.17**
Preparing for Class Discussion and Case Analysis **23.17**

IN CONCLUSION **23.17**
Debrief **23.17** ■ Suggested Readings and References **23.18** ■ Relevant Web Sites **23.18** Critical Thinking Questions **23.18** ■ Exercises **23.19**

INDEX **23.20**

24 Managing Careers **24.1**

Carrie R. Leana ▪ *Daniel C. Feldman*

MODULE OVERVIEW **24.4**

OBJECTIVES **24.4**

RELATION TO THE FRAME **24.4**

CORE CONCEPTS IN MANAGING CAREERS **24.5**
Career Stages **24.5** ▪ Life Stages **24.7** ▪ The Formation of Stable Career Interests **24.7**

MAJOR CAREER TRANSITIONS **24.10**
Organizational Entry and Socialization **24.10** ▪ Transfers, Promotions, and Relocation **24.12** ▪ Downsizings and Layoffs **24.13**

STRATEGIC ISSUES IN MANAGING CAREERS **24.14**
Individual Strategies for Managing Careers **24.14** ▪ Organizational Strategies for Developing Employees' Careers **24.16**

IN CONCLUSION **24.16**
Debrief **24.16** ▪ Suggested Readings **24.17** ▪ Relevant Web Sites **24.18** Critical Thinking Questions **24.18** ▪ Exercises **24.18**

INDEX **24.19**

PART 5 GROWING HUMAN RESOURCE CHALLENGES FOR THE MILLENNIUM AND BEYOND

25 Globally Managing Human Resources **25.1**

Jennifer Palthe

MODULE OVERVIEW **25.4**

OBJECTIVES **25.4**

RELATION TO THE FRAME **25.4**

CORE CONCEPTS IN GLOBALLY MANAGING HUMAN RESOURCES **25.5**
Global Megatrends Impacting HR Management **25.5** ▪ The Difference Between Global and Domestic HR **25.6** ▪ Global Corporate Evolution **25.8** ▪ Implications of Globalization for the HR Function **25.9** ▪ Competencies Necessary for Success as a Global Manager **25.13**

STRATEGIC ISSUES IN GLOBALLY MANAGING HUMAN RESOURCES **25.13**
Global Strategic Options: Creating Synergy Amongst Diverse Cultures **25.14**
Global Strategic HR Orientations: Managing Integration and Differentiation **25.15**

APPLICATION **25.15**

IN CONCLUSION **25.16**
Debrief **25.16** ▪ Suggested Readings **25.16** ▪ Relevant Web Sites **25.17** Critical Thinking Questions **25.18** ▪ Exercises **25.18** ▪ Optional Exercises **25.18**

APPENDIX **25.19**
Case Study Exercises **25.27** ▪ Notes **25.28** ▪ References **25.28**

INDEX **25.29**

26 Comparative Industrial Relations **26.1**

Peter Berg ■ *Eunmi Chang*

MODULE OVERVIEW **26.4**

RELATION TO THE FRAME **26.4**

CORE CONCEPTS IN COMPARATIVE EMPLOYMENT RELATIONS **26.5**
Employees and Labor Unions **26.5** ■ Employers and Their Associations **26.7**
Government **26.7** ■ Collective Bargaining **26.8** ■ Culture **26.9**

STRATEGIC ISSUES IN COMPARATIVE EMPLOYMENT RELATIONS **26.10**

APPLICATION **26.12**
The Case of Korea **26.12** ■ The Case of Germany **26.14**

IN CONCLUSION **26.17**
Debrief **26.17** ■ Suggested Readings **26.18** ■ Critical Thinking Questions **26.18**
References **26.18**

INDEX **26.17**

27 Ethical Perspectives in Employment Relations and Human Resources **27.1**

John L. Revitte ■ *Jerry C. Lazar*

MODULE OVERVIEW **27.4**

OBJECTIVES **27.4**

RELATION TO THE FRAME **27.4**

CORE CONCEPTS IN WORKPLACE ETHICS **27.6**
Ethics, Morals, and Philosophy **27.6** ■ Law and Legality **27.6** ■ Political
Correctness **27.7** ■ Good Manners, Etiquette, and Civility **27.7** ■ Western
Traditions and Judeo-Christian Values **27.7** ■ Gender Differences and Ethical
Systems **27.8** ■ Conflicts at Work Regarding What Is and Is Not Ethical **27.8** ■
Intergroup Conflicts **27.8** ■ Intragroup Conflicts **27.9**

STRATEGIC ISSUES IN WORKPLACE ETHICS **27.9**
Selection and Promotion of Employees and Supervisors **27.10** ■ Rights to Collect
Information Versus Rights of Privacy **27.10** ■ Income Differentials within
Workplaces and in Society **27.11** ■ Punishments, Progressivity, and "Just Cause"
in Discipline Cases **27.12** ■ Occupational Health and Safety **27.13** ■ Employee
Involvement and Quality of Worklife Enhancement **27.14** ■ Labor-Management
Relations **27.14** ■ Affirmative Action Programs Versus Seniority and Other
Systems **27.16** ■ Workforce Reductions Versus Job Creation Efforts **27.16**

APPLICATIONS **27.18**
Application 1: Light Versus Regular Duty Work **27.18** ■ Questions for Group
Discussion **27.18** ■ Application 2: Work-Family Conflicts **27.19** ■ Questions for
Group Discussion **27.19**

IN CONCLUSION **27.19**
Debrief **27.19** ■ Suggested Readings **27.20** ■ Critical Thinking Questions **27.20**
Exercises **27.21** ■ References **27.21**

INDEX **27.22**

GENERAL INDEX **I.1**

OVERVIEW AND PREFACE

This is the first edition of *Managing Human Resources in the 21st Century: From Core Concepts to Strategic Choice.* The book stresses how the human resource management function and its contemporary activities contribute to organizational effectiveness and the achievement of strategic business objectives. It is grounded in the assumption that traditional human resource management practices need to be reconsidered in light of the transformed employment relationships of the twenty-first century.

An engaging human resource management course should cover many contemporary topics. These include: the changing employment relations contract of lessened job security, the spiraling demands for continuous high performance, the outsourcing of many functions (including human resources), the increasing use of temporary or contingent workers, the growing multiculturalism of the workplace, the increasing blurring of the lines between work and personal life, the growth in the use of computer technology to perform work, the rise of work teams as a basic job design element, flattened careers, global employment systems, and the rise of variable pay and risk sharing in compensation for employees at all levels. These are just some of the current topics covered in this book.

This book considers human resource management issues from both the employer and employee perspectives (as well as that of other stakeholders where appropriate). It is delivered in a modular format to reflect current trends in degreed education. It is geared toward graduate-level students, and also would be appropriate for advanced undergraduates in business and the social sciences. Courses in human resource management, as well as those in organizational behavior, management, and the social sciences that examine any of the topics in this book—e.g., managing diversity, cultural support of work and family, managing change, scenario planning, mergers and acquisitions, and strategy, to name a few—will benefit from the exciting content and flexibility the modules provide. Another relevant audience is practicing managers and professionals in continuing management and executive education delivered by corporations or business schools.

Origins of This Book

This text was motivated by discussions among the faculty at the School of Labor and Industrial Relations at Michigan State University. The school has an internationally recognized Master of Labor Relations and Human Resources program and a respected Ph.D. degree program in social sciences. Both the faculty and student population represent a wide variety of experience, interest, and expertise. Our doctoral students teach at many industrial relations and business schools. The faculty hold degrees from such universities as Cornell, Notre Dame, Yale, Massachusetts Institute of Technology (MIT), Minnesota, Michigan, Maryland, and Wisconsin. Nearly all also have international experience teaching or conducting research in global corporations or other international organizations. With degrees ranging from management to labor and industrial relations, organizational behavior to economics, these faculty as a group provide multiple perspectives to graduate students in human resources through an integrated curriculum that has distinguished the school. The modules in this book reflect the key competencies and wisdom that we impart throughout our curriculum.

This book reflects a particular research and teaching perspective on the employer-employee relationship that is held at Michigan State's School of Labor and Industrial Relations. First, the school's faculty believe it is important to consider multiple views of the employment relationship, including both the employer view and the employee view. Shareholder and societal views are also often discussed. All of these stakeholder views are considered legitimate. On occasion, these views are in conflict; sometimes they coincide. For example, while lessened job security may serve employer and shareholder interests by helping to reduce labor costs in the short run, it may create uncertainty for employees' income stream and the surrounding communities' economic well-being. Managers need to understand these competing perspectives in order to develop strategy, policies, and practices that recognize how these perspectives affect employing organizations. This book was conceived to present the issues grounding these multiple perspectives.

Second, the school has substantial contacts with the practitioner community. Practitioners inform our teaching and research, and the vast majority of our students pursue careers as practitioners. A key question that we ask in our teaching is, "What is a proper mix of theory and practice?" We felt that a human resource management text that would incorporate a balance between the employer and employee and other perspectives, written by a mix of academics and practitioners, would be a useful teaching tool both inside and outside Michigan State University. In addition to our own faculty writers, we have enlisted over two dozen leading experts in the research and practice of human resources so that each module is written by a contributor who is an authority in his or her field. Teaching excellence is highly valued in our culture, and this book reflects that commitment.

Overall, our specific substantive and pedagogical objectives for this book and the courses it supports are as follows:

1. To provide an understanding of the current theory, principles, and practices associated with human resource management decision making and strategy.

2. To offer individuals an appreciation of how the human resource function can contribute to organizational effectiveness and the achievement of strategic business objectives.

3. To present a balanced view of human resource issues from the employer and employee perspectives.

4. To present the material using a modular approach mirroring how many professors and managers teach today.

5. To offer flexibility by offering 27 modules for teachers to customize their courses.

Features of This Book

The text has several features that are rare, if not unique, among human resources management (HRM) texts.

A Balanced Perspective on the Employment Relationship.   It is important for students to recognize that human resource (HR) practices and strategies vary in their impact and implications for multiple constituencies such as employers, employees, and shareholders. When students become managers and professionals, they will need to consider the views of all of these groups in order to develop and implement policies effectively. Most HRM texts are written from a micro-organizational/industrial psychology viewpoint that evaluates practices normatively from the employer perspective. Because the HRM field is based on this important perspective, our book likewise utilizes this approach. Nonetheless, even though it is written predominantly from the standpoint of the employer, general manager, or organization, we also integrate employee and or societal perspectives where appropriate. Balance is provided by having editors and contributors to this book who view employment issues from management or labor/employee perspectives.

Recognized Experts Writing in Their Specialty.   Unlike some texts, where the authors must write on topics on which they are not expert, this text draws on multiple authors who are experts in their field. In this way, each module in this book reflects the very best of each contributor's intellect. Authors were invited to write modules because they had taught or done research in the assigned topic area. We invited leading scholars and practitioners from far and wide to contribute material to the book. (This includes an international case on the implications of the 1997 Asian economic crisis for Korean employment systems.)

Integration of Practice with Scholarly Views on HRM.   The authors represent a mix of academics and practitioners consistent with the industrial relations and human resource management view of the importance of practitioners. Since HR and collective bargaining involve the practice of employment relations, we felt it was critical to invite a few insightful practitioners (all with graduate degrees, some including Ph.D.s) to contribute. This view reflects what many leading business schools have done today. Increasingly, leading business executives are being invited to teach after they have retired from industry. We believe it was important to draw on the insights of successful practitioners while they were at the peak of their careers.

Unparalleled Flexibility in a Human Resource Text.   This text consists of 27 modules. Some modules cover core or fundamental knowledge on basic human resource management issues ranging from equal employment opportunity law to compensation. Other modules include material on a specialized topic such as the Family Medical Leave Act (FMLA), using the Internet for training, mergers and acquisitions, and how scenario planning can be used for strategic analysis. The combination of core concepts and specialized modules will allow instructors to tailor their course to their curriculum and to their students' learning needs.

A Guiding Framework on Human Resource Decision Making.   To ensure continuity between the modules, the book was written around an overarching guiding "framework"—a universal chart illustrated in each module as Figure 1, A Frame for Understanding Human Resource Strategy: Context, Roles, and Constraints. HR practitioners can use this model as an analytical tool to break down HR decisions and processes into their basic component parts. In each module, the author(s) begins with a section relating the module to this framework. The framework divides HR processes into four roles: the *transaction* role, the *translation* role, the *transition* role, and the *transformation* role. Increasingly, it is important for managers to understand not only HR *activities,* such as hiring and firing people, but also what HR *delivers* (its roles) for organizational effectiveness. Human resource management activities—from recruitment to selection to compensation to performance appraisal—occur in all of these roles.

Equally important, the framework recognizes that management carries out these roles under various constraints. While management may on occasion act unilaterally in what it deems is the best interest of the firm's constituents, on other occasions its actions must be negotiated with a union. In still other situations, its actions are mandated by the government. Furthermore, these roles are influenced by the economic environment, business strategy, and HR strategy. In the sample illustration on the following page, the framework has been filled in to show how different, common HR functions and decisions can be classified according to the diagnostic variables explained above. In Module 1—New Employment Relations—these sample HR decisions are explained in further detail and in a more extensive introduction to the overall framework; Module 2—Human Resource Strategy—and Module 3—Leadership by Human Resources—elaborate on the model. These three modules provide the foundation for the frame that informs the entire book.

Modular Teaching Format.   Each module is designed to be taught in either two one-and one-half hour classes or one three-hour class. In this way the course material could be appropriate for either business and social science students in classes for credit or in classes designed for practicing managers. Each student module has its own table of contents, and is divided into the following sections: Module Overview; Objectives;

ENVIRONMENTAL CONTEXT				
ORGANIZATIONAL		BUSINESS		

More ← **Managerial Discretion** → Less

		Unilateral Decisions	Negotiated Decisions	Imposed Decisions
HR STRATEGY / HR Roles	Transaction	Hiring Decision Entry Level	Selection of Arbitrator	Payment per Fair Labor Standards Act Minimum Wage and Overtime
	Translation	Explain Benefits Outsourcing	Summarizing Collective Bargaining Agreement	Explanation of Fair Labor Standards Act to Management and Employees
	Transition	Retirement Benefits Change	Negotiating Retirement Plan	Adjustment of Sick Leave Policy to Family Medical Leave Act
	Transformation	Merger and Acquisition	Change Labor Relations Strategy	Culture Change with Equal Employment Opportunity Laws, mid-1960s

STRATEGY

APPLICATION OF GUIDING FRAME TO COMMON HUMAN RESOURCE DECISIONS.
The completed framework shows how various HR functions can be classified according to different diagnostic variables. A blank copy of the frame is included in each module so that students can complete the model for the particular topic being discussed.

Relation to the HR Decision-Making Framework; Core Concepts and Strategic Issues in the topic area; Application—e.g., a role play, case study, game, simulation, exercise, computer assignment, or debate—and Conclusions. Modules conclude with a Debrief, Suggested Readings, Relevant Web Sites, Critical Thinking Questions, Exercises, and References. Pre- and postclass assignments are suggested. It is our assumption that most instructors could teach the class without assigning students any additional readings, unless the instructor chooses to select from the suggested reading lists.

Many Original New Current Cases, Exercises, and Simulations. Even though few instructors today exclusively lecture to students, detailed lecture notes are provided in the teacher's edition. This book includes many original contemporary applications to enable instructors to teach human resource management in an engaging way. A specific goal of the book was to integrate experiential exercises, role play, games, and exercises into each module so that HR topics will be discussed in a lively and memorable manner. Module 11 on cultural support of work and family even features an original board game of work and family strategy that had been developed for teaching managers by Tower Perrin, the international human resources consulting firm. It is included with their permission.

Teachers' Manuals and Transparency Masters on the Web. Excellent teaching support is provided for each module through a corresponding teacher's module consisting of lecture notes and a PowerPoint slide presentation that can be used electronically or to create transparency masters. These instructor components are available for download on the book's Web site at *http:\\kossek.swcollege.com*. Each instructor module has been tailored to work effectively with its companion student module. Instructor modules all provide an overview of the concepts presented and a teaching plan, plus more to aid in the development of an effective lesson plan for the topic to be covered.

Overview of Modules and Contributors

Below we provide a brief summary of what each module contains and relevant background on the contributor. The book is divided into five thematic sections and includes a mix of basic and specialized modules in human resource management.

Part 1   Overarching Employer Principles for Managing Human Resources

The modules in this section are on general topics or macro-organizational issues in the field of human resource management today.

Module 1— New Employment Relations: Challenges and Basic Assumptions

This module discusses the basic propositions underlying the text. It notes that the most noticeable feature of employment relations in the United States is variation, with the "commitment" and "labor transactional" approaches at either end of the continuum. Module 1 provides examples of this variation, a history of human resource management, and also the basic framework for analyzing HR decision making. Authored by the editors of this volume, **Ellen Ernst Kossek** and **Richard N. Block**, Module 1 introduces and develops the guiding framework. It is based on the assumption that students should not only understand HR's functions in terms of its traditional activities (e.g., selection, equal employment opportunity, appraisal) but also more broadly what purpose or roles the activities serve and how they contribute to the firms' effectiveness. The framework recognizes that management has varying amounts of discretion to carry out these roles, and these roles are influenced by the economic environment, business strategy, and HR strategy. An original case and simulation, Kensi Commitment Manufacturing, Inc., is provided.

Module 2—Human Resource Strategy: From Transactions to Transformation

This module examines human resource strategy and how to ensure that HR systems are fully integrated with the strategic and organizational change needs of the firm. Since human resource strategy is derived from business strategy, the chapter begins with a discussion of core concepts in organizational strategy. The activities and key issues and principles involved in developing human resource strategy and alternative perspectives on how human resource strategy can be used to gain competitive advantage are then discussed. The module includes an original case study of the Daehan Corporation written by ByeongCheol Lee and YoungMyon Lee, who are professors in the College of Management and Economics at Dongguk University in South Korea. Professor Byeong-Choel Lee was a visiting scholar at Michigan State and holds a Ph.D. from MIT. The case describes how change in the international economy of the Far East Pacific Basin prompted a major employer in South Korea to fundamentally revise its human resource strategy. The module also includes original vignettes on strategic HR issues developed by Lisa Copeland, a former graduate at Michigan State University who now works as a change management analyst for Andersen Consulting Group. **Ellen Ernst Kossek,** the module's author, has taught a course on human resource strategies and decisions at Michigan State for over a decade.

Module 3— Leadership by Human Resources: Organizational Roles and Choices

This module provides an understanding of HR roles, responsibilities, and objectives via leadership by the human resource function in the strategic organization. The module develops the HR roles used in the guiding framework: transactions, translations, transitions, and transformation. Students will be introduced to examples of how traditional HR activities ranging from selection to compensation to training can be carried out to serve these different roles. HR activities can be organized into five main clusters: human resource strategy and organization, talent identification and deployment, human capital development, reward management, and employee relations and voice. Examples of forces influencing the degree of management discretion in HR decision making, current and historical developments shaping the nature and power and delivery (including outsourcing) of the HR function, and the competencies needed for the delivery of HR are provided. The module concludes with an original exercise where students are asked to quantify the value added from HR activities. A case on AT&T and other exercises are offered as options. The module was written by **Ellen Ernst Kossek** and **Karen S. Markel,** a doctoral student in the School of Labor and Industrial Relations at Michigan State University. Ms. Markel, who formerly worked for Andersen Consulting, currently does research in the areas of human resource management, labor markets, and institutional economics.

Module 4—Managing Change: Scenario Planning and Other Tools

Most organizations operate in environments demanding constant adaptation, so they must remain capable of changing to survive. This module examines how HR can create a change capability within organizations. The basic premise is that HR must assure that organizations are prepared for strategic changes and create systems that can adapt to these changes, both within the HR function and in other functions with which HR interacts. The module includes a strategic planning exercise where students complete a consumer lifestyle worksheet and consider the pressing people management implications of various market scenarios. This exercise was adapted from the Royal Dutch Shell corporate planning group, which was one of the originators of scenario planning. Author **Steve S. Fitzgerald** is a Vice President of Human Resources at Fairlane Credit LLC (a start-up venture of Ford Credit). Steve has designed and deployed the corporate strategic planning process currently used at Fairlane Credit LLC. In the mid-1990s he was a member of the five-person team that created Ford's global human resources strategy activity, where he led the development and use of environmental scanning, scenario planning, and other strategic planning tools. Subsequently, he partnered with Michigan State in bringing this tool to students of human resource strategy. He holds a master's degree from Michigan State University.

Module 5—Mergers and Human Resources

Mergers and acquisitions have been a dominant feature of corporate life in the United States since the early 1980s. This module discusses the role of HR in facilitating the success of a merger or reorganization. It lays out a series of key human resource tasks that must be performed in order to support leadership tasks. These tasks include reconciling cultural differences between organizations, educating the workforce regarding the cultural change integration, and helping to make the changes and to create a smooth integration. It includes a merger and acquisition brainstorming exercise. Author **Susan K. Graff** is Director of Integration Management at Integrated Changeware Systems (ICWS), Inc. Graff's background includes intensive work in international and domestic organizations in the areas of strategic planning, business structure design, leadership profiles and development performance system and skill and its alignment, productivity commitment, and cultural integration. Her graduate and postgraduate work is in organization analysis and the behavioral sciences. She is currently on the teaching staff of Central Washington University and Seattle University's Albers School of Business. Professor Graff was a former instructor of organizational development at Michigan State. Author **William N. Case** is Managing Partner of ICWS, Inc. He supervises major client projects in merger integration and strategic change and has a wide variety of industry and management experience, from start-ups to Fortune 100 businesses (e.g., Atlantic Richfield Company and Price Waterhouse). He has served as business owner, executive, and senior consultant for major change initiatives including mergers and acquisitions, outsourcing redesign, reengineering/change integration, technology architecture development, strategic systems, and contingency planning.

Module 6—Collective Bargaining, Industrial Relations, and Human Resource Systems: Managing in Environments

This module focuses on the basis of collectively bargained employment relations in the United States. It points out the differences between the greater managerial discretion that exists in the absence of a union and the lesser managerial discretion that exists when the firm's employees are represented by a union. It discusses the core concepts of workplace rules, the bargaining process, labor unionism, and employer and employee perspectives on the employment relationship, and it presents the strategic options for firms in collective bargaining. The module offers the original Comp-U-Car case. The company is a maker of computer chips in the auto industry that has to decide how to improve productivity on three shifts, comparing decision making under unionized and nonunionized scenarios. Author **Richard N. Block** has taught collective bargaining at Michigan State for many years and is an active arbitrator and scholar.

Module 7—Human Resource Information Systems

This module makes students aware of the fundamental concepts in using and designing information systems in the human resource context. As human resource information systems become increasingly sophisticated and increasingly user-friendly, they will be used not only to process HR transactions, but also to support management in its strategic decision making. A distinction is made between transaction processing systems, workflow systems (with multiple individuals), reporting systems, decision support systems, and executive support systems. This module includes an application on Web-based recruiting. Author **Brian T. Pentland** is an assistant professor at Michigan State who regularly teaches a graduate course in human resource information systems. He received his Ph.D. in organizational behavior from MIT.

Part 2   Building the Human Resource Base: Recruitment and Selection Strategies and Legal Concerns in Constructing the Workforce

The modules in this section relate to the legal selection and recruitment of workers. Workforce planning for flexibility, and managing diversity and the legal and cultural integration of work and family concerns are additional topics related to constructing and keeping the requisite workforce.

Module 8—EEO in the Workplace: Employment Law Challenges

This module provides an overview of what may be the most important public policy factor to affect the employment relationship in the last 40 years—the panoply of laws prohibiting discrimination on the basis of race, gender, age, and other protected classes of employees. This module provides understanding of the basics of the legal structure of antidiscrimination law in the United States, and also key legal concepts of disparate impact, treatment, and affirmative action. The employer's state of mind is irrelevant; it is the results, not the intent, of the employment practice that is of interest to the courts. The module includes some original cases on common EEO issues that can be used for small-group discussion. Author **Ben Wolkinson** has taught employment law for many years at Michigan State. An accomplished scholar in this area who has published many refereed articles, he is coauthor with volume coeditor Richard N. Block, of *Employment Law: The Workplace Rights of Employers and Employees* (Blackwell, 1995). He is an active arbitrator and received his Ph.D. from Cornell University. Dr. Wolkinson had a Fulbright Fellowship to Israel, where he studied ethnic discrimination and recently published a book on this topic.

Module 9—Managing Diversity: Human Resource Issues

Module 9 teaches the student about managing the diverse workforce that, to some extent, was created by antidiscrimination laws discussed in Module 8. Law, demographics, and globalization are making the workforce more diverse than ever. A demographically heterogeneous workforce presents challenges and opportunities to firm management. While a diverse workforce may have different needs that must be met, such a workforce often brings new ideas and ways of thinking to an organization. The module defines diversity, managing diversity, and how managing diversity differs from equal employment opportunity and affirmative action. It considers the implications of managing diversity for human resource outcomes, managing diversity paradigms, and the major stages in managing diversity. It includes some original vignettes highlighting the complex issues involved in managing diversity on issues ranging from telecommuting to sexual orientation. Author **Stella M. Nkomo,** a professor in the Department of Management at the University of North Carolina at Charlotte, is one of the most recognized scholars today on managing diversity. Her research focuses on race and gender and diversity issues in the workplace. Dr. Nkomo serves as a officer for the National Academy of Management. She holds a Ph.D. from the University of Massachusetts at Amherst. Author **Ellen Ernst Kossek** has published a book entitled *Managing Diversity: Human Resource Strategies for Transforming the Workplace* (Blackwell, 1996 with Sharon Lobel) and articles on human resource issues related to diversity.

Module 10—Administering the Family Medical Leave Act

This module discusses issues in implementing FMLA of 1993. This act provides up to 12 weeks of unpaid job-protected leave for certain family and medical reasons and provides for the continuation of group health benefits. The module helps individuals understand the strategic implications of FMLA, and how to develop human resource policies that comply with the requirements of the act. It discusses how to coordinate compliance with FMLA with other employment statutes such as workers' compensation and the Americans with Disabilities Act. An exercise where students have to work in teams to design a leave policy for employees that is in accordance with FMLA is included. Author **Tina M. Riley** is a doctoral candidate in the School of Education at Michigan State. She has taught many courses to human resource practitioners and is the Associate Director of the Human Resources Education and Training Center at Michigan State University.

Module 11—Support of Work-Life Integration: Cultural Issues Facing the Employer

Module 11 discusses the evolution in corporate policies that attempts to encourage a balance between work and life issues among employees. Progressive firms have come to realize that work/life policies benefit both the employee and the firm. The key is for management to understand the cultural values inherent in both the human-relations and rational-goals approaches to management, and to balance these competing but essential models of management. The module considers the stages of organizational development of work/life cultural maturation, cultural assumptions regarding work and family integration in the United States and other countries, and alternative organizational approaches for managing employer involvement in employees' personal lives. The module includes an original board game of work and family strategy that was originally developed for teaching managers by Tower Perrin. Author **Ellen Ernst Kossek** has published widely on work and family issues and is a member of the Wharton Work Life Roundtable.

Module 12—Workforce Planning for Flexibility: Staffing with Temporary Employees

As firms have attempted to reduce the costs of employment in order to compete, contingent employment—or employment that is other than traditional, permanent, full-time employment—has become increasingly common. This module provides an overview of contingent work in the United States and discusses the benefits and costs of using contingent workers to meet an organization's strategic goals. An organization needs to define its core competencies and its other needs; the former may require permanent employees, while the latter may be able to accommodate contingent workers. It provides an application tool that shows how to use cost/benefit analysis to make strategic staffing decisions. It reviews the strategic issues employers must consider when planning for flexibility. A spreadsheet exercise is presented that demonstrates the use of the module's concepts in determining the cost-effectiveness of using contingent workers. Author **Karen Roberts** holds a Ph.D. from MIT and teaches courses in labor markets and data sources in human resource management at Michigan State University. She has published extensively on human resource management, worker's compensation, and labor market issues. Professor **Sandra E. Gleason** holds a Ph.D. from Michigan State University and taught at the School of Labor and Industrial Relations for many years. Currently she is the Associate Dean for Faculty Research of the Commonwealth College of The Pennsylvania State University. Her areas of expertise include policy issues in labor economics, contingent work, dispute resolution, and long-range planning in higher education. Both authors have served as associate directors of the academic graduate programs at Michigan State University.

Module 13—Recruitment and Selections: Hiring for the Job or the Organization?

In this module, **Mark L. Lengnick-Hall** points out that firms that do business in a rapidly changing, highly competitive global market must hire for the organization rather than for the job. Recruitment and selection is an expensive and time-consuming process, and the firm must make sure that, as it continually adapts—and if necessary, transforms—itself, the employees it has recruited and selected are also able to adapt and transform themselves. As the nature of the "job" changes, the individuals in those jobs must also have the ability and flexibility to change. The module includes a model of the recruitment and selection process. It discusses organization and job analysis, person-job fit, person-environment fit, and recruitment and selection. The module includes an exercise where students apply their knowledge by developing a recruitment plan, a selection plan, and an interview protocol that yields the quantity and quality of employees needed to make the business successful. Professor Lengnick-Hall has taught human resource management courses for many years at Wichita State University's W. Frank Barton School of Business. Widely published in the area of human resource management, he holds a Ph.D. from Purdue University. He currently teaches and conducts research in the areas of HRM and organizational behavior.

Module 14—Selecting Employees Strategically Today: What Managers Need to Know

This module examines the implementation of selection. Selection procedures and criteria must be job- and performance-related. The module discusses several statistical concepts, among them reliability and validity, that support these relatedness requirements. The expanding definition of job performance, including adaptability and contextual performance, is examined. Simple yet thought-provoking exercises to encourage students to think about how to apply these new performance concepts are offered. The module also discusses the relationships between strategic direction and selection methods. Authors **Sandra L. Fisher** and **Michael E. Wasserman** both have doctorates from Michigan State University. Dr. Fisher is a research scientist with Personnel Decisions Research Institute and has published articles in such journals as *Personnel Psychology*. Her research interests include individuals' motivation to learn and adapt and the implementation of strategic HR systems in large organizations. Professor Wasserman currently teaches strategic management at George Mason University. His current research interests include the strategic role of human capital development—specifically, examining the role of knowledge management, organizational learning, and management cognition.

Part 3   Socializing, Motivating, and Developing Employees to Compete

Once employees are selected, they must be motivated and developed to perform so as to enhance the corporation's goals. Adequate systems must also be in place to reward and develop employees so they are motivated and able to perform their jobs.

Module 15—Moving from Performance Appraisal to Performance Management

This module discusses organizational, managerial, and legal issues in the performance appraisal and performance management processes. It places the function of employee performance appraisal in the broader context of performance management. This module first describes the principal goals that most employers have for the performance management process within their organization. These goals are not mutually exclusive, and their importance and relevance vary from employer to employer. The module then details legal issues in performance management. The performance management cycle is continuous and is introduced as a major tool for making decisions, identifying and resolving problems, and developing employees and the organization. Changing issues in performance management and implementation suggestions are provided. The module includes exercises to demonstrate the difficulty in developing objective performance measures and using them for evaluation. Author **Theodore H. Curry II** is the Director of the School of Labor and Industrial Relations. In his many years as the director of Michigan State's Human Resources Education and Training Center, Professor Curry has developed, presented, and managed development programs in human resources for thousands of managers. He holds graduate and undergraduate degrees in business administration from the University of Kansas.

Module 16—Compensation Fundamentals and Linkage to Organizational Performance

This module focuses on the major components of pay and options for the design of pay systems. The module discusses the legal framework surrounding compensation decisions in the United States, competing models of best practices in pay design, the elements of direct and indirect pay, strategic options in designing compensation for job-based versus skill-based systems, and the forms of equity necessary for successful compensation systems. The module includes many optional exercises including visiting the American Compensation Association Web site, developing job descriptions, identifying compensable factors, and selecting relevant organizations for salary surveys. Author **Michael L. Moore** was the director of the School of Labor and Industrial Relations from 1993 to 1998. He holds a Ph.D. from the University of Michigan and has taught compensation at Michigan State University for many years.

Module 17—Pay and Incentive Systems: Transitional, Transformational, and Nontraditional

This module addresses nontraditional compensation systems. To a large extent, organizational change requires a rethinking of individual performance as employees are increasingly working in groups, as part of a team, often for short periods of time. Compensation and incentive systems must be aligned with these new ways of organizing work. This module provides an understanding of the meaning of the term "group incentive" and the motivational and organizational change impacts of group incentives. A ten-stage process for deploying group incentives and aligning them with business and organizational strategies is provided. Author **Edilberto F. Montemayor** holds a Ph.D. from the University of Minnesota and has taught compensation for many years to graduate students at Michigan State University and in seminars for managers. Professor

Montemayor has worked with the American Compensation Association, presenting at their meetings, and has published articles on compensation.

Module 18—Benefits: Current Challenges in Providing Cost-Effective Employee Supports

In this module, **MaryAnne Hyland** examines one of the biggest cost challenges facing employers today: managing costs while still offering competitive benefits. A major theme throughout is the shift in viewing employee benefits as an entitlement. Basic definitions of benefits and their role in total compensation are provided. The main benefits laws, regulation, and social insurance programs are discussed. Employer benefits plans including retirement benefits, health and welfare, and work/life and miscellaneous benefits are discussed as well as the design, funding, and administration of benefits plans. The module includes an exercise on flexible benefits and another exercise on the role of benefits in recruitment. The author received her Ph.D. from Rutgers University, where she taught courses in benefits. She currently is an assistant professor at Adelphi University. Previously she worked for the Hay Group, an international compensation and benefits and human resources consulting firm.

Module 19—Training and Employee Development

This module examines the process of training and employee development and workplace learning. The module sets the context for organizational learning in the new millennium and introduces key terms related to training and employee development. It discusses when training is and is not an appropriate strategy. The different models of planning and designing training and their strengths and weaknesses are considered. Adult learning principles, the nuts and bolts of training delivery, facilitation and transfer strategies, and strategic issues are also examined. The module includes a simple but important exercise where students working in small groups consider the multiple perspectives on the training process from the roles of trainee, trainer, and client or stakeholder. Author **Laura L. Bierema** received her Ph.D. from the University of Georgia. She is an assistant professor in the Human Resource Management and Education Training Center. She has taught many human resources management courses to managers and has published on training and development. Professor Bierema recently received a fellowship for education scholars from the Kellogg Foundation. She currently does research on workplace learning, more specifically adult learning, career development, women's development, and organizational development.

Module 20—Using the Internet for Training and Development

To keep pace with rapidly advancing technology and its impact on training, a module on Internet-based training (IBT) has been developed. This module provides an overview of IBT, a comprehensive list of resources, and hands-on experience with IBT. It defines Internet-based training and how theories of learning and instructional design relate to IBT. It discusses the steps in implementing IBT, its typologies, and critical issues for the future. Two scenarios are provided at the end of module where students consider whether to implement IBT or not. Students are also encouraged to explore IBT through "hands-on" experience. Author **Linda A. Jackson** is a professor of psychology at Michigan State University. She holds a Ph.D. from the University of Rochester. Professor Jackson is currently conducting research on Internet-based training and has previously taken Internet-based training courses to inform her scholarly endeavors.

Part 4: Continuous Improvement of Organizational Processes and Work Relationships

It is critical that organizations strive to continuously improve work processes and help individuals and the firm grow productively. The modules in this section are focused on these topics.

Module 21—Systems Approaches to Human Resource Management: New Assumptions

This module provides HR practitioners and students with a heuristic method for designing human resource systems, including practices, processes, and policies that align with desired organization culture and business strategies. All HR systems are based on underlying assumptions. The module presents a normative view on how human resource systems ought to be designed to have a healthier workplace. Strategic issues in redesigning human resource systems are discussed. A case study based on Dr. W. Edwards Deming's work with GM Powertrain is included. Students are asked to apply systems theory to examine traditional associations with performance appraisal and consider how performance appraisal systems might be redesigned. Author **Mary Jenkins** holds a master's degree in labor and industrial relations from Michigan State University. Ms. Jenkins worked for many years in human resources at General Motors Powertrain, rising to key manager positions before she left to become an independent consultant. Author **Tom Coens** received a J.D. degree from the John Marshall School of Law. Mr. Coens is a lawyer on many issues including labor law, and also regularly consults to employers. Both Jenkins and Coens have taught graduate courses at Michigan State University.

Module 22—Organizational Development and Change: The Role of Human Resources

This module outlines ways that the HR function can aid the rest of the organization by providing more transformational support, taking project ownership, reducing infrastructure costs of core services, and strategizing to anticipate the organizational change issues that comprise today's dynamic business environment. The module discusses strategic issues in human resource's role in organizational development and change. It discusses how the HR organization should be modified to improve and streamline itself and become more connected to critical organizational change initiatives. A case study on Ford Motor Company's human resource function is provided. **Ben B. Bensen** is a principal in change management at Andersen Consulting and has taught as a professor of human resources at local colleges while working full-time. **Angela Endres** is a change management analyst at Andersen Consulting and received her master's from Michigan State University.

Module 23—Employee Safety and Health

This module by **Scott H. Tobey** examines the legal and strategic managerial issues in the highly regulated area of employee safety and health. He distinguishes between immediate safety issues caused by barriers and noise, and longer-term health issues often caused by exposure to toxic substances. Most important is the difference between improving safety and health by changing employee behaviors and improving them through managerial and strategic decisions. A case for discussion is provided where students consider the problems in implementing safety policies, using the simple example of a hairnet requirement. The Occupational Safety and Health Administration Web page and how to contact the National Institute of Health and Safety are also discussed. Professor Tobey is the Associate Director of the Labor Education Program, School of Labor and Industrial Relations, at Michigan State University. Through Michigan State University, Tobey has worked with Ford Motor Company and many other firms in developing joint health and safety programs. He holds a master's degree from Michigan State University.

Module 24—Managing Careers

This module recognizes the diversity of career paths available to individuals today. It discusses the employee and organizational factors that influence people to change jobs, employers, and careers. The individual strategies and organizational practices that help people make successful transitions into new careers, jobs, and organizations are identified. The dynamics of career transitions over the career life cycle from entry to departure, and strategies for managing careers, are discussed. The module includes some reflective career planning exercises for individuals. Author **Carrie R. Leana** is a professor at the University of Pittsburgh Katz School of Business. She holds a Ph.D. from the University of Houston. Author **Daniel C. Feldman** is Distinguished Business Partnership Foundation Fellow and Professor of Management at the University of South Carolina. Professor Feldman received his Ph.D. in organizational behavior from Yale, and has served on the faculties of Yale College, the University of Minnesota, Northwestern University, and the University of Florida. Feldman is the author of five books and has won many teaching awards. His current research interests include unemployment, underemployment, expatriation, early retirement, and bridge employment. Leana and Feldman have published numerous refereed articles on managing careers and layoffs. Leana has a new book coming out, *Relational Wealth: Managing Employment for Competitive Advantage* (Oxford 2000), which she contributed to and coedited with Denise Rousseau.

Part 5 Growing Human Resource Challenges for the Millennium and Beyond.

This section includes modules on global challenges and ethical issues in the workplace.

Module 25—Globally Managing Human Resources

This module examines the global trends influencing HR practices and policies, the nature of global enterprises, and the challenges of managing a cross-culturally diverse workforce. The module discusses the differences between global and domestic human resources; the difference between international, multinational, and global corporations; and the implications of globalization for the HR function and practices. Competencies needed to manage globally and related strategic issues are also discussed. The module includes the Amoco case study on the globalization of human resource practices at this firm, written by Ellen Ernst Kossek. Author **Jennifer Palthe** is a doctoral student at Michigan State University. She has worked for Andersen Consulting in South Africa and consulted to British Airways and General Motors in Europe. Her dissertation is on the role of global human resources practices in socialization.

Module 26—Comparative Industrial Relations

This module exposes students to employment relations issues in countries outside the United States. Most other countries have a structure of domestic institutions, such as employer organizations, rooted in collective bargaining that mediate the relationship between the firm and its employees, and these institutions are more developed than those institutions in the United States. Cultural differences are found across countries, and these differences affect the institutions of the employment relations system and the day-to-day interactions of employers and employees. The module uses examples from Germany and Korea. Author **Peter Berg** teaches comparative industrial relations at Michigan State. Professor Berg received his Ph.D. from the University of Notre Dame and formerly worked for the Economic Policy Institute in Washington, D.C. Professor Berg currently does research on the areas of organizational change in the United States and Germany, comparative industrial relations, high-performance work systems, and worker training. Author **Eunmi Chang** received her Ph.D. from the University of Maryland while on a Fulbright Fellowship. Her dissertation and published research includes a study of the implementation of strategic human resource management practices in multinational companies. Prior to coming to Michigan State University, she worked for Hyundai Research Institute and taught university courses in South Korea.

Module 27—Ethical Perspectives in Employment Relations and HR

This module explores ethical issues in labor relations and human resources. It points out the distinction between moral, ethical, and unlawful behavior. Ethical behavior at the workplace is in the context of such basic HR issues as the selection and promotion of employees; wage, salary, and income differentials; employee privacy and the interest of the firm in monitoring employees on the job; discipline; occupational safety and health; employee involvement; labor and management relations; and firm downsizing. **John L. Revitte** is a professor of labor education at Michigan State University. He has taught labor leaders and graduate students on collective bargaining and human resource issues for many years. He holds a master's degree from the University of Massachusetts at Amherst. Author **Jerry C. Lazar** holds a master's degree from Northern Illinois University in classical political philosophy. He has taught business ethics for 20 years. He has an adjunct faculty appointment in the Center for Ethics and Life Sciences at Michigan State University's College of Human Medicine, and is on the State of Michigan Board of Medical Ethics.

About the Editors

Ellen Ernst Kossek is a professor of human resources and organizational behavior at Michigan State University. She teaches and does research on human resource management, organizational behavior, and managing work/life and diversity challenges. Her work has been published in many scholarly outlets including *Journal of Applied Psychology; Personnel Psychology; Journal of Organizational Behavior* (best paper award); *Journal of Applied Behavioral Science; Human Relations; Academy of Management Executive; Organizational Dynamics; Human Resource Planning; Human Resource Management; American Psychological Association; Journal of Community, Work, and Family;* and *Center for Creative Leadership.* She is the author of several books including *Managing Diversity: Human Resource Strategies for Transforming the Workplace* (with Sharon Lobel-Blackwell, 1996); *Child Care Challenges for Employers* (LRP Publications, 1991), and *The Acceptance of Human Resource Innovation: Lessons for Managers* (Quorum, 1989). She is on the editorial boards of *Human Resource Planning,* the *Journal of Organizational Behavior,* the *Journal of Applied Behavioral Science,* and reviews for many other journals. She was a visiting scholar at the University of Michigan's Institute for Social Research. She is the year 2000 program chair of the National Academy of Management Gender and Diversity Division. Professor Kossek holds a Ph.D. in organizational behavior from Yale University, an M.B.A. from the University of Michigan, and an A.B. in psychology (cum laude) from Mount Holyoke. Prior to becoming a professor, she worked in human resources for Hitachi, IBM, GTE, and John Deere & Co. in Japan, Geneva, Switzerland, and the United States.

Richard N. Block is Professor of Labor and Industrial Relations at Michigan State University. He is the author of numerous articles and books (most recently, *Labor Law, Industrial Relations, and Employee Choice: The State of the Workplace in the 1990s,* published in 1996 by the W.E. Upjohn Institute for Employment Research) on such issues as the relationship between law and practice in industrial relations in the United States and Canada, industrial relations and structural economic change, employment law, and employee training. His research has appeared in all the major journals in the industrial relations field. He is an experienced labor-management neutral currently listed on all major arbitrator rosters, on several permanent panels, and on the panel on matters related to the implementation of the North American Agreement on Labor Cooperation, the labor side agreement of North American Free Trade Agreement. He also served as Director of the School of Labor and Industrial Relations at Michigan State University from July 1985 through June 1993 and as a member of the Executive Board of the Industrial Relations Research Association from 1990 to 1993. He has been a visiting faculty member at the Graduate School of Business at Columbia University and the Centre for Industrial Relations at the University of Toronto. Professor Block received a B.S. (1971) and M.S. (1973) in economics from the University of Illinois at Urbana Champaign, and a Ph.D. in industrial and labor relations from Cornell University in 1977.

Acknowledgments

We would like to express our appreciation to individuals who have made this book possible. The South-Western College Publishing team was a joy to work with. We appreciated the professionalism and high-quality yet pleasant work style that was evinced by all members of the team. Thanks to John Szilagyi, the acquisitions editor, for believing in our project and providing the grant that enabled us to complete it. Thanks to Jamie Gleich Bryant for her wonderful and thoughtful editorial support. As development editor, she kept us on task and organized (even sticking with us after the birth of her first child and life as a freelancer). Jamie was very adept at working with the multitude of personalities and working styles of the contributors to this book. Thanks to Tamborah Moore of the production division and the team at The Left Coast Group for ensuring the smooth production of the book under a tight deadline. Thanks to the School of Labor and Industrial Relations of Michigan State University for providing administrative support of this book. Special thanks goes to Kay Beach, D. Lydia Reed, Alison Grieve, and Klerissa Smith for their administrative work on this project.

Dedication

Ellen Ernst Kossek would like to dedicate this book to her family. This includes her husband, Sandy Kossek, and children Dylan, Haley, Sarah, and Andrew; inspiring siblings Dan and Ruth Ernst; and her mother and father, Dan and Ann Ernst. The book is also dedicated to the memory of her deceased grandparents: Sigmund and Elinor Robinson, and Dan and Elaine Ernst.

    Richard N. Block dedicates this book to his wife, Marcia Horan, and his daughters, Talia Horan-Block and Jessica Horan-Block; his parents, Henry and Ferne Block; and his sister, Diane Covertone. The book is also dedicated to the memory of his brother Gerald Block, and Marcia's mother, Harriet Horan.

OVERARCHING EMPLOYER PRINCIPLES FOR MANAGING HUMAN RESOURCES

MANAGING HUMAN RESOURCES
IN THE 21st CENTURY

From Core Concepts to Strategic Choice

MODULE 1

New Employment Relations

Challenges and Basic Assumptions

Ellen Ernst Kossek
MICHIGAN STATE UNIVERSITY

Richard N. Block
MICHIGAN STATE UNIVERSITY

Managing Human Resources in the 21st Century: From Core Concepts to Strategic Choice,
by Kossek and Block

Publisher: Dave Shaut
Executive Editor: John Szilagyi
Developmental Editor: Bryant Editorial Development
Marketing Manager: Joseph A. Sabatino
Production Editor: Tamborah E. Moore
Manufacturing Coordinator: Dana Began Schwartz
Cover Design: Tin Box Studio
Cover Photographs: Copyright Shoji Sato/Photonica
Production House: The Left Coast Group, Inc.
Printer: West Group

Printed in the United States of America
1 2 3 4 5 02 01 00 99

For more information contact South-Western College Publishing, 5101 Madison Road, Cincinnati, Ohio, 45227 or find us on the Internet at *http://www.swcollege.com*
For permission to use material from this text or product, contact us by
- telephone: 1-800-730-2214
- fax: 1-800-730-2215
- web: *http://www.thomsonrights.com*

ISBN: 0–324–01800–2

This book is printed on acid-free paper.

Contents

MODULE OVERVIEW 1.4
Pressure on Human Resources to Demonstrate Value Added 1.4
Variation in Employment Strategies 1.5

OBJECTIVES 1.6

A FRAMEWORK FOR UNDERSTANDING HUMAN RESOURCE
MANAGEMENT DECISION MAKING AND CAPABILITIES:
STRATEGIC ROLES AND CHOICES 1.6
HR Roles: The Four "Ts" 1.8
Roles Delivered by Many Sources and Reflected in All Policy Domains 1.9
Managerial Discretion in HR Decision Making 1.10
Using the Framework as a Managerial Diagnostic Tool 1.11

CORE CONCEPTS IN NEW EMPLOYMENT RELATIONS 1.13
Historical Roots of Organizational Approaches to Managing
Employment Relationship 1.14
Current Variation in Employment Relations 1.16
Workforce Commitment Employment Model 1.17
Labor Transactional Employment Model 1.20
Mixed Approach: Core-Noncore Workforce Model 1.22
Summary of Contrasting Approaches to Employment 1.23

STRATEGIC ISSUES IN NEW EMPLOYMENT RELATIONS 1.24
Determining a Firm's Place on the Transactional Continuum 1.24
Alignment Between Business and Human Resource Strategy 1.25

APPLICATION 1.25
Chainsaw Al Dunlap at Scott Paper 1.25
High Commitment at Starbucks Coffee 1.26

IN CONCLUSION 1.27
Debrief 1.27
Suggested Readings 1.27
Relevant Web Sites 1.28
Critical Thinking Questions 1.28
Expanded Exercise 1.28
Exercise 1.30
References 1.31

INDEX 1.34

MODULE OVERVIEW

> We invested in our people in competitive wages, benefits, activities, working conditions, and other rewards and recognize that our strategy of empowering people required a corresponding system of rewards for great business results. We expect that our employees will give us their thoughts, ideas, and improvement suggestions, in addition to their time and their physical effort. To help them do this, we empower our employees.[1]

> (It is) readily apparent that the old employment contract is no longer sustainable: the past decade . . . downsizing and reengineering efforts mark a systematic and permanent change in the relationships between corporations and employees.[2]

> America has entered the age of contingent or temporary worker, of the consultant and subcontractor, of the just-in-time work force—fluid, flexible, disposable. This is the future. You are on your own. For good (sometimes) and ill (often), the workers of the future will constantly have to sell their skills, invest new relationships with employers who must themselves change and adapt constantly in order to survive in a ruthless global market.[3]

As the foregoing quotes suggest, firms use a range of approaches to manage human resources in organizations today. This module is designed to make managers aware of these different approaches. A major premise is that there has been a dramatic increase in options for managing employment. With increasing globalization since the mid-1980s, corporations—especially those in industrialized countries—have faced increased competition. Senior management looked inward at all business functions in a continuing quest to find ways to become more efficient in the new marketplace. Human resource management (HRM) did not escape this scrutiny. The overall purpose of the HRM function is to enable management to enhance the individual and collective contribution of employees to the success of the enterprise.[4] Human resource strategy is an organization's fundamental approach to managing employees in a way that ensures achievement of the firm's business objectives in the marketplace. The separate activities such as selection, recruitment, compensation and benefits, performance appraisal, training, collective bargaining, and others that comprise the human resource function are integrated to provide a unified pattern to the employment relationship and are directly related to environmental and business conditions.[5] The question now is, what can management do to improve the efficiency of the human resource function?

Pressure on Human Resources to Demonstrate Value Added

Reorganization of the Delivery of HR Services. Management started by placing increased pressures on HR to visibly contribute more value to business performance and demonstrate its functional efficiency. In many firms, the way human resource services were delivered began to be reorganized to make the added value of HR activities more visible. For example, some of the tasks associated with the delivery of human resource activities, such as greater involvement in selection and interviewing, were transferred to line management. Other HR tasks such as pension and benefit administration were outsourced to external suppliers. By updating their own personnel records and initiating benefits service approvals when needed, even employees started to perform tasks that had formerly been part of the HR department. Actions such as these helped to streamline human resource departments and forced them to better demonstrate their contribution to the bottom line as a business partner of management. However, reorganizing how HR services were delivered, while valuable, resulted in mainly cosmetic changes to HR, which historically had begun as an administrative record-keeping function. In light of increasing competitive pressures, major transformation of the HR mission and roles were needed.

Variation in Employment Strategies

Management began to explore far broader options related to overall human resource strategy and the transformation of the employment relationship. The result of these explorations was the development of a range of management strategies toward employment. For many years, the dominant model of employment at major U.S. employers was what might be called a *long-term labor purchase* model. Under this model, firms would employ workers, implicitly, for as long as they performed well and the company was financially able to maintain the employment relationship. But when profits declined, labor costs would be the first to be cut via layoffs.

Besides ad hoc downsizing, firms began to consider other employment models to address long-term competitiveness issues. Some companies shifted to a *workforce commitment* model that was associated with explicit employer commitment to employees often providing job security for regular employees on the principle that this would encourage greater commitment from workers with enhanced productivity. The *commitment* approach takes a long-term perspective on employment relations and focuses on developing social and intellectual capital within the boundaries of the firm.

Other firms adopted an internal labor minimization strategy, moving toward a *labor transactional* model. This model seeks to minimize wage and benefit costs and transactions, and employment levels within organizational boundaries. Some scholars have referred to this strategy as the *externalization* of employment.[6] Under the transactional approach, the employer transacts or buys only the employee services it currently needs from the marketplace at the best cost available.

Still other employers follow a *mixed model* approach with different employment models for *core and noncore* workers. Under a mixed model, workers who support the core businesses or have skills that are viewed as supportive of the core competencies of the firm (the unique attributes that make the company special in competing in the marketplace) may be employed under policies supporting the commitment approach. Yet this same employer may also employ workers who are viewed as noncore, or who have been hired under temporary status or under different negotiated hiring rules in a multi-tier wage setting. These noncore workers have employment policies more reflective of the transactional approach. They may have few, if any, of the benefits enjoyed by core workforce employees.[7]

This module is intended to encourage the reader to consider the different types of employment relationships, the sources of variation in the employer-employee relationship, and factors associated with the adoption and usage of different types of human resource practices. For present purposes, major distinctions can be made between the *commitment,* the *transactional,* and the *mixed* or *core-noncore* approaches to employment introduced above. In this module you are introduced to some of the pros and cons of contrasting strategies for managing human resources as a basis of this book.

The module includes several case study applications illustrating the different human resource policies and practices that are associated with a commitment or a transactional contingent approach to the employer-employee relationship. Also provided is an overview of the historical development of human resources and labor relations in employing organizations. You are encouraged to reflect on your own experience in relation to the management of human resources in employing organizations. The assignments, readings, and in-class materials are designed to develop your analytical skills and fluency in discussing and evaluating current trends in managing employment relations. The module ends with an original case study at Kensi Manufacturing and exercises to illustrate how human resource decision making might be conducted in a high-commitment setting.

Objectives

In this module, we will examine new employment relations that enable the reader:

- To understand that there are different approaches to managing human resources in organizations and that these may vary over time

- To identify the causes of variation, such as differing organizational business and strategic objectives, market pressures, and management views regarding the importance of having highly committed employees

- To become aware of how the nature of the psychological contract varies for employee groups as an organization moves from a transactional to a commitment approach to employment, or alternatively, from a commitment to a transactional approach

- To develop analytical skills in identifying emerging employment relations trends and factors influencing their adoption that students become aware of by either (1) reflecting on their past organizational experience, (2) reading the business press, or (3) assessing cases

A Framework for Understanding Human Resource Management Decision Making and Capabilities: Strategic Roles and Choices

Figure 1.1 introduces the framework and model that will be used to help the student understand human resource management decisions and strategies. Its purpose is to point out how the environmental context and strategy of an organization influence how it makes human resource decisions and designs employment practices and strategies while balancing multiple roles and constraints. Each module will use this framework as a lens to understanding the content. The purpose of this summary is to expose the reader to the unifying framework that will be used in the volume. Module 2 on Human Resource Strategy contains more in-depth discussion of the relationship between human resource strategy and the environmental context. Module 3 further explains human resource roles and choices.

On the outside of the model is the environmental context in which the firm operates. The *environmental context* includes all the trends and environmental forces that shape business decisions. These include such factors as market conditions, technology, the diversity of the labor force, globalization, and government regulations that are imposed on the firm from outside. For example, consider the deregulation of the United States telecommunications industry in the early 1980s. Prior to deregulation, all long-distance services were provided by one carrier, American Telephone &Telegraph (AT&T), and prices were regulated by the government. Price adjustments and rates of return on investment were stable and predictable. Following deregulation, multiple players entered the long-distance market. The market was now characterized by intense price competition and many new entrants. Add to this such fast-changing technology as fiber optics and the Internet. Consider, even briefly, how different management of human resource practices would be in a market of stable, predictable prices and no new entrants compared with a market characterized by severe price competition and multiple entrants exerting constant competitive pressures. As a strategic business partner with line management, the human resource leader must understand how changes in the environment affect the firm.

Between the end of World War II and the early 1980s, human resource and labor relations professionals in firms were primarily interested in such employment-specific environmental factors as the strength of unionization, government policies regulating

FIGURE 1.1 *A Frame for Understanding Human Resource Strategy:*
Context, Roles, and Constraints

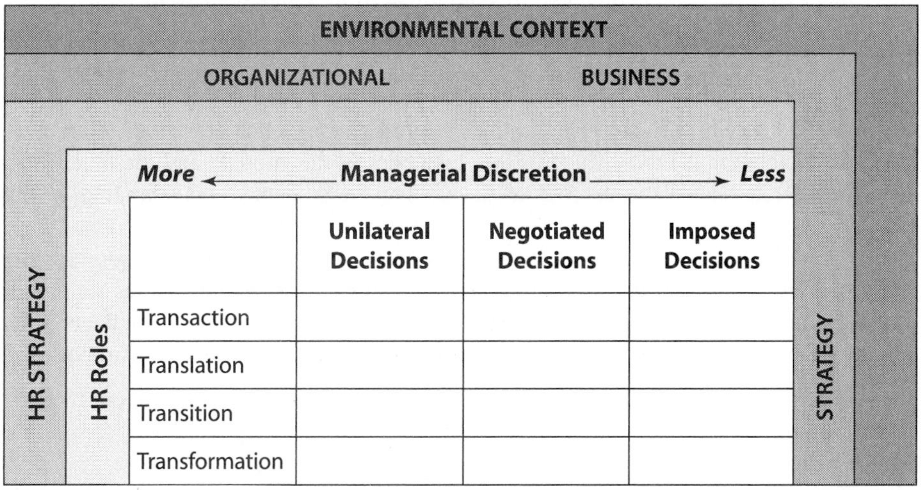

	ENVIRONMENTAL CONTEXT			
	ORGANIZATIONAL		BUSINESS	
	More ←——— Managerial Discretion ———→ **Less**			
		Unilateral Decisions	**Negotiated Decisions**	**Imposed Decisions**
Transaction				
Translation				
Transition				
Transformation				

(Left axis: HR STRATEGY / HR Roles; Right axis: STRATEGY)

© 2000 by Ellen Kossek and Richard Block. Thanks to Brian Pentland, Karen Markel, and John Beck for helpful comments and discussions that enhanced the model.

employment relations, or the tightness of labor markets due to economic growth increasing the demand for labor.[8] Beginning in the 1980s, however, human resource and labor relations professionals have been expected to pay equal attention to product market competitiveness and to the increased power and activism of shareholders and financial institutions. Indeed, the human resource function now must strive toward adding strategic value to the firm. It is increasingly becoming an agent of and advisor to management rather than a mere provider of staff support to management. Recently, HR has served as management agent by designing and implementing employment practices that decreased job security, increased outsourcing of work and layoffs, and improved quality and productivity.[9]

MODULE
1

A level below the environmental context is the organizational and business strategy. This represents the firm's business response to the environment. In 1982, at the trough of a deep recession in the steel industry, U.S. Steel spent over $6 billion to purchase the Marathon Oil Company. Imagine yourself as a steelworker buffeted by an industry hit by a downturn in the demand for steel and increased foreign competition (reflecting changes in the organizational context, as discussed above). Now, in the midst of these hard times, your company finds $6 billion to buy an oil company, seemingly an unrelated business. This might suggest to you a reduced level of commitment to the line of business in which you work. What would it say about your future job security in the steel industry?

Alternatively, picture yourself as a Ford Motor Company employee in 1983. The company lost over $1 billion the previous year, but it is investing in new vehicle models and has made a commitment to stay in the automotive business. What does this imply about your future job security in this industry?

These examples represent different organizational business strategic responses to a newly competitive environment. U.S. Steel decided that it could best serve its shareholders by diversifying its assets into the petroleum industry, thereby reducing its stake in its (former) core business. Ford decided that it could best serve its shareholders by investing in its core business.

Differences in business strategy will be associated with differences in human resources strategy, and it is HR strategy that is at the third level of the framework and, to a substantial extent, at the heart of the modules in this book. Strategic human resource management is the linking of all aspects of human resource practices with the strategic goals of the organization. Human resource programs, practices, and systems must be organized and integrated so they continue to fit a company as its strategic and business objectives change. Once the firm has determined the nature of its environment and settled on a business strategy, the HR professional must develop a human resources strategy to complement the business. Whether the HR strategy is developed as part of the business strategy or is conveyed to the HR professionals once developed, there must be a match between the two. Much of the remainder of this module and the other modules in the volume will be devoted to developing the student's understanding of this linkage.

The lowest level in the framework incorporates the roles human resources professionals must play and the discretion they have to play those roles. Roles reflect the functions and activities human resources is expected to deliver. Overall, HR activities are conducted to help add value to the business and support the implementation of business and strategic objectives.

HR Roles: The Four "T's"

The framework shows that there are four major HR roles: transactions, translations, transitions, and transformations. HR roles vary along the focus from a short- to long-term emphasis. They also vary in the degree to which they emphasize processes and people.[10] The transaction and translation roles are largely focused on people and have a short-term view. The transition and transformation roles are oriented more toward improvement or transformation of new processes, whereas organizational processes (and the employees involved in them) are realigned to support customer and market demands, and have a future orientation.

The *transaction* role refers to the routine yet essential subfunctions of human resource management that assures that the day-to-day tasks are carried out. The transaction roles include the traditional personnel or HR administration activities: hiring and firing, making sure employees are paid in a timely and accurate manner, and handling grievances. These day-to-day activities of personnel administration are important ongoing administrative roles, but may not necessarily transform the firm to meet future competitive business pressures. A helpful analogy is to think of personnel transactions as being like a single bank transaction to cash a check. Like cashing a check, it takes a one-time action to cut a payroll check, initiate a title change to promote someone to a new job, or process a payment covered under a benefits plan. Management expectations of the transaction role implicitly come from transaction cost theory from institutional economics.[11] The goal of HR activities associated with the transaction role is to reduce administrative people costs associated with accomplishing work tasks.[12] It is focused on ensuring administrative efficiency, cost-effectiveness, and customer service[13] (in this case, serving employees and line managers as internal customers).

The *translation* role refers to the communication responsibilities associated with listening and responding to employees' and customers' concerns, as well as explaining to and implementing for employees the policies established by higher management. Examples of translation activities might include the communication of any HR policy such as equal employment opportunity laws, business operating objectives, or customer needs to employees. These can also include the cross-cultural translation of activities, such as adapting a new performance appraisal system developed at the U.S. headquarters to fit with the cultural mores of the subsidiary in Egypt.

If employees and management understand each other well and have a common line of sight regarding organizational and individual goals (i.e., employees view the achievement of organizational and personal objectives as in line with one another), operational excellence is likely to occur. For example, one reason Dell Computer is among the most admired companies in 1999, according to *Fortune* magazine, is that the translation of customer needs to employees via middle men is eliminated. Says Dell vice chairman Kevin Rollins: "Our only religion is the direct model." Even Chairman Michael Dell's new book is entitled *Direct from Dell.* Being direct has made Dell a very successful firm, as employees are in constant touch with customers, can respond immediately to problems, and receive ongoing customer feedback. For example, the Internet is Dell's ultimate direct translation tool, accounting for about 20 percent of its business, and it is expected eventually to represent half of its revenues. In 1997, the company started Premier Pages, web sites that let customer-authorized employees research, configure, and price personal computers the customers plan to buy. By allowing translation of customer needs to be directly communicated to employees, Dell cut down processing errors and saves money because fewer purchasing and data entry people are needed.[14]

The *transition* role refers to execution of human resource activities, policies, and practices to make the necessary ongoing changes to support or improve business operational and strategic objectives. Typically, this role focuses on the implementation of new or revised HR practices and substantive and procedural changes in HR policies and practices. For example, starting in 1993, HR strategies to support improved quality processes were introduced at Motoring Services, a small business in Richland, Washington, that is focused on car repairs. These included open-book management, giving employees a greater understanding of the financial position of the firm, encouraging them to continue learning, supporting them in personal development, and increasing employee involvement and participation in decision making. Based on these newly implemented HR policies to support the business, revenues had increased the 1990 revenue by three times to nearly a million dollars by 1997 with a net profit of 15 percent.[15]

Under the *transformation* role, HR serves a leadership change agent role. Here, new HR practices and systems typically accompany new organizational structures, and may also accompany organizational cultural transformation. This occurs when a firm decides to make a fundamental change in the nature of its human resource management practices, work systems based on how jobs are designed and organized, organizational structures, and cultures to support major strategic change. Examples of transformation activities might include the globalization of all policies and practices, instigating a high-commitment work culture with team-based work systems, merging and transforming two organizations involved in a merger and acquisition or an international joint venture, or developing a more collaborative and less militant relationship with a union. As an example of the latter—as will be discussed in Module 6, "Collective Bargaining, Industrial Relations, and Human Resource Systems: Managing in Environments"—Ford, in the early 1980s, determined to make fundamental changes in its relationship with the United Automobile Workers, the union representing its production employees. This relationship changed from highly adversarial to cooperative. This change truly represented a transformation in Ford's human resource management practice. It was also accompanied by strategic and organizational changes such as a major transformation toward a quality culture and greater teamwork, and a greater use of suppliers and just-in-time methods of lean production in the manufacturing of automobiles.

MODULE
1

Roles Delivered by Many Sources and Reflected in All Policy Domains

Delivery of HR Roles.　From time to time, employees, line managers, the HR department, and external vendors or experts from consulting firms are involved in delivery of HR roles. It is a strategic choice for management in determining whether internal or external resources (e.g., an in-house HR department or an external consulting HR firm), or line managers or employees are empowered to deliver these roles. Who delivers the roles may have an impact on their acceptance. Furthermore, the degree to which HR roles are outsourced or mainstreamed into the organization as tasks anyone can do (whether they are trained or have the expertise to do so or not) may also influence the degree of excellence in the delivery of HR roles and the likelihood of whether they are developed as core competencies of the firm. If external vendors, for example, develop more expertise in a firm's HR needs in compensation and benefits than internal HR leaders possess, then the firm risks losing expertise in this area and becomes overly resource dependent on the external consultants. This is not to suggest that the use of external vendors is necessarily bad in itself. It just means that the firm must take care to not outsource an HR capability that is critical intellectual or social capital and a core competency for competing in the marketplace.

Roles Occur in All HR Policy Domains.   In every HR policy domain, such as compensation, selection, training, and development, activities may be conducted reflecting each role. Take employee compensation and benefits, for example. The processing of paychecks and day-to-day salary and benefits administration are examples of HR activities associated with transactional roles. The communication to employees of how business goals and customer marketing objectives are tied to the annual pay plan or increased global competitive pressures due to the Asian economic flu in 1997–1998 reflect the translation role. The initiation of a new flextime program and an on-site company childcare center are new benefits supporting the transitional role. Changing or enhancing HR policy to reflect a new company's strategy aimed to improve the degree to which employees' nonwork roles are integrated with their work roles is a means to continuously enhance on-the-job performance. Instigating group-based variable pay, where a portion of employees' pay is placed at risk for various international workgroups in the firm—especially when the payout is based on the degree to which teams accomplished goals to support organizational transformation to a more team-oriented global culture—reflects transformational roles.

Managerial Discretion in HR Decision Making

While the roles that HR activities can serve are found on the left-hand side of the framework (Figure 1.1), the constraints and choices that employers have in making decisions within each role can be found along the top (labeled managerial discretion). These roles are carried out with a range of management discretion over the determination of human resource strategies and decisions. On occasion, employers have full *unilateral discretion* over human resource matters, and may act as they believe is in the best interest of shareholders, employees, management, or other constituents. In other situations, the implementation of HR issues must be *negotiated* with employees, either formally via legal or union representatives, or informally with each individual worker. In still other cases, constraints are *imposed* from the outside, usually because of laws and legal regulations of governments.

The most obvious example of a range of discretion may be seen when comparing the enactment of HR activities and roles affecting unionized and nonunion groups of employees. In 1998, in the United States, 15.4 percent of all workers were represented by unions in a collective bargaining relationship. If this figure is broken down into private- and public-sector jobs, we find that 10.3 percent of private-sector workers are represented by unions, while 42.5 percent of public-sector workers are represented by a union. The employer is legally obligated to negotiate with a union over terms and conditions of employment germane to the working environment. Even routine transactions that are unilaterally controlled by management in the absence of a union often must be *negotiated* when a union is present to represent the affected workers. For example, suppose that the firm finds it necessary for an employee to work overtime for two hours one day. In a nonunion situation, this transaction may be as simple as asking the desired employee to stay two hours after work. For workers covered by a union, however, there may be established negotiated rules in the collective bargaining agreement for the distribution of overtime. Those rules, rather than unconstrained management choice, will determine who receives the overtime. Sometimes the range of management discretion in HR decision making must be negotiated even in a nonunion situation. For example, if the employee is a highly valued, respected worker (having some market power, as he or she could turnover if mistreated), even in a nonunion setting some negotiation may occur. The employee may implicitly bargain by stating, "If I work late tonight, then I want to be able to take the afternoon off tomorrow."

HR activities reflecting translation and transition roles may also be negotiated when a union is present. For example, the implementation of a new employee suggestion system would likely require negotiation with the union regarding its communication (translation) and design and implementation (transition), particularly if that suggestion system included matters involving employment. Such a system would create an alternative communication system and opportunity for employee voice and governance to the one established through the union.

An example of an *imposed* decision in the transaction role may be seen when an employee requests a leave for pregnancy purposes. The length of the leave is not within the discretion of management. It is 12 weeks, and it is imposed by the Family and Medical Leave Act for employers with 50 or more employees.

Using the Framework as a Managerial Diagnostic Tool

Figure 1.2 on page 1.12 presents examples of common types of HR decisions as they would be explained by the model. The model provides a useful diagnostic framework for managers to assess the level of discretion and role associated with common HR decisions. An example is provided in each inner box for the reader, and almost any HR decision can be analyzed using the framework. Managers need to understand their level of discretion and the HR role involved in any HR decision to effectively develop policy and strategy.

The "Unilateral Decisions" Column as It Applies to HR Roles.
The column under unilateral decisions depicts firm decisions under each of the HR roles. An example of a unilateral decision in the *transaction* role is the hiring of an entry level employee. Even in a unionized firm, management has the right to hire whomever it wishes. An example of a unilateral decision in the *translation* role is explaining how benefits administration will operate under a newly outsourced system. Many firms have recently chosen to outsource benefits to expert consulting firms in order to reduce costs and obtain expertise. This normally requires communication about the rationale for the change and the operation of the new system, since this decision will likely affect how employees understand and receive benefits.

An example of a unilateral decision in the HR *transition* role is changing a retirement benefit plan from defined benefit to defined contribution. Under defined benefit plans, employees are paid a fixed benefit at the time they retire, with the firm remaining responsible for managing the employee portfolio. Under a defined contribution plan, a specified amount is contributed each month with the employee responsible for managing the portfolio. This involves a fundamental shift in retirement philosophy, moving responsibility from the firm to the employee. The retirement benefits policy is changed to follow a firm's cost reduction business strategy.

Finally, an example of unilateral decision making in the HR *transformation* role occurs before and during a merger or acquisition. Firm management almost always has the unilateral discretion to purchase a business (subject to anti-trust requirements). Such a change often requires cultural and systems transformation, as two companies with different cultures and different systems come together.

FIGURE 1.2 *Application of Decision-Making Framework to Common HR Decisions*

ENVIRONMENTAL CONTEXT

ORGANIZATIONAL BUSINESS

HR STRATEGY — HR Roles — STRATEGY

More ← **Managerial Discretion** → *Less*

	Unilateral Decisions	**Negotiated Decisions**	**Imposed Decisions**
Transaction	Hiring Decision Entry Level	Selection of Arbitrator	Payment per Fair Labor Standards Act Minimum Wage and Overtime
Translation	Explain Benefits Outsourcing	Summarizing Collective Bargaining Agreement	Explanation of Fair Labor Standards Act to Management and Employees
Transition	Retirement Benefits Change	Negotiating Retirement Plan	Adjustment of Sick Leave Policy to Family Medical Leave Act
Transformation	Merger and Acquisition	Change Labor Relations Strategy	Culture Change with Equal Employment Opportunity Laws, mid-1960s

MODULE 1

 Thanks to Brian Pentland, Karen Markel, and John Beck for helpful comments and discussions that enhanced the model.

The "Negotiated Decisions" Column as It Applies to HR Roles. Turning to the column under negotiated decisions, an example of this type of decision in the *transaction* role is the selection of an arbitrator according to a collective bargaining agreement. Typically, the agreement specifies a process that the parties must follow: submission of the case to an agency, receipt of a list with an odd number of names, selection from the names (often by alternate striking), and notification of the agency, with a forthcoming appointment. The process for managing the transaction of selecting an arbitrator has been negotiated. An example of a negotiated decision in the *translation* role is the summarization of a new collective bargaining agreement to employees and management. Once negotiations are completed, the negotiators are obliged to explain the changes to their constituents. Otherwise the new agreement cannot be effectively implemented by workers and management.

Regarding a negotiated decision in the *transition* role, an example is negotiation of a new retirement plan. In the absence of a union, a firm can simply impose the changed plan, albeit usually with an explanation. In a unionized firm, firm management must convince the union that it will be better off with one plan rather than the other. An example of a negotiated decision in the *transformation* role occurs when the firm's labor relations strategy changes from adversarial to cooperative. Such a decision represents a fundamental cultural change in the firm's philosophy toward the union representing its employees, and is often associated with concessions to prove the firm's good faith.

The "Imposed Decisions" Column as It Applies to HR Roles.   Turning now to the column labeled imposed decision, an example of this type of decision in the *transaction* role is paying employees in accordance with minimum wage and overtime requirements as delineated in the Fair Labor Standards Act. Although all employees are subject to the minimum wage requirements, it is HR's role to ensure management establishes a pay policy that correctly denotes which classifications are exempt from overtime requirements, and which classifications must receive overtime for all hours worked in a week in excess of forty. An example of an imposed decision in the *translation* role is explaining Fair Labor Standards Act requirements (or the requirements of any statute) to employees and managers, to avoid penalties if supervisors inadvertently violate the law.

An example of an imposed decision in the *transition* role occurs when a sick leave policy is adjusted for consistency with the Family Medical Leave Act (FMLA). The firm must decide the extent to which it will dovetail its sick leave policies with the FMLA requirements, supervisors must make arrangements to replace employees during longer absences, and HR must advise management on how to assure that workers receive comparable employment upon return.

Though examples of an imposed decision in the *transformation* role are rare, an excellent illustration occurred in the mid-1960s and thereafter, when the enactment of Equal Employment Opportunity legislation imposed new labor requirements. Firms were required to undergo major cultural change due to new legal prohibitions on treating some employees as "second class" citizens in the workplace. Even today, it is the basis for managing cultural diversity in employment.

CORE CONCEPTS IN NEW EMPLOYMENT RELATIONS

In the sections that follow, we will discuss each of the following six core concepts:

MODULE
1

- Historical roots of personnel department's role in U.S. employment policies

- Variations in employment relations

- Workforce commitment employment model

- Labor transactional employment model

- Mixed approach: core-noncore workforce model

- Pros and cons of contrasting approaches

Few would argue with the contention that fundamental changes have occurred in employment relations practices over the past several decades, particularly among (but not limited to) U.S. multinationals. As former U.S. Secretary of Labor Robert Reich recently observed, "The overarching trend in employment relations is to make everything contingent," from jobs to benefits to organizational relationships.[16] Growing competitive pressures have had a major influence on the employment relationship between companies and their people. Rapid technological innovation, particularly in computer-based technology, the rise of customer-driven markets, and increasing deregulation are dictating new skills for a company to be successful.[17] Though products can be copied and training and technology can be duplicated, no one can match having highly charged, motivated people who care. Consequently, having inspired employees who possess valuable knowledge and skills are main ingredients for a company to effectively compete. How did human resource management systems and employment approaches evolve to where they are today? It is helpful to briefly consider the historical roots of human resources and labor relations in the United States. Over time, three main external environmental pressures have a critical influence on management strategy for the personnel and labor relations departments in organizations: (1) market pressures or the economy; (2) unions, and (3) government.[18]

Historical Roots of Organizational Approaches to Managing Employment Relationship

Pre-Personnel Departments: Little Variation with Foreman Ruling Employment Relations.   As the factory system of manufacturing and the Industrial Revolution grew in the United States from 1880 to about 1915, regardless of industry, the foreman historically was in control of employment matters. According to historian Sanford Jacoby, whether in the machine shop, the steel or textile mill, or on the assembly line, the foreman was given free rein by owners in hiring, pay, job assignments, and supervision. Because of the latitude they were given in determining wage rates and hiring, the foremen were expected to hold down labor costs at the same time they were to keep worker effort up.[19] The methods they used were known as the "drive system," where workers were driven to be productive. This system was based on the fear of unemployment as a way to ensure obedience. In fact, a basic management assumption of the drive system was that if workers perceived they had job security, motivation would be reduced and they would not work as hard.[20]

Birth of Personnel Departments: Market Pressures of World War I.   Historically, personnel departments began to first appear in the United States after 1910 largely due to the market pressures of World War I for wartime production.[21] Another reason for their appearance was the increased availability of human engineering and other techniques growing out of Frederick Taylor's notions of scientific management determining the optimal way for jobs to be performed regardless of the individual in them. According to Sanford Jacoby, the *creation of personnel departments signaled that employment policy would now be treated as an end in itself rather than a means to the production divisions' ends.*[22] Many early personnel managers thought of themselves as neutral professionals whose job was to reconcile opposing industrial interests between labor and management and make employment practices more scientific and humane. A main task of personnel managers was to stabilize labor relations, relieve labor shortages, and improve productivity—all at the same time![23] This often meant keeping line managers such as production foremen in check, a historically combative relationship that may explain how some line managers interact with human resources managers even today.

Personnel Departments Rebirth: Union Avoidance Tools.   Due to the great economic depression after the stock market crash of 1929, which removed many of the economic pressures that helped personnel departments evolve, many of the newly formed personnel departments were downgraded in size and responsibility and sometimes even abolished. Some of the human relations advances that had occurred in some firms prior to the crash—such as the provision of stock ownership, pensions, and other employee benefits of welfare capitalism—became undone.[24] Then in 1933, as part of President Franklin D. Roosevelt's New Deal of economic recovery that aimed to increase worker purchasing power and reduce unemployment, the National Industrial Recovery Act was passed. In 1935, the passage of the National Labor Relations Act, also known as the Wagner Act, gave employees the right to organize and bargain collectively through representatives of their own choosing and without the interference, restraint, or coercion of employers. At the time, over half of major U.S. firms still allowed the foremen to be the sole arbiters of dismissal, which could result in arbitrary decisions. Most firms still lacked systematic rules for managing layoffs or dismissals, rules on issues such as severance pay and how to deal with seniority. Foremen also were likely to discriminate against older workers and those favoring union activity. In the thirties, a personnel program was often viewed as a means to prevent unionization in nonunion firms. And even in unionized firms, the personnel department was seen as a vehicle for weakening or keeping the union under control. If a union was voted in or made gains, it was usually viewed by management as a result of ineffective personnel administration programs.[25] Despite this, personnel departments that were likely to be more sympathetic to the human relations concerns of the workforce than the firm owners and senior management were often helpful in getting reforms implemented that unions and social employment reformers wanted.

From 1935–1960, as union membership grew, industrial relations and the labor relations subgroups rose to prominence within personnel and industrial relations departments in major U.S. companies.[26] In companies that had both personnel and labor relations departments, the labor relations staff and its focus on collective bargaining issues often was much more powerful than its personnel cousins. The risk of labor instability hindering or shutting down firm operations and the constant pressure for pay and benefits increases made management elevate labor relations issues to strategic importance.

Historian Jacoby notes that as the unionized sector grew in the United States, a new employment doctrine was introduced. The doctrine was that once management hired an employee who "makes good it must continue to give employment" or preference for employment to that individual.[27] Over the last half of the twentieth century, the effects of unions on employment relations have been that wages, benefits, work rules, and promotion and job security structure are more clearly known to applicants. Unions have also fostered a preference for the use of internal labor markets for promotion, and seniority is a positive factor in managing layoffs. Within an industry, employees in unionized firms usually get about 15 percent higher wages.

Starting in the 1950s, many post-World War II Americans conceived of employment as a long-term, stable relationship with a single or a few employers, and reaped many personal and societal benefits from this model of employment. These included regular economic livelihood, psychological advantages such as personal security and positive individual self worth, and access to employer-supported benefits, including healthcare, pensions, paid vacations, and disability insurance.[28]

MODULE
1

1960–1980: Government Regulations Increased Prominence of Human Resource Policy.

From 1960–1980, as labor relations departments sought to stabilize collective bargaining, personnel programs once again grew in prominence largely due to the dramatic increase in government regulations during this period.[29] During this time, for example, Title VII of the Civil Rights Act of 1964 was passed, as well as regulations governing health and safety, pensions, and labor standards, with increased employer penalties for noncompliance. The growth in personnel's power was also due to the growth in workers such as managers, professionals, and technical staff who were often not covered by collective bargaining agreements.[30] Union membership in the United States had fallen from a peak of 33 percent of the nonfarm labor force in the mid-1950s to about 24 percent by the late 1970s.[31]

From World War II to the mid-1980s, the dominant model of employment at major U.S. employers was the long-term labor purchase model discussed earlier in this module. One of the largest nonunion companies historically renowned for offering this type of employment relationship was IBM. Starting in the 1950s, IBM would hire bright young employees out of school and invest considerable resources in training and developing them over the course of their careers. This model worked well and was not questioned as long as the employer was profitable. (And for many years, IBM consistently was one of the most profitable companies in the world.) However, in the mid-1980s, when personal computers started to displace mainframes, even IBM began to conduct layoffs. Over the next decade, it downsized nearly half of its workforce from a high of 405,500 to 225,000 by the mid-1990s.[32] Similarly, many major companies around the globe began to trim workforce levels.

Mid-1980s Through the New Millennium: Global Product Market Pressures Paramount.   Now at the end of the twentieth century, as we approach the new millennium, there is great variation in organizational approaches to managing employer-employee relations. This variation is largely due to the current mix of union, government, and economic pressures. With increasing globalization since the mid-1970s, corporations—especially those in industrialized countries—have faced increased competition. These global market pressures have placed tremendous demands on human resources to improve productivity and at least hold labor costs constant. Regarding government pressures, the deregulation of industries such as telecommunications and natural gas, for example, helped spawn great economic growth and demand for new employees. As a result of these competitive pressures, the employment model based on a long term employee-employer relationship began to erode.

To a large extent, union power has waned in the United States, though there have been some major strikes that received significant attention in the media in the late 1990s. Highly publicized work stoppages included the United Parcel Workers (UPS) strike over part-time work and pension plan funding, and the 1998 Northwest pilots' strike. Currently, as noted previously, only 15.4 percent of the U.S. workforce is unionized. Yet the costs of unstable labor relations systems have increased due to today's more competitive economic environment. As price competition increases in the global product markets, and unions have been unable to organize them, union and firms are regularly challenged by the lower labor cost of developing countries.[33] It has become more and more difficult for employers to pass on to customers the cost increases (e.g., regular pay raises and benefits increases, and no layoffs during slack times) associated with a more stable labor relations system. Yet certainly the effects of the threat of unionization on the waxing and waning of the power and influence of the human resources department are important to consider when assessing its current role in employing organizations. Further, in many countries around the world, the percentage of workers unionized is much higher than in the United States.

Current Variation in Employment Relations

Consider the following recent headlines and article titles from recent newspaper and journal clippings, which provide insight into the current state of employer and employee relations:

"Oil Rigs Hanging onto Workers"

—New York Times, Feb. 16, 1999, p. C2.

"At Whirlpool, 4,700 Workers to Lose Jobs"

—New York Times, Sept. 19, 1997.

"Nerds in Gilded Cubicles: In Silicon Valley, Free Diet Coke Is Out, Gourmet Meals and Private Gyms Are In"

—New York Times, Feb. 4, 1999, p. D1.

"Angered by H.M.O.'s Treatment: More Doctors Are Joining Unions"

—New York Times, Feb. 4, 1999, p. A1.

"Bank of Montreal Invests in Its Workers"

—Workforce, Dec. 4. 1997, pp. 30–38.

"Shin Nippon Steel Lays Off Thousands of Employees"

—Nihon Keizai Shimbun, Oct. 29, 1996, p. 2.

"Pluralism Under Golden Arches: From Abroad, McDonald's Finds Value in Local Control"

—*New York Times,* Feb., 12, 1999, p. C1.

"Minnesota's Proposed Tenure Changes Lead to Union Drive"

—*New York Times,* Sept. 22, 1996.

"How Starbuck's Impassions Workers to Drive Growth"

—Workforce, August 1998, pp. 60–64.

As these examples from industry illustrate, there are considerable differences in how various firms view employees as critical components of business growth. In this book, you will read about the many different practices companies use in all aspects of employment, including how people are recruited and selected, trained and appraised, and paid and promoted. We argue in this chapter that employment relations strategies generally fall along three main types: the workforce commitment model, the labor transactional model, and the mixed core-noncore approach. These alternative approaches to the employment exchange relationship have varying business and psychological implications for not only how employees, workgroups, and organizations behave, but also how they think and feel. In regard to the latter, a psychological contract is the unwritten expectations that the employer has of the employee—such as that the worker will work hard in return for wages—and that the employee has of the employer—such as she or he will not be fired arbitrarily or mistreated.

Many observers of United States and global employment relations believe that fundamental changes have occurred in the employer-employee relationship over the past several decades, particularly among (but not limited to) U. S. multinationals. In fact, the popular press makes it seem that lifetime employment in exchange for hard work and loyalty does not exist anymore. The following summaries of recent employer actions appearing in the business press illustrate the transformation in employment relations that is occurring. While it is true that many firms have shifted toward greater contingency in the employment relationship, the excerpts below and the headlines noted above show that great variation exists in managing the employment relationship. These variations range from the transactional approach to the commitment approach to employment. A paradox facing many employers seeking to compete in increasingly competitive labor markets is the demand for flexibility in the employment and layoff of employees, versus the flexibility and benefits accruing from having highly committed employees who are willing to do whatever tasks the employer needs.

Workforce Commitment Employment Model

Some companies today have shifted to a model that is associated with explicit commitment to employees, on the principle that this would encourage greater commitment from workers with enhanced productivity. The *employee commitment* approach takes a long-term perspective on employment relations and focuses on developing social and intellectual capital within the boundaries of the firm. It focuses on developing and investing in social and human capital within the boundaries of the firm in a manner that is difficult for competitors to imitate over time. In doing so, it treats its human resource assets as a core competency, a unique organizational capability that differentiates the firm from other competitors in the marketplace.

Many employees who desire a long-term employment relationship are likely to view a firm adopting the commitment approach as an "employer of choice." Employers of choice generally treat employees well by training them, offering opportunities for personal development, and striving to avoid using layoffs as a way to manage labor costs unless absolutely necessary. Examples of human resource practices supporting a commitment approach include but are not limited to job security, incentives for performance, regular training and investment in employee skills, measurement of managers' skill in developing and motivating workers, information sharing of detailed performance and financial information with employees, sincere caring about employees as "whole people"—ensuring their well-being both on and off the job, a culture that minimizes status differences between workers and managers, flexible job assignments, and job design using teams. In essence, high-commitment human resource practices have a real impact (not just on paper) on the development of employees' job knowledge, well being, and business literacy, and the sharing of information, decision-making power, and reward related to firm performance.

This model of employment relationship is "organization-focused, which has the advantage of greater employee flexibility in assignment."[34] Employers are willing to offer employment security and training in return for employee commitment and flexibility in terms of accepting different tasks and working at different geographic locations. Employees in these firms, which tend to have fewer hierarchical levels, are "empowered."[35] In order to ensure that the employees exercise their autonomy in the employer's interests, employers try to give job security to the workers in return for high employee commitment to the firm. Employees are willing to forgo short-term advantages in return for long-term employment security.[36] These advantages might include being willing to learn a variety of general tasks that are specific to the employer but may not be highly transferable in the external market; and being willing to work overtime.

Stanford Business School professor Jeff Pfeffer[37] gives a cogent rationale for following the commitment approach as a best practice. He argues that high-commitment work practices result in employees working harder because of the increased involvement that comes from having more say over their work. Also, administrative overhead costs are reduced because fewer managers are needed as more responsibility is placed in the hands of workers and less energy needs to be allocated to adversarial labor-management relations. Further, people are more motivated to work smarter and engage in skill building that is focused on enhancing organizational performance. Pfeffer clearly delineates how common labor-cost minimization practices such as downsizing, outsourcing, and heavy use of temporary employees may ultimately undermine competitiveness. Across the board, constant layoffs of employees can undermine their trust in their employer—an essential ingredient for innovation and productivity gains. Traditional outsourcing of work pitting one supplier against another in a bidding war, while driving down short-term costs, can create longer-term problems with quality and reliability. Pfeffer believes that a widespread use of temporary employees as a thinly disguised way to replace regular workers with lower-paid temps also undermines trust, innovation, and quality over the long haul.[38]

Indeed, in one study of 702 large firms in many different industries, being one standard deviation better on an index of high-commitment human resource management practices resulted in an increase in shareholder wealth of $41,000 per employee.[39] Another study of the productivity effects of high-commitment employment practices in the steel industry showed that firms using a set of these innovative practices (e.g., employment security, teams, incentives, training) achieved substantially higher productivity than firms following the labor minimization approach.[40] Still another study in the automobile industry by John-Paul MacDuffie of the Wharton School showed that motor vehicle manufacturing firms that implemented flexible production processes with commitment practices for managing people enjoyed 47 percent better quality and 43 percent better productivity than firms relying on traditional mass-production approaches.[41] The key is not to adopt a few of these innovative practices piecemeal, such as having teams or incentives, and then combining them with a labor minimization approach. Rather, the adoption of innovative human resource practices supporting a commitment approach must be done as a "bundle." Innovative workplace practices fostering workforce commitment can increase performance, primarily through systems of related practices that enhance worker participation, make work design less rigid, and decentralize managerial tasks.[42]

Below are two case studies of firms following a commitment approach. One is on State Farm Insurance; the other is Birkenstock, which followed a workforce commitment approach to employment even in the face of economic adversity. The Starbuck's case in the Application section, and the Denso case in the Exercise section are also examples of the workforce commitment approach. As these studies indicate, the pattern of human resource practices adopted gave a coherent and consistent message to employees that people mattered: management gave the sincere message that employees were seen as key to long-term competitive success.

State Farm Insurance: How Promoting Employee Loyalty Adds Value.   State Farm Insurance demonstrates the "Royalty of Loyalty" for employer profitability.[43] State Farm insures 20 percent of U.S. households and continues to enjoy growing market share. State Farm has a loyalty-based human resource management system that results in agents staying with State Farm at a rate more than twice as long as agents at competitor companies. It also has the lowest sales and distribution costs among all insurers of its type. State Farm enjoys a tenure advantage: its employees are farther down the learning curve than competitors'. Consequently, since it doesn't deal with constant turnover, its agents are on average 40 percent more productive than agents at other companies. It is a well-known fact that new employees are generally less productive than seasoned workers, yet many employers often overlook this. The key to State Farm's agent retention is the company's commission structure, which shares higher revenues with the agents to a greater extent than do competitors. It has highly selective hiring strategies, developed career paths for internal labor markets, training, and the generous compensation system noted above. These practices combine into a human resource system that adds employee capability as an intangible that is difficult for competitors to imitate. Employee loyalty, through the commitment strategy, is a core competency of the firm of the business strategy.

Birkenstock Braces to Fight the Competition.   "As the marketplace changes, we need to be flexible enough to change with it," says the human resources manager at Birkenstock,[44] the two-strap footprint sandal company. Birkenstock is a smaller California-based company with 130 employees that has grown steadily since it was incorporated in 1971. Its mission statement reads: "Birkenstock's purpose is to share with the American people our heartfelt belief that comfortable, healthy footwear is important to everyone because it can contribute to happiness and well-being. Through our distribution of high quality Birkenstock footwear, we strive to creative positive, harmonious relationships with employees, customers, and vendors, emphasizing integrity and honesty in all we do. Within our company, our goal is to provide an atmosphere that stimulates growth and creativity among employees and rewards and encourages their contributions."

The firm is now facing increasing competition. It has been an industry leader for a long time and would like to stay there. Birkenstock competes by expanding its product line, increasing its employees' skills, and hiring workers who fit with the culture. The human resource manager explains, "We're looking for individuals with a nonprofit mentality in a for-profit world." Teamwork plays a major part in the interview process. Depending on the level and skill of the position, an interview team can consist of 3 to 12 people. Teamwork is also involved in the performance review process where supervisors, employees, and peers rate each other. Even management is rated at Birkenstock. Four areas are rated: performance management, delegation/accessibility, coaching/guiding, and team building.

In 1993, the company faced its first layoff. It was the most difficult year the company ever had, as it had too much inventory due to a volatile economy and a series of natural disasters. As the HR manager commented, "When you have a major flood in the Midwest, that stops sandal sales. People can barely afford to buy sandals, much less find the store in the flood." Though the Worker Adjustment and Retraining Notification (WARN) Act requires that employees be given a minimum of 60 days notice before layoffs, six months before the layoffs all employees were told that the firm was struggling to meet it sales goals. Fourteen employees eventually had to be laid off. Birkenstock brought in a temporary unemployment service agency and counseling services to help the affected employees. All received severance packages based on seniority with the firm, and most of them quickly found other jobs. As a way to ensure that the remaining employees kept their jobs, contingent workers were now kept to a minimum, though they had been used more heavily in the 1980s. One of the innovative ways Birkenstock managed to minimize the hiring of contingent workers was through the Help Program. Employees throughout the company volunteered four hours a week in a department other than their own. Employees from advertising, human resources, marketing, and customer service volunteered, for example, in shipping and receiving. The Help Program not only forged camaraderie between departments; it gave the company more flexibility during fluctuating economic conditions. Birkenstock's small size may help support the commitment strategy to employment. The employees like the feeling of smallness in which an individual person matters. It is interesting to note that by the year 2000, 85 percent of the American workforce will work for companies with less than one hundred employees.[45]

Labor Transactional Employment Model

Many firms today have not followed a workforce commitment strategy to manage the employment relationship. Rather, they have adopted an internal labor minimization strategy, moving toward a *labor transactional* model. This model seeks to minimize wage and benefit costs and transactions, and employment levels within organizational boundaries. Some scholars have referred to this strategy as the externalization of employment.[46] Under the transactional approach, the employer transacts or buys only the employee services it currently needs from the marketplace at minimal cost.

The labor transactional approach is chiefly driven by economic product market pressures and the power of shareholders and financial institutions.[47] Its main strategy is to purchase the requisite human resources available from individuals or suppliers in the marketplace at minimal short-term cost, in order to maximize flexibility and minimize ownership of human resource assets within internal organizational boundaries. Simply put, these two models—commitment and transaction—can be viewed as contrasting "make-versus-buy" decision-making approaches to human resource management. Under the commitment approach described above, human resources are viewed as an organizational asset, the return on which will be maximized through investment in it—i.e., the firm "makes" the human resources it needs. In contrast, the labor transactional approach assumes that human resources—employees—are primarily a cost, and seeks to minimize that cost of doing business. The firm "buys" only the employee services it needs, as it needs them ("just in time"), and at minimal cost.[48] In the short run, it is likely that the labor transactional approach will cost less in terms of labor than the commitment approach.

The labor transactional approach is "job-focused" and has the advantage of flexibility in employment when product or service demands fluctuate. This employment relationship seeks to foster a high level of task performance from employees, without requiring their commitment to or concern for the long-term success or survival of the firm.[49] Another benefit to the employer is that job responsibilities are clearly defined. However, a downside may be that a change in the task demands may be inflexible and may require a formal renegotiation of the labor contract.[50]

Layoffs and downsizing have become more frequent in fact because these practices have become normatively valued. When Xerox announced in 1993 that it would lay off 10 percent of its workforce, the fact that it was aggressively ahead of the competitive curve made its stock price go up by 7 percent by the end of the day. Between 1983 and 1993, most Fortune 500 firms had had layoffs, reducing the workforce by 2.5 million, or nearly 18 percent.[51] The following case studies depict firms following the labor transactional approach.

Job Losses in BP-Amoco Merger Could Be Three Times Projected Figure.

When a British Petroleum and Amoco merger initiated in 1998 is completed, it is estimated that up to 20,000 workers could lose their jobs. This figure is a lot higher than the executives of these oil companies claimed when the global merger and acquisition was first announced. Twenty percent of both companies' employees will lose their jobs. Although BP is a British company, most of its job losses will affect American workers. Under the new deal of employment relations, workers do not have the job stability they once had. Because the two firms' workforces are combining and both are global companies, there is a decrease in the jobs needed. The two companies have to combine and reorganize their workers in order to streamline redundant operations and overlapping positions, and become more efficient. With global mergers, jobs are less secure than they once were.[52]

At Whirlpool, 4, 700 Workers to Lose Jobs.

In September 1997, Whirlpool Corporation announced it would dismiss 4,700 or 10 percent of its workforce and take a $350 million charge against earnings as part of a plan to improve profits.[53] The reorganization plan mainly affected its European operations, where Whirlpool has run into strong local competition, made marketing missteps, and faced adverse exchange rates in Italy, its European manufacturing hub. The company also said it planned to seek strategic alliances or other alternatives to get out of money-losing joint ventures that make refrigerators and air conditioners in China; there is a problem of severe overcapacity in China. However, the company will continue to make washing machines in China, where it is the leading brand, as well as microwave ovens, which is third in the market in China.

As the chairman of the Benton Harbor, Michigan-headquartered company explained, "We're addressing the realities of the marketplaces in which we operate." Whirlpool has concluded that high unemployment rates and low levels of consumer confidence point to poor market conditions in Europe for many years to come. The move to cut losses in China and Europe sent Whirlpool's shares soaring up 14.2 percent to a 52-week high on the New York Stock Exchange. The company's moves came just months after Electrolux, its largest European competitor, announced a reorganization that cut up to 12,000 jobs and closed 25 plants. Similarly, Maytag, which invested heavily in Europe, finally gave up in 1995, suffering a $135 million loss on the sale of its operations there.

Cost Minimization at the Extreme: Imperial Food Products.

On September 3, 1991, 25 workers died in a fire at an Imperial Food Products chicken processing plant in Hamilton, North Carolina. The workers, who generally were paid from $5 to $7 per hour, were trapped inside the plant because all but two of the doors, including some fire exits, were locked from the inside. Within a week of the fire, a congressional investigation was launched, as lawmakers criticized the company and government regulation that failed to prevent the tragedy. One congressman observed that the poultry industry "decided they could subsidize their profits with the broken lives, limbs and lacerations and decapitations of their workers."

Another view was expressed by a maintenance worker at the plant who stated, "This is not an unsafe plant. They go by all the standards; they even go out of their way to do better than the standards. They don't lock doors. They don't make people work like dogs." An official of the local chamber of commerce said, "That plant brought a lot of jobs to the county; we were fortunate to get them. A lot of them are unskilled jobs. You don't have to be a rocket scientist. But there's a need for $6-an-hour jobs—for teenagers, retired older people who have to work, migrant workers."

A congressional report, released the following December, found that "officials at the plant . . . were preoccupied with production and profits at the expense of safety." The report concluded that plant managers acted "recklessly" by locking exit doors, which prevented workers from escaping. "Common sense should have suggested to management that locked fire exit doors could be deadly. But Imperial Food ignored common sense and the (government) regulation."

In an editorial published within a few days of the fire, the *St. Louis Post-Dispatch* observed: "Can this be an American factory in the 1990s? The stories of the two Imperial plants sound more like something Upton Sinclair might have written about at the turn of the century. But here we are, just nine years away from the turn of another century, and workers struggling to get by on little more than the minimum wage are still taking their lives into their hands when they go to work each day to feed, clothe and house their families. No reasons can excuse their deaths."[54]

(Upton Sinclair's 1906 novel *The Jungle* created a storm of indignation from the American public against the meatpacking industry for its arrogant disregard of basic health standards and led to government regulation of food and drugs. The novel told the story of a Lithuanian immigrant who worked in the meatpacking plant and was unable to speak English—like many other millions of immigrants—and so made a good target for exploitation by employers.[55])

Mixed Approach: Core-Noncore Workforce Model

Of course, few employers are purists following only a workforce commitment or a labor transactional cost minimization approach. Many follow a *mixed model* approach with different employment models for *core* and *noncore* workers. Under a mixed model, workers who support the core businesses or have skills that are viewed as supportive of the core competencies of the firm—those unique attributes that make the company special in competing in the marketplace—may be employed under policies supporting the commitment approach. Yet this same employer may also employ workers who are viewed as noncore, or who have been hired under temporary status or under different negotiated hiring rules in a two-tier wage setting such as a number of airlines have. The employment policies for these noncore workers are more reflective of the transactional approach. They may have few, if any, of the benefits enjoyed by the core workforce employees.[56] Widely recognized human resource professor Dave Ulrich of the University of Michigan has argued that having different employment systems for core and noncore workers may in fact be a means of gaining competitive advantage. He notes that a key risk of a build strategy, where firms invest heavily in general workforce skill development, is that significant time and money may be expended on training that becomes an end in itself and doesn't create value.[57]

The shift to a core-noncore model first began to appear in the late 1970s when the long-term employment relationship model began to erode. To be globally competitive, employers—first in manufacturing and blue collar jobs, and then in white-collar professional jobs such as financial services, healthcare, and education—downsized and then "rightsized" to reduce labor costs, often replacing employees (from blue collar and clerical workers to managers and professionals) with temps, part-timers, or contract workers. It is now estimated that 25–30 percent of the U. S. labor force are contingent workers—a figure that is growing. Further, the trend is a global one as subcontracting is starting to substantially increase in many other countries such as the United Kingdom and even Japan.[58]

Some scholars argue that when temps are used strictly for short-term purposes, either to perform work of a one-time, nonrepeating type (i.e., noncore) or to help carry firms through a period of peak temporary demands, the mixed model can in fact help preserve the employment security of regular full-time employees.[59] Hewlett-Packard in some ways follows a core-noncore model to ensure employment stability for its regular full-time workers. Japan's largest companies followed this model for many decades following post-World War II. Unfortunately, the dual economy in Japan also resulted in more women and minorities being hired at the smaller firms following temporary practices and rarely able to become full-time regular employees at the most prestigious firms.

The airline industry has been renowned for the use of two tiers of workers. Often, newly hired employees have less generous wages and benefits than more senior workers. In some firms, the second tier eventually is able to "graduate" to the better-paying upper tier, after a certain period of time. In other cases, the two tiers are permanently maintained.

In early February 1999, American Airlines' pilots union staged a major sick-out over the way the company was handling its acquisition of Reno Airlines. Union officials were concerned that American planned to transfer some of its routes to Reno Air, where pilots earn about half of American's pilots' salaries, and that American pilots might lose some work as a result. Currently American pilots earn an average of $140,000 per year. Though American officials denied they planned to do this, stating they intended to integrate Reno Air into the larger network over an 18-month period, many workers noted that the airline decided to make a modest reduction in the number of flights for March. As one pilot commented: "I'm really angry at the company right now. My personal feeling is that I'm going to work to rule and not fly any overtime now." A judge ruled that the union was in contempt for calling the sick-out and ordered it to pay $10 million in fines.[60]

Summary of Contrasting Approaches to Employment

Below are two tables analyzing the contrasting approaches to the employment relationship discussed in this module. Table 1.1 is a summary table. (The mixed model is not shown since it reflects the concomitant use of both commitment and cost-minimization strategies.) Table 1.2 on page 1.24 shows pros and cons of long-term employment relationships.

TABLE 1.1 *Summary of Contrasting Employment Approaches*

	Workforce Commitment Model	**Labor Transaction Model**
Philosophy	Make or invest in developing human assets within the firm	Buy labor available in the market for a specific job
Goal	Maximize commitment, employee empowerment, quality, and assignment flexibility	Maximize employment flexibility via minimization of ownership
Human Capital Development Responsibility	Joint employee-employer investments in developing organizational human and social capital	Employee solely responsible for ensuring employability and development
Outsourcing Stance	Only work considered to be related to noncore competencies outsourced	Extensive outsourcing and fluid work arrangements
Employment Relationship Focus	Long-term, organization focused, employees viewed primarily as "resources for doing business"	Short-term, job focused, employees viewed primarily as "costs of doing business"
Economic Risk for Product Market Fluctuations	Joint Responsibility (employee and employer share)	Employee takes on all risk

TABLE 1.2 *Pros and Cons of Long-Term Employment Relationships*

Pros	Cons
Amortize costs of training	Risk of variable demands for labor
Ease of performance evaluation	Dark side of loyalty
Incentives may work better since both employee and employer assume a long-term relationship	Dysfunctional behavior possible; problem of dead wood
Greater loyalty to employer/coworkers	Familiarity can breed contempt
Greater job assignment flexibility and willingness to work overtime	Difficulty in getting rid of workers when not needed
Enhanced social and intellectual capital over time	Risk of skill gaps

STRATEGIC ISSUES IN NEW EMPLOYMENT RELATIONS

The previous parts of the module have shown that there is great variation in employment relations and human resources systems in the United States. The transactional approach views human resources and employees as costs, and attempts to minimize those costs. This is generally done through direct means, such as reducing wage and benefit costs. The commitment approach, on the other hand, views employees as an asset. Under this approach, the company can generate the highest rate of return on that asset by investing in the employee. The assumption is that the employee will return in productivity more than the company invests.

There are two interrelated strategic questions that will be addressed throughout the book. The first is "What determines where the firm will choose to be located on the transactional-commitment continuum?" The second is "How does a firm assure that there is alignment between its human resources strategy and its business strategy?"

Determining a Firm's Place on the Transactional Continuum

The first question, involving the determinants of human resources strategy, is addressed by a range of factors, which are discussed below.

Management Values.   How one approaches human resources is often a question of the values of management. How does a firm wish to treat its employees? Those firms that believe employees should be treated with fairness and equity, and that favor balanced decision making by employees and management, are likely to be on the commitment end of the continuum. Those firms that focus more on employee costs and high management discretion are likely to be on the transactional end.

Size.   Size can be a key determinant of human resources strategy. In fact, many mergers and acquisitions occur as firms try to seek economies of scale. Yet in terms of payoff, research by Pfeffer of Stanford shows that across industries, the correlation between size and two measures of profitability—return on assets and return on shareholder equity—was only 0.1, meaning size is almost completely unrelated to profitability.[61] It may be that large firms have the resources to utilize a commitment approach to employment, if they so choose.

The Nature of the Firm's Production Process. On occasion, the nature of the firm's production process will determine the human resources strategy of a firm. It is likely that one reason that the auto industry continues to maintain a sophisticated collective bargaining relationship in the United States with the United Auto Workers is because of the power of the union to shut down a highly integrated and complex production and assembly process by striking one key plant. On the other hand, U.S. automakers have not abandoned a cost minimization strategy. They have invested large amounts of money in production capacity in Mexico, where wage costs are substantially lower than in the United States. In addition, the automakers have established alliances with firms outside the United States to produce low-priced vehicles. Such firms normally pay lower wages than are paid in the United States.

Nature of the Product. Firms that produce a product that is technologically sophisticated or in which labor adds a great deal of value are often closer to the commitment end of the continuum. One reason for this is that such firms require stable employment to work with the technology. On the other hand, firms that make products in which labor does not work with sophisticated technology, such as apparel, are more likely to be on the transactional end of the continuum, since labor is viewed as less firm specific. Workers are viewed as easily exchangeable—it is held that "almost anyone can do the job."

Alignment Between Business and Human Resource Strategy

The second question that must be addressed is the matter of alignment between human resources strategy and business strategy. If the firm's business strategy involves a long-term investment in its current product line, and the product incorporates a technologically sophisticated, engineering-intensive design and production process, that firm is more likely to adopt a human resources strategy on the commitment end of the continuum. Employment stability is likely to be important for such a firm, as investments often are necessary in substantial employee training in order to meet the demands of rapid changes in both market conditions and technology. High rates of technological change have made the workplace more complex. This requires employees to be highly flexible, to be able and motivated to perform different tasks everyday.[62] The workforce commitment strategy is more likely than the transactional strategy to be used in this situation.

MODULE
1

On the other hand, a firm that sees its strategy as direct labor cost minimization for an undifferentiated product that is produced with a static technology is most likely to implement a transactional strategy. This approach tends to result in immediate cost minimization. Moreover, given what will probably be a minimal investment in training, such firms are less likely to be concerned about the turnover associated with such a strategy. At this point, it is unnecessary to discuss in detail different human resources strategies, since these will be examined in the subsequent module. It is sufficient to point out that firms will normally have a great deal of flexibility in designing human resources strategies. This is an additional factor leading to variation in human resource practices.

APPLICATION

Below, the reader will find two brief case studies of the workforce commitment and labor transaction approaches.

Chainsaw Al Dunlap at Scott Paper

In his new book, *The New Deal at Work: Managing the Market-Driven Workforce,* Wharton professor Peter Cappelli discusses the application of a cost-minimization approach to Scott Paper company.[63] The inventor of the paper towel, Scott Paper was founded outside of Philadelphia toward the end of the nineteenth century. By the late 1980s and early 1990s, the company had grown into the largest tissue manufacturer in the world, operating in over 21 countries.

A highly cyclical business, the paper industry suffered its worst recession since the Great Depression starting in 1989, when a 15 percent decline in tissue prices cost the firm over $275 million. (Many consumers had become unwilling to pay higher prices for a brand name, and generic tissue had taken a large part of the market.) Like many U.S. paper companies in the early 1990s, Scott Paper got a new CEO. The first outside CEO to run the firm, Al Dunlap was renowned for ruthless cost-costing at troubled companies. The company had already had massive layoffs, and some felt a morale builder should have been brought in to help with the turnaround. Dunlap made an additional 34 percent reduction in staff including laying off three out of every four workers at headquarters. Rather than waiting for attrition or early retirements to minimize the trauma for employees, Dunlap laid off 11,000 employees, probably the largest reduction in the history of U.S. firms. He sold off many of Scott's assets, including a printing company and real estate holdings. He also eliminated all corporate contributions to the community, and reneged on the last payment to the Philadelphia Art Museum. As a result of these actions, the stock price went up an incredible 225 percent in about a year. Cost-cutting clearly contributed to the firm's financial success at the expense of employees and the community. Now Dunlap is looking for a buyer to take over what is left of Scott Paper.

High Commitment at Starbucks Coffee

Bucking the trend in managing the employment relationship in the food service industry, which is notorious for low wages, high turnover, and little or no benefits, is nothing new for Starbucks Coffee Company. It was listed in 1997 on *Fortune* magazine's "100 Best Companies to work for in America." Founded in 1971, the company has over 27,000 employees and is growing with the goal of becoming a $1 billion dollar company by the turn of the century. Its stock has gone up more than 800 percent since going public in 1992. The Starbucks commitment approach to the employment relationship and the loyalty of its employees have helped build a company that has more than 1,700 stores worldwide with a goal of expanding at 35 to 40 percent per year.[64]

The first line in Starbucks mission statement is "Provide a work environment where we treat each other with dignity and respect." The staffing of committed human resources played a key role in the company's growth strategy. It competes not only by offering great products, but also by creating a warm and inviting place through hiring great people. Turnover is only 65 percent, which is typically double in the restaurant industry. All workers begin at $6.25, which when started was $2 better than the required minimum wage. All partners who work at least 20 hours per week get full benefits. They also are eligible for Bean Stock, which is granted at 14 percent of base pay. After two stock splits, employees have the opportunity to build wealth. The way partners are treated in the employment relationship makes a supreme difference in how they treat customers. The HR policies and procedures are designed so partners are treated well as a given, the assumption being that great customer service will follow from this employment relationship. Training and orientation are a key part of Starbucks' commitment strategy. Each new partner goes through 24 hours of orientation in retail skills, customer service, and home brewing and coffee information. Each market, which is about 100 stores, has a learning development leader who is responsible for quality assurance of core training and succession planning for talented partners. Starbucks has a policy of promoting from within. These are just some of the many human resource practices at the company that are designed to foster a flexible, loyal, and committed workforce.

In Conclusion

Debrief

This module has argued that major distinctions can be made between the *commitment,* the *transactional,* and the *mixed* or *core-noncore* approaches to the management of employment relations. It has also introduced a framework for understanding managerial decision making and strategy development. The framework holds that HR decisions and strategies vary in their level of management discretion and in the nature of their organizational roles.

The greater prevalence of labor transactional cost minimization and mixed model approaches has heralded a fundamental shift in the attitudes or schema of senior managers and employees in many firms about the centrality of having committed employees engaged in a long-term employment relationship. Employees at all levels and job types are increasingly being viewed as mainly labor costs as opposed to human resources. The practical implications of such a shift in mental framing are significant: *it is typically assumed that organizations should increase their investment in resources, while limiting and reducing costs.*[65] Taken to an extreme, such changes may have a long-range negative effect resulting in reduced loyalty and commitment between employees and employers in these relationships.

It is interesting to note that research by a Harvard Business School professor John Kotter following the careers of the school's graduates found that many are opting away from jobs at major established U.S. corporations, preferring entrepreneurial work. If many of the best and brightest are unsure about working for America's biggest employers, the ramifications of the growing use of labor transactional cost minimization approaches are not necessarily positive for U.S. competitiveness, let alone society as a whole. The shift toward new workplace practices such as this, and transformed employment relationships have significant ramifications not only for employers and employees, but also for the competitiveness of nations in the global marketplace.

Although the popular press might lead one to believe that nearly all firms have shifted toward employment relations geared toward labor cost minimization, this module, which sets the stage for those that follow, is grounded in the assumption that variation exists in the management of the employment relationship. Managers and employing organizations have a high degree of choice about the importance of investing in human resources as a core competency. There are still a significant number of organizations such as Southwest Airlines, Starbucks, Birkenstock, and State Farm, among others, that follow a high-commitment approach to the employment relationship. They view employees as long-term assets, train and invest in them, pay them well, and strive to offer long-term job security.

Suggested Readings

Bridges, W. 1994. The end of the job. *Fortune,* Sept. 19, 1994, 62–74.

> *This article discusses how employment has become "dejobbed" and increasingly boundaryless between organizations.*

Kochan, T. 1997. Rebalancing the role of human resources. *Human Resource Management,* Spring 1997, 121–128.

> *This article discusses how, in its efforts to become more strategic and serve line management, human resource management may be reducing its role in protecting employee rights and the long-term well-being of society.*

Cappelli, P. 1999. *The New Deal at Work: Managing the Market-Driven Workplace.* Boston: Harvard Business School Press, Ch. 1, pp. 17–48.

> *This chapter discusses the new employment relationship that has emerged from corporate restructuring and how it has changed the way employees are managed. The growth of the labor market has begun to allow employment relationships to mirror that of product market competitive pressures.*

Relevant Web Sites

There are many web sites that can augment the information in this module. Here are a few examples:

BUREAU OF LABOR STATISTICS
http://stats.bls.gov

MSU LABOR AND INDUSTRIAL RELATIONS LIBRARY
http://www.lib.msu.edu/coll/main/lir

INDUSTRIAL RELATIONS COLLECTION (MIT)
http://nimrod.mit.edu/depts/dewey/indrel/html

SOCIETY FOR HUMAN RESOURCE MANAGEMENT
http://www.shrm.org

YAHOO LIST OF HUMAN RESOURCES
http://www.yahoo.com/Business/Corporations/CorporateServices/
Human Resources/

WORKFORCE ONLINE
http://www.workforceonline.com/

Critical Thinking Questions

1. Define the three main models for managing the employment relationship. Which do you most identify with and why? Are there pros and cons to each approach? If so, what are they?

2. What are examples of human resource practices that you can think of that you view as supporting the labor transactional approach, the workforce commitment approach, or the mixed model? Review the applications and cases in this module, and search the Internet and library to find examples of these practices at both U.S. companies and firms headquartered outside of the United States. Be sure to explain how these practices support a particular approach to the employment relationship.

MODULE
1

3. Discuss how the human resources and labor relations function have historically evolved over time and the main pressures on how management has used them to manage the employment relationship.

4. Discuss the framework presented for understanding human resource management decision making. Give examples of human resource decisions that vary in levels of managerial discretion. Give examples of human resource activities reflecting the four roles presented. Are some roles more important than others? Why or why not?

Expanded Exercise

The following exercise includes a case study and a team exercise. In preparation for the exercise, you will need to carefully read the Kensi Manufacturing Inc. case that follows.[66]

***Kensi Manufacturing Inc. Case* and Exercise.** "Open the hood of a car made anywhere in the world. You are bound to find Kensi-made components. The company is a world leader in supplying components that make cars run safely, cleanly, and economically."

This quote can be found on the first page of Kensi's 1997 annual report. It is the automotive parts that Kensi is most recognized for. They develop, produce, manufacture, and market products including but not limited to air conditioners and heaters, radiators, and filters. However, through today's technology, Kensi has expanded into nonautomotive products as well, such as telecommunications and information systems. Their air conditioning and heating systems and related components maintain their largest percent of net sales (34 percent).

Established in December 1949, the corporate headquarters of Kensi is located in Kariya, Japan. Kensi has grown into a worldwide organization with locations throughout Asia, North America, Europe, Australia, and South America. This case will focus on Kensi Manufacturing Inc. (KMI), in production since 1986. KMI services over 15 customers including Chrysler, Toyota, and Mercedes-Benz. The company concentrates on designing and producing advanced automotive heating and cooling systems. It employs over 1,650 associates in 1998, and net sales as of 1995 were $703 million.

Furthermore, KMI has won over 50 awards since its establishment. A KMI brochure states that "companies all over the world seek us out as a benchmark of excellence, and *Industry Week* magazine has named us one of the 10 best manufacturers in the United States." This plant has been recognized for many outstanding accomplishments from quality and customer service to a strong dedication to the community and the environment.

Plant Tour

A unique architectural entrance greets both employees of and visitors to KMI. The front lobby and the hallways are typical of most plant office areas. However, upon entering the professional workers' area, peculiar layout is revealed. There is one large room containing an army of desks for those working in areas such as HR and finance. No cubicle walls exist. Each person has his or her desk, chair, and one file cabinet. Each department shares a table or two as well as a community computer. Signs hang down from the ceiling indicating the territories of each department. With no partitions the noise level is a bit distracting, which probably takes new employees some getting used to. A separate office does not distinguish the managers of each department. Their status is shown by the placement of their desks on the outskirts of the room and their possession of a gray chair versus the red chairs of the other employees.

Before entering the plant floor where production is taking place, one is required to wear safety goggles. Ear plugs are also available to those interested because, despite the fact that Kensi's noise level is 15 percent better than OSHA standards, it is nevertheless necessary to yell if one is expected to be heard. Along two sides of the plant are long runways that allow trucks to actually drive through the plant for shipping and receiving. The center of the floor is filled with machines, assembly lines, materials, and workers. Spuriously located are small areas containing two tables. These areas are referred to as the Hot Spots. This is where each production team meets for breaks and their daily 5–10 minute meetings. The walls of these areas contain a Job Knowledge Matrix, which informs everyone exactly what each worker is trained on. An Overtime Rotation is also posted noting who is next in line to perform overtime. Finally, the walls display any awards that the team may have received in order to give them the recognition that they deserve.

The plant provides a 24-hour cafeteria for the employees of all three shifts. Job posting boards are hanging throughout the plant listing any open positions for which KMI is actively recruiting. There is also a medical department with nurses on staff 24 hours a day. A recreation center is located in a separate building just outside of the plant. This benefit includes everything from cardiovascular equipment to on-site fitness experts to their very own baseball diamond.

Communication Channels

The associates of KMI have numerous systems in place for their communication needs. Initially, when employees reach an obstacle, they are encouraged to speak with their team leader. If an associate prefers to speak with HR, they may do so with their assigned

MODULE
1

associate relations representative. The A/R Rep. spends time on the floor each day, allowing the associates to ask questions.

Each production team also assigns a delegate to attend at least two vice president meetings each year. These meetings are held every three to four months and last about one hour. Before each meeting the delegate collects questions and concerns from teammates to bring up for discussion. If not all of these concerns are addressed in the meeting, they are collected and answered in writing through the meeting minutes.

The vice president of human resources has a direct line, known as the "red phone," solely devoted to the concerns of the associates. The VP of HR is the only individual permitted to answer it, and if he or she is directly unavailable at any point in time, an answering machine will take messages that will be addressed as soon as possible.

The president of KMI has a comment box, commonly referred to as "George's Box." It is conveniently located at the employee entrance so that workers can address any of their concerns. The box is emptied twice a week by the president's administrative assistant, and is in turn presented to the president. His response is typically in writing.

Focal point committees are also an important resource for the associates to tap regarding their concerns. These committees are conceived when major policy emerge that require associate input. The committee members must be in good standing with the company. For example, any individual under written discipline would be excluded from participation in a focal point committee.

There are many other means of communication within KMI. *Shop Talk,* the quarterly newsletter, keeps Associates informed of issues arising within the company. Televisions, scrolling signs, and "hot news" boards located throughout the plant, as well as e-mail and voice mail, are other ways to inform employees of current events, issues, and important information within KMI.

Issues Facing KMI

Through conversations with employees and managers as well as through the KMI quarterly newsletter, *Shop Talk,* a huge issue facing this plant becomes abundantly apparent. The frequent long workdays are allowing employees to accrue quite a bit of overtime. The 1998 Special Edition of *Shop Talk* in its cover story claims that "while the extra money is nice, it's still hard to put your personal life (and your loved ones) on hold for long stretches." Due to the extensive demand today for KMI products and the large number of new products, the overtime level has hit a record rate. With the need for overtime comes the need for more employees as well as temporary workers to reduce that time. However, unemployment is at a low percentage nationally (4.7 percent as of December 1997). Thus absences are another major concern within KMI. A balance is essential in order to simultaneously satisfy the organizational objectives and the needs of the employees. The question is, What are managers and human resources doing about this need?

Exercise

KMI human resources is faced with the problem of managing production schedules while allowing associates time off. Over the next six months, 48 hours of overtime per month need to be worked by all associates in order to satisfy the tremendous demand for KMI products. The manager of HR needs to collect data and gather advice, meeting with a self-managed work team consisting of four employees in order to overcome this obstacle. Your instructor will give you an exercise where you will be a member of a decision-making group at KMI to develop a solution to this problem. As preparation for class, please consider the following question:

1. To what extent does KMI's strategy in regard to the employment relationship reflect a workforce commitment, labor transactional, or mixed approach? Be sure to identify the HR practices that support your rationale for your thinking.

2. What are alternatives that you think KMI should consider to manage the overtime problem? What are preferred solutions from the employee perspective? from the management perspective? Is the overtime decision an example of an HR activity reflecting transactions, transitions, translations, or transformations? Is it a unilateral, negotiated, or imposed decision?

References

1. Mahron, William D., President and CEO, Whirlpool Corporation. Nov. 8, 1993. Testimony before the Commission on the Future of Worker-Management Relations, U.S. Depts. of Commerce and Labor, Washington, D.C., 95.
2. Corporate Leadership Council. August 1996. *Compelling Careers: Workforce Management Structures of the 'New Employers of Choice.'*
3. Morrow, L. March 29, 1993. "The Temping of America," *Time,* 40–41.
4. Smilansky, J. 1997. *The New HR.* Detroit: ITT.
5. Milkovich, G. and Bourdreau, J. 1997. *Human Resource Management,* 8th ed. Chicago: Irwin.
6. Pfeffer, J. and Baron, J. 1988. "Taking the Workers Back Out: Recent Trends in the Structuring of Employment," in *Research in Organizational Behavior,* vol. 10., B. Staw and L. Cummings, eds. Greenwich, CT: JAI Press, 257–303.
7. Tsui, A., Pearce, J., Porter, L., and Hite, J. 1995. "Choice of the Employee-Organization Relationship: Influence of External and Internal Factors," in *Research in Personnel and Human Resources Management,* vol. 13. Greenwich, CT: JAI Press, 117–151.
8. Kochan, T. and Cappelli, P. 1984. "The Transformation of the Industrial Relations and Personnel Function," in *Internal Labor Markets,* Paul Osterman, ed. Cambridge, MA: MIT Press, 133–190.
9. Kochan, T. Oct. 3–4, 1997. "Beyond Myopia: Human Resources and the Changing Social Contract." Paper prepared for a conference on Research and Theory in Strategic Human Resource Management: An Agenda for the 21st Century. Cornell University School of Industrial and Labor Relations, Center for Advanced Human Resource Studies.
10. Adapted from Ulrich, D. 1997. *Human Resource Champions.* Boston: Harvard Business School Press. Also see Kossek, E. and Markel, K. "Leadership by Human Resources: Organizational Roles and Choices," in E. Kossek and R. Block, 2000, *Managing Human Resources in the 21st Century: From Core Concepts to Strategic Choice.* South-Western College Publishing.
11. See, for example, Oliver Williamson's 1975 book *Markets and Hierarchies: Analysis and Antitrust Implications.* New York: Free Press.
12. Ulrich, D. 1997. *Human Resource Champions.* Boston: Harvard Business School Press.
13. Senge, Peter. Nov. 19, 1997. Keynote address to the 3d Annual HR Consulting Skills and Tools Conference. Orlando, FL.
14. Brown, E. Mar. 1, 1999. "America's Most Admired Companies," *Fortune,* 68–73.
15. Bartholomew, D. Nov./Dec. 1998. "Small Business: Driving Success." *The Journal for Quality and Participation,* 21:56–57.
16. Keynote speech, Oct. 23–25, 1997. Conference on 21st Century Employment Practices: Organizational Behavior, Public Policy, and New Employment Relations. D. Rousseau and C. Leana, cosponsors. Pittsburgh.
17. Pasternack, B. A., Keller, S., and Viscio, A. J. 1996. *The Triumph of People Power and the New Economy.* New York: Booz Allen, Inc., 1–12.
18. Kochan and Cappelli, "Transformation of Industrial Relations."
19. Jacoby, S. M. 1985. *Employing Bureaucracy: Managers, Unions, and the Transformation of Work in American Industry, 1900–1945.* New York: Columbia University Press, 16–20.
20. Ibid, 20.
21. Kochan and Cappelli, "Transformation of Industrial Relations."
22. Jacoby, *Employing Bureaucracy,* 7.
23. Ibid, 137.
24. Ibid, 221.
25. Ibid, 255.
26. Kochan and Cappelli, "Transformation of Industrial Relations."
27. Jacoby, 243.

MODULE
1

28. Gutek, B. and Murrell, A. Nov. 18–20, 1995. Conference on Human Resources Versus Labor Costs: The Changing Role of People at Work. Tucson: The University of Arizona.

29. Kochan and Cappelli, "Transformation of Industrial Relations."

30. Ibid.

31. Ibid.

32. Cappelli, P. 1999. *The New Deal at Work: Managing the Market-Driven Workforce.* Boston: Harvard Business School Press.

33. Kochan and Cappelli, "Transformation of Industrial Relations."

34. Tsui et al., "Choice of the Employee-Organization Relationship."

35. Ibid.

36. Ibid.

37. Pfeffer, J. 1998. *The Human Equation: Building Profits by Putting People First.* Boston: Harvard Business School Press.

38. Ibid.

39. Huselid, M. and Becker, B. 1997. "The Impact of High Performance Work Systems, Implementation Effectiveness, and Alignment with Strategy on Shareholder Wealth." Unpublished paper, Brunswick, NJ.

40. Ichiniowski, C., Shaw, K., and Prennushi, G. 1997. "The Effects of Human Resource Management Practices on Productivity: A Study of Steel Finishing Lines." *The American Economic Review.*

41. MacDuffie, J. P. 1994. "Human Resource Bundles and Manufacturing Performance: Organizational Logic and Flexible Production Systems in the World Auto Industry." *Industrial and Labor Relations Review,* 48:197–221.

42. Ichiniowski, C., Kochan, T., Levine, D., Olson, C., and Strauss, G. 1996. "What Works at Work: Overview and Assessment." *Industrial Relations,* 35:3, 299–333.

43. Reichheld, F. 1996. *The Loyalty Effect: The Hidden Force Behind Growth, Profits, and Lasting Value.* Boston: Harvard Business School Press.

44. Sunoo, B. P. August 1994. "Birkenstock Braces to Fight the Competition." *Personnel Journal,* 73:68–75.

45. Ibid.

46. Pfeffer and Baron, "Taking the Workers Back Out."

47. Kochan, "Beyond Myopia."

48. While subcontracted employees who are professionals and managers frequently get higher wages than full-time regular employees, the overall cost to the employer is still often lower for subcontracted workers since the employer usually does not pay benefits or many other indirect labor costs, and can more easily terminate the employment relationship. Subcontracted employees are more likely to be nonunion workers who typically make less than union workers doing the same job.

49. Tsui et al., "Choice of the Employee-Organization Relationship."

50. Ibid.

51. Pfeffer, J. *The Human Equation.*

52. Barnett, A. Aug. 16, 1998. "BP-Amoco Merge Could Be Three Times Projected Figure," London: *The Observer.*

53. Feder, B. J. Sept. 19, 1997. "At Whirlpool, 4,700 Workers to Lose Jobs," *The New York Times.*

54. This example is taken from the following sources: Bronstein, S. and Torpy, B., "Congress to Probe Poultry Plants' Safety in Wake of Fatal N.C. Fire," *Atlanta Journal-Constitution,* Sept. 6, 1991, 2B; "Editorial: Death by Negligence," *St. Louis Post-Dispatch,* Sept. 9, 1991, 2B; Bronstein, S., "Plant Safety Largely Ignored, Report Says; Company, Government Agencies Blamed for Fatal N.C. Fire," *Atlanta Journal-Constitution,* Dec. 4, 1991, 3.

55. Axelrod, A. and Phillips, C. 1992. *What Every American Should Know About American History: 200 Events That Shaped the Nation.* Holbrook, MA: Bob Adams, Inc., 230–231.

56. Tsui et al., "Choice of the Employee-Organization Relationship."

57. Ulrich, *Human Resource Champions.*

58. Belous, R. S. 1989. *The Contingent Economy.* Washington, D.C.: National Planning Association.

59. Lawrence, P. 1998. Book review of *The Human Equation: Building Profits by Putting People First,* in *Administrative Science Quarterly,* 43:4, 956–958.

60. Greenhouse, S. Feb. 16, 1999. "Most Pilots at American Are Now Back in the Cockpit." *The New York Times,* C1, C8.

61. Pfeffer, J. 1998. "The Real Keys to High Performance," in *Leader to Leader.* Drucker Foundation, 23–29.
62. Tsui et al., "Choice of the Employee-Organization Relationship."
63. Cappelli, P. *The New Deal at Work.*
64. Weiss, N. August 1998. "How Starbucks Impassions Workers to Drive Growth," *WorkForce,* 60–64.
65. Gutek and Murrell, Conference on Human Resources.
66. The KMI case was based on an independent study done for Dr. Ellen Ernst Kossek by Jennifer Cook, a former master's student at Michigan State University. Kensi is a fictitious name.

MODULE
1

Index

....

Adversarial labor-management relations, 1.12, 1.18

Arbitrary decisions, 1.14

Business environment, 1.4

Business strategy, 17, 1.8, 1.12

Change-agent role, 1.9. *See also* Human resource role

Civil Rights Act of 1964, 1.15

Collective bargaining, 1.11, 1.12, 1.14, 1.15

Combative relationship, 1.14

Commitment approach. *See* Workforce commitment model

Communication, as translation role, 1.8, 1.11

Competitive environment, 1.7, 1.13, 1.16

Competitiveness, 1.5, 1.7, 1.17, 1.18, 1.22, 1.27

Computer-based technology, 1.13, 1.15

Contingent workers, 1.20, 1.21

Cooperative relations, 1.12

Core competency, 1.5, 1.10, 1.17, 1.19

Core-noncore approach, 1.5, 1.22, 1.27. *See also* Employment strategies, Labor transactional model, Mixed model approach

Cost minimization, 1.11, 1.18, 1.21, 1.23, 1.25, 1.27. *See also* Labor transactional model

Cultural change, 1.11, 1.12, 1.13

Decision-making, employee, 1.9, 1.18

Decision-making, HR, 1.7, 1.10, 1.11. *See also* Human resource roles

Decision-making, managerial, 1.6, 1.12, 1.24, 1.27

Deregulation, 1.6, 1.13, 1.16

Diagnostic framework, 1.12, 1.27

Diversity, of labor force, 1.6

Downsizing, 1.4, 1.5, 1.15, 1.18, 1.20, 1.22

Drive system, 1.14

Economic factors, 1.8, 1.14, 1.19, 1.20, 1.23

Employee benefits, 1.10, 1.17

Employee commitment approach. *See* Workforce commitment model

Employee compensation, 1.10

Employee selection, 1.17. *See also* Employment practices

Employee work/nonwork roles, 1.10

Employer commitment, 1.5, 1.17

Employer of choice, 1.17

Employer/employee partnership, 1.26

Employer/employee relations. *See* Employment relationship

Employment practices (policies, systems), 1.4, 1.11, 1.22

Employment relations, 1.13–17, 1.20

Employment relationship, 1.4, 1.5, 1.13, 1.14, 1.16–17, 1.18, 1.20, 1.23, 1.26, 1.27

Employment security. *See* Job security

Employment strategies, 1.4, 1.5–7, 1.14, 1.17, 1.19

Empowering employees, 1.4, 1.18

Environmental change, 1.5, 1.6

Environmental factors, 1.6, 1.7, 1.12, 1.13–14

Equal employment opportunity, 1.8, 1.13

External resources, 1.9–10

Fair Labor Standards Act, 1.13

Family and Medical Leave Act (FMLA), 1.11, 1.13

Flexible work options, 1.18

Global marketplace, 1.16, 1.27

Globalization, 1.4, 1.6, 1.9, 1.16

Government regulations, 1.6, 1.10, 1.15, 1.21, 1.22

Hiring strategies. *See* Employment strategies

Human resource function. *See* Human resource roles

Human resource leader or manager. *See* Human resource professional

Human resource management (HRM). *See* Managing human resources

Human resource policy domain, 1.10

Human resource practices, 1.4, 1.5–7, 1.8, 1.9, 1.18–19

Human resource professional (manager), 1.5, 1.6–7, 1.8, 1.14, 1.19

Human resource roles, 1.4, 1.7, 1.8–14, 1.16. *See also* Transactional role, Translationsal role, Transitionsal role, and Transformational role

Human resource strategies (policies, systems), 1.4, 1.5, 1.7–8, 1.10, 1.12, 1.15, 1.19, 1.24, 1.25

Imposed decision, 1.7, 1.10, 1.11, 1.12, 1.13. *See also* Decision making, HR; Government regulations

Incentives, 1.17. *See also* Job performance

Information sharing, 1.18

Intellectual capital, 1.5, 1.10, 1.17

Internal customers, 1.8

Internal labor, 1.5, 1.15, 1.19, 1.20

Internal resources, 1.9–10

Involvement, worker (employee), 1.9, 1.18

Jacoby, Sanford, 1.14, 1.15

Job design, 1.18

Job security, 1.5, 1.14, 1.15, 1.18, 1.23, 1.27

Job-focused approach, 1.20. *See also* Labor transactional model

Labor relations, 1.5, 1.12, 1.13, 1.16. *See also* Employment relationship, Human resource practices
Labor transactional model, 1.5, 1.20–21, 1.22, 1.23, 1.27
Layoffs, 1.5, 1.7, 1.15, 1.17, 1.19, 1.20–21, 1.26
Level of discretion, 1.11. *See also* Managerial discretion
Long-term employment, 1.5, 1.15, 1.17, 1.22, 1.24, 1.27
Loyalty, 1.19, 1.26, 1.27

Management values, 1.24
Managerial discretion, 1.7, 1.10, 1.11, 1.12, 1.24
Managing human resources, 1.4, 1.5–9, 1.18, 1.20
Marketplace, 1.4, 1.5, 1.17, 1.20, 1.21, 1.25
Minimum wage, 1.13, 1.22, 1.26
Mixed model approach, 1.5, 1.22–23, 1.27. *See also* Employment strategies
Morale, employee, 1.26
Motivation, 1.13, 1.14

National Labor Relations Act, 1.14
Negotiated decision, 1.7, 1.10, 1.11, 1.12. *See also* Decision making, HR; Managing human resources
New company strategy, 1.10
New employee suggestion system, 1.11
New employees, 1.19
Noncore workers, 1.5. *See also* Core-noncore approach
Nonunion firm or employee, 1.10, 1.11, 1.12, 1.15

Older workers, 1.14
Organizational approach, 1.14. *See also* Employment relationship
Organizational culture, 1.9
Organizational objectives, 1.8
Outsourcing, 1.7, 1.9, 1.10, 1.11, 1.18, 1.23
Overtime, 1.10, 1.11, 1.18
    requirements, 1.13

Performance appraisal system, 1.8
Personal development, 1.9. *See also* Employment relationship, Human resource practices
Personal objectives, 1.8
Personnel department, 1.14, 1.15
Private-sector workforce, 1.10

Productivity, 1.5, 1.7, 1.14, 1.16, 1.18
Public-sector jobs, 1.10

Reorganization plan, 1.21
Responsibility, worker, 1.18

Scientific management, 1.14
Seniority, 1.14, 1.15, 1.20
Severance, 1.14, 1.20
Systems transformation, 1.11

Taylor, Frederick, 1.14
Teamwork, 1.9, 1.19
Technological advances, 1.6, 1.13, 1.25
Telecommunications, 1.6, 1.16, 1.29
Temporary workers, 1.4, 1.18, 1.21. *See also* Contingent workers
The New Deal at Work: Managing the Market-Driven Workforce, Peter Cappelli, 1.25
Title VII, 1.15
Transaction cost theory, 1.8
Transactional (contingent) approach, 1.5, 1.20, 1.22, 1.23, 1.24, 1.25, 1.27. *See also* Labor transactional model
Transactional role, 1.8, 1.11, 1.12, 1.13
Transformational role, 1.4, 1.8–9, 1.10, 1.11, 1.12, 1.13
Transitional role, 1.8–9, 1.10, 1.11, 1.12
Translational role, 1.8–9, 1.11, 1.12, 1.13
Trends, business, 1.6

Unilateral decision, 1.7, 1.11, 1.12
Unilateral discretion, 1.10. *See also* Managing human resources
Union avoidance tools, 1.14
Union membership, 1.15, 1.16
Union power, 1.16, 1.25
Union representative, 1.10
Unionization, 1.15, 1.16
Unionized firm or employee, 1.10, 1.11, 1.12, 1.15
United Auto Workers, 1.25

Wagner Act. *See* National Labor Relations Act
Work environment, 1.10, 1.26
Work systems, 1.9. *See also* Organizational culture
Workforce, employees, 1.5, 1.15, 1.20–21. *See also* Core-noncore approach
Workforce commitment model, 1.5, 1.17, 1.18–20, 1.22, 1.23, 1.24, 1.25, 1.27
Workforce skill development, 1.22
Workgroups (teams), 1.10

MODULE
1

Managing Human Resources
in the 21st Century

From Core Concepts to Strategic Choice

MODULE 2

Human Resource Strategy

From Transactions to
Transformation

Ellen Ernst Kossek
MICHIGAN STATE UNIVERSITY

Managing Human Resources in the 21st Century: From Core Concepts to Strategic Choice,
by Kossek and Block

Publisher: Dave Shaut
Executive Editor: John Szilagyi
Developmental Editor: Bryant Editorial Development
Marketing Manager: Joseph A. Sabatino
Production Editor: Tamborah E. Moore
Manufacturing Coordinator: Dana Began Schwartz
Cover Design: Tin Box Studio
Cover Photographs: Copyright Shoji Sato/Photonica
Production House: The Left Coast Group, Inc.
Printer: West Group

Printed in the United States of America
1 2 3 4 5 02 01 00 99

For more information contact South-Western College Publishing, 5101 Madison Road, Cincinnati, Ohio, 45227 or find us on the Internet at *http://www.swcollege.com*
For permission to use material from this text or product, contact us by
- telephone: 1-800-730-2214
- fax: 1-800-730-2215
- web: *http://www.thomsonrights.com*

ISBN: 0–324–01801–0

This book is printed on acid-free paper.

Contents

MODULE OVERVIEW   2.4

OBJECTIVES   2.5

RELATION TO THE FRAME   2.5

CORE CONCEPTS IN HUMAN RESOURCE
NEW EMPLOYMENT RELATIONS   2.7

Organizational Strategy   2.7

Human Resource Strategy   2.15

Allocated Resources and Develop Processes and Systems
to Support HR Delivery   2.27

Organizational Adaptation and Performance Outcomes   2.27

Alternative Strategic HR Perspectives   2.28

STRATEGIC ISSUES IN CREATING COMPETITIVE ADVANTAGE
THROUGH PEOPLE   2.31

APPLICATION   2.31

Daehan Corporation   2.31

Company Background   2.37

The Staff Meeting   2.40

IN CONCLUSION   2.42

Debrief   2.42

Suggested Readings   2.42

Relevant Web Sites   2.42

Critical Thinking Questions   2.43

Exercises: Strategic HRM Vignettes   2.43

References   2.48

INDEX   2.52

MODULE OVERVIEW

Consider the following questions on future trends likely to affect the management of human resources (HR) into the new millennium:[1]

- Have you ever worked for a learning organization?

- Do you think business process reengineering is a good idea?

- Do most companies leverage their core competencies?

- What is sound organizational architecture?

- Do you believe in time-based competition?

A *learning organization* is one whose members view learning as central to success. *Business process reengineering* is the rethinking and radical redesign of work. This could take the form, for example, of organizing around process—say, the filling of a customer order—instead of by functional departments such as finance, marketing, and human resources. This involves overhauling job designs, organizational structures, and management systems to *organize work around outcomes, not tasks or functions.* *Core competencies* are bundles of skills and technologies that enable a company to provide a particular benefit to customers. They are difficult for competitors to imitate and often provide access to more than one market.[2] Increasingly it is being argued that corporate strategy should be based not on products or markets, but on competencies that give an organization access to several markets and are difficult for competitors to imitate. *Organizational architecture* is a metaphor that forces managers to think more broadly about organization in terms of how work, people, and formal and informal structures fit together. This involves thinking architecturally about how firms must be more fluid to accommodate new organizational forms that are more virtual and flexible and can evolve around autonomous work teams in higher-performance work systems built on strategic alliances. Organizational structures are generally being revised to have wider spans and fewer levels, to balance autonomy, integration, and teamwork. *Time-based competition* involves using speed for a competitive advantage and paying attention to "cycle times" in every process. It is based on the belief that time is the equivalent of money, productivity, quality, and innovation. Time, like costs, is manageable and a source of competitive advantage through every process in the organization.

As organizations experience the need to implement new business strategies, capabilities, cultures, and structures to accommodate changes such as these, their leaders develop HR strategies, policies, and programs to align the organization with these changing conditions. The goal of this module is to examine the role of HR strategy, which involves processes and activities, to ensure HR systems are fully integrated with the strategic and organizational change needs of the firm. Since HR strategy is derived from business strategy, the module begins with a discussion of core concepts in organizational strategy. The activities, key issues, and principles involved in developing HR strategy, and alternative perspectives on how HR strategy can be used to gain competitive advantage, are then discussed. The module includes an original case study of the Daehan Corporation (fictional name) written by ByeongCheol Lee and YoungMyon Lee, who are professors in the department of management at Dongguk University in South Korea. The case describes how change in the international economy of the Far East Pacific Basin prompted a major employer in South Korea to fundamentally revise its HR strategy. The module also includes original vignettes developed by Lisa Copeland, a former graduate student in human resources at Michigan State University. The case and exercises found at the end of the module are designed to develop your diagnostic and analytical skills in identifying obstacles and developing solutions related to HR strategy implementation.

As Stanford business professor Jeffrey Pfeffer points out, most business leaders will say that managing their people is a top priority; yet the reality is that smart organizations often do very dumb things with how they recruit, manage, and retain their people. Although knowledge and intellectual capital are repeatedly proclaimed as being critical for business success, the truth is that most business leaders pay lip service to managing people effectively—but worship the bottom line.[3]

A recent study of manufacturing firms in the United Kingdom found that strategic human resource management (HRM) practices accounted for 19 percent of the variance in performance and 18 percent of productivity improvements. HRM practices explained more of the variation in the bottom line than any other factors such as other functional activities and the business environment. The study concluded that despite its potential positive impact, research and practitioner emphasis on strategic HRM is one of the most neglected areas of management.[4] Yet as this module will show, how people are managed can provide competitive advantage—assuming business and HR strategies are effectively integrated.

OBJECTIVES

- To understand the core concepts and principles related to business strategies and HR strategies for organizational growth and goal achievement

- To review a framework that can be used to analyze and develop HR strategy

- To be aware of alternative perspectives on how HR strategy should be designed to support business strategy

- To be aware of current HR strategy trends such as high-performance work systems and organizational strategy for managing flexibility and new organizational forms

RELATION TO THE FRAME

The belief that external environmental pressures are the main source of organizational changes is fundamental to strategic human resource management thinking.[5] As Figure 2.1 on page 2.6 shows, the environmental context in which the firm operates shapes organizational and business strategy. The environmental context includes all the trends and environmental forces that drive business decisions such as market conditions, technology, labor market pressures, globalization, unions, and government regulations. Strategy reflects a firm's business response, or how it will adapt to major environmental change. Human resource strategy is an organization's fundamental approach toward the management of employees to ensure that the firm achieves its business objectives in the marketplace. Historically, business and human resource strategies have been influenced by environmental drivers such as the tightness of external labor markets and the threat of labor unrest and government regulations. Most recently, these external forces have been overshadowed by global product market pressures and the increased power of shareholders—both drivers of significant changes in the employment relationship and human resource strategy. Increased ratcheting of employee performance demands, lessening of job security, and heightened requirements for increasing shareholder value, customer responsiveness, and quality, are all now imperative for the achievement of strategic business objectives. These performance requirements are being demanded *at the same time* that firms must control labor costs, restructure, and downsize in order to focus on core competencies.[6]

The *transitional* role of HR pertains to HR strategy execution, whereas the *transformational* role involves strategic cultural change. Cisco Systems, Inc., the global leader in networking for the Internet, is an example of the strategy execution or the transition role, where HR practices are implemented to transition the firm to execute business strategy. Cisco reads the external market well and knows how to harness high technology

FIGURE 2.1   *A Frame for Understanding Human Resource Strategy:
Context, Roles, and Constraints*

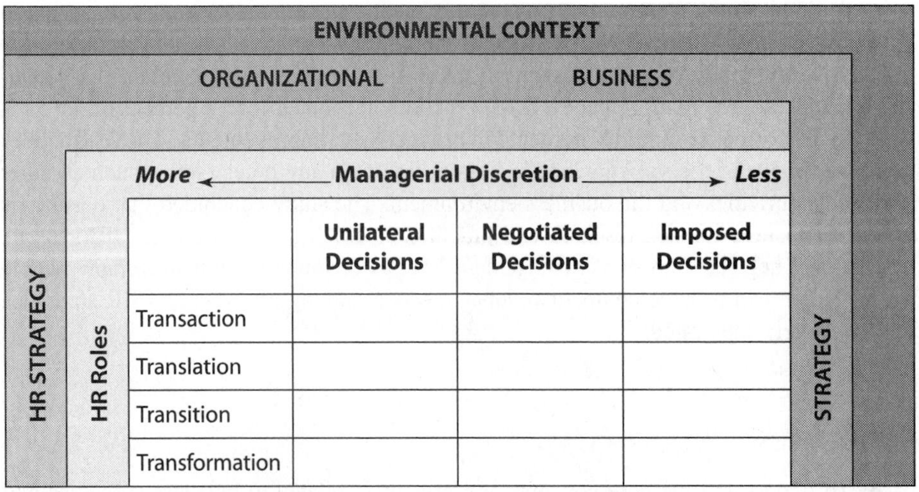

ENVIRONMENTAL CONTEXT			
ORGANIZATIONAL		BUSINESS	

More ← Managerial Discretion → Less			
	Unilateral Decisions	**Negotiated Decisions**	**Imposed Decisions**
Transaction			
Translation			
Transition			
Transformation			

(HR STRATEGY / HR Roles on left axis; STRATEGY on right axis)

© 2000 by Ellen Kossek and Richard Block. Thanks to Brian Pentland, Karen Markel, and John Beck for helpful comments and discussions that enhanced the model.

and use people systems to achieve business effectiveness. At Cisco, seven out of ten customer requests for technical support are filled electronically at satisfaction rates that are much higher than those involving human interaction. Using the network for tech support has saved Cisco money estimated to equal the cost of 1,000 engineers, which allows the company to take those engineers, and instead of putting them in support, put them into building new products. This gives Cisco a tremendous competitive advantage.

IBM Corporation provides an example of the transformational role of human resources strategies. Back in the early 1980s, IBM had become bloated and unable to adapt to customer and technological demands transforming the computer industry. The company's corporate culture was seen as a key barrier to strategic change. Organizations such as IBM originally became successful in the 1950s, '60s, and '70s by building a culture supported by human resource systems based on models of homogeneity (promoting similarity), not diversity.[7] IBM had training programs for new managers to foster similar ways of thinking. It had implicit lifetime employment and requirements such that employees dressed alike wearing the famous white shirt. It prided itself on what sociologists have called "homosocial production"[8]—the tendency of selection and promotion systems to allow only those employees to rise who fit with the characteristics of the dominant coalition. In this case that meant the white-shirted, white male, IBM company man.

Unfortunately, these HR systems inculcated a culture of arrogance—with the IBM way always seen as superior to the customer's or the competitor's way. This inhibited IBM's ability to adapt to differential customer demands in the business environment and read diverse competitive strategic thrusts, let alone be able to respond to these new demands with internal structures and processes. When business flagged, IBM conducted a culture audit to assess what barriers in its culture were getting in the way of managing diversity and becoming more multicultural. Developing a strategy for managing diversity became viewed as critical to changing the culture to allow it to be more customer oriented and able to adapt to different niches in the marketplace. Becoming more multicultural was also viewed as a means to transform IBM from being highly paternalistic in a traditional hierarchical family model to more of a co-op culture where different groups of employees could band together to serve the market in unique, flexible, and new ways. Putting in new HR systems of communication, rewards, training, and performance also helped transform the culture to be less entitlement based and individually oriented, and more performance and teamwork oriented.[9]

In sum, people strategies such as these and the use of human capital are increasingly being viewed as core competencies that are central to the formation and delivery of most business strategies today. Products can be cloned and technology and training can be copied, but no one can match highly charged, motivated people who care. Organizations need people who have the knowledge, skills, and abilities to be able to deliver at the frontier of performance—who understand where the company is going and are able to influence its path.[10]

CORE CONCEPTS IN HUMAN RESOURCE STRATEGY

- Organizational strategy
  - ✓ Porter's Five Forces framework
  - ✓ Strategies for gaining competitive advantage
  - ✓ Assessing value: Core competencies, resources, and activity streams
- Human resource strategy
  - ✓ Strategy and structure linkages: Evolving strategic HR roles
  - ✓ HR strategy framework
  - ✓ HR congruence: Vertical and horizontal fit
- Alternative strategic HR perspectives
  - ✓ Universal/best practices
  - ✓ Strategic contingency behavioral perspective
  - ✓ HR bundles: The case of high-performance work systems

MODULE
2

Each of these core concepts will be discussed in the sections that follow.

Organizational Strategy

A strategy is an organization's plan for interacting with the competitive environment to achieve its long-term goals and objectives. It involves choosing courses of action and the allocation of resources necessary for carrying out those goals.[11] Strategy has also been referred to as all the things necessary for the successful functioning of an organization as an adaptive mechanism.[12] Strategy implementation is the use of managerial and organizational resources and systems to direct and allocate resources to achieve strategic objectives.[13] In this section, we discuss the competitive forces that shape industry strategy, the notion of core competencies and key success factors, and the main business strategies for gaining competitive advantage.

Porter's Five Forces Framework.   Since the purpose of HR strategy is to align the organization with business strategy, it is important to begin with an understanding of how competitive forces shape business strategy. A popular strategy model is Harvard Business School Professor Michael Porter's Five Forces model.[14] Porter holds that the essence of strategy formulation is coping with industry competition, which depends on five competitive pressures. Below I review these pressures and give examples of the strategic HRM implications of each.

Force 1: Intensity of Competitor Rivalry

The degree of rivalry among competitors determines the extent to which value created by an industry will be dissipated through head-to-head competition.[15] The more intense the rivalry, the more likely firms will use tactics like price competition to gain market share, new product introduction to try to increase product differentiation, and adversarial slugfests. Intense rivalry is correlated with the presence of several of the following factors. When the industry is concentrated so that competitors are roughly equal in size and power, there is likely to be price rivalry. Price cutting is also likely to occur when industry growth is slow, the product is perishable, or the product or services lack differentiation or switching costs, which make it difficult to distinguish one competitor from another. Rivalry also increases when there are high barriers to exiting an industry. Examples of exit barriers are high fixed costs and specialized assets such as the high capital intensity of an auto or steel plant, as well as high management loyalty to a business. Factors such as these keep a firm competing even when return on investment is low or negative.[16] Rivalry is also likely when industry capacity is allocated in large increments, creating imbalances in demand and supply and causing intermittent periods of overcapacity. When overcapacity and high capital intensity exists, the ratio of fixed capital costs to value added is high. When this occurs, profitability is likely to be low and labor costs high, which will create pressures for firms to reduce operating costs.

Competitive pressures from intense rivalry can produce three types of organizational challenges.[17] The first is demand risk from a reduction in the market or an increase in competition from rivalry forces. High demand risk leads to a need for organizational flexibility responsiveness and improved quality. Innovation risk stems from the failure to be able to match competitors' innovations. Inefficiency risk is the risk of being unable to match a competitor's costs. Some human resource management implications of intense rivalry mean that pressures to hold or reduce labor costs will be high. Firms are also more likely to adopt a labor-transaction, cost-minimization approach to the employment relationship or pursue HR strategies to support product differentiation on quality or innovation.

Force 2: Threat of Entry

The average profitability of an industry is also affected by how easy it is for competitors to enter the market and add new industry capacity and rivalry to market share. High entry barriers occur when the scale and investment required to efficiently compete in an industry are high or when the existing competitors have high brand identity and differentiated products. It also occurs because of high legal barriers to entry such as patents or licensing limits, or physical barriers such as limited availability of new gates for landing at an airport. Barriers to entry are also high when there are high economies of scale in production, marketing, customer service, or research, making it difficult for others to enter the market and compete efficiently.

The experience curve, which assumes that costs of competing decline with experience as workers achieve more efficiency and volumes increase, can be but is not always related to economies of scale. Whether being high on the experience curve pays off may vary by industry. In industries where those who compete by having the newest, largest, and most efficient plant have the lowest costs, and there are high barriers to getting rid of old capital and replacing it with new, high experience (and an aging workforce) may not necessarily be a cost advantage. Having the largest, most efficient plant is a different concept than the economies of scale notion where a firm strives to cumulatively produce as much as it can of a product in order to reduce costs.[18]

After World War II, the rise of reduced barriers to global entry in the auto market, and the fact that experience on the learning curve did not always lead to price competitiveness, illustrate why U.S. companies today can no longer compete only on low cost and economies of scale based on mass production. Historically, U.S. auto companies benefited from a market where having economies of scale was the major competitive advantage. For example, in the 1950s and 1960s, the U.S. auto companies followed a market-push approach. They produced as much as they could to gain economies of scale and then were able to push the product from the dealer lots onto the buyers. Then in the late 1970s and early 1980s, the bottom dropped out of the

U.S. auto industry as newly built auto plants in Japan and later Korea began to build cars that had not only lower cost due to newer and more efficient plants but also higher quality and lower costs from a younger and more flexible workforce. Customers in the U.S. auto market and other developed countries also began to demand more product differentiation. Successful auto producers now needed to compete by being able to accommodate frequent model changes, having vertical integration (e.g., owning not only the plant but now the steel mill or suppliers to the plant or the distribution systems to sell the cars), and lower material and labor costs. The change in the industry conditions transformed the *critical success factors*—those capabilities firms need to even be a player or *begin* to compete in the industry.

In their book on the new American workplace, Appelbaum and Batt[19] discuss the human resource implications of these new competitive demands. U.S. work systems in manufacturing industries such as auto and steel have become transformed since there is now a need for less direct employee supervision as firms try to reduce labor costs through attrition and make the existing employees more flexible, multiskilled, and productive. Having younger, newly trained workers who knew how to work in new manufacturing approaches using flexible teams, and just-in-time inventories to reduce material and fixed labor costs, was also helpful. The increased capacity for product customization and diversity inherent in the rise of microprocessor technologies also reduced the cost advantages of mass production and increased competition in quality-conscious markets. Consequently, firms in newly industrialized countries and less industrialized countries are competing successfully in price-conscious U.S. markets by offering much lower wages and having more efficient plants. Competing on the basis of cost alone was no longer a viable single strategy for U.S. auto companies. The U.S. auto firms must now be able to compete not only on cost reduction based on cumulative gains in productivity from high-volume mass production of standardized products, but also innovation and/or quality at the same time. Yet for U.S.—and many European—firms it was difficult if not impossible to increase quality and variety without increasing costs. The rise of new global auto producers in the market transformed the requisite business and human resource strategies needed to compete.

Force 3: Threat of Substitutes

The more that an industry has conditions where many product substitutes are available to compete with its products or services, the greater the threat of substitutes. When a threat of substitutes exists and the cost of customer switching to new products is low, it is more likely that a ceiling exists on the prices that can be charged. High substitutability limits an industry's potential for profitability of earnings and growth. Unless a firm is able to increase the quality of the product or differentiate it via intense marketing—e.g., campaigns by Coke and Pepsi, and by McDonald's and Burger King—the threat of substitutes limit profit potential even in boom times.[20] The higher the threat of substitutes, the more important it may be to compete by lowering costs. For example, steel used to be the main product used in manufacturing cars. Now the threat of substitution from plastics and many other materials has increased price-competitive pressures on the steel industry.[21]

A human resource implication of high substitutability is the greater likelihood of increased pressures to reduce or hold labor costs and externalize conditions of employment—e.g., limit job security, use contingent workers, etc. HR strategies may also be adopted to differentiate services based on quality or innovation, assuming labor costs can be kept in line. For a company to be viewed as offering products that have no substitute, human resources is likely to be critical. For example, without great employees, Nordstrom's department store would be unable to offer extraordinary customer service. Without productive employees, Southwest Airlines would be unable to turn its planes so rapidly and have great on-time landing records. Without committed, knowledgeable employees, Toyota would be unable to produce cars of the highest quality.

Forces 4 and 5: Power of Suppliers and Buyers

Buyer power affects potential value creation across many industries. The greater their power, the more customers can force competitors to reduce price or increase the level of service without commensurate remuneration. Buyers tend to be more powerful the more concentrated they are (few in number) and when they buy in volume so that the importance of their purchases in the industry is high. High substitutability for a supplier's product may increase buyers' power to influence the human resource strategies of suppliers. The U.S. Big Three auto companies provide a good example of buyer power. The Big Three have placed intense pressure on suppliers to implement ISO 9000 and other types of quality improvement training. Many suppliers are forced to limit labor costs in order to meet buyers' demands of lower product costs. Buyer power can also affect the supplier's labor relations strategy. For example, Ford Motor Company has reached an agreement with the United Auto Workers (UAW) that its suppliers preferably must be members of the UAW.

Some critics argue that the Big Three have tried to remain profitable more by squeezing suppliers than by actually improving the efficiency of their own work processes. Buyers' pressures on suppliers to reduce costs are most likely to be high when the suppliers provide a material that is a major share of the purchasing cost in the industry— as purchasing decisions naturally first focus on reducing the costs of bigger ticket items.

Like buyer power, suppliers are more powerful if they are dominated by a few companies and are more concentrated than the industry to which they sell. Suppliers also have high power when the products or services they sell are unique and highly differentiated, with few substitutes. For example, the suppliers of many patented drugs in the pharmaceutical industry are often very powerful since there are few substitutes and in some cases a single manufacturer when a patent is held. When suppliers are able to charge customers different prices in accordance with differences in the value created for each buyer, supplier power is high.[22] Because the most important suppliers to the U.S. integrated steel industry are unionized by the United Steel Workers, these suppliers have wielded so much power that labor costs take up to 25 percent of the steel industry's total revenues.[23] Suppliers are also powerful when the industry's buyers are not an important customer of the supplier group or if a buyer's costs of switching to a different supplier are high. For example, IBM has patented a chip used in Powerbook laptop computers that only it and Motorola manufacture. When Apple Computer buys this chip, it must pay dearly for it; this helps IBM to have lower materials costs on the laptop it produces to compete with the similar model made by Apple. When suppliers have a specialized product that is not easily substitutable, they are able to charge a premium for their product. This forces buyers to try to reduce costs in other areas such as labor costs. If the buyer also has high switching costs—for example, perhaps it has invested a lot of training to help employees learn how to operate a supplier's product, such as computer software[24]—the switching costs of retraining employees in a new supplier's system may also be high. These circumstances may escalate buyers' need to continue organizational partnering with powerful suppliers, even costly ones.

The "Sixth" Force: Complementors

Complementors do not show up in Porter's original model, yet they increase customers' or buyers' willingness to purchase a product. Their availability can affect the volume demanded for suppliers' products. Complementors are groups from which buyers purchase complementary services or groups from which suppliers sell complementary products.[25] Complementors affect industry cooperation and are a very different competitive force than the first five forces. Instead of thinking about competitors as deciding how to divide a fixed industry pie, complementors' forces try to make the industry pie bigger for everyone.[26]

Most buyers of a new computer would not view themselves as a customer of Wintel—a colloquial reference to in the computer industry to the Microsoft Windows 98/Intel virtual monopoly on many personal computer products. Yet these complementors have high power—Intel's Pentium chip and the Windows 98 operating system are bundled on most of the computers sold in the United States. (The more that complementors are easily unbundled from products or service, the less their power.) The high concentration of these complementors in the computer industry, the extremely limited substitutability of their products, and the very high costs of switching to other complementors have given Intel and Microsoft tremendous industry power. In 1999, Microsoft was in a bitter antitrust lawsuit with the U.S. government on whether its Internet browser, among other features, should be unbundled from Windows' operating systems. In 1999, Intel did not go to trial but also was involved (and settled) on antitrust matters with the government. An example of an HR strategy implication for powerful complementors is that Intel now trains all its employees in antitrust law to prevent future lawsuits.

In the auto industry, the U.S. Big Three firms had historically ignored dealers, which were run as separate entities, underestimating their role as important complementors affecting the purchase, service, and repeat purchase of a car. Saturn Corporation challenged this assumption by making Saturn car dealers become certified in human resource strategies—especially selection, training, and rewards—to promote excellent customer service. They also required dealers to use nonpressure sales tactics with full information disclosure of costs to all purchasers as a means to gain competitive advantage.

Buyers' or suppliers' need to balance complementors' power can sometimes create cooperative organizational relationships between firms that may also be competitors. This happens in part because, if complementors are too powerful, they also have more license in the market and the freedom to choose not to cooperate with buyers or suppliers. Microsoft and Intel are notorious for cooperating on projects to the extent that Intel has been known to pull out of projects if Microsoft has indicated that it would prefer Intel does. This may have fostered cooperative relationships between other computer competitors. For example, in 1999 Dell and IBM consummated a seven-year deal to have many of Dell's personal computer components manufactured by arch-rival IBM. This may be a way for IBM and Dell to gain market power against not only other competitors, but also powerful complementors such as Intel and Microsoft.

MODULE
2

Strategies for Gaining Competitive Advantage.   Having assessed competitive industry forces, a firm can begin to consider strategies to compete in the marketplace. Corporate strategies involve decisions on the mix of businesses a firm holds and the allocation of resources among these businesses. Within a firm, different strategies can be pursued across business units to gain competitive advantage.

A *cost leadership* strategy involves developing operational efficiency so that products or services can be priced generally lower than average than the industry competition. A company following this strategy might strive to reduce or hold administrative expenses and labor and material costs, implement efficient technology for the development of products and services, and seek high volume to support economies of scale. Firms are profitable by being able to both charge lower prices and experience a higher volume, or charge average prices for the industry but enjoy higher profit margins.[27] An example is discount retailers such as Wal-Mart, K-Mart, or Target, which have eroded department store profits by offering name-brand merchandise in less plush surroundings with little sales service but lower prices.

Having lower costs and offering lower prices is not the only way to compete. Another way is to compete through product *differentiation*. Firm's charge a premium for their products or services because they offer the customer services that are extraordinary or better than the competition or are unique or innovative in the market. The nature of the industry may influence the success of a differentiation strategy. For example, in bulk commodities, it might be very difficult to compete on differentiation—being low cost is all that matters to the customer.[28]

Some strategists believe that firms need to choose between competing on lower costs or on differentiated products or services. For example, many customers are willing to pay more for a Toyota than a Hyundai, but the costs of manufacturing a Toyota are higher than a Hyundai. Toyota's profits are based on the fact that the premium it charges for its cars enables higher profit margins, despite the higher incremental costs associated with production.[29]

A *focus strategy*[30] is where a firm competes by carving out a market niche and serving customers that the market underserves or ignores. These companies can charge a premium for their services since the market has overlooked these segments. Examples might include companies that give loans to individuals with poor credit backgrounds, a retailer that focuses on gourmet take-out dinners for working parents, or a clothes manufacturer focusing on petite women.

Another way to gain competitive advantage using a hybrid of differentiation and operational efficiency is through *speed to market*. Here, firms differentiate themselves by having operational excellence that enables them to deliver services or develop new products faster than their competitors. They are able to charge higher prices since they deliver these services or new products ahead of others in the industry. For example DaimlerChrysler, has gained competitive advantage by by having a product cycle design and manufacturing time for a new car from the engineering drawing board to the dealer lot for some of its products such as minivans that is half the time (at least a year or more shorter) than General Motors.

Assessing Value: Core Competencies, Resources, and Activity Streams. In developing organizational strategy, it is critical for a firm to conduct strategic analysis to identify its core competencies, most valuable resources, and how workflow activity streams add value to customers.

Core Competencies: A Resource-Based View

Professors Prahalad and Hamel developed the notion of *core competencies,*[31] the idea that companies should identify and organize around what they do best. Corporate strategy should not be based on products or services but on competencies that give a company access to several markets and are difficult for competitors to imitate. Core competencies should reflect the diverse learning of the organization, especially how to coordinate diverse skills and production streams and organizational systems. Core competencies are the collective learning of the corporation that provide access to multiple markets, add substantial value to the end product received by customers, and are difficult for competitors to imitate.

For example, Disney Co.'s strategy is not based on the products of theme parks, toys, or movies per se. More aptly, its unique market capability or core competency is being one of the best mass communication companies in the world and having employees who are talented in communicating with customers. Disney is able to communicate entertainment better than most of its rivals, and customers are willing to pay a premium for the Disney experience—whether in their parks, at their movies, or in their retail stores. The company also places a good deal of emphasis on communications in its human resource strategy from management to cast member (theme park employee), from cast member to guest (customer), and from cast member to management.[32] Because Disney is able to communicate entertainment better than most firms, it has achieved access to market share in many arenas.[33]

Core competencies reflect people-embodied skills[34] and a resource-based view of strategy. Resource-based theorists argue that human assets can be a source of sustainable competitive advantage because tacit knowledge and social complexity are hard to imitate.[35] Strategic HRM involves the identification, development, and deployment of organizational competencies and capable human assets, which are used as the basis for strategy development. Core competencies involve the way people work together, cooperate, and cross functional and business-unit boundaries. Core competencies relate to how the organization works as a whole, which is why they are difficult for competitors to develop and copy.[36] The skills that constitute core competencies must cluster around individuals so that efforts are not so narrowly focused that members cannot recognize opportunities for blending functional expertise with others in new and interesting ways."[37] The management culture must be one where unit managers recognize they are "stewards" rather than "owners" of human resources.[38]

Prahalad and Hamel note that although many executives will proclaim that "people are our most important asset," the focus on human capital as core competencies has generally been undervalued by many U.S. firms in comparison to firms in other countries such as Japan. For example, in the United States, the head of finance typically has more status and power than the head of personnel. Yet in Japanese companies, typically the situation is reversed—access to competencies via people rather than access to cash are considered the primary drivers of growth.[39] It is also not uncommon in Japanese companies such as Hitachi for senior HR executives to have senior line management experience. Most senior HR executives in the United States rarely move laterally into senior line management positions.

Value Chain Analysis of Workflow Activity Stream

Another approach to formulating competitive strategy involves analysis of the activity streams related to the producing and delivery of a product or service. Activity analysis focuses on the resources expended in production or service delivery and often involves competitive cost analysis related to the firm's activity stream. Value chain analysis is based on the idea that firms should expend the most financial and managerial resources on activities that add a lot of value to its goods or services. It focuses on "doing the right things" as opposed to simply "doing things right" (e.g., being efficient).[40]

Classic value chain analysis shows the series of primary and support activities that are performed to transform inputs (raw materials, components supplies) into a product delivered to a customer (see Figure 2.2).[41] Based on this analysis, a firm would attempt to reduce or eliminate activities that add the least value. Unfortunately, for human resources, value chain analysis has led to the outsourcing of some administrative transaction-based activities of human resources (e.g. payroll, benefits).

While Figure 2.2 best fits manufacturing firms and focuses on what the firm *does* in producing the product, a customer-focused value chain analysis begins with identification of customer needs and delineates all direct and indirect activities associated

MODULE
2

FIGURE 2.2 *Sample Activity Value Chain: Primary and Support Activities*[42]

Primary Activities of a Mass-Production Manufacturing Firm

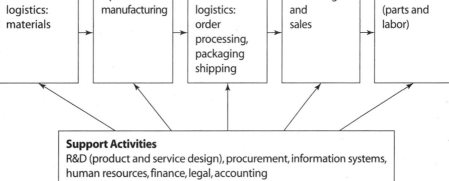

FIGURE 2.3 *Customer-Focused Value Chain*

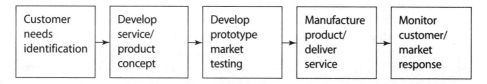

Source: Adapted from Fahye, *Competitors.*

with customer interaction (see Figure 2.3).[43] This analysis is relevant for customized products and for activity analysis of service delivery businesses such as publishing, insurance, systems integration, software, and advertising. For example, Dell Computer Company tries to fill as many computer orders as possible via employees who directly interface with customers who order over the Internet. This enables Dell to eliminate hundreds of purchasing jobs, thereby minimizing human resources devoted only to procurement activities in the activity stream. The processing of a purchasing form adds limited value to the perceived customer value of the end product. The organizational resources that would have been allocated to procurement can now be reallocated to research and development of future products, thereby giving Dell a competitive advantage. The elimination of middlemen between the customer and employees not only gives Dell a speed-to-market advantage, but also improves service quality, since fewer processing mistakes are likely to be made due to miscommunication. Even when a mistake does occur, an employee can respond to it immediately without waiting to be told.

HR is also a service delivery business. It serves internal customers, the firm's employees and managers. The customer-focused view of value chain as shown in Figure 2.3 could also be adapted for the HR function. How efficiently HR is organized for service delivery has increasingly been viewed as critical for the support of business financial and strategic objectives.[44]

Adding More Value-Through Benefits Customer Service at IBM: HR as a Business[45]

IBM's reengineering of its HR function is based on the principles of value chain analysis. It enabled IBM to reduce costs by 50 percent, but also improve services. Rather than outsourcing, the company centralized its benefits function into a national benefits service center. HR had become a very expensive, bloated staff function at IBM. It was not adding sufficient value in relation to the activities and resources that were being expended. The ratio of HR staff to employees was extraordinarily high (1:61), when on average it is 1:100 for all companies in a Bureau of National Affairs survey. IBM had a large number of benefits experts—220 benefits administrators alone. Technology was not being used effectively, as paper-driven processes were still in heavy use. Even when computers were used, there were more than 2,200 HR computer applications. Additionally, customers (employees and managers) were not being well served. There were inconsistent interpretations to the same benefits questions as staff members in business units across the country had different answers, leading employees to "shop around" even within the company until they got the answer they wanted. Multiple layers of staff review at the local, division, and corporate level slowed new program implementation. When IBM experienced a $3.4 billion loss in 1991, the company restructured into autonomous business units. Expanding HR to provide staff support for each of the decentralized business units would have been counter to the firm's competitive strategy of cost reduction.

IBM first tinkered with ways to reduce costs within HR and even outsourcing of activities. The company realized that its HR staff had the skills and competencies to compete effectively with outside vendors. It appeared that IBM could make profits by selling its HR services to other companies, which could help offset internal expenses. The firm implemented transfer pricing that made IBM's HR services competitive with external vendors and a stand-alone business. After a nine-month waiting period, if IBM vendors were not competitive, managers were free to source services externally.

In 1995, IBM decided to consolidate regional benefits centers in a National Resource Service Center in Raleigh, North Carolina. It was estimated that after start-up costs, centralization would reduce HR labor expenses by 40 percent. Employees and managers can access benefits information and process transactions though the Internet or automated voice response. If they need more assistance, there is a three-tiered structure. Tier 1 customer service generalists use an online HR knowledge-based system to locate answers and find solutions for customers. More difficult questions are passed on to Tier 2 subject matter specialists. Tier 3 involves experts who deal with policy and program design issues and critical incidents. A survey showed 90 percent satisfaction with the benefits services.[46]

Complementary Activity and Resource-Based Strategic Analysis: The Case of Southwest Airlines

Although resource- and activity-based views of the firm have sometimes been depicted as opposing views, Harvard Business School Professor Pankaj Ghemawat views them as complementary. Activity-based views focus on the activities the firm does, while resource-based views focus on the resources the firm deploys. If a firm's activity chain fits together in a way that is difficult to imitate, it can provide competitive advantage. Similarly, if a firm is able to develop and deploy resources that are unique, capable, well linked, and difficult to imitate, competitive advantage can also be achieved. Ghemawat discusses the case of Southwest Airlines to show how it gains competitive advantage through both its activity stream and resources.[47]

Southwest Airlines is the only U.S. airlines that has been consistently profitable over the past 25 years. It has grown at an annual rate of 20–30 percent over the past five years. Although Southwest specializes in short-haul flights, its operational efficiency enables it to fly its planes an average of 11.5 hours a day, compared with an average 8.6 hours for the industry. Because of this resource utilization advantage, Southwest is able to operate with a third fewer planes than competitors. And it leads the industry in customer service ratings.

Southwest is able to conduct the activities of frequent reliable departures because it has simplified the activities employee perform at the gate such as delivering food service and baggage transfer. It also employs more human resources but less information technology than its rivals in its turnaround process. While Southwest dedicates a "case manager" operations agent to turnaround each flight, a competitor might assign an operations agent 10 to 15 flights to turn around at a time. Southwest's approach to resource deployment on the right activities reduces turnaround time by facilitating employee control, coaching, and coordination of interdependent activities. The lean, highly productive ground crews are a source of competitive advantage, because Southwest deploys human resources efficiently to do the right activities that add the most value.

Human resources and the way they are deployed are clearly core competencies. They are firm specific, and labor costs account for a large share of the value added to the airline industry. Despite being unionized and following a low cost strategy, Southwest has high levels of productivity and is consistently viewed as one of the best companies to work for in the United States.

Human Resource Strategy

Strategy and Structure Linkages: Evolving Strategic HR Roles

> Strategic human resource management is the pattern of planned human resource deployments and activities intended to help an organization achieve its goals.
> —Wright and McMahan[48]

MODULE
2

> A business enterprise has an external strategy; a chosen way of competing in the marketplace. It also needs an internal strategy: a strategy for how its internal resources are to be developed, deployed, motivated, and controlled . . . external and internal strategies must be linked.
>
> —Beer and Spector[49]

> Human resource strategy is an organization's fundamental approach toward the management of employees to ensure that the firm achieves its business objectives in the marketplace. The separate activities such as selection, recruitment, compensation and benefits, performance appraisal, training, collective bargaining and others that comprise the human resource function are integrated to provide a unified pattern to the employment relationship and are directly related to environmental and business conditions.
>
> —Milkovich and Boudreau[50]

There are many definitions of strategic human resource management (SHRM). The definitions offered above are based on the traditional view of SHRM. They are grounded in the philosophy that structures, cultures, and systems follow strategy. This follows early historical analysis of strategy by Alfred Chandler,[51] who maintained that the structure of an organization (which includes HR policies and systems) followed from its strategy.[52] He found that different growth strategies and stages such as expansion of volume, geographic dispersion, vertical integration between the firm and it suppliers or distributors, and product diversification evolved to different structures. As organizations such as General Motors and other major U.S. firms grew and became larger and more complex, they underwent structural transformation from functional to product to multidivisional structural forms. Firms that failed to align their structures with their new strategies for growth faced inefficiencies that eventually forced them to either adapt or go out of business.[53]

SHRM's main goal is to enhance corporate capability to implement corporate strategy. Just as firms will be faced with inefficiencies when they try to implement new strategies with outmoded structures, they will face problems of inappropriate implementation when they try to effect new strategies with incongruent HR systems. The main management task of SHRM is to align the formal structure and the HR systems so they can drive strategic objectives.[54] This view is essentially the organizational transition or strategy execution role noted in this book's framework.

Of course, HR activities must be designed and implemented to support business and strategic objectives. Yet consider the following strategic expectations of human resources that have arisen:

> HRM (has) a role in creating competitive advantage, in which the skills and motivation of a company's people and the way they are deployed can be a major source of competitive advantage. A company can methodically identify where its HR strengths lie, and gear its HRM policies and business strategies toward utilizing and developing these advantages. The HR skills that will be crucial for the future in its industry can be identified, and (the company) can take steps to acquire these.
>
> —Hendry and Pettigrew[55]

> HR should become an agent of continuous transformation, shaping processes and a culture that together can improve an organization's capacity for change. . . . HR can be the architect of new cultures.
>
> —Ulrich[56]

These definitions show increasing emphasis on the transformational role. They also imply a resource-based view of SHRM analogous to core competencies discussed earlier in this chapter. The firm is seen as a bundle of tangible and intangible resources and capabilities required for market competition.[57] Both quotations imply that HR can help identify and organize core competencies and/or can shape cultural transformation. SHRM involves the identification, development, and deployment of organizational capabilities, which are used as the basis for strategy development.

Thus, SHRM can sometimes involve fitting structures to strategies (the classic strategy execution transition role). It can also align strategies to structures or competencies (the transformational role).[58] The latter asks "What core competencies do we have, or can we have that will make or sustain our competitive strategy and enable individual business to adapt to changing conditions?"[59]

Human Resource Strategy Framework.   The human resource strategy framework (Figure 2.4 on page 2.18) shows the steps in strategic HRM formation.[60] While the framework is linear as depicted, in reality it is a fluid, iterative process involving continuous interaction between the firm's organizational response and its environmental pressures. As the model shows, the first SHRM stage is strategic analysis and organizational strategy formulation. The next stage is human resource strategy development and execution. The last stage involves organizational adaptation and performance outcomes. The model shows that organizational culture is the mechanism through which HR practices effect employee group and organizational outcomes.[61] The factors in each of these stages will be examined briefly below with examples provided.

Firm Strategic Analysis and Formulation

External Environment Scan

INDUSTRY COMPETITIVE PRESSURES.   Because the external environments in which it operates have become increasingly complex, the firm must scan the external environment to assess current and forecast future trends. These trends relate to the industry, stakeholders, and situational factors. The firm should first conduct a *strategic analysis of industry competitive pressures,* the six forces that were discussed in detail toward the beginning of this module and need not be repeated here. In essence, this analysis should answer the questions: "How is our market changing and why do we exist?" and "What are key success factors needed to compete?"

STAKEHOLDER ANALYSIS.   Next the firm should also conduct stakeholder analysis. A stakeholder is any group that has a stake in the firm's performance.[62] These may include but are not limited to shareholders, employees, owners, government, communities, unions, customers, suppliers, and managers. Each of these different groups will have different interests and expectations of organizational effectiveness and performance. For example, while shareholders may see performance as being most effective if profits are maximized, employees as a group may have different views. Workers may want the business goals of efficiency, growth, and investment balanced with their needs for job security, equity, job satisfaction, and economic and family well-being. Managers must shape organizational and HR strategy in a way that effectively minimizes differences between stakeholders, and contains conflict should it arise.[63]

The case of Iowa Beef Packers' (IBP) opening of a new meat packing plant in a small town in Iowa shows how HR policies can differentially affect stakeholders. The new plant created 1,300 jobs, bringing a payroll of $23 million to a town of only 1,400. Initially, the community was happy as the plant brought new stores, new roads, and prosperity. The Teamsters Union was happy because IBP had a good safety record and the plant created jobs for many surrounding unionized suppliers. However, in order to fill many of the jobs, the company imported poor and underprivileged people from Michigan, Texas, and Chicago. Many individuals, some African-American and Hispanic, came to this formerly nearly all-white town with no more than the clothes they were wearing. The company had to provide housing and transportation for many. Since the work was hard, many employees left after only a few months. Crime rose by 400 percent in the town, and school pupil turnover was as high as 25 percent per semester. The company realized it needed to make more donations to the United Way. This case illustrates how multiple stakeholder analysis is critical to effective strategy development.[64]

FIGURE 2.4 *The Human Resource Strategy Framework*

Organizational Adaptation and Performance Outcomes

Firm Strategic Analysis and Formulation
1. External environment scan/forecast
   - Competitor/industry
   - Stakeholder analysis
   - Environmental situational factors (e.g., social, political, technological, legal)
2. Internal capital assessment
   - Financial
   - Physical and technological
   - Human
     ✓ Workforce skills, abilities, competencies, culture management/style values
3. Identify competencies and sources of competitive advantage
4. Organizational strategy formulation
   - Mission and vision
   - Strategic thrusts:
     ✓ Financial
     ✓ Human capital
     ✓ Technological
     ✓ Research and Development
     ✓ Marketing

Human Resource Strategy Development and Execution
5. Management choices and constraints regarding the HR and people deployment
6. HR planning and organization design of policy clusters
   - HR strategy and work organization
   - Talent ID and deployment
   - Human capital development
   - Reward management
   - Employee relations, quality of work environment, and voice
7. Allocate resources and develop processes and systems for HR role delivery
   - Transactions
   - Translation
   - Transition
   - Transformation

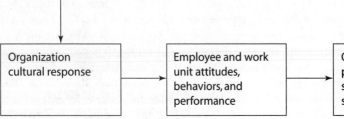

Situational Environmental Analysis of Key Workplace Trends.   Organizational and human resource strategies are shaped by external environments. The complexity, heterogeneity, and turbulence of these environments affect a firm's need for environmental information and demand for resources from the environment.[65] In order to develop appropriate operating, financial, and people components of the overarching business strategy, the firm must understand the many environmental factors that affect these resources. Table 2.1 shows sample environmental trends shaping human resource strategy in the future workplace. Examples of how technological, social, political, and economic forces might interact with the human resource component of the business strategy are discussed below. This same analysis could be done for the financial or other components of business strategy.

Technological forces, such as the tremendous growth of the Internet and intranets (in-house electronic computer communication systems) have demolished time and distance between employees. This certainly influences HR strategy, as it has transformed the workplace and the way that work is done. It has shrunken markets and workplaces, increased the rapidity of doing business, and reduced product life cycles. Each firm needs to identify the workplace trends that are most relevant for their industry and

TABLE 2.1   *Sample Environmental Trends Shaping SHRM: Workplace of the Future*

Traditional Workplace	Future HR Trend
Technology controlled by experts	Employees have greater control over technology
Segmented work/life boundaries	Increased blurring work/life boundaries
U.S. culturally dominated HR policies in multinationals	Global best practices of HR policies
Basic compliance with U.S. equal employment opportunity and affirmative action laws	Manage diversity toward multiculturalism
Long-term employment relationship	Greater contingency and variation in employment relationships
Only HR delivers HR services	Greater line management and employee involvement in service delivery; more outsourcing
Assumption of workforce homogeneity	HR systems designed with attention to heterogeneity (ethnicity, language, country, age, family structure)
HR policies mandated for groups	HR policies individually negotiated
Jobs designed for individual work	Jobs designed for individuals *and* teamwork
Standardized worksites and schedules	Flexiplace (work may be done at home, or customer or firm); employees have greater control over where, when, and how work is done
Explicit management-determined formal HR policies	Implicit systems (more of HR work is culturally driven)
Hired to fit a specific job	Hired to fit culture
Company-driven careers	Boundaryless careers—self-driven

MODULE
2

employees. Take the example of "Java Round the Clock at IBM." A group of programmers at the Tsinghua University in Beijing writes software using Java technology and then sends their work over the Internet to an IBM facility in Seattle. From there programmers work on it and send it to the Institute of Computer Science in Belarus and a software house in Latvia. The work is then sent to the Tata Group in India and then back to Beijing by morning, continuing the global relay that never ceases until the work is done. As the head of IBM's Internet division commented: "Once you're on the Web, going global is a natural. The difference between Peoria and Romania on the Web is not very large."[66]

The advent of new technology such as point-of-sale (POS) computer and network systems has revolutionized the way work is done and the types of human resources needed. Applebee's Restaurants, owned by Darden Restaurants, Inc., have a POS computer system known as OSCAR, which stands for Operating Strategically Competitive Applebee's Restaurants. OSCAR has reduced administrative work as the system is able to do automatic labor scheduling, perpetual inventory, and all sales audit and cash management tasks. It enables management to compare, for example, the sales from the most recent previous 20 Saturdays or Sundays with sales for the same period a year ago. This means managers can plan better for how many workers are needed, how much food to order, and what customers are likely to demand. The new PosiTouch screen registers have item descriptions so server takers are no longer required to memorize prices or look up item numbers to place an order. This proves to be very fast and accurate, and reduces the time and money spent on training. ProHost numeric pagers keep a restaurant or beverage manager only a page away if a problem occurs. Technology has also changed hiring practices. Today's new hires know that technology and the ability to use it effectively are part of the job. The intranet is used to convey company policies, procedures, customer comments, and business forms. It also has an in-house chat room, and allows ordering inventory directly from distributors.[67]

Technology has had *social* implications by increasingly blurring the boundaries between work and home for some employees who have jobs suitable for telecommuting. Work-at-home alternatives via technology can empower some employees to live where they want and have greater control over when, where, and how work is done—creating a *flexiplace*. With the ability of some employees to increasingly do work at home without ever or rarely coming into the office, many key issues related to supervision and the measurement of performance and productivity are in flux. Issues such as "What is the work day?," "What is the workplace?," "What is absenteeism?," "How should performance be measured when the employee is not visible to the manager most of the day?" are raised. "How does one create a cohesive workplace culture among employees and managers who have less face-to-face interaction than ever before?" is also made salient. A study by the General Accounting Office of the U.S. government notes that some federal managers are having difficulties in changing from managing by observation to managing by results. The report found that some managers and supervisors resisted allowing staff to participate in flexiplace policies such as telecommuting because they could not believe employees were working unless they could see them.[68]

Many other alternative work schedules are being used besides work-at-home options. At McDonald's, for example, employees at all levels are supported with alternative work schedules. There are many part-time managers who work 20 hours a week. These employees maintain benefits and vacation days and keep a prorated salary. McDonald's is also experimenting with job sharing and a flex week (3–4 days).[69]

Growing workforce diversity is another important social trend. By the year 2020, white non-Hispanics will account for only 68 percent of the U.S. population. General Motors' current strategy is to sell more vehicles to a diverse customer group. It therefore has adopted HR and organizational systems to better link the firm to diverse markets. For example, GM now tries to incorporate women and minorities into the vehicle engineering and design processes. Changing buyer demographics have driven GM's efforts to form new alliances with diverse groups. For example, the company has been very successful with its minority- and women-owned dealerships. Its Minority Dealer Development Academy Program has had a high success rate across the country in preparing well-operating automotive dealerships that survive.[70]

Economic forces such as the 1998 economic crisis in the Far East can lead to industry overcapacity and low earnings. For example, although Japan has had a jobs-for-life policy for employees working for the most prestigious companies, in 1999 many began instituting massive layoffs. Payrolls and wages may have to be cut by 7 percent before companies return to health, as plants are still operating far under capacity. Sony Electronics will shed 17,000 workers and close 20 percent of its factories by 2003. It will also restructure to become leaner and more centralized. Sony's ten internal companies will be regrouped into four autonomous units focused on products and networks. Each will be allocated research funds and will be forced to justify its existence by profits. The home office's function in Japan will shift to oversee but not manage the company's units. It will also scout for investments. Consequently, by 2003 headquarters staff will be cut from 2,500 to several hundred employees. Similarly, NEC Corporation will shed 15,000 employees worldwide by 2003. Hitachi has already made 4,000 cuts, and more are coming. Japan's top 15 banks have agreed to cut almost 20,000 jobs by 2004.[71]

Political and legal environmental pressures have induced many multinational firms to hire a workforce that is representative of the host country. Some countries will simply not let the multinational have access to new markets unless an agreement is made to hire local labor. The rise of global corporations and product markets means that the days when companies could create products domestically and ship them abroad "as is" are gone. Now employees need to "think globally but act locally." This means employees must strive to constantly remain literate in international commerce, customers, and cultures more than ever before.

New legal developments are constantly occurring. The U.S. Supreme Court recently ruled in *Burlington Industries v. Ellerth* [118 S. Ct. 2257, Sup. Ct. 1998], for example, that in sexual harassment cases, an employer can no longer use the "we didn't know" defense. Training employees and managers on legal trends is imperative unless a business wants to expose itself to large legal liability. The company can also save money in settlement costs if it has a clear, concise sexual harassment policy that is accessible to all employees. Having a policy in an employee handbook it does not distribute will not insulate a company from liability. The U.S. foodchain, Ruby Tuesday restaurants, for example, requires all employees to watch a video on sexual harassment prior to starting work.

MODULE
2

Internal Capital Assessment   A business strategy must conduct an internal assessment of its strengths and weaknesses for competing in the market. Internal capital includes several components: financial, physical, technological, and human. The human component includes an evaluation of the workforce, the organization's culture and management values, and current organizational structure, and the technology used in production.

WORKFORCE, PRODUCT DEMANDS, CULTURE, MANAGEMENT VALUES, STRUCTURE. *Workforce analysis* assesses the degree to which the workforce possesses the individual and group capabilities needed to win. How technologically up-to-date is the workforce? What is the mix of values and skills, and how do these relate to critical success factors needed to compete in the market? *Cultural analysis* assesses the firm's unwritten values and assumptions about how to operate in its environment. Are these values based on cooperation or competitiveness? Are we hierarchical or egalitarian? Do we value conformity or diversity? Is work viewed as a job or drudgery?[72] Do we value promotion from within, or are outsiders viewed as innovative leaders for hire?

The nature of labor relations is another important workforce consideration. For years, Saturn Corporation had a competitive advantage due to its revolutionary partnership between management and the United Auto Workers. The 28-page Memorandum of Agreement, one that fits in a shirt pocket instead of the usual three-inch binder, gave Saturn tremendous workforce flexibility.[73] For example, Saturn promotes high quality via self-directed work teams, which would have been impossible under a traditional UAW agreement with rigid job classifications. Unfortunately in spring 1999, when sales of Saturns dipped in the market, the workers at Saturn voted in militant union leaders and voted out leaders who had cooperated with management. The effects of this change on Saturn's ability to continue to use a committed workforce as a means to build extraordinary customer loyalty for repeat purchases remains to be seen.

Certainly the *nature of the product* sold often correlates with the predominant nature of the workforce. Firms that produce a product that is technologically sophisticated or in which labor adds a great deal of value are more likely to have cultures and management values that support heavy investment in firm-specific human assets, such as SAS Corporation in the computer software industry. One reason for this is that such firms require stable employment and employees with the necessary intellectual capital to work with the sophisticated technology. On the other hand, firms that produce products in which labor does not work with sophisticated technology, such as apparel manufacturing, are more likely to be able to be competitive with labor that is viewed as less firm specific. Workers are viewed as more exchangeable, as management may believe that "almost anyone can do the job." The more that the product made is susceptible to cost differentiation pressures, the less likely the firm is to adopt bundles of human resource practices that are a high investment and based on a long-term employment relationship.

Clearly, an organization's cultural approach for managing its workforce employees has implications for a firm's long-term success. The Hay Group, the Philadelphia-based management consulting firm, developed the 1998 list of *Fortune* magazine's most globally admired companies by interviewing executives from firms that ranked at or near the top of their industries. The companies—which were consistently highly profitable and highly admired for how their organizations were run—included among others Asea Brown Boveri, Toyota, 3M, Intel, Southwest Airlines, Bristol Meyers Squibb, Dow Chemical, and J. P. Morgan. The results of the study found that the single best predictor of excellence was a company's ability to attract, motivate, and retain talent. The CEOs interviewed invariably stated that their corporate culture was their most important business lever. What kind of corporate culture works? The main values of corporate cultures of high-performing companies were: teamwork, fair treatment of employees, initiative, innovation, and customer focus.[74] Human resource practices policies and the way they shape the culture send a powerful message to employees about how to act, think, and feel at work.

Sometimes cultural values and the workforce will need to be adapted to support strategic change. For example, Hewlett-Packard (HP), which was the cornerstone of California's Silicon Valley, had a culture that valued innovation and entrepreneurship. Its management values were that the firm should engage in adaptive practices that fit a sensible strategy for the business context (the needs and expectations of stakeholders). HP started out as a scientific instruments company. The original HP culture was a promote-from-within culture. When it entered the computer business, it altered this practice. Why? To do well in computers (and HP's principles stated that firms are not to enter businesses in which they can't do well and make money), the firm needed to have people who knew the customers and the computer business. There were simply not enough HP managers who did. HP was able to change the norm of promotion from within because it also had management values that supported adaptation.[75]

Sometimes current organizational structures are not appropriate for the strategy needed to compete in the industry. Responding to the ever-shifting fortune of high-technology companies, HP announced in spring 1999 that it needed to split into two independent companies in an effort to have organizational structures that would allow the firm to compete in a more market-focused way. Two independent companies were formed: one focusing on computers, printers, and scanners, and the other on electronic test equipment and medical technology products. The latter, while prestigious and the one on which the company had been founded, had recently been marked by higher overhead and slower growth than the company had realized in computers, printers, and scanners. The computer business is one in which HP faces tougher industry pressures and intense rivalry, which has resulted in heavy price cutting. While HP's computer business revenues grew 3 percent in 1998 to $10.2 billion, in contrast, Dell's sales grew by 38 percent in the same period. Also, Dell has grabbed market share from HP with the direct sales model that eliminates the overhead of dealers and distributors and allows it to sell machines at higher profit margins. The new structure will enable each HP business to focus on its core competencies. The complexity and confusion of having so many businesses under one roof outweighed the synergy of having them all together.[76]

In sum, the current assessment of the firm's human assets is critical for strategy development. It is also critical that strategies are designed with the understanding that human assets, while a strategic asset like an oil field, are different from other forms of capital. Human assets involve tacit knowledge and social complexity that is hard to imitate. They are also difficult to manage as a strategic asset. Strategist Russell Coff points out that "once acquired, an oil field (1) cannot quit and move to a competing firm, (2) cannot demand higher or more equitable wages, (3) cannot reject the firms authority or become unmotivated, (4) need not be satisfied with supervision, coworkers, or advancement opportunities."[77]

Identify Competencies and Sources of Competitive Advantage   The concierge at any Four Seasons hotel will tell you how proud he or she is to work for a firm that delivers world-class service at all levels of the hotel in all locations. An employee at Red Storm Entertainment (named after the American spy novel of the same name by author Tom Clancy) will tell you how much fun it is to work for firm a that is able to not only develop Clancylike military games but also other kinds of top-notch computer software games year after year.[78] As discussed earlier in this chapter, companies that know how to coordinate their collective learning of diverse organizational activities from research and development to production to supplier management have core competencies that are a competitive advantage.

MODULE
2

Competitive analysis should identify core competencies such as these and other sources of competitive advantage. Core competencies are likely to involve people, since deploying organizational learning across functions and a firm's ability to embrace organizational learning involve human capabilities.

Other sources of competitive advantage may be the ability to vertically or horizontally integrate key players in the industry chain. Besides a great culture that treats employees well, Starbucks Coffee has been able to successfully grow because it has access to suppliers and technology that give it great control over the quality and delivery of its product. Supply Chain Operations (SPO) is a unit of Starbucks that involves three roasting plants. Keeping up with the growth of the company has been an incredible challenge. SPO developed technology that pushed the envelope to keep coffee fresh, which has now enabled Starbucks to move into new markets that it could never service before. Prior to SPO, Starbucks' stringent standards on freshness never allowed them to grind their coffee before selling it. Now with enhanced technology such as the flavor-lock seal, the wholly enclosed roasting and grinding process that prevents oxygen from being introduced into the coffee, and control over the supply of quality coffee, Starbucks can now serve customers in new venues. (Recall that a core competency gives a firm access to multiple markets and is difficult for competitors to imitate.) The new types of markets Starbucks is serving range from United Airlines to Barnes and Noble Cafe, from Westin hotels to an international catalog mail order group that meets customer demands in locations that do not have any retail stores.[79]

Organizational Strategy Formulation

Once the organization has assessed its current internal and external situation, the key to any successful business plan is to have a vision of where the company wants to be in the future. A mission statement is present-oriented and describes what the company does—its purpose. A vision statement is future-oriented and defines what the firm wants to become in the next three to ten years. The vision statement is a very important part of the business plan because it defines the company's direction. A good vision statement ought to paint a picture in all employees' minds of where the organization wants to be. For example, Starbucks had a brief but highly effective vision statement of "2000 stores by 2000." A vision should be verifiable—i.e., measurable. Slick words like "world class" may sound impressive but do not give the firm anything to measure. The vision statement's purpose is to ensure that the firm's strategy can be communicated to every employee. It should be in language that employees can understand. It should also be inspirational. It should make employees feel good about the company direction, so they are motivated to help ensure that the vision comes true. Cargill provides a good example of a motivating vision statement: "Raise the standard of living in every country where we do business and double in size every five to ten years." This vision statement is inspirational yet measurable.[80]

Having developed the mission and vision, management will develop organizational projections including how each function or business unit will be affected by projected changes in the marketplace and business. The projections help identify gaps between the current situation and the desired future. Then the plan can identify areas for improvement or opportunities to gain competitive advantage, as well as obstacles (e.g., competitors' or suppliers' actions, etc.) or barriers to be removed.[81] These can be organized into broad strategic thrusts regarding the firms' operating, technological, financial, marketing, and people strategy. The methods the company will use to operationalize these strategic thrusts, with a timetable and measures of each objective, can be delineated. The plan should also state how much it will cost as well as how much it will generate in revenues and profit.[82]

Human Resource Strategy Development and Execution

Management Choices and Constraints Regarding the Deployment of People

In order for successful deployment of the business plan to occur, leaders must hold themselves responsible to disseminate information about the role of employees in achieving the strategy. Management must be visionary leaders as well as transformational leaders, and be able to obtain members' commitment to achieving that vision.[83]

James Walker, the founder of the Human Resource Planning Society, has written extensively on the human resource strategy component. Business executives and managers working with the human resource department leadership should develop long-term strategies to answer important people issues. Some strategies may utilize multiple programs and functions. Human resource strategies are broadly stated, before they can be translated into specific HR policies and action plans. He gives a number of examples: "Become the preferred employer (or employer of choice) of quality talent in the markets in which we compete for talent." Another possibility: "Become an industry leader in improving teamwork and enhancing productivity." Still another: " Establish performance management as a way of life, aligning individual and team objectives with business goals and customer requirements, evaluating results achieved, and coaching for continual improvement." Alternatively, some firms select strategic HR focus areas such as managing diversity, or retooling the workforce to enhance technological capability.[84]

In developing the human resource strategy, it is important for management to be clear about its values pertaining to the firm's overarching approach to the employment relationship as discussed in Module 1 of this book. According to the first module, employment relations strategies generally fall into three main types: the workforce commitment model, the labor transactional model, and the mixed core-noncore approach. These alternative approaches to the employment exchange relationship have varying business and psychological implications for not only how employees, workgroups, and organizations behave, but also how they think and feel in performing their jobs. These approaches have tremendous implications for the design and delivery of HR policies and the amount of organizational resources devoted to developing people as asset-specific resources. For example, Howard Schultz, the CEO of Starbucks Coffee Company had a very different philosophy about how to treat people in the restaurant retail industry, which historically says the customer always comes first. At Starbucks, Schultz says, "The employee comes first." The first line in Starbucks' mission statement is "Provide a work environment where we treat each other with dignity and respect." The result: great benefits for workers and security for the employee. The average turnover of a Starbucks employee is 50 percent in an industry where the norm is 400 percent. Less turnover means less training time and costs. Taking a commitment approach to the employment relationship has paid off for Starbucks. Since 1989, Starbucks has reported a compounded annual revenue growth rate of 80 percent. Profit margins have also improved each quarter. Customers keep coming back for more. Some store sales are often up 10 percent from the previous year—which is double the 5 percent most retailers would be happy to achieve.[85]

HR strategy decisions occur not in a vacuum but in a business context. As argued in Module 1, there are levels of constraints that affect the degree to which management has discretion over the determination of human resource strategies and decisions. On occasion, employers have full *unilateral discretion* over human resource matters, and may act as they believe is in the best interest of shareholders, employees, management, or other constituents. In other situations, the implementation of HR issues must be *negotiated* with employees, either formally via legal or union representatives, or informally with each individual worker. In still other cases, constraints are *imposed* from the outside, usually because of laws and legal regulations of governments. These constraints must be considered in HR strategy development.

HR Planning and Design of HR Policy Clusters   Having developed HR strategies, managerial systems and action plans need to be developed. The action plans specify what will be done by whom, how, when, and at what cost. The human resource plans ideally should be integrated with the business plans at each business level (e.g., corporate, division, plant, or sales office, etc.). Alternatively, when they are developed as separate functional plans in a process parallel to business plan development, they tend to be viewed as owned by only the human resources function, as opposed to the entire business team.[86]

HR Policy Congruence: Achieving Vertical and Horizontal Fit.

A very important concept in HR strategy development is the notion that HR strategies must be congruent or integrated with business strategy as well as with each other. There are five main clusters of HR decisions and activities: human resource strategy and organization; talent identification and deployment; human capital development; reward management; and employee relations, quality of work environment, and voice.[87] (See Module 3 for further detail.) These policy areas will be emphasized to varying degrees depending on the HR strategy chosen. When these policy clusters are designed to support HR strategies in a way that is congruent with the overarching business strategy, they have *vertical fit or congruence.* When they are aligned with each other to create powerful connections, there is *horizontal fit or congruence.* For some readers, it may be useful to picture the "Pillsbury Doughboy," the puffy little man with a white baker's hat appearing in Pillsbury commercials, as a metaphor for the organizational system. If one part of the organizational system is changed and emphasized, pushing on one part of the little man's body, the other part of his puffy figure must respond with change. So if the firm has a new business strategy regarding its organization's fundamental direction and how it will compete, assessment must be done regarding fit of HR strategies. Does the firm have the right mix of HR activities and organizational structure to successfully implement the strategy (vertical fit)? And do the different policy clusters fit with each other (horizontal fit), or do they send mixed messages or act in a "deadly combination"?[88] For example, what if a firm wants to implement a team-based work system, yet it is reluctant to change the existing pay system, which still largely rewards people based on individual performance?

To illustrate the concepts of vertical and horizontal fit, consider how human resource strategies supported Netscape's achievement of business strategy. Netscape had 60 percent of the Internet browser market less than two months after it was founded and grew to a $7 billion company less than two years after founding. How did this occur? A core operating principle of Netscape was to "hire and acquire managerial expertise, in addition to technical expertise."[89] Netscape had a very different talent identification and hiring strategy than its arch-rival Microsoft. Compare the following case study developed by Professors Cusumano and Yoffie in their book on Netscape. In the summer of 1997, the average employee age at Netscape was 37. In contrast, the average age at Microsoft was 27 in the mid-1990s and 34 by 1997, while the average employee age at Intel was 33. Unlike Microsoft, which often hired recent college graduates and developed talent, Netscape's start-up strategy emphasized hiring experienced managers who understand the Internet and information technology. Most of Netscape's engineers and managers had "grey hair," having previously worked in major companies in computer software, hardware, or communications technology. These employees also had high levels of expertise in the development and usage of fundamental Internet technologies.[90] In order to ensure that Netscape's business strategy of immediately appearing as a dominant industry player was successful, Netscape had to have an human resource strategy with *vertical fit:* Identify and hire experience. With experienced people, Netscape could ask people to be aggressive self-starters and jump in working and adding value immediately.

In order to be able to successfully identify and buy talent, the human resource policy clusters also had to have *horizontal fit.* For example, the reward systems at Netscape had to fit with the talent identification and selection systems. They also may need to be tailored to fit the human resource strategy specific to different employee groups. The philosophy of compensation at Netscape was markedly different than the philosophy typically taken at other start-ups and by rival Microsoft. Often companies in the computer industry offer very low base pay relative to many of their direct competitors but compensate their employees with stock options tied to their long-term performance. For example, in the 1990s at Microsoft, the average salaried worker earned one-third less than the average of his or her human resource Silicon Valley peer in cash compensation, but total compensation was 140 percent of the average due to the high rapid growth of Microsoft stock. Netscape's senior managers were paid like their Microsoft counterparts with relatively low cash compensation and stock options comprising most of their total compensation package. A number of them even deferred their salaries in 1997 because of the wealth they garnered from their stock. However, Netscape paid middle and lower level employees quite differently in cash compensation. In order to get experienced people in the Silicon Valley, where living costs are among the highest in the United States, Netscape had to pay people high salaries. Its human resource strategy was "to be competitive with the big companies where we want to recruit from, and take salary away as a recruiting barrier."[91] Additionally, Netscape offered spot bonuses and weekends away for completing business milestones. Noncash work/life supports were also offered to help people cope with their busy lives. Netscape offered services ranging from an on-site dentist to banking to a corporate concierge to help arrange employee errands and other personal needs.[92]

MODULE
2

Allocate Resources and Develop Processes and Systems to Support HR Delivery

Having determined the strategic thrusts, the final step is to allocate organizational resources and develop processes and systems to support HR role delivery. These decisions relate to what HR roles need to be emphasized, how they will be delivered, and by whom. Module 3 gives many examples of how HR roles of transactions (administrative human resources), translation (communicating policy), transition (executing strategy), and transformation (managing culture and organizational change) occur in all policy clusters and can be delivered by employees, HR, managers, and vendors. A key HR role to achieving business strategy is translation—communicating to employees the reason for action plans and how each policy cluster and any policy changes support the business strategy.

Open-book management is an organizational technique supporting the policy translation role that directs employees not only to quality or efficiency but also to the success of the business. Significant company information must be shared and understood by all employees. This includes the business plan, financial goals, income statements, and forecasts. Managers must influence employees to be responsible and accountable for not only performing their own work and meeting targets but for making their unit's budget or profit goals. In order for this to work, financial resources must be allocated to the compensation plan. The compensation plan must reward employees for the success of the business, often involving sizeable bonuses augmented by stock ownership. Wal-Mart is a successful implementer of open-book management. Its employees receive financial information, are rewarded with stock, and are encouraged to act and think as if they are running the store.[93] The gourmet food retailer Whole Foods provides another example. Every Whole Foods store has a book that lists the previous year's salary and bonus for each of the tens of thousands of employees in the company. Every week, each store receives a fax of how all the stores in the region performed broken down by team in comparison to the previous year. Once a month, each store gets a business report that is available to all employees. The business report analyzes sales, product costs, wages and salaries, and operating profits for all stores in the company.[94] These are just several examples of how communication of policies helps promote a strategic mindset where employees act and feel like owners of the business.

MODULE
2

Organizational Adaptation and Performance Outcomes

HR strategy and policy thrusts will support strategy only to the extent that the HR practices are supported by the *organizational culture*. All the fancy HR practices in the world will not be very effective if the organizational culture does not support employee performance of business objectives. If the culture gives the message that employees aren't valued and that their efforts don't really matter in regard to the achievement of business strategy, then HR practices will not favorably influence individual and organizational performance. It is also important to look at the relationship between policy use and the culture. Some companies have cultures that hinder the potential effectiveness of new HR policies for performance enhancement due to the hypocrisy effect. Classic labor theorist Karl Marx once pointed out that management sometimes adopts human resource policies that are contradictory with reality in order to fool the workers. Nonfamily-friendly companies can have some family-friendly policies on the books, for example, but management discourages their use. Even Mitsubishi Corporation, which repeatedly lost legal battles due to its poor climate for women and problems with sexual harassment, countered its image in the media with the adoption of new anti-sexual harassment policies.

Granted, investing organizational resources to develop and adopt new formal HR policies is a challenging, albeit important step to cultural change. However, management must immediately reshape its behaviors and values to act in a way that supports the new policies' intent or the policies will have little real performance. Otherwise, the policies will mainly exist on paper. Unfortunately, most of the studies in the current literature have overlooked culture as a key mediating variable between HR policy adoption and business performance outcomes. The strategic HR studies generally have not moved beyond measuring adoption of practices, overlooking how long they have been in place and the degree to which there is agreement by multiple stakeholders feel that these practices are culturally supported.

Assuming the corporate culture is congruent with or positively adapts to the HR practices needed to support strategy, then the attitudes and behaviors of employees, workgroups and work unit attitudes, and behaviors and performance will be favorably affected. Higher commitment, job satisfaction, and productivity lead to lower absenteeism, turnover, and better performance. These employee outcomes have positive ramifications not only for the bottom line and shareholders, but for all societal stakeholders who have a stake in organizational performance. Dave Ulrich—one of the top consultants to major corporations on human resource strategy today—discusses the current research on links between human resources and financial performance. A study of 260 firms, sponsored by the Society of Human Resource Management and CCH Incorporated, correlated the quality of HRM practices to four financial measures. These were: *market/book value,* which is the market value of the firm based on its stock price divided by those assets reflecting value added by management; *productivity,* which is the dollar value of sales divided by number of employees; *market value,* which is stock price multiplied by outstanding shares; and *sales.* The study found that these financial indicators increased dramatically with the quality of the human resource practices and when they had good vertical fit. Research by Mark Huselid of Rutgers University and his colleagues has examined the financial effects of high-performance work practices, which are bundles of HR practices designed to promote high commitment. One Huselid study found that turnover was significantly reduced by these practices, productivity went up 16 percent, and sales and market value increased dramatically—$27,044 (sales) and $18,641 and $3,814 (profits), respectively.[95]

Alternative Strategic HR Perspectives

Research on SHRM has identified three main perspectives on the relationship between HRM strategy and firm level outcomes. These are the universal or best practices approach, the strategic contingency view, and the HR bundles or configurational approach. High-performance work systems are the most widely studied example of the bundles approach.

Universal/Best Practices   Stanford professor Jeff Pfeffer[96] argues that there is a business case for managing people right. He holds that assuming the existence of certain conditions, there are some ways for managing employees that, regardless of industry, may be universally better than others. Relying on Wharton researcher MacDuffie's work, he notes that three conditions must be met for innovative HR practices to operate as universally best practices that contribute to economic performance. First, employees must possess knowledge and skills that managers lack. Second, employees must be motivated to apply this skill and knowledge through discretionary effort on their jobs. Third, the firm's business strategy can only be achieved when employees contribute this discretionary effort.[97] Assuming these conditions exist, then treating employees well and having HR policies that align the individual employee interests and performance with those of the firm are likely to pay off financially. HR policies under the universal approach give the message that employees are assets, should be invested in to develop their skills, and assume a long-term mutually committed employment relationship.

What are the best practices? Pfeffer cites seven.

1. *Employment security* is essential because innovations in work practices, productivity improvement, and other forms of labor-management cooperation are unlikely to be sustained over time if workers fear that by increasing productivity they will work themselves out of jobs.

2. *Selectivity in hiring* new personnel is important because it is much more cost-effective to select people who have those important characteristics that are needed for job success than to train or try to change them. In order for selectivity to work, there must be a large applicant pool so that the firm can hire the best. Screening must be done for cultural fit and attitude and critical skills. Senior management should be involved in the process. At Disney, for example, the casting department in the HR operation may invite a candidate to meet with anywhere from 1 to 15 line managers before an offer might be made. Outsiders view the selectivity in recruitment as a barrier to getting a job. Cast members, however, view this experience as an unforgettable socialization experience, and Disney ensures it is hiring the best!

3. *Self-management work teams* and *decentralization of decision making* as a basic element of organizational design is a third important element. One recent study found a 38 percent decrease in defects and a 20 percent increase in productivity following the advent of teams.[98]

4. *High compensation contingent on organizational performance* is the fourth best practice. As Pfeffer points out, the level of salaries given to workers sends a message as to whether their efforts are valued or not. Contingent rewards can take many forms: gain sharing, profit sharing, stock ownership, pay for skill, and team incentives. All of these encourage members to act like owners.

5. *Extensive training* can pay off, though U.S. firms provide the least in comparison to most major European or Asian firms. Having a multiskilled, motivated, and flexible workforce and an organizational culture that values learning is essential to compete for future markets.

6. *Reducing status differences and barriers* through HR practices is another best practice. These practices relate to rules for how different employee groups are to dress, office arrangements, language used to refer to employee groups, wage differentials across levels, and parking and cafeteria privileges. Practices such as these send a signal that all employees share a common fate and must work together to achieve the vision.

7. *Information sharing* is the seventh best practice. Pfeffer believes that information sharing on financials and sensitive business data gives the message that employees are trusted. It also is important because motivated and trained people will not be able to contribute to organizational performance if they don't have information on important dimensions of performance.

Strategic Contingency Behavioral Perspective. While the best-practices approach in essence assumes that strategy follows structure (HR practices), the strategic contingency perspective holds that structure (which includes human resource policies) follows strategy. Specific HR practices are believed to be aligned with specific business strategies.[99] Taking the notion of vertical fit between HR and overarching business strategy to the maximum, the strategic contingency view holds that organizations adopting a particular business strategy require different HR practices than those adopting alternative strategies. Different HR strategies are required for different strategic positions. This is to promote a core workforce mindset. Some of the main ways of competing include: operational excellence (e.g. cost), product leadership (innovation) or competing on customer excellence (offering the best quality or solutions).[100] In essence, this perspective argues that for any business strategy there is one best human resource policy or practice for each of the policy clusters.

A cost leadership strategy for competitive advantage seeks to have a workforce that is highly efficient in production so that economies of scale can be experienced.[101] Workers are focused on cost reduction and effectiveness, and worker performance measures should be linked to these goals. Performance appraisals are used to counsel or fire poor performers. Job descriptions are narrow so that workers become proficient at performing them, and pay may be closely linked to the specific job performed. Individuals are more likely to be hired because they possess job-specific skills. Training is also likely to be very job-specific and often occurs on the job. Management systems plan and control the flow of work for smooth, efficient operations. K-Mart, WalMart, and Meiers discount stores follow these kinds of HR strategies to support cost leadership.

A product leadership or differentiation strategy would emphasize a different HR approach.[102] Product engineering and research and development would be viewed as critical to success, and HR strategies would be tailored to attract a highly capable and skilled workforce for these areas. Workers would be rewarded for innovation and flexibility in performing their jobs. Individual-based training would be emphasized to keep workers up-to-date. External recruitment might be needed to buy talent. Performance appraisals might be more developmental than control oriented in nature. 3M and Apple Computer are examples of firms that successfully follow as a product leadership form of differentiation strategy.

Competing on having the best customer service or quality is another form of differentiation. Here the HR policies are designed to promote and reward extraordinary quality. Teamwork and quality successes that surpass customer needs are likely to be highly rewarded. Suggestion systems are highly valued. For example, at Toyota Motor Manufacturing in Kentucky, last year over 75,000 suggestions were offered by its team members. Of these, 99.8 percent were implemented. Team involvement is also likely to be used to improve quality. According to the manager of the assembly line, "(Team member) input is a key factor in our success. No one knows processes on the line better than our team members. They are very open, honest, and willing to share their ideas."[103]

MODULE
2
HR Bundles: The Case of High-Performance Work Systems.
Like the strategic contingency theorists, configurational or bundles theorists also use the notion of fit—but in a horizontal fashion. They maintain that certain bundles of HR practices that are consistent or hold together enhance firm performance.[104] The theory proposes that there are ideal types of configurations of HR practices that promote synergies. One well known ideal type—high-performance work systems (HPWS)—is based on the concept of increasing employee skills and commitment. HPWS share many of the best practices that Pfeffer identified as universally beneficial. These include information sharing, decentralized decision making via teams, joint labor-management structures at the operational, tactical, and strategic levels, extensive training to nonmanagerial employees, and incentives contingent on group and firm performance. One study by Huselid and Becker found that the presence of a high-performance work system that was aligned effectively resulted in a $42,000-per-employee increase in market value.[105] Lincoln Electric Company is probably the best-known long-term example of an HWPS in the United States.

Unfortunately, a recent review concluded it is very difficult for older firms to change strategies and adopt HPWS at "brownfield" or existing companies. As the review "What Works at Work" notes: "The diffusion of new workplace innovations is limited, especially among older U.S. businesses. Firms face a number of obstacles . . . the abandonment of organizational change initiatives after limited policy changes have little effect on performance, the costs of other organizational practices that are needed to make new work practices effective, long histories of labor-management conflict and mistrust, resistance of supervisors, and other workers who might not fare as well under the newer practices, and the lack of a supportive institutional and public policy environment."[106] Perhaps the greatest barrier to making HPWS work is that managers tend to be highly focused on the short term, and a long-term vision is needed to make HPWS succeed.

It may be that a hybrid of these strategic approaches might work best. One recent study of HPWS found that even for HPWS systems, sometimes the way the work was structured directly varied by the nature of the customer served. For the banking industry, for example, the SHRM systems differed by market segmentation. *Who* the employees interacted with, even though the industry was the same (banking), had a great influence on the way the work was structured. Employees serving high-end customers in banks offering a lot of services (differentiation) were given greater discretion in decision making, needed more and higher level skills, and had higher pay. In contrast, employees in banks serving low-end customers had less discretion; more repetitive, narrower tasks; and lower pay.[107]

STRATEGIC ISSUES IN CREATING COMPETITIVE ADVANTAGE THROUGH PEOPLE

One of the most critical strategic issues relates to the development of HR strategies that promote organizational flexibility, given the rapidity of environmental change in many industries. Increasingly many firms have externalized employment for many types of workers. Particularly common is the growing outsourcing of work that is considered to be of a noncritical nature. The risk firms face is if they outsource work in an area that later is identified as a core competency critical for competing for future market share.

The rise of virtual organizations creates other strategic HR challenges. A virtual organization is defined as a temporary network of companies that come together to exploit fast-changing opportunities. Some key HR challenges are to assess cultural fit between entities considering virtual partnerships, and ensuring that the organizational performance and measurement systems are appropriately aligned. Another dilemma is to determine how to plan careers for employees who are likely to move across organizational boundaries. With horizontal moves more likely to be the norm, how should compensation systems be redesigned? Could benefits and compensation become portable as contractors move from place to place? And, more importantly, should firms have the flexibility to develop rewards to retain valuable contributors regardless of who they worked for?[108]

APPLICATION

Daehan Corporation

Original case written by ByeongCheol Lee & YoungMyon Lee
Department of Management, Dongguk University, South Korea

Looking down from the window of his twenty-first floor office, Manjo Kim, the director in charge of the human resource department of Daehan Corp., was recollecting his meeting yesterday with Senior Vice President Jihan Park. It was early September afternoon in 1998, and the streets of downtown Seoul were filled with cars and people as usual, but that familiar scene looked a little bit different to him now. It was approaching half past three, and he realized that there was not much time left before the staff meeting he had called at four o'clock. What Senior Vice President Park told him yesterday had been disturbing Kim all day. In short, Park told him that Daehan Corp. would need to reduce the total number of employees by 20 percent by the end of year. This task was the biggest and most difficult challenge of Director Kim's whole career. Even though there had been some minor layoffs during the previous economic downturns, a reduction of this magnitude had never happened at Daehan Corp. before. As one of the largest conglomerates in Korea, Daehan had grown rapidly since the early 1970s. Since Kim joined the company in 1976 right after graduating from college, Daehan had grown about 15 times in number of employees and about 60 times in sales volume. Kim had spent most of his career working in the HR department, except a few years when he was sent to the Los Angeles office of Daehan America. During his tenure, the most important tasks of the HR department had been to recruit as many quality employees as possible and train them to fit into the Daehan culture. Although Korea had an abundant supply of college graduates, attracting first-quality managerial talent was not an easy task for any company, because for the last three decades the Korean economy had rapidly expanded at a rate of about 8 percent annually in terms of gross national product (GNP). This period had seen many changes in terms of recruitment criteria and promotion and pay policies, but the company always took pride in the fact that it attracted the best people and retained most of them for their entire career.

After the whole Korean economy was jostled by the foreign exchange crisis beginning in the fall of 1997, most companies including Daehan experienced enormous difficulties in their business operations. Sales figures were down, and the Korean government, backed by International Monetary Fund (IMF) recommendations for crisis management, strongly demanded the restructuring of the Korean chaebols. By September 1998, already 5 of the top 30 chaebols had gone bankrupt due to higher interest costs and lower demand from a weakened economy. Even though the Korean Federation of Unions emphasized that laying off employees was not the best solution to cope with this emergency situation, the national unemployment rate was already reaching 7 percent (compared to 2.5 percent before the foreign currency crisis). In 1998, almost 200,000 people lost their jobs every month. Even for those who still had their jobs, wages were cut more than 20 percent on average, which had never happened before in the boom economy.

Mr. Kim entered the conference room at five minutes to four, wondering how he could devise the necessary action plans for this difficult task.

The Korean Economy and Employment System. The Korean economy became the eleventh largest in the world in 1996 with a real gross domestic product (GDP) of $484.6 billion, 4.9 percent inflation, and 2.0 percent unemployment rate. The Korean economy entered a period of stable growth in the 1990s after rapid growth during the 1970s and 1980s. From 1990–1996, Korea's real GDP grew 7.4 percent annually, compared to an annual rate of 9.1 percent in the 1980s. Per-capita GNP was $10,537 in 1995, and $10,548 in 1996. These figures were praised as the advent of the five-digit per capita income era.[109]

MODULE
2

Korea is well known for its country-specific growth pattern. It sustained a high growth rate through government-guided economic policy that was outward oriented, industry oriented, and growth oriented. Export promotion, industrial targeting, and close coordination between government and big business have been the main ingredients of economic policy and success. Korea's strong economic performance is attributed largely to the effective combination of the abundant, high-quality labor supply with the cheap foreign capital and technology under the government-guided system. However, international pressure for the deregulation and opening of domestic markets coupled with ongoing democratization since 1987 accelerated the movement of the Korean economy toward a more market-oriented economy.

The Korean government has supported companies financially if they followed the export-oriented government policies. Chaebols benefited tremendously from government

TABLE 2.2 *Korea's Top Chaebols*

Chaebol	Sales*	Major Products
Samsung	$63	Electronics, semiconductors, aerospace, food, machinery, apparel, trading, insurance
Hyundai	$63	Construction, autos, shipbuilding, electronics
LG	$48	Electronics, semiconductors, chemicals, oil
Daewoo	$40	Electronics, machinery, autos, shipbuilding

*U.S. $ in billions, as of 1995.

policies, and their growth accelerated since the early 1970s, which fueled the economic growth in Korea. The chaebol is a type of conglomerate where the relationship among the companies is financial rather than product or service related. Most of the large companies in Korea belong to one of chaebols, such as Hyundai, Samsung, Daewoo, LG, and so on. The top ten chaebols, for example, account for about a quarter of the GNP (see Table 2.2).

However, the Korean economy ran into trouble in mid-1997, due to enormous short-term foreign debts of business and financial institutions that far exceeded Korea's foreign exchange reserve. The Asian economic crisis, which started in Thailand and Indonesia, made foreign creditors nervous, and they started to lose confidence in Korea's ability to pay off debts. This lowered the value of Korea's currency, the *won,* and caused foreign creditors to call in short-term debts. This resulted in the standby loan agreement with the IMF. Recently, chaebols have been under strong pressure to restructure from the government, since they were blamed for being partly responsible for the foreign currency crisis.

Korean Labor Market.   The Korean workforce amounted to 21.2 million persons in 1996, with a registered labor force participation rate of 62 percent. With a fast-growing economy, the unemployment rate had continuously dropped to 2.0 percent in 1996 (see Table 2.3). One distinctive characteristic of unemployment statistics is the

TABLE 2.3   *Unemployment Statistics (Unit: Thousand, percent)*

Year	Unemployed (highly educated): A	Unemployed (total): B	A/B (%)	Unemployment Rate (highly educated): C	Unemployment Rate (total): D	C/D %
1980	60	749	8.0	6.6	5.5	1.2
1981	63	661	9.5	6.6	4.7	1.4
1982	71	656	10.8	6.4	4.5	1.4
1983	77	613	12.6	6.5	4.2	1.5
1984	82	567	14.5	6.1	3.9	1.6
1985	109	619	17.6	7.1	4.1	1.7
1986	124	611	20.3	7.5	3.9	1.9
1987	111	519	21.4	6.1	3.2	1.9
1988	101	435	23.2	4.9	2.6	1.6
1989	116	460	25.2	5.1	2.6	2.0
1990	114	451	25.3	4.6	2.5	1.8
1991	101	436	23.2	3.8	2.3	1.7
1992	109	463	23.5	3.6	2.4	1.5
1993	141	551	25.6	4.2	2.8	1.4
1994	130	489	26.5	3.6	2.4	1.5
1995	108	419	25.8	2.7	2.0	1.4
1996	110	425	25.9	2.6	2.0	1.3

Highly educated is defined as junior college graduate or beyond.

Source: South Korea National Statistical Office, *Economically Active Population Survey,* various years.

TABLE 2.4   *Unions, Union Members, and Strikes in Korea: 1980-1997*

YEAR	NUMBER OF UNIONS		UNION MEMBERS		STRIKES
	Industry	**Company Level**	**Numbers**	**Density***	
1980	16	2,635	948,134	20.1	206
1985	16	2,551	1,004,398	15.7	265
1986	16	2,675	1,035,890	15.5	276
1987	16	4,103	1,267,457	17.3	3,749
1988	21	6,164	1,707,456	22.0	1,873
1989	21	7,883	1,932,415	23.3	1,616
1990	21	7,698	1,886,884	21.5	322
1991	21	7,656	1,803,408	19.7	234
1992	21	7,527	1,734,598	18.4	235
1993	26	7,147	1,667,373	17.2	144
1994	26	7,025	1,659,011	16.3	121
1995	26	6,606	1,614,800	15.3	88
1996	26	6,424	1,598,558	14.7	85
1997	—	—	—	—	78

*Density = union member/nonfarm regular workers
Source: Ministry of Labor

fact that the unemployment rate of the highly educated (defined as the junior college graduate or beyond) has been greater than the total unemployment rate. The proportion of highly educated workers among the unemployed increased from 8 percent in 1980 to 25.4 percent in 1996. The unemployment rate, however, is expected to rise rapidly in coming years due to the current economic crisis and the agreement with the IMF to curtail the economic growth rate. In fact, the unemployment rate surged to 7 percent in November 1998.

Labor Relations in Korea.

Before 1987, it was very difficult to organize a union, let alone strike in Korea. The government's export-oriented policy for economic growth limited the rights of workers over 30 years until June 1987, when Rho, Tae Woo, the presidential candidate, declared the movement toward social democracy in Korea. This declaration evoked a deep change in Korean labor relations.

For the two years from 1987 to 1989, the number of unions and union members almost doubled (see Table 2.4). This is the result of a great number of strikes for union recognition and the union's internal democracy.

Wage increases were a key issue. The real wage rate increase was 11.3 percent on average over five straight years since 1987. (Comparisons with the labor productivity increases for the same period are provided in Table 2.5). However, since the mid-1990s, the labor relations have been relatively stable as the number of strikes has been reduced to less than 100. Korea also faced an economic growth slowdown, slow growth in exports, an increase in the foreign currency deficit, and the massive failure of small and medium businesses. The Korean government realized that fundamental changes in industrial relations were necessary in order to recover the competitiveness of Korean industries.

The government issued an announcement entitled "Vision for New Industrial Relations" in April 1996, and a month later established an organization called "The Presidential Commission on Industrial Relations Reform." Before the end of 1996, tripartite

TABLE 2.5   *CPI, Wage Increase, and Labor Productivity: 1980–1997*

Year	Gross National Product[1] (billion U.S. dollars)	Consumer Price Index[2] (1990=100)	Nominal Wage Levels in Manufacturing	Real Wage Index in Manufacturing Sector[3]	Labor Productivity Increase in Manufacturing
1980	60.5	54.5	147	45.6	46.9
1985	91.1	76.8	270	59.4	64.0
1986	105.4	79.0	294 (9.2)	63.2 (6.2)	69.9 (9.2)
1987	133.4	81.3	329 (11.6)	68.4 (8.3)	75.3 (8.1)
1988	179.8	87.1	393 (19.6)	76.4 (11.6)	83.0 (10.6)
1989	220.4	92.1	492 (25.1)	90.4 (18.3)	88.8 (7.1)
1990	251.8	100.0	591 (20.2)	100.0 (10.7)	100.0 (12.5)
1991	292.0	109.3	690 (16.9)	106.9 (6.9)	114.0 (14.0)
1992	305.7	116.1	799 (15.7)	116.4 (8.8)	126.7 (10.9)
1993	330.8	121.7	885 (10.9)	123.2 (5.8)	136.5 (7.8)
1994	378.0	129.3	1,022 (15.5)	133.9 (8.7)	150.3 (9.8)
1995	452.6	135.1	1,124 (9.9)	140.8 (5.2)	166.4 (10.7)
1996	480.2	141.8	1,261 (12.2)	150.6 (7.0)	187.9 (12.9)
1997	437.4	—	1,326 (5.2)	—	—

Source: [1]Bank of Korea, National Account, 1997.
[2]Ministry of Labor, *Monthly Labor Survey,* various issues.
[3]Korea Productivity Center, *Review on Productivity,* various issues.

representatives from labor, management, and the public sector at the Commission reached a consensus that the current labor-management relations must be changed and that a new mindset and practices be established. This reform effort was closely related to the new launch of the World Trade Organization and Korea's participation in the Organisation for Economic Co-operation and Development. Korea's economy had to appropriately respond to the changes in international economic conditions. International expectations and demands on Korea are expected to be greatly heightened in light of its industrial relations law and institutions. Under these circumstances, Korea could not avoid international criticism if it retained the current and inadequate labor laws in comparison to internationally adopted labor standards.

In 1997, Kia Motor Company went bankrupt and the consequent failure of many chaebols heightened deepening feelings of economic crisis in Korea. The government, in its inability to effectively deal with the massive failures of businesses in time, worsened the financial and currency crisis. The Korean government finally requested much-needed relief from the IMF. Under IMF surveillance, Korea was forced at first to reduce expenditures and restructure its banking industry. In addition, institutional reforms were called for in order to increase the flexibility of the labor market. This labor flexibility was considered to be an essential factor in receiving IMF funds and attracting foreign capital. As a result, another "Commission" was established. The Commission was composed of representatives from employees, employers, and the ruling party of the government as an advisory committee to the new President-elect Kim Dae Jung. The Commission formed a consensus to increase employment flexibility and enlarge labor movement rights. In February 1998, the national assembly legislated and revised labor-related laws based on this consensus.

Under IMF surveillance, Korean industrial relations experienced a deep change toward a new direction. First, to cope with the economic crisis, the major bodies of the Korean economy gathered and formed the Commission mentioned above. A decision-making mechanism committed to a new social order, this Commission deals with colliding social matters. Second, trade unions, whose greatest power lies in collective bargaining and related activities, are geared to devise a new strategy due to the economic crisis. Trade unions tend to gather and form industrial unions that play an important role in industrial relations. Third, the increasing number of bankruptcies due to the economic crisis create a cooperative relationship between employees and employers.[110]

Employment Relations in Chaebols.   Chaebols not only play a dominant role in Korean economy but also provide typical models in employment relations. Other companies in Korea, to a large extent, follow HRM policies implemented by these chaebols, such as wage structure, promotion system, and evaluation criteria. Traditional chaebol HRM systems can be characterized as paternalistic, with practices such as lifelong employment, seniority system, and group training based on strong collectivist values.[111] Under the traditional Korean employment system, most of the regular workers have assumed lifelong employment. The companies they work for also harbor the same assumption. This employment system was compatible with the Korean value system of loyalty, but makes it difficult for workers to move from one company to another. Until recently, moving between companies was regarded as disloyal by both individuals and the companies they worked for. Consequently, lateral moves in the labor market were rare. In Korea, 20 or 30 years of service with one company were common for both white- and blue-collar workers.

However, Korean chaebols started to realize that the management systems that fueled Korean economy growth in the past several decades were not as effective as they used to be. Since the 1990s, chaebols were trying to implement new employment systems that could secure their global competitiveness in a rapidly changing environment. Their attention was focused on the transformation of the current seniority-based HR system into a human capital-enhancing and performance-based HR system in order to increase their competitiveness through lean and flexible organizations. These changes were mainly triggered by two factors. The first is a change in employee needs and values. The traditional paternalistic approach does not have the same appeal to the younger generation, whose environment was quite different from their predecessors. The young were strongly influenced by a world that emphasizes individual talents and success. They prefer HR policies based on merit and performance to a traditional seniority-based system. The second factor is the changing nature of world markets that chaebols have to compete in. To survive in the globalized market, chaebols will have to enhance their global competitiveness through greater efficiency, higher individual wages, and lower total labor costs. To attract younger and better employees, they need to restructure their hierarchical organizations and develop their employees into specialists with adequate skills for a changing world market. During the implementation of these changes, the real challenge for the chaebols will be how to balance the seniority-based system that older workers depend on, with the performance-based system that the younger workers prefer.

Economic Crisis and Changes in Job Security.   The foreign exchange crisis since November 1997 has profoundly changed the Korean economy. In 1997 and 1998, a lot of companies including chaebols have gone bankrupt. Many of the chaebols, whose survival and prosperity depended mainly on the government's and banks' support in the past, have collapsed. This caused the unemployment rate to surge rapidly from 2.5 percent in November of 1997 to 7.0 percent in November of 1998.

In addition, the economic crisis also accelerated changes in many aspects of the employment system and labor relations. The custom of lifetime employment in Korea started to wane. Many companies started to reduce their workforces based on the workers' performance. This was new to Koreans because Korean companies traditionally seldom fired workers due to poor performances. The salary for white-collar workers is now determined largely by performance rather than seniority. The most important criterion for promotion has also changed from seniority to performance. All of these changes are very new and uncomfortable to Korean workers and unions. But they have spread rapidly to many companies despite the resistance of workers and unions due to the economic crisis.

Moreover, massive layoffs are legally allowed for the first time if the following four conditions are met:

1. An urgent business necessity shall be required to dismiss employees due to business reasons. Urgent business reasons shall be deemed to exist in case of a business transfer and merger and acquisition (M&A) to prevent deterioration of the business.

2. Every effort shall be made to avoid dismissals.

3. Reasonable and fair criteria shall be used to select employees to be dismissed. Gender discrimination is strictly prohibited.

4. Sixty days' prior notice to the employee representative or the union which represents the majority of the employees and good faith consultation in connection thereto as to the measures to avoid dismissals and the selection criteria for such dismissals is required.

Two additional conditions were added later: (1) A report to the Ministry of Labor is required for administrative purposes 30 days prior to the layoffs, and (2) employers must rehire previously dismissed employees within two years of their dismissal if the employer rehires for these positions.

Company Background

Daehan Corporation.   Daehan Corp. was established in 1972 and grew rapidly with the Korean economy. Currently it produces mainly electronics products such as computers, monitors, TVs, VCRs, camcorders, refrigerators, and microwave ovens, but in the beginning Daehan manufactured radios and black-and-white TVs. In the 1970s, their major product line changed to color TVs, refrigerators, and washing machines. Daehan began to export color TVs to Japan in 1982 and established overseas subsidiaries in America, Germany, and the United Kingdom. In the 1990s, the company focused its efforts on increasing market share in former communist countries such as Russia and other emerging markets. Also, the company works to enhance its competitive advantage by restructuring and maintain cost-effectiveness by increasing the product quality.

The number of employees increased from 389 at the end of 1972 to 29,791 by the end of 1997 (see Table 2.6 on page 2.38). Until the foreign currency crisis at the end of 1997, the company enjoyed continuous increases in sales and stability in operating profits. This led the company to invest heavily in research and development since the 1980s.

Daehan's Human Resource Management.   The working conditions at Daehan, including wage and salary levels, are among the best in Korea. HRM practices of chaebols such as Daehan have become models in Korean HRM practice and program development. This includes recruiting and selection practices, wage structures, and promotion systems. The traditional paternalistic approaches for employment relations began to change when Daehan realized that the seniority-based HR system was not fully compatible with its new strategies to enhance global competitiveness. Recent organizational restructuring from a hierarchical authoritative structure to a flat, team-oriented one called for new competencies for all employees. Accordingly, a new HRM vision and strategy

TABLE 2.6 *Daehan Corporation: Number of Employees, Sales, and Profits*

Year	Number of Employees	Sales (million dollars)	Net Profits (million dollars)
1972	389	2.7	0
1975	1628	81.2	0.9
1980	2573	185.2	3.3
1985	7013	843.7	10.8
1986	8752	977.5	15.2
1987	10366	1190.6	16.1
1988	11785	1514.1	50.6
1989	14267	2000.3	78.1
1990	20650	2260.8	36.1
1991	22978	2613.7	32.3
1992	22310	3051.8	34.2
1993	23797	4072.3	74.6
1994	25926	5709.4	120.3
1995	28499	6744.9	155.3
1996	29086	6337.2	95.4
1997	29791	n/a	n/a

MODULE
2

was established in 1995 (see Table 2.7). New HRM policies that strive to balance the former seniority based-system and the new ability-based system are being implemented.

Recruitment and Hiring. Daehan has always emphasized the importance of hiring the best people. Their definition of "best," however, was mostly limited to past scholastic achievements of the candidates. In addtion, an emphasis on the "attitudinal" aspect of the candidate resulted in recruiting homogeneous and conforming employees. To resolve this problem, Daehan is now trying to implement drastically new hiring processes. First of all, more attention was directed to identifying the applicant's abilities based on their creative, energetic, aggressive positive thinking and global point of view. An interview process, instead of written examinations, was given more weight in the new system in order to determine the applicant's ability. Also, deliberate effort

TABLE 2.7 *Daehan's New HRM Vision*

Our HRM policy and practices strive for the realization of a fair system for all our employees through continuous professional development, which can be beneficial both for individuals and the organization.

- Encouraging Creativity and Individual Initiatives
- Developing Adequate Human Capital for the Twenty-First Century
- Open and Effective Communication
- Fair Treatment of Employees
- Harmonious Industrial Relations Based on Mutual Trust and Sharing Common Goals

TABLE 2.8 *Number of Employees by Position at Daehan*

Position	Number of Employees	Percentage	Average Year of Employment at Daehan
Director or Above	215	0.7%	24 years
General Manager	1,254	4.2%	21 years
Deputy General Manager	2,375	8.0%	16 years
Manager	3,615	12.1%	11 years
Assistant Manager	3,926	13.2%	8 years
Staff or Below	18,406	61.8%	3 years
Total	**29,791**	**100%**	

was made to pay much less attention to the universities and colleges the applicants attended. These changes were specifically made to ensure that Daehan can attract a new kind of manager who will work more effectively with the new organizational strategy and culture.

Pay System. Compensation in Daehan is composed of base pay, bonuses, and allowances/benefits. In the old pay system, employees' salaries were composed of monthly salaries and bonuses. Monthly salaries were divided into a base pay and extra benefits: base pay is determined by position within the company, educational background, experience, and performance record; benefits include an overtime work allowance, long-service allowance, and family allowance.

In the past, employees' pay was not related to either job evaluation or individual performance but closely related to job grade or seniority based on length of service in the organization. But increased globalization and market competition forced the chaebols to move toward ability- and performance-based pay from seniority-based pay. Daehan changed its pay system to common pay and merit pay. Common pay consists of the cost of living and increases at a preset rate each year. The percentage of common pay decreases drastically as the employee moves up to higher-level positions. (See Tabel 2.8 for the number of employees by position at Daehan.) Merit pay consists of ability-based pay reflecting an individual display of ability and performance-based pay reflecting personal performance. Thus Daehan is trying to change its pay system to one that is more merit based while minimizing resistance from older employees.

Training and Development. Since the early 1980s, Daehan invested heavily in developing their human resources in accordance with their organizational value of "having the best people." The company strongly believed that human assets are one of the least costly and most predictable sources of productivity gains in the fast-changing business environment. Training and development not only helps individual employees' smooth adjustment into new jobs, but also enhances employee productivity for maintaining corporate competitiveness.

Daehan's training programs can be classified into three categories: grade education, managerial skill education, and global training. Grade education tries to develop appropriate abilities to carry out grade-specific work. Newcomer orientations, middle-level manager programs, and top management programs are major programs of this kind. Diverse topics at different levels, such as marketing, accounting, and production, are offered in managerial skill education. Realizing that their managers are weak at working in the globalized business environment, Daehan was determined to overcome this problem. Recently, more efforts were put into developing new programs to enhance

MODULE
2

global skills for their employees, including foreign language proficiency. Outcomes of these training programs were added as a new criterion for managerial evaluation. Foreign language proficiency such as in English or Japanese became a prerequisite for every manager in the organization, and a specific level of language skill must be shown to be promoted to middle-level managerial positions.

As past training programs were criticized for emphasizing too much conformity and uniformity, Daehan is trying to implement new training programs. For example, major changes have been made in the orientations about proper work attitude and company culture. New programs emphasized self-learning and autonomous workgroup building, compared to old programs known as "boot camp" and "indoctrination center." They aimed to foster a new progressive organizational culture, to create an environment where employees can work with autonomy and freedom. Also, they intended to promote innovativeness and creativity—values that are gaining importance as Daehan's organizational structure becomes flatter.

The Staff Meeting

Director Kim first thanked every manager for attending this emergency meeting on such a short notice and explained why he had to call this meeting in such a hurry. The main agenda of this meeting, he explained, was to come up with a specific plan to cut about 20 percent of all employees at Daehan. Sluggish economic performance in addition to strong pressure from the Korean government to restructure chaebols mandated downsizing of the company. Top management had decided to spin off some business divisions that showed unpromising financial performance for the last few years. Also, negative economic forecasts for the next few years seemed to require changing Daehan's traditional human resources policy to retain slack resources for anticipated future growth.

More specifically, higher-level managerial employees needed to be cut more deeply since that would be the quickest way of saving ever-increasing personnel costs and coping with current adverse economic conditions facing Daehan. Three seniors managers, who are respectively in charge of human resource planning, human resource administration, and industrial relations, attended this meeting with other major staffs in the department.

After listening quietly to Kim's explanation, Senior Manager Doosung Lee expressed his opinion.

> Don't you think cutting 20 percent of our employees is not only impossible but also immoral? I believe that we, as one of the largest employers in this country, cannot let these people go at this difficult time. These people were working 70 to 90 hours every week for this company and without their effort, this company could not be what it is now. They have sacrificed all their lives to build this company. What can they do if they are asked to leave now? These were the best people when we hired them, and they are still very competent managers. Yet it will be almost impossible for them to find new jobs in this kind of labor market. Especially for those who are over 40, their options will be very limited.

Senior manager Kwon disagreed.

> I can understand how you feel about this task. Certainly without their tremendous contributions, we could not be what we are now. Yet even before this crisis didn't we brood over how we could devise better human resource strategies to adapt to rapidly changing business environments? When we changed our organizational structure a few years ago from a hierarchical one to a flat and more flexible team structure, many of our older managers resisted this kind of change. We tried very hard to retrain these senior managers to adapt themselves to a new team-oriented structure and to make them better team players. Still, many of them had a lot of trouble changing from an authoritarian managerial role of simply giving orders to their subordinates and trying to control everything. I think they also lack essential competencies for being an effective manager in a globalized economy such as necessary

language skills and cross-cultural understandings. Our efforts to change our company culture, which will make us more effective in a globalization era, largely depend on what we do with these people. I think now is the time to let them go with proper compensation, since everybody expects that we will cut some employees.

Manager Cho added to what Kwon had said.

Our business paradigm is changing now. We used to compete with the cheapest products in the world market. Now China and all of the Southeast Asian countries can provide a cheaper product than we can. I think we needed to implement a whole new business and HRM strategy in this regard. Those people who cannot adapt to the new paradigm have to leave regardless of this foreign exchange crisis. Since our future competitiveness and eventually our survival are dependent on this issue, we need to go on and reinforce our new HRM strategy at this time.

Senior manager Jung, who is in charge of labor relations, expressed his view.

I don't know whether cutting 20 percent of our entire workforce will be possible. With the new labor law, we can lay them off legally. But certainly the union will try to prevent this in every possible way. They may try a wildcat strike like the ones that troubled us so much during the 1980s. If strikes go on for a long time with the support and participation of most of the union members, we may lose a lot of things: not only lost business but also our reputation for the best workplace. This in turn may lead to lower morale and motivation in those who will stay after the layoff. I think this is why none of the other big five chaebols has tried large-scale layoffs yet. We will need a contingency plan for all these possibilities.

Manager Cho tried to express his view.

How about using a voluntary early retirement program? Most of our employees are aware that some kind of layoff is imminent. If we let them go with attractive financial packages, many of them may volunteer for early retirement. I think that especially senior people will find this idea more attractive, because they are starting to realize that their future in the organization is not promising given the new organizational culture and flat structure. With their experience and knowledge, they may want to start their own small business with their lump sum severance pay. Since incentive packages are mainly dependent on seniority, early retirement will look more attractive to senior people.

Manager Jun cautioned.

Wouldn't it cost too much if we use only the early retirement plan with financial incentives? In the past, we used to give two years' full compensation as a financial incentive. I don't think we can afford to give that much in this difficult financial situation. Also, it is not easy to avoid having only the best people take advantage of this opportunity, while those poor performers show a tendency to refuse this kind of offer. If we chose this option, we will need to devise a very careful plan.

After listening carefully to his staff, Director Kim commented.

Certainly firing any of our colleagues is very painful. However, we also need to consider the interests of our other stakeholders. For the last few years, we emphasized and tried to implement new HRM strategies to become more competitive in the changing global market. For example, we changed our recruiting criteria to hire more flexible and team-oriented people who can be better managers in our new flat organizational structure, which is quite a different model from our traditional authoritative one. However, the foreign currency crisis and subsequent IMF intervention dramatically changed our economic landscape. It showed that our previous efforts were not good enough and also showed how vulnerable we are in the globalized market. We are expecting another dismal financial performance report in addition to last year's red ink. Our stock value keeps declining in the market. We cannot let this situation continue. I think this situation requires some drastic measures. Since everybody is now fully aware of what we have to do, we will have another meeting tomorrow afternoon. I hope each of you can come up with a specific plan for how we can reduce 20 percent of our workforce with minimum negative consequences.

What should the management at Daehan do? What do you think the union leaders will want Daehan to do? How about the Korean government?

IN CONCLUSION

Debrief

The chapter has examined the role of human resource strategy, which involve processes and activities, to ensure that HR systems are fully integrated with the strategic and organizational change needs of the firm. The chapter began with a discussion of core concepts in organizational strategy and value chain analysis. It developed a framework of SHRM formulation and deployment. The activities and key issues and principles involved in developing human resource strategy and alternative perspectives on how human resource strategy can be used to gain competitive advantage were then discussed.

The future challenges for HR strategy development are substantial. A survey of nearly 3,000 companies identified the strategic human resource management priorities to help firms achieve competitive advantage. The survey identified the following future HR imperatives: HR needs to be responsive to a highly competitive marketplace and global business structures. It needs to be closely linked to strategic business plans, and jointly conceived by line and HR managers. It must focus on HR strategies to improve customer service, quality, employee involvement, productivity, workforce flexibility, and teamwork.[112]

MODULE
2

Suggested Readings

Beatty, R. and Schneier, C. 1997. "New HR roles to impact organizational performance: From partners to players," *Human Resource Management,* 36: 29–37.

Becker, B., Huselid, M., Pickus, P., and Spratt, M. 1997. "HR as a source of shareholder value: Research and recommendations," *Human Resource Planning,* 36: 39–48.

Eichinger, B. and Ulrich, D. "Are you future agile?" 1995. *Human Resource Planning Journal.* 18(4): 30–41.

Pfeffer. J. 1995. "Producing sustainable competitive advantage through the effective management of people,* " Academy of Management Executive,* 9: 55–69.

Relevant Web Sites

HUMAN RESOURCE PLANNING SOCIETY
http://www.hrps.org

BUREAU OF LABOR STATISTICS
http://stats.bls.gov

MSU LABOR AND INDUSTRIAL RELATIONS LIBRARY
http://www.lib.msu.edu/coll/main/lir

INDUSTRIAL RELATIONS COLLECTION (MIT)
http://nimrod.mit.edu/depts/dewey/indrel/html

SOCIETY FOR HUMAN RESOURCE MANAGEMENT
http://www.shrm.org

YAHOO LIST OF HUMAN RESOURCES
  http://www.yahoo.com/Business/Corporations/CorporateServices/Human Resources/

WORKFORCE ONLINE
  http://www.workforceonline.com/

Critical Thinking Questions

1.   Define business strategy and HR strategy. Consider examples of companies that you have worked for or that you know of. To what degree did activities/ functions add value? To what extent was there vertical or horizontal fit? What were the main industry pressures shaping the firm's mission and strategy?

2.   Compare the strategic contingency and universal SHRM approaches. Think about how these theories apply to firms you are familiar with from your work experience or the press. Is it more important to have best practices or to have vertical fit? Which perspective do you most identify with and why? Be sure to give clear rationale for your thinking.

3.   Does HR strategy really matter for shareholder value? Why or why not? How might high performance work systems affect shareholder value?

Exercises: Strategic HRM Vignettes

By Lisa Copeland
Michigan State University, School of Labor & Industrial Relations
(Now employed at Andersen Consulting)

MODULE
2

Situation 1: Giant Manufacturing.   Giant Manufacturing is a large manufacturing company with approximately 350,000 employees worldwide. Through its six divisions, Giant manufactures a variety of products. The divisions were established over the last 100 years through internal growth as well as acquisition of external organizations. The Giant culture is one in which each division has historically operated with a great deal of decision-making autonomy. As a result, there has been wide variation throughout Giant in relation to its human resources practices. The rationale behind this is that each division is distinctive and has different needs as well as purposes. This last assumption is definitely true due to the fact that some divisions compete within their markets on a high-quality basis, while others compete as low-cost producers. Still others are innovators, both within their markets and within the company. Its customers are all very different, with wide variation in their demographic and psychographic characteristics. Giant's laissez-faire strategy has worked well in the past when it dominated its various markets, in part due to size and resources alone. However, in this era of global competition, Giant leadership has found that it must reexamine its strategy on every level.

Therefore, in recent years, a much greater effort has been put into aligning the company's divisions and strategies. The divisions have, with greater frequency, been asked, if not ordered, to implement "common" initiatives designed by Corporate Headquarters. This is an incredible amount of change for divisional Giant management, and has been very difficult; resistance at times has been very high. Therefore, corporate leadership has tried to ease the transition where it can by allowing divisional leadership to retain some decision-making authority.

In addition, when designing common practices and initiatives, it is difficult, if not impossible, to anticipate all the different ways in which practices and initiatives will have to accommodate the specific needs and individual cultures of the divisions. Moreover, the company tries to allow enough latitude to each unit to optimize buy-in from its stakeholders. Otherwise, implementation of new policies, practices, and procedures would be a much longer and more arduous process.

In relation to HR practices and initiatives, this approach has been played out in some very interesting ways. For example, in its efforts to encourage lateral movement and cross-training, Corporate Headquarters is moving toward broadbanding as opposed to its traditional salary grade system. However, some divisions have squawked at this idea, and more time is needed to achieve buy-in with them, while others have embraced the concept and are ready to carry it forward to their employees. Therefore, HQ has allowed broadbanding implementation to be done on a voluntary basis for the next two years, with the understanding that all divisions will be at least in the process of implementation after that.

As another example, a rigorous, three-hurdle, common selection process has been implemented organizationwide for entry-level salaried personnel. However, between divisions there is variation on cutoff scores, resulting in greater ease or difficulty in clearing the hurdles and being selected for a position depending on the testing unit. In addition, some divisions will allow applicants to retest after a specific period of time has passed, while at least one will not allow applicants to ever test again if they failed to clear part or all of the hurdles. This situation has arisen, in part, due to the different applicant pool sizes and amount of interest in each division.

Situation 1: Giant Manufacturing Questions

1.   What are the implications for strategic HR practices and change management in large organizations with distinctly different divisional-level "personalities" (subcultures, climates, histories)?

2.   How do you implement common HR strategies in an organization with wide variation in competitive business strategy (high-quality producer vs. low-cost producer vs. innovator)?

3.   What are the implications for allowing parts of the organization to implement initiatives on a "voluntary" basis? Is this ever appropriate?

4.   If different companies can have different selection needs, can different divisions within an organization have variation in selection needs as well? If so, should they be allowed to alter a "common" selection procedure to fit unique needs and/or realities? Are there any foreseeable problems and/or advantages associated with this approach from an organizational perspective?

Situation 2: Lean Manufacturing, Inc.

Lean Manufacturing is a well-established firm and is known as an innovator in its market. The company has gained incremental market share in the last decade in a tough market, and has undergone an incredible amount of planned change. It has four divisions and 180,000 employees worldwide. Its strength as an organization is based, in part, on centralized control and common processes throughout its divisions. World Headquarters shares a great deal of information with its divisions. In a recent climate survey, employees generally considered employee relations to be positive, and indicated that they felt they understood the strategy and further direction of the company.

Another hallmark of Lean is that employees are very knowledgeable in where they stand on a performance basis. Performance appraisals are conducted regularly and in a timely fashion. There are four categories into which salaried Lean, Inc., employees can possibly fit: high potential (HP), high development potential (HDP), development potential (DP), and low potential (LP). An employee's category fit is determined by management/leadership, and is focused on an employee's potential for promotion and advancement. It is separate from the performance appraisal system, and is a tool used by management to identify "fast-track" or highly promotable employees. Only about 10 percent of employees fall into this category. Management, *if asked,* will give employees information on their categories and rationale behind category placement.

Most salaried employees are aware of this categorization, and many have taken advantage of the opportunity to receive this information in order to help them make career decisions and/or performance changes.

In the past few years, leadership has communicated to employees the need to make Lean even leaner. Most downsizing has taken place through natural attrition and retirement. However, 18 months ago, the company made its employees well aware that it would still have to eliminate 10,000 positions. Leadership has decided to eliminate the jobs based on performance. Appraisals, as well as promotion-potential categorizations, have been reviewed. It has been decided that 10,000 of those employees who have the lowest performance appraisal ratings combined with lower potential for promotion will be laid off. In addition, Lean has communicated its intentions and rationale to the media.

Upon the day of the announcement that the company would be laying off 10,000 low-performing employees, Wall Street reacted favorably and Lean's stocks reached an all-time high that would persist for months afterward.

Situation 2: Lean Manufacturing Questions

1.   What are your thoughts on Lean's communication policy with its employees, specifically as it relates to promotion potential?

2.   Did Lean do an effective job of balancing all the interests of its stakeholders? If so, how? If not, why not?

3.   What are the implications for the 10,000 laid-off Lean employees? Should this concern the company's leadership?

4.   Do you think Lean's actions were aligned with its strategy?

Situation 3: Fair Company.   Fair Company is a large manufacturing firm with a significant unionized workforce, but the management-union relationship is generally considered to be fair to poor. It is widely known that while recently acknowledged as the most important job, the first-line supervisor position throughout the company is the most difficult and least rewarding job in the firm. In recent years, with a tight labor market, it has been extremely difficult to attract and retain a talented pool of first-line supervisors. Often, young first-line supervisors turn over within two years to accept a different position within the company. At the same time, there is an increasing rate of retirement as the workforce ages, although there is still a sizable group of older and more experienced floor supervisors at Fair Company.

In the past, the company's floor supervisors were primarily high-school educated, with a moderate percentage of college-educated people. In the past few years, though, Fair Company has implemented a very stringent selection system, only considering college graduates for application. Those who make it through the selection system successfully have been hailed as the best and brightest. In addition, an increasing number of initiatives aimed at retention have been created. Management is very interested in retaining this talented group—not just within the company, but on the floor as well.

The most recent retention initiative is the creation of the Supervisory Leadership Council, which annually honors the top new supervisors (those on the floor for no less than 12 months and no more than 24 months after training has been completed) with a dinner and gift. Selection is by leadership nomination from various facilities and centralized evaluation and approval. Furthermore, it provides council members an opportunity for time away from the plant to meet six to eight times a year to mentor each other, share experiences, and interact with guest speakers. This initiative has been well communicated to the supervisors, and in turn has been very well received by them. They do not speak of this as just another program, but are eager to participate and welcome the attention that management is showing them.

MODULE
2

However, there are quite a few older, more experienced supervisors around, and they have increasingly begun to feel resentment toward the very same attention that new supervisors enjoy. Their opportunities for advancement are very slim, but most prefer their current jobs anyhow. They have been disturbed by the ambition and expectations of many of these "young kids" to move ahead quickly, and their attitude that their time "in the trenches" is a temporary but necessary evil. These older workers have remained loyal to the company and committed to their roles throughout their career at Fair Company, even when there was no acknowledgment of the significance of their positions. They never had the same opportunities as the younger workers, but have even served as good mentors and role models to the "young kids." They have enjoyed great benefits and compensation from Fair Company, although both have been scaled back for new recruits. However, management is beginning to fear that these seasoned veterans may retire early—too early for Fair Company's needs—due to their disgruntlement.

Situation 3: Fair Company Questions

1. What are the implications of introducing strategic initiatives aimed at new or recent hires only? Is this ever appropriate? If so, when? If not, why not?

2. How do you secure buy-in and support from groups who will not ever directly benefit from the new initiative?

3. Are there any strategic misalignments in Fair Company's approach to its new recruits or new hires? If so, where?

4. How do you implement new cutting-edge programs and still keep "old-guard" solid performers motivated?

5. How should the success of these new initiatives be measured, and how long over time should they be measured for effects?

Situation 4: Money Matters, Inc.

Money Matters, Inc. (MMI) is a global financial services firm with over 80,000 employees worldwide. The company provides its employees a great deal of opportunity for business unit and geographical movement. It has a more "relaxed" culture than many of its competitors in financial services, and tries very hard to implement shared practices globally that will benefit its employees.

Recently, there has been more attention paid by MMI to the work/life balance of its workforce. With the advent and greater usage of e-mail and the Internet, employees have more flexibility than in the past regarding working long hours. The use of e-mail is strongly encouraged, especially given the wide variation in time zones and the difficulty in communicating organizationwide at common times during business hours.

The company has just completed a climate survey, which has revealed some disturbing discrepancies, in part arising from both different time zones and casual overtime on the weekends. In relation to work/life balance, the company has found that U.S., Latin American, and European employees overall are receiving the work/life balance message, and are gradually taking advantage of new work/life initiatives. In contrast, however, many Asian employees are not practicing it very well, although they have received the same type and amount of communication on this subject. In fact, in recent years, time spent at the office has actually increased.

Upon further investigation with focus groups throughout Asia, it is discovered that as the use of e-mail has increased, so have hours in the office. Apparently, due to cultural differences, many Asian employees feel compelled to respond to e-mail immediately, especially when it is tagged as "high priority." They routinely will stay late or come in on the weekends to read and respond to e-mail. This certainly was not leadership's intent behind promulgating wide usage of e-mail. Even after Asian managers and employees have received communication that this type of vigilance is not necessary, the behavior persists.

Situation 4: Money Matters Questions

1. How should strategic practices and HR initiatives/policies be addressed globally within the same organization?

2. How do you prevent (unforeseen?) situations like this in the future?

3. Should strategic HR practices even be implemented globally? If so, why? If not, why not?

4. How do you check for true alignment throughout the system? Are periodic climate surveys the only means? Are there any other measures?

5. Is this simply an "Asian" issue to be addressed locally in this case, or is it a problem that should be addressed throughout the system? How should the problem be corrected?

Situation 5: Flying High.

Flying High is a well-established firm in the transportation industry. It has approximately 65,000 employees domestically and internationally. Recently, they have undertaken a great deal of planned change, including various HR strategic initiatives such as: succession development, leadership development, performance appraisal re-design, selection re-design, a climate survey, and 360-degree feedback. The 360-degree initiative, in particular, was handled very delicately by Flying High. The climate survey indicated that there was a great deal of distrust of management by employees. Therefore, every effort was made to help employees feel at ease about the 360-degree process. In addition, the first level of management to go through the 360-degree process was the executive level, including the CEO and president.

An outside consulting firm contracted to codesign, collect, analyze, and distribute the feedback. In addition, while Flying High could deliver the reports to its management employees or have them come to Headquarters to receive them, leadership decided to conduct feedback sessions at each location for the convenience of its employees (a first!). The 360-degree reports were distributed at this time, delivered by a professional delivery firm in shrinkwrapped plastic. No one at Flying High had access to the completed 360-degree forms, results, or the reports.

The process went over very well, and was pushed down through the different levels of management, with each level serving as a role model for the next. Managers were required to complete action plans based on their results, and to share their plans—but not results—with their supervisors and reporting employees. The tool was used for developmental purposes only for the first two years, with success, judging by the increase of overall ratings each year over the last. Employees undergoing 360-degree feedback indicated that they felt the received constructive and honest feedback. This was quite an achievement for a company that had two years previously overall indicated a significant amount of distrust from one level of management to another. However, leadership felt that due to the improvements achieved through the 360-degree process, the company could receive even greater benefits by converting this developmental tool into a performance tool, on which all managers' pay increases and promotions would be based.

Situation 5: Flying High Questions

1. How could the use of the 360-degree feedback as a performance appraisal system be an advantage ? How could it be a disadvantage?

2. Is it ever appropriate to convert a strategic initiative tool from one purpose into another? If so, when? If not, why not?

3. What are the implications of using a developmental tool for reward/punishment?

4. What implications does this conversion have for the climate and/or morale of this or any organization?

References

1. Some of these ideas were adapted from the Business Week article, "The horizontal corporation: It's about managing across, not up or down," December 20, 1993: 76–81.

2. Hamel, G. and Prahalad, C. K. 1994. *Competing for the Future,* Boston: Harvard Business School Press.

3. Pfeffer, J. 1998. *The Human Equation: Putting People First,* Boston: Harvard Business School Press.

4. ERSC Centre for Organization and Innovation. "The use and effectiveness of modern manufacturing techniques in the United Kingdom." Institute of Work Psychology: University of Sheffield.

5. Mabey, C., Salaman, G., and Storey, J. 1998. *Human Resource Management: A Strategic Introduction,* Malden, MA: Blackwell.

6. Kochan, T. 1997, Oct. 3–4. Beyond myopia: Human resources and the changing social contract. Paper prepared for the conference "Research and theory in strategic human resource management: An agenda for the 21st century," Cornell University, School of Industrial and Labor Relations.

7. Kossek, E. and Lobel, S. 1996. "Introduction: Transforming human resource systems to manage diversity—an introduction and orienting framework," in E. Kossek and S. Lobel (eds.), *Managing Diversity: Human Resource Strategies for Transforming the Workplace,* Oxford: Blackwell, pp. 1–20.

8. Kanter, R. 1977. *Men and Women of the Corporation.* NY: Basic Books.

9. Kossek, E. 1996. "Managing Diversity as a Vehicle for Culture Change: Confronting Monocultural Dominance at IBM," in E. Kossek and S. Lobel (eds.), *Field Guide of Managing Diversity: Human Resource Strategies for Transforming the Workplace,* Oxford: Blackwell, pp. 1–20.

10. Pasternack, B. A., Keller, S. S. and Viscio, A. 1996. "The triumph of people power and the new economy." New York: Booz Allen, Second quarter report.

11. Chandler, A. 1962. *Strategy and Structure.* Cambridge, MA: MIT Press.

12. Cited in Walker, J. W. 1996. "The ultimate human resources planning: Integrating the human resources function with the business," in G. Ferris, S. Rosen, and D. Barnum (eds.), Handbook of Human Resource Management, Oxford: Blackwell:429–445.

13. Hrebiniak, L. G. and Joyce, W. 1984. Implementing Strategy. New York: Macmillan.

14. Porter, M. 1979. "How competitive forces shape strategy," *Harvard Business Review,* 57:137–145.

15. Ghemawat, G. and Collis, D. 1999. "Mapping the business landscape, " in P. Ghemawat, *Strategy and the Business Landscape,* Boston: Addison-Wesley.

16. Porter, "How competitive forces shape strategy."

17. Child, J. 1987. "Information technology, organization, and response to strategic challenges," *California Management Review,* 30:33–50.

18. Porter, "How competitive forces shape strategy."

19. Appelbaum, E. and Batt, R. 1994. *The New American Workplace.* Ithaca, NY: ILR Press.

20. Porter, "How competitive forces shape strategy."

21. Ghemawat, G. and Collis, D. "Mapping the business landscape."

22. Ibid.

23. Ibid.

24. Porter, "How competitive forces shape strategy."

25. Ghemawat, G. and Collis, D. "Mapping the business landscape. "

26. Brandenburger, A. and Harborne, S. W. 1996. "Value-based business strategy," *Journal of Economics,* 5:5–29.

27. Daft, R. 1992. *Organization Theory and Design.* Saint Paul, MN: West Publishing.

28. Porter, M. 1980. *Competitive Strategy.* New York: Free Press.

29. P. Ghemawat and Rivkin, J. 1999. "Creating competitive advantage." In Ghemawat, *Strategy and the Business Landscape,* Boston: Addison-Wesley.

30. Daft, *Organization Theory and Design.*

31. Prahalad, C. K. and Hamel, G. 1990, May-June. "The core competence of the corporation," *Harvard Business Review.*

32. Peters, T. and Waterman, R. H. 1982. *In Search of Excellence.* New York: Harper & Row.

33. Though Disney stumbled initially in Euro Disney as it tried to take American cultural approaches and plop them in France, it has largely recovered.

MODULE
2

34.   Prahalad and Hamel. "The core competence of the corporation."

35.   Coff, R. 1997. "Human assets and management dilemmas: Coping with hazards on the road to resource-based theory," *The Academy of Management Review,* 22:374–402.

36.   Mabey, et al. *Human Resource Management: A Strategic Introduction.*

37.   Prahalad and Hamel. "The core competence of the corporation."

38.   Hamel and Prahalad. 1994. *Competing for the Future.*

39.   Ibid.

40.   Ghemawat, P. and Pisano, G. 1999. "Building and sustaining success," in P. Ghemawat, *Strategy and the Business Landscape,* Boston: Addison-Wesley.

41.   Fahye, L. 1999. *Competitors.* New York: John Wiley & Sons.

42.   Adapted from P. Ghemawat and J. Rivkin, 1999. "Creating competitive advantage," in P. Ghemawat, *Strategy and the Business Landscape;* and Fahye, L. 1999. *Competitors.* New York: John Wiley & Sons.

43.   Ibid.

44.   Ibid.

45.   Shrugrue, E., Berland, J., Gonzales, B., and Duke, K. 1997, March-April. *Compensation and Benefits Review.* Case Study: How IBM reenginered its benefits center into a national HR service center. 41–48.

46.   For more information on HR role delivery, please see Module 3.

47.   Ghemawat, P. and Pisano, G. 1999. "Building and sustaining success," and Porter, M. 1996, November-December. "What is strategy?" *Harvard Business Review.*

48.   Wright, P. and McMahan, G. C. 1992. "Theoretical perspectives for strategic human resource management," *Journal of Management, 18*(2), 295–320.

49.   Beer, M. and Spector, B. (eds.). *Readings in Human Resource Management,* New York: Free Press.

50.   Milkovich, G and Boudreau, J. 1997. *Human Resource Management.* (8th ed.) Chicago: Irwin.

51.   Chandler, A. 1963. *Strategy and Structure.* Cambridge, MA: MIT Press; Mabey et al. *Human Resource Management.*

52.   Chandler, A. 1962. *Strategy and Structure.* Cambridge, Mass.: MIT Press.

53.   DeVanna, M., Fombrun, C. and Tichy, N. 1984. "A framework for strategic HRM," in C. Fombrun, N. Tichy, M. DeVanna, (eds), *Strategic Human Resource Management.* New York: John Wiley & Sons, 33–51.

54.   Tichy, N., Fombrun, C., DeVanna, M. 1984. "The organizational context of strategic management," in C. Fombrun, N. Tichy, and M. DeVanna, (eds.), *Strategic Human Resource Management.* New York: John Wiley & Sons, pp. 19–31.

55.   Hendry, C. and Pettigrew, A. 1986. "The practice of strategic human resource management," *Personnel Review,* 15:3–8. Cited in Mabey et al., *Human Resource Management.*

56.   Ulrich, D. 1998. "A new mandate for human resources," *Harvard Business Review.* January-February.

57.   Kamoche, K. "Strategic human resource management within a resource-capability view of the firm," *Journal of Management Studies,* 313–331.

58.   Mabey et al. *Human Resource Management.*

59.   Prahalad and Hamel. "The core competence of the corporation."

60.   Copyright Ellen Ernst Kossek.

61.   Kossek, E. E. and Yakura, E. 1998. "Opening the black box of strategic HMR fit," a paper presented at the National Academy of Management Meetings, San Diego.

62.   Daft. *Organization Theory and Design.*

63.   Beer, M., Spector, B., Lawrence, P., Mills, D., and Walton, R. 1984, *Managing Human Assets.* New York: Free Press.

64.   Farney, D. 1990, April 3. "A town in Iowa finds big new packing plant destroys its old calm." *The Wall Street Journal,* A1, A14. Cited in Daft. *Organization Theory and Design.*

65.   Daft. *Organization Theory and Design.*

66.   "Technology is 'demolishing' time, distance." 1997, April 24. *USA Today,* 1B.

67.   O'Connell, T., Sebastian, M., Stoloff, M., and Stormes, R. 1998, December. "Workplace of the Future" Student Project. Prepared for Ellen Ernst Kossek's Human Resource Strategies and Decisions Course, Michigan State University, School of Labor and Industrial Relations.

68.   "The future of flexiplace," 1997, September. *Government Executive,* Washington: GAO, 9:12.

69. Baldwin, H., Brueker, K., Lee, A., and Levine. L. 1998, Dec. 10. "Workplace of the Future" Student Project. Prepared for Ellen Ernst Kossek's Human Resource Strategies and Decisions Course, Michigan State University, School of Labor and Industrial Relations.

70. Addison, M., Hall, C., Keipper, E., Krayer, J., and Reed, L. 1998, Dec. 10. "Workplace of the Future" Student Project. Prepared for Ellen Ernst Kossek's Human Resource Strategies and Decisions Course, Michigan State University, School of Labor and Industrial Relations.

71. "Sony's shakeup." 1999, March 22. *Business Week,* pp. 52–53.

72. Baron, J. and Kreps, J. 1999. *Human Resource Management for General Managers.* Manuscript draft. New York: John Wiley & Sons.

73. Lenz, V. 1999. *The Saturn Difference: Creating Customer Loyalty in Your Company.* New York: John Wiley & Sons.

74. Kahn, J. 1998, Oct. 26. "The world's most admired companies," *Fortune,* 206–226.

75. Kotter, J. and Heskett, J. 1992. *Corporate Culture and Performance.* New York: Free Press.

76. Fisher, L. 1999, March 2. "Hewlett plans to split in 2 in revamping," *The New York Times,* C1, C5.

77. Coff, R. W. 1997. "Human assets and management dilemmas: Coping with hazards on the way to resource-based theory," *Academy of Management Review.* April, 22:374–402.

78. Reich, R. B. 1998, Nov. "The company of the future," *Fast Company,* 124–150.

79. Browning, M. Nov. 1996. Speech to American Society of Quality Control. Atlanta, Georgia Chapter.

80. Brown, M. 1998. "Improving your organization's vision," *The Journal for Quality and Participation,* 21:18–21; Copeland, L., Howell, F., Fernandez, M., McCoskey, C., and Marcano, C. 1999. "Business plan deployment," paper prepared for Ellen Ernst Kossek's Quality of Work Life Class, Michigan State University, School of Labor and Industrial Relations.

81. Walker, J. 1996. "The ultimate human resources planning: Integrating the human resources function with the business," in G. Ferris, S. Rosen, and D. Barnum, *Handbook of Human Resource Management,* Oxford: Blackwell, 429–445.

82. Siegel, M. 1999. "How to create a business plan," *The Magazine for Magazine Management,* 27:191–192.

83. Hitt, M., Keats, B., and DeMaire, S. 1998. "Navigating the new competitive landscape: Building strategic flexibility and competitive advantage in the 21st century," *Academy of Management Executive,* 12:22–42.

84. Walker. "The ultimate human resources planning," 433.

85. Scott, M. 1995, November-December. "An interview with Howard Schultz, CEO of Starbucks Coffee Co.," *Business Ethics Magazine.*

86. Walker. Op cit.

87. Adapted from Smilansky, J. 1997, *The New HR,* London: ITT

88. Becker, B., Huselid, M., Pickus, P., and Spratt, M. 1997. "HR as a source of shareholder value: Research and recommendations," *Human Resource Planning,* 36:39–48.

89. Cusumano, M., and Yofife, D. 1998. *Competing on Internet Time.* New York: Free Press.

90. Ibid

91. Ibid, p. 53.

92. Ibid.

93. Case, J. 1997. "Open book management," *Harvard Business Review,* 12:118.

94. Fishman, C. 1998. "Whole Foods is all teams," *Fast Company,* in The New Rules of Business, Greatest Hits, 1:102–109.

95. Ulrich, D. 1998. "Introduction," *Delivering Results: A New Mandate for Human Resource Professionals,* Boston: Harvard Business Review Press.

96. Pfeffer. *The Human Equation: Putting People First.*

97. MacDuffie, J. 1995. "Human resource bundles and manufacturing performance: Organizational logic and flexible production systems in the world auto industry," *Industrial and Labor Relations Review,* 48:199.

98. Banker, R., Field, J., Schoeder, R., and Sinha, K. 1996. "The impact of work teams on manufacturing performance: A longitudinal design," *Academy of Management Journal,* 867–890.

99. Jackson, S., Schuler, R. and Rivero. C. "Organizational characteristics as predictors of personnel practices." *Personnel Psychology.* 42:727–786.

100. Beatty, R. and Schneier, C. "New HR roles to impact organizational performance: From partners to players," *Human Resource Management,* 36:29–37.

101. Gomez-Mejia, L., Balkin, D., Cardy, R. 1998. *Managing Human Resources.* New Jersey: Prentice Hall.

102. Ibid.

103. "The Toyota Sienna . . . manufacturing ideas," 1998, September 7. *The Times@Toyota, http://www.toyota.com/times*

104. MacDuffie. "Human resource bundles and manufacturing performance."

105. Huselid, M. and Becker, B. 1997. "The impact of high performance work systems, implementation effectiveness, and alignment with strategy on shareholder wealth," a paper presented at the 1997 National Academy of Management meetings, Boston.

106. Ichiniowski, C., Kochan, T., Levine, D., Olson, C., and Strauss, G. 1996. "What works at work," *Industrial Relations,* 35:299–333.

107. Berg, P. 1999, March. Talk given to Ellen Ernst Kossek's Quality of Work Life Class, Michigan State University, School of Labor and Industrial Relations.

108. Coyle, J., and Schnarr, N. 1995. "The soft-side challenges of the 'virtual corporation,'" *Human Resource Planning,* 41, 42.

109. Ko, S. 1998. "Human resources management profile of Korea," a paper prepared for the APEC project, *Global Advantage Through People, Human Resources Management Policies and Practices in APEC Economies.*

110. Park, J. 1998. "Historical perspective on Korean industrial relations," in *Korean Labor and Employment Law: An Ongoing Evolution,* Korean Labor Institute, and Kim and Chang Law Offices.

111. Lim, J. and Pucik, V. 1997, March. "Human resource management in Korea: The changing roles of Korean chaebols' HRM system," a paper presented at the Korean Academy of Management.

112. Towers Perrin. 1990. *Priorities for competitive advantage.* New York: Towers Perrin.

Index

Activity stream (analysis), 2.12, 2.13, 2.15
Adding value, 2.14, 2.15
Autonomous business units, 2.14

Best practices approach, 2.28, 2.30
Bureau of National Affairs, 2.14
Business strategy, 2.4, 2.15–16, 2.19, 2.24. *See also* Mission statement, Vision statement
Buyer power, 2.10–11. *See also* Supplier power

Chaebols (conglomerates), 2.32–33
Communication of policies, 2.27. *See also* Open-book management
Competitive advantage, 2.6, 2.7–8, 2.9, 2.11–12, 2.14, 2.15, 2.23, 2.24, 2.29, 2.31
Complementors (complementary products), 2.10–11
Configurational approach, 2.28, 2.30. *See also* Strategic contingency behavioral approach
Congruence, vertical and horizontal fit, 2.25–26
Core competencies, 2.4, 2.5, 2.7, 2.12–13, 2.16, 2.23
Cost leadership strategy, 2.11, 2.29–30
Cost-minimization approach. *See* Labor transaction model
Critical success factors, 2.9
Cultural values, 2.21, 2.22
Customer-focused activities, 2.13–14

Decentralization, of decision making, 2.29
Decentralized business units. *See* Autonomous business units
Deployment of people, 2.24–25
Differentiation. *See* Product differentiation
Diverse learning, 2.12
Diversity, 2.6. *See also* Multiculturalism
Dominant culture, 2.6

Economic forces, 2.21
Economies of scale, 2.8, 2.11
Employment relations, Korean chaebols, 2.36
Employment relations strategies, 2.24–25
Employment relationship, 2.5, 2.8, 2.19, 2.22, 2.24–25, 2.28
Environmental context, 2.5, 2.17
Environmental forces (drivers), 2.5, 2.21
Experience curve, 2.8
External environment, 2.17, 2.19, 2.24

Flexibility, workforce. *See* Workforce flexibility
Flexiplace, 2.19, 2.20
Focus strategy, 2.12
Frontier of performance, 2.7

Heterogeneity, 2.19
High-performance work system (HPWS), 2.30
Homogeneity model, 2.6, 2.19
Horizontal congruence or fit, 2.25. *See* Congruence
Horizontal integration. *See* Integration
HR bundles, 2.30–31
Human capital (assets), 2.7, 2.13, 2.23
Human resource departmen, 2.24, 2.31
Human resource function, 2.14
    Korean, 2.37–39
Human resource management (HRM), 2.5, 2.8, 2.15
        practices, 2.28
Human Resource Planning Society, 2.24
Human resource policies and practices, 2.22, 2.24, 2.27, 2.29
Human resource role delivery, 2.27
Human resource strategy, 2.4, 2.5, 2.8, 2.12, 2.19, 2.24–25, 2.42
    core concepts, 2.7
    development framework, 2.17–25
    structure linkages, 2.15–17
Human resource systems, 2.6, 2.16, 2.20, 2.25, 2.42
Human resources, 2.13, 2.16
Hypocrisy effect, 2.27

Imposed decision, 2.25
Industry competitive pressures, 2.17. *See also* Competitive advantage
Industry cooperation, 2.10–11
Industry power, 2.11
Integration, vertical/horizontal, 2.9, 2.16, 2.23
Internal assessment, 2.21, 2.24
Internal customers, 2.14
International Monetary Fund (IMF), 2.32–33
Internet/Intranet, 2.20, 2.26

Java Round the Clock at IBM, 2.20
Job security, Korean, 2.36–37

Korean employment system, 2.32–33

Labor relations, Korean, 2.34–36
Labor transactional model, 2.8, 2.25

Management culture, 2.13, 2.22
Market entry, 2.8
Market power, 2.11
Mission statement, 2.24, 2.25. *See also* Business strategy
Mixed core-noncore approach, 2.25
Multiculturalism, 2.6, 2.19. *See also* Diversity

Negotiated decision, 2.25

Open-book management, 2.27
Operational excellence, 2.11, 2.12
Organizational architecture. *See* Organizational structure
Organizational change, 2.5
Organizational cooperation, 2.10, 211
Organizational culture, 2.27–28
Organizational learning, 2.4
Organizational partnering, 2.10
Organizational strategy, 2.7, 2.12, 2.16, 2.24
Organizational structure, 2.4, 2.16, 2.22

Performance contingent compensation, 2.29
Performance management systems, 2.24, 2.31
Performance requirements, 2.5, 2.28–29
Porter's five forces framework, 2.7, 2.10
Power. *See* Buyer power, Industry power, Market power, Supplier power
Power of shareholders, 2.5
Price rivalry, 2.8, 2.23
Primary activities, 2.13. *See also* Activity stream
Product differentiation, 2.11
Product diversification, 2.9, 2.16
Product life cycles, 2.19
Production streams. *See* Activity stream
Profitability, 2.8, 2.9, 2.10, 2.11

Resource-based theorists, 2.12
Rewards, 2.31

Self-directed (self-managed) work teams, 2.22, 2.29
Senior management, 2.13, 2.29
Situational environmental analysis, 2.19
Sixth force. *See* Complementors
Social implications of technology, 2.20
Speed to market, 2.12
Stakeholder analysis, 2.17
Status differences and barriers reduction, 2.29
Strategic contingency behavioral approach, 2.29, 2.30. *See also* Business strategy

Strategic human resource management (SHRM), 2.16–17, 2.28–31
Strategy, internal/external, 2.16. *See also* Business strategy, Human resource strategy
Substitutability, 2.9, 2.10
Supplier power, 2.10–11. *See also* Buyer power
Support activities, 2.13. *See also* Activity stream

Team member, input, 2.30
Technological advances, 2.9, 2.19–20, 2.23
Telecommuting employees, 2.20
Training, employees, 2.29
Transformational role, 2.5, 2.6
Transitional role, 2.5
Trends, workplace. *See* Workplace trends

Unemployment, Korean statistics, 2.33–34
Unilateral discretion, 2.25
Union members, Korean statistics, 2.34, 2.37
United Auto Workers (UAW), 2.10, 2.22

Value chain activity (analysis). *See* Activity stream, Customer-focused activities
Value-added management, 2.27. *See also* Adding value
Vertical congruence or fit. *See* Congruence
Vertical integration. *See* Integration
Virtual partnerships, 2.31
Vision statement, 2.24. *See also* Business strategy

Work/life balance, 2.19
Workflow activity streams. *See* Activity streams
Workforce analysis, 2.21
Workforce commitment model, 2.25
Workforce diversity, 2.20. *See also* Diversity, Multiculturalism
Workforce flexibility, 2.22, 2.42
Workplace culture, 2.20. *See also* Organizational culture
Workplace trends, 2.5, 2.19

MODULE
2

KOSSEK ■ BLOCK

Managing Human Resources
in the 21st Century

From Core Concepts to Strategic Choice

MODULE 3

Leadership by Human Resources

Organizational Roles and Choices

Ellen Ernst Kossek
MICHIGAN STATE UNIVERSITY

Karen S. Markel
MICHIGAN STATE UNIVERSITY

Managing Human Resources in the 21st Century: From Core Concepts to Strategic Choice,
by Kossek and Block

Publisher: Dave Shaut
Executive Editor: John Szilagyi
Developmental Editor: Bryant Editorial Development
Marketing Manager: Joseph A. Sabatino
Production Editor: Tamborah E. Moore
Manufacturing Coordinator: Dana Began Schwartz
Cover Design: Tin Box Studio
Cover Photographs: Copyright Shoji Sato/Photonica
Production House: The Left Coast Group, Inc.
Printer: West Group

Printed in the United States of America
1 2 3 4 5 02 01 00 99

For more information contact South-Western College Publishing, 5101 Madison Road, Cincinnati, Ohio, 45227 or find us on the Internet at *http://www.swcollege.com*
For permission to use material from this text or product, contact us by
- telephone: 1-800-730-2214
- fax: 1-800-730-2215
- web: *http://www.thomsonrights.com*

ISBN: 0–324–01804–5

This book is printed on acid-free paper.

Contents

....

MODULE OVERVIEW   3.5

INTRODUCTION   3.6

OBJECTIVES   3.7

RELATION TO THE FRAME   3.8

CORE CONCEPTS IN HR LEADERSHIP ROLES AND CHOICES   3.9
What Is HRM? Responsibilities and Objectives   3.10

HUMAN RESOURCE ROLES: THE FOUR "Ts"   3.18
The Transaction Role   3.18
The Translation Role   3.19
The Transition Role   3.20
The Transformation Role   3.21
Roles Occur in All HR Policy Domains   3.21

MANAGEMENT DECISION-MAKING CONSTRAINTS AND CHOICES   3.22
Unilateral   3.22
Negotiated   3.23
Imposed   3.23

DELIVERY OF HUMAN RESOURCE ROLES   3.24
Basic Organizational Criteria for Effective Role Delivery   3.24
Integrated Line-Staff Role Delivery   3.26
Reengineering the Mix and Structure of HR   3.26
Centralizing HR Role Delivery: Shared Services   3.28
Outsourcing   3.28

HUMAN RESOURCE EFFECTIVENESS: CONTRASTING APPROACHES   3.28
People Poll: How Do You Measure HR's Impact on the Bottom Line?   3.28
Stakeholder/Multiple Constituency   3.29
Business Consulting   3.29
Utility Approaches: Assessing Quantitative Value Added   3.30

STRATEGIC ISSUES IN HUMAN RESOURCE LEADERSHIP ROLES AND CHOICES   3.30
Strategic Challenges Across HR Policy Clusters   3.30
HR Roles: Strategic Issues   3.31
HR Outsourcing and Role Delivery   3.31

APPLICATION: AT&T CASE   **3.32**

Case Study Exercises   3.33

IN CONCLUSION   **3.34**

Debrief   3.34

Required Readings   3.34

Relevant Web Sites   3.34

Critical Thinking Questions   3.35

Exercises   3.35

References   3.40

INDEX   **3.44**

MODULE
3

MODULE OVERVIEW

The telephone rang at 3 A.M., and the human resource manager awoke in a panic as she reached for the receiver: "No one calls with good news at 3 A.M.!" The shift supervisor at her company's plant apologized for waking her. "We have a sexual harassment problem here"—and he plunged into his story. The HR manager agreed to meet with him first thing in the morning.[1]

A corporate headhunter complained that he was constantly trying to recruit people from 360° Communications, but that no one ever wanted to leave. Back in 1996, 4,000 employees from Sprint Cellular faced an uncertain future; it was likely that they were going to be spun off, which usually meant reorganizing and downsizing. The senior vice president of human resources believes the TRUST principles are the core of 360°'s success in retaining employees in 1999. TRUST is an acronym that stands for teamwork, respect, understanding, support, and tenacity. When the new company was created, HR had most of the responsibility for communicating the reasons for the spin-off to all associates. Openness in communications with employees, and the use of employee input in coming up with a name for the new corporation was carried out by HR using the TRUST principles.[2]

On the wall in the human resource director's office is a plaque from her company president at Celedyne, a manufacturer of advanced technical ceramics for industry and consumers. The plaque thanks the human resource director for her successful contribution in creating a safety-awareness culture that resulted in huge company savings (about $300,000) last year in workers' compensation.[3]

The vice president/relationship leader of human resources for Corporate Services at American Express leads a meeting to review what is known as "The Stand." This vision statement is based on an annual employee satisfaction and morale survey. Its three main goals: to make people incredibly successful, inspire intense customer loyalty, and continually transform entire industries. These must be aligned with the drivers for leadership and development, which are what employees say they want most from their employer, such as "I feel I can grow and progress with my company." The vice president of human resources explains to his colleagues that The Stand leads to competencies, which in turn lead to employee behaviors.[4]

MODULE
3

As the preceding examples show, the human resource function delivers various organizational roles to manage employees. The goal of this module is to develop an understanding of the ways in which the human resources (HR) department can deliver activities that support organizational effectiveness. As today's business environment becomes increasingly competitive, leadership by HR to ensure that all of its services provide value to the firm is necessary to organizational survival. HR departments require visionary leadership to facilitate their role as a partner with line management in the organization.

What were the HR roles depicted in the opening vignettes? Solving the sexual harassment problem faced by the night shift manager is an example of an HR *transaction role,* which refers to the routine but essential problem-solving tasks HR carries out on in a timely and effective manner on a daily basis. Resolving the sexual harassment grievance serves an important role, but may not necessarily transform the firm to meet future competitive business pressures. HR's role in communicating to employees the spin-off of their company by Sprint to create 360° Communications is an example of HR's *translation role.* This refers to the communication responsibilities associated with listening and responding to employees' concerns, advocating for these issues and ensuring two-way employee and management dialogue, and explaining to and implementing for employees the policies established by higher management. Implementing

HR programs to change Celedyne's culture to be more safety aware, while not transforming the entire firm, is an example of HR's *transition role*. This refers to execution of human resource activities in a focused HR policy domain to make the necessary ongoing changes to support or improve business operational and strategic objectives. Typically this role focuses on the delivery of new or revised HR practices and substantive and procedural changes in HR policies and practices. Developing "The Stand," the HR Vision at American Express, and ensuring it is aligned with business drivers, is an example of the *transformational role* of HR. In this case, HR serves a leadership change agent role. Here new HR practices and systems typically accompany new organizational structures, and may also accompany organizational cultural transformation. In this module, we review each of these roles as well as how HR policy areas and objective have evolved over time.

Introduction

The growing competitiveness of global product markets in the early 1990s forced many organizations to consider reengineering or radically redesigning business processes to ensure corporate survival. The goal of reengineering, which is often conducted by cross-functional teams, is to improve the quality and speed of the delivery of services to customers and to cut costs and staff.[5] As noted in Module 1, the human resources function has not remained unaffected by reengineering efforts. Nearly three in five companies reported in a 1996 survey by the Society for Human Resource Management that they have dramatically changed the structure of their human resources departments over the past several years. More than 50 percent anticipate major future organizational change in their human resources departments.[6]

Why does HR need to change? In many organizations, the HR department has a history of being viewed as ineffective. Evidence of this is provided by results from a recent survey by the Human Resource Planning Society headquartered in New York. The survey was designed to scan the business environment on issues related to the future of human resources. The survey sampled leading organizations where the HR function developed systems and strategies to support competitive advantage. These companies had an overall approach to their workforce and HR systems that had a clear positive impact on both the bottom line and employees, was innovative or creative, and contributed to growth and/or customer loyalty. Even in these leading companies where HR was viewed as being strategically oriented, five top issues were identified as keeping HR from providing effective leadership. The most frequently mentioned problem was that HR and its employees lacked a working understanding of the business and the strategic intent of their firms. Another common problem was that the HR executives did not have a personal leadership presence where they were respected by senior top line management. HR often seemed to be holding on too much to the HR of the past— the administrative or old-style paper-pushing aspects of HR. HR also appeared incapable or unwilling to take the lead in facilitating revolutionary change in their firms. Lastly, HR was viewed as being too preoccupied with chasing fads, quick fixes, and benchmarking "me too" practices that didn't fit their firms' needs.[7]

As these critical comments show, human resources is facing greater pressure from line management to show increased leadership and serve as a strategic partner to enhance organizational effectiveness. Companies are realizing that with the fast pace of technological advancement and change in global markets, the human capital within their companies is a main source of competitive advantage. How effectively people systems are managed clearly impacts the success of an organization. Because human resources' contribution to revenue enhancement is not easily measured, HR departments must increasingly focus on assessing the value they add to a company's success. This increased scrutiny has required HR to become a more progressive part of any organization by continually balancing the needs of its customers with environmental constraints on its processes and activities. The goal of this module is to provide an understanding of HR roles, responsibilities, and objectives via leadership by the human resource function in the strategic organization.

For purposes of this module, distinctions can be made among the four human resource roles: *transaction, translation, transition, and transformation,* as introduced above. The reader is also introduced to how traditional HR activities ranging from selection to compensation to training can be carried out to serve these different roles. Examples of forces influencing the degree of management discretion in HR decision making, current and historical developments shaping the nature and power of the HR function, and the competencies needed for the delivery of HR are discussed. The module concludes with a case study from AT&T and an original exercise where you will be able to practice quantifying the value added from HR activities. Throughout the module you are also encouraged to reflect on your own experience in relation to the management of human resources in employing organizations.

OBJECTIVES

- To understand the main responsibilities and objectives of the human resource function and how these policy areas and roles have evolved over time

- To develop an understanding of the main HR roles (transaction, translation, transition, transformation)

- To understand the ways HR roles are enacted across HR policy areas (human resource strategy and organization; talent identification and development; human capital deployment; reward management; employee relations; quality of work environment and voice)

- To understand the varying levels of discretion and constraint on managerial HR decision making

- To examine variation in how HR roles are delivered by HR and others within and external to organizational boundaries and basic effectiveness criteria

- To be aware of the competencies needed for HR functional expertise

- To examine the various approaches for evaluating HR effectiveness, which range from the level of responsiveness to multiple stakeholders or constituents, to adding financial value or utility, to serving as a strategic business partner for strategy execution or cultural transformation

MODULE
3

RELATION TO THE FRAME

Figure 3.1 shows the framework and model that will be used to understand human resource management decisions and strategies, which was introduced in the first module of this series. Its purpose is to show that the environmental context and strategy of an organization influence how management makes human resource decisions and designs employment practices and strategies (explained further in the Human Resource Strategy Module of this series), while balancing multiple roles and constraints.

On the outside of the model is the environmental context in which the firm operates. The *environmental context* includes all the trends and environmental forces that shape business decisions such as market conditions, technology, labor market pressures, globalization, unions, and government regulations that are imposed on the firm from outside. A level below the environmental context is the organizational and business strategy. This represents the firm's business response to the environment. *Human resource strategy* is an organization's fundamental approach toward the management of employees to ensure that it achieves its business objectives in the marketplace.

The external environmental drivers noted above have led to the monitoring and reshaping of business strategy and the human resource strategy. Historically, HR strategy and supporting roles have been largely influenced by the tightness of external labor markets, and the threat of labor unrest and government regulations. Since the early 1980s, these external forces have taken a back seat to global product market pressures and the increased power of shareholders—both drivers of significant changes in the employment relationship and human resource strategy. Increased ratcheting of employee performance demands, and heightened customer responsiveness and quality and adaptability are needed to enable the achievement of strategic business objectives *at the same time* that firms are being asked to control labor costs, restructure, and downsize in order to focus on core competencies.[8]

Core competencies are the collective learning of the corporation that provide access to multiple markets, add value to the end product received by customers, and are difficult for competitors to imitate.[9] People strategies and the use of human capital are increasingly being viewed as core competencies that are central to the formation and delivery of most business strategies today. Products can be cloned and technology and training can be copied, but no one can match highly charged, motivated people who care. Organizations need people who have the knowledge, skills, and abilities to be able to deliver at the frontier of performance—who understand where the company is going and are able to influence its path.[10] Decisions about the delivery of human resource services and what is supposed to be accomplished via human resource policies and practices have become increasingly complex. HR and line managers must make sure that HR roles are simultaneously delivered to support organizational effectiveness.

Like the organization in which it is embedded, the HR department does not deliver its activities in a vacuum but is affected by the same environmental forces as organizational strategy. Organizations are open systems that respond to external pressures by changing elements in the organizational-environment relationship. Employing organizations have permeable boundaries, and HR deals with transactions between the organization's systems and the environment and is located in what is known as a *boundary-spanning function*.[11] For example, HR allows individuals to enter (hire) or leave (fire or retire) from the organization's boundary. HR helps the firm continually adapt to new environmental pressures such as the growing diversity and cross-cultural nature of the labor market. The fact that HR serves a boundary-spanning capacity for the employer's dealings with the external environment can help it gain power, particularly if it is effective in dealing with external threats such as unions, government regulation, labor market shifts, and the economy.[12] HR's power and organizational effectiveness depend on how well it deals with these threats and helps management handle environmental uncertainty.

Globalization and technological change are examples of external environmental changes that have made HR strategy and roles matter now more than ever before. University of Michigan Business School Professor Dave Ulrich notes that the rise of global product markets means that the days when companies could create products domestically and ship them abroad "as is" are gone. Now employees need to "think globally but act locally." This means employees must strive to constantly remain literate in international commerce, customers, and cultures more than ever before. Technology has served to heighten the importance of HR to business strategy execution by making the world smaller via the Internet. It has increased the pace and complexity of information that employees must process and use to make business decisions. Ulrich argues that employees need to stay ahead of the information curve and leverage appropriate data for business results.[13]

The lowest level in the framework (Figure 3.1) incorporates the roles human resource activities play and the level of discretion or constraints management has in

FIGURE 3.1 *A Frame for Understanding Human Resource Strategy: Context, Roles, and Constraints*

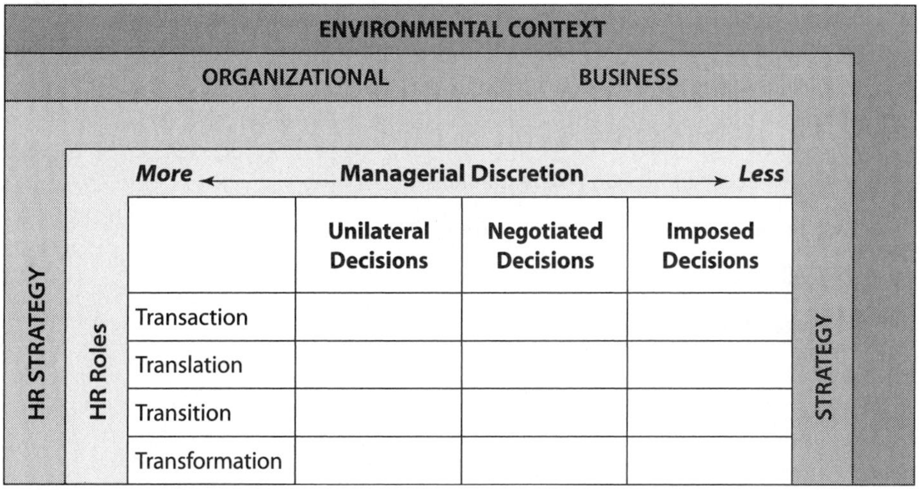

		More ← Managerial Discretion → Less		
		Unilateral Decisions	**Negotiated Decisions**	**Imposed Decisions**
HR STRATEGY / HR Roles	Transaction			
	Translation			
	Transition			
	Transformation			

ENVIRONMENTAL CONTEXT — ORGANIZATIONAL / BUSINESS — STRATEGY

© 2000 by Ellen Ernst Kossek and Richard Block. Thanks to Brian Pentland, Karen Markel, and John Beck for helpful comments and discussions that enhanced the model.

making decisions related to these roles. *Roles* are the expectations associated with a position or in this case an organizational function. While the roles that HR activities can serve are found on the left-hand side of the framework, the *constraints* or level of discretion that employers have in making decisions within each role can be found along the top (labeled Managerial Discretion). As noted in Module 1, HR roles are carried out in a wide variety of situations. Unlike the management of a firm's financial or physical resources, which are normally under complete management control or unilaterally determined, the management of human resources may be subject to constraints of varying degrees. For example, the level of bargaining power of unions or individual talented employees may cause management to negotiate some HR issues. In other cases, constraints are *imposed* from the outside, usually because of laws and legal regulations of governments. The objective of this module is to explain these multiple roles and the constraints on their delivery, which will be covered in detail in the next section.

MODULE 3

Overall, HR activities are conducted to help add value to the business and support the implementation of business and strategic objectives. Management increasingly expects HR to focus less on just being busy or *doing* staff activities, and more on *creating value* that contributes to the bottom line and to general organizational effectiveness. The shift in emphasis is from activity-based measures of HR performance to those related to adding value to the firm. For example, managers are less concerned with the numbers of individuals interviewed or recruited by HR as an annual performance measure, and more concerned with HR's ability to attract and retain quality talent who have the capabilities needed to effectively compete in future markets.

CORE CONCEPTS IN HR LEADERSHIP ROLES AND CHOICES

- What is human resource management (HRM)? HR responsibilities and objectives
  - ✓ Creating productive workplaces through HRM
  - ✓ HRM policy clusters
  - ✓ HR at critical historical juncture: evolutionary stages

- HR roles: The Four "Ts"
  - ✓ The Transaction Role
  - ✓ The Translation Role
  - ✓ The Transition Role
  - ✓ The Transformation Role
  - ✓ Roles occur in all HR policy domains
- Management decision-making constraints/choices
  - ✓ Unilateral
  - ✓ Negotiated
  - ✓ Imposed
- Delivery of HR roles
  - ✓ Basic organizational criteria for effective role delivery
  - ✓ Integrated line-staff delivery
  - ✓ Reengineering the mix and structure of HR
  - ✓ Centralizing HR role delivery: shared services
  - ✓ Outsourcing
- Human resource effectiveness: contrasting approaches
  - ✓ Stakeholder/Multiple Constituency
  - ✓ Business consulting
  - ✓ Utility/HR financial value

MODULE
3

What Is HRM? Responsibilities and Objectives

Creating Productive Workplaces Through HRM.   Take a moment to think about companies you know about or have heard about as being wonderful places to work. Perhaps companies such as SAS Institute, Southwest Airlines, Deloitte and Touche, or Hewlett-Packard come to mind. These companies were in the 1999 top ten of *Fortune* magazine's "The 100 Best Companies to Work For" list conducted by the management consulting firm Hewitt Associates.[14] What is it about particular companies' human resource policies and practices that might lead you or experts to rate them as being especially effective?

The most important characteristic is having HR policies that support a corporate culture giving the message that *employees are valued.* Management ardently believes the firm's people are its most important assets and treats them with respect. Continual training and humane treatment are the most effective policies to ensure that the best employees stay.[15] While in many companies when economic times are tough, employees are the first to be laid off as a means to reduce costs, this is not typical of most of the 100 best companies. Three-fourths have never had a mass layoff and nearly half (40 percent) formally or informally maintain a no-layoff policy.[16] If employers are willing to commit to employees, employees are often much more likely to dig in and commit even in tough times, which is how loyalty affects the bottom line.[17]

Besides not viewing workers as easily expendable, other signals of valuing employees also might include HR policies that minimize artificial distinctions in the workforce, offer the same dining and parking privileges for all, and give equal career development opportunities.[18] At Intel, in order to maintain the cooperative and egalitarian culture that started it, there are no reserved parking spaces, no executive lunchrooms, and no corner offices, and everyone can get stock options.[19] It is important to have stock options and gain sharing for everyone, not just managers. For example, in 1999, record profit-sharing checks of $6,100 were handed out to each of Ford Motor Company's 160,000 U.S. employees. In the same year, $7,400 was given to Daimler Chrysler AG's hourly U.S. workers.

The second most critical characteristic of HR at these companies was having *innovative HR policies that invested in employees and were responsive to their personal development both on and off the job.* Most of these companies (81 percent) offered career counseling, and over half (60 percent) had mentoring programs. Paid educational sabbaticals were available at 17 percent, and unpaid at nearly a third (31 percent). Over a third of these companies offered on-site childcare, and over half had flextime (59 percent). Telecommuting and job sharing was available at about a fifth (18 percent) of the firms. Other good benefits included: group home-owners' and auto insurance, individual financial counseling, college planning assistance, subsidized cafeterias and take-home meals, home purchasing assistance, group prepaid legal services, and personal concierge services where errands and personal needs were taken care of so employees could give more energy to work and family demands.[20]

The third most important characteristic of HR at the best companies was having a *strategic HR orientation.* HR policies, practices, and systems were linked to business and strategic plans. The role of HR in these firms was *to make the business successful.* For example, a longitudinal study of a unionized paper mill in the United States with a history of bitter employment relations showed how the implementation of the "team concept" turned around the company. Based on a new contract that realigned HR policy with strategy, reducing job classifications from 96 job titles to 4, and giving workers extensive training and guaranteed job security helped triple annual profitability.[21]

HRM Policy Clusters. The overall purpose of the human resource function is to design systems and policies to manage human assets in a way that enhances the individual and collective contribution of people to the short- and long-term success of the enterprise.[22] To accomplish these objectives, HR delivers services. Traditionally, the primary objectives of the HR function are to assist management (which implies that all managers of the firm are involved in delivering HR roles) in attracting, retaining, and motivating people to support business and organizational objectives through the development of HR policies, programs, and practices. HR also provides advice and counsel to line management to ensure that the employee relations principles and beliefs of the organization are embodied in business actions.

Why is the effectiveness of the human resource function critical to organizational success? First, labor costs are a major organizational expense. They average 40 percent in manufacturing firms and can go as high as 85 percent of operating expenses in service-intensive companies. Second, people affect productivity. People are more likely to be productive if they are motivated to perform well and believe they are treated equitably.[23] Third, having a skilled, motivated, and adaptable workforce or "people-embodied skills"[24] is directly related to firm profitability. Possessing people capability and intellectual capital enables organizations to be able to learn and capitalize on new growth opportunities in the marketplace.[25]

There are five main clusters of HR decisions and activities (see Figure 3.2 on page 3.2):

- Human resource strategy and organization
- Talent identification and deployment
- Human capital development
- Reward management
- Employee relations and voice[26]

FIGURE 3.1A *HRM Policy Clusters*

Human Resource Strategy and Organization

This cluster involves planning and decision making to ensure that HR activities and organizational structures support a unified approach to the employment relationship that enables the firm to achieve its business strategy. This policy area anticipates the question "How can the pattern of HR decisions made by managers be developed to reflect business strategies and explicitly recognize the competition and the impact of external environmental forces?"[27] HR decisions in this cluster ensure that organizational structures, technology, culture, and work processes support organizational effectiveness strategy execution. Throughout the firm, management must face the task of arranging people, information, activities, and technology, and design individual and group jobs and work systems. In other words, it must define and organize work systems to support strategy.[28] For example, the workforce commitment model to the employment relationship introduced in Module 1 often uses clusters of HR practices to support a quality enhancement business strategy. Extensive selection processes to identify individuals who are adaptable and able to work in teams, continuous training, job security, and group incentives are likely to be used. These types of practices are also often part of high-performance work systems. In contrast, the labor transaction approach to the employment relationship might use clusters of HR activities to support a strategy where the firm competes by being a lower-cost producer. Here the HR practices might support overall minimal investment in human resources, such as inexpensive selection strategies, limited training, and incentive systems that reward individuals for high quantity of performance output.

Often a new business strategy requires a new human resource strategy to support its enactment. Take the example of the organization that wants to increase the speed at which services are delivered to the customer. What if the company currently had reward systems that paid managers based mainly on the number of employees and levels they supervised, had decision-making rules that were very hierarchical and formal, and did not give all employees access to e-mail or the company's intranet? These current HR and organizational practices would be barriers to implementing the business strategy emphasizing speed to market. A new HR strategy should ensure that pay systems are redesigned to focus more on management contribution to rapid product delivery and less on status. Organizational structures should be flattened so information flows more quickly through fewer levels. Jobs and work processes should be revised to empower workers to take on some decision-making authority that previously required supervisor approval before implementation. Employees in all jobs and at all levels should be given e-mail and easy access to the company's intranet.

Talent Identification and Deployment

This second HR cluster involves managing the flow of human resources into, through, and out of the firm.[29] The main objective of this cluster is "How can HR ensure the firm has the right people are at the right place at the right time?" This entails attracting, deploying, and releasing people, both permanent and contingent workers. Just-in-time sourcing and deploying of talent is increasingly being used by HR through a wide range of employee types including temporary help, part-time employees, contract workers, consultants, and regular full-time employees. Because of the changing role of people and human resources in many firms where increased emphasis is being placed on developing a knowledge-leveraging culture, employees are viewed as being more critical than ever before in impacting the bottom line. Employees are increasingly being hired to fit the company, not just a specific job. Companies that are selecting individuals to fit into a high-performance work culture are likely to screen for the following capabilities:

- Comfort with change and ambiguous assignments

- Creativity and problem-solving abilities

- A skill set with competencies that are applicable in a wide variety of assignments

- Recognition that career development is less of a vertical path and more horizontal and zig-zagging in nature

- Willingness to take responsibility for self development.[30]

Many companies may hope to hire the "Michael Jordan" of marketing or programming, but talented people like these do not come along every day. Most talented people have a job or many options, and are likely to be happy where they are. Why should they join a new company's team? What should a company do to compete?[31] First, companies need to develop a clear understanding of what makes a "great" and "not so good or bad" employee and explicitly communicate these attributes to all members involved in selection decisions. At AES, which develops electric power plants, a bad hire is "someone who always complains, is unhappy, blames others, isn't honest or trusting, needs specific direction and waits to be told what to do, is inflexible, and doesn't take responsibility."[32] It is also important to build relationships with talented potential employees, avoid coincidence hiring, and try to constantly improve and develop innovative ways to recruit top talent. According to research done by John Sullivan, the head of the human resources department at San Francisco State, companies like Cisco, Hewlett Packard, Microsoft, Nike, and Schwab try to mirror how they market their business and products in their recruitment. In these firms, senior management makes it clear that hiring great people is the responsibility not only of HR but of every single manager. They train their managers to spot the best people and remember the names of impressive people they meet at conferences or in the field. Cisco uses e-mail to try to attract talented people. The Make Friends@Cisco program matches Cisco employees with people who have expressed an interest in the company to create a learning relationship. The message is "We're going to be friends with you because you're smart. Let's try to learn from each other. If we wind up hiring you, even better."[33] Great companies focus on not only hiring talent, but keeping it. Executives are measured and rewarded for attracting and retaining the best people in the company. Attracting and *retaining* top talent is a vital talked-about subject in the company. Individuals are frequently asked, "Are you challenged, listened to, recognized, and rewarded?"[34]

Human Capital Development

The activities in this third HR cluster include formulating and implementing HR strategies to manage individual and group socialization, development, and performance. It also involves enabling training that enhances individuals' and teams' abilities to not only perform current responsibilities, but also develop capabilities to perform future demands. The key objective of this cluster is "How can HR practices promote and renew a learning- and performance-driven culture to support business objectives?"

Regarding performance, historically many companies have done a better job of focusing on performance *appraisal*—looking back over the previous year and judging how well one did—and less on performance *management*—looking forward and planning for future skill enhancement while taking account of an individual's context. Often individuals and teams have too many objectives to keep employees focused on top priorities, and performance objectives are often not linked to requisite changes in employee skills and behaviors.[35] Further, performance appraisal systems have been largely individually based and overlooked links between individual and team or group performance. Traditionally, the manager only did the appraising. Now, with 360-degree appraisal systems in many firms, managers, employees, team members or peers, subordinates, and even customers are giving performance input. At the Whole Foods Company, a specialty gourmet supermarket, for example, peers are critical to the performance process. Teams from around the country benchmark each other by visiting stores conducting a two-day performance review, and giving feedback.[36]

Turning to training, many companies have not placed a high value on training employees at all levels, or training has usually not been strongly linked to strategy or transfer on the job. Yet increasingly, companies are seeing training as a strategic lever. If a firm's employees are better trained and trained ahead of its competitors, those employees are likely to be more productive in a way that offers competitive advantage. Edward Jones, an operator of more than 4,000 stock brokerage offices, spends a minimum of $50,000 on training per employee. Twenty-seven percent of employees are partners, earning recent returns of 20 to 27 percent. Companies such as Edward Jones strive to create cultures where employees want to continually improve. Similarly, the USAA insurance company for military officers has very low turnover. Employees receive 80 hours of training per year, and one out of four voluntarily participates in educational reimbursement programs.[37] Besides caring about training and development on the job, some companies take a "whole people approach" to human capital development. Using a software program called a "life-cycle program" at one company that was identified as having state-of-the-art HR practices, employees engaged in self-assessments to identify personal and professional goals. Based on this information, the individual and the firm developed career planning to fit with the person's aspirations. The firm did not view development as only a one time on-the-job transaction; rather, it sent the message that it cared if you have a child in school or need to take a sabbatical over your career span.[38]

Reward Management

This fourth HR cluster involves the management of the total pay system including benefits, as well as recognition and intrinsic reward systems. The key issue of reward management is "How can reward systems be communicated and fairly distributed to promote the performance needed to compete now and in the future?" Reward systems send a powerful message to employees as to the kind of firm management seeks to create and maintain and the type of attitudes and behaviors management expects from employees.[39] For example, Whole Foods has an open salary plan where each store has a book that lists the previous year's salary and bonuses for all employees from around the country by name. This was done to help eliminate mistrust over who makes what. The goal of having an open salary system was for people to have a clear understanding of how pay is distributed, to focus less time wondering what others are making and more time on team goals.

TABLE 3.1 *Stages of Evolution of the Human Resource Function*

Time Period	Primary Human Resource Stage	Key Environmental Pressure
Late nineteenth century U. S. Industrial Revolution	Pre-personnel department	Market pressures, immigration
Early 1900s–1930s	File drawer maintenance	Market pressures and World War I
1930s–1960s	Union avoidance/functional specialization	Unions
1960s–1970s	Government accountability	Government
1970s–1990s	Strategic business partner	Global market pressures
1990s–2000+	Strategic player: adding value	Global market pressures, technological change

Teams and individuals are rewarded for performance by bonuses, recognition, and promotion of members. The adage "What gets rewarded, gets done!" is very apt.[40]

Management needs to make choices about the degree to which compensation should be used as an incentive, the balance between intrinsic rewards and financial rewards—pay and benefits—and the mix of rewards allocation based on individual, group, and organizational performance.[41] In the United States, many reward systems are out of sync with the greater movement toward teamwork and empowerment, as work cultures have traditionally rewarded individualism. Yet rewards must be given for both individual and teamwork if they are going to fit with the workplace trend toward greater teamwork. Most firms have traditionally mainly rewarded individual behavior even when teams are in place. The credit card company MBNA has countered this problem by making *individuals or teams* eligible to receive $15,000 for the best idea made to a suggestion plan.[42] Another key critical challenge facing organizations is that rewards are too often tied to promotions that are increasingly unavailable due to the flattening of organization structures and an aging workforce that is retiring later in life.

Employee Relations, Quality of Work Environment, and Voice

This fifth and final HR cluster includes developing labor agreements with groups such as unions and individuals, determining the appropriate level of employee influence and participation in decision making, managing grievances and discipline, maintaining a work environment that ensures high quality of work life such as equal opportunity and health and safety. It also involves implementing communication and organizational development initiatives to manage organizational change processes. The Bank of Montreal is a good example of how improving employee relations can pay off for an organization. Regarding the importance of ensuring equal opportunity, in 1991 executives became aware of an alarming statistic. Though women constituted 75 percent of the workforce, 91 percent were in nonmanagement positions. Executives created a task force to identify barriers to women's advancement. The task force surveyed over 9,000 workers and found the following results. First, many at the bank had false assumptions about women, believing they automatically quit when there were family demands. Second, women lacked advancement opportunities. Third, all employees faced a culture unsupportive of work and family commitments. To counter these problems, the bank publicized that women on average had higher service records than men, despite the myth. The bank created better access to job opportunities through an improved job vacancy posting system, and trained managers and employees in career development. Flexible work arrangements were also implemented. By 1997, the bank enjoyed record profits, and nearly a quarter of its executives

MODULE
3

are now women. This is just one example of how managing employee relations effectively can support business and organizational effectiveness.

HR at a Critical Historical Juncture: Evolutionary Stages.   *"Human Resources must be defined by what it delivers, not by what it does!"*[43] The role of the human resource management function in many firms is at an important juncture. On the one hand, in some firms HR budgets are being cut and responsibilities are being outsourced to experts or contingent workers. On the other hand, organizations are facing an important opportunity to renew and redesign their HR systems as strategic assets to add shareholder value and intellectual capital.[44] The sources of intellectual capital come from having a highly skilled, motivated, and adaptable workforce, and HR systems that maintain and revitalize these competencies.

In order to understand the roles and activities of the function today, it is useful to briefly examine the historical evolution of HR, depicted in Table 3.1. The reader also may find it helpful to refer to Module 1 for a discussion of HR's historical influence on the employment relationship.

Pre-Personnel Department: The Foreman Ruled

From the late nineteenth century until about 1915, when the United States was undergoing the Industrial Revolution and massive immigration, and the factory system of manufacturing grew regardless of industry, the foreman historically was in control of employment matters. The foreman was given free rein by owners in hiring, pay, job assignments, and supervision in order to "drive" workers to be productive.[45] Labor was viewed as a commodity to be bought and sold, and the government did little to control the worker's lot. See Module 1 for further historical elaboration.

File Drawer Maintenance: Emergence of Personnel Departments

Even today, when an entrepreneurial organization starts up, the personnel department doesn't usually exist until the firm becomes sufficiently large that the owner needs functional specialization in human resources. Often the first duties given to the personnel department are clerical functions like selecting and paying employees, processing benefits, or keeping track of years of service. This is known as the *file drawer maintenance stage*.[46] While these are all useful activities, they carry little organizational prestige or sense of critical importance. Historically, personnel departments began to first appear and take on file drawer maintenance activities in the United States after 1910. They arose largely due to the market pressures of World War I for wartime production, which caused many organizations to grow.[47] Also, there was increased availability of human engineering and other techniques related to Frederick Taylor's notions of scientific management determining the optimal way for jobs to be performed regardless of the individual in them. The human relations movement, which began in 1923 and continued until the early 1930s, also supported the growth of personnel. The Hawthorne Works of Western Electric in Chicago provided a famous setting where research was conducted to identify work factors influencing productivity. The human relations movement found that if management paid attention to workers, productivity went up. Coffee rooms, company picnics, and other perks to improve the workplace as a social system were managed by personnel departments.[48]

Union Avoidance and Functional Specialization Stage

Supported by the passage of the National Labor Relations Act in 1935, union membership grew in the United States from 1935–1960. Industrial relations and the labor relations subgroups rose to prominence within personnel and industrial relations departments in major U.S. companies.[49] HR helped management deal with the negative impact of labor strife on business. In companies that had both a personnel and labor relations department, the labor relations staff with its focus on collective bargaining issues often was more powerful than personnel. The risk of labor instability hindering or shutting down firm operations, and the constant pressure for pay and benefits increases, made management elevate labor relations issues to strategic importance. As unions became successful in negotiating pensions, healthcare, and so forth, functionally specialized human resource department subfunctions such as recruitment, labor relations, benefits, and wages began to appear.[50]

Government Accountability Stage

During the 1960s–1970s, beginning with the passage of Title VII of the Civil Rights Act of 1964, government regulations were passed demanding employer accountability for virtually every aspect of employment. Besides discrimination laws, laws governing health and safety, pensions, and labor standards were written. Once again, HR helped management deal with negative environmental pressures—in this case the threat of legal fines. In 1973, for example, a consent decree by AT&T with the federal government to bring the pay of women in line with the pay of men cost the company over $30 million.[51] Many managers viewed the HR activities devoted to compliance as a drain on organizational resources.

Strategic Partner Stage

Many U.S. firms were struggling to survive economically by the early 1980s, due to high interest rates, growing foreign competition, more mergers and acquisitions, and lagging U.S. productivity. Due to these competitive pressures, Personnel began to be renamed in many firms as "Human Resources" to reflect an increased emphasis on employees as valued human resources. In many firms even employees began to be called new names to reflect this change—for example, "associates," "partners," or "members."

One of the most popular HR roles to emerge in the 1980s and 1990s is that of strategic business partner.[52] All organizations conduct strategic planning, which is the process of positioning the organization in the competitive environment and implementing actions to compete successfully. Forming a strategy is an interactive process where senior managers select goals to define corporate success, form these goals into a vision, target the vision within the firms' internal and external environment, and develop a tactical plan to accomplish this vision.[53] The strategic plan typically has designated functional strategies for marketing, finance, engineering, etc., to support the organizational strategy. Human resource professionals historically have not been viewed as players in this arena. For an HR professional, being a strategist means shedding the once traditional image of managing only the human side of business operations—"people management" and policy enforcement.

Strategic Player Stage: Adding Value

Although the business *partner* stage is valuable because it signifies HR is part of the management team that develops strategy, it has a risk of not being realized if HR is seen as an organizational part that indirectly helps out but does not directly add value. HR in the strategic *player* stage seeks to enhance competitive advantage by adding real measured economic value to the firm.[54] Using a basketball player analogy, it is no longer enough for HR to *assist* in achieving business goals as being part of the team (strategic *partner*); HR must now actually *score* some baskets as a strategic *player*. A value-based focus is now placed on HR where like other functions, if the customer is unwilling to pay for the work, the organization should not provide it. Besides partners and players, other metaphors for HR are architects, leaders, and stewards. Names are important as they shape images that affect behavior of HR and managers.[55] Further, these new labels are certainly more positive than file drawer maintainers, government compliers, policy police, or bureaucrats.

MODULE
3

Management is currently placing increased pressures on HR to become more cost-effective and visibly contribute more added value to business performance. As a means to improve its functional efficiency, the way human resource services are delivered is being reorganized and transferred from HR. For instance, line management is becoming more involved in selection, payroll is increasingly being outsourced (see later in this module) to external vendors, and employees are even updating their own personnel records. Actions such as these have helped streamline human resource departments, forcing the function to better demonstrate its contribution to the bottom line. According to a recent survey of executives on their human resource department practices and expenditures conducted by the Society for Human Resource Management and The Bureau of National Affairs, Inc., currently the median ratio of human resource staff members to total employee headcount is 1:100.[56] Over the next decade, it is not unlikely that this ratio will rise as HR seeks to increase efficiency.

HUMAN RESOURCE ROLES: THE FOUR "TS"

Given the new emphasis on adding value as an organizational player, the role of the human resources department has become considerably more multidimensional in many firms.[57] A value chain perspective holds that it is unwise for an organization to expend managerial or financial resources on activities that add little to the final value of products or services. A value chain consists of primary activities—those related to the physical creation of a product or service, its sales or distribution, and support activities that assist primary activities in creating value.[58] Most HR activities are support activities in that they indirectly contribute to the creation of value in the eyes of the customer (effective selection processes do not directly create a better car or computer, they indirectly do so). Yet it is useful to classify HR activities into distinct roles that add value and contribute to organizational effectiveness. It is also important to note that HR activities can directly affect internal customers (employees or management) as well as external ones.

The framework in Figure 3.1 on page 3.9 shows that there are four major HR roles—transactions, translations, transitions, and transformations—which are subject to not only constraints, but also organizational and strategic factors. Figure 3.3 shows how these specific roles are different in focus from short to long term and in the degree to which the nature of activities emphasize processes (which support strategy execution and customer service) or people.[59] The transaction and translation roles are more focused on people and have a short-term view. The transition and transformation roles are more oriented toward improvement or transformation of new processes, where organizational processes (and the employees involved in them) are realigned to support customer and market demands, and have a future orientation. HR is responsible for the daily ongoing activities to manage an organization's employees (e.g., payroll and benefit administration) and simultaneously monitoring and forecasting future responsibilities. HR must balance its efficient infrastructure without comprising its position as an employee advocate or strategic partner. It is important to note that while HR has multiple roles, they are not necessarily executed one at a time but may be performed simultaneously across policy domains. These roles can be delivered not only by HR, but also line managers, employees, and vendors.

The Transaction Role

The *transaction role* refers to the routine but essential traditional personnel or HR administration activities emanating from earlier historical stages such as the file drawer maintenance or government accountability. These activities include hiring and firing of people, making sure that employees are paid in a timely and accurate manner, and

FIGURE 3.3 *Human Resource Roles*

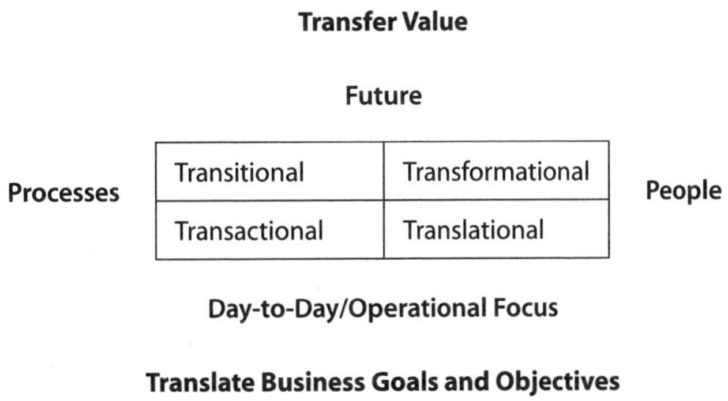

Transfer Value

Future

Processes	Transitional	Transformational	People
	Transactional	Translational	

Day-to-Day/Operational Focus

Translate Business Goals and Objectives

Source: Adapted from Ulrich. *Human Resource Champions,* 24.

handling grievances. In this role, HR works to build an efficient infrastructure by acting as an administrative expert. As illustrated in Figure 3.3, the activities in this role are focused on the day-to-day/operational processes. In order to ensure that the administrative duties are executed properly, HR experts strive to improve the functioning of their own department as well as that of the entire organization.

The National Semiconductor Company traditionally used a paper-based system to track more than 50,000 resumes per year. Now, with scanning and data storage software, all resumes can be searched electronically. Additionally, using the company electronic intranet, HR can e-mail a candidate's resume to a hiring manager for review. This system, along with a supplemental job opening system, contributed to the reduction in hiring cycle time from 110 to 62 days.[60]

Screening resumes and hiring people are examples of day-to-day activities of personnel administration and important ongoing administrative roles, but they may not necessarily transform the firm to meet future competitive business pressures. A helpful analogy is to think of personnel transactions similar to a single bank transaction of cashing a check. Like cashing a check, it takes an administrative action to cut a payroll check, initiate a title change to promote someone to a new job, or process a payment covered under a benefits plan. Management expectations of the transaction role come from transaction cost theory from institutional economics.[61] The goal of HR activities associated with the transaction role is to improve administrative efficiency and reduce costs associated with accomplishing tasks.[62]

The Translation Role

The *translation role* refers to the communication responsibilities associated with listening and responding to employees and customer concerns, as well as explaining to and implementing for employees the policies established by higher management. As shown in Figure 3.3, the activities in this role are focused on the day-to-day/operational focus in relation to people. These activities are designed to promote employee commitment, improve morale, and enhance the capability to respond to customer demands. By facilitating two-way communication between employees and management, HR also serves the role of employee champion and advocate by ensuring their views and rights are addressed.

Examples of translation activities might include communicating to employees human resource policy relating to such matters as equal employment opportunity laws, or business operating objectives and customer needs. These can also include the cross-cultural translation of activities, such as the adaptation of a new performance appraisal system developed at the U.S. headquarters to fit with the cultural mores of the subsidiary in Egypt, as Amoco Corporation did.

If employees and management understand each other well and have a common line of sight (view that the achievement of individual and organizational goals will be mutually beneficial), operational excellence is likely to occur. Making the low-cost, high-service strategy of Southwest Airlines work by supporting translation is part of CEO Herb Kelleher's daily job. In the employee newsletter, *LUV Lines,* a segment entitled "So, What Was Herb Doing All This Time?" highlights the major activities in which Kelleher participates. Examples include station visits, days in the field, Ronald McDonald suppers, conferences, and special employee events, such as birthdays, weddings, interviews, and television programs. While most airlines have struggled to turn a profit in recent years, Southwest Airlines has excelled in this area. The company flew more passengers per employee and had the fewest employees per aircraft in 1991, and had the second lowest cost per available seat mile in 1993. Moreover, the company's employee turnover rate is just 7 percent—the lowest in the industry—and for four years running (1993–1996), the U.S. Department of Transportation has determined that Southwest has had the most on-time flights, the best baggage handling rating, and the highest customer satisfaction ratings. It uses a six-person ground crew to ready a plane in 15 minutes versus an average of one hour for other airlines. Southwest has a workplace with few rigid rules since Kelleher has done such a good job of translating business and HR strategy. It also rewards employees through a profit-sharing plan, and performance appraisals and communications emphasize customer service.[63]

Similarly, Dell Computer directly translates customer needs to employees by letting them communicate directly with customers without going through purchasing departments. Employees can respond immediately to problems without processing errors, and are given constant customer feedback. For example, Dell uses the Internet as the ultimate direct translation tool; it now accounts for about 20 percent of Dell's business.[64]

The Transition Role

The *transition role* refers to execution of human resource activities, policies, and practices to make the necessary ongoing changes to support or improve business operational and strategic objectives. Typically, this role focuses on the implementation of new or revised HR practices and long-term procedural changes in HR policies and practices. Besides ensuring *vertical fit* between the HR and business strategy—HR supports the overarching strategy—the transition role also involves assessing *horizontal fit* or congruence between HR activities. For example, in a study of employee involvement in the global auto industry, higher performance was associated with the bundling of human resource practices as a cluster with business strategy.[65] For example, if a firm just put in a single HR practice such as quality circles that fit vertically with a business strategy toward quality enhancement, without linking them to the simultaneous availability of supportive training and changes in pay systems to support teamwork, it had less positive results than firms following the bundling approach.

At the Sprint Corporation, their performance management system (known as LINK) was implemented in order to make specific links between individual employee behavior and corporate strategy.[66] Through LINK, HR aligns Sprint's corporate objectives vertically and horizontally throughout the company, creating the basis for setting each employee's performance objectives. Additionally, LINK provides a set of behavior-based parameters used to measure performance improvements and professional development. Performance is assessed in relation to employees' progress toward their own goals (which ultimately tie into Sprint's goals). Sprint's development of LINK supports its goals to maximize profitable market share and appropriately reduce unit costs. In this instance, individuals received evaluations as to how well they reached goals related to maximizing profitable market share and reducing unit costs.

MODULE
3

The Transformation Role

Under the *transformation role,* HR acts as a change agent and realigns systems to support massive organizational change. Here new HR practices and systems typically accompany new organizational structures and cultural transformation. Transformation occurs when a firm's top management makes a fundamental change in the nature of its human resource management practices and work systems that shape the way work task and jobs are designed and organized. Additionally, organizational structures and cultures are altered to support major strategic change in the way the firm competes in the marketplace.

For example, one widely publicized shift is the transformation taking place at Sears. Under the direction of the chief executive officer (CEO), the key components of Sears' strategy have been to refocus on the core retail business, improve its stores' look, and provide superior service. The core competencies needed to drive the Sears strategy include improving employee customer service and selling skills, and management's ability to provide coaching and feedback to employees on these skills. To build these competencies and create a more customer-driven culture, the CEO has realigned many HR activities, ranging from performance to pay to communication to organizational structures. For example, the company has a redesigned performance management system. Managers now receive 360-degree feedback, and bonuses for the top 200 executives are no longer solely based on financial measures. Revenues, return on assets, and operating margins are the basis for only half of executive incentives. The other half is based on customer satisfaction measures and employee ratings of management. Sears also changed its physical environment by converting individual department supervisors' offices in their stores to a shared team space, encouraging supervisors to spend more time out on the selling floor providing feedback and coaching sales associates about sales behaviors and techniques. The company has also utilized PSE (pure selling environment) employee events. These events are designed to disseminate to employees information about what the company is doing in such areas as customer service. Training on customer service has also been provided to management, supervisors, and employees across the company. New job descriptions and operating structures have been implemented to place decision making closer to the customer. The old policy manual at Sears, laden with rules and procedures, has been replaced with a brief folder called "Freedoms and Obligations." It measures about one-eighth of an inch thick, and contains a one-page letter from the CEO, a one-page list of "shared beliefs," a 16-page booklet outlining leadership principles for managers (e.g., reward people who add value to Sears), and a 17-page code of business conduct that applies to every employee. This transformation is leading to improved performance for the company. Since 1992, Sears has seen its market share, operating margins, and inventory turns all rise, while overhead as a percent of sales has fallen.[67]

Another example comes from United Airlines' response to deregulation of the industry, which required airlines to move to a more customer-centered approach in order to remain competitive in capturing market share. The company changed its culture by realigning HR systems to support an employee-owned firm, when it was bought by its employees. Stock ownership is part of every employee's benefit package and increases with years of company service. The culture became more customer driven by each employee having a vested interest in performance.

Roles Occur in All HR Policy Domains

In every HR policy domain, activities may be conducted that reflect each role. To illustrate, let's take the cluster of activities associated with talent identification and deployment. The hiring of a new employee and processing related paperwork are examples of HR activities associated with transaction roles. The communication to employees that all current workers had to go through a reselection process to validate that they have the

MODULE
3

current skills needed to hold onto their jobs, as General Motors recently did with some employees, is an example of the translation role. The validating and development of new assessment centers and selection systems to identify engineers with team-based skills, as Chrysler and AON HR consulting group implemented in 1997 and 1998 for both hourly and professional workers, reflects the transition role. Chrysler's implementation of these new selection systems changed the past practice of largely hiring workers because they were related to individuals who had worked for Chrysler. In order to support the business strategy of increasing speed to market, quality, and innovation, Chrysler wanted new systems where individuals would be selected not on the basis of being historically linked to the Chrysler family but rather on their ability to work and communicate in teams. Choosing the new management team to successfully transform Chrysler's culture to be more global in the Daimler-Benz Chrysler merger and acquisition is an example of how talent identification activities support the transformation role.

MANAGEMENT DECISION-MAKING CONSTRAINTS AND CHOICES

While the roles that human resource activities can serve are found on the left-hand side of the framework (see Figure 3.1 on page 3.9), the constraints and choices that employers have in making decisions within each role can be found along the top (labeled Managerial Discretion). These constraints can be grouped into three types (unilateral, negotiated, and imposed) that vary in the degree to which they are proscribed. As noted in Module 1, on occasion, employers have full *unilateral discretion* over human resource matters, and may act as they believe is in the best interest of shareholders, employees, management, or other constituents. In other situations, the implementation of human resource issues must be *negotiated* with employees, either formally via legal or union representatives, or informally with each worker. In still other cases, constraints are *imposed* from the outside, usually because of laws and legal regulations of governments.

Unilateral

Many human resource decisions are made unilaterally by the firm. Examples of this include determining how much financial and managerial attention to allocate to human resource matters, the making and communicating of human resource decisions, the employer's overall philosophy on managing the employment relationship, and choosing the role that HR will play in the current and future goals of the company.

A top management decision to hire contingent workers to accommodate labor shortages due to the labor market or unforeseen production demands is typically done unilaterally. Due to the increasing costs of benefits and other fixed labor costs associated with offering long-term job security, more and more companies (especially nonunion) are using contingent workers where they might have previously hired a permanent employee. Peter Cappelli of the Wharton School has reviewed the research on the changing employment relationship. His review shows how this change is generally a unilateral employer decision that *transforms* the employment relationship.[68] Relying on several national surveys, Cappelli notes that currently 25 percent of the workforce are either part-time, temporary, or contract employees, and that 57 percent of the firms surveyed used contractors to provide services that could be performed by their employees. Regarding job security, a 1994 survey on downsizing practices by the American Management Association found that workforce reductions are increasingly strategic or structural in nature as opposed to a response to a short-term economic condition as only 5 percent of firms in a 1996 survey cited economic conditions as the sole reason for reductions in workforce.[69]

Negotiated

A key constraint on human resource management is market power, which can often cause employers to negotiate HR decisions with employees or a union.[70] Some employees or groups of employees, because of the nature or level of their skills or knowledge (intellectual or human capital), may bring substantial market power to bear on the employment relationship. This market power in turn constrains the flexibility of the organization vis-à-vis these individuals or groups of individuals. Well-known examples of individuals with substantial market power are experienced executives, famous athletes, and movie stars. Sometimes local labor market situations may give some employees bargaining power. Skilled tradespeople in manufacturing industries are examples of such individuals. Groups of individuals can sometimes have substantial power that can constrain HR decisions even if individuals do not. A group of engineers may possess special knowledge over a production process that may make them difficult to replace, especially if this knowledge was obtained over a substantial period of time and is essential to producing many of the firm's products. In a unionized setting, under the National Labor Relations Act, the employer is legally obligated to negotiate with a union over terms and conditions of employment germane to the working environment. Even routine transactions that are unilaterally controlled by management in the absence of a union often must be *negotiated* when a union is present to represent the affected workers. For example, suppose the firm finds it necessary for an employee to work overtime for two hours one day. This simple *transaction* may be as seemingly routine as asking the desired employee to stay two hours after work in a nonunion situation. For workers covered by a union, however, there may be established negotiated rules in the collective bargaining agreement for the distribution of overtime. Those rules, rather than unconstrained management choice, will determine who receives the overtime.

Regardless of whether a group is unionized or not, it may be increasingly valuable for employers to negotiate HR decisions. Research shows that if an individual or group participates in the decision-making process, they are more likely to accept—and be committed to help implement—a decision.[71] As organizations are restructuring to become more flexible in the ways work is accomplished—whether team-based or through adopting telecommuting or new reward systems—such decisions may be best implemented jointly. The key to managing negotiated constraints and making the most valuable and effective choices rests on management and HR's ability to effectively communicate (the *translation* role) with employees (internal customers). When managers are able to create and communicate a joint vision that becomes accepted and enacted by employees, unity and internal strength facilitate a competitive edge.

Imposed

Constraints at the imposed level are out of scope of either the HR or firm's control. Often these are through market or governmental constraints. The employment relationship in the twenty-first century is covered by a web of regulations protecting workers' rights. Numerous statutes have been passed covering labor standards, employment discrimination, employee benefits, plant closings, and occupational safety and health. Some of these regulations are procedural.[72] (Under the WARN [Worker Adjustment and Retraining Notification] Act, if a plant is to close, workers have a right to have at least 60 days notice). Others are substantive. (Under Title VII of the Civil Rights Act, employers may not discriminate on the basis of gender, race, ethnicity, age, or religion.) For example, the Family Medical Leave Act of 1993 mandates that employees in firms with 50 or more workers have a right to take up to 12 weeks unpaid leave without threat of job loss. Provisions and procedures for managing this employee *transaction had* to be developed. An example relating to market power is that of a powerful customer. If a company's success is contingent on satisfying a specific client's needs, the firm has no choice but to accommodate their needs or risk total failure. For example, the Big Three U.S. auto companies mandated that many of their suppliers had to implement quality and statistical process training if they wanted to remain suppliers. Management had little or no choice but to implement these HR systems, or lose a substantial part of their business.

DELIVERY OF HUMAN RESOURCE ROLES

From time to time, employees, line managers, the HR department, and external vendors or experts from consulting firms are involved in delivery of HR roles. *Who* delivers the roles and *how* they are delivered may have an impact on their acceptance and can affect an organization's development of competency in these HR roles and policy areas. Thus, management faces strategic choices in determining whether internal or external resources (e.g. an in-house department, line managers or employees, or an external vendor) are empowered to deliver these roles. There are four management choices related to delivery. The first is, assuming basic criteria are met for effective HR decision-making, how should the firm balance the line management, employee, and HR partnership in HR role delivery? Second, what is the appropriate mix or balance of roles from transactional to transformational? Third, what is the extent to which HR activities should be centralized into shared services? Fourth, to what extent, if any, should HR services be outsourced? Before considering these questions, it is important to review the basic organizational criteria for an effective HR decision-making environment.

Basic Organizational Criteria for Effective Role Delivery

Before deciding who and how HR roles should be delivered, some basic organizational requirements for HR decision making must be met.[73] These are an effective line-staff relationship between HR, employees, and managers; top management commitment to HR; an employee relations climate of openness and respect; a strong HR department with competent professionals, and an implementation approach that balances key HR decision-making tensions.

Integrated Line-Staff Relationship. HR is mainly a staff function—it is not primarily or directly involved in the actual production of the firm's good or service. In contrast, line managers and workers are directly involved in processes related to the production and delivery of the firm's good or service to the customer. The notion of line versus staff has its historical roots in the ancient Greek Army. Those who were in battle literally were on the "firing line." Those who planned where and when the battles took place and when people would fight were considered "staff" and were in safe places far behind the line of fire. The concept carries over to the staff-line or operating relationship between HR and the line today. Staff functions often lack the ultimate authority to implement decisions; they can only plan for them. They are often perceived as being removed from the "firing line," i.e., the direct or actual production of the firm's economic goods valued in the market—the true service of the firm.

Necessity of Top Management Commitment to HR. In order for HR decisions to be implemented, top management has to be actively committed to HR. Senior management has to participate in and support policy development. In essence, HR issues have to be considered a management priority and given adequate resources and support to deliver services. To facilitate this, the senior HR professional needs to have a direct reporting relationship to the CEO. Top management must reward managers not only for making profit objectives, but also for being good managers of people at the same time.

Employee Relations Climate of Openness and Respect.   HR can develop all the quality programs in the world, but if HR policies are to be effectively implemented, it is critical to have an employee relations climate of openness and respect. That is, employees must believe they are able to express dissatisfaction and concerns without fear of reprisal. This can only occur when they have a high degree of confidence and trust in line management.

Competent HR Department.   It is critical for the HR department to be staffed by competent, respected professionals who have educational expertise in HR. HR must not be viewed as a dumping ground for individuals who were ineffective in other functions. The competencies required from HR professionals to manage the roles of transaction, translation, transition, and transformation have evolved over time. The challenge in identifying HR competencies is to start not with the function's activities, but with the business results.[74,75] HR professionals must possess the following knowledge, skills, and abilities to be an integral part of any global organization's corporate strategy. These are: global operating skills; business expertise; the ability to leverage technology; communications expertise; an employee champion; and change management capabilities.

Masters of Global Operating Skills

Almost all of the real economic growth over the next decade will occur outside the United States and Western Europe. In the 1960s, 6 percent of the U.S. economy was exposed to international competition. In the 1980s, that number surpassed 70 percent.[76] To meet the challenges of globalization successfully, employers must educate employees to do business in environments with individuals of different cultural backgrounds and perspectives. HR leaders must develop both internal and external networks of contacts who can help them identify and evaluate global best practices for adoption within the company.

MODULE
3

Business Experts

HR professionals must be able to understand firm financial reports, goals, and investors. HR does not need to replace general managers, but knowledge of the business operations will assist in the department's ability to develop initiatives and value. Two sets of information should form the basis of human resource leadership: an analysis of employees' requirements for the products and services the department provides, and a review of the organization's objectives.

Technology Leveragers

HR professionals must evaluate how new technology will change the nature of work in the organization, both for the human resources department and as it relates to the organization. Examples of this include the use of portable computers and shared data sources, which might facilitate worker telecommuting. Advances in technology might also influence future labor demand or changes in the skills required by the workforce.

For example, a case study on the planned implementation of a new human resource information system[77] illustrates how the human resource leader must be able to communicate and understand the value of new system implementation. In this example, the company identified four business issues that drove the need for this system: the regulatory environments, the labor market, decision modeling support, and reporting systems capabilities and ability to change. After conducting interviews with human resource professionals over time, it was apparent that human resource leadership needed to drive new system implementation through its commitment to ongoing training and coordination of system activities within the HR function.

Expert Communicators, Employee Champions, and Change Managers

HR professionals must be able to effectively communicate with employees, managers, and vendors. In conjunction with effective communication, HR must "walk the talk," acting with integrity and honesty in all business transactions. Further, since work is more demanding than ever and employees are constantly being asked to do more with less, HR professionals must be held accountable for ensuring that employees are engaged and committed to fully performing their jobs. HR must take responsibility for educating line management about the importance of high employee morale. Management must understand the importance of giving employees opportunities for personal growth and sufficient resources to meet their work demands.[78] HR also has the responsibility to help the firm embrace and capitalize on change. To do this HR needs the skills to be able to identify what needs to be altered in the culture to support change, clearly articulate why change is vital to business success, identify the gap between the current and desired culture, and develop approaches for creating cultural transformation.[79]

Ability to Balance Tensions in HR Decision Making. The final criteria for the effective delivery of HR roles is to ensure that systems are developed to balance two main tensions. The first tension is balancing equity with efficiency. HR decisions are equitable when employees believe that procedures and outcomes are fair. HR decisions are efficient when they are cost-effective and help maximize profitability. Yet it is not always easy to achieve both objectives simultaneously. For example, when allocating overtime, it might be most efficient to give all the overtime to your best worker in the short run. Over the long run, morale might drop due to equity problems. Other workers might resent the lack of opportunity to make extra money, and the best worker might become overworked and overstressed.

The second tension is the need to balance consistency with flexibility. Consistency is when policies are designed to treat employees or groups of employees the same across the board. Flexibility is when policies are administered in a way to meet the unique individual needs of the diverse workforce. It is often difficult to meet both of these objectives at the same time. Yet flexibility is important. As famed former football coach Lou Holtz once said: "You don't begin by motivating the group, you begin by motivating individuals." In other words, before an organization can foster teamwork, individual employees' needs must be met so they will be motivated to work with others. (This is true at least in an individualized culture such as America's.)

Integrated Line-Staff Role Delivery

Assuming basic criteria are met for effective HR decision making, a key problem is how should the firm balance role delivery among line management, employee, and human resources? Increasingly, some believe HR's main role is to design policies and then educate managers and employees on how to use them. Ceridien Performance Partners headquartered in Minneapolis has developed a Web-Based Manager Coach Protype for line management decision-support. Take the example of employee discipline. If a manager needed to discipline a worker, she or he could go to the Web, put in the facts of the problem, and be coached on how to handle it. Although senior managers usually are highly enthusiastic about this product and feel that this was exactly what was needed to improve efficiency, HR generalists had some resistance. They felt they would be held accountable if the line manager made a mistake, and did not like the message that "anyone could do human resources."

Reengineering the Mix and Structure of HR

A second key choice in delivery is determining the appropriate mix of roles from transactional to transformational. Human resource departments have typically been structured to support their most well-known stages: file maintenance and government accountability. Consequently, HR has been mainly seen as maintaining employee work records, ensuring compliance to both internal and external regulations, and implementing HR practices. As HR added new subfunctions and these responsibilities grew sufficiently, new managers or directors would be added to head them who typically reported to a director or HR vice president.

Ford Motor Company provides a good example of the reorganization that is occurring in the structure of HR in many firms. At Ford in 1998, a manager or director headed the following functions, which reported to the vice president of human resources. The functions included: organization and personnel planning (staffing); labor and union affairs; education and training and development; compensation planning; strategy and process planning; and personnel services/occupational health and safety. By the year 2000, when Ford implements an organizational change program called Ford 2000, the structuring and mix of HR roles will be transformed.

Under Ford 2000, HR will be reorganized to better focus on critical HR areas that had been buried under large HR subgroups. The proposed new HR functions include: diversity/work/life planning; employee advocacy; strategic planning; reward and recognition; organizational learning and development; labor relations; HR business operations; and HR services, which has HR Centers of Expertise and Shared Service Centers (see the next section).

Ford 2000 is also designed to realign HR's focus from being mainly transactional to being strategic and transformational. Ford surveyed its HR professionals and found that 70 percent of the HR function was devoted to conducting transactions and translational) and information processing activities, and only 30 percent had a strategic or transformational focus. The goal was to reverse these percentages. By the year 2000, Ford wants 70 percent of HR's time to be spent on strategic (transitional and transformational or organizational change issues, and only 30 percent on transactional work. The following shows how Ford wants to shift HR time and resources to where HR provides the greatest value to the business.[80]

1998 HR Focus	$\rightarrow$	*HR Ford 2000 Focus*
∇ 30% strategic or transformational	$\rightarrow$	70% strategic or transformational
70% transactional	$\rightarrow$	∇ 30% transactional

This change in the emphasis of activities does not imply that these traditional roles have declined in importance. It just means that HR needs to be able to do more: to support these traditional or transactional roles while adopting strategic and other new roles. Like Ford, increasingly, the traditional human resource department function and structure are shifting toward being more of a strategic business partner and player in many firms. The shift in the time spent on various human resources activities over a five to seven year period is shown in Table 3.2.

TABLE 3.2 *Percent of Time Spent on Various Human Resources Activities*

Human Resource Activity	5 to 7 Years Ago	Current
Maintaining records	23.0	15.4
Auditing/controlling	19.5	12.2
Implementing/administering HR practices	34.3	31.3
Developing HR service systems and practices	14.3	18.6
Strategic business partner	10.3	22.2

Source: Gary C. McMahan. 1996. "The current practice of the human resources function." *Human Resource Planning.*

Centralizing HR Role Delivery: Shared Services

Another key management choice in role delivery is the degree to which HR decision making should be centralized. Historically, many worksites had a HR generalist who was expected to be knowledgeable on all HR matters, from pensions to labor disputes to selection. Now some companies feel that it may be more efficient to reorganize and centralize how some HR decisions are delivered. These may be centralized in two ways.

Shared service centers involve the consolidation of HR services in an organization. Transaction-based HR roles—payroll, benefits administration, training enrollment, corporate and employee contributions to charities, and staffing paperwork—are easily combined into shared services. Sometimes shared services are in service centers, which are effective if they help reduce the costs of HR transactions and provide good customer service to employees and managers. Typically, shared services require fewer positions (which often appeals to downsizing organizations) to perform the same function through the consolidation of expertise and knowledge transfer across group members.

HR centers of excellence offer centralized HR functional expertise to solve innovative issues. Here HR professionals serve as consultants, troubleshooters, or coaches to HR generalists, managers, or employees in the field or to corporate staff. Typically nonroutine and nonadministrative HR activities that help transition or transform a firm are the most suitable for centers of excellence. Examples of HR activities might include succession planning, talent assessment and screening of key hires via sophisticated selection systems, executive development, performance management, gain sharing and recognition, pay for performance, organizational development, and new labor agreements.[81]

Outsourcing

Given the complexity, cost, and highly regulated nature of the HR function, thousands of companies have started to outsource HR activities. Many companies are looking to cut administrative costs in HR and view this as a short-run cost-effective solution. Also, some companies simply do not have the technology or expertise needed to conduct some HR activities.[82] As businesses look for the competitive edge, outsourcing emerges as an effective way for them to be more strategic by helping to meet the often overwhelming demand for time- and cost-effective solutions to other HR problems. Transactional roles such as payroll or benefits administration are the most easily outsourced. Outsourcing involves a long-term contractual relationship for business services from an external provider. Unlike contracting, which is often utilized for short-term activities (for example, a rush or special project), outsourcing requires both the integration and coordination of the vendor selected to provide a successful relationship for both parties. With the growth in HR consulting, some firms are also outsourcing transitional and transformational roles. Experts from consulting firms ranging from Andersen Consulting to Towers Perrin to Hay Associates are just a few of the many international HR consulting firms that have grown over recent years. Yet as noted in the strategic issues section at the end of this module, there is a risk to outsourcing capability in HR roles that might provide a competitive advantage.

HUMAN RESOURCE EFFECTIVENESS: CONTRASTING APPROACHES

People Poll: How Do You Measure HR's Impact on the Bottom Line?[83]

"We do that every six months. HR is part of senior planning session with the company owner, the president and top function levels. We measure ourselves against other companies of our size."

—HR Manager, Deutsch Metal Components, Gardena, CA

"Now, one of the biggest hurdles I have is that it takes an average of 84 days to hire someone because of the bureaucracy. I want to reduce that to a maximum 30 days by reengineering, technology and process improvement. Taxpayers do not want a lot of staff. We have to make sure resources go to services."

—Director of the Michigan Department of Civil Service, Lansing

"We're getting away from the traditional, what I call the 'tenderfoot,' side of HR. We've got six companywide performance standards we use, developed annually. We measure productivity, overall salary-and-benefit expense per employee, and a baseline ratio for turnover. We also do customer surveys."

—Senior Vice President of Business Services, Farm Credit Bank of Texas, Austin

"At our company, we are an internal HR service provider and a provider of HR services to client organizations. Therefore, we are a revenue generator without outsourcing, and have been for 10 years."

—Senior HR Officer, National Computer Systems P.T.E., Singapore

"Once a year, we solicit information from internal customers as to how we're doing—how much each percentage of turnover costs us, the cost of HR as a percentage of sales."

—Director of HR, Brodart Co., Williamsport, PA

As these examples show, there are many perspectives on how to measure human resource's impact.

Given the growing importance of demonstrating how HR adds value, this module ends with a brief discussion of alternative perspectives for evaluating HR effectiveness. There are three main approaches: stakeholder, business consulting, and utility or HR financial value. To be effective, all HR departments need to be successful to some extent from each of these perspectives. Companies vary in the degree to which they adhere to a particular approach depending on their organizational stance toward HR effectiveness.

Stakeholder/Multiple Constituency

Under the stakeholder approach, HR is successful as long as multiple constituents perceive the organization as effective. The strength of this approach is that it encourages a service orientation. However, it may not be possible for HR or organizations to please everyone at the same time, and the approach may keep HR from being very strategic. The Bank of Montreal uses a scorecard that illustrates this perspective. In order to be competitive, executives decided that the bank had to meet goals of four stakeholders: shareholders, customers, employees, and communities. Shareholders want return on equity. Customers want good service. Employees want to feel loyal and satisfied. Communities want to feel the bank makes a difference in their neighborhoods. Each employee's and each department's performance ratings are now dependent on their contribution toward each goal. Employees in the customer service department, for example, are rated on their return on equity (judged by their cost-effectiveness), customer satisfaction (judged by customer feedback) , and their community involvement (judged by outreach programs or increase in customers). HR is in charge of ensuring the employees are loyal, satisfied, and high performing. Training and education are used to ensure employee competency, work/life and career development programs ensure commitment, and HR must use cost-effectiveness in delivery. Indices are developed at the end of the year where all of HR is measured on how well it does on competency, commitment, and cost-effectiveness for all of its constituents.[84]

Business Consulting

Under this model, HR is effective if it is successful in acting as business consultants that create policies valued by management. Lotus Corporation, the software firm, provides an example of an effective HR function under this model. The Lotus HR department's vision statement is as follows: "We view ourselves as a business dedicated to helping our customers achieve maximum value from our products and services." Dave Ulrich points out the importance of this statement: HR sees itself as a business, it supports employees and managers as customers, its activities must add financial value, and it provides products and services rather than just policies. At Lotus, HR was reengineered to focus less on policy creation and more on consulting. Each line manager was given a compact disc with answers to common HR questions on it, and employees increasingly went to their mangers to get these questions answered.

Utility Approaches: Assessing Quantitative Value Added

Quantitative measures of HR effectiveness translate HR activities into financial indices and assess the financial utility of HR services. Though numbers are the language of business, HR historically has not done a very good job of quantifying how its activities improve profits, reduce costs, or add financial value. Many HR professionals do not know how to measure the costs of employee attitudes and behaviors. Also, some top managers have accepted the myth that personnel activities cannot be quantified in financial terms.[85] Yet the competitive advantage of an organization's human resources rests in the creative ways HR professionals can organize to deliver value-added services and demonstrate their financial value or utility. In order to become a strategic business player, HR needs to determine what to measure, and how to capture the most useful data.[86] Neglecting to analyze data to quantify the value from HR activities and roles has perpetuated the myth that HR activities are not core competencies or can be outsourced.

Human resource accounting involves several utility approaches. The *asset method* assesses the costs of HRM activities, treats employees as assets, and determines the value of employees as capitalized resources.[87] The costs of each employee are amortized over the expected working life of the individual. Unamortized costs are written off. The organization's investment in each employee (the asset) is measured by the costs incurred in developing that employee. A problem of the asset model is that it does not consider the return on investment from each employee's contributions. While the asset model of HR accounting treats the value of employees as capitalized resources, the *expense model* determines the economic effects of employee behavior such as the costs of turnover, absenteeism, and job performance. New initiatives can be assessed in the degree to which they favorably influence controllable costs such as preventing undesirable behaviors (e.g., voluntary turnover) or fostering good ones (e.g., increased employee suggestions). Another way to show the utility of HR is to measure employees' contribution to company *profitability*. For example, developing a compensation plan that rewards employees for increasing profits improves profitability more than a plan that, while competitive with the labor market, pays employees contingent on only showing up for work. HR can justify new programs by demonstrating the *cost/benefit* ratio of activities. This is determined by comparing the benefits of an HR activity to the costs incurred in delivering it. It is similar to calculating a return on investment.

Strategic Issues in Human Resource Leadership Roles and Choices

Strategic Challenges Across HR Policy Clusters

There are many critical future challenges that organizations face in the *HR strategy and organization* cluster. How should firms redesign human resource systems to support new organizational structures and growing variations in employment relationships? How should human resource policies be used as levers for contingent or contract workers, who might not view themselves as employees of the company? How should issues of measuring performance and absenteeism be assessed when more and more work is taking place away from a centralized workplace? Increasing numbers of workers are working at home or at the customer's site. How can human resource strategies be better adapted to support globalization, where U.S.-designed practices run counter to another country's culture? Or what about the growth in joint ventures and virtual organizations, where a company might partner with another for a single project as IBM has done with Dell? IBM components will increasingly be in Dell computers—highly unusual in the computer industry where rapid technological changes occur and Dell is one of IBM's major competitors. How should HR systems support this unique business strategy?

A strategic issue in the *talent identification and deployment* cluster is how an organization ensures that its workforce has the right mix of skills to meet future needs. Developing appropriate assessment tools to identify employees who will fit and adapt to knowledge-creating cultures is also a challenge. Reducing long hiring-cycle times and costs per hire and making succession planning to identify top management talent less bureaucratic are other concerns.[88]

In the *human capital development* cluster, a strategic challenge is how to realign performance and learning systems to fit with new organizational structures such as team-based and virtual organization forms. Employees also need to be resocialized to continually develop themselves as a condition of employment and take personal accountability for this development. At the same time, the firm needs to renew its commitment to and resources devoted to training and development.[89] Further, individuals and teams often have too many objectives to keep employees focused on top priorities, and performance objectives are not tightly linked to requisite changes in employee skills and behaviors.[90] *Reward management* has similar strategic issues. Rewards systems are not well aligned with these new organizational structures and are not linked as closely as they should be to performance. In the *employee relations* cluster, a critical strategic challenge is how to create a workplace that fosters high performance, yet respects employees' needs for work/life balance and outside work commitments. Obtaining high employee commitment and job satisfaction when job security is limited at many firms is another future dilemma.

HR Roles: Strategic Issues

As a result of increased competitive external environmental pressures, HR's cultural transformation role has become especially critical as strategies are constantly being reassessed to achieve higher performance. A recent survey of leaders in the HR field cited "Helping their organization reinvent/redesign itself to compete more effectively" as the top priority that HR executives should be addressing today.[91] In order to do this, HR systems must be designed to continually foster complex employee behaviors to support high performance from the workforce. Since organizations need employees to simultaneously do many things to compete, HR policies must foster cultures that simultaneously respect competing values. For example, it is not enough to compete solely on cost alone or quality alone. Companies often need to compete on quality, cost, innovation, variety, and speed to market. Yet HR policies, organizational cultures, and functional directives often give employees the message that some one mission or corporate objective is to be met at the expense of others when in reality competing values must be supported in order to drive complex performance demands.

HR Outsourcing and Role Delivery

The degree to which HR roles are outsourced may affect whether they are developed as core competencies of the firm. If external vendors develop more expertise in a firm's HR needs in compensation and benefits than internal HR leaders possess, then the firm risks losing expertise in this area and becomes overly resource dependent on the external consultants. This is not to suggest that use of external vendors is necessarily bad in itself. It just means that the firm must take care to not outsource an HR capability that is critical intellectual or social capital and a core competency for competing in the marketplace. Similarly, if HR tasks are mainstreamed into the firm as tasks anyone can do—whether they are trained or have the expertise to do so or not—may also influence the degree of excellence in HR role delivery.

APPLICATION: AT&T CASE[92, 93]

AT&T began with the greatest invention: the telephone by Alexander Graham Bell, in 1876. By 1902, 1,500 firms controlled more than a million phones. However, only the Bell System sold long-distance service, and it refused to connect a local exchange on its network until the local phone company complied with AT&T's terms—the first signs of raw monopoly power. The core of AT&T was established through vertical integration, protected in the union between technology and equipment, and the sprawling phone network. AT&T employees still take pride in the extent of the network, praising its ability to fulfill its well-understood mission: to provide low-cost, high-quality telephone service to every American household.

For many years, this system operated as a fully self-contained world. However, by the 1960s, political and technological change had doomed the company's monopoly. In 1968, a landmark Federal Communication Commission decision seriously compromised AT&T's control in the industry. Companies could now attach non-AT&T equipment into the system. Soon, competitors were entering the telecommunications industry, and the deregulation of the U.S. telecommunications industry had begun. In 1974, the Justice Department filed suit against AT&T, alleging the company had violated the Sherman Act of 1890 by its conspiracy to monopolize the supply of the industry. After spending a fortune fighting this suit, in 1982, as part of a settlement, the company finally sacrificed its manufacturing and local telephone groups. However, the company was now free to start selling computers—a new right gained in their court settlement. The company initiated its line of personal computers with six models developed with Olivetti. None of them sold well.

The human resource function did not experience these changes without negative effects. In November 1983, a few months before the actual divestiture of the manufacturing group, the company offered early retirement deals to 13,000 employees. No one was actually fired; instead, called into an executive's office, an employee would be told that it was perhaps time to leave AT&T. There was widespread suspicion that the resignation offers would only become less generous as time passed (and they did). Between 1984 and 1995, about 120,000 people disappeared from the company payrolls—some voluntary, but an increasingly visible number not. However, over time, these layoffs had a distinguishing feature: while layoffs in the 1980s were primarily due to technology's elimination of blue-collar jobs, those of the 1990s began to move into the white-collar positions.

In 1995, AT&T announced that it would be splitting into three companies: AT&T, which would continue to provide communication services; Lucent Technologies, which would provide communications systems and technologies; and NCR Corporation, which would concentrate on transaction-intensive computing. This move was designed to take full advantage of changes in the global information industry by focusing each company's market segment. AT&T hoped to create even stronger businesses and market position in each area to add greater value to its customers, employees, and investors. Wall Street cheered the breakup, driving the stock up more than 10 percent on the day the news broke. This split was a strategic business move, which presented the task of

MODULE
3

splitting $79 billion in revenue and approximately 300,000 employees into three companies over a 15-month period.

With the company's now long history and recent experience with competing in a dynamic market of technological, market, regulatory, and global change, all current and future organizational leaders were able to draw on their previous experiences to implement the latest transformation, the trivestiture. During the fall of 1995, a team of senior leaders worked almost full-time developing AT&T's strategic direction and recommending a new organizational structure designed to support its execution. A new governance process was created to guide how the company would operate and make decisions; it was rolled out in January 1996. Two important business decisions influenced the development of all transition processes. First, the company decided to assess all employees in the support departments and determine if their skills and experiences qualified them for jobs with the new companies. Second, each new company was to use the transition as an opportunity to reduce costs. During this time, the human resource department had to reallocate the corporate support staff of 16,000 into the three organizations. A transition team was created within HR. This team was led by an HR department representative to ensure alignment with the overall corporate direction. The guiding objectives listed in Figure 3.4 were developed for their reorganization process. Following are some examples of human resource programs that would support the objectives:

1.   Talent assessment within each function across the company

2.   Selection of people to positions based on the skill requirements and the needs of the new companies

3.   Identification of those who were going to be left without job assignments within the new organization (deselection)

4.   Design of career transition and employee support programs.

Case Study Exercises

In the business environment of AT&T today, the company is living through a time when its technology, financial resource, and business strategies may be replicated by competitors. AT&T must maintain its most powerful resource in this reorganization, its employees. Imagine you are a member of the human resource department's transition team. What actions would you take to address the challenges unique to this restructuring and develop a recommendation plan for its implementation. Make sure you include

FIGURE 3.4.   *Human Resource Guiding Objectives*

The Vision
Create exciting and successful high-performing businesses where people are valued and valuable.

The Objectives
1.   Design, size, and staff each new company to meet its future business requirements and strengthen its ability to compete successfully.

2.   Oversee the equitable distribution of talent among the entities and discourage unilateral "talent raiding."

3.   Retain critical skills and key talent throughout the transition.

in your plan the reasoning behind the elements of your plan. Some examples of these elements might be:

- Honor all existing collective bargaining and labor agreements.

- Employees will have the opportunity to express their job preferences.

- Provide employees whose jobs are at risk a standard set of resources and tools that enable them to move to new careers either within or outside AT&T.

IN CONCLUSION

Debrief

It is important to realize that in order for HR to become a business partner, its initiatives must be supported throughout the organization. HR cannot forget that without the fulfillment of its transactional and translational roles, the roles that focus on future change, transitional and transformational, will be initiated in an antagonistic environment. Paying employees on time, enrolling new employees for benefits accurately, and having a stream of qualified applicants available must be carried out in order for company functioning. Once the administrative activities are conducted efficiently, HR will be more successful in the fulfillment of its transitional and transformational role responsibilities.

In order to become strategic business players, HR departments must demonstrate a willingness to collaborate and understanding of how to motivate and address organizational members and their goals. Currently, the multiple roles and constraints HR must juggle are difficult to manage. On the one hand, HR needs to become more strategic and transformational. On the other hand, other functions of the organization might be resistant to HR adopting a more active role in overall business strategy. By behaving as a change agent, HR can ultimately take responsibility for its own destiny, dramatically redefine its own role, and lead others by example to a culture that fosters organizational change and sustained improvement.

Required Readings

Stewart, T. "Taking on the Last Bureaucracy." *Fortune,* January 15, 1996, pp. 105–107.

Ulrich, Dave. "A New Mandate for Human Resources," *Harvard Business Review,* January-February, 1998.

Suggested Readings

Becker, B. E., Huselid, M. A., Pickus, P., and Spratt, M. 1997. HR as a Source of Shareholder Value Research and Recommendations, *Human Resource Management,* 36:39–47.

Ehrlich, C. 1997. Human Resource Management: A Changing Script for a Changing World. *Human Resource Management,* 36:85–89.

Relevant Web Sites

THE SOCIETY FOR HUMAN RESOURCE MANAGEMENT
http://www.shrm.org

This is the major human resource professional organization in the United States. This Web site contains information on both current human resource practices and future development issues. This organization publishes the monthly publication *HR* magazine.

HUMAN RESOURCE PLANNING SOCIETY
http://www.hrp.org

The Human Resource Planning Society is a nonprofit organization dedicated to human resource issues. This organization publishes the *Human Resource Planning Journal,* a good source of HR development information.

THE BUREAU OF NATIONAL AFFAIRS
http://www.bna.org

The Bureau of National Affairs is a privately held, wholly employee-owned company in the United States. A leading publisher of print and electronic media reporting on developments in business, labor relations, law, health-care, and in many other public policy areas and regulatory issues.

Critical Thinking Questions

1.   What are the four HR roles? Choose one of the five HR policy clusters (e.g., organization and strategy, talent identification and deployment, etc.) and give two types of HR roles in this cluster. Then give an example of a type of constraint (unilateral, negotiated, imposed) that might influence HR decision making in the roles you selected.

2.   In your opinion, what human resource roles are most critical for managing in the twenty-first century and why? Consider the required knowledge, skills, and abilities as they relate to these roles.

3.   If you had to choose, would you rather see human resource professionals be "employee advocates" or "corporate strategy partners"? Defend your choice.

MODULE
3

Exercises

Read the article: T.A. Stewart. (1996), "Taking on the Last Bureaucracy," *Fortune,* January 15, 1996, 105–107.

- Build three pros and three cons for or against outsourcing HR. Does HR add any direct value to the organization? Could organizations run efficiently if HR is outsourced? Why or why not? Choose a side and come to class with arguments ready to debate your perspective.

- How about shared services and the idea of 1-800-HR, where employees or managers call in with HR issues? Do you think this is a good idea? Why or why not? Be prepared to discuss your view.

Human Resource Professional and Line Manager Interview

Interview a human resource professional and if possible a line manager in the same organization to determine if and what processes and activities are being conducted to manage the roles discussed in this module in their organization. Write a summary report that outlines the information gathered for each role category. The following questions may be useful in your interview.[94]

1.   What factors make an employee want to stay at your company?

2.   What HR strategies have been developed to accommodate future changes in the company?

3.   What is HR doing to provide value-added services to internal and external clients?

4. What are the three most important HR activities currently conducted to improve employee commitment?

5. What kind of investment has management made in the HR department so that its activities are better than your competitors?

6. What should the HR department do to improve the company's marketplace position?

7. What can the HR department do to add to the bottom line?

8. How does the HR department measure its effectiveness?

9. What is the best change the HR department could make to prepare for the future?

10. What is the biggest impediment to HR performance?

11. How does HR promote employee and organizational learning?

Calculating Cost of Turnover Exercises[95]

You are a human resource professional for a $10 billion corporation that specializes in selling consulting services to Fortune 500 companies across the United States. Building strong and long-term relationships with customers has been the key to increased revenue throughout the years. However, within the last three years, as unemployment has decreased to historical lows, your organization has incurred historical highs in employee turnover. Most troubling to you is the fact that the highest number of employees leaving the corporation are those that work directly with the customer, the consultants. You are concerned that customer loyalty will decrease as customers see that your company has a difficult time retaining good employees. Employee morale, as measured by the corporation's employee survey, has steadily declined due in part to long hours, no overtime pay, and the stress associated with being understaffed.

Executives within the company are not concerned with the high turnover (45 percent this year) nor the decline in employee morale. They believe that the high turnover is good for keeping costs down because the executives believe that by hiring experienced employees below market wages, they are getting better value than their competitors. They feel that the high employee turnover decreases costs because they do not have to pay expenses related to benefits such as retirement and vacation pay.

As a human resource professional skilled in cost-justifying HR initiatives and allocating costs for various human resource behaviors, you have been assigned the task

MODULE
3

FIGURE 3.5 *Turnover of Key Staff Positions by Year*

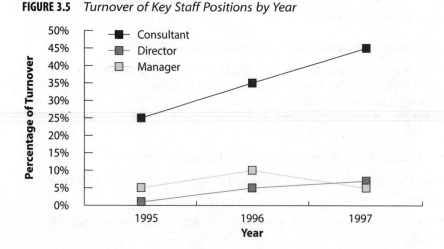

FIGURE 3.6 *Contracts Not Renewed Due to Employee Turnover*

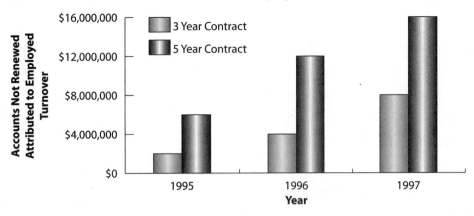

of calculating the costs of turnover for 1997. You are expected to present your findings to the executives at their next executive staff meeting.

Attached is information you have collected in order to determine the costs of turnover at your organization. A great deal of additional data could be analyzed to account for all possible costs associated with turnover. The scope of your assignment, however, is to determine the impact of turnover by focusing on the traditional costs of turnover, i.e., separation, replacement, and training.

Will your analysis point toward the views of the executives, or will you be able to show them that high turnover actually increases costs to their corporation?

MODULE
3

TABLE 3.3 *1997 Turnover Data Elements*

Wages/Benefits

Average hourly wage/benefits of human resource professional	$28
Average hourly wage/benefits of consultant	$25
Average hourly wage/benefits of departmental staff	$35

Time Estimates

Average amount of time performing separation administrative functions per consultant	30 minutes
Average amount of time obtaining advertising/recruiting per position	3 hours
Average amount of time performing preemployment administrative functions per consultant	5 hours
Average amount of time preparing for an interview	15 minutes
Average length of an interview	45 minutes
Average amount of time administering aptitude tests	30 minutes
Average amount of time in staff meetings per candidate	25 minutes
Average amount of time spent disseminating information	1 hour
Average amount of on-the-job training per new consultant	8 hours

TABLE 3.3 *continued*

Cost Estimates

Average amount of separation paid per consultant	$500
Average cost per exit interview	$125
Advertising/recruiting fees per position	$450
Cost per aptitude test	$35
Cost per background check	$65
Cost per drug test	$25
Average travel costs per applicant	$200
Average moving expenses per new consultant	$6000
Training materials per new consultant	$50
Formal training costs per session	$225

Counts/Numbers

Number of consultants replaced in 1997	100
Average number of unused vacation days paid out	4
Number of applicants in 1997	500
Number of departmental staff conducting interviews	3
Number of aptitude tests conducted annually	500
Number of departmental staff meetings per open position	2
Number of background screens conducted	105
Number of drug tests per year	110
Number of replacement training programs conducted annually	4
Proportional reduction in productivity due to training	.5

TABLE 3.4 *Turnover Calculation Worksheet*

Separation Cost Formulas

Administrative costs	=	(Average hourly wage/benefits of HR professional) × (Average amount of time performing separation administrative functions per consultant) × (Number of consultants replaced in 1997)
Exit interview costs	=	(Average cost per exit interview) × (Number of consultants replaced in 1997)
Separation costs	=	(Average amount of separation paid per consultant) × (Number of consultants replaced in 1997)
Unused vacation	=	(Average number of unused vacation days) × (8 hours per day) × (Average hourly wage/benefits of consultant) × (Number of consultants replaced in 1997)

TABLE 3.4   *continued*

Replacement Cost Formulas

Communicating open position = [(Advertising/recruiting fees per position) + {(Average hourly wage/benefits of human resource professional) × (Average amount of time obtaining advertising/recruiting per position)}] × (Number of consultants replaced in 1997)

Preemployment administrative functions = (Average amount of time performing preemployment administrative functions) × (Average hourly wage/benefits of human resource professional) × (Number of applicants in 1997)

Interview with HR = (Average length of an interview) × (Average hourly wage/benefits of human resource professional) × (Number of applicants in 1997)

Interview with department staff = (Average length of an interview) × (Average hourly
staff filling position   wage/benefits of department staff conducting interviews) × (Number of applicants in 1997)

Testing = (Cost per aptitude test) × (Average hourly wage/benefits of human resource professional) × (Average amount of time administering tests) × (Number of aptitude tests conducted annually)

Staff meeting = {(Average hourly wage/benefits of human resource professional) + (Average hourly wage/benefits of departmental staff conducting interviews)} × {(Average amount of time in staff meetings per candidate) × (Number of staff meetings per open position) × (Number of consultants replaced in 1997)}

Travel/moving expense = {(Average travel costs per applicant) × (Number of applicants in 1997)} + {(Average moving expenses per new consultant) × (Number of consultants replaced in 1997)}

Postemployment acquisition and = (Average amount of time spent disseminating infor-
dissemination of information   mation) × (Average hourly wage/benefits of human resource professional) × (Number of consultants replaced in 1997)

Background screens = (Cost per background check) × (Number of background screens conducted)

Drug testing = (Cost per new hire)

Training Cost Formulas

Training materials = (Training materials per new consultant) × (Number of consultants replaced in 1997)

Formalized training program = (Formal training costs per session) × (Number of replacement training programs conducted annually)

On-the-job training = {(Average amount of on-the-job training per new consultant) × (Number of consultants replaced in 1997)} × {(Average hourly wage/benefits of consultant) + (Average hourly wage/benefits of department staff conducting interviews) × (Proportional reduction in productivity due to training)}

MODULE
3

TABLE 3.4 *continued*

1997 Total Turnover Cost Worksheet

Separation Costs

Administrative Cost	$_____
Exit Interview Cost	$_____
Separation Pay	$_____
Unused Vacation Paid Out	$_____
Total Separation Costs	$_____

Replacement Costs

Communicating Open Position	$_____
Preemployment Administrative Functions	$_____
Entrance Interview	$_____
Testing	$_____
Staff Meeting	$_____
Travel/Moving Expense	$_____
Postemployment Acquisition and Dissemination of Information	$_____
Background Screens	$_____
Drug Testing/Medical Testing	$_____
Total Replacement Costs	$_____

Training Costs

Training Materials	$_____
New Hire Orientation	$_____
Formalized Training Program	$_____
On-the-Job Training	$_____
Total Training Costs	$_____

MODULE 3

References

1. Halcrow, A. 1998, June. "A day in the life of Kathy Davis: Just another day in HR," *Workforce,* 77:56.
2. Leonard, B. 1998, Feb. "Spin-off makes heads turn," *HRM magazine,* 108–114.
3. Anfuso, D. 1998, June. "A day in the life of Linda Duffy: Putting fun into work," *Workforce,* 77:69–70.
4. Sunoo, B. P. 1998, June. "A day in the life of John Harvey: Positioning HR for the fast track," *Workforce,* 77:64.
5. Champy, J. and Hammer, M. 1993. *Re-engineering the Corporation.* New York: Harper-Collins.
6. Research done through an independent study by Julie Watkins supervised by Ellen Ernst Kossek while she was a master's student in labor and industrial relations at Michigan State University.

7. Eichinger, B. and Ulrich, D. 1996. *Human Resource Challenges: Today and Tomorrow.* New York: State of the Art Council. Human Resource Planning Society.

8. Kochan, T. 1997, Oct. 3–4. Beyond myopia: Human resources and the changing social contract. Paper prepared for the conference "Research and theory in strategic human resource management: An agenda for the 21st century," Cornell University, School of Industrial and Labor Relations.

9. Prahalad, C. K. and Hamel, G. 1990, May–June. "The core competence of the corporation," *Harvard Business Review.*

10. Pasternack, B. A., Keller, S. S. and Viscio, A. 1996, "The triumph of people power and the new economy." New York: Booz Allen, second quarter report.

11. Kossek, E. 1990. "Why personnel practices are likely to fail," *Personnel.*

12. Kochan, T., and Cappelli, P. 1984. "The transformation of the industrial relations and personnel function." In Paul Osterman, Editor, *Internal Labor Markets.* Cambridge, MA: MIT Press, 133–190.

13. Ulrich, D. 1998, Jan.–Feb. "A new mandate for human resources," *Harvard Business Review.*

14. Branch, D. 1999, Jan. 11. "The 100 best companies to work for in America." *Fortune,* 118–144.

15. Ibid., 118.

16. Ibid., 134.

17. Reichheld, F. 1996. *The Loyalty Effect: The Hidden Force Behind Growth, Profits, and Lasting Value.* Boston: Harvard Business School Press.

18. "Ford workers get checks." 1999, March 4. *Lansing State Journal,* 5B.

19. "What makes a company great?" 1998, Oct. 28. *Fortune,* 218.

20. Ibid., 118–144.

21. Ichniowski, C. 1992. "Human resource practices and productive labor-management relations." In *Research Frontiers in Industrial Relations and Human Resources,* edited by David Lewin, Olivia Mitchell, and Peter Sherer, 239–271, Madison, WI: Industrial Relations Research Association.

22. Milkovich, G. and Boudreau, J. 1997. *Human Resource Management.* Chicago: Irwin.

23. Hamel, G. and Prahalad, C. K. 1994. *Competing for the Future,* Boston: Harvard Business School Press.

24. Becker, B., Huselid, M., Pickus, P., and Spratt, M. 1997. "HR as a source of shareholder value: research and recommendations." *Human Resource Management,* 36:39–47.

25. Smilansky, J. 1997, *The New HR.* London: ITT.

26. Adapted from Smilansky, *The New HR.*

27. Milkovich and Boudreau, *Human Resource Management.*

28. Beer, M., Spector, B., Lawrence, P., Mills, D. Q., and Walton, R. 1984. *Managing Human Assets.* New York: The Free Press.

29. Ibid.

30. Society for Human Resource Management. Nov./Dec. 1996. *Workplace Visions,* 6.

31. Imperato, G. 1998, Dec. "How to hire the next Michael Jordan," *Fast Company,* 212–219.

32. Pfeffer, J. 1998. *The Human Equation.* Boston: Harvard Business School Press.

33. Ibid.

34. Ibid.

35. Ibid.

36. Fishman, C. 1996, April–May. "Whole Foods is all teams," *Fast Company,* 100–109.

37. Branch, D. 1999. "The 100 best companies to work for in America." *Fortune,* Jan. 11, 1999: 118–144.

38. Caimano, V., Canavan, P., and Hill, L. 1998. *The State-of-the-Art and Practice Council Report.* New York: Human Resource Planning Society.

39. Beer et al. *Managing Human Assets.*

40. Fishman. "Whole Foods is all teams."

41. Ibid.

42. Branch. "The 100 best companies to work for in America."

43. Leyda, M. 1998, March 10. Ford 2000 handout. Presentation made at Michigan State University School of Labor and Industrial Relations, Ellen Kossek's HR Strategies and Decisions class; Ulrich, D. 1997. *Human Resource Champions.* Boston: Harvard Business School Press.

44. Stewart, T. A. 1996. "Taking on the last bureaucracy." *Fortune,* Jan. 15: 105–107; Becker et al. "HR as a source of shareholder value: research and recommendations."

45. Jacoby, S. M. 1985. *Employing Bureaucracy: Managers, Unions, and the Transformation of Work in American Industry, 1900–1945.* New York: Columbia University Press, 16–20.

46. Cascio, W. 1992. *Managing Human Resources* (3rd edition). New York: McGraw-Hill.

47. Kochan and Cappelli. "The transformation of the industrial relations and personnel function."

48. Cascio. *Managing Human Resources.*

49. Kochan and Cappelli. "The transformation of the industrial relations and personnel function."

50. Freedman, A. 1991. "The changing human resource function." Report 950. New York: The Conference Board.

51. Cascio. *Managing Human Resources.*

52. . Ibid.

53. Schermerhorn, J., Hunt, J., and Osborn, R. 1997. *Organizational Behavior.* New York: John Wiley & Sons.

54. Beatty, R. W. and Schnneier, C. 1997, Spring. "New HR roles to impact organizational performance: From "partners" to "players," *Human Resource Management,* 36: 29–37.

55. Ulrich, D. 1998, Jan. "The future calls for change." *Workforce,* Costa Mesa.

56. Source: *www.shrm.org/press/releases/bna.htm.*

57. Ulrich. *Human Resource Champions.*

58. Dess, G., Rasheed, A., McLaughlin, K., and Priem, R. 1995. "The new corporate architecture," *Academy of Management Executive,* 9:7–18.

59. Adapted from Ulrich, D. *Human Resource Champions.*

60. Ibid.

61. See, for example, Oliver Williamson's 1975 book *Markets and Hierarchies: Analysis and Antitrust Implications.* New York: Free Press.

62. Ulrich. *Human Resource Champions.*

63. Galpin, Timothy. 1998. "When leaders really walk the talk: Making strategy work through people." *HR Human Resource Planning:* 21:38–45.

64. Brown, E. 1999, March 1. "America's most admired companies." *Fortune,* 68–73; Leyda, M. Ford 2000 handout.

65. MacDuffie, J. P. 1995. "Human resource bundles and manufacturing performance: Organizational logic and flexible production systems in the world auto industry." *Industrial Labor Relations Review,* 48:197–221.

66. Mailliard, K. (1997) "Linking performance to the bottom line," *HR Focus,* 74:17–18.

67. Galpin. "When leaders really walk the talk."

68. Cappelli, P. 1997, July/Aug. "Rethinking the nature of work: A look at the research evidence." *Compensation and Benefits Review.*

69. The reader may find it useful to refer to the module by Roberts and Gleason in this book on deciding when to hire contingent workers.

70. We are indebted to Richard Block of Michigan State for the market power examples in this section.

71. Vroom, V. and Jago, A. *The New Leadership: Managing Participation in Organizations.* 1998. Englewood Cliffs, NJ: Prentice Hall.

72. We are indebted to Richard Block of Michigan State for the notions of procedural and substantive constraints in this section.

73. These ideas were adapted from a combination of the following sources: F. Foulkes. 1980. *Human Resource Management.* Englewood Cliffs, NJ: Prentice Hall; an IBM Corporation Personnel Manual from the early 1980s; and Milkovich and Boudreau. *Human Resource Management.* Personal notes developed in Martha Miller's Managing Organizational Systems class while the first author was a doctoral student at Yale University.

74. Eichinger, B. and Ulrich, D. (1996) "Are you future agile?" *State-of-the-Art Council Report.* Presented at the Human Resources Planning Society Annual Conference, Palm Desert, CA.

75. Yeung, A., Woolcock, P., and Sullivan, J. 1996. "Identifying and developing HR competencies for the future: Keys to sustaining the transformation of HR functions." *Human Resource Planning,* 19:48–58.

MODULE
3

76. Martinez, M. N. 1996. "3 strategies for successful business partners." *HR magazine,* 41(supplement): 1–4.

77. Kossek, E. E., Young, W., Gash, D.C., and Nichol, V. 1994. "Waiting for innovation in the human resources department: Godot implements a human resource information system." *Human Resource Management,* 33(1):135–159.

78. Ulrich. "A new mandate for human resources."

79. Ibid.

80. Leyda. Ford 2000 handout.

81. Ulrich, D. 1989. "Shared services: From vogue to value," *Human Resource Planning,* 12:301–315.

82. Cook, M. 1999. *Outsourcing Human Resources Functions.* New York: American Management Association.

83. Pasternack et al. "The triumph of people power and the new economy."

84. Flynn, G. 1997, Dec. "Bank of Montreal invests in its workers," *Workforce,* 30–38.

85. Cascio, W. 1991. *Costing human resources—The Financial Impact of Behavior in Organizations.* Boston: PWS-Kent.

86. Martinez. "3 Strategies for successful business partners."

87. This paragraph is based on a literature review conducted by Michele Rodier entitled "Quantifying Human Resources," during an independent study she conducted with Professor Ellen Ernst Kossek while a master's student at Michigan State University's School of Labor and Industrial Relations.

88. Ettorre, B. and Capowski, G. 1997. "Value-added HR: people, performance, and the bottom line." *HR Focus,* 74:9–12.

89. Ibid.

90. Ibid.

91. Eichinger, B. and Ulrich, D. 1996. *Human Resource Challenges: Today and Tomorrow.* New York: HR Planning Society.

92. AT&T Corporate History. Adapted from the AT&T Web site, *www.att.com.*

93. AT&T Human Resource department information adapted from: Rudolph, Barbara. 1998. *Disconnected: How Six People from AT&T Discovered the New Meaning of Work in a Downsized Corporate America.* New York, NY: The Free Press; Graddick, M. M. and Cairo, P. C. 1998. "Helping people and organizations deal with the impact of competitive change: An AT&T Case Study." In Gowing, M. K., Kraft, J. D., and Quick, J. C. (Eds.) *The New Organizational Reality: Downsizing, Restructuring, and Revitalization.* Washington, DC: The American Psychological Association; Connor, J. and Wirtenberg, J. 1993. "Managing the transformation of human resources work." *Human Resource Planning,* 16(2):17–35.

94. Adapted from Halcrow, A. 1998. "HR at the table: Best questions posed to HR by CEOs," *Workforce,* 77:74.

95. Developed by Michelle Rodier as part of an independent study conducted with Dr. Ellen Ernst Kossek. This application was developed while Ms. Rodier was completing her master's degree in the School of Labor and Industrial Relations at Michigan State University.

MODULE
3

Index

Adding value, 3.6, 3.8, 3.9, 3.17–18, 3.29, 3.30
Administrative roles (HR), 3.19, 3.34
AT&T/telecommunications industry deregulation, 3.32–34
Attracting/retaining employees, 3.13. *See also* Recruiting top talent

Boundary-spanning function, 3.8. *See also* Organizational-environmental relationship
Bundling approach, 3.20. *See also* Business strategy, Human resource policies and practices
Bureau of National Affairs, 3.18
Business strategy, 3.8, 3.12

Career planning, 3.14
Centers of excellence (HR), 3.27
Centralized decision making, 3.28
Change managers, 3.26. *See also* Human resources, as change agent
Collective bargaining, 3.17
Communication effectiveness (HR), 3.5, 3.19–20, 3.23, 3.26. *See also* Translation role
Competitive advantage, 3.6, 3.28
Congruence (horizontal and vertical fit), 3.20
Continuous training, 3.10
Core competencies, 3.8, 3.21, 3.32
Creating value. *See* Adding value
Cultural change, 3.26

Decision-making (HR), 3.8, 3.11–12, 3.22–24, 3.26
Downsizing, 3.22, 3.28

Educational reimbursement programs, 3.14
Employee relations, 3.11, 3.15–16, 3.31
Employees, expendable vs. valued, 3.10, 3.30
Employer of choice, 3.10
Employment practices and strategies, 3.7
Employment relationship, 3.12, 3.22, 3.23, 3.30
labor transaction approach, 3.12
Empowered workers, 3.12
Environmental context, 3.7–8
Environmental forces, 3.7
Equity/efficiency balance, 3.26
External resources, 3.18, 3.24, 3.32

Flexibility, HR professionals, 3.26
Flexibility, organizational, 3.23
Flexibility-consistency balance, 3.26
Frontier of performance, 3.8
Functional specialization stage, 3.16

Global product market pressures, 3.8
Globalization, 3.31
Government regulation, 3.17, 3.23
Government regulation stage, 3.17

HRM policy clusters, 3.12–16, 3.30–31
Human capital development cluster, 3.31. *See also* Training and development, human capital
Human relations movement (1923–1930s), 3.16
Human resource effectiveness, 3.8, 3.28–30
Human resource function, 3.5, 3.6, 3.11, 3.16, 3.27
time spent on activities, 3.27
Human resource leadership roles, 3.25, 3.30–32
stages of evolution, 3.15–17
Human resource management (HRM), 3.7, 3.8, 3.10
Human Resource Planning Society, 3.6
Human resource policies and practices, 3.6, 3.8, 3.10–12, 3.14, 3.20, 3.21
Human resource policy domain, 3.21–22
Human resource professional, 3.24–25
as strategic player, 3.17, 3.24–28, 3.31–32
centralizing, 3.26
organizational criteria, 3.24–26
Human resource roles, 3.5, 3.7, 3.8–11, 3.18–21, 3.24–28, 3.31
Human resource strategy, 3.8, 3.12, 3.14, 3.30
Human resource systems, 3.16, 3.25, 3.30–31
Human resources department, 3.5, 3.6, 3.8, 3.17, 3.24, 3.26, 3.29, 3.34

Imposed decision, 3.23
Integrated line staff, 3.24, 3.26
Intellectual capital, 3.8, 3.16, 3.32. *See also* Training and development, human capital
Internal resources, 3.24

Knowledge-leveraging culture, 3.13

Labor relations, 3.16–17
Line manager, 3.6, 3.26

Management discretion, 3.7, 3.9
Market power, 3.23
Morale, employee, 3.26

National Labor Relations Act, 3.16, 3.23
Negotiated decision, 3.23
No-layoff policy, 3.10

Open salary system, 3.14
Operational excellence, 3.20

Organizational culture, 3.31
Organizational effectiveness strategy, 3.8, 3.12, 3.18
Organizational-environment relationship, 3.8
Outsourcing, HR activities, 3.28, 3.31–32

People management, 3.17
People systems/strategies, 3.6, 3.8, 3.13
Performance appraisal system, 3.14. *See also* 360-degree appraisal systems
Performance management, 3.14, 3.20, 3.21
Performance-driven work culture, 3.13–14
Personal development, 3.11
Personnel department, 3.16
Power of groups, 3.23
Power of shareholders, 3.8
Pre-personnel department, 3.16
Productivity, 3.10, 3.11, 3.16
Professional development, employees, 3.20
Profitability, HRM activities, 3.11, 3.26, 3.30

Quantitative measures, HRM activities, 3.30

Recruiting top talent, 3.13
Revenue enhancement. *See* Adding value
Reward management, 3.14–15, 3.31

Shared service centers, 3.28
Short-run cost-effective solution, 3.28
Society for Human Resource Management, 3.6, 3.18
Stakeholder/multiple constituency approach, 3.29

Strategic partner vs. strategic player, 3.17, 3.27, 3.34

Talent identification and deployment, 3.12, 3.21, 3.31. *See also* Recruiting top talent
Teamwork, workplace trend, 3.15
Technological advances, 3.6, 3.8
360-degree appraisal systems, 3.5, 3.14
Top management commitment to HR, 3.24
Total pay system, 3.14
Training and development, human capital, 3.14, 3.29, 3.31. *See also* Intellectual capital
Transaction role, 3.5, 3.7, 3.18–19, 3.21, 3.23, 3.27
Transformational role, 3.6, 3.7, 3.18, 3.21
Transition role, 3.6, 3.7, 3.18, 3.20
Translation role, 3.5, 3.7, 3.18–20
Twenty-first century, 3.23

Unilateral discretion, 3.9, 3.22
Union avoidance, 3.16
Unionized companies, 3.23
Utility approaches, 3.30

Valuing employees. *See* Employees, expendable vs. valued

Women in the workforce, nonmanagement position, 3.15
Work/life balance, 3.31
Workforce commitment model, 3.12
Workforce reductions, 3.22

MODULE
3

Mᴀɴᴀɢɪɴɢ Hᴜᴍᴀɴ Rᴇsᴏᴜʀᴄᴇs
ɪɴ ᴛʜᴇ 21ˢᵗ CENTURY

From Core Concepts to Strategic Choice

MODULE 4

Managing Change

Scenario Planning and Other Tools

Steve S. Fitzgerald
FORD MOTOR COMPANY

Managing Human Resources in the 21st Century: From Core Concepts to Strategic Choice,
by Kossek and Block

Publisher: Dave Shaut
Executive Editor: John Szilagyi
Developmental Editor: Bryant Editorial Development
Marketing Manager: Joseph A. Sabatino
Production Editor: Tamborah E. Moore
Manufacturing Coordinator: Dana Began Schwartz
Cover Design: Tin Box Studio
Cover Photographs: Copyright Shoji Sato/Photonica
Production House: The Left Coast Group, Inc.
Printer: West Group

Printed in the United States of America
1 2 3 4 5 02 01 00 99

For more information contact South-Western College Publishing, 5101 Madison Road, Cincinnati, Ohio, 45227 or find us on the Internet at *http://www.swcollege.com*
For permission to use material from this text or product, contact us by
- telephone: 1-800-730-2214
- fax: 1-800-730-2215
- web: *http://www.thomsonrights.com*

ISBN: 0–324–01803–7

This book is printed on acid-free paper.

Contents

MODULE OVERVIEW 4.4

RELATION TO THE FRAME 4.4

CORE CONCEPTS IN MANAGING CHANGE 4.5

The Pace and Impact of Rapid Change 4.6

Building the Change-Ready Culture 4.8

HR's Emerging Role in the Formulation and Execution of Strategy 4.12

Scenario Planning 4.17

IN CONCLUSION 4.26

Debrief 4.26

Suggested Readings 4.26

Relevant Web Sites and Other Resources 4.27

Critical Thinking Questions 4.27

Student Class Assignment 4.28

Consumer Lifestyle Worksheet 4.29

References 4.31

APPENDIX 4.32

Developing Scenarios for HR 4.32

How the Scenarios Were Created 4.32

The "Just Do It" World in 2020 4.34

INDEX 4.39

MODULE
4

MODULE OVERVIEW

This module will explore the necessity for organizational change-readiness and describe how human resource (HR) professionals should be leading the effort to cultivate it. To effectively instill a change-ready mindset, HR will need to assume a greater role in organizational strategic planning with a particular emphasis on enhancing the execution and quality of strategies. To accomplish this objective, HR must reinvent itself and assume a role to which it is largely unaccustomed. New tools—such as scenario planning—are needed to help instill a change-ready mentality throughout the organization. Unfortunately, there is a problem: The skills required to grow a change-ready culture are largely unfamiliar to most contemporary HR professionals. That will have to change—the ability to hardwire change-readiness into an organization will be a critical differentiator amongst practitioners of HR.

RELATION TO THE FRAME

This module examines HR's role and capacity to ensure the implementation of strategy, core to the business execution/unilateral portion of the model (Figure 4.1). Business execution, scenario planning, and the creation of a change-ready culture all fall under the managerial discretion segment of the model, although they are often best accomplished with strong participation from all levels and business units within the firm. Scenario planning and the creation of a change-ready organization are strategic issues, thus falling in the strategic objective and business execution segments of the contextual model for this textbook.

This module has been written with the time-starved practitioner and/or student in mind, with an emphasis on density of content and economy of text. Those seeking more complete examinations of the concepts or strategies contained herein should consult the suggested readings and references at the end of the module.

FIGURE 4.1 *A Frame for Understanding Human Resource Strategy: Context, Roles, and Constraints*

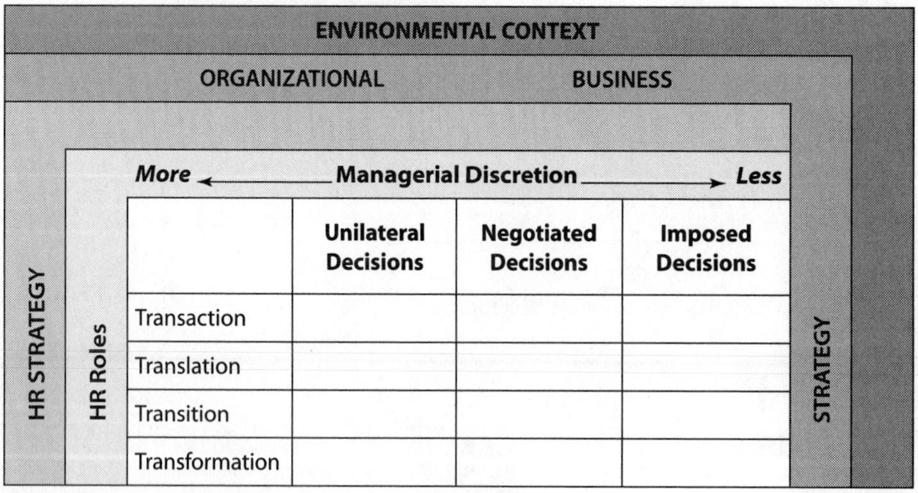

ENVIRONMENTAL CONTEXT		
ORGANIZATIONAL		BUSINESS

More ← Managerial Discretion → Less		
	Unilateral Decisions	Negotiated Decisions	Imposed Decisions
Transaction			
Translation			
Transition			
Transformation			

(Left axis: HR STRATEGY / HR Roles; Right axis: STRATEGY)

© 2000 by Ellen Kossek and Richard Block. Thanks to Brian Pentland, Karen Markel, and John Beck for helpful comments and discussions that enhanced the model.

CORE CONCEPTS IN MANAGING CHANGE

This module will explore the following core concepts:

- *The Necessity of Building a Change-Ready Organization.* The pace and scope of change in virtually all walks of life have been increasing and will continue to do so. In this climate, wise firms resist the urge to try and predict the future and instead focus their energies on building the organizational capability for managing change.

  - ✓ With a few notable exceptions (Microsoft, GE, Intel), organizations across the world are struggling to adjust to today's change-intensive environment.

  - ✓ Sustainable competitive advantage is no longer possible for firms that lack the ability to manage change.

  - ✓ Because of the pace of change, the intellectual capital of an organization is increasing in importance vis-à-vis its physical capital. As a result of this shift, a new paradigm for HR work is emerging.

  - ✓ Many in the HR function are ill prepared for the demands of this new model and are struggling to adapt.

  - ✓ Pundits call for HR to become "more strategic," but few define what that means. HR can become more strategic by (1) ensuring that the organization executes its strategies, and (2) building better strategies in the first place—strategies that embrace the likelihood of constant change.

- *HR's Emerging Role in the Execution of Corporate Strategies.* Many well-conceived strategies are poorly executed. Interestingly, many of the tools used by organizations to reinforce the execution of strategy fall within the traditional purview of the human resources function. A large part of the reason why organizations struggle to effectively execute their strategies is because of the failure to align their people processes with strategic intent.

  - ✓ In order to align HR tools and processes with organizational objectives, HR professionals need to *understand* the strategic intent of the organization.

  - ✓ Accomplishing this objective will require greater involvement in the process of strategic planning.

  - ✓ HR professionals should lead, perhaps even guarantee, the execution of organizational strategies.

- *The Practice of Scenario Planning.* In itself, the improved ability to execute strategies does not help the organization improve its change-readiness. It is, however, the requisite first step in that direction. Once the firm can do what it sets out to do, however, it is time to then turn its attention to improving the strategies themselves. That is where scenarios come in. Scenarios help build better strategies by:

  - ✓ Testing current strategies.

  - ✓ Testing the conventional wisdom or "worldview" of the organization.

  - ✓ Cultivating a change-ready mindset in the organization.

This module examines each of these concepts in turn. In this respect it differs slightly from other modules, where core concepts and strategic issues are considered separately. This difference is simply due to the fact that the entire subject matter of this module is strategic in nature. As in a pyramid, each concept is the foundation for those above it, and a complete examination is required before placing the next block on the pile.

The Pace and Impact of Rapid Change

Change, change, and more change. Perhaps the greatest competitive challenge companies face is adjusting to—indeed, embracing—nonstop change. They must be able to learn rapidly and continuously, innovate ceaselessly, and take on new strategic imperatives faster and more comfortably. Constant change means organizations must create a healthy discomfort with the status quo, an ability to detect emerging trends quicker than the competition, an ability to make rapid decisions, and the agility to seek new ways of doing business. To thrive, in other words, companies will need to be in a never-ending state of transformation, perpetually creating fundamental, enduring change. . . .

In the new economy, winning will spring from organizational capabilities such as speed, responsiveness, agility, learning capacity, and employee competence. Successful organizations will be those that are able to quickly turn strategy into action; to manage processes intelligently and efficiently; to maximize employee contribution and commitment; and to create the conditions for seamless change. (Ulrich 1998)

At its root, the need to manage change is not a just a scientific, engineering, product development, marketing, or leadership challenge. Instead, firms that thrive in a change-intense environment have developed *cultures* and *processes* that make them flexible, nimble, and change-ready. They are adept at the seemingly simple discipline of deciding which path they want to take, and then rigorously ensuring that they take it.

These organizations realize that while they cannot predict the future, they can and must develop the capacity to respond faster then their competition. Members of these organizations come to innately understand that change is a constant; they expect it, prepare for it, and realize that their strategies, tactics, products, and processes cannot remain static. When the time for change comes, they accept and embrace it and are passionate and relentless about executing the tactics necessary to effect the change.

Microsoft's well-documented about-face on the strategic importance of the Internet is a perfect case in point. Despite discounting the significance of the Internet and being late to the Web browser game, Microsoft was able to recognize *and acknowledge* their strategic miscalculation and embrace a new direction. It then ruthlessly executed its revised Internet strategy so effectively that those firms with huge head starts, like Netscape, have been unable to withstand the onslaught (Wallace 1997). The Microsoft example illustrates the central themes of this module:

MODULE
4

- Today, the only constant is change.

- A change-intensive environment requires the organizational capability to quickly alter strategy and rigorously execute it.

- Organizations adept at change management actively prepare their members for the inevitability of change.

(T)he kinds of changes companies are experiencing now are unexpected and unanticipatable. The pace of change has accelerated; the time horizon has been foreshortened. By the time companies can sight an approaching change its effects are already upon them. By the time most companies work out what's going to happen, it already has.

Will the business agenda for 1996 also be the business agenda for 2006? No one knows. Those who say they do know are fools or charlatans. The next decade will see change every bit as mind-boggling and ornery as has the last one. The old business version of Newton's first law of motion—that a company that did a billion dollars last year will do more or less a billion this year—has been repealed. The rate of change in the economic environment has become exponential. Organizations built for yesterday can't and don't work today, and today's organizations may not work tomorrow.

Then what on earth should be done? How can companies prepare to meet the business issues of the next decade if they're unpredictable? The answer is that they

> can accommodate the forces of change only by creating and institutionalizing a capacity for changing themselves. The secret of success is not predicting the future; it is creating an organization that will thrive in a future that cannot be predicted. (Hammer 1996)

Change has become a constant companion in modern organizational life. The pace of that change has been escalating, and that escalation shows no near-term signs of abating. Moreover, much of the change we are experiencing is chaotic, thus *by definition* the lessons and models of the past may no longer be very predictive of the future (Hammer 1996; Johansen and Swigart 1994). When asked what he would like to leave as his legacy, Jack Welch, CEO of General Electric, said, "a company that's able to change at least as fast as the world is changing, and people whose real income is secure because they're winning and whose psychic income is rising because every person is participating" (Welch, interviewed by Stewart, 1991).

Wal-Mart serves as another example of a change-conscious organization that has been successfully able to attack several icons of American business, namely, Sears and K-Mart. It was not lower prices, better service, or Wal-Mart's vaunted logistical processes that gave it an advantage. Instead, founder Sam Walton asserted that his company vanquished the competition because it was better at *making changes*. During weekly meetings Wal-Mart senior managers from around the country gather to review successes and failures from the prior week. They then decide what to do based on what they had just learned, and proceed to alter their practices as required. Thus, Wal-Mart never allows itself to become prisoner to an outdated paradigm (Hammer 1996).

Walton, Welch, and other leaders have come to recognize a premise that is elegant in its simplicity: While we can't predict change, we can be certain that change itself will be a constant. Knowing this, these leaders have structured their organizations to be change-sensitive, change-ready. Most importantly, they ensure that the people within those organizations face the world with the expectation of constant, rapid change.

Perhaps the most dramatic impact of our change-intensive environment is that intellectual capital is rising in importance relative to physical capital. Throughout the history of the industrial revolution, competitive advantage was most often gained by having superior technology, product, and/or access to capital, and then leveraging those advantages via mass production. Today, however, organizations are finding that they are increasingly dependent on the creativity, innovation, and intellectual capacity of their people and processes. Despite (or perhaps because of) advances in technology, people simply matter *more* today than ever before. New products or technologies can be readily replicated, but the knowledge and abilities of key value contributors in an organization cannot. Increasingly, therefore, developing and managing human intellect and skills will be the dominant concerns of managers in successful companies (Quinn 1992).

When Skandia of Sweden published their first *Annual Report on Intellectual Capital* in the early 1990s, prominent Wall Street pundits suggested that the report would soon have more relevance to investors than the traditional annual report. Much to the surprise of many on the "Street," lightning did not strike these observers dead.

> People . . . are now becoming more than mere 'hands' or 'temporary role occupants.' They increasingly represent valuable 'intellectual property.' Slowly the auction ring for companies is realizing that assets don't have to be made of bricks or steel but can be made of brain . . . (P)ut people on the balance sheets as assets, not in the profit and loss as costs. It happens in the auction ring where companies are valued way beyond the worth of their physical assets and you cannot account for the difference with 'goodwill' or 'Research and Development in the pipeline' or 'patents pending' or 'brands,' all of which are also part of intellectual property. People matter more now. (Handy 1996)

Like many others, Charles Handy realizes that it is no longer possible to sustain an enterprise on the profits generated by a single great product or innovation. Today, product life cycles dwindle by the hour. A company's current "cash cow" may be made obsolete overnight with the introduction of a new chip, format, or platform—perhaps from a firm that heretofore was not even considered a competitor. Your best strategy is, like Intel, to ensure that this happens by being the one to make your *own* products obsolete.

Building the Change-Ready Culture

What has change-readiness to do with the business of HR, of managing people? Firms such as Wal-Mart, Intel, Microsoft, Hewlett-Packard, Disney, and others appreciate the need to institutionalize a receptivity to, and capacity for, change. Simply put, they strive to be good at changing. Sometimes this is accomplished through installing innovation and change processes ("Workout" at GE, "RAPIDS" at Ford), strategic planning, or rewards for creativity—in other instances it is achieved via less tangible means. For example, at Fairlane Credit, a start-up affiliate of Ford Motor Credit Company, the notion of change-readiness is embodied in a document called the Fairlane Commitment, an articulation of the value system for the company. This document is shown in Figure 4.2.

At Fairlane, the notion of change-readiness is cultivated as part of every employee's assimilation into the culture. The Fairlane Commitment articulates the expectation of change, and it is posted on walls, mousepads, screen savers, and notepads throughout the company. All hiring, reinforcement, reward, and feedback tools are aligned with it. Employees cite it in presentations and casual conversation. During orientation, Fairlane goes to great pains to ensure that every new employee is introduced to the idea that change will be a constant companion. Thereafter, the president and other leaders reinforce the notion in business updates, corporate learning sessions, and a variety of other ways.

The emphasis at Fairlane Credit is on receptivity and openness to change—not specific methodologies to manage it. Do the words translate into action? In early 1998 Fairlane suddenly dropped an intensive, well-funded and -staffed effort to acquire portfolios from other firms. Why? Because certain legal guidelines had changed, making other—potentially more lucrative—initiatives possible. Shortly after the decision was reached, a new cross-functional team was well underway in planning the pilot for the new initiative, work had been redeployed, and budgets revised. Within a month a pilot was launched, and after three months the complete process was in place. "Mooning" and griping over the change were minimal. Fairlane was able to change quickly because its people had a fundamental receptivity to change; embracing it is an expectation of the culture.

HR's Role in Cultivating a Change-Ready Culture.

What should HR's role in this be? Simply stated, to champion the spirit of change-readiness within the organization. HR professionals should be striving to ensure that members of the organization will *embrace* change—not just tolerate it, manage it, or even "take it in stride." Today's change-rich environment requires the hiring, development, and retention of those people who *enjoy* dealing with change. A culture receptive of change can assist the organization in surviving an uncertain, rapidly changing, and perhaps even chaotic future.

Why HR? In many ways, HR is best positioned to champion this shift in strategic thinking, as it has traditionally been responsible for the delivery of programs designed to align individual and corporate objectives. A 1996 Human Resources Institute (HRI) study asked HR professionals to speculate on their current vs. future roles. The results are shown in Table 4.1 on page 4.10.

In its 1998 study entitled *Major Issues Impacting People Management,* HRI elaborated:

> The role of change agent is becoming more important for HR professionals. HRI's research shows that in the future, HR professionals will be expected to play a much larger role in the continual transformation of the business to enhance its global

competitiveness. It is no wonder that this role is becoming so important. In today's business environment, significant organizational change is no longer an infrequent, special event. Today and even more so in the future, organizations must continually change and adapt to the competitive environment. (HRI 1998)

These sentiments were echoed by Dave Ulrich and Robert Eichinger at the 1996 Human Resources Planning Society Annual Conference. They presented the results of their conversations with a variety of European and American "thought leaders" from across industry and academia. Topping the list of competitive challenges that HR must meet was the need to "create(e) an adaptive culture with a capacity for rapid change." This challenge for HR stemmed from the identification of the ability to "adapt to needed external requirements/changes rapidly and comfortably" as the single most important organizational capability for the future.

FIGURE 4.2 *The Fairlane Commitment.*

FAIRLANE CREDIT LLC

The Fairlane Commitment...

Every community has certain values that shape it. Fairlane Credit is no exception. In the early days of our company, the following principles were identified as being critical to our long-term success. Please join us in our absolute commitment to these values.

I will...

Never compromise in my dedication to
- **integrity,**
- **superb customer service, and**
- **teamwork.**

I know that these cornerstone values will separate Fairlane from our sub-or non-prime automotive financing competitors.

Deliver.

Within the context of our cornerstone values, I'll do whatever it takes to get the job done.

Know my "water line" and continuously seek to lower it.

I understand that when I do this, small failures are possible. As long as they aren't frequent events, that's OK.

Build Fairlane to last.

I am now part of an enterprise with nearly a century of tradition. I'll help make it two.

Take responsibility.

For my work, for my actions, for my career, and for my professional development.

Be both an exceptional leader *and* an assertive follower.

I understand that being part of a team means playing offense and defense.

Value diversity.

I recognize that our differences make us stronger.

Embrace change.

I know that our prosperity may depend upon our ability to "turn on a dime."

Never utter the words, "It's not my job."

I am a team player and will help advance the interests of the Company whenever the opportunity presents itself.

TABLE 4.1   *Relative Importance of Various HR Roles*

1996	2001
1. HR policy setting	1. Change Agent
2. Functional HR Expert	2. HR Strategist
3. Consultant/Confidant	3. Strategic think(er)

Source: Human Resources Institute 1996

However, when asked how well organizations have succeeded in creating a change-ready culture, the performance was poor—the combined European and U.S. grade on creating a change-ready culture was the worst of the aptitudes surveyed. While participants on both sides of the Atlantic felt that change management was going to be the most important HR practice of the future, they also ranked it 17th (of 19) when asked, "In general, how good is HR *now*?" (emphasis added) (Ulrich & Eichinger 1996).

Thus, the good news is that a strong demand exists for an activity that can help the organization cultivate change-readiness. Unfortunately, there's also bad news—few HR practitioners have the necessary skills to build that change-ready culture, and even fewer HR activities are focused on delivering it.

HR is Ill—Is Radical Surgery Required?   Stated bluntly, for the most part HR as a function has failed to deliver the value-added services that today's organizations require. The Human Resources Institute noted that, when asked about future roles for HR, operating managers rarely mentioned strategic thinking, strategist, or change agent. This should not come as a surprise: Because HR has been performing its traditionally administrative role for so long, line management has been "conditioned" to identify HR with that narrow role. Even more distressing is the fact that most HR professionals have contributed to this stereotype by showing little interest or aptitude for the business (HRI 1998).

Fortune editor Tom Stewart was more direct:

> There's a reason that more and more new HR executives come to the post with backgrounds in line management or consulting rather than from HR's own ranks . . . (M)any people doing the work now can't cut it in the HR of the future. Clearly, companies need a place to think about the skills they need and will need, about executive development, about a way to focus on human capital. This is precisely why they should ask the do-or-die question of their human resource departments. The prospect of hanging, as Dr. Johnson said, is a sure way of concentrating the mind. (Stewart 1996)

As Stewart and HRI suggest, the function of HR is not meeting the challenges being asked of it in the Knowledge Age. Sadly, this should not surprise us. After decades of being rewarded and counted on to control, stabilize, and regulate the organization, HR and most of the professionals in it have outmoded skill sets and, even worse, outdated paradigms. Today, many practitioners acknowledge that it's logical and necessary to become "business partners" but struggle with the organizational diagnosis, operational effectiveness, and change-management skills required to be one. The barriers to achieving the partnership model include:

- HR professionals who can differentiate the strategic from the more operational and reactive aspects of HR jobs.

- An understanding of, and role in, planning the growth of the business. The competencies that enable one to excel at contract negotiations or compensation and benefits administration do not necessarily prepare an HR professional to solve business problems.

- A shift in focus from reacting to problems toward the enhancement of operational effectiveness (HRI 1998).

The dilemma with the new HR paradigm is that few HR people are skilled at the disciplines required for it. Most are far more adept at functional specialties such as benefit administration, staffing, employee relations, succession planning, and training. Worse yet, many have become jack-of-all-trades, master-of-none generalists in the administrative and transactional components of these disciplines. While elements of these disciplines are still required in the organization, they are no longer at the core of the function. The strategic HR role transcends them.

At their root, most traditional HR disciplines are simply "tools" intended to *align* people with the strategies of the organization. However, they often fail to do so. The root cause of the failure is systemic: human resource professionals have rarely been active participants in the formulation of corporate strategy. Thus they have often failed to align the tools of the trade with strategic intent because they too often have little idea what that intent is. All that most HR practitioners know about strategic intent is what they see on the model put out by the strategic planning activity. This "disconnect" is largely responsible for the function's failure to help organizations manage the demands of the burgeoning Knowledge Age.

There are exceptions to this rule—at National Semiconductor, PepsiCo, Texas Instruments, IBM, Ford Motor Company, Fairlane Credit, Intel, Bechtel, GE, and other businesses, HR operates under a different paradigm. The emphasis within HR in these organizations is decreasingly on its historical strengths of benefits administration, employee relations, staffing, labor relations, diversity management, recruiting, and task-specific training. Instead, the focus is on:

- Change management

- Strategic HR planning

- Executive development

- Organizational effectiveness

- Culture management (Ulrich and Eichinger 1996)

These practices require the HR practitioner to be an advisor or "business partner" to management, spending the majority of the time on those aspects of the business that are *transformational* to the organization, not transactional. Examples include:

- Aligning corporate goals to team and individual behavior

- Managing intellectual capital

- Performing organizational diagnosis and brokering solutions

- Promoting creativity, innovation, and empowerment

- Coaching managers on how to accomplish the above

- Building organizational systems that ensure that the organization is nimble and executes its strategies

An effective people-focused function has never been more important. Movements in organizational learning, quality, teamwork, and reengineering are all primarily focused on attaining organizational excellence *through people.* Ensuring success on this front should be the primary work of HR. The University of Michigan's Dave Ulrich identifies four ways for HR to deliver organizational excellence:

- First, HR should become a partner with senior and line managers in strategy execution, helping to move planning from the conference room to the marketplace.

MODULE
4

- Second, it should become an expert in the way work is organized and executed, delivering administrative efficiency to ensure that costs are reduced while quality is maintained.

- Third, it should become a champion for employees. . . .

- And finally, HR should become an agent of continuous transformation, shaping processes and a culture that together improve an organization's capacity for change.

(Ulrich 1998)

As Ulrich notes, this new agenda for HR is a radical departure from the status quo. Rather than just quoting policy, the new paradigm for HR requires practitioners to concretely help the company serve its customers or otherwise increase shareholder value.

In many organizations, HR already excels at championing employee needs, designing organizations, and delivering efficient administrative service. These elements *are* important. In fact, the credibility of the function often starts with the ability to process merit pay, bonus, and stock options correctly. If those simple administrative tasks cannot be delivered, why should operating managers believe that HR can make a meaningful contribution on the strategic level? The point is that administrative efficiency, however necessary, is no longer "enough." Indeed, the participants in Ulrich and Eichinger's study gave HR high marks for delivering in these administrative and transactional areas . . . and then placed them squarely at the bottom of the list in terms of future importance (Ulrich & Eichinger 1996).

HR functions ready to adopt the new paradigm know that the primary challenge they face is to transform *themselves* to be able to deliver a culture of change-readiness and lead the organizational effort to ensure that strategies are executed. In these two objectives, the opportunity exists for HR to radically transform its role (and prominence). They are the keys to survival and prosperity for the function and its practitioners. As *Fortune* editor Thomas Stewart wrote: "People need people—but do they need Personnel? It's time for human resources departments to put up or shut up" (Stewart 1996).

MODULE 4

HR's Emerging Role in the Formulation and Execution of Strategy

Many firms share similar strategies, but only a subset succeed. Why does Southwest Airlines thrive where others—with roughly the same strategy—have struggled or failed? Better execution of that strategy is usually the reason. In fact, when one cannot out-strategize the competition, the only other viable alternative in most instances is to out-execute them (Prahalad & Hamel 1990). What does this have to do with HR? Why should it concern itself with corporate or business unit strategy? HR must understand the strategic intent of the organization in order to properly align the tools in HR's kit with them. Unfortunately, this understanding is often limited to a singular HR leader or a very small cohort within the function and does not permeate the organization deeply enough to reach those charged with deploying the tools of strategic execution.

The culture of the organization, the reward structure, the policies, the rewards, and the management of the firm's intellectual capital should all be aligned with, and designed to direct behavior towards, the strategic intent of the company. In many respects, the execution of strategy should be the core of what HR does. In their 1992 book *Strategy Formulation and Implementation,* Thompson and Strickland identified twenty components of effective strategic execution or implementation. Revealingly, sixteen of those twenty components fall within the traditional purview of the human resources function:

1. Creating a strategy-supportive organization structure.

2. Developing the skills and core competencies needed to execute the strategy successfully.

3. Selecting people for key positions.

4. Developing administrative and operating systems to give the organization strategy-critical capabilities.

5. Motivating organizational units and individuals to do their best to make the strategy work.

6. Designing rewards and incentives that induce employees to do the very things needed for successful strategy execution.

7. Promoting a results orientation.

8. Establishing shared values.

9. Setting ethical standards.

10. Creating a strategy-supportive work environment.

11. Building a spirit of high performance into the culture.

12. Leading the process of shaping values, molding culture, and energizing strategy accomplishment.

13. Keeping the organization innovative, responsive, and opportunistic.

14. Dealing with the politics of strategy, coping with power struggles, and building consensus.

15. Enforcing ethical standards and behavior.

16. Initiating corrective actions to improve strategy execution.

These elements of strategic execution all fall within the realm of HR's traditional practice: organizational structure, competency development, selection, policy, motivation, rewards and incentives, corporate culture and values, ethical standards, work environment, morale, managing politics, and so on. Despite this, HR has historically been—at best—a tangential participant in the development of the organizations' business strategy. Thus, the organizational component most directly responsible for aligning individual or team behavior with strategic intent is not intimately involved in the development of the strategy. Too often, HR leaders don't know the "why," just the "what."

This is a systemic "disconnect" that causes many firms to struggle to implement their strategies. To effectively align employees with the desired future direction of the firm, HR must understand not just the *words* on the strategy summary, but the strategic *intent* as well. That way, the tools of strategy execution (organizational structure and rewards, for example) can be aligned with that intent.

> More business strategies are declared than delivered. HR professionals should play a proactive partnership role in ensuring strategy execution. They (should be able to) guarantee that strategies (will) happen. (Ulrich 1995)

In order to successfully make the guarantee, HR must be intimately involved in the *process* of corporate, or business unit-level, strategic planning. After all, how can the function reasonably expect to ensure execution without a thorough understanding of not just the final strategy, but of all the thinking that went into it, the debates that took place, the alternatives that were adopted and those that were rejected, and the overarching *intent* of the plan? The answer is simple—it can't.

HR's Role in the Formulation of the Strategic Plan. Despite the aforementioned limitations of many HR practitioners, most do possess skills and occupy roles that are unique within their organizations. They:

- Manage the tools that link corporate goals to those of the individual or team (hiring criteria, rewards, reinforcement tools, evaluation and feedback, career pathing, promotion criteria, and policy deployment).

- Tend to be, with the possible exception of marketing and public relations personnel, the sole organizational repository of trained expertise in human behavior, organizational learning, systems design, *and* group facilitation techniques.

- Are accustomed to "working between the boxes" on the organizational chart, using interpersonal contact, relationships, and influence to obtain information and exert their agendas. The most effective HR personnel use their personal credibility, sound advice, and understanding of interpersonal and team dynamics to exert their influence on the organization. They rarely accomplish this influence based on the limited power vested in their position. Stated simply, effective HR practitioners are almost always savvy politicians.

These skills are exactly those required of a good facilitator, especially for a sensitive, politics-laden subject like strategic planning. However, the role of facilitator is too often an afterthought and filled by a financial analyst or engineer with little or no formal education or experience in interpersonal and group dynamics. These substitutes may have enormous technical knowledge, but they do not know how to quickly create a high-performance team, ensure open debate, build a risk-taking environment, draw out important but silent perspectives, and communicate and ensure common perceptions of important conclusions. This puts them at a significant disadvantage when it comes to helping the strategic planning team succeed.

When positioned as the coordinator of the planning process, HR can set out to deliver planning processes that prevent functional, product, or other types of myopia. HR practitioners best understand the principles of system thinking (anyone who manages human cultural systems completely understands the cascading impact of one small individual change on a total population), organizational learning, and the challenge of managing complex political issues.

Is this to say that HR should strive to formulate corporate strategy? Hardly. That is the role of the leadership of the enterprise, of which HR is presumably a part. So-called business partners, however, should guide the consideration of how the company should be organized to carry out its strategy (Ulrich 1998).

HR should attempt to garner the responsibility to facilitate the *process* of strategic planning. In this capacity, it could:

- Coordinate with the other functional areas to design a robust process.

- Schedule the meetings and invite the participants.

- Provide the process facilitators, scribes, and logistics support for planning sessions.

- Lead the deployment or communication of the strategies to the workforce.

- Carefully track and manage the organization's success in implementing what it set out to do.

This immersion in the process is a key step in ensuring that the broad HR function, not just one or two people, completely understand the strategic intent of the organization. Once armed with this knowledge, the alignment of HR systems and processes (rewards, structure, and culture) with strategic intent is far more likely.

As a start-up enterprise, Fairlane Credit has had the luxury of constructing its planning cycle from scratch, as shown in Figure 4.3 and Figure 4.4. It embodies many of the principles articulated above. Note that:

- Elements of strategic execution, including the communication to and involvement of every employee, are considered to be part of the planning process, not outside of it.

- HR is responsible for facilitating strategic planning sessions as well as linking rewards and other internal reinforcements to the strategic intent.

FIGURE 4.3 *Fairlane Credit Strategic Planning Cycle*

Phase	STRATEGIC PLANNING—JANUARY (PLANNING FOR NEXT 5 YEARS BEGINNING IN JANUARY OF THE *UPCOMING* YEAR)					TEST THE STRATEGY	REVISE THE STRATEGY
Timing	Prior to Strategic Planning Workshop (SPW)	SPW Day 1	SPW Day 1	SPW Day 2–3	SPW Day 2–3	SPW Day 3–4	SPW Day 5
Step	*Environmental Scan (SWOT)*	*Competitive Assessment*	*Sister Company Strategy Briefing*	*Rework the Strategic Plan*	*Recommendations and Strategic Agenda*	*Scenario Planning*	*Rework the Strategic Plan Again*
Champion	VP-Marketing	VP-Marketing	President	VP-Marketing	VP-Marketing	VP-Human Resources	VP-Marketing
Actors	Management Committee	Management Committee	Leaders of respective Ford Credit sister firms	Management Committee	Management Committee	Management Committee	Management Committee
Schedule and Facilitate	HR	HR	HR	HR	HR	HR	HR
What Is It?	Pre-work: Identify internal strengths and weaknesses, external opportunities and threats. Examine significant social, political, economic, and technological trends.	Assess strengths, weaknesses, opportunities and threats of Fairlane and our major competitors. Discuss core competencies and how to leverage them. Develop action plans for weaknesses (internal) and threats (external).	Strategy update from our sister companies within Ford Credit. Focus on synergies that optimize return for overall enterprise.	Recheck our current strategy and revise for next five years. How did the SWOT exercise change our thinking? Then shift emphasis to the next calendar year. Where do we want to go, what are we going to do, when will we do it, and why? Debate important, encourage it.	Given SWOT and strategy consensus, determine list of things to study. Narrow list of potential "Vital Few" initiatives required to execute the strategy. Determine which require more study (Strategic Agenda—name teams to investigate). More precise the better.	Test strategic plan—what would we do if "x" happened? Use plausible yet productive scenarios. Emphasis less on actual action planning than "practice" in thinking through the company response to the scenario.	What did we learn from the scenario exercise? Are there any actions we took across all or most scenarios? If so, shouldn't we do them now? What should we change based on what we learned, if anything? Is our plan robust enough to withstand the alternative futures we explored? Achieve tentative consensus on Vital Few initiatives required to execute the strategy.

MODULE
4

FIGURE 4.4 *Fairlane Credit Strategic Planning Cycle*

Phase	**STRATEGY ALIGNMENT AND FINE-TUNING**			**EXECUTION**			
Timing	**Day 5 of SPW and February/March**	**May–September**	**October–November**	**November–December**	**December**	**December**	**December**
Step	***Develop Business Plan and Budget***	***Revise Incentive Pay and Bonus Targets***	***Revisit and Fine-tune the Strategy***	***Ensure Alignment***	***Policy Deployment***	***Communication of Fairlane Objectives, Business Plan, Balanced Scorecard***	***Employee Letter (to home)***
Champion	CFO	VP-Human Resources	VP-Marketing	VP-Human Resources	VP-Human Resources	President	President
Actors	Finance Activity	HR	Management Committee	Miscellaneous depending on need	All Business Units	To all employees	To all employees
Schedule and Facilitate	HR	HR	HR	HR	HR	HR	HR
What Is It?	Prepare a budget that allocates resources to key issues, growth plan, and top priorities, *all based on the strategy.* Resource priority should be directed to the Vital Few.	For the upcoming year, determine the milestones that must be met for incentive pay payouts. Use budget/business plan objectives as targets for rewards. This helps ensure alignment between company strategy and employee priorities.	Recheck the strategy, revisit scenarios, receive and discuss the results of the research that's taken place (Strategic Agenda), and then finalize the Vital Few for the upcoming year. The Vital Few should be just that—preferably no more than one or two key initiatives, never more than five.	Review budgets, incentives, business metrics in light of any changes made during fine-tuning of the strategy. Make sure rewards, organizational structure, policy, core competencies, culture, leadership are aligned with the Vital Few and the strategy about to be deployed.	Use policy deployment process to involve and communicate the vital few to all employees. Policy Deployment serves to link the objectives of each business unit and individual to some part of the Vital Few.	Explain where we're headed, why, and how. Post new metrics on incentive pay charts, websites, and other key communication points. Have president hold "all hands" meetings to explain and discuss the strategic intent, not just the strategy itself. Talk about the alternatives that were rejected and why. Discuss plausible scenarios that could change the company's approach.	Letter congratulating employees for their contributions throughout the year; reminder of Vital Few for next year. Wish all a great holiday season.

- HR does not have lead responsibility for any of the planning steps until long after the business plan is created. The focus, instead, is on the planning process, not the content of the plan. In many organizations, this nuance is not recognized (or valued), and poor management of interpersonal and/or group dynamics lead to suboptimal outcomes.

Once HR has immersed itself in the planning process and enhanced the organization's ability to execute, the job is not done. After all, with new responsibilities comes a higher standard of duty. HR must strive to do more than facilitate the process and execute strategies; it should aim to improve the planning process. In particular, it should assist organizations in making their processes more robust in the face of the ever-changing world. As the number of variables generating change increase, the pace of change escalates, and thus planning becomes even more difficult. "Traditional planning was based on forecasts, which worked reasonably well in the relatively stable 1950s and 1960s," writes Pierre Wack, formerly of the Royal Dutch/Shell planning activity. "Since the early 1970s, however, forecasting errors have become more frequent and occasionally of dramatic and unprecedented magnitude" (Wack 1985a). What is an organization to do?

Organizations need tools to help them manage the change-intensive environment. One such tool is the discipline of scenario planning. Scenario planning is readily made to help both improve planning and cultivate a receptivity to change within the organization. By their nature, scenarios acknowledge that the only reliable constant is change itself and that attempts to consistently predict the future are folly. Scenarios make the planning process more robust by:

- Assisting the organization in imagining multiple futures and their potential reaction to them.

- Being invaluable tools in helping shift the worldview, paradigms, or mental models of the members of the organization.

- Reinforcing the certainty of change and the need to prepare for it.

It is to this subject that the remainder of this module is dedicated.

Scenario Planning

The basic assumption of traditional planning is that the future can be predicted. Conventional forecasting focuses on analyzing an existing situation and determining how it might be projected into the future. The underlying paradigm that rules this activity is that the best strategy comes from the most accurate forecast of the future. Unfortunately, the problem with this approach is that *consistently* accurate forecasts of the future are simply not possible. As an old Arabian proverb wryly notes, "Those who pretend to know the future lie, even if they accidentally speak truth."

Too many forces work against the possibility of getting the "right" forecast, largely because no single "correct" projection can be deduced from past behavior. Moreover, classical forecasting approaches often fail to account for the unpredictable influence of the external environment (Wack 1985a). Traditional planning techniques are susceptible to the following errors:

- Firm faith in forecasting methods that are based on historical data and assume unbroken economic growth as well as continuous and uninterrupted economic development.

- Inadequate observation and assimilation of developments taking place on the political, social, and economic levels, as well as of newly arising crisis points. Paradigm-shifting developments (like the Internet) are rarely anticipated by extrapolating from historical trend data.

- Inadequate observation of developing societal trends and processes likely to shape public opinion . . . (von Reibnitz 1987)

Should we therefore abandon forecasts? Of course not—but they must be augmented with the reality that consumer preferences shift quickly, new products emerge from out of the blue, and new competitors pop up not only from exotic locales, but even from previously "unrelated" industries. For example, who in 1990 would have thought that the biggest threat to, *and* opportunity for, the long-distance telephone industry could be the World Wide Web? that the same medium could also threaten to dramatically alter the way cars, books, and other goods and services were distributed?

Classical forecasts are only of relevance today to well-defined and limited subjects. They need to be made more robust by using techniques that embrace the certainty of an uncertain future and make it part of our reasoning. As scenario pioneer Pierre Wack notes, "uncertainty today is not just an occasional, temporary deviation from a reasonable predictability, it is a basic structural feature of the business environment. The method used to think about and plan for the future must be made appropriate to a changed business environment" (Wack 1985a). Michael Hammer sums it up nicely: ". . . the best strategy is not one that tries to divine the future but one that responds rapidly to the present (1996)."

This is particularly important in a time when last year's success has little bearing on tomorrow's performance; traditional linear economic projections from established data rarely hold value in a dynamic world. It is critical to guard against planning for the Information Age with paradigms drawn from the industrial era (Davis 1987). Echoing this theme, C. K. Prahalad and Gary Hamel detailed the "failure of one-time leaders to keep up with the accelerating pace of industry change. For decades the changes that confronted Sears, General Motors, IBM, Westinghouse, Volkswagen, and other incumbents were, if not exactly glacial in speed, at least more or less linear extrapolations of the past" (Hamel and Prahalad 1994). These firms were all caught napping as their worldview betrayed them—the world had changed when they weren't paying attention—the long-held "truths" of their business environments were no longer absolutes.

MODULE
4

Given the unpredictability of change, traditional methods of future planning are, if not obsolete, then certainly inadequate for today. They need to be augmented by new techniques to help manage the likelihood and impact of change. We need to add the discipline of scenario planning to our toolkit. As Royal Dutch/Shell's former group managing director Andre Benard commented: "Experience has taught us that the scenario technique is much more conducive to forcing people to think about the future than the forecasting techniques we formerly used" (Wack 1985a).

The earliest uses of scenario planning were concerned primarily with military conquest and defense. Often called "war games," military organizations around the world have long practiced the art of trying to prepare for the unpredictable movements of their opposition by attempting to anticipate their next move(s) and then imagining how their side would best respond. While the context is clearly different, nonmilitary uses of scenario planning include many of the key approaches of this early work, including:

- Attack your enemy where it is weakest.

- Build on your strengths.

- Focus on the long-term objective of the campaign, not just the battle at hand. One may elect to lose a battle to win the war. (von Reibnitz 1987)

To improve their forecasting abilities and to cultivate a culture of change-readiness, many organizations employ scenario planning techniques. Examples include Royal Dutch/Shell, Chrysler Motors, the U.S. Air Force, British Petroleum, AMP, Ford Motor Company, Boeing, Daimler-Benz, IBM, 3M, Kodak, Hewlett-Packard, Procter & Gamble, Sears Roebuck and Company, Skandia, Toshiba, The Club of Rome, the Datar Institute (French Institute for Regional Planning and Development), and the Battelle

Institute in Frankfurt, Germany (Swartz 1991; von Rebnitz 1987; Fost 1998; Wack 1985a). Contemporary growth in the use of scenarios stems largely from dissatisfaction with conventional methods in managing the unpredictability of the future. As Bell Atlantic's CEO Raymond Smith reports:

> If you make all your investment and marketing decisions based upon a single view of the future, you put your company at risk if your assumptions turn out to be invalid. On the other hand, if you make a decision that is correct across a wide range of outcomes, you reduce your risk while maximizing your exposure to growth opportunities. (Smith 1996)

Scenarios are stories about plausible alternative futures that are used in a wide variety of ways, but most often to test and refine existing strategies. Planners use scenarios to seek tactics, strategies, or products that transcend a variety of futures and consider them to be the most robust of an array of options. After all, if there is a demand for a given product in four of five plausible scenarios of the future (*especially* if for different reasons), it would seem to be an investment worth making.

Why the emphasis on stories? First of all, lists are too generic; they are intentionally terse summaries of far more substantive ideas, especially in a strategic planning context. While brevity is always of value in the fast-paced environment of today, complex issues simply require more detail. When an organization communicates its strategy in list form, the most important part of the equation—the rationale behind the statements, the intent behind the strategy—is left out. The unintended consequence of this approach is that those not involved in crafting the strategy will only gain a superficial grasp of it. This impedes the execution of the strategy and the alignment of organizational processes with it.

Moreover, a considerable body of psychological research indicates that lists are difficult to remember largely because of various cognitive biases, such as the recency and primacy effects (Shaw, Brown, and Bromiley 1998). Stories also play an important role in learning: Researchers studying learning amongst high school students found that the students learned best from story-like formats like those found in the periodicals *Time* and *Newsweek*. To test this finding, when history textbooks were translated into a story format, student recall improved by a factor of three (as compared to the retention associated with traditional textbooks). Thus, a good strategic plan should read like a good story—it defines relationships, a sequence of events, cause and effect, and a priority among items—and those elements are likely to be remembered as a complex whole. That likelihood, supported by a substantial amount of cognitive science, argues strongly for strategic planning through storytelling. Indeed, at 3M, stories have become a central tool in strategic planning specifically because of their educational value (Shaw, Brown, and Bromiley 1998).

Finally, numbers and lists usually fail to connect emotionally with the reader. Vivid stories or metaphors are often the best means to galvanize a robust image of the writer's intent. Research indicates that those individuals who are the most effective at persuasion in their respective organizations rely less on spreadsheets and more on the use of vivid stories and metaphors to communicate their positions (Conger 1998). To illustrate the educational power of stories, let us consider a business classic: The introduction and use of scenarios at Royal Dutch/Shell.

Scenarios at Royal Dutch/Shell.   In the early 1970s, scenarios were introduced at Royal Dutch/Shell (RD/S) and used effectively to confront the conventional wisdom inherent in their base-planning forecast. The paradigm of Shell, and the rest of the oil industry, had been that crude oil prices would continue to inflate consistent with historical trends. Planners at RD/S, including Pierre Wack and Arie DeGues, noticed some interesting trends and began to build scenarios to test this assumption. They observed that:

- U.S. oil reserves were almost depleted.

- Western demand for oil was steadily increasing.

- OPEC was maturing politically.

- Several of the key members of OPEC strongly opposed Western influence, religious beliefs, and social norms, a situation exacerbated by western support of Israel during the Six Day War in 1967 (Wack 1985a and b; Swartz 1991).

These and other economic, political, social, and technological trends were important component pieces to planners at Shell in determining that a highly plausible scenario of their future was a world in which the price of oil went up dramatically. This contrasted sharply with decades of experience to the contrary—historically, the price of oil had been so stable that few could conceive of a world in which the price went up at an accelerated rate. Such behavior was not only foreign to the experience of RD/S's managers, it was also beyond their imagination. To help shift the paradigm of the firm and prepare managers for the possibility of this environment, Shell constructed robust scenarios that painted a very different world for oil companies, a world in which the price of oil had exploded.

In order to be able to think about a world in which the price of oil defied all previous experience, mangers first had to "feel" what that world would be like. The RD/S scenarios were created to depict that plausible future and to make it more tangible. RD/S planners used them to change the firm's perception of reality. "The first step was to question and destroy their existing view of the world in which oil demand expanded in orderly and predictable fashion, and Shell routinely could add oil fields, refineries, tankers, and marketing outlets. . . . But exposing and invalidating an obsolete worldview is not where scenario analysis stops. Reconstructing a new model is the most important job and is the responsibility of the managers themselves" (Wack 1995b). Using scenarios, the planners at Shell successfully altered the paradigm or mental model of the firm's managers and then began to build a shared vision for how the firm would respond in such an environment.

Wack and other former RD/S planners report that the real challenge was not constructing the scenarios, analyzing them, or even deciding what to do, but instead was the expansion of the worldview of the people in the organization. Achieving that shift in worldview must be the goal of scenario exercises. Accomplishing this is not done with meetings, slick PowerPoint presentations, or other traditional means. Instead, it requires one to paint pictures with words, vividly depict future states, and challenge managers to think through what they would do. It is storytelling with a purpose: Managers must be confronted with the future on more than an intellectual level—they must be made to feel the problems and associated emotions that the future state would engender. To derive the greatest value from scenarios as a learning tool, people must "live" in the future state for awhile. To wit:

> We told our upstream managers, engaged in exploration and production, that the unthinkable was going to happen: "Be careful! You are about to lose the major part of your concessions and mining rents . . ." To the downstream world of refiners, transports, and marketers, we said something equally alarming: "Prepare! You are about to become a low-growth industry." (Wack 1995a).

Shell's scenarios prepared it for the change. When OPEC dramatically raised the price of oil following the Yom Kippur War in 1973, RD/S moved aggressively to embrace the opportunities inherent in the new environment. In so doing, RD/S dramatically improved its competitive position, an improvement that it has sustained to this day. They were able to do this because they had *already thought about* the consequences of such an environment, where the opportunities were, and they had *reacted faster* than anyone else could.

MODULE
4

Prior to the oil crunch, Royal Dutch/Shell was generally regarded as one of the weakest of the big oil firms. Today, it is widely viewed as not only the preeminent oil company in the world, but one of the foremost firms regardless of industry. Royal Dutch/Shell executives attribute a significant part of this improvement to the disciplined use of scenario planning tools. Scenario techniques helped Royal Dutch/Shell "out-change" its competition. While RD/S was developing tools to become more nimble and change-ready, its competitors were focused on plans based on more linear models. When the rules of the game changed in fundamental ways, the other oil firms had to first get over the shock of the change, sort through the situation to determine their array of potential responses, decide amongst them, and only then could they react. Conversely, RD/S was ready to react as soon as it became clear that the world was changing, primarily because it already had thought about what it would do in such a context.

> Shell executives didn't predict those changes. They reacted faster and better than their rivals when the changes happened, because scenario-planning exercises had prepared them to respond well to change. "It's not about predictions," says Peter Schwartz, president of the Global Business Network. "Scenarios are about trying to avoid getting the future wrong in fundamental ways." (Fost 1998)

Was Royal Dutch/Shell really any better at predicting the future than its competitors? No—but the disciplined use of scenarios helped make it ready for a future that it thought highly plausible. Scenarios made Royal Dutch/Shell's planning process better. As a direct result, RD/S reacted so much faster than its competition that it garnered sustainable competitive advantage.

The Importance of Challenging the Worldview of the Organization.
As the RD/S story illustrates, a central tenet of scenario planning is that while *predicting* the future may not be possible, *preparing* for it certainly is. Moreover, it is the analysis of scenario implications—and the introspection that the firm and its members undergo—that builds change-readiness. Wise organizations use scenarios not to predict the future, but to test their current strategies, determine how their organization might be affected, and *stimulate thought* about how they would respond against the array of futures. Brian Marsh of RD/S put it succinctly: "The real misunderstanding about scenarios is that they are not a tool for helping our managers predict what will happen, but a means by which we can explore about what we should do if it happens!" (Tenaglia and Noonan 1992).

The organizational mindset of change-readiness is the ultimate goal of scenario planning. Scenarios help build change-readiness by institutionalizing a repeatable process to challenge the underlying mental models of the organization. They make it less likely that the organization will be victimized by its own paradigm.

> A Company's perception of its business environment is as important as its investment infrastructure because its strategy comes from this perception. I cannot overemphasize this point: Unless the corporate microcosm changes, managerial behavior will not change—the internal compass must be recalibrated. . . . (U)nless we influenced the mental image, the picture of reality held by critical decision makers, our scenarios would be like water on a stone. (Wack 1985a)

As Wack, Swartz, and others have chronicled, scenario planners in the early 1970s at RD/S succeeded admirably in this respect. RD/S managers came to not only understand that the price of oil might increase significantly, but to almost expect it. When it did happen, there was not the same sense of confusion, bewilderment, and despair that plagued management with regard to competitors. What changed at RD/S were the mental models of those in the firm, a shift that made them more receptive to the dramatic change with which they were confronted. This intangible was the key to RD/S's successful response to the oil crisis and is the real value in scenario processes.

In his book *Beyond Reengineering* (1996), Michael Hammer makes a similar observation about the importance of the underlying paradigm or "conventional wisdom" of the organization. He asserts that every firm has:

- *Surface systems:* The organized tasks of the business processes, with their attendant jobs, structures, systems, and values—the things that create customer value.

- *Deep systems:* The paradigms or mental models of the organization. In his words, "A company's deep system bears the responsibility for detecting external changes, determining what those changes mean, and intervening to modify or transform the surface system accordingly. The deep system, working beneath the surface, embodies the capacity to change" (Hammer, 1996).

The deep system could be called the mental model, paradigm, or worldview of the firm. Change in the deep system leads to the evolution of the surface system. Using slightly different terminology, the University of Michigan's C. K. Prahalad writes about the "dominant logic" of the organization. Like Hammer, he asserts that our deeply held beliefs significantly shape and influence organizational thinking. "We need to understand the 'cognitive maps' of people inside the organisation, the processes by which those maps evolve, and the processes of collective learning and socialisation. Then how to *forget this past* becomes a more important prerequisite to learning about the future. Our problem is not learning new things per se; rather, it is letting go of what we know. It is managing the 'forgetting curve' as well" (Prahalad 1995).

> During stable times, the mental model of a successful decision-maker and unfolding reality match. Some adjustment and fine tuning will do. Decision scenarios have little or no leverage.
>
> In times of rapid change and increased complexity, however, the manager's mental model becomes a dangerously mixed bag: rich detail and understanding can coexist with dubious assumptions, selective inattention to alternative ways of interpreting evidence, and illusory projections. In these times, the scenario approach has leverage and can make a difference.
>
> In today's world, a management microcosm shaped by the past and sustained by the usual types of forecasts is inherently suspect and inadequate. Yet it is extremely difficult for managers to break out of their worldview while operating within it. When they are committed to a certain way of framing an issue, it is difficult for them to see solutions that lie outside this framework. By presenting other ways of seeing the world, decision scenarios allow managers to break out of an one-eyed view. (Wack 1995b)

It's clear that underpinning an organization's mission statement, strategic plan, and perhaps even culture is a less tangible but pervasive sense of what is "true." Hammer calls it the "deep system," Wack the "worldview," Peter Senge the "mental model" (Senge 1990; Senge et al 1994), and Prahalad the "dominant logic." Regardless of label, what is important is that they all recognize its existence. The practice of scenario planning helps "hardwire" into the organization a healthy wariness of its deeply ingrained assumptions. In fact, scenarios exist to deliberately challenge the conventional wisdom of the organization's deep system. By institutionalizing this constant reexamination of its base assumptions, the firm is positioned for constant redesign and rebirth. The intentional reevaluation and redesign of the deep system and subsequent transition of the surface system are the hallmarks of a learning, change-ready organization and are the most desirable outcome of the practice of scenario planning.

Using Scenarios. The most prevalent way in which scenarios are used is to critically evaluate an organization's current strategy against an array of plausible futures. Amongst other things, the Royal Dutch/Shell example illustrates this application of the tool, and that of identifying strategic weaknesses. However, other applications exist. For example, scenarios can be used to identify those decisions, actions, or products that appear promising across *multiple* futures and thus appear to be the most robust of an array of strategic options. Smith and Hawken is a mail-order firm that sells high-quality gardening equipment. The founders of the firm started it with the idea of selling high-quality, high-priced garden tools. They created three scenarios for the business: a world of high economic growth, a worldwide depression, and a major social transformation marked by more holistic thinking. In each scenario, the founders identified the potential for increased interest in gardening, and a need for durable, high-quality tools (Fost 1998). Since their idea made sense across an array of possible futures, the product strategy of Smith and Hawken appeared robust to the founders of the firm. Peter Swartz is former scenario planner at Royal Dutch/Shell, current president of the Global Business Network (a leading firm in the construction of scenarios), author of the preeminent text on the subject, *The Art of the Long View,* and one of Smith and Hawken's founders. He said:

> We were preparing for a world with a very poor economy. We got a world of high wealth, and Smith and Hawken changed its strategy. We were orienting ourselves to hippies growing vegetables in a depression. Instead Reagan took office, and we altered our strategy to a premium market. Scenarios enabled us to recognize and act on the change. (Fost 1998)

While this module has focused on the use of scenarios to test existing strategies, many other nuances or techniques exist for optimizing scenarios. They include:

- Identifying "early warnings" of deviations from a base planning scenario and contingency plans for the most likely deviations. Once early warning events are identified, some organizations constantly scan the environment for signs that these events are taking place. In many ways, this is similar to the Royal Dutch/Shell experience in the early 1970s. (Wack, 1995a and b)

- Assigning teams to attack one's current strategy by assuming the role of a competitor in one of the future scenarios.

- Identifying possibilities for new products or new niche markets.

- Creating a videotape depicting a near-term future in which yet-to-be-invented company products are being used. Focus the creative energy of the workforce in a common direction by demonstrating the type of products that the organization believes will be desirable to consumers in the future. Hewlett-Packard employs this technique to great effect.

- Deciding between various strategic options. "Future mapping . . . is a way of looking at different scenarios for the future. We look at several alternative futures, or 'end states,' for our business, assign a probability to each one, and identify the forces that will determine whether a scenario will happen. The key is to select those actions with the biggest returns, the least risk, or both." (Smith 1996)

- Education. One European automaker has established a close relationship with California's Institute for the Future to develop and explore future scenarios. It also rotates a few key senior staff monthly through an outpost in Silicon Valley, simply to stay abreast of emerging developments in that hotbed of innovation. This is despite the fact that the firm has virtually no production or product development facilities in the area.

- Exploring the implications of "wild card events" such as "Toyota buys Hyundai" or "a very stringent CO_2 limit treaty is signed."

- Developing robust implementation plans for strategies already in place.

- Anticipating competitor action/reaction to new products, trends, other changes.

- Testing new strategic initiatives, current trend analysis and forecasts, and the robustness of brand images.

- Examining the relevancy of current consumer profiles or segmentation schemes.

- Exploring future competency requirements, both for the corporation and for individuals within it.

- Enhancing manager and executive training.

- Prioritizing technology investments.

- Testing the current strategic intent of the organization and its underlying deep system.

- Determining when and where to attack competitors and/or where your firm is most vulnerable.

- Determining the way the organization would prefer the future to unfold, then working to bring it about. This is not implausible given the resources of some organizations, their partners, and their stakeholders.

- Exploring demographic trends and the social changes they may engender. Demographic change is very predictable, as we know that people at age 20 today will be 30 in 10 years.

- Evaluating cohorts vis-à-vis employment needs. For example, is it entirely unexpected that the children of the 1970s and 80s insist on a work/life balance when they grew up with dual-career parents, childcare, and high rates of divorce?

- Evaluating the core competencies of the organization:

  ✓ Are current ones adequate?

  ✓ Will all of our core competencies remain relevant?

  ✓ Will some of those competencies become obsolete; will new ones be required?

  ✓ How will the organization divest itself of outdated competencies and/or acquire new ones?

These uses can be viable, value-adding endeavors for the organizations that undertake them. Remember, however, that the real value of scenario planning is not in the specific answers that come out of off-site meetings. Instead, the optimal outcome is decision makers with an expanded worldview, leaders who have thought seriously about how to manage plausible future events. Arie DeGeus, a pioneer in the use of scenarios in a corporate setting, wrote, "The real purpose of effective planning is not to make plans but to change the microcosm, the mental models that . . . decision-makers carry in their heads." (DeGeus 1988)

Scenarios institutionalize the mindset that:

- The long-term viability of the business is influenced by social, political, economic, and technological trends, not just yesterday's stock price.

- All plans are tenuous, dynamic, and unstable.

- All of us are part of the early warning system.

- We are prepared for the unpredictability of the future because we have spent time thinking about it.

- The world *will* change and thus requires at least a reexamination of strategy.

- Some responses to anticipated changes seem promising, others do not, but there is opportunity in every future.

Scenario work teaches participants to understand that their plans are held hostage by their current assumptions, and in all probability, those assumptions will not hold. They learn to *expect* to have to reevaluate the current plan. They feel comfortable with that prospect because they have already thought about what they would do in the event of some of the more plausible changes that might come along. They resist change less because they expect it, understand that it is part of the "deal," and have rehearsed ways in which they might respond to it (Swartz 1991; Wack 1995a and b). For this reason, scenario exercises should be a participative, high-involvement exercise for as many key people as possible.

Challenges in Introducing Scenarios to Your Organization.

Reflecting the "past predicts the future" mindset, many traditional planners insist on identifying which scenario is the most likely, completely missing the point of scenario work. They often see little value in testing the baseline strategy of the firm against future scenarios that seem more science fiction than probable reality. This is especially true when the output of such exercises is often limited to intense conversation, thought-provoking questions, and other intangible outcomes. Leaders of these conventional planning processes often point out that their forecasts have been, more often than not, reasonably accurate.

> And that is what makes (conventional forecasts) so dangerous. They are usually constructed on the assumption that tomorrow's world will be much like today's. They often work because the world does not always change. But sooner or later forecasts will fail when they are needed most: in anticipating major shifts in the business environment that make whole strategies obsolete. Most managers know from experience how inaccurate forecasts can be. On this point, there is probably a large consensus. (Wack 1985a)

MODULE 4

Moreover, many proponents of the traditional linear planning models reject the complexity and uncertainty of scenario planning, preferring their more "specific and predictive" forecasts. In today's environment, that's dangerous. As Peter Swartz notes: "If (organizations) want a simple answer of what will happen, and believe they can get it, we don't work with them. A great majority of companies follow a relatively simpler model. They get it wrong, and they fail" (Swartz, in Fost, 1998).

The greatest receptivity to scenarios tends to be in industries with extremely long lead times and high-risk product development cycles (big oil, pharmaceuticals) or in industries at the other extreme, with extremely short lead times and product life spans (computer hardware and software). The traditional smokestack industries generally appear to be the slowest to convert to the scenario mentality, unless threatened. When one considers the relatively ponderous nature of change in rust-belt industries, their paradigm is understandable, but dangerous nonetheless. Another reason for this resistance is that scenarios are often misused as a tool for *creating* strategy. Unless wielded by experts, scenario planning is a tool best used for testing strategies, not creating them. Bob Frish, former head of corporate strategy at Sears Roebuck and Company, notes that scenarios are commonly subverted by the natural tendency to try and predict the future. Scenario exercises often end up with the participants "feeling like they are at a casino, asking themselves how many chips to put on each method" (Fost 1998).

Many corporate planners are also uncomfortable with investing time and energy in scenario planning when the desired outcome—an expanded mental model—is intangible and unmeasurable. Given that this outcome deviates so completely from the paradigm they have developed over years of more "predictive" planning, that's understandable. That doesn't mean, however, that they are correct to dismiss scenario techniques. The traditional icons of strategic planning—reams of economic data, volume trends, market analysis, and careful examination of economic, political, and technological trends—are no longer adequate for the challenge. To them one must add creative, almost intuitive evaluations of social trends, the ability to detect and link together seemingly unrelated events, and the testing of potential strategies against plausible future scenarios (Hammer 1996).

Scenarios are essential tools in testing current strategies, identifying weak spots, and then thinking about and preparing potential responses. They can be the foundation for building a change-ready strategy and culture.

IN CONCLUSION

Debrief

HR as a function and its practitioners are at a crossroads. Firms abound to supply organizations with the transactional services that have traditionally been provided by internal HR functions. Pundits are challenging CEOs to dismantle the function, while at the same time others claim it has never been more necessary. C. K. Prahalad writes, "I believe from the work I have done in the area of strategy that the biggest underleveraged skill in a large company is in HR. The question is what you as a professional group can do to make your services more valuable to your companies" (Prahalad 1995). The irony is that this turmoil is occurring at a time when intellectual capital has become more important then ever before.

As in every such situation, there is real opportunity in this change for the savvy practitioner. Mastery of the core concepts of this chapter will position the aspiring HR practitioner to deliver considerable value to the organization by cultivating a change-ready culture. By being more intimately involved in the strategic planning process, HR can position itself to significantly help the organization by:

- Making better strategies.

- Executing those strategies once they are formulated.

Moreover, the scenario process helps make the organization change-ready. Not only have they thought about the future, they have anticipated how they might respond to it and how they might execute that response. Better strategies that can be executed: These are outcomes that any organization would prize.

Remember that these new skills can only complement a sound foundation in the fundamentals of the function. HR must deliver on the mundane to have the opportunity to aspire to new heights. Flawless processing of the annual bonus payments may not be exciting or especially noteworthy, but it builds credibility. Make no mistake, however, that being a sound administrator is enough: The time has come for HR to assert itself in new ways, some of which are described in this module. Anything less is a disservice to the organization and *especially* the people in it.

Suggested Readings

The Pace of Change and Its Impact on HR and/or the Organization

Ulrich, D. 1998. "A New Mandate for Human Resources." *Harvard Business Review* (January-February): 124–134.

The Current Perception of HR's Capabilities

Stewart, T., and Woods, W. 1996. "Taking on the Last Bureaucracy." *Fortune* (January 15).

Ulrich, D., and Eichinger, R. 1996. "SOTA96: It's De-Ja Future All Over Again." Presentation to the *Annual Meeting of the Human Resources Planning Society* (April 2).

Scenario Planning—Overview and Examples

Wack, P. 1985a. "Scenarios: Uncharted Waters Ahead." *Harvard Business Review* (September-October): 72–89.

Wack, P. 1985b. "Scenarios: Shooting the Rapids." *Harvard Business Review* (November-December): 139–150.

Swartz, P. 1991. *Art of the Long View.* New York: Currency Doubleday.

Scenario Construction and Uses—Detailed

von Reibnitz, U. (translated by Rosenthal, P. A. W.) 1988. *Scenario Techniques.* Hamburg: McGraw-Hill.

Fahey, L., and Randall, R. (eds.). 1988. *Learning from the Future: Competitive Foresight Scenarios.* New York: John Wiley and Sons.

Relevant Web Sites and Other Resources

Coates & Jarratt, Inc., Scenario construction and research on the future of issues germane to HR and many other disciplines. *cji@tmn.com,* 202-966-9307

The Futures Group, Scenario construction and strategic planning. *http://www.tfg.com,* 203-633-3501

Gemini Consulting (Bob Frish), Scenarios and strategic planning. 973-285-9009

Global Business Network (Peter Swartz, President), Construction of and education about scenarios. *http://www.gbn.org,* 510-547-6822

The Human Resources Institute, Comprehensive literature reviews, trend research, scenarios, and other data on the practice of HR. *http://hri.eckerd.edu,* 727-864-8330

The Institute for the Future (Bob Johansen), Scenarios and strategic planning. *http://www.iftf.org,* 415-854-6322

The Millenium Project (and its 1997 & 1998 State of the Future Reports), An international, multidisciplinary attempt to build global scenarios and to refine the methodology to do so. Led by the United Nations University. *http://millennium-project.org*

The Santa Fe Institute, A private, nonprofit research and education center, founded in 1984. SFI uses a multidisciplinary approach to projects to break down traditional barriers between disciplines. It focuses on emerging science. *http://www.santafe.edu/,* 505-984-8800

University of Houston at Clear Lake, Future Studies Program (including an M.S. degree in Future Studies). *http://cl.uh.edu/futureweb/*

World Future Society, An organization dedicated to the exploration and study of the future. *www.wfs.org,* 800-989-8274

Critical Thinking Questions

1. Is the pace of change today really faster than it was 50 or 100 years ago? Why or why not?

2. Do you accept the premise that HR should seek to facilitate the process of corporate strategic planning? If not, why? If so, what do HR practitioners have to offer that others do not?

3. David Ulrich argues that HR should be able to guarantee that corporate strategies will be executed. Do you agree? How can it do so?

4. If, as is asserted in this module, it is not possible to predict the future, why spend time on scenario planning?

5. Do you agree with the premise that HR has failed to meet the challenges of today's environment? If so, in what ways? If not, why?

6. How readily would the organizations you know embrace the practice of scenario planning? What could you do to overcome any resistance?

7. Do you agree that an *effective* HR activity is more necessary today than ever before? Why?

8. Discuss ways in which HR can facilitate the alignment of employee behavior with corporate strategy.

9. Is HR an "endangered species"?

10. Why is it important to challenge the worldview (or paradigm) of the managers in an organization? What role can scenarios play in that?

Student Class Assignment

In November 1997, members of the Human Resources Institute developed scenarios around "burning people-management issues." This process was led by Pam Hurley of the Royal Dutch/Shell corporate planning group. The scenario that follows, in the Appendix starting on page 4.32, is a result of this work, abridged and used with the gracious permission of the Institute.

Individually, read and analyze the scenario using the provided Consumer Lifestyle Worksheet that follows on pages 4.29 and 4.30. Identify potential people-management implications inherent in the scenario. Do this portion of the analysis individually, then do the remainder of the work with a group of your peers.

In your group:

1. Agree on the perspective from which your group will evaluate the scenario. Choose the viewpoint of the leaders of a union or corporation.

2. Complete a consensus version of the Consumer Lifestyle Worksheet for your chosen scenario. The worksheet will help your group better understand the scenario's consumer environment.

3. Discuss the people-management implications you identified individually and add any new ideas that emerge. Perform this analysis from your chosen perspective.

4. Determine what people-management action(s) your chosen organization should take. As best you can, figuratively put yourselves into the scenario and identify what you would do.

5. Identify the group dynamics that enhanced or inhibited your collaboration. In retrospect, what could the group have done to anticipate or overcome them?

6. Prepare a written paper and/or oral report to the specifications of your instructor.

MODULE
4

Consumer Lifestyle Worksheet

Imagine living in the scenario. What would be important to you and why? What would influence your purchasing decisions? Where and how do you live, work, learn, and shop? What are the political, social, economic, and technological challenges in your world? How would organizations respond to the demands of consumers like you, and what would those organizations be like? Use the matrix below to assist you in your analysis. You and/or your group may find it useful to complete one Worksheet for emerging markets and another for mature ones.

	Affluent Consumers	Middle-Income Consumers	Low-Income Consumers	The People-Management Impact on Organizations
Event #1				
Event #2				

MODULE
4

Consumer Lifestyle Worksheet—Page Two

Imagine living in the scenario. What would be important to you and why? What would influence your purchasing decisions? Where and how do you live, work, learn, and shop? What are the political, social, economic, and technological challenges in your world? How would organizations respond to the demands of consumers like you, and what would those organizations be like? Use the matrix below to assist you in your analysis. You and/or your group may find it useful to complete one Worksheet for emerging markets and another for mature ones.

	Affluent Consumers	Middle-Income Consumers	Low-Income Consumers	The People-Management Impact on Organizations
Event #3				
Event #4				

References

Bertsche, D., Crawford, C., and Macadam, S. 1996. "Is Simulation Better Than Experience?" *The McKinsey Quarterly* (Number 1): 50–57.

Conger, J. A. 1998. "The Necessary Art of Persuasion." *Harvard Business Review* (May–June).

Davis, S. M. 1987. *Future Perfect.* Reading, MA: Addison-Wesley.

De Gues, A. P. 1988. "Planning as Learning." *Harvard Business Review* (March–April): 70–74.

Fahey, L., and Randall, R. (eds) 1988. *Learning from the Future: Competitive Foresight Scenarios.* New York: John Wiley and Sons.

Fost, D. 1988. "How to Think About the Future." *American Demographics* (February): 6–9.

Hamel, G., and Prahalad, C. K. 1994. *Competing for the Future.* Cambridge, MA: Harvard Business School Press.

Human Resource Institute. 1998. *Major Issues Impacting People Management.* (March): 1-727-864-8330.

Hammer, M. 1996. *Beyond Reengineering.* New York: HarperCollins Publishers, Inc.

Handy, C. B. 1996. *Beyond Certainty: The Changing Worlds of Organizations.* Boston: Harvard Business School Press. vii, 221 p. 22 cm.

Johansen, R., and Swigart, R. 1994. *Upsizing the Individual in the Downsized Organization.* Reading, MA: Addison-Wesley.

Leemhuis, J. P. 1985. "Using Scenarios to Develop Strategies." *Long Range Planning* (2): 30–37.

Prahalad, C. K., and Hamel, G. 1990. "The Core Competence of the Corporation." *Harvard Business Review,* (May–June): v. 68, no. 3 79–93.

Quinn, J. B. 1992. *Intelligent Enterprise: A Knowledge and Service Based Paradigm for Industry.* New York: The Free Press.

Randall, D., and Wilson, R. 1996. "Building Bridges Among Diverse Scenarios." *Strategic Scenarios-Learning From the Future.* New York: John Wiley and Sons.

Senge, P., Kleiner, A., Roberts, C., Ross, R., and Smith, B. 1994. *The Fifth Discipline Fieldbook.* New York: Currency Doubleday.

Senge, P. M. 1990. *The Fifth Discipline: The Art and Practice of the Learning Organization.* New York: Currency Doubleday.

Shaw, G., Brown, R., and Bromiley, P. 1998. "Strategic Stories: How 3M is Rewriting Business Planning." *Harvard Business Review* (May–June).

Smith, R. W. 1996. "Business as War Game: A Report from the Battlefront." *Fortune* (September 30).

Stewart, T. and Woods, W. 1996. "Taking on the Last Bureaucracy." *Fortune* (January 15).

Swartz, P. 1991. *Art of the Long View.* New York: Currency Doubleday.

Tenaglia, M., and Noonan, P. 1992. "Scenario-Based Strategic Planning: A Process for Building Top Management Consensus." *Planning Review* (March–April).

Thompson, A., and Strickland, A. 1992. *Strategy Formulation and Implementation.* Burr Ridge, IL: Irwin. 218.

Ulrich, D. 1998. "A New Mandate for Human Resources." *Harvard Business Review* (January–February): 124–134.

Ulrich, D. 1995. "Shared Services: From Vogue to Value." *Human Resource Planning.*

Ulrich, D., and Eichinger, R. 1996. "SOTA96: It's De-Ja Future All Over Again." *Presentation to the Annual Meeting of the Human Resources Planning Society* (April 2).

Ulrich, D., and Lake, D. 1990. *Organizational Capability: Competing from the Inside Out.* New York: John Wiley & Sons.

von Reibnitz, U. (translated by Rosenthal, P. A. W.) 1988. *Scenario Techniques.* Hamburg: McGraw-Hill.

Wack, P. 1985a. "Scenarios: Uncharted Waters Ahead." *Harvard Business Review* (September–October): 72–89.

Wack, P. 1985b. "Scenarios: Shooting the Rapids." *Harvard Business Review* (November-December): 139–150.

Wallace, J. 1997. *Overdrive: Bill Gates and the Race to Control Cyberspace.* New York: John Wiley and Sons.

Welch, J. 1991. Quoted in "GE Keeps Those Ideas Coming," by Stewart, Thomas A. *Fortune* (August 12): 49.

Wilkinson, L. 1985. "How to Build Scenarios." *Wired* (Special Scenarios Edition): 74–81.

APPENDIX: RESULTS OF THE HRI AND ROYAL DUTCH/ SHELL HUMAN RESOURCE SCENARIO DEVELOPMENT WORKSHOP*

Held on November 20–21, 1997
Don CeSar Beach Resort and Spa
St. Pete Beach, FL, USA
December 1997
Human Resource Institute
Eckerd College
4200 54th Avenue So.
St. Petersburg, FL 33711 USA
Telephone (813) 864-8330; Fax (813) 864-1432

Developing Scenarios for HR

Participating Organization List

American Express	Ford Motor Company
Armstrong World Industries	Goodyear Tire & Rubber Co.
AVNET	Hughes Space & Communications
BellSouth Corporation	IBM
BHP Petroleum	Johnson & Johnson
Chevron Corporation	Lucent Technologies
CPC International Inc.	Metropolitan P&C
C. R. Bard Inc.	PacifiCare Health Systems
Digital Equipment Corp.	PSE&G
EMC Corporation	Texaco Inc.
Exxon Corporation	Unisys Corporation
Federal Reserve Board	

How the Scenarios Were Created

The workshop participants were divided into four groups of eight. Each group was asked to select one "burning people-management issue" to use for developing scenarios. To begin the discussion, Jay Jamrog, Executive Director of Research at HRI, presented the results from HRI's annual survey of *Major Issues Impacting People Management,* which was compiled by over 325 senior executives worldwide. The top 10 issues for managing people in the future were (1) Information technology; (2) Leadership; (3) Focus on the customer; (4) Skill level of the workforce; (5) Managing change; (6) Electronic transfer of information; (7) The information superhighway; (8) Innovation and creativity; (9) Improving productivity; and (10) Quality of technical education. After a short discussion, the following issues were selected:

- *Group A—Organizational Culture Change* with related topics including leadership transformation and global diversity. The group identified the following business challenges:

  ✓ Given that the employer/employee relationship is now more tenuous, the challenge becomes redefining that relationship.

Source: Human Resource Institute, *Major Issues Impacting People Management,* March 1998. Abridged and used with the permission of the Institute.

✓ How to sustain positive behavioral change in an increasingly demanding environment.

✓ How to expand our customer base and be socially responsible as a corporation. One way of viewing the situation is that by expanding the consumer base, the socioeconomic gap in a society will narrow. Reversing the statement—by narrowing the socioeconomic gap, you help expand the consumer base. This illustrates two goals with perhaps different priorities and approaches. As an HR challenge, the goal is to help management understand these linkages.

- *Group B—Leverage Global Talent* with major subtopics to include capabilities, partnership/alliances, and inclusion issues. The group identified the following business challenges:

✓ Global education

✓ Experience/skills

✓ Immigration patterns

✓ Political stability

✓ Mobility—matching opportunities with talent

✓ Communication infrastructures; language skills

✓ Economic stability

✓ Economic dispersion—haves/have-nots

✓ Cultural diversity

✓ Legal issues, ethics and values

✓ Education—standards and consistency

✓ Business processes

✓ Establish business relationships—partnerships/alliances

✓ Managing volatility

✓ Structural flexibility

✓ Global mindset—getting rid of ethnocentricity

✓ Competing for talent

✓ Alignment of strategies—linking globally

- *Group C—Global skills/competencies* with major subtopics to include recruitment, retention, and quality of education. This group identified the following business challenges:

✓ How to keep leadership skill sets "evolving" in organizations. How to keep leaders from becoming "cloggers" who actually impede organizational progress. How to create an atmosphere that allows managers to evolve into leaders.

✓ How to address an organization's imbalance between the skill sets (not limited to leadership skill sets) it has and the skill sets it needs. This includes two parts: identifying and assessing such imbalances. Important factors to consider include competence identification; gap analysis; the dynamic/continuing imbalance that is due to changing technologies; the time frame needed for skills development; the conflict/choice between "hiring" and "developing" the people with the right skill sets; and global imbalances in skill sets.

MODULE
4

✓ How to acquire and retain people with the required skill sets. Important factors to consider include diversity (retaining people in different population groups and whether to "make," "buy," or "lease" skill sets), specific retention methods (compensation, contracts, etc.), and the integration of divergent systems.

- *Group D—Focus on the customer* with a major subtopic including the "new social contract." The group identified the following business challenges:

✓ Identify the common value proposition. (What is our mission?)

✓ Achieve global customer intimacy.

✓ Align the workforce with customer requirements.

These "burning" people-management issues are the basis for the scenario that follows.

The "Just Do It" World in 2020

The year is 2020, and the world in which business operates is best characterized by the following:

- *Individualism*

✓ Innovative, entrepreneurial spirit

- Libertarianism

✓ Privatization of industry worldwide

✓ Power devolves

- Hypercompetition

✓ Relentless competition

- *"Empty Core"*—Describes a market with no competitive equilibrium.

✓ Undifferentiated products, free market entry

✓ Economies of scale, fixed plant capacities

✓ Plant capacity large relative to demand

✓ Demand is uncertain, cyclical, volatile

- *Dematerialization*—More is done with less, and "the sinews" of economic development are computer bits rather than atoms.

- *Bubbles of Value*—Exceptional returns arise from exploitation of market, political, and technological discontinuities, including

✓ Market (de)regulation

✓ Breakthrough technologies

✓ Emergence of new growth markets

✓ Restructuring and divestment by other players

✓ Stock market over(under)-valuation

✓ Environmental pressures

- *Blurring boundaries*

✓ Geography doesn't matter, clustering does

✓ Open regionalism/borderless world

✓ Liberalization of networks

✓ Key players are mainly not governments

✓ Political visions risk getting in the way

● *Corporate values and success factors*

✓ Creating value

—Innovation and speed

—Spotting and creating deals

—Accountability and personal reward

—Contract out non-core activities

✓ Working together

—Informal project teams, inside and outside

—Minimum hierarchy, minimum rules

—Networked with IT, distributed working systems

—Inspire via achievement, excitement, opportunity for development

✓ Relationship with society

—Highly responsive to customers and shareholders

—Aware of "outrage"

—Network/dialogue with pressure groups

—First rate lawyers

Group A—"Just Do It" Scenario
Issue: Organizational Culture Change

Event #1—Decision to exploit the Chinese market: The year is 2020 and senior management has decided to more fully exploit the huge market in mainland China. Ten years ago, our company's share of that market was less than 1% and we initiated a strategy to invest nearly 25% of our development funds in this emerging market. Unfortunately, we have yet to receive a decent return from this investment. Indeed, over the past 10 years, while China was slowly opening its markets, our firm's share of the Chinese market increased just 4 percentage points.

In the past, the political environment in China has been confusing and full of contradictions. The central government has been stable, with very little turnover of key figures. But, they tend to be very conservative, often pushing for various forms of isolation and/or market protection using the argument that open markets are destroying the Chinese culture. On the other hand, as you get farther away from the central government, the political environment seems to become unstable. Although the government leaders are younger and eager to embrace foreign investment, they also must struggle with growing social unrest as the gap between the haves and have-nots widens. Over the past three years, this situation has escalated as gangs of have-nots have resorted to terrorism and, on a couple of occasions, specifically targeted foreign companies for bombings and kidnappings. At times, this conflicting political environment has caused the Chinese economy to nearly collapse. In addition, a recent series of natural disasters and a growing AIDS crisis in China have hurt their economic growth. It is also important to note that in 2010, China officially ended its one-child policy, although in the countryside people have been ignoring it for years.

Group B—"Just Do It" Scenario
Issue: Leveraging Global Talent

Event #2—Unrestricted Immigration/Mobility. The business world in 2020 is becoming more and more difficult to manage, especially for human resource professionals. Over the past 20 years, the boundaries between countries and regions have been slowly disappearing. In 2015, this trend led to a major trade agreement between the 26 industrial nations to eliminate restrictions to immigration. The very next year, the General Assembly of the United Nations embraced this development and passed a resolution to not only eliminate immigration barriers, but also to develop strategies to increase the mobility of workers around the world, with priority being given to skilled labor. However, while governments agreed to no longer restrict the movement of labor, they also agreed to create common employment standards that would apply to all employers worldwide to ensure fair and equitable treatment of workers. There are rumors that pressure groups want the UN to set up a governing board that would hold companies accountable for common employment standards.

The major driving force behind this development has been the rapid advancement in technology. At first, technology made it easier to relocate facilities anywhere in the world. During the early part of the twenty-first century, the Internet made it possible for our shoe factory to search through the whole world for workers who would give us the highest productivity and quality for the lowest wage. In addition, the Internet made communications with distant factories much easier. As a result, we set up plants in emerging countries like China, San Salvador, and India, giving extra pay and benefits, until another emerging nation offered a more attractive environment for relocation. This strategy became very popular and very successful for more and more companies, but it was very disruptive to local economies. The strain of firms constantly moving into an area one year and moving out the next became too much for their governments to handle. In theory, however, unrestricted mobility of workers will eventually stabilize labor cost worldwide, and there will be little or no advantage to moving facilities to a new location.

The technology used to advance the manufacture of shoes also has changed. While the factory still needs humans, newer technology requires fewer low-skilled laborers and more highly skilled technicians. With the demand for skilled workers far outreaching the local supply, we were forced to alter our strategy. We still would search the world for highly productive, low-wage workers, but we also needed to consider the availability of highly skilled technicians. Again, in theory, the new unrestricted immigration policy should make it easier to source scarce talent worldwide.

Group C—"Just Do It" Scenario
Issue: Competencies

Event #3—A Global Economy. During the first two decades of the twenty-first century, the world has been slowly moving toward a truly global economy. By 2020, trade barriers have been eliminated and there is a single global market with one global currency. The customer base also has become more global with the Internet serving as the primary marketing system for most goods and services. Most customers around the world are aware that there is a severe scarcity of natural resources. As a result, there has been much greater emphasis placed on creating products that can be recycled and that are environmentally safe, and there has been a proliferation of new technologies that enable communities and societies to do more with less.

During the past ten years, most government services have been privatized or pushed down to the local level. Indeed, one of the principal functions of the central government has been to set minimum standards to protect individuals and to aggregate and provide economic and labor force data. Many of the most important government decisions now are being made at the local level, since they are best able to adapt to a faster-changing world. The judicial branch is the one government institution to become more powerful, with some arguing it has swung too far toward protecting the individual. The court system seems to be overwhelmed with settling social conflicts and contract disputes among individuals and large organizations.

There is a global pool of workers from which businesses can easily select qualified people via the Internet. There are more and more "virtual employees" in the sense that qualified people step into a company on an as-needed basis and then leave after a specific project is completed. Such workers—many of whom are professionals and knowledge workers—are contingent workers, and most perform much of their work via electronic media rather than by moving to a specific geographic location.

Increasingly, education is more competency based, and schools are becoming virtual learning organizations, with much education occurring via the Internet. To the degree that traditional schools still exist, they are "privatized," financed with a voucher system. In 2015, the UN adopted international education standards to facilitate people moving into or out of jobs quickly and efficiently.

Unfortunately, there is not much interest in providing quality education to everyone; people are on their own in terms of finding the right education, and many are not able to afford the best-quality education, resulting in a "Education Have" and "Education Have-not" population.

Group D—"Just Do It" Scenario
Issue: Focus on the Customer

Event #4—The Virtual Mall.   In the twenty-first century, shopping on the Internet has become very popular, despite many problems. Today, there are limitless bandwidths, with very secure methods for transactions. On August 22, 2020, our chairman, CEO, and founder, Galactic Gates, announced that the company has developed a revolutionary new software program that will turn the Internet into the ultimate Virtual Mall. This mall is the product of more than five years of planning, programming, and negotiations that have resulted in over 70,000 joint ventures with vendors from all corners of the world. This couch-based shopping system has eliminated the need to go out to purchase goods anymore. Customers have products available from the entire world at their fingertips. No one is limited to the display of goods on hand at a single source. "Hours of operation" do not exist anymore. People can shop from their homes or offices. Consumers also are able to design the products that they want. If they need assistance, virtual salespeople will come through the device (television, PC terminal, whatever) to demonstrate their virtual products. In a clothing store, you are able to enter in your size requirements and a virtual model shows you how it will look or makes fashion comments if you want.

With over 70,000 vendors in the mall, name-brand recognition will be very difficult. Yet our research shows that consumers who buy regularly on the Internet want the assurances of name-brand quality, since they are buying without opportunity to personally inspect. Consumers tend to use the Internet to shop for goods that they already have in mind. As a result, there is less opportunity to expose them to new goods. Companies find that they are focusing too much on selling the customers what they want and they are not investing enough in breakthrough thinking and in developing innovative goods and services for their customers. How do we create customers' needs in this environment?

In addition, customer demands and expectations have been escalating in recent years. They have preconceived ideas of what they want and how much it should cost, and then they go to the Internet and search for the desired product. Customers expect price competitiveness as a given. Significantly, we see evidence of a growing desire to return to face-to-face transactions and personal services. Customers long for a sense of village. How do we achieve a sense of intimacy with customers in the virtual mall?

MODULE
4

The growing need for privacy has become a major block to marketing efforts. Customers want to control the access of sellers to them. They want to be able to decide when and if to shop, and how to keep unwanted sales calls away. Indeed, Internet customers tend to assume multiple levels of identity. People do not want to divulge everything about themselves to every vendor they contact on the Internet. They want to be able to control this. How do we understand/anticipate our customers' needs and capture and measure customer satisfaction in this environment?

MODULE
4

Index

Ability to adapt, 4.9
Administrative efficiency, 4.12
Aligning individual and corporate objectives, 4.8, 4.11, 4.13
Altered mental model, 4.20
Alternative futures (plausible), 4.19, 4.21, 4.22, 4.23, 4.24
Anticipating competitor action/reaction, 4.23

Barriers to partnership, 4.10
Base assumptions, 4.22, 4.25
Beyond Reengineering, Michael Hammer, 4.22
Business environment, 4.9, 4.18, 4.21

Certainty of uncertain future, 4.18
Championing employees, 4.12
Change management, 4.11
Change-conscious organization, 4.7
Change-intensive environment, 4.5, 4.6, 4.7, 4.17
Change-readiness, 4.4, 4.8, 4.18, 4.21, 4.26
Competitive advantage, 4.5, 4.7, 4.20
Constancy of change, 4.6, 4.7, 4.17
Contingency plans, 4.23
Conventional wisdom of organizations, 4.5, 4.19, 4.22
Core competencies, 4.24
Corporate strategy, 4.5, 4.11
Creativity, 4.7, 4.11
Culture change, organizational, 4.4, 4.8, 4.10, 4.18, 4.26, 4.32, 4.35
Culture management, 4.11

Deep systems, 4.22

Economic environment, 4.6, 4.36
Effective at persuasion, 4.19
Employee selection, 4.12
Empowerment, promoting, 4.11
Ethical standards, 4.13
Executive development, 4.11

Facilitating, strategic planning, 4.14
Fairlane Commitment, 4.8, 4.9
Focus, common direction, 4.23, 4.34, 4.37
Forecasting, classical planning, 4.17, 4.18, 4.19, 4.24, 4.25
Formulate corporate strategy, 4.14
Formulation, strategic plan, 4.13
Functional specialists, 4.11
Future planning (mapping), 4.18, 4.23

Global competitiveness, 4.8–9, 4.36
Global skills/competencies, 4.33–34

Group dynamics, 4.14, 4.17
Group facilitation, 4.14

High performance, 4.13
High-involvement exercise, 4.25
HR function, 4.5, 4.12, 4.13, 4.14, 4.26
HR professional (practitioner), 4.4, 4.8, 4.10, 4.11, 4.13–14, 4.26
HR's emerging role, 4.5, 4.8, 4.10, 4.12
Human behavior expertise, 4.14
Human resource systems, 4.14
Human Resources Institute (HRI), 4.8, 4.10, 4.32

Identifying strategic weaknesses, 4.22
Implementing strategic plan, 4.14
Information Age. *See* Knowledge Age
Innovation, 4.7, 4.8, 4.11, 4.23
Institutionalizing change, 4.7, 4.24
Intellectual capital, 4.5, 4.7, 4.11, 4.26

Knowledge Age, 4.10, 4.11, 4.18

Leveraging advantages, 4.7, 4.33

Major Issues Impacting People Management, HRI, 4.8, 4.32
Managerial discretion, 4.4
Managing change, core concepts, 4.5, 4.11
Mental model, 4.20, 4.21, 4.22, 4.24, 4.25
Multiple futures. *See* Alternative futures

Need to manage change, 4.6
New economy (environment), 4.6, 4.20
New HR paradigm, 4.5, 4.11, 4.12

Obsolete worldview, 4.10
Openness to change. *See* Receptivity
Operational effectiveness, 4.11
Organizational change-readiness, 4.4, 4.5, 4.21
Organizational learning, 4.14
Organizational objectives, and HR function, 4.5
Outdated paradigm, 4.7, 4.10
Outmoded skill sets, 4.20

Pace of change, 4.5, 4.6, 4.7, 4.18
Partnership model, 4.10, 4.11
People-focused function, 4.11
People-management issues, 4.34
Pervasive culture, 4.22
Physical capital, 4.5, 4.7
Planning for growth, 4.10
Policy deployment, 4.13
Predicting change, 4.7, 4.21

MODULE
4

Predictive planning, 4.25
Primary priority, 4.11
Principles of system thinking, 4.14
Privacy, need for, 4.38
Product obsolescence, 4.7–8

Receptivity to change, 4.8, 4.17
Resistance to scenario planning, 4.25
Results orientation, 4.13
Rewards and incentives, 4.13, 4.14
Risk-taking environment, 4.14
Robust implementation plans, 4.23

Scenario planning approach, 4.4, 4.8, 4.11,
    4.15, 4.17, 4.18, 4.19, 4.20–21, 4.22, 4.24,
    4.25, 4.26
Shared values, 4.13
Shared vision, 4.20
Socially responsible, 4.33
Standard of duty, 4.17
Status quo, departure from, 4.6, 4.12
Story-like formats, 4.19
Strategic intent, 4.5, 4.12, 4.13
Strategic miscalculation, 4.6
Strategic planning, 4.4, 4.11, 4.13, 4.14,
    4.15–16, 4.19, 4.22
        through storytelling, 4.19

Strategy execution, 4.12, 4.13
Strategy Formulation and Implementation,
    Thompson and Strickland, 4.12
Strategy-critical capabilities, 4.13
Surface systems, 4.22

Technological advances, 4.7, 4.17, 4.36
The Art of the Long View, Peter Swartz, 4.23
Traditional (HR) role, 4.10, 4.11, 4.13
Traditional planning, 4.17
Transactional aspects, 4.11, 4.12
Transformational aspect, 4.6, 4.11
Trend analysis, 4.18, 4.24

Unpredictability of the future, 4.19

Value system, 4.8
Virtual Mall, 4.37

Wild card events, 4.23
Work environment, 4.13
Work/life balance, 4.24
Worldview, organizational, 4.5, 4.17, 4.20,
    4.21, 4.22, 4.24

MANAGING HUMAN RESOURCES IN THE 21st CENTURY

From Core Concepts to Strategic Choice

MODULE 5

Mergers and Human Resources

Susan K. Graaff
INTEGRATED CHANGEWARE SYSTEMS, INC.

William N. Case
INTEGRATED CHANGEWARE SYSTEMS, INC.

Managing Human Resources in the 21st Century: From Core Concepts to Strategic Choice,
by Kossek and Block

Publisher: Dave Shaut
Executive Editor: John Szilagyi
Developmental Editor: Bryant Editorial Development
Marketing Manager: Joseph A. Sabatino
Production Editor: Tamborah E. Moore
Manufacturing Coordinator: Dana Began Schwartz
Cover Design: Tin Box Studio
Cover Photographs: Copyright Shoji Sato/Photonica
Production House: The Left Coast Group, Inc.
Printer: West Group

Printed in the United States of America
1 2 3 4 5 02 01 00 99

For more information contact South-Western College Publishing, 5101 Madison Road, Cincinnati, Ohio, 45227 or find us on the Internet at *http://www.swcollege.com*
For permission to use material from this text or product, contact us by
- telephone: 1-800-730-2214
- fax: 1-800-730-2215
- web: *http://www.thomsonrights.com*

ISBN: 0–324–01802–9

This book is printed on acid-free paper.

Contents

MODULE OVERVIEW 5.4

OBJECTIVES 5.4

RELATION TO THE FRAME 5.4

CORE CONCEPTS IN MERGERS AND ACQUISITIONS 5.5

Key Distinctions between Mergers and Acquisitions 5.5

Mergers and Acquisitions: A Brief History 5.6

Relevant Legislation 5.7

General Categories of Mergers and Acquisitions 5.7

Characteristics of Merger and Acquisition Types 5.8

After the Financial and Legal Hurdles:
The Integration of Multiple Organizations 5.9

The Role of the Human Resource Professional 5.10

Critical Tasks in Integrating Organizations 5.11

STRATEGIC ISSUES IN MERGERS AND ACQUISITIONS 5.12

The Process of Integration 5.12

Predictable Dynamics of Mergers and Acquisitions 5.12

APPLICATION 5.13

Failure Case Study: Great Southern Railroad 5.14

Task Force Integration Examples 5.15

Success Case Study: Star-Excel Building Corporation 5.17

IN CONCLUSION 5.18

Debrief 5.18

Suggested Readings 5.19

Critical Thinking Questions 5.19

Exercises 5.19

APPENDIX 5.20

Task Force Integration Application Case Forms 5.20

INDEX 5.24

MODULE OVERVIEW

This module is intended to link the strategies and outcomes of mergers and acquisitions with the human resource management (HRM) function to show the impact on that function and the areas in which HRM plays the most critical leadership and support role. The following quote will set the tone for our discussions:

> When you define the Human Resource function's critical responsibility as being the technical expert for consulting to management on ways to achieve the highest performance of the workforce, then the Human Resource professional must care about the dramatic impact on productivity of a merger or acquisition. Human Resources must advise management on how to mitigate the productivity drop and how to speed up the return to high performance. Loss of productivity comes from people focusing on their own issues relative to retention; integration into the new company; clarity of where they fit, what they will be doing, who they will be working for, and how they will be expected to perform; how their career track will be affected; and if they can retain their compensation and benefits. Many business managers view a merger as a strategic business initiative involving primarily legal or financial considerations. And while these are critical to "make the deal," what will actually make the newly combined organization operate successfully is the people. Human Resources must understand how to gather, interpret and act on information from the total workforce and how to counsel management on keeping their employees connected and committed through the period of change. The most important service a human resource professional can provide is making sure all relevant human resource related questions have been asked, and related decisions thoroughly thought through. The premier theme to remember is that the work begins before the deal is completed and continues long after the merger structure is established. (Jeffrey D. Gard, Director, Human Resources, Millipore Corporation, Microelectronics Division, Bedford, MA)

MODULE
5

OBJECTIVES

1. Describe what mergers and acquisitions are and the distinctions between types

2. Analyze the background of mergers and acquisitions—what they are and why they occur

3. Discuss the role human resources plays in the integration of multiple organizations in mergers and acquisitions

4. Explore the key issues of mergers and acquisitions within the context of the whole organization

5. Use case studies to look at merger and acquisition interventions that have the highest probability of impact on human resources

RELATION TO THE FRAME

The HR function generally plays all four roles in a merger and acquisition process. The *transaction* role may be as simple, but nonetheless important—as assuring that record-keeping systems for payroll and benefits are consistent across all sectors of the newly merged organization. In its *translation* role, HR assures that employees in the new organization are aware of the changes that will occur as the merger or acquisition unfolds throughout the organization. In addition to this communication role, HR may be called upon to support corporate management by providing advice that facilitates the desired *transition* from two separate organizations to one new organization. Finally, in its *transformation* role, HR may be involved in the actual merger negotiations as it advises corporate management on the employment-relations implications of and barriers to a successful merger.

FIGURE 5.1 *A Frame for Understanding Human Resource Strategy:*
Context, Roles, and Constraints

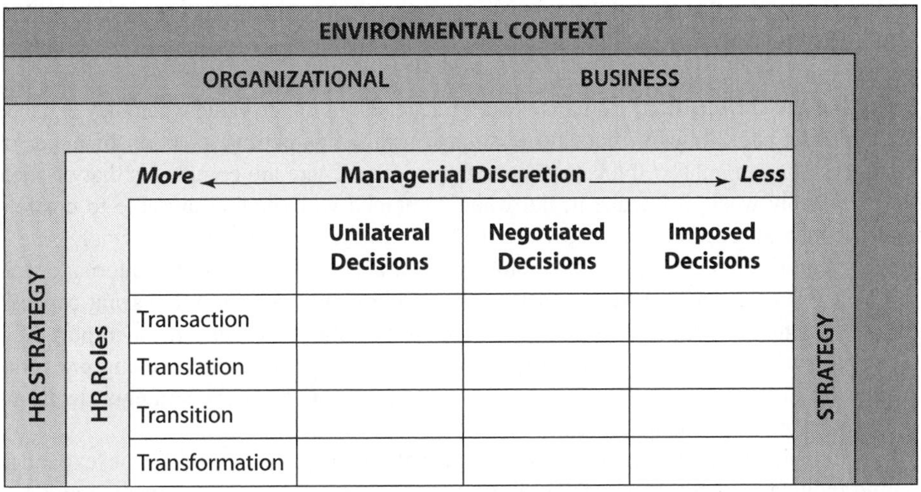

ENVIRONMENTAL CONTEXT			
ORGANIZATIONAL		BUSINESS	

HR STRATEGY	HR Roles	More ← Managerial Discretion → Less			STRATEGY
			Unilateral Decisions	Negotiated Decisions	Imposed Decisions
		Transaction			
		Translation			
		Transition			
		Transformation			

© 2000 by Ellen Ernst Kossek and Richard Block. Thanks to Brian Pentland, Karen Markel, and John Beck for helpful comments and discussions that enhanced the model.

As for the discretionary aspects allowed management in the merger process, in general management has a great deal of discretion about how it wants to implement a merger. Thus, most of its HR decisions during a merger are likely to be unilateral. However, if the "new" firm is acquiring unionized facilities, some decisions may require negotiation with a labor organization. For example, many airlines that merge often have long and complicated negotiations with the unions representing pilots and flight attendants because under collective agreements, choice of routes and domicile is usually determined by seniority (length of service) with a single airline. If two airlines merge, how is seniority measured? Finally, some HR decisions may be imposed during a merger—such as how the pension plans of the two companies will be merged, because pensions are regulated by law. Of course, unilateral decisions may also be constrained by law, to prevent discrimination on the basis of such characteristics as race, gender, and age. Figure 5.1 depicts the various ways that HRM can play an important role in the blending of two organizations.

MODULE
5

Core Concepts in Mergers and Acquisitions

Key Distinctions between Mergers and Acquisitions

What Is a Merger?   A merger occurs when one company is combined with and totally absorbs another. The only way to determine if a merger has occurred is by examining the documents required to be filed and recorded. Operations, facilities, and functions are rationalized and combined for maximum efficiency. The cultural beliefs, norms, and infrastructures of the acquired organization generally defer to the acquiring culture for integration purposes.

What Is an Acquisition?   Acquisition is the process used to transfer stocks or assets from one company to another (from seller to buyer). The process of acquisition can take place as a purchase of stock, a purchase of assets, or a merger.

What Is the Difference?   Acquisition is a generic term used to communicate the transfer of ownership. A merger may or may not be a part of an acquisition. You can do an acquisition *followed by a merger* or *by means of a merger,* or you can do an acquisition *in which no merger occurs.* In the language of business there is usually little or no distinction made about the way in which transfer of ownership is going to occur. Generally all such activity, whether technically an acquisition or a merger, is simply referred to as a merger.

Why Merge or Acquire?   Fundamentally, acquisitions create value when they enhance the strategic capabilities of both firms, improving the competitive position of either or both, resulting in improved financial operating results. There are companies that on their own probably would not make it, but when combined with another are able to create a much better set of products or services than could have been offered otherwise.

Acquisitions can help renew a company's market position faster than internal development strategies and can realize benefits from combining assets and sharing capabilities not achievable through joint ventures or partnerships. Possibly most importantly, acquisitions provide a way to bring in new capabilities and leverage existing ones that would be difficult without the synergy of an acquisition. They are strategic decisions that shore up or change a company's direction.

Considerations of ways that the organization's capabilities might be expanded could include operational benefits such as improvement of marketing coverage and distribution networks, expansion of product line, economies of scale, increased purchasing power, cost reductions, maximum utilization of physical and human resources, acquisition of specific talents or skills, or augmentation of management practices. Considerations might also include nonoperational benefits such as the ability to raise capital, improvement in innovative thinking, or lowered taxes.

Hard data on merger and acquisition success rates is difficult to come by. One reason is that the Federal Trade Commission (FTC) indicates that approximately 60 percent of merger activity is never publicized or takes place in a series of small transactions that are not tracked formally.

What seems to be consistent in merger and acquisition studies is the fact that 75 percent of these occurrences fail to meet the expectations for benefit or are outright failures; that the organization often experiences a 50 percent dropoff in productivity in the first 4–8 months of the integration; that 47 percent of senior executives in the acquired firm leave within the first year; and that 75 percent of senior executives leave within the next three years. The failure rate could potentially be attributed to changes in the economic environment, the inaccurate calculation of benefit, or a mismatch of product or culture. The majority, however, can be traced to unskilled, unprepared, or uncommitted management and the resulting "people problems." Even with proper calculations, a healthy economic environment, and a good match of product and culture, poor management can cause the integration effort to fail through the inability to capitalize on the human resources of the two organizations.

Mergers and Acquisitions: A Brief History

Prior to the 1980s, acquisitions came in distinct cycles or waves. In the 1990s, however, they became a consistent tool by which firms renewed their competitive positions and restructured for efficiency.

In 1989, acquisition transactions were in excess of $1 billion. In the first ten months of 1997, they produced $698 billion in domestic deals. Half of those $698 billion in deals were stock for stock, the highest percentage ever. By 1998, the value of mergers and acquisitions had topped $1 trillion in the United States alone. This record-setting volume reflects changes in government regulation, technological evolution, and forces for globalization. The market is demanding 10–20 percent growth, and mergers are the logical choice to get that bottom-line expansion. To find a similar period of economic change and merger activity, you would need to go all the way back to the 1890s. The late 1800s witnessed waves of consolidations spurred by changes in the

FIGURE 5.2   *Number of Mergers per Billion Dollars of Real GNP*

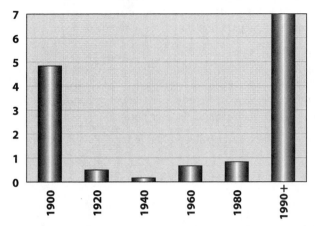

regulatory structures and an increasingly volatile business environment. Out of that activity arose such companies as Standard Oil and American Tobacco, examples of the vertically integrated "modern" corporation. Figure 5.2 traces the increasing number of mergers across the twentieth century.

Merger activity will remain a viable way to grow a business. As long as there is a rising stock market, low interest rates, a liberal regulatory environment, and a healthy economy, intense merger activity can be expected to continue.

Relevant Legislation

In acquisitions and mergers, firms must comply with regulatory barriers and governing laws such as the Hart-Scott-Rodino Antitrust Improvements Act of 1976. Hart-Scott-Rodino requires that information be supplied to the U.S. Department of Justice and the FTC prior to completion of the merger.

Hart-Scott-Rodino covers any transaction with a prescribed minimum in gross assets or annual sales; where the acquiring company will own more than $15 million of the acquired voting securities of a company with annual sales or gross assets of $25 million or more; or where one of the companies involved is engaged in U.S. commerce or activity affecting U.S. commerce. The parties considering a merger or acquisition are required to provide a description of the companies, current financial information, and a breakdown of all revenues.

Competitive considerations as viewed by legislation might include vertical acquisitions of suppliers or customers that could foreclose markets to competitors, horizontal acquisitions between competitors that may result in monopoly power or cause over-concentration of the market, and conglomerate acquisitions between firms in different fields that may remove potential competitors.

General Categories of Mergers and Acquisitions

Mergers fall into four general categories: rescue, partnership, adversarial, and hostile takeover:

- A *rescue* is the response to a raid that has been initiated by another firm or a financial bailout by another firm. The acquiring organization is viewed in a generally positive light by the acquired organization. It might not be what the company would choose, but it is the best of what is available.

- The majority of mergers and acquisitions fall into the *partnership* category, where both parties actively desire the combination of the two organizations.

MODULE
5

- In the *adversarial* situation, only one firm has a strong interest in the deal or the two parties want very different kinds of deals. This type of merger may develop when there are multiple hunters in the pack and the stakes continue to be increased for the desired company.

- The *hostile takeover* is the most intense of the merger types, with the maximum of resistance in both of the organizations. The acquisition target actively resists being taken over by the other company or investor. The target generally feels it is better off operating as it is than as a part of another entity.

Each category carries its own characteristics, as described in the following sections.

Characteristics of Merger and Acquisition Types

Rescue

- Major weaknesses in operations or management

- Top management generally requested to leave

- Requires tremendous attention by acquiring firm to keep employees focused and on board

- Cooperation tends to be high between companies

- Data gathering and auditing often rushed, requiring more energy to integrate once deal is complete

- Significant issues often not dealt with during negotiations, requiring compromises later on

- Management doesn't have to sell the benefits of the deal

Partnership

- Surprises or heavy-handed tactics are rare

- Goodwill and respect prevail

- Top management is positive about the deal, but often forgets to sell the benefit to the employees

- Once the financial deal is closed, management often forgets to attend to the integration details

- Communication plays a significant part in the organization's acceptance of the deal

- Management packages and agreements to keep key talent is critical

Adversarial

- Negotiations become aggressive, resistance extreme

- "Us versus them" atmosphere prevails

- Win-win is possible if both parties work at it

- High probability acquired management can come out as heroes through their cooperation

- Employee job security issues intensify as the ambiguity of negotiations continues

- Talk of consolidations, layoffs, and closures surface

- Productivity may drop and resistance rise significantly prior to actual closure of the deal

Hostile Takeover

- Communication often can't overcome the rumor mill

- Common practice is for target company to generate animosity toward the raider, leaving substantial residue of ill will once the deal is completed

- There is a strong win-lose atmosphere

- Talent leaves first in this type of merger, leaving critical gaps in the ability to manage the integration and reassure remaining employees

- Resisted takeovers are most likely to experience human resource failures

After the Financial and Legal Hurdles: The Integration of Multiple Organizations

Acquisition decisions are not made without considerable care and expenditure of resources. Even when the acquisition opportunity is solid, the synergies are realized only in a successful integration. Value is created when capabilities are transferred or combined and people from both organizations collaborate on expected and unanticipated benefits. Success depends heavily on the commitment of managers from both sides to work together toward the new strategy and the required new interactions. In addition to considering and valuing a complex acquisition, management must develop a common view of the expected synergies and costs. Leadership must provide a vision for the combined entity to bond to and form energy around.

The approaches to the integration can be seen as an *assimilation* where the two organizations become one; as a type of *protectorate* that protects the cultural identity of the acquired organization; or as an *adaptation* that envisions separate entities that adapt to one another.

In an *assimilation,* a high degree of interdependence is needed in order to create the desired value, combined with a low need for autonomy to achieve the interdependence. The biggest reason to merge in this manner is to realize the synergies of the people skills. Technology and product gains are important as well, but in the end the technology is operated by people and the product is sold by people. Management seldom has an appreciation for the magnitude of the challenge and impact of integrating multiple organizational cultures, rituals, and practices. Even when attention is paid to forging a new and singular identity, most people continue to identify with the old company and remain loyal to their original products and services. Particularly where the objective is to blend multiple organizations, the sheer weight of the activity will challenge the human resource professional to understand the integration needs and anticipate methods to implement that need.

In a *protectorate,* there is a high need for autonomy with low need for interdependence among the firms involved. Even when the cultures are to remain the same and there is no requirement to help people understand and work within new policies, procedures, and philosophies of work, it is still little different than hiring a whole new workforce, including orientation, expectation setting, signing up and administering compensation and benefit packages, and waiting through learning curves.

In an *adaptation,* there is a high need for interdependence because of the amount of capability transfer required coupled with high need for autonomy because the acquired capability must be preserved in an organizational context. This approach does not require the level of energy necessary in the other two in integrating the administrative aspects of the workforce, but it requires an equal level of energy in understanding how each organization has worked in the past and how that translates across the boundaries as they plan and coordinate their work in the future. Human resource professionals, as an example, must help their management understand whether the organizations are achievement oriented or affiliation oriented in order to plan effectively the coordinating activities desired.

The actual integration process determines the ultimate success of the merger. Value is not created until the two entities come together and begin to interact around strategic and operational issues. Managers reported being least comfortable in this phase of acquisition activity. Dealing with the numbers in the decision making and due diligence phases was a recognizable activity for them. Facing the issues that arise from human resource interactions was often unfamiliar territory and uncomfortable due to its lack of specificity and predictability.

The Role of the Human Resource Professional

Human Resources must focus on the fact that it is their role, by definition of their title, to be involved in any process that causes the organization to effectively manage its people. The strategic human resource professional will view the role and take responsibility in a macro sense for the strategy of the organization and how the capabilities of the organization best fulfill that strategy. The administrative human resource or personnel practitioner looks at the micro segments of the profession such as policy, compensation and benefit administration or training, and implements them as programs once they have been directed to do so. The strategic HR professional can direct the organization in understanding both destination clarity and role clarity in times of change such as merger integrations. They can represent the due diligence of the people and cultures to ensure it isn't just a numbers exercise, create a catalyst that will cause people to join together in effective ways, tell people where they will play, and provide a deliberate, well planned strategy to accelerate populating the organization against the new structures. The point of a merger integration is to populate the organization with the fewest number of great, well-paid players possible. The strategic HR professional can also influence the structure of the language and the approach that will be used to integrate multiple companies if they are viewed as partners by the top executives of their organization. To be recognized as a partner, HR must learn to talk and think in strategic business and operational terms as well as cultural and people terms. (James B. Alleman, Vice President Human Resources, Global Industrial Technologies, Inc., Dallas)

Having considered the variables that can add value to the merger and result in sufficient synergy to make the deal worthwhile, management often forgets some of the key costs that occur during the merging process. The visible costs (profitability, assets, stocks, deal price, customer and vendor base, facilities) are ones that managers would normally deal with in the course of business, so they are generally considered during the deliberations. The hidden costs (cost of FTC compliance, replacement of key talent, productivity drop-off, loss of competitive position, customer attrition due to uncertainties about the deal, power struggles, staffing decisions, cultural differences) are often overlooked or underappreciated for the magnitude of their impact on the deal itself and on the integration process. One of the most significant of the hidden costs is related to people. As much as 80–95 percent of the cost of a deal can often be attributed directly to the base wages of the employees involved. If they view themselves as strategic partners with the organization, human resources can play a key role in the success of the integration by conveying the value of employees. In those areas where there are opportunities to become a high-performing organization through people, human resources can lead the way in understanding the capacity of the workforce, how they serve the strategic intent of the merger, where the key talent resides and how to best retain that capability, the level and type of risk involved in failing to retain critical capability, and what types of performance incentives will ensure that the right resources remain. HR professionals who view themselves as strategic partners will raise the compelling business issues linked to people, will quantify that value in operational and financial terms, and will clearly understand how the capacity and capability of the workforce impacts the process and outcomes. On the other hand, HR professionals who view themselves as the administrative arm of the organization will generally focus on the policies, systems, and programs that must be modified or implemented as part of the merger activity passed on to them from the leadership.

Critical Tasks in Integrating Organizations

Table 5.1 shows the organizational leadership tasks and human resource tasks that are critical in the process of integrating two organizations.

TABLE 5.1 *Critical Tasks in Integrating Organizations*

Critical Organizational Leadership Tasks	Critical Human Resource Tasks
Establish key management for the transition and later for the new operating business structure; address ambiguities in power and authority.	Integrate policies and programs from both organizations. Define and add functions that are needed such as risk management.
Instill a sense of meaning for the changes.	Recognize customs, symbols, language, and ceremonies needed to help the cultures assimilate.
Assess the situation and establish direction; determine degree of strategic alignment; recognize concurrent pressures.	Design performance and reward systems.
Assimilate the capabilities from the acquired organization; determine depth of management talent; assess business performance.	Process retention, compensation, and benefits packages using creative and humane methods.
Communicate the vision and establish a common language for talking about the future.	Vary communication types and increase frequency. Create strategies to communicate quickly the important information about the integration and systems to process the information.
Establish credibility of the leaders and the process.	Identify key talents and expertise.
Protect shareholders' interests.	Educate organization on predictable dynamics of the process as well as business issues and practices, strategic plans, and job changes.
Communicate with the marketplace.	Advise top managers on the potential issues and tactics needed.
Determine level of integration desired and relative dominance in the market. Provide liaison, project manager for third-party consulting assistance.	Advise leaders on the state of the organization's resources relative to resistance, cooperation, need for communication, etc.
Recognize the collaboration or hostility quotient.	Act as truth teller, coordinator, administrator, counselor, and coach for the leaders and the organization.

STRATEGIC ISSUES IN MERGERS AND ACQUISITIONS

The Process of Integration

The faster the integration is completed, the greater the chances of its ultimate vitality and success. The basic phases of an integration that need to be recognized and planned through include due diligence, organize, mobilize, implement, and perform.

- The *due diligence* process includes the quantification of the risks, assessment of the operational and cultural assets, and the contribution potential of the existing workforce.

- In the *organize* phase, the leadership must be educated relative to the predictable human dynamics and emotions of change events such as mergers and acquisitions, an interim infrastructure must be determined to guide the ongoing business while the integration is being planned, and retention plans must be defined.

- In the *mobilize* phase, generally a human resource task force is designated, along with other functional task forces, to identify success measures, rationalize operational issues, assess the available workforce, identify synergies, launch communication campaigns, and plan the integration details.

- As the organization moves to the *implement* phase, it begins to prioritize the critical integration activities and define the means by which the synergies will be realized.

- At this point, the *perform* phase activates the integration plans by installing the new operating structure for the combined companies, initiating the detailed integration plans completed by the task forces, establishing the new performance and management feedback systems, and introducing organizationwide skills training.

While much of the work of planning for the integration of multiple companies can be formalized and standardized by the use of planning tools, there are distinct human experiences that sideline the best efforts of managers to be scientific and analytic about the process. The human condition provides an infinite variety of interesting reactions to change. Fortunately, there are some predictable dynamics that occur in all groups undergoing upheaval in their environment that the strategic human resource professional can utilize to educate the organization about what it is going to experience in an integration.

Predictable Dynamics of Mergers and Acquisitions

A merger or acquisition may be associated with an increase in uncertainty causing communications to deteriorate. People lose touch with each other and with the overall purpose of the business. Productivity may drop, and people and processes lose momentum. There is a decline in trust. Cooperation suffers and people begin to focus internally, losing sight of the competition and the customers. Turf wars and power struggles surface for perceived scarce resources and to position within the new organization. Self-preservation surfaces. Morale falls, and people feel less commitment and satisfaction with their work and with the organization. Good people may begin to jump ship to what looks more like a "sure thing." People focus on what is most important to them, their job security, pay and benefits, chain of command, and maintenance of the safety of the status quo.

FIGURE 5.3 *Integration Phases*

Due Diligence	Organize	Mobilize	Implement	Perform

When these dynamics occur, they are often manifested outwardly as resistance. Studies have shown that all human beings, when confronted with a significant change in their lives—whether in their personal life, community life, or work life—will move through a resistance curve that is predictable. They may move back and forth through the four stages of resistance depending on the situation they are operating in and the intensity of new changes that are loaded on top of one another. These stages are betrayal, denial, identifying crises, and search for solutions.

In the *betrayal* stage, you would tend to hear statements such as, "How could they do this to me?" "Who do they think they are?" "How could they pull this?" The *denial* stage would produce statements such as, "If I just keep doing a good job, everything will be fine." "We've been through this type of thing before and things will get back to normal soon." At the *identifying crises* stage, people will begin to explore possible solutions, and you would be more likely to hear statements such as, "I wonder where my job fits in the new organization." "What would a plan like this look like when it is implemented?" "What skills will I need to work in the new structure?" And by the time people reach the *search for solutions* stage, you would tend to hear statements such as, "If I get involved, I could use my skill and experience to move toward the targets." "It would be more effective if we tried doing it a new way." "My background would offer a chance to address issues in a better way."

Even within rescues, there is likely to be passive resistance to changing the way business is carried out within the organization; and in hostile takeovers, the other extreme witnessed is resistance manifested as hostile and defensive behavior. The higher the level of resistance experienced, the more personally attached each side becomes to its own history. The higher the level of resistance, the longer it takes to subside and move into cooperation. Rather than ignoring the resistance, organizations must recognize it, name it, and design strategies to take advantage of the energy it creates.

As diverse groups within the organization begin to be introduced to the idea of change, they will begin their movement through the stages of resistance. An organization will then have groups of its members moving through the stages at varying times and in varying degrees of intensity. The result is a staggered experience of change in the organization as a whole.

MODULE
5

The function in any organization most conversant with the macro-culture of the organization as well as the individual and group motivators and incentives is the human resource function. Existing within that function as well is all of the information necessary relative to the employees of the organization to assess capability, to understand compensation and benefit complexities and needs, and to plan for communication to the diverse groups that will require reassurance and information about the anticipated changes. Human resources generally serves as the clearinghouse for information flow among and between groups and is in a unique position to hear first where resistance may be causing problems and why, and to structure events and programs that will quickly supply the information needed for people to move through the stages of resistance into a constructive and committed role.

To bring the organizations through change faster, human resources often will supply tools that help the management, planning task forces, and employee groups, work through the issues more collaboratively and more quickly. These tools can include assessments and surveys, project planning skills, communication guides, change awareness training, and templates for information gathering purposes.

Application

Integration presents tremendous challenges and opportunities for the organizations involved. Read the following Star-Excel and Great Southern case studies. Using the information and examples provided for the Great Southern case, complete the integration worksheets for Star-Excel. Blank worksheets can be found in the Appendix on pages 5.20–5.23. After you complete the case study, consider the following questions:

- What key factors can you identify that differentiated the success and failure in the Star-Excel and Great Southern case studies?

- How might consideration of these different factors help an organization considering a merger or acquisition be successful?

Failure Case Study: Great Southern Railroad

Since deregulation of railroads in 1980, the industry has dramatically reshaped itself to meet the challenges of customer demand. For the prior 25 years, Great Southern had led the way with the industry's first centralized customer service center and one of its most advanced computerized dispatching centers, followed by the most innovative equipment tracking techniques and the most efficient, and powerful, locomotive fleet. Along with its campaign to improve transit times, productivity, and reliability, the railroads had employed the strategy of broadening its geographic and competitive reach.

From 1980 through 1995, Great Southern acquired five other railroads, most recently, the Northern Tier. In 1869, these two railroads had united America after the Civil War with the driving of the Golden Spike in Promontory, Utah. Now the two railroads were merged into one. These consolidations created the largest railroad in North America with 36,000 route miles in 23 states.

Stated objectives for the merger of Great Southern and Northern Tier included:

- Shorter routes, elimination of congestion and delays, and more efficient traffic flows

- Improved on-time performance for shippers and faster transit times

- Reduced costs through operating efficiencies, better equipment, and more reliable service

- Faster, more dependable intermodal service and specialized use of parallel routes

- Elimination of inefficiencies and limitations and increased capacity

- Reduced train conflicts and upgraded service through substantial capital investment programs

- Provision of the fastest westbound trains

- Concentration of priority trains on one line and mixed-freight trains on another

- Establishment of a directional network

- Assignment of freight yards to specialized functions to improve service

- Increased number of automotive trains

Great Southern had traditionally been managed in a centralized and autocratic style. Its acquisition strategy generally followed the pattern of meetings among the top management of the company, removed from the operations of the railroad and isolated from communication with the organization. Months were spent in closed-door deliberations at the top levels and when the plans were revealed, they were simply mandated as directives that were to be carried out in successive levels of the acquiring and the acquired organizations. Information was generally not shared with levels of management below the executive suite, and information seeking a way to move up the chain of command seldom made it to the top. No systems existed for resolution of concerns or problems in the integration of the tremendous resources, facilities, and holdings of the two companies and decision making was lengthy as it was passed up and down the hierarchy.

Great Southern had enjoyed preeminence in the railroad industry for many years and felt justified in taking the position that it knew best what would make the combined railroads successful. The railroad unions, representing the majority of the workforce, were neither consulted nor engaged in the planning or decision making for the integration. The managers were not involved in the discussions or plans either and became increasingly discouraged and unwilling to enforce new policies and schedules.

Press Releases in 1998

March 11: Letter to Shareholders of The Great Southern Railroad. At last year's annual meeting we were actively tackling the integration of the Northern Tier into the Great Southern, confident of quickly realizing the tremendous synergy of the combined railroads. Since then, we have experienced a number of unprecedented challenges. As this year's annual meeting approaches, we wanted to update you on current developments and assure you that our company is resilient and has a great future. We know many of you are concerned by our recent announcements on expectations for a first-quarter loss and the actions to reduce the dividend. We know these are strong measures, but it is absolutely essential that we provide the funds needed for capital spending on the railroad's critical merger-related projects. We ask for your continued support and understanding as we work to fix our operations and to restore the confidence our shareholders and customers have in our ability to provide good financial returns and the best rail service in the business.

June 1: Great Southern announced today that the Executive Vice President-Finance and a member of the Corporation's Board of Directors resigned.

July 23: Great Southern reported a $520 million loss on Thursday, the third straight quarterly loss for the nation's largest railroad. The loss was primarily attributed to the railroad's settlements with customers angry over massive congestion problems that began on the tracks last summer. Since that time, the railroad has been plagued by a service backlog that critics have blamed on its merger with Northern Tier. The railroad said it had also been hurt by traffic slowdowns related to major track maintenance and capacity expansion. The company is spending nearly $1 billion this year in improving and maintaining its 35,000 miles of track in 23 states.

MODULE
5

July 27: Great Southern has settled a lawsuit filed by Organic Chemical Co., the second agreement the nation's largest railroad has reached with a major customer disgruntled over poor service. In its breach of contract suit Organic Chemical stated that it was frustrated with disruptions in rail service that had cost more than $25 million in lost revenue and extra shipping expenses. Chemical and plastics producers claimed they were particularly hard hit because of the rail slowdown, losing as much as $100 million a month. The railroad is also in settlement talks with Cal-Carbide Corp., Mason Petroleum Co., the Maxim Co., the railroad's own shareholder group, and 300-plus customers who say congestion on the railroad delayed, or in some cases lost, their shipments.

December 5: U.S. Transportation Secretary says federal controls on Great Southern should remain in place as the company wrestles with the worst railroad freight traffic jam in recent U.S. history. The nation's largest railroad has been operating under the scrutiny of the U.S. Surface Transportation Board for six months. The board imposed special restrictions on the railroad. Shippers' groups have asked the board to extend its oversight of Great Southern, while the railroad maintains the year-long traffic jam has been resolved and the restriction should be lifted.

Task Force Integration Examples

Tables 5.2–5.6 on pages 5.16–5.17 show examples of Great Southern's task force integration in the areas of key integration initiatives, risk assessment and contingency plan, strategy for communication, strategy for retention of key talent, and cultural change plan.

TABLE 5.2 *Key Integration Initiatives*

Prioritized Initiatives and Sub-Tasks	Start	End	Resp.	Cost
1.0 Consolidate outplacement services	12/1	2/3	CR	
2.0 Consolidate 401K plan	12/1	1/15	DB	
3.0 Develop labor contract	1/30	3/15	FW	
4.0 Develop synergy savings/cost tracking system	1/30	2/30	FW	
5.0 Evaluate existing HR systems and programs	2/1	4/30	DB	

TABLE 5.3 *Risk Assessment and Contingency Plan*

Description of Risk to Each Key Initiative	Mitigation Strategy for Each Risk	Timing
1.0 Conflicting philosophy	Discussion groups	12/15
2.0 Cost of plan too high	Fact-finding task force	12/15
3.0 Unable to meet deadlines	Forge interim agreement	2/30
4.0 Lack of target clarity	Task force collaboration	1/30
5.0 Resource availability	Hire interns or consultant	2/1

TABLE 5.4 *Strategy for Communication*

Stakeholders	Objective (Why?)	Message (What?)	Vehicle (How?)	Frequency (When?)
Executive Management	Inform/ rationale	Dates/plan	Meeting	Once
All employees	Inform/ prepare	Dates/work assignments/ training	Newsletter/ e-mail Managers	First two weeks
Customers	Inform/ prepare	Dates/contacts/ schedule	Phone calls/ letters/visits	First two weeks
Community	Inform	Reason/plan	Press release/ letter to Mayor	Once

TABLE 5.5 *Strategy for Retention of Key Talent*

Key Groups or Individuals	Cost of Loss	Motivators to Retain	Time Frame	Responsibility to Contact
Top Ten Names	$2.5 MM	Stay bonus/ promotion Involvement	30 days	CEO
Other Key People	$35 MM	Pay increase Involvement	90 days	Direct Manager
Key Groups	$14 MM	Involvement	90 days	Project Manager
Technical Experts	$22 MM	Stay bonus Pay increase	30 days	Project Team

TABLE 5.6 *Cultural Change Plan*

Element	Supporting Features	Conflicting Features	Action Required	Person(s) Responsible	Completion Date
Rules and Policies	Flextime	Dress code	Focus Group	HR Manager	
Goals and Measures	Quality plan, net profit	Parts out the door	Task Force	Operations Manager	
Training	Individual development plans	Voluntary and not tracked	Task Force	HR Manager	
Ceremonies and Events	Annual picnic and family day		Task Force	HR Manager	
Reward and Recognition	Quality Day	No consistent system	Design system	HR Manager	
Physical Environment	Rural	Isolated	Focus Group	Operations Manager	

Success Case Study: Star-Excel Building Corporation

Star Foundry and Excel Brick share more than 200 years of rich history. Star Foundry opened in the mid-1800s to supply the ceaseless demand of post-Civil War America for refractory brick. The company today has manufacturing facilities at 14 plants in five countries with over 5,000 employees worldwide.

Excel Brick began in the early 1900s and many revolutionary ideas and new products followed. For nearly 50 years the firm was a single-plant operation. A new president in the 1950s led the company to become a multiplant operation with 14 plants in the United States and Canada. Soon Excel products were being manufactured at 35 international plants in 17 countries with nearly 4,000 employees.

Star Foundry announced its determination to acquire Excel Brick in a partnership style of merger; it hired an outside consulting firm to guide the process. It set up a project management structure for the integration planning process with an Executive Sponsor group made up of the CEOs of both companies, the presidents of both companies, and a project manager. Reporting to them for the duration of the project, approximately three months, was an Acquisition Team made up of the president of Star Foundry and executive management from both companies that acted as the operational decision-making body for the transition period. It directed the data gathering and recommending activities of Task Force Teams made up of selected functional managers from both organizations. The Acquisition Team's primary function was to coordinate all the acquisition activities and make decisions based on recommendations of the 14 Task Force Teams that were created by the Acquisition Team. It sought input from the Task Force Teams because they were closest to the business processes and knew best how to integrate the two companies. The goal was to achieve a fast integration process, completing all of the major organizational and integration tasks within 90 days following FTC approval. Then the project structure would be disbanded and the completed integration plans and recommendations handed off to the identified managers in the new company for execution and implementation.

The acquisition process was organized into a fast 30-60-90 day timetable of events that began in mid-March. During the first 30 days, the Acquisition Team began developing an interim infrastructure to run the companies during the transition and a new business design that would represent the combined company. The Task Force Teams met weekly, identifying synergies, efficiencies, and business growth opportunities, and developing integration recommendations that would benefit from the strengths of each company. The Task Force Teams provided the Acquisition Team with weekly progress updates. The Acquisition Team, in turn, provided the teams with guidance and direction based on these updates.

The Sales Task Force Team quickly identified several areas that could grow the business by establishing a larger selection of products. In addition, several opportunities were identified for each company to buy and resell products to each other when products are not available from one company. The Product Transfer Team also quickly identified numerous opportunities to move products between the two companies that would result in more efficient production operations. The Human Resource team reports concentrated on eight fronts: Human Resources Information Systems, welfare plans, 401(k) plans, pension plans, travel, labor negotiation planning, HR staffing, and communication to all employees throughout the integration process.

Synergies identified at the outset of the merger agreement were $30 million in cost reductions, 600 reductions in headcount from a workforce of 3,200 between the two companies, and several plant closings. As a result of the actual integration process, synergies of $42 million in cost reductions were realized. Once the workforce capability was accurately assessed, talent retained in key positions, and capabilities deployed effectively, the necessity for headcount reduction to realize the net synergy was reduced to 450 total. In addition, during the integration period, rather than a decline in sales, the combining organizations saw a rise in revenue of nearly 30 percent overall as the sales and administrative teams joined forces to bring their products and services to market. Those involved attributed the concurrent decrease in cost and increase in revenue to intensive employee training about the culture, vision, products, and projects; to solid customer education, image campaigns, cross-selling, and attention to quality; and to shareholder awareness of the consolidation progress and results.

IN CONCLUSION

Debrief

In the integration process, people from the two organizations become familiar with each other's values, styles, and cultures and begin to forge ways to work together cooperatively. Resources, capabilities, and management skill must be transferred, shared, or learned during this transition period. These transitions take place at the operational, functional, and management levels and include combinations of sales and manufacturing skills, physical space, distribution channels and brand names, concerns imbedded in the disparate procedures and cultures, and in such things as financial planning and human resource management processes. Both institutional and interpersonal leadership must be available and accessible or the transfer of the necessary capabilities is limited.

Unless cultural differences are examined, understood, and addressed as an integral part of the merger process, the risk of failure increases dramatically. Culture is a blend of organization values, traditions, ceremonies, myths, beliefs, and history. Culture shapes organizational structures, systems, philosophies, and behaviors. It establishes the formal policies and procedures and dictates the norms and unwritten rules that tell organization members what is acceptable, rewarded, and valued, and what is not.

When two cultures collide in a merger or acquisition, people find that behaviors that once reaped reward, recognition, and promotion may no longer be valued or rewarded. People may be put on the defensive as they attempt to understand how to react to the new expectations and the changed environment. As tension mounts and confusion and uncertainty gain ground, people begin to protect themselves. One of the manifestations of this self-protection is resistance.

In other cases, the cultures may be compatible and easily assimilated, but the operating strategies and practices may be discrepant, as when strong centralization meets a decentralized structure. One of management's first decisions is whether there is a need to reconcile the two organizations' structures, strategies, and cultures and to what extent.

Shareholders and analysts look into the eye of the top managers and ask, "Do they have the operating capability to integrate these two companies?" It requires operating skill beyond tax synergies and financial synergies. Investors look for real operating improvements before they indicate confidence in the management. Many deals make sense because the acquirer will run the target company's business better than the current management and investors will be looking closely at the talent in the target company. The strength of the human resource manager is often a key consideration of organizations that are experienced in merging and acquiring. There is a recognition of the critical role a strategic human resource professional can play in helping the organizations integrate successfully. The human resource function can be the best interpreter and translator of the organizations capabilities, style, and culture because of their day-to-day proximity to the people and cultural issues.

Suggested Readings

The Art of Merger and Acquisition Integration: A Guide to Merging Resources, Processes, and Responsibilities. Alexandra R. Lajoux. New York: McGraw-Hill. 1997.

Organizational Culture in the Management of Mergers. Afsaneh Nahavandi and Ali R. Malekzadeh. Westport, CT: Greenwood Publishing Group. 1993.

Managing Transitions: Making the Most of Change. William Bridges. Reading, MA: Addison-Wesley. 1991.

Five Frogs on a Log: A CEO's Guide to Accelerating the Transition in Mergers, Acquisitions, and Gut Wrenching Change. Mark L. Feldman and Michael F. Spratt. New York: Harper Business. 1999.

MODULE
5

Critical Thinking Questions

1. Why should management in mergers and acquisitions care about human resource issues?

2. Why should the human resource function care about merger and acquisition activity?

3. What distinguishes a strategic human resource professional from an administrative one?

4. Where can human resources make the most dramatic impact in a merger or acquisition?

Exercises

1. List all the major market segments you can think of (example: aerospace, electronics, manufacturing, retail, automotive, etc.). List as many companies as you can think of that fall within each market segment. Then discuss which companies might realistically want to combine their resources by merging or acquiring in order to increase their value. Give your rationale for why these combinations might make sense in the next few years. See Example on the following page.

Market Segment	Companies Within Segment	Potential Combinations

Example:

With deregulation erasing the line between commercial banks, brokerage houses, insurers, finance companies, and credit card issuers, the message is that only the biggest and strongest will prosper. In banking, the biggest merger to date at publication—the $13.8 billion acquisition of Barnett Banks by NationsBank—showed that even a big, strong regional bank like Florida's Barnett needed the national muscle of a NationsBank to survive. In telecommunications, GTE's bid for MCI presaged the evaporation of distinctions between local and long-distance phone companies and the bid for WorldCom, one of the country's largest owners of Internet networks, showed how phone companies and Internet-oriented companies will compete to own what in just a few years could become a single network carrying both voice and data.

2. Consult your notes from the Success case in the Application section. What specifics of the situation seem to have contributed to the success? Discuss the case in small groups, and compile the top ten most likely contributors to the success. Be prepared to share your rationale with the rest of the group.

3. Consult your notes from the Failure case in the Application section. What specifics of the situations do you perceive as having significantly contributed to the failure? Be prepared to share your rationale with the rest of the group.

APPENDIX

Task Force Integration Application Case Forms

Tables 5.7–5.11 show templates for Great Southern's task force integration application case forms in the areas of key integration initiatives, risk assessment and contingency plan, strategy for communication, strategy for retention of key talent, and cultural change plan. Complete the forms using the parts of the Star-Excel case. How do the forms differ?

TABLE 5.7   *Key Integration Initiatives*

Prioritized Initiatives and Sub-Tasks	Start	End	Resp.	Cost

TABLE 5.8   *Risk Assessment and Contingency Plan*

Description of Risk to Each Key Initiative	Mitigation Strategy for Each Risk	Timing

TABLE 5.9   *Strategy for Communication*

Stakeholders	Objective (Why?)	Message (What?)	Vehicle (How?)	Frequency (When?)

TABLE 5.10   *Strategy for Retention of Key Talent*

Key Groups or Individuals	Cost of Loss	Motivators	Time Frame to Retain	Responsibility to Contact

TABLE 5.11   *Cultural Change Plan*

Element	Supporting Features	Conflicting Features	Action Required	Person(s) Responsible	Completion Date
Rules and Policies					
Goals and Measures					
Training					
Ceremonies and Events					
Reward and Recognition					
Physical Environment					

MODULE
5

Index

Acquired firm, 5.6
Acquisition, 5.4–7, 5.14
Acquisition target, 5.8
Acquisition team, 5.17–18
Adaptation (integration), 5.9
Adversarial (mergers), 5.8–9
Ambiguity of negotiations, 5.8
Assessments and surveys, 5.13
Assimilation (integration), 5.9

Betrayal stage (mergers and acquisitions), 5.13
Breach of contract suit, 5.15

Centralized/autocratic management style, 5.14
Change awareness training, 5.13
Collective agreements, 5.5
Colliding cultures, 5.18. *See also* Mismatch of
  culture
Combined assets, 5.6
Commitment of managers, 5.9
Communication role. *See* Translation role
Communication strategy, 5.16
Communications guides, 5.13
Conglomerate acquisitions, 5.7
Consolidation, 5.6, 5.18
Corporate culture, 5.5, 5.18
Cultural change plan, 5.17

Defensive behavior, 5.13
Denial stage (mergers and acquisitions), 5.13
Due diligence (integration), 5.12

Economic environment, 5.6
Economics of scale, 5.6
Employment relations, 5.4

Federal Trade Commission (FTC), 5.6
FTC compliance, 5.10

Globalization, 5.6
Government regulation, mergers and acquisitions, 5.6–7

Hart-Scott-Rodino Antitrust Improvements Act
  of 1976, 5.7
Hidden costs, 5.10
High-performing organization, 5.10
Hostile takeover (mergers), 5.8–9, 5.13
HR decisions management, 5.5
Human resource function, 5.4, 5.19
Human resource management (HRM), 5.4–5
Human resource professional, 5.4, 5.10–12
Human resource professional's role, 5.10–12,
  5.19

Human resource tasks, 5.11
Human Resources, 5.4, 5.10

Identifying crises stage (mergers and acquisitions), 5.13
Implement phase (integration), 5.12
Information gathering templates, 5.13
Integration, 5.6, 5.9–12, 5.17–19
  phases of, 5.2
Interdependence, 5.9–10
Internal development strategies, 5.6

Key integration initiatives, 5.16
Key talent, 5.10
Key talent retention strategy, 5.16

Leverage, 5.6
Liberal regulatory environment, 5.7

Management tools, 5.13
Market position, 5.6
Merger, Great Southern and Northern Tier railroads, 5.14
Merger activity, 5.6–7
  categories and characteristics, 5.7–10
Mergers and acquisitions, 5.4–7
  dynamics of, 5.12–13
  key distinctions, 5.5–6
Mismatch of culture, 5.6. *See also* Colliding
  cultures
Mobilize phase (integration), 5.12
Monopoly power, 5.7
Morale (employee), 5.12

Nonoperational benefits, 5.6

Organizational change, 5.13
Organizational culture, 5.13
Organizational leadership tasks, 5.11
Organizational strategy, 5.10
Organize phase (integration), 5.12

Partnership (mergers), 5.6–8, 5.17
People problems, 5.6
Perform phase (integration), 5.12
Power struggles, 5.12
Product mismatch, 5.6
Project planning skills, 5.13
Protectorate (integration), 5.9

Raider company, 5.9
Rescue (mergers), 5.7–8, 5.13
Resistance to change, 5.13, 5.19
Resisted takeovers, 5.9

MODULE
5

Restructuring, 5.6
Risk assessment, 5.16
Role of human resource professional. *See* Human resource professional's role

Search for solutions stage (mergers and acquisitions), 5.13
Status quo, 5.12
Strategic partners, 5.10–11
Synergy, 5.6, 5.10, 5.18

Task force teams, 5.17–18
Technological advances, 5.6

Transaction role, 5.4
Transformation role, 5.4
Transitional activities, 5.18
Translation role, 5.4
Turf wars, 5.12

Unilateral decisions, 5.5
Unionized facilities, 5.5

Vertically integrated corporation, 5.7
Visible costs, 5.10

Workforce capacity, 5.11

MODULE
5

Managing Human Resources in the 21st Century

From Core Concepts to Strategic Choice

MODULE **6**

Collective Bargaining, Industrial Relations, and Human Resource Systems

Managing in Environments

Richard N. Block
MICHIGAN STATE UNIVERSITY

Managing Human Resources in the 21st Century: From Core Concepts to Strategic Choice,
by Kossek and Block

Publisher: Dave Shaut
Executive Editor: John Szilagyi
Developmental Editor: Bryant Editorial Development
Marketing Manager: Joseph A. Sabatino
Production Editor: Tamborah E. Moore
Manufacturing Coordinator: Dana Began Schwartz
Cover Design: Tin Box Studio
Cover Photographs: Copyright Shoji Sato/Photonica
Production House: The Left Coast Group, Inc.
Printer: West Group

Printed in the United States of America
1 2 3 4 5 02 01 00 99

For more information contact South-Western College Publishing, 5101 Madison Road, Cincinnati, Ohio, 45227 or find us on the Internet at *http://www.swcollege.com*
For permission to use material from this text or product, contact us by
- telephone: 1-800-730-2214
- fax: 1-800-730-2215
- web: *http://www.thomsonrights.com*

ISBN: 0–324–01805–3

This book is printed on acid-free paper.

Contents

MODULE OVERVIEW   6.4

OBJECTIVES   6.4

RELATION TO THE FRAME   6.4

CORE CONCEPTS IN COLLECTIVE BARGAINING   6.5
Workplace Rules   6.5
Collective Bargaining   6.6
Labor Unions   6.7
Multiple Perspectives on the Employment Relationship   6.9

STRATEGIC ISSUES IN COLLECTIVE BARGAINING   6.9
Institutionalized Adversarialism Through the 1970s   6.9
Collective Bargaining Since the 1970s   6.11

FIRM CHOICES IN LABOR RELATIONS   6.12
Deunionization   6.12
Cooperation   6.13
Traditional Adversarialism   6.14

APPLICATION 1   6.14
Deunionization Strategy in Labor Relations: The Case of Phelps Dodge
and the United Steelworkers of America   6.14
Other Examples of Conflict   6.15
Deunionization in the Rubber Tire Industry   6.16

APPLICATION 2   6.16
Traditional Adversarialism in Labor Relations: The Case of
United Parcel Service and the International Brotherhood of Teamsters   6.16

APPLICATION 3   6.18
Cooperation in Collective Bargaining: Ford and the UAW   6.18

IN CONCLUSION   6.19
Debrief   6.19
Suggested Readings   6.19
Critical Thinking Questions   6.19
Exercise   6.20
Reference   6.20

INDEX   6.22

MODULE OVERVIEW

Union-management conflict receives a great deal of attention in the United States. Strikes were a dominant news story in the summer of 1997, when the International Brotherhood of Teamsters struck United Parcel Service, and again in the summer of 1998, when two locals of the United Auto Workers Union struck General Motors, effectively halting production at the giant automaker. The GM strike was followed by a pilot's strike against Northwest Airlines, inconveniencing large numbers of air travelers during the Labor Day weekend. The first half of the 1998–1999 National Basketball Association season was canceled because the owners locked out the union representing the players.

Routine union-management relations are regularly covered in the business press, and rarely does a week go by without several news stories about collective bargaining and unions. A sampling of these stories carried in fall 1998 is instructive:

- The reaction of the unions representing employees at Boeing to job cuts for financial reasons

- The reaction of the unions representing employees at Exxon and Mobil to job reductions caused by the merger of the two companies

- A lockout of its broadcast technicians by the American Broadcasting Company

- The strained negotiations between Federal Express and the union representing its pilots

These stories indicate the importance of understanding collective bargaining. *Collective bargaining* is the regulated model of negotiated employment relations in the United States. It is the legal process by which a company and the legal representative of its employees, generally a labor union, negotiate the terms and conditions of employment that will be applied to the legally designated group of employees, called the *bargaining unit*. This module discusses the fundamental concepts and structures associated with collective bargaining in the United States.

MODULE
6

OBJECTIVES

This module will first focus on four concepts or institutions that are crucial to understanding negotiated employment relations in the United States:

- The concept of workplace rules

- The institutions and processes of collective bargaining

- The nature of a labor union

- The principle of multiple perspectives on the employment relationship

Following this, the module will apply the concepts to the key strategic human resource management question: what type of collective bargaining relationship should a company develop with the union representing its employees? The final section will discuss examples of firms and unions that have experienced each type of relationship.

RELATION TO THE FRAME

Collective bargaining in the United States would fall primarily in the middle column in the framework (see Figure 6.1), although the legal regulation of collective bargaining means that some process requirements are imposed.

FIGURE 6.1 *A Frame for Understanding Human Resource Strategy: Context, Roles, and Constraints*

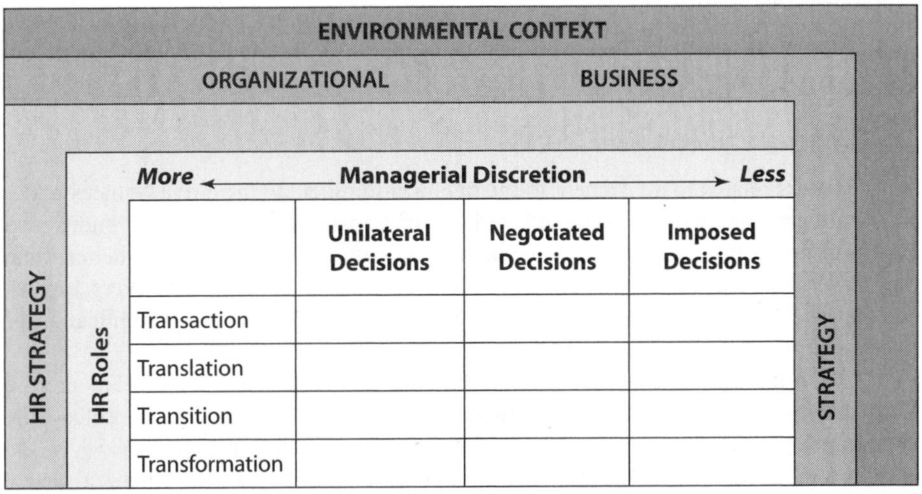

		Managerial Discretion		
		Unilateral Decisions	Negotiated Decisions	Imposed Decisions
	Transaction			
	Translation			
	Transition			
	Transformation			

ENVIRONMENTAL CONTEXT
ORGANIZATIONAL · BUSINESS
HR STRATEGY · HR Roles · STRATEGY
More ← Managerial Discretion → Less

© 2000 by Ellen Ernst Kossek and Richard Block. Thanks to Brian Pentland, Karen Markel, and John Beck for helpful comments and discussions that enhanced the model.

As will be discussed, collective bargaining as it is practiced in the United States is a highly decentralized institution that varies across regions, industries, and even across firms in the same industry and region. While collective bargaining will almost always impact the HR roles of transacting, building, developing, and governing, in some cases, it may even impact how the business is executed.

CORE CONCEPTS IN COLLECTIVE BARGAINING

There are four core concepts—workplace rules, collective bargaining, labor unions, and multiple perspectives on the employment relationship—that must be understood if collective bargaining is to be properly studied. Each of these will be examined in the following sections.

Workplace Rules

The workplace can be viewed as a small society. Just as the citizens of a country must establish a set of rules so that they can live with one another and the society can function, a workplace must also have rules. These rules dictate how the members of the workplace society interact with each other, and they establish behaviors necessary for the society/organization to accomplish its mission.

What are these workplace rules? They cover such matters as compensation, employee responsibilities, and attachment to the workplace or the organization.

Most people are familiar with rules covering compensation. Examples include:

- The wage or salary to be paid an employee

- The frequency of pay adjustments

- The criteria for receiving pay adjustments (merit or across-the-board)

- Eligibility for bonuses, stock options, and profit sharing

- Benefits such as health insurance, life insurance, and dental insurance

Matters involving responsibilities include such issues as:

- The tasks to be performed

- Amount of supervision

- Receipt of training

- Criteria for promotions

Matters related to attachment to the organization include the circumstances under which an employee will be dismissed, laid off, or transferred. Some organizations also have procedural rules that include a complaint process for employees who believe that they have not been treated properly or within the rules. Put differently, every organizational decision that is made vis-à-vis an employee involves either the application or interpretation of a workplace rule.

Given the daily importance of these rules, a logical question arises: how are the rules determined and how are they altered? In a democratic society, the rules—the laws—are created by the representatives of the citizenry. In the workplace, however, the rules are generally established and altered through a mixture of firm unilateral determination and individual bargaining.

Firm unilateralism is the most common method of determining the rules of the workplace. Under unilateralism, management, as the representative of the shareholders (in private organizations), determines the rules based on its perception of their best interests. Thus, typically, when a person takes a position in a corporation, most of the terms and conditions of employment are predetermined. Moreover, the job responsibilities and grounds for termination are also determined by management.

On occasion, there is some room for individual bargaining. Employees at entry- or low-level positions in some industries, such as retailing, may be able to negotiate the hours to be worked (e.g., weekends, evenings, etc.). Employees entering the organization in professional positions may find that there is some flexibility in the starting salary or the initial assignment. Employees at very high level positions often have substantial freedom to negotiate salary, termination benefits, etc. However, the fact remains that firm unilateralism is the dominant method of determining the rules of the workplace in the United States.

Collective Bargaining

Although firm unilateralism with some flexibility for individual bargaining is the dominant method of rulemaking in U.S. workplaces, it is not the only method. Roughly 10 percent of the private-sector workforce in the United States has its terms and conditions of employment and many of the workplace rules determined by collective bargaining. Moreover, some of the largest and most important corporations in the United States use this approach. Thus, it is crucial to understand the collective bargaining process.

What is collective bargaining? It is the process in which the firm negotiates terms and conditions of employment—the workplace rules—with the legal representative of a specified group of employees. It is *collective* bargaining because, unlike individual bargaining, the legal representative negotiates for the employees it represents on a collective, or group, basis.

There are several key components to collective bargaining. First, it is a process by which the workplace rules are *negotiated*. Firms that engage in collective bargaining are not in a position to unilaterally determine the terms and conditions of employment for the employees who are represented. These must be negotiated with the employees' legal representative.

Second, collective bargaining in the United States, and in most other countries, is a legal process. Before the terms and conditions of employment can be collectively negotiated, there must be an established legal representative of the employees. This is generally determined through a government process administered by the National Labor Relations Board in which an election is held to determine if the majority of a specified group of positions, a legal "bargaining unit," desire collective representation by a petitioning labor organization (a labor union). If the employees in the bargaining unit vote in favor of representation, the firm has a legal obligation to bargain in good faith with that labor organization. Thus, the law determines when a bargaining obligation exists, and the bargain determines the terms and conditions of employment for the positions in the firm.

In the United States, that labor organization in turn represents all the employees in the bargaining unit, including those who voted against collective representation. Thus, the terms and conditions of employment negotiated by the union are applied to all employees in the bargaining unit, and the firm may not agree with any individual employee on a term or condition of employment that is different from that negotiated by the union. This is called the principle of *exclusive representation.*

There is also a legal obligation on the part of the company and the employees' representative to negotiate in good faith. This means that once a union is certified as the employees' legal representative, the company may no longer unilaterally determine the rules of the workplace for those employees in the bargaining unit. Rather, those rules are subject to negotiation with the labor organization, and they cannot be changed or altered by the firm without first negotiating in good faith with that labor organization. The obligation to bargain in good faith requires that both the company and the employees' representative meet at reasonable times and confer about terms and conditions of employment.

Although neither the company nor the union may engage in "surface bargaining" or attempt to impede the bargaining process, there is no obligation on either party to agree to a proposal by the other. If the parties, after good-faith negotiations, are unable to reach an agreement and have irreconcilable differences, they are considered to be at "impasse." At that point, either side may use its economic weapons to influence the other party to change its position. The major economic weapon of the labor organization is, of course, the strike. However, the company may lock out its employees and permanently replace striking workers, provided the strike is an economic one to improve terms and conditions of employment, and not a strike either caused by or called to protest a company's alleged unlawful practice. The company may also implement its final pre-impasse proposal for all employees.

Although the strike remains the traditional economic weapon for a labor organization, unions have developed other strategies as well. A union dissatisfied with the progress of negotiations may engage in a slowdown, in which employees remain on the job but give less than 100 percent effort or structure the job based on their interests. Occasionally, a union will engage in a corporate campaign in which it puts pressure on other firms with which the company does business.

Once an agreement is reached, it must be set down in writing in a legally enforceable contract. Although collective agreements may be enforced in court, most are enforced through a negotiated grievance procedure culminating in final and binding third-party arbitration.

MODULE
6

Labor Unions

Although the law requires only that employees be represented by a "labor organization" on which few constraints are placed, the vast majority of employees covered by a collective bargaining agreement are represented by a union. A *union* is a formal organization established to represent employees in collective bargaining and to further their interests. The best-known unions are large organizations that may have over half a million members. The International Brotherhood of Teamsters, the United Auto Workers, and the United Steelworkers of America are three of the better-known unions representing large numbers of employees in the private sector.

Unions are fundamentally different from corporations in several ways. Although in theory corporations are shareholder democracies that are run by an elected board of directors, in reality they are highly hierarchical organizations. On a day-to-day basis, they are run by their management.

Unions, on the other hand, are usually administered by elected officials rather than hired managers, since their mission is to *represent* employees. The governing structure of a union is determined by its constitution. The constitution determines the election process for the officers of the union and the terms of office. All unions must have a convention, at which the constitution may be amended. Federal law places requirements on unions for frequency of elections and conventions, and maximum requirements for terms of office of union officials.

Unions function at two basic levels—the international or national, and the local. The international level establishes fundamental policies, aggregates and coordinates the activities of the local unions, and provides varying levels of service and support to them, depending on the nature of the union. The international union may also approve local action and, on occasion, provides oversight to the local.

The local union is chartered by the international union. It is the union entity closest to the membership. In general, a person becomes a member of the local union, and through that, a member of the international union. Local unions vary in size depending on the chartering practices and history of the national unions. Some unions, such as the Teamsters and the Service Employees International Union, chartered their locals on a geographic basis. A geographic jurisdiction makes it possible for a local to grow quite large, a process that to some extent keeps its size within its control. Such locals often have multiple collective agreements.

Other unions, such as the United Auto Workers and the United Steelworkers, were organized from the international level on a firm-by-firm or plant-by-plant basis. As each firm or plant was organized, its membership was granted a local union charter. Therefore, large plants result in large locals (e.g., UAW Local 652 in Lansing, Michigan, represents all hourly employees at the General Motors assembly plants in Lansing, a total of approximately 8,000 employees). On the other hand, a small plant of only 50 persons would also be a local union. Single-facility locals typically administer only one collective agreement.

In a large local of several thousand people, the officers may be full-time employees of the local union. In a small local, however, the officers are normally working employees who either administer the local during their nonworking hours or are reimbursed by the local for any working time lost for union activities.

Because a union is a democratic organization, there may be tension between the local and international level. For instance, when the actions of one local are perceived as adversely affecting the interests of other locals because the local is acting independently in the best interests of its local membership, the international union may see its role as protecting the broader interests of the union. This may mean placing constraints on the local.

Most unions have also created intermediate bodies between the local and international union. These have two purposes, governance and collective bargaining. Governance intermediate bodies are usually locals that are combined for the purposes of representative government. They are usually geographic in scope. The United Auto Workers, for example, has also created separate corporate councils for the locals that represent employees at each of the automobile companies.

Multiple Perspectives on the Employment Relationship

The principles underlying collective bargaining cannot be truly understood unless one understands that there are two perspectives to the employment relationship—the firm perspective and the employee perspective. Collective bargaining views each as equally legitimate.

The firm perspective on the employment relationship is, in general, comparable to that of a purchaser of a product or service. The employee who is being paid must add value to the firm or further its mission or purpose in some way. In other words, the firm's interest in the employment is based on what the employee can contribute to the firm. The greater the level of pay, the greater the contribution expected. Moreover, if, after a period of time, the firm management believes the employee can no longer make an appropriate contribution, the firm would see it as appropriate to sever the employment relationship.

From the perspective of the employee, the employment relationship is fundamentally the means by which the employee earns a living and attains a status in society. Thus, the employee's interest is in the job as a source of income and as a contribution to his or her well-being. The employee has an interest in being treated fairly and in maintaining an attachment to the firm.

This is not to say that firms and employees do not, in some sense, share each other's perspective. Both want the firm to prosper and succeed. But this does suggest that, at the core, firms and employees have different perspectives on the employment relationship.

These different perspectives carry the seed of potential conflict. As these different perspectives are both seen as equally legitimate, this conflict is an inherent part of the employment system. Therefore, the purpose of collective bargaining is to manage this conflict and find a way to resolve it.

The negotiated employment relations system, then, recognizes a blend of coinciding and conflicting interests. To the extent that shareholders and employees both benefit if the organization is successful, the interests of the parties coincide. On the other hand, to the extent that higher pay and a higher standard of living for employees are associated with higher labor costs and lower profits for the firm and its shareholders, the interests of employees and firms conflict.

Strategic Issues In Collective Bargaining

Collective bargaining places constraints on management that do not exist in the absence of the requirement to recognize and negotiate with the union. In the absence of this obligation, management has unilateral discretion over matters involving terms and conditions. A collective bargaining relationship removes that discretion.

A major strategic question in collective bargaining is the response of management and the nature of the collective bargaining relationship. Through the 1970s, the only management strategy was acceptance of the union in an arm's length relationship—institutionalized adversarialism. Beginning in the 1980s, however, management began to develop other options for structuring collective bargaining—cooperation and conflict/ deunionization.

Institutionalized Adversarialism Through the 1970s

The basic legal structure for collective bargaining and the characteristics of the collective bargaining system in the United States through the 1970s were created in the late 1930s following the passage of the National Labor Relations Act in 1935. These characteristics were reinforced during World War II, when the War Labor Board, in order to avoid work stoppages during the war, institutionalized practices that were to dominate collective bargaining through the late 1970s, and that still exist today.

The system that grew between 1935 and 1945 can be called *institutionalized adversarialism*—"institutionalized" because it recognized the role of unions as the protector of employees and management as the protector of the shareholders, and "adversarialism" because it created an arm's length relationship between the union and the firm. Each party accepted the legitimacy of the other party's role, and neither showed any interest in becoming involved in the institutional prerogatives of the other.

The characteristics of the system included detailed, long-term (generally three years) written contracts, often running several hundred pages in length, and structured communications. Included in the contract were detailed provisions covering such issues as recognition (which occupations or classifications of employees were covered by the agreement), management rights, union or agency shop provisions, wage rates, fringe benefits, hours of work, call-in pay, and pay for time not worked (vacations, holidays, etc.). The contract also covered such issues as posting and bidding on vacancies, role of length of service (seniority) in promotions and layoffs, protection from discharge or discipline without just cause, and the method of resolving disputes over the interpretation of a contract—generally a multistep grievance procedure culminating in third-party final and binding arbitration as a quid pro quo for a union waiver of its right to strike during the term of the agreement.

The amount of detail that can be incorporated into a collective agreement is illustrated by this excerpt from the job bidding provision in an agreement between a major petroleum producer and its union. The provision governs the procedure for filling vacancies.

MODULE
6

ARTICLE 10
Job Bidding

Section 10.1. Except as otherwise provided in this Article, the principle of seniority and ability shall be the determining factors in filling permanent job vacancies.

(a) When a permanent job vacancy occurs on an existing unit in the Operations Department the employees currently assigned to the unit where the vacancy occurs shall have the opportunity to bid the vacancy. If no one on the unit elects to take the vacancy, it shall be assigned to the junior qualified person assigned to the unit where the vacancy occurs.

(b) When a permanent job vacancy occurs with the Maintenance, Safety and Laboratory departments, employees of the respective department where the vacancy occurs shall have the first opportunity to fill the vacancy. If not filled from within the respective department (Maintenance or Lab) the vacancy shall then be posted for plantwide bid in accordance with Section 10.9. of this Article.

(c) When Tester I Positions for the Laboratory Department are posted for bid, the job will be awarded to the senior eligible bidder. If the senior eligible bidder disqualifies, the position will be awarded to the next high eligible bidder. In the event the second high eligible bidder disqualifies, the position may be filled by outside hire.

Section 10.2. The Company's refinery shall be divided into four (4) departments as follows:

(a) The Operating Department
(b) The Maintenance Department
(c) The Laboratory Department
(d) The Safety Department

Communications between the parties were typically structured into two forums—negotiations for a new agreement at the expiration of the previous one, and union protests over management decisions during the term of the agreement. The latter would normally go through the grievance procedure.

From the union point of view, the purpose of such detailed agreements was to limit the discretion of management and to clarify what it could and could not do vis-à-vis terms and conditions of employment. Such detailed agreements would prevent arbitrary, capricious, and unfair decision making on the part of management. Moreover, because the agreements could be enforced through the grievance procedure, arbitration, and, ultimately, in court, management could not renege on that to which it had agreed.

Such agreements had clear advantages for unions, and management learned to live with them. For management, they had the advantage of limiting the incursion of unions on its right to make the fundamental decisions about the business, and the length of the contract provided stability in the company's day-to-day operations.

One disadvantage of such a system of long-term structured agreements is their inflexibility, with the firm limited in making changes in terms and conditions of employment during the term of the agreement without the consent of the union. This was not, however, generally noticeable through the 1970s. The lack of foreign competition in manufacturing and the regulated environment in transportation meant that whatever inefficiencies resulted from such a system could be passed on to customers. Moreover, because unions had often organized for the important firms in the industry, the unionized firm's competitors were generally under the same constraints. Thus, no firm was disadvantaged.

Collective Bargaining Since the 1970s

By the late 1970s, the underlying conditions that had made institutionalized adversarialism acceptable to management began to break down, causing many firms to question that system. The most noticeable change was an increase in foreign competition in manufacturing, the heart of the unionized sector. Foreign firms began to make inroads in such markets as automobiles, basic steel, and electrical equipment. These firms often operated under different labor relations systems, or perhaps they were not unionized. In steel, for example, an increase in worldwide capacity resulted in a reduction in capacity and diversification for U.S. firms and the rise of nonunion "minimills" that successfully took part of the market.

As a result, the management of many firms began to question the efficacy of traditional adversarialism. While they could accept it so long as markets were generally sheltered and their competitors had to operate under the same system, the increase in foreign competition meant that this was no longer the case. Therefore, management began to seek other choices for structuring their labor relations. The result was a movement toward extremes, with some firms embracing cooperation and others engaging in open conflict with unions. This choice is illustrated in Figure 6.2. Here, the traditional

FIGURE 6.2   *Management Labor Relations Strategies Since Late 1970s*

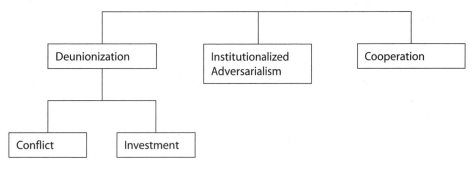

model of institutionalized adversarialism is depicted as middle ground between union-management cooperation and conflict at either extreme.

What drove the choices? In some cases, it was a desire to control costs in the production process. In others, it was part of a broad product market strategy in response to changing competitive conditions. In still others, it was the result of activation of long-dormant preferences to operate without the constraints of the traditional adversarial collective bargaining process.

FIRM CHOICES IN LABOR RELATIONS

Deunionization

Processes for Deunionization.   Some firms viewed the presence of the traditional adversarial system as an obstacle to successfully competing in a newly competitive environment. These firms made the strategic choice to either eliminate union representation or, at least so weaken the union that the constraints on the firm would be minimized.

There were two basic strategies by which a firm could deunionize—conflict and investment. A firm engaging in the conflict was able to use its rights in the legal system to accomplish deunionization. The process was, and is, straightforward. At the expiration of the contract, the firm notified the union that it wished to make changes in the collective agreement. During negotiations, the firm would make proposals that were acceptable to it but were deemed unacceptable to the union. As the law requires simply good-faith bargaining but not necessarily concessions, the firm could adhere to its proposals.

At some point during the process, the negotiations would reach legal impasse, that state at which the parties had irreconcilable differences after good-faith negotiations. At that point, the company would be legally free to implement its final pre-impasse proposal. The choice of the union would be to accept the proposal or to strike. If the union accepted the proposal, the firm was successful in obtaining its terms and conditions of employment.

If the union struck, however, the firm would have the right to hire permanent replacements, provided all strikers are given the opportunity to return to their former positions. If the firm can successfully operate with crossovers and replacements ("scabs," in union terminology), then at some point it may claim that it has a legal "good faith doubt" about whether the employees want the union to represent them.

The other deunionization strategy is investment away from the union. A firm that engages in this strategy establishes nonunion facilities in geographic areas distant from the unionized facilities. Because the nonunion facilities, by choice, have more modern, more productive capital equipment than the unionized facilities, it is difficult for the unionized facilities to compete with the nonunion facilities for internal business. The result is that the unionized facilities continue to lose business, leaving the organization with a unionized sector that is greatly reduced in size.

Advantages and Disadvantages of Deunionization.   From the point of view of the firm, the major advantage of deunionization is eliminating the obligation to negotiate with the union over terms and conditions of employment and the reestablishment of unilateralism and flexibility. This allows costs to be controlled through the adjustment of wages and the elimination of day-to-day rigidities in the work process.

The major concerns about deunionization are the costs associated with the process. Deunionization through the use of strike replacements carries both human and legal costs. If strikers perceive that they will lose their jobs, they are often willing to resort to physical confrontation. The result can be violence and injuries. Other human costs include interpersonal conflict and morale problems in the workplace as replacements and often disgruntled crossovers must work side by side.

Legal costs include the inevitable charges of unfair labor practice, as the union will likely argue that the strike was provoked by the firm's unfair labor practice rather than its good-faith refusal to accede to the union's position. This not only generates legal fees associated with defending the charge, but it also raises the possibility of a large back pay liability should the firm be found guilty and be required to reinstate the strikers. Thus, even though it obtains control over direct labor costs, the firm may expose itself to the uncertainties associated with a lawsuit. These legal challenges also mean that an attempt to deunionize may not be successful.

The physical confrontations that may occur when replacements and picketing strikers are in physical proximity to each other often result in additional legal costs. The firm may find it necessary to go to court to obtain an injunction to limit the picketing.

Investing away from the union has the advantage of gradualness, occurring over a period of time. This advantage may be enhanced if the union is a less militant one. Nonetheless, it can also be a disadvantage if the union uses its leverage in facilities that are older, but still operating. A union anticipating the firm's long-term strategy may believe it has nothing to lose by putting pressure on the firm's vulnerable areas in the unionized facilities.

Cooperation

Process of Cooperation.   Deunionization is one extreme response by a firm to new competitive pressures. On the other end of the spectrum is cooperation. In this situation, management takes the position that the major costs of unionization are associated not with unionism per se but with the rigidities associated with institutionalized adversarialism. Organizations taking this approach have moved toward cooperative relationships with the unions representing their employees, changing from rigid, adversarial structures to flexible, cooperative ones. Costs are reduced not through the direct method of reducing terms and conditions of employment, but through the indirect method of reducing the costs of adversarialism.

Firms that have taken the cooperative approach work jointly with the union to create nontraditional, nonadversarial structures for communication, such as in-plant committees. Thus, structures for continuous communication are created as an alternative to the structured communication in institutionalized adversarialism. This permits the firm to more effectively exploit the knowledge base of its workers. It is based on notions of commonality of interest between the firm and the employee. If the firm is successful, the wealth of the shareholders increases and the employee retains a well-paying job.

With increased cooperation, not only does communication change, but generally, the nature of bargaining changes. Traditional bargaining can be thought of as "positional" bargaining, with each party taking a position and then modifying it based on each side's perception of its bargaining power relative to the bargaining power of the other party. Cooperative bargaining is often "interest-based" in the sense that discussions focus on the needs of the party that proposes a change, but it often becomes a joint search for solutions. A classic trade-off is job security for workers in exchange for work-rule flexibility and moderation in compensation.

Advantages and Disadvantages of Cooperation.   As can be expected, the major advantage of cooperative structures are a reduction in conflict and rigid work rules. The firm obtains its flexibility not through open conflict and deunionization, but through working with the union. In addition, as noted, cooperation has the benefit of taking full advantage of the knowledge and expertise of workers and developing a commonality of interest between workers and management. It generally means a nonlegalistic relationship.

The major disadvantage to cooperation is the conflict between the necessities of cooperation and the legal status of the parties. Management's legal responsibility is to

MODULE
6

its shareholders, and the union's legal responsibility is to its members. To the extent that cooperation blurs these legal lines, role conflict can occur. By cooperating with the union and sharing information, does management compromise the interests of the shareholders? For example, if management shares financial information with the union, will the union take advantage of that by demanding more than it otherwise might?

By the same token, by cooperating with rather than resisting management, does the union compromise the interests of the members? For example, by sacrificing some compensation for job security, is the union sacrificing the standard of living of its members, especially if there was little risk to the job security of employees?

Traditional Adversarialism

Not all firms and unions have moved toward the extremes. Many relationships in this realm continue to bear the characteristics of traditional adversarialism. The parties continue to bargain on an arm's-length basis. The union makes concessions when it believes it is in its interest to do so, and will attempt to regain those concessions.

Parties who have maintained a traditional adversarial relationship have decided, implicitly, that they are comfortable in their traditional roles. They prefer to maintain the separation that is the hallmark of traditional adversarialism. At the same time, the firm is unwilling to challenge the status of the union as the legitimate representative of its employees. It accepts the union and deals with it.

This section has demonstrated that collective bargaining and industrial relations in the United States are characterized by variation. The archetypes in Figure 6.2 on page 6.11 represent the opposite ends of the spectrum. The following section will focus on examples of each of the strategies.[1]

APPLICATION 1

Deunionization Strategy in Labor Relations: The Case of Phelps Dodge and the United Steelworkers of America

Phelps Dodge and the unions representing employees at its Arizona copper mining and smelting operations had long had a contentious relationship. Indeed, labor strife in the copper mines can be traced to 1917, when county law enforcement officials placed 1,200 strikers in boxcars and forced them to stay in the desert for 36 hours without food or water. Every negotiation since 1959 had been associated with a strike. The 1983 strike, however, represented a new level of conflict. Phelps Dodge was negotiating with a coalition of 12 labor unions led by the United Steelworkers of America for its facilities in Arizona. The company refused to accept the industrywide contract pattern and sign a contract comparable to that which had been negotiated with other copper companies. Phelps Dodge claimed that it was far more dependent on copper than the other companies; as a result, it could not offset low earnings in copper with other income, it was not comparable to those companies, and it required relief the other companies did not.

On July 1, 1983, 2,300 unionized employees struck at the Arizona facilities in Aho, Clifton, Morenci, and Douglas. Unlike in previous strikes, where it had ceased production, Phelps Dodge maintained production with management workers, office personnel, and picket line crossovers.

The decision to maintain production raised the stakes in the dispute. If the company could maintain production during the strike, the strikers were placed at a substantial disadvantage. Moreover, the company's willingness to permit union members to cross picket lines threatened to cause divisiveness in the small towns.

Phelps Dodge was apparently aware of the possibility of violence. By mid-July, working employees were congregating at company offices and traveling to work in convoys, often past jeering strikers. By July 26, the company had obtained restraining orders to stop minor violence, limiting to five the number of picketers on each side of the state road leading to the Morenci facility. On July 27, the 3-year-old daughter of a copper worker was shot in the head while she slept. Law enforcement officials believed the shooting was "union-related," but the union denied any involvement. Other violent episodes included the burning of company-owned railroad bridges and window breakage.

On August 5, Phelps Dodge announced that it was seeking to fill 1,500 positions, meaning that if the union did not return to work, the strikers would be permanently replaced. This announcement escalated the situation. The strikers were no longer in a dispute over terms and conditions of employment, but over their jobs. On August 9, Phelps Dodge announced it was closing its Morenci facility for ten days after approximately 1,000 strikers and supporters holding baseball bats, ax handles, and pipes congregated around the entrance to the mine.

The Morenci facility reopened on August 20, this time under the watchful eye of 500 state troopers, including sharpshooters stationed in the surrounding hills. Negotiations also resumed that day. On August 29, the company announced it had rejected a union proposal. The strike continued.

In December, the company began to evict strikers who were living in company-owned housing but were unable to pay their rent. In January 1984, state troopers were again called out to prevent violence following a union meeting. On May 6, Governor Bruce Babbitt called out the National Guard after 11 people were arrested in a strike-related rock-throwing incident. On June 30, police used tear gas canisters to disperse a crowd after they claimed they were the target of a Molotov cocktail.

By late July 1984, a year after the strike began, with the facilities running at full capacity with crossovers and permanent replacements, efforts were underway to decertify the union on the grounds that it no longer had the support of a majority of the persons employed in the facilities. It was estimated that of the 2,400 Phelps Dodge employees on the payroll in Arizona, roughly 1,350 were employed before the strike and 1,050 had been hired since the strike began. The company had declined a union offer to forgo cost-of-living increases in return for a company agreement to rehire strikers and terminate replacements. The company believed the union no longer represented a majority of the employees. Wages had been cut, with the hourly rate of about $13 before the strike dropping to $10 for continuing workers and $7 for new hires.

On September 12, 1984, the regional director of the National Labor Relations Board ruled that the Phelps Dodge replacements were permanent and were eligible to vote in a decertification election. Strikers were ineligible to vote because of the length of time they had not been working. On January 27, 1985, the employees voted 1,098 to 87 to end union representation at the company's Arizona facilities. Union objections to the election were not upheld.

Phelps Dodge attributed its survival in the mid-1980s, when copper prices were low, to the reductions in labor costs associated with its labor relations strategy. By 1987, the industry's fortunes were improving, and unionized employees at copper firms Kennecott, Asarco, and Magma were either receiving negotiated bonuses or having wage reductions restored.

By 1993, Phelps Dodge, which had been described by analysts and its management as "ailing" a decade before, was healthy. The company's financial success was attributed to the lower wage costs and greater flexibility associated with operating without the union.

Other Examples of Conflict

Phelps Dodge is an example of a replacement strategy that ended in the elimination of the union. Caterpillar was involved in a nearly seven-year struggle with the UAW involving approximately 12,000 workers in Illinois, Tennessee, Colorado, and Pennsylvania.

The dispute started in November 1991 after Caterpillar declined a UAW proposal for a contract similar to that between other agricultural and heavy equipment manufacturers. The dispute led to a work stoppage, a threat to hire permanent replacements, large-scale picket line crossing of union members, and, eventually, a return to work by the UAW, the union representing Caterpillar workers. As a result of the strike, the UAW filed hundreds of charges with the National Labor Relations Board alleging that Caterpillar had violated the law. In March 1998, the UAW and Caterpillar reached an agreement that gave Caterpillar much of what it had proposed in 1991 but maintained the UAW as the representative of the employees.

At the time of this writing, the Detroit Newspaper Agency, representing the Detroit News and Detroit Free Press, is in a labor dispute with a coalition of unions representing its employees. The strike began in July 1995. Soon after that, the papers hired replacement workers and resumed publishing using replacements and picket line crossovers. The union filed unfair labor practice charges against the papers, and in August 1998, the newspapers were found to have acted unlawfully. As this book goes to press, the newspapers have appealed the decision, all the unions do not have contracts, and the papers continue to publish.

Deunionization in the Rubber Tire Industry

Although deunionization through conflict is the most noticeable method of eliminating a union, a second strategy is the use of investment—specifically, how and where new investments are made and placed. In the late 1970s and early 1980s, when the rubber tire industry shifted from bias-ply to radial tires, the companies installed the new equipment required by this shift in the newer plants in which the United Rubber Workers Union was not the bargaining agent. As a consequence, where in the early 1970s, roughly 90 percent of the industry's capacity was governed by collective agreements, that percentage had dropped to about 45 percent by 1982.

APPLICATION 2

Traditional Adversarialism in Labor Relations: The Case of United Parcel Service and the International Brotherhood of Teamsters

The 1997 strike by the International Brotherhood of Teamsters against United Parcel Service (UPS) was the latest chapter in a sometimes rocky collective bargaining relationship. The 1997 strike, which the parties claimed was driven primarily by differences over part-time workers, grew from seeds planted at least seven years earlier. In 1990, the Teamsters and UPS were unable to agree on pay rates for part-time employees. Although that agreement was eventually ratified by the membership against the recommendation of the Teamsters leadership, the union served notice that the issue was on the table.

In 1992, Teamsters president Ron Carey had publicly criticized the trucking industry for its reliance on part-time workers. Although the part-time workforce was not an issue in the 1993 negotiations between the parties, Carey's comments the previous year indicated that the matter had not been forgotten.

The parties again clashed in 1994. On February 7 of that year, the union called a one-day strike over a decision of UPS to increase the weight limit on packages from 70 pounds to 150 pounds. Just prior to the strike, UPS had filed a $50 million damage suit against the union, a suit that was ultimately dismissed. The union filed a countersuit several weeks later, which was also dismissed.

Despite this stormy relationship with the union representing its employees, UPS prospered. In 1996, it earned $1.15 billion on sales of $22.4 billion. By late 1996 and early 1997, it was estimated that UPS handled approximately 12 million packages per day, constituting approximately 80 percent of the U.S. market for ground deliveries. To an extent, UPS had ridden the boom in catalog sales. It was able to do this due in large part to low prices on deliveries made within three days, the provision of pickup services for large numbers of smaller packages, contracts with many large shippers, a substantial capital investment in tracking and sorting equipment, a management system that decomposed each work task into its component parts, and a disciplined, flexible workforce. The company's part-time workforce was a contributor to this flexibility. In mid-1997, roughly 60 percent of UPS's workforce of 185,000 was part-time, earning between $8 and $12 per hour, while full-time UPS employees earned approximately $20 per hour.

As the July 31, 1997, expiration date of the 1993 collective agreement grew closer, it was apparent that this large, part-time, relatively low-paid workforce constituted a pivotal issue in the negotiations. Negotiating past the strike deadline of 12:01 A.M. on Friday, August 1, the union finally walked off the job on Monday, August 4.

Given the notoriety of both UPS and the Teamsters, the strike was soon played out in the national media. The national news shows featured both sides of the strike on a daily basis. Both parties provided material for the media. The union portrayed its position in the strike as defending low-wage part-time workers, making the point that the success of UPS—and U.S. corporations in general—had been attained by denying workers a decent standard of living. Indeed, the Teamsters leadership encouraged their membership by stating that they were striking not just for themselves, but for all working people.

UPS, perhaps hoping for a repeat of 1994 when the membership had rejected a leadership call to strike, made its case based on worker choice, pointing out that the union was denying its members the right to vote on what it believed was a generous and fair proposal. The company made its case through advertisements, columns, and public statements on the news broadcasts.

Polling results suggested that the Teamsters had won the public relations battle. A CNN/USA Today poll found that 55 percent of respondents supported the union, as compared to only 27 percent supporting the company. This was consistent with informal interviews conducted by news correspondents. Pondering the apparent inconsistency between the inconvenience being suffered by the public and their support of the strikers, *The Wall Street Journal* ran a story attributing this support to, among other things, the warm feelings between customers and the UPS drivers who delivered and picked up from their workplaces twice a day.

The parties also differed on the wisdom of presidential intervention. UPS, with the open support of the Republican congressional leadership, publicly called for presidential involvement to resolve the dispute, using emergency dispute authority under the Taft-Hartley Act. The Teamsters, supported by the AFL-CIO, opposed presidential intervention. President Clinton took the position that he had no legal authority to intervene, as the strike did not constitute a national emergency under the Taft-Hartley Act.

On the other hand, the administration took what could be called a compromise position on intervention. President Clinton directed Alexis Herman, the Secretary of Labor, to work with the parties. Thus, although there was no statutory presidential intervention, the administration was involved.

By the eleventh day of the strike, it was clear that the tone of the dispute was beginning to change. The parties ceased their daily public posturing and, in the presence of Secretary Herman and Federal Mediation and Conciliation Service Director John Wells, began serious discussions. On August 19, the parties announced that they had reached agreement.

The outcome of the strike seemed to be a classic compromise. UPS dropped a pension proposal opposed by the union, and agreed to convert 10,000 (of approximately 110,000) part-time jobs into full-time jobs. UPS, however, retained the right to determine which jobs would be converted, and would not be required to convert the jobs if there were a substantial decrease in sales volume below the immediate prestrike levels. UPS also obtained increased flexibility on work rules.

As often happens during a strike, competitors benefited, and questions lingered regarding the costs of the strike to UPS and the Teamsters. The U.S. Postal Service experienced a substantial increase in business. Federal Express experienced a growth in revenues for the year ending August 31, 1997, from $2.69 billion to $3.3 billion, $170 million of which it attributed to the UPS strike. It had retained about 15 percent of that business through the end of November 1997. During the last week of that month, UPS's volume was down 2 percent compared to the last week in November 1996.

APPLICATION 3

Cooperation in Collective Bargaining: Ford and the UAW

The roots of the cooperative relationship between Ford and the UAW can be traced to the early 1970s and the "Quality of Worklife" (QWL) movement. QWL was an attempt to shift the model of labor relations in the United States from one of adversarialism and viewing employees as a cost to a model in which they were viewed as an asset, whose knowledge could benefit the company.

Although QWL in the 1970s had its greatest impact on General Motors, it was a matter for discussion at Ford as well. Ford's QWL program, called Employee Involvement (EI), was triggered in 1979 with the signing of a national Letter of Understanding between Ford and the UAW. Equally important as a motivating factor to the parties were Ford's enormous financial losses in the early 1980s. Ford lost $1 billion in 1980 and $1.5 billion in 1981. An integral aspect of the company's comeback strategy was cost reductions and quality improvements in the assembly process. In order to accomplish this, Ford believed that it was necessary to gain the cooperation of the UAW.

By the mid-1980s, Ford was enormously profitable. In 1978, the company's pretax earnings were $2.8 billion on sales of 6.6 million vehicles. In 1985, that figure was $3.6 billion on 5.6 million vehicles. During this time, Ford reduced employment by 28 percent, or 143,000, with management and labor sharing the cuts equally. Clearly, Ford's EI process was a major contributor to its successful strategy to reduce the costs of building cars. Ford was able to make the employment reductions while still maintaining credibility with the union.

Although the EI process, of necessity, was created with the commitment of the company's senior management, its initial contribution to Ford's turnaround was its effectiveness at the local level. An excellent example can be found at Ford's Sharonville plant, near Cincinnati. Employing 2,000 people, the Sharonville plant built automatic transmissions for Ford pickup trucks and vans. Ford had been seriously considering closing Sharonville when the local union and management established an EI process. A plantwide steering committee consisting of plant management and a bargaining committee was established. EI coordinators and area subcommittees were appointed throughout the plant. Self-directed work teams were established in 1985.

As a result, and indicative of the commitment of top management to EI, Ford awarded Sharonville a new truck transmission. With the award, cross-functional teams consisting of electrical, hydraulic, machine repair, and tool and die were formed. Training was provided so that each trade could learn the basics of the other trades.

Manufacturing classifications were collapsed into one overarching classification—manufacturing technician, permitting maximum flexibility in assignments. Teams were formed that reported to the plant superintendent. They established production schedules, relief, vacations, overtime, training needs, and daily job assignments. At the national level, Ford provided substantial training support, offering 151 courses at the plant. As a result of the EI program, there was a 53 percent improvement in quality between 1988 and 1992, and a 57 percent decline in safety costs.

Ford's commitment to its program at the national level was illustrated by its decisions in a 1997 UAW dispute with a Ford supplier, Johnson Controls, Inc. (JCI). On January 29, 1997, the UAW struck two JCI plants in Michigan and Ohio. The plants produced seats for the highly profitable Ford Expedition sport utility vehicle as well as for full-size vans. Although JCI announced that it would hire replacements for the striking workers, Ford, acting in support of the UAW, announced that it would not accept any seats from Johnson Controls if those seats were made with nonunion labor. As the strike continued, the seat shortage caused Ford to lay off 6,000 workers at two plants on February 6 and 7. On February 10, Ford announced it was moving its equipment from the JCI plant to a unionized Lear plant in Kentucky. This announcement by Ford was the spark that encouraged JCI and the UAW to engage in serious negotiations. On February 20, they reached a tentative three-year agreement covering the employees at the Michigan and Ohio plants. The agreement was ratified on February 23, and production resumed.

IN CONCLUSION

Debrief

Collective bargaining and the negotiation of workplace rules and terms and conditions of employment is a fundamentally different process than the (primarily) unilateral determination of workplace rules and terms and conditions of employment that is the "default" system in most U.S. workplaces. It involves an understanding of the nature of the workplace rules, the process and institutions of collective bargaining, the nature of the union, and the meaning of multiple perspectives on the employment relationship.

Because collective bargaining in the United States is highly decentralized, three basic management strategies have developed: deunionization, acceptance of institutionalized adversarialism, and cooperation. While a successful deunionization may result in the disappearance of the collective bargaining relationship, the process often means substantial human and legal costs. Institutionalized adversarialism retains some inflexibility, but it maintains the legal distinctiveness of each party. Cooperation minimizes industrial conflict but can result in some role conflicts for the parties involved.

MODULE
6

Suggested Readings

Bemstein, Irving. *Turbulent Years: A History of the American Worker,* Boston: Houghton Mifflin, 1971.

Block, Richard N., John Beck, and Daniel H. Kruger. *Labor Law, Industrial Relations, and Employee Choice: The State of the Workplace in the 1990s,* Kalamazoo, MI: W. E. Upjohn Institute for Employment Research, 1996.

Dunlop, John T. *Industrial Relations Systems,* Boston: Harvard Business School Press, 1993.

Kochan, Thomas A., Harry Katz, and Robert B. McKersie. *The Transformation of American Industrial Relations,* New York: Basic Books, 1986.

Voos, Paula V., ed. *Contemporary Collective Bargaining in the Private Sector,* Madison, WI: Industrial Relations Research Association, 1994.

Critical Thinking Questions

1. When considering the nature of collective bargaining, factor in your personal views and values. Think about places you have worked. Did you have "solidarity" with your coworkers and colleagues? Would you ever have been willing to strike, sacrificing your short-term interests for the broader concerns of your fellow workers? For how long would you be willing to strike?

2. Reread the sample contract language on job bidding on page 6.10. What do you think might be the purpose of such detail?

3. The National Labor Relations Board is the administrative agency that interprets and enforces collective bargaining law in the United States. As discussed, its members serve five-year terms and are appointed by the president with the advice and consent of the Senate. Compare this term limit with the lifetime appointments of federal judges in the United States. What are the advantages and disadvantages of the five-year terms for board members?

4. Consider the three management strategies of deunionization, institutionalized adversarialism, and cooperation. If you were a manager and had total control over the labor relations strategy of your company, which of the three would you favor? Why?

5. If available, read newspaper articles covering the GM-UAW strike that occurred in the summer of 1998. Compare GM-UAW labor relations with Ford-UAW labor relations. What accounts for the differences?

Exercise

Compu-Car has, for the past 19 years, manufactured computer chips for the automobile industry. Between 1982, when the company was established, and late 1994, its production employment remained stable at 40 production employees, all on one shift. This was due to stable demand for its product and the nature of the work; the company determined that it took approximately three years of experience for production employees to perform at the expected level. The company experienced limited turnover with its extremely competitive pay and benefit packages, and it hired new employees sparingly.

Beginning in early 1995, however, demand for its chips increased dramatically, as the auto manufacturers computerized an increasing number of functions in the automobile (e.g., seat positioning, antilock braking systems, engine monitoring systems, etc.). Indeed, by mid-1996, demand had increased so much that the company had moved from a one-shift to a three-shift operation in order to more efficiently use its plant and equipment. When the company added shifts, it hired new employees. The new employees were assigned disproportionately to the second, and then to the third, shift.

Because the company kept excellent production records, by late 1997 it determined that productivity on the second shift was lower than on the first shift, with lower output and lower quality, and productivity on the third shift was even lower than on the second shift. The company concluded that there were three possible reasons for this discrepancy: (1) the best, most experienced employees were on the first shift, and the least experienced employees were on the second and third shifts; (2) the company may have lowered its hiring standards when staffing the second and third shifts due to the demands of production; and (3) the working hours for company management are from 8:00 A.M. to 6:00 P.M., overlapping with most of the first shift, and some of the second shift. The company does a better job of monitoring and correcting problems when company management is in the plant. [Note that first shift is 7:00 A.M. to 3:00 P.M., second shift is 3:00 P.M. to 11:00 P.M., and third shift is 11:00 P.M. to 7:00 A.M.]

Scenario 1: Discuss how management would address this problem under the assumption that the employees are not covered by a collective bargaining agreement and management has complete discretion to make unilateral decisions in what it believes is the best interest of the firm.

Scenario 2: Develop a solution to this problem under the assumption that the employees are covered by a union-management collective bargaining agreement that contains the provisions indicated below.

MODULE
6

1.   Shift preference is determined by seniority, with the longest-service employees having the right to choose their shift.

2.   Management has the right to determine the number of employees per shift.

3.   Discipline and discharge must be for just cause.

4.   Management has the right to determine the production methods and number of supervisors on a shift.

5.   Wage rates for all employees are established by the collective bargaining agreement and do not differ by shift (e.g., employees receive no extra pay solely because they work on a specific shift).

6.   All disputes over the interpretation of the collective bargaining agreement and conditions of employment may be taken to outside arbitration that is final and binding.

7.   An arbitrator is required to make his or her decision based on the language of the collective agreement, regardless of whether he or she believes that a "better" solution is contrary to the language of the agreement.

8.   The agreement expires on April 30, 2000.

You may assume that these discussions are occurring in early 1999 and that no provisions of the agreement can be changed during the term of the collective agreement without the consent of the company and the union. On the other hand, if the company and union agree, any provision may be changed.

Reference

1.   The material in this section is based on contemporary accounts of these events in the general and business press (*New York Times, Wall Street Journal, Detroit News, Detroit Free Press* and *Business Week.*)

Index

Adversarialism. *See* Institutionalized adversarialism
Arbitration, 6.11
Arm's length relationship, 6.9, 6.10

Bargaining unit, 6.4, 6.7

Chartering practices, (unions), 6.8
Collective agreement, 6.7, 6.8, 6.10, 6.12, 6.19
Collective bargaining, 6.4–5, 6.6–7, 6.9, 6.14, 6.16
Collective representation, 6.7
Commonality of interest, 6.13
Compensation, 6.5
Competitive environment, 6.12
Conditions of employment, 6.4, 6.11
    collective bargaining, 6.6, 6.7, 6.12, 6.13, 6.19
Conflict, deunionization, 6.9, 6.11, 6.15–16
Cooperation. *See* Cooperative bargaining
Cooperative bargaining, 6.9, 6.11, 6.13, 6.19
Cross-functional teams, 6.18
Crossovers, 6.14, 6.15. *See also* Permanent re-placements, Picketing, Scabs

Decentralized institution, 6.5
Default system, 6.19
Democratic organization of unions, 6.8
Deunionization, 6.11, 6.12–14
    labor relations strategy, 6.14
    management strategy, 6.19
Discretion of management, 6.11

Economic weapons (collective bargaining), 6.7
Effort to decertify union, 6.14
Employee Involvement (EI), 6.18
Employee perspective (employment relationship), 6.9
Employee representative, collective bargaining, 6.7, 6.8, 6.14. *See also* Union representation
Employee responsibilities, 6.5, 6.6
Employment relationship, 6.8, 6.9
Exclusive representation, 6.7
Expertise of workers, 6.13

Federal Mediation and Conciliation Service, 6.17
Firm perspective, 6.9. *See also* Employment re-lationship
Firm unilateralism, 6.6
Flexibility, conditions of employment, 6.6, 6.12
    cooperative relationships, 6.13, 6.15
    work rules, 6.18
Flexible workforce, 6.17

Ford Motor, 6.18–19
Foreign competition, 6.11

General Motors, 6.18
Geographic jurisdiction, 6.8
Good faith bargaining, 6.7, 6.12
Governance intermediate bodies, 6.8
Grievance procedure, 6.11

Human resource roles, 6.5
Human resource management, 6.4

Impasse, 6.12
Individual bargaining, 6.6
Industrial relations, 6.14, 6.19
Industrywide contract, 6.14
Inflexibility. *See* Institutionalized adversarialism
Institutionalized adversarialism, 6.9–11, 6.13, 6.14, 6.18, 6.19
Investment, and deunionization, 6.11, 6.12, 6.16

Job bidding, 6.10. *See also* Collective agreement

Labor organization, 6.7. *See also* Collective bargaining, Unions
Labor relations, 6.12, 6.15, 6.18
Labor relations systems, 6.11
Labor unions, 6.4, 6.8
    collective bargaining, 6.5, 6.7
    responsibility to members, 6.14
Legal representative, 6.7, 6.15. *See also* Collective bargaining, Unions
Legal responsibility, of unions to members, 6.14
Level of conflict, 6.14
Leverage, of unions, 6.13
Local union, 6.8, 6.18
Lockout, 6.4

Management labor relations strategies, 6.11
Management response, collective bargaining, 6.9
Management strategies, 6.19. *See also* Deunionization, Institutionalized adversari-alism, Cooperative bargaining
Management workers, 6.14
Multiple perspectives, 6.5. *See also* Collective bargaining, Unions

National Labor Relations Act, 6.9
National Labor Relations Board, 6.7, 6.15
Negotiated employment relations system, 6.9

MODULE
6

Negotiated grievance, 6.7. *See also* Collective bargaining, Unions
Negotiating, 6.6–7, 6.15, 6.16–17. *See also* Collective bargaining, Unions
Nonunion facilities, 6.12
    minimills, 6.11
Nonunion labor, 6.19

Obligation, (collective bargaining), 6.7. *See also* Legal responsibility
Organizational procedure, rules, 6.6
Overarching classification, 6.18

Part-time workforce, 6.16–17
Permanent replacements, 6.14, 6.19
Physical confrontation, 6.12, 6.13
Picketing, 6.13, 6.14. *See also* Crossovers, Permanent replacements, Scabs
Positional bargaining, 6.13
Presidential intervention, 6.17
Private-sector workforce, 6.6, 6.8
Professional positions, 6.6

Quality of worklife (QWL), 6.18

Regulated model, 6.4
Replacements. *See* Permanent replacements
Role conflict, 6.14, 6.19

Scabs, 6.12, 6.14–15. *See also* Crossovers, Permanent replacements, Picketing, Strikes
Self-directed work teams, 6.18
Separate corporate councils, 6.8
Single-facility local, 6.8
Slowdown, 6.7

Strike, 6.7, 6.12,
    Teamsters & UPS, 6.16
    United Steelworkers & Phelps Dodge, 6.14–15
Surface bargaining, (collective bargaining), 6.7

Teamsters (International Brotherhood of Teamsters), 6.4, 6.8, 6.16–18
Third-party arbitration, (collective bargaining), 6.7
Traditional bargaining, 6.13

Unfair labor practice, 6.11, 6.13
Unilateral discretion, (collective bargaining), 6.9
Union, 6.7–8, 6.11–12, 6.16–17. *See also* Deunionization, Labor unions
Union facilities, 6.12
Union representation, 6.14, 6.15
Union-management cooperation, 6.12
Union-management relations, 6.4, 6.15
Unionized employees, 6.14
Unionized plant, 6.19
Unionized sector, 6.11, 6.12
United Auto Workers (UAW), 6.4, 6.8, 6.15–16, 6.18–19
United Parcel Service, strike, 6.16–18
United Rubber Workers, 6.16
United Steelworkers, 6.8, 6.14–15

War Labor Board, 6.9
Workplace
    employee attachment to, 6.5, 6.6
    problems, 6.12
Workplace rules, and labor relations, 6.5, 6.6–7, 6.12, 6.13, 6.18, 6.19

MODULE
6

Managing Human Resources
in the 21st Century

From Core Concepts to Strategic Choice

MODULE 7

Human Resource
Information Systems

Brian T. Pentland
MICHIGAN STATE UNIVERSITY

Managing Human Resources in the 21st Century: From Core Concepts to Strategic Choice,
by Kossek and Block

Publisher: Dave Shaut
Executive Editor: John Szilagyi
Developmental Editor: Bryant Editorial Development
Marketing Manager: Joseph A. Sabatino
Production Editor: Tamborah E. Moore
Manufacturing Coordinator: Dana Began Schwartz
Cover Design: Tin Box Studio
Cover Photographs: Copyright Shoji Sato/Photonica
Production House: The Left Coast Group, Inc.
Printer: West Group

Printed in the United States of America
1 2 3 4 5 02 01 00 99

For more information contact South-Western College Publishing, 5101 Madison Road, Cincinnati, Ohio, 45227 or find us on the Internet at *http://www.swcollege.com*
For permission to use material from this text or product, contact us by
- telephone: 1-800-730-2214
- fax: 1-800-730-2215
- web: *http://www.thomsonrights.com*

ISBN: 0–324–01806–1

This book is printed on acid-free paper.

Contents

MODULE OVERVIEW 7.4

OBJECTIVES 7.4

RELATION TO THE FRAME 7.4

CORE CONCEPTS IN HUMAN RESOURCE INFORMATION SYSTEMS 7.5

Kinds of Systems in the HR Function 7.6

Storing and Retrieving Information: Relational Database Technology 7.10

Distributing Information: Network Technology 7.14

Implementing and Maintaining Systems: The Software Life Cycle 7.16

Requirements 7.16

STRATEGIC ISSUES IN HUMAN RESOURCE INFORMATION SYSTEMS 7.18

Organizational Design and System Design 7.19

APPLICATION: WEB-BASED RECRUITING 7.19

IN CONCLUSION 7.23

Debrief 7.23

Suggested Readings 7.23

Relevant Web Sites 7.24

Critical Thinking Questions 7.24

Exercises 7.24

Endnote 7.25

INDEX 7.26

MODULE OVERVIEW

Cisco Systems Inc., a Menlo Park, Calif., maker of computer network hardware, uses Internet technology to connect with its 12,000 employees in 45 countries. Workers key in their own information on everything from benefits enrollment to performance-review responses. "About the only things still done on paper are vacation-request forms, and that's changing soon," says Norman Snell, senior director of global compensation and benefits. (*Wall Street Journal,* February 17, 1998, p. A1)

High-tech companies like Cisco Systems aren't the only ones making innovative use of information technology in the human resources function. Companies of all sizes are using intranets and sophisticated database systems to automate and support all aspects of the HR function. Policies and procedures, recruiting, applicant management, compensation, benefits, and training are all moving online. Where information systems were once limited to payroll, now they are everywhere.

The growth of information systems in human resources makes sense because:

- Storing, retrieving, distributing and reporting information is a practical necessity in nearly every aspect of human resource administration.

- The cost of information technology continues to decline.

- The quality and availability of HR software continues to improve.

Indeed, there is a vast array of different products on the market that can be used to support core tasks such as applicant management, benefits, compensation, and more. While some specialized applications will always require customized development, it is increasingly possible to purchase ready-made solutions to HR technology problems. Getting these systems to work successfully in your organization, however, is still a challenging problem. To be a competent HR person in the twenty-first century, you must understand how to apply information systems technology to your work.

OBJECTIVES

This module is designed to provide you with an introduction to some of the basic concepts you will need to understand information systems in the HR context. Our objective here is awareness, not expertise. To gain expertise in the technology itself requires a significant investment of time and experience. This module assumes that you have not had a course in management information systems, but that you may already be familiar with some aspects of the technology, such as databases or networks, since they are widely used for many other purposes. These technologies are the core of any computer-based information system, and human resource information systems are no exception. Our purpose here is to make you aware of how these technologies can be used to support the human resource function.

RELATION TO THE FRAME

In the past, information systems were primarily used to support basic transaction processing. Payroll was the earliest and probably still the best example of pure transaction processing in the HR function. In payroll, of course, many aspects of system design are imposed by law, such as tax withholding and W-2 processing. Benefits administration is another area that is very transaction oriented and was also an early candidate for automation. Some kinds of benefit programs, such as COBRA and FMLA, are required by law as well. But as systems move into other aspects of the human resources function, such as training and development, recruiting, grievance handling, or workers'

FIGURE 7.1   *A Frame for Understanding Human Resource Strategy:*
Context, Roles, and Constraints

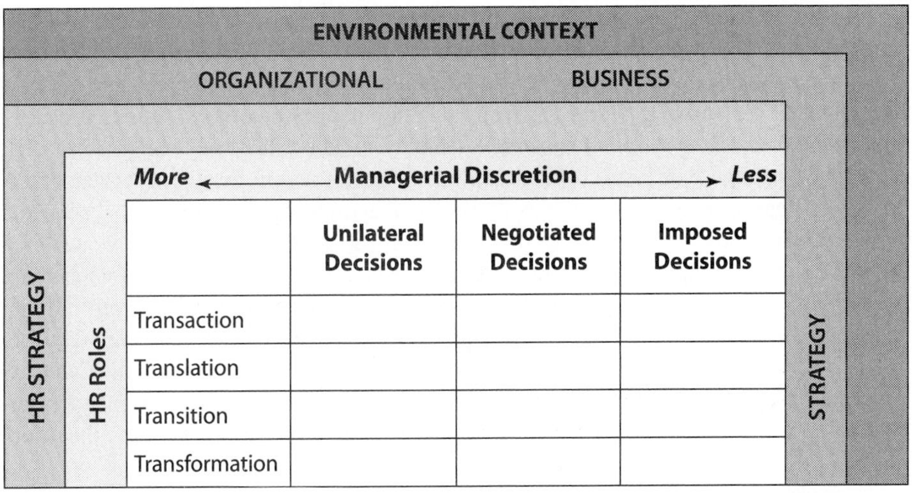

ENVIRONMENTAL CONTEXT				
	ORGANIZATIONAL		BUSINESS	
	More ← **Managerial Discretion** → *Less*			
		Unilateral Decisions	**Negotiated Decisions**	**Imposed Decisions**
HR STRATEGY / HR Roles	Transaction			
	Translation			
	Transition			
	Transformation			

STRATEGY

© 2000 by Ellen Ernst Kossek and Richard Block. Thanks to Brian Pentland, Karen Markel, and John Beck for helpful comments and discussions that enhanced the model.

compensation, they are increasingly used to build, develop, and govern. These applications are generally subject to managerial discretion. Management can choose what kind of system to implement, what its features should be, and who gets to use it.

Human resource information systems are following a trajectory similar to that of information systems in general: from basic transaction processing towards more strategic aspects of the business. To the extent that companies depend on their workforce to provide distinctive competencies, systems for recruiting, training, and developing must serve those needs. But as Broderick and Bourdreau (1992) argue, HR systems must go beyond simply improving the management of routine tasks, such as record keeping. They must connect to strategic objectives of the organization. For example, if an organization wants to expand internationally, the human resource system must support multiple currencies, multiple regulatory environments, and multiple languages. Ideally, these systems can also facilitate more effective recruiting, training, communicating, planning, and other core HR processes. While this module is too short to examine all these processes in detail, it should be clear that there is more to human resource information systems (HRIS) than just payroll. See Figure 7.1, A Frame for Understanding Human Resource Strategy.

CORE CONCEPTS IN HUMAN RESOURCE INFORMATION SYSTEMS

To understand HRIS and to be an effective member of an HRIS implementation team, there are several key ideas that you will find useful:

- Kinds of systems and their interrelationships

- Storing and retrieving information: relational database technology

- Distributing information: network technology

- Implementing and maintaining systems: the software life cycle

These concepts are applicable to information systems in any business function. In the sections that follow, we will explore each of these concepts using examples from the human resource function.

Kinds of Systems Used in the HR Function

A human resource information system includes more than just the computer-based technology. It also includes organizational practices and policies, paper-based forms of information flows, and decision making procedures. Unless all of these components are in place, the computer-based part of the system cannot function. Thus, when someone talks about "installing an HRIS," they are really talking about a major organizational change initiative. At Cisco Systems, for example, employees know that they can do basic HR transactions online, via their corporate intranet. The forms are mostly computer based. In other organizations, however, the forms for the same transactions might be paper based, or might involve a mix. The overall system includes all of these components.

Very few software applications are truly "stand-alone." Most programs store or retrieve information over a network, or share data with other programs. Even individual word processing programs and spreadsheets can share documents, read e-mail attachments, and so on. Seen from this perspective, the applications we use as individuals are only the tip of a huge computational iceberg. Most organizations have extensive information system infrastructures that involve layers of interconnected systems that work (or too often, don't work) together.

Figure 7.2 shows the several basic kinds of systems in the human resource function and the way they are typically interrelated. The arrows in the figure indicate the flow of information between systems. The most basic functions involve entering transactions (such as time and attendance) and creating reports (such as absenteeism). There are all kinds of routine transactions in an HR department (such as benefits enrollment, address changes, forms requests, and so on), all of which are candidates for automation. Automating these basic tasks does more than just save direct labor and improve service; it provides the core information needed for other systems. As shown in Figure 7.2, transaction processing systems feed data into basic management reports, but they can also feed data into more sophisticated workflow and decision support systems. To understand how these pieces fit together, let's look at some examples of these systems in some more detail.

MODULE
7

FIGURE 7.2   *Relationships between Different Kinds of Information Systems in Human Resources*

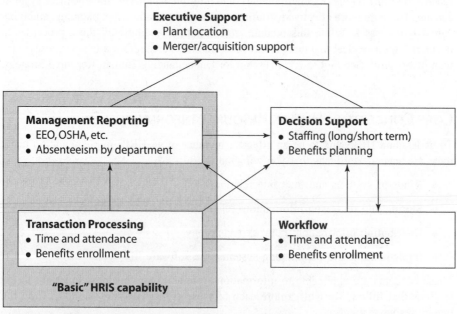

Source: Adapted from Laudon and Laudon 1994.

Transaction Processing Systems.   When you go to an automated teller machine, the system reads information from your bank card and records your transaction. Likewise, when an employee files a time sheet, or takes time off, or misses work, the information must be recorded and tracked in the appropriate place. Figure 7.3 (a typical screen from a system called HR/Vantage), shows how transactions can be entered into an HRIS. It shows that a hypothetical employee named Hal Smith was absent for 8 hours on April 5, 1996. Because the reason for the absence was jury duty, it was "excused" and "paid." It also shows that he has already missed two days due to jury duty so far this year. If this employee had a pattern of missing work for other reasons, however, the problem could be easily identified.

Time and attendance tracking is a good example of transaction processing, because employees make routine "deposits" and "withdrawals" in accordance with well-defined rules. In factory settings, a variety of automated time-clock systems are available that read an employee's ID badge like a credit card and enter the time-in and time-out information directly into a database.

Such systems can be used to provide security, as well, by functioning as access control to secure areas. In professional settings, such as law firms or consulting firms, employees usually track their time by project so that clients can be billed appropriately. Each day or week, the time spent on each project is recorded, often in 15-minute increments. Systems that allow employees to fill out these time-sheets online are a huge improvement over the traditional paper-based systems.

Time and attendance data are an excellent example of where transaction processing feeds into other systems. Consider the following uses for time and attendance data:

- Payroll: How much should we pay this person this period?

- Vacation scheduling: Has this person accrued enough vacation days?

- FMLA compliance: Is this employee legally entitled to time off, and has the employee used his or her full entitlement yet?

- Billing: How many hours of direct labor should we charge this client?

- Absenteeism: Are we having a problem in this department?

MODULE
7

FIGURE 7.3   *Typical Attendance Tracking Screen*

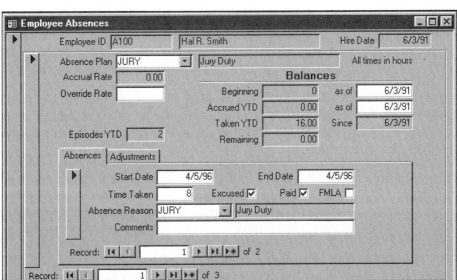

Source: © Spectrum, Inc. Used by permission.

In the context of the human resource function, even the most basic transaction (e.g., recording how many hours someone worked) feeds into a host of other systems, such as reporting systems or workflow systems.

Workflow Systems. Office automation or "workflow" systems are used to support work processes where more than one individual is involved. When forms or paperwork must be transferred from person to person, or department to department, workflow systems can facilitate the routing and transfer. For example, in a recruiting process, paperwork must go from a hiring manager and to various points in the HR function and elsewhere in the organization.

The decision to hire is only the first step of a long and often cumbersome process. There are typically routine procedures for getting approval to hire and creating an "open position." Once the position has been authorized and a job description is available, there are usually procedures for posting it internally, or advertising it externally, or otherwise generating appropriate applicants (such as campus recruiting or executive search consultants). Given a pool of applications, there is usually a screening process that involves more paperwork (interviews, tests, rankings, etc.). Once an individual has been selected for hiring, there are several steps required to initiate the employment relationship. This may include verification of eligibility for employment (the federal I-9 form), benefits enrollment, payroll setup (e.g., tax withholding), assignment of office space or equipment, and so on. A simple transaction processing system could be used to record certain steps in this process (e.g., contact information, benefits enrollment, etc.), but a workflow system is intended to support the process from one step to the next. Many workflow systems are inspired by the vision of the "paperless office"—everything stays online. While few systems currently meet this ideal, it is increasingly feasible and cost-effective to keep actual paper to a minimum.

Companies like Texas Instruments, for example, have taken great strides to streamline this process and make it more effective (Flynn 1998). Chuck Nielson, Vice President of HR at TI, explains that recruiting is key: "Just to be pragmatic, it's damn competitive right now for the kind of people we're needing. You can't get the best if you don't have an excellent recruitment product. We're wrestling like crazy to get the best people in instead of just filling slots." (Flynn 1998, p. 31). In a tight labor market, they need to identify those individuals and close the deal quickly, before the candidate goes elsewhere. This is a good example of how an effective HRIS can support the strategic goals of the organization.

Reporting Systems. The generation of standard reports is a basic function in any human resource information system. The data accumulated as a result of transactions is stored and used as the basis for reports. For example, a time and attendance system could be used to generate reports on sick time utilization by department, or to identify areas with high absenteeism. A major reason for installing information systems in the human resource function is to facilitate this kind of reporting. In addition to standard reports, even the most basic HRIS allows customized or ad hoc reporting. The ability to produce such reports is quite valuable because it facilitates improved decision making.

While HR data can be valuable by itself, its utility in management decision making is greatly enhanced when it is combined with data from other functions, such as manufacturing or sales. The capability to make these linkages is a feature of so-called "enterprise resource planning" systems from vendors like SAP, Peoplesoft, or Baan (Edmondson, Baker, and Cortese 1997). If fully implemented throughout an organization, these systems can provide the capability of matching HR data with production and financial data. This matching makes it possible to answer questions like, "What is our direct labor cost for this sub-assembly?" and "Will we have to add a third shift if our sales increase 20 percent? What will that cost?" These kinds of data can be built into standardized reports (showing production and direct labor by facility, for example), or they can be fed into systems that are specifically designed to support decision making.

Decision Support Systems. Decision support systems rely on transaction data as well, but they go further than simply reporting information; they typically incorporate rules, formulae, or specialized displays that are designed to help end users make decisions. Decision support systems can be as simple as a spreadsheet or a graph, or they can incorporate complex optimization procedures. Because they can incorporate decision-making rules, they can be used to restrict users to following prescribed corporate policies or procedures.

Scheduling and staffing are areas where decision support can be especially useful. In scheduling, a routine question is how many people to schedule for a given time period. If there are seasonal variations, or changes in workload due to increasing or decreasing sales, it may be helpful to have a model that recommends the number of people in each job category that should be scheduled. Supermarkets and other retail operations use these systems to schedule cashiers, baggers, and so on.

The same kinds of questions emerge over the longer term with respect to recruitment and staffing. If increased sales are anticipated, what kinds of people need to be hired and how many? To get the right answer to that question, one has to factor in turnover rates and promotions as well. Of course, unless the basic human resource and benefits are already online, such a system could not function. More sophisticated analytical problems, such as benefits planning and analysis, are also excellent candidates for decision support.

Of course, decision support does not always work smoothly, as demonstrated by a recent "fiasco" at FedEx (Blackmon 1998). Airline scheduling is extremely complex, and the objective is to keep on schedule with the most efficient use of planes, fuel, and human resources. Pilot schedules are constrained by FAA rules concerning mandatory rest periods between flights, and also by company work rules. At most airlines, these work rules are the product of collective bargaining with the pilot's union. FedEx implemented the same computerized decision support software that had been used successfully at other airlines. But while those carriers worked closely with pilot unions to ensure that pilot's interests were maintained, FedEx rushed ahead without taking their employees' needs into account. The system recommended legally feasible but grueling flight plans. Pilots found themselves "blasting across the time zones of two hemispheres, pulling back to back transpacific and transatlantic flights . . . Worst of all, the Altitude Pairing system, commonly called the "Optimizer," wrecked many pilots' cherished hometown layovers." (Blackmon 1998, p.1). As a result, union representation rose from 60 percent to 94 percent in a few months and the union board held a membership vote to authorize a strike. A major issue in the negotiation was an overhaul of the work rules that govern the assignment of pilots to flights. The FedEx case is an excellent example of the details of a human resource system ultimately being determined through a collective bargaining process.

Executive Support Systems. Some organizations provide decision support for top management decision making, as well. The difference between so-called executive support systems and traditional decision support is not just the rank or title of the people using the system. While traditional decision support systems are usually directed at fairly well-defined, narrowly focused problems, executive support systems bring together data from diverse sources to help assess broader strategic questions. Human resource issues figure prominently in some of these decisions.

For example, if an organization is trying to decide where to locate a new facility, it is helpful to have comparative data on the availability of the relevant occupational groups, prevailing wages, education levels, labor standards, and so on. When considering a merger or an acquisition, labor costs (including pensions and benefits) are usually a significant concern. The ability to provide timely, accurate information is one way that the HR function can become a more valuable strategic partner in top management decision making. When seen from this perspective, human resource information systems take on added significance. Automating routine transactions like time and attendance may be a valuable end in itself, but it provides a foundation for other systems that may be of even greater value to the organization.

Storing and Retrieving Information: Relational Database Technology

All of the systems described above depend on the ability to store and retrieve information. In most human resource information systems, this basic function is handled by a relational database. But what makes a relational database special? Figure 7.4A– Figure 7.4C shows a typical form for entering the detailed qualifications and credentials of an employee. In Figure 7.4A, the "Certification" part of the form is showing, but by clicking on the "tabs," one could also view or update records of employee education or other training, as shown in Figures 7.4B and 7.4C.

The screens shown in Figures 7.4A, 7.4B, and 7.4C are used to record some of the basic information needed to keep track of employee skills, training, and development. For example, imagine that you are planning on opening a new facility and you need 15 people trained in a particular technology. Does your current workforce already have these skills? If not, how many more people need training? Or imagine that your workforce includes dozens of certified technicians who must periodically get recertified or get "continuing education" classes to keep their certification current. This database helps you track and schedule the necessary training. Certifications are frequently required by law; failing to keep current would expose your organization to fines or legal liability.

Note that for each employee, there are multiple kinds of credentials to keep track of (education, training, certification, skills). To make matters worse, there are different numbers of related items—not everyone has the same number of educational credentials or certifications. Some people may have several credentials, while others may have none. This kind of data cannot be stored or retrieved efficiently if it is stored in a simple "flat file," like a spreadsheet.

FIGURE 7.4A *Training and Development: Certifications*

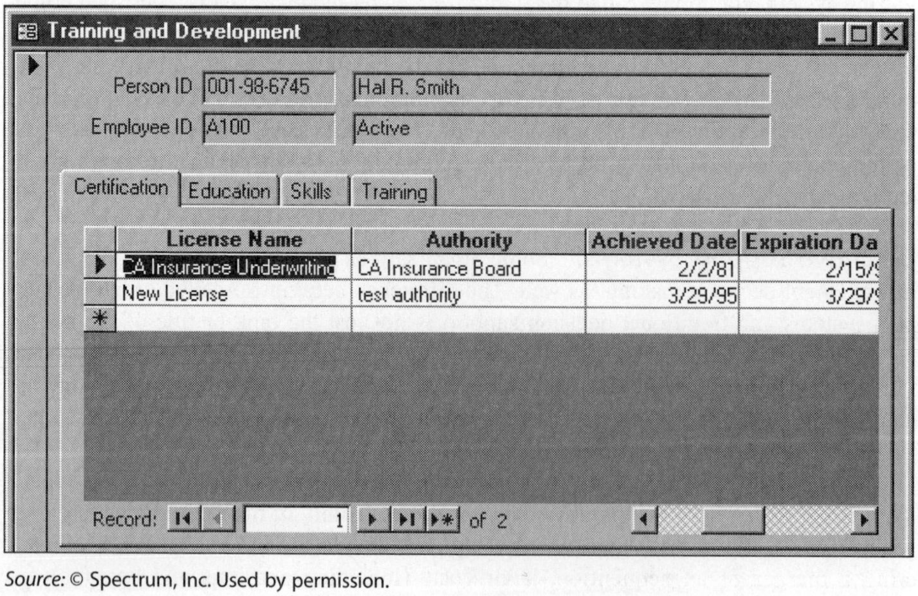

Source: © Spectrum, Inc. Used by permission.

FIGURE 7.4B   *Training and Development: Education*

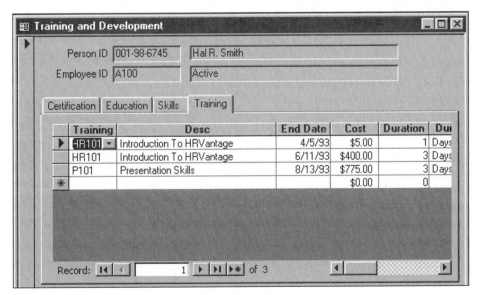

Training and Development

Person ID [001-98-6745]   [Hal R. Smith]

Employee ID [A100]   [Active]

| Certification | Education | Skills | Training |

School Name	Major	Start Date	End Date	Assistance	GPA
College San Mateo	LIB	9/16/63	6/15/65	$0.00	3
Univ. Calif. Berkeley	BUS	9/15/65	6/15/67	$0.00	3.5
Stanford University	PSYC	2/14/69	6/15/71	$0.00	3.8
				$0.00	0

Record: |◄ ◄ | 1 | ► ►| ►* | of 3

Source: © Spectrum, Inc. Used by permission.

To handle this kind of data, HR systems use a relational database. This kind of database gets its name from its structure, which consists of entities and the relations among them. Entities can be almost anything, such as people, or locations, or departments, or jobs. In this example, some of the entities are educational or training credentials. Relations are used to indicate which people have which jobs, in which departments, in which locations, and so on. The most common kind of relation in an HR database is one-to-many relationship. There are innumerable examples: one person may have many credentials, many dependents, or many benefit plans. One department may have many employees, many locations, and so on.

Figure 7.5 on page 7.12 shows the entity relationship model required to store the data from the employee training and development forms shown in Figure 7.4. Note that the data for "education" is different than the data for "training" or "certification." The

FIGURE 7.4C   *Training and Development: Training*

Training and Development

Person ID [001-98-6745]   [Hal R. Smith]

Employee ID [A100]   [Active]

| Certification | Education | Skills | Training |

Training	Desc	End Date	Cost	Duration	Dur
HR101 ▼	Introduction To HRVantage	4/5/93	$5.00	1	Days
HR101	Introduction To HRVantage	6/11/93	$400.00	3	Days
P101	Presentation Skills	8/13/93	$775.00	3	Days
			$0.00	0	

Record: |◄ ◄ | 1 | ► ►| ►* | of 3

Source: © Spectrum, Inc. Used by permission.

FIGURE 7.5 *Relational Model for Training and Development Data*

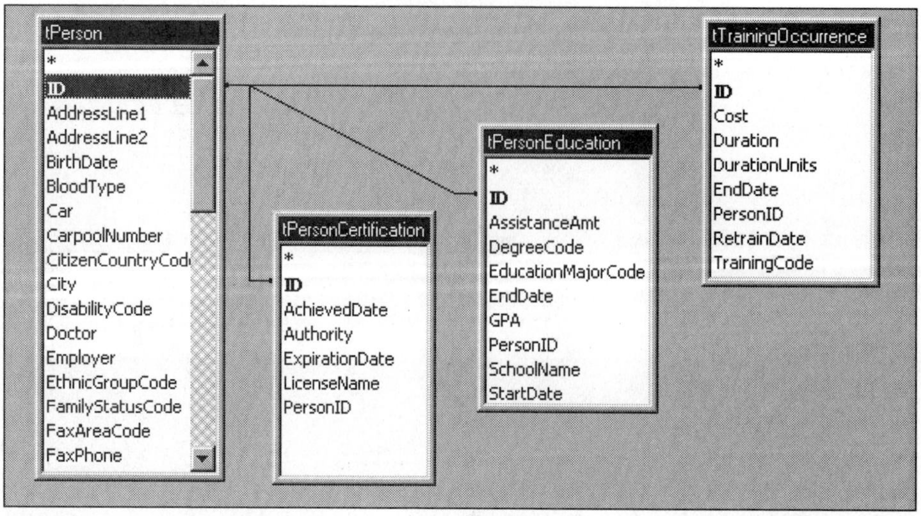

Source: © Spectrum, Inc. Used by permission.

MODULE
7

ability to tailor the information associated with entity is a key part of what makes relational databases so useful in human resources.

Now let's look at another example of how a relational database can be used to create a report for job postings. Nearly every large organization maintains a system of internal job postings to make employees aware of opportunities for transfers or promotions. Figure 7.6 shows a typical list of job openings for a hypothetical company. Note that it includes information on the salary range for each position, as well as the grade level, and posting date. Where does the information for these postings come from?

The job openings report is created using the relational database shown in Figure 7.7. While this figure may seem confusing at first, take a minute to look it over. The large table near the middle describes the job itself, including the desired education, desired experience, essential functions, primary responsibilities, tasks performed, and so

FIGURE 7.6 *Job Openings Report*

Job Opening Notice

Date Printed: *23-Apr-98*

The following jobs are currently open. Contact the employment office for further information.

Post Date	Job Code	Title	Overtime	Grade	Annual Minimum	Midpoint	Maximum
Job Family:	**Clerical And Support- General**						
6/30/95	2607	Clerk-Personnel	Non-exempt	04	$8,819.20	$12,272.00	$15,308.80
Job Family:	**Computer Operations**						
	0003	EEO - General Technical	Exempt	09	$14,801.40	$21,145.32	$27,489.24
Job Family:	**General Management**						
	0001	EEO - General Management	Exempt	09	$14,801.40	$21,145.32	$27,489.24
Job Family:	**Underwriting**						
6/30/95	8605	Underwriter-Senior Workers C	Exempt	14	$36,832.32	$52,617.60	$68,403.96

Source: © Spectrum, Inc. Used by permission.

on. Note that some of these attributes, such as the FLSA status code, are required by law. Job descriptions like this can be used for all kinds of purposes, such as recruiting, compensation analysis, and ADA compliance. But the organization has many jobs, only some of which are currently open, so there is a separate table (in the upper left corner) that describes the specific job opening. This table includes the approval date, the posting date, and other information needed to administer the internal recruiting process. There is a one-to-many relationship between job descriptions and job openings; for any job, there may be many openings, but for each job opening, there is only one job description.

Likewise, on the right side of Figure 7.7, there is a table that stores information on the grade level for the job. This includes the minimum, mid-point, and maximum base pay rates, as shown in the job openings report. Why are these pay rates stored in a separate table instead of being stored with each job, or with each employee? The answer is that it simplifies making changes and helps keep all information accurate and up-to-date.

Imagine that you have just negotiated a new contract with one of your labor unions. The contract calls for a new minimum base pay for employees in certain grade levels. To make this change correctly and implement the new salary agreement, you need to know which jobs are in those grade levels, and which employees are in those jobs. In a paper-based system, this would mean leafing through employee folders (which are probably stored alphabetically), searching for the affected individuals and making each change individually (and then notifying payroll). In the relational database structure, all of this can be handled automatically. Just change the information for the affected grade levels, and all related jobs will pick up the new pay rates. And of course, the correct information will show up in the job openings report the next time it is printed. Perhaps more important, however, is the ability to use the database to do "what-if" scenarios while you are in the process of negotiating the new contract. For example, what would be the cost of a 3 percent increase to certain grade levels? As discussed in the previous section, many applications are interdependent. This is an example of how a transaction-based system can also be used for reporting and decision support.

FIGURE 7.7 *Relational Database for Job Posting Report*

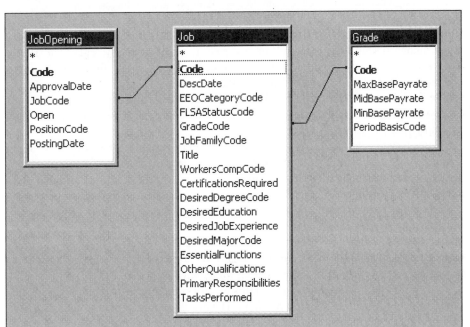

Source: © Spectrum, Inc. Used by permission.

Distributing Information: Network Technology

To make information useful, it must be available where it is needed. In many systems, distribution is just as important as storage and retrieval. In the past, human resource applications, such as payroll, were usually centralized on a single computer and used by a small group of authorized users (e.g., the payroll department). The trend today is toward distributing human resource applications throughout the organization. The example of Cisco Systems, where employees can do routine transactions themselves, via a network, is becoming increasingly common.

Networking has several benefits for human resource systems. First, it puts information where it is needed. Take the example of job postings from the previous section: a list of available openings is pointless unless it can be distributed to interested candidates. Many organizations are finding that once the network is in place, it is easier, faster, and cheaper to distribute information via computer than with paper. The more numerous and widely distributed the locations, the greater the potential benefits. Second, information can be more up-to-date. Consider the job postings again; as positions get filled, a computer based listing can change automatically. A paper-based listing (for example, in a newsletter) inevitably becomes obsolete and inaccurate as positions are filled. This problem is especially difficult for such taken-for-granted activities as internal telephone lists. Think of any organization where you have worked. How frequently were updated phone lists distributed? Was the list *ever* complete and up-to-date for more than a few days?

More generally, networked applications make it possible to decentralize decision making while keeping data centralized. In human resources, there are many examples where this is useful, such as hiring. Consider a geographically dispersed organization, with operations in several locations around the country (or around the world). It is valuable to keep track of all personnel, in all locations, in a common database. Centralizing HR data makes it possible to create a complete organizational address book, to continue the previous example. Even before applicants are hired, it is useful to share resumes across locations, so that applicants can be matched against the full range of opportunities. At the same time, it is very helpful to decentralize some aspects of the hiring process, such as interviews and final selection. This balance between centralized data storage and decentralized decision making is made possible with networks.

Client-Server Systems in Human Resources.

In an effort to strike this balance, many human resource applications are designed as client-server systems (The 1995). The "server" typically provides centralized storage of data, while the "client" allows end-users access to the portions of the data that they need. There are many ways to distribute data storage and computational work between clients and servers. The details of these arrangements are beyond the scope of this module. The important concept here is simply that processing is decentralized.

Because the client-side software is a full-fledged program (instead of just a "dumb terminal"), it can be designed to perform a wide variety of different functions. Client-server systems can be used for transaction processing, workflow automation, and decision support, as well as basic reporting functions. Also, client software can be configured to allow varying levels of access to different categories of users. For example, individual employees can be given access to view or update portions of their own data, while supervisors can have access to data on their direct reports. The ability to tailor data access depending on each organizational role is a key part of what makes client-server software so helpful in implementing a modern HR system.

The difficulty with client-server software lies primarily in its complexity. Traditional systems reside on a single machine. Having the entire program and all of the data in a single location simplifies installation and maintenance, whether it's a personal computer or a mainframe. When software and data are distributed across a network, however, different parts can get "out of synch." For example, upgrading any part of the system or the underlying network can potentially introduce problems. Also, distributed systems create problems for security. When legitimate users could come from anywhere in the organization, it becomes more difficult to filter out the illegitimate ones.

Intranets and the World Wide Web in Human Resources.   Alongside their customized client-server applications, many human resource organizations are taking advantage of the generic technology used on the Internet and the World Wide Web (WWW). Web-based systems are also client-server in their design, using a "web server" and "web browsers" such as Netscape or Internet Explorer. But unlike a client-server system designed specifically for human resources, WWW systems can be used for nearly anything. When used on a private network that is available only to members of an organization, this kind of system is referred to an "intranet." When used between organizations, on the Internet, the term "extranet" is sometimes used. Either way, the technology is the same.

Internet technology is evolving very quickly, so it is difficult to write about anything that will not become obsolete just as quickly. For example:

- Creating web pages used to require a good working knowledge of Hypertext Markup Language (HTML). Now, any typical word processing or spreadsheet program can "publish" documents to the WWW. Specialized HTML editors are available that make it easy to create entire web sites.

- Web pages used to contain only static information, such as text or graphics. Now, they frequently contain dynamic data retrieved from a database.

- Web clients (like Netscape) had very limited processing capabilities, such as buttons and links to other documents. Now, through the use of programming languages like Java, they can execute elaborate programs of any kind.

- Hundreds (probably thousands) of new web sites that are of potential interest to HR managers and unions have been created. These include a variety of sites for recruiting and placement, as well as many excellent informational resources. A few of these sites are listed at the end of this chapter.

These changes (and others) occurred over a period of only about three years, during which time the cost of the technology dropped dramatically as well. It is difficult to predict what the future holds, but even these changes have significant implications for HRIS.

First, the ease of creating WWW documents means that anyone can do it. It is entirely realistic for HR departments to create and maintain their own portion of the corporate web site. Many organizations post policies and procedures on the web to reduce printing costs and keep them up-to-date.

Second, the ability to retrieve and display information from a database means that WWW technology is a viable way to distribute that information. The job postings report shown in Figure 7.5, for example, is an excellent candidate for a corporate intranet.

Third, the ability to create customized, secure client software means that WWW technology can be used for all kinds of core HR processes, from benefits enrollment to recruiting.

Finally, the growing number of resources on the WWW makes it an increasingly useful tool for human resources and labor relations. A recent book (Moran and Padro 1997) lists hundreds of web sites and discussion groups of interest to human resource managers. The resources are already vast, and they are constantly growing and changing.

In other words, web technology is quickly becoming a critical tool for HR departments. Whether you are creating your own web site or just browsing, these tools are likely to become part of your daily work routine. Like the other technologies mentioned in this chapter, becoming a "web guru" takes a significant investment of time and effort. But if the trends in technology continue, human resource and labor relations professionals may find that it is an investment they need to make.

Implementing and Maintaining Systems: The Software Life Cycle

The availability of good software packages makes it less and less common that anyone develops HR software from scratch. Still, software is a large, complicated investment. In many respects, it is more like getting married than it is like making a purchase. In particular, implementing an HRIS is a long-term commitment. It takes a lot of work to get started, and once you cross the threshold, it's very hard to throw it out and start over. Plus, your vendor must be able to support you over time as your needs change and evolve. Like selecting a mate, selecting an HRIS is a decision worth taking seriously.

Unfortunately, even a seemingly sensible relationship sometimes ends in failure. FoxMeyer Drug Co, the nation's fourth largest distributor of pharmaceuticals, was expecting to save $40 million per year after implementing SAP's R/3 enterprise resource planning software. The system was intended as a complete overhaul of the company's warehousing and distribution process, as well as other aspects of the business. But after spending over $100 million, the system was still not operational and FoxMeyer was eventually forced to file for bankruptcy. While this is an extreme example in terms of both size and severity of the failure, it is a useful reminder that implementing new systems is not always easy. Many implementation efforts, even small-scale ones, yield disappointing results in terms of schedule, budget, or functionality. To minimize this risk, it is important to understand what is required to get a system up and running.

Figure 7.8 depicts a typical software life cycle, modified to reflect the fact that very few HR systems are developed from scratch.[1] Rather, after requirements are worked out, a vendor is selected and the basic package is purchased and then customized. Unlike a "shrink-wrapped" application, such as a word processing program, even a simple HRIS requires extensive planning, implementation, and support if it is going to be successful. The software may arrive on a CD-ROM, but you can't expect to just install it and start using it. A minimum of six months will be required (and typically more like 12–18 months) to get the system working. This is because the installation of any system raises a number of questions that usually do not have easy or obvious answers. For example, who controls the data in the system? Who has access to which pieces of information? Because systems can affect so many different parts of an organization, these kinds of issues take time to resolve. The following sections describe some of the most important steps to a successful implementation.

Requirements

Before purchasing or installing a new system, it is worth taking time to define the problem that the system is intended to address. The "requirements" phase of the life cycle is intended to answer the question: What are our needs?

Functionality is obviously the most important consideration, but since you usually can't have everything you want, you have to identify priorities. What is *really* needed, by whom, for what purpose? For example, does your system need to handle multiple currencies? multiple languages? multiple tax systems? These kinds of

FIGURE 7.8 *System Life for Purchased HR Software*

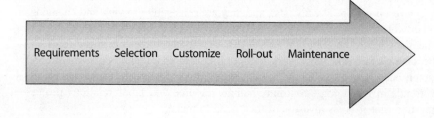

Requirements Selection Customize Roll-out Maintenance

questions interact with the strategic issues identified in the next section because system requirements should be decided in relation to the overall design and strategic objectives of the organization. Ideally, determining requirements is much more than an exercise in automating existing processes. Rather, it should include some consideration of what your processes should be and a redesign of those processes, if necessary. Even when large strategic changes are not envisioned, it may still be easier (and cheaper) to redesign existing processes to match the available software rather than customizing the software to match your existing processes (Williamson 1997).

Whether redesigning processes or not, it is important to keep an eye on what is feasible from a technical, economic, and operational point of view. For example, are there technical limitations on the kinds of software your current computer systems can host? Such limitations become an important part of the requirements. For example, if all the computers in your organization run Windows/NT, any new application must run on Windows/NT. Economic feasibility centers around costs: you have to stay within your budget, both for the initial investment and the ongoing maintenance and operations. If a new system requires an additional full-time staff member to maintain it, for example, that might be difficult to justify. Finally, not all systems are operationally feasible. For example, it might make sense to allow employees to view and update their own records (e.g., selecting a benefit plan). But such a plan would not be feasible unless everyone had access to a terminal or a computer that is connected to the network and training on how to use it.

The requirements process does not necessarily result in the decision to purchase a new system. One can decide to leave well enough alone and do nothing, or to upgrade an existing system in some way. But if the decision is made to invest in a new system, the requirements process should generate a list of specific things that the new system should be able to do. This list becomes the basis for screening vendors and selecting a system.

Selection.   Once you have developed a basic set of requirements and decided that a new system is needed, it is time to proceed to selection. Selecting a vendor is often done through a "request for proposal" (RFP) process. Depending on the sophistication and availability of your own information systems staff, you may or may not need to select a consultant to assist in the implementation, as well as a vendor for the product. The early stages of the process involve identifying a "short list" of vendors that are capable of (and interested in) supplying the necessary software. This may involve checking references and basic qualifications. For example, does the vendor have satisfied clients with requirements similar to your own? The later stages involve working out the details and making a final choice. This should involve demonstrations of the software and extensive review of the specific technical capabilities and requirements.

Customization.   In the past, most HR software was completely customized and available only to large organizations that had an information systems department capable of undertaking large programming efforts. Today, a wide range of packaged applications are available to address many aspects of the HR function. It is increasingly unlikely that an organization would build the core parts of an HRIS (e.g., payroll, benefits, applicant management, etc.) from scratch. However, packaged applications may not meet all the needs of a specific organization, and they never include all the detailed descriptions of departments, pay rates, vacation plans, and benefit options that are needed to operate. One also needs to design the procedures for its use, including data security and access rights. As a result, even if you are purchasing a "vanilla" system, it will require significant setup and customization. Simply defining these parameters can take weeks or even months.

The big trade-off here is the extent to which you customize the software versus customizing your operations. The prevailing wisdom today is increasingly leaning toward the latter: buying packaged applications and customizing your operations to fit. In many cases, the software embodies "best practices" that are worth adopting. In other cases, it is simply cheaper and easier over the long run to adapt your business. This is especially true when you are installing software in multiple locations that currently use different procedures (for example, you are installing applicant tracking software in several divisions that have traditionally handled this function separately). In that situation, most of the locations would have to make changes in any case. They may as well adapt to the same software.

Roll-out. Just because a system is ready for use does not mean that the organization is ready to use it. There are a large number of activities required to get a complex system into productive use. For example, what training will be required, and for whom? It is critical to plan for these needs in advance because they consume a lot of resources and take a lot of time and attention. Insufficient, inappropriate, or badly timed training is a common problem in systems implementation, and the costs of training are often underestimated (Stedman 1998).

Also, in most cases there will be existing data that needs to be converted. If so, a conversion strategy must be planned. Will the old system continue to operate in parallel with the new system until the bugs are worked out? Or will operations cut over from one system to the other all at once? Parallel operation is safer, but more expensive. These decisions need to be made based on the constraints of time and available resources.

Throughout the roll-out process, and even before, communication with stakeholders is critical. One needs to make sure that people are prepared for the change and that rumors or negative impressions are managed appropriately. It is also important to develop and put in place an appropriate support plan. Will telephone support be required? If so, who will handle the phone calls and how will they be trained?

In a large organization, or with a large system, it is nearly impossible to get everyone using a new system at the same time. The question arises, then, how to proceed. Should the new system be implemented by location? Or, if the software is divided into modules, should it be implemented one module at a time? These are difficult choices, but they are key to the success of a large project. The complexity of the roll-out phase is one reason why consultants with appropriate experience can be an important asset.

Maintenance. Once a system is in operation, it needs to be maintained. Estimates suggest that roughly half the cost of a system is incurred after it is fully operational. There are always problems that emerge, either because they were present all along or because conditions change and the software needs to change, too. At some point, if conditions change enough, one has to revisit the question of requirements: should the current system be upgraded? Is a new system needed? The important point here is that system implementation is never really "done."

STRATEGIC ISSUES IN HUMAN RESOURCE INFORMATION SYSTEMS

It should be clear from the examples given so far that human resource information systems affect critical resources in the organization. System design interacts with organizational design, and gives rise to a wide range of issues. While many of the issues involved in HRIS implementation are operational in nature, the basic decisions of what to automate and how to adapt the technology to the organization are clearly strategic. This is particularly true if the technology is used to facilitate increased flexibility, better recruiting and retention, and workforce development.

MODULE
7

TABLE 7.1 *Effects of Organizational Structure on HRIS Capabilities*

Structure	Implications for HRIS
One location	Everything can be centralized
	Communication is fast and inexpensive
	Single language, currency, and legal environment
Multiple locations (all in the United States)	Need local HR for some processes
	Communication is more difficult
	Single language and currency but differing legal environments at the state level (e.g., state taxes)
International locations	Need local HR for most processes
	Communication is much more difficult
	Multiple languages, currencies, and legal environments

Organizational Design and System Design

Ideally, system structure and organization structure go hand in hand: the way a system is designed supports and complements choices about how a business is organized. Too often, however, they can be in conflict. As an example, consider the differing issues that face organizations with differing degrees of geographic dispersion. The question of where to locate operations is clearly a key strategic issue for any organization. If an organization chooses to respond to competitive pressures by "going global," it would benefit from a human resource information system that supports this strategy. Table 7.1 shows, in very general terms, how this strategic choice might affect HRIS operations.

Geographic decentralization is only one dimension of organizational design that affects HRIS. If an organization includes multiple business units, these may have rather different business requirements and operational needs. Imagine a high-tech organization where one division focuses on manufacturing and distribution of products, while a separate division focuses on service (technical support, repair, etc.). The two divisions will very likely have different policies concerning travel, time reporting, career paths, and compensation. In addition, the field service division will need to track the assignment of vehicles and equipment (such as portable computers) to employees, and may have a greater need to monitor and update the training of their personnel. As the mix of business units in the organization gets more diverse, the task of implementing a single, centralized system to meet all of their needs becomes more challenging.

APPLICATION: WEB-BASED RECRUITING

So far, we have talked about a wide variety of different HR systems. In this section, let's focus on an application that brings together all of the concepts we have discussed: web-based recruiting. There are a number of specialized web sites that provide a clearinghouse for resumes and job opportunities, such as *www.monster.com* and *www.career-mosaic.com*.

At the same time, more and more companies are adding "job applications" to their own corporate web sites (Mottl 1998). These customized sites can do much more than just collect resumes. For example, Texas Instruments provides an online "compatibility" test, called "Fit Check," that prospective applicants can fill out to see whether they would be good candidates for a job at TI (see *www.ti.com*). Cisco Systems uses its web site to let prospective applicants "Make friends @ Cisco" (see *www.cisco.com*). Applicants are put in touch (via electronic mail) with current employees and hear about what it's really like to work at the company. Even companies that are not in high-tech industries have had great success in recruiting online. Humana Inc., an HMO with over 20,000 employees, based in Louisville, Kentucky, used to spend $128 in advertising per qualified resume. Today, the figure has dropped to six cents. Reginald Barefield, Humana's Executive Director of Talent Resources, says, "A major paradigm shift is taking place. The way companies recruited only a few years ago is much different than how they must recruit today." (Greengard 1998)

At a minimum, a recruiting web site requires the basic technologies described in this module. Database technology is needed for storing and retrieving the applicant and job information, and network technology for collecting the information and making it available. But making it successful takes more than just good technology. The following article provides some useful advice on how companies can make the most effective use of Internet technology in online recruiting.

Ten Easy Tips for Recruiting Online

Mark Williams and Ben Klau

Building a recruitment center within your company's Web site is a popular way of increasing the visibility of job announcements at a reasonable cost. But posting a job online is not as simple as running a classified ad in your local paper. Two experts in online recruiting offer these tips to help you get started.

So you've decided to expand your company's Web site to include recruiting capability. Or maybe you're just taking your first steps toward setting up the heavily traveled information superhighway. Either way, before plunging head first into cyberworld, here are a few pointers on building an effective and lasting Internet recruiting center.

Tip One: Consider whether you really need a Web site. If you're not yet convinced that you need a corporate Web site, consider this fact: According to the 400 HR professionals who in the past two years have participated in Austin Knight's "Internet Recruitment Survey" (which you can view online at *www.austinknight.com*), the number of companies with corporate Web sites has jumped 400 percent since 1996. Unlike the early days of Web recruiting, when most recruiters took their first cybersteps via a third-party career hub like On-line Career Center (*www.occ.com*), today's successful cybercruiters also are incorporating online recruitment pages into their corporate Web sites. In fact, nearly 70 percent of respondents to the Austin Knight survey reported that corporate homepages are effective places to recruit candidates. Only half that number said career hubs were equally effective. It's clear that you need to include

your company homepage if your goal is a well-rounded online recruiting strategy.

If you're lucky enough to work for a well-known organization—like Federal Express Corp., Digital Equipment Corp. or Yahoo!—chances are your company homepage is drawing significant online traffic from customers and vendors. So you'll want to be sure that visitors to the site have an opportunity to review the company's career opportunities. Our research has shown that, when available, "jobs" is among the most accessed parts of any corporate site. But don't fret, even if your business isn't a household name, there's still plenty to be said for advertising job opportunities to online visitors: Just think about all the times you've checked out your competitors' Web sites.

Is reducing the cost of advertising jobs one of your primary goals? Classified ads are notoriously costly and sometimes ineffective. Corporate Web sites, on the other hand, can be updated easily with few outside costs. In fact, respondents to the 1997 Internet recruitment survey, like those who participated in an earlier version in 1996, rated the cost-effectiveness of Web recruiting very highly: 80 percent reported it's the most cost-effective recruitment method. Add to this the fact that your marketing department is probably spending time and money promoting the company's Web address, and you've got an unbeatable deal.

Tip Two: Figure out what you want to communicate and how you want to do it. At a minimum, visitors should be able to review your postings and apply online, if interested. If you already have an existing site, review options for getting candidates to job postings quickly and easily. You may find it obvious to look behind the "corporate" or "human resources" button, but don't count on candidates being that savvy. Remember, only the dedicated job seeker will take the time to hunt for job listings. An "employment" button in a prominent location on your homepage is a great way to convert curious visitors into applicants.

Next, consider how you'll provide potential recruits with some form of electronic application process. It's relatively easy to create an online resume builder; and for those with proprietary resume-management software, you may be able to upgrade your system to allow downloading from the Web. Alternatively, you can outsource the job to a third-party resume manager like job-fair specialist The Lendman Group based in Virginia Beach, Virginia. Through Lendman's online resume system (*www.lendman.com*), recruiters have access to a password-protected database and can avoid maintaining an onsite database.

Another alternative is the innovative new technology pioneered by start-up Network Recruiting (*www.engdir.com*) in San Rafael, California. Network Recruiting's Employment Packet Language (EPL) software automatically matches applicants with job openings. The EPL software immediately informs applicants of their suitability for a position and sends an e-mail to the hiring authority.

You also need to think about how to deal with electronic dialogue. An online recruitment site is a two-way channel of communication open 24 hours a day, 365 days a year. The question is how long do you want candidates to wait for a response? It's true that this new communication channel, as one pundit noted, "offers incredible new opportunities to disappoint." If it's possible to apply for a position in seconds, candidates will expect a quick response. One thing you can try is giving candidates the option to e-mail comments directly to the relevant hiring manager in addition to applying online.

Tip Three: Think about the involvement of HR and the hiring managers. Many Web surfers expect fresh new content on a regular basis. The work involved with this aspect of Web recruiting is easy to underestimate. For any who've struggled with writing employment ads, it should be simple to

imagine how challenging it will be to develop and maintain an accurate and up-to-date employment-opportunity database. And don't even think about posting job requisitions to the Web. At the best of times, a requisition is hard to decipher. Bottom line: Keeping a Web site up-to-date is a big job. If you're not prepared to deal with it, sign on with a company that is.

Using a Web site is an entirely new way to run a recruiting department. Advanced Web sites can automate many of the routine tasks and even can deal with some pretty complex challenges as well. For example, Dallas-based Texas Instruments Inc. (TI) has been using a candidate profiler for four years (*www.ti.com/recruit/docs/fitcheck.htm*). Here, visitors to TI's site have the opportunity to take a "FitCheck" before applying for a position. Participants answer a series of questions designed to gauge whether they would fit into TI's culture. But TI's real innovation is allowing candidates to review the results of their fit check before deciding to submit it to TI. Now, your dream of providing a steady stream of pre-screened, interested and qualified candidates to hiring managers is possible.

Tip Four: Decide how high-tech you want your site to be. Not everyone will be accessing your site via high-speed ISDN or T1 lines. Non-technical visitors or people surfing from home could be using a range of browsers. Many of the most successful recruiting sites— like Maynard, Massachusetts-based Digital Equipment Corp.'s (*www.digital.com/info/careers*)—are very basic and eschew the latest multimedia enhancements like Java or Shockwave. Our advice is save the bells and whistles and aim your site at the rank and file. But don't carry this philosophy too far. All of us on the Web are knee-deep in sites that never should've seen the light of day. If you have any doubts about the quality of your intended site, benchmark it against competitors' at the start of your project.

Tip Five: Content is king. If your Web site isn't going to contribute anything of value and substance, why bother? Don't fall into the trap of putting everything online just because you can. A company's annual report is usually the first thing to go up on a Web site, and we all know what a scintillating read that can be. If you're downsizing, expect a storm of disdain online if your new Web site fails to explain why you're busy posting so many jobs. Instead of just bragging about the benefits of working at your company, consider Redmond, Washington-based Microsoft Corp.'s approach (*www.microsoft.com/jobs/pnwfaq.htm*) and address the reasons people might not be applying (such as the interminable rain in Seattle).

Tip Six: Coordinate your efforts with your marketing and communications department. Never before has it been so important—and so difficult—to present a consistent, logical and coherent identity to possible workers. At the same time, be aware that an online recruitment center comes with its own set of needs and requirements which your coworkers in marketing may not understand. If they have no interest in writing recruitment ads, they may not be familiar enough with your objectives to take on your Web recruitment pages.

Tip Seven: Learn more from your online visitors. OK, you've established your site, and people are swinging by to see what you're offering. So, what kind of things would you like to know about your online visitors? Employment applications are only part of the story. As the New York City consulting firm McKinsey and Co. recently pointed out, prior to incorporating Web marketing, retail stores only could capture information on products they sold and the customers they sold them to. People who just came in to browse were unaccounted for. Electronic traffic is much more measurable. Everything surfers touch, click or view on a site can be measured. Did you know many Internet services can provide you with a list of the companies, schools and organizations that visited your Web site, along with details on all the pages they looked at? Why not go one step further like Bay Networks in Santa Clara, California *(www.baynetworks.com/talentquest)*, and reward visitors for passing on the e-mail addresses of their friends. Or take a leaf out of Netstart's Career Builder's book (billed as "Your Comprehensive Career Achievement Site" at *www.careerbuilder.com*) and give visitors the opportunity to register their career preferences. This way you can e-mail appropriate jobs directly to them whenever positions at your company become available.

Tip Eight: Build relationships with job seekers. Use the information online candidates provide to add value to their experience. Think about how you might build a relationship with a candidate who decides to pass on your offer and joins a rival company. After all, today's newly graduated systems engineer is tomorrow's senior systems engineer. Like Bay Networks, use your presence to gather e-mail addresses, and then use that list to create an ongoing dialogue.

Tip Nine: Make your site memorable and talk it up. The Web won't replace traditional advertising just yet, but it's already reshaping the way HR thinks about recruitment communications. According to the 1997 "Internet Recruitment Survey," companies that use their existing materials to promote their Web sites enjoy a much greater return than those that don't. Consider incorporating your new URL (Web address) into all recruiting materials including ads, coffee mugs, T-shirts and knickknacks.

And when it comes to your address, you don't need to stick with *www.your company.com*. It only costs $100 or so to register a unique URL. Why not adopt a more memorable URL like one drawn from your tag line? That's what semiconductor leader LSI Logic, based in Milpitas, California, did with *www.godeep.com,* for example. And for heaven's sake don't let anyone push you into a hard-to-remember string such as *www.gsc.gte.com*, the URL for GTE Government Services.

Tip Ten: Listen and learn from feedback. As any good marketer will confirm, Nature gave us two ears and one mouth for a reason. Forget this and you'll miss out on the true promise of cyberspace. Listen to what people have to say about your site and continually reevaluate your presence. Only then will you be able to stay on the forefront of this fast-moving wave.

Ben Klau has been actively involved in the development of interactive recruiting solutions for many Fortune 500 clients for more than six years. He's currently the head of Sausalito, California-based Austin Knight's Interactive Services Group.

Mark Williams has 10 years of high-tech recruiting experience in the United Kingdom and North America. He has been involved in developing worldwide sourcing strategies for a wide range of clients as the vice president of sales and marketing for Austin Knight.

Mark Williams and Ben Klau are part of Austin Knight's Interactive Services Group, which specializes in the development of cutting-edge interactive recruiting strategies. E-mail frazeev@workforcemag.com to forward comments to the editor.

In Conclusion

Debrief

Human resource information systems are complex. They are also expensive to implement, expensive to maintain, and they require a commitment on the part of the organization to particular ways of working. For these reasons, it is important not to rush in and install the best-looking system that comes along. In weighing the alternatives, it is important to look carefully at system benefits. The most obvious benefits arise from direct savings (e.g., reduced labor cost, less paperwork) and from "intangibles" such as better decisions. However, intangible benefits can be hard to document. It is usually much easier to specify the costs. In this situation, some HR systems can be difficult to justify on economic terms alone.

Increasingly, organizations are realizing that they need modern human resource systems just to stay in business. To some extent, this is driven by the increasing globalization, which is a strategic choice. But as operations span multiple legal and economic boundaries, very sophisticated systems are required even for seemingly simple tasks, such as computing total labor costs (i.e., when employees in various locations have different taxes, different benefits, and are paid in different currencies). Also, compliance with legal requirements (e.g., FMLA) requires careful documentation. Technological change also drives the need to implement new HR technology. If your personnel records system runs on a mainframe that is being taken out of service and replaced with a network of personal computers and servers, it is time to start investigating a new system!

In this module, we have focused on the technology that underlies any modern HRIS. But in closing, it is important to emphasize that information systems are more than just collections of computers and databases. Rather, they become part of the fabric of the organization. Systems affect the job descriptions and decision-making responsibilities of the individuals who use them. Systems can enable new workflows, new structures, and new jobs. In doing so, old workflows, structures, and jobs need to be abandoned. For this reason, information technology is rarely neutral. Almost inevitably, it tends to create winners and losers. So, when you find yourself getting infatuated with the latest and greatest new technology, it may be worthwhile to step back and get a little perspective. As one consultant puts it, "Too often technology is seen as the do-all and end-all. But if you don't take care of the people and the process pieces, the technology won't do you any good. You wind up with a $6 million paperweight." (Roberts 1998).

MODULE
7

Suggested Readings

Blackmon, Douglas A. 1998. "Optimizer" Schedule Fiasco Strengthens Union at FedEx. *Wall Street Journal Interactive Edition,* 19 October.

Boehm, Barry. 1988. A Spiral Model of Software Development and Enhancement. *IEEE Computer,* 5: 61–72.

Broderick, Renae and John W. Bourdreau. 1992. Human Resource Management, Information Technology and the Competitive Edge. *Academy of Management Executive,* 6: 7–17.

Ceriello, Vincent R. and Christine Freeman. 1991. *Human Resource Management Systems: Strategies, Tactics, and Techniques.* New York: Lexington Books.

Edmondson, Gail, Stephen Baker and Amy Cortese. 1997. Silicon Valley on the Rhine. *Business Week.* 3 November, 162–166.

Flynn, Gillian. 1998. Texas Instruments Engineers a Holistic HR. *Workforce Magazine,* February, 30–35.

Forsberg, Kevin, Hal Nooz and Howard Cotterman. 1997. *Visualizing Project Management.* New York: Wiley.

Frame, J. Davidson. 1995. *Managing Projects in Organizations: How to Make the Best Use of Time, Techniques, and People.* San Francisco: Jossey-Bass.

Greengard, Samuel. 1998. Humana Takes Online Recruiting to a Hire Level. *Personnel Journal.* August, 75–77.

Laudon, Kenneth C. and Jane P. Laudon. 1994. *Management Information Systems: Organization and Technology.* New York: Macmillan.

Moran, Mark M. and Alexander M. Padro. 1997. *The Internet Answer Book for HR Professionals.* Orange Park, FL: Moran Associates.

Mottl, Judith N. 1998. Employers Head to the Web. *Internetweek,* 10 August, 29.

Roberts, Bill. 1998. The New HRIS: Good Deal or $6 Million Paperweight? *HR Magazine.* February, 40–46.

Sabherwal, R. and D. Robey. 1993. An Empirical Taxonomy of Implementation Processes Based on Sequences of Events in Information System Development. *Organization Science.* 4: 548–576.

Stedman, Craig. 1998. ERP User Interfaces Drive Workers Nuts. *Computerworld.* 2 November, 1, 24.

Thé, Lee. 1995. Retool Human Resources. *Datamation.* 15 June, 66–75.

Williams, Mark and Ben Klau. 1997. 10 Easy Tips for On-line Recruiting. *Workforce Magazine.* August, 13–14.

Williamson, Miryam. 1997. From SAP to nuts. *Computerworld.* 10 November, 68–69.

MODULE
7

Relevant Web Sites

There are a large number of web sites available that are of interest to HR students and professionals. Several of the corporate recruiting sites have been mentioned already. Moran and Padro (1997) provide a good printed reference. But the best way to find web sites is on the web; printed lists are quickly out of date. For an extensive listing of web sites related to human resources, unions, labor relations, and government statistics, please visit the School of Labor and Industrial Relations at Michigan State University: *www.lir.msu.edu/hotlinks/.* This list of web sites is constantly maintained and updated, and will be much more current than anything we might include here.

Critical Thinking Questions

1. We are putting more and more information online, which always raises questions about privacy. What rights should employees have to control (view, approve, modify) their employment records? Who should have access to those records?

2. Many organizations already outsource basic functions like payroll and benefits. Some organizations even outsource their entire information systems function. Do you think that the increased use of information systems in HR could lead firms to outsource their whole HR function as well? Why or why not?

Exercises

1. Visit two (or more) recruiting database sites on the Internet. They can be for single organizations (like Humana) or for one of the clearinghouses (like the Monster Board). Compare and contrast (a) the kinds of data they are asking applicants to provide and (b) the kind of information they provide about jobs that may be available. What features do you think are most effective?

2.   Imagine that you are in charge of a training center for a large organization. You handle many different kinds of courses, from basic computer courses to leadership development. In a small group, brainstorm about the kinds of system(s) you would need to support your operations and make a list of "requirements."

Endnote

1.   Research has shown that the classic "waterfall" model depicted in Figure 7.8 is not necessarily descriptive of actual implementation processes (Sabherwal and Robey 1993). Also, leading experts on project management suggest that it should not be the normative ideal either. Other project management models, such as the "spiral," are more likely to produce successful results (Boehm, 1988). Readers who plan to undertake an actual HRIS implementation project would be well advised to invest in a good book on project management, such as Frame (1995), or Forsberg, Nooz and Cotterman (1997).

MODULE
7

Index

Absenteeism, 7.7, 7.8

Benefits administration (IS), 7.4
Benefits planning and analysis, 7.9
Billing, 7.7. *See also* Transaction processing (HRIS)

Centralized data storage, 7.14, 7.19
Certification (training and development systems), 7.10
COBRA, 7.4
Collective bargaining, 7.9
Credentials, employee, 7.10
Customization phase (HRIS implementation), 7.16, 7.17–18

Data access, 7.14
Database technology. *See* Relational database technology
Decentralized decision making, 7.14
Decision support systems (HRIS), 7.6, 7.9, 7.13, 7.14

Economic feasibility (HRIS), 7.17
Education (training and development systems), 7.11
Enterprise resource planning, 7.8
Entity relationship model, 7.11. *See also* Relational database technology
Executive support systems (HRIS), 7.9

Flat file or spreadsheet, 7.10
FLSA status code, 7.13
FMLA compliance, 7.4, 7.7, 7.23
Functionality (HRIS), 7.16

Human resource information systems (HRIS), 7.4–6, 7.8–13, 7.16–19, 7.23
　implementation, 7.16–18
　implications of organizational structure, 7.19
Human resource information systems (HRIS), system design, 7.19
Human resource manager, 7.4, 7.15
Human resource system, 7.9, 7.14, 7.16. *See also* Human resource information systems
Human resources function, 7.4, 7.6–8, 7.15
　process technology, 7.15, 7.17. *See also* Customization phase (HRIS implementation)
Hypertext Markup Language (HTML), 7.15

Implementation of HRIS, 7.16–18, 7.23
Information systems (IS) technology, 7.4, 7.23
Internal recruiting process, 7.13

Internet and HRIS, 7.5, 7.20
Intranet and HRIS, 7.5, 7.15

Job posting, 7.12–13, 7.14, 7.19. *See also* Recruiting online

Labor standards, 7.9

Maintenance phase (HRIS implementation), 7.18
Management decision making, 7.8–10
Management discretion, 7.5
Management information systems, 7.4
Management reporting (HRIS), 7.6

Network technology, 7.4, 7.14

One-to-many relationship, 7.11, 7.13. *See also* Relational database technology
Organizational change, 7.5
Organizational practices and policies, 7.5
Organizational strategy, 7.5, 7.17
Organizational structure and HRIS system design, 7.19, 7.23
Out-of-synch data, 7.14–15

Paperless office, 7.8
Parallel operation (system implemention), 7.18
Payroll systems, 7.5, 7.7, 7.14

Recruiting online, 7.20–22. *See also* Job posting
Recruitment and staffing, 7.4, 7.8, 7.9, 7.13, 7.19
Relational database technology, 7.5, 7.10–13. *See* Database technology
Reporting systems, 7.8, 7.14
Request for proposal (RFP) process, 7.17
Requirements phase (HRIS implementation), 7.16–17
Resource planning software, 7.16
Retrieving information, 7.10–12, 7.15
Roll-out phase (HRIS implementation), 7.18

Security problems (HRIS), 7.15
Selection phase (HRIS implementation), 7.17
Simple transaction processing system, 7.7. *See also* Transaction processing (HRIS)
$6 million paperweight, 7.23
Software life cycle, 7.5, 7.16–18
Standardized reports, 7.8. *See also* Reporting systems
Storing and retrieving information, 7.10–12, 7.15
System design (HRIS), 7.19
System interrelationships, 7.5

Systems implementation (HRIS), 7.16–18

Technological advances, 7.15, 7.23
Tracking systems, 7.7, 7.8, 7.18
Training and development systems, IS, 7.4,
    7.10–12
Training (training and development systems),
    7.11
Transaction processing (HRIS), 7.6–7, 7.8–9,
    7.13, 7.14
Twenty-first century, 7.4

Union contract, 7.13
Union representation, 7.9

Vacation scheduling, 7.7
Vanilla system (HRIS software), 7.17

Web-based HR systems, 7.15, 7.19
Workflow automation systems, 7.8, 7.14. *See
    also* Human resource information systems
Workflow (HRIS), 7.6, 7.23
WWW systems, 7.15

MODULE
7

PART

2

BUILDING THE HUMAN RESOURCE BASE

Recruitment and Selection Strategies and Legal Concerns in Constructing the Workforce

Managing Human Resources in the 21st Century

From Core Concepts to Strategic Choice

MODULE 8

EEO in the Workplace

Employment Law Challenges

Ben Wolkinson
MICHIGAN STATE UNIVERSITY

Managing Human Resources in the 21st Century: From Core Concepts to Strategic Choice,
by Kossek and Block

Publisher: Dave Shaut
Executive Editor: John Szilagyi
Developmental Editor: Bryant Editorial Development
Marketing Manager: Joseph A. Sabatino
Production Editor: Tamborah E. Moore
Manufacturing Coordinator: Dana Began Schwartz
Cover Design: Tin Box Studio
Cover Photographs: Copyright Shoji Sato/Photonica
Production House: The Left Coast Group, Inc.
Printer: West Group

Printed in the United States of America
1 2 3 4 5 02 01 00 99

For more information contact South-Western College Publishing, 5101 Madison Road, Cincinnati, Ohio, 45227 or find us on the Internet at *http://www.swcollege.com*
For permission to use material from this text or product, contact us by
- telephone: 1-800-730-2214
- fax: 1-800-730-2215
- web: *http://www.thomsonrights.com*

ISBN: 0–324–01807–X

This book is printed on acid-free paper.

Contents

MODULE OVERVIEW   8.4

OBJECTIVES   8.4

RELATION TO THE FRAME   8.4

CORE CONCEPTS IN EQUAL EMPLOYMENT OPPORTUNITY   8.5
    Who Is Covered Under Title VII   8.5
    Prohibited Acts of Discrimination   8.6
    Administration and Enforcement of Title VII   8.6
    Remedies   8.7
    Evidence and Proof in Equal Employment Opportunity Cases   8.8
    Affirmative Action   8.13
    Religious Discrimination   8.13
    Sex Discrimination   8.15
    Sexual Harassment   8.16
    National Origin Discrimination   8.18

APPLICATION   8.19

IN CONCLUSION   8.20
    Debrief   8.20
    Suggested Readings   8.20
    Critical Thinking Questions   8.20
    Exercises   8.21
    References   8.21

INDEX   8.24

MODULE
8

MODULE OVERVIEW

The 1964 Civil Rights Act was enacted against a background of serious economic inequality between white and minority workers in the United States. In the early 1960s, only 17 percent of nonwhite workers were in white-collar occupations and professions, as compared with 47 percent of white employees. Additionally, approximately half of the minorities employed were concentrated in the lower-paying, less skilled labor and service occupations. As a result of these occupational patterns, nonwhite families earned only half that of white families, and black unemployment rates doubled those of white families.[1]

Many factors can account for these patterns of inequities. In part they were the result of the substandard schooling and educational opportunities afforded minority students. Another factor was employment discrimination against minorities.[2]

Likewise, women confronted major barriers to equal employment opportunities. In 1964, 40 states and the District of Columbia restricted the number of hours women could work in many occupations. Many jurisdictions limited the weight women workers could lift or carry. Even in the absence of these governmental restrictions, firms acting on the basis of stereotypical judgments excluded women from many jobs. As a result, women were concentrated in a small number of occupations traditionally open to them: clerical, retail trade, nursing, teaching, bookkeeping, and waitressing.

In an attempt to create equality in the workplace, Congress passed Title VII of the Civil Rights Act of 1964. Title VII remains today the most important piece of legislation ever enacted by Congress to guarantee American workers equal employment. With the passage of Title VII Congress made it unlawful to discriminate on the basis of race, sex, religion, or national origin.

MODULE
8

OBJECTIVES

In this module, we will examine the following issues:

- The jurisdictional scope of the statute as it impacts on employers, unions, and employees

- The primary role of the Equal Employment Opportunity Commission and the courts in administering Title VII

- The major principles of equal employment opportunity as they have evolved as a result of judicial interpretations

RELATION TO THE FRAME

With the passage of Title VII Congress made it illegal to discriminate against workers on the basis of race, religion, sex, or national origin. Title VII applies to nearly all aspects of the employment relationship, including hiring, promoting, dismissal, pay raises, benefits, work assignments, and leaves of absence. Its requirements are statutorily imposed upon organizations by federal law. Therefore an HR department has no choice but to comply with the mandates directed by Title VII.

However, even though organizations are required to conform with the law, human resources (HR) has the strategic function of building, developing, and administering employment policies and procedures that attempt to ensure compliance. Through appropriate preventive and educational efforts, an HR department can greatly reduce a company's potential liability associated with a Title VII violation. See Figure 8.1, A Frame for Understanding Human Resource Strategy.

FIGURE 8.1   *A Frame for Understanding Human Resource Strategy:*
Context, Roles, and Constraints

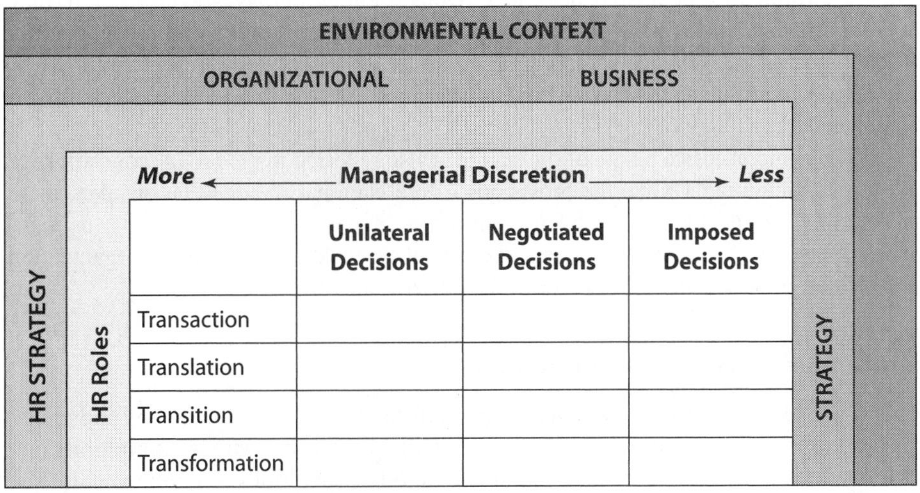

| | | More ← **Managerial Discretion** → Less | | |
		Unilateral Decisions	**Negotiated Decisions**	**Imposed Decisions**
	Transaction			
	Translation			
	Transition			
	Transformation			

ENVIRONMENTAL CONTEXT — ORGANIZATIONAL — BUSINESS — HR STRATEGY — HR Roles — STRATEGY

© 2000 by Ellen Ernst Kossek and Richard Block. Thanks to Brian Pentland, Karen Markel, and John Beck for helpful comments and discussions that enhanced the model.

CORE CONCEPTS IN EQUAL EMPLOYMENT OPPORTUNITY

The following core concepts must be understood to effectively apply and comprehend the legal requirements imposed by Title VII:

- Who is covered under Title VII

- Prohibited acts of discrimination

- Administration and enforcement of Title VII

- Remedies under Title VII

- Evidence and proof in equal employment opportunity cases

- Affirmative action

- Religious discrimination

- Sex discrimination

- Sexual harassment

- National origin discrimination

Who Is Covered Under Title VII

Title VII is one of the most comprehensive pieces of employment legislation ever enacted by the U.S. Congress; it applies to nearly all employers, labor unions, and employment agencies in the country. All firms and organizations with at least 15 workers who have been employed for a period of 20 weeks in a calendar year are covered. Even the smallest employer would be covered under the statute. Additionally, the term "employer" applies not only to firms operating in the private sector, but also to all governmental units whether operating at the local, city, or state level.[3] In 1991, Title VII was amended to extend protection to American employees working abroad for American companies. Consequently, foreign operations controlled by an American employer are also barred from discriminating against American citizens.[4] Labor unions are covered if they operate a hiring hall or have 15 or more members and are certified or recognized by an employer as an exclusive bargaining representative or seek to represent employees.[5] All employment agencies are covered if their role is to procure employees for an employer.

The comprehensive nature of the statute is also reflected in the broad scope afforded the term "employee." Unlike the provisions of the National Labor Relations Act, there is no exclusion afforded independent contractors, supervisors, professionals, or managerial personnel.[6] All employees regardless of their rank or stature in an organization are entitled to seek relief from employment discrimination.

Prohibited Acts of Discrimination

Title VII makes it illegal for an employer to refuse to hire or discharge any individual because of a person's race, religion, sex, or national origin. In addition, it prohibits discrimination with respect to compensation and all other conditions of employment.[7] The use of the term "conditions of employment" imposes on an organization the duty to afford workers equal employment opportunity with regard to all matters affecting their job, including promotions, benefits, and layoffs. Employment agencies are prohibited from refusing to refer individuals to employers because of considerations of race, national origin, religion, or sex.[8] Similarly, labor unions are prohibited from excluding or expelling individuals due to their race, national origin, religion, and sex, and from discriminating in the admission of individuals into apprenticeship training programs or in the referral of workers from hiring halls.[9] Title VII also provides protection for workers who have opposed any unlawful practice and have made a charge, testified, assisted, or participated in an investigation, proceeding, or hearing under the act.[10] Under this provision workers are afforded protection against employer retaliation for exercising their rights under Title VII.

Administration and Enforcement of Title VII

In order to ensure even application of its articles, Title VII created the Equal Employment Opportunity Commission (EEOC) and charged it with responsibility to administer the statute. One of its primary responsibilities is to process complaints of employment discrimination. The process of enforcing the statute itself is divided into three components: investigation, conciliation, and litigation.

The process of investigation commences when an individual files a charge with a local EEOC office. Normally an individual must file a charge within 180 days of the date of the alleged act of discrimination.[11] This requirement is of critical importance, as untimely charges will be rejected. If the charge is filed in a timely manner, the EEOC will begin its investigation. During this process the EEOC questions the charging party, management representatives, and other relevant parties to determine the facts and circumstances surrounding the charge. To assist in the investigation, the EEOC typically requests records and documents. If the employer rejects this request, the EEOC is authorized to seek subpoenas in federal court.[12] Because of the huge backlog of cases pending investigation and decision, the EEOC has introduced a procedure of inviting the parties to attend a fact-finding conference for the purpose of resolving any disputed issue even prior to the completion of its investigation.

If this fails to resolve the issue, the EEOC will pursue its investigation until completion, upon which it determines whether or not there is probable cause to believe that the employer has violated Title VII. If the EEOC finds no probable cause, it will dismiss the charge. The charging party, however, retains the right to seek relief in federal court. Thus, the premise of Title VII is the notion that individuals will be guaranteed their day in court.

Alternatively, if the charge of discrimination is deemed meritorious, the EEOC will attempt to conciliate.[13] In conciliation the EEOC representative will meet with the respondent and the charging parties and attempt to work out a settlement that will remedy the discriminatory practice as well as compensate the charging party for any losses sustained. As an incentive to the organization for settling, the EEOC and the charging party normally will waive their right to sue in the event a settlement agreement is executed.

If the conciliation effort is unsuccessful, either the charging party or the EEOC may initiate a lawsuit in federal court against the defendant employer, labor union, or employment agency.[14] It is important to note that if the respondent is a public employer, the EEOC lacks authority to initiate a suit. In such situations, suit can be brought by the attorney general.[15] Regardless of whether the suit is initiated by an individual charging party, the EEOC, or the Department of Justice, suits are first tried at the district court level and are appealable to the courts of appeal and ultimately to the United States Supreme Court.

Given the multiple layers of governmental intervention, it is not surprising that years may lapse between the initiation of the charge and ultimate judicial resolution. The EEOC itself may take many months to begin investigating a charge, particularly as it is confronted with a backlog of thousands of charges pending investigation and decision. Such delays impose serious problems for both the charging party and the defendant organization. The charging party is potentially denied relief, and the defendant organization must maintain operations while the scope and nature of legal liability that may evolve from pending charges is uncertain. Further complicating relief for the charging party is the limited facility of the EEOC and the Justice Department to initiate lawsuits. Litigation is a very expensive proposition requiring the commitment of vast resources. Given the limited litigation funds available to those agencies, litigation typically is limited to critically important cases in which the agency feels there is a strong prospect of vindication. Consequently, the ultimate burden of compliance may fall on the individual charging party. Because the average individual may lack the necessary resources to pursue a legal remedy for employment discrimination, often the charging party fails to initiate a suit against the employer or labor union. This occurs in most cases where conciliation fails.

Remedies

Although the likelihood of litigation is rather limited, employers today have more incentives than ever to ensure that their policies and actions are well reasoned, business related, and justifiable. If an employee wins a Title VII complaint, he or she is entitled to reinstatement, retroactive seniority and injunctive relief, and back pay for up to two years prior to the filing of the Title VII charge.[16] Additionally, a charging party may be entitled to front pay. This occurs where reinstatement may be denied because of extreme feelings of hostility between the parties. In such a circumstance, the courts will award pay to the employee for a reasonable period of time to permit the charging party to gain other employment.

In 1991, the Civil Rights Act was amended to permit charging parties to recover compensatory and punitive damages where a defendant organization has engaged in "unlawful intentional discrimination."[17] Compensatory damages are defined to include future monetary losses, emotional pain, suffering, inconvenience, mental anguish, and loss of enjoyment of life that may be realized by the discriminated. If it is deemed that the defendant acted with malice and reckless indifference to another person's rights, punitive damages may be imposed. The 1991 statute placed a cap of $300,000 on the amount of damages that can be levied on a defendant organization as well as a sliding scale of fines that increase according to an organization's size.[18]

Number of Employees	Maximum Award
15–100 employees	$ 50,000
101–200 employees	$100,000
201–500 employees	$200,000
501 or more	$300,000

The availability of compensatory and punitive damages under Title VII makes it likely that litigation will increase, and the prospect that Title VII suits can now be brought before juries who may be more sympathetic to individual plaintiffs may widen business exposure to liability. Increased liability has enhanced the incentive for employers to settle Title VII complaints in order to avoid not only costly litigation but also large damage awards. Consequently, the best defense to costly litigation and liability will remain good workplace policies.

Evidence and Proof in Equal Employment Opportunity Cases

Although Title VII does not define the term "discrimination," through judicial interpretation the courts have developed two distinct principles that identify discrimination: disparate treatment and disparate impact.

Disparate Treatment. As the Supreme Court has noted, disparate treatment is the most easily understood type of discrimination. In this situation employers treat individuals less favorably than others because of their race, religion, sex, age, or national origin.[19] To win a disparate treatment case, a charging party must demonstrate that the employer's conduct was intentionally discriminatory. Occasionally, a company through its own statement may provide direct evidence that a particular employment decision was motivated by a legal consideration. For example, in *EEOC v. M.D. Pneumatics,* direct evidence of an employer's discriminatory intent was based on the company president's statement, "It's going to be a cold day in hell before we really have women."[20] A supervisor's routine use of racial slurs has also been viewed by the court as constituting direct evidence that racial animus is a motivating factor in a contested disciplinary decision.[21]

In the absence of direct evidence, illegal motive may be established through circumstantial evidence that incorporates a three-step order and allocation of proof. In *McDonnell Douglas v. Green,*[22] the Supreme Court held that a complainant may establish a prima facie case of discrimination by showing the following:

1. He or she belongs to a racial minority.

2. He or she applied and was qualified for the job for which the employer was seeking applicants.

3. Despite his or her qualifications, the applicant was rejected.

4. After the person's rejection the position remained open, and the employer continued to seek applicants from persons of the complainant's qualifications.

The existence of these facts establishes an inference of discrimination. The burden of proof would then shift to the employer "to articulate some legitimate nondiscriminatory reason for the employee's rejection."[23] Here the courts have recognized factors that would operate to dispel the inference of discrimination created by the prima facie case. These might include any of the following situations:

- An applicant's participation in unlawful conduct against the firm[24]

- The chosen candidate had more experience[25]

- Considerations of personal patronage[26]

- Budgetary consideration[27]

- Application of employee seniority rights[28]

Where the employer has presented legitimate reasons for its actions, the charging party may prove intentional discrimination by presenting evidence that the reasons advanced by the employer for his or her rejection were pretextural in nature. Evidence relevant to a showing of pretext might include examples of different treatment of minority and nonminority employees and of the company's general policy and practices with regard to minority employment.

In subsequent cases the Supreme Court has emphasized that the ultimate burden of persuasion remains on the charging party to demonstrate that he or she was a victim of intentional discrimination. As a result, the falsity of an employer's explanation by itself may not be sufficient to establish that it was a pretext for racial discrimination. In *St. Mary's Honor Center v. Hicks,*[29] the Supreme Court dealt with a prison guard who was dismissed for violating various prison rules. At trial, it was discovered that other guards had engaged in similar and more serious violations that had been ignored by management or had been treated more leniently. Nonetheless, the Supreme Court upheld the district court's dismissal of the charge on the basis of the district court's determination that "although the charging party had proven the existence of a crusade to terminate him he had not proven that the crusade was racially rather than personally motivated."[30] In short, in disparate treatment cases the charging party must always persuade the court that the adverse action was motivated by unlawful hostility rather than some other factor such as personal animosity toward the complainant.

Disparate Impact

Selection Instruments, Testing

The decision by the United States Supreme Court in *Griggs v. Duke Power Co.*[31] established the disparate impact paradigm for proving employment discrimination. In the *Griggs* case, minority employees challenged the employer's requirement that applicants possess a high school diploma and pass two professionally developed tests for placement in particular jobs. These requirements screened out a disproportionately greater number of minorities than white applicants and employees. Notwithstanding the absence of any evidence of hostile intent towards minorities, the Supreme Court found that the use of selection instruments, although neutral on their face, that have an adverse impact on minorities were nonetheless illegal if they were not job related. Thus, the court noted:

> The act prescribes not only overt discrimination but also practices that are fair in form but discriminatory in operation. The touchstone is business necessity. If an employment practice which operates to exclude Negroes cannot be shown to be related to job performance, the practice is prohibited.[32]

The 1991 amendment of the Civil Rights Act made clear that Title VII is not violated in a disparate impact case unless the evidence indicates that the challenged device causes a disparate impact. This means that the charging party must point to a specific practice that produces a disparate impact, such as requiring experience or a college education rather than through the decisional process as a whole. In imposing this burden, Congress was apparently sensitive to organizational concerns that a "bottom line" attack would impose on firms the impossible burden of defending and validating all their employment practices. This outcome is avoided by preventing charging parties from relying on the cumulative effects of a selection process as a basis for a disparate impact claim.[33] The act, however, does provide for an exception where the "elements of the respondent's decision making process are not capable of separation for analysis."[34] This situation may arise where the employer's decision-making process is entirely subjective in nature. Alternatively, where the employer relies on or utilizes functionally integrated practices, such as a combination of height and weight requirements to measure strength, then the charging party may challenge the overall results of utilizing the combination of height and weight as a screening device.[35]

There are two general means used by charging parties to prove that a particular selection device has an adverse impact on minorities. The first is applicant flow data that identifies the specific impact of a device upon those who have actually applied for a job. For example, assume the challenged device is a paper and pencil test given to 100 white and 100 black applicants. Fifty of the white applicants passed the test, but only 25 of the black applicants passed. The applicant flow selection rate then is 50 percent for whites but only 25 percent for minorities. This difference raises the question whether a test has an adverse impact as it seemingly screens out more minorities than whites.

A second method is to determine whether the challenge selection device has a negative impact on the applicant pool. Here the charging party would seem to demonstrate the effect of the requirement on the relevant population from which the employer would be expected to draw its workforce. For example, in *Griggs v. Duke Power Co.* it was demonstrated that 34 percent of white males but only 12 percent of black males had completed high school. Similarly, in *Dothard v. Rawlinson,* in evaluating the potential discriminatory effect of a height and weight requirement, the Supreme Court noted or relied upon census data demonstrating that approximately 99 percent of the men in the United States but only 59 percent of the women would qualify.[36]

The courts have never definitively determined the degree of disparity necessary to establish disparate impact. The EEOC, however, has promulgated what has been called the four-fifths rule. This rule stipulates that:

> A selection rate for any race, sex or ethnic group which is less than four-fifths of the rate for the group with the highest rate would generally be regarded by federal enforcement agencies as evidence of adverse impact while a greater than four-fifths rate will generally not be regarded by federal agencies as evidence of adverse impact.[37]

For example, in a situation where test scores are used as a basis for hiring, if 25 percent of minority applicants pass a test as compared with 50 percent of white males, adverse impact is demonstrated by a selection rate that for minorities is only 50 percent that for whites. The four-fifths or 80 percent rule is, however, only a rule of thumb. Differences of more than 20 percent in passage rates may not be viewed as significant where the differences are based upon very small sample sizes. Alternatively, differences in selection rates of less than 20 percent might be considered critical where the data is drawn from a large sample and where differences in selection over time might be significant for both statistical and practical purposes.[38] For example, in *Green v. Missouri Pacific Railroad Company,*[39] the appellate court found unlawful an employer's policy not to employ any applicant with any type of conviction besides a minor traffic offense. As a result of this policy, 5.3 percent of black applicants but only 2.23 percent of white applicants were rejected because of conviction records. Although the four-fifths rule was satisfied, the rejection rate for blacks was nonetheless 2½ times that of whites. Consequently, the court determined that this policy over time created a disparate impact against minorities.

In *Connecticut v. Teal,*[40] the Supreme Court addressed the question of whether the overall or bottom line results of the selection process, if favorable to minorities, would immunize the employer from liability in the event that any component of that process has an adverse impact on minorities. Here each applicant was first given a written examination to qualify for the position of social worker. Those who failed to achieve a minimum score were eliminated from further consideration. Those who passed were subject to further evaluation based on other criteria including seniority, prior experience, supervisory evaluation, and affirmative action considerations. Eighty percent of the white applicants, but only 54 percent of the black applicants, passed, producing a passage rate for minorities that breached the four-fifths rule. At the same time the bottom line results of the selection process was more favorable to minorities than others, as approximately 23 percent of black applicants and 13 percent of white applicants were promoted to the position of social worker. Despite the bottom line results, the Supreme Court held that the state of Connecticut breached Title VII by using a screening test that disproportionately eliminated black applicants from consideration.

Once a selection instrument has been proven to have a disparate impact, the employer is obliged to demonstrate that the exclusionary device is job related. In 1978, federal enforcement agencies including the U.S. Department of Labor, the Justice Department, and the EEOC promulgated the uniform guidelines on employee selection procedures.[41] These guidelines require validation of tests in accordance with standards formulated by the American Psychological Association. According to the United States Supreme Court in *Albemarle Paper Company v. Moody*,[42] these guidelines are entitled to significant judicial deference. These guidelines recognize three types of validation: content validity, criterion-related validity, and construct validity.

Content Validity.   Content validity may be appropriate where the test is a representative sample of the content of the job for which the person is being tested. A common example would be a test measuring a secretary's typing or dictation speed or an electrical wiring test for an electrician. Although the test need not assess all elements of job performance, the matters tested must be important aspects of the job. The content validity approach is normally inappropriate if used to assess personality, intelligence, or aptitude.

Criterion-Related Validity.   Criterion-related validity views a selection instrument as valid when there is empirical evidence demonstrating a statistical relationship between performance on a particular test and objective measures of job success. In performing this validity analysis, employers may follow one of two approaches: predictive and concurrent analysis. In predictive study, job applicants rather than job incumbents are used as a source of data. Tests are given to all job applicants rather than current employees. Test scores are analyzed, but applicants are hired on the basis of other available selection instruments. After the applicants have been hired, trained, and have had time to learn their job adequately, data on their job performance is collected. Subsequently the two sets of scores, scores on the test and on job performance, are analyzed to see if there is any meaningful relationship between the two. If applicants who achieve high test scores perform well on the job and those who achieve low test scores perform poorly, the test is viewed as valid. Alternatively, if those who score high on the test perform no better than those who have scored poorly, the test is not a good predictor of job performance and therefore is not valid.

Predicted validation may not be feasible where there are too few job applicants to permit testing. Where this is the case, the employers might engage in a concurrent validation. Here only incumbent employees are tested and their scores measured against the evaluation of their job performance. One advantage of a concurrent validation approach is that the employer has almost immediate information on the utility of a selection device. However, there are disadvantages that can affect its usefulness. First, the experience of employees on the job may influence their scores. Second, applicants may differ from job incumbents in terms of educational background. As a result, the relationship between the predictor and performance criteria (validity coefficient) for incumbent employees may not be the same for applicants.

Construct Validity.   Construct validity involves identifying traits or characteristics (the construct) that are considered important for successful job performance.[43] Employers need to validate tests measuring constructs according to standards established for criterion-related studies. This means that a thorough job analysis must be performed to demonstrate that the construct required is a critical element in job performance.

MODULE
8

Additionally, the test must demonstrate that it accurately measures the required trait.[44] Finally, validation requires proof that the construct itself is statistically correlated to the quality of the job.[45]

Previously, in order to minimize the potential adverse effect of various tests, some employers engaged in a practice of using different cutoff scores for different racial or ethnic groups. Alternatively, the employer might add points to scores received by minorities. These practices are now unlawful under section 703(L) of the 1991 act, which makes it illegal for an organization to adjust or use different cutoff scores or to otherwise alter the results of employment-related tests on the basis of race, religion, sex, or national origin. This prohibition places additional pressure on employers to either validate their tests or abandon those that screen out disproportionately greater numbers of minorities than other employees.

Other Selection Criteria

It is hard to exaggerate the significant implications and effects of the commission's testing guidelines and the Supreme Court's decision in *Griggs v. Duke Powe Co.* As a result of these decisions and policies, employers have had to reevaluate a whole range of selection criteria used to assess the fitness of candidates for employment. For example, employers can no longer rely on arrest records to screen out job applicants, since statistical data often demonstrates that minorities are arrested at a far greater rate than others. Moreover, arrest records do not by themselves prove job fitness since they are an inadequate means to establish a person's guilt.[46] Even with regard to conviction records, the courts have held that a personnel policy that excludes from employment all individuals who have ever been convicted of any crime with the exception of misdemeanors might also be unlawful. Underlying this determination are the general absence of evidence that such policies are job related and the concern that the rigid application of a conviction policy would have an adverse effect on minority employment.[47] At the same time, courts have acknowledged the employer's legitimate right on a case-by-case basis to determine whether applicants convicted of a particular crime are eligible for employment. Such factors to be considered include the nature of the crime committed, the type of job to be performed, the age at which the person was convicted, and an individual's record of employment since the initial conviction. Employers should also be careful not to utilize experience requirements that are set at an artificially high level that tends to exclude minorities at a significantly higher rate.

While normally affording firms broad authority to establish grooming requirements, courts have been responsive to the problems that minorities might confront from the application of a no-beard policy. Thus, minorities suffering from the skin condition pseudofolliculitis barbae (PFB) may have a very difficult time shaving. As a result, unless justified by compelling business considerations, courts have struck down no-beard policies where the evidence has indicated a disparate effect on blacks.[48]

There is one type of selection system that may have a disparate impact on minorities that is nevertheless immune from challenge. This involves the application of seniority systems. Under section 703(H) of Title VII, Congress declared that "it shall not be an unlawful employment practice for an employer to apply different standards of compensation or different terms, conditions or privileges of employment pursuant to a bona fide seniority system."[49] It is not unusual to find blacks and women disproportionately occupying lower-paid, less skilled job classifications in particular departments. Their capacity to move out into better-paying departments may be hindered by the application of seniority arrangements. Thus, if employees accrue seniority only in the departments in which they currently work, they may lack the relevant seniority credits to bid for positions in the better-paying departments. Further exacerbating this situation is their unwillingness to move when seniority arrangements require the forfeiture of accrued seniority when these employees move into new departments. Notwithstanding these considerations, the Supreme Court has recognized the right of employers and labor unions to negotiate and establish rules for the administration of seniority systems.[50] Thus, unless the evidence clearly indicates that seniority systems were deliberately implemented to penalize minority workers, seniority systems may normally be used to determine the job rights of employees with regard to promotions, layoffs, and transfer workers. On the other hand, in cases where a minority employee has been a victim of discrimination in hiring, the Supreme Court has upheld relief granting an applicant seniority credit retroactive to the date the employee should have been hired.[51]

Affirmative Action

In *United Steelworkers v. Weber*,[52] the Supreme Court identified the legal parameters surrounding the implementation of affirmative action programs. To be lawful, the plan must comply with a number of criteria:

- It must be designed to open employment opportunities for minorities in occupations that had been traditionally closed to them.

- The plan must be temporary. Attempts to afford preferences to minorities after underrepresentation has been rectified would constitute an unlawful quota.

- The plan must not unnecessarily trammel the interests of white employees. In this regard, plans that bar white males, reserve certain positions to minority employees, or operate to displace incumbent white employees would be considered unlawful. For example, in *Wygant v. Jackson Board of Education*,[53] a school district was found to have violated the equal protection clause of the Fourteenth Amendment when nonminority teachers with greater seniority were laid off in order to secure employment for minority teachers. Similarly, in the *United States v. Board of Education of Piscataway*[54] the Third Circuit held that race could not be used as a tie-breaker to choose which employee would be subject to layoff.

To ensure the legality of affirmative action programs, employers should narrowly tailor preferences and employment goals to address the specific problems of minority underutilization. In *Johnson v. Transportation Agency, Santa Clara County*,[55] the Supreme Court noted that goals should reflect the availability of qualified minorities within the relevant labor market. An affirmative action program designed to remedy the underrepresentation of minorities would not justify preferences for Hispanics if they did not suffer any underutilization in the workforce. Plans are also more likely to be upheld when preferences are just one of and not the only determining factor in the selection process. Finally, those making the hiring or promotion decisions should have the discretion to select candidates from a given list and to reject those lacking requisite qualifications.

Religious Discrimination

Title VII prohibits adverse treatment of an individual because of that person's religion. For example, it would be unlawful for an organization to refuse to hire Catholics or Jews into managerial positions while affording preference to members of a particular church.[56] Most court cases involving religious discrimination do not address problems of overt discrimination but rather the use of employment practices that may limit or interfere with the job opportunities of members of certain religious faiths. A typical problem involves the question of work on a person's Sabbath. Orthodox Jews, Seventh Day Adventists, and members of the Worldwide Church of God are required by their religion to refrain from working between Friday sunset and Saturday sundown. Members of the Dutch Reform Church and smaller Christian sects have beliefs that preclude them from working on Sunday. Conflicts arise where employer requirements to work on a Sabbath conflict with an employee's desire to be off that day because of religious beliefs.

Title VII seeks to promote the employment rights and opportunities of religious minorities by requiring employers to accommodate an individual employee's religious beliefs or practices unless through accommodation the employer would sustain undo hardship to its business operations.[57] Whether or not an employer can accommodate and under what circumstances it will cause an employer undo hardship has spawned a significant amount of litigation.

According to the EEOC and the courts, whether or not an employer can accommodate an individual must be evaluated on a case-by-case basis. However, there are several factors that all employers need to consider:

1. The nature of the employer's operations. Some companies or organizations operate on a seven-day-a-week, 24-hour basis. The critical nature of the job the individual performs—particularly those involving safety-sensitive functions such as police and firefighters—may make it difficult for an employer to accommodate an individual's request to be off from work.

2. The size of the organization. If the employer is a large company, there may be a much greater number of people who can substitute for the employee who needs time off. Alternatively, in a larger company the employer may be able to transfer the employee to a different position in which the conflict between the employer's production requirements and the individual's religious beliefs would not arise.

3. The number of employees seeking accommodation. Inherently, the fewer the number of employees requiring accommodation, the easier it might be for the employer to accommodate.

4. The employee's good-faith efforts in reaching accommodation. The employer capacity to accommodate will certainly be facilitated where the employee gives appropriate notice to management of the need for time off.

The most significant case addressing the scope and nature of an employer's duty to accommodate is the Supreme Court's decision in *Trans World Airlines v. Hardison.*[58] There the Supreme Court held that the duty to accommodate does not take precedence over or supersede a seniority provision of a collective bargaining agreement. Consequently, an employer need not require an employee with greater seniority and job preference rights to work a less desirable shift, such as Saturday, in order to accommodate a particular employee's desire not to work on a particular shift because of religious beliefs. Additionally, the Supreme Court held that undue hardship exists and the duty to accommodate is liquidated whenever an employer would suffer more than a *de minimis* cost. In *Hardison,* the court found that an accommodation that requires an employer to replace a Sabbath observer with supervisory personnel who otherwise would not be able to perform their normal functions or with another employee who would have to be paid overtime constitutes undue hardship. Similarly, accommodations that impose serious burdens on coworkers may not be required. Thus, for example, a hospital that must schedule a substantial amount of overtime on the weekends need not excuse a Sabbath observer from this obligation where the exclusive imposition of overtime assignment on other employees increases employees' complaints and lowers their morale.[59]

At the same time, the duty to accommodate cannot be justified on the basis of speculative considerations. For example, in *Brown v. General Motors,*[60] the court of appeals found illegal the dismissal of an automobile worker who was a member of the Worldwide Church of God and refused to work on Friday evenings. While the plant management complained that the nonavailability of Brown would create all kinds of production problems, the court found that the cost of replacing Brown was negligible as the plant had maintained relief crews available at no extra cost to fill in for employees otherwise absent from work.

An employer's dress and grooming requirement may also conflict with an employee's religious beliefs. For example, Sikhs and some Orthodox Jewish sects require their members to wear beards. Women of the Moslem faith, because of considerations of modesty, may object to wearing short skirts. The obligation of an employer to accommodate in these circumstances is controlled by the *Hardison* decision. Where an employer can demonstrate more than *de minimis* costs as would arise, for example, where non-conformity with a grooming requirement would create a safety hazard, the employer's grooming requirements would be upheld. For example, in *Batia v. Chevron, Incorporated,* the company upheld the employer's policy of requiring all employees potentially exposed to toxic chemicals to shave any facial hair that might interfere with their wearing a respirator. Finding that his beard would interfere with the use of his respirator, the court found that the employer had acted properly in removing Batia from his machinist position.[61] On the other hand, in *EEOC v. Electronic Data Systems,*[62] the district court found unlawful the dismissal of a computer programmer because of his refusal to shave for religious reasons because the organization failed to provide evidence that accommodating that person's religious beliefs would impose upon the organization any undue hardship.

Sex Discrimination

Although Title VII prohibits discrimination on the basis of sex, it also permits employers to consider an applicant's gender where "sex is a bona fide occupational qualification reasonably related to the performance of the job." In construing the BFOQ exception, the courts have noted that there exists only a small range of jobs were employers are permitted to consider the sex of the individual in making an employment offer. In *Weeks v. Southern Bell Telephone Company,* the Fifth Circuit ruled that an employer could rely on the BFOQ exception only by demonstrating "a factual basis for believing that all or substantially all workers would be unable to perform safely and efficiently the duty of the job involved."[63] Similarly, the same court subsequently held that the BFOQ exemption can be maintained only when "the essence of a business operation would be undermined by not hiring members of one sex exclusively."[64] In effect, only where sex determines a person's ability to do the job satisfactorily can it be considered in employment conditions. As a result, it is illegal to rely on stereotypical characterization or assumptions more common in one sex than another as a basis for excluding men or women from positions. For example, an employer could not exclude women on the basis of a stereotypical characterization that women would not wish to work in difficult or dangerous circumstances. Similarly, the preferences of coworkers, employers, clients, or customers normally are not a basis for establishing a BFOQ, since that would afford employers the license to discriminate.

The Supreme Court most recently interpreted the BFOQ exemption in *International Union, United Automobile Workers v. Johnson Controls.*[65] There the employer had adopted a gender-based fetal protection policy that excluded all women of reproductive age from jobs involving their exposure to lead substances on the grounds that women in the event of pregnancy would suffer harm either to themselves or to the fetuses that they might carry. Since the health concerns raised by Johnson Controls—protecting the fetus—did not relate to a woman's ability to perform the job, the Supreme Court found the exclusion of women from these positions unlawful.

Only in a small range of job opportunities will it be held that a BFOQ exemption is justified. For example, the Commission has held that it may be permissible to hire men or women when necessary for purposes of authenticity. For example, an employer may give preferences to female actresses to play female roles.[66] Unique problems arise in the context of penal institutions where employment of guards of the opposite gender may threaten the privacy interest of inmates. Yet the courts have been unwilling to establish blanket BFOQ exemptions on this basis. For example, in *Torres v. Wisconsin Department of Health and Social Services,* the court found that the privacy interest of female inmates was insufficient to establish a BFOQ. At the same time, it sought to harmonize the employment rights of individuals under Title VII and the privacy rights of inmates by recommending that prison officials adopt measures to afford privacy to inmates whenever possible to do so. In *Torres,* it was suggested that female inmates could cover the windows to their cells during certain hours to allow them privacy when dressing or using toilet facilities. Similarly, the courts have upheld the right of prisons to use only guards of the same sex to perform strip searches of inmates.

In 1978, Congress enacted the Pregnancy Discrimination Act as an amendment to Title VII. Under it:

> Women affected by pregnancy, childbirth or related medical conditions shall be treated the same for employment related purposes including receipt of benefits under fringe benefit programs as other persons not so affected but similar in their ability or inability to work.[67]

While not affording pregnant women any special set of rights, this law prohibits disparate treatment of pregnant women for employment-related purposes. Pregnancy alone cannot be a basis for making decisions concerning the hiring, promotion, assignment, or dismissal of employees. Additionally, pregnant women are entitled to the same benefits that other workers receive when unable to work. For example, if an employer provides cancer or stroke victims up to six months of paid leave, it must grant a similar amount of paid leave to women unable to work because of pregnancy and childbirth. Similarly, if individuals on sick leave are entitled to return to their original jobs with no loss of seniority, the same treatment must be afforded a pregnant employee on leave because of her inability to work.

The new amendment also prohibits employers from arbitrarily establishing a time when women must go on maternity leave or remain home following childbirth. These decisions normally should be made exclusively on the basis of the individual's ability or inability to work. Limited exceptions may be established for safety considerations. On this basis, the courts have permitted companies to prohibit female flight attendants from flying during the last trimester of their pregnancy.[68]

In seeming contrast, the Supreme Court has held that an employer need not provide the same level of benefits for the pregnancy-related medical conditions of spouses of employees in the same way it does for its female workers.[69] Also, a disability plan covering employees' children may exclude or limit maternity benefits. At the same time, an employer would violate Title VII if it failed to provide dependents of employees coverage for pregnancy while affording them otherwise comprehensive medical care for all other illnesses or disabilities. Additionally, if an employer's insurance program covers the medical expenses of spouses of female employees, it cannot exclude from coverage pregnancy-related conditions affecting the spouses of male workers.

The only exception to the mandate of equal employment opportunity in the treatment of pregnant workers is the provision that employers are not required to pay the health insurance benefits of female employees seeking abortion. An exception would arise where the life of the mother would be in danger if the fetus was carried to term or medical complications develop from the abortion.[70] In such circumstances, female employees' medical payments, disability, and sick leave benefits would have to be covered by an employer's comprehensive health and disability program. Furthermore, an employer cannot discriminate in employment against a woman because she has had an abortion.

Sexual Harassment

The Equal Employment Opportunity Commission defines sexual harassment as:

> unwelcome sexual advances, requests for sexual favors, and other verbal or physical conduct of a sexual nature . . . when (1) submission to such conduct is made either explicitly or implicitly a term or condition of an individual's employment, (2) submission to or rejection of such conduct by an individual is used as a basis

for employment decisions affecting such individual, or (3) such conduct has the purpose or effect of unreasonably interfering with an individual's work or performance by creating an intimidating, hostile or offensive working environment.[71]

Two forms of sexual harassment have been recognized, quid pro quo and hostile environment. The former type of harassment exists when a supervisor conditions receipt of tangible job benefits such as promotion, more favorable fringe benefits, and job security on the employee's acquiescence to the supervisor's sexual demands or advances. Even a single act of sexual harassment of this nature may be sufficient to impose liability on an employer. Furthermore, an employer will normally be held strictly liable for the quid pro quo sexual harassment engaged in by supervisors.

Not all harassment is linked to supervisory threats to retaliate against workers. An employer may nonetheless create a hostile environment by subjecting employees to offensive remarks, sexual innuendoes of a verbal or nonverbal nature, and unwelcome physical contact. In *Meritor Savings Bank v. Vinson,* the Supreme Court held that sexual harassment that creates a hostile and abusive working environment violates Title VII even when the harassed employee suffers no tangible job loss.[72] The court, however, did place limits on what kinds of conduct would be actionable. Not every isolated incident would result in employer liability. For such harassment to be unlawful it must be sufficiently severe or pervasive to alter the conditions of the victim's employment and create an abusive working environment.

Subsequently in *Harris v. Forklift Systems,*[73] the Supreme Court identified the following factors that will be considered in determining whether work environment harassment is sufficiently severe or pervasive to be unlawful. These include:

- The frequency of the harassing conduct

- Its severity; for example, whether it is physically threatening or humiliating or merely an offensive remark

- Whether it unreasonably interferes with an employee's work performance

- The effect of the harassment on the employee's psychological well-being

MODULE
8

However, the Court pointed out that while all factors are relevant, no single one is required. Furthermore, the Court specifically rejected the contention that evidence of psychological injury must be demonstrated to prove the existence of an abusive environment.

The Supreme Court has relied also on a reasonable person standard. Thus in *Harris v. Forklift Systems,*[74] the Court noted that for sexual harassment to be unlawful it must create an environment that a reasonable person would find hostile or abusive. This standard has been utilized more recently to prevent hypersensitive employees from barraging the workplace and courts with complaints. As a result sporadic use of abusive language, gender related jokes, and occasional teasing normally do not constitute illegal harassment.

In two recent Supreme Court decisions, *Fragher v. Boca Raton*[75] and *Burlington Industries v. Ellerth,*[76] the Court has developed a new standard for determining employer liability in cases of hostile environment. Here it held that where supervisors create a hostile environment, the employer will be liable unless the employer can demonstrate by a preponderance of the evidence that (a) it exercised reasonable care to prevent and promptly correct the sexually harassing behavior and (b) the employee unreasonably failed to take advantage of any preventive or corrective opportunities to avoid harm.

These decisions reemphasize the need for employers to adopt policies against sexual harassment. Where an employer has established, widely disseminated, and vigorously enforced a complaint mechanism against sexual harassment, an employee's failure to utilize it may immunize management from liability in cases of hostile environment charges. The need to adopt sexual harassment policies is reinforced by the serious financial liability that may be assessed against an employer in such cases. Plaintiffs are now permitted to recover not only back pay but also compensatory and punitive damages. Furthermore, employers may also be subject to tort suits for such harassment, and this exposure can make them vulnerable to damage judgments. Consequently, firms must act vigorously to adopt mechanisms to address and deter such conduct.

A comprehensive policy against sexual harassment should contain at the very least the following ingredients.

1. The policy should identify for workers what constitutes sexual harassment. It should note that sexual harassment is not limited to demands for sexual favors in return for job benefits but can also include verbal abuse, gestures, and other forms of pressure such as intentional touching, patting, and other unwelcome physical contact.

2. The policy must clearly communicate the message that sexual harassment will not be tolerated at the workplace. Workers should be informed that the employer has remedies available and that they should be directed to report any allegations to their supervisors or higher-level managers.

3. It may be useful to designate a particular employee such as a high-level management individual or officer to serve as an EEO officer to whom complaints of sexual harassment may be made and who can advise employees of the confidential nature of this process. The policy should also establish alternative mechanisms in the event complaints are about the designated EEO officer.

4. Investigate complaints immediately and thoroughly. All facts supporting or refuting the complaints should be documented carefully at each step of the investigation process, including the names of all interviewed, what they said, and what personnel records were reviewed.[77]

5. Take vigorous disciplinary measures. Where egregious harassment has occurred, a guilty employee may have to be removed. Alternatively, lesser forms of punishment, including warnings or nondisciplinary transfers to similar jobs in other departments, may be appropriate.

6. Train managers and workers. Harassment frequently arises because employees may be ignorant that others will perceive their actions as offensive. Training is necessary to sensitize employees to the kinds of language, attitudes, and behaviors that are not only objectionable but unlawful. Such awareness training can be expected to reduce the incidence of sexual harassment complaints.[78]

7. Sexual harassment policies should be a component of the employee manual. Changes in policy must be communicated to all employees, and human resources staff must be kept current on legal developments.

National Origin Discrimination

Over the last several decades, the United States has experienced substantial increases in population among groups with ancestral ties to countries from Asia, Central America, and South America. Within the next 25 years, persons of Hispanic origin may surpass blacks as the single largest minority group in the country.[79] Under Title VII it is unlawful to discriminate on the basis of an individual's national origin. Thus, it would be illegal to favor persons of Western European heritage over those whose forebears were of Eastern European origin. It is also unlawful to discriminate on the basis of physical, cultural, or linguistic characteristics of national origin groups.[80] For example, the application of a height requirement may exclude disproportionately a greater number of Hispanics, and unless validated, this requirement would be found unlawful. Similarly, requirements to speak with accent-free English would be held discriminatory where a person's accent did not interfere with his or her ability to be understood by coworkers or supervisors.

Considering the millions of Americans whose native language is not English, the EEOC has issued guidelines restricting an employer's right to promulgate English-only rules at the worksite. Viewing language as an essential national origin characteristic, the EEOC has held that restricting the right to speak one's native language is presumptively unlawful unless justified by considerations of business necessity. Most recently, the appellate courts have rejected EEOC guidelines as they relate to bilingual employees. Thus, courts have held that employees fluent in both English and Spanish were not adversely impacted by a requirement to speak only English during worktime, because they readily could comply with such a directive.[81] Yet preventing workers who have difficulty with English from speaking in their native language might well be considered unlawful unless justified by considerations of safety or efficiency. Finally, there does not appear any justification to extend English-only rules to an employee's free time such as lunch or work breaks.

Following the Second World War, the United States and some foreign countries executed commercial and navigation treaties whereby foreign corporations operating in the United States would have the right to employ experts, executive personnel, agents, attorneys, and other specialists of their choice. On the basis of such treaties, courts have upheld the right of foreign corporations in the United States to afford job preferences to their own citizens. For example, in *MacNamara v. Korean Airlines,*[82] the court upheld the right of Korean Airlines to replace an American citizen in an executive position with a Korean national. Nonetheless, the same foreign corporation cannot rely on this treaty to permit discrimination on the basis of other considerations such as race, sex, or age. Although foreign corporations in the United States may select individuals on the basis of citizenship concerns, their right to prefer foreign nationals cannot be used to effect intentional discrimination against American workers on the basis of race, age, sex, or religion.

APPLICATION

Title VII of the Civil Rights Act of 1964 is the cornerstone of the federal civil rights enforcement effort. While the process of compliance is bureaucratically cumbersome, employers subject to Title VII have substantially increased their employment of minority workers particularly in professional and management positions. Most significantly, through the threat of costly litigation and the establishment of sweeping legal precedents, employers throughout the United States have been compelled to eliminate employment practices that discriminate on the basis of race, religion, sex, or national origin.

Title VII requires managers not only to refrain from overt discriminatory behavior, but also to ensure that personnel practices, neutral on their face, not have a discriminatory effect unless such practices prove to be job related and essential to safety, efficiency, and productivity considerations. Such efforts have undoubtedly required the allocation and expenditure of considerable resources, as managers must collect and review demographic data, maintain personnel records, and use more comprehensive job evaluation and hiring techniques. Yet the failure to engage in such efforts may impose even greater costs on organizations, which run the risk of costly legal judgments.

It must be remembered that Title VII does not require an organization to employ unqualified workers merely because they are members of a protected class. Title VII compels only the elimination of discriminatory employment practices against workers who are qualified. Consequently, an organization's commitment to equal employment opportunity not only promotes the social and economic integration of minorities within our society, but by its emphasis on the implementation of job-related personnel practices should help facilitate the organization's critical goal of maintaining a qualified workforce.

IN CONCLUSION

Debrief

Title VII is the most broadly based and influential statute prohibiting discrimination in employment. It prohibits discrimination based on race, sex, religion, or national origin, and its coverage extends to all "terms, conditions or privileges" of employment. The breadth of Title VII was greatly expanded in *Griggs v. Duke Power Co.,* in which the Supreme Court held the employer's state of mind is irrelevant. The crucial question is the ultimate effect of employment practices. If a practice has a discriminatory effect on minority group opportunities, the employer must show that the employment practice is required by considerations of "business necessity."

With the enactment of Title VII of the Civil Rights Act, a new era in human resource management began. Previously, managers were free to rely on whatever recruitment, selection, and promotion criteria they desired. Currently, however, they must scrutinize each decision and organizational practice for compliance with Title VII. As a human resource manager, you undoubtedly will encounter many Title VII issues. It may take the form of an employee refusing to work a certain day due to religious reasons, complaints of sexual harassment, or the rejection of a minority person's application for employment or promotion. Understanding the requirements of Title VII will facilitate personnel decisions that will help immunize the employer from liability.

Although this module provides an overview of Title VII, the centerpiece of employment discrimination law, the reader should understand that significant statutes impose other equal employment opportunity obligations on management and unions. These include the Age Discrimination in Employment Act (ADEA), the Americans With Disabilities Act (ADA), the Equal Pay Act (EPA), and the Immigration Reform and Control Act. Compliance with all these statutes is certainly in an organization's best interest. Through such compliance, an organization will be better able to recruit a diverse and qualified workforce and promote good morale and productivity among its workers.

MODULE
8

Suggested Readings

Wolkinson, Benjamin, & Richard Block. *Employment Law,* New York: Blackwell, 1996.

Cadwell, P. W. "A Hair Piece: Perspectives on the Intersection of Race and Gender," *Duke Law Journal,* 1991: 365–396.

Levin-Epstein, Michael D. *Equal Employment Opportunity,* Washington D.C.: The Bureau of National Affairs, Inc., 1987.

Steingold, Fred, S. *The Employer's Legal Handbook,* Berkeley, CA: Nolo Press, 1994.

Critical Thinking Questions

1. Jane Sparks believes that she was discriminatorily bypassed for promotion. Acting on a recommendation of a coworker, John Eager, she files charges with the EEOC. Upon discovering that Eager had advised Sparks to file charges, the company's labor relations director suspends him for instigating an EEOC investigation of the company's personnel practices. Is Eager's suspension lawful?

2. What factors may influence a city to impose residency requirements on job applicants or employees? Are such requirements lawful?

3. Areo Airlines is attempting to increase the number of male business passengers. As part of its marketing campaign, it imposes a 120-pound weight limitation on female flight cabin attendants. Additionally, it requires them to wear short skirts and low-cut blouses. Subsequent to the implementation of this policy, Aero experiences a 15 percent increase in male passenger traffic. Are the company's grooming requirements lawful?

Exercises

1. At ABC, Incorporated, a successful job applicant has to complete a favorable interview and pass an aptitude test. Jane Good, a black female, fails the test and is not employed. Joseph Friend, a black male, is rejected because of his performance at an interview in which company officials determined that he lacked common sense and good judgment. Of 100 black and 200 white applicants, 20 blacks and 40 whites are hired. Of the 300 candidates, 40 blacks and 130 whites have passed the aptitude test. Following Good's and Friend's rejection, they file Title VII charges. In response, the company attempts to promote minority employment by adding ten points to the interview and test scores of minority applicants. Examine the legality of the company's conduct under Title VII.

2. Identify whether any employee conduct is objectionable or unlawful.

   Case A. For monthly staff meetings, Barry, the department head, always asks Jane to set up the meeting room, arrange for refreshments, and take the minutes. The work group is made up of engineers: Jane, John, Jorge, and Kumar.

   Case B. When Harriet walks over to the department's computers, she has to pass Larry's door. Larry frequently wheels his chair to the opening, and as he watches her he often says things like, "Hey, sweetie, let me know when you finish so I don't miss the show on your way back."

   Case C. Jack supervises Lillian. Lillian complains of sexually oriented jokes, innuendoes, and pictures from coworkers. No other female employee complains and no action is taken.

   Case D. Marty is a new, recently relocated manager. He asks his secretary, Louise, to rent him an apartment because he's too busy with his new job. While Louise is at the apartment checking that everything has been done as requested, Marty shows up and suggests they try out the bed. She refuses. Nothing else happens. Two months later there is a reduction in force and Louise is laid off. The official reason is her inability to get along with coworkers.

MODULE

8

References

1. Lloyd Reynolds, *Labor Economics and Labor Relations,* Englewood Cliffs, NJ: Prentice-Hall, 1964, 401.
2. Arthur Ross, "The Negro in the American Economy," in *Employment, Race and Poverty,* ed. Arthur Ross and Herbert Hill, New York: Harcourt, Brace and World, 1967, 3–47.
3. Section 701(b).
4. Sections 109(a), 109(c)(1), and 109(c)(3).
5. Section 701(c) (1–5).
6. There is no express exception for independent contractors under Title VII. However, some courts have construed the term "employee" to exclude independent contractors from coverage. See, for example, *Cobb v. Sun Papers, Inc.* 673 F.2d 337 (11th Cir.), cert denied 103 S.

Ct. 163 (1982); see also *Falls v. Sporting News,* 714 F.Supp. 843 (ED Mich), aff'd w/o opinion, 899 F.2d 1221 (6th Cir. 1990).

7. Section 703(a)(1).
8. Section 703(b).
9. Section 703(c)(1).
10. Section 704(a).
11. Section 706(e).
12. 29 CFR, section 1601.16, July 1, 1988.
13. 29 CFR, section 1601.24, July 1, 1988.
14. Section 706(f), 1964 Civil Rights Act.
15. Ibid.
16. Section 706(g).
17. Section 102(a)(1).
18. Section 102(b)(3).
19. *Teamsters v. US,* 14 FEP 1514, fn. 15, at 1519, 431 US 324 (1977).
20. 44 FEP 530, 779 F.2d 21 (8th Cir. 1985).
21. *Brown v. East Mississippi Electric Power Association,* 989 F.2d 858(1993).
22. *McDonnell Douglas v. Green,* 5 FEP 965 (1973).
23. Ibid., at 969.
24. Ibid.
25. *Colon-Sanchez v. March,* 34 FEP 1144, 733 F.2d 78 (10th Cir. 1984).
26. *Lombard v. School District,* 19 FEP 72, 463 F.Supp. 566 (1978).
27. *Davis v. Weidner,* 19 FEP 668, 596 F.2d 726 (7th Cir. 1979).
28. *Kelly v. Atlantic Richfield,* 17 FEP 823, 468 F.Supp. 712 (1979).
29. 62 FEP 96 (1993).
30. 55 FEP 131, 756 Fupp. 1244 (1991), at 137.
31. 3 FEP 175, 401 US 424 (1971).
32. Ibid., at 178.
33. David Lathcart and Mark Snyderman, "The Civil Rights Act of 1991," 8 *Labor Lawyer* 849, 1992, 862–869.
34. Section 105(B)(i).
35. Congressional record of October 25, 1991, S15, 276.
36. *Dothard v. Rawlinson,* 15 FEP 10, 433 US 321 (1977).
37. 29 CFR section 1607.4(D)(1978).
38. "Questions and Answers on the Uniform Guidelines," March 2, 1979, question 20, *BNA Fair Employment Practice Manual,* at section 403.437.
39. *Green v. Pacific Railroad Company,* 10 FEP 1409 (1975).
40. 457 U.S. 400 (1982).
41. 29 CFR, part 1607.
42. 10 FEP 1181, 422 US 405 (1975).
43. Dale Yoder and Paul Staudham, "Testing and EEOC," *Personnel Administrator,* February 1984, 80.
44. 29 CFR section 1607.14D(3).
45. Mark A. Rothstein, *Employment Law West,* 1994, P. 138.
46. *Gregory v. Litton Systems, Inc.,* 5 FEP 267, 472 F.2d 631 (9th Cir. 1972).
47. *Green v. Missouri Pacific Railroad* 10 FEP 1409, 523 F.2d 1290 (1975).
48. *EEOC v. Trailways,* 27 FEP 801, 530 F.Supp. 54 (1981); *Johnson v. Memphis Police Department,* 50 FEP 211, 1713 F.Supp. 244 (1989). *Bradley v. Pazacco of Nebraska,* 55 FEP 347, 926 F.2d 714 (8th Cir. 1991).
49. 42 USCA, paragraph 2000E-2H.
50. *Teamsters v. United States,* 431 US 324 (1977); *California Brewers Association v. Bryant* 444 US 598 (1980); *American Tobacco Corporation v. Patterson* 456 US 63 (1982).
51. *Franks v. Bowman Transportation, Incorporated,* 424 US 747 (1976).
52. 20 FEP 1, 443 US 193 (1979).
53. 40 FEP 1321, 476 US 267 (1986).
54. 91 F.3d 547 (3rd Cir. 1996).
55. 480 US 616 (1987).
56. See, for example, *Smith v. University of North Carolina,* 18 FEP 913 (1978).
57. Section 701(j), Title VII.

58. 14 FEP 1697, 432 US 63 (1977).
59. *Brener v. Diagnostic Center,* 28 FEP 907, 671 F.2d 141 (5th Cir. 1982).
60. 20 FEP 94, 601 F.2d 956 (8th Cir. 1979).
61. 34 FEP 1816, 734 F.2d 1382 (9th Cir. 1984).
62. 31 FEP 588 (1988).
63. 1 FEP 656, 408 F.2d 228 (5th Cir. 1969), at 661.
64. *Diaz v. Pan American Airways,* 3 FEP 337, 442 F.2d 385 (5th Cir. 1971), at 339.
65. 55 FEP 365, 499 US 187 (1991).
66. Guidelines on Discrimination Because of Sex, 29 CFR, section 1604.2(a)(2).
67. Section 701K.
68. *Gardner v. National Airlines,* 14 FEP 1806, 434 F.Supp. 249 (1977).
69. *California Federal Savings and Loan Association v. Guerra,* 42 FEP 1073, 479 US 272 (1987).
70. Section 701(k), Public Law 95-555 (1978).
71. 29 CFR 160411
72. 40 FEP 1822, 477 US 57 (1986).
73. 63 FEP 225 (1993).
74. Ibid at 21.
75. 118 S.Ct. 2275 (1998).
76. 118 S.Ct. 2257 (1998).
77. Mary E. Kurz, "Investigating Sexual Harassment Complaints," Michigan State University, September 2, 1993.
78. Frederick L. Sullivan, "Sexual harassment: the Supreme Court ruling," *Personnel,* December 1986, 42–45.
79. Gregory DeFreitas, *Inequality at Work: Hispanics in the US Labor Force,* New York: Oxford University Press, 1991, 65–66.
80. EEOC Guidelines on Discrimination Because of National Origin, 29 CFR 1606.1 (1980).
81. *Garcia v. Moore,* 618 F.2d 264 (5th Cir. 1980); *Garcia v. Spunsteak Company,* 998 F.2d 1580 (9th Cir. 1993).
82. 48 FEP 980, 863 F.2d 1135 (3rd Cir. 1988).

MODULE
8

Index

....

Abusive environment. *See* Hostile environment

Affirmative action, 8.5, 8.13

Americans working abroad, 8.6

BFOQ, bona fide occupational qualification, 8.15

Burden of proof, 8.8

Citizenship requirement, and employment, 8.19

Civil Rights Act, Title VII, 8.4, 8.20

Civil Rights Act of 1964, 8.4, 8.19

Civil Rights Act of 1991, 8.5–6, 8.7, 8.9

Compensatory damages, 8.7–8

Compliance, Title VII, burden of, 8.4, 8.13

Conciliation, and EEOC, 8.7

Conditions of employment, 8.6. *See also* Discrimination, Employment tests, Sex discrimination, Validity of tests
   sexual harassment, 8.17

Construct validity, employment tests, 8.11

Content validity, employment tests, 8.11

Contested disciplinary decision, discrimination, 8.8

Criterion-Related validity, employment tests, 8.11

Damage awards, compensatory and punitive, 8.7

Discrimination, in employment, 8.4. *See also* Conditions of employment

Discriminatory practice, 8.7

Disparate impact, 8.9–11

Disparate treatment, 8.8–9, 8.12

Dress and grooming requirement, 8.14–15

Duty to accommodate, employer's, 8.14–15

Economic inequality, 8.4

EEOC (Equal Employment Opportunity Commission).
   bilingual guidelines, 8.19
   conciliation, 8.7
   employer duty to accommodate, 8.14
   enforcement of Title VII, 8.6
   sexual harassment, 8.16
   uniform guidelines, 8.11
   v. Electronic Data Systems, 8.15
   v. M.D. Pneumatics, 8.8

Employee, term defined, 8.6

Employer liability
   sexual harassment, 8.17
   under Title VII, 8.7, 8.8, 8.10

Employer retaliation, protection of workers, 8.6
   sexual harassment, 8.17
   Employer's duty to accommodate, 8.14

Employers, and seniority, 8.12
   Title VII compliance, 8.5

Employment agencies, Title VII compliance, 8.5

Employment discrimination, 8.4, 8.9, 8.19. *See also* Minority workers, Women workers

Employment policies, harassment, 8.18
   Title VII compliance, 8.4, 8.12

Employment practices, 8.9, 8.19
   religious discrimination, 8.13
   selection criteria, 8.12
   uniform guidelines, 8.11

Employment tests, vs. job performance, 8.11

Enforcement, Title VII, 8.6, 8.19

English-only rules, and employment, 8.18

Environmental context, 8.5

Equal employment opportunity, 8.5, 8.8
   pregnant workers, 8.16
   statutes, 8.20
   women and barriers to, 8.4

Equal Employment Opportunity Commission. *See* EEOC

Equality in workplace, 8.4

Exclusionary device, 8.11

Experience requirements, 8.12

Hiring techniques. *See* Employment practices

Hostile environment, sexual harassment, 8.17

Human Relations (HR), 8.4

Human relations roles, 8.5

Human Relations Strategy, 8.5

Illegal motive, discrimination, 8.8

Inference of discrimination, 8.8

Intentional discrimination, 8.7, 8.9

Job analysis, 8.11

Labor unions, 8.20
   and seniority, 8.12–13
   Title VII compliance, 8.5, 8.7

Language requirements, 8.19

Litigation, Title VII, 8.7

Management obligations, under Title VII, 8.20. *See also* Employer liability

Managerial discretion, 8.5

Minority workers, discrimination, 8.4, 8.8–11
   employment test scores, 8.12
   professional and management positions, 8.19

National Labor Relations Act, 8.6

National origin discrimination. *See* Racial discrimination

Negative impact, Title VII compliance, 8.10

MODULE
8

Paid leave, 8.16
Pregnancy Discrimination Act, 8.16
Pregnant workers, level of benefits, 8.16
Prima facie case, discrimination, 8.8
Privacy, right of, 8.15–16
Prohibited acts, Title VII, 8.6
Punitive damages, 8.7–8

Quid pro quo sexual harassment, 8.17

Racial discrimination, 8.4, 8.5, 8.8–9
Religious discrimination, 8.4, 8.13
Remedies, sexual harassment, 8.18
    Title VII, 8.5, 8.7–8
Retaliation, 8.17. *See* Employer retaliation
Reverse discrimination, 8.13
Right to sue, Title VII, 8.7

Seniority, 8.12
    loss of, 8.16
    retroactive, 8.7
    rights, 8.9

Sex discrimination, 8.4, 8.15
Sexual harassment, 8.16–17
Sexual harassment policies, 8.18
Stereotypical assumptions
    sex discrimination, 8.15
    women workers, 8.4

Terms, conditions or privileges, of
    employment, 8.20
Title VII, 8.4–20

Uniform guidelines, employment, 8.11

Validity of tests, employee selection, 8.11–12
Violation of Title VII, 8.6, 8.9

Weight lifting, Women workers, 8.4
White collar occupations, 8.4
Women workers, employment
    discrimination, 8.4
Workplace policies, 8.8
    sexual harassment, 8.17

MODULE
8

Managing Human Resources in the 21st Century

From Core Concepts to Strategic Choice

MODULE 9

Managing Diversity

Human Resource Issues

Stella M. Nkomo
UNIVERSITY OF
NORTH CAROLINA AT CHARLOTTE

Ellen Ernst Kossek
MICHIGAN STATE UNIVERSITY

Managing Human Resources in the 21st Century: From Core Concepts to Strategic Choice,
by Kossek and Block

Publisher: Dave Shaut
Executive Editor: John Szilagyi
Developmental Editor: Bryant Editorial Development
Marketing Manager: Joseph A. Sabatino
Production Editor: Tamborah E. Moore
Manufacturing Coordinator: Dana Began Schwartz
Cover Design: Tin Box Studio
Cover Photographs: Copyright Shoji Sato/Photonica
Production House: The Left Coast Group, Inc.
Printer: West Group

Printed in the United States of America
1 2 3 4 5 02 01 00 99

For more information contact South-Western College Publishing, 5101 Madison Road, Cincinnati,
Ohio, 45227 or find us on the Internet at *http://www.swcollege.com*
For permission to use material from this text or product, contact us by
- telephone: 1-800-730-2214
- fax: 1-800-730-2215
- web: *http://www.thomsonrights.com*

ISBN: 0–324–01808–8

This book is printed on acid-free paper.

Contents

MODULE OVERVIEW   9.4

RELATION TO THE FRAME   9.4
External Environmental Forces Contributing to a Diverse Workplace   9.5
Why Employers Seek to Manage Diversity   9.7

CORE CONCEPTS IN MANAGING DIVERSITY   9.7
Primary and Secondary Dimensions of Diversity   9.7
Identity   9.8
How Managing Diversity Differs from AA/EEO   9.9
Multiculturalism   9.10
Managing Diversity Paradigms   9.10
Diversity Processes   9.12

STRATEGIC ISSUES IN MANAGING DIVERSITY   9.13

APPLICATION   9.14

IN CONCLUSION   9.15
Debrief   9.15
Suggested Readings   9.15
Relevant Web Sites   9.16
Critical Thinking Questions   9.16
Exercises   9.16
References   9.19

INDEX   9.21

MODULE
9

MODULE OVERVIEW

This module discusses the fundamental concepts and processes associated with human resource issues related to managing diversity in organizations. In recent years, employing organizations have become increasingly aware of changing labor market demographics and the need to effectively manage a diversity of perspectives and talents. Workforce demographics for the United States and many other nations of the world indicate increasing racial, ethnic, and gender diversity of employees. Building the competencies and human resource systems needed to manage diversity has become a major strategic issue for organizations. Human resource professionals carry the primary responsibility for leading organizational initiatives to manage diversity.

This module will first describe why many employers today seek to manage diversity. First and foremost, significant demographic, economic, and cultural external environmental changes have made an employer's ability to effectively manage workplace diversity a critical organizational core competency and a strategic business issue for many firms. A brief discussion of three significant trends will illustrate how environmental factors are pressuring organizations to address workplace diversity issues. These include the changing demographic nature of the workforce, the growing service economy, and increasing globalization. Many firms are beginning to recognize that effectively adapting human resource and organizational systems to these trends will affect the degree to which an organization will be able to (1) be viewed as an employer of choice, (2) achieve high levels of profitability, and (3) be able to transform its work culture to capitalize on the organizational benefits of managing diversity.

The module defines diversity and managing diversity. Specifically, it focuses on the meanings of important concepts associated with the management of diversity. These concepts include diversity and the notions of primary and secondary dimensions of diversity, identity, multiculturalism, how managing diversity differs from equal employment opportunity (EEO) and affirmative action (AA), and the implications of managing diversity for human resource outcomes. Following this, the module will describe two different diversity paradigms and explain the major stages of managing diversity. The final section provides exercises to demonstrate the complexity of the issues involved in managing diversity in organizations.

RELATION TO THE FRAME

A firm's culture can impede organizational performance if it inhibits the ability to adapt to changing environmental conditions such as shifting market conditions, new technologies and ideas, societal shifts, or the changing expectations of the workforce. If a firm is able to change its culture to be multicultural in a way that links the effective management of diversity to organizational performance, then managing diversity serves a transformational human resource role. If managing diversity activities changes the culture in such a way that the firm better taps into the potential of employees of all backgrounds to the benefit of its customers, then it transforms the culture into a more performance-driven entity. What is accomplished is more important than individual differences in *how* it is accomplished. Teaming and group work are enhanced because the talents of many are better utilized in the development of the final product for the customer.

An example of the transformational role of managing diversity occurred when IBM Corporation conducted a cultural audit as a means of enhancing its ability to improve not only how it manages diversity but also its performance capabilities. For decades IBM led the computer market with a strong company culture typified by employees wearing white button-down collar shirts, learning the IBM way, and selling large mainframe computers. Then in the early 1980s, when the computer industry underwent major technological and economic upheaval, IBM's strong monoculture was no longer

FIGURE 9.1   *A Frame for Understanding Human Resource Strategy:*
Context, Roles, and Constraints

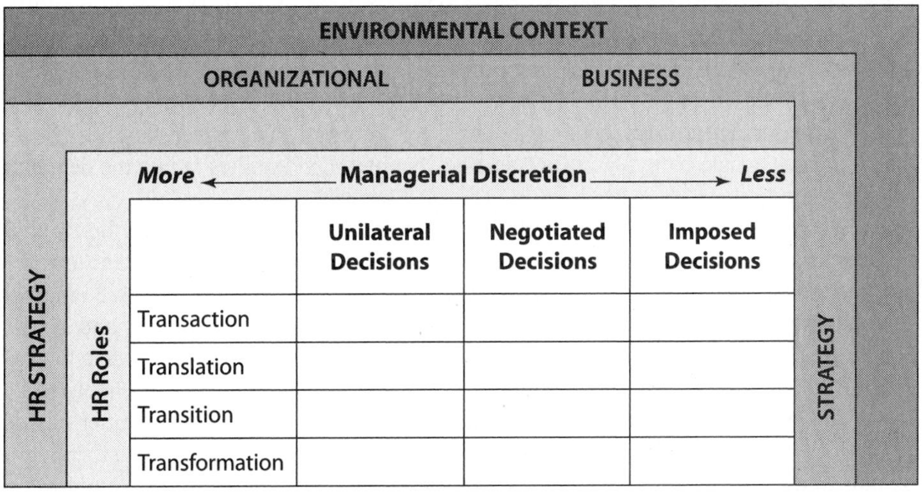

ENVIRONMENTAL CONTEXT			
ORGANIZATIONAL		BUSINESS	

HR STRATEGY	HR Roles	More ← Managerial Discretion → Less			STRATEGY
		Unilateral Decisions	**Negotiated Decisions**	**Imposed Decisions**	
	Transaction				
	Translation				
	Transition				
	Transformation				

© 2000 by Ellen Ernst Kossek and Richard Block. Thanks to Brian Pentland, Karen Markel, and John Beck for helpful comments and discussions that enhanced the model.

seen as a competitive strength but as a major weakness inhibiting its ability to compete. The inability of IBM to embrace multiculturalism in the late 1980s and early 1990s was viewed by all employee groups, from white males over 40, to African-American men and women, to working mothers, to new hires, as a major inhibitor to utilizing their unique attributes and skills. By the mid- to late 1990s, IBM had successfully transformed its culture to better utilize employee talents from many different backgrounds. This cultural change has allowed the company to once again put the customer first and allowed individuals of all backgrounds to feel that they could contribute to the maximum of their potential to support this renewed direction.[1] (See Figure 9.1, A Frame for Understanding Human Resource Strategy.)

MODULE
9

External Environmental Forces Contributing to a Diverse Workplace

Demographic Changes.   The major impetus for the current attention to managing diversity was the demographic and economic forecasts contained in the now infamous *Workforce 2000 Report* published by the Hudson Institute in 1987.[2] This report offered a number of projections about the changing nature of the workforce. It is predicted that the workforce of the twenty-first century will have greater cultural, gender, and age diversity than ever before. *Workforce 2000* indicated that five-sixths of the net additions to the workforce between 1985 and 2000 would be nonwhites, women, and immigrants. Only 58 percent of the new entrants into the labor force would come from the majority group population of white Americans.

Most demographic forecasts also indicate high levels of immigration in the United States from Asian and Hispanic groups during the twenty-first century. Hispanics are projected to represent the largest minority group in the United States, surpassing African-Americans, who have traditionally been the largest minority group population. It is believed that the workforce will consist of a larger percentage of older workers compared to previous decades. The average age of the workforce will climb from age 36 to 39 by the year 2000.

While women made up 43 percent of the total workforce in 1980, it was predicted that by the year 2000, women would account for more than 47 percent of the total workforce, and 61 percent of all American women would be employed. More recent forecasts indicate a continuing decrease in the percentage of white males in the labor force. Their numbers were 43 percent in 1990 but would decline to 38 percent by 2005. The movement of large numbers of women into the workplace has also come with significant changes in family roles for both men and women. Workers are demanding greater flexibility to achieve balance between work and family demands. The workforce is also experiencing a dramatic increase in the number of dual-career families (many with children), single-parent families, same-sex couples, and families facing the demands of elder care.

Taken together, these demographic changes indicate the workforce of the twenty-first century will be more heterogeneous than ever before. It is also important to point out that the changing nature of the workforce is not simply numerical. Diverse employees also bring different perspectives, cultures, lifestyles, values, attitudes, and needs. For example, it is estimated that gay men and lesbians constitute between 4 and 17 percent of the workforce.[3] The concentration of gay and lesbian employees is likely to be higher in key urban areas such as San Francisco, where many high-tech computer related companies are located. Organizations are faced with the challenge of transforming a homogenous work environment into a heterogeneous one that values all employees. Unquestioned company loyalty is a thing of past.

Economic Changes. The United States economy is shifting from a manufacturing base to a service and information base. While manufacturing produced some 30 percent of all goods and services in 1955, its share is predicted to drop to less than 17 percent by the year 2000. The twenty-first century is being viewed as the century of the knowledge worker. Producing and delivering services requires a different set of knowledge, skills, and abilities in addition to work structures. In a service economy, person-to-person contact dominates, whether it consists of employee to employee or employee to customer. The ability of companies to interact effectively with a diverse marketplace will become increasingly important to an organization's success. Avon, for example, was able to turn around its unprofitable inner city markets by diversifying its sales force to include more Hispanic and African-American managers in charge of marketing to these groups.[4]

Globalization. A third trend contributing to workforce diversity is the increasing emphasis on global marketing and multinational business operations. Many United States corporations now derive more than half of their revenues from overseas markets. U. S. direct investment has almost doubled since 1994. With growing proportions of a firm's revenues coming from foreign sales, the ability to understand the market needs and preferences of different cultures becomes essential to profitability. As global boundaries fall, more companies are operating in different cultural contexts and are also employing more foreign employees. Consequently, their workforces are more diverse in gender and ethnic composition. For example, the International Labor Organization reports the percentage of women managers increased in 39 of 41 countries studied between 1985 and 1991.[5]

Honda Corporation's global network reflects an international viewpoint with a solid commitment to local markets and economies. A local approach with a global outlook best meets the individual needs of diverse markets. Honda's philosophy is to produce where there is market demand. By integrating work processes with local customs and cultures and making use of local management resources, Honda has been better able to serve the people of the regions in which it operates. Products that meet the specific needs of four world market regions (the Americas; Europe; the Middle East and Africa; and Asia, and Oceania, and Japan) are developed, produced, and sold in those regions. This practice ensures a higher level of creativity in Honda's technology and products.[6]

Why Employers Seek to Manage Diversity

Besides the environmental changes described below, additional business reasons most employers today seek to manage diversity include employer of choice, profitability, and organizational benefits. If an employer is able to attract a very large labor pool of qualified individuals, it can have greater selectivity in choosing future employees. In general, the more choosy an employer can be, the higher the quality of the applicant. If a company is going to be able to constantly attract and hire the best workers, it is critical to avoid cultivating a reputation of not being a good place for individuals of a certain minority or gender or other backgrounds to work.

Diversity can also affect a company's bottom line. Competence in serving diverse customers has direct implications for market share and customer satisfaction. An example of how profitability is linked to diversity issues is provided by the Tiger Woods phenomenon in the PGA. In the year he won the Masters, PGA profits were up a record 185 percent, a $653 million dollar increase from the previous year. Another effect on the bottom line relates to cost. If a firm manages diversity well, organizational waste should decrease due to fewer lawsuits, less conflict, and improved morale. For example, in 1997, over $500 million was paid to settle discrimination suits in the United States. The organizational benefits of managing diversity include greater creativity, better teamwork and group problem-solving, greater system flexibility, and enhanced ability to manage globalization.[7]

CORE CONCEPTS IN MANAGING DIVERSITY

Diversity is a relatively new concept in organizations, and a difficult one to define because it is multidimensional. In its broadest sense, diversity refers to a mixture of people with different group identities operating within the same social system.[8] For example, in any organization there may be diversity based on gender, race/ethnicity, religion, age, sexual orientation, etc. The focus is on diversity in identities based on membership in social and demographic groups and how differences in identities affect social relations in organizations.

A key point is that diversity, as defined in this module, does not refer to one individual—an employer does not hire a "diverse" employee—but to a labor pool. Diversity involves a group as a whole; it involves the concepts of relationships and differences within a group. There are six core concepts that must be understood to grasp the complexity of managing diversity:

- Primary and secondary dimensions of diversity
- Identity
- How managing diversity differs from affirmative action and equal employment opportunity (AA/EEO)
- Multiculturalism
- Managing diversity paradigms
- Diversity processes

Primary and Secondary Dimensions of Diversity

It is important to distinguish between primary and secondary dimensions of diversity. Primary dimensions of diversity consist of immutable human differences that are inherent and significant. They represent core dimensions of our identity. Race and ethnicity, nationality, age, gender, physical abilities, and sexual orientation are generally considered to be primary dimensions of human difference.[9] They have a profound effect on our self-definition and how others categorize us, and they have the most direct and salient influence on our status in society and in organizations. These core dimensions are viewed as socially meaningful categorizations and are generally known by others who interact with us. For example, coworkers can usually easily and explicitly see if someone is a man or woman, white or African-American, or speaks English as a second language. Differences between people based on these dimensions are often grounded within structures of power inequalities and unequal access to resources. For example, racial/ethnic minorities and women often experience subordinate status and exclusion from opportunities and resources.

Like primary dimensions, secondary dimensions also distinguish one human being from another. However, these differences are mutable; we acquire and can modify them through our actions or other changes. For example, when people join organizations, they are placed in different positions and different levels. Where they are placed distinguishes one individual from another. Secondary dimensions include organization level/function, work experience, abilities, educational background, values, and tenure. Relative to the primary dimensions, secondary dimensions are viewed as having an indirect and less salient effect on our self-concept and organization experiences.

In employing organizations, it is not unusual for primary and secondary dimensions of diversity to be correlated among workgroups. For example, the top management group in many firms typically consists of white males over 35 years. The secretarial group is still often female. If an organization's HR policies to manage diversity are effective in changing the culture over time, the tendency to be able to characterize workgroups as being typified by primary dimensions of diversity will be reduced.

Identity

At the root of diversity is the concept of identity. Both of the primary and secondary dimensions described above help shape our identity. We can talk about our gender identity, racial identity, ethnic identity, or professional identity. According to Brewer and Miller (1984), an individual's identity is highly differentiated and based in part on membership in significant social categories, along with the value and emotional significance attached to that membership. Social identity theory points out that our self-concept is partly defined by various group affiliations.[10] In answer to the question, "Who am I?" a person might respond in terms of a group identity (e.g., "I am a woman") or an individual characteristic (e.g., "I am an introverted person"). It is even more complicated because individuals have multiple identities, not just a single identity.[11] People may view themselves in terms of their membership in many different identity groups at once, and also may vary in the importance they assign each group in their overall self-concept. Race and gender can interact with each other as well as with other aspects of an individual's identity. For example, a worker can be assigned to a work team because of particular education and functional knowledge, but the individual also will come with an identity based on his or her race and gender. Identities are not fixed but can change.

The significance or salience of an identity also depends on the context. All individuals have gender, race, ethnicity, age, sexual orientation, educational background, etc. Sometimes, individuals may stress one of these identities over others. For example, if you are in a workgroup consisting of a single gender group (e.g., all men), differences in age or education may become more significant than gender in defining group interactions. If the group is dominated by younger males, the older males in the group may experience "feeling different" and being treated differently. Because employees have multiple identities, each identity can lead to experiences of relative privilege or relative exclusion in different contexts.

HR Implications of Diversity and Identity.   The diversity and identities of employees as individual and group members in work organizations have a number of HR implications. They have implications for power—that is, the experience of being oppressed or dominant in organizational life. A key definition of power often involves access to resources, networks, and assimilation demands. For example, some primary identities bring higher costs (or benefits) to an individual because of their social, historical, and cultural status. In the United States, the historical experience of African-Americans is one of stereotyping, discrimination, and racism. Consequently, as a group, African-Americans have had less access to educational opportunities and upper-level positions in organizations. In contrast, as a group, white males have enjoyed a privileged status with greater access to the best positions in organizations because of their race and gender. Dominant identity groups generally hold greater power in organizations.

Diversity and identity also influence the subjective perceptions of group members. They influence individuals' and groups' framing of how they experience the world; perceptions of justice, and the degree to which they feel their contributions are likely to be valued. When people with different identities work together, differences in culture, perspectives, and values can result in misunderstandings, ultimately affecting work and organization performance. Diversity and identity have also affected objective outcomes of individuals and groups, such as career experiences, and the likelihood of experiencing workplace discrimination in areas such as pay, promotion, access to mentors, and general conflict in day-to-day interaction with members of the dominant culture.

Perhaps more important to understand is how organization structures and human resource practices disadvantage certain groups and advantage others. The challenge of managing diversity is to develop human resource practices and organizational systems that value and reinforce rather than hinder the full participation of all organizational members regardless of identity.

How Managing Diversity Differs from AA/EEO

Organizations make a very clear distinction between affirmative action/Equal Employment Opportunity and managing diversity. There are not only different assumptions but also very different practices. AA/EEO came about in response to laws prohibiting discrimination against women and minorities—specifically, to Title VII of the Civil Rights Act of 1964, which prohibited discrimination based on race, color, sex, national origin, and religion. It required that employers not discriminate in the area of selection, pay, promotion, or access to training, and decreed that they show that HR decisions are made on valid job-related criteria. Affirmative action resulted from a series of executive orders issued by Presidents Johnson and Nixon. The orders required companies to adopt policies and practices to recruit and employ women and minorities when their representation in an organization was inadequate and underutilized. Despite its lofty origins, affirmative action has largely been a remedial tool as practiced by organizations. It presupposes that previously excluded groups should assimilate into the organization and adapt to existing organizational norms and practices.

Affirmative action and EEO primarily focus on recruitment, staffing, and promotion policies within organizations rather than focus on culture change to ensure employees are utilized to the maximum of their potential.

Researchers and organizational practitioners argue that managing diversity goes far beyond affirmative action/EEO.[12] Managing diversity is viewed as a strategic issue that has profound implications for the productivity and strategic success of organizations. It emphasizes the building of skills and human resource practices to ensure that differences among employees are a valued, integral part of an organization's very mission, strategies, and day-to-day operations. Emphasis is placed on incorporating different employee perspectives into the main work of the organization, and enhancing work

TABLE 9.1 *Some Ways Managing Diversity Differs from AA/EEO*[13]

AA/EEO	Managing Diversity
Special program	Change culture
For the disadvantaged	For the manager and the organization's benefit
Focus: hiring, retention, promotion	Focus: utilization, tapping potential
Legally mandated	Not legally mandated

by rethinking primary tasks and redefining markets, products, strategies, management and human resource practices, and organization culture. While affirmative action/EEO stresses assimilation, managing diversity strives for multiculturalism. Table 9.1 summarizes the differences between AA/EEO initiatives and managing diversity.

It should be pointed out that managing diversity does not replace affirmative action/EEO initiatives in organizations. Most organizations still recognize the need for such initiatives to address the glass-ceiling barriers that prevent women and minorities from being fairly represented in upper-level managerial positions.

Currently, a national debate is occurring in state and local governments and in public universities over affirmative action as a long-term remedy. For example, California's Proposition 209 abolished affirmative action in a number of state programs, leaving cities and universities uncertain whether to dismantle affirmative action. Most private-sector employers have adopted a wait-and-see attitude until future actions are taken by the U.S. Supreme Court.

Multiculturalism

Multiculturalism assumes that each culture group can preserve its original culture without assimilating into a dominant culture. Each culture is valued, and no judgment is made that one culture is better than another. In the context of organization diversity, a multicultural organization is one where no one group dominates. Each cultural group is fully involved in all aspects of the organization, and there is an absence of prejudice and discrimination. Diverse organizational members work with little intergroup conflict. Intergroup conflict in the context of diversity has two distinguishing features: (1) group boundaries and group differences that are involved, and (2) differences that occur because of differences in group identities.[14] Another characteristic that should be examined is how jobs are distributed within an organization. In a multicultural organization, this is not done according to group membership. All groups have equal representation in the organizational hierarchy, and all individuals appreciate and value other cultures. Here, human resource practices are designed to accommodate the needs of a diverse set of employees.

Managing Diversity Paradigms

Thomas and Ely[15] identify three approaches guiding diversity initiatives in organizations: the discrimination-and-fairness paradigm, the access-and-legitimacy paradigm, and the learning-and-effectiveness paradigm. Each has different assumptions and approaches to managing diversity. According to Thomas and Ely, organizations that view diversity through a discrimination-and-fairness perspective focus on equal opportunity, fair treatment, recruitment, and compliance with state and federal equal employment opportunity legislation. Human resource practices within this perspective include mentoring and career development programs targeted toward women and minorities. Emphasis is placed on recruiting strategies that increase the number of these groups in the organization. Training programs focus on teaching other employees to respect cultural differences. Under this model, diversity effectiveness is measured by how well the

TABLE 9.2 *Diversity Paradigms*

	Discrimination-Fairness	Access-Legitimacy	Learning-Effectiveness
Focus	Creating equal opportunity, assuring fair treatment, and compliance with state and federal equal opportunity laws	Matching internal employee demographics to customers and marketplace served	Incorporating diversity into the heart and fabric of the mission, work, and culture of the organization
HR Practices	Recruitment of women and minorities, mentoring and career development programs for women and minorities, written affirmative action plans	Recruitment of diverse set of employees, Knowledge, Skills, Abilities, and Other (KSAO) to match external demands	Redesigned and transformed to be flexible to enhance performance of all employees; reward diverse teams, creative career paths
Effectiveness Measure	Recruitment numbers, retention rates of women and minorities	Niche markets captured, degree of diversity among employees	All employees feel respected, valued, and included; quality of work
Weaknesses	Does not capitalize on diversity of all employees, emphasis on assimilation	Does not affect mainstream of company business, diversity confined to the specific market segments	Requires a long-term effort

Based on Thomas and Ely (1996).

organization meets recruitment and retention targets, but the work and culture of the organization is not diversified. Indeed, differences among employees are downplayed, and assimilation to a standard way of operating for all employees is valued.

In contrast, the access-and-legitimacy paradigm seeks to capitalize on the diversity that exists in the marketplace. Organizations subscribing to this perspective seek to match internal employee demographics with its diverse customers in the marketplace. For example, a number of consumer product companies create segmented markets to serve different racial, ethnic, and gender groups. The underlying assumption of the access-and-legitimacy paradigm is that an organization needs a diverse workforce to help it compete in a multicultural marketplace. As noted earlier, Avon was very successful in hiring African-American women to market a new line of cosmetics to an African-American market in the New York City area.[16] In short, managing diversity is viewed as good business. Human resource practices under this paradigm would also emphasize the recruitment of a diverse set of employees. The search would be for employees with multicultural knowledge, skills, and abilities. The goal, however, would not be to assimilate these employees into the organization, but to maintain the distinct perspectives they bring. Job assignments would seek to match employee diversity to market diversity so that employee's capabilities could be used to capture niche markets. Efforts are not made to understand how a set of diverse skills could be integrated into the mainstream of the company.

Finally, the learning-and-effectiveness perspective attempts to incorporate the diversity of employees into the very fabric of the work and culture of the organization.

Organizations using this perspective seek ways to enhance the primary work of the company by redefining markets, tasks, products, strategies, missions, business practices, and organization cultures.[17]

Diversity Processes

Organizations have developed a number of different processes for managing diversity. These processes can be arranged on a continuum from single programmatic interventions, such as one-time cultural audits and awareness training, to comprehensive diversity processes involving major changes in human resource practices and organizational systems. Some organizations utilize only one of the processes, while a few have implemented comprehensive strategies that incorporate continuous cultural audits, awareness training, skill building, redesigned human resources practices, and organizational systems. Unfortunately, when a firm uses only a couple of these processes as isolated human resource strategies, the tendency is to put more emphasis on adopting formal HR activities without obtaining support from senior management in a way that links these HR practices to how the company does business. If diversity management efforts consist mainly of programs, their long-term effectiveness in transforming the organization's culture to embrace multiculturalism in a way that shapes business strategy is likely to be diminished.[18] Each of the major diversity processes is described below.

Cultural Audits/Surveys.   Regardless of the process ultimately used by an organization, most diversity processes begin with a cultural audit. It might be easier to think of this as being similar to a needs assessment done before designing training programs. Large amounts of data are collected to assess the dominant corporate culture and how different employee groups experience it. These audits cover individual attitudes and beliefs about diversity, organizational values and norms, and the status of different identity groups in the organization. They also assess management and human resource practices to uncover cultural barriers that may hinder the full participation of all employees regardless of their identity.

Awareness Training.   Awareness training focuses on teaching employees about cultural differences through training sessions. Training topics typically include stereotyping, prejudice, and the role of culture in understanding individual and group behavior. Many of these programs involve self-assessments of perceived similarities and differences between different groups of employees, communication styles, attitudes toward affirmative action programs, and the success and failure of members of different groups. Awareness training is built on the assumption that awareness will help sensitize employees to differences that exist among people.[19]

Skill-Building Training.   Skill-building training goes one step beyond awareness training. It focuses on teaching managers and employees the behaviors and skills needed to function in a heterogeneous work environment. These include interpersonal communication, performance feedback, cross-cultural conflict resolution, and managing and working in diverse teams.[20]

Diversity Enlargement Hiring Strategies.   Diversity enlargement strategies focus on hiring individuals of different backgrounds in order to develop a more diverse workforce. This assumes that an organization will become more multicultural if it increases the level of diversity in the firm. Employees are generally expected to assimilate into the dominant corporate cultural background. Natural processes are assumed to allow members of nontraditional managerial backgrounds to be able to move up the corporate hierarchy.[21]

TABLE 9.3 *Sample Human Resource Diversity Initiatives*

- Parental leave policy
- Alternative career paths
- Flexible work schedules
- Support groups (singles, minorities, women, etc.)
- Elder care
- Job redesign to allow for greater employee opportunities for employees with disabilities
- Internships to attract underrepresented groups
- Training in English as a second language
- Explicit promotion opportunities to break through glass ceiling
- Cultural/ethnic days

- Company-paid literacy training
- Telecommuting
- Phased retirement for older workers
- Physical access for employees with disabilities
- In-house day care
- Allowing greater flexibility with respect to absences for religious holidays
- Mentoring programs for women and minorities
- Bilingual training for managers and employees
- Measuring the management of diversity performance of managers

Redesigning Human Resource Policies and Practices. The emphasis here is on transforming human resource policies designed for a homogenous workforce into policies and practices responsive to a heterogeneous workforce. Efforts are made to design human resource policies and practices that support the diversity employees bring to the workplace. Human resource managers play a critical role in the redesign process. Their role includes: (1) creating the awareness of the need to value diversity; (2) making the business case for developing a diversity initiative in the organization; (3) gaining top management commitment; (4) developing a diversity plan of action; and (5) identifying the needed changes in human resource management functions (e.g., staffing, training and development, compensation and benefits, performance appraisal, etc.) and organization culture to assure diversity is valued.[22] Table 9.3 gives a sample of human resource programs and policies that have been created to respond to the growing diversity of the workforce.

MODULE
9

STRATEGIC ISSUES IN MANAGING DIVERSITY

Despite good intentions (and there are exceptions such as Denny's restaurants, which is discussed below), many employers today have not been highly successful in managing diversity. A primary reason for this is that most of the common employer approaches reviewed in the previous section are often implemented in a piecemeal fashion with little or no integration with each other or with broader HR systems (e.g., reward, selection, etc.). They also fail to address core organizational work processes, culture change, and business decisions. Most organizations today have viewed managing diversity as an end in itself as opposed to a means to an end.[23] Too often diversity is viewed as a "program" and not as a major organization change process. Yet if diversity management is viewed strategically, it is a key ongoing component of organizational change processes—not a one-time program or event—aimed at making an organization more competitive by capitalizing on the rich talents and competencies of diverse individuals. Managing diversity has become even more of a strategic issue because the twenty-first century will be the century of the knowledge worker. Competitive advantage will rely increasingly on the knowledge, talents, and skills of a company's workforce. Diversity represents a distinct company resource that can make a difference to goal attainment. To be successful, managing diversity must be tied to the organization's business strategy and mission.

APPLICATION

James B. Adamson is the chairman and chief executive of Advantica Restaurant Group, the parent company of Denny's, headquartered in Spartanburg, South Carolina. He has discussed how his company has transformed itself to be more multicultural. His comments illustrate the importance of viewing managing diversity as a strategic business issue.[24] In 1993, many writers in the media and the press had labeled Denny's "racist," largely due to two highly publicized class-action suits that were settled in 1994. It is unlikely that a company's customer base or employee morale will be improved with such negative publicity. Then several years later, the National Association for Colored People awarded the Advantica Group its Corporate Fair Share Award for Minority Business Development and named Adamson "CEO of the Year." By 1998, *Fortune* magazine ranked the Advantica Restaurant Group second in the country in its annual survey of "The 50 Best Companies for Asians, Blacks, & Hispanics." How did Denny's transform itself and overhaul its corporate culture? The human resource and business strategies it followed are discussed below.

First, it diversified its board of directors. Among Fortune 500 firms, minorities lack representation on 97 percent of boards of directors, and women on 94 percent. In five years, from 1993 to 1998, the company's board of directors went from one minority member to being 42 percent women and people of color. Since a firm's CEO establishes the values, expectations, and operating philosophies of a company, a second strategy was for Adamson to actively communicate his commitment to developing a diverse and inclusive company as a business strategy. Implementing this strategy has resulted in 30 percent of Advantica's and 40 percent of Denny's senior management being members of minority groups.

Since it is critical to make a senior manager accountable for diversity, Adamson appointed a chief diversity officer. He made sure she had sufficient power and authority to be able to get things done. A clear expectation was set that anyone who discriminated was fired. Diversity performance began to be monitored and measured and reported so that employees and managers knew it was a senior management priority. Improvement and progress in diversity management was tied to reward and recognition systems. Up to 25 percent of senior officers' bonuses is tied to how well they value and manage their diversity, which, as Adamson remarked, "certainly got their attention!" Individuals who are successful in championing diversity are publicly celebrated and recognized.

Another tactic Denny's followed was to make 35 percent of its franchise system minority owned. If a third of a franchise's owners are minority, it is much more likely that there will be commitment to and ownership of diversity management principles. Business practices were changed so that now up to $125 million in annual business are awarded in minority purchasing contracts.

Human resource systems and management practices were audited to ensure they did not impede inclusion. Those policies that hindered inclusion were abolished or modified. While it may sound strange to say that employees need to be trained to treat others equally, Adamson felt it was critical to invest the necessary financial resources to train over 70,000 managers, hosts, servers, and other employees in racial sensitivity. The goal of the training was to provide Denny's employees the knowledge and tools necessary to deliver on Adamson's promise of equal treatment for each of the one million customers served each day.

While certainly each company trying to manage diversity strategically must diagnose its own unique circumstances, Adamson's approach provides some clear examples of strategies that a firm can use to manage diversity effectively from the top.

IN CONCLUSION

Debrief

Managing diversity is a complex issue. The changing demographic characteristics of the workforce present both challenges and opportunities for managing human resources in organizations. Managing diversity should not be viewed as a substitute for companies addressing discrimination in the workplace. Managers must understand the need to rectify discrimination and also to work toward creating a workplace that values the contributions of a diverse group of employees. Designing human resource management practices and policies that allow all employees to perform at their best is easier to state than to put into practice. Part of the difficulty is that sensitive issues get raised in organizations with a diverse workforce. As this module pointed out, diversity is a multidimensional concept, and some of our identities have greater influence on human behavior and attitudes than others. Organizations that manage diversity well stand to benefit on a number of fronts. Drawing a broader talent pool into an organization means more high-quality employees. Cultural diversity can enhance creativity, innovation, and productivity. On the other hand, if it is not well managed, it can have negative results. Diversity management is not a program. In the end, managing diversity is a change process that requires a long-term strategy involving redesigning management and human resource management practices and ultimately the organization's culture. Diversity management has to be linked to the organization's strategic business goals if it is to succeed.

MODULE
9

Suggested Readings

Chemers, M. M., Oskamp, S., and Costanzo, M. (eds.) (1995). *Diversity in Organizations: New Perspectives for a Changing Workplace.* Thousand Oaks, CA: Sage Publications.

Cox, Taylor. (1993). *Cultural Diversity in Organizations: Theory, Research, and Practice.* San Francisco: Berrett-Koehler.

Ferdman, B. (1995). Cultural identity and diversity in organizations. In Chemers, M. M., Oskamp, S., and Costanzo, M. (eds.) (1995). *Diversity in Organizations: New Perspectives for a Changing Workplace.* Thousand Oaks, CA: Sage Publications, 37–61.

Friedman, J. and DiTomaso, N. (1996). Myths about Diversity: What Managers Need to Know about Changes in the U. S. Labor Force. *California Management Review,* 38, 54–77.

Gardenswartz, L. and Rowe, A. (1998). *Managing Diversity: A Complete Desk Reference and Planning Guide.* New York: Business One-Irwin.

Johnnston, W. and Packer, A. (1987). *Work Force 2000.* Indianapolis: Hudson Institute.

Johnson, W. (1991, March/April). "Global Work Force 2000: The New World Labor Market." *Harvard Business Review,* 69, 115–127.

Kossek, E. E. and Lobel, S. (eds.). (1996). *Managing Diversity: Human Resource Strategies for Transforming the Workplace.* Cambridge, MA: Blackwell Publishers.

Nkomo, S. M. and Cox T., Jr. (1996). Diverse Identities in Organizations. In S. Clegg, C. Hardy, and W. Nord (eds.) *Handbook of Organization Studies.* London: Sage Publications, 338–356.

Thomas, David and Ely, Robin. (1996, September/October), "Making Differences Matter: A New Paradigm for Managing Diversity," *Harvard Business Review,* 79–90.

Thomas, R. R., Jr. (1990, March/April). "From Affirmative Action to Affirming Diversity." *Harvard Business Review,* 68 (2), 107-117.

Relevant Web Sites

Here are two excellent web sources for current information on diversity issues:

http://www.equalopportunity.on.ca./enggraf/forum./manage.html

http://www.yforum.com

Critical Thinking Questions

1. How does managing diversity differ from affirmative action and EEO?

2. What are the business and strategic reasons for managing diversity?

3. How successful have U.S. employers been in managing diversity? What are the typical strategies used and how much impact have they had on corporate culture?

4. Some people argue that emphasizing differences among employees actually encourages stereotyping instead of valuing differences. Do you agree or disagree? Why?

Exercises

Diversity Incidents. One of the actions Denny's management took was to examine whether current human resource practices helped or hindered the management of diversity. Below you will find some employee incidents that should be reviewed in terms of their human resource implications for class discussion. Read each of the following incidents and be prepared to answer three questions: (1) What is the major issue to be resolved? (2) What actions do you recommend to resolve the issue? (3) Does the incident suggest a needed change in human resource practices or policies? If so, how should they be changed?

1. In the last year, Hedges Manufacturing located in Raleigh, North Carolina, had hired about a dozen Mexican immigrants. One Monday morning, Claude Vance, a shift supervisor at Hedges, found a note on his desk saying that Hector Morales would be absent because he had to take his wife to the doctor. The next day when Claude saw Hector, he inquired about his wife's health. Hector responded that his wife wasn't sick and that he had merely taken her for a regularly scheduled physical. Claude became very upset; it was the third time Hector had used a sick day to accompany his wife to an appointment that was not an emergency. A month ago he was absent because he took his wife to the dentist to have her teeth cleaned. Employees are allowed one sick day per month. Company policy specifically states that sick days are to be used for the illness of an employee or the illness of a member of his/her immediate family. When Claude confronted Hector about missing work to take his wife to the doctor, Hector told him he didn't understand all the fuss. As the head of the family, it was his responsibility to see to the well-being of his wife. Claude felt he should take some action. Exasperated, Claude went to speak with Mary Henderson, the human resource manager, about his dilemma.

2. Gateway Publishing Company is located in a large metropolitan area on the West Coast. It specializes in publishing popular business books marketed to a

MODULE
9

professional audience. Its most recent bestseller sold over 300,000 copies. The company has about 450 employees in its offices. The publisher, Johnson Houston, is the great-grandson of the original founder of the business. The company's culture is rather conservative. Office decor resembles that of a staid legal firm rather than what might be expected in a publishing house. Sherita Jackson, a 24-year-old African-American woman was hired last month as a receptionist. The receptionist's desk is the first place that all visitors stop at when they enter Gateway.

One Monday morning, Sherita arrived at the office with her hair in long braids decorated with purple, white, and lavender beads. When Mr. Houston arrived at work, he greeted Sherita with the statement, "What have you done to your hair?" He went immediately to see the director of human resources. He instructed the director to talk with Sherita and to let her know that her hairstyle was inappropriate for Gateway Publishing. The director called Sherita into her office and told her this. Sherita became quite agitated and told the director that the hairstyle was part of her culture and she felt that she should have the right to wear her hair in braids. She also complained that no one had said anything to the two assistant editors who had pierced noses and multiple earrings. The director pointed out that they did not directly interact with the public. As Sherita left the office in tears, the director wondered how she should handle the whole situation.

3. Debra Knight is the human resource manager for a medium-sized hotel located in Atlanta. It has been very difficult in the last few years to recruit workers for their housekeeping and janitorial departments. Recently, the hotel has hired a number of Mexican immigrants. They now constitute about 20 percent of the hotel's staff. The company has an excellent history of management-employee relations. One day a group of five employees came to talk to Debra about a problem they were experiencing. They complained that the Mexican workers would chatter among themselves in Spanish. The group felt the Mexicans were talking about them or just wasting time. They wanted Debra to require the workers to speak only English at work.

4. In three years, Data Management Systems experienced 150 percent growth in its employees, going from 250 to over 600 employees. John Ferguson, the director of human resources, recognized the increasing diversity of the employees coming into the company and convinced the company's president of the need for diversity training. After talking with a number of consulting firms, Mr. Ferguson signed a contract with Diversity Consultants, Inc., to conduct training sessions with the managerial staff of 50 employees. The managerial staff was primarily white males but did include 8 women and 5 minority employees. The three-day training program was designed to increase sensitivity to employee diversity. Mr. Ferguson sat in on the first few hours of the first training session and was generally pleased with what he observed. Unfortunately, he had to leave for a business trip that would cause him to miss the remaining two days of training.

When Mr. Ferguson returned to the office two days after the end of the training sessions, he found an urgent message from the president of the company. When he went to see the president, he learned that a number of employees had walked out of the training on the afternoon of the second day. They complained that the training had become abusive and unbearable. They had been forced to call each other by stereotypical names and to reveal their biases against others. At one point in the training program, the men had to walk a gauntlet consisting of a line of the women managers who were given the opportunity to verbally insult the men. It was at this point that the training broke down and a number of the trainees stormed out of the training sessions, refusing to continue. Soon the episode was known throughout the company.

5. A white male (Henry), a woman who is confined to a wheelchair as a result of a childhood car accident (Mary), and an employee with two preschool children (Harriet) are all employed as software designers in the R&D department of CompuSoft, a software development company. As software designers, they are represented by the United Auto Workers.

   Mary and Harriet request permission from their department head to work at home three days a week. Mary makes the request because she finds it difficult to load herself into her specially equipped van and to get from the parking garage to the office every day, particularly in the winter. However, she doesn't assert that she can't make it into the office; indeed, her attendance is excellent. Harriet explains to the department head that she has been having problems arranging reliable childcare. She wants to work at home so that she will be available in an emergency and will be able to spend her lunch hour, and the extra time in the morning and the evening that she will save by not commuting into the office, with her children. Harriet does not say that she cannot be physically present. Her previous attendance record is excellent. Henry's attendance record has been good but not as good as Harriet's and Mary's record.

   The company has had a culture of long hours on-site and ready availability to meet face-to-face with clients and customers. Nevertheless, in an effort to be supportive of employees, management decided to allow both Mary and Harriet to work at home. The union also agreed that management had the right to allow them to do so. Henry is neither disabled nor a parent. He too, however, would like to work at home occasionally. Henry was delighted to learn that his colleagues could work at home until he was informed that his request was denied because someone was needed in the office to meet with clients. As the weeks went by, Henry grew increasingly upset with management's decision. Henry is complaining about "reverse" discrimination and unfair treatment. He believes that all three workers should be treated equally because they all have the same positions and the same salary grade.[25]

6. Jill and Bob are respected reporters at a major U.S. metropolitan newspaper on the East Coast. When Jill, an African-American woman, was found to have combined parts of interviews in her final article write-up to develop strong fictitious characters, she was immediately fired. In later interviews, Jill commented that she was only trying to emphasize a point that she found in her investigative reporting. By taking composite quotations and characteristics of her various interviews, she molded illustrative individuals to make a point more compelling and her storytelling more effective. Bob is a senior white male reporter who wrote a feature column. When it was discovered that Bob had "borrowed" considerable material from a well-known comedian's book for his column without attribution, he was suspended for several months. The male columnist was quoted as saying, "You can accuse me of sloppiness, and I plead guilty. You can accuse me of intellectual laziness, and I plead guilty. But plagiarism, no." Later, after an outcry regarding the difference in treatment of the two reporters, Bob eventually resigned under pressure.

7. A major Fortune 100 employer has worked with a human resource consulting firm to identify the core management competencies desired in newly hired high-potential employees. Some of these included decisiveness, change management skills, oral and written communication skills, and team leadership capabilities. The company is sure it has identified candidate profiles that mirror the background of its most outstanding current managers.

MODULE 9

Recently, the company conducted interviews at a leading MBA program. It invited five outstanding students to go through a second step in the selection process, which involves spending one day in an assessment center where applicants are rated on these competencies. The applicants include Fen-we (a female Chinese national from Hong Kong), Yim (a male Korean National from Seoul), Peter (a white male from Westport, Connecticut), James (an African-American male from Detroit), and Susan, a white female from Santa Fe. The applicant backgrounds were typical of most groups brought in for the assessment. Over time, the company was noticing that the U.S. white males and females were consistently being rated as performing better in the assessment process than candidates with other backgrounds. A significantly higher proportion of offers to join the company was being made to these white applicants. The company is sure it has developed a valid selection system that is based on job-related criteria.

8. Sarah is the human resource manager of employee benefits at a high technology firm. She is noticing that many talented workers who are gay or lesbian are not joining the company. She also noticed that one of the top marketing managers who she believes is gay never brings a partner to any company events and is reluctant to talk about his family. Sarah has heard rumors that a head-hunting company has contacted the top marketing manager. She knows that some Christian religious right groups will sell off the company stock if domestic partner benefits are added. They reflect a sizable stockholder group, and the chairman respects their views greatly.

9. Sam is a 60-year-old white male executive who has worked for your company for over three decades. He has wonderful ideas, is still very hardworking, and is a dedicated employee who is respected by many in the firm. Sam has just been promoted to head of applicant recruiting. He feels uncomfortable using e-mail and simply does not wish to use it to do his job. Yet many college and graduate students now like to contact the company by e-mail. It is suspected that some potential new hires are being dissuaded by the lack of e-mail contact.

References

1. Kossek, E. (1996). Managing Diversity as a Vehicle for Culture Change: Confronting Mono-Cultural Dominance at IBM. In E. Kossek, S. Lobel, and R. Oh (eds.), *Managing Diversity: Human Resource Strategies for Transforming the Workplace: A Field Guide,* Oxford, England: Blackwell, 49–67.
2. Johnston, W. B., & Packer, A. E. (1987). *Workforce 2000: Work and Workers for the 21st Century,* Indianapolis: Hudson Institute.
3. Gonsiorek, J. and Weinrich, James D. (1991). *Homosexuality: Research Implications for Public Policy.* Thousand Oaks, CA: Sage Publications.
4. Robinson, G., and Dechant, K. (1997). "Building the Business Case for Diversity." *Academy of Management Executive,* 11, 21–31.
5. International Labor Organizations. (1993). *The Unequal Race to the Top.* World of Work—U.S. 2:6–7.
6. ————. (Aug. 1, 1998). Thanks to Overseas Sales: Honda Reports Big Profit Gain. *New York Times.*
7. Cox, T. (1993). *Cultural Diversity in Organizations: Theory, Research and Practice.* San Francisco: Berrett-Koehler.
8. Cox, T. and Nkomo, S. (1996). Diverse Identities in Organizations in S. Clegg, C. Hardy, and W. Nord (eds.) *Handbook of Organization Studies.* London: Sage Publications, 338–356
9. Loden, M. and Rosener, J. (1991). *Workforce America.* Homewood, IL: Business One-Irwin.

10. Tajfel, H. (1982). *Social Identity and Intergroup Relations.* Cambridge: Cambridge University Press.

11. Nkomo, S. M. (1995). Identities and the Complexity of Diversity. In Susan E. Jackson and M. Ruderman (eds.). *Diversity in Work Teams: Research Paradigms for a Changing Workplace,* 247–253.

12. Thomas, R. (1991). *Beyond Race and Gender: Unleashing the Power of Your Total Work Force by Managing Diversity.* New York: AMACOM.

13. Access by the second author to some of Roosevelt Thomas's materials from his consulting work for the American Institute on Managing Diversity at Morehouse College contributed to some of the ideas in this table.

14. Cox, T., p. 137.

15. Thomas, David and Ely, Robin. (September/October, 1996). "Making Differences Matter: A New Paradigm for Managing Diversity," *Harvard Business Review,* 79–90.

16. Robinson and Dechant, Ibid.

17. Kossek, E. E. and Lobel, S. A. (1996). Introduction: Transforming Human Resource Systems to Manage Diversity—An Introduction and Orienting Framework. In E. Kossek and S. Lobel (eds.). *Managing Diversity: Human Resource Strategies for Transforming the Workplace.* Oxford, England: Blackwell, 1–19.

18. Kossek and Lobel, Ibid.

19. Ford, J. K. and Fisher, S. (1996). The Role of Training in a Changing Workplace and Workforce: New Perspectives and Approaches. In E. Kossek and S. Lobel (eds.). *Managing Diversity: Human Resource Strategies for Transforming the Workplace.* Oxford, England: Blackwell, 164–193.

20. Ibid.

21. Kossek and Lobel, 1–19.

22. Ibid.

23. Ibid.

24. Adamson, J. B. (Oct. 5, 1998). "The Denny's Discrimination Story—And Ways to Avoid It In Your Operation." *Nation's Restaurant News,* 40, 151.

25. We would like to thank the Chicago Kent School of Law Illinois Institute of Technology for development of the basic hypothetical of the telecommuting case for a 1998 Members Forum at the Center for Law and the Workplace that Ellen Kossek participated in at Chicago. The contributors were Peggy Smith and Mary Rose Stroebner.

Index

Access-legitimacy paradigm, 9.10–11. *See also* Diversity paradigms

Affirmative action (AA), 9.4, 9.7, 9.9, 9.10

Awareness training, 9.12

Changing environment, 9.4, 9.7

Chief diversity officer, 9.14

Civil Rights Act of 1964, 9.9

Company loyalty, 9.6

Context of identity, 9.8

Core competency, 9.4

Corporate culture. *See* Organizational culture

Corporate hierarchy. *See* Organizational hierarchy

Cultural audit, 9.4, 9.12

Cultural change, 9.5, 9.8, 9.9

Cultural diversity. *See* Diversity

Demographics, 9.5, 9.6, 9.7, 9.11, 9.15

Discrimination, 9.7, 9.9, 9.15

Discrimination-fairness paradigm, 9.10–11. *See also* Diversity paradigms

Diverse workforce, 9.5–6, 9.11, 9.12

Diversity, 9.4, 9.7, 9.9, 9.10
management, *See* Managing diversity processes, 9.12–13

Diversity enlargement hiring strategies, 9.12. *See also* Human resource systems

Dominant culture or identity group, 9.9, 9.10, 9.12. *See also* Identity issues, Minority group, Organizational culture

Employee demographics, 9.11

Employee morale. *See* Morale, employee

Employee perspectives, 9.9, 9.11

Employer of choice, 9.4, 9.7

Environmental forces, 9.4, 9.5

Equal employment opportunity (EEO), 9.4, 9.7, 9.9, 9.10

Exclusion, 9.8

Flexible work options, 9.6, 9.13

Glass-ceiling barriers, 9.10, 9.13

Globalization, 9.4, 9.6, 9.7

Group identity, 9.8, 9.9

Heterogeneous workforce, 9.6, 9.12, 9.13. *See also* Workforce

High-tech companies, 9.6

Human resource management, 9.13, 9.15. *See also* Human resource systems

Human resource professionals, 9.4, 9.13

Human resource strategy, 9.4, 9.14

Human resource systems and practices, 9.4, 9.9, 9.11, 9.12, 9.13

Identity issues, 9.7, 9.9, 9.12, 9.15

Immigrant population, 9.5

Immutable human differences, 9.7

Inclusion, 9.14

Individual identity, 9.8, 9.9, 9.12. *See also* Identity issues

Job redesign, 9.13

Labor force or labor pool. *See* Workforce

Labor market demographics, 9.4. *See also* Demographics

Learning-effectiveness paradigm, 9.10–11. *See also* Diversity paradigms

Managing diversity, 9.4, 9.7, 9.9, 9.10, 9.12, 9.13, 9.14, 9.15
paradigms, 9.10–13

Marketplace diversity, 9.6, 9.11

Maximize potential, 9.9, 9.10

Minority group, 9.5. *See also* Identity issues, Dominant culture or identity group, Organizational culture

Monoculture, 9.4. *See also* Diversity, Multiculturalism, Organizational culture

Morale, employee, 9.7, 9.14

Multicultural marketplace, 9.11

Multiculturalism, 9.4, 9.5, 9.7, 9.10, 9.12

Multiple identities, 9.8. *See also* Identity issues

National Association for Colored People, 9.14

Niche markets, 9.11

Objective outcomes, 9.9

Older workers, 9.5

Organizational change, 9.13. *See also* Cultural change

Organizational culture, 9.4, 9.8, 9.11–12, 9.14, 9.15. *See also* Dominant culture

Organizational hierarchy, 9.10, 9.12

Organizational initiatives, 9.4, 9.10

Performance-driven entity, 9.4

Power in organizations, 9.9

Primary dimension, 9.4, 9.7–8. *See also* Diversity

Primary identity, 9.9. *See also* Identity issues

Private-sector employers, 9.10

Privilege, 9.8

Profitability, 9.4, 9.6, 9.7

Recruiting strategies, 9.10. *See also* Human resource systems
Relationships, diverse groups, 9.7
Reward and recognition system, 9.14

Secondary dimension, 9.4, 9.7–8. *See also* Diversity
Self-concept, 9.8
Service economy, 9.4, 9.6
Skill-building training, 9.12
Social identity theory, 9.8. *See also* Identity issues
Strategic business issue, 9.4, 9.14
Subjective perceptions, 9.9

Teamwork, 9.7. *See also* Workgroups
Telecommuting employees, 9.13
Title VII, 9.9

Transformational role, 9.4, 9.12. *See also* Human resource management
Twenty-first century, 9.5, 9.6, 9.13

Upper-level managerial positions, 9.10

Work culture, 9.4. *See also* Organizational culture
Work team, 9.8
Work/family balance, 9.6
Workforce, 9.4, 9.5, 9.6, 9.7, 9.14
    demographics, 9.4
    diversity, 9.5–6, 9.11, 9.15
    expectations, 9.4
Workforce 2000 Report, Hudson Institute, 9.5
Workgroups, 9.8
Working mothers, 9.5

MODULE
9

KOSSEK ■ BLOCK

Managing Human Resources
in the 21st Century

From Core Concepts to Strategic Choice

MODULE 10

Administering the Family and Medical Leave Act

Tina M. Riley
MIGHIGAN STATE UNIVERSITY

Managing Human Resources in the 21st Century: From Core Concepts to Strategic Choice,
by Kossek and Block

Publisher: Dave Shaut
Executive Editor: John Szilagyi
Developmental Editor: Bryant Editorial Development
Marketing Manager: Joseph A. Sabatino
Production Editor: Tamborah E. Moore
Manufacturing Coordinator: Dana Began Schwartz
Cover Design: Tin Box Studio
Cover Photographs: Copyright Shoji Sato/Photonica
Production House: The Left Coast Group, Inc.
Printer: West Group

Printed in the United States of America
1 2 3 4 5 02 01 00 99

For more information contact South-Western College Publishing, 5101 Madison Road, Cincinnati, Ohio, 45227 or find us on the Internet at *http://www.swcollege.com*
For permission to use material from this text or product, contact us by
- telephone: 1-800-730-2214
- fax: 1-800-730-2215
- web: *http://www.thomsonrights.com*

ISBN: 0–324–01809–6

This book is printed on acid-free paper.

Contents

MODULE OVERVIEW   10.4

OBJECTIVES   10.4

RELATION TO THE FRAME   10.4

CORE CONCEPTS IN ADMINISTERING THE FAMILY AND MEDICAL LEAVE ACT   10.5

Enforcement   10.5

Covered Employers   10.5

Joint Employment   10.6

Eligible Employees   10.6

Continuation of Benefits   10.6

Job Restoration   10.6

Leave Entitlement   10.7

Determining the Amount of Leave Used   10.7

Limitations and Exceptions   10.7

Serious Health Condition   10.7

Intermittent or Reduced Schedule Leave   10.8

Obligations and Policy Issues   10.8

Defining the "12-Month Period"   10.10

Substitution of Paid Leave   10.12

Coordination with Other Statutes   10.12

STRATEGIC ISSUES IN ADMINISTERING THE FAMILY AND MEDICAL LEAVE ACT   10.12

APPLICATION   10.13

IN CONCLUSION   10.14

Debrief   10.14

Suggested Readings   10.14

Critical Thinking Questions   10.14

Exercises   10.14

References   10.15

INDEX   10.16

MODULE
10

MODULE OVERVIEW

In today's tight labor market, recruiting and retaining employees is more critical than ever. The quality of worklife that an organization provides is often the determining factor in an individual's choice of employer. Human resources (HR) policies that acknowledge employees' responsibilities outside of work can have a direct impact on an organization's ability to attract and retain high-quality employees. One tool that can help employers accommodate employee needs, and meet organizational objectives regarding recruitment and retention, is the Family and Medical Leave Act (FMLA) of 1993.

The FMLA is designed to help employees balance work and family responsibilities by granting up to 12 workweeks of unpaid, job-protected leave for certain family and medical reasons while providing for continuation of group health benefits.

OBJECTIVES

The objectives of this module are to provide the learner with the knowledge and skills necessary to:

- Understand the strategic implications of the FMLA on organizational objectives, organizational effectiveness, and organizational constituencies.

- Develop human resources policies that comply with the requirements of the act and facilitate the achievement of organizational goals and objectives.

- Coordinate compliance of the FMLA and other employment statutes such as workers' compensation, the Americans with Disabilities Act, and state leave laws.

- Utilize various resources to enhance his or her ability to effectively administer the act within an organization and stay abreast of proposed changes to it.

RELATION TO THE FRAME

When family and medical responsibilities necessitate the taking of a FMLA leave, a number of transactions occur. Employees are given specific notice of their rights and responsibilities under the act as well as any relevant employer policies. Certification of Health Care Provider forms are often given to employees to be filled out by their medical practitioner and returned to the employer. All of this must occur within the timelines laid out in the act. HR is generally responsible for tracking this paperwork, ensuring time limits are met, and notifying employees of the consequences of failing to meet time limits. HR is also responsible for tracking the actual amount of leave taken and keeping this separate from other absences. Ensuring the payment of insurance premiums, again within required time frames and with proper employee notices, and coordinating other types of leave such as employer short-term disability and workers compensation, also fall to HR.

Given the large number transactions precipitated by the taking of FMLA leave, it's important to remember that the goal of the act is not to create a paperwork nightmare for HR. Its goal is to help employees balance work and family, thereby promoting economic security. Administered proactively, the act benefits employers as well as employees. Proactive administration means explaining to employees how the act can help them balance the myriad responsibilities of work and family. Educational efforts for managers and supervisors must focus on the link between a work/family balance and increased morale and productivity. Organizations that fail to make explicit this connection risk having managers subtly discourage the taking of FMLA leave, negating the benefits that would otherwise accrue to the organization.

FIGURE 10.1   *A Frame for Understanding Human Resource Strategy: Context, Roles, and Constraints*

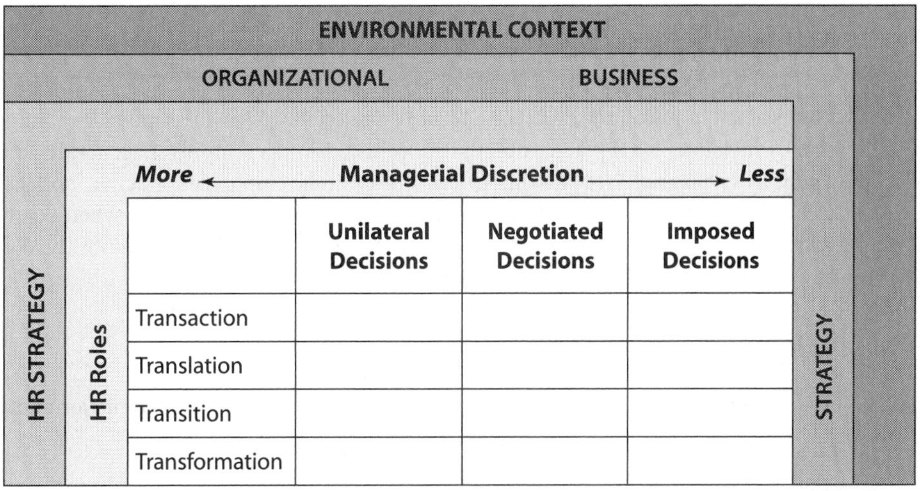

		More ←——— Managerial Discretion ———→ Less		
		Unilateral Decisions	**Negotiated Decisions**	**Imposed Decisions**
	Transaction			
	Translation			
	Transition			
	Transformation			

ENVIRONMENTAL CONTEXT — ORGANIZATIONAL / BUSINESS

HR STRATEGY / HR Roles / STRATEGY

© 2000 by Ellen Ernst Kossek and Richard Block. Thanks to Brian Pentland, Karen Markel, and John Beck for helpful comments and discussions that enhanced the model.

Core Concepts in Administering the Family and Medical Leave Act

The Family and Medical Leave Act provides eligible employees of covered employers up to 12 workweeks of unpaid, job-protected leave per year for family and medical reasons, and requires group health benefits to be maintained during the leave. To effectively administer the act in an organization, managers need to have a clear understanding of several core concepts embodied within it.

Under the FMLA, requests for leave must be evaluated on a case-by-case basis. In order to make proper determination of leave, HR professionals and managers must be able to use the Department of Labor's (DOL) "Final Rules on Implementing the Family and Medical Leave Act" as a reference. To this end, the relevant section numbers have been provided. Managers should familiarize themselves with the various sections of this publication.

Enforcement (825.400–825.404)

The Office of Personnel Management enforces the FMLA for employees of the U.S. government. For all other employers, the Wage and Hour division of the Department of Labor enforces the act. Employees may file a complaint with the department or file a private lawsuit. In either case, the employee must file within two years of the violation, three years if the violation was willful.

Covered Employers (825.105–825.106)

Private companies that employ 50 or more employees during 20 or more weeks in the current or preceding calendar year are covered by the FMLA. When counting employees to determine coverage, the employer must include any employee whose name appears on the payroll, regardless of whether or not they received compensation. Leased, temporary, and part-time employees are counted when determining whether the employer meets the 50-employee threshold. All public employers are covered by the act regardless of the number of employees.

Joint Employment (825.106)

According to the DOL's Final Rules:

> Where two or more businesses exercise some control over the work or working conditions of the employee, the businesses may be joint employers under the FMLA.[1]

Clearly, temporary employees hired through a temp agency will fall under the "joint employment provision" of the act. Although only the primary employer, generally the temp agency, is responsible for providing leave to eligible employees, posting notices, and maintaining health benefits, both employers must count the employees when determining whether or not the employer is covered by the act and employee eligibility. Job restoration is also the responsibility of the primary employer.

Eligible Employees (825.110)

To be eligible for FMLA leave, an employee must work for a covered employer and:

- Have worked for that employer for at least 12 months.

  ✓ It need not be 12 consecutive months.

  ✓ The 12 months is measured by counting the number of weeks their name appears on the payroll.

  ✓ Employees on leave, provided the employer has a reasonable expectation that they will return to work, are considered employed.

- Have worked at least 1,250 hours during the 12 months prior to the start of the leave.

  ✓ Measure the 1,250 hours as of the date the leave is to begin; this may be projected.

  ✓ For exempt employees for whom the employer does not track hours worked, the employer must show that the employee does not meet the hours requirement or otherwise assume that the employee is eligible.

  ✓ Full-time teachers are assumed to meet the 1,250 hours test.

- Work at a location where at least 50 employees are employed at the site or within 75 miles of it.

Continuation of Benefits (825.209)

The act requires employers to continue the employee's group healthcare coverage as if the employee were not out on leave. Employees on leave are also entitled to any new plan the employer offers, again, as if the employee were not out on leave. There are extensive regulations regarding the continuation of benefits, payment of premiums while on leave, and the potential consequences of failing to make premium payments. Managers are urged to refer to the Final Rules for guidance.

Job Restoration (825.214–825.216)

One of the basic provisions of the act is that of job protection. As long as an employee returning from FMLA leave is able to perform the essential functions of the job held prior to taking leave, he or she is entitled to return to that same, or an equivalent, position. The DOL's Final Rules explain:

> An equivalent position is one that is virtually identical to the employee's former position in terms of pay, benefits, and working conditions, including privileges,

perquisites and status. It must involve the same or substantially equivalent skill, effort, responsibility, and authority.[2]

Leave Entitlement (825.112)

Eligible employees are entitled to up to 12 workweeks of unpaid leave for:

- The birth of a child, and to care for the newborn child.

- Placement with the employee of a child for adoption or foster care, and to care for the newly adopted or placed child.

    ✓ The leave must conclude within 12 months of the birth or placement (825.201)

- To care for an immediate family member with a serious health condition.

    ✓ The act defines immediate family member as the employee's spouse, child, or parent. State leave laws may provide a broader coverage.

- The employee's own serious health condition.

Determining the Amount of Leave Used (825.205)

Leave usage is based on the employee's normal workweek. For example, an employee who regularly works 40 hours per week requests one day of leave. One day of leave for a 40-hour, five-day week would equal one-fifth of the leave for each full day of leave taken. Similarly, the leave entitlement for part-time workers is determined by the number of hours that they normally work each week. Leave entitlement for employees who work variable schedules is determined by averaging the number of hours worked each week during the 12 weeks prior to taking leave.

MODULE
10

Limitations and Exceptions (825.202, 825.217, 825.302)

Under certain circumstances, limitations or exceptions to the act may apply.

- Spouses employed by the same employer may be limited to a combined total of 12 workweeks of family leave for:

    ✓ The birth and care of a child

    ✓ Placement for adoption or foster care, and to care for the newly placed child

    ✓ Care of an employee's parent who has a serious health condition.

- If the employee fails to provide requested medical certification, the employer may delay continuation of FMLA leave until the employee provides the certification.

- If the employee fails to give timely advance notice when the need for leave is foreseeable, the employer may delay the taking of leave until 30 days after notice is given.

Reinstatement of employment may be denied to certain "key employees." To be designated a "key employee," the individual must be a salaried employee who is among the highest-paid 10 percent of all employees. The employer may only deny job reinstatement to the "key employee" if such reinstatement would cause "substantial and grievous economic injury" to the employer.[3]

Serious Health Condition (825.114)

The FMLA grants leave for a serious health condition of either the employee or the employee's immediate family members. It is therefore necessary for the manager to understand what types of conditions are considered a "serious health condition" under the act.

A "serious health condition" is defined as an injury, illness, impairment, or physical or mental condition that involves any of the following:

- Any period of incapacity or treatment connected with inpatient care in a hospital, hospice, or residential medical-care facility, and any period of incapacity or subsequent treatment in connection with such inpatient care.

- Continuing treatment by a healthcare provider that includes any period of incapacity (i.e., inability to work, attend school, or perform other regular daily activities) due to:

  ✓ A health condition lasting more than three consecutive days, and any subsequent treatment of incapacity relating to the same condition, that also includes treatment two or more times by or under the supervision of a healthcare provider; or one treatment by a healthcare provider with a continuing regimen of treatment

- Pregnancy or prenatal care.

- A chronic serious health condition that continues over an extended period of time, requires periodic visits to a healthcare provider, and may involve occasional episodes of incapacity.

- A permanent or long-term condition for which treatment may not be effective.

- Any absences to receive multiple treatments for restorative surgery or for a condition that would likely result in a period of incapacity of more than three days if not treated.[4]

Intermittent or Reduced Schedule Leave (825.117)

Under certain conditions an employee may take FMLA leave on an intermittent or reduced schedule basis. The employer is required to grant intermittent or reduced schedule leave when medically necessary. The employer may *elect* to grant such leave requests to allow an employee to care for a newborn child, a newly placed adopted child, or a foster child.

When requesting this type of leave, the employee is required to work with the employer to minimize disruption to the employer's operations.

Obligations and Policy Issues (825.302)

Both the employer and employees have certain obligations regarding the act. Employees must provide the employer with 30 days advance notice when planning to take FMLA leave. When such notice is not possible, the employee is required to give notice as soon as is practical, generally within two business days. When requesting leave, the employee must provide sufficient information to make the employer aware that the leave may qualify for FMLA leave. It is up to the employer to ask for more information to make this determination.

When an employee requests leave that may qualify as FMLA leave, the employer must notify the employee within two days that the leave may be counted as FMLA leave. A sample of the optional "Employer Response to Employee Request for Family or Medical Leave" has been provided in Figure 10.2 on pages 10.9 and 10.10. The employer must also review the general employee rights and responsibilities under the act at this time. Among the employer's general notice obligations is the posting of a notice of employee rights under the act (Figure 10.3), including FMLA-related information in employee handbooks, collective bargaining agreements, and other written materials.

- The employer's FMLA policies should include:
  - ✓ Employee's rights or requirements to use accrued paid leave
  - ✓ Requirements to provide medical certification and fitness-for-duty certifications
  - ✓ Employee rights to job restoration
  - ✓ Key employee restrictions
  - ✓ Requirements regarding the payment of insurance co-premiums while on leave
  - ✓ Consequences of failing to return from leave

FIGURE 10.2   *Employer Response to Employee Request for Family or Medical Leave*

Employer Response to Employee
Request for Family or Medical Leave
(Optional use form - see 29 CFR § 825.301

U.S. Department of Labor
Employment Standards Administration
Wage and Hour Division

(Family and Medical Leave Act of 1993)

(Date)

TO: _____
(Employee's Name)

FROM: _____
(Name of appropriate employer representative)

SUBJECT: Request for Family/Medical Leave

On _____ , you notified us of your need to take family/medical leave due to:
(date)

☐ the birth of a child, or the placement of a child with you for adoption or foster care; or

☐ a serious health condition that makes you unable to perform the essential functions of your job; or

☐ a serious health condition affecting your ☐ spouse, ☐ child, ☐ parent, for which you are needed to provide care.

You notified us that you need this leave beginning on _____ and that you expect leave to continue until on or
about _____ .   (date)
(date)

Except as explained below, you have a right under the FMLA for up to 12 weeks of unpaid leave in a 12-month
period for the reasons listed above. Also, your health benefits must be maintained during any period of
unpaid leave under the same conditions as if you continued to work, and you must be reinstated to the same
or an equivalent job with the same pay, benefits, and terms and conditions of employment on your return
from leave. If you do not return to work following FMLA leave for a reason other than: (1) the continuation,
recurrence, or onset of a serious health condition which would entitle you to FMLA leave; or (2) other
circumstances beyond your control, you may be required to reimburse us for our share of health insurance
premiums paid on your behalf during your FMLA leave.

This is to inform you that: *(check appropriate boxes; explain where indicated)*

1. You are ☐ eligible ☐ not eligible for leave under the FMLA.

2. The requested leave ☐ will ☐ will not be counted against your annual FMLA leave entitlement.

3. You ☐ will ☐ will not be required to furnish medical certification of a serious health condition.
   If required, you must furnish certification by _____ *(insert date)* (must be at least 15 days after you are
   notified of this requirement) or we may delay the commencement of your leave until the
   certification is submitted.

Form WH-381
March 1995

continued

FIGURE 10.2   *continued*

---

4.   You may elect to substitute accrued paid leave for unpaid FMLA leave. We ☐ will ☐ will not require that you substitute accrued paid leave for unpaid FMLA leave. If paid leave will be used, the following conditions will apply: *(Explain)*

5(a).   If you normally pay a portion of the premiums for your health insurance, these payments will continue during the period of FMLA leave. Arrangements for payment have been discussed with you and it is agreed that you will make premium payments as follows: *(Set forth dates; e.g., the 10th of each month, or pay periods, etc. that specifically cover the agreement with the employee.)*

(b)   You have a minimum 30-day *(or, indicate longer period, if applicable)* grace period in which to make premium payments. If payment is not made timely, your group health insurance may be cancelled, <u>provided</u> we notify you in writing at least 15 days before the date that your health coverage will lapse, or, at our option, we may pay your share of the premiums during FMLA leave, and recover these payments from you upon your return to work.   We ☐ will ☐ will not pay your share of health insurance premiums while you are on leave.

(c)   We ☐ will ☐ will not do the same with other benefits (e.g., life insurance, disability insurance, etc.) while you are on FMLA leave. If we do pay your premiums for other benefits, when you return from leave you ☐ will ☐ will not be expected to reimburse us for the payments made on your behalf.

6.   You ☐ will ☐ will not be required to present a fitness-for-duty certificate prior to being restored to employment. If such certification is required but not received, your return to work may be delayed until certification is provided.

7(a).   You ☐ are ☐ are not a "key employee" as described in § 825.218 of the FMLA regulations. If you are a "key employee," restoration to employment may be denied following FMLA leave on the grounds that such restoration will cause substantial and grievous economic injury to us.

(b)   We ☐ have ☐ have not determined that restoring you to employment at the conclusion of FMLA leave will cause substantial and grievous economic harm to us. *(Explain (a) and/or (b) below. See § 825.219 of the FMLA regulations.)*

8.   While on leave, you ☐ will ☐ will not be required to furnish us with periodic reports every ____ *(indicate interval of periodic reports, as appropriate for the particular leave situation)* of your status and intent to return to work *(see § 825.309 of the FMLA regulations).* If the circumstances of your leave change and you are able to return to work earlier than the date indicated on the reverse side of this form, you ☐ will ☐ will not be required to notify us at least two work days prior to the date you intend to report for work.

9.   You ☐ will ☐ will not be required to furnish recertification relating to a serious health condition. *(Explain below, if necessary), including the interval between certifications as prescribed in § 825.308 of the FMLA regulations.)*

Source: http://www.dol.gov/dol/esa/public/regs/cfr/fmla/wh.pdf

> ✓ Any other requirements as potential consequences of failure to comply with employer policies
>
> ✓ Clear explanation of how the employer defines the "12-month period" for purposes of the act

Defining the "12-Month Period" (825.200)

It is critical that employers develop and disseminate a written policy stating how the 12-month period will be defined. If an employer has not officially adopted and announced this information, each employee may apply whichever definition is most advantageous

FIGURE 10.3   *Sample Notification of Employee Rights under the Family and Medical Leave Act of 1993*

Your Rights
Under The
Family and Medical Leave Act of 1993

FMLA requires covered employers to provide up to 12 weeks of unpaid, job-protected leave to "eligible" employees for certain family and medical reasons.

Employees are eligible if they have worked for a covered employer for at least one year, and for 1,250 hours over the previous 12 months, and if there are at least 50 employees within 75 miles.

Reasons For Taking Leave:

Unpaid leave must be granted for *any* of the following reasons:

• to care for the employee's child after birth, or placement for adoption or foster care;

• to care for the employee's spouse, son or daughter, or parent, who has a serious health condition; or

• for a serious health condition that makes the employee unable to perform the employee's job.

At the employee's or employer's option, certain kinds of *paid* leave may be substituted for unpaid leave.

Advance Notice and Medical Certification:

The employee may be required to provide advance leave notice and medical certification. Taking of leave may be denied if requirements are not met.

• The employee ordinarily must provide 30 days advance notice when the leave is "foreseeable."

• An employer may require medical certification to support a request for leave because of a serious health condition, and may require second or third opinions (at the employer's expense) and a fitness for duty report to return to work.

Job Benefits and Protection:

• For the duration of FMLA leave, the employer must maintain the employee's health coverage under any "group health plan."

• Upon return from FMLA leave, most employees must be restored to their original or equivalent positions with equivalent pay, benefits, and other employment terms.

• The use of FMLA leave cannot result in the loss of any employment benefit that accrued prior to the start of an employee's leave.

Unlawful Acts By Employers:

FMLA makes it unlawful for any employer to:

• interfere with, restrain, or deny the exercise of any right provided under FMLA:

• discharge or discriminate against any person for opposing any practice made unlawful by FMLA or for involvement in any proceeding under or relating to FMLA.

Enforcement:

• The U.S. Department of Labor is authorized to investigate and resolve complaints of violations.

• An eligible employee may bring a civil action against an employer for violations.

FMLA does not affect any Federal or State law prohibiting discrimination, or supersede any State or local law or collective bargaining agreement which provides greater family or medical leave rights.

For Additional Information:

Contact the nearest office of the Wage and Hour Division, listed in most telephone directories under U.S. Government, Department of Labor.

U.S. Department of Labor
Employment Standards Administration
Wage and Hour Division
Washington, D.C. 20210

WH Publication 1420
June 1993

U.S. GOVERNMENT PRINTING OFFICE:1996 171-169

Source: http://www.dol.gov/dol/esa/public/regs/compliance/posters/pdf/fmlaenbw.pdf

to him or herself for each absence. The employer must provide 60 days notice when implementing or changing policies regarding this calculation.

● Under the act, there are several different ways to calculate the 12-month period. The employer may elect to use:

✓ The calendar year

✓ Any fixed year such as fiscal or anniversary date

✓ 12 months forward from the start date of the first FMLA leave

✓ A rolling 12-month period measured back from each date of FMLA leave

The rolling 12-month period is the only calculation that prevents "leave stacking," the taking of 12 weeks of leave at the end of one calendar and 12 more weeks at the start of the next calendar year. By giving careful thought to selecting the 12-month period, an employer can minimize potential attendance problems. As with all employer policies, the 12-month calculation policy should be clearly explained to employees to avoid misunderstandings and ill will that may lead to legal action, reduced morale, and increased turnover.

Substitution of Paid Leave (825.207)

The act allows an employee to choose, or an employer to require, the use of accrued paid leave for some or all of the FMLA leave. The employer should carefully consider the decision to require employees to use accrued paid leave. While such a requirement would reduce time away from work, it may be seen as punishing employees for taking FMLA leave. The employer should consider the organization's underlying human resource philosophy and culture.

- Limitations to the substitution of accrued paid leave include the following:

    ✓ No substitution of paid leave is allowed if the employee is receiving disability or workers' compensation benefits.

    ✓ Public employers may not require the substitution of compensatory time.

    ✓ The employee must be notified that the paid leave will be counted against the employee's 12-week FMLA leave entitlement.

    ✓ Substitution of paid leave is limited by the employer's policies. If there is no such policy in place, the employer may not require an employee to use accrued paid time off for the FMLA leave.

Coordination with Other Statutes

When assessing absences, employers need to consider more than the FMLA. The specific circumstances may require consideration of the Americans with Disabilities Act, Title VII of the Civil Rights Act, workers' compensation, and state and local leave laws.

- Key points for coordination of the FMLA and other statutes include the following:

    ✓ The act does not affect any federal or state law prohibiting discrimination.

    ✓ Where state and local laws provide for family and medical leave, the employee is entitled to the most generous leave provided under either law.

    ✓ FMLA leave and workers' compensation leave can run concurrently.

    ✓ Unlike workers' compensation, an employee cannot be required to accept a light duty assignment under the FMLA.

Strategic Issues in Administering the Family and Medical Leave Act

Effectively administering the FMLA involves more than simply maintaining legal compliance. Carefully thought out policies can be developed that help the organization achieve its strategic objectives, increase organizational effectiveness, and benefit the various constituent groups. While most employers can easily point out the act's benefits to employees, they often fail to consider the benefits that accrue to the organization. The author recently conducted an FMLA training seminar for managers and human resources professionals. Seminar participants were asked to identify employer benefits of the act. Participant responses to the question "How does the FMLA benefit employers?" included:

- Absences can be planned for due to advance notice requirements.

- Since employees know that they can take time off when they really need it, they are more focused when they are at work, meaning less scrap and fewer errors.

- Reduced turnover.

These comments are supported by survey findings that many organizations experienced improved morale and lower turnover after they implemented family leave policies.[5]

One policy that has the potential to greatly benefit both the employer and employees is the development of a Leave Dispute Resolution System (LDRS). Adopting and implementing a system whereby employees can request an impartial review of their leave request can allow for low-level conflict resolution. Employees who feel that they have been improperly denied rights under the act can either file a complaint with the Department of Labor or file a private lawsuit. The LDRS provides for internal resolution that may avert costly litigation. If a mistake has been made in the determination of leave, the LDRS provides a formal system to make appropriate changes. Other steps that can be taken to improve the administration of the act within an organization include using software to track FMLA leaves and training supervisors to ensure understanding of the act and related employer policies.

APPLICATION

Organizations are required to include FMLA policies in their employee handbooks, policies and procedures manuals, and other written communications to employees. As we've already seen, it is in the employer's best interests to determine company policies regarding the use of paid time off and how the 12-month period is to be defined. The following is the FMLA policy of one organization, Cartright Laboratories, that produces vaccines for various diseases such as ebola and anthrax. They employ approximately 120,000 individuals in the United States, the United Kingdom, and Malaysia.

Roughly 30 percent of the workforce are classified as exempt from the overtime provisions of the Fair Labor Standards Act. Exempt employees are not required to track the number of hours worked each week. It is not uncommon for exempt employees to work 55 to 60 hours per week. Cartright Labs also employs full-time and part-time nonexempt employees. Full-time employees are scheduled to work 40 hours each week. Part-time employees are defined as "employees who are regularly scheduled to work up to 30 hours each week." Hours worked for all nonexempt employees are tracked by computerized time clocks.

Department managers and supervisors are required to take the FMLA training provided by human resources. All other employees may take FMLA training on a voluntary basis.

Cartright Laboratories' FMLA policy is as follows:

Eligible employees of Cartright Laboratories may request a total of 12 workweeks of FMLA leave during the 12-month calendar year (January 1 through December 31).

FMLA leave is concurrent with existing maternity and other paid/unpaid absences.

Nonexempt employees are required to use any accrued paid time off for FMLA leaves.

FMLA leave may be taken intermittently or on a reduced schedule when medically necessary. Intermittent or reduced schedule leave may be taken for other FMLA qualified reasons ONLY with the approval of the department.

Whenever possible, an employee must provide his or her department 30 days notice of need for FMLA leave. When the need for leave is unforeseen, the employee must provide at least verbal notice to the department within two business days of when the need for leave became known.

Employees may need to provide medical certification for certain leave requests and will be required to inform their department how they wish to use their accrued time off to cover the FMLA leave.

The department will maintain medical certification forms as a confidential medical record. These records are to be kept separate and confidential for duration of employment plus 30 years.

The department may require an employee to report on his or her status and intent to return to work. The department may request recertification once every 30 days. The department may require a return-to-work certification from the employee's healthcare provider.

In Conclusion

Debrief

The Family and Medical Leave Act helps employees balance work and family responsibilities by providing up to 12 workweeks of unpaid, job-protected leave for specified family and medical reasons. The act also requires continuation of healthcare benefits. Although the act's benefits to employees are more obvious, employers also benefit from thoughtful implementation of the FMLA.

Suggested Readings

"Final Rules Implementing the Family and Medical Leave Act," The Bureau of National Affairs, Inc., 1995.

Critical Thinking Questions

1. Many families live "paycheck to paycheck" and cannot afford to take time off without pay. The bipartisan Commission on Leave reported in 1996 that nearly two-thirds of employees who needed leave did not take it simply because they couldn't afford to go without pay.[6] Should this be of concern to employers? How would you attempt to resolve this dilemma?

2. Identify the various organizational constituent groups and how they might benefit from the FMLA. What groups might resist the FMLA and other policies aimed at enhancing employees' quality of work life? Why?

Exercises

1. Identify the specific reasons for which an eligible employee may take FMLA leave.

2. An employee comes to you requesting FMLA leave for plastic surgery. Using the Department of Labor's Final Rules, determine whether or not the leave should be counted as FMLA leave.

3. After the death of her parents, one of your employees was raised by her aunt. The aunt is now seriously ill. Is the employee entitled to take FMLA leave to

care for her? Refer to the Final Rules to check your answer.

4. You are the human resources manager for ABC, Inc., a manufacturing company with 1,500 employees. You and your team need to design a leave policy for your employees that is in accordance with the FMLA. There should be 3–5 people per team. You will have (30) minutes to design the policy, summarize it, and prepare a short presentation to the class. The following items should be taken into consideration when designing your plan:

- To whom does the policy apply? Are there any exceptions? Are the exceptions clearly identified in the policy?

- How much leave will be available? What is the maximum duration of allowable leave? Under what conditions is intermittent leave permissible? Under what conditions may a couple who are both employees of the company split or alternate available leave?

- What are the eligibility requirements for leave taking? For example, does the policy include a length-of-service requirement, and does it apply to both full-time and part-time employees?

- Does the policy clearly define all terms such as "serious health condition"? Does that terminology conform to terminology in the FMLA, or, if appropriate, state law?

- Is the leave to be granted paid or unpaid? If paid and unpaid may be combined, does the policy state the conditions under which an employee may use both types of leave?

- How does a family or medical leave affect other employee benefits?

- In the case of medical leave, must an employee first exhaust all forms of other available leave, such as paid vacation or sick leave? Is medical certification and/or periodic recertification required? If certification is required, under what conditions may the company require a second or third opinion from a healthcare provider?

- What other restrictions, if any, apply to employees who wish to take family or medical leave?

- What procedures will employees have to follow to notify the employer that they wish to take or return from leave?

- What discretion will a supervisor have to approve or disapprove a requested leave?

MODULE
10

References

1. Labor Department: Final Rules Implementing the Family and Medical Leave Act, Bureau of National Affairs, Inc., 1995, section 825.106.
2. Labor Department: Final Rules Implementing the Family and Medical Leave Act, Bureau of National Affairs, Inc., 1995, section 825.214–825.216.
3. Department of Labor-ESA, "Fact sheet on Family and Medical Leave Act," July 22, 1993, BNA *Fair Employment Practice Manual,* section 405:201.
4. Ibid.
5. Benjamin Wolkinson and Richard Block, *Employment Law: The Workplace Rights of Employees and Employers* (Blackwell Business, Cambridge, MA, 1996), p. 70.
6. Commission on Leave, "A Workable Balance: Report to Congress on Family and Medical Leave Policies," 1996.

Index

Accrued paid leave, 10.12
Administering FMLA, 10.12–13
Advance notice (FMLA), 10.11
Americans with Disabilities Act, 10.4
Amount of leave used, 10.7

Case-by-case basis, 10.5
Changing policies (under FMLA), 10.11
Collective bargaining, 10.8
Complaint filing (FMLA), 10.5
Compliance, 10.4
Continuation of benefits, 10.6
Continuing treatment (regimen), 10.8. *See also* Short-term treatment
Covered employers, 10.5

Department of Labor (DOL), 10.5, 10.6
Discrimination, 10.12

Elective conditions (FMLA), 10.8
Eligible employees, 10.5–6
Employee rights and responsibilities (FMLA), 10.4, 10.8–9, 10.11
Employer obligations (FMLA), 10.8
Enforcement (FMLA), 10.5
Entitlement (FMLA). *See* Leave entitlement
Exempt employees (FMLA), 10.6, 10.13. *See also* Nonexempt employees

Failure to comply (FMLA), 10.9–10
Family and Medical Leave Act (FMLA), 10.4–7, 10.12, 10.14
50-employee threshold, 10.5, 10.6
Final Rules (DOL's), 10.5–12
FMLA leave, 10.4–8, 10.11–12, 10.13–14
FMLA policies, 10.9–10, 10.12, 10.13
FMLA training, 10.13
Full-time employees, 10.13

Healthcare coverage, 10.6
Healthcare provider, 10.8
Human resource professional, 10.5, 10.13
Human resource strategy, 10.5

Immediate family member, 10.7
Intermittent or reduced-schedule leave, 10.8

Job restoration, 10.6, 10.9
Job-protected leave, 10.5, 10.14
Joint employment, 10.6

Key employees, 10.7

Leased employees, 10.5
Leave Dispute Resolution System (LDRS), 10.13
Leave entitlement, 10.7, 10.12
Light duty assignment, 10.12
Limitations and exceptions (FMLA), 10.7

Medical certification (FMLA), 10.7, 10.9, 10.11, 10.14
Morale (employee), 10.4, 10.13

Nonexempt employees (FMLA), 10.13. *See also* Exempt employees
Notification (FMLA), 10.4, 10.6, 10.11

Organizational strategy, 10.12

Part-time employees, 10.5, 10.13
Period of incapacity, 10.8
Permanent condition, 10.8
Policies and procedures manual, 10.8, 10.13. *See also* Notification (FMLA)
Primary employer, 10.6
Private companies, 10.5
Proactive administration, 10.4
Productivity (employee), 10.4
Public employers, 10.5

Quality of worklife, 10.4

Reasonable expectation, 10.6
Reinstatement of employment, 10.7
Request for leave, 10.9–10

Serious health condition (FMLA), 10.7–8
Short-term disability, 10.4. *See also* Continuing treatment (regimen)
Substitution of paid leave, 10.12

Temporary employees, 10.5
Title VII, 10.12
Training for managers (FMLA), 10.13
12-month period (FMLA), 10.6, 10.10–12

Work/family balance, 10.4, 10.14
Workers' compensation, 10.4, 10.12
Working conditions, 10.6

MANAGING HUMAN RESOURCES
IN THE 21st CENTURY

From Core Concepts to Strategic Choice

MODULE 11

Support of Work/Life Integration

Cultural Issues Facing the Employer

Ellen Ernst Kossek
MICHIGAN STATE UNIVERSITY

Managing Human Resources in the 21st Century: From Core Concepts to Strategic Choice,
by Kossek and Block

Publisher: Dave Shaut
Executive Editor: John Szilagyi
Developmental Editor: Bryant Editorial Development
Marketing Manager: Joseph A. Sabatino
Production Editor: Tamborah E. Moore
Manufacturing Coordinator: Dana Began Schwartz
Cover Design: Tin Box Studio
Cover Photographs: Copyright Shoji Sato/Photonica
Production House: The Left Coast Group, Inc.
Printer: West Group

Printed in the United States of America
1 2 3 4 5 02 01 00 99

For more information contact South-Western College Publishing, 5101 Madison Road, Cincinnati,
Ohio, 45227 or find us on the Internet at *http://www.swcollege.com*
For permission to use material from this text or product, contact us by

- telephone: 1-800-730-2214
- fax: 1-800-730-2215
- web: *http://www.thomsonrights.com*

ISBN: 0–324–01810–X

This book is printed on acid-free paper.

Contents

MODULE OVERVIEW 11.4

OBJECTIVES 11.5

RELATION TO THE FRAME 11.6

CORE CONCEPTS IN MANAGING CULTURAL SUPPORT OF
WORK/LIFE POLICIES 11.7

Traditional U.S. Business Cultural Assumptions Regarding the
Integration of Work and the Family 11.7

Common U.S. Cultural Assumptions Regarding Work and Family 11.8

Stages in the Organizational Development of Work/Life Programs 11.9

Cultural Assumptions Regarding Work and Family Integration
Outside of the United States 11.10

Alternative Organizational Approaches for Managing Employer
Involvement in Employees' Personal Lives: Competing Values 11.10

Importance of Encouraging Employee Self-Reflection on
Work/Life Integration Preferences 11.14

STRATEGIC ISSUES IN MANAGING CULTURAL SUPPORT OF
WORK/LIFE POLICIES 11.15

Work/Life Responsiveness Is a Critical Management Challenge 11.15

Employer-Concern for Personal Needs On and Off the Job:
A Strategic Investment in Human and Social Capital and
High-Performance Work Systems? 11.15

APPLICATION 11.16

IN CONCLUSION 11.17

Debrief 11.17

Suggested Readings 11.17

Critical Thinking Questions 11.18

Exercises 11.18

References 11.19

INDEX 11.21

MODULE OVERVIEW

"One of Chevron's competitive strategies is to build a committed employee team . . . Helping employees balance work and personal life is a crucial factor in achieving the cultural change necessary to empower the work force and enhance productivity," reports Sue Osborn, the company's work-family coordinator. For example, Chevron's 8,000 employees now have compressed workweeks, with most working nine hours a day with every other Friday off. Part-time workers receive pro-rated health benefits based on the number of hours they work. Osborn concludes, "Like most companies, we can no longer afford to offer the level of job security that used to be a given. But we are investing in programs that give our people opportunities they need to manage their careers and be more effective contributors."[1]

The preceding Chevron quote suggests that the effective implementation of human resource strategies to enable employees to balance their work and personal lives involves more than legally complying with the Family and Medical Leave Act. It also suggests that the issue of work and personal life integration affects all workers, not just those with young children, as was the case when work/family policies first appeared in the corporate world. The quality of work/life that an organization provides is often the determining factor in many individuals' choice of employer. Human resource policies designed to help employees balance their work and family lives can also affect turnover, performance, absenteeism, organizational commitment, and employee willingness to go the extra mile on behalf of their employers.

Formal policies can be categorized into four main types of employer support:

1. *Time and place flexibility.* This includes part-time work, emergency leave, compressed workweeks, job sharing, leaves of absence, flextime and telecommuting, and other policies enabling employees to work at home if desired.

2. *Information.* This includes resource and referral programs where employees are given information about licensed dependent-caregiving options in their area, stress management seminars, child- and elder-care provider support groups, dependent-care provider fairs, preretirement planning, and supervisor training on how to effectively manage subordinates' work/family integration needs.

3. *Financial.* This includes flexible spending accounts in which employees set aside pretax money each year into an account from which they will be reimbursed, vouchers offering employees a stipend toward caregiving expenses, company discounts negotiated at local providers, well-baby care, tuition reimbursement, college scholarship, health benefits for dependents, and long-term care insurance.

4. *Direct.* This includes on- or near-site company-sponsored day-care centers, sick care, company support of in-home day-care providers, family day-care networks where relatives of employees provide licensed home-based care, concierge services to run errands for busy employees such as dry cleaning, grocery shopping, etc. Additional services in this area include employee assistance programs that provide mental health, substance abuse, family counseling and other services, domestic partner benefits, legal counseling, adoption support, personal financial planning, emergency backup childcare centers or in-home care, before and after school programs, holiday and vacation care, and lactation programs.[2]

Towers Perrin, an international human resources consulting firm, surveyed over 100 large employers in various industries to see which work/life programs form a baseline of programs that are the most frequently adopted. The most frequently offered policies were:

- unpaid personal leave of absence (90%)

- employee assistance plans (88%)

- coverage for routine gynecological exams (79%)

- dependent-care spending account (79%)

- coverage for well-baby care (73%)

- personal days (62%)

- vacation days carryover into the next year (59%)

- closing-cost assistance with house purchases (59%)

- wellness programs (58%)

- paid time off for relocation (52%)

- gradual return to work after a personal leave (50%)

- on- or near-site banking (50%)

- employee attitude surveys (49%)

- health coverage for adult dependents of full-time employees (47%)

- housing resource and referral (47%)

- preretirement planning (47%)

- health benefits for part-time workers (45%)

- narrow-banded flextime (44%)[3]

MODULE
11

Unfortunately, family-supportive policies often are underutilized by employees or face cultural barriers in their effective implementation.[4] One reason for this is that many firms' have workaholic cultures. For example, when a senior editor at *The New York Times,* Joyce Purnick, gave a commencement address at her alma mater, Barnard College, she stated that she was absolutely convinced she "would not be the metro editor of the *Times* if I had had a family ... With rare exception, women who have children get off track and lose ground." While juggling family and careers is difficult in many professions, it is especially hard in professions such as journalism where there are last-minute deadlines and late-breaking news. Many women staffers with young children at the *Times* are on four-day schedules, or have jobs with regular hours such as editing weekly sections. When a woman at a staff meeting later asked Purnick, "Do you actually think because we're mothers we contribute less?," Purnick's painful answer was "You contribute differently."[5] True or not, perception is often reality. A main goal of this module is to help the learner understand that there is a big difference between simply offering work/life programs and ensuring that they are used effectively and valued by organizational members.[6]

OBJECTIVES

- To spark reflection and discussion on the organizational cultural realities faced by employees striving to integrate work and personal lives

- To encourage learners to contemplate work/life interventions as a form of cultural change that could be linked to broader organizational improvement efforts as opposed to simply a program or benefit

- To increase awareness of how the cultural assumptions regarding the separation of work and family may be idiosyncratic to the U.S. culture

- To enable learners to enter into dialogue with peers and to explore differences in values

- To understand that it is vital that employers implement work/family policies that are congruent with their firm's culture and the unique needs of their workforce

RELATION TO THE FRAME

Work/life policies can cover the range of HR roles shown in Figure 11.1, ranging from transactions (one-time personnel changes such as a maternity leave) to transformation of the corporate culture (i.e., a balanced work/life environment). Historically, work/family policies have been thought of as a benefit to help employees to manage short-term or occasional family (e.g., childbirth, illness) demands in a reactive way. After a family demand becomes apparent or an employee makes a request to invoke a policy to support family needs, human resources (often with supervisor permission) would process a transaction to help an employee meet the family demand. For example, paperwork would be processed to enable an employee to take a leave of absence, enroll for medical benefits, and so forth. Most recently, with the passage of the Family and Medical Leave Act, if an employee requests, all employers will invoke the leave as a transaction to comply with the law that allows workers to take up to 12 workweeks of unpaid, job-protected leave for specific family and medical reasons.

Work/family policies were originally developed based on the assumption that work should be the primary priority in a person's life. Policies often were designed to minimize family intrusions on work that compete for an employee's time and energy. Examples might include a sick-care program or encouraging employees with heavy family demands to take a leave of absence until they are ready to enter the workforce again on a full-time basis. Programs tended to be directed at employees with the most visible kinds of work and personal-life conflict. For instance, programs exist to allow a working mother to take a leave to care for a newborn, while programs to help a single workaholic with a crumbling relationship with a significant other probably do not.[7]

Today, progressive organizations have moved beyond focusing policies on mainly child-related or a nonworking spouse's healthcare demands (often the most visible family needs) to involve eldercare, as well as to acknowledge an increasing diversity of lifestyles, workstyles, and the need to accommodate many different types of work and

FIGURE 11.1 *A Frame for Understanding Human Resource Strategy:
Context, Roles, and Constraints*

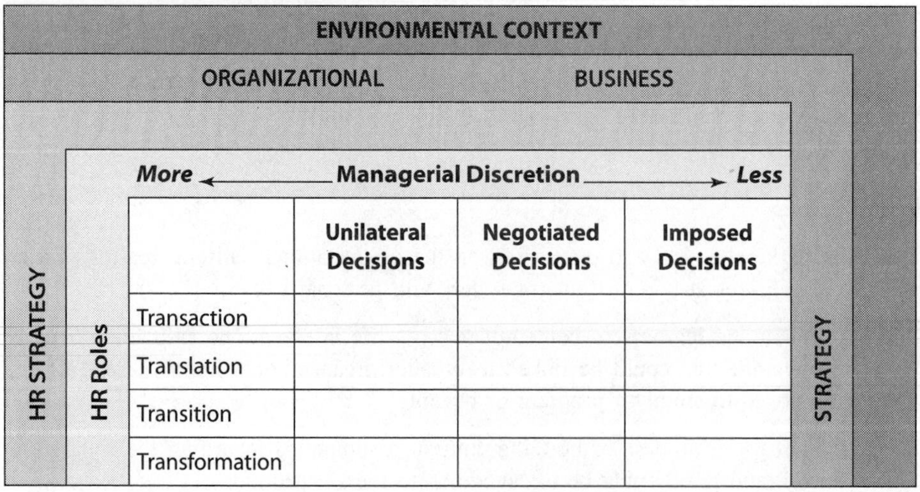

ENVIRONMENTAL CONTEXT			
ORGANIZATIONAL		BUSINESS	

HR STRATEGY	HR Roles	More ← Managerial Discretion → Less			STRATEGY
		Unilateral Decisions	**Negotiated Decisions**	**Imposed Decisions**	
	Transaction				
	Translation				
	Transition				
	Transformation				

© 2000 by Ellen Ernst Kossek and Richard Block. Thanks to Brian Pentland, Karen Markel, and John Beck for helpful comments and discussions that enhanced the model.

personal-life interactions. Progressive organizations realize that adopting all the family-friendly policies in the world will not enable employees to balance their work and personal lives if they are afraid to use the policies because their supervisors, peers, or general work culture do not support their use. Or the policies that are available may not fit their personal needs. Work cultures are becoming transformed via support of work/family policies to enable employees of many different backgrounds to be able to effectively integrate their work and nonwork lives. The movement is from framing these issues as involving "work/family" toward a broader concept of "work/life" integration. Thus, when they first appeared, work/life decisions mainly involved HR transactions related to childbearing. Over time, as companies recognized the strategic importance of work/life integration activities, many firms have increased their emphasis on cultural or transformational HR initiatives. See Figure 11.1, A Frame for Understanding Human Resource Strategy.

CORE CONCEPTS IN MANAGING CULTURAL SUPPORT OF WORK/LIFE POLICIES

In the sections that follow, we will discuss each of these five core concepts:

- Traditional U.S. business cultural assumptions regarding the integration of work and family

- Stages of organizational development of work/life programs

- Cultural assumptions regarding work and family integration outside the United States

- Alternative organizational approaches for managing employer involvement in employees' personal lives: competing values

- Importance of encouraging employee self-reflection on work/life integration preferences

Traditional U.S. Business Cultural Assumptions Regarding the Integration of Work and Family

Growing evidence suggests that the adoption of workplace supports for family does not necessarily result in the reduction of the level of work/family conflict experienced by employees.[8] The leading U.S. business magazine *Fortune* had a cover story proclaiming: "Is Your Family Wrecking Your Career?" Despite a lot of politically correct talk currently being conducted at many U.S. corporations about the importance of being "family friendly," most companies have not fully determined how to move beyond formal policy adoption. Employers are struggling with how to implement work/life balance policies to really make them work well and equally benefit the employer and employee. There will always be employees willing to put their career before their family and personal needs, and these employees will be the most promotable, since they will be willing to do whatever the company needs without taking family considerations into account.

Evidence suggests that in many companies, the use of work/life integration policies is seen as benefiting the individual employee far more than the firm. Meeting employees' personal needs is often not yet seen as meeting customers' needs. Yet employees are the ultimate internal customers of a firm. Mixed messages are sent when workers are viewed as a resource to use up as opposed to invest in. Companies need to communicate to their managers (i.e., translate) how work/life policies enable the firm to attract and retain satisfied, nonstressed workers who are able to perform to the best of their abilities to serve the customer.[9]

Consider the following equation:

$$\text{Performance} = f \text{ (motivation, opportunity, and ability)}$$

This equation states that performance is a function of employee ability, motivation, and opportunity to perform. An employee's ability is generally the province of selection; hopefully, good selection systems are in place to ensure that a firm hires employees who have the ability to perform their jobs. An employee is likely to be motivated to perform his or her job if a company reward system fairly pays people based on their performance. An employee who needs to manage caregiving or other personal life demads while on the job will have the opportunity to perform well if she or he is able to attend work and focus on the job. Cultural support of policies where employees perceive that norms give the message that it is acceptable to use flextime or take work home to care for a sick child or elder will give affected employees the opportunity to perform their job.

Picture the starting line in a footrace as representing an employee's starting point for performing his or her job. If an individual is not able to use work/family policies due to either their nonexistence or norms discouraging their use, the runner (employee) is five paces behind the starting line before even starting the race (beginning to do his or her job). Work/family policies help employees with family demands to be at the same starting line as all other workers when beginning to perform the job competition.

Some employees fear that if they reduce work hours, they will be put on a mommy or daddy track and hindered in their career path. A 1992 study of 902 women graduates of the Harvard law, business, and medical schools found that 85 percent felt that reducing hours of work was detrimental to their careers. Similarly, Catalyst, the nonprofit organization that does research on issues affecting senior women in business, found in a study that one-fourth of human resource managers felt that use of flexible policies such as part-time work had a negative impact on career advancement. A study by Work/Family Directions, a major consulting firm providing work/life services to employees, found that though many firms offer flexible work options, barriers to use persist. These most notably include supervisor resistance and fear about hurting career advancement.[10]

Recognition of the need to shift the cultural assumption that work/life policies benefit the employee more than the employer is reflected in the philosophy of The Partnership Group, an innovative work/life consulting firm (now merged into Ceridian Performance Partners, Inc.) that works with Nike and Avon and other leading companies. Rather than labeling these services work and family benefits, the company stresses that employees and employers are "in partnership" together to manage work and family responsibilities in a way that makes a productive workplace and society. If work/family policies are going to be used to their fullest potential, common U.S. business assumptions regarding work/life issues that may serve as barriers to use must be identified and challenged where appropriate. Some of these assumptions are listed below.[11]

Common U.S. Cultural Assumptions Regarding Work and Family

- Employees cannot be equally committed to the family and the workplace.

- The workplace can be designed without regard to employees' nonwork lives.

- Society as a whole doesn't necessarily benefit when we help individuals with family needs.

- Nurturance activities such as child- and eldercare are mainly the province of women.

- In an individualistic culture, achieving balance between work and family is not necessarily highly valued.

- Personal problems should be kept at home.

- Benefit programs can only satisfy workers and make them happier, not more productive.

- Face time (or hours present at the office) equals output/performance.

- Equitable means identical.

- Families and children are private matters. The choice to have children is personal and should neither be sanctioned nor discouraged.

- The workplace can be designed without regard to employees' nonwork lives.

- When work/family conflicts occur, work demands must prevail.

- Work/family conflicts are seen as a form of special-cause variance (a deviance resulting from an individual employee's problem) as opposed to common cause variance (resulting from not optimizing the design of workplace systems to accommodate work/life integration issues for all employees).

Employers who offer new work/life programs without assessing how the prevailing corporate culture may send signals that block their use will be disappointed by the results. Similarly, companies that introduce work/life policies mainly as a reaction to what other companies are doing also are unlikely to reap the full potential of their investment. In order for these programs to make a significant difference in employee perceptions about work/life integration and productivity, they must be supported by the work environment and the company culture.[12]

Towers Perrin poses some key questions for employers to use to assess their cultural support for programs. For example, does the firm reinforce the programs and policies with employee research such as attitude surveys and focus groups, management training, and other supports? Does the culture truly allow and encourage employees to use work/life benefits? Do these benefits fully recognize diversity in the workforce?[13] Are managers held accountable for effective support of work/life integration? In order to plan for improved long-term success, it may be useful for a company to assess each stage in the organizational development of cultural support for work/life initiatives.

Stages in the Organizational Development of Work/Life Programs

The Families and Work Institute in New York has developed stages in the organizational development of work/family programs. At stage one, a company has adopted a few work/family programs and takes a programmatic approach to employees' family needs. Separate initiatives are adopted in a piecemeal manner that do not challenge existing work norms about the primacy of the work role over the family role at all times. Policies are mainly seen as benefits that will be used by noncareer-oriented employees.

At stage two, top management begins to champion some programs, and a work/family manager is named. All human resource management policies are evaluated for their contribution to work/family issues. The company by now is likely to have a plethora of work/family policies in place. These programs are perceived to comprise a core human resource management policy stream. Company productivity and bottom-line impact are starting to be measured.

At stage three, the successful integration of work/family policies is seen as a competitive issue. The company sees that having a culture receptive to employees' work/family needs will enable them to attract the best workers. Company mission statements may be changed to reflect values supporting personal employee needs. Managers may have their performance evaluated on how well they handled work/family needs. Work/family issues are mainstreamed and integrated with other HR policies such as diversity or total quality management.[14]

Sustained top management commitment is necessary for long-term success. What chief executive officers need to do, with the help of human resource executives, is address the broader issues that have emerged in the evolution of the new social contract between employer and employee. As the meaning of work itself becomes redefined to exclude the idea of long-term employment with one company and the concept that work must always supersede caregiving and other nonwork demands, work/family programs need to be translated into practice in a manner that shows that support of "soft issues" such as work/life balance is truly credible and not merely talk.[15]

Cultural Assumptions Regarding Work and Family Integration Outside of the United States

MIT professor Lotte Bailyn has researched cultural assumptions on work and family integration in countries outside of the United States. She found that in Great Britain, it was more culturally acceptable for women to acknowledge that family is a priority. Great Britain has been an international pioneer in the implementation of work-at-home arrangements and career breaks. Yet she found that these arrangements tend to promote separate gender-based spheres and continued male corporate domination in Britain.

In Sweden, culturally there is a social consensus of equality (women should have jobs and men should be involved in the family sphere). Care of the family is seen as a responsibility of the state or government. In Sweden (and also Haiti), being a child-care worker has more cultural value than in the United States. Although Sweden makes it easier for women to combine work and family than in the United States, with shorter workdays and greater availability of part-time work, the cultural career rules for moving up in the corporation still stress long hours at work. Therefore, women still lag behind men in career progress.[16]

In France, the birth of a child is celebrated by society as the birth of a new French citizen. The well-known statement "It takes a village to raise a child" has its origin in Africa. Thus, global U.S. corporations should be aware that the U.S. cultural assumptions regarding the relations of work and family are not necessarily transnational.

Alternative Organizational Approaches for Managing Employer Involvement in Employees' Personal Lives: Competing Values

A key issue in cultural assessment involves employers choosing the level of corporate involvement in employees' personal lives that fits with the company business mission and way of doing business. Firms need to select broad policy approaches that fit with their corporate culture, managerial values, and workforce needs.

There is a continuum of employer approaches to work/life involvement. These range from cautious social arbiters to whole persons to omniscient organizational philosophies. This section will describe each of these approaches, offer company examples, and the pros and cons of each. First, a brief overview of University of Michigan professor Bob Quinn's competing values perspective[17] is useful in providing a broad framework for discussion of these approaches.

Managing the Competing Demands of High Performance in Work and Family Life: Are There Fundamental Conflicts Between Employees' Personal Needs for Balance and Corporations' Needs for Productivity?   The efficiency- and productivity-oriented values of organizations that sell a product or service and the work/life needs of employees may have some fundamental conflicts that are not easily resolved. For example, Fran Rodgers, the president of Work/Family Directions, notes that these competing demands result in companies sending mixed signals to employees. Though companies are often willing to delegate responsibility for redesigning

products to workers, they are often uneasy about allowing greater employee control over flexibility and other things that would help them balance their work and family lives.[18]

One explanation of the mixed messages given to employees on how to balance work with family may be that organizations often have to jointly manage competing values. A long-term view of human resource development sees investment in employees' work/life integration needs as way to promote productivity through caring about workers; this fits with the *human relations model* of management. This model is concerned with the development of human resources and longer timelines. The assumption is that if you give an employee some slack over the short term to deal with personal needs, over the long run, productivity will be maximized due to higher employee morale and commitment. The human resources department as the unit that helps ensure employees have a voice in the company has historically reflected human relations philosophies. In contrast, most companies also have managers in other functions such as production or marketing, or even top management, who hold values consistent with the *rational goal approach*. This approach is concerned with quarterly maximization of output and shorter timelines. Under this view, employee needs for company support of nonwork demands may be viewed as hurting efficiency over the short run. For example, if an employee takes a leave of absence for personal needs, efficiency is hurt over the short run since she or he is not at work producing.

Effective organizations learn how to simultaneously manage these competing values. The company need to efficiently produce must be managed concurrently with individual employees' needs to have organizational responsiveness to personal off-the-job demands. If such approaches are not jointly implemented, companies may be effective over the short run (and be efficient) but over the long run they will have burned-out, stressed employees who are unhappy in their nonwork lives and also on the job.

Some forward-thinking organizations learn how to link work/life interventions to other organizational change initiatives such as total quality improvement and organizational redesign to promote greater flexibility (e.g., the virtual workplace). Work/life change efforts could also be linked to globalization efforts and strategies to transform corporate cultures to become more cross-cultural. For example, U.S. efforts to become global and more multicultural are likely to fail if greater tolerance of competing values and approaches to work are not accepted and encouraged.

MODULE
11

Currently, most organizations do not manage competing values very well. They tend to have a predominant cultural approach to managing work and family, which will be discussed below.

Social Arbiter Approach: Work/Life Issues Are Private and Employer Should Only Get Involved in Cases of Poor Performance.

The *social arbiter approach* suggests that employers should tread cautiously in managing nonwork issues. The premise is that employers are increasingly sending signals to employees that have social meaning for how individual workers ought to manage their personal lives or should behave. For example, a sick-care program that takes care of a sick child so a parent can continue working sends the message that children should not interfere with work. Other common messages through smoking cessation programs or spot drug testing are that employees should not smoke or use illegal drugs.

What about issues of genetic testing and personal medical histories? What if employees had to work with hazardous materials that could affect fertility in those with certain medical family backgrounds? These jobs may be financially attractive and high paying. Some workers may be sure they are not planning to have any children, and want to work in these jobs even if their medical histories suggest they might have fertility problems down the line. Should the company require all workers to be tested and share their medical histories, and forbid employees with certain backgrounds from taking the jobs? In an article published several years ago with my labor relations colleague, Rich

Block, we argued no. We maintain that employers should only get involved if the employee requests help or if the company becomes aware that nonwork issues are getting in the way of performance.[19]

Reflecting this philosophy, some firms emphasize a separation between work and family. As a U.S. West manager comments: "We believe very strongly in the separation of church and state—between work and family. Our salaries are higher than the national average and our benefits far exceed the national average. We are not going to start subsidizing child care. That's not our target. We believe in strengthening the community—it's an important key to how we do business." Though U.S. West does not have company-sponsored childcare centers, it has contributed over $7 billion during a two-year period to community-based childcare initiatives in 14 states where it does business.[20]

Whole Persons and Systems Approach: Work/Family Policies Sensitive to the Needs of Workers as Internal Customers Can Serve to Enhance Quality and Cultural Change.

Fred Freidlander argues a "whole systems" and "whole persons" approach to employment. He believes that the world would be better off if all employers were more sensitive to work/life integration needs. His view is that good employers should strive to have greater sensitivity to personal needs for all workers.[21] The whole persons perspective is consistent with the human relations approach to management. As a manager at Steelcase, the furniture company, comments: "If employees are truly empowered to not only pinpoint and voice work problems, but also develop and implement solutions for both work and family issues, they will have more ownership, and thus will be more loyal and committed to their jobs, departments, and to the company overall."[22]

Some managers argue that implementing holistic work/life programs in a manner that challenges corporate cultural values to be sensitive to employees as internal customers can also shape the corporate culture to be more quality oriented for its external customers. As one manager at Dow commented: "A corporation's success depends on a quality, innovative and dedicated workforce. If you don't get the people thing right, you won't get the customer thing right."[23] Similarly, a manager interviewed at Motorola said: "To get high quality you need to be sensitive to the personal needs that employees have. There should not be a division between personal needs and what is going on at work."[24]

A manager at Corning discussed the whole persons or integrative approach to work and family: "(You must believe) that people are worth developing and that you manage by prevention. Think about the fact that you've got this valuable commodity—this human being—who works for the company. You want to continually develop this. Hopefully . . . you will gain a long-term employee who is flexible, creative, and gives a lot to the organization . . . There are very few managers who are really good at managing the human resource and looking at the long-term picture of career development, work/family issues, and dealing with diversity. When these become integrated things—instead of add-ons—that's when I think we have gotten close to arriving."[25]

Omniscient Organization: Too Little Separation.

With the growth of computer technology, electronic beepers, telecommuting, and other workplace developments, a third approach is the omniscient organization.[26] Under this approach, technological advances and flexible workplace options result in a blurring of the boundaries between the work and personal domains. There is virtually no separation between work and personal life.

Employees who work at home full-time often experience this dilemma. Issues such as "What is the workday" and "What is the workweek?" are in flux. An employee's boss can send an e-mail overnight that the employee knows is waiting at his or her home terminal when he or she wakes up at 6 a.m. A father with a newborn baby who is in charge of a global project can hear faxes print out on his home fax machine when he is up at 2 A.M. with the baby. A human resource manager who turned off her beeper while on vacation blames herself when an incidence of workplace violence occurs, even though someone else was on duty to cover for her. A father going out to take his child ice skating at 6 P.M. feels guilty for not taking a phone call someone returned to him in response to a 1 P.M. query. A professional with an elderly parent visiting from out of town feels the strain of juggling heavy workload demands that keep piling up while trying to work shorter days to take care of the parent she rarely sees during a two-week visit.

Privacy concerns are also heightened, and basic human resource policy administration is put into flux. For example: What if an employee's home computer needs to be seized when she or he is fired for misconduct? How should performance appraisal be measured if the boss rarely sees the telecommuter face-to-face? What is considered absenteeism when one works at home? What if a work call comes in and a customer hears a child wailing (or wildly barking dogs) in the background? The whole human resource management system based on direct supervision and face time at work in the office is up in the air. When is it okay for an employee to request more separation, or say it is too early or late to take a phone call?

The omniscient organization runs the risk of having the rational goal value that organizational efficiency objectives must always take precedence even if it does not fit with the employees' work/life needs and values.

Pros and Cons of Each Approach.   Certainly there is no one best way to manage employees' rising work and family demands. There are pros and cons to each approach, and individual employees and their work organizations need to have dialogue over the fundamental conflicts that exist.

Some of the pros and cons of each approach are listed in Table 11.1 below.

TABLE 11.1 *Comparison of the Pros and Cons of Alternative Approaches to Managing Employer Involvement in Employees' Personal Lives*

Cautious Social Arbiter	Whole Persons and Systems	Omniscient Organization
Pros		
Individual employee rights are protected.	Promotes systems thinking.	Considers the total employee.
Management intervenes in personal problems only when there is a clear performance issue.	Contends work/life balance should be an organizational goal.	Attempts to make work a home to employees.
The focus of organizational involvement is to help manage an individual person's circumstances to facilitate doing one's job well.	Suggests a new paradigm focused on values.	Management shows it cares about its workers' personal lives by allowing greater flexibility.
Management has awareness of how norms and social pressures may affect use of so-called "voluntary programs."	Recognizes the importance of the nonwork domain to most employees.	Technology and human resources are tightly integrated.
		Work is rationalized and there is an attempt to make it fair (e.g., all employees treated alike).

(continued)

TABLE 11.1 *continued*

Cautious Social Arbiter	Whole Persons and Systems	Omniscient Organization
Cons		
Management's hands-off approach is reactive. The organization doesn't get involved until there is a performance problem, which may be too late. Earlier intervention might have avoided a problem.	Light on specifics as to how to manage whole persons	Invasive.
	Danger of overinvolvement of omniscient organization exists.	Risk exists for management invasion of privacy.
The approach is a very conservative, overly cautious one. It will lead more firms against involvement in nonwork issues than the alternatives.	Naive view of the reality of spiralling work and family demands.	Technology is used to control people's lives in coercive ways.
		Employee may feel dehumanized.
It may be difficult to discern when there is an actual performance problem or risk to an employee.		Not all employees have personality, work styles, and family situations suitable for effective self-management of telecommuting arrangements.
The approach relies heavily on supervisory judgment. Not all supervisors may be equally adept at reading and diagnosing the needs of their subordinates.		Lack of separation between work and family may cause additional stress and work overload.
		Onus is on employee to set boundaries.

Importance of Encouraging Employee Self-Reflection on Work/Life Integration Preferences

Not only do employers need to assess their values and philosophies regarding work and family integration, employees themselves need to be encouraged to self-reflect on their values for managing the integration of work and personal life. A book by a major sociologist, Arlie Hochschild, entitled *The Time Bind: When Home Becomes Work and Work Becomes Home,* highlights the importance of encouraging workers to self-reflect on their values and preferred work/family integration strategies. Hochschild found that many professional workers are too attached to their jobs to take advantage of many work/life policies and spend more time at home. Consciously or unconsciously, many career-minded employees choose to work longer hours because they feel more valued and receive more recognition at work than they do for being a good parent, elder caregiver, or taking care of themselves. With the divorce rate skyrocketing, and growing family and nonwork demands, many employees feel that doing these chores are psychologically difficult and draining after a hard day's work. "The greedy workplace" is a widespread way of describing a major U.S. employer in the 1990s.

In the United States, there are several mechanisms employees are using to cope with the rising family and personal demands they face off the job. One coping mechanism is emotional asceticism—psychologically minimizing the care our families or we actually need. Another coping vehicle is to pay other people to meet many of our family demands. Hochschild asks pointedly: "Is the world we are shaping in the U.S. one where everyone works and leaves the family side of work and family to 'hired hands'?" A third psychological mechanism is the potential self, where workers dream that someday they'll take the time to have a rich and rewarding family life.[27] But unfortunately, unless workers develop strategies to do so, "someday" may never come until retirement, which may be too late.

STRATEGIC ISSUES IN MANAGING CULTURAL SUPPORT OF WORK/LIFE POLICIES

Work/Life Responsiveness Is a Critical Management Challenge

Despite increasing evidence that family issues have critical implications for the workplace, senior managers have given relatively little attention to this major societal and organizational change. Statistics show that currently less than 7 percent of American families are "traditional" families.[28] The growing diversity in family structures and caregiving demands and arrangements is also supported by findings from the just-released National Study of the Changing Workforce.[29] The number of single working parents has jumped nearly 50 percent—from 13 percent in 1977 to 19 percent in 1997 and surprisingly, a quarter (27 percent) of the single parents are men (i.e., they had at least 50 percent custody). Nearly half (42 percent) of full-time workers expect to provide eldercare for an older parent or relative in the next five years, and one in four employees—equally men and women—already informally do so for an average of 11 hours per week. These trends reflect employees at all levels as nearly half of the managers in Fortune 500 companies are in dual-career families,[30] and reports indicate that men and women professionals are both concerned with decision making and assessment of alternatives on how to integrate work and family caregiving demands.[31]

Why should senior managers care about these trends? The development that nearly all individuals at some point during their careers will be employed caregivers has significance because work/family demands have been consistently shown to influence key work and personal outcomes ranging from job, life, and family satisfaction[32] to performance[33] to turnover.[34] The growing work/life integration pressures on employees also may affect employers' ability to realize the potential of their future labor force. Reports indicate that for growing numbers of college graduates about to enter the labor market, nearly half (45 percent) say that their top consideration in selecting a first employer is the ability to achieve a balance between work and a rewarding life outside of work.[35] Research also shows that family problems can have major financial costs for employers. For example, analysis of data from a national panel study conducted by the University of Michigan's Institute for Social Research indicates that family and marital problems translate into work loss of approximately $6.8 billion per year.[36]

Work/life programs that are effectively supported by the work culture can also have financial implications for other factors typically not included in benefits calculations. These include financial improvements associated with reduced recruiting, training, and related replacement costs, since employees who are satisfied with their work/life situation are less likely to turn over. There also may be increased productivity due to employees' heightened ability to perform their jobs since they are not distracted by constant dependent-care or other nonwork problems.[37]

Employer-Concern for Personal Needs On and Off the Job: A Strategic Investment in Human and Social Capital and High-Performance Work Systems?

Employer concern for personal needs, whether on or off the job, is likely to be increasingly important to growing numbers of employees, yet many management studies do not view employer responsiveness to personal needs as a key part of HR strategy or the design of high-performance work systems. When work/life policies are studied,

MODULE
11

research tends to be programmatic—studying the effects of single work-family policies in isolation and lacking integration to general job design and HR policy relationships.[38]

The linkage of work/life policies to bundles of HR practices indicative of high-performance work systems[39] and high employer investments in workers (e.g., extensive selection systems, good training, etc.) has been overlooked by most managers and leading HR scholars. The idea of "bundles in strategic human resource management" is that groups of human resource practices have congruence and should be adopted as bundles to send employees a coherent human resource management message. If policies to invest in employees' work/life balance needs over the life span are adopted as part of a package of other high-performance HR policies that invest in attracting and keeping the best workers, then employees will be feel valued and will be motivated to stay with the employer over the long term. The employer benefits because top talent is less likely to leave.

Lotus Development Corporation, for example, extended domestic partner benefits to its 3,000-employee North American workforce. According to Russ Campenello, Vice President of Human Resources at Lotus, "We think of diversity as a way for us to continue to attract and retain the best people the industry has to offer. . . . We're trying to position ourselves as the employer of choice in a competitive market for workers."[40] While it is currently in vogue in the management literature to focus on creating intellectual and social capital as a means of building a stable base of human assets,[41] the role of HR policies in responding to personal needs (e.g., work/life supports) and in developing this capital is still overlooked. Yet it is interesting to note that a recent article[42] on HR strategy found that the adoption of work/life policies was statistically related to the HR strategies adopted.

APPLICATION

A recent study supported by the Ford Foundation examined the linkages between work and life integration and business demands at Xerox Corporation, Corning Inc., and Tandem Computers. The researchers believed that the process of linking work and personal concerns demanded viewing work though a work/family perspective, linking these relationships through a work/family frame, and then fostering change. They developed case studies by asking three main questions:

1. "How does work get done around here?"

2. "What are the employees' personal stories of work-family integration?" and

3. "What is it about the way that work gets done around here that makes it difficult (or easy) to juggle work and personal life so that neither one suffers?"[43]

One of the case studies involved a sales and service district with over 600 employees. In the sales district, half of the workers were men and half were women. The service district's workers were mostly men who serviced the machines. The administrative staff was mostly women. The management team included four men and one woman. While formally (on paper), the company had many work/family programs including flextime, compressed workweeks, and job sharing, these policies were rarely utilized. Informally, some managers were willing to allow unofficial flextime beyond the formal policy mostly for administrative workers. Work/family issues were rarely openly talked about at work, but were subtly apparent in many conversations.

The interviews with men and women revealed that work/life integration was an emotional issue for many, and many workers talked about the high stress that influenced their work quality. One manager, who was the one most liked by his subordinates, talked about the devastating toll his divorce the previous year had on his work and how worried he was about his ratings. Some workers felt women's concerns for work/family issues were part of women's greed for higher and more expensive lifestyles.

A recent survey on customer satisfaction showed that customer relations were going downhill and that improving these relationships would improve sales. The research team found that the same cultural issues that were hurting customer sales were also related to the lack of company partnership in helping employees integrate work and family issues. There was an individualistic culture involving serving customers. Rather than working together to solve problems, each employee had to identify his or her individual contribution. Similarly, solving work and family problems was viewed as an individual employee's problem and not a companywide systems issue. Establishing greater cultural support of cross-functional collaboration would motivate more people to help each other out, not only for business integration problems, but also for work/family integration needs.[44]

IN CONCLUSION

Debrief

The effective integration of work/life interventions into the organizational culture can best be achieved by addressing potential conflicts and congruencies between work/life policies and other ongoing business initiatives.

Work/life interventions ultimately have the greatest chance for long-term success if they are viewed in terms of their capacity for fostering change in organizational cultural assumptions as opposed to being largely programmatic efforts.

Suggested Readings

Cutcher-Gershenfeld, J., Kossek, E. E., and Sandling, H. (Jan. 1997). "Managing Multiple Concurrent Change Initiatives: Integrating Quality and Work/Family Strategies." *Organizational Dynamics.*

> *This article examines conflicts and synergies associated through the introduction of multiple change initiatives in nine leading organizations using work/family and total quality management programs as examples.*

Friedlander, F. (1994). "Toward Whole People and Whole Systems." *Organization:* vol. 1, 59–64.

Friedman, S., Christensen, P., and DeGroot, J. (Nov./Dec. 1997). "Work and Life: The End of the Zero-Sum Game," *Harvard Business Review.*

> *This article highlights the competencies managers need to manage work and family. It is based on the thinking of scholars and practitioners associated with the Wharton Work/Life Roundtable.*

Kossek, E. E., Barber, A. E., and Winters, D. (1999). "Using Flexible Schedules in the Managerial world: The Power of Peers." *Human Resource Management Journal,* 38:33–46.

> *This practitioner-friendly article examines how business and social context influenced the use of different types of flexible schedules. Practical tips for getting cultural support of flexibility are provided in the discussion.*

Kossek, E. and Block, R. (1993). "The Employer as Social Arbiter: Considerations in Limiting Employer Involvement in Off-the-Job Behavior." In *Employee Rights and Responsibilities,* 6:2, 139–155.

Lewin, T. (Oct. 12, 1994). "Men Whose Wives Work Earn Less, Studies Show." *New York Times.*

This article reports findings from several recent studies showing that men from traditional families in which the wives stay home to care for their children earn more and get higher raises than men do from two-career families. The pay gap can be debated as being attributed to either greater effort or longer hours and more work/life supports of sole breadwinners or to corporate prejudice.

Marx, Gary. The Omniscient Organization (Mar./April 1990). *Harvard Business Review,* 12–16.

Senge, P. (1990). "Ending the War Between Work and Family." In *The Fifth Discipline: The Art and Practice of the Learning Organization.* New York: Doubleday.

This is a wonderful chapter that discusses how work and family are viewed as separate competing roles in the business world.

Selected excerpts from Quinn, R. E. (1988). *Beyond Rational Management: Mastering the Paradoxes and Competing Demands of High Performance.* San Francisco: Jossey-Bass.

Towers Perrin. (1994). Work/Life Programs: Supporting a New Employer/Employee "Deal." Boston: Towers Perrin.

This is an excellent overview of the many HR policies available to support work and life integration.

Critical Thinking Questions

1. *Work/Family Interventions as Cultural Change Initiatives:* Based on your reading of the article by Cutcher-Gershenfeld, Kossek, and Sandling, the chapters by Senge, the Families and Work Institute article, and the *Wall Street Journal* excerpt:

   a. Is support for work/family integration a business issue? Why or why not?

   b. In what ways are the basic assumptions of quality improvement and work/family change initiatives congruent with each other, and in what ways are they in conflict? (Hint: See Table 2 of the Cutcher-Gershenfeld, Kossek, Sandling paper listed as reference 18.)

   c. If an organization only had enough resources to put in one change initiative, work/family or a quality improvement, which would you choose to support and why?

2. *Political Correctness of Being Family Friendly:* Should all companies strive to improve their cultures to be stage three companies as described in the Families and Work Institute model? Explain your thinking.

Exercises

1. *Competing Values:* Based on your reading of the sections in this module on the various employer approaches to managing the work/life interface (social arbiter, whole systems and persons, and omniscient) and on managing the work and nonwork interface, along with your reading of Senge's chapter, write a short essay discussing which cultural approach you prefer and self-assess your personal and professional goals in regard to work/life integration.

   a. What are your professional goals relative to work?

   b. What are your personal goals relative to your private and family life?

    c. Which organizational approach (social arbiter, whole person, or omniscient) would you most likely see followed by your future employer to help you achieve them both and why?

2. *U.S. Cultural Assumptions of Employing Organizations:*

    a. Based on your reading of Lewin's *New York Times* article, do you believe that organizations pay employees differently depending on their family type and extent of family responsibility? Be prepared to explain your thinking on this issue using both theory and any experiences you may have had.

    b. Is having a nonworking spouse a legitimate career resource in large employing organizations in the U.S.? Why or why not?

    c. Based on your reading of the Bailyn article, what changes, if any, would you like to see U.S. companies make to counter prevailing U.S. cultural assumptions regarding the work/family interface?

    d. Be ready to debate pro or con on any of these questions with your classmates.

3. *Work/Life HR Strategy:* What factors should an organization consider in developing HR strategies for the adoption of specific work/life policies? (Your instructor may opt to have you participate on a team in a work/life strategy game as a class exercise. As preparation for the game, you may want to review the Towers Perrin report listed in the Suggested Readings of this module in order to be aware of the many available options.)

References

1. Towers Perrin. 1994. *Work/Life Programs: Supporting a New Employer/Employee "Deal."* Boston: Towers Perrin.
2. Lobel, S. A. and Kossek, E. E. 1996. "Human Resource Strategies to Support Diversity in Work and Personal Lifestyles: Beyond the 'Family Friendly' Organization." In E. E. Kossek and S. A. Lobel, eds. *Human Resource Strategies for Transforming the Workplace.* Cambridge, MA.: Blackwell, 221–244.
3. Towers Perrin, *Work/Life Programs.*
4. Kofodimos, J. 1995. *Beyond Work-Family Programs: Confronting and Resolving the Underlying Causes of Work-Family Conflict.* Greensboro, NC: Center for Creative Leadership.
5. Gideonse, T. June 1, 1998. "Mommy Track at the Times." *Newsweek,* 61.
6. Towers Perrin. *Work/Life Programs.*
7. Lobel and Kossek, "Human Resource Strategies."
8. Morris, B. March 17, 1997. "Is your family wrecking your career?" *Fortune,* 70–90.
9. M. Dunnette's theory of motivation applied in Kossek, E. E. & Nichol, V. 1992. "The Effects of On Site Child Care on Employee Attitudes and Performance." *Personnel Psychology.* 45: 485–509.
10. Kossek, E. E. April 1997. "Linking Work/Life Strategies to On-going Organizational Improvement" speech. The University of Michigan.
11. Some of the ideas in this table built on work by L. Baliyn (1992). "Issues of Work and Family in Different National Contexts: How the United States, Britain, and Sweden Respond." *Human Resource Management Journal,* 201–208. And Galinsky, E., Friedman, D. & Hernandez, C. 1992. "Stages in the Development of Work-Family Programs." *The Corporate Reference Guide of Work-Family Programs.* New York: Families and Work Institute. 9–15.
12. Towers Perrin, *Work/Life Programs.*
13. Ibid.
14. Galinsky, E., Friedman, D. and Hernandez, C. 1992. "Stages in the Development of Work-Family Programs." *The Corporate Reference Guide of Work-Family Programs.* New York: Families and Work Institute. 9–15.
15. Budd, J. 1994, Oct. "Selling Work/Life Agendas to CEOs." *HR* magazine, 136.
16. Bailyn, L. 1992. "Issues of Work and Family in Different National Contexts: How the United States, Britain, and Sweden Respond." *Human Resource Management Journal,* 201–208.

17. Quinn, R. E. 1988. *Beyond Rational Management: Mastering the Paradoxes and Competing Demands of High Performance.* San Francisco: Jossey-Bass.

18. Cutcher-Gershenfeld, J., Kossek, E., & Sandling, H. 1997. "Managing Multiple Concurrent Change Initiatives; Integrating Quality and Work-Family Strategies." *Organizational Dynamics.*

19. Kossek, E. and Block, R. "The Employer as Social Arbiter: Considerations in Limiting Employer Involvement in Off-the-Job Behavior." In *Employee Rights and Responsibilities,* 6:2, 139–155.

20. Cutcher-Gershenfeld, et al. "Managing Multiple Concurrent Change Initiatives."

21. Friedlander, F. 1994. "Toward Whole People and Whole Systems." *Organization,* 1:59–64.

22. Cutcher-Gershenfeld, et al. "Managing Multiple Concurrent Change Initiatives."

23. Ibid.

24. Ibid.

25. Ibid.

26. Marx, Gary. March-Apr. 1990. "The Omniscient Organization." *Harvard Business Review,* 12–16.

27. Shellenbarger, S. April 16, 1997. "Epilogue: Work and Family Column." *The Wall Street Journal,* B1.

28. Kwasha, L. 1996. In "When Work and Private Life Collide: Fascinating Facts." Minneapolis: Ceridian Performance Partners. Handout.

29. Bond, J., Galinsky, E., and Swanberg, J. 1998. *The 1997 National Study of the Changing Workforce.* New York, NY: Families and Work Institute.

30. Brett, J., Stroh, L., and Reilly, A. 1992. "What Is It Like Being a Dual-Career Manager in the 1990s?" In S. Zedeck, ed., *Work, Families, and Organizations.* San Francisco: Jossey-Bass, 138–167.

31. Shellenbarger, S. Apr. 15, 1998. "Good News at Last in the Battle of the Sexes: Men are Helping More." Work and Family Column, *The Wall Street Journal,* B1.

32. Duxbury, L. and Higgins, C. 1991. Gender Differences in Work-Family Conflict. *Journal of Applied Psychology,* 76:60–74; Rice, R., Frone, M., and McFarlin, D. 1992. "Work-Nonwork Conflict and the Perceived Quality of Life." *Journal of Organizational Behavior,* 13:155–168.

33. Kossek, E. E. and Nichol, V. 1992. "The Effects of On Site Child Care on Employee Attitudes and Performance." *Personnel Psychology,* 45:485–509.

34. Rothausen, T. J. 1994. "Job Satisfaction and the Parent Worker: The Role of Flexibility and Rewards." *Journal of Vocational Behavior,* 44:317–336.

35. *HR News.* 1997. In "When Work and Private Life Collide: Fascinating Facts." Minneapolis: Ceridian Performance Partners. Handout.

36. Forthofer, M. S., Markman, H., Cox, M., Stanley, S., Kessler, R. 1996. "Associations Between Martial Distress and Work-Loss in a National Sample." *Journal of Marriage and the Family,* 58:597–605.

37. Towers Perrin, *Work/Life Programs.*

38. Kossek, E. E. and Ozeki, C. 1998. "Work-Family Conflict, Policies, and the Job-Life Satisfaction Relationship: A Review and Directions for OB/HR Research." *Journal of Applied Psychology,* 83:139–149. Kossek, E.E. and Ozeki, C. 1999. "Bridging the Work-Family Policy and Productivity Gap." *International Journal of Community Work and Family,* 2(1): 7–32.

39. MacDuffie, J. P. 1995. "Human Resource Bundles and Manufacturing Performance: Flexible Production Systems in the World Auto Industry." *Industrial Relations,* 34:2, 147–168.

40. Lawrence, S. and Fadel, J. 1993. "Total Compensation Plan Design: The Dollars and Sense of Adding Domestic Partner Health Coverage." *Compensation and Benefits Management,* 82–86.

41. Pennings, J., Lee, K., Witteloostuijn, A. 1998. "Human Capital, Social Capital, and Firm Dissolution." *Academy of Management Journal,* 41(4):425–440; Reichheld, F. 1996. *The Loyalty Effect.* Cambridge, MA: Harvard Business School Press.

42. Huselid M. A., Jackson, S. E., Schuler, R. 1997. Technical and Strategic Human Resource Management Effectiveness as Determinants of Firm Performance, *Academy of Management Journal,* 40:171–188.

43. Rapport R., and Bailyn, L. (1996). *Rethinking Life and Work: Toward a Better Future.* New York: Ford Foundation.

44. Ibid.

Index

....

Absenteeism, 11.13

Barriers to change, 11.8
Benefit programs, 11.9

Career issues, 11.8, 11.10, 11.14
Company-sponsored day-care, 11.4, 11.12
Competing demand conflict, 11.10–11
Compressed workweeks, 11.4
Computers, 11.12
Corporate involvement, 11.10
Cross-functional collaboration, 11.17
Cultural change, 11.4, 11.5, 11.12
Cultural issues, 11.7, 11.8, 11.10, 11.17
Cultural support, 11.9, 11.15

Diversity, 11.9, 11.11, 11.12, 11.15

Efficiency objectives (organizational), 11.13
Employee ability, 11.8
Employee assistance, 11.4
Employee selection, 11.8
Employees as internal customers, 11.12
Employer support, 11.4
Employer/employee partnership, 11.8, 11.10
Empowered workforce, 11.4, 11.12

Family and Medical Leave Act, 11.4, 11.6
Family friendly, 11.7
Family needs, 11.6, 11.7, 11.8, 11.9
Family-supportive policies, 11.5
Flexible spending accounts, 11.4
Flexible work options, 11.8, 11.11, 11.12
Flextime, 11.8
Full-time workers, 11.15

Greedy workplace, 11.14

Hand-off approach (management), 11.14
Hochschild, Arlie: *The Time Bind: When Home
    Becomes Work and Work Becomes Home,*
    11.14
Holistic work/life programs, 11.12. *See also*
    Work/life policies
Human relations model of management, 11.11,
    11.12
Human resource management, 11.8, 11.9,
    11.10, 11.11, 11.12, 11.13
Human resource policies, 11.4, 11.9, 11.16.
    See also Work/life policies
Human resource roles, 11.6
Human resource strategy, 11.6, 11.15

Individualistic culture, 11.8, 11.17. *See also*
    Cultural issues
Invasion of privacy, 11.14

Job security, 11.4
Juggling workload demands, 11.13

Leave of absence, 11.6, 11.11
Lifestyles, 11.6, 11.17

Management commitment, 11.10
Mixed messages, 11.10, 11.11

National Study of the Changing Workforce,
    11.15
Noncareer-oriented employees, 11.9
Nonwork issues, 11.8, 11.10, 11.11, 11.12–15.
    See also Work/life balance, Workplace
    issues

Omniscient organization, 11.13–14
Organizational culture, 11.5, 11.17. *See also*
    Cultural issues
Organizational perspective, 11.10

Part-time work, 11.4, 11.8
Performance, 11.8, 11.10, 11.11. 11.14, 11.16
Personal life, employer involvement in, 11.10,
    11.13
Personal life needs, 11.7, 11.9, 11.12, 11.13,
    11.16
Potential self, 11.14
Primary priority, 11.6
Privacy concerns, 11.13, 11.14
Productivity issues, 11.8, 11.9, 11.10, 11.11,
    11.15

Quality management, 11.9, 11.11

Rational goal approach, 11.11. *See also*
    Work/life policies
Recognition, career-minded employees, 11.14
Referral programs, 11.4
Responsiveness as management challenge,
    11.15
Reward system, 11.8
Rewarding family life, 11.15. *See also*
    Work/family issues

Self-management, telecommuting employees,
    11.14
Senior women in business, 11.8

Separation of work and family, 11.12. *See also* Work/family issues

Single working parents, 11.15, 11.16

Social arbiter approach, 11.11, 11.13–14. *See also* Work/life policies

Social capital, 11.15–16

Soft issues, 11.10

Strategic issues, 11.15

Stressed employees, 11.11, 11.17

Supervisor resistance, 11.8

Supervisory judgment, 11.14

Systems approach, 11.12. *See also* Work/life policies

Technological issues, 11.12, 11.13

Telecommunicating employees, 11.14

The Time Bind: When Home Becomes Work and Work Becomes Home, by Arlie Hochschild, 11.14

Time and place flexibility, 11.4. *See also* Flexible work options

Unpaid personal leave, 11.4

Virtual workplace, 11.11. *See also* Telecommunicating employees

Whole-person approach, 11.12, 11.13-14. *See also* Work/life policies

Work culture, 11.7, 11.15. *See also* Cultural issues

Work overload, 11.14

Work-at-home, 11.8, 11.13. *See also* Telecommuting employees

Work/family issues, 11.4, 11.6–7, 11.8, 11.9, 11.10, 11.11, 11.12, 11.14, 11.17

Work/family perspective, 11.16. *See also* Work/life policies

Work/life balance, 11.6, 11.7, 11.9, 11.10–11, 11.12, 11.13, 11.14–16

Work/life policies, 11.4, 11.6, 11.7, 11.9, 11.11–12, 11.13–14, 11.15–16

Workaholic cultures, 11.5

Workforce diversity, 11.9. *See also* Diversity

Workplace issues, 11.9, 11.10

Workstyles, 11.6, 11.14

MODULE
11

MANAGING HUMAN RESOURCES
IN THE 21st CENTURY

From Core Concepts to Strategic Choice

MODULE 12

Workforce Planning for Flexibility
Staffing with Temporary Employees

Karen Roberts
MICHIGAN STATE UNIVERSITY

Sandra E. Gleason
THE PENNSYLVANIA STATE UNIVERSITY

Managing Human Resources in the 21st Century: From Core Concepts to Strategic Choice,
by Kossek and Block

Publisher: Dave Shaut
Executive Editor: John Szilagyi
Developmental Editor: Bryant Editorial Development
Marketing Manager: Joseph A. Sabatino
Production Editor: Tamborah E. Moore
Manufacturing Coordinator: Dana Began Schwartz
Cover Design: Tin Box Studio
Cover Photographs: Copyright Shoji Sato/Photonica
Production House: The Left Coast Group, Inc.
Printer: West Group

Printed in the United States of America
1 2 3 4 5 02 01 00 99

For more information contact South-Western College Publishing, 5101 Madison Road, Cincinnati,
Ohio, 45227 or find us on the Internet at *http://www.swcollege.com*
For permission to use material from this text or product, contact us by
- telephone: 1-800-730-2214
- fax: 1-800-730-2215
- web: *http://www.thomsonrights.com*

ISBN: 0–324–01811–8

This book is printed on acid-free paper.

Contents

MODULE OVERVIEW   12.4

OBJECTIVES   12.4

RELATION TO THE FRAME   12.4

CORE CONCEPTS IN WORFORCE PLANNING   12.5

What Is Contingent Work? Types of Alternative Employment Arrangements   12.5

Who Are Contingent Workers? Characteristics of the Workforce
in Alternative Employment Arrangements   12.6

How to Use Alternative Work Arrangements to Advance Organizational
Strategic Goals   12.10

STRATEGIC ISSUES IN WORKFORCE PLANNING   12.11

Contingent Workers as Strategic Response   12.12

APPLICATION   12.13

Step 1: Calculate the Costs of Using Core (Core Cost) and Temporary
(Contingent) Workers (Temp Cost)   12.16

Step 2: Calculate Per-Unit-of-Time Productivity for Core Workers
(Core Productivity)   12.16

Step 3: Calculate the Productivity Needed from Contingent Workers   12.17

Step 4: Calculate the Cost of Training Contingent Workers   12.19

Step 5: Calculate How Long It Will Take to Recover Training Costs   12.19

IN CONCLUSION   12.20

Debrief   12.20

Suggested Readings   12.21

Relevant Web Sites   12.21

Critical Thinking Questions   12.22

INDEX   12.23

MODULE
12

12.3

MODULE OVERVIEW

This module discusses the concepts needed to make decisions about the use of temporary or contingent employees to achieve operational flexibility. Contingent workers can be hired in a wide variety of employment arrangements ranging from low-skilled part-time employees hired day to day to engineers and computer programmers hired on annual contracts. However, they are distinguished by a nontraditional employment arrangement, i.e., they are not permanent, full-time employees of a single organization.

The module discusses the three core concepts needed to make flexible staffing decisions: What contingent work is, who the contingent workers are, and how contingent workers can be used to achieve strategic objectives. It then provides an application tool that shows how to use cost-benefit analysis to make strategic staffing decisions. It reviews the strategic issues that employers must consider when planning for flexibility. A spreadsheet exercise is then presented that demonstrates the use of these concepts in determining the cost-effectiveness of using contingent workers. This exercise demonstrates that cost-effectiveness will vary with the type of job and skills needed, as well as by company due to different cost structures.

OBJECTIVES

This module has four objectives, each of which correspond to the core concepts related to the use of contingent workers and the application tool. Before discussing those objectives, a few points about terminology should be noted. There are multiple synonyms for contingent work and the activities surrounding the use of contingent workers. Among those most commonly heard are "strategic staffing," "market-mediated work arrangements," "temporary help," and "alternative work arrangements." In this module, "contingent work" and "alternative work" (or employment) arrangements are used interchangeably. A full definition is provided in the section "What Is Contingent Work?" In addition, the terms "employer," "organization," and "firm" are used interchangeably in this module. In the discussion of using temporary help or contract workers, the term "client firm" refers to the organization that contracts with the contingent worker (or temporary agency) for some purpose.

By the end of this module, the reader should be familiar with three central concepts related to the use of contingent workers and know how to use the application tool. The module objectives are:

- To provide readers with an in-depth definition of contingent work

- To familiarize readers with the characteristics of contingent workers and what they want

- To present a framework for integrating the use of contingent workers into the firm's strategic plan

- To present a tool for analyzing the cost-effectiveness of using contingent workers

RELATION TO THE FRAME

As practiced by most employers, flexible staffing represents an example of *transformation* activities since it is designed to assist the organization in adapting to its rapidly changing competitive environment. It also includes some *transition* activities since it must be planned in conjunction with "right sizing"—training current permanent employees in multiple skills and training contingent employees to be most effective in the organization. Unless the organization is unionized, these activities are largely *unilateral* on the part of the employer. In the presence of a union, the parties would be required to

FIGURE 12.1 *A Frame for Understanding Human Resource Strategy:*
Context, Roles, and Constraints

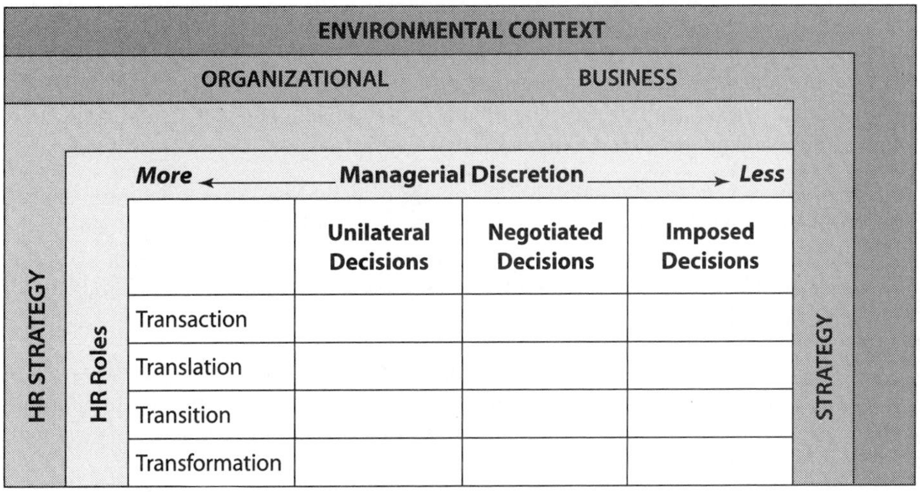

ENVIRONMENTAL CONTEXT			
ORGANIZATIONAL		BUSINESS	

More ← ———— **Managerial Discretion** ———— → *Less*

HR STRATEGY	HR Roles		Unilateral Decisions	Negotiated Decisions	Imposed Decisions	STRATEGY
		Transaction				
		Translation				
		Transition				
		Transformation				

© 2000 by Ellen Ernst Kossek and Richard Block. Thanks to Brian Pentland, Karen Markel, and John Beck for helpful comments and discussions that enhanced the model.

negotiate the conditions under which temporary workers could be hired to do work that was traditionally done by employees in the bargaining unit. For example, some collective agreements permit the employer to hire temporary workers only if there are no regular employees on layoff. Outsourcing has typically been a highly contentious issue between employers and unions due to the loss of unionized jobs that usually results. See Figure 12.1, A Frame for Understanding Human Resource Strategy.

CORE CONCEPTS IN WORKFORCE PLANNING

There are three core concepts that must be understood prior to strategically planning for flexibility in a constantly changing competitive environment:

- What is contingent work? Types of alternative work arrangements

- Who are the contingent workers? Characteristics of the workforce in alternative work arrangements

- How to use alternative work arrangements to advance organizational strategic goals

    Each of these core concepts is discussed in detail below.

What Is Contingent Work? Types of Alternative Employment Arrangements

The phrase "contingent workers" was coined by Audrey Freedman in 1985 to refer to workers whose work is contingent on the employer's need for them (Nollen and Axel 1996). While contingent employment takes many forms, it is best understood by what it is not—permanent, full-time employment with a single employer—as indicated in the two definitions below:

> Any job in which an individual does not have an explicit or implicit contract for long term employment and where minimum hours worked can vary in an unsystematic manner. (Polivka and Nardone 1989)

Contingent workers are people who have little or no attachment to the company at which they work. Whether they work, when they work, and how much they work depends on the company's need for them. They have neither an explicit nor implicit contract for continuing employment. (Nollen and Axel 1996)

Contingent work arrangements can take multiple forms including temporary help service workers, leased employees, on-call day workers, independent contractors, self-employed consultants, and part-time workers.

- *Temporary help service employees* are those directly hired by a temporary staffing firm or perhaps part of an in-house temporary staffing pool. Assignments, pay, and scheduling are determined by the staffing firm. Usually, assignments are short-term, and schedules are erratic. Often, temporary workers will be comingled with regular workers during the assignment.

- *Leased employees* are also employed by an outside firm. Typically, their assignments are longer term than those of temporary help service workers. In addition, leased workers are assigned to a discrete function and are not comingled with regular workers.

- *On-call day workers* are employees called upon on an as-needed basis usually from an informally constituted hiring pool associated with a particular employer or group of employers. They may have specialized skills that are used intermittently for which the employer pays a daily or hourly rate. Or they may be relatively unskilled labor.

- *Independent contractors* are employees working according to a specific contract. Usually they know precisely when their assignment will be completed. They may be brought in for a specific task or project, but they are not employees of any firm.

- *Self-employed consultants* are much like independent contractors in that they do not work for a particular employer. They are more likely to offer services to multiple employers as opposed to working full-time on a specific job. Further, they usually do not work on-site.

- *Part-time workers* are not always considered to be contingent workers because they may work on a regular or permanent basis for a single employer. Some have job security, benefits, and regular schedules. Others are treated as on-call workers. In the United States, a worker who works fewer than 35 hours a week is considered a part-time employee.

Thus, the key features of contingent work arrangements are that they are associated with job insecurity and irregular work schedules. Although often these workers have a strong attachment to the labor force, there is usually a lack of attachment to a particular company.

Who Are Contingent Workers? Characteristics of the Workforce in Alternative Employment Arrangements

One of the difficulties in assessing the extent of contingent work arrangements arises out of the instability of the employment relationship and the frequent movement in and out of contingent work status. Until 1995, contingent work was typically measured as employment in the temporary help industry, SIC 731, and part-time workers, and in February of the same year, the U.S. Bureau of Labor Statistics (BLS) initiated a special survey as part of the February Current Population Survey in February 1995. This survey was designed to measure change in the use of alternative work arrangements over time, and so it was readministered again in February 1997.

The BLS used two different approaches to measuring contingent work. The first measure was based on alternative employment arrangements. Four types of arrangements were included:

- Independent contractors

- On-call workers

- Workers paid by temporary help agencies

- Contract workers

The second measure focused on the degree of job insecurity in the workforce by dividing the workforce into three categories:

- Wage and salary workers who expect their jobs to last an additional year or less and who have worked at their jobs for less than one year

- Workers including self-employed and independent contractors who expect employment to last no more than one year and who have been at the jobs for less than one year

- Workers who do not expect their job to last more than one year even if they have been on the job for more than one year.

The findings are reported in Tables 12.1 and 12.2 for 1997 and discussed below.

Using the first measure of alternative employment arrangements, 9.9 percent of the workforce was found to be working under such conditions in 1997. Of these, the largest group was independent contractors, 6.7 percent of the workforce. Those employed by temporary help agencies only account for about 1 percent of the workforce, despite the rapid growth in that industry. Table 12.1 on page xx shows the composition of those employed in both alternative and traditional arrangements by race, education level, gender, and age as of the February 1997 survey. That table shows that independent contractors are disproportionately white male college graduates between the ages of 35 and 55. Women under the age of 55 and black workers are disproportionately represented in the temporary help services industry.

Table 12.1 also shows the occupational composition of workers in both alternative and traditional work arrangements. Some of the traditional patterns hold: temporary help agency workers are disproportionately concentrated in administrative support occupations. Twenty-one percent of the on-call and day laborers are in professional occupations compared with 15 percent in traditional arrangements, suggesting that this category includes many self-employed professionals. Similarly, professional and technical occupations are disproportionately represented among contract workers.

Using the second measure based on job insecurity, 4.9 percent of the workforce who might reasonably expect employment security describe themselves as facing employment insecurity. Two and two-tenths (2.2) percent could be classified as working under a traditional arrangement but have worked in their current job for under a year and expect that they will not be in the same job for another year. Two and eight-tenths (2.8) percent of those working in nontraditional arrangements that could possibly last for a long time, self-employed and independent contractors, have been at their current assignment for less than a year and do not expect it will last another year. Four and nine-tenths (4.9) percent have been at their current jobs for more than one year in either traditional or alternative work arrangements, but do not expect the job to last another year.

In general, individuals in alternative employment arrangements are paid less than those in traditional arrangements and are less likely to be receiving nonwage benefits. According to the Bureau of Labor Statistics, in February 1997, the average weekly earnings for all workers in traditional work arrangements were $510. Contract workers and independent contractors, on average, earned more than that: $619 and $523, respectively. However, on-call workers and those from temporary help agencies earned

TABLE 12.1 *Characteristics of Contingent Workers, 1997*

	Contract Workers	Temporary Help Services	On-Call and Day Laborers	Independent Contractors	Traditional Arrangements
Race					
White	82%	75%	89%	91%	85%
Black	13%	21%	8%	5%	11%
Hispanic origin	6%	12%	13%	7%	10%
Education					
Less than high school	7%	11%	13%	9%	10%
High school graduate	37%	31%	29%	30%	33%
Some college	23%	36%	32%	27%	28%
College graduate	33%	22%	26%	34%	30%
Gender and Age					
Males					
20 to 24	8%	10%	6%	2%	5%
25 to 34	24%	15%	12%	11%	14%
35 to 44	22%	7%	12%	21%	15%
45 to 54	9%	6%	7%	18%	11%
55 to 64	5%	2%	4%	10%	5%
65 +	9%	2%	3%	5%	1%
Females					
20 to 24	0%	7%	5%	1%	5%
25 to 34	10%	15%	11%	7%	12%
35 to 44	9%	15%	13%	10%	13%
45 to 54	5%	10%	8%	9%	10%
55 to 64	3%	4%	6%	4%	4%
65 +	2%	1%	4%	2%	1%
Occupation					
Executive, Administrative, Managerial	8%	7%	3%	21%	14%
Professional	20%	8%	21%	18%	15%
Technicians	7%	4%	4%	1%	3%
Sales	3%	3%	7%	18%	12%
Administrative support	5%	30%	9%	4%	15%
Service occupations	28%	9%	20%	9%	14%
Precision production, craft, repair	20%	6%	15%	18%	10%
Operators, fabricators, laborers	9%	33%	19%	7%	14%
Farm, fish, and forest	0%	1%	3%	5%	2%

Source: http://www.bls.gov/news.release/conemp.toc.htm

considerably less than the average for traditional employment arrangement workers and noncontingent workers: $432 and $329, respectively. This variation is primarily a function of patterns among white male workers. Women and black workers both male and female in alternative work arrangements earned less than their traditional counterparts regardless of the type of alternative arrangement. Independent contractors of Hispanic origin earned more than traditional Hispanic-origin workers, but those in other alternative work arrangements earned less.

Table 12.2A, below, and Table 12.2B on page 12.10 show the availability of pension coverage and health insurance coverage for contingent and noncontingent workers. As Table 12.2A shows, the differences in pension coverage are fairly dramatic: workers in traditional employment arrangements are three times more likely to have pension coverage than those in nontraditional arrangements. Further, this does not seem to vary much by gender, race/national heritage, or educational level of the worker. Table 12.2B shows that the gap between workers in traditional and nontraditional arrangements in health insurance coverage is not nearly so great as with pensions. However, Table 12.2B also shows this gap widening significantly if the question of coverage is framed in terms of employer-provided insurance. Then traditional workers tend to be about two times more likely to have employer-provided insurance.

There is always some discussion about the extent to which workers in alternative work arrangements would prefer to be working in traditional arrangements. In general, alternative work arrangements are thought to be beneficial for working mothers, college students, retirees, the short-run unemployed, and those moving back into or gradually out of the labor market by choice. To some extent, the share of workers preferring contingent work is sensitive to the business cycle: the tighter the labor market, the more likely that those in alternative arrangements prefer to be there.

TABLE 12.2A *Pension and Health Insurance Coverage, 1997*

	CONTINGENT WORKERS		NONCONTINGENT WORKERS	
	Percent with Pension Coverage	Percent Eligible for Employer Provided Pension	Percent with Pension Coverage	Percent Eligible for Employer Provided Pension
Total	15.3	22.2	49.5	56.5
Male	16.8	24.5	51.4	57.7
Female	13.9	19.9	47.3	55.1
White	16.8	23.7	49.9	56.8
Black	10.7	18.3	49.5	57.5
Hispanic Origin	5	8	32	37.9
Full-time	22	31.2	56.7	63.9
Part-time	6.6	10.6	16.7	22.8
HS Grads	14	22.7	46.3	54
Some College	16.6	21.4	51.4	58.6
AA degree	19.9	27.4	58.8	66.4
BA degree	28.2	38	67.9	73.6

Source: http://www.bls.gov/news.release/conemp.toc.htm

TABLE 12.2B   *Wage and Salary Workers with Health Insurance Coverage, 1997*

	CONTINGENT WORKERS			NONCONTINGENT WORKERS		
	Percent with Health Insurance	Percent Insured Through Employer	Percent Eligible for Employer Provided Insurance	Percent with Health Insurance	Percent Insured Through Employer	Percent Eligible for Employer Provided Insurance
Total	65.1	22.4	34.1	82.9	61.6	73.9
Male	62.8	26.1	36.9	82.2	66.6	76.5
Female	67.5	18.7	31.4	83.7	56	71.1
White	69.1	22.8	34.5	84.3	61.8	74.2
Black	48.9	19.3	31.4	75.9	61	73.5
Hispanic Origin	27.4	10.6	15.5	63	50.1	60
Full-time	62.7	32.2	46.1	85.2	71.4	83
Part-time	68.3	10	19	72.9	17.4	33.1
High School Graduates	59.4	20.2	33.8	80.2	60.3	73.7
Some College	61.6	21.8	31.7	84.3	64.3	77.9
AA degree	69.8	28.7	38.9	89.7	69.1	82.3
BA degree	80.3	40.9	54.2	93.5	77.3	87.2

Source: http://www.bls.gov/news.release/conemp.toc.htm

   Table 12.3 shows the preferences by type of arrangement according to the BLS February 1997 survey. What is clear is that preferences vary depending on type of contingent arrangement. For those jobs where the pay tends to be lower and where there are more women and minorities, there is a greater preference for traditional employment. Having said that, less than two-thirds of temporary help workers and only slightly more than half of on-call workers prefer traditional arrangements.

TABLE 12.3   *Work Arrangement Preferences of Contingent Workers, 1997 (Percent)*

	Independent Contractors	On-Call/Day Laborers	Temporary Agency Workers
Prefer Traditional Arrangement	9.8	57.9	63.3
Prefer Alternative Arrangement	82.5	35.8	26.6

Source: http://www.bls.gov/news.release/conemp.toc.htm

How to Use Alternative Work Arrangements to Advance Organizational Strategic Goals

Organizations need to engage in strategic staffing, not crisis management. This involves the application of strategic human resource planning to decisions about use of core versus contingent workers. As discussed below in more detail, an organization's core employees are those who provide the skills and expertise to support the basic, or core, competencies needed to keep its primary business activities competitive. Employees needed to perform other work are more peripheral and therefore are potential candidates for alternative employment arrangements. For example, a core employee for a computer software company would be an expert in software development, while a janitor needed to keep the offices clean would be a peripheral employee.

Strategic human resources management refers to integrating decisions about human resources with specific strategic choices made by the organization. The rationale for managing human resources strategically is fourfold (Lengnick-Hall and Lengnick-Hall 1998):

- It allows the organization to solve more complex problems.

- The use of a variety of resource types is considered simultaneously (financial, technological, human).

- The skills and abilities of the current workforce are taken into consideration.

- Strategic goals are less likely to be subordinated to the limits of the current human resources within the organization.

Strategic human resource planning requires a focus on both the short-term and long-term goals. In applying strategic human resource planning to contingent employment, three dimensions must be considered: the strategic goals of the organization, core competencies, and organizational culture.

STRATEGIC ISSUES IN WORKFORCE PLANNING

The economy of the United States has been undergoing a fundamental restructuring since the early 1950s. Following World War II, the nation was still heavily rural, but it began to reduce its dependence on jobs linked to agriculture due to technological changes in the agricultural sector, thereby shifting employment to nonfarm sectors. The technological changes more recently set in motion by new developments in information technology since the 1980s have again fomented dramatic changes in the mix of industries and the structure of employment and occupations. In addition, technology has allowed competition to become increasingly global, thereby adding new types of uncertainties and risks to the competitive environment of many firms. Technology is expected to continue to generate increasingly rapid changes well into the twenty-first century. The organizations that adapt to the forces of change will have new opportunities to grow and expand, while those ignoring or resisting change will find it increasingly difficult to compete and survive (Deavers 1997).

MODULE
12

These new stresses are occurring simultaneously in the United States with two other forces for change. First, fixed employment costs have increased as legally required benefits (social security, workers' compensation, and unemployment insurance contributions) and other nonwage benefits have risen as a share of total compensation. Second, greater workforce diversity has generated new demands on employers to become more family-friendly and more tolerant of differences among employees.

The basic strategy issue, therefore, is: How can an organization plan its staffing in a flexible manner to continuously and smoothly adapt in a rapidly changing environment? Employers are interested in three types of flexibility. *Functional* flexibility permits the rapid deployment of employees between different activities and assigned tasks. This permits the labor force to change as products and production methods change. *Numerical* flexibility allows the number of employees and hours and patterns of work to be changed quickly in response to product demand changes. Finally, *financial* flexibility includes seeking both ways to hire labor to reduce costs and new systems of compensation such as outsourcing.

Contingent Workers as Strategic Response

There are at least five situations commonly cited by employers in which the use of contingent workers reflects a strategic response in this environment, as follows.

Handling Fluctuations In Business Activity.   First, having some work done by a contingent workforce allows the organization to more easily handle fluctuations in business activity—whether increases or decreases. It makes it easier to adjust both the number and types of employees, as well as the hours and patterns of work, to meet changes in demand. Such staffing also allows core employees to concentrate on those activities critical to the competitive health of the firm.

Reducing Labor Costs.   In addition, using a contingent workforce can reduce labor costs. For example, the employer may be able to avoid paying some payroll costs such as social security contributions, unemployment insurance, and workers' compensation insurance, as well as more selectively offering fringe benefits such as health and life insurance, vacation and holiday pay, paid sick leave, pension contributions, and bonuses. In some situations this may lead an organization to hire workers in other countries employed at wages lower than those in the United States. This, however, is not necessarily a solution to reducing labor cost. Lower wages often reflect lower levels of labor productivity.

Reducing Time Spent In-House on Administrative Functions.   Another variation on the theme of reducing labor cost is reducing the in-house time spent on the administration of human resource activities and monitoring workplace regulations. Examples of the former include hiring, record keeping for pay and benefits, etc. A high-quality temporary staffing firm may more cost-effectively provide these services for some employee groups such as secretaries and word processing staff. This also may provide a way for both the temporary employee and the employer to mutually screen prior to changing to a permanent employment arrangement. In the case of workplace regulations, if the core employee group is kept small enough, then the organization may be exempt from some regulations. An example is the Americans with Disabilities Act of 1990 (ADA) that applies only if an organization has 15 or more employees, or the Family Medical and Leave Act of 1993 (FMLA) which requires 50 or more employees.

Subcontracting for a Specific Project.   Fourth, for a specific and limited time period the organization may need to hire a special set of skills for which there will be no further need after a project is completed. A common example is hiring highly skilled computer programmers to develop and install customized software. This type of contingent worker often can be hired by subcontracting with another organization. For example, subcontracting may provide access to more highly qualified personnel than a small firm could afford to hire as permanent employees.

Avoiding Layoffs and Protecting Workers' Security.   Finally, the use of contingent workers can protect the organization's core employees from job insecurity and help the organization avoid painful and expensive layoffs. This can be important for the morale and productivity of the core employee group, particularly in an era marked by employee concerns about job loss through downsizing. It also may improve the reputation of the organization as one that treats its employees well.

To decide whether to pursue one or more of the strategic uses of alternative work just discussed, an organization must first identify its core competencies and consider its culture. The core competencies of an organization are those that are difficult for competitors to imitate and that make a significant contribution to meeting customer

MODULE
12

needs in the end product and provide access to a wide variety of markets. Consequently, an employer should keep as core employees those who provide the skills and expertise to support its core competencies. Employees needed to perform other work are potential candidates for contingent employment in a wide array of employment arrangements.

The following questions will help identify an organization's core competencies:

- What do we do best? What is our primary business?

- Which functions support our organizational strategy?

- What critical knowledge/skills do we need to maintain within our organization?

- What are our current and future staffing needs?

- What are the direct business reasons for using contingent work arrangements?

By carefully considering each of these issues, the organization can identify those jobs that require core workers with a strong commitment to the employer's success. This, in turn, permits an organization to effectively use the many varieties of contingent work arrangements. For example, if significant in-depth, firm-specific knowledge is needed, then core workers, permanent part-time employees, or leased workers can be used. If much independence on the job is needed, then an independent contractor who is usually self-employed and used to working without supervision can be hired. If the staffing need is long term but cyclical, temporary help or on-call part-timers can be used. If the need is for a short-term and nonrecurring employee, a temporary firm worker is indicated.

Decisions about which arrangement to use should be based on a clear knowledge of the needs of a business. In some cases, achieving flexibility may be more important; in others, cost-effectiveness may be the major objective. Using contingent workers is not always the best solution and therefore must be evaluated carefully. The presence of a union will further complicate this decision-making process, since the union contract may place limitations on options in the short term. Similarly, tensions over pay differences between part-time and full-time employees can precipitate tensions and even a strike as in the case of the UPS strike in 1997.

Even though an organization desires staffing flexibility, it has to consider the expectations of its organizational culture in determining how to achieve this flexibility. In some cultures the use of temporary workers is unacceptable. If there is a strong hire-from-within culture, then it may be necessary to use an internal temporary pool of workers rather than going outside the organization. Where there is a strong "people matter" culture, then approaches should be selected that support this value. Examples include an internal temporary pool, forming a close relationship with a staffing firm so some "regular" temporary employees are supplied, and/or a commitment to training temporary employees even if it is possible that the "temp" will leave before the project is completed.

MODULE
12

APPLICATION

The cost-effectiveness of using temporary, leased, or on-call workers as compared to in-house employees will vary from job to job and across organizations. What is a strategically logical decision in one setting may not be so in another. Part of thinking strategically about human resources management is the rational evaluation of the relative costs and benefits of having work done by core employers compared to using contingent workers.

This section of the module presents a five-step process for analyzing the cost-effectiveness of using workers under alternative versus traditional work arrangements for a particular job. The process is presented in Figure 12.2, "Calculating the Cost-Effectiveness of Using a Temporary Employee." This figure reproduces an Excel spreadsheet that is used to make the necessary calculations.

Figure 12.2 presents an example where the employer needs software to be written and is trying to decide between using in-house software engineers who would have to work and thus be paid overtime in order to get the work done in a timely fashion; and contract software engineers who would be temporary employees of a temporary help firm specializing in computer-related occupations. It is assumed in this example that the engineers are paid on an hourly basis. The calculations can be adapted to some other unit of time such as weekly, monthly, or a custom unit tailored to reflect expected project length.

FIGURE 12.2   *Calculating the Cost-Effectiveness of Using a Temporary Employee*

FIGURE 12.2 *continued*

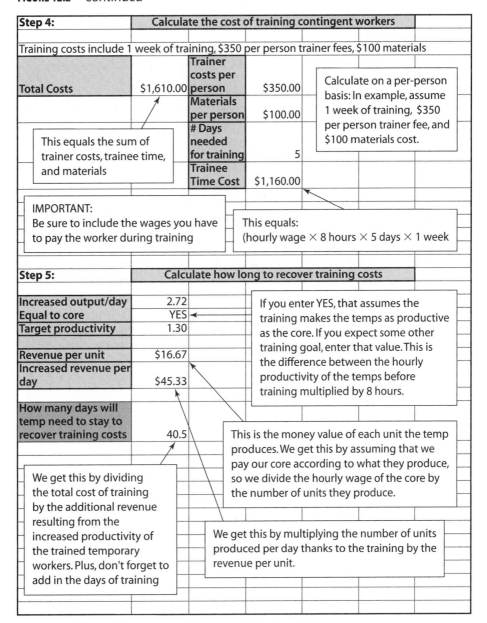

Step 4:		Calculate the cost of training contingent workers		
Training costs include 1 week of training, $350 per person trainer fees, $100 materials				
Total Costs	$1,610.00	Trainer costs per person	$350.00	Calculate on a per-person basis: In example, assume 1 week of training, $350 per person trainer fee, and $100 materials cost.
		Materials per person	$100.00	
This equals the sum of trainer costs, trainee time, and materials		# Days needed for training	5	
		Trainee Time Cost	$1,160.00	
IMPORTANT: Be sure to include the wages you have to pay the worker during training		This equals: (hourly wage × 8 hours × 5 days × 1 week		

Step 5:		Calculate how long to recover training costs		
Increased output/day	2.72	If you enter YES, that assumes the training makes the temps as productive as the core. If you expect some other training goal, enter that value. This is the difference between the hourly productivity of the temps before training multiplied by 8 hours.		
Equal to core	YES			
Target productivity	1.30			
Revenue per unit	$16.67			
Increased revenue per day	$45.33			
How many days will temp need to stay to recover training costs	40.5	This is the money value of each unit the temp produces. We get this by assuming that we pay our core according to what they produce, so we divide the hourly wage of the core by the number of units they produce.		
We get this by dividing the total cost of training by the additional revenue resulting from the increased productivity of the trained temporary workers. Plus, don't forget to add in the days of training		We get this by multiplying the number of units produced per day thanks to the training by the revenue per unit.		

MODULE
12

The steps in the process are:

Step 1. Calculate the costs of using core and contingent workers.

Step 2. Calculate the per-unit-of-time productivity of core workers.

Step 3. Calculate the per hour productivity needed from contingent workers.

Step 4. Calculate the training costs for contingent workers, if training is needed.

Step 5. Calculate how long it will take to recover training costs (if contingent workers are to be trained).

Step 1: *Calculate the Costs of Using Core (Core Cost) and Temporary (Contingent) Workers (Temp Cost)*

These are the data you will need:

- The hourly rate for your core workers for each job category (from your own payroll data)

- The hourly rate for temporary workers (from the temporary help firm or the workers themselves, if using a direct contract)

- Cost of paying your core employees overtime if overtime is incurred by not using contingent workers

The cost calculation in the example is based on the simplifying assumption that the only cost associated with both core and contingent workers is the hourly wage. To improve the accuracy of the analysis, more realistic cost estimates can easily be incorporated into the spreadsheet. The obvious additional costs are the nonwage payroll costs associated with core workers. These include the benefits required by statute (unemployment insurance, workers' compensation, and social security) as well as other nonrequired benefits that the employer may offer its employees (health, life, and/or disability insurance, pension contributions, paid time off, and perhaps others). The information necessary to calculate the true hourly costs for core workers is available from the organization's own human resources (HR) department. In the example, it is assumed that core employees would have to work overtime to complete the project, so the overtime cell is set equal to YES. Per-unit costs of temporary workers can be easily obtained either from the temporary help agency, if that is the hiring mechanism, or from the temporary worker directly if using independent contractors or self-employed consultants.

The worksheet shows the hourly wage as the only cost; however, according to the Bureau of Labor Statistics, nonwage benefits add approximately 30 percent to the cost of core employees. In addition, there are likely to be other noncompensation costs associated with core employees that may not be readily quantified by an HR department, such as morale costs associated with overtime or additional workload. Similarly, there may be nonwage costs associated with using contingent workers. These take multiple forms. If the work is done on-site, there may be costs associated with the provision of workspace, equipment, and other materials. It is likely that the temporary worker will need some orientation, some ongoing supervision, and perhaps some training. Training is explicitly incorporated into the analysis in Steps 4 and 5.

There are two common ways to handle uncertainty about difficult-to-quantify costs (or benefits) in a cost/benefit analysis. One is to estimate several cases to show a range of cost estimates. Typically, this would include a base- or average-cost case, a low-cost case, and a high-cost case. You can then examine the sensitivity (variability) of the results to whichever case is assumed. The other, more qualitative, method is to incorporate the nonquantifiable effects into the interpretation of the results and the final decisions that are made based on the quantified results. If benefits and costs are approximately equal, assumptions about the difficult-to-quantify costs and benefits can be determining factors.

Step 2: *Calculate the Per-Unit-of-Time Productivity of Core Workers (Core Productivity)*

For this step you will need to know the productivity of the core workers in your organization. These are data you will need.

- The per-unit-of-time (for example, hourly or daily) productivity of the core workers in your organization. Our example uses hours as the unit of time.

- You will need to generate at least three estimates to handle the associated uncertainty: a base- or average-productivity case, a higher-productivity scenario, and a lower-productivity scenario.

Depending on the type of work involved, this information may be very straightforward or riddled with uncertainty. For jobs where the output from a particular individual can be readily measured, this calculation is fairly straightforward. Examples might be in manufacturing where a certain number of parts are made or assembled per hour, or in data processing where a certain number of data items are to be entered per hour. In cases like these, it is known how many person-hours go into each unit produced. In other cases where the tasks are integrated with those of other jobs, attributing levels of output to any particular person or job is more difficult. Nevertheless, it is necessary to estimate what the productivity of your core workers is, or would be, at the job for which you are considering using contingent workers.

There are several potential sources for this information within your organization: data from a quality control system, supervisors, performance evaluation reports either at the individual or unit level, and the workers themselves. In cost-benefit analysis, both benefits and costs are commonly enumerated in dollars. In this case, that is not necessary. The time unit of output, however, must be the same as that used for the compensation cost estimates. In the example in Figure 12.2, costs are estimated in dollars per hour; and productivity is estimated in output per hour, in this case, units of code written and tested per hour. Again, if there is uncertainty about this estimate, calculate several scenarios: a base case, a low-productivity scenario, and a high-productivity scenario.

Step 3: *Calculate the Productivity Needed from Contingent Workers*

This is a calculation based on a decision rule commonly used in labor economics. To use this rule you will need the unit costs calculated in Step 1 as well as the productivity figure from Step 2. Make sure your time units are the same. This example uses hours, so for our purposes here, we need to know the following:

- Hourly cost of core workers (Core Cost): calculated in Step 1

- Hourly cost of temporary (contingent) workers (Temp Cost): calculated in Step 1

- Hourly productivity of core workers (Core Productivity): calculated in Step 2

- Hourly productivity of temporary (contingent) workers (Temp Productivity): to be calculated in Step 3

This decision rule, or efficiency condition, states that for a firm to be operating efficiently, the ratio of the marginal productivity of two inputs must equal the ratio of the marginal revenue product of those two inputs. The marginal revenue product is calculated by multiplying extra or marginal output produced by the extra revenue when that output is sold. This efficiency condition means that the firm cannot further adjust its usage of either input to further reduce the cost of production, so it is in a least-cost position. Applying a simplified version of this rule indicates how productive the contingent workers must be for the firm to use them rather than core workers and continue to operate using the most efficient combination of employees.

In this case, the two inputs are the two types of workers, core and contingent. The efficiency condition can be rewritten as:

$$\frac{\text{Temp Productivity}}{\text{Core Productivity}} = \frac{\text{Temp Cost}}{\text{Core Cost}}$$

As noted above, three of the four parts of the rule have already been determined in Steps 1 and 2. The purpose of Step 3 is to solve for Temp Productivity:

$$\text{Temp Productivity} = \text{Temp Cost} \times \frac{\text{Core Productivity}}{\text{Core Cost}}$$

The solution to this equation tells how productive the contingent workers must be to justify their use.

The decision rule used here is based on the efficiency condition commonly applied in models of long-run demand for labor, where firms are deciding on the maximally efficient levels of capital and labor. This rule assumes conditions of perfect competition and zero profits for the firm. While it is unlikely that those conditions will hold, the efficiency condition does provide a reasonable, if not perfect, guideline for deciding between the use of core and contingent workers.

Looking at the engineering example in Figure 12.2, the hourly cost of core engineers is $37.50 per hour, assuming payment of overtime but not additional nonwage costs, and the hourly cost of temporary engineers is $29 per hour. The hourly productivity of your core workers is 1.5 (a measure of software code written in an hour). To find the productivity needed from temporary workers, substitute in the above equation:

$$\text{Temp Productivity} = (\frac{29}{37.5}) \times 1.5 = 1.16$$

This determines the minimum level of productivity that should be expected from the contingent workers to justify their use. That is, a temporary worker should produce at least 1.16 units of software code per hour to be considered cost-effective under this set of cost conditions. If less software code is produced, then the firm is not operating in a least-cost mode relative to its labor costs.

A client or hiring organization may use this information in several ways. First, it may simply find out from either the temporary help firm (if using one) or the workers themselves (if using independent contractors or self-employed consultants) about expected productivity and make a decision. Second, the organization may specify this level of productivity as a minimum standard in a contract with the contingent workers or their employment agency and structure the contract in such a way that any costs associated with not meeting this standard are not borne by the organization. At this point, you should be able to ask the temporary agency (or the contingent workers themselves) if the contingent employees can produce at a high enough level to justify their use.

As has been noted throughout this process, there may be some uncertainty about the estimates of either the costs or productivity of the two types of workers. Assuming that there is some uncertainty, consider the results of the analysis under different cases. Returning to the engineering example, it was estimated that core engineers produced 1.5 units of code per hour. Using that as the base case, the contingent engineers would have to produce 1.16 units of code per hour to justify using them. In contrast, if the low-productivity scenario indicated that core engineers produced 1 unit of code, the contingent engineers would only have to produce .77 units. Similarly, if the high-productivity scenario indicated that the core engineers produced 2 units of code, the contingent engineers would have to write 1.55 units per hour. Thus, the estimated necessary productivity of the contingent engineers is sensitive to changes in the assumptions about the core workers. Therefore, it is especially important to accurately estimate both groups' likely productivity.

Finally, the organization may decide to train the contingent workers to assure the necessary level of productivity. If this decision is made, then the organization must proceed to Steps 4 and 5 below to estimate the costs of training and the time required for the employer to recover the training costs.

Step 4: *Calculate the Cost of Training Contingent Workers*

This is the information you will need:

- Direct costs of training

- Indirect costs of training

If training is needed for contingent workers, these costs also must be considered while evaluating whether or not to use contingent workers for a particular job. To estimate direct training costs, you need four types of information: trainer cost per trainee, total materials costs per trainee for the entire training, the length of time needed for the training, and the number of hours per day spent in training. Where you will get this information will depend on whether or not the training is being done internally or subcontracted to an external training firm.

In the example, it is assumed that the contingent engineers will need one full week of training, that the per-trainee cost is $350, and that materials will cost $100. The largest single component of the total training costs is the time cost of the trainees. Assuming the $29 per hour contingent worker cost, payments for the trainees' training time equal $1160 (based on a 40 hour week).

There may also be indirect training costs. They can take several forms and may be directly related to the project and/or take the form of lowered productivity while learning, even after formal training. Contingent workers may have questions or need help from core workers, so core worker time costs should be estimated. There may be firm-specific nonproject costs if the work is done on-site, such as time costs associated with learning where materials are kept, offices for certain personnel, and so on. These indirect costs may be very difficult to estimate, and the best way to handle them may be to use these difficult-to-quantify costs in interpreting final results.

Step 5: *Calculate How Long It Will Take to Recover Training Costs*

If a training investment is made in the contingent workers, it is necessary to estimate how long those workers need to stay on the job to get a positive return on that investment. The essence of this step is to calculate the value of the additional revenue per day attributable to training and divide total training costs by that revenue figure to determine how many days beyond the training period contingent workers would have to stay for the organization to recover its training investment.

You will need the following information for this calculation:

- Increased output per day due to training

- Revenue per unit

- Increased revenue per day due to training

- Total cost of training: calculated in Step 4

The basic definition of investment is the decision to forgo income in the present period for expected greater gain in future periods. An important component, then, of investment is the degree of uncertainty associated with securing that future gain. In the context of training contingent workers, the chief source of uncertainty is whether or not they will stay on the job long enough and at a high enough level of productivity to recover the training costs.

In the engineering example, it is assumed that the objective of the training is to raise the productivity of contingent workers so it is equal to that of the core workers. Admittedly, there are many alternative training objectives and different expectations for the training may be held. For example if the task involves the use of skills that core employees do not have and that the organization expects to need only for a short time, it may be more cost-effective to train contingent workers. The important point is that there be a clear and quantified expectation about how much more productive the contingent workers will be as a result of the training.

Returning to the example, Figure 12.2 shows the increase in temporary workers' output per day due to the training. Recall that the training objective in the example is to bring the productivity level of the temporary workers up to that of the core workers. The hourly increase in output due to the training is thus:

Increased Temporary Productivity = Core Productivity − (Pre-training) Temp Productivity

We know the productivities needed for this calculation from Step 3, so:

Increased Temporary Productivity = 1.5 − 1.16 = .34

Since we are ultimately interested in how many days contingent workers must stay to cover the training investment, we calculate this increase in output on a daily basis:

Increased Temporary Productivity due to Training = 8 × .34

= 2.72

The important feature about the training objective is that it is specified in quantitative terms, that is, in terms of additional units of output per unit of time.

The next step is to calculate revenue per unit that will result from the increased productivity of the contingent worker. In the engineering example, this figure is based upon a version of the economic efficiency assumption that core workers are paid according to what they produce. Therefore, the core worker hourly wage is divided by their output per hour:

$$\text{Revenue per Unit of Output} = \frac{\text{Core Cost (per hour)}}{\text{Core Productivity per hour)}}$$

Depending on the product, a more precise measure of the revenue associated with selling another unit may be available from the marketing unit of the organization. In the engineering example, the engineers are paid $25 per hour and produce 1.5 units (using the base-case productivity estimate from Step 2), so the per-unit value of their product is $16.67 ($25 ÷ 1.5). Increased revenue per day is simply the product of the additional revenue per unit ($16.67) and the additional units produced per day due to the training (2.72) or $45.33 per day.

The number of days the contingent workers must stay on the job in order to recover the cost of training is calculated by dividing total training costs by the additional revenue per day plus the number of days spent in training. In this example, the contingent workers would have to stay on the job 40.5 workdays to justify the training. If it is reasonable to assume that they will stay at least that long, then training is a good decision. If there is reason to expect that they will leave before that, then the training investment may be lost.

In Conclusion

Debrief

There have been several changes over time in the role of contingent work in U.S. workplaces. As noted, one of the biggest changes has been in the composition of occupations. Although support occupations are still the model category for contingent employment, employers are considering a much broader set of skills and tasks that can be handled through nontraditional employment. As a result, there has been a shift toward the increased use of contingent workers in professional, technical, and managerial occupations. This module has provided an overview of what constitutes contingent work, who the contingent workers are, how an organization staffs strategically with contingent workers, and how to evaluate the cost-effectiveness of using contingent workers.

Despite some of these changes, many organizations are still in the early stages of thinking strategically about the use of alternative work arrangements. Using temporary employees is often a short-term response to a crisis. As organizations begin to implement strategic HR planning, they will develop an in-depth understanding of their core competencies. Specifically, they will learn which human resources give them a competitive advantage. The tool for analyzing cost-effectiveness provided in this chapter is a first step toward thinking rationally about the core competencies of the organization and the best way to staff to secure those competencies. Even under conditions of uncertainty, the use of base-, high-, and low-expectation scenarios allows HR professionals to think logically about alternative employment staffing decisions.

Suggested Readings

Abraham, Katherine and Susan Taylor. "Firm's Use of Outside Contractors: Theory and Evidence," *Journal of Labor Economics,* 14 July 1996, pp. 394–421.

Belous, Richard S. "How Human Resource Systems Adjust to the Shift Toward Contingent Workers," *Monthly Labor Review,* March 1989, pp. 7–12.

Deavers, Kenneth L. "Outsourcing: A Corporate Competitiveness Strategy, Not a Search for Low Wages." *Journal of Labor Research,* 18(4), Fall 1997, pp. 504–517.

Kosters, Marvin. "New Employment Relationships and the Labor Market," *Journal of Labor Research,* 18(4), Fall 1997, pp. 551–559.

Lengnick-Hall, Cynthia and Mark Lengnick-Hall. 1998. "Strategic Human Resources Management: A Review of the Literature and a Proposed Typology," *Academy of Management Review,* 13(3), pp. 454–470.

Nollen, Stanley and Helen Axel. 1996. *Managing Contingent Workers,* New York, AMACOM.

Polivka, Anne. "Contingent and Alternative Work Arrangements, Defined," *Monthly Labor Review,* October 1996, pp. 3–21.

Polivka, Anne E. and Thomas Nardone, "On the Definition of 'Contingent Work,'" *Monthly Labor Review,* December 1989.

Relevant Web Sites

There are several sorts of resources available on the Internet. Below is a list of sites that are particularly useful as of this writing.

Government Information

BUREAU OF LABOR STATISTICS
http://stats.bls.gov/blshome.htm
http://www.bls.gov/news.release/occomp.toc.htm

Professional Associations

NATIONAL ASSOCIATION OF TEMPORARY AND STAFFING SERVICES (NATSS)
http://www.nats.org

HR NET—THE MANAGEMENT ARCHIVE
http://ursus.un.alaska.edu/archives/hrnet/msg00434.html

SOCIETY FOR HUMAN RESOURCE MANAGEMENT (SHRM)
http://www.shrm.org

Temporary Help Agency Web Sites

MANPOWER
> *http://www.manpower.com*

SNELLING
> *http://www.snelling.com*

COMFORCE
> *http://www.comforce.com*

KELLY SERVICES
> *http://www.kellyservices.com*

Critical Thinking Questions

1. What, if any, ethical issues should an employer consider when planning for staffing flexibility by using contingent workers? Should an employer's decision to hire or not hire contingent workers be made entirely based on a "rational" cost/benefit analysis?

2. What factors must you consider when determining which type(s) of staffing flexibility is (are) most important to your organization? How does knowing the most important type of flexibility affect your cost/benefit analysis?

3. When is the use of contingent workers a good idea?

4. What additional risk factors must be considered when an employer is considering outsourcing outside the United States?

Index

Alternative employment arrangements. *See* Contingent work arrangements

Americans with Disabilities Act (ADA), 12.12

Base-case scenario, 12.17, 12.18, 12.20, 12.21
Benefits (legally required), 12.11
Bureau of Labor Statistics (BLS), 12.6–7, 12.16

Client firm, 12.4
Collective agreements, 12.5
Competitive environment, 12.11
Contingent work (employment) arrangements, 12.4, 12.5–6, 12.7, 12.9, 12.11, 12.13, 12.20
Contingent workers, 12.4, 12.5–9, 12.12, 12.16, 12.18–20. *See also* Temporary employees, characteristics of, 12.7
Contingent workers, pension and health insurance coverage, 12.9
Contract workers, 12.4, 12.7
Core competencies, 12.10, 12.12–13
Core employees, 12.10, 12.12–13, 12.16
Cost-benefit analysis, of core vs. contingent workers, 12.4, 12.13–16, 12.20

Day laborers, 12.5, 12.7

Efficiency condition, 12.17–18.
Employer-provided insurance, 12.9
Employment insecurity. *See* Job insecurity
Employment security. *See* Job security

Family Medical Leave Act (FMLA), 12.12
Financial flexibility (staffing), 12.11
Fixed employment costs, 12.11
Flexible staffing, 12.11
Full-time employees, tension over part-timers, 12.13
Functional flexibility (staffing), 12.11

Health insurance coverage, 12.9
High-productivity scenario, 12.17, 12.18, 12.21
Hire-from-within culture, 12.13
Human resource department, 12.16
Human resource management.
    administrative functions, 12.12
    strategic planning, 12.11, 12.13, 12.21
Human resource strategy, 12.5

Independent contractors, 12.5, 12.7, 12.13, 12.16, 12.18. *See also* Contingent workers
Information technology, 12.11
Internal temporary worker pool, 12.13
Irregular work schedules, 12.5

Job insecurity, 12.5, 12.7, 12.12
Job security, 12.7

Labor cost reduction, 12.12
Layoffs, avoiding, 12.12–12
Leased employees, 12.5, 12.13
Low-productivity scenario, 12.17, 12.18, 12.21

Noncontingent workers, 12.9–10. *See also* Contingent workers
Nonrecurring employees, 12.13
Nontraditional employment. *See* Contingent work
Nonwage costs/benefits, 12.7, 12.11, 12.16
Numerical flexibility (staffing), 12.11

On-call workers, 12.5, 12.7, 12.13
Operational flexibility, 12.4
Organizational strategy, 12.5, 12.10–11, 12.13
Outsourcing, 12.5
Overtime costs, 12.16

Part-time workers, 12.5, 12.13
Pension coverage, 12.9
    contingent/noncontingent workers, 12.9
Permanent part-time employees, 12.13
Productivity.
    contingent workers, 12.17–18, 12.20
    core workers, 12.16–17, 12.20
Professionals, self-employed, 12.5, 12.7

Self-employed consultants, 12.5, 12.7, 12.13, 12.16
Social security, contributions, 12.11, 12.12
Strategic staffing decision, 12.4
Subcontracting, specific project, 12.12

Technological advances, 12.11
Temporary employees, 12.4, 12.5, 12.7, 12.13, 12.16, 12.20, 12.21. *See also* Contingent workers
Temporary help services, 12.7
    Web sites, 12.22
Traditional work arrangements, 12.10, 12.13
Training investment, contingent workers, 12.18–20
Transformation activities, 12.4
Transition activities, 12.4
Twenty-first century, 12.11

Unemployed workers, 12.9
Unemployment insurance, contributions, 12.11, 12.12
Union workers, 12.4–5, 12.13

MODULE
12

Wage and salary workers, 12.5, 12.10
Workers' compensation, contributions, 12.11, 12.12
Workforce diversity, 12.11
Workforce planning, 12.5, 12.11–13
Working mothers, 12.9

MODULE
12

Managing Human Resources
in the 21st Century

From Core Concepts to Strategic Choice

MODULE 13

Recruitment and Selections

Hiring for the Job
or the Organization?

Mark L. Lengnick-Hall
WICHITA STATE UNIVERSITY

Managing Human Resources in the 21st Century: From Core Concepts to Strategic Choice,
by Kossek and Block

Publisher: Dave Shaut
Executive Editor: John Szilagyi
Developmental Editor: Bryant Editorial Development
Marketing Manager: Joseph A. Sabatino
Production Editor: Tamborah E. Moore
Manufacturing Coordinator: Dana Began Schwartz
Cover Design: Tin Box Studio
Cover Photographs: Copyright Shoji Sato/Photonica
Production House: The Left Coast Group, Inc.
Printer: West Group

Printed in the United States of America
1 2 3 4 5 02 01 00 99

For more information contact South-Western College Publishing, 5101 Madison Road, Cincinnati, Ohio, 45227 or find us on the Internet at *http://www.swcollege.com*
For permission to use material from this text or product, contact us by

- telephone: 1-800-730-2214
- fax: 1-800-730-2215
- web: *http://www.thomsonrights.com*

ISBN: 0–324–01812–6

This book is printed on acid-free paper.

Contents

MODULE OVERVIEW 13.4

OBJECTIVES 13.4

RELATION TO THE FRAME 13.4

CORE CONCEPTS IN RECRUITMENT AND SELECTION 13.5

Staffing Matches Individual and Organizational Needs 13.5

Recruitment and Selection Are Processes 13.7

Organization and Job Analyses Are Prerequisites to the
Recruitment and Selection Process 13.9

Hiring for the Job Requires Person-Job Fit 13.12

Hiring for the Organization Requires Person-Organization Fit 13.13

Recruiting Involves Identifying and Attracting Applicants 13.17

Selecting Involves Assessing and Evaluating Applicants 13.20

The Legal Environment Constrains Recruitment and Selection 13.24

STRATEGIC ISSUES IN RECRUITMENT AND SELECTION 13.25

The Strategic Impact of Human Resources 13.25

Traditional Approaches 13.25

Staffing as Strategy Implementation 13.25

Staffing as Strategy Formation 13.26

Melding the Three Strategic Approaches 13.27

Make vs. Buy Human Resources 13.27

Summary 13.29

APPLICATION 13.29

Preparing for Class Discussion 13.29

IN CONCLUSION 13.30

Debrief 13.30

Suggested Readings 13.31

Critical Thinking Questions 13.31

Exercises 13.32

References 13.33

MODULE OVERVIEW

This module discusses the process of recruitment and selection in organizations—identifying and attracting applicants; assessing their knowledge, skills, abilities, and other characteristics (KSAOs); evaluating those KSAOs; and making decisions on whom to hire. A major theme of this module is that in a rapidly changing global market, organizations will need to place a greater emphasis on hiring for the organization and not just for the job. However, recruitment and selection is not a one-way process in which organizations have complete control and make all of the decisions. Applicants, too, are "recruiting" organizations that they would like to work for, selling their KSAOs, and finally, "selecting" where to work based upon their needs and desires. Therefore, recruitment and selection is a mutual process in which organizations and applicants take actions and make decisions about each other.

First, this module focuses on the matching process—matching organizational and individual needs. Next, a model of the recruitment and selection process is described. Then specific components of that model are discussed in more detail: (1) organization and job analysis, (2) person-job fit, (3) person-organization fit, (4) recruitment, and (5) selection. Since the legal environment imposes constraints on the recruitment and selection process, it is examined also. Finally, strategic issues associated with recruiting and selection are discussed. The role business strategy plays in recruitment and selection is increasingly important as businesses discover that human resources are one of the last frontiers for gaining competitive advantage in the global marketplace.

The final section provides opportunities for you to apply your knowledge to a recruitment and selection situation. You will get information about an organization as well as the descriptions of jobs for which the organization wishes to recruit applicants and hire employees. With this information, your task will be to develop a recruitment plan, a selection plan, and an interview protocol that yields the quantity and quality of employees needed to make the business successful.

OBJECTIVES

Key objectives of this module include:

- To discuss how recruitment and selection is a mutual matching process between individuals and organizations

- To identify the five stages in the recruitment and selection process

- To distinguish between organization and job analysis

- To distinguish between person-job fit and person-organization fit

- To explain the major issues involved in recruiting applicants

- To explain the major issues involved in selecting applicants

- To describe how the legal environment constrains recruitment and selection

- To identify the strategic issues involved in staffing organizations

RELATION TO THE FRAME

Recruitment and selection in the United States falls primarily in the first column in the framework (unilateral HR choices), although the legal regulation of recruitment and selection imposes some constraints. For example, organizations are prohibited from using race, color, religion, sex, national origin, age, disability, handicap, or ancestry in

FIGURE 13.1   *A Frame for Understanding Human Resource Strategy: Context, Roles, and Constraints*

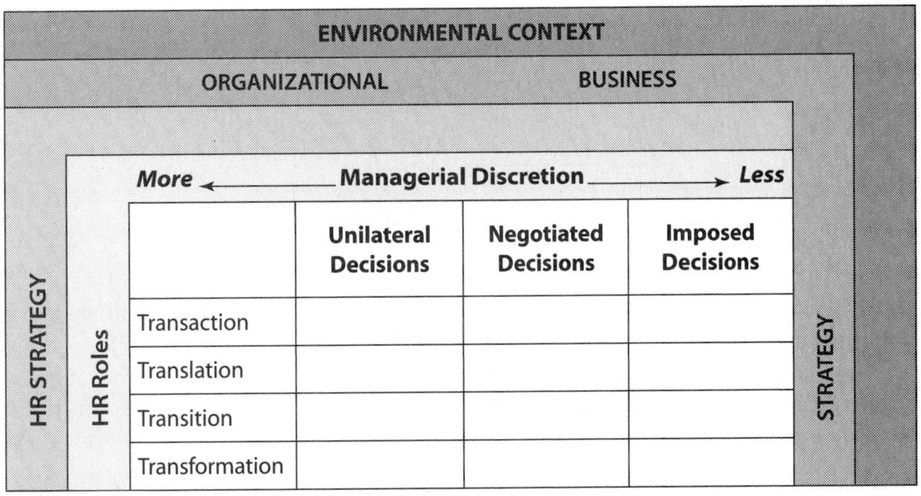

ENVIRONMENTAL CONTEXT			
ORGANIZATIONAL		BUSINESS	
More ← Managerial Discretion → Less			
	Unilateral Decisions	Negotiated Decisions	Imposed Decisions
Transaction			
Translation			
Transition			
Transformation			

© 2000 by Ellen Ernst Kossek and Richard Block. Thanks to Brian Pentland, Karen Markel, and John Beck for helpful comments and discussions that enhanced the model.

hiring decisions. Furthermore, in a unionized environment, many aspects of the recruitment and selection process are negotiated.

Some selection activities are transactional, such as conducting a job analysis. Others are managerial, for example, validating selection methods. Finally, some selection activities are transformational, such as specifying the organizational capabilities needed to run the business in the long term. See Figure 13.1, A Frame for Understanding Human Resource Strategy.

MODULE
13

CORE CONCEPTS IN RECRUITMENT AND SELECTION

There are eight core concepts that must be understood in order to successfully recruit and select individuals for an organization:

- Staffing matches individual and organizational needs
- Recruitment and selection are processes
- Organization and job analyses are prerequisites to the recruitment and selection process
- Hiring for the job requires person-job fit
- Hiring for the organization requires person-organization fit
- Recruiting involves identifying and attracting applicants
- Selecting involves assessing and evaluating applicants
- The legal environment constrains recruitment and selection

Let's look at these in more detail.

Staffing Matches Individual and Organizational Needs

Staffing is a mutual matching process: organizations seek individuals who will help them achieve goals such as profitability, growth, and in some cases survival;

FIGURE 13.2   *The Mutual Matching Process*

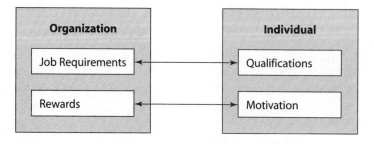

individuals seek organizations that will help them achieve goals such as fulfilling needs and obtaining rewards (Dawis, 1991; Heneman, Heneman, and Judge 1997).

As shown in Figure 13.2, the recruitment and selection process matches requirements of the job to the qualifications of the individual, and rewards of the job to the motivation of the individual. Several degrees of match may occur:

- *An organization's job requirements and job rewards match both the individual's qualifications and motivation needs.* For example, an Internet technology organization needs to fill a job that requires web-based computer programming skills. The organization offers applicants a competitive base salary with above-market, performance-based bonus pay opportunities. A woman who has several years' experience with the desired programming skills applies for the job. In addition, she has a strong desire to make a high salary in a work environment that places greater emphasis on job performance than on seniority. Here, the match is complete across all dimensions: the applicant's qualifications match the organization's job requirements and the organization's reward system matches the individual's motivation needs. Both the organization and the individual benefit from this match.

- *An organization's job requirements match the individual's qualifications, but the organization's reward system does not match the individual's motivation needs.* For example, a man with the desired programming skills applies for the same programming job. However, he prefers a work environment that places greater emphasis on seniority and less on performance. While the organization may benefit from this match (i.e., the applicant can perform the job), the individual will not have his motivation needs fulfilled.

- *An organization's reward system matches the individual's motivation needs, but the organization's job requirements do not match the individual's job qualifications.* For example, another woman applies for the same programming job, but she has no web-based computer programming experience. She, too, is motivated by a work environment that places greater emphasis on performance than on seniority. Thus, the organization's reward system matches her motivation needs, but the organization's job requirements do not match her qualifications. Neither party would achieve its goals: the organization would not have needed tasks completed (without an additional training investment), and the individual would not be able to obtain performance-based bonuses, since she would be unable to complete the needed tasks.

The consequences of a good match are beneficial to both the organization and the individual. Furthermore, a good match makes it possible for the organization and the individual to establish a long-term relationship in which both parties maximize the returns on their investments in each other. On the other hand, any mismatch between the organization's job requirements and rewards and the individual's qualifications and motivation needs will lead to less desirable consequences for one or both parties.

TABLE 13.1 *Stages of the Recruitment and Selection Process*

	Stage 1	Stage 2	Stage 3	Stage 4	Stage 5
Organization	Identify and attract applicants	Narrow pool to minimally qualified applicants	Further narrow pool to those who best fit the job	Further narrow pool to those who best fit job and organization	Decide whom to hire
Individual	Identify and attract organizations	Narrow pool to minimally acceptable organizations	Further narrow pool to those who best fit with needs/career goals	Further narrow pool to those who have desirable jobs and desirable cultures	Decide which job offer to accept

Recruitment and Selection Are Processes

The actual recruitment/selection process consists of five stages, depicted in Table 13.1.

Stage 1: Recruitment   In this stage, the organization's goal is to identify and attract applicants in order to create an applicant pool for vacant jobs, while the applicant's goal is to identify and attract organizations in order to create an organization pool of potential places to work.

In our previous computer programming job example, the Internet technology organization may identify educational institutions and professional associations as the primary sources for applicants with the needed skills. In order to attract applicants, the organization may send recruiters to college campuses and professional association meetings. Additionally, the organization may recruit applicants over the Internet, since those with needed skills will likely use the Internet in their job search.

Applicants for the computer programming job will probably identify organizations to work for through referrals from friends and relatives, job and company information available at college campuses, and job and company information provided by their professional associations. In addition, these same applicants will likely use resources on the Internet in their job search. To attract organizations, applicants will send them their resumes and complete application blanks. Some applicants may use personal networks (e.g., friends and family members) to gain the interest of the organization.

Stage 2: Screening   In this stage, the organization's goal is to narrow the overall applicant pool to only those who are minimally qualified for the job(s). The applicant's goal is to narrow the overall organization pool to those that provide the minimal job and organizational characteristics he or she will accept in a workplace.

The Internet technology organization will probably obtain resumes, application blanks, and reference reports from applicants in order to narrow the pool to those individuals with the minimum qualifications for the job. The organization will likely use scanners to enter resumes into their human resource information system (HRIS), and their application blanks may either be computerized themselves or scanned into the HRIS as well. Once basic applicant information is in the HRIS, screening on minimum qualifications can be a fast and efficient process.

MODULE
13

On the other hand, applicants will likely narrow their pool of potential organizations to work for by obtaining information from libraries and the Internet, and talking to friends and others whom they trust to learn about organizations and job characteristics. Applicants will then narrow down the pool of potential employers to those that meet personal criteria, such as type of industry, location, career opportunities, etc.

Stage 3: Person-Job Fit In this stage, the organization's goal is to narrow further the applicant pool to those who are best qualified (i.e., fit best with the requirements for the job[s]). Likewise, the applicant's goal is to narrow his or her organization pool to those who offer the best job fit with his or her needs and career goals.

The Internet technology organization may use a number of selection methods to assess person-job fit. These methods include personality tests, ability tests, job knowledge tests, performance tests and work samples, integrity tests, and structured interviews. Information obtained from these selection methods will enable the organization to identify those applicants who could best fit with the requirements of the job.

Applicants for the web-based computer programming job may use a number of information sources to assess their person-job fit. For example, during the selection interview, applicants learn about the job, and in some cases, may be provided with a job description. Facilities tours and interviews with potential peers may also bring additional information that helps the applicant assess person-job fit.

Stage 4: Person-Organization Fit In this stage, the organization's goal is to narrow further the applicant pool to those who *both* fit the requirements of the job well *and* fit the climate and culture of the organization well. The applicant's goal is similar in that he or she wants to narrow the organization pool to include only those organizations that have *both* a desirable climate/culture *and* desirable work to perform.

The Internet technology organization will likely rely upon multiple sources of information to determine whether applicants are a "good" person-organization fit: responses to interview questions, reactions to discussions of "what it's like to work at this place," interactions with potential peers and supervisors, as well as, in some cases, personality assessments. The selection technology to assist organizational decision makers is not as well developed in the area of person-organization fit, but achieving this type of fit may be crucial to organizational functioning.

Applicants for the programming job will be exposed to many overt manifestations of the organization's culture: the physical structure, the organization structure, the recruitment process, observations of how employees behave, what they wear to work, etc. Furthermore, applicants may assess person-organization fit by collecting information from what is not said and from nonverbal behaviors they witness during the recruitment/selection process. From both objective sources of information and "gut reactions" to how they are treated, applicants determine whether they could feel comfortable working for the organization.

Stage 5: Decision Making In the final stage, the organization must make a decision or decisions about whom to hire from the narrowed-down applicant pool. The decision may hinge upon subtle perceptions of which applicants are better fits with the organizational culture when many applicants are considered "good" person-job fits. Once the organization decides whom to hire, it offers the job(s) to the selected applicants.

On the other hand, the applicant makes either a yes-no decision (if there is only one offer) or compares offers from several organizations to select the most desirable one. Applicants, too, may make their final decisions based on which organization "feels" like a better person-organization fit, especially when the jobs are very similar and other job rewards are comparable across organizations.

When both the organization selects the applicant and the applicant selects the organization, the recruitment and selection process ends. Failure to reach a mutual selection means that both parties have to reconsider other offers or begin the entire process anew.

The recruitment and selection process can take place over several months for some jobs. If the job is important enough and time permits, a thorough but lengthy process may yield the best hires. Alternatively, if a job must be filled quickly in order to ensure uninterrupted operations, the recruitment and selection process may be compressed into a very short time period. Thus, situational variables dictate the pace of the process.

Organization and Job Analyses Are Prerequisites to the Recruitment and Selection Process

Organization Analysis.   Prior to the beginning of the recruitment/selection process, it is necessary to conduct two types of analyses: an organization analysis, and a job analysis.

The purpose of an organizational analysis (Bowen, Ledford, and Nathan 1991) is to identify:

- *The long- and short-term goals of the organization*

  ✓ What strategy or strategies is the organization pursuing to compete in its marketplace?

  ✓ What types of capabilities does the organization need in order to implement its chosen strategy?

- *The organization's staffing needs*

  ✓ What are the organization's human resource needs?

  ✓ How many employees does the organization need?

  ✓ What tasks does the organization need to accomplish?

  ✓ What knowledge, skills, abilities, and other characteristics (KSAOs) does the organization need for job performance?

- *The nature of the organization's environment*

  ✓ What aspects of the organization's environment (product and labor markets, legal, social, political, etc.) affect the management of its human resources?

- *The organization's climate/culture*

  ✓ What characterizes the climate/culture that exists in the organization?

  ✓ What is it like to work for this organization?

The transformation of Sears from an "organizational dinosaur" operating under old assumptions and headed for extinction to a rejuvenated competitor able to challenge marketplace giants such as Wal-Mart provides a vivid example of why organization analysis is an important prerequisite to the recruitment/selection process (this description is drawn from Ulrich 1997).

Prior to the recent changes initiated at Sears, the company operated in the retail environment it had helped to create: catalog sales supplemented with full-service retail outlets merchandising store-brand products throughout the United States. Innovative retailers, particularly Wal-Mart, changed the retail landscape to favor high-volume, technology-driven stores with low costs. Sears had no choice but to change.

Under the leadership of Arthur Martinez, Sears began the transformation process toward the organization it is today. Unprofitable operations were closed, the catalog business was discontinued, and Allstate was divested so that Sears could better focus its strategy. Brands other than Sears' own were introduced into the merchandise offerings, and customer service became a major theme through the creation of a positive sales environment among all store employees. Sears' advertising began to focus on the "softer side of Sears" with an emphasis on apparel and accessories. In addition, global expansion was begun by opening new stores throughout North America.

Anthony Rucci, the senior vice president of administration, led the team that implemented the new strategy using a simple but powerful vision encompassing "3 C's:" a compelling place to shop, work, and invest. Rucci's team then integrated Sears' new initiatives into this vision, providing a clear focus for the organization's future. To become a compelling place to shop, Sears placed emphasis on consistent in-stock performance, customer-service training, brand-name merchandise, competitive pricing, and better advertising. To become a compelling place to work, Sears undertook efforts to improve communication, education, training, and involvement of all sales associates in decision making. To become a compelling place to invest, Sears focused on reducing inventories, lowering administrative costs, strategic sourcing, better costing, and store remodeling.

Their careful organizational analysis led Sears' top decision makers to develop a competitive strategy that has specific implications for recruitment and selection. Stores need to be staffed sufficiently to meet customers' expectations for service, but also staffed with an eye toward lowering administrative costs. Recruiting and selection efforts need to produce employees with customer-service orientations and the ability to contribute to business decision making. Additionally, the new emphasis on the "softer side of Sears" means that employees must have a broader product knowledge base. And finally, the culture of the organization has to change in ways to nurture these new expectations. Neither Sears nor any other company can effectively compete in the long run if it is unable to attract and select employees with the needed capabilities to realize the chosen business strategy.

Job Analysis.   The purpose of job analysis in recruitment and selection is to identify the tasks that comprise a job and the context that those tasks are performed in, and to identify the KSAOs necessary to perform them. Each of these factors is defined below along with an example for a sales associate job (like one you might find at the new Sears!).

A *task* is a work activity that produces a single meaningful work product or outcome (Harvey 1997). A task for a sales associate job might be: *Develop a seasonal display of lawn furniture and garden tools to encourage customers to purchase a variety of related products.*

Job context refers to the physical demands of the job and the environmental conditions in which it is performed (Heneman, Heneman, and Judge 1997). For the sales associate job, the job context might be described as: *No excessive physical demands; mostly indoors; safe; occasionally noisy work environment.*

Knowledge refers to a body of information, usually of a conceptual, factual, or procedural nature, that makes for successful performance of the job (Gatewood and Feild 1998). For the sales associate job, a required knowledge might be: *Knowledge of store products and characteristics in order to answer customer questions and encourage purchases.*

A *skill* is an individual's level of proficiency or competency (either mental or physical) in performing a specific task (Gatewood and Feild 1998). For the sales associate job, a required skill might be: *Skill in communicating technical product information so it is understood.*

Ability is a more general, enduring trait or capability (cognitive, psychomotor, physical, or sensory/perceptual) an individual possesses when he or she first begins to perform a task (Gatewood and Feild 1998). For the sales associate job, a required ability might be: *Tolerates stress; bounces back quickly when frustrated.*

Other refers to personal characteristics including attitudes, beliefs, personality traits, temperaments, and values (Spector 1997). For the sales associate job, a required *other* characteristic might be: *Is patient with customers; controls temper.*

While jobs require certain KSAOs for successful performance, they also provide individuals with rewards for their performance. Therefore, to attract applicants it is necessary to understand what kinds of rewards a job can offer. Two types of rewards are available in a work context: extrinsic and intrinsic (Steers and Porter 1991). *Extrinsic rewards* are those the organization provides to the individual (e.g., pay and benefits). *Intrinsic rewards* are those the individual provides himself or herself (e.g., feelings of accomplishment) as a result of performing a task. Organizations have direct influence over extrinsic rewards and indirect influence over intrinsic rewards (i.e., the organization can create conditions to make intrinsic rewards available through such means as job design). While no list is comprehensive, the following represents the range of job rewards (Milkovich and Newman 1996):

- Compensation (wages, commissions, bonuses)
- Benefits (vacations, health insurance, etc.)
- Social interaction (friendly workplace)
- Security (stable, consistent position and rewards)
- Status/recognition (respect, prominence due to work)
- Work variety (opportunity to experience different things)
- Workload (right amount of work)
- Work importance (work valued by society)
- Authority/control/autonomy (ability to influence others; control own destiny)
- Advancement (chance to get ahead)
- Feedback (receive information to improve performance)
- Work conditions (hazard free)
- Development opportunity (formal and informal training to learn knowledge/skills/abilities)

MODULE
13

The nature of jobs and organizations has changed dramatically in recent years. Some authors describe "fields of work" rather than jobs (Bridges 1994). The permanent and static nature that characterized jobs in the past has changed to a temporary and dynamic one today. Likewise, the emphasis on individual contributors in the past has changed to an emphasis on team members today.

These changes in how we conceptualize and design jobs will pose significant challenges for recruitment and selection in the future. One consequence of these trends is a move away from relying solely on the classic selection model of creating a tight fit between the qualifications of the job and the qualifications of the individual (person-job fit). Instead, more organizations are moving toward a new model that focuses less on a tight person-job fit and more on a person-organization fit. The differences between these two approaches as well as how they can be used together will be discussed next.

Hiring for the Job Requires Person-Job Fit

Person-job fit is a state of congruence between job demands and resources on the one hand, and individual abilities and proclivities on the other (Villanova and Muchinsky 1997). You can assess person-job fit by answering two questions: (1) To what extent is there congruence between the demands of the job and the capabilities of the employee? (2) To what extent is there congruence between a person's desires and the job's ability to satisfy those desires?

A "tight" person-job fit—i.e., a good match between the demands of the job and the capabilities of the employee, and between the employee's desires and the job's ability to satisfy them—means that minimal training is necessary for the organization to obtain a return on its human resource investment. The employee can "hit the ground running" and quickly make value-added contributions to the organization.

A "loose" person-job fit can mean one of two possibilities: the demands of the job are greater than the capabilities of the employee or less than the capabilities of the employee. In the first case, the employee is "underqualified" for the job, and he or she may need extensive training for the organization to achieve a return on its investment. Alternatively, the organization may have to terminate an "underqualified" employee if it is not possible to train him or her to perform the job. In the second case, the employee is "overqualified" and the organization may not obtain a return on its investment if the employee leaves the organization prematurely due to boredom, job dissatisfaction, or better opportunities elsewhere.

How can you assess person-job fit? Two key methods are ability tests that measure the capacity for task/job performance and work sample tests that measure current job/task performance. However, other selection methods to obtain KSAO information are available, and the choice of specific methods depends on the nature of the organization and the job (see Fisher and Wasserman, Module 14).

Hiring for person-job fit has both potential benefits and costs for an organization. The potential benefits of hiring are: (1) higher job performance, (2) higher job satisfaction, (3) lower absenteeism, and (4) lower turnover. However, a singular focus on person-job fit may result in problems as well. These may include: (1) less staffing flexibility, since individuals are hired for their match with a particular job's qualifications rather than for multiple jobs; and (2) the fact that it is difficult to achieve a precise match in a more dynamic job environment where, for example, rapid technological advances make some tasks and skills obsolete literally overnight.

Orlando Behling (1998) has identified five circumstances where achieving a precise match between the person and the job is appropriate:

- When the new employee will be called on to do little or no problem solving

- When the new employee will be closely monitored or performance problems will be otherwise obvious to his or her superior

- When the skills and abilities that the new employee brings to the job are more important than the things he or she will learn on the job

- When the new employee will have plenty of time to learn the job and can expect to deal with few, gradual changes, if any

- When one job candidate is clearly superior to the others in terms of key skills and abilities

These five circumstances describe many manufacturing jobs dating back to the turn of the century, but are becoming less applicable to the technologically driven, rapidly changing, global environment of the present and the future.

In short, a "good" person-job fit does not guarantee benefits for both the organization and the individual. In fact, in a dynamic job environment, trying to achieve a "tight" person-job fit is like trying to hit a constantly moving target: even if you achieve the fit, the benefits may be very short-term. This helps explain why many organizations are placing less emphasis on a particular person-job fit and more on hiring people who fit with the organization and can perform multiple duties as needs change. This new trend in employee selection will be discussed next.

Hiring for the Organization Requires Person-Organization Fit

Person-organization fit is a state of congruence between the overall personality, goals, values, and interpersonal skills of the individual and the climate/culture of the organization (Bowen, Ledford, and Nathan 1991). People whose values fit the values of the organizational culture are more committed to the organization (Schneider and Smith 1997). More committed employees display higher levels of *contextual performance* (Borman and Motowidlo 1992). This takes the form of (1) persisting with enthusiasm and extra effort as necessary to complete their own task activities successfully, (2) volunteering to carry out task activities that are not formally part of their own job, (3) helping and cooperating with others, (4) following organizational rules and procedures, and (5) endorsing, supporting, and defending organizational objectives.

The importance of person-organization fit is illustrated by the story of engineer Kathy Wheeler (from Siegel 1998). In 1992, she had a successful career at Hewlett-Packard when Apple Computer offered her an enticing job opportunity: sole responsibility for a product team and an increase in salary. At Hewlett-Packard, Kathy had been one of three managers running a 40-person product design team, and while she liked her job, the Apple opportunity was too good to pass up. She took the job and looked forward to a long-term relationship with her new employer.

Unfortunately, things didn't work out as Kathy had anticipated. The skills that propelled her career at Hewlett-Packard were not the same ones valued by the organizational culture at Apple. Instead of the collaboration, consensus seeking, and rock-solid engineering emphasis she had grown accustomed to at Hewlett-Packard, Apple placed more value on slick user interfaces and exalted heroes who were more "evangelists," brashly marketing Apple's products to the outside world. As Kathy said, "When you're used to being valued for one set of accomplishments and what's actually being valued are accomplishments you either don't feel comfortable with or just aren't able to deliver on, the discomfort is pretty profound."

After just 14 months, Kathy quit her job at Apple and returned to Hewlett-Packard. "I admire Apple to a large extent, but I wouldn't work there again because of the cultural issues." Kathy's lament is an indication of just how important person-organization fit is to a successful selection decision, from the perspective of both the organization and the individual. The difficulty is in determining how good that person-organization fit will be in the future—when the selection decision must be made using limited information and usually in a relatively short time frame.

MODULE
13

Selection Methods for Person-Organization Fit.
There are four major methods to assess person-organization fit (Bowen, Ledford, and Nathan 1991):

1. Ability tests (cognitive abilities, motor abilities, and interpersonal abilities)

2. Personality tests

3. Interviews (with potential coworkers and others)

4. Realistic job previews/work sample tests

Using a combination of all of these methods is probably the best approach to accurately assess person-organization fit, since no single method has been shown to be superior for this purpose.

Cognitive ability tests (i.e., those that measure intelligence) are promising tools for hiring for the organization. Since hiring for the organization typically implies seeking individuals with multiple skills or the ability to learn quickly, cognitive ability tests can provide useful information to aid in making that decision.

Personality tests, especially those that assess the trait conscientiousness, have also been found to be useful in hiring for the organization. Conscientiousness is the degree to which an individual is achievement oriented, careful, hardworking, organized, persevering, responsible, and thorough (Behling 1998). Individuals high on this trait can become good organizational citizens.

Behling (1998) has identified several circumstances where hiring primarily on the basis of cognitive ability and conscientiousness is most appropriate:

- When the new employee will be called on to do a great deal of problem solving

- When the new employee will have a high degree of autonomy, i.e., will work pretty much on his or her own

- When the skills and abilities the new employee will learn on the job are more important than those he or she brings to the job

- When the new employee must learn the job rapidly and adapt equally rapidly to job changes

- When two or more top job candidates are practically equal in terms of key skills and abilities

Interviews with potential coworkers and other organizational members are another important method for hiring for the organization. Both the applicant and the potential coworkers get a chance to "look each other over" to assess compatibility. While brief encounters in the recruitment process are inadequate to fully judge compatibility, they do provide opportunities to eliminate clearly "bad" fits, and at least get some confirming evidence where a "good" fit is most likely.

Realistic job previews and work sample tests provide applicants the opportunity to experience what it is "really like" working for the organization. Providing a more balanced picture of organizational realities helps applicants determine if they could fit in, and helps the organization observe applicant reactions to typical job situations.

The Organizational Culture Profile (OCP) (O'Reilly, Chatman, and Caldwell 1991) is one method specifically designed to assess person-organization fit (see Figure 13.3). Research evidence suggests that the OCP can predict job performance, employee satisfaction, commitment, and turnover. This instrument offers organizations a simple, easy-to-use method to obtain person-organization fit data during the recruitment process.

Hiring for the Organization: How Southwest Airlines Does It.

Southwest Airlines is one of the most successful companies in the airline industry. (This description of Southwest Airlines' practices is drawn from Freiberg and Freiberg 1996.) Its net profit margins, averaging over 5 percent since 1991, have been the highest among its competitors. How do they consistently post such impressive results? Their success is due, in large part, to their ability to hire the right kind of people—those who fit the Southwest Airlines culture, which is sustained by a simple but effective business strategy.

What is the organizational culture at Southwest Airlines? It can be summed up in one word: fun. "Fun is taken very seriously at Southwest Airlines, and the company's recruiting and hiring practices are built on the idea that humor can help people thrive during change, remain creative under pressure, work more effectively, play more enthusiastically, and stay healthier in the process" (Freiberg and Freiberg 1996). Southwest seeks to make a profit by serving people and making life more fun. In addition, the company places a great deal of importance on authenticity—employees are expected to express themselves in real, creative ways, and to project their own individuality into their jobs.

FIGURE 13.3 *The Organizational Culture Profile (from Siegel, 1998)*

The Organizational Culture Profile

O'Reilly, Chatman, and Caldwell (1991) have identified 54 items that can be used to profile an organization's culture. Using your own organization as an example, identify the top 10 items that are most characteristic of your organization's culture and the bottom 10 items that are least characteristic of your organization's culture. This task can best be achieved by first dividing the 54 items into two groups: 27 that would be most characteristic of your workplace and 27 that would be least characteristic. Keep halving the groups until you can identify your top and bottom 10 choices.

Top Ten Choices

1. ___ 2. ___ 3. ___ 4. ___ 5. ___ 6. ___ 7. ___ 8. ___ 9. ___ 10.___

Bottom Ten Choices

1. ___ 2. ___ 3. ___ 4. ___ 5. ___ 6. ___ 7. ___ 8. ___ 9. ___ 10.___

You Are

1. Flexible
2. Adaptable
3. Innovative
4. Able to seize opportunities
5. Willing to experiment
6. Risk-taking
7. Careful
8. Autonomy-seeking
9. Comfortable with rules
10. Analytical
11. Attentive to detail
12. Precise
13. Team-oriented
14. Ready to share information
15. People-oriented
16. Easygoing
17. Calm
18. Supportive
19. Aggressive
20. Decisive
21. Action-oriented
22. Eager to take initiative
23. Reflective
24. Achievement-oriented
25. Demanding
26. Comfortable with individual responsibility
27. Comfortable with conflict
28. Competitive
29. Highly organized
30. Results-oriented
31. Interested in making friends at work
32. Collaborative
33. Eager to fit in with colleagues
34. Enthusiastic about the job

Your Company Offers

35. Stability
36. Predictability
37. High expectations of performance
38. Opportunities for professional growth
39. High pay for good performance
40. Job security
41. Praise for good performance
42. A clear guiding philosophy
43. A low level of conflict
44. An emphasis on quality
45. A good reputation
46. Respect for the individual's rights
47. Tolerance
48. Informality
49. Fairness
50. A unitary culture throughout the organization
51. A sense of social responsibility
52. Long hours
53. Relative freedom from rules
54. The opportunity to be distinctive, or different from others

How does Southwest select people that fit its organizational culture? They "hire for attitude and train for skills." As CEO Herb Kelleher says, "We look for attitudes; people with a sense of humor who don't take themselves too seriously. We'll train you on whatever it is you have to do, but the one thing Southwest cannot change in people is inherent attitudes." The kind of people who fit Southwest's culture are other-oriented, outgoing personalities, individuals who become part of an extended family of people who work hard and have fun at the same time. Some typical interview questions include: "Tell me how you recently used your sense of humor in a work environment." "Tell me how you recently used humor to defuse a difficult situation." Answers to these and other similar questions help Southwest identify those applicants who will likely fit their culture.

Southwest uses a novel approach to measure selflessness, a key value of their culture. Interviewers ask a group of applicants to prepare a five-minute presentation about themselves. During the presentations, Southwest's interviewers watch the audience as well as the speakers. What are they looking for in the audience? They want to determine which applicants are using the time to prepare for their own presentations and which are enthusiastically cheering and providing support for the presenters. Interviewers consider the cheering, supportive applicants a better fit with Southwest's culture than the fastidious applicants who continue to prepare up until their presentations.

Will Southwest turn down an applicant who is a good person-job fit? The answer is yes—if the applicant is not a good fit with the organization's culture. For example, a highly decorated military pilot applied for a position at Southwest and was turned down because of several episodes that occurred during the interview process: he was rude to the customer service agent at the ticket counter where he received his transfer pass, and he was cold and arrogant to the receptionist when he arrived for the interview. These behaviors were considered indicators that this pilot would not fit in at Southwest.

How can Southwest afford to turn away applicants with impeccable credentials like the military pilot? The company has created a desirable culture that attracts huge numbers of applicants to apply for a limited number of jobs. For example, in 1995, Southwest received 124,000 external applications, interviewed 38,000 people for 5,473 jobs, and hired 5,444. They have a large applicant pool to choose from, and they invest the time and other resources necessary to find just the "right" person who fits with their philosophy.

The Benefits and Costs of Hiring for the Organization.   As can be seen in the Southwest Airlines example, hiring for person-organization fit has both potential benefits and potential problems for an organization. Potential benefits include:

- More favorable attitudes (such as greater job satisfaction, organization commitment, and team spirit)

- More desirable individual behaviors (such as better job performance and lower absenteeism and turnover)

- Reinforcement of organizational design (such as support for work design and desired organizational culture)

  Potential problems include:

- Greater investment of resources for the hiring process

- Relatively undeveloped and unproved supporting selection technology

- Individual stress created by the process

- Difficulty of use in some organizations (i.e., it is easier to use in start-ups and new plants than in existing organizations)

- Lack of organizational adaptation (if everyone has the same personality profile, the organization may become stagnant)

- Unvalidated assessments of fit may create adverse impact (screening out a disproportionate number of minority and women applicants)

A "good" person-organization fit does not guarantee benefits for both the organization and the individual. An employee who fits the organization but cannot perform a specific job or cluster of tasks effectively is like a good team player who has no KSAOs to help the team: he may be a good cheerleader, but he can't contribute to the team's success. Therefore, if you place more emphasis on person-organization fit, you must also place more emphasis on hiring individuals who either have multiple skills and talents or can be trained to do different tasks as organizational needs change (Behling 1998).

Recruiting Involves Identifying and Attracting Applicants

Recruiting consists of organizational activities that provide a pool of applicants for the purpose of filling job openings (Breaugh 1997). Organizations can assess the effectiveness of their recruiting efforts by examining three things (Rynes and Barber 1990):

1. The quantity of applicants attracted

2. The quality of applicants attracted

3. Spillover effects (e.g., positive or negative comments applicants make to other applicants or to customers of the organization).

Not long ago, Texas Instruments found its college recruitment strategy was not attracting a sufficient number of the high-quality students it needed (Flynn 1994). And to make matters worse, the recruitment program had many negative spillover effects. Neither students nor college deans liked Texas Instruments' recruiting approach. Armed with an assessment battery that took more than three hours for students to complete—and resembled a final exam—company recruiters were able to visit only a limited number of college campuses. Their recruitment strategy needed revamping.

MODULE
13

With the help of Personnel Decisions Inc., Texas Instruments created a tool to use in its recruiting efforts that proved effective in increasing the quantity and quality of applicants, while promoting positive spillover effects. "Engineer Your Career" is contained on a disk and was initially distributed to students on campuses where Texas Instruments had not previously recruited (thus expanding the reach of their recruitment efforts). The disk provides students with several things:

- Information about the company, its products, its history, and its values

- A self-selection tool that gives students the opportunity to assess their fit with the organizational culture by responding to 32 questions about work preferences, such as work environment, working conditions, and relationships

- A built-in resume writer

- A listing of current job opportunities (that can be updated each time a new disk is issued)

- A "career mapper" section that supplies the company with more information about the applicant's skills and interests in order to facilitate matching with job opportunities

Students who complete the assessments and return the disks to Texas Instruments receive direct feedback on their fit with the company as well as a manual on getting started in the workforce. The company sees three benefits from this recruiting approach: First, assessments returned by students on the disks allow the company to determine whom they want to interview when visiting campuses. Second, the personality assessment helps screen out individuals who would not fit well with the organization's culture. Third, by honestly presenting the values and culture of the company, applicants are given a realistic preview of what to expect if they accept a job. This realistic job preview is in contrast to the typical recruitment message that focuses only on positive organizational characteristics, leaving the negative aspects to be discovered only after employment.

Organizations must address several issues in order to create a successful recruiting process that attracts a sufficient number of qualified applicants (Breaugh 1997). First, which recruiting sources should the organization use: internal (within the organization) or external (outside of the organization), or both? Second, how broadly and intensively must the organization recruit in order to obtain applicants? Third, what recruitment message does the organization want to convey? And fourth, what recruitment medium(s) will the organization use to communicate its message?

Internal Versus External Recruiting Sources.   The choice of internal vs. external recruiting sources depends on the organization's goals and its culture. One approach is to recruit externally for entry-level jobs and internally for all other jobs. Here, a premium is placed on maintaining a stable, loyal, and committed workforce over a long period of time. However, there may not be enough qualified and willing applicants internally for all positions, so sometimes organizations must recruit externally for these positions as well. Another approach is to recruit externally for virtually all positions. Here, no premium is placed on organizational loyalty and commitment. Instead, the goal is to recruit the best person for the job even if this means bypassing a more senior internal candidate.

There are numerous external recruitment sources. For most jobs, organizations use multiple sources to recruit applicants. The choice of a particular recruitment source depends on (1) the quantity of labor needed, (2) the quality of labor needed, (3) the availability of sources, (4) past or promised experiences with sources, (5) budget constraints, (6) contractual obligations, and (7) the effectiveness of sources (e.g., on measures such as satisfaction, job performance, and retention) (Heneman, Heneman, and Judge 1997).

Organizations recruit internally through either an open or a closed process. In an open recruitment process, internal candidates have the opportunity to apply or bid for available jobs. This usually is accomplished through some form of job posting system. In a closed recruitment process, internal candidates are not provided an opportunity to apply for available jobs. Instead, managers evaluate employee information (without the employees' knowledge that they are being considered) to identify possible candidates. This usually is accomplished through some form of (computerized nowadays) employee skill bank.

Recruiting Scope and Intensity.   The relevant labor market determines the scope and intensity of recruiting efforts. The relevant labor market for a job may be local, county, regional, state, national, or international. For example, the Boeing Company in Wichita, Kansas, needs to use only local recruiting sources for secretarial and clerical positions. Furthermore, an advertisement in the paper is all that is necessary to generate a sufficient supply of applicants. However, for specialized aerospace engineers, Boeing must recruit from an international labor market. The company will send recruiters all over the world in search of the best applicants. Thus, the relevant labor market depends on many variables such as the complexity of the job, the availability of qualified applicants, willingness of people to relocate or commute, etc.

Recruitment Message.   There are four types of recruitment messages an organization may use (Heneman, Heneman, and Judge 1997): traditional, realistic, attractive, and targeted. *Traditional recruitment messages* provide applicants with very little concrete or accurate information (e.g., "salary potential unlimited"). *Realistic recruitment* *messages* present the organization and the job as it really is, providing both positive and negative information. Texas Instruments provides students with a realistic job preview through their "Engineer Your Career" recruitment program described previously. An *attractive recruitment message* focuses solely on positive information about the organization and the job in order to induce applicants to join. *Targeted recruitment messages* focus on particular audiences (e.g., electrical engineers).

The choice of a recruitment message in large part depends on the demand for and supply of labor in the market. In a high-demand–low-supply labor market, employers must make greater efforts to attract sufficient qualified applicants. Consequently, an attractive or targeted recruitment message is most appropriate. In a low-demand–high-supply labor market, employers may use realistic recruitment messages to ensure better person-job and person-organization fits. Those who don't fit well will self-select out during the recruitment stage.

Recruitment Media.   Organizations may use numerous recruitment media to convey their recruitment message (Heneman, Heneman, and Judge 1997), such as recruitment brochures, advertisements, phone messaging systems, videos and videoconferencing, and online services using the Internet. Most organizations use more than one medium, and the controlling factors in choosing media are typically cost and ability to reach desired audiences.

Humana, the Louisville, Kentucky-based HMO with 20,000 employees serving six million members, is in the forefront of using the Internet for recruiting (Greengard 1998). Rather than having recruiters scan job sites such as The Monster Board, E.Span, etc., Humana uses a sophisticated smart-agent software, workflow, and back-end Oracle database that systematically checks personal web pages, Usenet sites, and other places people post resumes. The program uses company criteria to identify resumes to index and include in the database. Hot Jobs' Softshoe program manages the process, which frees up recruiters' time for other activities. Before implementing their Internet recruitment strategy, Humana was spending $128 in advertising per qualified resume. Internet recruiting has dropped that cost to six cents per qualified resume, saving the company $8.3 million per year.

MODULE
13

Evaluating the Recruitment Process.   In order to pinpoint problem areas in a recruitment process, many organizations use yield ratios. A *yield ratio* reflects the percentage of job candidates at the beginning of a step in the recruitment/selection process who move on to the next step in that process (Breaugh, 1997). For example, Figure 13.4 provides applicant flow data: the number of applicants who continue at each stage in the process.

The candidates-to-applicants yield ratio is 50/100 = 50 percent; the finalists-to-candidates ratio is 20/50 = 40 percent; the offer receivers-to-finalists ratio is 10/20 = 50 percent; the offer-acceptance to offer-receivers ratio is 8/10 = 80 percent; the

FIGURE 13.4 *Applicant Flow Data*

Applicant Flow Data

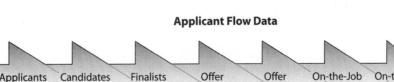
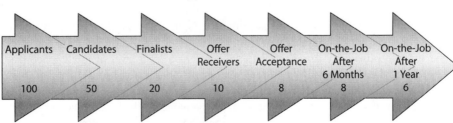

Applicants	Candidates	Finalists	Offer Receivers	Offer Acceptance	On-the-Job After 6 Months	On-the-Job After 1 Year
100	50	20	10	8	8	6

six-month retention ratio is 8/8 = 100 percent; and the one-year retention rate is 6/8 = 75 percent. Depending on specific organizational conditions, the candidates-to-applicants ratio of 50 percent may be considered low and suggest identifying alternative recruiting sources. The one-year retention rate of 75 percent may suggest additional problems related to the recruitment/selection process—for example, unrealistic expectations created by an overly positive recruitment message.

Summary.   Recruiting is a crucial prerequisite to a successful selection process. The quality of the applicant pool produced from the recruiting process sets an upper limit on the quality of selection decisions that an organization can make. A sophisticated selection procedure applied to a low-quality applicant pool can only pick the "best of the worst." On the other hand, a sophisticated selection procedure applied to a high-quality applicant pool can help an organization pick the "best of the best." Once you have an applicant pool, the next step is to select whom to hire.

Selecting Involves Assessing and Evaluating Applicants

Selecting employees involves several steps:

- Gathering information about applicants through the use of various selection methods in order to assess KSAOs and motivation

- Evaluating applicant KSAO and motivation data against job requirements to determine the likely degree of person-job fit

- Evaluating applicant KSAO and motivation data against organizational climate/culture assessments to determine the likely degree of person-organization fit

- Deciding which applicants to consider further and which to reject

- Making a job offer or offers

Selection Methods.   Numerous selection methods are available for gathering KSAO and motivation data on applicants. These methods can be categorized (Heneman, Heneman, and Judge 1997) as: initial assessment methods, substantive assessment methods, and contingent assessment methods as shown in Table 13.2.

Organizations use *initial assessment methods* primarily as screening devices in order to reduce the number of people assessed by more costly substantive methods administered later in the selection process. At a minimum, unqualified applicants are eliminated from the applicant pool. Commonly used initial assessment methods include resumes and cover letters, application blanks, biographical information, reference reports, and screening interviews.

Organizations use *substantive assessment methods* to further reduce the applicant pool in order to make final hiring decisions. Commonly used substantive assessment methods include ability tests, personality tests, job knowledge tests, performance tests and work samples, integrity tests, and interviews.

Organizations use *contingent assessment methods* as a final screen to ensure that those applicants offered jobs meet certain additional requirements. The two most commonly used contingent assessment methods are drug tests and medical exams.

From a practical standpoint, the following rules of thumb are helpful in gathering and evaluating applicant KSAO information. First, use multiple methods to gather KSAO information on applicants. For example, resumes, application blanks, and interviews may all provide evidence that an applicant has a high level of intelligence (see, e.g., Behling 1998). If you have several pieces of evidence collected from different sources showing that someone has the KSAOs (e.g., intelligence), it is more likely that you have measured them accurately. Second, past behavior is the best predictor of future behavior, so use information from resumes, application blanks, and interviews (as well

MODULE
13

TABLE 13.2 *Selection Methods: Average Validity Coefficients*

Initial Assessment Methods		Substantive Assessment Methods		Contingent Assessment Methods	
Resumes and cover letters	no data	Ability tests	.50	Drug tests	no data
Application blanks	.10–.20	Personality tests	.31	Medical exams	no data
Biographical information	.32–.37	Job knowledge tests	.45		
Reference reports	.16–.26	Performance tests and work samples	.54		
Screening interviews	no data	Integrity tests	.33–.35		
		Interviews	.37		

The validity coefficients in the table represent the ability of the selection methods to predict job performance. The ability of the same methods to predict other criteria, such as training performance, may vary. Validity coefficients can range from 0.00 (no validity) to 1.00 (highest possible validity). Generally, validity coefficients for selection methods do not exceed 0.50–0.60. Consequently, rules of thumb for judging the validity of selection methods typically consider those methods with average validities from 0.00–0.15 to have low validity, those with average validities from 0.16–0.30 to have moderate validity, and those with average validities from 0.31 and above to have high validity.

Source: Data from Heneman, Heneman, and Judge 1997

as other sources) to identify patterns of behavior. Third, hire based on how applicants actually behave in the hiring process, not simply on what they say they can do (Schneider and Bowen 1995). Rather than assume (based on an application blank or interview data) that an applicant can perform a task, devise some way to simulate real job situations when possible. Simulations create standardized conditions requiring applicants to display the kinds of behaviors needed to perform the job successfully. For example, you could role play an angry customer and observe how an applicant behaves to assess a customer service orientation. The applicant could then be asked to write a memo to her supervisor describing the incident (Schneider and Bowen 1995). These three rules of thumb improve the odds of making effective selection decisions.

Evaluating Selection Methods. The choice of specific selection methods for a particular situation depends upon several factors (Heneman, Heneman, and Judge 1997): reliability, validity, utility, applicant reactions, and adverse impact.

- *Reliability* refers to consistency of measurement:

  ✓ Does the selection method produce consistent information regarding applicant KSAOs? For example, unstructured job interviews are usually unreliable because two people assessing the same applicant will frequently disagree in their evaluations. Furthermore, the same applicant interviewed by the same interviewer at two different times is often evaluated differently as well.

- *Validity* refers to the ability of the selection method to predict a criterion (usually job performance). It is typically expressed as a correlation coefficient—see Table 13.2.

  ✓ Does use of the selection method help predict job performance accurately? For example, handwriting analysis (graphology) is widely used in western Europe, despite the fact that there is virtually no evidence that it predicts job performance!

- *Utility* refers to the cost/benefit analysis of using the selection method:

  ✓ Do the benefits of using the selection method outweigh the costs? For example, a department store currently hires store managers using an ability test, a personality test, and several structured interviews. Ninety percent of store managers hired using this procedure have been successful in the job (i.e., there is a high base rate of success). A consultant has offered to develop an assessment center for selecting store managers; however, the assessment center would be very expensive to develop and use and would only increase the base rate of success from 90 percent to 93 percent. Therefore, the utility (i.e., costs are greater than expected benefits) of the proposed assessment center probably does not justify its creation.

- *Applicant reactions* refers to the favorability or receptivity of applicants toward the use of the selection method:

  ✓ Do applicants respond favorably toward the selection method, and do they perceive it to be fair? Personality tests, while valid predictors of success in many jobs, are often viewed unfavorably by applicants. Applicants typically complain that such assessments don't appear to be related to job performance. Surprisingly, applicants often have unfavorable reactions to some of the more valid predictors of job performance, such as personality tests.

- *Adverse impact* refers to a selection method's likelihood of screening out a disproportionate number of applicants from a legally protected group:

  ✓ Does use of this selection method screen out proportionally more of a legally protected group compared to others? Even though cognitive ability tests are among the most valid of all selection methods, they do create adverse impact against some minorities. Consequently, most selection experts recommend using cognitive ability tests in conjunction with other selection methods that produce less adverse impact.

In summary, a useful selection method is one that is reliable, valid, with benefits that outweigh the costs of using it, favorable response from applicants to its use, and without a disproportionate number of legally protected group members screened out.

Selection Decision Making.   Once information on applicant KSAOs has been collected through the use of the various assessment methods previously described, the organization must combine that information to form an overall evaluation of the applicant in order to make decisions. Should we reject this applicant from further consideration? Should we make an offer to this applicant? If our first choice candidate turns us down, should we offer the job to our second choice candidate or should we reopen the recruitment process?

There are two primary approaches organizations can use to combine applicant KSAO information in order to form an overall evaluation of an applicant: compensatory or noncompensatory. A *compensatory* approach assumes that high levels on one KSAO can compensate for lower levels on another KSAO. Thus, two applicants could have the same overall evaluation derived from different combinations of strengths and weaknesses across KSAOs. In contrast, a *noncompensatory* approach assumes that high levels on one KSAO cannot compensate for lower levels on another KSAO. Typically, scores below some prespecified cutoff on a selection method eliminate an applicant from further consideration in a noncompensatory approach.

Once applicant KSAO information has been combined (through either a compensatory or noncompensatory approach), an overall evaluation score allows decision makers to select one or more applicants using decision rules. Two commonly used decision rules (Heneman, Heneman, and Judge 1997) are: (1) ranking from most to least desirable with top-down selection, and (2) grouping applicants into rank-ordered categories (e.g., top choices, acceptable choices, and last-resort choices) with top-down selection by groups.

The final step in the selection process is to make a job offer to a selected applicant or applicants. A job offer should include (Heneman, Heneman, and Judge 1997) starting date, duration of contract (fixed vs. indeterminate), compensation (starting pay, incentives and bonuses, benefits), hours of work, special hiring inducements (e.g., bonuses, relocation assistance), and acceptance terms.

Validation.   Both for legal protection and to ensure sound decision making, organizations should validate their selection practices. *Validation* is the process of gathering information to demonstrate that the inferences regarding applicants' job capabilities will lead to correct employment decisions. Validated selection practices are fair to all applicants and increase the odds that the best candidate is chosen for the job.

Three strategies can be used to document the validity of selection practices (Kleiman 1997): a content-oriented strategy, a criterion-related strategy, and a validity generalization strategy. The choice of validation strategy depends on both technical (e.g., sample size) and organizational (e.g., budgetary) constraints.

A *content-oriented strategy* focuses on demonstrating that "proper" procedures were followed in the development and use of selection devices. For example, a fire department that uses a ladder-climbing test as part of its selection process could show through a well-documented job analysis that climbing ladders is an essential component of the job. By demonstrating a one-to-one correspondence between important tasks of the job and important KSAOs assessed by the test, the fire department could establish the content validity of its practice.

A *criterion-related strategy* focuses on providing statistical evidence that shows a relationship between applicant selection scores and subsequent job performance levels. Ideally, an organization would collect data on a particular selection practice from applicants, but not use the data for making actual hiring decisions, at least not until the practice had been validated. This is called a *predictive validation design.* For example, a hospital wants to validate a new job knowledge test to be used in selecting medical records clerks. The test assesses applicants' knowledge of basic medical terminology. The hospital collects job knowledge test scores, interview scores, and application blank data from applicants. However, only the interview scores and application blank data are used to make hiring decisions (the job knowledge test scores are filed away for later use). After six months or a year, the job performance of those hired (who took the job knowledge test but were hired on the basis of the interview and application data) is assessed. If high and low scores on the job knowledge test were correlated with, respectively, high and low scores on the job performance measures, a statistical relationship would provide evidence of validity. Once validity evidence was established, the organization could then begin using the job knowledge test scores to help make selection decisions.

An alternative criterion-related strategy, called a *concurrent validation design,* does not require hiring employees without the use of the selection method being validated. Currently employed medical records clerks would be given the job knowledge test. Then their scores on the job knowledge test would be correlated with their most recent scores on job performance measures. Consequently, the organization would not have to wait six months to a year before evaluating the data. As with the predictive approach, a correlation between test scores and job performance measures would establish empirical evidence of validity.

A *validity generalization strategy* focuses on demonstrating that the validity of the selection procedures used have already been established by other organizations.

Validity generalization evidence consists of studies summarizing a selection measure's validity for similar jobs in other settings (Gatewood and Feild 1998). To use this published validity data in lieu of collecting validity data for itself, an organization must establish that (1) its job is similar to the same job or groups of jobs included in the validity generalization study, and (2) its selection measure is similar to the selection measure included in the validity generalization study.

Validation is a process that ensures organizations are using only selection methods that have some ability to predict job performance. Without validation data supporting the use of its selection methods, an organization would not know whether its selection practices were actually working as intended. Furthermore, without validation data to support its use of selection methods, an organization is in a more precarious legal position should its selection practices lead to adverse impact. This and other legal issues that form the context for selection will be discussed next.

The Legal Environment Constrains Recruitment and Selection

The legal environment in the United States imposes specific requirements on government organizations and on companies that do business with the federal government. In addition, the legal environment prohibits the use of certain criteria in recruitment and selection in both the public and private sectors and provides individuals and groups with recourse when they believe they have been victims of illegal discrimination.

The legal environment consists of federal laws, state laws, local laws, executive orders (issued by the President of the United States), and agency guidelines (issued by enforcement agencies). Federal laws take precedence over state laws unless the state laws are more restrictive. Major federal equal employment opportunity laws and executive orders affecting recruitment and selection include:

- The Civil Rights Act (1964, 1991)

- The Age Discrimination in Employment Act (1967)

- The Americans with Disabilities Act (1990)

- The Rehabilitation Act (1973)

- Executive Order 11246 (1965)

Several criteria are specifically prohibited from use in recruitment and selection: race, color, religion, sex, national origin, age, disability, handicap, and ancestry. Either direct or indirect consideration of these factors in recruitment and selection can lead to costly lawsuits for organizations and stressful experiences for individuals involved.

The two types of illegal discrimination are disparate treatment and disparate impact. *Disparate treatment discrimination* involves intentionally (either overtly or covertly) treating applicants differently based on illegal criteria (e.g., race, color, religion, etc.). *Disparate impact discrimination* occurs when employment practices (e.g., recruitment and selection) exclude a disproportionate number of a legally protected group (e.g., Native Americans, females, etc.) from consideration for a particular job.

While there are no guaranteed legally "safe" recruitment and selection practices, there are two ways to minimize legal liability. First, use recruitment and selection criteria that are (1) job related (focused on "essential job functions," major and nontrivial tasks), and (2) used because they are necessary for the safe and efficient operation of the business (i.e., "business necessity" based). Second, use recruitment and selection practices that are standardized (in content, administration, and scoring). Make sure that all applicants receive the same opportunities and are treated in a consistent and fair manner. By following these two prescriptions, it is possible to both comply with the law and make effective recruitment and selection decisions.

STRATEGIC ISSUES IN RECRUITMENT AND SELECTION

There are two major strategic issues in recruitment and selection to consider: (1) How can human resource selection affect the ability of an organization to formulate and implement a successful business strategy? (2) Should an organization "make" (develop internally) or "buy" (hire externally) its needed human resources? The answers to both of these questions provide direction for the development of an integrated staffing system.

The Strategic Impact of Human Resources

How can human resource selection affect the ability of an organization to formulate and implement a successful business strategy? There are three possible answers to this question (much of this discussion is drawn from Snow and Snell 1993):

1. *Traditional approaches* imply that there is no direct relationship between business strategy and human resource selection.

2. *Staffing as strategy implementation* implies that human resource selection influences business strategy implementation. A good match between human resources and business strategy leads to a successful strategy implementation, which increases the odds that the strategy will succeed in the marketplace.

3. *Staffing as strategy formation* implies that human resource selection influences business strategy formation. By matching strategy to human resource capabilities (instead of human resources to strategy as in the previous approach), the organization is able to fully capitalize on one of its core competencies.

Traditional Approaches

Traditional approaches to recruitment and selection have ignored or downplayed strategic issues. In these approaches, organizations view business strategy as a contextual feature, much like the legal, social, and political environment, and while it can't be ignored, it does not directly affect the fundamental goal of achieving a tight person-job fit (see, e.g., Pfeffer 1994). Traditional approaches to recruitment and selection assume that organizations and jobs can be separated into individual components, that people and jobs are stable, and that job performance can be measured validly and reliably. The practical implications of this approach are: (1) analyze the organization and jobs, (2) assess person-job fit, and (3) recruit, select, and staff the best qualified person for a specific job.

The traditional approach to recruitment and selection was probably best exemplified during World War I. The armies of the United States, England, and France used cognitive ability tests to select soldiers and place them where they fit the job best, regardless of particular military strategies. After the war, the practice of using cognitive ability tests in hiring spilled over into private industry. While organizations have gained much from the traditional approach, the rapidly changing current environment has caused concern that downplaying strategic issues may lead to disastrous results. Consequently, two new approaches to recruitment and selection have emerged that bring business strategy out of context and more directly into the foreground: staffing as strategy implementation and staffing as strategy formation.

Staffing as Strategy Implementation

This approach focuses on the need to recruit, select, and staff in a manner that makes it possible for an organization to achieve its chosen business strategy. Therefore, organizations must fit their recruitment and selection processes to their business strategy(ies).

MODULE
13

This approach assumes that the organization's business strategy is well defined and stable, that organizations can quickly deploy their human resources after choosing a strategic direction, and that fit between strategy and human resources is desirable. The practical implications of this model are: (1) Identify the organization's business strategy, (2) deduce the organizational capabilities needed to implement the strategy, and (3) recruit, select, and staff the organization with employees who have the needed organizational capabilities to implement the business strategy.

For example, Chaparral Steel is one of the five lowest-cost steel plants in the world (Garvin 1993). They are able to achieve this through continuous process improvements and organizational learning. This requires ongoing programs that involve everyone in the organization. First-line supervisors are sent on sabbaticals around the world where they visit university and industry leaders to develop knowledge of new work practices and technology. These supervisors are responsible for teaching other employees what they learn and embedding these advances in daily operations. This means that Chaparral's recruitment and selection must focus on hiring people who are good students, teachers, innovators, and experimenters.

Staffing as Strategy Formation

This approach focuses on the need to adapt organizations to rapidly changing environmental threats and opportunities. Rather than viewing strategy as fixed and staffing as variable (whereby staffing aligns with strategy), this approach proposes that staffing can influence strategy formation (i.e., both strategy and staffing are variable) (Lengnick-Hall and Lengnick-Hall 1988). Staffing as strategy formation can succeed by developing strategic capability among an organization's human resources. Rather than hiring a person for a specific job, the goal is to hire a person on a "value-added" basis, someone who offers KSAOs unique or different from the organization's current stock of human talent. This makes it possible for an organization to implement a wide array of strategies with minimal response times. In sports, this approach is equivalent to hiring "the best athletes" and building a strategy based on their skills rather than starting with a predetermined strategy and finding athletes with specific skills to implement the strategy.

Staffing as strategy formation makes several assumptions. First, it assumes that organizations can create successful business strategies from their pool of human resources, but there is no way to forecast the particular strategy that will emerge from a specific combination of human resources. Second, it assumes that staffing has equal status with other resource acquisition and allocation decisions in a firm. And third, it assumes that the fit between an organization's current strategy and human resources must be "loose" in order to provide the flexibility to adapt to the environment with minimal response time (i.e., human resource slack is a necessary component of organizational success).

The practical implications of staffing as strategy formation are threefold. First, the organization needs to hire the "best" people, emphasizing person-organization fit over person-job fit; and it needs to hire people with unique or complementary KSAOs compared to the organization's current human resources. As part of this staffing process, the organization should develop a broad base of organizational KSAOs in order to have the capability of implementing a wide array of potential business strategies. Finally, creating business strategies that capitalize on the human resource talents of the organization will ensure that an organization considers all possible directions it might take.

Becton Dickinson is a good example of the staffing as strategy formation approach. The company is a manufacturer of medical diagnostic equipment (Snow and Snell 1993). Its corporate executives identify broad guidelines and let product market strategies emerge from the bottom up in its 15 divisions. Within each division, a cross-functional team that includes division members, vendors, suppliers, and people from other divisions conceive strategies and then carry them out. While Becton Dickinson allows business strategies to emerge from its own divisions, network organizations take a different approach.

Network organizations consist of brokers who subcontract needed services to designers, suppliers, producers, and distributors linked by full disclosure information systems and coordinated by market mechanisms (Kolb, Oslund, and Rubin 1995). For example, Nike, Apple Computer, Reebok, and Benetton do very little manufacturing themselves. Each organization in the network has particular capabilities (human as well as others) to contribute for a specific purpose. Once that purpose has been fulfilled, the network reforms around, frequently, different contributing organizations. Because the participants in their networks may change with each product cycle, staffing involves nurturing relationships with many organizations.

Melding the Three Strategic Approaches

All three models discussed have potential benefits for an organization. The traditional approach implies that person-job fit can lead to greater efficiency and higher productivity. However, organizations must consider person-job fit in light of their business strategy(ies). Employees who perform their jobs well are not useful unless the jobs they perform support an effective business strategy. Furthermore, in the long run, an organization wedded to a particular strategy may encounter competitive realities that force change. Consequently having a broad base of KSAOs in the human resource pool may provide an organization with the capabilities to successfully adapt and survive. The assumptions and practical implications of each of the three staffing approaches are shown in Table 13.3 on page 13.28.

Make vs. Buy Human Resources

Should an organization "make" or "buy" its human resources? A "make" approach can best be described as a *pure development strategy:* hire just about anyone as long as they are willing and able to learn the KSAOs required by the job (Heneman, Heneman, and Judge 1997). The "make" approach is most associated with the staffing as strategy formation approach, where a long-term committed relationship is established between the organization and its employees. Careful hiring (e.g., using cognitive ability tests to assess ability to learn, and personality tests to assess important traits such as conscientiousness) is necessary to create a collection of employees who can easily adapt to changing business circumstances. Furthermore, employees who have multiple skills and abilities provide the organization with more options for creating a successful business strategy around their competencies.

A "buy" approach can best be described as a *pure staffing strategy:* the organization concentrates on hiring new employees who can "hit the ground running" and be at peak performance the moment they arrive (Heneman, Heneman, and Judge 1997). The "buy" approach is most associated with the staffing as strategy implementation approach, where employees with particular competencies are needed in order to effectively implement the chosen strategy. Time delays in implementation could lead to failure in the marketplace, so acquiring employees who can "hit the ground running" is often very desirable.

A combined "make" and "buy" approach may be appropriate in many organizations. For example, critical jobs that demand the latest technological skills may be filled using the "buy" approach, while less critical and less dynamic jobs may be filled using the "make" approach. The combined "make" and "buy" approach allows organizations to take advantage of the benefits of both approaches, but may send mixed signals

TABLE 13.3   *Three Approaches to Staffing Strategy*

Staffing Approach	Assumptions	Practical Implications
Traditional	Organizations and jobs can be separated into individual components.	Analyze the organization and jobs.
	People and jobs are stable.	Assess person-job fit.
	Job performance can be measured validly and reliably.	Recruit, select, and staff the best-qualified person for a specific job.
Staffing as Strategy Implementation	Business strategies are well defined and stable.	Identify the organization's business strategy(ies).
	Human resources can be quickly aligned with business strategy.	Deduce the organizational capabilities needed to implement the strategy.
	A fit between human resources and strategy is desirable.	Recruit, select, and staff the organization with employees who have needed organizational capabilities for strategy implementation.
Staffing as Strategy Formation	Organizations can create successful business strategies from their pool of human resources.	Hire the "best" people emphasizing person-organization fit over person-job fit.
	Staffing has equal status with other resource decisions of the firm.	Develop a broad base of organizational KSAOs for strategic adaptability.
	There must be a "loose" fit between an organization's strategy and its human resources.	Create business strategies that capitalize on the organization's human resource talents.

to employees about career opportunities. If hard work and loyalty are rewarded with promotions at one level but downplayed at another, the organization may experience greater turnover among its best employees.

Organizations are dynamic systems utilizing inputs (such as human resources) for transformation processes (such as adding value to products or services) that result in outputs (products or services). To remain competitive, organizations must develop "healthy" (i.e., functional) human resource flows. *Human resource flows* include the addition of new hires from outside of the organization, the movement of employees within the organization (upward, downward, and laterally), and the movement of employees out of the organization (voluntary and involuntary terminations, retirements, etc.). For example, too much turnover of high-performing employees is like a patient who loses too much blood in a surgical operation—the prognosis for the future is not promising. On the other hand, too little turnover of low-performing employees may cause an organization to become rigidly inflexible, and thus incapable of adapting to changing environments—the prognosis for its future is not good either. Recruiting and selection processes are like valves that regulate the human resource flows of an organization. Consequently, careful attention must be paid to how they affect organizational functioning in the long term.

Summary

Countless individual recruitment and selection decisions ultimately add up to a collection of human resources in an organization. The make-up (KSAOs) of an organization's human resources is critical to both its short-term and long-term success. Consequently, managers today have to see both the forest (strategy) and the trees (individual decisions) in order to successfully recruit and select people for their organizations.

APPLICATION

There is a wealth of useful organization and job information on the Internet. Most large companies, and increasingly many smaller ones as well, are establishing a presence on the Internet for recruiting job applicants.

This exercise is based on information available at Citibank's web site for their Global Management Associates program. Citibank has over 3,400 offices located in almost 100 countries providing a wide range of financial services. Their Global Management Associates program provides job/career opportunities that vary by the nature of specific businesses in terms of education, experience, and language requirements as well as functional emphasis, but they share a common purpose: to bring fresh talent to be developed into the future leaders of the Citibank organization. Citibank encourages their managers to acquire cross-business, cross-functional, and cross-geographical experiences to better meet the demands of leading a complex global business.

The success of the Global Management Associates program can be measured by the quality of their senior management team. A majority of Citibank's senior management team began their careers in either a Global Management Associate (MA) or Technical Associate (TA) Program. In fact, John S. Reed, the company's current chairman, began his career over 30 years ago as a Global Management Associate.

MODULE
13

Preparing for Class Discussion

Students should complete the following steps before coming to class:

Part I: Background Information on the Organization

1. Find Citibank's Global Management Associates web site on the Internet *(www.citicorp.com/hr)*.

2. Click on "CEO John Reed Talks About Citibank" and the "Chairman's Letter."

   ✓ Print a copy of each for your reference.

   ✓ What is the overall strategy of the company?

3. Click on "Organization Chart."

   ✓ Print a copy of the organization chart for your reference.

4. Click on "Citibank Businesses" and read it.

   ✓ What are Citibank's core business franchises? (Click on each one and print a copy for your reference.)

   ✓ What are Citibank's support businesses? (Click on each one and print a copy for your reference.)

5. Click on "Corporate Citizenship" and read it.

6. Click on "History of Citibank" and read it.

7. Click on "Management Bios" and read them.

   ✓ Are there any commonalities in backgrounds, education, and experience among these managers?

Part II: Background Information on the Job

1. Click on "You and Citibank" and read it.

   ✓ What 8 to 10 attributes (knowledge, skills, abilities, and other characteristics) should Citibank use to assess applicants for its Global Management Associates Program?

   ✓ For each of the attributes, identify three indicators/evidence you would obtain from applicants in order to assess their level of those attributes. For each of those indicators/evidence of attributes, identify how you would obtain that information from applicants (e.g., application blank, resume, interview, etc.).

2. Click on "Citibank on the Road" and read it.

   ✓ Looking over the list of colleges and universities where Citibank recruits, how would you describe their recruiting strategy in terms of sources, scope, and intensity?

3. Click on "Career Development" and read it. Also click on the "Wet Feet Press" link and read it.

   ✓ What do these documents tell you about potential rewards offered by a Global Management Associates job?

   ✓ What do these documents tell you about careers and career development at Citibank?

4. Click on "A Day in the Life" and read the testimonials about the Global Management Associates Program.

   ✓ As a recruiting method, what type of message is conveyed: traditional, realistic, attractive, or targeted?

   ✓ How effective is this approach to recruiting?

In Conclusion

Debrief

Recruitment and selection are key human resource activities in every organization. You cannot have an organization until you hire some employees. Furthermore, you cannot sustain an organization unless you replenish your human resources when they are depleted. Whenever a current employee moves either within the organization (through promotions, demotions, or transfers) or outside the organization (through voluntary turnover, involuntary turnover, retirement, death, etc.), it creates a job vacancy. Therefore, recruitment (internal and external) and selection (internal and external) are continuous processes in organizational life.

A key issue faced by all organizations is whom to hire—applicants who fit a specific job well or applicants who fit the organization well? This module demonstrated that organizations must achieve both types of fit in order to be maximally effective. Organizations need employees who can both perform specific jobs well, and share values and goals with the organization's culture. However, as the pace of change in global markets continues, more organizations will place greater emphasis on hiring multiskilled (or trainable) employees who are compatible with the organization's culture and less emphasis on specific person-job fits.

Both recruitment and selection involve systematic planning and decision making. This module highlights the importance of recruitment in setting upper limits for the quality of selection decision making. An applicant pool must contain sufficient quantity and quality in order to provide the opportunity to choose those applicants who best fit both available jobs and the organization.

The legal environment places some constraints on recruitment and selection. Legislation prohibits specific criteria from use in recruitment and selection: race, color, religion, sex, national origin, age, handicap, disability, and ancestry. However, organizations that recruit and select employees with job-related criteria and procedures that are applied consistently can achieve both legal compliance and high-quality hires.

Finally, strategic issues in recruitment and selection have become more important as markets have become both more global and more competitive. Traditional approaches to recruitment and selection in which employees were hired to fit a specific job regardless of the organization's strategy are being replaced by new approaches. Organizations must align their recruitment and selection practices with their business strategy(ies); organizations must have the human capabilities that enable them to effectively implement their chosen strategy(ies). Moreover, some organizations even consider their human resource talents as a source for competitive advantage and adapt business strategies to fit those organizational capabilities. This is especially true for the increasing number of network organizations.

The future will challenge organizations and their management—more networked arrangements, more team-based operations, more rapidly changing jobs, and more rapidly evolving markets. Human resource professionals will need to adapt fundamental recruitment and selection principles in order to meet this challenge. Indeed, organizational success or failure will rest heavily on the ability to attract and select the best employees.

Suggested Readings

Bridges, W. 1994. The end of the job. *Fortune* 130(6): 62–74.

Bowen, D. E., G. E. Ledford, and B. R. Nathan. 1991. Hiring for the organization, not the job. *Academy of Management Executive* 5: 35–51.

Judge, T. A., and G. R. Ferris. 1992. The elusive criterion of fit in human resources staffing decisions. *Human Resource Planning* 15: 47–67.

Powell, G. N. 1998. The simultaneous pursuit of person-organization fit and diversity. *Organizational Dynamics* Winter: 50–61.

Critical Thinking Questions

1. Assume that there is a "good fit" between employee qualifications and job requirements. What other HR factors could inhibit job performance and make an employee who was a "good fit" perform poorly?

2. Assume that there is a "poor fit" between employee qualifications and job requirements. What other HR factors could facilitate job performance and make an employee who was a "poor fit" perform well?

3. What KSAOs are necessary for effective team members?

4. What aspects of a recruitment and selection process are likely to affect applicant reactions (either favorably or unfavorably)?

5. Identify two jobs for which a compensatory approach to combining applicant KSAOs would be appropriate. Explain your rationale. Identify two jobs for which a noncompensatory approach to combining applicant KSAOs would be appropriate. Explain your rationale.

Exercises

1. It is Monday morning. Your Administrative Assistant quit last Friday. You need to fill this job by Wednesday; a large amount of specialized paperwork will need to be completed by the end of the week, so it is imperative that you fill the position as quickly as possible with the right person for the job. Unfortunately, there is no job description for the job, and the previous jobholder tailored the job to fit his particular strengths and preferences.

   - In a small group (e.g., five people), detail all of the steps you would take to recruit and select someone to fill the job opening.

2. Exercise 2 can be done either individually or in small groups.

   A small general contracting firm builds about 60 single-family homes and 6 multifamily projects a year. It draws plans for buildings and makes cost estimates. Then the firm invites subcontractors to bid for various aspects of the work. The firm employs 10 people. Company personnel supervise construction and then sell the properties to others or keep them for investment purposes. The company president feels that it is time to hire an additional construction superintendent. The superintendent's tasks include:

   ✓ Ensure prompt adherence to oral commitments

   ✓ Do a walk-through inspection with customer of production supervisor

   ✓ Complete superintendent's quality control checklist at specified intervals or phase of construction

   ✓ Differentiate between possible and impossible conditions on the various classifications of construction (Section 8, custom, commercial, etc.)

   ✓ Schedule work and materials in accordance with critical path set by company

   ✓ Inspect work progress daily and determine adherence to critical path

   ✓ Adjust schedule in accordance with work progress/delays

   ✓ Notify subcontractors and suppliers of accelerated or delayed progress to negotiate their time in

   ✓ Read and interpret plans and specifications

   ✓ Correct and document errors in plans

   ✓ Recognize when on-site changes create problems in other areas of the building

   ✓ Identify common errors made by layout person or architect

   ✓ Recognize deviations from the plans or code

   ✓ Call for subcontractor when job is ready for that phase of operation

   ✓ Ask subcontractor about work methods, production, availability of workmen

   ✓ Inspect a subcontractor's work

   ✓ Identify opportunities for theft and vandalism, and specify or take countermeasures, depending on costs/benefits

✓ Recognize violations of OSHA safety standards

✓ Keep an inventory of company equipment and tools

- Group the tasks into three or four related KSAO dimensions (e.g., communication skills, memory, etc.) for selection purposes. Name the dimensions.

- What applicant KSAOs would you assess with an interview?

- How would you assess applicants on the remaining dimensions? Develop a selection plan for this job in which you specify how applicant KSAOs will be assessed for each task.

3. A customer sales representative in a department store has "front-line" contact with customers. A "moment of truth" occurs whenever a customer comes into contact with any aspect of the service and draws conclusions about its overall service quality. One good way to assess applicants for such positions is to use a behavioral simulation. A behavioral simulation creates standardized conditions requiring applicants to display the kinds of behavior needed for successful job performance. A good place to start in creating a behavioral simulation is to identify a critical incident from your own personal experience with customer sales representatives. Here's a format to help you. Try to think of several positive experiences and several negative experiences you have had with customer sales representatives in a department store. For each experience, write your answers to the following questions:

- What were the circumstances leading to the incident?

- What did the customer sales representative do that made you think he or she was a good/average/poor performer?

- What were the consequences of the customer sales representative's behavior in this incident?

MODULE
13

Next, create a role-play simulation in which the interviewer plays the role of the customer and the applicant plays the role of the customer sales representative. Write out the script for the customer and develop a method for scoring applicant responses.

References

Behling, O. 1998. Employee selection: Will intelligence and conscientiousness do the job? *The Academy of Management Executive* 12: 77–86.

Borman, W. C., and S. J. Motowidlo. 1993. Expanding the criterion domain to include elements of contextual performance. In *Personnel selection in organizations,* ed. N. Schmitt, and W. Borman, 71–98. San Francisco: Jossey-Bass.

Bowen, D. E., G. E. Ledford, and B. R. Nathan. 1991. Hiring for the organization, not the job. *The Academy of Management Executive* 5: 35–51.

Breaugh, J. A. 1997. Recruiting. In *The Blackwell encyclopedic dictionary of human resource management,* ed. L. H. Peters, C. R. Greer, and S. A. Youngblood, 286–287. Oxford, England: Blackwell Publishers, Inc.

Breaugh, J. A. 1997. Yield ratios. In *The Blackwell encyclopedic dictionary of human resource management,* ed. L. H. Peters, C. R. Greer, and S. A. Youngblood, 402. Oxford, England: Blackwell Publishers, Inc.

Bridges, W. 1994. The end of the job. *Fortune* 130(6): 62–74.

Dawis, R. V. 1991. A psychological theory of work adjustment. In *Applying Psychology in business: The handbook for managers and human resource professionals,* ed. J. W. Jones, B. D. Steffy, and D. W. Bray, 535-541. Lexington, MA: Lexington Books.

Flynn, G. 1994. Attracting the right employees and keeping them. *Personnel Journal,* 73(12): 44–49.

Freiberg, K, and J. Freiberg 1996. *Nuts! Southwest Airlines' crazy recipe for business and personal success.* Austin: Bard Press.

Garvin, D. A. 1993. Building a learning organization. *Harvard Business Review.* 71 (4): 42–55.

Gatewood, R. D., and H. S. Feild. 1998. *Human resource selection.* Fourth ed. 342. Fort Worth: The Dryden Press.

Greengard, S. 1998. Humana takes online recruiting to a hire level. *Workforce* 77(8): 73–76.

Harvey, R. J. 1997. Task. In *The Blackwell encyclopedic dictionary of human resource management,* ed. L. H. Peters, C. R. Greer, and S.A. Youngblood, 344. Oxford, England: Blackwell Publishers, Inc.

Heneman, H. G., III, R. L. Heneman, and T. A. Judge. 1997. *Staffing organizations.* Second ed. Chicago: Irwin.

Kleiman, L. S. 1997. *Human resource management: A tool for competitive advantage.* 144–147. Minneapolis: West Publishing Co.

Kolb, D. A., J. S. Osland, and I. M. Rubin. 1995. *Organizational behavior: An experiential approach.* Sixth ed. 527. Englewood Cliffs, NJ: Prentice-Hall.

Lengnick-Hall, C. A., and M. L. Lengnick-Hall 1988. Strategic human resources management: A review of the literature and a proposed typology. *Academy of Management Review* 13: 454–470.

Milkovich, G. T., and J. M. Newman 1996. *Compensation.* Fifth ed. 305. Chicago: Irwin.

O'Reilly, C. A., J. Chatman, and D. F. Caldwell 1991. People and organizational culture: A profile-comparison approach to assessing person-organization fit. *Academy of Management Journal* 34: 487–516.

Pfeffer, J. 1994. *Competitive advantage through people: Unleashing the power of the workforce.* Boston: Harvard Business School Press.

Rynes, S. L., and A. E. Barber 1990. Applicant attraction strategies: An organizational perspective. *Academy of Management Review* 15: 286–310.

Schneider, B., and D. E. Bowen 1995. *Winning the service game.* Boston: Harvard Business School Press.

Schneider, B., and D. B. Smith 1997. Organizational culture and selection. In *The Blackwell encyclopedic dictionary of human resource management,* ed. L. H. Peters, C. R. Greer, and S. A. Youngblood, 240–241. Oxford, England: Blackwell Publishers, Inc.

Siegel, M. November 9, 1998. The perils of culture conflict. *Fortune,* 257–262.

Snow, C. C., and S. A. Snell 1993. Staffing as Strategy. In *Personnel selection in organizations,* ed. N. Schmitt, and W. Borman, 448–478. San Francisco: Jossey-Bass.

Spector, P. E. 1997. KSAOs. In *The Blackwell encyclopedic dictionary of human resource management,* ed. L. H. Peters, C. R. Greer, and S.A. Youngblood, 197. Oxford, England: Blackwell Publishers, Inc.

Steers, R. M., and L. W. Porter 1991. *Motivation and work behavior.* 478. New York: McGraw-Hill.

Ulrich, D. 1997. *Human resource champions: The next agenda for adding value and delivering results.* 154–156. Boston: Harvard Business School Press.

Villanova, P., and P. M. Muchinsky. 1997. Person-job fit. In *The Blackwell encyclopedic dictionary of human resource management,* ed. L. H. Peters, C. R. Greer, and S. A. Youngblood, 257–258. Oxford, England: Blackwell Publishers, Inc.

MODULE
13

Index

Ability, 13.11, 13.12

Ability tests, 13.8, 13.13. *See also* Cognitive ability tests

Adverse impact, evaluating selection methods, 13.22

Applicant flow data, evaluating the recruitment process, 13.19–20

Applicant pool, 13.7, 13.8, 13.16, 13.17, 13.20

Applicant reactions, evaluating selection methods, 13.22

Assessment methods, 13.22

Attracting applicants, 13.4, 13.11, 13.17

Attractive recruitment messages, 13.19

Business strategy, 13.4, 13.10, 13.14, 13.25, 13.26, 13.27, 13.31

Classic selection model, 13.11

Climate/culture. *See* Organizational culture

Closed recruitment process, 13.18

Cognitive ability tests, 13.13–14, 13.27

Compensatory approach, applicant evaluation, 13.22

Congruence, 13.12, 13.13

Conscientiousness, 13.13

Content-oriented strategy, 13.23. *See also* Validition of selection practices

Contextual performance, 13.13

Contingent assessment methods, 13.20–21

Criterion-oriented strategy, 13.23. *See also* Validition of selection practices

Customer service orientation, 13.21

Decision making, recruitment and selection process, 13.8, 13.10

Decision rules, applicant evaluation, 13.22–23

Discrimination, employment practices, 13.24

Disparate impact, discrimination, 13.24

Disparate treatment, discrimination, 13.24

Equal employment opportunity laws, 13.24

External recruiting sources, 13.18

Extrinsic rewards, 13.11

Grouping, applicant evaluation, 13.23

"Hire for attitude, train for skills," 13.16

Human resource information system (HRIS), 13.7

Human resource investment, 13.12

Human resource selection, strategic impact, 13.25

Human resources, 13.27–29

Individual qualifications, 13.11, 13.12

Initial assessment methods, 13.20–21

Internal recruiting sources, 13.18

Internet, use in recruiting, 13.7, 13.8, 13.19, 13.29

Interview protocol, 13.4

Interviews, coworker, 13.13, 13.14

Intrinsic rewards, 13.11

Job analysis, 13.4, 13.5, 13.9, 13.10, 13.25,

Job context, job analysis, 13.10

Job preview, 13.13, 13.14, 13.18. *See also* Work sample tests

Job requirements-qualifications match, 13.6, 13.20

Job rewards, 13.8, 13.11

Knowledge, job analysis, 13.10

Knowledge tests, 13.8, 13.23

KSAOs (knowledge, skills, abilities, and other characteristics), 13.4, 13.10–11, 13.12, 13.17, 13.20, 13.21, 13.22, 13.23, 13.29

Legal compliance, recruitment and selection, 13.24, 13.31

Level of proficiency, job analysis, 13.10

Long-term employment relationship, 13.6

Managerial activities, 13.5

Matching process, 13.4, 13.6, 13.12

Motivation, evaluating applicants, 13.20

Motivation-rewards match, 13.6

Multiple assessment methods, 13.20–21

Multiple skills and talents, 13.17, 13.30–31

Network organizations, 13.27, 13.31

Noncompensatory approach, applicant evaluation, 13.22

Organization analysis, 13.4, 13.9, 13.10, 13.25

Organization climate/culture. *See* Organizational culture

Organizational capabilities, 13.5, 13.9, 13.26

Organizational citizens, 13.14

Organizational culture, 13.8, 13.9, 13.10, 13.13, 13.14, 13.15, 13.16, 13.17, 13.30 profile, 13.15

Organizational Culture Profile (OCP), 13.14

Organizational goals/objectives, 13.9, 13.13

Overall evaluation, 13.22

Overqualified employee, 13.12

Performance (job), 13.10, 13.14, 13.23, 13.25

Performance tests, 13.8

Person-job fit, 13.4, 13.5, 13.8, 13.12–13,
    13.19, 13.25
    hiring for, 13.13
Person-organization fit, 13.4, 13.5, 13.8,
    13.13–14, 13.16–17, 13.19
    benefits and costs of hiring for, 13.16–17
    selection methods, 13.13
Personality assessment tests, 13.8, 13.13,
    13.14, 13.17, 13.18, 13.27
Predictive validation design, 13.23
Predictor of behavior, 13.20
Predictor of performance, 13.14, 13.24

Qualifications, 13.11. *See also* Person-job fit
Qualifications-job requirements match, 13.6

Ranking, applicant evaluation, 13.23
Realistic recruitment messages, 13.18–19
Recruiting sources, 13.18
Recruitment, 13.7, 13.17
    scope and intensity, 13.18
Recruitment and selection.
    core concepts, 13.5
    legal regulation, 13.4, 13.5, 13.24
    process, 13.6–11, 13.20
    strategic issues, 13.4, 13.10, 13.25, 13.31
    traditional approaches, 13.25
Recruitment media, 13.19
Recruitment message, 13.18
Reliability, evaluating selection methods, 13.21
Rewards, 13.11
Rewards-motivation match, 13.6

Screening, 13.7
Selection decision making, 13.22, 13.29
Selection methods, 13.8, 13.20–22, 13.24
Simulations of job situations, 13.21
Skill, job analysis, 13.10
Staffing, 13.5, 13.9, 13.25
Staffing strategies, 13.25–28
Standardized selection practices, 13.24
Strategy formation approach, 13.25, 13.26,
    13.28
Strategy implementation approach, 13.25–26,
    13.28
Structured interviews, 13.8
Substantive assessment methods, 13.20–21

Targeted recruitment messages, 13.19
Task, job analysis, 13.10
Traditional approach, recruitment and
    selection, 13.25, 13.28, 13.31
Traditional recruitment messages, 13.18
Transactional activities, 13.5
Transformational activities, 13.5, 13.10

Underqualified employee, 13.12
Utility, evaluating selection methods, 13.22

Validation of selection practices, 13.23–24
Validity, evaluating selection methods, 13.21
Validity generalization strategy, 13.23–24. *See
    also* validition of selection practices

Work sample tests, 13.8, 13.13, 13.14

MANAGING HUMAN RESOURCES
IN THE 21ST CENTURY

From Core Concepts to Strategic Choice

MODULE 14

Selecting Employees Today

What Managers Need to Know

Sandra L. Fisher
PERSONNEL DECISIONS RESEARCH INSTITUTE

Michael E. Wasserman
GEORGE MASON UNIVERSITY

Managing Human Resources in the 21st Century: From Core Concepts to Strategic Choice,
by Kossek and Block

Publisher: Dave Shaut
Executive Editor: John Szilagyi
Developmental Editor: Bryant Editorial Development
Marketing Manager: Joseph A. Sabatino
Production Editor: Tamborah E. Moore
Manufacturing Coordinator: Dana Began Schwartz
Cover Design: Tin Box Studio
Cover Photographs: Copyright Shoji Sato/Photonica
Production House: The Left Coast Group, Inc.
Printer: West Group

Printed in the United States of America
1 2 3 4 5 02 01 00 99

For more information contact South-Western College Publishing, 5101 Madison Road, Cincinnati, Ohio, 45227 or find us on the Internet at *http://www.swcollege.com*
For permission to use material from this text or product, contact us by
- telephone: 1-800-730-2214
- fax: 1-800-730-2215
- web: *http://www.thomsonrights.com*

ISBN: 0–324–01813–4

This book is printed on acid-free paper.

Contents

MODULE OVERVIEW   14.4

OBJECTIVES   14.4

RELATION TO THE FRAME   14.4

CORE CONCEPTS IN SELECTION SYSTEMS   14.5
    Traditional Core Concepts   14.6
    Emerging Core Concepts   14.12

STRATEGIC ISSUES IN SELECTION SYSTEMS   14.15
    Selection for Competitive Advantage:
    Developing Organizational Capabilities   14.15

APPLICATION   14.16
    Selecting for Information Technology Jobs   14.16
    Developing "Internal" Selection Systems   14.17
    Adaptability in the Army   14.17

IN CONCLUSION   14.18
    Debrief   14.18
    Suggested Readings   14.18
    Critical Thinking Questions   14.21
    Exercises   14.21

INDEX   14.23

MODULE
14

14.3

MODULE OVERVIEW

As made clear by the popular press and business newspapers and magazines over the past several years, the manner in which organizations compete is rapidly changing. These shifts in how firms compete have naturally driven changes in the content and structure of the work that people do. The expectations employers and employees have about the nature of the job have changed, and uncertainty about the role of the individual within the organization has increased (Cascio 1995; Howard 1995). This module is designed to help shed light on the impact of workplace changes on selection practices, and to help managers decide how to undertake most effectively the important task of staffing their organizations.

OBJECTIVES

Some of the key learning objectives of this module are for students to understand and be able to apply the following concepts:

- Important statistical and legal issues related to developing and evaluating the usefulness of selection measures

- The expanding definition of job performance, including adaptability and contextual performance

- Relationships between strategic direction and selection methods

RELATION TO THE FRAME

Selection has traditionally been considered a transactional HR role. The process of choosing which applicants will join the organization is often viewed as a standard function that is simply carried out on a regular basis, depending on how frequently the organization needs new employees. However, this chapter suggests that selection should play a transitional role in organizations. The selection process should be used to help the organization continually adjust to rapidly changing environmental forces. The current shift from a manufacturing- to an intellectual capital-based economy puts a premium on knowledge and expertise. Selection plays a pivotal role in enabling organizations to develop and maintain intellectual capital. Selection can also help support transformational activities. For example, when organizations move to team-based work systems, procedures especially designed to identify team players can be implemented. Selection can also be used strategically to identify individuals with characteristics aligned with an organization's strategic direction. Human Resource roles can be categorized as transactional, translational, transitional, or transformational (Figure 14.1).

Employers generally have unilateral control over selection procedures and decisions. Organizations conduct their own job analyses, develop selection tests, and implement selection procedures with minimal outside influence. External standards exist for the process that organizations should follow to develop their selection tests (the *Principles for the Validation and Use of Personnel Selection Procedures* [SIOP 1987] and the *Standards for Educational and Psychological Testing*), but specific decisions concerning which tests to use and how to use them are made by the employer. Additionally, the government exerts some control over the outcomes of selection procedures. Organizations are held to certain standards of societal fairness in their hiring practices. As you will see later in the module, the concept of adverse impact is a concern for many organizations as they develop and implement their selection systems.

FIGURE 14.1   *A Frame for Understanding Human Resource Strategy:*
Context, Roles, and Constraints

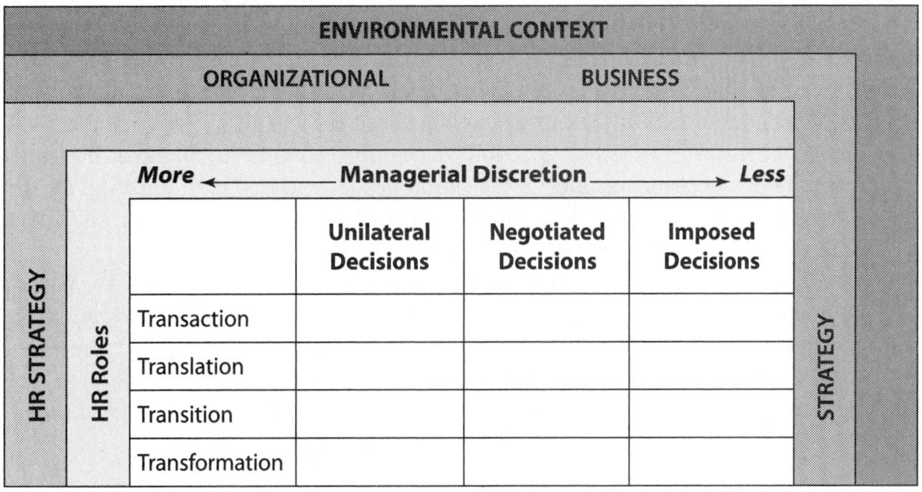

		More ← Managerial Discretion → Less		
		Unilateral Decisions	**Negotiated Decisions**	**Imposed Decisions**
	Transaction			
	Translation			
	Transition			
	Transformation			

ENVIRONMENTAL CONTEXT — ORGANIZATIONAL — BUSINESS — HR STRATEGY — HR Roles — STRATEGY

© 2000 by Ellen Ernst Kossek and Richard Block. Thanks to Brian Pentland, Karen Markel, and John Beck for helpful comments and discussions that enhanced the model.

CORE CONCEPTS IN SELECTION SYSTEMS

Employee selection is the process of matching an individual's characteristics and capabilities to the requirements of a job. Job requirements are determined through a process called *job analysis* (see Lengnick-Hall, Module 13, pp. 13.1–36 for a review), which involves outlining the tasks performed on the job and defining the knowledge, skills, abilities, and other characteristics (KSAOs) needed to perform those tasks. Hiring managers must then find a way to determine which applicants have the KSAOs required for the job. An applicant must possess certain levels of these important characteristics, or selection criteria, to be hired for the job. As you will see throughout this module, managers and researchers look at many different characteristics of prospective employees and use many different methods to determine which applicants have those characteristics.

In this section, we will discuss traditional selection concepts by first reviewing several issues relevant to the measurement of selection criteria and the legal and ethical use of those measures. It is critical to understand the statistical concepts of reliability and validity in relationship to selection tests. Reliability and validity are key issues in test development, but are equally critical to a manager's ability to be a good consumer of selection methodologies. Test developers should always document evidence of reliability and validity so that potential test users can evaluate the test. Additionally, managers must understand the legal issues inherent in selection, most notably the concept of adverse impact.

After laying the foundation of employee selection with the statistical and legal concepts, we will review some of the individual differences that tend to predict job performance and discuss traditional ways in which these individual differences are measured. Finally, we will address ways in which the selection process is evolving to keep up with changes in the business environment. Two emerging core concepts are discussed in this section: the adaptability of employees to the changing world of work, and contextual performance.

Traditional Core Concepts

Statistical and Legal Issues. To apply a consistent, strategic approach to selecting employees, and to comply with legal and professional selection standards, managers use a variety of selection methods to choose which employees to hire. These selection methods can include interviews, personality tests, cognitive ability tests, motor skill tests, and work samples. But before discussing these tests in detail, statistical principles that are relevant to any test or selection procedure need to be highlighted. Throughout this module, whenever we refer to the properties of a test, we are referring to any selection procedure, whether it is a paper-and-pencil test, an interview, or any other procedure used to make employment decisions.

These statistical principles, often referred to as psychometric properties, are important for many reasons. Managers need to ensure that selection tests measure precisely what managers intend that they measure, and to ensure that the tests work consistently among candidates. The two key statistical issues that managers need to be aware of with regard to employment testing are reliability and validity. One important legal aspect of selection—adverse impact—is also discussed in this section.

Reliability

Reliability is an index of the consistency of a measure. When using any kind of measure to select employees, organizations must ensure that the characteristics of each candidate are measured in the same way. Reliability is an index of the extent to which an individual's score on a test is caused by the actual characteristic being measured rather than factors that are irrelevant to the characteristic. These irrelevant factors are considered error. Several of the models that can be used to determine the reliability of a measure are discussed below.

The first model is *test-retest reliability*. In this model, we want to know if a person's test scores would change over time even if the characteristic we are measuring does not change. Error is simply attributed to the passage of time. The index of test-retest reliability is a correlation. Test-retest reliability is examined by computing the correlation between scores on the exact same test administered at two different times. Unless the characteristic actually changes between the two occasions, the two test scores should be exactly the same. However, the scores often differ based on error, or irrelevant factors such as the temperature in the testing room, the time of day when the test is administered, and the other people present in the room.

Test-retest reliability is most appropriate for characteristics that are not expected to change easily or quickly, such as cognitive ability and personality traits. For example, if an applicant takes a test that measures his conscientiousness (a personality trait), he should have approximately the same score on that test on Friday as he did on Wednesday. The passage of time alone should not affect the test scores. Test-retest would not be an appropriate index of the reliability of a test that measures mood, as mood can change several times a day.

The second model of reliability is *parallel forms*. In this model, we want to know if two different forms of a test are measuring the same concept or characteristic. Error is attributed to the particular items that were chosen for the test. When researchers are designing a test, they cannot ask every possible question that is relevant to the construct of interest. They must select a sample of items to actually include in the test. With parallel forms, we are looking to see if the specific items that were chosen for the test make a difference in a person's test score. Ideally, many different sets of items should be able to measure a construct equally well. The index of parallel forms reliability is the correlation, and is computed by correlating the scores on two versions of tests measuring the same concept.

Parallel forms reliability is often a very important form of reliability in terms of the security of selection tests. Organizations typically test a group of applicants for a position over a period of several days, if not weeks. Parallel forms of tests, especially knowledge tests or interview questions, help minimize the possibility that the testing process will be compromised.

The third model of reliability is *internal consistency.* Like parallel forms reliability, internal consistency reliability looks at the specific items that were chosen for the test. In this model, we want to know if different halves of a test are measuring the same concept or characteristic. The primary advantage of internal consistency reliability over the other forms is that an estimate of reliability can be computed with only one form of the test (unlike parallel forms) and with only one administration of the test (unlike test-retest). The most popular way to compute an index of a measure's internal consistency reliability is with coefficient alpha. Coefficient alpha is not a correlation, but it normally ranges from 0–1. The guideline for acceptable internal consistency reliability is .70.

Another form of reliability that is often relevant to selection situations is *interrater reliability.* Essentially, interrater reliability tells us if two or more raters agree on a candidate's characteristics. Each rater is treated like a test, and the scores of the raters are correlated to check for consistency. Differences between the raters are considered error. For example, in a group interview situation, all the interviewers were present for the same interview, and therefore should agree on their ratings of the applicant's experience and qualifications. Interrater reliability is also important in assessment centers, where multiple raters assess a candidate's capabilities in several different situations.

Validity

The use of a selection test or procedure should allow managers to hire better people than if no test or procedure were used. This seems obvious both from a business standpoint (why pay to administer a test that fails to help select better employees) and from a legal standpoint (tests need to fairly distinguish among candidates based on relevant knowledge, skills, and abilities rather than gender, racial, or physical attributes as protected by law). But there is a catch. The hiring organization must be able to prove with statistical evidence that the selection procedure did indeed result in hiring better employees. For example, managers should be able to prove that computer help desk personnel hired based in part on high scores on a test of problem solving abilities would be better at their jobs than those with low scores on the problem solving test.

Although it sounds simple, assessing validity properly is complicated. Statistical tests of validity do not provide a yes-or-no answer; they provide a number that can be compared to other known validity numbers or professional standards. The validity statistic itself can change based on the type of test, the nature of the applicants, or the testing conditions. Validity is not a characteristic of a test but of how a test is used. A test that measures cognitive ability can be a highly valid predictor of how well a person will pilot an airplane. The very same test can be an invalid predictor of the number of touchdowns scored by a wide receiver in his rookie season in the National Football League.

The *Principles for the Validation and Use of Personnel Selection Procedures* (SIOP 1987) and the *Standards for Educational and Psychological Testing* outline the types of evidence necessary to establish validity. Although this information is too detailed for this module, these two guides are excellent sources for managers wishing to find out more about this important and useful concept.

There are several different ways to demonstrate the validity of a test, including content, construct, and criterion-related strategies. Each method is discussed below. Two special cases of validity are also discussed: validity generalization and face validity.

The *content validation* strategy documents the extent to which a test adequately covers an area of interest. Content validity is especially important in regard to knowledge tests and job sample tests. For example, if you were hiring a history teacher, you might have all the candidates deliver a sample lecture as your selection test. Certainly, delivering lectures is a critical part of a teacher's job. However, a good teacher also must be able to create a structured lesson plan, interact with students, answer questions, and so on. For a test to demonstrate content validity, it must contain a representative sample of the area of interest. A content valid test for selecting teachers would measure applicants' ability to conduct all these different activities; lecturing, creating lesson plans, interacting with students, and answering questions.

In the selection of employees, the area of interest should be defined with a systematic job analysis (Goldstein, Zedeck, and Schneider 1993). A content-valid test should contain nothing that is not part of the area of interest, and it should not focus on just one small aspect of that area of interest. Content validity is determined primarily through a series of structured, expert judgments. The percentage of judges who agree that a concept is covered in the test is recorded. Using our teacher example, a panel of experienced teachers would provide ratings on the extent to which each component of a selection test for teachers was relevant to the job. Typically, if fewer than two-thirds of the experts agree, the question will be removed from the test.

Construct validity examines the extent to which a test measures a given theoretical construct. Construct validity is especially important with tests that measure "unseen" characteristics such as cognitive ability and personality. One way to establish construct validity is to examine correlations between the test of interest and established tests of other constructs. If the correlations fit the theory about this construct, then there is evidence of construct validity.

For example, imagine that an analysis of a customer service representative's job found that "friendliness" was a critical component of the job. How could a manager determine which job applicants were friendly? One way would be to develop a written test of that characteristic. The manager could write ten questions that each fit her definition of things a friendly person would do. But how would that manager really know that the test measured friendliness? She could look at correlations between measures of extraversion and friendliness. She could look at correlations between her measure of friendliness and observations of people acting in a friendly way toward others. If the correlations between these similar measures were high and positive, she would have some evidence of the construct validity of her measure. Test manuals of personality measures should all contain evidence of construct validity.

Criterion-related validity examines the relationship between a test (the predictor) and some measure of performance (the criterion). To demonstrate evidence of criterion-related validity, a researcher or manager must show that scores on the selection measure are significantly related to job performance. Again, a correlation is often used to document this. For example, scores on a cognitive ability test could be correlated .45 with supervisory performance ratings. Because of this moderate, positive correlation, we could conclude that this cognitive ability test is a valid predictor of performance in the job. For selection purposes, criterion-related validity should be researched and documented even if content or construct validation evidence exists.

For many years, validity was considered situation specific. This means that each organization would have to establish the validity of a selection test for every new use. Schmidt and Hunter (1977) contended that this situation specificity was due to errors in conducting criterion-related validity studies such as low reliability (an example of measurement error) and small sample sizes (an example of sampling error). Based on this premise, Schmidt and Hunter advocated the concept of validity generalization. Most often applied with cognitive ability tests, *validity generalization* is a special case in which a test can be considered valid for use in selecting employees for a job when other organizations have demonstrated that the test was valid for selecting employees in a very similar job. A major advantage of validity generalization is that it results in considerable cost savings for organizations (especially small firms), which no longer need to pay for expensive validation studies in all testing situations.

One other concept that is often mentioned in relation to validity is *face validity*. This is not technically a form of validity, but rather refers to the extent to which a test appears to measure what it is supposed to measure. For example, if a real estate company is using a mathematical ability test to hire a new bookkeeper, the math problems on the test should refer to assets and liabilities rather than the distance two trains would have to travel to pass each other in a certain city, or the cost of seven oranges and three apples. Research has shown that a lack of face validity can reduce test-taker motivation, and thus test-taker performance (Chan, Schmitt, DeShon, Clause, and Delbridge 1997).

Adverse Impact

Even though they are key statistical tools in assessing the usefulness of a test in the selection process, validity and reliability are not the only concepts that help researchers and managers judge testing devices. In addition to meeting standards of statistical quality, selection tests should also meet standards of social fairness. Employment law suggests that any selection procedure should result in relatively equal hiring rates for majority and minority applicant groups. For example, if 20 percent of the Caucasian applicant group is hired, then approximately 20 percent of the African-American or Asian-American applicant groups should also be hired. If the hiring rate for the minority group is substantially lower than the hiring rate for the majority group, the selection procedure has resulted in *adverse impact.*

The test for adverse impact is known as the four-fifths rule. This rule states that if the hiring rates for a minority group are below four-fifths the hiring rate for the majority group, potential evidence of unfairness in the hiring procedures exists (Schmitt and Klimoski 1991). If a selection procedure does result in adverse impact, the organization must demonstrate that use of the procedure is justified by business reasons. For example, physical ability tests, particularly those measuring strength, often result in adverse impact against women. If an employer can demonstrate that a certain amount of physical strength is a business necessity, and that the selection process is a valid predictor of job performance, use of the test can still be supported. The concept of adverse impact is based on the societal value that relatively equal demographic representation in the workplace is desirable.

Traditional Predictors.   A second traditional core topic in selection is the concept of predictors. Predictors are the variables that are used to forecast how well an individual will perform on the job. Predictors typically used in selection include cognitive ability, personality traits, biographical data, and past performance.

Cognitive ability is an important, frequently used predictor of job performance. Several different types of cognitive ability are used. General cognitive ability, also known simply as *g,* is an individual's ability to acquire, store, retrieve, manipulate, and use information (Kanfer and Ackerman 1989). General cognitive ability encompasses such concepts as reasoning, and is related to individuals' capability to learn, perform most tasks that require thought, and deal with complexity on the job. Other types of cognitive ability are defined more specifically, including verbal, numerical, and spatial abilities. These more specific instances of cognitive ability tend to predict more specific components of job performance. For example, trainees with strong spatial abilities performed well in naval aviation training, while verbal abilities were not directly related to training performance (Gordon and Leighty 1988).

Cognitive ability has two primary benefits in selection. First, it can be measured reliably. Commonly used tests of general cognitive ability such as the Wonderlic and the GATB have test-retest reliabilities in the .8–.9 range, and the Wonderlic has demonstrated internal consistency reliability estimates of .88 (Hartigan and Wigdor 1989; User's Manual 1992). These reliability estimates are quite high, given that the upper bound of reliability is 1.0. Second, cognitive ability is a valid predictor of performance in virtually all jobs (Schmidt, Ones, and Hunter 1992). The primary drawback of using cognitive ability to predict job performance is adverse impact. Minority groups tend to score .5–1 standard deviation lower than whites on cognitive ability tests (Ackerman and Humphries 1990). The reasons for this difference are currently being hotly debated by managers, researchers, and politicians.

As these three groups grapple with the fairness and validity of using cognitive ability as a selection tool, *personality* has recently enjoyed a resurgence in popularity as a predictor of performance (see Hogan, Hogan, and Roberts 1996 for a review). Early uses of personality tests showed low validities when used to select employees for most jobs (e.g., Guion and Gottier 1965), which as discussed above, means these tests did not predict performance very well. However, in the past 15 years, several events have led to increased usage.

First, a common personality framework, known as the Big Five, evolved (Digman 1990; McCrae and Costa 1997). This framework suggests that there are five primary components of personality: conscientiousness, agreeableness, neuroticism, openness, and extraversion. The use of this common framework led to the discovery that some aspects of personality tended to predict performance in some jobs (Barrick and Mount 1991). For example, extraversion was found to consistently predict performance in sales jobs. Other personality characteristics can be used to predict performance in a wide range of jobs. Ones, Viswesvaran, and Schmidt (1993) documented that tests of integrity, also known as the Big Five dimension *conscientiousness,* consistently predict job performance across many jobs.

A second reason for the increased use of personality as a predictor is that personnel psychologists and HR managers started using tests that were developed specifically for selection rather than the assessment of personality disorders. Companies were finding themselves in legal battles after using tests such as the Minnesota Multiphasic Psychological Inventory (MMPI) that contained items deemed not relevant to job performance. For example, job applicants sued Target Stores over their use of a test battery based on the MMPI and the California Psychological Inventory (CPI). Applicants felt that several of the test questions dealing with religious beliefs and sexual preference invaded the applicants' rights of privacy (Jackson and Kovacheff 1993). The case was eventually settled out of court. However, given the potential for adverse applicant reactions to sensitive test questions, it is generally best to avoid using these kinds of test questions whenever possible. Tests such as the Hogan Personality Inventory and the NEO Five Factor Inventory that were developed to measure the Big Five traits in normal populations tend not to contain the invasive, highly personal kinds of items to which applicants object.

Third, in addition to the finding that some personality traits are related to performance, researchers found that most personality traits are not correlated with cognitive ability. The use of a second valid predictor (in this case, personality) that is uncorrelated with the first valid predictor (in many cases, cognitive ability) results in the ability to better predict which applicants will succeed on the job (Schmitt, Rogers, Chan, Sheppard, and Jennings 1997). This concept is known as *incremental validity.* Finally, and perhaps most important to organizations making selection decisions, adverse impact is less of a problem with personality traits. Minority and majority applicant groups generally do not have major differences in personality measures (Ryan, Ployhart, and Friedel 1998). These last two issues make the use of personality in selection particularly attractive to managers.

Another traditional predictor of job performance is the *work sample,* or the performance of a small sample of the tasks required on the job. A work sample essentially demonstrates that the applicant has the requisite procedural knowledge, or the ability to perform specific tasks. For example, a work sample test may require applicants for electrician jobs to assemble a circuit. For administrative or managerial positions, work sample tests are often called "in-basket tests." With this type of test, applicants are asked to work their way through a series of office tasks typical of the job such as responding to mail, using word processing software, and answering phones.

Work sample tests are also used as selection tests in jobs that require physical performance. Applicants for firefighter jobs are asked to carry hoses and climb ladders. Work samples are usually content valid, as they actually sample a portion of the performance domain.

Biodata, or autobiographical information about an applicant that is objectively scored, is another traditional predictor of performance (Schmidt, Ones, and Hunter 1992). The underlying theory behind biodata suggests that past life experiences, captured by relatively easy-to-collect biographical information such as socioeconomic status, academic achievement, relationship with parents, and work experience can predict an individual's behavior, and thus can be used to predict job performance (Owens and Schoenfeldt 1979). Biodata measures tend to show high reliability, as well as useful validity (in the .30 range), according to Schmidt et al. (1992). Furthermore, biodata has been shown to predict job choice, vocational preferences, job turnover, and job performance across a wide range of job types and over time (Russell, Mattson, Devlin, and Atwater 1990).

Traditional Measurement Methods.   We will now review traditional ways in which predictors are measured during the selection process. While some predictors are typically measured in a certain way, any of the predictors discussed above can be measured using any of these methods. For example, the personality construct of agreeableness can be assessed via an interview, a paper-and-pencil test, or in an assessment center. It is important to remember that any method used to select individuals into an organization or promote them within the organization is considered a selection test.

Interviews have consistently been the most popular selection method in all types of organizations (Pulakos and Schmitt 1995). Unfortunately, interviews tend to be among the least reliable and valid of all frequently used selection devices. One explanation for this poor psychometric showing is that many interviews are unique to the interviewer. Each manager asks the questions he or she wants to ask, and provides ratings according to his or her own needs and perceptions. In other words, most interviews are unstructured. Research has consistently shown that structured interviews are more valid than unstructured ones (Landy, Shankster, and Kohler 1994). The more an interview is structured (i.e., interviewers use the same questions, rate the applicants against the same rating scale, and so on), the higher the reliability and validity of the interview. High-quality, structured interviews can have validities in the range of .40–.50 for predicting job performance.

Structured interview questions can either be experiential or situational. Experiential questions ask applicants to draw on past experiences to demonstrate certain characteristics or abilities, while situational questions ask applicants to imagine how they might react in a particular situation. One potential benefit of situational interviews is that the applicant need not have experienced something in order to answer a question about it. Experiential questions rely on the same conceptual background as biodata, that past life experiences are a good predictor of future performance. Indeed, research evidence suggests that experiential interviews have higher validity than situational interviews (Pulakos and Schmitt 1995).

For many years, selection tests have been primarily administered in a format using *paper and pencil.* The test items are presented on paper, and the test taker uses the pencil to mark her responses on the paper. One of the first selection and placement tests, the Army Alpha, was an objectively scored, mass-administered, paper-and-pencil test (Hakel 1998). Most college students have taken one or both of the largest paper-and-pencil tests administered each year: the SAT or ACT. Many cognitive ability, personality, and knowledge tests are administered via paper and pencil. This type of test administration has many benefits. It is generally inexpensive, requires little in the way of specialized equipment or technology, and can handle many different types of questions.

As computers become more and more pervasive in the workplace, *computerized testing* has become a common way of administering selection tests. Some kinds of computerized tests are simply electronic versions of paper-and-pencil tests, with the added benefits of automated administration and scoring. Computers can be used to present test takers with more elaborate questions that include audio and video. Computerized tests can even select specific test items that are most appropriate for the test taker's level of ability (see Hambleton, Swaminathan, and Rogers 1991 for a review), often resulting in a shorter test. Some people have expressed concerns that testing via computer can change the results of the test, as people might have different levels of computer skill or computer anxiety. So far, research has demonstrated very few differences between the results of computerized tests and paper-and-pencil tests in their adequacy as measures (Burke 1993; Hough and Schneider 1996).

Some selection procedures combine several of the methods discussed above. One example of a multimethod selection procedure is the *assessment center,* in which job applicants participate in a series of exercises designed to measure a number of job-related characteristics or abilities. One assessment center may use a leaderless group problem solving activity, an in-basket exercise, an interview, and a battery of paper-and-pencil tests to measure predictors such as extraversion, conscientiousness, verbal ability, and leadership skills. Applicants typically participate in centers in groups, and are assessed by several trained assessors. These centers are often two or three days long, and consequently can be quite costly. Because of the cost and degree of involvement by the applicant, the use of assessment centers is frequently limited to internal selection processes, such as selecting individuals for promotions to managerial ranks (Klimoski 1993).

Emerging Core Concepts

Changes in the workplace such as the use of teams, the emphasis on information technology, downsizing, and the emergence of truly global markets, have not eliminated the need for a high-quality selection program. Managers still need to identify people who can successfully perform work in the organization. However, one result of the changes in organizations is that managers' expectations of successful work performance have changed. The traditional model of performance has been oriented toward task performance. Organizations have been most interested in the extent to which an employee can perform a set of well-defined tasks. Consequently, selection methods have focused on identifying individuals who can meet task performance expectations.

Elements of performance that are outside the traditional task-related criteria are becoming increasingly important. Campbell's theory of job performance (Campbell 1990; Campbell, McCloy, Oppler, and Sager 1993) notes that effective performance is comprised of many different components. One important performance criterion is certainly job-specific task performance, but other criteria such as demonstrating effort, maintaining personal discipline, and facilitating peer and team performance are also important. Two such performance criteria will be discussed in this module; adaptability and contextual performance. This section will define these criteria and discuss predictors that will help organizations select employees who will meet these criteria.

Adaptability.   One performance criterion that is rapidly becoming more important in organizations is adaptability. As workers increase the range and depth of job responsibilities (due to team-based structures, downsizing, and decentralization), the need for flexibility and adaptability in performing a range of work activities, responding to unpredictable changes, and learning new skills and job duties is becoming more salient. The changes that call for employee adaptability vary widely in scope. For example, military organizations are experiencing major changes in their primary mission as a result of the collapse of the Soviet Union. The military must now be prepared to defend against a variety of uncertain threats such as terrorism. At the other end of the spectrum, employees in virtually all organizations must adapt to continual changes in office tools, such as new hardware and software systems (Coovert 1995). Managers need workers who can successfully work in a changing environment, learn new concepts and techniques, and adjust to constantly shifting customers, suppliers, and competitors.

Adaptability Research Findings

Adaptability is a multidimensional construct (Pulakos, Arad, Plamondon, and Kiechel 1996). Dimensions of adaptability include handling emergencies and work stress, dealing with changing work situations, learning new tasks and technologies, and displaying interpersonal and cultural adaptability. Research has shown that jobs vary on the extent to which a person is required to display adaptability (Donovan and Pulakos 1998). Preliminary results suggest that supervisory jobs generally require more adaptability than nonsupervisory jobs. Additionally, jobs differ in the extent to which particular dimensions of adaptability are required within that particular job. For example, military police jobs require extensive adaptability in terms of handling emergencies, but much less in terms of cultural adaptability. Jobs in which employees work in teams may require substantial interpersonal adaptability, while a salesperson for a multinational corporation would likely need to display more cultural adaptability. Before deciding to select employees on the basis of adaptability, managers should conduct an adaptability job analysis. That is, they should determine the extent to which adaptability is an important part of the job in question, and which dimensions of adaptability are most needed.

Predictors of Adaptability

As discussed above, adaptability is a multidimensional construct. Consequently, many individual characteristics have been suggested to predict adaptability on the job (Pulakos et al. 1996). These predictors include cognitive abilities, noncognitive characteristics, and physical abilities. The *cognitive abilities* that have been suggested to predict adaptability include general abilities such as verbal and quantitative abilities. Certainly, the capability to learn new tasks and technologies is related to these general cognitive abilities (e.g., Kanfer and Ackerman 1989). More specific abilities should also predict adaptability, including reasoning ability, problem solving ability, and practical intelligence. These specific abilities should allow individuals to deal with rapidly changing situations.

Many noncognitive predictors of adaptability have been proposed. These include *openness,* which is one of the Big Five personality factors (Barrick and Mount 1991). Openness includes curiosity and tolerance of new ideas. Scoring high on openness suggests a decreased likelihood of perceiving change as stressful. Another predictor, *locus of control,* deals with whether a person believes he is in control of what happens to him. People with an internal locus of control are likely to be more adaptive because they are better at coping. They are likely to believe that they have the capability to have an impact on the situation, regardless of uncertainty or change. *Risk aversion* is another noncognitive predictor of adaptability. Risk aversion addresses a person's willingness or unwillingness to take risks. Judge, Thoresen, and Pucik (1996) found that people who are risk averse have a hard time coping with change. Often people must take intelligent risks to solve a new problem or deal with an emergency situation. Another noncognitive characteristic suggested to predict adaptable behavior is *self-efficacy,* or a person's perception that he or she can accomplish things. Individuals with high self-efficacy tend to perform better, simply as a function of their own expectations of success. Low self-efficacy is related to an inability to handle change.

The measurement of both adaptability and the constructs that predict on-the-job adaptability are still very much under development. We have seen organizations measure adaptability using structured interview questions that ask applicants to describe situations in which they have demonstrated adaptable behaviors. This approach is

MODULE
14

consistent with research on characteristics of effective employment interviews (Pulakos and Schmitt 1995). The development of other measures of adaptability and its predictors are described later in the Application section of this module.

Contextual performance. Task performance is the static set of behaviors that people have traditionally associated with "what the job entails." These discrete tasks have traditionally been determined using job analysis, which then form the basis of job descriptions, and the development of selection tests. Recently, the definition of performance has been expanded beyond task performance (Campbell 1990; Landy, Shankster, and Kohler 1994; Borman, Hanson, and Hedge 1997). Contextual performance includes behaviors that fall outside the specific behaviors involved in completing an assigned task, but are behaviors that are still helpful to the organization. These include persistence, volunteering, cooperating with others, helping, following organizational rules, and endorsing, supporting, and defending organizational objectives (Borman and Motowidlo 1993; Borman and Motowidlo 1997; Motowidlo, Borman, and Schmit 1997). Contextual performance is similar to earlier concepts such as organizational citizenship behaviors and prosocial organizational behavior (Smith, Organ, and Near 1983; Brief and Motowidlo 1986).

As a result of the changes in the nature of work, the relationship between employers and employees has changed, making contextual performance an even more important selection criterion. Until the mid-1980s, individuals could typically count on staying with the same employer for many years, moving up the career ladder with regular promotions (Arthur and Rousseau 1996). There was an implicit agreement, or psychological contract, between employees and employers (Rousseau and Wade-Benzoni 1995). The organization would provide long-term, secure employment, and in return, the employee would perform his or her job and exhibit a certain amount of commitment to the organization. But in the modern business climate, the psychological contract has changed. The assumption that employees will stay with one company for an entire career no longer exists. As employers are less able (and willing) to offer long-term employment, employees are less able and willing to be highly committed to the organization.

With the changed psychological contract between the employees and employers, employers can no longer expect employees to exhibit the behaviors consistent with high organizational commitment. Many of the attitudes and behaviors associated with organizational commitment, including willingness to exert extra effort for the organization and a strong belief in its goals (Meyer and Allen 1984), are similar to aspects of contextual performance. In the past, employees could be expected to display these positive behaviors because of their commitment to the organization. Now it appears that organizations may need to focus on contextual performance to select employees who are likely to display these behaviors that are good for business but not part of traditional performance criteria (Borman et al. 1997).

Contextual Performance Research Findings

Contextual performance appears to be recognized by managers as an important piece of job performance. Research has shown that it is a key component of actual job performance ratings. In a study by Motowidlo and Van Scotter (1994), individuals were rated by three different supervisors, each using a different type of performance measure. For each employee, one supervisor rated the employee's task performance, one supervisor rated contextual performance, and the third supervisor rated overall performance. Task performance and contextual performance were each related to overall performance, but each, as hypothesized, measured a different piece of the overall performance puzzle. This relationship is demonstrated in Figure 14.2. Both task performance and contextual performance are important components of overall performance, but neither component tells the whole story by itself.

FIGURE 14.2   *Relationship of Contextual Performance with Overall Performance*

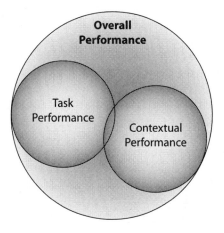

Predictors of Contextual Performance

The best predictors of contextual performance tend to be in the personality domain. Some of the personality factors related to contextual performance are dependability, cooperativeness, extraversion, and agreeableness. People who have these characteristics tend to display contextual performance behaviors. Conversely, the best predictors of task performance tend to be in the ability domain. There is some cross-over between the two (Motowidlo et al. 1997). Including contextual performance as a selection criterion, then, has two main benefits regarding validity and adverse impact. First, the overall validity of the selection process should increase as personality tests that tend to be unrelated to ability tests are used to predict contextual performance. Second, because personality tests tend not to have adverse impact, including contextual performance as part of the performance criteria can help reduce the adverse impact of the overall selection process (Ryan et al. 1998).

STRATEGIC ISSUES IN SELECTION SYSTEMS

Selection for Competitive Advantage: Developing Organizational Capabilities

Managers and researchers both take great interest in the strategic aspects of human resource management (Wright and McMahan 1992). The fundamental question that stems from this interest is how can the human resource function boost firm performance, as measured by such variables as profits and market share? Traditional theories explaining firm-level performance have strongly suggested that economic forces are the primary drivers of firm performance (see Porter 1980 for more detailed discussion). Under this theoretical approach, human resource managers play merely a supporting role, making little direct contribution to a firm's bottom line. Over the past several years, however, attention has focused on the need to develop firm-specific capabilities that managers can use as competitive weapons against rivals, such as flexibility, reputation, and capacity for innovation (Dierickx and Cool 1989).

These capabilities, often labeled core competencies (Prahalad and Hamel 1990) or organizational competencies (Lado and Wilson 1994), have been defined as collections of interrelated resources that are developed over time and, ideally, are difficult for rivals to imitate. Thus, managers now strive to outperform rivals consistently over time by developing rare and valuable capabilities by combining several types of resources together (Dierickx and Cool 1989). For instance, human resources are developed in conjunction with other types of resources, including technological (such as database management software and company intranets), physical (such as raw materials, machinery, and cash), and intangible (such as brand loyalty and reputation) resources.

The consensus among managers and researchers is that human resources indeed are an important part of the resource "mix" from which these organizational capabilities develop (Lado and Wilson 1994). People, rather than economic forces, provide such valuable competitive resources as expertise, creativity, and relationships with customers and suppliers. Given the centrality of the human resources function in developing organizational capabilities, it should be clear that, contrary to traditional strategic theories, the effective management of human resources indeed can directly boost firm performance. In fact, effective human resource management is most likely a necessary component of strong organizational performance (Lado and Wilson 1994).

An example of a valuable organizational capability that impacts key organizational outcomes is Wal-Mart's distribution system. This system combines human expertise with information technology and physical facilities to get products to stores faster and at lower cost than rivals. Wal-Mart's strategy is to continuously upgrade this distribution system in an effort to stay ahead of rivals such as Target and K-Mart and to leverage this system by applying it in global markets. In order to continue to build this distribution capability, Wal-Mart's managers must select employees who have expertise, can learn, and fit into Wal-Mart's unique culture. How can human resource managers help?

An emerging perspective in strategic management is that the selection process can and should help identify and develop such critical organizational resources as expertise, flexibility, and creativity by identifying and assessing adaptability and contextual performance, as discussed above. Human resource managers have the opportunity to manage the newly developed intersection between the changing nature of work and the increasing focus on capability development as the key to improving firm performance. This important role has many practical applications, which will be discussed next.

MODULE
14

APPLICATION

Selecting for Information Technology Jobs

As the economy shifts from an industrial base to an information base, we are seeing a corresponding shift in the demands of work. The number and types of jobs that require technical skills are rapidly increasing. In 1996, approximately 1.2 million jobs existed in the information technology and data processing industry. By 2005, that number is expected to increase by over 100 percent to 2.5 million jobs (Silvestri 1997). Even jobs that traditionally were considered "manual labor" now require the use of sophisticated computer hardware and software. Examples include workers who operate complex machinery to assemble cars, and warehouse workers who track inventory.

This shift creates a particular challenge for human resource managers. The content domain of tasks associated with information technology jobs changes so rapidly that firms cannot expect to select information technology workers solely on the basis of their current knowledge. Computer hardware, software, and even whole paradigms shift extremely rapidly. In these jobs, the ability to adapt and learn becomes at least as important as the current technical skill set for effective long-term job performance. Selecting employees who can adapt and learn becomes a critical component of the human resource function. Managers can use predictors of adaptability to select employees who can thrive in this new economic reality.

Developing "Internal" Selection Systems

A second practical implication of expanding the performance criterion domain to include adaptability and contextual performance is the development of an internal selection system. An internal selection system can be used to identify employees who are qualified to fulfill a variety of internal roles including serving on cross-functional project teams or working with strategic alliance partners.

This kind of system can be useful for both large and small organizations. Many large organizations have downsized their workforces over the past ten years. Downsizing has reduced the total skill complement available to many organizations, and has eliminated the existence of specialists in others. Small organizations need to leverage the skills available in the few employees they do have. Employees who are able and willing to adapt to a variety of job assignments, and who demonstrate contextual performance behaviors such as volunteering and helping, are particularly useful to employers who wish to implement a flexible, internal staffing system.

One large government organization is in the process of developing an internal selection system. This organization conducted a job analysis to determine the skills needed by employees in different job categories across the organization. The organization is now conducting a survey of current employee skill levels. The skill data will be kept in a database that can be searched to locate employees with the skills needed for important projects, task forces, and so on.

While this skills database can be a powerful tool, we expect that having the skills needed for projects and task forces may not be enough for employees to be successful in a variety of different assignments. Those employees who are called upon to serve on these projects and task forces will need to have a certain amount of adaptability in order to perform well under rapidly changing circumstances. Asking an employee to change jobs or interrupt individual career plans to fill an important role for the organization is an example of contextual performance. The success of an internal selection system will rely not only on employee skills, but also on their adaptability and willingness to display contextual performance.

MODULE
14

Adaptability in the Army

A project is currently underway to measure and predict adaptability in the Army (Pulakos et al. 1996). The Army is undergoing drastic changes in the way it meets its mission. Rather than focusing efforts on one easily identifiable enemy, the Army must now be able to respond to many potential threats. Consequently, the Army is very interested in being able to identify potential recruits who will display adaptable behaviors. The Army also needs to identify the current soldiers who have the capability to adapt so appropriate placement and promotion decisions can be made.

Several different tests to predict adaptability are being developed for this particular situation. The first predictor test is a situational judgment test. This test presents individuals with a series of realistic situations that represent each of the eight adaptability dimensions. For each situation, four or five potential actions a person could take in that situation are listed. The test-taker is asked to choose the response that he or she would be most likely to engage in. The items are intended to measure the different individual characteristics that are related to adaptability. The correct response would be one that demonstrates a characteristic such as sociability or cooperativeness.

The second proposed test is a self-report profile of several different noncognitive predictors, including openness, cooperativeness, achievement motivation, internal locus of control, and self-efficacy. This test consists of a series of statements such as "I don't like things to change frequently." The test-taker is asked to indicate the extent to which each statement describes him- or herself. This test will be similar to a paper-and-pencil personality test.

The third proposed test is a biodata inventory. The biodata inventory will consist of a series of statements related to each of the eight adaptability dimensions that describe a situation the test-taker may have encountered. One example item is "You quickly develop an effective plan to deal with an emergency." The test-taker is asked to indicate how frequently he or she has experienced each event.

Each of these tests, while based on many traditional predictor constructs, will be specially designed to predict adaptability. With these three new tests, along with standard cognitive ability and physical ability tests, the Army hopes to be able to reliably identify soldiers who are willing and able to adapt to new situations. These new tests should predict soldier performance above and beyond the selection tests currently in use.

IN CONCLUSION

Debrief

Traditional selection predictors and methods have enabled managers to effectively select employees for many years. However, the changes in the workplace over the past decade have also changed the definition of successful performance. It is no longer enough for employees to perform one well-defined job over the course of a career. They now must display adaptability and contextual performance behaviors for many organizations to compete. Human resource managers must also adapt to the new organizational realities by developing and implementing new selection processes that can identify individuals who can meet the new workplace challenges.

Suggested Readings

Main Readings

Borman, W. C., Hanson, M., and Hedge, J. W. 1997. Personnel selection. *Annual Review of Psychology* 48: 299–337.

Borman, W. C., and Motowidlo, S. J. 1997. Task Performance and Contextual Performance: The Meaning for Personnel Selection Research. *Human Performance* 10(2): 99–109.

Campbell, J. P., McCloy, R. A., Oppler, S. H., and Sager, C. E. 1993. "A Theory of Performance." Pp. 35-70 in *Personnel Selection in Organizations*, ed. N. Schmitt and W. C. Borman. San Francisco: Jossey-Bass.

Hogan, R., Hogan, J., and Roberts, B. W. 1996. Personality Measurement and Employment Decisions: Questions and Answers. *American Psychologist* 51 (May): 469–477.

Howard, Ann (Ed). 1995. *The Changing Nature of Work*. San Francisco: Jossey-Bass.

Supplementary Readings

Ackerman, P. L. and Humphries, L. G. 1990. "Individual Differences Theory in Industrial and Organizational Psychology." Pp. 223–282 in *Handbook of Industrial and Organizational Psychology (2nd Ed.)*, ed. M. D. Dunnette and L. M. Hough. Palo Alto, CA: Consulting Psychologists Press.

Arthur, M. B., and Rousseau, D. M. 1996. "Introduction: The Boundaryless Career as a New Employment Principle." Pp. 3–19 in *The Boundaryless Career: A New Employment Principle for a New Organizational Era*, ed. M. Arthur and D. Rousseau. New York: Oxford University Press.

Barrick, M. R., and Mount, M. K. 1991. The Big Five Personality Dimensions and Job Performance: A Meta-Analysis. *Personnel Psychology* 44(1): 1–26.

Borman, W. C., and Motowidlo, S. J. 1993. "Expanding the Criterion Domain to Include Elements of Contextual Performance." Pp. 71–98 in *Personnel Selection in Organizations,* ed. N. Schmitt and W. C. Borman. San Francisco: Jossey-Bass.

Brief, A. P., and Motowidlo, S. J. 1986. Prosocial Organizational Behaviors. *Academy of Management Review* 11:710–725.

Burke, M. J. 1993. "Computerized Psychological Testing: Impacts on Measuring Predictor Constructs and Future Job Behavior." Pp. 203–239 in *Personnel Selection in Organizations,* ed. N. Schmitt and W. C. Borman. San Francisco: Jossey-Bass.

Campbell, J. P. 1990. "Modeling the Performance Prediction Problem in Industrial and Organizational Psychology." Pp. 687–732 in *Handbook of Industrial and Organizational Psychology (2nd Ed.),* ed. M. D. Dunnette and L. M. Hough. Palo Alto, CA: Consulting Psychologists Press.

Cascio, W. 1995. Whither Industrial and Organizational Psychology in a Changing World of Work? *American Psychologist* 50(11): 928–939.

Chan, D., Schmitt, N., DeShon, R. P., Clause, C. S., and Delbridge, K. 1997. Reactions to Cognitive Ability Tests: The Relationships Between Race, Test Performance, Face Validity Perceptions, and Test-Taking Motivation. *Journal of Applied Psychology* 82(2): 300–310.

Coovert, M. 1995. "Technological Changes in Office Jobs: What We Know and What We Can Expect." Pp. 175-208 in *The Changing Nature of Work,* ed. A. Howard. San Francisco: Jossey-Bass.

Dierickx, I., and Cool, K. 1989. "Asset Stock Accumulation and Sustainability of Competitive Advantage. *Management Science* 35: 1504–1511.

Digman, J. M. 1990. Personality Structure: Emergence of the Five-Factor Model. Pp. 417–440 in *Annual Review of Psychology* (Vol. 41), ed. M. R. Rosenwieg and L. W. Porter. Palo Alto, CA: Annual Reviews.

Donovan, M. A., and Pulakos, E. D. 1998. *The Development, Administration, and Analysis of the Job Adaptability Inventory.* Technical Report. Arlington, VA: Personnel Decisions Research Institutes.

Goldstein, I. L., Zedeck, S., and Schneider, B. 1993. "An Exploration of Job Analysis-Content Validity Process." Pp. 3–34 in *Personnel Selection in Organizations,* ed. N. Schmitt and W. C. Borman. San Francisco: Jossey-Bass.

Gordon, H. W., and Leighty R. 1988. Importance of Specialized Cognitive Function in the Selection of Military Pilots. *Journal of Applied Psychology* 73(1): 38–45.

Guion, R. M., and Gottier, R. F. 1965. Validity of Personality Measures in Personnel Selection. *Personnel Psychology* 18: 135–164.

Hakel, M. 1998. "Into the Great Beyond." Pp. 1–6 in *Beyond Multiple Choice: Evaluating Alternatives to Traditional Testing for Selection,* ed. M. Hakel, Mahwah, NJ: Lawrence Erlbaum Associates.

Hambleton, R. K., Swaminathan, H., and Rogers, H. J.. 1991. *Fundamentals of Item Response Theory.* Newbury Park, CA: Sage Publications.

Hartigan, J. A. and Wigdor, A. K. (Eds.). 1989. *Fairness in Employment Testing: Validity Generalization, Minority Issues, and the General Aptitude Battery.* Washington, D.C.: National Academy Press.

Hough, L. M., and Schneider, R. 1996. "Personality Traits, Taxonomies, and Applications in Organizations." Pp. 31–88 in ed. K. R. Murphy, *Individual Differences and Behavior in Organizations.* San Francisco: Jossey-Bass.

Jackson, D. N., and Kovacheff, J. D. 1993. Personality Questionnaires in Selection: Privacy Issues and the Soroka Case. *The Industrial-Organizational Psychologist:* 45–50.

Judge, T. A., Thoreson, C. J., and Pucik, V. 1996. Managerial Coping with Organizational Change: A Dispositional Perspective. *Presentation at the 1996 Annual Academy of Management Meetings,* Cincinnati.

Kanfer, R., and Ackerman, P. L. 1989. Motivation and Cognitive Abilities: An Integrative/Aptitude-Treatment Interaction Approach to Skill Acquisition. *Journal of Applied Psychology* 74(4): 657–690.

Klimoski, R. J. 1993. "Predictor Constructs and Their Measurement." Pp. 99–134 in *Personnel Selection in Organizations,* ed. N. Schmitt and W. C. Borman. San Francisco: Jossey-Bass.

Lado, A. A., and Wilson, M. C. 1994. Human Resource Systems and Sustained Competitive Advantage: A Competency-Based Perspective. *Academy of Management Review* 19(4): 699–727.

Landy, F. J., Shankster, L. J., and Kohler, S. S. 1994. Personnel Selection and Placement. *Annual Review of Psychology* 45: 261–296.

McCrae, R. R., and Costa, P. T. 1997. Personality Trait Structure as a Human Universal. *American Psychologist* 52(5): 509–516.

Meyer, J. P., and Allen, N. J. 1984. Testing the "Side-bet" Theory of Organizational Commitment: Some Methodological Considerations. *Journal of Applied Psychology* 69:372–378.

Motowidlo, S. J., Borman, W. C., and Schmit, M. J. 1997. A Theory of Individual Differences in Task and Contextual Performance. *Human Performance* 10(2): 71–83.

Motowidlo, S. J., and Van Scotter, J. R. 1994. Evidence That Task Performance Should Be Distinguished from Contextual Performance. *Journal of Applied Psychology* 79:475–480.

Ones, D., Viswesvaran, C., and Schmidt, F. 1993. "Meta-Analysis of Integrity Test Validities: Findings and Implications for Personnel Selection and Theories of Job Performance." *Journal of Applied Psychology* 78(4): 679–703.

Owens, W. A., and Schoenfeldt, L. F. 1979. Toward a Classification of Persons. *Journal of Applied Psychology* 65(5): 569–607.

Porter, M. E. 1980. *Competitive Strategy.* New York: Free Press.

Prahalad, C. K., and Hamel G. 1990. The Core Competence of the Corporation. *Harvard Business Review* 68 (May/June): 79–91.

Pulakos, E. D., and Schmitt, N. 1995. Experience-Based and Situational Interview Questions: Studies of Validity. *Personnel Psychology* 48(2): 289–308.

Pulakos, E. D., Arad, S., Plamondon, K. E., and Kiechel. K. L. 1996. Examining the Feasibility of Developing Measures of Stress Adaptability. Technical Report No. 288. Arlington, VA: Personnel Decisions Research Institutes.

Rousseau, D. M., and Wade-Benzoni, K. A. 1995. "Changing Individual-Organizational Attachments: A Two-Way Street." Pp. 290–322 in *The Changing Nature of Work,* ed. A. Howard. San Francisco: Jossey-Bass.

Russell, C. J., Mattson, J., Devlin, S. E., and Atwater, D. 1990. Predictive Validity of Biodata Items Generated from Retrospective Life Experience Essays. *Journal of Applied Psychology* 75(5): 569–580.

Ryan, A. M., Ployhart, R., and Friedel, L. 1998. Using Personality Testing to Reduce Adverse Impact: A Cautionary Note. *Journal of Applied Psychology* 83(2): 298–307.

Schmidt, F. L., and Hunter, J. E. (1977). Development of a General Solution to the Problem of Validity Generalization. *Journal of Applied Psychology* 62: 529–540.

MODULE
14

Schmidt, F. L., Ones, D. S., and Hunter, John E.. 1992. Personnel Selection. *Annual Review of Psychology* 43: 627–670.

Schmitt, N. J., and Klimoski, R. J. (Eds.) 1991. *Research Methods in Human Resource Management.* Cincinnati: Southwest.

Schmitt, N., Rogers, W., Chan, D., Sheppard, L., and Jennings, D. 1997. Adverse Impact and Predictive Efficiency of Various Predictor Combinations. *Journal of Applied Psychology* 82(5): 719–730.

Silvestri, G. T. 1997. Occupational Employment Projections to 2006. *Monthly Labor Review* November:58–83.

SIOP (Society for Industrial and Organizational Psychology, Inc.) 1987. *Principles for the Validation and Use of Personnel Selection Procedures* (3rd ed.). College Park, MD: Author.

Smith, C. A., Organ, D. W., and Near, J. P. 1983. Organizational Citizenship Behavior: Its Nature and Antecedents. *Journal of Applied Psychology* 68(4): 653–663.

User's Manual for the Wonderlic Personnel Test and the Scholastic Level Exam. (1992). Libertyville, IL: Wonderlic Personnel Test, Inc..

Wright, P. M., and McMahan, G. C. 1992. Theoretical Perspectives for Strategic Human Resource Management. *Journal of Management* 18(2): 295–320.

Critical Thinking Questions

1. Why must organizations make every effort to minimize test compromise (i.e., cheating)? What could happen to the validity of the selection test if some applicants cheated on the test?

2. Why do you think laws around adverse impact exist? Desires for equal demographic representation in the workplace can conflict with desires to select the best employees. Which is more important, maximizing validity of selection procedures or ensuring equal racial representation? Why?

3. Why do you think cognitive ability is a valid predictor of performance in almost all jobs? Can you think of any jobs in which cognitive ability might not be a valid predictor of performance?

4. Paper-and-pencil tests have many benefits for organizations, including cost and efficiency. What are the potential limitations of paper-and-pencil tests?

5. For years, companies have hired people to perform a specific set of tasks. Including adaptability as part of job performance changes many traditional assumptions about performance. What risks do you see in selecting individuals in part on their ability to adapt?

6. Some researchers have suggested that contextual performance is not actually part of the job, but rather "extra" things employees can do to benefit the organization. Should employers select employees based on these "extras"? Why or why not?

MODULE
14

Exercises

Individual Exercise

Think about your current job, or a job you have recently held. How does that job require you to adapt? What are the important components of contextual performance for that job?

Team Exercise

Pick a job with which the whole group is familiar. Spend ten minutes on an informal job analysis by listing 10 or 15 major activities an employee in that job would perform. Which of those activities are task related? Which are contextual?

Library or Web Exercise

Find a current article in the business press that discusses a company that is pursuing a strategy that requires its employees to be adaptable. What challenges might this company face in selecting and retaining its workforce?

MODULE
14

Index

Ability domain, 14.15

Ability test, 14.15. *See also* Job-specific task performance; Work sample text

Adaptability.
　　as performance criterion, 14.12–13, 14.16
　　of employees, 14.5

Adaptability, in the Army, 14.17

Adaptability, predictors of, 14.13. *See also* Cognitive ability, Locus of control, Openness, Practical intelligence, Problem-solving ability, Reasoning ability, Risk aversion, and Self-efficacy

Adverse impact, 14.5, 14.6, 14.9, 14.10, 14.15

Area of interest, 14.7, 14.8

Assessment center, 14.12

Assessors, trained, 14.12

Big Five framework (tests of integrity), 14.10

Biodata inventory, 14.11, 14.18

Business environment, 14.5, 14.6, 14.9–10, 14.11

Cognitive ability, as predictor of adaptability, 14.13, 14.18

Commitment (organizational), 14.14

Computerized testing, 14.11–12

Construct of interest, 14.6

Construct validity, 14.7, 14.8

Content domain (of tasks), 14.16

Content validity, 14.7–8

Contextual performance, 14.5, 14.14, 14.17, 14.18

Contextual performance, predictors of, 14.15

Core competencies (organizational, 14.15

Correlations between measures, (test validity), 14.8

Criterion-related validity, 14.7, 14.8

Critical component, 14.8

Downsizing, 14.12, 14.17

Effective employment interviews, 14.14

Employer/employee expectations, 14.4

Employment relationship, 14.14

Error in selection tests, 14.6

Experiential questions as predictors, 14.11

Face validity, 14.7, 14.8-9

Fairness, 14.10. *See also* Validity

Flexibility, as performance criterion, 14.12, 14.17

Four-fifths rule, 14.9

Global markets, 14.12

Group interview, 14.7

Hiring managers. *See* Human Resource management

Hiring standards, 14.4

Human resource management, 14.15, 14.16, 14.18

Human resource roles, 14.4–5

Implicit agreement, 14.14

In-basket test, 14.10

Incremental validity, 14.10

Information technology, 14.12, 14.16

Intellectual capital, 14.4

Internal consistency, 14.7, 14.9. *See also* Reliability

Internal selection system, 14.17. *See also* Selection process

Interrater reliability, 14.7

Interrelated resources, 14.15–16

Interviews (as measurement method), 14.11

Irrelevant factors, 14.6

Job analysis, 14.5, 14.8, 14.14, 14.17

Job descriptions, 14.14

Job performance, 14.5, 14.9

Job performance (overall), 14.14

Job requirements, 14.5

Job sample test, 14.7

Job-specific task performance, 14.12

Knowledge test, 14.7, 14.11

KSAOs (knowledge, skills, abilities, and other characteristics), 14.5

Level of ability, 14.12

Locus of control, as predictor of adaptability, 14.13

Measuring strength, 14.9

MMPI (Minnesota Multiphasic Psychological Inventory), 14.10

New economic reality, 14.16

Openness, as predictor of adaptability, 14.13

Paper and pencil tests, 14.11

Parallel forms model, 14.6

Personality tests, 14.9, 14.10, 14.11, 14.15

Personality traits, 14.6

Physical performance, 14.11

Practical intelligence, as predictor of adaptability, 14.13

Predictor of performance, 14.8, 14.9, 14.11

Problem-solving ability, as predictor of adaptability, 14.13

MODULE
14

Procedural knowledge, 14.10
Project teams, 14.17
Promotions, 14.12, 14.17
Psychological contract, 14.14
Psychometric properties, 14.6, 14.11

Reasoning ability, as predictor of adaptability, 14.13
Relationship, employer/employee. *See* Employment relationship
Reliability, 14.5, 14.6–7, 14.11. *See also* Validity of tests
Resources, technological, physical, and intangible, 14.16
Right of privacy, 14.10
Risk aversion, as predictor of adaptability, 14.13

Security, of selection tests, 14.6
Selection criteria, 14.5
Selection practices, 14.4
Selection process (or method), 14.6, 14.7, 14.18
Self-efficacy, as predictor of adaptability, 14.13
Self-report profile, 14.17
Situation specific validity, 14.8
Skills database, 14.17
Social fairness, 14.9

Standards in hiring, 14.4
Statistical principles, and test validity, 14.6, 14.9
Strategic direction, 14.4
Strategic management, 14.16
Structured interview, 14.11
Supervisory jobs and adaptability, 14.13

Task performance component, 14.14
Task performance expectations, 14.12. *See also* Predictor of performance
Team-based work systems, 14.4
Technological change, 14.13
Test development, 14.5, 14.6, 14.14
Test evaluation, 14.5. *See* Validity of tests
Test standards, 14.7
Test-retest reliability model, 14.6
Test-taker performance, 14.9
Traditional model of performance, 14.12

Unseen characteristics, 14.8. *See also* Cognitive ability and personality

Validity generalization, 14.7, 14.8
Validity of tests, 14.5, 14.7, 14.11, 14.15

Work sample test, 14.10
Work teams and adaptability, 14.13

MODULE
14

SOCIALIZING, MOTIVATING, AND DEVELOPING EMPLOYEES TO COMPETE

KOSSEK ■ BLOCK

Managing Human Resources in the 21st Century

From Core Concepts to Strategic Choice

MODULE 15

Moving from Performance Appraisal to Performance Management

Theodore H. Curry II
MICHIGAN STATE UNIVERSITY

Managing Human Resources in the 21st Century: From Core Concepts to Strategic Choice,
by Kossek and Block

Publisher: Dave Shaut
Executive Editor: John Szilagyi
Developmental Editor: Bryant Editorial Development
Marketing Manager: Joseph A. Sabatino
Production Editor: Tamborah E. Moore
Manufacturing Coordinator: Dana Began Schwartz
Cover Design: Tin Box Studio
Cover Photographs: Copyright Shoji Sato/Photonica
Production House: The Left Coast Group, Inc.
Printer: West Group

Printed in the United States of America
1 2 3 4 5 02 01 00 99

For more information contact South-Western College Publishing, 5101 Madison Road, Cincinnati, Ohio, 45227 or find us on the Internet at *http://www.swcollege.com*
For permission to use material from this text or product, contact us by

- telephone: 1-800-730-2214
- fax: 1-800-730-2215
- web: *http://www.thomsonrights.com*

ISBN: 0–324–01814–2

Contents

MODULE OVERVIEW 15.4

OBJECTIVES 15.4

RELATION TO THE FRAME 15.4

CORE CONCEPTS IN MOVING FROM PERFORMANCE APPRAISAL
TO PERFORMANCE MANAGEMENT 15.5

Performance Appraisal and Performance Management Defined 15.5

Principal Goals of Performance Management 15.5

Legal Issues in Performance Management 15.7

The Performance Management Cycle 15.8

New Developments in Employee Performance Management 15.14

STRATEGIC ISSUES IN MOVING FROM PERFORMANCE APPRAISAL
TO PERFORMANCE MANAGEMENT 15.16

Involvement of Users in Development 15.16

Alternative Implementation Models 15.17

IN CONCLUSION 15.19

Debrief 15.19

Suggested Readings 15.19

Critical Thinking Questions 15.19

Exercises 15.20

References 15.20

INDEX 15.21

MODULE OVERVIEW

This module places the function of employee performance appraisal in the broader context of performance management. For many years, both employees and their managers have complained about the performance appraisal process. Organizational responses have ranged from revising the performance appraisal processes, to creating completely new processes, to discarding formal performance appraisals altogether. Yet few argue with the concept of ensuring that employees are clear about what is expected of them and that they receive some feedback about how they are doing. A high-performing organization can only succeed in accomplishing its mission, goals, and objectives if its employees perform at high levels on priority activities. Human resource professionals carry the primary responsibility for the development of processes that assist managers in helping their employees accomplish important organizational objectives.

This module will first describe the principal goals that most employers have for the performance management process within their organization. These goals are not mutually exclusive, and their importance and relevance varies from employer to employer. Next, the module details legal issues in performance management. It then describes the performance management process as a continuing cycle, which includes employee performance feedback and appraisal, among other core components. Each of these core components is described in detail. Changing issues in performance management are next addressed. Finally, implementation suggestions for human resources professionals are provided, along with exercises to demonstrate the difficulty in developing objective performance measures and using them for evaluation.

OBJECTIVES

By the end of this module, the reader should have a clear understanding of:

- Major goals of the performance management process and the importance of an employer identifying its specific objectives to effectively design its process

- The legal issues that affect the performance management process

- The components of the performance management process, including setting and clarifying expectations, monitoring performance, providing ongoing feedback, conducting performance appraisal interviews, and using the performance appraisal results individually and organizationally

- Implementation strategies for creating and introducing a new or revised performance management/appraisal process

RELATION TO THE FRAME

Performance management is critical to key human resources transactions. The compensation program of many employers includes performance-based or merit pay, in which past performance, as documented in a performance appraisal, is a key determinant of the size of an employee's pay increase. Promotional decisions are often based in part on past performance as documented in a performance appraisal. And performance appraisals often serve as a critical tool in validating an employer's selection process.

But more importantly, performance management can serve as a key transformation tool for the employer. It can help transform the employer's stated mission, vision, and values into specifics for employees—specific results expected or specific behaviors required. In fact, any organizational initiatives must eventually become the responsibility of an individual or individuals. Any program or process created to accomplish

FIGURE 15.1   *A Frame for Understanding Human Resource Strategy: Context, Roles, and Constraints*

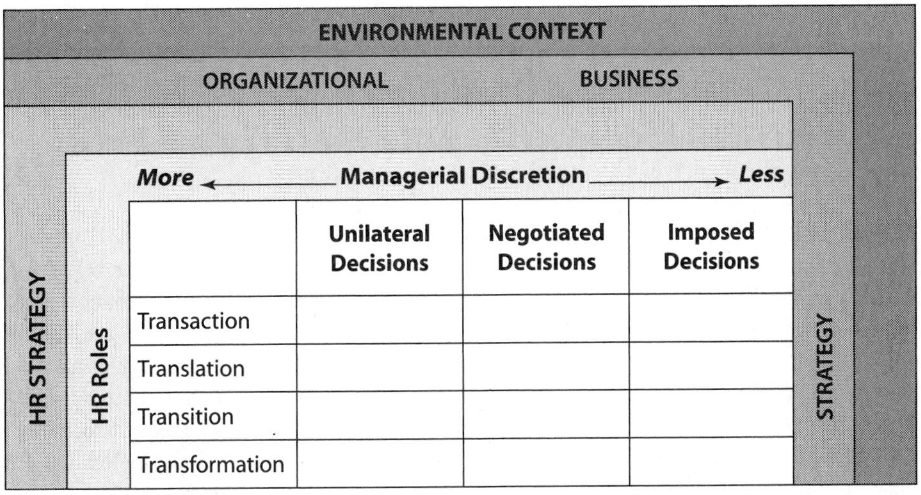

© 2000 by Ellen Ernst Kossek and Richard Block. Thanks to Brian Pentland, Karen Markel, and John Beck for helpful comments and discussions that enhanced the model.

the initiative must be somehow communicated to individual(s), action plans developed and implemented, and progress monitored. The relationship between these roles is depicted by the frame in Figure 15.1.

MODULE
15

CORE CONCEPTS IN MOVING FROM PERFORMANCE APPRAISAL TO PERFORMANCE MANAGEMENT

Performance Appraisal and Performance Management Defined

Performance appraisal as an informal process has no doubt existed among employers since the point at which the first employee began working. The formal process of evaluating or appraisal is newer, growing in use in the 1940s. It can be defined as "the process of establishing written standards of performance criteria and both telling employees about those standards and frequently informing them how they are performing in relation to the standards." (Myers 1992). Performance management can be defined as all of those processes, led by managers, that help employees perform as effectively as possible. Included are defining responsibilities, setting expectations, providing the necessary resources, giving ongoing feedback, periodically appraising performance, and utilizing the resulting information. Uses include making human resources decisions, solving individual and organizational problems, and developing people and organizational systems. The appraisal of performance is but one aspect of the broader process of performance management. Performance appraisal looks back and asks the question, "How well was the work done?" Follow-up issues might include what can be done to improve future performance. Performance management, by contrast, asks a future oriented question: "What can be done to help employees perform as effectively as possible?"

Principal Goals of Performance Management

In order to assess or develop an effective performance management process, an employer must ask and answer two questions: "What do we want to accomplish from this process?" and, "What are our intended purposes for its use?" The major goals of performance management are discussed in the following sections.

Improve Employee Performance.   Most employers adopt performance management processes primarily to help employees perform more effectively in their current positions and to be more successful in accomplishing organizational goals. Traditional performance appraisal methods have performed poorly against this goal by taking a "rearview mirror" approach to management. They focus more attention on past performance than on the present and future. Performance management processes include a future orientation designed to paint a clear picture of what is expected from employees and how the employer will support them in their efforts.

Develop People for Promotional Opportunities.   Neither traditional performance appraisal nor performance management processes are well suited for achieving a goal of *identifying* employees for promotional opportunities. Past performance is no guarantee of success on a new job assignment involving duties that require a different skill set. Identifying candidates for promotion or new organizational assignments is a selection decision that requires a thorough look at the extent to which a candidate possesses the necessary competencies to perform well in the new job. Past performance may provide a good indication of likely success where the required competencies are very similar, but will likely provide little guidance if different competencies are necessary. For example, the promotion into a supervisory assignment may require new competencies like team-building, interpersonal communications, conflict resolution, planning, and decision making, which may not have been so essential in the previous nonsupervisory assignment. Performance management processes can serve to help develop people for new assignments and promotional opportunities. If the company sets expectations with and for employees in areas that require some "stretch," employees can be helped to develop the competencies required for new positions. Where similar competencies are required in the present and future position, providing feedback, training, and support helps develop people for those new assignments.

Meet Employees' Need for Feedback.   Most agree that the majority of employees want to know how they are doing on the job. They would like positive feedback from their employer about their accomplishments and suggestions on how they can improve. It is clear, however, that most employees do not look forward to performance review sessions, nor do most managers look forward to conducting them. While the reasons for this disconnect are numerous and varied, the principal answer seems to be that employees want regular feedback on their job performance, not a once-a-year review. A well-designed and well-implemented performance management process helps accomplish this goal, by providing the tools with which employees can monitor their own performance and engage in self-feedback.

Ensure That Employees Are Working Toward Organizational Goals.   Some traditional performance appraisal programs ask the question, "Are you performing well?" More effective performance management approaches rephrase it as "Are you performing well on the right things?" Performance management programs can serve to link the organization's strategic planning process to individual efforts. The identification of strategic initiatives, goals, and objectives is meaningless without individuals being held accountable for their accomplishment. Employees must have a sense of the relative importance or priority of the many duties and projects to which they are assigned. Similarly, organizational values are meaningless without those values being made real to employees and translated into behavioral expectations. Performance management serves this function.

Provide the Information Needed to Make and Defend Important Human Resources Decisions.   At its core, the process of making job-related or valid human resources decisions involves assessing the extent to which the decision made actually predicted success on the job. Performance appraisal results often provide the dependent variable for determining the validity of the hiring or promotion processes. The performance appraisal usually serves as the information source when an employer chooses to use performance or merit as a basis for allocating salary increases. Finally, when discipline and dismissal decisions are made because of poor performance, the performance appraisal is often the employer's most critical document.

At the same time, employers are increasingly required to defend their human resources decisions—before federal, state, and local fair employment practices commissions; before unemployment compensation boards; and in court. The performance appraisal can serve as an essential information source documenting not only past employee performance, but also that the employee had been made aware of her or his performance and the consequences of not improving.

Legal Issues in Performance Management

In our increasingly litigious society, employer human resources decisions are more frequently challenged. The many exceptions to the employment-at-will doctrine and the explosion of fair employment practices statutes (Title VII of the Civil Rights Act, the Age Discrimination in Employment Act, the Americans with Disabilities Act, etc.) have forced employers into court to defend their decisions. "Because performance appraisals are often the only tangible evidence by which a jury can determine the employee's worth, appraisals potentially provide either a devastating weapon for the employee or an impenetrable shield for the employer" (Davidson 1995). The design of the performance management and appraisal process as well as its implementation and use provide critical indicators as to whether the performance appraisal will be an employee weapon or employer shield supporting the employer's performance-based decisions. To develop a defensible performance management and appraisal program, an employer must consider these factors.

Job Related or Valid. The factors being assessed should be relevant, given the tasks and duties expected of the employee. An employer attempting to use the same set of performance criteria for vastly different jobs might have difficulty proving that an individual's performance appraisal is an accurate reflection of his or her performance. As a result, some employers identify not only core performance factors, perhaps reflecting identified organizational values that are required of all its employees, but also individual performance factors unique to each position and/or employee. Examples of core organizational performance factors could include behaving ethically, having a customer focus, or being a good team player. The same employer may also identify other performance factors or expectations that are specific to the job of the individual employee, such as "increase market penetration by 5 percent by the end of the year."

Minimum Subjectivity. Defensibility of performance-based decisions is enhanced when performance expectations are clear and unambiguous. Objective standards of performance that are specific, measurable, and with clear timelines help minimize subjectivity and the possibility of misunderstanding. An example is "reduce the time required to fill employment requisitions by five days by the end of the third quarter." Similarly, clearly provided examples of expected behaviors give much better guidance than general statements like "be a good team player." Such a clear behavior example of teamwork could include:

- Treats all team members with respect

- Supports teams decisions even when the decision my not entirely reflect one's own position

- Tries different approaches to work with people that will create better results and working relationships

Consistent Application/Procedural Fairness.   The essence of a discrimination charge is that one was treated inconsistently because of race, sex, age, disability, or some other prohibited characteristic. Unjust dismissal claims in state courts often require establishing that there was an implied employment contract created through an employer handbook or oral promise and that the contract was breached when the employer did not do what it promised. Employers must be diligent, therefore, in ensuring that the procedures it enunciates in policies and handbooks are scrupulously followed by all appraisers. If required, employees must be notified of performance standards or expectations, must receive feedback about their performance, and must have an improvement plan if their performance is substandard. Required signatures must be provided. Consistency in the administration of the process is critical to employee perceptions of a fair process, which is critical to the process having the desired impact.

Instructions and Training for Appraisers.   For a system to be administered consistently and in line with its stated objectives, those required to appraise must, at a minimum, receive training on the process. Such training should include not only the mechanics of the particular system, but also performance planning, problem solving, coaching, and feedback skills. Perceptions of fairness are maximized when the employer trains not only appraisers, but also those whose performance is being appraised on the process and their role in it.

Forewarning.   Perhaps the most important requirement for developing a defensible performance management process is that those whose performance is to be appraised receive forewarning. Forewarning includes prior knowledge of the results and behaviors expected of them, and of the process and their role in it. Forewarning includes communication of performance or behavior problems early, while there is time for correction. And finally, it includes a clear message that adverse employment consequences (e.g., discipline, dismissal) can result if the employee does not improve within a set time frame.

The Performance Management Cycle

The process of performance management is summarized in the performance management cycle illustrated in Figure 15.2, which incorporates the major components involved.

Define the Job: Relate to Employer Goals, Values, and Customer Expectations.   The process of performance management begins with ensuring that each individual's activities are aligned and organized to effectively accomplish the goals and objectives of the employer. Effective performance management requires the proper organizational structure so that the effort of both individuals and groups is positioned to achieve organizational ends. It does little good if an employee is working diligently, but on tasks that are not high priority for the organization. Job analysis and job descriptions can serve to capture and summarize the broad parameters of expected employee activities, but they have often hindered an employer's ability to properly direct employee effort. Flexible job descriptions incorporating key competencies for job success and highlighting important organizational values can provide a critical tool for effective performance management. Such a job description lays a foundation for effective individual performance and performance management.

Set Expectations: Paint a Picture of a Good Job.   Perhaps the most significant component of the performance management cycle is to "set expectations." When thousands of managers have been asked in hundreds of seminars by the author for the number-one reason employees do not do what they are supposed to do, the most frequent response given is "They don't know what they are supposed to do." Performance management requires, therefore, that performance planning occur. There must be a

FIGURE 15.2 *The Performance Management Cycle*

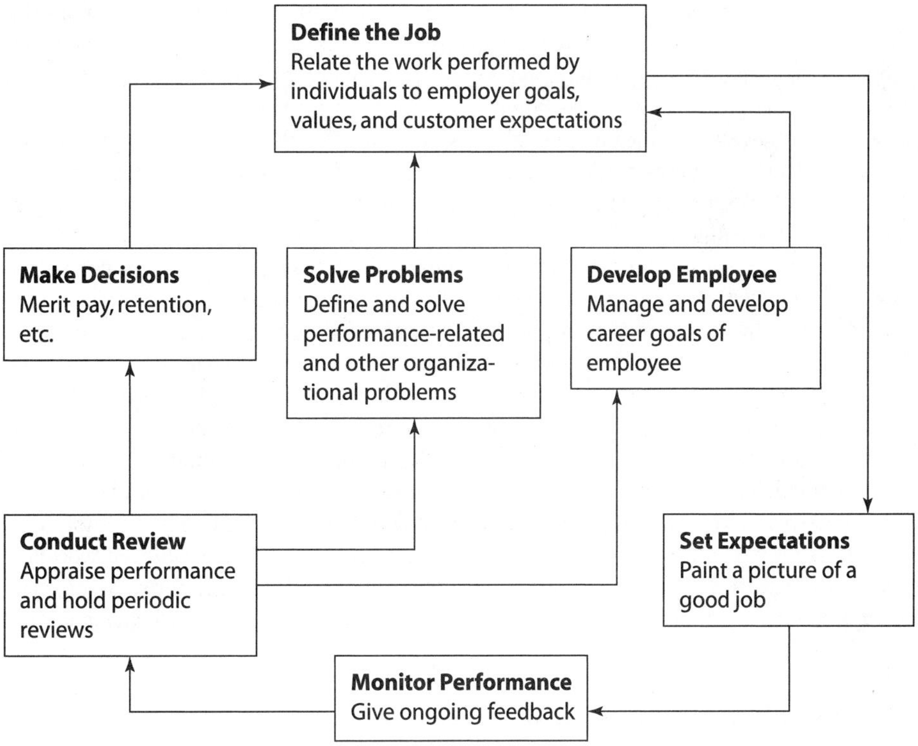

```
                    ┌─────────────────────────────┐
                    │ Define the Job              │
                    │ Relate the work performed by│
                    │ individuals to employer     │
                    │ goals, values, and customer │
                    │ expectations                │
                    └─────────────────────────────┘

┌──────────────┐   ┌──────────────────┐   ┌──────────────────┐
│ Make         │   │ Solve Problems   │   │ Develop Employee │
│ Decisions    │   │ Define and solve │   │ Manage and       │
│ Merit pay,   │   │ performance-     │   │ develop career   │
│ retention,   │   │ related and      │   │ goals of         │
│ etc.         │   │ other organiza-  │   │ employee         │
│              │   │ tional problems  │   │                  │
└──────────────┘   └──────────────────┘   └──────────────────┘

┌──────────────┐                        ┌──────────────────┐
│ Conduct      │                        │ Set Expectations │
│ Review       │                        │ Paint a picture  │
│ Appraise     │                        │ of a good job    │
│ performance  │                        │                  │
│ and hold     │                        │                  │
│ periodic     │                        │                  │
│ reviews      │                        │                  │
└──────────────┘   ┌──────────────────┐ └──────────────────┘
                   │ Monitor          │
                   │ Performance      │
                   │ Give ongoing     │
                   │ feedback         │
                   └──────────────────┘
```

meeting of the minds between each employee and her or his manager about the expected duties and norms for performing those duties. Setting expectations requires the following steps:

1.   Review organizational and unit goals and individual performance expectations.

2.   Identify objectives, duties, and projects.

3.   Describe performance measures and standards.

4.   Identify performance factors.

5.   Develop a monitoring plan.

Review Organizational and Unit Goals and Individual Performance Expectations

Organizational goals serve as the starting point for individual performance planning by describing the specific areas in which the organization expects accomplishment. Department or unit goals, and ultimately individual goals all serve to support the accomplishment of the employer's goals. These larger organizational and departmental goals must be reviewed to identify individual and team accomplishments necessary for their achievement. When individual and/or team performance expectations are established, they must be checked against employer goals to ensure that they served to support those goals.

Identify Objectives, Duties, and Projects

At higher levels of an organization, the objectives or performance expectations of managers duplicate those of the manager's unit. The manager of a department is responsible for accomplishing the goals of that department. Therefore, for those individuals higher in the organizational hierarchy, setting unit expectations serves to establish individual expectations at the same time. Because others within the organization may find themselves directly responsible for some portion of the unit's goals, a review of the organizational and unit goals is essential in performance planning for all employees. However, a careful review of the individual's job description often proves more useful as a performance planning impetus for those at lower levels within the organizational hierarchy. Relevant duties and tasks for which the employee is responsible can be identified from the description. Any special projects to which the employee has been assigned must also be identified.

In identifying objectives for which an individual or team is responsible, it is important to focus first on finding those important areas of expected accomplishment. The methods by which they will be measured or assessed is not of concern yet. Difficulty in measurement should not be a determining factor in deciding what are the important things that an employee is to do. In preparing a list of objectives, it is usually helpful to keep the list relatively short (fewer than ten items) so that an employee's efforts can be concentrated. Just as a job description usually summarizes the hundreds of tasks that an individual may perform into a smaller list of major job duties, the goal in identifying objectives is to highlight the key or major results areas for each employee that constitute 75–90 percent of the job. Finally, active involvement of the employee who is to perform the work contributes to successful performance planning efforts. Many managers allow or encourage the employee to prepare the first draft of performance duties and objectives.

Describe Performance Measures and Standards

Performance measures provide ways of describing a "good job" on each objective, duty, or project. As part of the process of setting expectations, agreement must be reached on measures that will be used to appraise how well the employee did with regard to each objective, duty, or project. It is important to identify more than one success indicator for each objective. Normally, quality will always be one of the measures or methods for judging success. Other measures usually relate to quantity, timeliness, and/or cost/budget. Where feasible, it is helpful to focus on objective, quantifiable measures rather than subjective ones. Often, however, quantifiable measures are difficult or costly to obtain. The cost of measuring must not exceed the value added from measuring.

Effective objectives and measures are consistent with and support the organization's mission and goals as well as the mission and goals of the relevant department or unit. They should cover achievement areas within the scope of control of the employee. Effective objectives and measures should reflect the more important, or key, responsibility areas of the employee and should be specific in stating end results and the timing expected. In other words, good objectives are "SMART":

- **Specific**

- **Measurable**

- **Aligned** with organizational and unit goals

- **Realistic** and results oriented

- **Time** limited

When developing objectives and measures, active involvement of the employee leads to greater employee commitment to accomplishing the objectives. Therefore, a manager should be willing to discuss the objectives with the employee. In fact, many managers let the employee prepare the first draft of objectives and measures. In doing so, the manager must share with the employee any constraints under which the manager (and, therefore, the employee) must work. For example, if the human resources director has already decided that the time to fill vacant positions must be reduced by at least five days by the end of the first quarter, it would be counterproductive to let the HR department's staffing specialist draft her or his own set of objectives without that advance knowledge. At the same time, managers should be willing to experiment by allowing for employee creativity, so long as important organizational and unit objectives are covered.

Performance levels or standards conclude the process of describing a "good job." Standards communicate in advance to the employee what must be accomplished to achieve each rating level. Standards usually define and describe the performance level that meets expectations, as well as what added behaviors and results are needed for a rating that exceeds expectations. For example:

- Exceeds expectations—The average of participant seminar evaluations must exceed 4.6 out of 5.0.

- Meets expectations—The average of participant seminar evaluations is 4.2 to 4.59.

- Fails to meet expectations—The average of participant seminar evaluations is less than 4.2.

Like objectives/duties/projects, standards may change over time due to new work methods, a changed resource picture, or changed priorities. Consistency and fairness in the performance management process require that standards be the same for employees having the same responsibilities. In the absence of clearly specified performance standards, disagreements or disputes over ratings are more likely to occur and ratings inflation tends to result.

Identify Performance Factors

A process of setting expectations that includes the identification of specific and measurable performance objectives but not the communication of expectations about how those objectives are to be accomplished implies that "the ends justify the means." This is rarely the case in organizations. If an employer, through its strategic planning process, has identified important organizational values, then that employer's performance management process should require and support employees behaving in line with those values. Performance factors provide this direction through identification, discussion, and agreement on the methods by which objectives are to be attained. Such performance factors could include customer service, embracing diversity, maintaining job expertise, attention to detail, planning and organizing, teamwork, open communications, etc. Ideally, the performance management process includes the identification of specific behavioral examples to describe any relevant performance factors.

Develop a Monitoring Plan

The final phase of setting expectations is developing a plan to monitor employee performance. Setting expectations without some system in place for regular monitoring is "performance wishing," not performance management. Monitoring requires discussion and agreement on the methods and tools for tracking employee performance. What will be the data sources and reporting mechanisms to ensure that progress is being made toward performance objectives? Will there be a cycle for mid-period review sessions? The development of a monitoring plan allows the employee as well as the manager to track employee progress and take corrective actions throughout the performance period.

Conduct Review: Appraise Performance and Hold Periodic Reviews. The performance management cycle includes a periodic, scheduled review of performance; a discussion with the employee; and the rating or appraising of the employee's performance if required. Organizational planning and goal setting generally occur on a regular cycle, most often annually. Because goals and objectives have expected completion dates, it is important to review the performance of individuals in attaining those goals on a regular cycle in line with those completion dates. Additionally, some employer human resources decisions are administratively easier if done at one time, e.g., merit pay increases. The most frequent cycle used by employers for conducting performance reviews is annually. Some employers use a shorter cycle, quarterly or semi-annually. More frequent cycles, while undoubtedly contributing to a better understanding of expectations and performance, often lead to supervisor complaints about the time required to rate performance and conduct reviews. In any case, the periodic review session should be in addition to, not in lieu of, regular discussions about employee performance.

Conducting the Performance Appraisal Interview

In many respects the key to a successful performance feedback session relates more to what occurs before the interview than during it. If the manager and employee have not reached a clear understanding of performance expectations and standards, disagreements are more likely to occur during the review session. If there has not been regular communication about progress during the appraisal period, and if performance improvements have not been initiated before the appraisal interview, the session is likely to be difficult. Therefore, performance planning and constant feedback are the keys to a good review session and improved performance.

In preparing for the interview, the supervisor should notify the employee well in advance of the session. The employee should be allowed the opportunity for self-appraisal—accomplishments, areas in need of improvement, supervisor support required. The subject matter of the review should never be left to chance. The appraiser should review the employee's objectives and gather all available data about his or her progress toward those objectives. Each objective should be analyzed—too difficult, too easy, adequate organizational support, factors beyond the control of the employee, etc. Performance factors should also be examined. Has the employee behaved in line with employer values? Were the right things accomplished in the right ways? In preparing, the appraiser should also look forward. Are job changes anticipated in the future? Are there new directions for the organization or unit? What changes need to occur for future success?

In preparing for the review session, the supervisor should also arrange for a private, comfortable meeting place. Moving out from behind a desk often contributes to more open communication. Better review sessions are conducted from a coaching or helping approach, rather than a judgmental one. The appraiser must concentrate on active listening and encouraging feedback from the employee. Finally, because most employees are performing well in more areas than those in which they are performing poorly, a balanced session would normally include more discussion of strengths and accomplishments than areas in need of improvement.

In conducting the session, the attitude of the appraiser is critical. If she or he sincerely views the session as a helpful opportunity to discuss the employee's accomplishments and areas in need of improvement relative to the employer's goals, this attitude is likely to be translated to the employee, leading to a more positive interview. The session should begin with a review of the purposes of the session:

- To discuss employee accomplishments and areas in need of improvement relative to organizational and unit goals

- To discuss ways in which the supervisor and organization can be more supportive in helping the employee perform

- To develop performance improvement strategies where required

- To begin to discuss expectations for the upcoming performance period

It is usually advisable to begin with a discussion of an employee's accomplishments; this helps create a positive platform on which the rest of the review session can be built. As the discussion moves to areas in need of improvement, a useful initial

MODULE
15

strategy is to encourage the employee to identify such areas. If she or he has ideas, move to a discussion of how improvement can be made. If the employee does not offer ideas, the supervisor should offer areas to consider: "How are you doing on...?" If the employee does not acknowledge or disagrees that an area needs improvement, the supervisor should be prepared to share specific data, facts, and examples to support the appraiser position—hence the importance of thorough preparation. If the employee cannot be persuaded with facts and arguments that improvement is needed, the supervisor must move forward and begin the discussion of strategies for performance improvement. If ratings are required, the appraiser and appraisee should try to reach agreement on these ratings, recognizing that the supervisor is always ultimately responsible for a fair and accurate appraisal. Finally, the review process should be summarized and the discussion of expectations for the upcoming performance period should commence.

Common Rating Errors

There are a number of common biases that affect the rating process.

- *Halo*—the tendency to rate appraisee highly in many performance areas because of good performance in one area

- *Horns*—the tendency to rate apraisee poorly on most performance areas because of one or a few areas in which he or she performs poorly

- *Recency*—the tendency to let recent events (performance or behavior) unduly affect the appraisal

- *Leniency/Severity*—the tendency toward "easy" or "tough" ratings

- *Central Tendency*—the inability of the rater to distinguish different levels of performance, so everyone gets rated as average

- *Similarity*—rating people high who are like the appraiser or do things in the same way as the appraiser

- *Stereotypes*—viewing people with certain characteristics the same way

- *Contrast Effect*—comparing an employee to other employees rather than to a standard

- *Selective Perception*—the tendency to see and hear what we want to see and hear

These common rater errors can be minimized. If raters recognize the tendencies they have, they can be more cognizant as they begin the appraisal process. Good use of the performance planning process can help minimize biases through clear performance expectations and mutually understood standards and levels of performance. Finally, regular discussion between the appraiser and appraisee during the performance period may be the most important factor in minimizing these common errors.

Is There a Need for Ratings?

Although rating or placing a label on employee performance is the normal practice by those employers using traditional performance appraisal methods, must this occur? The employer must first ask the critical questions, "What are we trying to accomplish with the process? What is our objective?" If an employer has decided that its primary purpose in the performance management and review process is to improve performance, enhance communication, and/or develop employees, there may be no need to rate employee performance. In fact, the discussion and, at times, disagreements over ratings may be counterproductive. The value added from doing the ratings may not equal the cost of doing so in terms of employee and supervisor morale, if not performance. Rating performance becomes important when the employer will use the process to make

MODULE
15

human resources decisions. If the program is to be used for merit pay increases, for example, it becomes necessary to label or classify the performance of employees to distinguish those receiving raises of various levels from those who will not. Many employers seem to assign ratings simply because "we've always done it that way," without real thought to the need for doing so.

Use of Performance Management Information—To Make Decisions, Identify and Solve Problems, and Develop Employees and the Organization

Making Decisions

Employers have historically used performance appraisal data for a variety of human resources decisions—merit pay, promotion, layoff. As discussed above, legal implications arise when such decisions are made. The system design, including factors used, must support the decision being made. For example, a performance management process that has focused on the accomplishment of specific employee objectives in the current job may not be a good predictor of success in a higher-level job. Promotion decisions require a system that looks not only at past performance, but also at the competencies required for successful performance in the new assignment. Similarly, if the process is to be used for rightsizing with some employees assigned to new responsibilities, then some assessment of the extent to which employees possess the required competencies for new positions must occur.

Identify and Solve Problems

The performance management process identifies problems, both employee specific and organizational. Appraisers must take responsibility for these problems. When the problems relate to an individual employee, the manager must work with that employee to develop a performance improvement plan for its resolution. Often, however, the performance management process highlights widespread rather than individual problems. This could be caused perhaps by a system deficiency rather than poor performance. At fault could be the selection process, the method by which work is assigned, training, technology, or even the supervisor her- or himself. Once such problems are identified, actions must be taken for their resolution.

Development

In the fast-paced environment faced by all employers, performance management must have a forward focus, helping employees perform excellently not only at the moment, but in the future. The performance management process can serve to identify individual and system needs for growth. Development plans and strategies should include steps required for employees to maintain their current competencies required for success, and also to acquire those skills and competencies needed in the changing environment. Such development objectives, like other objectives, should be SMART—specific, measurable, aligned with employer/unit goals, realistic, and time limited.

New Developments in Employee Performance Management

While few argue with the importance of performance planning and feedback for successful individual and organizational performance, employee performance management programs have been criticized on many grounds.

The Focus on Ratings and Rewards. By focusing on ratings and rewards, the axiom "You get what you reward" often applies with devastating consequences. Employees and their managers spend too much time arguing over ratings at the expense of productive time directed toward accomplishing employer objectives. The rewards sought are often short term (one year or less), but may have long-term consequences for the employer. Rewards may be achieved in counterproductive ways, i.e., "the ends justify the means."

There Is Too Much for One Rater to Appraise.

Supervisory and management jobs are becoming more complex. As organizations downsize, the span of control of managers and supervisors often increases. It becomes more difficult to monitor and track what a manager's staff is doing. Remaining managers often find themselves leading a group of employees who are more diverse in their required duties and skills. It becomes more difficult for the manager to assess or appraise the performance of such a diverse team as their duties and skills are often quite different from those of the manager.

The System Is Too Top Down.

Among the many charges leveled by those being appraised, the complaint that the system is too heavily controlled by the supervisor without adequate employee participation is a common one. As a result, general charges of unfairness—favoritism, discrimination, etc.—arise.

Team-Based Work Systems.

As employers organize their workforces into teams for more effective accomplishment of organizational objectives, the traditional performance appraisal system may not fit. The focus on individual effort and rewards is likely to be incongruent with the team-based structure being utilized. And the supervisor of the team may not be able to appraise the use of the correct teamwork behaviors by team members.

Total Quality Management.

Total Quality Management proponents argue that traditional performance appraisal programs focus on individual performance, often blaming low level individuals for errors in organizational systems. In this view, performance appraisal programs are inherently in conflict with achieving product or service quality. Employers have responded to these criticisms with program modifications and innovations.

Increased Employee Involvement.

Consistent with the general trend toward more employee participation in workplace issues that affect them, there has been an increase in employee involvement in the performance management process. Such involvement can include employee participation in the development of his or her performance expectations and measures, more active employee monitoring and initiation of changes during the performance period, and self-appraisal by the employee as part of the review process.

Less Focus on Ratings and Rewards.

If an employer decides that the major purpose of its performance management program is feedback, rather than making pay or downsizing decisions, then the employer may have no need to affix a rating or label to the performance of an employee over the performance period. Similarly, if an employer's compensation program calls for skill-based pay, gain-sharing, or simple across-the-board increases, there is little need for an individual rating beyond, perhaps, that the employee is somehow eligible for the increase.

Multirater Systems.

Perhaps the most significant recent innovation in performance management has been the use of multirater systems. Bottom-up appraisals, peer reviews, and 360-degree feedback systems are examples. The underlying premise of each of these approaches is that a more accurate and fairer appraisal will result if an individual's performance is assessed by those in the best position to do so. Such systems are more frequently used for developmental purposes than to make evaluative human resources decisions. Because such programs require substantially more administrative effort, their success requires a supportive organizational culture, training and skill development for all program participants, and a clear top management commitment.

Bottom-up appraisals, usually used in conjunction with a traditional manager-conducted process, are used to provide a more complete picture of the performance of a supervisor. Direct reports of the supervisor are used to provide performance feedback. To minimize the possibility of retaliation, employees often complete the instrument anonymously; where a supervisor has a very small number of direct reports, ensuring confidentiality may be impossible. Feedback is often summarized, perhaps by an outside consultant or human resources representative, before it is provided to the supervisor. The focus is on specific supervisor behaviors the employee should be positioned to see, e.g., "the extent to which my supervisor lets me know what is expected of me." Such feedback is provided to help the supervisor improve.

In order to assess the extent to which team members utilize teamwork skills, *peer review* is often required. In the most commonly used peer review systems, team members are asked to assess the behaviors of fellow team members. Because of the possibility of such systems evolving into a popularity contest, they are usually used for developmental purposes rather than to make human resources decisions. The content is usually behaviorally focused, concentrating on behaviors observable to fellow employees.

Another approach is the *360-degree feedback* system, which includes both bottom-up appraisals and peer reviews. The premise is that in order to get a complete picture of the performance of an individual, one must gather information from all those having a relevant view of the employee's performance. Such information may come from external customers or internal customers (direct reports, peers, etc.), and is usually gathered through surveys, either online or paper and pencil. The process normally involves the identification of key customers to be surveyed. Often, both the appraisee and supervisor have input into the selection of those to be surveyed. Steps are usually taken to ensure confidentiality, both in data gathering and in feedback. Results are most often used for developmental purposes, as many from whom information is sought may be unwilling to provide honest information knowing that important human resources decisions may result. The 360-degree feedback process is often used, therefore, in conjunction with another system for assessing performance results if important human resources decisions are to be made.

MODULE
15

STRATEGIC ISSUES IN MOVING FROM PERFORMANCE APPRAISAL TO PERFORMANCE MANAGEMENT

Successful implementation of a sound performance management process is as important as is the development of the process. Too often employers give too little thought and devote too little effort to developing an implementation strategy after having given considerable attention to developing the instrument. Successful implementation of a new or revised performance management process is an organizational change that demands the same planned effort required by other large-scale organizational changes. Implementation issues and strategies are discussed in the following sections.

Involvement of Users in Development

While human resources professionals usually take the lead in developing or revising performance management processes and instruments, employers are wise to involve system users in the development process. Such involvement can take many forms—development team members, participants in focus groups, and respondents to surveys, for example. Involving those who will be affected by the system—appraisers and appraisees—in the development process serves a number of useful purposes. First, their perspective and insights will likely lead to a better process being created. Second, there may be less resistance to the new or revised program because people are more likely to be supportive of things they have some involvement in creating. Third, involvement during the development process facilitates the notion that the performance management program objectives are truly about helping individuals and the organization achieve success.

Alternative Implementation Models

It is unrealistic to assume that an employer will design the perfect process that requires no revisions. Therefore, employers are well advised to consider alternatives to full-blown adoption of a new system as soon as it has been developed. Such alternatives can include the following.

- *Pilot program.* Starting the program on a pilot or trial basis for a limited period allows for time to study system successes and areas in need of improvement and to make needed modifications. Perceptions of fairness with the system are also enhanced through use of a pilot program, especially when feedback is solicited from pilot participants, no permanent records are kept concerning individual performance appraisals, and no individual human resources decisions are made using the process. Often during pilot programs, however, the current system must be utilized simultaneously, creating double effort for managers and employees in the pilot program. For this reason, when an employer has an existing performance management program, the pilot program for the new program is often limited to a section of the workforce—sample, unit, department, etc.

- *Implement in one unit.* At times, an employer finds that one unit has a strong need for a new or revised system or has characteristics that reflect the larger organization. In such cases it may be wise to develop the program for that unit(s), making necessary improvements, before widespread implementation.

- *Staggered implementation.* The key to successful implementation is support from top management. Therefore, some employers choose a strategy that cascades down from the top of the organization to its lower levels. During the first year, the top management team would be covered by the program. In the second year, the next lower one of two levels of the organization would be covered, and so on until all organizational levels are covered.

- *Obstacles to successful implementation.* There are a number of common obstacles to successful implementation of new or revised performance management systems. These include:

  ✓ *Lack of commitment from those at the top.* Performance management efforts are at their core simply good leadership practices, e.g., ensuring that employees know what is expected from them and how they are doing. But the creation of a formal process, which requires documented actions by appraisers, often leads to resistance from those appraisers. Not only legitimate resistance ("I am stretched too thin now"), but also simple resistance to change arise initially and through the program's use. It must be clear that the employer's leaders support the program fully if it is to become a priority for busy managers. Such commitment can be demonstrated through written statements, presentations, and appearances (live or on videotape) during training programs as the program is being introduced. But this commitment is most vividly demonstrated when top management requires that subordinate managers follow the requirements of the system and take corrective actions against those who do not.

  ✓ *Overselling the program.* Performance management will not cure an employer's problems of poor employee performance. The root cause of the problems often lie outside the scope of performance planning, feedback, and development. An employee may be performing poorly because of any of a number of factors—e.g., a lack of necessary skills, barriers beyond the employee's control that prevent successful performance, the organizational structure being out of line with its mission and objectives, stressful situations in the employee's personal life, etc. Frequently, supervisors and managers simply lack adequate leadership and managerial skills, leading to poor performance from their subordinates. The performance management process will not correct the problem of employee poor performance caused because his or her supervisor lacks basic communication, decision making, or planning skills.

✓ *Developing a program excessive in paperwork and administrative requirements.* A performance management program that does not add value to the organization is counterproductive. At its core, the cost of administering the performance management system should not exceed the value gained from its use. The system must contribute to assisting managers in helping their staff perform at their highest levels. Unnecessary administrative requirements not only fail to add this value, they also serve to undermine commitment to the performance management process and other human resources programs.

✓ *Failing to train and retrain appraisers.* Performance planning, feedback, and development are not innate skills possessed by everyone asked to plan or appraise another's performance. Skill development is often required. Additionally, one involved in the system must understand the system being utilized. What are its rules, regulations, and requirements? Such training needs are not a one-time event, occurring only when a new program is introduced. Managers and employees come and go, and those who stay may need skill redevelopment or upgrading.

✓ *Changing the system.* Employers that too frequently change their performance management process find that some participants become skeptical about the employer's commitment to the new program. Employees may question how much effort they should invest in a program that is likely to change soon. However, failing to make necessary changes to a program also leads to employee distrust and lack of commitment.

✓ *Failing to monitor the program and deal with those who fail to comply.* An important human resources responsibility for success of a performance management program is monitoring the program. Ideally, such monitoring includes careful study of program results to find improvement opportunities for the employer—training needs, system changes, selection system revisions, etc. A successful program must also be monitored to ensure that program guidelines are being followed—e.g. that reviews are being conducted on time and properly. Human resources may or may not handle that responsibility. In some organizations, such monitoring is conducted through the organizational hierarchy; i.e., higher-level managers ensure that their subordinate managers are in compliance. Regardless of who does such monitoring, failure to correct the behavior of those who do not comply with the performance management program and to get them on board leads to a lack of commitment to the program from others.

In the final analysis, successful implementation requires commitment from appraisers and appraisees. This commitment is more likely to arise when they see benefit from the process—it helps them perform better, leads to organizational rewards, improves the quality of worklife, etc.

IN CONCLUSION

Debrief

Developing a performance management process that will work effectively to help the employer accomplish its goals and objectives through its employees is a complex process. There is no one right way to do so. The process must match the objectives of the employer for its use, and it must fit the culture and character of the organization. Many performance management and/or appraisal efforts have failed for not addressing these two critical issues. A process cannot simply be transplanted from one employer to another without gauging its fit and modifying it as needed. Additionally, as the module points out, there are not only legal issues in using performance appraisal results to make and/or defend human resources decisions, but also practical challenges in identifying value-added strategies for planning and managing employee performance. However, as employers struggle to continually improve their products, services, and processes, the performance management process can serve as an essential organizational tool. When done well, performance management serves to align the efforts of employees with employer goals and values, helps ensure that employees have a clear understanding of what is expected of them, and makes certain that employees receive continuous feedback about their performance. Finally, the results of such a program can serve to develop not only individuals, but also organizational systems and processes.

Suggested Readings

Bader, G. E. and Bloom, A. E. (1992, June). How to do peer review. *Training & Development Journal,* 45 (6), 61–66.

Gebelein, S. H. (1996, January). Employee development: Multi-rater feedback goes strategic. *HR Focus,* 73 (1).

Vinson, M. N. (1996, April). The pros and cons of 360-degree feedback: Making it work. *Training & Development Journal,* 50 (4), 11–12.

Edwards, M. R. and Ewen, A. J. (1996, May/June). How to manage performance and pay with 360-degree feedback. *Compensation and Benefits Review,* 28 (3), 41–46.

Brotherton, P. (1966, May). Candid feedback spurs changes in culture. *HR Magazine,* 41 (5), 47–50.

Phipps, P. A. (1996, March). Due-process performance appraisals. *Monthly Labor Review,* 119 (3), 34–39.

MODULE
15

Critical Thinking Questions

1. How can the performance management process help both employees and the employer?

2. What are important factors in constructing and administering a performance management process to maximize its ability to operate within legal challenges when used in making human resources decisions?

3. The use of multirater appraisal systems is increasing. What are the characteristics of an organizational culture necessary for a successful multirater feedback system?

4. Some argue that the process of formal performance appraisals should be abandoned given the difficulties that employers face in successfully administering them. Do you agree or disagree? Why?

Exercises

1. You have just been hired as a consultant to the human resources department of a four-year-old, fast-growing, 500-person financial services firm located outside of Chicago. Your consulting assignment is to develop a performance management system for the firm. What critical questions will you need to ask and answer before deciding how to proceed? What implementation strategies will you consider? If the firm is committed to continuous quality improvement, is nonunion, and employs team-based work systems, what performance management approaches might be most appropriate? If the firm has a more traditional organizational structure and philosophy and the CEO believes in performance-based pay, what performance management approaches might be more appropriate?

2. You are the human resources advisor in a manufacturing facility of an automobile supplier. Chris Johnson, a newly hired supervisor, has come to you complaining about Pat Roland. In fact, Chris wants to fire Pat for poor performance. However, as you and Chris review Pat's personnel file, you discover no record of prior disciplinary actions or notices. In fact, Pat's performance reviews, completed by Chris's predecessor, all state that Pat is a performer who has consistently met or exceeded expectations. What advice do you give Chris for dealing with this situation?

3. Which of the following performance objectives are "SMART"?

   - Exit interview summaries will be submitted to the director of human resources monthly.

   - Training programs for departments will be conducted within 60 days of requests.

   - The time needed to fill vacant positions will be reduced to 22 days on average by December 31.

   - An acceptable workforce diversity program will be submitted to the Executive Committee.

   - All monthly status reports will be submitted and approved by the third working day of the following month.

   - The pilot test of the new performance management system will be successfully completed by the end of the third quarter.

References

Myers, D. W. (1992). *Human Resources Management,* 2nd ed., Chicago: Commerce Clearing House.

Davidson, J. E. (1995, Spring). Temptation of performance appraisal abuse in employment litigation, *Virginia Law Review,* 81 (1605–1629).

Index

Appraiser attitude, 15.12
Appraiser training, 15.8, 15.18

Bottom-up appraisals, 15.16

Central tendency (bias), 15.13
Clarifying expectations, 15.4, 15.7
Coaching approach, 15.12
Commitment to change, 15.18
Competencies (required), 15.6, 15.14
Complexity of appraisal criteria, 15.15
Consequences of performance, 15.7. *See also* Forewarning
Consistency/fairness (appraisal), 15.8, 15.11
Contrast effect (bias), 15.13
Core organizational performance factors, 15.7

Developing people for promotion, 15.6
Discipline and dismissal decisions, 15.7
Discussion of strengths, 15.12

Employee involvement, 15.15, 15.16–17
Employee objectives/accomplishments, 15.12, 15.14
Employee performance, 15.6
Employee performance appraisal. *See* Performance appraisal
Expectations, performance standards, 15.8–12
External customers, 15.16

Fair employment practices, 15.7
Feedback, employees' need for, 15.6, 15.8, 15.12
Flexible job descriptions, 15.8
Focus on ratings and rewards, 15.14
Forewarning, 15.8. *See also* Consequences of performance
Future orientation (appraisal), 15.6

Halo or horns biases, 15.13
HR department staff, 15.11
Human resource decisions, 15.5, 15.6–7, 15.12, 15.14, 15.16
Human resource development, 15.14
Human resource professional, 15.4, 15.10, 15.16
Human resource strategy, 15.5
Human resources representative, 15.16

Implied employment contract, 15.8
Individual performance expectations, 15.9
Internal customers, 15.16

Job descriptions, 15.8
Job-related criteria (appraisal), 15.7

Legitimate resistance, 15.17
Leniency/severity (bias), 15.13
List of objectives, 15.10

Manager responsibilities/skills, 15.9–11, 15.18
Measurable criteria (appraisal), 15.7
Merit increases in salary, 15.7
Mid-period review, 15.11
Minimum subjectivity, 15.7. *See also* Human resource decisions
Monitoring performance, 15.4, 15.5. *See also* Performance review, Performance management process
Monitoring plan, 15.9, 15.11, 15.18
Multirater systems, 15.14

Needs for growth, 15.14

Objective performance measures, 15.4
Objectives, individual and team, 15.10, 15.14
One-unit implementation, 15.17. *See also* Performance management implementation, Performance management process
Organizational culture, supportive, 15.16, 15.19
Organizational goals, 15.6, 15.9–11
Organizational initiatives, 15.4
Organizational structure, 15.8, 15.18
Organizational values, 15.8, 15.11
Overselling the program, 15.17

Past performance (appraisal), 15.6
Peer review, 15.16
Performance appraisal, 15.7. *See also* Performance management
interview, 15.4–5, 15.12–14
process, 15.4–5
Performance appraisal, use of results, 15.6–8, 15.19
Performance factors/rating, 15.11
Performance management
cycle, 15.8–14
implementation, 15.8–18
goals, 15.4–5
legal issues, 15.7–8
new developments, 15.14–16
process, 15.4–5, 15.6, 15.11
Performance planning, 15.8, 15.10, 15.14
Performance review, 15.6
Performance-based decisions, 15.7
Periodic review, 15.11
Pilot program, 15.17. *See also* Performance management process, Performance management implementation
Planning (performance), 15.8

Problem identification, 15.14
Promotion decisions, 15.14
Providing ongoing feedback, 15.4

Ratings inflation/rating errors, 15.11, 15.13–14
Recency (bias), 15.13
Resistance to change, 15.17
Retaliation, possibility of, 15.16
Review cycle, 15.11
Review session, 15.12. *See also* Performance
    appraisal interview

Selective perception (bias), 15.13
Self-feedback, 15.6
Similarity (bias), 15.13
SMART objectives, 15.10, 15.14
Staggered implementation, 15.17. *See also*
    Performance management implementation,
    Performance management process

Standards of performance, 15.7–8, 15.11
Stereotype (bias), 15.13
System deficiency, 15.14

Team performance expectations, 15.9
Team player, 15.7
Team-based work systems, 15.14
360-degree feedback, 15.14–15
Top management commitment (lack of), 15.17
Total quality management, 15.14
Traditional manager-conducted process, 15.16.
    See also Performance management
Traditional performance appraisal, 15.6
Training and skill development, 15.16
Transactional role, 15.4
Transformational role, 15.4

Unjust dismissal claims, 15.8

Workforce feedback, 15.17

MODULE
15

KOSSEK ■ BLOCK

MANAGING HUMAN RESOURCES
IN THE 21st CENTURY

From Core Concepts to Strategic Choice

MODULE **16**

Compensation Fundamentals and Linkages to Organizational Performance

Michael L. Moore
MICHIGAN STATE UNIVERSITY

Managing Human Resources in the 21st Century: From Core Concepts to Strategic Choice,
by Kossek and Block

Publisher: Dave Shaut
Executive Editor: John Szilagyi
Developmental Editor: Bryant Editorial Development
Marketing Manager: Joseph A. Sabatino
Production Editor: Tamborah E. Moore
Manufacturing Coordinator: Dana Began Schwartz
Cover Design: Tin Box Studio
Cover Photographs: Copyright Shoji Sato/Photonica
Production House: The Left Coast Group, Inc.
Printer: West Group

Printed in the United States of America
1 2 3 4 5 02 01 00 99

For more information contact South-Western College Publishing, 5101 Madison Road, Cincinnati, Ohio, 45227 or find us on the Internet at *http://www.swcollege.com*
For permission to use material from this text or product, contact us by
- telephone: 1-800-730-2214
- fax: 1-800-730-2215
- web: *http://www.thomsonrights.com*

ISBN: 0–324–01815–0

This book is printed on acid-free paper.

Contents

MODULE OVERVIEW   16.4

OBJECTIVES   16.4

RELATION TO THE FRAME   16.4

MODELS OF BEST PRACTICES IN PAY SYSTEM DESIGN   16.6

CORE CONCEPTS IN COMPENSATING EMPLOYEES   16.8
   Types of Pay   16.8
   Direct Pay Components: Basic Elements of the Work-Reward Exchange   16.8
   Indirect Pay Elements   16.9

STRATEGIC ISSUES OF JOB-BASED PAY COMPARED TO SKILL/COMPETENCY-BASED PAY   16.10
   Internal Equity Tools   16.11
   Job Evaluation Methods for Internal Equity   16.12
   Person-Based Pay Methods for Internal Equity   16.16
   External Equity Issues   16.16
   Individual Equity   16.18
   Disadvantages of Each System   16.19
   Balance of Pay Elements Over the Organization's Life Cycle   16.19
   Tangibles and Intangibles   16.20

IN CONCLUSION   16.20
   Debrief   16.20
   Suggested Readings   16.20
   Relevant Web Sites   16.20
   Critical Thinking Questions   16.21
   Exercises   16.21
   Application Exercises   16.21
   References   16.21

INDEX   16.23

MODULE OVERVIEW

Compensation systems that determine how pay is handled in organizations are major strategic levers in determining the culture of the firm. Managers of compensation face the major challenge of efficiently allocating the financial returns for work in a manner viewed as equitable by all stakeholders of the enterprise. To make these decisions even more difficult, options for distributing pay are almost infinitely varied. This module will attempt to provide an overview of the major components of pay and options for the design of pay systems.

OBJECTIVES

The major objectives for this module are to help you:

- Understand the scope of "compensation"

- Appreciate the legal framework surrounding compensation decisions in the United States

- Understand how legal compliance is an important aspect of compensation administration

- Consider competing models of best practices in pay system design

- Understand the elements of both direct pay and indirect pay

- Learn the strategic options of designing compensation as a job-based versus a skill-based system

- Understand the three forms of equity necessary for successful compensation systems

- Be sensitive to the intangible elements of pay as well as the more frequently assessed tangible elements

RELATION TO THE FRAME

Compensation systems fall in all three columns of the model shown in Figure 16.1. Most of the strategic and tactical pay decisions discussed in this model are unilateral in the sense that they are designed by compensation experts in-house who may work with external consultants. Pay decisions and policies are discussed and coordinated with upper management and executives. In the case of executive compensation, a special committee of the board of directors is established to set criteria and performance expectations for executives. In most organizations in the United States, pay for salaried employees who are not represented by a union would be unilaterally designed at management's discretion. If the organization has employees represented by a union, pay practices and pay levels would be negotiated by representatives of management and employees. After normal negotiations, a written agreement is signed by the parties. This contract or bargaining agreement forms the basis of a legal understanding of the agreements reached in terms of wages (pay), hours, and working conditions. Other aspects of pay are imposed by the U.S. government via a wide variety of employment laws at federal and state levels that influence compensation practices. Federal laws have been enacted that affect four aspects of compensation systems:

- Income maintenance

- Discrimination

FIGURE 16.1   *A Frame for Understanding Human Resource Strategy:*
Context, Roles, and Constraints

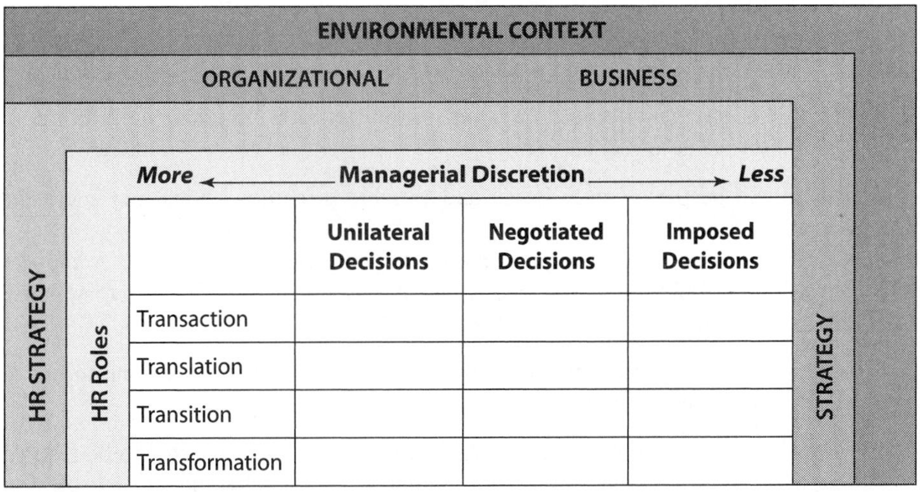

ENVIRONMENTAL CONTEXT			
ORGANIZATIONAL		BUSINESS	

		Unilateral Decisions	Negotiated Decisions	Imposed Decisions
	Transaction			
	Translation			
	Transition			
	Transformation			

More ← ———— Managerial Discretion ———— → Less

HR STRATEGY · HR Roles · STRATEGY

© 2000 by Ellen Ernst Kossek and Richard Block. Thanks to Brian Pentland, Karen Markel, and John Beck for helpful comments and discussions that enhanced the model.

- Prevailing wages

- Accommodation of disabilities and family situations

Income maintenance laws are extremely important to compensation professionals. The best-known law in this category is the Social Security Act of 1935 that sets out fundamental protections for workers who became unemployed, injured, or otherwise unable to work. Its provisions cover old age, disability, health insurance, and income continuation for most U.S. workers and their dependents. Another Great Depression-inspired piece of legislation was the Fair Labor Standards Act of 1938 (FLSA). This act provided for a federal minimum wage, regulation of hours worked, and exemption conditions for overtime pay, and also regulated conditions for the employment of children. This act is enforced by the U.S. Department of Labor. Another category of laws enacted in the Depression years were the "prevailing wage laws" such as the Davis-Bacon (construction contracts), Walsh-Healey (government contracts), and the McNamara-O'Hara Act of 1965 (service and consulting contracts). These laws emphasize the role of the U.S. government as a purchaser of services and require those firms doing business with the government to pay prevailing (labor union) wages and to adhere to the FLSA. This generally keeps wages high.

The major law covering pay discrimination is the Equal Pay Act of 1963. This act is enforced by the Equal Employment Opportunity Commission (EEOC), which focuses on equal pay for women and men in the workplace. Pay for men and women must be the same when their jobs are equal or "substantially equal" in terms of the task skill, effort, responsibilities, and working conditions required.

Accommodation of disabled workers and family needs is required by the Pregnancy Discrimination Act of 1978, which amends the Civil Rights Act of 1964; the Americans with Disabilities Act (ADA) of 1990; and the Family and Medical Leave Act of 1993. Each act requires employers to structure jobs or leaves in ways that do not penalize employees in the affected groups. These laws do impose constraints on employer ability to design pay systems and employer-union ability to negotiate pay systems, but they leave adequate room for the parties to design distinctive pay arrangements to meet strategic objectives.

Before focusing on specific building blocks of basic pay systems, it may be helpful to consider some best practices in looking at pay systems.

MODULE
16

MODELS OF BEST PRACTICES IN PAY SYSTEM DESIGN

Schuster and Zingheim (1992) and Lawler (1990) describe a bundle of practices best conceptualized as "new pay." These practices include the following pay system elements:

- Pay that is externally focused on labor market pay rates. Internal equity in pay is deemphasized as less important.

- Pay should be performance based and variable in nature: annual pay increases should be deemphasized or eliminated. Variable pay puts employee pay "at risk" if the firm fails to meet its performance targets. On the other hand, employees have the possibility of earning above market pay if the firm "makes its numbers" and achieves financial returns and/or revenue targets.

- Risk sharing is the basis for pay relationships between employees and the firm. Pay is not treated as entitlement.

- Formal job descriptions are deemphasized. Employees are expected to be flexible and to look for opportunities to contribute in both functional duties and work on projects and initiatives.

- Formal hierarchical promotions are replaced by enhancement of lateral opportunities to contribute. Pay is more linked to responsibilities than job titles. Career paths and specific stepping-stones on a route to the top are deemphasized.

- Job security is deemphasized. Firms encourage employee "employability" rather than career commitments. Employability means that the firm will try to provide many opportunities such as working on cutting-edge projects or building state-of-the-art systems that enable employees to continuously enhance their skills and thus protect their future employment potential. This is quite different from firms that approach each hire as a potential career-long commitment to the employee by the organization with the expectation that the employee will reciprocate with loyalty and a career-long desire to learn, improve, and maximize his or her contribution to the firm's objectives.

- Teams rather than individuals are increasingly seen as the relevant unit of contribution.

Proponents of the "new pay" precepts would argue that these bundled pay strategies optimize business competitiveness strategies by keeping labor costs in check in times of economic hardship and allowing the firm maximum flexibility in paying, developing, and moving its employees to high value-adding tasks and projects. However, another bundle of pay practices exists as a best-practice alternative.

Jeffrey Pfeffer (1994) offers a set of best practices that he identifies as "High Commitment Pay" and argues that these practices will optimize human resource contributions. Pfeffer's list of practices include:

- Paying high wages: High-wage policies allow the firm to attract, retain, and motivate the best people at all levels of the enterprise. This strategy is grounded in the belief that you get what you pay for.

- Employment security should be valued and guaranteed. Since few employees are independently wealthy, firms that threaten layoffs and downsizing will not be seen as "employers of choice" and will force employees to devote time to seeking work elsewhere. Employment security is seen as the bedrock for high-quality work and a willingness to be flexible and innovative in performing tasks for the enterprise.

- Use incentives wisely: Focus on encouraging employees to innovate and work hard by sharing gains while insulating them from downside risk.

- Encourage employee ownership of the enterprise in terms of stock gifts, thrift plans [401(k)s], options of company, and employee stock ownership plans (ESOPs) that link enterprise success and increases in employee wealth over the long run.

- Build a culture where leaders engage in high levels of participation and use empowering practices to involve employees at all levels. Encourage employees to identify their success with the success of the enterprise.

- Teams, not individuals, should be seen as the unit of work practices and leadership.

- Pay differentials across jobs and minimize levels. Everyone should be made to feel that they are succeeding and are successful. Efforts are made to avoid a "we-they" mentality.

- Promotion from within is emphasized to encourage employee commitment to the organization.

- Recruiting and staffing practices are distinctive and highly selective. Willingness to adopt the firm's culture and values is encouraged in addition to customary knowledge, skill, and ability criteria.

- Information sharing is valued at all levels and across the enterprise. Power games and function-based "chimneys" are not encouraged.

- Training, cross-training, and skill development are seen as fundamental to enterprise success.

- Egalitarian symbols and perquisites are common. Everyone eating in the same cafeteria, parking in the same lot, uniforms, etc., are deliberately used to reduce status distinctions.

- A long-term focus is fundamental. The enterprise does not move people around without good reason or change fundamental strategies based on Wall Street's perception of quarterly earnings.

- Processes and systems are studied closely and are subjected to a continuous improvement philosophy. Close attention is paid to policy deployment and measurement issues.

MODULE
16

Looking at these two sets of best practices poses a cognitive dilemma: each appears plausible. The "High Commitment" set of practices emphasizes a psychological and social contract between employer and employees and uses security-oriented pay as its foundation. The "New Pay" emphasizes the interplay between the employer and the shareholders of the enterprise and sees the roles of employees as being more expedient to the changing needs of the organization. Which bundle is the best? Little research exists on these matters, although the work of MacDuffie (1995), Huselid (1995), and Becker and Gerhart (1996) provides support for the idea that high-performance work and pay practices can be best viewed as bundles rather than in a piecemeal manner.

The alternative approach to looking for best practices is to choose pay practices that seem to "fit" with the business strategy (Montemayor 1994). Since most business strategies fall under cost control/cost leadership or differentiation/innovation rubrics, pay policy can be seen as fitting or not fitting these overarching frameworks. Having discussed pay practices from the 40,000-foot level, it is now time to lay out the core concepts of compensation/pay administration.

CORE CONCEPTS IN COMPENSATING EMPLOYEES

Sprinkled through the discussion of best practices were specific goals for compensation systems. These include aspects of organization performance such as being able to (1) attract, retain, and motivate the highest-quality human resource talent; (2) support organization design elements such as teams, lateral careers, and project management; (3) encourage a focus on customers and doing quality work; and (4) promoting efficiency by keeping pay costs low in relation to outputs achieved. An additional objective (5) would be to be in legal compliance with federal and state laws, while another (6) would be to have a system that promotes equity in all its facets.

Looking at the equity objective in greater detail reveals the need to consider several levels of equity. These are:

- *Internal Equity:* Are jobs within the organization that are equal on skill, effort, responsibility, working conditions, and other valid compensable factors paid the same in terms of placement in pay grades or bands?

- *External Equity:* Are jobs in the firm paid as well as identical jobs found in firms in the relevant labor market? Firms have the strategic option of paying "above market," "at market," or "below market" wages. Are employees satisfied with their pay relative to pay available in the competitive labor market?

- *Individual Equity:* Do employees who produce more and/or better work receive recognition in the form of merit increases or incentive pay for their contributions?

Making all three forms of equity seem acceptable to employees requires continuous administrative vigilance over the total compensation system. Let us now turn our attention to the components of a total compensation system.

Types of Pay

Having examined pay issues along dimensions of strategies and best practices, pay objectives, and equity considerations, it is now appropriate to move from the context of pay to the ground-level aspects of pay that must be considered in doing compensation tasks. A good place to begin is by defining compensation. *Compensation* in the professional sense "refers to all forms of financial returns and tangible services and benefits employees receive as part of an employment relationship." (Milkovitch and Newman 1999, p. 6). A broadened view of compensation would include the psychological, social, and cultural benefits employees derive from the work tasks, team accomplishments, and organizational prestige, respectively. This module will focus on the financial remuneration elements of pay systems. These elements are customarily seen as composed of two groups of factors: "direct pay elements" and "indirect pay elements." Each will now be described.

Direct Pay Components: Basic Elements of the Work-Reward Exchange

The complete exchange of the employee contribution of time, effort, and creativity for inducements offered by the organization is varied and endless but can be segmented into several major categories. In this module, compensation is defined as tangible financial returns and benefits an employee receives from an organization as part of a contract or formal employment relationship. Components of a tangible nature include the following:

- *Direct pay:* Cash payments that include a base wage, merit pay adjustment, cost-of-living adjustments, individual incentives, group incentives, organization-wide incentives, short-term bonuses, and long-term incentives including executive or employee stock ownership plans. The major components of direct pay administration include the following:

✓ *Base pay:* This is the financial compensation the employer pays for each job. It tends to be anchored to the specific collection of tasks customarily viewed as a job. It sounds like this: "My new job pays me $75,000 per year."

✓ *Merit pay:* Merit pay is the adjustment to base pay that is allocated by the organization as a result of using a subjective performance appraisal system. Merit increases can be paid as a lump sum, where employees receive a raise but their base pay remains unchanged, or as merit pay "baked in," where the amount of the raise is used to adjust the employee's base salary upward by the raise amount.

✓ *Incentives:* Incentives are additional payments earned by objectively exceeding standards set up as a written plan. By selling more, producing more, contributing more to earnings, etc., employees earn payments that are distributed on a lump-sum basis as bonuses, commissions, or simply incentive payouts.

✓ *Cost-of-living adjustments* (COLAs): These direct pay adjustments raise employee pay on a lump sum basis to reflect negotiated pay adjustments for changes in the Consumer Price Index or CPI. These are typically found in unionized workplaces or in government income maintenance programs such as social security.

Indirect Pay Elements

All direct pay components are reflected in actual remuneration flowing into employee paychecks. Indirect compensation elements reflect valuable considerations to employees that are not paid as money in the paycheck.

- *Indirect compensation:* This term includes benefits and employee services such as protection programs including pensions, various insurances such as disability insurance, life insurance, and health insurance. Another category of indirect compensation is pay for time not worked on the job (breaks, wash up time, meal times) and off the job (vacations, holidays, sabbaticals, and leaves). A final aspect of indirect compensation is perquisites, services, and allowances such as attractive work places, health clubs, on-site day care, product discounts, and similar benefits valued by employees.

Additional examples reflecting the detail of indirect compensation will now be provided. For a more thorough treatment of this topic, see Module 18 on Benefits.

Examples. Benefits are viewed as protecting the employee's standard of living created by the direct pay package. Benefits protect the employee from hazards that can befall workers. For example, Table 16.1 on page 16.10 identifies typical workplace hazards and the type of private and public benefits designed to protect the worker or worker's family income flow.

- *Payments for time not worked:* These payments include remuneration for time not worked on the job such as wash-up time, rest breaks, paid lunch time, and payments for time not worked off the job such as vacations and holidays.

- *Employee services and perquisites:* These payments include items like cafeteria food subsidies, discounts on employer merchandise, counseling, and financial planning.

- *Intrinsically motivating aspects of compensation:* The tangible elements of pay are defined as compensation because they are provided by the organization to employees. Because they come from outside the person, they are seen as forms

TABLE 16.1   *Workplace Hazards and Benefit Response/Tools*

Hazard	Benefit Response/Tools/Private	Benefit Response/Tools/Public
Retirement	• Defined benefit pensions • Defined contribution pensions • Money purchase and thrift plans (401(k)s and ESOPs)	• Social security old age benefits
Death	• Group term life insurance (including accidental death and travel insurance) • Payouts from profit-sharing, pension, and/or thrift plans • Dependent survivors' benefits	• Social security survivors' benefits
Disability	• Short-term accident and sickness insurance • Long-term disability insurance • Wellness programs	• Workers' compensation • Social security disability benefits • State disability benefits
Unemployment	• Supplemental unemployment benefits and/or severance pay	• Unemployment benefits
Medical/dental expenses	• Hospital/surgical insurance • Other medical insurance • Dental insurance • Vision insurance	• Workers' compensation • Medicare

of extrinsic motivation. Other rewards are termed intrinsic motivation because they only work to motivate if individual employees perceive them as doing so. Examples include exciting work, recognition, the chance to learn, and various forms of recognition and status.

These reward elements are important in fully understanding the psychological contract between individuals and the organization but will not be the focus of this module. The concern here is creating a better understanding of the direct and indirect pay elements and systems.

Having covered the major components of compensation systems, it is now appropriate to consider the next major strategic question of whether to design our system based on job-based pay, or on some type of skill- or competency-based pay system.

STRATEGIC ISSUES OF JOB-BASED PAY COMPARED TO SKILL/COMPETENCY-BASED PAY

The choice of basing a firm's compensation system on job factors versus employee skill factors merits serious thought. A brief summary of the advantages and disadvantages of each approach will be offered within the equity framework provided earlier in this module. Tools necessary to implement each approach will also be identified as options are discussed. The fundamental issue is one of control over the system. In a job-based system, the organization possesses greater control over pay levels and ultimately labor costs. A skill-based pay or pay-for-knowledge system puts more control in employees' hands in a practical way. Employees can increase their pay by learning more skills/job duties identified as valuable by the employer. Attention now turns to the tools used to implement each type of equity (internal, external, individual) under job- and skill-based pay systems.

Internal Equity Tools

Both the job-based and the skilled-based approaches rely on extensive study of jobs and tasks. Work analysis is used to codify practices into job descriptions and to validate the existence of specific skill elements and clusters existing in each job. A job-based system creates internal equity by devising job evaluation systems for assessing the relative worth of jobs in terms of the amount of skill, effort, responsibility, and working conditions factors any incumbent faces in the job. Job information is obtained from various sources. These include:

- Prior job descriptions
- Supervisors
- Current job incumbents
- Published job descriptions in the Dictionary of Occupational Titles (DOT)
- Experts and consultants
- Customers and clients

Methods for obtaining job data include questionnaires, group interviews, individual interviews, work observation, and maintenance of task diaries of work performed. Once job data are obtained, organized, and codified, the process of job evaluation can begin.

Once the work tasks are assessed and summarized, a job description can be created. The job description is the foundation of the job-based pay system. The job description format is usually standardized and contains the following elements:

MODULE
16

- *Job title:* describes the nature and level of the work performed without inflating its importance, and without implying the gender of the current jobholder.

- *FLSA status:* exempt or nonexempt.

- *Department:* administrative to technical.

- *Job number:* the number assigned to the job by the firm.

- *General summary:* states the general nature, level, and purpose of the job; recommended length is under four sentences.

- *Principal duties and responsibilities:* lists duties crucial to successful job performance; written in present tense, focuses on verbs and verb objects, and includes explanatory phrases (tells why each duty is performed).

- *Knowledge, skills, and abilities required:* lists specific elements required of an employee to perform the job; includes mental requirements, and levels of skill, knowledge, education, and experience.

- *Working conditions:* describes work environment and any safety hazards encountered in performing the job (includes degree and frequency of exposure).

- *Approvals and dates:* verification that a jobholder, supervisor, and human resource member agree that the description is accurate; dates are included to ensure that the description is current.

- *Disclaimer statement:* states that the job description is not intended to be an exhaustive list of all job duties and/or knowledge, skills, and abilities required, but a description of the job's most important elements. Such a statement helps maintain flexibility. Figure 16.2 illustrates a completed job description suitable for use in pay system development.

Job Evaluation Methods for Internal Equity

Having summarized work in the job description, the next task is to determine the compensable factors inherent in the work. In the simplest sense, this involves asking key stakeholders in the organization the question "What do we want to pay for?" Typical compensable factors include knowledge, amount of supervision required, complexity of work, responsibilities of various kinds (for money, equipment, etc.), contacts inside and outside the firm, as well as physical demands and/or exposure to hazards. The choice of compensable factors may be the basis of an extensive organization development

FIGURE 16.2   *Job Description*

MODULE
16

Title: Secretary A   FLSA: Nonexempt

General Summary:
Under general direction, performs administrative support tasks and general office duties.

Principal Duties and Responsibilities
1. Creates and processes routine correspondence, some of which is sensitive in nature.
2. Maintains files of various records including correspondence.
3. Reviews and routes incoming mail. Enters and reviews e-mail messages.
4. Receives incoming telephone calls. Answers questions and/or routes incoming calls to the appropriate party.
5. Responsible for the maintenance and scheduling of staff appointments and travel arrangements.
6. Maintains knowledge of company and secretarial policies and procedures.

Knowledge, Skills, and Abilities Required
1. Ability to use current word processing software and type 60 WPM with 100 percent accuracy.
2. Completion of courses in secretarial science through high school, a community college, or other special training.
3. Three years of related clerical experience.
4. Ability to use standard office equipment such as copier, fax machine and personal computer.
5. Strong organizational and interpersonal skills with potential to work on teams.

Working Conditions
Normal office setting where there is no physical discomfort due to temperature, dust, noise, lighting, etc.

Approvals

_____	_____	_____
Name	Title	Date
_____	_____	_____
Name	Title	Date

The above describes the general type and level of work to be performed. It is not an exhaustive list of responsibilities, duties, or skills required to adequately perform the duties and responsibilities of the position.

---

exercise involving focus groups and surveys of various groups culminating in recommendations to the officer group. Alternatively, sets of compensable factors seen as "plausible" for the firm are presented to executives by compensation consultants who then "tweak" their basic plans as necessary to achieve buy-in from executives. Figure 16.3 shows a list of compensable factors used by a large automobile-related company in the United States.

FIGURE 16.3 *Categories*

Skill
1. Specialized or technical knowledge required
2. Experience required
3. Manual skill or dexterity required

Effort
4. Physical effort
5. Mental/visual effort

Responsibility
6. Complexity and difficulty of duties
7. Seriousness of error
8. Contacts with customers, the general public, and other companies*
9. Contacts with other departments (within the company)
10. Responsibility for safety of others
11. Responsibility for company funds or property
12. Responsibility for confidential information
13. Responsibility for performance of work without immediate supervisor
14. Responsibility for the work of others

Working Conditions
15. Environment/surroundings
16. Unavoidable hazards

*Throughout the plan, the words "company" and "companies" are used to refer to business firms, governmental agencies, and work organizations of all types.

Most plans choose seven or fewer factors to minimize complexity and bureaucracy. Figure 16.4 on page 16.14 illustrates a typical compensable factor used in a "point plan." Note: the levels of the factor and the allocation of points in this example.

Job evaluation is the process of determining the relative worth of jobs. Which of the following jobs should be paid more: supermarket cashier or the delivery person who carries groceries to your car and retrieves shopping carts? The cashier handles money, talks with customers, must be accurate, and works indoors albeit standing up for an entire shift. The delivery person handles purchased merchandise, talks with customers, lifts heavy packages, and spends much of his or her time outside braving extreme heat or cold as determined by climate and season. Which job is "heaviest" in terms of internal equity? Job evaluation processes can provide an answer.

Job evaluation methods include (1) simply assessing whole jobs head to head (ranking method), (2) comparing duties against prewritten job criteria (classification method), and (3) comparing job elements across a set of compensable factors that allow assessment of level of job requirements. Typical compensable factors include skill factors such as analytical skills, education, and experience; responsibility factors such as responsibility for money, for tools, for external contacts, for internal contacts; effort factors such as visual effort, accuracy, physical effort; and working conditions and hazard

FIGURE 16.4 *Factor 6: Complexity and Difficulty of Duties*

Under this factor, measure: (1) the extent to which decisions made and actions taken are controlled by precedents, prescribed work practices, and regulations or other guidelines; (2) the degree of originality, versatility, judgment, and developmental work actually required in the work performed.

Degree	Job Requirements	Point Value
A	Work of some variety, as opposed to simple repetitive operations, but within the range of fairly simple clerical or manual operations.	25
B	Work of a substantial variety of the same kind of routine clerical or manual operations requiring the exercise of comparative judgments to make easy routine decisions.	50
C	Work involving a number of different kinds of clerical operations or the performance of specialized duties calling for the exercise of some judgment based on precedent in carrying out such operations or duties according to established standards, specifications, or prescribed routines and instructions.	75
D	Work requiring either the handling and coordinating of a number of involved clerical operations or the performance of specialized and/or technical duties, calling for the exercise of independent judgment to make decisions in carrying out such operations or duties within the limits of general practices and standards.	100
E	Work of a difficult and complex nature in a professional or technical field, requiring the exercise of considerable independent judgment to make the decisions necessary to carry out this work.	130
F	Work requiring the handling of matters of a complicated technical or professional character, necessitating thorough analysis and the exercise of a large degree of independent judgment in making decisions as to these operations, projects, or policies, usually in an area where methods and practices are not completely or fully established.	180

factors. These comparisons across compensable factors enable each job to be given a point score. Thus the cashier job may earn a score of 275 points while the delivery job earns a score of 175 points when compared across the same factors. This score difference could lead to the cashier job being placed in salary structure grade two, while the delivery job would likely end up being placed in grade one. The pay grade controls maximum pay levels for the jobs within a grade, and thus job evaluation makes a great difference to employees.

Once jobs have been analyzed and described and compensable factors chosen, these compensable factors must be turned into a metric suitable for weighing jobs in the job evaluation process. To convert compensable factors into measurement tools takes several steps. First, using an organization development or consultant-based approach such as mentioned earlier, executives, employees, design teams, and focus groups are asked to allocate one hundred percentage (100%) points across all of the chosen factors. Through discussion and argument, a plan may look like this:

Compensable Factor	
Analytical skills	25%
Education/experience	20%
Responsibility for money	10%
Responsibility for tools	10%
External contacts	15%
Internal contacts	10%
Hazards/environment	10%
	100%

Percentages are then converted to points (enough to adequately cover all levels of each factor). To provide an easy example, in a 1,000-point plan each of the above factors would be converted to points by multiplying its percentage of the total plan by 1,000 points. Thus, analytical skills would be a factor worth 250 points. This factor could then have five levels ranging form 50 to 250 points for jobs containing requirements for the highest levels of analytical skills. This process is repeated to give a point value to each compensable factor in the plan. Now that a 1,000-point job evaluation plan has been created, actual job evaluation can begin using this "point plan." Figure 16.5 shows an example of a complete job evaluation plan.

Evaluating a Job Using a "Point Plan". The compensation analyst or HR specialist performs a job evaluation by using the latest information from the job description and relating it to the levels and definitions within each compensable factor. Once the appropriate level or degree of each factor is assessed in terms of the actual work performed, points are assigned from the job evaluation plan. A job may be at level three of the first factor for 75 points, level two of the second factor for 40 points, level one of the third factor for zero (0) points, and level four of the fourth factor for 60 points, for a total of 175 points. In like manner, every job covered by the job evaluation plan can then be given a point total using the job evaluation measurement tool.

MODULE
16

FIGURE 16.5 *Job Evaluation Plan: Compensable Factors*

Compensable Factors	Weight	Points
Skill		
Education/Experience	22%	220
Innovation	22%	220
Analysis/Problem Solving	18%	180
Effort		
Mental Effort	5%	50
Responsibility		
Autonomy	10%	100
Customer Contacts	13%	130
Working Conditions		
Working Conditions	10%	100
TOTAL	**100%**	**1000**

Jobs can then be grouped into salary grades according to their similar point totals. When this task is done, the organization now possesses a structure of jobs that reflects their internal equity dimensions. We now know how each job in the firm ranks relative to all other jobs covered by this job evaluation plan. The method just described, a point plan, represents the most common method of determining internal equity. It is common in the United States, Europe, England, and former British Commonwealth nations such as Canada, Australia, and South Africa. Having just seen how internal equity is achieved with a job-based system, it is now appropriate to see how skill and/or competency-based systems achieve this goal.

Person-Based Pay Methods for Internal Equity

The skill- or competency-based pay system would not take job data along the job evaluation route. Instead it would use job data to develop skill tests and comprehensive tests to certify that employees have mastered all job skills. Employers typically create job circles of six to eight related jobs. Employees earn higher pay by mastering more jobs and by maintaining their skill levels. Employees are usually expected to work on a job for at least six months before attempting the test. This approach is positive in that it sends a strong signal to employees that their learning is desired and recognized as valuable by allocating pay for learning. Employees like skill-based pay initially because they see it as enabling them to raise their own pay through their own efforts and willingness to learn. Both systems, however, are useful for assessing and creating internal equity. Several writers have led the way for promoting a changeover from job-based to skill- or competency-based plans (Lawler 1994; O'Neill and Doig 1997).

Creating a skill- or competency-based internal structure requires the following steps that are in many ways parallel to those involved in the job-based system discussed above. The first step is to perform a skill analysis or competency analysis. This task is analogous to doing a job analysis and preparing a job description. The next step is to create skill blocks or competencies much like the creation of compensable factors. Then, just as the compensable factors had to be broken into levels and degrees and assigned weights, so must skill levels and competency levels be scaled. The final task is to develop tests and criterion behaviors to enable the firm to certify that the person truly possesses the skill or competency level being assessed. Having gone through a certification process, the skill blocks and competency levels must be market priced. This brings us to the need to establish external equity now that we have created mechanisms to clarify our internal equity structure. Skill- and competency-based structures were not treated at the same level of detail as job-based structures because job-based systems are far more prevalent. One way to learn more about competency systems is to examine the Mercer Consulting firm Web site at *http://www.mercer.com* and to read its posting on *Global Competencies, Performance, and Pay.*

External Equity Issues

Creating external equity is more problematic. The tools for doing this are labor market definitions, pay surveys, choice of policy lines, and the creation of pay structures. The important issue here is that virtually all pay surveys of relevant labor markets are based on job description data, market analysis of numbers of incumbents, minimums, maximums, weighted average pay, etc., that can be used to place pay rates on various jobs in the skill hierarchy and to choose starting rates of pay and maximum rates of pay. Stepping-stones for learning a skill curriculum could then be developed. The basic point to be made here is that skill-based pay depends on having most employers using job-based pay so surveys can be used. Each approach is equally complex and bureaucratic. Whereas job-based pay uses job evaluation plans, skill-based pay uses multiple levels of tests to assess progress. Job-based pay ultimately produces a pay structure consisting of pay grades that reflect job evaluation scores (internal equity) and pay rates (external equity) and ultimately produce a graded pay structure. Jobs are placed in pay grades based on their job evaluation points. Pay grades have a minimum, a maximum, and midpoint pay rates based on pay surveys. Once created, a structure of salary grades is useful for pay equity and for recognizing merit and promotion. A promotion must move an individual to a higher grade to be a true promotion.

External equity procedures involve tasks related to assessing pay rates in the labor markets surrounding the organization and relating then to the organization's strategic decisions regarding its pay policy. Pay policy decisions focus on whether the organization should set its pay levels (1) above the market, (2) at the market, or (3) below the market; (4) try to be an "employer of choice" that can attract talent for reasons other than high pay; or (5) adopt some sort of a hybrid strategy where some jobs receive above market pay while other job categories are paid at or below the market. To calibrate these policy decisions requires data on how other firms pay for similar types of jobs.

The tasks for establishing external equity include:

1. Defining the appropriate labor market for the types of jobs being surveyed

2. Defining the purpose of a survey (new hire pay, college recruit pay, basic pay, benefits, vacation and leave options, availability of incentive pay, etc.)

3. Conducting or purchasing an appropriate survey

4. Analyzing the data and applying the results to the current pay structure

5. Interpreting and assessing the implications of external pay rates for the current structure given the pay policy adopted by organization leadership

Adding external data (averages, weighted averages, modes, ranges, medians) to the internal equity point scores already obtained from the job evaluation process allows the analyst to calculate a trend line that can serve as the backbone of a salary structure. Think about it this way. If jobs with 150 job evaluation points tend to be paid $15 per hour in the labor market and jobs with 300 job evaluation points tend to be paid about $30 per hour in the labor market, a relationship is clear that for this firm, one job evaluation point tends to be worth $.10 or ten cents. Once relationships are found for benchmark jobs (common, well-known jobs) used in a survey, then other non-benchmark jobs can be assigned appropriate pay rates. Knowing the Y axis (dollar pay rates from the survey) and the X axis (job evaluation points) allows a structure of pay grades to be constructed to facilitate individual pay decisions. Figure 16.6 on page 16.18 shows a salary structure with pay grades.

With decisions made reflecting strategies for internal equity (job evaluation points) and external equity (survey pay rates), it is finally time to look at mechanisms for delivering pay to individual employees.

Individual Pay Decisions. Employees can have their pay adjusted through several mechanisms. General adjustments include (1) *structural adjustments,* where compensation experts simply move everyone's pay upward by a like percentage to keep pace with the firm's desired position relative to the labor market; and (2) *a cost-of-living increase* (COLA) that adjusts pay according to a negotiated formula such as .3 percent change in the Consumer Price Index (CPI) equals a one cent per hour increase. Neither of these types of increases are performance related but instead are given to all members of the organization who qualify by being on the payroll as of a specific date.

Pay can also be adjusted to reflect *time* served in a position, or seniority. The U.S. government provides a system of automatic raises that reflect the longevity of those employees. Many collective bargaining agreements have provisions for automatic increases in pay for trainees as they successfully stay on the job for prescribed amounts of time.

FIGURE 16.6   *Salary Structure*

Maximum points given in job evaluation: **820**

Grade	Grade Points			Range		Range Dollars		
	Minimum	Maximum	Midpoint	% Below	% Above	Minimum	Maximum	Midpoint
1	200	270	235	35%	35%	$884	$1,837	$1,360
2	271	330	300.5	30%	30%	$1,487	$2,762	$2,125
3	331	400	365.5	25%	25%	$2,162	$3,604	$2,883
4	401	500	450.5	20%	20%	$3,100	$4,650	$3,875
5	501	600	550.5	20%	20%	$4,033	$6,050	$5,042
6	601	700	650.5	20%	20%	$4,967	$7,450	$6,208
7	701	800	750.5	20%	20%	$6,195	$9,293	$7,744
8	801	900	850.5	20%	30%	$7,175	$11,660	$8,969
9	901	1000	950.5	20%	40%	$8,155	$14,272	$10,194

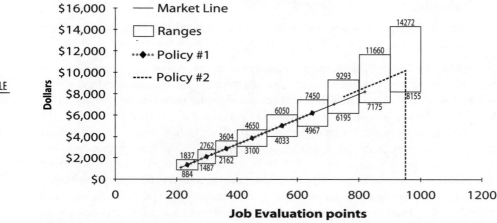

The most common merit-based system in private industry are merit increases. The process involves obtaining individual performance ratings from a subjective performance review system. (See Module 15 for descriptions of performance management and appraisal processes.) These ratings then correlate to increases to base pay by either fixed or variable percentages. For example, a performance rating descriptor of "excellent" may receive an increase of 10 percent or in other organizations an increase of 9–11 percent according to the judgment of the manager. Organizations do have the option of "baking in" an increase to an individual's base salary as in the above example or giving an equivalent amount as a "lump sum" that leaves the base salary unchanged. Figure 16.7 shows a merit increase "grid" that relates size of merit increase to the employee's position in pay grade and his or her performance rating.

Individual Equity

In assessing individual equity, the two approaches diverge dramatically. Job-based pay uses merit increases, seniority increases, and incentive programs to relate individual contributions to pay increases. Skill-based pay focuses on using learning systems, tests,

FIGURE 16.7 *Merit Increase Grid*

PERFORMANCE RATING (IN PERCENT)						
Range Quartile	**Far Exceeded**	**Exceeded**	**Met**	**Met Some**	**Did Not Meet**	**Total Employees**
Quartile 1	4.0	3.0	2.0	0.0	0.0	
Employees	6.0	13.5	7.5	3.0	0.0	30
Quartile 2	5.0	4.0	2.0	0.0	0.0	
Employees	4.0	9.0	5.0	2.0	0.0	20
Quartile 3	6.0	5.0	3.5	1.5	0.0	
Employees	4.0	9.0	5.0	2.0	0.0	20
Quartile 4	8.0	6.0	4.0	2.0	0.0	
Employees	6.0	13.5	7.5	3.0	0.0	30
Total Employees	20	45	25	10	0	100

retesting, and a job curriculum to raise an individual's pay through learning and passing tests. Each system is equally complex.

Skill-based pay systems are frequently viewed as more "fashionable" and modern than job-based pay systems. Their emphasis on learning and motivation of employees to learn is clearly of strategic relevance to modern organizations. They have frequently shown superior results in terms of quality, attendance, and employee satisfaction (Jenkins, Ledford, Gupta, and Doty 1992).

Disadvantages of Each System

Job-based pay systems have been criticized for being subject to manipulation by employees who wish to inflate the points attached to their jobs. Typical unproductive behaviors include providing inflated pictures of actual job responsibilities and constantly requesting job reevaluations as tasks change, thus greatly reducing employer flexibility. Skill-based systems also have a downside. Essentially employees like them only as long as pay increases are available. When an employee "maxes out" by learning all the jobs in a circle, he or she frequently becomes highly demotivated and negative. Skill-based systems often have to be reconverted to job-based plans after five years or so. Another problem is that skill-based plans may raise labor costs because the employer really does not need all employees to reach the high levels of skill available. A related set of issues is whether employees can maintain tested skill levels and whether employers must pay employees for skills that they are not using to perform their work tasks. Clearly, the choice of job-based or skill-based pay systems is not easy to make.

Balance of Pay Elements Over the Organization's Life Cycle

Pay policies and decisions send important signals about what the organization values most. The balance among base pay, incentives, and benefits is one of the most important decisions in terms of acceptability to employees. In many ways, the issue of balance is related to the life cycle of the organization. For example, a new organization can often ill afford to offer its first employees high salaries and complete benefits packages, so it emphasizes incentives such as stock options (if the business succeeds, we shall all become rich!). As the organization matures, it may increase pay and benefit levels and decrease the proportion of pay based on incentives except for strategic employees and top executives. Mature organizations are typically characterized by the prevalence of high levels of base pay and very complete packages of benefits with little or no use of incentives below executive ranks. Maintaining the proper balance of pay mechanisms relative to the organization's strategy is one of the most important jobs of a compensation person.

Tangibles and Intangibles

Pay administration reflects many important tangible aspects of the organization. Choice of pay mechanisms such as types, balance, and pay levels show up in a tangible way in terms of labor cost, ability to compete, and the quality of human resources the organization can attract and retain. In addition to cost and productivity aspects of pay, legal compliance is also an important tangible factor. Yet, in many ways, intangible factors are equally important in pay administration. Does pay empower employees to learn, to take risks, to innovate and offer suggestions, to continuously improve, to share their knowledge, to undertake training, and to make a commitment to pursue the organization's goals? The intangible aspects of pay include its fairness, its level, and its flexibility to incorporate employee input into the design of pay plans and benefit plans. The transparency of pay processes and the ability of individual employees to understand their pay are crucial aspects of pay satisfaction.

IN CONCLUSION

Debrief

The tasks of the compensation person are fascinating. Compensation work is deeply embedded in the organization's most important strategies. Mergers, acquisitions, right-sizing, globalization, reengineering, "greenfield" plant start-ups, conversion of "brown-field" operations, changes in manufacturing systems, and adoption of new technologies all change the work of the organization and thus require the compensation system to change. Compensation practitioners work with everyone in the organization from executives to shop floor employees. An appreciation for the entire business is obtained as jobs in manufacturing, marketing, finance, and engineering undergo change to meet customer and market demands. An understanding of compensation principles and tools is as much a key to business competence as an appreciation of generally accepted accounting principles. Other modules in this series deal with variable pay and with benefits. The modules can be invaluable in increasing our understanding of compensation tools and principles.

MODULE 16

Suggested Readings

Edward E. Lawler. *Strategic Compensation*. San Francisco: Jossey-Bass, 1992.

ACA Journal, published by the American Compensation Association in Scottsdale, AZ.

Relevant Web Sites

AMERICAN COMPENSATION ASSOCIATION
http://www.acaonline.org/

BUREAU OF LABOR STATISTICS
http://www.stats.bls.gov

CONSULTING FIRMS
http://www.haygroup.com   *http://www.towersperrin.com*
http://www.mercer.com   *http://www.radford.com.general.welcome.html.*

Critical Thinking Questions

1. What roles might compensation practitioners play if your firm acquires another firm?

2. If the executives of your firm are concerned about competitiveness, what pay proposals can you offer for their consideration?

3. Many firms have the compensation function reporting to the finance organization. Most have it reporting to human resources function. Argue the case for placing compensation responsibilities within the human resources function.

4. How might gender discrimination enter pay practice?

Exercises

1. Visit the American Compensation Association web site at *http://www.acaonline. org/*. Assess its certificate training programs in terms of coverage and cost. Do these courses provide useful opportunities for compensation professionals to keep their skills up-to-date?

2. Read any five issues of the *ACA Journal*. Understand and offer a critique of its editorial policies. Who is its intended audience? Is it a scholarly journal? Why? Why not?

3. Prepare a plan for a compensation practitioner who wishes to stay current in this field. What must a person do to expand and enhance his or her knowledge base after taking a permanent employment position on a full-time basis?

Application Exercises

4. Prepare a job description for a member of your school's staff using the process described in this module and illustrated in Figure 16.2.

5. Design one compensable factor that could be used in analyzing the job of technical support person for your computer lab. See Figure 16.3 for ideas and Figure 16.4 for an example.

6. Identify seven organizations in your community that you would include in a salary survey for the position of training specialist. Which organization may have the most incumbents? Which organization may pay the most? the least? What other job titles may encompass "training specialist" duties?

References

Becker, Brian and Gerhart, Barry. 1996. "The impact of human resource management on organizational performance: Progress and prospects." *Academy of Management Journal,* Vol. 39, No. 4, 779–801.

Huselid, Mark. 1995. "The impact of human resources management practices on turnover, productivity, and corporate financial performance." *Academy of Management Journal,* Vol. 38, No. 3, 635–672.

Jenkins, Douglas, G., Jr., Ledford, Gerald E., Jr., Gupta, Nina, and Doty, D. Harold. 1992. *Skill-Based Pay,* Scottsdale AZ: American Compensation Association.

Lawler, Edward E. III. 1994. "From job-based to competency-based organizations." *Journal of Organizational Behavior,* 15, 3–15.

Lawler, Edward E. III. 1990. *Strategic Pay: Aligning Organizational Strategies and Pay Systems.* San Francisco: Jossey-Bass.

MacDuffie, John Paul. 1995. "Human resource bundles and manufacturing performance: Organizational logic and flexible production systems in the world auto industry." *Industrial and Labor Relations Review,* Vol. 48, No. 2, 197–221.

Montemayor, Edilberto. 1994. "Aligning pay systems with market strategies," *ACA Journal,* Winter 1994, 44–53.

Milkovitch, George and Newman, Jerry. 1999. *Compensation,* Chicago: Irwin.

O'Neill, Graham and Doig, David (1997). "Definition and use of competencies by Australian organizations," *ACA Journal,* Winter, 45–56.

Pfeffer, Jeffrey. 1994. *Competitive Advantage Through People.* Boston: Howard University Press.

Schuster, Jay and Zingheim, P. K. 1992. *The New Pay: Linking Employee and Organizational Performance.* New York: Lexington Books.

MODULE
16

Index

....

Administration, pay systems, 16.8, 16.20

Balance of pay mechanisms, 16.19–20
Bargaining agreement. *See* Collective bargaining agreement
Base wage (salary), 16.8–9, 16.18, 16.19
Benefits packages, 16.19. *See also* Incentives
Bonuses, 16.8

Career-long commitment, 16.6
Collective bargaining agreement, 16.17
Compensable factor (job evaluation), 16.12–16. *See also* Point plan
Compensation, defined, 16.8
Compensation systems, 16.4, 16.6–10, 16.12, 16.20. *See also* Job-based pay systems, Merit-based pay systems, Skill-based pay systems
Competency-based pay system, 16.10. *See also* Skill-based pay system
Complexity and difficulty of duties factor (job evaluation), 16.14
Compliance, pay discrimination laws, 16.8
Continuous improvement philosophy, 16.7
Cost-of-living adjustments (COLAs), 16.8–9, 16.17. *See also* Structural adjustments (compensation)
Cross-training, 16.7

Dictionary of Occupational Titles (DOT), 16.11
Direct compensation, 16.8, 16.10
Disclaimer statement, 16.11
Discrimination, 16.4

Effort factors (job evaluation), 16.13. *See also* Compensable factor, Knowledge requirements, Responsibility factors, Skill factors
Egalitarian perquisites, 16.7
Employability, 16.6
Employee services/perquisites, 16.9
Employee skill factors, 16.10
Employee stock ownership plans (ESOPs), 16.7
Employee-employer relationship, 16.6
Employment relationship, 16.8
Employment security, 16.6
Enterprise success, 16.7
Entitlement, 16.6
Equal Employment Opportunity Commission (EEOC), 16.5
Equal Pay Act of 1963, 16.5
External equity, 16.8, 16.16–17
Extrinsic motivation, 16.10

401(k) plan, 16.7
Fair Labor Standards Act of 1938 (FLSA), 16.5

Flexibility, employee, 16.6
Flexibility, employer, 16.19
FLSA status (exempt/nonexempt), 16.11
Future employment potential, 16.6

Global Competencies, Performance, and Pay (Mercer Consulting Web site), 16.16
Grade (pay or salary), 16.14, 16.17–18

Hierarchical promotions, 16.6
High-commitment pay, 16.6, 16.7
High-wage policies, 16.6. *See also* Job security

Incentives, 16.7, 16.8–9, 16.19. *See also* Motivation of employees
Income maintenance, 16.4–5
Increases, pay. *See* Merit-based pay system, Skill-based pay system, Structural adjustments
Indirect compensation, 16.8, 16.9, 16.10
Individual contributions, 16.18
Individual equity, 16.8
Information sharing, 16.7
Intangibles (administration, pay systems), 16.20
Internal equity, 16.8, 16.11, 16.12, 16.16–17
Interviews, 16.11
Intrinsic motivation, 16.9–10

Job analysis (evaluation), 16.11–18. *See also* External equity, Individual equity, Internal equity, Point plan
Job description, 16.6, 16.12, 16.16
Job evaluation plan, 16.15–16. *See also* Job analysis (evaluation)
Job security, 16.6
Job-based pay systems, 16.10–11, 16.16, 16.18–19

Knowledge requirements, 16.12–13

Labor market pay rates, 16.6, 16.16. *See also* Market analysis
Lateral careers, 16.6, 16.8
Learning systems, 16.18
Long-term focus, 16.7
Lump-sum increase, 16.18. *See also* Merit-based pay system, Structural adjustments

Market analysis, 16.16. *See also* Labor market pay rates
McNamara-O'Hara Act of 1965, 16.5
Merit-based pay system, 16.8–9, 16.18–19. *See also* Job-based pay system, Skill-based pay system

Motivation of employees, 16.8, 16.19. *See also* Extrinsic motivation, Incentives, Intrinsic motivation, Rewards

Negotiations (employer-union), 16.5
New pay, 16.6, 16.7

Pay differentials, 16.7
Pay discrimination, 16.5
Pay for learning, 16.16
Pay systems. *See* Compensation systems
Pay-for-knowledge system, 16.10
Payment for time not worked, 16.9
Performance expectations, 16.4, 16.6
Performance ratings, 16.18
Perquisites, 16.7, 16.9
Person-based pay, 16.16
Pfeffer, Jeffrey, 16.6
Point plan, 16.13–15, 16.17–18. *See also* Compensable factors, Job analysis (evaluation)
Power games, 16.7
Prevailing wage laws, 16.5
Project management, 16.8
Promotion from within, 16.7

Recruiting and staffing practices, 16.7
Responsibility factors (job evaluation), 16.6, 16.12, 16.13. *See also* Compensable factor, Effort factors, Knowledge requirements, Skill factors
Rewards, 16.10
Risk sharing, 16.6

Seniority, 16.17
Skill development, 16.7
Skill factors (job evaluation), 16.13. *See also* Compensable factor, Knowledge requirements, Responsibility factors
Skill-based pay system, 16.10–11, 16.16, 16.18–19. *See also* Job-based pay system, Merit-based pay system
Social Security Act of 1935, 16.5
Standard of living, 16.9
Structural adjustments (pay), 16.17–18. *See also* Cost-of-living increase, Merit-based pay system, Seniority
Survey, labor market, 16.17

Tangibles (administration, pay systems), 16.20
Task assessment, 16.11. *See also* Job analysis
Team focus, 16.6, 16.7, 16.8
Time not worked, 16.9
Time served. *See* Seniority
Training, 16.7

Unilateral decisions, 16.4
Union wages, 16.5

Variable pay, 16.6

Wages, 16.5. *See also* Compensation
Weighted average pay, 16.16
Work analysis. *See* Job analysis
Working conditions, 16.11, 16.12
Workplace hazards, 16.9

MANAGING HUMAN RESOURCES
IN THE 21st CENTURY

From Core Concepts to Strategic Choice

MODULE 17

Pay and Incentive Systems

Transitional, Transformational, and Nontraditional

Edilberto F. Montemayor
MICHIGAN STATE UNIVERSITY

Managing Human Resources in the 21st Century: From Core Concepts to Strategic Choice,
by Kossek and Block

Publisher: Dave Shaut
Executive Editor: John Szilagyi
Developmental Editor: Bryant Editorial Development
Marketing Manager: Joseph A. Sabatino
Production Editor: Tamborah E. Moore
Manufacturing Coordinator: Dana Began Schwartz
Cover Design: Tin Box Studio
Cover Photographs: Copyright Shoji Sato/Photonica
Production House: The Left Coast Group, Inc.
Printer: West Group

Printed in the United States of America
1 2 3 4 5 02 01 00 99

For more information contact South-Western College Publishing, 5101 Madison Road, Cincinnati, Ohio, 45227 or find us on the Internet at *http://www.swcollege.com*
For permission to use material from this text or product, contact us by

- telephone: 1-800-730-2214
- fax: 1-800-730-2215
- web: *http://www.thomsonrights.com*

ISBN: 0–324–01816–9

Contents

MODULE OVERVIEW   17.4

OBJECTIVES   17.4

RELATION TO THE FRAME   17.4

CORE CONCEPTS BEHIND THE USE OF GROUP INCENTIVES   17.5

    The Nature of Group Incentives   17.5

    A Taxonomy for Group Incentive Plans   17.7

STRATEGIC ISSUES IN DEPLOYING GROUP INCENTIVES   17.9

    Need for Alignment with Business Strategy   17.10

    Group Incentives as an Organizational Change/Development Intervention   17.10

IN CONCLUSION   17.21

    Debrief   17.21

    Suggested Readings   17.21

    Critical Thinking Questions   17.21

    Exercises   17.22

    References   17.22

INDEX   17.24

Module Overview

The notion of "paying for results" has dominated the design of executive and management compensation plans in the United States for many years. One fundamental premise behind paying executives and managers for results is that this approach will align individual executive goals with the goals of the organization and its shareholders.

Since the mid-1980s, the notion of paying for results has been extending gradually to cover more and more nonmanagement employees in the United States. This clear trend toward the more frequent use of variable (incentive) pay-for-results schemas for nonmanagement employees reflects the growing realization that all human resource management policies and systems must be integrated with each other and with the organization's business strategy.

Objectives

As explained in this module, group incentives provide a very effective means for organizational change and for motivating employees to contribute to top organizational priorities. The major objectives for this chapter are to help you:

- Understand the meaning of the term "group incentive"

- Learn a taxonomy that illustrates the range of group incentive plans

- Understand the role of group incentives in leading or supporting organizational change

- Appreciate the similarity between the deployment of group incentives and other organizational change and development initiatives

- Learn major elements in a ten-stage process for designing and deploying group incentives that is anchored in the organization's business and HR strategies

Relation to the Frame

Although long-established group incentives may be limited to a transactional role, most organizations that have successfully used group incentives report significant changes in culture and internal work processes. For this reason, it is the contention of this module that group incentives can serve as a seed to energize or as a catalyst to support organizational change.

With respect to the columns in our framework (Figure 17.1), the design of group incentives could be approached as a unilateral decision in a nonunion organization. If the organization's workforce (or a portion of it) is unionized, then employers must bargain with the employee representatives over the decision to introduce a group incentive and/or over key features of the group incentive (provided the union, on behalf of the employees it represents, agrees to the idea of having a group incentive).

However, one of the many lessons we have learned over the last two decades, based on the considerable increase in the number of organizations that have developed (or at least attempted to develop) group incentive plans is: *Employee participation in the design of group incentive plans is a major contributor to their success.*[1] Thus, even if an organization does not have any unionized employees, it seems to be a very good idea to involve employees as much as possible in the design and implementation of group incentive plans.

FIGURE 17.1 *A Frame for Understanding Human Resource Strategy: Context, Roles, and Constraints*

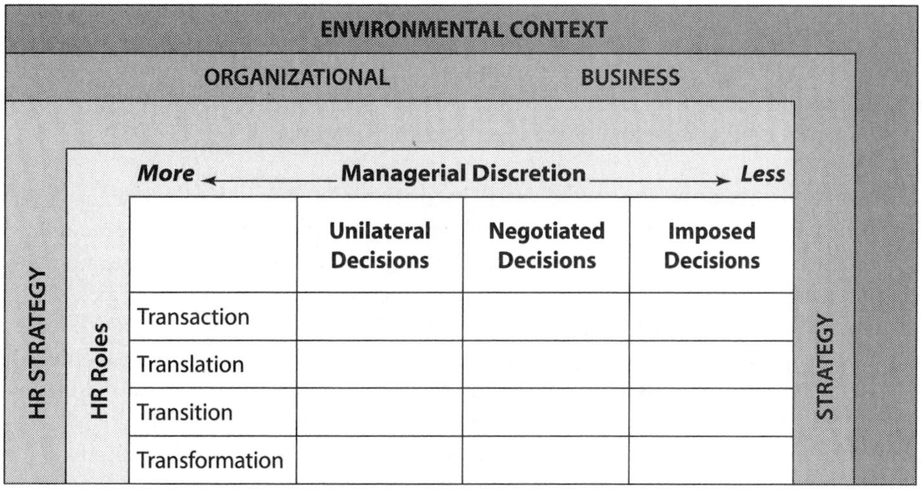
ENVIRONMENTAL CONTEXT
ORGANIZATIONAL
BUSINESS
More
Managerial Discretion
Less
Unilateral Decisions
Negotiated Decisions
Imposed Decisions
Transaction
Translation
Transition
Transformation
HR STRATEGY
HR Roles
STRATEGY

© 2000 by Ellen Ernst Kossek and Richard Block. Thanks to Brian Pentland, Karen Markel, and John Beck for helpful comments and discussions that enhanced the model.

Core Concepts Behind the Use of Group Incentives

Reviewing the following concepts is necessary to understand how group incentives can be used in organizations:

- The nature of group incentives
  - ✓ Definition
  - ✓ Difference between "rewards" and "incentives"
  - ✓ Incentive plans incorporate ideas from multiple motivation theories
- A taxonomy for group incentive plans
  - ✓ Differences in group incentive funding
  - ✓ Differences in the link between result levels and incentive payoffs
- Examples for six various cells in the taxonomy

The Nature of Group Incentives

Defining group incentives. For purposes of this chapter, we will define *group incentives* as *plans that offer a group of eligible employees the opportunity to earn variable payoffs contingent on the results achieved in key measurable outcomes.* Group incentives represent a form of variable pay. The amount of money employees receive in connection with the incentive plan changes from one period to the next depending on the results achieved.

As an illustration, let's consider the hypothetical case of XYZ, Inc., a company that needs to improve its record of on-time deliveries to customers in order to keep growing. Seeking to support such strategy, XYZ establishes a simple group incentive that offers production employees $15 per person for each 1 percent unit improvement in the monthly percent of items delivered to customers on time. This hypothetical plan would have a "baseline" of 90 percent—that is, employees would receive a bonus for those months when on-time deliveries exceed 90 percent. The bonus would be

Copyright © 2000 by Edilberto F. Montemayor. All Rights Reserved.

calculated as $15 times the difference between actual and baseline (90) percent of on-time deliveries for the month. Further assume the following XYZ results for the first three months last year: 93 percent deliveries on time in January, 89 percent on time in February, and 98 percent on time in March. Under this plan, each production employee at XYZ would receive a $45 bonus in January and a $120 bonus in March. No bonus would be paid in February because the actual result (89 percent deliveries on time) did not exceed the plan's baseline (90 percent deliveries on time).

Difference between "Rewards" and "Incentives." There are significant differences between the concepts of "reward" and "incentive" systems. These differences have important implications for the impact that elements of the employee compensation system may have on employee behavior and, consequently, on organizational success. The notion of "reward" implies the provision of something valuable. Discretionary bonuses granted by companies when revenues (or profits) are high represent examples of "rewards." Receiving a discretionary bonus at the end of the year because the organization did very well is a form of reward. Employees will probably be happy and satisfied; they may even feel indebted to the organization and try to do their best next year hoping the organization will perform well (or better) and grant the bonus again. However, rewards seldom focus and energize employee contributions. Employees do not know for sure what they need to do to receive the bonus. Moreover, there are no guarantees that employees will receive the same bonus if the organization does equally well next year. In contrast, group incentives focus and energize employee contributions because group incentive plans specify clearly and precisely what results need to be achieved for employees to receive a monetary reward. In the case of our hypothetical firm, XYZ production employees know that they will only receive the incentive bonus when monthly on-time deliveries exceed the 90 percent baseline. Under this incentive, employees are likely to direct their effort and cooperation to strive for the highest level of on-time deliveries they can achieve.

Incentive Plans Incorporate Ideas from Multiple Motivation Theories. Group incentive plans focus and energize employee contributions and add to organizational success because they embody the principles and lessons from multiple organizational theories, as follows.

- *Learning or reinforcement theories* suggest employees will engage in behaviors that lead to positive consequences. Organizations that deploy group incentives successfully provide a clear "line of sight" ensuring that employees understand how their jobs, their day-to-day dedication, and their cooperation with each other will lead to a valued financial reward (the incentive bonus).

- *Expectancy theory* suggests the maximum effort occurs when employees perceive their effort will lead to improved results, which in turn will lead to valued rewards. Organizations that deploy group incentives successfully ensure that employees believe they have the resources, skill, and expertise to earn a bonus by exceeding the minimum baseline(s) in the incentive plan and believe that their efforts will lead to significant economic payoff.

- *Goal-setting theory* suggests the best performance occurs when employees accept and pursue specific and challenging goals. Organizations that deploy group incentives successfully ensure that employees understand the outcomes measured in the incentive plan and perceive the minimum results levels (or baselines) required to earn a bonus as challenging but realistic and attainable goals.

- *Self-actualization and intrinsic motivation theories* suggest employees are motivated (or energized) when work is fun and allows them to develop and apply their talents. Organizations that deploy group incentives successfully use these incentives as one of multiple means to satisfy employee needs for interesting work, recognition, and validation of their sense of self-worth. Often, the deployment of group incentives is accompanied by work-redesign efforts, by substantial team-work and problem-solving training, and by enhanced emphasis in communications within and across teams and departments. Also, successful organizations provide opportunities for fun and celebration during the day-to-day pursuit of the goals contained within the incentive formulas and, more importantly, when the resulting bonuses are delivered to employees.

A Taxonomy for Group Incentive Plans

Overview. As illustrated in Figure 17.2, group incentive plans can be classified in terms of a two-dimensional taxonomy.[2] The classification used here focuses on differences among group incentive plans in two critical features: (1) the source of funds for incentive payoffs, and (2) the linkage between actual results and incentive payoffs.

Differences in Group Incentive Funding. The design of most group incentive plans is based on a "self-funding" principle. This means organizations using group incentives expect that incentive payoffs will be financed through improvements in organizational results. Few organizations, if any, view incentive plans as a means for delivering additional pay to employees without any benefit for the organization. The classification system used here recognizes three possible sources of funds for group incentive plans: (1) improvements in labor productivity (and the corresponding savings in labor costs), (2) savings in multiple-cost items (including but not limited to labor cost savings), and (3) financial statement results (such as revenues and/or various profit measures or indices).

Differences in the Link between Result Levels and Incentive Payoffs. Group incentive formulas also differ in the linkage between result levels and incentive payoffs. There are two possibilities in this respect: (1) gain sharing and (2) goal sharing.

FIGURE 17.2 *A Taxonomy for Group Incentive Plans*

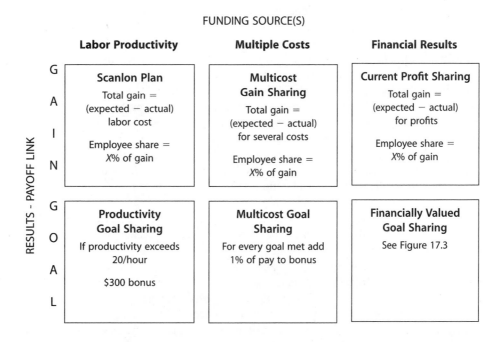

FUNDING SOURCE(S)

	Labor Productivity	Multiple Costs	Financial Results
GAIN	**Scanlon Plan** Total gain = (expected − actual) labor cost Employee share = X% of gain	**Multicost Gain Sharing** Total gain = (expected − actual) for several costs Employee share = X% of gain	**Current Profit Sharing** Total gain = (expected − actual) for profits Employee share = X% of gain
GOAL	**Productivity Goal Sharing** If productivity exceeds 20/hour $300 bonus	**Multicost Goal Sharing** For every goal met add 1% of pay to bonus	**Financially Valued Goal Sharing** See Figure 17.3

(RESULTS - PAYOFF LINK)

Gain-sharing incentive plans have been used longer than goal-sharing plans. In a gain-sharing plan, the incentive payoff formula computes explicitly the economic value of results improvements and then determines the total payoff for all employees as a share (proportion) of those "gains." In contrast, goal-sharing plans use formulas that directly link individual employee payoffs to the level of results achieved. The examples in the following section will illustrate these concepts and our taxonomy for group incentive plans.

Examples for Various Cells in the Taxonomy.   The top-left cell in our taxonomy (Figure 17.2) corresponds to *labor productivity gain-sharing plans*. Examples of these plans include the so-called Scanlon, Rucker, and Improshare plans. In labor productivity gain-sharing plans, the pool of money for incentive payoffs to employees is determined by a formula that involves the difference between "expected" and actual labor costs. Employees as a group will receive a certain proportion (the employees' share) of any positive difference between actual and expected labor costs. In the Scanlon plan, expected labor costs are computed in terms of a baseline (or standard) percentage of the sales value of production. Let's assume that an organization has a Scanlon plan with a baseline of 20 percent and an employee share of 25 percent of the savings. That is, expected labor costs are 20 percent of the sales value of production. Further, let's assume that for a given period (month or quarter), actual sales value of production was $7,000,000 and actual labor cost was $1,320,000. For this period, the expected labor costs would be $1,400,000 (or 20 percent of $7,000,000). This means the total gain (expected minus actual labor costs) for the period was $80,000. Because the plan shares 25 percent of the gains with employees, the total payoff pool would be $20,000. This pool would then be distributed among all eligible employees.

The top-middle cell in our taxonomy (Figure 17.2) corresponds to *multicost gain-sharing plans*. These plans follow a logic similar to that in labor productivity gain-sharing plans but consider gains (savings) in multiple-cost items. Examples of costs other than labor in a multicost gain-sharing plan may include the cost of materials, the cost of energy, the cost of waste, etc.

The top-right cell in our taxonomy corresponds to *"current" profit-sharing plans*. The term "current" is used here to contrast with the notion of "deferred" profit-sharing plans that delay payoffs until employees retire. Deferred profit-sharing plans are not considered a group incentive because their motivational impact is likely to be very weak given that it may take a long time for employees to enjoy the benefits from improved results (profits). Deferred profit-sharing plans are vehicles for funding retirement benefits. In contrast, current profit-sharing plans, where benefits are paid to employees annually once the level of profits is determined, represent another instance of group incentive plans as defined at the beginning of this chapter. In a current profit sharing plan, the total annual payoff, to be distributed among all eligible employees, would be a certain portion of the difference between actual and expected profits. That is, a current profit-sharing plan functions much like other gain-sharing plans, but in this case the focal measures are expected and actual profits.

The bottom cells in our taxonomy correspond to goal-sharing plans. As indicated before, these plans use formulas that directly link the payoff for individual employees to the level of results achieved. The bottom-left cell corresponds to *labor productivity goal-sharing plans*. An example of such a plan for a data processing group serving an insurance company would be to offer all employees a bonus of $300 every month that the organization exceeds a certain productivity target (say an average of 20 new policies processed per employee per hour).

The bottom-middle cell in our taxonomy corresponds to *multicost goal-sharing plans*. A Quaker Oats plant that produces pet foods, for instance, adopted an incentive that determines a bonus for eligible employees (as a percentage of pay) based on the number and difficulty of operational goals accomplished.[3] This incentive focuses on basic and "stretch" (more difficult) goals in four result areas: safety, quality, waste, and

FIGURE 17.3 *Financially Valued Goal Sharing*

OPERATIONAL SCORECARD

Measures

	Labor Productivity	Percent Scrap	Solder PPM	
Baseline	80%	0.90%	300	
1 point	80+ %	0.90% or less	300 or less ★	
2 points	82+ %	★ 0.85% or less	270 or less	
3 points	★ 84+ %	0.80% or less	240 or less	
4 points	86+ %	0.75% or less	210 or less	
9 points	96+ %	0.50% or less	60 or less	
10 points	98–100%	0.45% or less	30 or less	

- Goal Sharing bonuses will be based on the number of payable points scored in a given period.

- The bonus will be a fixed dollar amount for each point scored.

- Financial results will determine the maximum number of payable points.

- Performance in key operational results will determine the actual number of points scored.

- For each measure we may score up to 10 points.

- Doing better than the "baseline" (the average for the last 12 months) will result in the first point scored.

- Doing at the "best in class" level defined for the measure will result in 10 points scored.

- Performance between these two limits will result in a proportional number of points scored.

transformation costs. For each results area, achieving the basic goal has a value of 0.5 percent and achieving the stretch goal has a value of 1 percent. The incentive bonus employees receive is computed as the sum of the values for the goals achieved.

Finally, the bottom-right cell in our taxonomy corresponds to *financially valued goal-sharing plans*. These plans reward operational goal attainment while considering also the firm's financial performance. This author worked recently with a manufacturing firm that developed such a group incentive for employees in one of its Midwestern plants. Under this incentive, called "Success Sharing" by the company, employees earn points depending on the degree of improvement, between the current (baseline) level and the maximum possible, in each of five operational areas. Every six months, the points are transformed into a dollar payoff. The dollar value of each point depends on the firm's revenues and profits. Such a plan is depicted in Figure 17.3.

STRATEGIC ISSUES IN DEPLOYING GROUP INCENTIVES

As discussed below, the effective use of group incentives leads to significant improvements in organizational performance. The literature discussing the successful deployment of group incentives contains two overarching themes: (1) ensuring group incentives are aligned with the organization's strategy, and (2) approaching the deployment of group incentives as a priority organizational change initiative.

Need for Alignment with Business Strategy

Group incentives need to be aligned with the organization's business and human resources (HR) strategies because they have a powerful influence on employee behavior and effort level. Deploying the group incentive in the case of the hypothetical firm XYZ, Inc. (based on the monthly percentage of on-time deliveries) would only be a sound business decision if on-time delivery has a significant impact on customer satisfaction and contributes to sustaining or (better) increasing sales and profits. The same incentive could be counterproductive for XYZ if the firm's ability to compete depended on achieving high volume and/or low unit costs, and production volume or efficiency suffered when employees focused their attention solely on delivering on time. Organizations competing on high volume and/or low costs need an incentive plan that stresses volume or efficiency. The Scanlon plan, presented earlier as an illustration for labor productivity gain-sharing plans, provides a good example for the kind of group incentive that is suitable for high-volume/low-cost firms. If relevant, such firms can use on-time deliveries as a secondary (or modifying) factor in the incentive formula. This issue is explored in more detail below in the section that deals with Stage 6 in the process for developing group incentives.

Evidence of the Strategic Impact of Group Incentives.

There have been a few research studies that examine the connection between group incentives and strategic organizational results. Some of these studies focus on productivity and provide productivity gain estimates ranging from 10 percent for profit-sharing plans to 25 to 35 percent for labor or multicost gain-sharing plans.[4] Also, surveys of organizations with successful plans conclude that group incentives are associated with improvements in efficiency, quality, customer service, and employee morale.[5]

In addition to reinforcing organizational strategy, group incentives have proven to be a very useful vehicle for leading and/or supporting organizational change. Surveys find that group incentives often help organizations change and enhance core business processes including planning, communication, goal setting, coordination, and motivation processes. Respondents to surveys of organizations with group incentives report these plans improve the linkage between business performance and employee rewards, promote employee understanding of top business priorities, strengthen communications across teams and departments, foster teamwork and coordination, enhance employee morale, and lead to an empowering work environment.[6] Other studies find that success with group incentives is related to greater acceptance of involving employees in decision making among both managers and employees.[7]

Unlike many change programs such as TQM and "Employee Involvement" that promote specific activities and seek to advance a particular management philosophy, group incentives, by definition, focus on improving results in key priority areas. Results-centered change programs, such as group incentives, tend to be more successful because they (1) force people to engage in actions that are clearly and directly linked to results improvement; (2) provide tangible and precise feedback on the consequences of such actions; (3) allow frequent reinforcement through setting, pursuing, and accomplishing challenging objectives, and via financial payoffs; and (4) establish a continuous learning culture.[8]

Group Incentives as an Organizational Change/Development Intervention

All of us have probably heard the aphorism "the only constant is change" more than once. Organizations function in a constantly changing environment and must adapt accordingly. Two of the greatest challenges for modern work organizations are to align the interests of individual employees with those of the organization as a whole and to promote the maximum level of internal cooperation and teamwork that is possible. The deployment of a group incentive plan can assist organizations in handling these two challenges by changing or enhancing the organizational culture and internal processes in the direction of greater alignment and teamwork. Thus, we may consider the deployment of group incentives as a powerful organizational change and development (OCD) intervention.

OCD Defined and Parallel with the Deployment of Group Incentives.
The best-known textbook on the subject defines OCD as

> a top-management supported long-range effort to improve an organization's problem-solving and renewal processes through more effective and collaborative diagnosis and management of organizational culture, with an emphasis on formal work team, temporary team, and inter-group culture with the assistance of a consultant-facilitator and the use of theory and technology of applied behavioral science, including action research.[9] (p. 17)

In the same vein, the deployment of a group incentive usually represents an effort:

- Supported by top management

- Intended to improve an organization's results

- To change culture and work processes at the team and intergroup levels (with an emphasis on communications, goal setting, information and feedback, integration and cooperation, employee participation, and rewards)

- Sometimes assisted by a consultant-facilitator

- Following an action research model

Top-management support and involvement is essential to the successful deployment of a group incentive plan. Group incentive plans will not capture employees' attention unless employees see credible actions and symbols that communicate the group incentive is a top priority project for top management. Top management needs to be very public and constant in communicating support and in allocating the resources and changes needed to design and launch the group incentive plan.

As suggested in the previous section, group incentive plans must be aligned with the organization's business strategy. Incentive plan formulas emphasize outcome measures and, therefore, communicate top business priorities. Consequently, the measures chosen for a group incentive plan must represent substantial opportunities for improvement and must be consistent with the organization's strategy. A detailed discussion of this matter is presented below as the first stage in the process for deploying group incentives.

The deployment of a group incentive usually has a strong impact on the organization's culture. When properly designed and communicated, group incentives expand employees' view of the employee-organization relationship. Before an incentive exists (when total employee pay is based only on wage or salary rates), employees may view their employment relationship as an exchange of time worked for base pay. Deploying a group incentive expands this view to include a partnership relationship in which employees contribute not only time worked but also (and perhaps more importantly) effort and dedication to enhance organizational performance in key result areas (those included in the incentive formulas). Moreover, the design and deployment of a group incentive often involves changes to communication, goal setting, information and feedback, and employee participation processes.

In the hypothetical firm XYZ, Inc., introduced earlier, deploying a simple group incentive that offers production employees $15 per person for each 1 percent point improvement in monthly on-time deliveries over the baseline level of 90 percent, will likely motivate XYZ employees to ask how and why the baseline level of 90 percent was determined. It is also likely that deployment of such incentive will motivate

XYZ employees to ask for an information system that provides regular and timely information (perhaps daily or at least weekly) regarding the actual percentage of on-time deliveries. Employees would need such information to stay the course or make any adjustments necessary to reach and exceed the 90 percent baseline every month. Finally, such incentive should induce XYZ employees to seek ways to enhance the coordination within and between teams and departments to ensure that as many customer orders as possible are delivered on time.

An OCD Perspective on the Deployment of a Group Incentive. According to the experts, many OCD interventions follow an action research model.[10] This model involves several phases, requiring data gathering and analysis in order to:

- Establish the need for change

- Explore and understand the client organization

- Contract with the client organization about the scope of the OCD intervention

- Diagnose and examine alternatives.

The action research model also involves two levels of action taken by the customer organization: intervention and stabilization.

Likewise, the process for designing and deploying a group incentive involves ten critical stages, described in detail in the next section, that span the OCD action research model. Table 17.1 groups the ten stages in the design and deployment of group incentives in terms of the corresponding phase in the OCD action research model.

Factors Associated with OCD and with Group Incentive Success. Because the deployment of group incentives represents a major organizational change, you should not be surprised to learn that the list of factors associated with success (and/or failure) in the deployment of group incentives is very similar to the list of factors associated with the success (and/or failure) of OCD initiatives in general. The following eight recommendations are critical for success in the deployment of group incentives:[11]

1. Create a sense of importance for the project and build strong and pervasive commitment among all levels of employees affected.

2. Provide vision: articulate how the group incentive and its formula express the organization's mission and strategy.

3. Assign responsibility clearly: use a design team comprised of knowledgeable, respected, and motivated individuals.

4. Include individuals who are opposed (or not enthusiastic) to the idea of a group incentive in the design team.

5. Promote interaction among different employee groups (e.g., between employees in technical support and operations units).

6. Plan for short-term wins: verify that the economic environment is conducive to improvements in the results measured by the incentive formula.

7. Ensure that changes associated with the group incentive are institutionalized.

    a. Devote enough time and attention to help employees assimilate changes in behaviors and work systems associated with the new group incentive.

    b. Provide for ongoing employee involvement and participation in decisions.

    c. Communicate, communicate, and communicate more!

TABLE 17.1   *An OCD Perspective on the Deployment of Group Incentives*

Phases in Action Research	Ten Stages in Deploying Group Incentives
Establish need for change	1. Stipulate business and HR strategies to guide incentive plan design
Explore client organization	2. Determine organizational readiness and build support for incentive plan
Contract about intervention scope	3. Define incentive plan scope: duration, eligibility, and relation to base pay
Diagnose and examine alternatives	4. Choose between operational and accounting result measures
	5. Select plan type (see Figure 17.2)
	6. Define key plan parameters (see Table 17.2)
	7. Determine initial baselines and update criteria and procedures
	8. Plan simulation and fine-tuning
Intervention	9. Plan communication and start-up
Stabilization	10. Plan administration and renewal

8.   Make the incentive plan dynamic: group incentive plans need to be managed like any other system.

Ten Stages in Deploying Group Incentives.   The following sections describe the major decisions and considerations within each of the ten stages in the process for designing and deploying a group incentive. Several other books offer a more extended discussion of this process for readers interested in developing a group incentive for their own organization.[12]

Stage 1: Stipulate Business and HR Strategies to Guide Incentive Plan Design

As mentioned before, group incentive plans must be aligned with the organization's business and human resources (HR) strategies. Otherwise, the incentive plan is likely to fail because it would be promoting and/or reinforcing behaviors that are not related to the organization's top priorities.

A small steering committee, comprised of knowledgeable individuals who understand the organization's current needs and strategies, can be formed to consider the plan's objectives. It can be asked to rate (say on a 0–100 points scale) the importance of each of the following criteria for the organization's business success:

1.   Deliver within specifications.

2.   Keep costs under control.

3.   Achieve low prices.

4.   Minimize direct labor costs.

5.   Respond quickly to customer requests.

6.   Ensure financial stability.

The preceding list provides a simplified way for readers to characterize their organization's business strategy. Odd-numbered items in the list represent a business strategy aimed at *maximum responsiveness* vis-à-vis customers and markets. Even-numbered items in the list represent a business strategy aimed at *maximum operational efficiency*.

In addition to business strategy, the steering committee should rate (again on a 0–100 points scale) the relative importance of each of the following HR objectives:

1. Motivate the desired employee behavioral and/or organizational changes.

2. Link employee rewards to business results.

3. Promote teamwork.

4. Link employee rewards to our ability to pay.

5. Support employee involvement/empowerment initiatives.

6. Become more competitive in total pay.

This second list provides a simplified way to characterize the organization's HR strategy. Odd-numbered items in the list represent an HR strategy seeking to *enhance employee involvement and commitment*. Even-numbered items represent an HR strategy seeking to *control labor costs*.[13]

The definition of business and HR strategies achieved at this stage should be used throughout the design process, particularly in Stages 5 and 6 discussed below, to promote alignment between the incentive plan's motivational impact and the organization's top needs and priorities.

Stage 2: Determine Organizational Readiness and Build Support

Human beings tend to prefer established routines to system changes. A group incentive will affect total employee pay and the level of labor costs for the organization. Because these are critical outcomes, it is essential that the organization be ready to adapt its compensation system as well as the other processes connected to group incentive plans: communications, goal setting, information and feedback, integration and cooperation, and employee participation. The following list of critical self-assessment questions must be reviewed before proceeding with the actual development of a group incentive plan.[14]

- Do we have a strong and committed sponsor for this project among the top-management ranks of the organization?

- Can we identify key outcome/result areas that are critical to our business success and for which we think there is substantial room for improvement?

- Do we have (or at least can develop in the short run) good and understandable measures for such outcome/result areas?

- Could we identify and address actions to improve our performance in such critical outcome/result areas? Or is it simply a matter of motivating employees to work harder?

- Do we have the facilities, materials, and financial resources to handle an increased amount of volume?

- Can we sell more output?

- What have we learned from past experiences with significant organizational change?

- Do we have a strong and committed leader for this project (someone with the drive and connections to ensure different parts of the organization contribute to the project as needed)?

- Can we put together an effective design team involving a representative cross-section of employees? Can we include some knowledgeable and respected employees who are opposed to or not enthusiastic about the idea?

- Do we have effective two-way means and processes for communicating with employees? If not, what can we do about it in the short run?

- Do we have any major concerns regarding employee morale and trust? If so, what can we do about those concerns?

The more positive answers you find for the above questions, the more likely that your organization will be ready and receptive to the kinds of changes associated with a new group incentive plan. On the other hand, those questions for which you have less-than-ideal answers indicate areas that need attention while developing (and before deploying) the new incentive plan. At an extreme, trying to develop a new group incentive plan would not seem to be a good idea if you find pessimistic answers to the majority of the questions listed above.

Stage 3: Define Incentive Plan Scope

This stage involves three critical decisions regarding boundaries for the incentive plan to be developed:

1. *Plan duration.* No matter how hard and smart you work, you will not develop the permanent, eternal solution to your needs in the area of group incentives. The plan should have a predefined *"sunset date"* after which the plan may be terminated or seriously modified. By establishing and communicating such a date, employees will know from the beginning that the new plan (which represents a major organizational change) will be managed and subject to changes as warranted by business and/or organizational developments.

2. *Employee eligibility.* With respect to employee eligibility, you will need to decide who will participate in the incentive plan and, thus, receive bonuses when organizational results improve. In general it is a good idea to err on the side of inclusiveness. However, sometimes organizations decide to exclude some employee groups from the incentive plan—e.g., executives and top managers, or sales employees who may have their own incentive plan.

3. *Relationship to base pay.* You will also need to decide whether the new incentive plan will be simply an "add on" to the existing compensation package, or will represent *"pay at risk"* for employees. "Pay at risk" means employees invest some of their base pay in the new incentive plan. In order to do so, employees may: (a) take a pay cut; (b) give up negotiated pay increases scheduled for the future (as in the case of Chrysler corporation during the early 1980s when employees gave up collective contract pay increases in return for a new profit-sharing plan); or (c) accept that the organization will be more conservative regarding base wages and salaries in the future. A widely cited survey of existing group incentive plans study found the add-on approach is much more common. Only one in every six plans was found to represent a pay-at-risk situation.[15] Moreover, the same study concludes that, on average, the potential payoff in pay at risk plans tends to be twice as large as for add-on plans.

Stage 4: Choose Between Operational and Accounting Measures

With the exception of profit-sharing plans (top-right cell in Figure 17.2), most group incentive plans can be based on formulas that contain operational and/or accounting results measures. Obviously, profit-sharing plans are focused on accounting measures. The Scanlon plan described in the first section provides an example of a labor productivity gain-sharing incentive that uses accounting measures (labor costs and sales value of production). Other labor productivity gain-sharing plans do not require the disclosure of accounting information. For example, this author recently worked with a manufacturing firm to develop a labor productivity gain-sharing plan whose formula is based on the principle of paying employees an extra 10 cents per hour for each 1 percent improvement in the monthly level of productivity attained in their plant. Using operational rather than accounting measures allows organizations to deploy group incentives without disclosing financial information.

In addition to avoiding disclosure of financial information, using operational measures allow organizations to adapt to drastic changes in work mix and to send a "work harder" message to employees. It is easier to develop targets for operational measures for different types of products or services than for accounting measures. Accordingly, group incentive plans based on operational measures are helpful when the work mix may change drastically from one incentive period to the next. Also, operational measures are helpful when the organization seeks to motivate employees to sustain and/or increase their effort levels—that is, when the goal is to motivate employees to "work harder."

In contrast, using accounting measures seems best indicated when the group incentive is intended to link employee pay to the organization's financial position and/or ability to pay. Using accounting measures promotes employee education and understanding of "bottom-line" issues: the need for the organization to spend less money than it takes in. Incentive plans that use accounting measures seem most helpful when the purpose is to motivate employees to "work smarter" and/or when incentive payoffs must take into consideration the effect of price changes in the various inputs needed by the organization.

Stage 5: Select Plan Type

This stage involves selecting the type of formula to use in the incentive plan from the six possible cells illustrated in Figure 17.2. Conceptually, this stage requires choosing the type of results-payoff link (the row in Figure 17.2) and the kind of funding sources (the column in Figure 17.2) that best fit the organization's characteristics.

At first glance, the choice of row in Figure 17.2, i.e., choosing the type of results-payoff link—appears simple. Conceptually, gain-sharing plans appear superior to goal-sharing plans from the point of view of motivating employees. Let's consider two examples for the leftmost column in Figure 17.2. The first example would be a labor productivity gain-sharing plan like the Scanlon plan described earlier. Such plans yield incrementally higher payoffs in response to incremental improvements in productivity. Once productivity exceeds the plan's baseline, any small improvement in productivity will lead to a somewhat bigger payoff. Our second example, a labor productivity goal-sharing plan, would pay each employee $100, $300, and $500 per month for productivity improvements of 5, 10, and 20 percent, respectively. Goal-sharing plans differ from gain-sharing plans in that the latter work on a pass/fail basis. It is conceivable that once employees meet a lower-level productivity goal (say a 5 percent improvement in the current example), employees may not continue to strive for higher productivity because they find the next-higher-level goal (10 percent improvement in the current example) fairly difficult and, to make things worse, there would be no additional monetary payoff if employees failed to achieve the next-higher goal.

Therefore, it would seem logical to expect all organizations to prefer gain-sharing plans. However, there are other factors that prevent this. Under some circumstances, organizations may be better suited for a goal-sharing incentive plan. Two considerations should guide the choice between the two incentive types: (1) the organization's "maturity" in terms of its life cycle stage, technology, and markets; and (2) the degree of development and precision of the organization's information systems. Gain-sharing plans, which are based on a precise formula to calculate the economic value of results improvements, are best indicated for mature organizations using fixed technology and serving stable markets. Further, gain-sharing plans can be used best by organizations that count on well-established information systems that yield precise data. Thus, goal-sharing plans are best suited for growing organizations, for organizations whose technology or market(s) are changing drastically, and/or for organizations that have an information system in the development stages.

Similarly, the choice of column in Figure 17.2 (i.e., the choice of funding sources) should be based on three general considerations: (1) business strategy, (2) HR strategy, and (3) funding potential. At this point, the reader may find it useful to review the text related to Stage 1. This author's experience and research indicates that organizations whose business strategy is dominated by "external responsiveness" considerations should prefer incentive plans funded by financial results. Conversely, organizations whose business strategy is dominated by "operational efficiency" concerns should prefer incentive plans funded by labor cost or multicost factors. Further, organizations whose HR strategy is dominated by "involvement and commitment" objectives should prefer incentive plans funded by financial results. Conversely, organizations whose HR strategy is dominated by "control" objectives should prefer plans funded by labor cost or multicost factors. The third consideration relates to the potential for results improvements that would yield funds for incentive payoffs. Obviously, plans funded by labor or multicost factors should only be considered if there is substantial room for improvement in the cost factors considered in the incentive formula. By the same token, financially funded incentive plans can only be effective if there is potential for improvement in the financial items used to fund the incentive (typically revenues and/or profits).

Stage 6. Define Key Plan Parameters

Once the type of formula has been chosen, the design process involves defining the set of key plan parameters listed in Table 17.2 on page 17.18. For purposes of illustration, the following text is limited to a select portion of these parameters. Readers interested in a more extended discussion of these decisions should consult the readings suggested at the end of this module.

MODULE
17

In general, the principle "simple is better" applies to the design of incentive formulas. However, sometimes organizations find it necessary to include *threshold variables or criteria* in the incentive formula. These thresholds stipulate conditions, other than exceeding the formula baseline, before a payoff can occur. Threshold variables or criteria usually refer to the organization's financial health. For example, a labor productivity gain-sharing plan such as the Scanlon plan discussed earlier may have a baseline of 20 percent for the labor-cost-to-sales-value ratio. Without a threshold, this plan would result in a payoff anytime labor costs fall below 20 percent of the sales value of production. However, the plan could be modified to stipulate there would be no payoff (regardless of actual labor productivity improvements) if the organization loses money or its profits are less than the incentive payoff. Such threshold conditions would prevent incentive payoffs from causing (or augmenting) financial losses for the organization. There are many group incentive plans which do not contain threshold conditions. Obviously, adding threshold variables or criteria complicates the incentive formula and may dampen employee acceptance and motivation. Thresholds should only be considered when they are essential for approval of the incentive by management and/or shareholders.

Another important design decision concerns the *choice between additive and multiplicative formulas*. The examples discussed so far are based on additive formulas in which improved results add to the incentive payoff. Sometimes labor or multicost incentive plans are designed using a multiplicative formula. Multiplicative formulas include multiplier (or modifier) variables that affect employees' share in gains achieved or the dollar value of goals attained. This added component is intended to emphasize

TABLE 17.2 *Ten Key Plan Parameters*

1. Threshold variables or criteria

2. Measure selection

3. Formula type: additive or multiplicative?

4. Bonus pool (for gain sharing) or bonus (for goal sharing) formula

5. Reserve or time-smoothing mechanism

6. Criteria for individual employee payoffs

7. Caps on payoffs?

8. Payoff delivery: frequency, vehicle, etc.

9. Special employee cases

   - part-time employees

   - temporary employees

   - employed for less than full payoff period

   - separations before payoff

10. Employee involvement system

the need to focus on noncost results such as various customer-oriented measures. Figure 17.4 describes schematically a multiplicative formula used in some hospitals. It shows a modified multicost gain-sharing plan in which performance versus the baseline for several costs (labor, materials, etc.) is used to compute a cost savings pool. The employees' share in the cost savings pool, in turn, depends on quality and customer service considerations. This plan sends a simple yet thorough message to employees: "We should focus not only on cost savings but also on clinical quality and patient satisfaction."

Another critical design decision concerns the *criteria to be used for individual payoffs*. According to a widely cited study,[16] the most common choices, listed by descending frequency of use, are: (1) payoff is the same percent of base pay for all eligible employees; (2) same dollar payoff for all eligible employees; (3) payoffs vary according to individual employee performance; and (4) payoffs vary according to the employee's job or organizational level. The first option has been used for the longest time and reflects the assumption that those employees whose salary or wage rate is higher contribute proportionally more to the achievement of group results.[17] Some question this assumption, observing that when there are large differences in base pay among participating employees (common in U.S. organizations), there will be correspondingly large differences in dollar payoffs. These dollar payoff differences among employees may dampen the motivation to cooperate and work as a team. For this reason, the second option listed above (same dollar payoff for all eligible employees) is favored by those who advocate a more egalitarian, team-oriented design for group incentives. Supporters of this view argue that base salary and wages already recognize and reward individual differences in education, skill, and responsibility. They suggest that an egalitarian group incentive, which results in the same dollar payoffs for all participating employees, should have a stronger motivational impact on the majority of the organization's workforce. It should be noted that it is possible for organizations to choose a middle-of-the-road approach allocating half of the incentive dollars on an equal dollar basis and half on a percentage-of-pay basis. This approach reduces in half the difference in dollar payoffs between highly paid employees and those at the bottom of the base pay structure.

FIGURE 17.4   *Multicost Gain-sharing Plan with Multiplicative Formula*

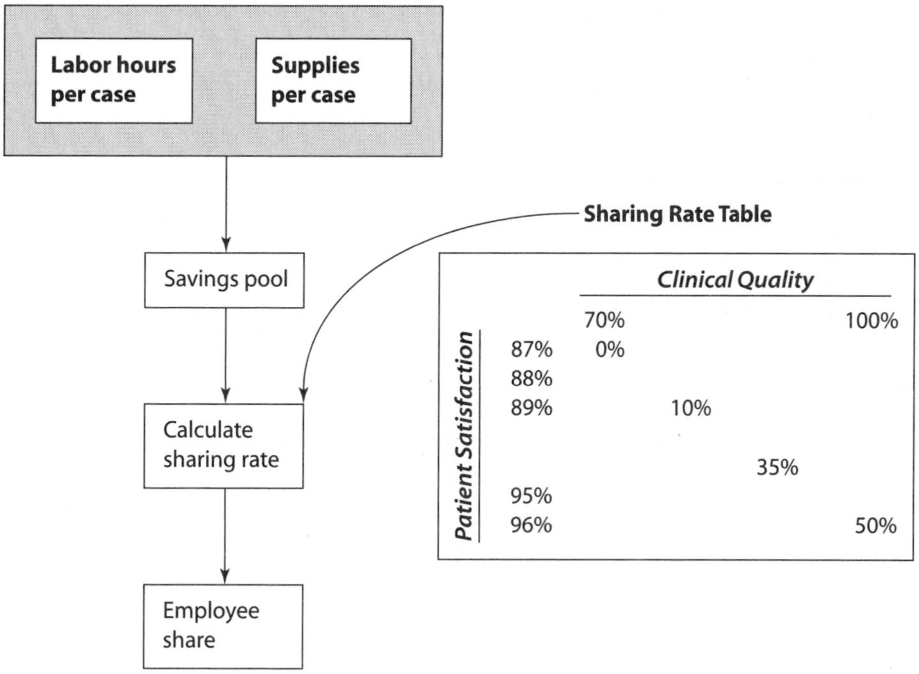

Figure showing flow: Labor hours per case and Supplies per case → Savings pool → Calculate sharing rate → Employee share. Connected to a Sharing Rate Table with Clinical Quality (columns 70% to 100%) and Patient Satisfaction (rows). Values in table: 87%/70% = 0%; 89% = 10%; 35%; 96%/100% = 50%.

Stage 7: Determine Initial Baselines and Update Procedure

Gain-sharing formulas require a baseline that must be exceeded before there is a pay-off. Goal-sharing plans require numerical values (or baselines) for the various goals included in the formula. Usually, baselines are determined after examining the history of results over the last three to five years. However, some organizations use competitive benchmarking information and/or budget planning values to determine baselines.

In addition, group incentives increasingly include a provision for the review and adjustment of plan baselines. Most organizations require and expect a positive trend in the level of results given that they continue to reinvest financial and human capital to improve their technology, systems, and business processes. Moreover, most organizations cannot afford to remain fixed at a certain level (of productivity, efficiency, and customer service) lest they risk being surpassed by their competitors. For these reasons, *group incentives tend to fail when baselines are not adjusted systematically.*

One approach to providing a mechanical, judgment-free review and update of plan baselines involves the use of rolling (or moving) averages. That is, the baseline(s) for next cycle are based on the average over several recent years. In this approach, the baseline follows the recent trend in organizational improvements. Alternatively, some organizations ask a team of knowledgeable employees to determine any changes to the baselines based on their judgment, recent experiences, and anticipated developments. Obviously, the mechanical approach does not involve human judgment and may be easier to sell to rank-and-file employees. However, the judgment of a knowledgeable team may be the better approach when the organization's business, market(s), and/or technology are evolving drastically.

Stage 8: Plan Simulation and Fine-Tuning

Once the formula and baselines have been chosen, the design process must proceed to assess whether the formula and baselines are likely to function as expected. If not, the design process should determine any necessary adjustments or fine-tuning to the plan's design. For this stage, it is useful to review historical data and the organization's record for the last three to five years, assuming the incentive plan was installed a few years ago. The following list identifies some of the most critical issues to examine during this simulation and fine-tuning stage:

- What size of payoffs does the formula generate?

- What happens when demand for our products or services changes drastically?

- What happens when we expand or add new equipment?

- Would there be payoffs even if we lost money? Can we live with this?

- What happens when prices change drastically?

- What if our customers' expectations (requirements) changed drastically?

Stage 9: Plan Communication and Start-up

After validating the design, it is time to prepare for launching the plan. Employee communication is critical to foster acceptance and, more importantly, to motivate employees to start thinking differently about their work and how they cooperate and coordinate with each other. A well-crafted communication strategy should probably involve multiple vehicles to help employees understand the new incentive plan and any associated changes to information systems and work processes. Communication means could include oral presentations, video presentations (if practical from a cost point of view), and some written materials that employees may consult at their leisure. At a minimum, these communications should focus the following key issues and principles:

- Why a group incentive? Why this type of group incentive?

- Who designed this group incentive?

- How long will the plan exist? (the sunset date issue)

- How does the entire formula work?

- How were the particular measures used in the formula chosen?

- How were baselines chosen?

- Will measures and/or baselines ever change? Why? When? How?

- Who is eligible to receive incentive payoffs?

- How will total payoff (for gain sharing) and individual payoffs be determined?

Stage 10: Plan Administration and Renewal

The final stage in the deployment process deals with maintaining the group incentive as a useful tool that supports and reinforces organizational success. It is common for organizations to create a team of employees that will administer and review the incentive plan periodically and make any necessary modifications. The administration part of this stage deals mostly with performing or monitoring payoff calculations and delivery. It may also involve making decisions in response to events or developments not considered in the plan's provisions. The renewal function, which is critical for the plan's long-term viability and success, deals with measure addition or deletion, changes to baselines (as suggested in the previous stage), and any needed revisions to plan parameters (see Stage 6).

IN CONCLUSION

Debrief

Group incentives can have a major impact on key organizational results including productivity, efficiency, quality, and customer service. Also, group incentives can serve as a seed to lead, or as a catalyst to support, organizational change and development. As illustrated by the taxonomy explained in this chapter (see Figure 17.2), organizations have considerable latitude in choosing the type of group incentive plan that fits their needs. Deploying a group incentive plan does not have to be an enormously challenging endeavor. This module described salient points in a ten-stage process for developing group incentive plans that are anchored on organizational business and HR strategies and discussed how group incentives can promote organizational success.

Suggested Readings

Abosch, Kenan S. 1998. "Variable pay: Do we have the basics in place?" *Compensation and Benefits Review,* 30(4): 12–22.

Beck, David. 1992. "Implementing a gainsharing plan: What companies need to know." *Compensation and Benefits Review,* 24(1): 21–33.

Belcher, John G., Jr. 1994. "Gainsharing and variable pay: The state of the art." *Compensation and Benefits Review,* 26(3): 50–60.

Belcher, John G., Jr. 1996. *How to Design and Implement a Results-Oriented Variable Pay System.* New York: Amacom.

Collins, Dennis. 1996. "Case study: 15 lessons learned from the death of a gainsharing plan." *Compensation and Benefits Review,* 28(2): 31–40.

Graham-Moore, Brian and Ross, Timothy L. 1995. *Gainsharing and employee involvement.* Washington, D.C.: Bureau of National Affairs.

Masternak, Robert. 1997. "How to make gainsharing successful: The collective experience of 17 facilities." *Compensation and Benefits Review,* 29(5): 43–52.

Masternak, Robert and Ross, Timothy L. 1992. "Gainsharing: A bonus plan or employee involvement?" *Compensation and Benefits Review,* 24(1): 46–54.

Critical Thinking Questions

1. The value of group incentives as a tool to help organizations succeed is easier to see for organizations in the private, for-profit sector of the economy. There is less agreement regarding the utility of group incentives for public-sector organizations. Identify and justify five *critical similarities between the private for-profit and the public sectors*—in terms of how organizations function, relate to their customers (or revenue sources), and define organizational success—that should *facilitate the use of group incentives in the public sector.*

2. Reconsider the frame from question 1, but now identify and justify five *critical differences between the private for-profit and the public sectors*—in terms of how organizations function, relate to their customers (or revenue sources), and define organizational success—that *complicate the use of group incentives in the public sector.*

3. At the conceptual level, some argue group incentives may encourage "free riding" attitudes and behavior among some group members who would benefit from group incentive payoffs without carrying their weight. Free riding may

discourage other employees in the same group and destroy the positive impact of group incentives. Prepare for a discussion with other students addressing the following issues:

a. What organization characteristics and kinds of work make free riding more likely?

b. What organization characteristics and kinds of work make free riding less likely?

c. What can organizations do to control and minimize the potential for free riding problems?

4. A paradox emerges when one considers the increasing popularity of group incentives in the United States: how can the country with the most individualistic culture in the world make such frequent use of group incentives (ignoring the case of countries where group payoffs like profit sharing are mandated by law)? What are we missing? Discuss the conditions and processes that allow group incentives to succeed in American organizations populated with highly individualistic employees.

Exercises

1. Lincoln Electric, Inc., and Springfield Remanufacturing, Inc., are two manufacturing firms whose use of group incentives has been described and reviewed extensively in the literature. Find three to five articles about group incentives in each of these two firms. Analyze and synthesize the information in those articles concerning the rationale, development, and use of group incentives in these firms. Discuss whether your findings verify, contradict, or extend the ideas discussed in this module.

2. Choose two adjacent cells in Figure 17.2—i.e., two rows from the same column or two adjacent columns from the same row. Search the professional and academic literature and locate two or three case analyses for examples of each type of group incentive. Read and analyze the articles you found comparing and contrasting the organizations that use each type of group incentive. Summarize your findings and discuss whether your findings verify, contradict, or extend the ideas discussed in this module.

3. Gain access to a small- or medium-sized organization that has only one site (plant, office) where it generates its products or services. Interview at least three people in the organization performing the business and HR strategy analyses discussed in Stage 1 in the ten-stage process described in this module. Then sketch the Stage 5 and Stage 6 implications of your strategy analyses.

References

1. See the articles by Collins (1996) and Masternak (1997) in the list of suggested readings.
2. A somewhat similar taxonomy, considering the second feature proposed here, can be found in Ledford, Gerald E. and Lawler, Edward E. III. 1994. "Reward systems that reinforce organizational change." *CEO Publication* G 94–32 (275). University of Southern California, Business School, Center for Effective Organizations.
3. Guthrie, J. P. and Cunningham, E. P. 1992. "Pay for performance for hourly workers: The Quaker Oats alternative." *Compensation and Benefits Review,* 24(2): 18–23.
4. Cooke, William N. 1994. "Employee participation programs, group-based incentives and company performance: A union-nonunion comparison." *Industrial and Labor Relations Review,* 47: 594–609. Jones, Derek C., Kato, Takao, and Pliskin, Jeffrey. 1997. "Profitsharing and gainsharing: A review of theory, incidence, and effects." In Lewin, David, Mitchell,

Daniel J. B., and Zaidi, Mahmood A. (Editors), *The Human Resource Management Handbook—Part I*. Greenwich, CT: JAI Press, pp. 153-173. Kaufman, Roger T. 1992. "The effects of IMPROSHARE on productivity." *Industrial and Labor Relations Review,* 45: 311–325.

5. Hammer, Tove H. 1988. "New developments in profit sharing, gainsharing and employee ownership." In John P. Campbell, Richard J. Campbell and Associates (Editors) *Productivity in Organizations.* San Francisco: Jossey-Bass, pp. 328–366. McAdams, Jerry L., and Hawk, Elizabeth J. 1992. *Capitalizing on Human Assets.* Scottsdale, AZ: American Compensation Association.

6. McAdams and Hawk, op cit.

7. Welbourne, Theresa M. & Gomez-Mejia, Luis R. 1995. "Gainsharing: A critical review and a future research agenda." *Journal of Management,* 21: 559–609.

8. Schaffer, Robert H. and Thomson, Harvey A. 1992. "Successful change programs begin with results." *Harvard Business Review,* 70(1): 80–89.

9. French, W. L. and Bell, C. H., Jr. 1990. *Organization Development* (Fourth Edition). Englewood Cliffs, NJ: Prentice-Hall.

10. French and Bell, Ibid. Burke, W. W. 1992. *Organization Development: A Process of Learning and Changing.* Reading, MA: Addison-Wesley.

11. This section is based on my loose adaptation of the ideas contained in the articles by Collins (1996) and Masternak (1997) cited in the suggested readings section and in Kotter, John P. 1995. "Leading change: Why transformation efforts fail." *Harvard Business Review,* 73(2): 59–67.

12. Interested readers may consult the books by Belcher (1996) and Graham-Moore and Ross (1995) listed with the suggested readings for this chapter.

13. A similar distinction between "control" and "commitment" oriented HR strategies can be found in Arthur, Jeffrey B. 1992. "The link between business strategy and industrial relations systems in American steel minimills." *Industrial and Labor Relations Review,* 43(5): 488–506.

14. Some of these questions are based on Stewart, T. A. 1994. "Rate your readiness to change." *Fortune.* February 7, pp. 106–110.

15. McAdams and Hawk, op. cit.

16. McAdams and Hawk, op. cit.

17. This option is also preferred because it simplifies handling of overtime premiums for those employees who are not exempt from the overtime provision in the current Fair Labor Standards Act when the payoff percentage is applied to the total of straight-time and overtime earnings. Readers interested in a more technical discussion of this issue should consult the recommended readings.

Index

Accounting/operational results measures, 17.15–16
Action research phases, 17.13. *See also* Group incentives, deployment
Annual payoff, 17.8

Baseline(s), 17.9, 17.18–19. *See also* Incentive bonus
Bonuses, 17.5, 17.6, 17.7. *See also* Rewards
Business strategy, and group incentives, 17.10, 17.13–14, 17.16

Change programs, 17.10
Communication strategy, and group incentive plans, 17.20
Communications, 17.7, 17.10, 17.12
Compensation plans, 17.4
Constancy of change, 17.10
Continuous learning culture, 17.10
Cost minimization, 17.7
Cultural change, 17.4, 17.11
Current profit-sharing plans, 17.8

Deferred profit-sharing plans, 17.8
Disclosure of financial information, 17.16
Discretionary bonus, 17.6

Economic factors, 17.17
Egalitarian group incentive, 17.18
Eligible employees, 17.5, 17.8
Employee commitment, 17.14, 17.20
Employee compensation system, 17.6
Employee contributions, 17.6, 17.11
Employee eligibility, 17.15
Employee involvement plan, 17.10, 17.14. *See also* Group incentives
Employee needs, 17.7
Employee participation, 17.4, 17.11, 17.14
Employee representative, 17.4
Employee-organization relationship, 17.11
Employment relationship, 17.11
Empowered workforce, 17.10
Expectancy theories, 17.6

Financially valued goal-sharing plans, 17.9
Funding potential, 17.17

Gain-sharing incentive plans, 17.8, 17.16–17
Goal-setting theory, 17.6
Goal-sharing incentive plans, 17.8, 17.16–17
Group incentive plans, 17.6–7, 17.8, 17.11, 17.15, 17.21

Group incentives, 17.4, 17.5, 17.9–20, 17.21
    core concepts, 17.5
    deployment strategies, 17.9–10, 17.11–13
    development strategies, 17.10, 17.12
    OCD perspective, 17.12
    strategic impact, 17.10
    success factors, 17.12

Human resource management systems and practices, 17.4
Human resource strategies, 17.4, 17.10, 17.13, 17.14, 17.16, 17.21

Incentive bonus, 17.6, 17.9
Incentive formulas (additive/multiplicative), 17.17–19
Incentive plan design, 17.13, 17.16. *See also* Ten stages
Incentives, 17.6, 17.7, 17.8. *See also* Group incentives
Information system, 17.16
Internal work process, 17.4
Involvement, worker (employee), 17.17

Judgment-free review, 17.19. *See also* Baseline(s)

Key measurable outcomes, 17.5
Key plan parameters, 17.17. *See also* Group incentives

Labor productivity gain-sharing plans, 17.8, 17.16. *See also* Gain-sharing incentive plans
Learning (reinforcement) theories, 17.6

Management employees, 17.4
Maximum operational efficiency, 17.14
Maximum responsiveness, 17.14
Morale, employee, 17.10, 17.15
Motivation of employees, 17.14, 17.16, 17.18
Motivation theories, 17.6
Multicost gain-sharing plans, 17.7–8, 17.16–17
Multicost goal-sharing plans, 17.7–8, 17.16–17

Nonmanagement employees, 17.4
Nonunion organization, 17.4

Operational efficiency, 17.17
Operational goals, 17.8
Organizational change and development (OCD), 17.11–12
Organizational culture, 17.11

Organizational performance, 17.11
Organizational readiness, 17.14

Partner relationship, 17.11
Payoffs, 17.5, 17.8, 17.16, 17.17, 17.18, 17.20
Performance-rewards link, 17.10
Plan administration, Group incentive plans, 17.20
Plan communication and start-up, 17.20
Plan duration, 17.15
Plan simulation, 17.19–20. *See also* Group incentives plan
Problem-solving training, 17.7
Productivity, 17.7
Productivity target, 17.8, 17.16
Profit-sharing plans, 17.8, 17.10, 17.15

Receptivity to change, 17.15
Relationship to base pay, 17.15
Results-payoff link, 17.7, 17.8, 17.10, 17.16
Rewards, 17.6. *See also* Bonuses

Scanlon plan, 17.8, 17.10, 17.15–16
Scope of incentive plan, 17.15
Self-actualization (intrinsic motivation) theories, 17.6
Self-assessment, 17.14
Self-funding principle, 17.7. *See also* Group incentive plans
Support, building, 17.14

Teamwork, 17.7, 17.10, 17.11
Ten key plan parameters, 17.18
Ten stages, group incentives, deployment, 17.13–20, 17.21
Top-management support, 17.11
Transactional role, 17.4

Unionized employees, 17.4
Update procedure, 17.19. *See also* Group incentives plan

Variable incentive schemas, 17.4
Variable payoffs, 17.5

MODULE
17

MANAGING HUMAN RESOURCES
IN THE 21st CENTURY

From Core Concepts to Strategic Choice

MODULE 18

Benefits

Current Challenges in Providing Cost-Effective Employee Supports

MaryAnne M. Hyland
ADELPHI UNIVERSITY

Managing Human Resources in the 21st Century: From Core Concepts to Strategic Choice,
by Kossek and Block

Publisher: Dave Shaut
Executive Editor: John Szilagyi
Developmental Editor: Bryant Editorial Development
Marketing Manager: Joseph A. Sabatino
Production Editor: Tamborah E. Moore
Manufacturing Coordinator: Dana Began Schwartz
Cover Design: Tin Box Studio
Cover Photographs: Copyright Shoji Sato/Photonica
Production House: The Left Coast Group, Inc.
Printer: West Group

Printed in the United States of America
1 2 3 4 5 02 01 00 99

For more information contact South-Western College Publishing, 5101 Madison Road, Cincinnati, Ohio, 45227 or find us on the Internet at *http://www.swcollege.com*
For permission to use material from this text or product, contact us by
- telephone: 1-800-730-2214
- fax: 1-800-730-2215
- web: *http://www.thomsonrights.com*

ISBN: 0–324–01817–7

This book is printed on acid-free paper.

Contents

MODULE OVERVIEW   18.4

RELATION TO THE FRAME   18.4

CORE CONCEPTS IN EMPLOYEE BENEFITS   18.5

    Benefit Basics   18.5

    The Regulatory Environment   18.7

    Social Insurance Programs   18.9

    Retirement Benefits   18.11

    Health and Welfare Benefits   18.13

    Work/Life and Miscellaneous Benefits   18.17

    Design   18.18

    Funding   18.19

    Administration   18.20

STRATEGIC ISSUES IN EMPLOYEE BENEFITS   18.21

APPLICATION   18.22

IN CONCLUSION   18.22

    Debrief   18.22

    Suggested Readings   18.23

    Critical Thinking Questions   18.23

    Exercise   18.23

    References   18.23

    Endnotes   18.24

INDEX   18.25

MODULE
18

MODULE OVERVIEW

Employee benefits have traditionally been a core component of human resource management. In recent years, rising benefit costs, an increasingly diverse workforce, and shorter-term employees have affected the type of benefits that are provided and how plans are administered. This module examines the effects of these changes on employee benefits by providing an overview of various benefit plans, how they are designed, and how they are administered.

In today's competitive business environment, employers face pressures to reduce the costs of benefits and benefit administration while still attracting and retaining valuable employees. This can be accomplished by offering benefits and benefit services that are perceived as valuable to today's workforce and thus providing maximum value per dollar spent on benefits. A theme that will be addressed throughout this module is the move away from employee benefits being viewed as an entitlement. Historically, employees often have not recognized the dollar value of their benefits and have not considered employer contributions toward their benefits to be part of their compensation. This was due in part to the fact that employers offered benefits "paternalistically," requiring no action or responsibility on the part of the employee. This perspective is shifting, as changing benefit needs and rising benefit costs have placed pressure on employers to offer a broader range of benefits and to share costs with employees. By communicating benefit objectives and having employees take a more active role in determining their benefits, employers can help employees better understand the value of their benefits.

Employers also can maximize their investment in benefits by minimizing administrative costs. Improvements in technology and the growth of outsourcing have changed the highly administrative nature of employee benefits departments in many organizations. This module addresses how employee benefits departments can become more strategic by focusing more on planning and design than on processing transactions. Regardless of whether employee benefit administration is outsourced or handled in-house, it is critical for human resource managers to understand the nature of employee benefit plans and how they add value for employees and the organization.

RELATION TO THE FRAME

Employee benefits have traditionally been a transaction-based area of human resource management. Benefit administration is an ongoing process that is constantly affected by transactions related to employees joining and leaving the organization, as well as employees and beneficiaries making changes to their benefits. In addition, legislative changes often require changes to plans and how they are administered.

This module relates to the other modules in this series by focusing not only on types of benefits, but on how plans are designed and administered. The design of individual benefits, as well as the overall employee benefits offering, is a strategic component of benefits management. Human resource managers must understand business needs and deliver effective benefit solutions that meet those needs. They also must consider the alignment of employee benefits with other functional areas within HR, such as compensation. Given the transaction-based nature of much of employee benefits, human resource managers also must ensure that the organization's human resource information system can support benefit needs. As human resource management moves into the twenty-first century, a strategic perspective of employee benefits will become increasingly critical to justify benefit offerings and services.

FIGURE 18.1 *A Frame for Understanding Human Resource Strategy:*
Context, Roles, and Constraints

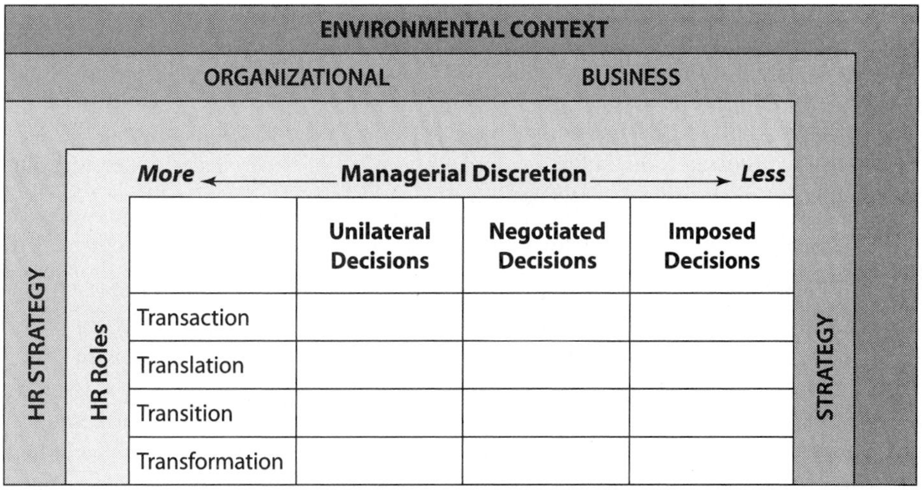

ENVIRONMENTAL CONTEXT			
ORGANIZATIONAL		BUSINESS	

HR STRATEGY / HR Roles	*More* ← **Managerial Discretion** → *Less*			STRATEGY
	Unilateral Decisions	**Negotiated Decisions**	**Imposed Decisions**	
Transaction				
Translation				
Transition				
Transformation				

© 2000 by Ellen Ernst Kossek and Richard Block. Thanks to Brian Pentland, Karen Markel, and John Beck for helpful comments and discussions that enhanced the model.

CORE CONCEPTS IN EMPLOYEE BENEFITS

A basic knowledge of employee benefits requires an understanding of the following key areas:

- Basic benefits definitions and the role of benefits in total compensation

- The role of the government:

  ✓ The regulatory environment

  ✓ Social insurance programs

- Employer-provided benefit plans:

  ✓ Retirement benefits

  ✓ Health and welfare benefits

  ✓ Work/life and miscellaneous benefits

- Design, funding, and administration of benefit plans

Benefit Basics

Before addressing core benefits concepts, a common understanding of the term "employee benefits" and the role of benefits in total compensation is needed. In addition, insight into employers' reasons for offering benefits and the parties eligible to receive these benefits will frame the discussion of individual benefit plans.

Employee Benefits Defined.   A common understanding of the term "employee benefits" is needed, as it is ordinarily conceptualized in two ways. A narrow definition of employee benefits includes employer-provided retirement, health, welfare, and other benefits. However, some would argue that benefits that are financed by employer contributions but are provided by social insurance programs should also be included. This latter, broader definition is used in this module as part of a total compensation perspective of employee benefits.

In defining employee benefits, it is useful to consider benefits as a component of total compensation. Rather than treating wages and benefits independently, a total compensation perspective treats both pieces as part of an employee's total compensation. Wages, bonuses, and the like generally are considered to be direct compensation, whereas benefits are considered to be indirect compensation. All of these pieces added together make up an employee's total compensation.

$$\text{Total compensation} = \text{Direct compensation} + \text{Indirect compensation}$$

From the employer's perspective, the same level of total compensation can be derived from different mixes of direct compensation and benefit levels that best meet employee needs. From the employee's perspective, this equation suggests that a job with lower wages may be more attractive than one with higher wages if the value of the benefits is high enough to result in a higher total compensation. Of course, the value that employees place on wages versus benefits will vary based on a number of factors, including the stage in the employee's life. Figure 18.2 shows the breakdown of total compensation as determined by the U.S. Chamber of Commerce for 1996.

FIGURE 18.2   *Total Compensation Components for 1996*

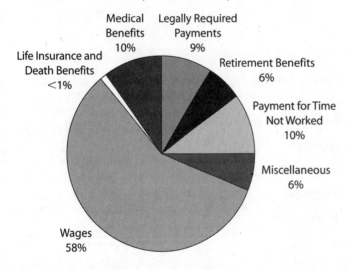

Why Do Employers Offer Benefits?

There are many reasons why employers offer employee benefits, ranging from economic reasons to social responsibility, including:

- *Attracting and retaining employees.* Benefits are a tool to attract and retain employees. They can be considered a reward to employees for beginning or continuing employment with an organization.

- *Favorable tax legislation.* Employer contributions to many benefits are tax deductible for the employer and do not count as taxable income to employees. Additional tax advantages exist for earned interest.

- *Regulatory compliance.* Employers are required by the federal or state governments to provide or contribute towards certain benefits, such as workers' compensation insurance.

- *Potential for increased mandatory programs.* Most benefits are provided voluntarily by employers. If employers did not provide these benefits, and the government perceived a need for such benefits, legislation could be passed that would require employers to provide or contribute toward benefits, taking away the flexibility that employers have when voluntarily providing the benefit.

- *Collective bargaining.* In unionized settings, employers are required to bargain in good faith over wages, hours, and other terms and conditions of employment, which includes retirement and welfare benefit plans.

- *"Right thing to do."* The cost and administrative burden of purchasing benefits privately can be quite high. Employers that see the need for and provide benefits may be motivated by ethical considerations.

Who Should Receive Benefits?   The term "employee benefits" is almost misleading because benefits affect a much broader audience than current employees. Benefit plan participants include:

- Active full-time employees and their dependents

- Retired employees and their dependents

- Part-time employees and their dependents

- Disabled employees and their dependents

- Survivors of deceased employees

- Employees who terminated employment and their dependents (e.g., COBRA)

- Employees on temporary leave and their dependents (e.g., FMLA)

A growing number of employers are beginning to include domestic partners as eligible dependents for benefits. Employer experiences suggest that the cost of covering domestic partners is comparable to that of covering spouses. However, tax must be paid on the value of domestic partner benefits due to the fact that the U.S. federal government does not recognize domestic partners as dependents. As the workforce continues to become more diverse, offering domestic partner benefits may become a key business decision related to attracting and retaining talented employees.

The Regulatory Environment

A variety of laws affect benefit offerings and administration. Some of these laws have been passed solely to address benefit-related issues, whereas other laws relate to broader social issues. Entire books have been written about the legal environment of employee benefits! Clearly, this module cannot go into the depth required for a detailed understanding of benefit legislation. This section will focus on some of the critical legislation, as well as some recent laws. It is not intended to serve as legal guidance.

ERISA.   The Employee Retirement Income Security Act (ERISA) of 1974 is the most comprehensive employee benefits legislation in the United States. Although ERISA primarily affects private retirement plans, health and welfare plans are also subject to certain provisions. One of the main goals of ERISA is to protect the interests of employees. Employers must meet standards under ERISA in order for their benefit plans to receive the tax advantages associated with ERISA. These standards include:

- *Reporting and disclosure.* The employer or the benefit plan sponsor must communicate the benefit plan to participants and must report information about the plan to the government. A summary plan description (SPD) is a communication piece required by ERISA that helps employees understand a benefit plan by ensuring that certain information, such as plan requirements for participation, is stated.

- *Funding.* Assets for certain benefit plans must be separated from the employer's general assets to protect the funds from misuse. Minimum funding standards also require the employer to accumulate these assets according to a schedule so that ample assets exist to pay benefits.

- *Fiduciary standards.* When operating the plan, anyone who has control or discretion in managing plan assets, known as a "fiduciary," must act only in the interests of the participants and beneficiaries. Fiduciaries also must diversify the plan's assets to reduce the risk of losses, and comply with the plan documents.

- *Employee eligibility.* For qualified retirement plans, employees are required to become eligible after a maximum of one year of employment and the attainment of age 21.

- *Vesting.* The time required for the employer's retirement benefit contributions to become nonforfeitable by the employee. If an employee terminates employment before becoming fully vested, a known percentage of his or her employer-provided retirement contributions will be revoked by the organization.

- *Plan termination insurance.* Sponsors of private-sector defined benefit plans must pay premiums for this insurance so that beneficiaries would still receive some payment if the plan were to terminate prematurely.

Not all plans are subject to the standards listed above. For example, health and welfare plans must meet the reporting and disclosure requirements, but not vesting requirements, to be qualified. Some nonqualified plans do not meet any of ERISA's standards; however, such plans are not eligible for tax-favored status. ERISA has been amended many times and has affected subsequent employee benefit legislation.

COBRA. The Consolidated Omnibus Reconciliation Act of 1985 (COBRA) was designed to enable individuals to continue their health coverage if they lost their job or experienced another event that resulted in a loss of coverage. Individuals electing health coverage through COBRA pay for the entire cost of the coverage (the premium) plus up to an additional 2 percent in administrative fees. Coverage is available for a finite period of time, ranging from 18 to 36 months. Most employers with 20 or more employees are required to comply with COBRA. However, the cost to employers is primarily administrative, since the individuals electing coverage pay the entire premium.

FMLA. The Family and Medical Leave Act of 1993 (FMLA) requires employers with 50 or more employees to allow an employee to take up to 12 weeks of unpaid leave per year for family and medical reasons. Qualified reasons for such leave include the birth or adoption of a child and the serious health condition of an immediate family member or of the employee. The law requires that covered employers maintain the health coverage that an individual received before the leave and that the individual be allowed to return to the same job or an equivalent job. The recognition at the federal level of the need for family and medical leave is consistent with the family needs of today's diverse workforce.

HIPAA. The Health Insurance Portability and Accountability Act of 1996 (HIPAA) affects individuals who lose health coverage or who experience difficulties gaining access to health coverage. Prior to HIPAA, individuals who had coverage for a medical condition could lose coverage for that condition if they switched medical plans due to preexisting condition exclusions. HIPAA restricts the use of preexisting condition exclusions, and also improves access to health coverage for all individuals with provisions for guaranteed access to coverage and guaranteed renewal.

Social Insurance Programs

Social insurance programs have been established by the federal and state governments to address social problems that affect a large number of people. In the United States, four main employment-related programs exist:

- Social security and medicare benefits

- Temporary disability insurance

- Unemployment insurance

- Workers' compensation insurance

All of these programs are prescribed by either federal or state law, although benefits vary by individual based on factors such as wage level. Social insurance programs are primarily based on the principle of social adequacy, which stresses the provision of a minimum benefit to all beneficiaries under the program regardless of their economic status. This differs from the principle of individual equity, which stresses that an individual's benefits from the program should be proportional to his or her contribution to the system. Some social insurance programs rely on high-income individuals or families to subsidize lower income individuals or families.

Social Security and Medicare.

The term *social security* used here is the meaning generally accepted in the United States, which is cash benefits from the federal Old Age, Survivors, and Disability Insurance Program (OASDI). Internationally, the term is used more broadly, including other types of economic risk, such as unemployment, short-term sickness, work-connected accidents and diseases, and medical care costs (Myers 1996).

OASDI is one of the programs resulting from the Social Security Act of 1935 and its amendments. The act was passed due to the Great Depression in an effort to provide economic security to those lacking it, such as the elderly. Medicare, which provides medical benefits, was added to the OASDI program in 1965.

Social security provides a monthly cash benefit to eligible individuals. This amount received, known as the Primary Insurance Amount (PIA), is based on a complex computation using average monthly wages. Medicare has traditionally provided two types of benefits. Hospital insurance (Part A) is for hospital services, such as daily room and board, and diagnostic services. Supplementary medical insurance (Part B), which is optional and requires payment of a monthly premium, provides partial reimbursement for the cost of physician services. Recently, the medicare program has begun to explore managed-care options that combine the benefits of Part A and Part B, and often provide additional benefits, such as prescription drug coverage.

Eligibility for social security benefits, known as fully insured status, is based on having a certain amount of covered employment, which is based on total yearly earnings. For 1999, individuals received one social security credit for each $740 of earnings, up to a maximum of four credits per year. A total of forty credits is required for eligibility.[1] The name of the OASDI program makes it easy to remember who can receive benefits:

- *Old age.* Full retirement benefits payable at the normal retirement age of 65, with reduced benefits available at age 62. The normal retirement age will gradually rise beginning in the year 2000 until it reaches 67 in 2027 for people born in 1960 or later.

- *Survivors.* The following family members of a deceased OASDI-insured individual are eligible: children under 18 and other children meeting certain conditions; widows and widowers who care for children that are under age 16 or disabled; widows and widowers age 60 or older, or age 50 or older if disabled.

MODULE
18

- *Disability.* People with severe physical or mental disabilities that prevent them from working are eligible to receive social security benefits.

Eligibility for medicare differs for Part A and Part B. Hospital insurance (Part A) is provided to all individuals age 65 and over who are eligible for social security benefits.[2] Supplementary medical insurance (Part B) is available to all individuals age 65 or over, regardless of their eligibility for social security benefits.[3]

The Federal Insurance Contributions Act (FICA) funds both social security and medicare. This tax rate (7.65 percent for 1999) can be broken down into a social security component and a medicare component. Employers and employees both pay social security tax and medicare tax on employee earnings for a total rate of 15.3 percent for 1999.[4]

Social security and medicare are facing a crisis due to projected costs exceeding income into the program. This issue is largely due to the expected retirement of the "baby boom" generation beginning around 2010 and to increased longevity. Although income to social security and medicare has never greatly exceeded costs, projections for the twenty-first century are not optimistic. Unless changes are made to the system, beneficiaries of the future will not have sufficient benefits available to them. The medicare program is using managed care options to address this problem, and the social security program is increasing the normal retirement age. Both programs also are considering additional measures.

Changes in the social security and medicare programs can be confusing to employees. Although these programs are sponsored by the federal government, employers often receive questions about social security and medicare and how they will be combined (if at all) with employer-provided retirement benefits. Many employers use printed communication materials as well as information sessions to educate employees nearing retirement about issues related to the government's retirement programs. Such a proactive measure may substantially reduce phone calls and missed deadlines related to retirement issues. In addition, employers may consider offering additional retirement benefits to supplement social security and medicare benefits.

Unemployment Insurance.　The Federal Unemployment Tax Act and state unemployment systems provide benefits to workers during periods of brief unemployment. Although each state has a separate program, most states offer a weekly cash benefit for 26 weeks that is based on a percentage of the worker's average wages. Individuals who had been working, are actively seeking work, and are able and available to work, are generally eligible to receive unemployment benefits. Employers pay 6.2 percent of the employee's first $7,000 of taxable wages in federal tax (this may be reduced by taxes paid to state programs). No employee contributions are required for unemployment insurance.

Workers' Compensation Insurance.　Workers' compensation is the oldest of the social insurance programs. The administration of workers' compensation has been left largely to the states, but similar federal laws exist. The program typically provides a cash benefit (a percentage of weekly earnings, e.g., 66.66 percent) as well as medical benefits and rehabilitation benefits to workers with injuries, illness, or death arising *out of and in the course of employment.* Workers generally forfeit their ability to sue their employer for the injury or illness by accepting the benefits. The program is financed by employer contributions. Employer rates are experience rated, which provides an incentive for employers to provide a safe working environment.

Temporary Disability Insurance.　Unlike unemployment insurance and workers' compensation programs, which are found in all 50 states within the United States, mandated temporary disability programs have only been put into law in five states (California, Hawaii, New Jersey, New York, and Rhode Island) and Puerto Rico.

Temporary disability insurance provides weekly wage replacement based on a percentage of the employee's average wage prior to the disability (up to a maximum amount). Given that the focus of the coverage is on *temporary* disability, there is a maximum coverage period, which is generally 26 weeks. Employees must have had sufficient earnings or have worked for a sufficient period of time according to the state law in order to be eligible to receive benefits. In addition, employees must meet the state's definition of disability and satisfy any waiting period (0–7 days). Most employers in the states and province with temporary disability laws are required to provide coverage for their employees. This generally can be done through the state program, through private insurance, or by a self-funded program. Depending on the state (or province), employers may be the sole financiers of their programs, employees may be the sole financiers, or both parties together may bear the costs of the program.

Retirement Benefits

An employee's retirement income generally comes from three sources, known as a "three legged stool" that can support a comfortable retirement. The three legs are:

- Social security

- Company retirement plan

- Personal savings or investments

Employer-sponsored retirement plans are changing their role in the three-legged stool due to cutbacks to social security, increased longevity of retirees, large numbers of soon-to-retire "baby boomers," and shorter lengths of service for many employees. Employers want to provide high-quality retirement programs to attract and retain employees, yet cost pressures make it necessary to find the most effective way to provide such a program without subjecting the organization to too great a level of risk. The two main categories of employer-provided retirement benefits are defined benefit plans and defined contribution plans. Although these two categories differ significantly, both types of plans offer various advantages to employers and employees. Recently, there has been an increase in the number of defined contribution plans offered by employers. Reasons for this trend should become clear as you read this section.

For both defined benefit and defined contribution plans, benefits generally become available upon:

- Retirement

- Death

- Disability

- Termination[5]

Benefit payments are available as either a lifetime annuity or a lump sum. An annuity is a stream of regular payments, usually on a monthly basis. A joint and survivor annuity option is required by law so that a surviving spouse continues to receive some benefit after the retiree's death. Lump-sum options, which are common for defined contribution plans, allocate the entire value of the benefit to the retiree at once. Lump sums offer the advantage of providing retirees with a large sum of money, with the disadvantage of having to carefully budget that money since there are no continuing payments.

Defined Benefit Plans. A defined benefit plan uses a formula to determine the actual retirement benefits that a retiree will receive. The amount of the benefit is defined by the formula, thus the name *defined benefit plan*. The formula generally is tied to the employee's earnings, age, or years of service. Employees generally do not contribute to a defined benefit plan. Employer contributions are placed in a fund designated for the defined benefit plan. The amount of money contributed to the plan will vary based on financial performance of the investments and other factors. The formulas and actuarial assumptions used to calculate how much to contribute to fund the benefit are quite complex. However, the formula used to determine an employee's benefit can be straightforward. Three examples of defined benefit plans are based on the following formulas:

- *Career average pay formula*—e.g., 2 percent of career average earnings for each year of service

- *Final average plan*—e.g., 2 percent of final average earnings for each year of service

- *Flat benefit*—e.g., $30 per month for each year of service (common for union plans or hourly employees)

In a defined benefit plan, the employer bears the risk of providing the level of benefit that is specified by the formula. Contributions needed over the years may increase or decrease depending on various factors in the economy, such as stock market performance. Some defined benefit plans also take into consideration the effects of inflation in their formulas, which is an additional type of risk that is then borne by the employer.

Defined Contribution Plans. A defined contribution plan establishes an individual employee account to which the employer and/or employee make annual or periodic contributions. Unlike a defined benefit plan, there is no guarantee of a certain level of benefit upon retirement. Rather, the *contribution* is defined, and the benefit payable at retirement reflects the balance of the employee's individual account. The employee bears the investment risk associated with the balance of the account, as well as the inflation risk. There are several types of defined contribution plans, some of which may be combined to incorporate the features of multiple plans:

- *Savings plan.* Also known as a thrift plan, a savings plan generally is funded by employee contributions that are made on an after-tax basis. Employers may design the plan to include a full or partial match on employee contributions to the plan, but employer contributions are not legally required for a savings plan.

- *401(k) plan.* Named after the section of the Internal Revenue Code referring to cash or deferred arrangements, a 401(k) plan enables employees to elect to have employer contributions and/or a portion of their compensation deposited on a pretax basis into an eligible defined contribution plan. Other plans, such as savings plans, can use the pretax contribution feature if they are compliant with the requirements of Section 401(k). The pretax feature is advantageous to both employees and employers because it reduces an employee's salary before federal and most state taxes are taken out. This creates a reduced taxable income for employees and reduced payroll taxes for employers.

- *Profit-sharing plan.* Discretionary employer contributions are made to an employee's individual account in a profit-sharing plan. Contributions are generally tied to the employer's annual profits, but there is no requirement for employers to make a contribution when they have profits. Rather, employers need only make substantial and recurring contributions. A typical profit-sharing award is a percentage of an employee's wages, such as 5 percent of annual salary.

- *Money purchase plan.* This plan uses mandatory employer contributions that are generally stated as a percentage of the employee's salary to fund the plan. Although an individual account is kept for administrative purposes, all employee accounts are usually combined for investment purposes.

MODULE
18

- *Employee stock ownership plan* (ESOP). An ESOP allows employees to share in the ownership of their employing organization through shares of stock that are awarded to them. ESOPS are required to invest primarily in the organization's stock. Two attractive features of ESOPs to employers are the ability to borrow money against the ESOP and tax advantages that can lower the cost of financing corporate transactions.

The growth trends in private retirement plans provide a good example of the move away from a paternalistic approach to benefits. Watson Wyatt Worldwide, a consulting firm specializing in employee benefits, reported that the total number of defined benefit plans has decreased from 168,000 in 1984 to 78,000 in 1995, whereas the number of defined contribution plans has grown from 436,000 to 660,000 in that same time period (Inglis 1997). However, defined benefit plans were not always replaced with defined contribution plans. Many larger employers have supplemented their defined benefit plan with a defined contribution plan. The latter are appealing to employers in today's business environment due to their ability to transfer the risk of providing a sufficient level of benefits to the employee. Rather than promising a predetermined level of benefits that may be difficult to fund given changing business conditions and increasing numbers of retirees, the employer commits to providing a contribution to employee accounts. The investment and inflation risk associated with that contribution is borne by the employee.

This shift away from paternalism and an entitlement mentality requires employees to take a more active role in planning for their retirement. Under traditionally defined benefit programs, employees generally were not concerned with the funding of their pensions because a certain benefit was guaranteed. Under defined contribution plans, employees are responsible for monitoring their accounts to ensure that their balances are sufficient. However, many employees are unaware of how much they will need to contribute to their accounts, and in those cases where the employee controls the investment of the account balance, how to invest the money. Retirees are generally able to maintain their preretirement standard of living if they are able to replace 50–80 percent of their preretirement income using social security, employer retirement plan(s), and personal savings. Many employers educate their workforce through booklets, information sessions, and interactive computer programs to help employees plan for their retirement. These types of education are advantageous to employers because they can increase employee satisfaction with their retirement plan and they protect employers from liability for employees' investment returns.

MODULE
18

Health and Welfare Benefits

Health and welfare benefits are commonly grouped together and are sometimes collectively referred to as welfare benefits. Although some health and welfare benefits can be extended into an employee's retirement, these benefits are targeted at providing coverage during an employee's working career.

Medical Benefits.   Health benefits have been facing a revolution since the early 1970s. In an attempt to control skyrocketing healthcare costs, employers have turned to managed-care options that alter the traditional approach to the delivery and financing of healthcare. Although many people think of managed care as a particular type of healthcare, there are a range of managed-care options. Managed care also applies to health plans in addition to medical plans, such as dental. Figure 18.3 identifies some of the major forms of managed care, although new forms are continually developing.

As Figure 18.3 demonstrates, managed-care plans trade beneficiary choice for increased cost control. A traditional fee-for-service plan provides beneficiaries with the greatest degree of choice in healthcare services and providers, but this level of choice is costly for employers. A managed-care plan uses a different manner of delivering

FIGURE 18.3 *Healthcare Delivery System Spectrum*

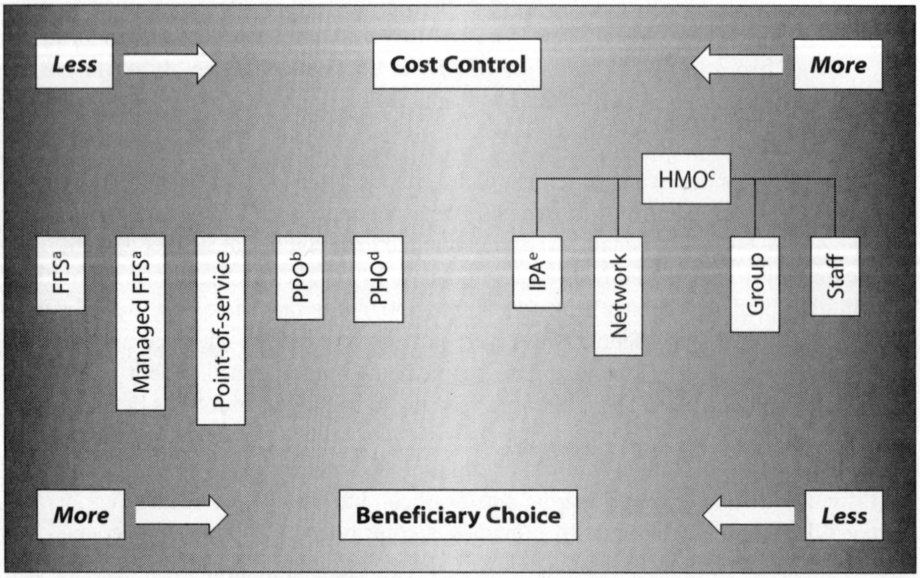

Source: Sarah Snider, "Features of Employer-Sponsored Health Plans," EBRI Issue Brief no. 128 (Employee Benefit Research Institute, August 1992).

[a]Fee-for-service   [d]Physician hospital organization
[b]Preferred provider organization   [e]Independent practice association
[c]Health maintenance organization

healthcare that results in reduced choice for the beneficiary, but also reduced costs. Sample cost saving features of managed-care plans include:

- *Preadmission certification*—participants must receive prior authorizations for non-emergency hospital admissions, elective surgery, and certain other procedures. This is one component of a larger program known as "utilization review" that is common to most forms of managed care.

- *Provider networks*—must be used by participants to receive a preferred "in network" level of benefits. Preferred provider organizations, physician hospital organizations, and point-of-service plans all offer more generous benefit levels for using network providers. For health maintenance organizations (HMOs), there generally are no out-of-network benefits.

- *Primary care physician*—plan participants must select a primary-care physician who coordinates their care. Participants must see the primary-care physician before seeing a specialist. Primary-care physicians are a feature used in point-of-service plans, PHOs, and HMOs.

The various provisions related to managed care and traditional medical coverage can be confusing to someone unfamiliar with healthcare plans. Employers should clearly communicate plan design features to employees. If employees can choose from amongst several medical options, it is critical that they understand the plans so that they can make informed benefit choices. Sample common terms related to managed care and medical coverage in general are listed in Table 18.1.

Managed care can be introduced gradually into an organization by offering a traditional fee-for-service plan and a managed care plan. Another approach would be to offer a managed-care plan that offers a fairly high level of beneficiary choice, such as a PPO. As with all benefit transitions, communication is critical. Employees are more

TABLE 18.1 *Common Health Care Terms*

Co-insurance	Participant cost sharing based on a percentage of costs incurred (e.g., 80 percent/20 percent would require employees to pay 20 percent of charges after meeting any applicable deductible)
Copayment	Participant cost sharing that is a flat dollar fee per service provided (e.g., $10 per office visit)
Deductible	The costs that a participant must incur before benefits are paid (e.g., a $500 deductible would require a participant to spend $500 on healthcare before being eligible for coinsurance)
In-network/Out-of-network	The distinction between providers that have contracted with the healthcare plan (in-network) and all other providers. Participants receive a more generous level of benefits for using network providers (e.g., 80 percent/20 percent coinsurance in-network; 70 percent/30 percent coinsurance out-of-network).
Premium	The cost of healthcare coverage for an insured plan. Employers may require employee contributions toward premium costs (e.g., $5,000 annual premium for individual indemnity coverage; employee may contribute $150 per month).
Primary-care physician	Chosen by participant as the coordinator of care for plans requiring a primary care physician. Participants must see the primary-care physician before seeing a specialist. Primary-care physicians are often referred to as "gatekeepers" because they monitor participant access to healthcare services.
Utilization review	An intervention into decisions related to healthcare in order to limit the inappropriate use of benefits under the plan (e.g., requiring a second opinion before performing a surgical procedure; preadmission certification for nonemergency hospital admissions, elective surgery, and certain other procedures)

likely to view managed care positively if the employer communicates the drastic increases in healthcare costs and that alternative approaches that maintained beneficiary choice would increase employee contributions to the healthcare plan.

The managed-care revolution has generated savings, but costs continue to rise. Some employers that have already implemented managed-care programs are now looking to pass costs along to employees through increased premium contributions and copayments. Although participants' choices have been restricted by managed-care plans, their use of healthcare services has not decreased, possibly due to the low copayments for routine services. Cost sharing may encourage participants to be more cautious in deciding when to use services.

Rising costs are not the only healthcare concern that employers face. Concerns about the quality of healthcare provided under managed-care plans also have become an important factor. The National Committee for Quality Assurance (NCQA) is a private, not-for-profit organization that assesses and reports on the quality of managed-care plans to enable purchasers and consumers of managed healthcare to make informed decisions. Several news magazines also rate managed-care plan quality. Continued attention in this area will drive managed-care companies to address issues of quality in order to remain competitive.

Although medical plans are the most costly of employer healthcare offerings, many employers offer additional health benefits to meet the needs of their employees. Dental, vision, and prescription drug plans are three such plans.

Dental Benefits. The two primary objectives of a dental plan are to help pay for dental care and to encourage participants to receive regular dental attention (EBRI 1997). Preventive care is critical to controlling dental costs, as standard examinations, x-rays, and cleanings are much less costly than procedures to correct serious problems, such as endodontics and crowns. Plans may pay a percentage of dental charges, a flat dollar amount per procedure, or the entire cost of services after a patient copayment. Preventive care is often covered at a more generous rate than corrective procedures.

Although the managed-care revolution has not affected dental plans to the extent that it has affected medical plans, preferred provider organizations and dental HMOs are growing in popularity. Costs for traditional indemnity dental plans have increased 8 to 10 percent annually, whereas dental HMO costs have increased only 5 percent or less per year (Harris 1997). Enrollment in managed dental plans is rising, and analysts predict that within ten years, more than half of all employees will be in a some form of managed dental plan (Harris 1997).

Vision Benefits. Traditional medical plans have offered little or no vision coverage, despite the fact that more than half of the population in the United States requires optometric care (EBRI 1997). Vision plans commonly cover routine eye examinations, eyeglasses, and contact lenses. Eye surgery and treatment of eye disease are generally covered by medical plans rather than vision plans.

Prescription Drug Benefits. Many medical plans offer prescription drug coverage, yet employers may choose to offer a separate prescription drug plan for price discounts or ease of use for beneficiaries. Cost-controlling features include the substitution of generic drugs for more expensive name brands and mail-in programs for maintenance drugs.

Group Life Insurance. Employers have traditionally provided group life insurance plans as a welfare benefit for their employees. The benefit provided by life insurance is a cash payment paid to the employee's beneficiary(ies) on his or her death. The amount of the benefit may vary by job level or an earnings schedule, or it may be a flat benefit amount for all employees.

The most common form of group life insurance is group term life insurance, which generally provides coverage that can be renewed annually by employees. This type of plan provides only a death benefit; premiums paid over the years do not develop any cash value.

Group universal life insurance is a newer form of life insurance that developed in the 1980s, partly due to the success of individual universal life insurance in the private market and changes to the tax treatment of traditional group term life insurance (employer-provided term life insurance greater than $50,000 is taxable after retirement). A group universal life insurance plan uses only employee contributions; participation is voluntary. The plan has two components: renewable term insurance and a cash accumulation fund. At the end of the covered period, the term price ends unless the coverage is continued. However, contributions to the cash accumulation fund remain with the employee. The portability of GUL is an advantage for employees who terminate or retire. A GUL policy can be continued by paying premiums directly to the insurance company. There are also loan and withdrawal features similar to those of some defined contribution retirement plans.

Accidental death and dismemberment (AD&D) insurance is often included with group life insurance. AD&D insurance provides benefits for the loss of a limb or an eye due to an accident, and it provides a larger benefit in the case of accidental death.

Disability Insurance. The two forms of disability insurance most commonly offered by employers are short-term disability (STD) insurance and long-term disability (LTD) insurance. STD plans generally provide up to six months of wage replacement for an employee with illness or injury that prevents the employee from working. LTD plans offer benefits to employees who have been unable to work for at least six months, thus picking up when STD plans generally terminate. Both STD and LTD only replace a portion of an employee's wages, providing an incentive for employees to return to work and receive full wages.

Long-Term Care Insurance.   Many employees must plan for the care of their parents and parents-in-law, as well as their own future long-term care. The growing number of dual-career families and increased life expectancies make long-term care insurance a potentially appealing mechanism to plan for the financial burden of long-term care. Long-term care includes a variety of health and social support services, including skilled nursing care, custodial care for activities of daily living, and home care for individuals who suffer from a cognitive impairment (such as Alzheimer's disease) or are unable to perform activities of daily living on their own. Such services are generally not covered by medicare, potentially creating a financial burden for the individual requiring care and his or her family. Employees are generally able to enroll themselves, their parents, or their parents-in-law for long-term care insurance.

Work/Life and Miscellaneous Benefits

When health, welfare, and retirement benefits were developed early in the twentieth century, one goal of these offerings was to meet the needs of the workforce. Employers also began to offer additional benefits that did not neatly fall into one of these three categories, such as paid time off and educational assistance, to meet workforce needs, and thus attract and retain employees.

The workforce of today is increasingly diverse, with different benefit needs than those of past employees. One dramatic change has been the presence of women in the workforce, and the resulting number of dual-career and single-parent families making up an organization's workforce. Although traditional health, welfare, and retirement benefits are important to today's workforce, these workers have additional needs. Benefits that assist with juggling work and family roles were initially called *work/family* benefits. Later acknowledgment that these benefits also are valuable to employees without families resulted in the more inclusive *work/life* term. Employers have begun to recognize that employees face personal issues that may affect them during their working time, such as childcare, eldercare, and home repairs. Work/life benefits can assist employees in balancing these needs by providing:

- *Adoption benefits.* An increasing number of employers offer reimbursement for the adoption of a child.

- *Child and elder care assistance.* Options include financial support, resource and referral services to assist in finding a provider, sick/emergency care, and on-site daycare centers.

- *Convenience benefits.* On-site services, such as dry cleaning, auto repair, and banking, enable employees to more easily accomplish routine tasks.

- *Employee assistance program (EAP).* These programs can exist as a resource and referral service, or they can include counseling to deal with issues that affect an employee's ability to concentrate at work. Substance abuse, family matters, and financial difficulties are among the issues dealt with by EAPs.

- *Flexibility.* Flexible work arrangements include the ability to work from a location that minimizes commuting time, such as the home; the ability to change start and stop times to better accommodate scheduling needs; and the ability to reduce the number of days or hours worked.

MODULE
18

This list identifies only the major types of work/life benefits. New forms of work/life benefits frequently emerge, and the number of programs employers include as work/life benefits varies. The following benefits are not always categorized as "work/life" benefits, yet they address work/life issues. (See Kossek, Module 11, for more on work/life issues.)

Paid Time Off.   Paid holidays, vacation time, sick time, and personal time existed before the term "work/life" came into existence. However, there are similarities between paid time off programs and other benefits aimed at meeting work/life needs. Some forms of time off are generally standard for all employees, such as holidays. However, other forms, such as vacation time, may increase with length of service. Time off for family and medical reasons now must be considered in conjunction with the Family and Medical Leave Act (FMLA), which requires employers to offer unpaid leave to employees for qualifying reasons. (See the section about FMLA on page 18.8. See also Riley, Module 10, on administering the provisions of the FMLA.)

Educational Assistance.   Employers offering educational assistance, also known as tuition reimbursement programs, pay for educational expenses, such as tuition, fees, and books. Existing legislation offers tax advantages to employers' educational assistance expenses, but it not clear that these advantages will continue (the section of the Internal Revenue Code related to this issue expires in the year 2000). However, this expiration date has been extended several times in the past, and could certainly be extended again.

Other miscellaneous benefits in addition to paid time off and educational assistance exist. Relocation expense reimbursement, company cars, and free or subsidized meals are only a few examples. Work/life and other benefits are a way to meet workforce needs with benefits that are valued. Although the employer's contribution to work/life and other benefits may be fairly low, the perceived value of such benefits can often be high, due to their ability to meet employee needs.

Design

The design of the employee benefits package should be consistent with the employer's total compensation philosophy, but it should also take into consideration the needs of the employee population. The types and levels of benefits offered, eligibility and participation requirements, and cost-sharing provisions all are part of employee benefit plan design. Given that the design of individual benefit offerings has already been discussed, this section focuses on the design of the overall benefit package—specifically, flexible benefit plans.

Flexible Benefit Plans.   Benefit plans were originally designed with a "one size fits" all approach. A standard package of health, retirement, and/or other benefits designed to meet the needs of a "traditional" family was offered to all employees. As discussed in relation to work/life benefits, a large portion of today's diverse workforce consists of single employees without children, dual-career couples, and single parents. The needs of today's workforce may not be best met with one standard package, but rather with a package that can be adjusted to each employee's needs.

A flexible benefits plan, also known as a *cafeteria plan,* allows employees to choose from a variety of benefit offerings. The amount of choice in a flexible benefits plan varies based on how the employer designs the flexible benefit plan. Some plans allow for choice only among several medical options, whereas other plans offer optional benefits, such as vision and long-term care insurance, that the employee can choose to elect if desired.

MODULE
18

Employers generally subsidize the cost of benefits. The cost that is passed along to the employee is the difference between the actual cost and the employer subsidy.

Total benefit cost = Employer subsidy + Employee contribution

Many employers using flexible benefits provide employees with credits or "benefit dollars" to be used for purchasing their benefits. The credits allocated to the employee are in effect the employer subsidy. If an employee wishes to "purchase" benefit coverage costing more than the value of his or her credits, additional money from the employee's salary can be put toward benefit costs. Federal legislation permits employees to use credits and salary reduction to purchase benefits without tax implications.

As an alternative to using a credit and price tag approach, employers can determine the net price an employee must pay for benefits after subtracting the employer subsidy. If the employer fully subsidizes a benefit, the net price for the employee would be zero. However, if the employer only partially subsidizes the full price of the benefit, the remaining net price will be passed along to the employee as a price tag. Rather than communicate the subsidy to the employee in the form of credits, the employer only communicates the necessary employee contribution for a particular benefit. If an employee chooses not to elect a certain benefit, he or she may be eligible to receive cash back. This is sometimes referred to as "opting out of coverage."

Employees may accumulate excess credits or cash from purchasing low levels of coverage or by opting out of coverage. Employers must determine how to distribute these excess amounts to employees. If employees receive cash for these amounts, they must be taxed on the full value. However, if employees roll the cash or credits into a tax-qualified plan, such as a flexible spending account (described below) or a 401(k) plan, they will not have tax consequences. Employees may also need to pay for their benefits using money from their salaries, especially if they purchase a high level of benefits. For tax-qualified plans, such as medical plans, employees do not have to pay tax on the money from their salary used to pay for benefits.

Healthcare spending accounts (also called healthcare flexible spending accounts) are a feature of flexible benefit plans that allow employees to set money aside on a pretax basis to pay for medically related expenses that are not covered by health insurance, such as copayments on contact lenses that are not covered by a vision plan. Employees simply specify an amount that they would like to set aside in the FSA and then submit claims against the balance throughout the year. The only cost to employers is the administration of the plan. The cost to employees is the risk of "losing" money that is put into the account if claims are not incurred within the year since the account has a "use it or lose it" rule.

A flexible benefit plan must follow certain requirements related to a plan year, which is often a calendar year. Once each year, employees must be given the opportunity to change their benefit elections. After the elections are made, the employee generally cannot change benefit options unless certain life events take place (e.g., birth or adoption of a child, change in spouse benefits).

Funding

The costs related to employee benefit plans can be funded in several ways. Employers can choose different funding approaches for the various plans they offer, depending on the cost and efficiency for each type of plan. Health and welfare plans are generally funded using an insurance arrangement or self-funding, whereas retirement plan funding involves making and investing employer contributions while taking into account legal and tax implications.

Insurance vs. Self-Funding.   When an employer purchases an insurance contract, premiums are paid to the insurance company in exchange for specific levels of benefits.

The risk of excessively high claims is borne primarily by the insurance provider (although employer premiums may be adjusted to reflect actual claims experience). Employers often choose an insurance contract to avoid this risk, even if premium costs may be higher than the costs an employer would incur to pay claims in a "typical" year. Some large employers prefer not to use an insurance contract, but rather to pay for claims themselves. This arrangement, known as self-funding, can be efficient for employers if the claims experience is generally less costly than premium payments.

Funding Retirement Benefits.   Funding requirements vary for qualified defined benefit and defined contribution plans, and also for different types of defined contribution plans. Defined benefit plans are subject to minimum funding standards under ERISA, which ensure that plans will have sufficient assets to pay benefits. Defined contribution plans are not subject to such minimum funding standards because the only benefit to which the beneficiary is entitled is that which has already been funded (i.e., the balance of the account). Retirement plan funds must be set aside from other company assets in one of several funding media, such as a trust.

Administration

Benefits is an administratively intense component of human resource management. Employee benefit administration involves the passage of information among the organization, plan participants, vendors. Benefit coverage changes daily as employees join the organization, terminate, retire, change their coverage options, and so on. In the past, most of these changes were made using paper forms that contained data that was manually entered into a payroll or human resources information system. Improvements in technology have reduced manual data entry, but have created a need for sophisticated information systems to collect, track, and report benefit information. Another administrative issue concerns regulatory compliance. Employers are required by law to produce certain reports for the government and for participants.

Figure 18.4 depicts a simplified model of the exchanges of data that take place as part of benefit administration. The human resources department provides the employee or other participant (e.g., retiree) with available benefit choices and reports of current elections and account balances. The employee/participant provides the human resources department with changes in coverage, mailing address, eligible dependents, and so on. After receiving employee data, the human resources department sends reports to the government in accordance with ERISA and provides election data to any plan vendors, such as a medical insurance company or a retirement plan administrator.

Outsourcing.   At the beginning of this module, we suggested that many employers are outsourcing the administration of benefits. Although outsourcing is not necessarily the right solution for every organization, deciding whether to do so is a key issue for human resource managers. Three goals of outsourcing are enhanced value, increased speed, and reduced costs (Jeffay, Bohannon, and Laspisa 1997).

- *Enhanced value.* By freeing up resources dedicated to benefit administration, outsourcing enables an organization to focus its areas of specialization, which are its core competencies. For an organization that specializes in human resources outsourcing, benefits administration *is* a core competency; therefore such an organization has top-notch systems and processes, as well as people whose primary focus is benefit administration who can build off of experiences with multiple client organizations.

- *Increased speed.* Technological, legislative, and other changes keep benefits administrators on their toes. Outsourcing providers can leverage the economies of scale associated with multiple client organizations to efficiently address changes. For

FIGURE 18.4   *Data Exchanges in Benefit Administration*

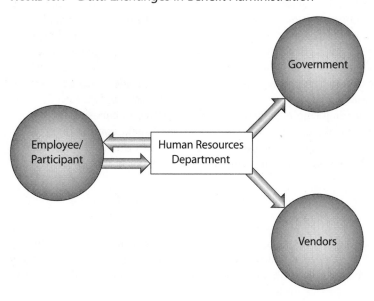

example, an outsourcing organization may have legal staff dedicated to benefits issues who serve all outsourcing clients. A client organization, on the other hand, will more likely have legal staff that specialize in issues related to its core competencies.

- *Reduced costs.* Outsourcing can reduce costs by improving efficiencies, which results in providing better service at a lower cost. The effects on overall costs will depend on the level of service and administrative efficiency provided before and after outsourcing. Given that part of the effectiveness of outsourcing is based on economies of scale, the size of the client organization may also play a role in the level of cost reduction, with larger organizations realizing greater reductions in costs.

In-House Administration.   An organization can effectively administer it own benefit programs if the proper systems exist and knowledgeable people understand the complexities of administration. Given that a single organization will not benefit from the economies of scale associated with outsourcing, in-house administration makes it difficult to match the speed or top-notch service of an outsourcing provider. However, in-house administration can be a viable and cost-effective solution.

STRATEGIC ISSUES IN EMPLOYEE BENEFITS

Benefits strategy should be part of the total compensation strategy in an organization that fosters a total compensation perspective. Benefits strategy may be separated from the strategy used for direct compensation, or it may flow from that strategy. The former approach allows employers to differentiate how competitive they wish to be in either direct compensation or benefits, and to raise or lower each component accordingly. Which of these two approaches an organization uses may vary on a number of factors, including the stage in the organization's life cycle. For example, a growing firm may offer average direct compensation but lower levels of benefits due to their short-term focus on growth. On the other hand, more mature organizations focused on security may offer higher levels of benefits to foster a long-term employment relationship.

MODULE
18

Thinking strategically requires analysis of the conditions inside the organization as well as the environment outside of the organization. Conducting a needs analysis is critical to determining benefit offerings. Employers also must examine competitor offerings, costs, and other factors. Benefits strategy involves an ongoing cycle of assessing needs, planning and implementing changes, gathering feedback, and reassessing needs.

The move away from paternalism and entitlement is strategic in nature. External pressures have encouraged employers to seek new ways to meet employee needs while controlling costs. Providing employees with a more active role in choosing their benefits empowers them to make the most of their employer's benefit contributions. Communication is needed to let employees know the advantages and the risks of such empowerment, as well as the reasons that many employers are moving in this direction.

APPLICATION

Imagine that you are the benefits director for a growing organization of approximately 2,000 employees. Your workforce is demographically diverse (e.g., age, gender, family responsibilities) in composition. Currently, your organization offers the following standard benefit package at no cost to its employees:

- Traditional indemnity medical plan for employee (family coverage available for an additional fee)

- Traditional indemnity dental plan for employee (family coverage available for a fee)

- Life insurance worth one times the employee's annual salary

- Long-term disability insurance worth 60 percent of employee's predisability salary

- 401(k) retirement plan with employer match for first $500 contributed by employee

Prepare a high-level proposal for the VP of Human Resources suggesting the implementation of a flexible benefits plan. Discuss changes you would make upon implementing the flexible benefits plan. Would you add additional benefits? Would employees share in the costs of the benefits? Make any necessary assumptions related to the current plan to justify your recommendations for the flexible benefit plan.

IN CONCLUSION

Debrief

Although employee benefits have traditionally been a highly administrative aspect of human resource management, changes in the workforce, business needs, and technology have compelled human resource managers to take a more strategic approach to employee benefits.

To offer a benefits package that is attractive to both employees and the organization, managers must consider both what employees perceive as valuable and the needs of the business. Keeping apprised of the types of available benefits, trends in benefit plan availability and use, and the regulatory environment is essential. Managers also must analyze how they can efficiently and effectively administer their benefits.

The overview provided in this module touches on major areas related to employee benefit management. Clearly, effective employee benefit management requires more in-depth knowledge. Although one could easily discuss the regulatory environment, plan design, and administration for an entire semester or more, the objective of this module is to create an understanding of key issues related to employee benefits. Keeping an eye on the big picture is essential to taking a strategic approach towards employee benefits. As human resource management moves into the twenty-first century, such a strategic perspective will become increasingly important to benefit management decisions and actions.

Suggested Readings

Ruth, Linda C., Bruner, Jack. E., and Chamernik, Aimee. L. "Benefits strategy: The new deal" *Compensation and Benefits Management,* Spring 1995, 7–15.

Critical Thinking Questions

1. Why would an employer want to communicate a total compensation perspective to employees?

2. How do defined benefit plans and defined contribution plans differ in terms of the amount of risk borne by the employer? Which type of plan exemplifies a move away from entitlement? Why?

3. Explain the trade-off between beneficiary choice and cost control in managed-care plans. Compare and contrast indemnity plans and HMOs as part of your answer.

Exercise

Imagine that you are a 40-year-old with a spouse and three young children. Your spouse is self-employed, and although the salary is adequate, he or she does not have any employee benefits (other than benefits he or she could purchase privately). You are considering the following two job offers. Assuming that all other features of the job are equivalent, which offer would you choose and why?

Offer A (annual compensation)
Salary:	$60,000
Bonus:	$5,000–$10,000
Dollar value of health benefits:	$6,000
Dollar value of retirement benefits:	$10,000

Offer B (annual compensation)
Salary:	$65,000
Bonus:	$5,000–$10,000
Dollar value of health benefits:	$2,000
Dollar value of retirement benefits:	$5,000

References

EBRI. *Fundamentals of Employee Benefit Programs (5th ed.)* Washington D.C.: Employee Benefit Research Institute, 1997.

Inglis, R. Evan. "Defined benefit plans still measure up." *HR Magazine,* June 1997, 123–128.

Harris, Lee J. "Smile: Vast changes in the dental industry means lower prices, better service and more options for employers." *HR Magazine,* August 1997.

Jeffay, Jason, Bohannon, Stephen, and Laspisa, Ester K. "Beyond benefits: The changing face of HR outsourcing." *Benefits Quarterly,* First Quarter, 1997.

Myers, Robert J. "Social Security and Medicare." In J. S. Rosenbloom (ed.) *The Handbook of Employee Benefits (4th ed.).* New York: McGraw-Hill. 1996.

Endnotes

1. Individuals born before 1929 need fewer credits.
2. Individuals also can be eligible for Medicare Part A by participating in the Railroad Retirement program.
3. Disabled OASDI and Railroad Retirement beneficiaries also are eligible for HI.
4. The social security tax is only applied to wages up to the taxable wage base. For 1999, the taxable wage base is $72,600.
5. For individuals below normal or early retirement age, penalties apply if the benefit is not rolled into another plan or an individual retirement account.

Index

···

Additional benefits, 18.10, 18.15, 18.17, 18.18
Adoption benefits, 18.17
Annuity, 18.11
Attracting/retaining employees, 18.6, 18.17

Beneficiary choice, 18.13, 18.14
Benefit administration, 18.4, 18.5, 18.20, 18.22
Benefit credits, 18.19. *See also* Employee contribution
Benefits regulations, 18.6, 18.7, 18.22

Career average pay formula, 18.12
Child and elder care assistance, 18.17
Co-insurance, 18.15
Collective bargaining, 18.7
Consolidated Omnibus Reconciliation Act (COBRA), 18.8
Contributions, employer, 18.12. *See also* Employee contribution, Employer-provided benefit plans
Convenience benefits, 18.17
Copayment, 18.15, 18.19
Cost sharing, 18.15, 18.18–19
Covered employment, 18.9

Defined benefit plans, 18.11, 18.13. *See also* Retirement plan benefits
Defined contributions plans, 18.11, 18.12, 18.13
Dental plan, 18.16
Direct compensation, 18.6
Disability insurance, 18.9, 18.16

Economic factors, 18.12
Educational assistance, 18.18
Eligibility for benefits, 18.8, 18.9–10
Eligible dependents, 18.7
Employee assistance program (EAP), 18.17
Employee benefit plan design, 18.18
Employee benefits, 18.4, 18.5–7, 18.13, 18.19, 18.21–22
Employee contribution, 18.19. *See also* Benefit credits
Employee Retirement Income Security Act (ERISA), 18.7–8, 18.20
Employee stock ownership plan (ESOP), 18.13
Employer-provided benefit plans, 18.5, 18.10, 18.11, 18.16
Employment-related insurance programs, 18.9
Entitlement, 18.4, 18.13, 18.22
Ethical considerations (benefits), 18.7
Experience rated, 18.10

401(k) plan, 18.12, 18.19
Family and Medical Leave Act (FMLA), 18.8, 18.18
Favorable tax legislation, 18.6
Federal Insurance Contributions Act (FICA), 18.10
Federal Unemployment Tax Act (FUTA), 18.10
Fee-for-service plan, 18.13, 18.14
Fiduciary standards (benefit plans), 18.8
Final average plan, 18.12
Flat benefit, 18.12
Flexible benefit plans, 18.18–19
Flexible spending account (FSA), 18.19
Flexible work arrangements, 18.17
Fully insured status, 18.9
Funding (benefit plans), 18.8, 18.12, 18.13, 18.19, 18.20

Government retirement programs, 18.10
Group life insurance, 18.16
Group universal life (GUL) insurance, 18.16

Health and welfare plans/benefits, 18.8, 18.13, 18.19
Health Insurance Portability and Accountability Act (HIPAA), 18.8
Healthcare, 18.13, 18.14, 18.15
Human resource management, 18.4, 18.20
Human resource manager, 18.4, 18.20
Human resources, 18.4

In-house administration, 18.21
In-network/Out-of-network, 18.15
Indirect compensation, 18.6
Individual equity principle, 18.9
Insurance contract, 18.19–20
Insurance provider, 18.20
Investment and inflation risk, 18.12, 18.13

Long-term care insurance, 18.17, 18.18
Long-term disability (LTD) insurance, 18.16–17
Long-term employment relationship, 18.21
Lump sum benefit payments, 18.11

Managed-care plans, 18.13, 18.14, 18.15
Mandatory contributions, 18.12
Medical coverage, 18.13, 18.14, 18.18, 18.19
Medicare program, 18.9, 18.10, 18.17
Minimum funding standards, 18.20
Money purchase plan, 18.12

National Committee for Quality Assurance (NCQA), 18.15
Normal retirement age, 18.10

Old Age, Survivors, and Disability Insurance Program (OASDI), 18.9
Optional benefits, 18.18. *See also* Additional benefits
Outsourcing, human resources, 18.20–21

Paid time off, 18.17, 18.18
Plan administrator, 18.20
Plan termination insurance, 18.8
PPO, 18.14
Predetermined level of benefits, 18.13
Preexisting condition exclusions, 18.8
Premium, 18.8, 18.15, 18.19–20
Preretirement income, 18.13
Prescription drug benefits, 18.16
Primary Insurance Amount (PIA), 18.9
Primary-care physician, 18.15
Private retirement plans, 18.13
Private-sector employers, 18.8
Profit-sharing plan, 18.12

Reporting and disclosure requirements, 18.7, 18.8, 18.20
Retirement plan benefits, 18.9, 18.11, 18.12, 18.13

Savings plan, 18.12
Self-funded program, 18.11, 18.19–20
Short-term disability (STD) insurance, 18.16–17
Social adequacy principle, 18.9
Social Insurance programs, 18.9
Social security, 18.9, 18.10, 18.13
Summary plan description (SPD), 18.7. *See also* ERISA
Supplementary medical insurance, 18.9, 18.10
Survivors benefits, 18.9

Tax-qualified plans, 18.19
Temporary disability insurance, 18.10–11
Three-legged stool retirement, 18.11
Total compensation perspective, 18.6, 18.18, 18.21
Tuition reimbursement programs. *See* Educational assistance
Twenty-first century, 18.4, 18.10

Unemployment insurance, 18.10
Utilization review, 18.15

Vesting (benefit plans), 18.8
Vision benefits, 18.16, 18.18, 18.19
Voluntary vs. mandatory benefits, 18.6

Weekly wage replacement, 18.11
Work/family benefits, 18.17
Work/life benefits, 18.17–18
Workers' compensation insurance, 18.6, 18.9, 18.10

MODULE
18

KOSSEK ■ BLOCK

MANAGING HUMAN RESOURCES IN THE 21st CENTURY

From Core Concepts to Strategic Choice

MODULE 19

Training and Employee Development

Laura L. Bierema
MICHIGAN STATE UNIVERSITY

Managing Human Resources in the 21st Century: From Core Concepts to Strategic Choice,
by Kossek and Block

Publisher: Dave Shaut
Executive Editor: John Szilagyi
Developmental Editor: Bryant Editorial Development
Marketing Manager: Joseph A. Sabatino
Production Editor: Tamborah E. Moore
Manufacturing Coordinator: Dana Began Schwartz
Cover Design: Tin Box Studio
Cover Photographs: Copyright Shoji Sato/Photonica
Production House: The Left Coast Group, Inc.
Printer: West Group

For more information contact South-Western College Publishing, 5101 Madison Road, Cincinnati,
Ohio, 45227 or find us on the Internet at *http://www.swcollege.com*
For permission to use material from this text or product, contact us by

- telephone: 1-800-730-2214
- fax: 1-800-730-2215
- web: *http://www.thomsonrights.com*

ISBN: 0–324–01818–5

This book is printed on acid-free paper.

Contents

MODULE OVERVIEW   19.4

OBJECTIVES   19.4

RELATION TO THE FRAME   19.5

SETTING THE CONTEXT FOR ORGANIZATIONAL LEARNING
IN A NEW MILLENNIUM   19.6

CORE CONCEPTS IN TRAINING AND EMPLOYEE DEVELOPMENT   19.7

Making the Decision to Train   19.8

Models of Training Planning and Design   19.9

The Role of Adult Learning in Training and Employee Development   19.14

Adult Learning: Establishing Goals for Learning and
Respecting Diverse Learning Styles   19.15

The Nuts and Bolts of Delivering Training   19.17

Effective Training Facilitation Strategies   19.20

Facilitating Training Transfer   19.23

Evaluating Training   19.24

STRATEGIC ISSUES IN TRAINING AND EMPLOYEE DEVELOPMENT   19.26

Linking Training to Organizational Strategy   19.26

The Shift from Training to Learning   19.26

The Learning Organization   19.26

Action Learning: Real Learning in Real Time   19.27

The Emergence of the "Learning Executive"   19.27

On-the-Job Training   19.28

Responding to a Rapidly Changing Environment   19.28

Deciding When to Hire a Consultant   19.28

Adopting a Customer Focus   19.28

Ethical Issues in Employee Training and Development   19.29

APPLICATION   19.29

IN CONCLUSION   19.29

Debrief   19.29

Suggested Readings   19.30

Relevant Web Sites   19.30

Critical Thinking Questions   19.30

Exercises   19.31

References   19.31

INDEX   19.33

MODULE
19

MODULE OVERVIEW

The purpose of this module is to introduce training and employee development. It is important for human resources professionals to be familiar with these concepts because the industrial age has shifted to the knowledge age, and the workforce is increasingly diverse and transforming from the physical to the virtual domain. Careers are becoming fluid with the expansion of the contingent workforce and the appearance of the free agent. Today, companies are competing as much for talent as for market share. Technological edge, market share, and good people are not enough, however, to make a company excel in a competitive environment. Competitiveness requires learning. The distinguishing feature between businesses that succeed and those that fail over hundreds of years lies in the ability to learn and adapt to the environment more effectively than the competition (deGeus 1997). Workplace learning has never been more important, and one strategy for surviving and thriving is learning. Marquardt observes that "A learning organization, systematically defined, is an organization which learns powerfully and collectively and is continually transforming itself to better collect, manage and use knowledge for corporate success" (1996, p. 19). Knowledge is doubling every two to three years, and communication mediums such as the Internet make it possible to exchange information as quickly as it is created. Learning is a powerful vehicle for fostering change. One way of cultivating it is through formal training and employee development.

Learning in the workplace is a major investment. The American Society for Training and Development (ASTD) reports that 1995 training expenditures in the United States totaled $55.3 billion. This is the equivalent of 1.46 percent of payroll or about $504 per employee. It is estimated that U.S. organizations spend over $200 billion annually on human resource development interventions (Training 1997), which include not only training, but also performance management, career development, and organizational development. These estimates do not account for lost time, which adds another $200 to $300 billion to the overall training investment (Robinson and Robinson 1998). Nor is training equally distributed among employees. Managerial-level employees receive the vast majority of training (ASTD 1998). Although there is a lot of money spent on training, not all of it is a sound investment. Robinson and Robinson (1998) estimate that less than 30 percent of what people learn is actually applied on the job, and that trainers tend to report activity (number of participant days, reactions to training), but not results. Trainers also tend to have an antagonistic relationship with management, reporting that one of their biggest challenges is lack of management support.

OBJECTIVES

HR leaders need to be discriminating in the selection, design, and delivery of training if they want a return on the training investment. Further, they need to understand the role of learning in the contemporary work context. Finally, they need to ensure that training is explicitly linked to organizational strategy. This module explores the process of training and employee development and workplace learning. The key learning objectives of this module are:

- To set the context for organizational learning in a new millennium

- To introduce the key terms related to training and employee development

- To understand when training is and is not an appropriate strategy

- To understand the different models of planning and designing training, including their strengths and weaknesses:

  ✓ Instructional Systems Design Model

  ✓ Human Performance Technology Model

- To understand the role of adult learning in training and employee development:
  - ✓ Understanding major principles
  - ✓ Identifying learning goals and objectives
  - ✓ Attending to different styles of learning

- To understand the nuts and bolts of delivering training:
  - ✓ Tips for designing training
  - ✓ Attending to the physical and psychological environment for training
  - ✓ Stimulating the senses

- To understand training facilitation strategies:
  - ✓ Instructional strategies
  - ✓ Starting training with style
  - ✓ Facilitating
  - ✓ Avoiding common training mistakes
  - ✓ Closing training
  - ✓ Evaluating training

- Facilitating training transfer:
  - ✓ Defining transfer
  - ✓ Building transfer strategies into training

- To understand strategic issues and future trends as they relate to training and employee development:
  - ✓ Linking training to organizational strategy
  - ✓ The shift from training to learning
  - ✓ The learning organization
  - ✓ Action learning
  - ✓ The emergence of the learning executive
  - ✓ On-the-job training
  - ✓ Responding to a rapidly changing environment
  - ✓ Deciding when to hire a consultant
  - ✓ Adopting a customer focus
  - ✓ Ethical issues

MODULE
19

RELATION TO THE FRAME

Learning plays a pivotal role at each level of the frame. Without learning, there would be no change, no performance improvement, and no innovation. Few companies could survive without change, performance, or innovation. Yet many companies fail to harness the resource that underlies sustained success: learning. Learning is regularly overlooked as a key resource in an organization. Learning is powerful, because every single employee has the capacity to learn. Smart organizations are finding ways to cultivate

FIGURE 19.1   *A Frame for Understanding Human Resource Strategy:*
Context, Roles, and Constraints

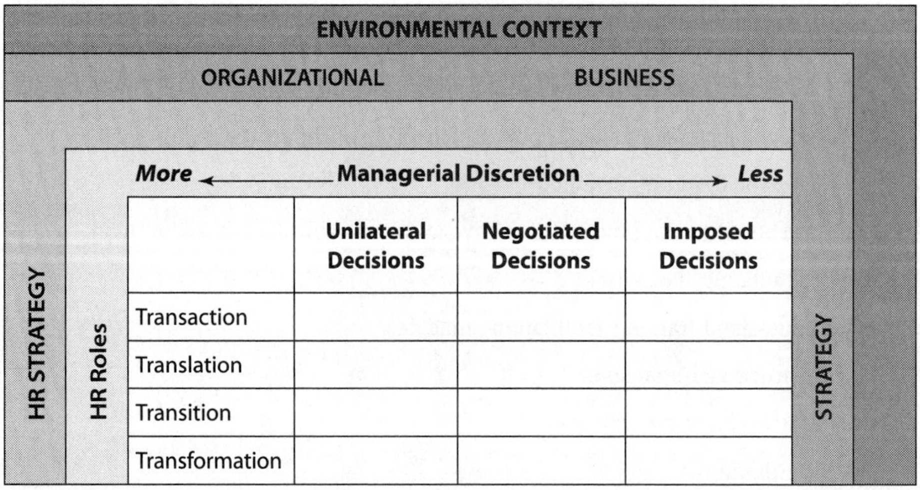

ENVIRONMENTAL CONTEXT			
ORGANIZATIONAL		**BUSINESS**	
More ← Managerial Discretion → *Less*			
	Unilateral Decisions	**Negotiated Decisions**	**Imposed Decisions**
Transaction			
Translation			
Transition			
Transformation			

(HR STRATEGY — HR Roles) ... (STRATEGY)

© 2000 by Ellen Ernst Kossek and Richard Block. Thanks to Brian Pentland, Karen Markel, and John Beck for helpful comments and discussions that enhanced the model.

MODULE
19

workplace learning, and capture and share lessons learned. After all, learning is the basis for individual and organizational change.

Training and employee development relate to the frame for HR roles and choices (Figure 19.1) in the following ways: training is a *transaction* that occurs with the goal of developing high-potential employees, building skill, complying with legislation and policy, and improving organizational performance. The *translation* aspect of training and employee development is the most challenging frame to accommodate, because learning occurring in the course of training will only be effective to the extent that it is accurately applied or *translated* to the work context. This is not an easy responsibility, as most training occurs in artificial contexts where employees are asked to simulate reality in their thinking and action. Bridging the gap between training and real life is often problematic. Effective training attends to transfer of learning. Training often serves a *transitional* role as organization policy changes, markets shift, and employees develop. Learning is the pivotal process in fostering any type of organizational *transformation;* thus training and learning play a key role here. It should be noted, however, that learning can be either formal (an organized session with specified goals), or informal (happening as a result of mistakes, experiences, and relationships). Finally, learning can only be transformational to the extent that it is tied to organizational strategy and transferred to the work context.

SETTING THE CONTEXT FOR ORGANIZATIONAL LEARNING IN A NEW MILLENNIUM

Learning is increasingly important as business globalizes, technology advances, and skills needed in the workplace constantly change and increase. Intense interest in the learning organization is not a mere coincidence. It comes at a time when learning is key to maintaining or improving competitive advantage. Training is one response organizations make to these demands. According to respondents to the July 1997 National HRD Executive Survey reported by the American Society for Training and Development, the trends shown in Table 19.1 are expected to influence training and employee development in the years to come.

TABLE 19.1 *Training Trends*

Currently	Next Three Years
1. Computer skills training	1. Shift from training to performance
2. Teamwork training	2. Computer skills training
3. Shift from training to performance	3. Shift from training to learning
4. Decision-making and problem-solving training	4. Virtual organizations
	5. Demonstrating training outcomes
5. Rapid development and deployment of training	6. Measuring performance outcomes
6. Systems-thinking training	7. Delivering training to meet specific needs
7. Demonstrating training outcomes	8. Emphasis on knowledge management
8. Measuring performance outcomes	9. Rapid development and deployment of training
9. Shift from training to learning	
10. Making a business case for training interventions	10. Teamwork training

Source: Selecting and Implementing Computer-Based Training, National Workforce Collaborative, 1997

CORE CONCEPTS IN TRAINING AND EMPLOYEE DEVELOPMENT

This section will define key terms in training and employee development. Employee training and development fall under the umbrella of the emerging field of human resource development, or HRD. In the following sections are some definitions to clarify the field.

Human Resource Development. HRD is concerned with learning and performance improvement for individuals, teams, and whole organizations. HRD integrates individual development, career development, performance management, and organization development with strategic goals and objectives.

Training. Training is any formal activity to improve current employee job performance, such as teaching employees new computer software, or orienting new employees to the policies and expectations of the company. Training also prepares employees for advancement. For instance, leadership training may be offered to develop employees' management potential, or tuition reimbursement programs may be provided to help employees build technical and administrative skills. Training provides performance enhancement to the organization, as well as growth for individuals on both the professional and personal level. Training is most effective when it is explicitly linked to organizational strategy, and is targeted at a problem that can be resolved by training.

Davis and Davis (1998, pp. 45–46) offer a comprehensive definition of training. Here are the key points of their definition:

- Training is always a process, not a program to be completed.

- Through training, skills are developed, information is provided, and attitudes are nurtured.

- Training helps the organization.

- Training usually contributes to the overall development of workers.

- Training helps workers qualify for a job, do the job, or advance.

- Training is also essential for enhancing and transforming the job.

- Training facilitates learning.

- Learning is not only a formal activity but also a more universal activity, and it is facilitated formally and informally by many types of people.

- Training should always hold forth the promise of maximizing learning.

Adult Education. Activity with the primary purpose of acquiring some type of knowledge, information, or skill that includes some type of instruction, including self-instruction. An adult is defined as anyone either age 21 or over, married, or the head of a household (Merriam and Caffarella 1999).

Individual Development. Individual development involves helping employees identify their strengths and weaknesses, build on those strengths, work at correcting their weaknesses. Through developing individually, employees will in turn contribute to the organization. Individual development issues are most often attended to through performance management processes.

Organization Development. Organization development (OD) is a planned change effort involving the total system managed from the top to increase organizational effectiveness through planned interventions using behavioral science knowledge (Bechart).

Career Development. Career development is concerned with the match between the individual and his or her job, and developing the individual over the career span.

Performance Management. The process of ensuring that employees understand what is expected of them in their jobs, and that managers provide the appropriate support and feedback to help them meet expectations.

Instructional Systems Development (ISD). A systematic process for designing training that is standard, comprehensive, internally consistent, and reliable. ISD incorporates tasks of analysis, design, development, implementation, and evaluation.

Human Performance Technology. Human performance technology (HPT) is "a practice that helps link business strategy and goals, and the capability of the workforce to achieve them, with a wide array of human resource interventions which include but are certainly not limited to education and training" (Rosenberg 1996). When considering options for improving performance, HPT considers three organization levels: the work, the workplace, and the worker. It also focuses on business, performance, learning, and work environment needs (Robinson and Robinson 1998).

Making the Decision to Train

Making the decision to train involves more than simply deciding problem-solving training would be a good idea for everyone in the organization to experience. While such training may indeed be useful, often training dollars are wasted because of failure to make a responsible decision to train. The first question human resource professionals should ask when someone declares "We need training!" is "Why?" In the case of problem solving, perhaps a manager wants to respond to a recent instance of inadequate problem solving. There are some key issues to consider when making the decision to train (Michalak and Yager 1979).

The first step is to identify a discrepancy between desired and actual performance. Once the gap is identified, then the organization needs to assess the costs and benefits of addressing the problem. If the cost of addressing the problem outweighs the potential benefit, then further action is probably not warranted. The next decision is to determine whether or not the deficiency is skill or knowledge based. If the answer is neither, then training is not the best response. If the answer to either is yes, then the organization needs to determine how to improve the skill or knowledge. Training is one of many approaches. Other responses may be to provide more information, practice, change the job, or transfer or terminate the employee. Training should never be used as a substitute for effective management. Proper feedback systems should be the heart of any organizational structure.

Models of Training Planning and Design

Lawson (1998) notes that successful training initiatives depend on taking a systematic approach to delivering instruction that is effective for both the participants and the organization. Training that has been designed to correspond with the organization's strategy and employees' needs is most effective. This result can happen only if attention is paid to the training system from the identification of a possible training need to assessment of organizational results. Nearly all instructional models incorporate the steps of analyzing needs and selecting solutions, designing and developing nontraining solutions, deriving instructional outcomes, designing and developing instruction, implementing instruction, and monitoring and improving the process (Mager 1997). Taking a systems approach to training design is the most conscientious way to proceed.

The instructional design process is the framework used to create training. It is rooted in program planning theory. Classical, rational program planning models developed by Ralph Tyler (1949) and Malcolm Knowles (1950) have been widely influential in the practice of designing instructional programs. Sork (1997) summarizes the contributions from these models:

- Honoring the learner's experience, perspective, and expectations

- Recognizing the importance of diversity

- Involving stakeholders in planning

- Understanding the importance of context in which planning occurs

- Basing programs on the needs of learners

- Clarifying the aims or goals of the workshop

- Incorporating workshop processes that actively involve learners

- Choosing facilitators or instructors and instructional resources with great care

- Promoting application of learning as a central theme

- Attending carefully to administrative details

- Caring for the physical and emotional needs of participants

- Assessing program outcomes in addition to learner satisfaction

Cervero and Wilson (1994) have recently criticized the classical models for being too technical. Their concern is that these models do not accurately reflect reality because they ignore the human element of power dynamics and the negotiation of interests in the planning process. Cervero and Wilson argue that the training planner's role is to negotiate often disparate and incompatible interests while simultaneously mitigating power dynamics. For instance, management may want to throw training at a performance problem, when in reality training will not resolve the issue because it is a result of a bad managerial decision. Training planners often find themselves confronted with the delicate task of investigating needs underlying assumptions that training is an appropriate course of action. When training is not the best choice, trainers must diplomatically sell the reason, which can be a political nightmare. Trainers may decide to forge ahead with training—even if it is not in the organization's or employees' best interests—if disagreeing with it is too problematic. Finally, even when everyone agrees on the purpose of training, the content and instructional design are often compromised to satisfy the interests of all stakeholders. I recall a total quality training in which one of our vice presidents demanded no group activities, because he did not want the training to appear "touchy-feely." Complying with this order and creating a meaningful experience for participants was a challenge. In spite of recent criticism, the classical model is widely applied. The next sections will explore the steps of designing training according to the business impact ISD models and human performance technology models.

The Instructional Systems Development Model.   The Instructional Systems Development (ISD) model is the most widely used framework for designing instruction. Molenda, Pershing, and Reigeluth (1996) describe this model's qualities as: *systematic* with sequential steps; *systemic* with attention to the whole organization; *reliable* or replicable from one site to another; *iterative* in that the design cycle repeats during a given project; and *empirical* in that data are collected and used to guide the design process. The ISD model is often referred to as "ADDIE," indicating the recurring steps of analysis, design, development, implementation, and evaluation (Figure 19.2), described in the following sections.

Analysis

Analysis is the first step of the ADDIE model. It involves identifying a need for intervention. This step identifies the problem to be solved and assesses whether or not training is the appropriate response. Deciding whether or not to train is vitally important, as training is often prescribed for problems that cannot be fixed by training, such as bad management, malfunctioning equipment, or unclear expectations. Nontraining interventions may be called for when the problem can more easily be solved by reassignment, job aids (e.g., simple instructions on equipment), management changes, or equipment modifications.

Once it is determined that training is a viable solution, performance deficiencies must be identified. Performance deficiencies are identified through needs analysis. Figure 19.3 on page 19.12 shows how to conduct and use the results of needs analysis. Needs analysis involves collecting data on the problem through individual or group assessments, observation, interviews, surveys, focus groups, professional literature, performance appraisal, or other data collection methods. The data help identify performance gaps between actual and desired performance. The learners, setting, and jobs may also be analyzed. For example: A plant supervisor works with the training manager to define a problem as rejected parts that are not meeting quality standards. They decide to analyze the problem and potential need for training by interviewing employees. They create a set of interview questions and identify a sample of employees to interview. After the interviews are conducted and answers are analyzed, the results reveal that new equipment was installed, but employees were never formally told how to operate it. Because the machinery is highly complex, training is identified as the best response to the problem. Other options would be less effective at improving quality performance.

Once the needs assessment is complete, the information should be presented to stakeholders and support for proceeding should be secured. Task analyses are often done at this point along with analyzing potential learners and writing training objectives. A training proposal should be developed that will guide the design process.

Design

Design is the second step of the ADDIE model. The design step assumes that the needs analysis identified a legitimate reason to invest in training. Design involves identifying learning objectives (based on the needs analysis), determining performance measures, and sequencing the objectives. Sequencing involves moving the learner from lower- to higher-level skills, and simple to complex concepts and tasks. For instance, in computer

FIGURE 19.2   *The ISD Model or ADDIE*

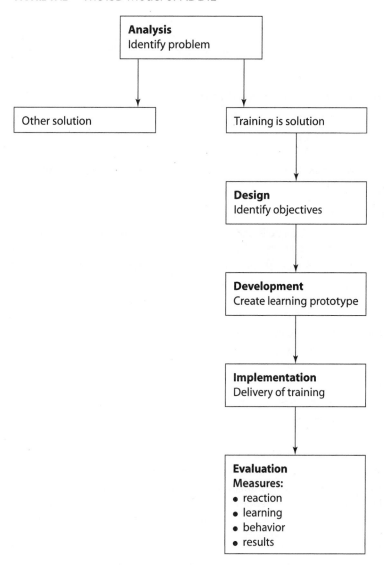

training, the learner would learn the simple task of how to navigate around a database before moving to the complex process of writing formulas. By the same token, the technical aspects of the computer operation would be investigated before ethical issues were evaluated.

Objectives writing is very important to the design step. Lawson (1998) suggests that training objectives fall into three categories of skill development: attitude (affective), skill (behavioral), and knowledge (cognitive). The instructional designer also has to make instructional and logistical decisions. These decisions include teaching or instructional strategies, participant grouping, training environment, teaching methods, and content. For example: The purpose of the training is to familiarize employees with new equipment. The objectives might be (1) to operate the equipment correctly and safely and (2) to understand basic repair and troubleshooting. The participants could be grouped according to shift or smaller groups of equipment operators in order to keep production moving during training. The environment could be in-plant, on the specific equipment, or at a technical training site. The methods might include lecture, demonstration, and practice. The sequencing would be from simple to complex, or from general operation to repair.

Development

Development is the next stage of the ADDIE model. During this step, a prototype of the learning process is created. This may include developing facilitation and participant manuals, audiovisual materials, and other tangible materials that will be used in

FIGURE 19.3   *Conducting and Using Needs Analysis*

Example of Needs Analysis Proposal

To conduct a needs assessment across the XYZ organization with the primary goals of analyzing gaps between desired performance and actual performance, and determining how best to address the gaps.

Outcomes of Needs Analysis

- Identify the critical knowledge, skills, and attributes required in the core job groups to be competitive in the workplace.
- Determine specific developmental needs for acceptable performance (e.g., training, experience, certifications).
- Determine promotional profile including knowledge, skills, and attributes for technical and managerial positions.
- Design a development plan, based on the data.
- Create profiles for employee advancement and development.

Rationale for Needs Analysis

Needs assessment is an important activity because it:

- Ensures that training and development dollars are spent where they have the most leverage.
- Lays the groundwork for training.
- Provides data to validate course of action.
- Identifies gaps between actual performance and desired performance. The analysis will identify how the company is performing versus how it *should* be performing; it will show what employees know and are capable of doing versus what they *should* know and be capable of doing; and it will show what people actually do everyday and what they *should* be doing.
- May result in increased quality and reduced turnover.

Assumptions for Needs Analysis Process

- There is managerial support to undertake this analysis.
- There is a desire for promotion from within.
- The organization has an established strategic planning process and intends to link future development programs to it.
- Growth is anticipated.
- The lack of a formalized training process was an issue in a recent survey.
- There is a framework for management development in existence.
- There is no clear "pipeline" for succession within the organization.
- Intervention must be linked to performance goals.
- A customer focus must be included in the analysis and resulting intervention.
- The needs analysis will consider the organizational system and strategic plan when making conclusions and recommendations.
- Specific measurables will be determined for this process.

training. It also involves determining program formats, schedules facilities, and staff needs during the event. Budgets and marketing issues need consideration as well. This phase may also include pilot testing of the materials and activities. There may be several revisions in the development of materials before the final materials are produced and ready for training. For example: A pilot group of machine operators could be trained to test the design. The participants provide feedback and improvement suggestions. The trainers would revise the training before the rest of the machine operators received training.

Implementation

Implementation is the next stage of the ADDIE model. Implementation involves the actual delivery of the training to the intended audience. For example: The training is rolled out to the machine operators.

Evaluation

Evaluation is the final stage of the ADDIE model. The most common framework of evaluation is Kirkpatrick's four-level model. This model measures reaction, learning, behavior, and results. Each level is increasingly difficult to measure. For example: Training participants could be asked how they liked the training (reaction). Learning and behavior might be assessed based on whether they operate machines correctly. Eventually, the organization would be able to measure results according to the quality performance of the operators. The four-level model of evaluation has been criticized for failing to measure return on investment (ROI) in training. Evaluation is increasingly being measured by looking for ROI performance. Human resource professionals need to ensure that training is evaluated, and that its value is communicated to the organization.

Human Performance Technology. The training profession is undergoing significant changes, one of which is a shift from learning as an output to performance improvement as the ultimate goal. This shift is grounded in a belief that training alone does not solve performance problems, nor is it a cure-all. Human performance technology, or HPT, views performance problems as created by multiple variables in the organization, including nontraining factors such as organization culture, reorganizing, job design, pay, and other organizational systems that affect organization performance. An HTP intervention yields a performance improvement plan when the needs analysis step is complete. Training is planned to correspond with other cyclical events in the organization's cycle, and is explicitly aligned with the business's strategic objectives. Usually, teams attend training together. Real-life simulation of work conditions is applied whenever possible, and there is regular follow-up to support transfer of the learning to the new environment.

HPT is a subset of the human resource development field. Robinson and Robinson (1998) suggest that the best structure for focusing on performance includes alignment of needs related to business, performance, learning, and work environment. The trainer becomes a performance consultant with the responsibility for partnering with learners to help them achieve improved performance. Robinson and Robinson (1998) contrast traditional training with a shift to performance in Table 19.2 on page 19.14.

While there is wild enthusiasm among HPT practitioners about the shift from training performance, many trainers view the HPT process as good training practice dressed in new clothes with a jazzy new vocabulary. Table 19.2 represents two extremes. HPT is also criticized for benefiting management interests, sometimes at the expense of employees.

TABLE 19.2   *Characteristics of a Traditional and Performance Focus*

Traditional Focus	Performance Focus
Focuses on what people need to learn; skill and knowledge is the end	Focuses on what people need to do; skill and knowledge is a means to an end
Event oriented	Process oriented
Reactive	Reactive and proactive
Seeks single solution through training	Open to multiple solutions of which training is a part
Sometimes independent of client	
	Based on partnership with client
Front-end assessment optional	
	Front-end assessment mandatory
Success measured on quality of solution (training event)	
	Success measured based on performance change and operational impact

The Role of Adult Learning in Training and Employee Development

Many educational experiences are designed without regard for the adult learner. Content-expert trainers sweep into the training session, dispense their infinite wisdom to the neophyte participants, and depart. Such instructor-centered training tends to both disregard the experience and knowledge that adult learners bring to the session, and slight the diverse learning needs of adults. HR professionals, whether designing or evaluating training, should be aware of adult learner needs and invest only in educational experiences that cater to adult learners. This is of vital importance as it is estimated that as much as 80 percent of training does not transfer from the training environment to the workplace (Broad and Newstrom 1992). Robinson (1994) summarizes various philosophical frameworks focusing on the purposes for adult learning. They are:

1. Personal growth and development

2. Personal and social improvement

3. Organizational effectiveness

4. Cultivation of the intellect

5. Social transformation

While most businesses may only be interested in learning for organizational effectiveness, they fail to realize that employees learn constantly, and that learning is usually beneficial to the organization regardless of the reason it is undertaken. Drawing on adult learning theory, I argued in 1996 that organizations sometimes fail to recognize the value of attending to employees' personal and professional development. Whole person development may help companies retain employees longer and keep them more productive. I suggested that organizations need to promote individual growth, cultivate cultures that value learning, and design an organizational infrastructure that supports learning as well as the capturing and sharing of it with the rest of the organization.

Caffarella (1994) has assembled several points related to adult learning that are important to consider to make the most of the training dollar (see Figure 19.4).

FIGURE 19.4   *Major Principles and Practices of Adult Learning*

- Adults can and do want to learn, regardless of their age.
- Adults have a rich background of knowledge and experience. They tend to learn best when this experience is acknowledged and when new information builds on their past knowledge and experience.
- Adults are motivated to learn by a mixture of internal and external factors.
- All adults have differing preferred styles of learning.
- For the most part, adults are pragmatic in their learning. They tend to want to apply their learning to real life.
- Adults are not likely to willingly engage in learning unless the content is meaningful to them.
- Adults come to a learning situation with their own personal goals and objectives, which may or may not be the same as those that underlie the learning situation.
- Adults prefer to be actively involved in the learning process than passive recipients of knowledge. In addition, they want the opportunity to be supportive of each other in the learning process.
- Adults learn both in independent, self-reliant modes and in interdependent, connected, and collaborative ways.
- Much of what adults learn tends to have an effect on others (for instance, on work colleagues and family).
- Adults are more receptive to the learning process in situations that are both physically and psychologically comfortable.
- What, how, and where adults learn is affected by the many roles they play as adults.
- Adults are often internally asking the questions, "Why am I learning this?" and "How will I use this in the future?" Be sure that this information is covered.
- Build in time for reflection.
- How does the content relate to the learner's experience? Often the learners will be able to answer this for themselves if asked.
- Attend to diverse learning needs.
- Conduct frequent process checks to ensure that learning needs are being met. Ask, "How could your learning be better supported by yourself? Your colleagues? Your learning facilitators?" Be sure to respond to any feedback offered by the participants.
- Vary the format to attend to multiple learning styles.
- Seek learner input to the design and flow of the learning.
- Challenge learners to consider how the wider context affects their learning. Think of this as a learning facilitator as you plan.

MODULE
19

Source: Adapted in part from Caffarella, R. S. (1994). *Planning programs for adult learners: A practical guide for educators, trainers, and staff developers.* San Francisco: Jossey-Bass.

Adult Learning: Establishing Goals for Learning and Respecting Diverse Learning Styles

There is no single formula for creating powerful instruction that will maximize learning for all learners. Yet, there are several things that trainers can do to ensure that each participant has an opportunity to learn from the experience. Educators of adults can begin this process by clearly identifying learning goals and objectives, and understanding learning styles.

ABC's or Affective, Behavioral, and Cognitive Learning Objectives. First and foremost, trainers must have a clear goal in mind for the training. A goal is an overarching vision or desired result of the training. For instance, a goal might be to train trainers, develop leadership skills, or value diversity. Learning objectives must consider the goal of the learning, but are much more explicit and framed in behavioral terms. There are three primary types of learning objectives:

- *Affective* learning involves the formation of attitudes, feelings, and preferences. This type of learning objective is best when you want to change attitudes or increase awareness or sensitivity. For example, a train-the-trainer affective training objective might be: "To reflect on individual style as a trainer and build self-confidence."

- *Behavioral* learning includes the development of competence in the actual performance of procedures, operations, methods, and techniques. This objective is best when employees have to learn a skill, task, or procedure, such as how to apply a total quality tool or test. A behavioral objective for a train-the-trainer training might be: "To design and present an eight-hour module of training incorporating at least three different instructional methods."

- *Cognitive* learning includes the acquisition of concepts or knowledge related to the course content. Cognitive objectives require that trainees demonstrate acquired knowledge, comprehend information, and analyze concepts. A cognitive objective for a train-the-trainer training might be: "To master the content of *xyz*."

When writing learning objectives, trainers must ensure that they are objective and measurable, results oriented, clearly worded, and specific. Objectives should be written in terms of performance, for instance, "demonstrate the proper, safe, and efficient operation of machinery." Well-written objectives describe ideal performance, conditions under which the participant will perform the activity, and criteria for acceptable levels of proficiency at the task.

MODULE
19

Learning Styles. Effective training is delivered with attention toward the diverse ways adults learn. To that end, training should at minimum be considerate of the kinds of learners as identified by Kolb (1991):

- *Feelers* are people-oriented and learn through expressing and focusing on feelings and emotions. They enjoy affective learning and thrive in open, unstructured learning environments. They also like group activities and the opportunity to share opinions and experiences.

- *Observers* like to watch and listen. They are reserved and quiet and slower to participate than others are. They like to consider various ideas and opinions, and enjoy learning through discovery.

- *Thinkers* appreciate logic and reason, and the opportunity to share ideas and concepts. They enjoy analysis and evaluation and will question the rationale behind activities. They are independent learners who will question the relevance of role plays and simulations.

- *Doers* like to be actively involved in the learning through group activities. They tend to dominate discussions and want opportunities to practice what is being learned. They want real-world information and get impatient when discussion goes on too long.

In addition to learning styles, Lawson (1998) identifies perceptual modalities, or the ways people assimilate information, as follows.

- *Visual* learners learn through the eyes. They like optical depictions of the concepts such as pictures, models, symbols, or demonstrations.

- *Auditory* learners learn through listening and hearing explanations of the concept. They respond well to lectures, audiotapes, and opportunities to take in information through their ears.

- *Print* learners like text. Paper-and-pencil exercises that help them absorb the written word are most effective.

- *Interactive* learners like group discussion, question-and-answer periods, and the opportunity to exchange ideas.

- *Tactile* learners like hands-on activities such as model building, object handling, or material assembly.

- *Kinesthetic* learners like role plays, physical games, applying psychomotor skills, and moving from one place to another.

The Nuts and Bolts of Delivering Training

Training Design Tips. There is no one "right" way of designing training, but there are several strategies that can streamline the process. First, training will only be effective to the extent training needs have been accurately identified. Need identification begins with thorough needs analysis, which is discussed earlier in this module.

All training should have a specific purpose and outcomes and a defined process of achieving them. I recommend that trainers create a "POP" for each training to ensure it is structured and true to the needs assessment. A POP is an acronym for purpose, outcomes, and process.

- *Purpose* indicates the core goal of the session, usually "to share and process information relative to . . ."

- *Outcomes* delineate learning objectives: "To understand, apply, distinguish, demonstrate . . ."

- *Process* describes the process of learning in terms of the outcome desired and content and activity necessary to achieve the outcome and goal.

It is recommended that designers create a plan that specifies the POP, as well as the time allotted, content, and learning points associated with each objective, methods and activities planned, and the materials or visual aids necessary for the module. Refer to Table 19.3 on page 19.18 for a brief example of what an introduction to a train-the-trainer workshop might look like.

Attending to the Physical and Psychological Environment for Training.
Creating an environment that is conducive to learning is more than just removing whatever might distract your participants from learning—it is proactively building an atmosphere that works with all the senses and brings them together into the learning process. These ideas will put you on the road to creating effective environments for learning.

Setting a comfortable physical environment involves creating a space that is conducive to learning for diverse learners. You should arrive early and assess the environment against your goals for the learning experience. Is the seating configuration most conducive to the exercises and activities you have planned? Will participants have enough "elbow room"? (If you are using three-ring binders, participants will need extra room to open them.) Can the screen be seen from every seat? How comfortable is the room temperature? Are there any external noises that will be distracting? Act to minimize them.

Once you have ensured that the physical environment is comfortable, you should attend to the psychological environment. This can be accomplished with lighting, soothing music, and welcoming signals such as signs or other directives to inform the

TABLE 19.3 *A Sample Train-the-Trainer Workshop Introduction*

Training Title:	*Train-the-Trainer Workshop Introduction*
Purpose:	Share and process information related to becoming an effective trainer.
Outcomes:	1. Explain the concepts of effective training and development.
	2. Reflect on your role as a trainer and articulate a teaching vision for yourself.
	3. Raise concerns and hopes about becoming a trainer.

Time	Learning Objective	Methods and Activities	Materials and Media
8:00	***Objective:*** Welcome everyone. Set stage for day. Conduct icebreaker.	1. Welcome participants. 2. Facilitate introductions. 3. Play the Name Game.	• Agenda • Koosh Ball
8:30	***Objective:*** Explain the concepts of effective training and development.	1. Lecture on core principles. 2. Paired reflections. Participants will teach each other core points from lecture.	• Workbook • Overhead projector • Transparencies 1–10
9:30	*Break*	*Break*	*Break*
9:45	***Objective:*** Reflect on your role as a trainer and articulate a teaching vision for yourself.	1. Participants individually draw a picture of their vision of themselves as trainers. 2. Participants will share pictures with table. Each table will share a brief summary of highlights. 3. Post pictures on the wall.	• CD/radio • Overhead projector • Transparency 11 • Crayons/paper
10:50	*Break*	*Break*	*Break*
11:00	***Objective:*** Raise concerns and hopes about becoming a trainer.	1. Dialogue about the issues.	• Dialogue ground rules • Chairs arranged in a circle • Koosh ball
11:45	***Objective:*** Share closing thoughts, comments, and feedback on the course content and facilitation.	1. Round-Robin sharing. Passing is okay.	
12:00	*Adjourn*	*Adjourn*	*Adjourn*

participant of what is expected (register, enjoy refreshments, take a seat). It is also recommended that you make some type of personal contact with each participant before the session begins. This can be accomplished by greeting them at the registration table or meeting them before you begin. Of course, this requires that you be ready to go *before* the participants arrive!

MODULE
19

FIGURE 19.5   *Checklist of Things to do **Before** the Participants Arrive*

Physical Environment

- ❏ Finish setting up the room.
- ❏ Ensure that name tags and/or name tents are provided.
- ❏ Advise the participants of when you will begin the workshop.
- ❏ Invite participants to make themselves comfortable.

Psychological Environment

- ❏ Play soothing music.
- ❏ Create a sign that welcomes participants and invites them to network and partake of refreshments (if provided).
- ❏ Smile.
- ❏ Greet participants as they walk in the door. Shake their hands and call them by name.

Stimulate the Senses.   To maximize learning, strive to stimulate the senses during the training. Here are some ideas for an environment that is stimulating to the senses and works with various learning styles.

- *Music.* Play music at the beginning of the session, and during breaks and exercises. If you are asking people to write, music without words is most helpful. If familiar songs are played, even without the words, participants my find themselves thinking of the words and become distracted. A caution when using music in training is to be aware of the copyright laws pertaining to such use.

- *Print.* Provide articles and printed material related to the information you are covering. It is recommended that you provide copies of all visual material shared. This will also appeal to learners who are visually oriented. A cautionary note: Be careful not to overwhelm participants with reams of printed material. If you do use printed material, be sure to refer to it.

- *Visual stimulation.* Use color in your overheads, flip charts, and anything you hang on the wall. Put quotes or commonly referred-to diagrams or models on the wall for participants to refer to often. They will also serve as a memory jogger of the information covered during the session. A cautionary note: Some learners may find visual props distracting.

- *Auditory.* Read a story, poem, or quote to participants. Play music and invite them to listen to the lyrics. A cautionary note: Be aware of participants who may have physical disabilities that prevent them from hearing. When working in international training, be aware that some participants may speak a different native language. In this case, provide written copy in the native language if possible. Also, provide written copy of spoken material for the less auditory learners.

- *Tactile Elements.* People often appreciate having something to hold on to or manipulate during the session. Use models to illustrate key points. Give participants items to "play with" during training. Placing Koosh™ balls on the table can serve as a tactile prop, as well as a "talking stick" for group activities. A cautionary note for using tactile props: Be careful that none of the props are noisy or distracting to the other participants.

MODULE
19

- *Interactive Training.* Involve participants by using a multitude of instructional strategies. A cautionary note: Some participants come to training expecting to be entertained and lectured to. Inform them either in advance or in the beginning about the activity level of the session.

- *Kinesthetic Elements.* Incorporate activities that get participants moving through role plays or activities that force them to move around the room. A cautionary note: Participants who are disabled may have difficulty moving around the room. Provide modified ways for them to participate.

- *Food.* Use food creatively, to reinforce learning points. For instance, in a creative thinking workshop, serve Chinese food with chopsticks to challenge learners to try something new. When making introductions, advise learners to take as many M&Ms as they need. Then have them introduce themselves sharing one bit of information for each piece taken. Use fortune cookies to add a creative twist to introductions. Participants have to explain why the fortune does or does not relate to them. When using food, be aware that you cannot please everyone. Make sure food items relate in some way to the key points of training.

Effective Training Facilitation Strategies

The implementation of training plans demands not only preparation of the content and facilities, but also planning to facilitate the process in an effective fashion. This section discusses instructional strategies, starting training with style, facilitating groups, facilitating exercises, avoiding common training mistakes, and closing the training.

Instructional Strategies. We have already discussed the importance of providing a diverse array of instructional strategies. Adult learners do not respond favorably to constant lecture. Research has also shown that passive instructional strategies, such as lecture, are less effective at helping learners retain information. Figure 19.6 shows a learning pyramid that predicts retention based on instructional strategy.

FIGURE 19.6 *Learning Pyramid or Cone of Experience*

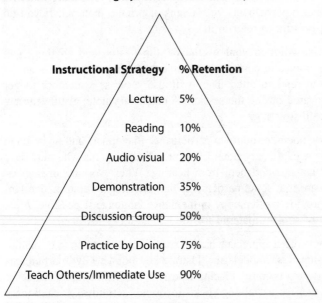

Instructional Strategy	% Retention
Lecture	5%
Reading	10%
Audio visual	20%
Demonstration	35%
Discussion Group	50%
Practice by Doing	75%
Teach Others/Immediate Use	90%

Source: Adapted from E. Dale, *Audiovisual methods in teaching* (New York: Dryden Press, 1954, p. 43).

Starting Training with Style.   How you begin the training session sets the tone for the entire session. You want to start the training in a fashion that both engages and informs the participants. It is a very good idea to use an exercise that gets people participating as soon as possible, versus talking at them and losing them at the beginning. There are many sources for beginning exercises, such as *Saying Hello: Getting Your Group Started* (Hart 1989), *The Winning Trainer* (Eitington 1996), and *101 Ways to Make Training Active* (Silberman 1995). One simple example of a group starter is to have the group pair off and interview each other based on a list of questions provided to all participants (e.g., hobbies, interests, learning expectations, and so forth). Each person introduces the person who was interviewed to the rest of the group. If the group is very large, have pairs meet up with two or three other pairs and have small group introductions.

In addition to using an icebreaker, you should also cover several items at the beginning of training to ensure the comfort of participants. Here is a checklist of the key information they will need at the start of training:

Things to Do at Start of Training

- ❑ Welcome participants
- ❑ Make introductions
- ❑ Explain POP
- ❑ Check for understanding of POP
- ❑ Explain logistics:
  - ○ Restrooms
  - ○ Telephones
  - ○ Breaks and meals
  - ○ Materials
  - ○ Emergency exits
  - ○ Other logistical items (context)

- ❑ Ensure that name tags are used
- ❑ Establish ground rules and expectations
- ❑ Describe your role as trainer
- ❑ Conduct a check-in or warm-up activity

Tips for Facilitating with Finesse.   Trainers need to manage multiple tasks to be effective. The following tips identify behaviors that accomplished trainers exhibit when delivering instruction. Trainers need to:

- Establish compatibility and credibility with the participants. This involves being courteous, polite, and knowledgeable.

- Demonstrate organization and competence throughout the session. This means they have to administer the training and master the content.

- Maintain leadership of the group—for instance, facilitating group discussion to allow maximal input without loss of control.

- Keep the energy level high. The energy level of the participants is usually proportional to that of the instructor.

- Project voice and check regularly that everyone can hear.

- Apply nonverbal communication effectively by making eye contact and gesturing appropriately.

- Respond adequately to questions and check with participants to confirm that the answer was satisfactory.

- Invite and encourage participation from all attendees.

- Manage time effectively, and monitor and adjust when time is limited.

- Ensure that the environment is comfortable for all participants.

Flawless Exercise Facilitation. Trainers often have trouble facilitating group exercises. Here are ten strategies for facilitating group exercises with ease:

1. Explain *WHY* the exercise is being done. Share objectives and benefits.

2. Specify *WHAT* participants are supposed to do. Visual backup is recommended. Demonstrate where needed.

3. Indicate *WHO* will do what.

4. Direct participants to *WHERE* the activity will take place.

5. Indicate *WHEN* the activity will end.

6. *SUMMARIZE* instructions (or ask a participant to do this).

7. *OBSERVE,* monitor, and adjust (to time and other unanticipated variables), and keep activity energized.

8. Conduct *PROCESS* and *TIME CHECKS* with groups.

9. *DEBRIEF* exercise for key points, feelings, insights, and learning.

10. Establish *SO WHAT'S* and summarize the highlights.

MODULE
19

Avoiding Common Training Mistakes. Every trainer remembers his or her mistakes, and while some of us may still cringe at the memory, each one served as a powerful lesson. Here are some common mistakes that trainers make:

- Covering too much information for the time available

- Failing to balance cognitive, behavioral, and affective learning objectives in instructional design

FIGURE 19.7 *Reflection Questions*

1. The most important thing I learned was . . .
2. If this experience were a song, a book, a quote, or a movie, then it would be . . .
3. The part of this course that I enjoyed the most was . . .
4. The part of this course that I will teach others is . . .
5. I will continue my learning by . . .
6. A metaphor for this experience is . . .
7. Something that I learned about myself is . . .
8. We laughed most when . . .
9. The best part was . . .
10. A disappointment was . . .
11. Before we go, I would like to tell all of you . . .
12. This experience has made me feel . . .
13. This experience has made me think . . .

- Lacking a variety of instructional strategies that cater to diverse learning styles

- Providing few opportunities for learner participation (lecturing)

- Failing to utilize the expertise of participants in relation to the content

- Failing to tie the training to "real life"

- Making no plans for learning transfer to the work setting

- Neglecting learner assessment at front end

- Failure to build in reflection

- Failure to tie new learning back to prior learning

- Lack of attention to details

- Not explaining the POP (purpose, outcomes, and process)

- Designing the training plan parallel to presenter's learning style

Closing Training.   Facilitating a strong closing to training is just as important as having a memorable, engaging opening. Solem and Pike, in their book *50 Creative Training Closers* (1997), suggest that training closers should review content, plan action, celebrate learning, or motivate future action and learning. Many trainers ignore the closing, but this leaves learners without closure or a plan for applying the learning. The final reflection is one strategy for closing the training. It works by asking participants to reflect on their learning during the course. Post the course purpose and outcomes to guide their thinking. Post the questions in Figure 19.7 as "thought starters" for their reflection. Ask participants to be prepared to share at least one "lesson" with the group at large. This works best if the group is seated in a circle without tables.

Facilitating Training Transfer

Some trainers may breathe a sigh of relief at the end of the training session. Yet getting through the training is not where it ends. It is the beginning for the learner. Responsible trainers are concerned with how effectively learning transfers from the training to the work setting. This section defines training transfer and offers strategies to enhance it.

Defining Training Transfer.   Learning transfer is the effective and continuing application of newly acquired knowledge, skills, and attitudes to the job. It is often referred to as the "so what," or "now what" phase of the learning process. "So what does all this mean and how can what was learned be applicable to my situation?" (Caffarella 1994).

Learning transfer is influenced by several factors including the learners, program design and execution, program content, changes required to apply learning, organizational context, and community and societal forces. Since adults wonder how they are going to use this information when they get back to work or back home, it is important that they be given some strategies to be sure this occurs.

One way that learners can be assisted in their application of training is to give them time to reflect on what they have learned and how they can use it after they leave. It is remarkable how in only five or ten minutes, participants will discover their own strategies to apply the tools they have discussed during the training. Reflection can be difficult, however, as many participants come from fast-paced environments where even stopping and gazing out a window for a few minutes to think is viewed as wasted time. They may need your acknowledgment that this is a difficult task for some people, and encouragement to stick with it. Trainers often sacrifice a few moments of reflection for the coverage of a few more points. This is to be avoided. Chances are, the participants have reached saturation point. Instead, have them consider how they will apply what they have learned and raise questions about points that may have been unclear.

Strategies for Training Transfer

Action Planning

The creation of a written action plan so that participants have a well thought-out strategy for applying their information will give them a jump-start toward application. Consider having participants complete the following matrix as they participate in the training:

Action Item	Interim/ Key Steps	Others Whose Help Is Needed	Target Date	Priority (Assess when sheet is full)

In addition to action planning, Figure 19.8 lists 25 tips for training transfer that I've assembled over the years.

Evaluating Training

Training evaluation is the step of the ADDIE model that is regularly overlooked or haphazardly applied. Evaluation many times is not considered until the training is nearly over. The time to think about evaluation is not at the end of training, but at the beginning of the design process. Why evaluate? Lawson (1998) identifies several reasons: to determine whether the training met its stated objectives, to assess the value of training, to identify areas where the training can be improved, to target appropriate audiences for future programs, to review and reinforce key learning points for participants, and to sell the program to management and participants. Evaluation can be done during the training, at the end of the session, or after the training. Building on Kirkpatrick's four-level model of evaluation, assessment usually considers:

Level 1: Reaction—Did participants like the program?

Level 2: Learning—What skills and knowledge did participants gain?

Level 3: Behavior—How are participants performing differently?

Level 4: Results—How was the bottom line impacted?

This model has been criticized. Organization management is also tasking trainers and HR professionals with assessing the cost/benefit ration of training, and demonstrating return on investment.

FIGURE 19.8 *25 Tips for Training Transfer*

1. Have participants develop an action plan, as discussed above.
2. Have participants craft a learning letter to their supervisor.
3. Create a network of course graduates (this could be electronic).
4. Schedule brown-bag lunch sessions to share lessons learned.
5. Create a slogan or acronym to reinforce key points. For instance, "Ya gotta be flexi-ble!" POP.
6. Create a job aid for reference back on the job.
7. Involve managers prior to the training with tips on how they can help trainees get the most out of training.
8. Hold the course over several weeks with application "homework" in between sessions and reports on progress at the sessions.
9. Have participants do a force-field analysis on applying learning at work before the end of the training.
10. Create post-training learning groups or "buddies" to help each other after the class.
11. Have participants keep a journal after the course and meet periodically to compare notes on what is and is not working.
12. Have teams from across the organization participate in the training.
13. Offer training to whole departments, and create collective strategies for application.
14. Have participants write letters to themselves and send them at a later date.
15. Have participants complete pre- and post-training assessments.
16. Hold a 30-day post-training debriefing on application with trainees and management.
17. Give managers a checklist of observable behaviors to look for after class.
18. Have participants create a vision or image of their learning.
19. Use music, poetry, or video clips to underscore points. These will serve as reminders of the training.
20. Have trainees "train" on what they learned.
21. Give participants a bibliography of books, periodicals, web sites, and video or au-diotape programs that will help them maintain and enhance their skill.
22. Encourage participants in keeping the information they want to focus on visible either in their planner, on their bulletin board, or on their screen saver.
23. Give the participants time with a "buddy"—someone they work with who will let them know when they are successfully using the skills.
24. Prior to the session, give the learning objectives to the participants' supervisor. Ask the supervisor to discuss with them what they would like them to learn during the session and why they are being sent to that particular class.
25. Use a Stop-Reflect time-out to consider how the learning can be applied to the job at various points throughout the session.

MODULE
19

Before administering an evaluation, the trainer needs to decide the purpose of the evaluation such as assessment of training, potential follow-up, or behavioral results. Once the purpose is determined, it must be decided what to measure in order to assess it, and what sources of information are appropriate. For instance, if you want to measure the results of a customer service training, you could measure number of complaints and could look at written complaints, or contact customers. You also have to decide how to gather information and determine when to conduct the evaluation. Finally, political issues must be assessed.

The previous sections have provided a general overview of the role, design, and facilitation of training. The next section introduces strategic issues in training and employee development.

STRATEGIC ISSUES IN TRAINING AND EMPLOYEE DEVELOPMENT

Managing training strategically is critically important if the investment is to pay off. There are several important trends in training and employee development including the shift from training to learning, which has precipitated the development of the learning organization, action learning, and chief learning officers in organizations. Trainers also have to respond to a rapidly changing environment characterized by technology advances, diversity, restructuring, and human performance management. Finally, training functions must adopt a customer focus.

Linking Training to Organizational Strategy

One of the problems with training is that, in spite of the investment of money and time, no change results over time. Unless explicitly linked to strategy, even the best-designed and executed training will fail. Of course, this assumes that the organization has a clear strategy to link training to. Often, organizations are unclear about their mission and vision. The first step is to clearly specify these. The second is to link all educational activities to them. In addition to strategic linkages, training should have a future focus. Rather than ensuring that employees have only the knowledge and skill that are helpful to the business today, organizations need to consider what information will help them in the future. Needs analysis takes on even greater importance when linking training to strategy. Needs analysis becomes an opportunity to assess how the organization is performing against its strategy, and to craft a performance-based plan to improve the situation. Strategic training is generally a team or collective process, because individuals who attend training often come up against cultural and political barriers that may prevent them from applying new knowledge to the organization.

The Shift from Training to Learning

Learning in the workplace is shifting from formalized, short-term instruction by an expert to informal, strategically focused learning facilitation by stakeholders and internal employees. This change parallels the JIT or just-in-time manufacturing movement. This JIT learning is evident in the development of learning organizations and action learning teams across corporate America, England, and Australia. Table 19.4 highlights these shifts. Training is also becoming more closely linked with organization strategy. This trend is expected to continue and become even more important when the results of training are being measured.

The Learning Organization

The "learning organization" has received steady attention since the 1990 publication of Peter Senge's book *The Fifth Discipline: The Art and Practice of the Learning Organization* (1990). Senge defines it as "Organizations where people continually expand their capacity to create the results they truly desire, where new and expansive patterns of thinking are nurtured, where collective aspiration is set free and where people are continually learning how to learn together." Watkins and Marsick (1993) note that "A learning organization is one that learns continuously and can transform itself." The Electronic

TABLE 19.4 *Elements of the Shift from Training to Learning*

From Training		To Learning
Focus on short term	➡	Focus on lifelong learning/development
Skill based	➡	Core competency based
Driven by individual request	➡	Driven by corporate strategy
Concentrates on managers and executives	➡	Concentrates on all employees
Assessment done by HR and/or managers	➡	Assessment done by affected individuals
Training happens off-site	➡	Learning happens anyplace
Training is scheduled periodically	➡	Learning happens in real time
Training based on knowledge delivery	➡	Learning based on creating new meaning about sharing experiences in workplace
Instructor driven; designed by specialists	➡	Self-directed
Generalized, prescriptions	➡	Specific, trainees determine
Trainers deliver, trainer centered	➡	Facilitated jointly, learner centered

and Fuel Handling Division (now a part of Visteon Automotive Systems, a division of Ford Motor Company) realized unprecedented performance in its new-product launch process through the application of learning organization principles to change their process. Their ability to launch new automotive component systems under budget, early, and of high quality resulted in a turnaround for the business (Bierema and Berdish 1996).

Action Learning: Real Learning in Real Time

Action learning teams are becoming common in organizations that have shifted from a traditional training to a learning orientation. They are referred to as "sets" in action learning terminology. A set comes together to work on a common problem or as individuals seeking to work on individual problems with the group. The set is assembled based on diversity and nonexperts. The set reflects on the problem, establishes a strategy to tackle it, and adjourns to take action. After a period of action, the set reconvenes to reflect on how the action worked, to consider lessons learned, and to chart strategy for further action. Sets can exist either until the problem is solved or indefinitely, based on organization need. The set is often facilitated by a set leader who assists the group in reflection on their actions. An example is the Electrical Fuel and Handling Division's Division Operating Committee (DOC). The general manager instituted weekly action learning sessions in place of one-on-one meetings with each of his executives. Through these sessions, the group was able to explore individual and collective issues related to managing the business, and learn in the process.

The Emergence of the "Learning Executive"

A scan of contemporary job titles hints that learning is taking hold in progressive organizations. Today titles like "chief learning officer" or "vice president of organizational learning" are becoming common. This shift is indicative of the heightened importance of learning in organizational life. Willis and May (1997) suggest that the concept of the chief learning officer (CLO) exceeds traditional concepts of training and development. These executive-level positions are usually charged with facilitating learning and change in the organization; improving the individual, team, and organizational effectiveness through integrated use of communication media, performance consulting, training, and organizational design; and supporting the business strategy and tactics.

On-the-Job Training

On-the-job training (OJT) is one of the oldest types of training. According to Levine (1997), OJT is a "just-in-time delivery system that dispenses training to employees when they need it" (p. 1). It is usually delivered one-on-one. OJT is classified as unstructured and structured. Unstructured OJT is the unstructured training that happens in the workplace, such as one employee teaching the other how to run a machine. The problem with unstructured OJT is that it is casual, haphazard, unmonitored, unrecorded, and hit-or-miss. Structured OJT has grown out of the quality movement and companies' quests to become ISO 9000 certified. Structured OJT has designated trainers, skill checklists, consistency of delivery, tracking recording, and evaluation. Levine outlines seven components of an OJT system: management support, formal trainer support process, checklists, OJT training materials, train-the-trainer program, tracking, and report generation. Effective OJT programs have structure, objectives, accountability, preparation, consistency, and sensitivity to learner needs.

Responding to a Rapidly Changing Environment

Technology. Technological advances show no evidence of slowing, and skill requirements will continue to change based on technological advances. Training must assist the workforce in learning new technology. Further, trainers must learn to use the new technology that is widely available to conduct training. Trainers need to be familiar with computer hardware, networking, multimedia software, and videoconferencing, and be able to manage multiple-site training delivery.

Diversity. The news that the workforce is diverse is hardly met with a raised brow. Trainers must design training that respects diverse cultures, learning styles, and needs, as well as deliver training that helps organizations address diversity issues effectively.

Restructuring. Corporate restructuring has kept a steady pace, and whether organizations are downsizing or reorganizing, training issues will result. Common restructuring training needs include new job skills, morale, outplacement, policy change, and change management.

Human Performance Management. ASTD (1997) predicts that emphasis on human performance management will accelerate in the future. They have noted comprehensive performance management approaches that include gain sharing, team-based performance evaluation, and employee performance evaluation tied to business goals.

Deciding When to Hire a Consultant

There will be occasions when it is desirable to hire a consultant to address training and development needs. Consultants are usually hired to help or advise the work of management. HR professionals may want a consultant when asked to do something they lack the competency to do, such as training of a technical nature that is beyond their scope of ability. Consultants are also appropriate if the organization lacks the time to develop and deliver training. Hiring a consultant is not a substitute for HR leadership. It will still take the HR manager time to brief the consultant and monitor and evaluate progress.

Adopting a Customer Focus

Training departments are increasingly tasked with having a strategic focus, producing high-quality training with a short cycle time, using the latest technology, linking multiple sites, and demonstrating a return on investment. These high expectations demand that training professionals adopt a customer focus. To best meet the needs of the customer, trainers must make strategic decisions related to needs analysis, outsourcing, design, delivery, and evaluation of training.

Ethical Issues in Employee Training and Development

As with many emerging fields of practice, HRD and training have undefined and sometimes conflicting ethical standards. Nadler and Nadler (1992) raise some of the ethical issues in the field. One concern is HRD's focus on behavioral change. Does the organization have a right to change people's behavior? What is to be done when HRD programs include controversial material? Is HRD a form of brainwashing or therapy? What if HRD is used with antiunion intentions? Is it ethical to force employees to learn? What is the organization's responsibility to support the community through learning efforts? How can HRD address the growing diversity of the workforce?

APPLICATION

Training and employee development are best understood in practice. Training can be perceived through the eyes of the participant, developer, deliverer, and evaluator. Progressive corporations are not only training, but also striving to create work environments that foster learning. The following application scenarios offer an opportunity for you to apply the concepts presented in this module.

1. You are in a strategic planning meeting. Make an argument for why the organization should pay attention to learning and training over the next five years.

2. The organization strategy is to improve quality, grow the business, expand into international markets, meet performance objectives, and become a learning organization. The strategy has been implemented, but the goals of quality and expansion into international markets are not even close to being met. The operations executive calls you and demands that you schedule a training on basic quality concepts for all employees and a globalization strategy class for executives ASAP. How should you respond to this request in light of the ADDIE model? How would you respond according to a human performance technology model?

3. You have conducted a needs analysis and have determined that you need to conduct a presentation skills workshop for midlevel managers. What steps will you take to design and develop the training? (Create a POP) What is your evaluation strategy?

4. Recall a training you recently attended, and critique it according to the principles of adult education (adult learning principles, learning objectives, learning styles), facilitation, and learning transfer.

MODULE
19

IN CONCLUSION

Debrief

This module has introduced the process of training and the role of learning in contemporary organizations. Key definitions were covered and various models of instructional development were explained. The role of adult learning in training was discussed and future trends were addressed. Whether designers, purchasers, or consumers of training, HR leaders need to make informed decisions about the selection, design, and delivery of training. HR also has the responsibility of assuring that training is explicitly linked with the organization's strategy.

Suggested Readings

Hodell, C. (1997). Basics of instructional systems development. *Info-line, 9706,* Alexandria, VA: American Society for Training and Development, June 1997.

Craig, R. L. (Ed.). (1996). *The ASTD training and development handbook: A guide to human resource development, 4th ed.* New York: McGraw-Hill.

Eitington, J. E. (1996). *The winning trainer: Winning ways to involve people in learning.* Houston: Gulf Publishing Co.

Goldstein, I. L. (1993). *Training in organizations: Needs assessment, development and evaluation, 3rd ed.* Pacific Grove, CA: Brooks/Cole Publishing Company.

Hart, L. B. (1989). *Saying hello: Getting your group started.* King of Prussia, PA: Organization Design and Development, Inc.

Lawson, K. (1998). *The trainer's handbook.* San Francisco: Jossey-Bass/Pfeiffer.

Mager, R. F. (1997). *Making instruction work or skillbloomers: A step-by-step guide to designing and developing instruction that works.* Atlanta: The Center for Effective Performance, Inc.

Merriam, S. B., and Caffarella, R. S. (1999). *Learning in adulthood: A comprehensive guide, 2nd ed.* San Francisco: Jossey-Bass.

Robinson, D. G., and Robinson, J. C. (1998). *Moving from training to performance: A practical guidebook.* San Francisco: Berrett-Koehler.

Relevant Web Sites

MODULE
19

ACADEMY OF HUMAN RESOURCE DEVELOPMENT
http://www.ahrd.org/

AMERICAN ASSOCIATION FOR TRAINING AND DEVELOPMENT
http://www.astd.org/

TRAINING & DEVELOPMENT RESOURCE CENTER
http://tcm.com/trdev/

LEARNING ORGANIZATIONS: A WEB BIBLIOGRAPHY
http://ads-sun2.ucsc.edu/learnorg.html

STANFORD LEARNING ORGANIZATION WEB
http://www.stanford.edu/group/SLOW/

THE FIFTH DISCIPLINE FIELDBOOK
http://www.fieldbook.com/

Critical Thinking Questions

1. What are the major trends driving training and employee development in organizations? Make an argument for why organizations need to pay attention to this area from a strategic viewpoint.

2. What model would you apply to designing a training (ADDIE or HPT)?

3. What is the difference between "learner-friendly" and "learner-unfriendly" training?

4. How would you evaluate training for effectiveness and results?

5. What is HR's role in training and employee development?

6. Under what circumstances would you discourage training?

7. Why is so little attention paid to transfer of learning from training to the work environment?

8. What does it mean to be a learning organization?

9. What are some of the ethical issues associated with training?

Exercises

1. Reflect on a significant learning experience you have had in the past year. What triggered it? What resources did you use? Where did you learn? Why was the learning important? How did your answers compare to Caffarella's principles of adult education?

2. What steps would you take to create a training program? Outline these. How do you think the instructional design models would work in real practice?

3. Working in groups of three, appoint the following roles:

   - Trainee

   - Trainer

   - Client or stakeholder

   Spend a few minutes identifying what is important for each person to get out of the training process. Share reflections and note the similarities and differences between the parities. Groups should select a reporter to summarize and share its reflections with the rest of the class.

References

American Society for Training and Development (ASTD) *http://www.astd.org/virtual_community/*

Bassi, L. J., and Van Buren, M. (1997). ASTD Training Trends 1997. Training and Development.

Bierema, L. L. (1996). Development of the individual leads to more productive workplaces. In R. W. Rowden (ed.) *Workplace learning: Debating the five critical questions of theory and practice. New Directions for Adult and Continuing Education, 72*, 21–30.

Bierema, L. L. and Berdish, D. M. (1996). Implementing the learning organization: A collaboration between business and education. In K. E. Watkins and V. J. Marsick (eds). In *Action, case studies: Creating the learning organization.* Alexandria, VA: ASTD Books, 1:179–190.

Broad, M. L. and Newstrom, J. W. (1992). *Transfer of training: Action-packed strategies to ensure high payoff from training investments.* Reading, MA: Addison-Wesley.

Caffarella, R. S. (1994). *Planning programs for adult learners: A practical guide for educators, trainers and staff developers.* San Francisco: Jossey-Bass.

Cervero, R. M., and Wilson, A. L. (1994). *Planning responsibly for adult education: A guide to negotiating power and interests.* San Francisco: Jossey-Bass.

Craig, R. L. (1996). *ASTD training and development handbook: A guide to human resource development.* New York: McGraw-Hill.

Dale, E. (1954). *Audiovisual methods in teaching.* New York: Dryden Press.

Davis, J. R., and Davis, A. B. (1998). *Effective training strategies: A comprehensive guide to maximizing learning in organizations.* San Francisco: Berrett-Koehler.

deGeus, A. (1997). *The living company: Habits for survival in a turbulent business environment.* Boston: Harvard Business School Press.

Knowles, M. S. (1950). *Informal adult education.* New York: Association Press.

Kolb, D. (1991). *Learning styles inventory.* Boston: McBer & Company.

Lawson, K. (1998). *The trainer's handbook.* San Francisco: Jossey-Bass/Pfeiffer.

Levine, C. I. (1997). On-the-job training. *Info-line, 9708,* Alexandria, VA: American Society for Training and Development, August 1997.

Mager, R. F. (1997). *Making instruction work or skillbloomers: A step-by-step guide to designing and developing instruction that works.* Atlanta: The Center for Effective Performance, Inc.

Marquardt, M. (1995). *Building the learning organization.* New York: McGraw-Hill.

Merriam, S. B. (1993). *An update on adult learning theory.* New Directions for Adult and Continuing Education, no. 57. San Francisco: Jossey-Bass.

Merriam, S. B., and Caffarella, R. S. (1999). *Learning in adulthood: A comprehensive Guide, 2nd ed.* San Francisco: Jossey-Bass.

Michalak, D. F., and Yager, E. G. (1979). *Making the training process work: A practical guide to better training programs.* New York: Harper & Row.

Molenda, M., Pershing, J. A., and Reigeluth, C. M. (1996). Designing instructional systems. In R. L. Craig (ed.) *The ASTD training and development handbook: A guide to human resource development.* Pp. 266–293. New York: McGraw-Hill.

Nadler, L., and Nadler, Z. (1992). *Every manager's guide to human resource development.* San Francisco: Jossey-Bass.

Robinson, D. G., and Robinson, J. C. (1998). *Moving from training to performance: A practical guidebook.* San Francisco: Berrett-Koehler.

Robinson, R. D. (1994). *An introduction to helping adults learn and change.* West Bend, WI: Omnibook.

Rosenberg, M. J. (1996). Human performance technology. In R. L. Craig (ed.), *The ASTD training and development handbook: A guide to human resource development.* New York: McGraw-Hill, 370–393.

Senge, P. M. (1990). *The fifth discipline: The art and practice of the learning organization.* New York: Doubleday Currency.

Solem, L., and Pike, B. (1997). *50 creative training closers: Innovative ways to end your training with impact.* San Francisco: Jossey-Bass/Pfeiffer.

Sork, T. J. (Winter 1997). Workshop planning. In J. Fleming (ed.), *New Directions for adult and continuing education,* no. 76, 5–17.

Training. (October 1997). 1997 Industry Report. *Training,* 33–75.

Tyler, R. W. (1949). *Basic principles of curriculum and instruction.* Chicago: University of Chicago Press.

Watkins and Marsick. (1993). *Sculpting the learning organization.* San Francisco: Jossey-Bass.

Willis, V. J., and May, G. L. (1997). A chief learning officer: A case study at Millbrook Distribution Services. In H. Preskill and R. L. Dilworth (eds.), *Human resource development in transition: Defining the cutting edge. Selected conference proceedings 1996,* 8–19. The International Society for Performance Improvement and the Academy for Human Resource Development.

Index

ABCs (learning objectives), 19.16
Action learning, 19.5, 19.27
ADDIE model, 19.10–13, 19.24, 19.29. *See also* ISD model
Adult learning, 19.5, 19.8, 19.14–15
Affective learning, 19.16
American Society for Training and Development (ASTD), 19.4, 19.6, 19.28
Analysis, ISD model, 19.10
Auditory learners, 19.17, 19.19

Behavioral learning, 19.16

Career development, 19.8
Changing environment, 19.26, 19.28
Chief learning officer (CLO), 19.27
Cognitive learning, 19.16
Competitiveness, 19.4
Cone of experience (learning pyramid), 19.20
Creative thinking workshop, 19.20
Customer focus, 19.5, 19.28

Design, ISD model, 19.10
Diversity (workforce), 19.28
Doers (learning styles), 19.16, 19.19

Empirical aspects, ISD model, 19.10
Employees' needs, 19.9
Ethical issues in training, 19.29
Evaluation, ISD model, 19.13, 19.24–26

Facilitating tips (training), 19.21
Feelers (learning styles), 19.16, 19.19
Fifth Discipline: The Art and Practice of the Learning Organization, Peter Senge, 19.26
50 Creative Training Closers, L. Solem and B. Pike, 19.23

Group exercises (training), 19.22

Human performance management, 19.28
Human performance technology (HPT), 19.8, 19.13
Human Resource Development (HRD), 19.4, 19.7, 19.13, 19.29
Human resource professional (manager), 19.8, 19.13, 19.14, 19.28–29

Implementation, ISD model, 19.13
Individual development, 19.8
Instructional strategies, 19.20
Instructional Systems Development (ISD), 19.8, 19.9, 19.10–11

Instructor-centered training, 19.14
Interactive learners, 19.17, 19.19
ISD model, 19.8, 19.10–13
Iterative aspects, ISD model, 19.10

Just-in-time (JIT) learning, 19.26, 19.28

Kinesthetic learners, 19.17, 19.19
Kirkpatrick's four-level model (evaluation), 19.24
Knowledge management, 19.7

Leadership training, 19.7
Learner-friendly/unfriendly, 19.30
Learning environment, 19.17, 19.29
Learning executive, 19.27
Learning organization, 19.5, 19.26
Learning pyramid (cone of experience), 19.20
Learning styles, 19.15–16, 19.19, 19.23
Learning transfer, 19.23. *See also* Training, transfer

Managerial-level employees, 19.4
Mistakes to avoid (training), 19.22

National HRD Executive Survey, 19.6
Needs analysis, training design, 19.12, 19.26
Nonverbal communication, 19.21

Objectives writing (training design), 19.11, 19.16
Observers (learning styles), 19.16, 19.19
On-the-job training (OJT), 19.5, 19.28
101 Ways to Make Training Active, Silberman, 19.21
Organizational change, 19.6, 19.14, 19.26
Organizational development, 19.8
Organizational strategy, 19.7, 19.9, 19.26, 19.29

Participation, 19.21–23, 19.25
Perceptual modalities, 19.16
Performance deficiencies, 19.10
Performance focus, training, 19.14
Performance management, 19.8
Physical environment, 19.17–19
POP (purpose, outcomes, process), 19.17, 19.23, 19.25, 19.29. *See also* Training, process design
Post-training learning groups, 19.25
Print learners, 19.17, 19.19
Problem-solving training, 19.8
Program planning theory, 19.9
Psychological environment, 19.17–18

Quality training, 19.10

Real-time learning, 19.27
Reflection questions, 19.22, 19.25
Reliable aspects, ISD model, 19.10
Restructuring (corporate), 19.28
Retention, 19.20
Return on investment (ROI), 19.13

Saying Hello: Getting Your Group Started,
  L. B. Hart, 19.21
Sequencing objectives, training design, 19.10
Systematic aspects, ISD model, 19.10
Systemic aspects, ISD model, 19.10

Tactile learners, 19.17, 19.19
Task analysis, 19.10
Teamwork training, 19.7
Technological advances, 19.26, 19.28
Thinkers (learning styles), 19.16, 19.19
To-do list (training), 19.21
Traditional focus, training, 19.14
Train-the-trainer training, 19.16, 19.18

Trainer/training manager, 19.10, 19.13, 19.21,
  19.23
Training,
  defined, 19.7–8
  environment, 19.17
  facilitation, 19.5, 19.20
  process design, 19.9–12, 19.17
  trends, 19.7
Training and employee development, core con-
  cepts, 19.7, 19.14, 19.26
Training planner's role, 19.9
Training transfer, 19.23–25
Training-to-learning shift, 19.26–27
Transaction role, 19.6
Transformational role, 19.6
Transitional role, 19.6
Translation role, 19.6

Visual learners, 19.16, 19.19

The Winning Trainer, J. E. Eitington, 19.21
Workplace learning, 19.4, 19.6

Managing Human Resources
in the 21st Century

From Core Concepts to Strategic Choice

MODULE 20

Using the Internet
for Training and
Development

Linda A. Jackson
MICHIGAN STATE UNIVERSITY

Managing Human Resources in the 21st Century: From Core Concepts to Strategic Choice,
by Kossek and Block

Publisher: Dave Shaut
Executive Editor: John Szilagyi
Developmental Editor: Bryant Editorial Development
Marketing Manager: Joseph A. Sabatino
Production Editor: Tamborah E. Moore
Manufacturing Coordinator: Dana Began Schwartz
Cover Design: Tin Box Studio
Cover Photographs: Copyright Shoji Sato/Photonica
Production House: The Left Coast Group, Inc.
Printer: West Group

Printed in the United States of America
1 2 3 4 5 02 01 00 99

MODULE
20

For more information contact South-Western College Publishing, 5101 Madison Road, Cincinnati, Ohio, 45227 or find us on the Internet at *http://www.swcollege.com*
For permission to use material from this text or product, contact us by
- telephone: 1-800-730-2214
- fax: 1-800-730-2215
- web: *http://www.thomsonrights.com*

ISBN: 0–324–01819–3

This book is printed on acid-free paper.

Contents

MODULE OVERVIEW 20.4

OBJECTIVES 20.4

RELATION TO THE FRAME 20.4

CORE CONCEPTS IN INTERNET TRAINING 20.5
What Is the Internet? 20.5
What Is Internet-Based Training? 20.7
Components of Internet-Based Training 20.7
Theories of Learning and Internet-Based Training 20.12
"Good" Internet-Based Training: Key Elements 20.14
Implementing Internet-Based Training 20.15

STRATEGIC ISSUES IN INTERNET-BASED TRAINING 20.17
Why Choose Internet-Based Training? 20.17
Why Not Choose Internet-Based Training? 20.17
What Type of Internet-Based Training? 20.18
Critical Issues for the Future of Internet-Based Training 20.19

APPLICATION 20.20

IN CONCLUSION 20.21
Debrief 20.21
Suggested Readings 20.23
Critical Thinking Questions 20.26
Exercises 20.26
References 20.27

INDEX 20.30

MODULE
20

MODULE OVERVIEW

The Internet is fast becoming a popular mode for the delivery of job training and development. Internet-based training (IBT) can deliver multimedia, interactive, self-paced instruction on demand, anytime, anywhere, and cost-effectively. Individuals at every level of an organization can obtain training in specific tasks, update skills, increase general or specific knowledge, or prepare for career advancement or change with minimal disruption to daily life activities. Potentially, IBT will revolutionize how we think about job training and development in the next century.

But what is IBT? What are the advantages of IBT for trainees? for organizations? How do principles of learning and instructional design apply to this new training delivery method and environment? This module will address these questions.

OBJECTIVES

The objective of this module is to provide an overview of IBT, a comprehensive list of resources for IBT, and hands-on experience with IBT. Specific objectives of the module are to:

- Define IBT and describe its components.

- Describe the key elements of "good" IBT.

- Describe the steps in implementing IBT.

- Discuss the advantages of IBT for trainees and organizations.

- Discuss critical issues for the future of IBT.

RELATION TO THE FRAME

As a specialized type of training, Internet-based training is related to the frame in much the same way as the general discussion of training found in Module 19. It is, however, most likely to affect the transaction and translation human resource roles. Like traditional training, it is designed to encourage employee development, skill building, and improved organizational performance. Computer-based training, however, is highly likely to have multiple uses, as most software runs on a similar platform. Thus, to the extent that employees become familiar with the Internet and the capabilities of computers, the number of transactions possible through this medium increases. In principle, such transactions as payroll reporting, acquisition of information on employee benefits, and the provision of various internal forms can be conducted through either the Internet or an intranet (i.e., an internet technology limited to a single organization).

Training via the Internet can also enhance the translation role. Internet-based tools such as e-mail, chat rooms, videoconferencing, and listservs can help employees to diffuse what they learn to colleagues throughout the organization. These tools can be tuned to reach as few or as many people as desired by the user. These tools often involve both asynchronous (at a different time) and synchronous (at the same time) feedback. In general, the Internet and an intranet are superb tools for disseminating information.

Normally, there are few constraints on the decision-making authority of firm management with respect to the Internet. Even unionized companies generally have the right to introduce new technologies. Unionized companies, however, will normally be required to bargain about the effects of a new technology on employees.

FIGURE 20.1   *A Frame for Understanding Human Resource Strategy:*
Context, Roles, and Constraints

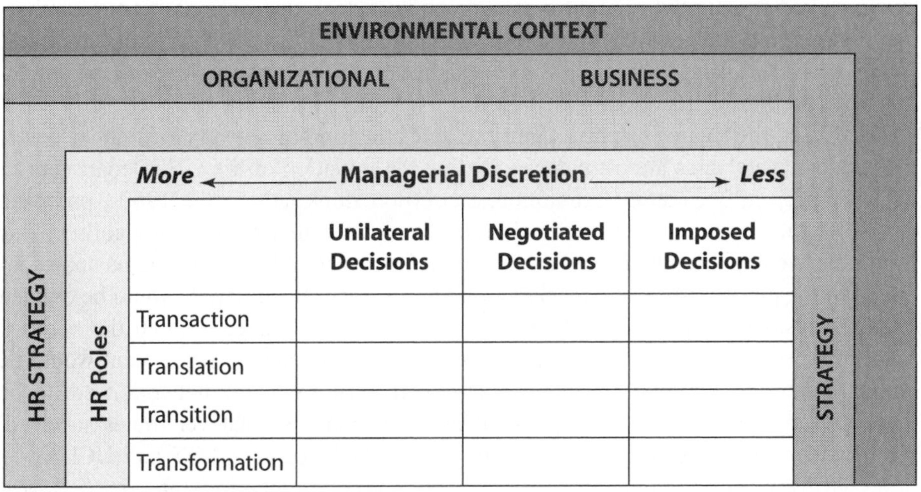

ENVIRONMENTAL CONTEXT			
ORGANIZATIONAL		BUSINESS	
More ← Managerial Discretion → *Less*			
	Unilateral Decisions	**Negotiated Decisions**	**Imposed Decisions**
Transaction			
Translation			
Transition			
Transformation			

(Left margin: HR STRATEGY, HR Roles; Right margin: STRATEGY)

© 2000 by Ellen Kossek and Richard Block. Thanks to Brian Pentland, Karen Markel, and John Beck for helpful comments and discussions that enhanced the model.

CORE CONCEPTS IN INTERNET TRAINING

What Is the Internet?

The Internet is the name given to an international network of interlinked computers, all of which use a common communications protocol called TCP/IP (transmission control protocol/Internet Protocol). TCP/IP is a standard way of formatting information and addressing computers so that information can be communicated between them. Any computer can be hooked to the Internet—it is "platform independent." It makes no difference what kind of computer is sending or receiving the information, or whether the information is transmitted by wire cable, satellite, or optical fiber. Another feature of the Internet is that it is decentralized; there is no central computer through which all communications must flow. TCP/IP and decentralization are at the core of the power of the Internet.

The term "the Internet" was first used in 1982 to refer to the enormous, growing collection of interconnected computer networks. Today, it is a global web of networked schools, businesses, libraries, federal agencies, private organizations, research facilities, individuals, and many other entities. The underlying connections that make up this network include terrestrial local area networks (LAN), wide area networks (WAN), plain old telephone service (POTS), and extraterrestrial services including satellite and microwave transmission. These connections now carry content, graphics, voice, and audio over the Internet to any connection on it.

The popularity of the Internet exploded with the invention of graphical "browsers" for the World Wide Web (the Web). The Web is a component of the Internet, or Internet "tool." Graphical browsers permit point-and-click navigation on the Web in ways understandable to most people. Other popular tools of the Internet are electronic mail (e-mail), file transfer protocol (FTP), and Usenet newsgroups, each of which is described in detail later.

A Short History of the Internet.   Historians of the Internet often begin its tale in 1973, although precursors of the Internet were in place long before then. It was in 1973 that the U.S. Defense Advanced Research Projects Agency (Darpa) initiated a research program to address a critical problem of the cold war era: How could the country's vital communications be maintained in the event of nuclear attack? A solution to this problem required an entirely different communication system, one with no "central authority," because a central authority would be the first target in the event of a nuclear attack. The new system would also need to be designed from the outset as capable of operating with portions of the system destroyed.

In fact, the idea of having a decentralized, attack-proof network was under development at several sites almost a decade before the initiation of the U.S. Department of Defense project. The Rand Corporation, a cold-war think tank in the 1960s, proposed a deliberately "unreliable" network designed to deal with its own unreliability. This would be accomplished by having all the nodes in the network of equal status and capable of originating, passing, and receiving information. The information would be divided into packets, each separately addressed and destined to meander through the network until reaching its final destination. The precise route from source to recipient would be unimportant. The important principle was that if portions of the network were to be destroyed, packets would still arrive at their destinations by whatever routes survived. Similar ideas were brewing at other technology hotbeds, namely, MIT and UCLA.

UCLA's supercomputer was the first node on the emerging Internet, followed shortly by other university and defense department computers. Together they formed Arpanet, named after the sponsoring agency (Advanced Research Projects Agency). Arpanet grew rapidly in the 1970s, sparked by the ease with which additional nodes could be added and by the network's indifference to the type of machine (i.e., computer) that wanted to join. All that was required to hook on to the network was that the computer/machine be capable of speaking the packet-switching language, known then as NCP (network control protocol), and now as TCP/IP, a more sophisticated language than NCP. TCP converts information into streams of packets at the source and reassembles them at the destination. IP handles the addressing and assures that packets will be routed across multiple nodes and multiple networks.

MODULE
20

In 1983, the military component of Arpanet separated from it and became known as MILNET. The remaining network, now less tightly controlled, was joined by other networks that had come into existence (e.g., BITNET) to form the network-of-networks now known as the Internet. The decentralized nature of the network and the fact that TCP/IP was public-domain software made connecting to the growing net easy. In fact, more connections meant more resources at no additional cost since each branch was independent.

It was the very next year, 1984, that the National Science Foundation, through its Office of Advanced Scientific Computing, decided to commit substantial resources to the development of NSFNET, which would connect bigger (capacity-wise), faster machines using bigger, faster links. The nodes of this network-of-networks, now recognizably the Internet, were denoted by either their geographic location (au for Australia) or by one of five Internet domain names: GOV (government), MIL (military), EDU (education), COM (commercial), ORG (nonprofit organizations). Arpanet, having accomplished its purpose, ceased to exist by 1989. NSFNET continues to exist, now funded by NSF, IBM, and MCI. But it is no longer "the" backbone of the Internet; there are now many backbones.

Growth of the Internet.   Internet watchers have been charting its growth since its emergence. But to quickly gain an appreciation of the Internet's phenomenal growth, consider the following statistics. In 1995, 22 million people accessed the Internet. In 1998, 70 million people did. In May 1998, it was estimated that there are 119 million people accessing the Internet worldwide. Projections are that 133 million people will be online by the year 2000, and this estimate is probably conservative (Commerce/Neilsen Internet Demographic Survey).

Equally impressive is growth in the number of Internet hosts. In 1981 there were 213 host computers. In January 1998, there were 30 million. More information about the history and growth of the Internet can be found at sites listed in the Suggested Readings section under Internet History and Growth on page 20.23.

What Is Internet-Based Training?

Internet-based training is a form of distance training that uses the Internet to deliver training materials. Similar to other forms of computer-mediated training (e.g., CD-ROMs), the trainee's primary tool is a personal computer located in the home, workplace, or training center. Training materials are typically created by professional instructional developers and delivered over high-speed networks.

Training materials vary in complexity from simple, text-only instruction to interactivity in virtual reality. In addition to Web pages—which constitute the core of most IBT—e-mail, chat rooms, and videoconferencing, described later, are often components of the training module.

IBT developers, professional or amateur, must have a "high-end" computer (i.e., fast processor, high capacity, fast modem) with a permanent IP (Internet Protocol) address, and an HTTP (hyper text transfer protocol) server software package. Professional developers generally provide the "server" computer, which "serves" the training module to trainees, or "end users." Computer requirements for the trainee depend on the sophistication of the training module. In general, any PC or MAC capable of handling browser software, having at least a 486 mhz processor, and a 28.8 kps modem will do. If the training module includes audio and video, additional hardware and software may be necessary that can be added easily on to most computer systems.

Components of Internet-Based Training

Training on the Internet involves the use of one or more Internet applications, or tools. More information about the Internet tools, described next, and about new tools coming to the market can be found in the Suggested Readings section (see Internet-Based Training (IBT): Foundations and Guidelines on page 20.24).

MODULE
20

The World Wide Web (the Web).

The *World Wide Web*, better known as the *Web*, is an Internet application that makes the Internet accessible to anyone, not just computer professionals. The Web was created in 1989 at CERN, the European Laboratory for Particle Physics, by Tim Berners-Lee. When people talk about the "Information Superhighway," they are talking about the Web.

To access information on the Web, you need a program called a *Web browser*, which communicates with a *Web "server"* that houses the information you want. The most popular Web browsers today are Netscape, Windows Explorer, and Mosaic. A *Web page* can be accessed either by clicking on the appropriate link on another Web page, or by typing its address, or uniform resource locator (URL), in the designated area of a Web browser.

To put information on the Web you must first have a *Web site*—a directory of files stored on a Web server. Space on a Web server may be obtained from an Internet Service Provider (ISP) or from your place of employment (e.g., universities typically provide server space for faculty and students). A Web site may consist of a single home (first) page or thousands of pages linked to the home page.

Web pages are written in hyper text markup language (HTML), a "soft" programming language used to "mark up" a document in a way that tells a Web browser how to display the information. Anyone can learn enough HTML to create a Web page. Alternatively, an HTML editor can be used to convert user input to HTML language. As of April 1998, there were approximately 350 million Web pages, with 1,000 new pages being added each day. Approximately 300,000 Web servers house these pages.

Web pages constitute the core of most IBT. The format of training Web pages varies considerably, from text-only to rich multimedia, interactive environments—e.g., videos, audio (voice, music, sound effects), photos/illustrations. But every training Web page, regardless of content, takes advantage of the "hyper" environment of the Web, that is, the ability to link to other information. *Hyperlinks* allow training Web pages to access information that can elaborate and extend the training module. Web pages also serve as gateways to other Internet applications, such as chat rooms, MUDS and MOOS, and videoconferencing, discussed next.

The contents of a training Web page obviously depend on the nature of the training activity and on how much an organization can invest in the professional development of training materials. Current estimates range from a few hundred dollars to $50,000 or more. Regardless of content and format, however, most training Web pages include the following elements:

- Information about the organization sponsoring the training, including mailing address, phone and fax numbers, and e-mail addresses of key personnel (e.g., training instructor, Webmaster).

- Title and brief description of the training module. The description should include information about the objectives of training, prerequisites (if any), nature of the training experience (e.g., text-only, interactive exercises), how performance will be evaluated (e.g., quizzes, task completion), approximate length of time to complete training, and answers to frequently asked questions (FAQs) about the organization and the training module.

- Links to Web pages and mailing lists/discussion groups relevant to the training module. Contents of links should be described in sufficient detail to allow the trainee to know what will be found there. It should also be clear whether a visit to a related site or discussion group is a required or optional part of training.

- Links to helper applications (tools) needed to complete the training module (e.g., Shockwave, Real Audio).

- Testing/evaluation tools and instructions on when and how to use them.

- Depending on expectations about trainees' familiarity with the Internet, it may be necessary to include on the training home page information about how to use links, including e-mail links, how to complete online quizzes/exercises and submit them, and how feedback will be delivered. If other Internet features are included in the training module, specific instructions about how to use them should also be provided on the training home page.

- A clear statement on relevant institutional policies and the roles and responsibilities of the trainer and trainee.

Electronic Mail.   Electronic mail *(e-mail)* is an easy-to-use IBT tool. Although many would consider it an underutilization of the Internet, training can be delivered entirely by e-mail since it is a highly effective way for trainers and trainees to communicate. Both can send messages and attachments (e.g., document files, photos) to one or many individuals simultaneously. E-mail links can be included in training Web pages so that trainees can send questions immediately, as they occur. Another advantage of e-mail in IBT is that most Internet users are familiar and comfortable with it.

Chat Rooms.   One way to facilitate interaction in real time (i.e., synchronous interaction) between trainer and trainees and among trainees is to include a *chat room* in the training module. Basically, a chat room is a place where any number of individuals currently online may enter and talk. The place is virtual, not physical, and talk is typed text, not spoken words. Professional instructional developers can create a chat room specifically for a training module. The room is then available only to trainees, unlike public chat rooms that are available to anyone. Recent advances in interactive technology now make it possible for the nonprofessional to create a chat room.

Chat rooms may be used for regular meetings between trainer and trainees— virtual office hours. Alternatively, trainees may meet with each other in the training chat room to share information, work on training projects, study together, or just chat. A chat room is always available to trainees but is used most effectively when visits are synchronized.

Multiuser Dimensions and Multiuser Object-Oriented Dimensions.

Multiuser dimensions (MUDS), like chat rooms, enable interpersonal communication in real time among multiple participants. MUDS vary from simple, text-only MUDS, where participants type in their contributions, to virtual realities, where participants may talk aloud, move their virtual bodies within virtual rooms, pick up objects, create objects, and leave objects for others. In the past, MUDS were primarily places where fantasy reigned; all-powerful participants would enter MUDS and engage in mortal battle with like-minded all-powerful participants. Today, MUDS are used in education and training as well. For example, they may be used to develop interpersonal skills, engage in group problem solving, and increase empathy for coworkers, to name but a few. *Multiuser object-oriented* dimensions (MOOS) are a variant of MUDS, adding to them the virtual reality dimension. Interpersonal communication in virtual reality contributes to the *edutainment* value of the training module, which may increase motivation to persist with training.

To date, IBT has not made much use of MUDS and MOOS, in part because they are more difficult to construct than other components of IBT, and in part because they require greater technical sophistication on the part of trainees. Expect this to change as the level of technical sophistication in the general population increases, and as trainees become aware of the learning and motivational advantages of the synchronous group activities that are possible in MUDS and MOOS.

MODULE
20

Mailing Lists/Listserv Discussion Groups.

Mailing lists, referred to as *listserv discussion groups* on the Internet, provide a means of asynchronous communication. There are thousands of public mailing lists covering almost every conceivable topic. Typically, a subscriber to the mailing list/listserv discussion group posts a question or comment which is sent via e-mail to every member of the group. Any member may respond, and all members receive all responses via e-mail.

Trainers can set up a mailing list/listserv for the exclusive use of their training group. The advantage of public mailing lists/listservs, however, is that they offer more information from a variety of sources, including experts on the training topic. Public listservs can inform trainees about current issues and hot topics. A list of public mailing lists/listservs that discuss IBT can be found on page 20.21).

Conference Rooms.

Another option for asynchronous communication between trainer and trainee and among trainees is the *conference room.* Trainer and trainees post questions and comments in the conference room, and respond to the questions and comments of others. All postings remains in the conference room (i.e., they are not distributed to participants via e-mail) for a predetermined period of time. The advantage of a conference room over a private listserv discussion group for training is that questions and comments may be elaborated, multiple topics may be considered simultaneously, and all postings remain available for as long as the conference room is in use. The disadvantage is that postings do not arrive conveniently by e-mail, but must instead be sought by visiting the conference room.

Newsgroups. *Newsgroup* is the name given to a listserv discussion group on Usenet. Usenet is a worldwide system of discussion groups that passes information among hundreds of thousands of computers. Not all USENET computers are on the Internet (maybe half). Like the Internet, Usenet is completely decentralized. There are now over 65,000 newsgroups hosting 10 million posts by 1.2 million people (Mediamark Research Inc. 1999).

Videoconferencing. Internet *videoconferencing* allows trainers and trainees to see and hear each other as they interact in real time. Also called desktop videoconferencing, participants are seen by a camera and heard by a microphone attached to their computers, which must also be equipped with conferencing software. Videoconferencing has numerous advantages. In addition to real-time interaction, new videoconferencing software allows participants to exchange material (e.g., files, e-mail) during the conference. The material appears in a video window on the participant's computer screen. Videoconferencing must be synchronized, although it is possible to call a conference at the spur of the moment.

Ideally, videoconferencing comes impressively close to classroom interaction, and will doubtless come closer as technology advances. The disadvantage of videoconferencing, at least at this time, is that it requires additional hardware (camera, microphone) and software that may be too costly for some trainees. In addition, bandwidth restrictions may limit video quality, and thus the quality of the videoconferencing experience.

Telnet. *Telnet* is an Internet protocol (i.e., program) for making a connection to a remote (physically distant) computer. Typically, it is necessary to have an account on the remote computer to access it via telnet. In the context of IBT, telnet is a convenient feature for trainers or trainees when they are away from home (i.e., training center, office, or home computer). Training can continue regardless of physical location by telneting to the host computer.

File Transfer Protocol. *File transfer protocol* (FTP) is the primary method for transferring files over the Internet. On many systems, it is also the name of the program that accomplishes this task (e.g., WS-FTP is an FTP program for Windows). Thus, it is another method, in addition to e-mail and videoconferencing, for trainees and trainers to exchange documents. For example, trainers can FTP an assignment to the training module server, where it can be accessed by trainees.

Another use of FTP is to obtain files from public-access FTP servers—remote host computers (or portions thereof) dedicated to maintaining and serving up files to the general public. Using a procedure known as *anonymous FTP*, trainees can bring a wealth of information about the training topic to their desktops. All that is needed is the name of the host computer and a few simple commands.

All of the major computer software giants (e.g., Microsoft, Netscape) maintain FTP servers containing public archives of shareware, freeware, and information. Many major universities also maintain vast archives of information available to the public via FTP. An extensive list of anonymous FTP sites is available at the University of Illinois, Urbana–Champagne. Also useful is a document titled "Internet Accessible Library Catalogs and Databases," available on many anonymous FTP servers (INTERNET.LIB). This document can be searched for information relevant to the training topic.

Intranets. *Intranet* is a term used to describe the implementation of Internet technologies within an organization, rather than by external connection to the global Internet. The advantages of an intranet are its ability to focus content on a particular purpose and provide a secure electronic environment for the organization. Because a corporate intranet can limit access to specified organizational members, sensitive information can be posted and shared. Intranets also provide more control over bandwidth reservation, assuring a quality connection that is not always obtainable with the Internet.

The disadvantage of intranets is that the wealth of information on the Internet is not available to the trainee. However, systems can be devised to permit calling out without permitting calling in to the organization's intranet.

Bulletin Board Systems. *Bulletin board systems* (BBSs) are networked computers that typically offer additional features and better performance over true Internet networks. Examples of commercial BBSs include America Online, CompuServe, and Prodigy.

Integrated Distributed Learning Environments. *Integrated distributed learning environments* (IDLEs) are professionally prepared training modules that are based on a collaborative learning model rather than a self-instructional model. As such, they make extensive use of the asynchronous and synchronous collaborative tools available via the Internet (e.g., chat, videoconferencing). IDLEs are designed specifically for training and education, and attempt to mirror the traditional instructional process (i.e., classrooms). Currently, IDLEs are being used both to deliver entire courses to remote learners (i.e., distance education) and to enhance classroom-based instruction. Examples of IDLEs can be found at the vendor sites listed in the Suggested Readings section under the Professional Instructional Developers/Vendor Sites heading (page 20.25).

Electronic Performance Support System. *An electronic performance support system* (EPSS) is a system designed to provide integrated, on-demand access to information, advice, learning experiences, and tools. The purpose of an EPSS is to enable a high level of job performance with a minimum of support from people (Gery 1991; Raybould 1990). Raybould (1995) defines it as an "... electronic infrastructure that captures, stores, and distributes individual and corporate knowledge assets throughout an organization, to enable individuals to achieve required levels of performance in the fastest possible time with a minimum of support from other people" (p. 11). An EPSS provides information at the moment it is needed, sometimes referred to as just-in-time training, while simultaneously building the knowledge infrastructure of the organization.

MODULE
20

EPSS is typically accessed through a graphical user interface (GUI) such as Windows. It consists of the following components:

- *Tools:* software (e.g., word processing) used with templates and forms.

- *Information base:* reference information, help facilities; statistical databases, multimedia databases; case history databases (all online).

- *Advisor:* an interactive expert system, case-based reasoning system, or intelligent tutor that guides the trainee through procedures and decisions.

- *Learning experience:* a multimedia interactive training module that uses simulations, case studies, scenarios.

An EPSS can be thought of as a high-tech job aid that combines tutorials, reference libraries, and computer-based training (CBT) into a single system that is accessible to workers as needed. Workers can ask questions, look up information, or participate in training without leaving their worksites.

Of course, the most difficult aspect of creating an EPSS is developing an intelligent advisor. The advisor must be capable of doing what a human advisor would do— e.g., model the behavior to be performed, help the worker establish goals and structure subtasks, and provide hints and reminders (Collins, Brown, and Newman 1990). If this difficulty can be overcome, an EPSS can be an invaluable aid for delivering just-in-time training—training delivered where it is needed, when it is needed, and without human assistance.

Theories of Learning and Internet-Based Training

IBT is a means to an end. That end is learning. A professional instructional developer can rather easily create a training module that uses interactivity and multimedia on the Web, and incorporates e-mail, chat rooms, telnet, FTP, and mailing/discussion groups. Whether the module optimizes learning is another matter. It is important to consider how principles of learning and instructional design apply to IBT, although the scope of this issue extends well beyond the objectives of this module.

In a thoughtful discussion about delivering instruction on the Web, McManus (1995) distinguished between instructional systems designs that focus on learning objectives, referred to as *traditionalist* designs, and those that focus on the interaction between the learner and learning content, referred to as *constructionist* designs (e.g., cognitive flexibility theory; Spiro, Feltovich, Jacobson, and Coulson 1991). Designs that focus on learning objectives typically adopt a step-by-step approach to producing and completing the training module, regardless of whether it is to be delivered over the Internet or in a traditional classroom. Traditionalist designs focus on teaching the learner to do X, rather than on increasing the learner's knowledge and understanding of X. McManus argues that these traditionalist designs are perfectly appropriate when training is about procedural knowledge that the trainee must ultimately exhibit. For example, if the objective of training is to "learn how to screw in a lightbulb," then these designs work just fine.

The traditionalist design model consists of seven steps, which may be completed in any order (McManus 1995):

- Identify the desired terminal behavior.

- Identify subordinate behaviors that must be achieved in order to achieve the terminal behavior.

- Based on the identification of subordinate behaviors, decide on prerequisites (i.e., behaviors that learners must bring to the instructional setting).

- Specify performance objectives for subordinate behaviors.

- Develop test items for the specific performance objectives.

- Develop the instructional materials.

- Evaluate the effectiveness of instruction (i.e., "Can the trainee do X?").

Consider, for example, the training of clerical staff to use a new word processing program. The traditionalist design model is appropriate in this case because the objective of training is easily stated in terms of the procedural knowledge that trainees should have upon completion of the training module. Specifically, trainees should be able to use the new word processing program to accomplish their job tasks. Subordinate behaviors are also relatively easy to identify. Trainees should be able to use the new word processing program to prepare letters, manuscripts, tables, attachments for e-mail communication, and any other products that are typically produced by the organization's clerical staff. Prerequisites for training would obviously include typing skills, but may also include familiarity with the clerical staff's typical products and with the word processing program used in the past to produce them.

Performance objectives for subordinate behaviors follow directly from each behavior. For example, if the subordinate behavior is "prepare technical reports submitted by field staff," the performance objective for this behavior may be stated as follows: "Trainees will be able to prepare technical reports submitted by field staff that are error-free within two days of receipt of report."

Testing the efficacy of training in this example would likely include both the development of specific test items (e.g., "Which keys are used to set margins for corporate letters?") and observations of on-the-job behavior and products (e.g., "Can the trainee produce an error-free technical report within two days of receipt?"). An additional and frequently overlooked issue with regard to testing, whether it be IBT or traditional classroom training, is the need to establish in advance what constitutes successful training. For example, is an overall score of 80 percent an indication of successful or unsuccessful training? If trainees can complete an error-free technical report in 2.4 days rather than 2 days, does this mean that training has been unsuccessful? It is very important that all parties (i.e., trainers, trainees, instructional development designers) be aware of the criteria for success at the outset of training.

Suppose that instead of training on how to use a new word processing program, for which specific behavioral objectives can be stated, the objective of training is to develop awareness of sexual harassment in the workplace. The traditionalist design model would be less well suited for this type of training than models based on constructionist theories of learning. Briefly, constructionist theories emphasize a nonlinear approach to learning, one in which knowledge is represented in multiple dimensions, with multiple interconnections among knowledge components (Spiro et al. 1991). An essential ingredient of this approach is user control over the sequencing and content of learning. The hypertext, hypermedia environment of the Internet is well suited for this approach.

How might a constructionist design model be used to develop awareness of sexual harassment in the workplace? The first step, according to McManus (1995), is to define the learning goals. Thus, the introduction to the training module should focus on what is and what is not sexual harassment. To help trainees think about this distinction, the second step in the model is to identify cases applicable to learning goals. Actual cases in which claims of sexual harassment were supported could be presented and compared with cases in which claims were not supported.

MODULE
20

At this point, constructionist models, unlike traditionalist ones, suggest that training be split into two paths—one predetermined and one learner-determined. Importantly, trainees decide which path to take, or whether to take both. The predetermined path should identify the most important themes and illustrate each with specific cases. In the context of our example, important themes might include the nature of the prior relationship between the accused and accuser, the power differential between them, and so on. To illustrate these themes, training might include a case in which a prior relationship between the accused and accuser existed and sexual harassment was not proved, a case in which a prior relationship existed and sexual harassment was proved, a case in which no prior relationship existed and sexual harassment was not proved, and a case in which no prior relationship existed and sexual harassment was proved. Similarly, cases could be selected to illustrate how the power differential between the accused and accuser is related to judgments about whether or not sexual harassment occurred. In this way, the trainee is encouraged to construct his own understanding of sexual harassment, an understanding that cannot be developed by simply providing a definition of the construct and a few examples.

On the learner-controlled path, the trainee can develop further her own understanding of sexual harassment by selecting cases and themes to explore. Thus, unlike the predetermined path, important themes are not identified first. Rather, it is left to the trainee to discover these themes for herself. Advocates of the constructionist approach (e.g., Harel and Papert 1991) insist that this discovery process is essential to true understanding. Trainees are of course free to return to the predetermined path to verify and refine their understanding (i.e., to reconstruct it).

The final step on both paths is to encourage trainees to reflect on what has been learned. Reflection can be incorporated into the evaluation component of training. In our example, trainees can be given actual cases in which sexual harassment has been alleged, and asked to decide whether harassment has occurred, and why. Alternatively, or in addition, trainees can be asked to construct hypothetical cases that illustrate harassment or not, and justify their illustration. Thus, the efficacy of training, from a constructionist perspective, is demonstrated by applying constructed understandings, not by reciting the understanding that others have provided.

Clear from this discussion is that the Internet is well suited for a constructionist approach to learning. The Internet encourages the creation of rich multimedia environments in which learners interact directly with the learning materials. Learners can choose their own paths to learning, constructing knowledge along the way. Learning materials can be arranged hierarchically (as well as linearly), allowing learners to move from broad inclusive concepts to specific examples. The learner controls the learning environment in a number of ways. She can practice new material immediately; repeat and review material as needed; and enter, exit, and reenter the environment at will. She can determine the pace and to some extent the difficulty level of material, and decide when material has been mastered based on feedback from the learning environment. Intelligent tutoring systems can help in this regard by providing feedback about the nature of the learner's mistakes and advice about how to correct them. Moreover, the learner can easily go beyond the training material by following hyperlinks to the wealth of resources on the Internet (Tennyson and Elmore 1997).

Based on his review of learning theories and instructional design, McManus (1995) concluded that which theory/design is best depends on the type of learning expected to occur. Learning that involves low-level cognitive processing, such as rote memorization, may best be accomplished by instructional designs developed from behaviorist perspectives. Learning that requires high-level cognitive processing, such as problem solving, may best be accomplished by instructional designs developed from constructionist perspectives. Learner characteristics must also be considered in the design of training. For example, visual learners might benefit most from graphic material in the training module; auditory learners from hearing the training material; and kinesthetic learners from hands-on, interactive exercises in the training module (Wave Technologies International, Inc. 1998).

Realistically, few organizations may be able or willing to first measure the learning styles of potential trainees, and then develop multiple training modules on the same topic, one module for each learning style. Moreover, research on learning styles has yet to produce a coherent set of findings and recommendations. Thus, the best recommendation for organizations is to build flexibility and redundancy into their training modules so that all learning styles will be accommodated. The nature of the Internet makes this recommendation relatively easy to implement.

"Good" Internet-Based Training: Key Elements

IBT should take into account motivational, cognitive, and behavioral aspects of learning. Essentially, IBT should motivate trainees to participate in the training module, facilitate knowledge and skill acquisition, and enable them to apply their knowledge and skills on the job. The following are suggestions for enhancing each of these three aspects of learning in the context of IBT.

- To enhance motivation for training:

  ✓ Use training materials that are appropriate for the ability/skill level of trainees.

  ✓ Organize material into learnable units (chunks).

  ✓ Provide opportunities for learner self-evaluation.

  ✓ Clarify the job relevance of training.

MODULE
20

- ✓ Reward successes.

- ✓ Use involving experiences in training (e.g., multimedia, interactive).

- To enhance cognitive outcomes (i.e., knowledge and skills):

  - ✓ Training materials should capture and retain attention.

  - ✓ Clarify learning objectives.

  - ✓ Adjust complexity and speed of materials to the ability/skill level of trainees.

  - ✓ Provide the "big picture" and return to it frequently.

  - ✓ Organize material into learnable units (chunks).

- To encourage the desired behavior:

  - ✓ Model the desired behavior in the training module.

  - ✓ Provide feedback and reinforcement during training.

  - ✓ Have trainees role-play the desired behavior during training.

- To accomplish training objectives in general:

  - ✓ Focus on the trainee. Consider the trainee's needs, abilities, and interests. Choose technology appropriate to them.

  - ✓ Focus on how to accomplish the learning objectives. Choose technology that facilitates this learning.

  - ✓ Maximize the trainee's opportunity to interact with the learning material. Learning is an active process. Avoid turning IBT into electronic page turning.

  - ✓ Maximize feedback to the trainee. Offer alternative paths, contingent on the trainee's responses. Provide contingent repetition.

  - ✓ Provide alternative ways of learning the same concept or task. Alternatives could be geared to different learning styles, mentioned earlier. For example, visual learners may benefit most from graphic representations, whereas auditory learners might benefit most from sound presentations of the same material.

  - ✓ Let the trainee determine the path of learning. Make the navigational alternatives clear. For example, trainees who successfully complete a pretest should be able to skip that unit and know where to go from there.

  - ✓ Be considerate of the trainee. Feedback should be constructive, not mocking. Avoid information that distracts rather than instructs. Avoid information that contributes to download time but not learning.

  - ✓ Invite feedback from trainees on how to improve training.

MODULE
20

Implementing Internet-Based Training

How does an organization implement IBT? While specific steps depend on characteristics of the organization (e.g., financial resources, current level of connectivity), the nature of the training material (e.g., skill acquisition, conceptual knowledge), and characteristics of trainees (e.g., number, computer literacy, location), discussed elsewhere, there are nevertheless a number of steps common to all implementation efforts:

- *Provide a clear statement of objectives.* What does the organization hope to accomplish with IBT? What specific outcomes will be used to indicate that the organization's objectives have been accomplished? For example, what specific skills, knowledge, or attitudes should trainees have as a result of IBT?

- *Identify existing and needed computing resources.* What hardware, software, and technical assistance are available now? What will be needed to implement IBT? What resources within and beyond the organization are available to move from current resources to those needed to implement IBT?

- *Design the interface.* Interface design is one of the most crucial steps in implementing IBT. The interface must be designed so that the trainee can navigate through the training material easily. Too many features will distract the trainee; too few will thwart progress. The trainees' previous experience with computers should be taken into account at this stage. A professional interface designer may be needed for implementing this step.

- *Test the interface.* Test the model interface on a sample of trainees or their equivalents, in terms of skill and knowledge about the training material and computer familiarity. Time spent to modify and retest at this stage is time well spent.

- *Prepare a design document.* As for interface design, it may be wise to hire professionals to work with organizational staff at this step. A technical group (systems analysts) is needed to establish the technical standards (e.g., required software, file-naming conventions). A project site manager or Webmaster is needed to establish the procedures and standards for server compatibility, security, and user access. Instructional designers are needed to clarify how the instructional design will accomplish the learning objectives.

- *Prepare the interface template.* The technical group (systems analysts) prepares the interface template, which consists of pages with prepositioned and coded navigational controls and repeating screen elements.

- *Prepare the training material.* A professional instructional developer may be helpful at this step also. She should work with the content experts to assure that the training material meets the training objectives.

- *Add multimedia.* Add graphics, movies, animations, etc., making sure that these additions are compatible with the user interface.

- *Create the HTML documents.* At this step, training content is added to the template's blank pages by writing HTML directly, or by using a WYSIWIG (what you see is what you get) editor.

- *CGI scripting.* CGI (common gateway interface) scripts turn static Web pages into dynamic ones. Dynamic pages allow for test taking, record keeping, updating, and security procedures within the training module. A professional programmer is usually needed to write CGI scripts.

- *Add interactivity.* Interactivity is becoming almost standard in IBT. Indeed, Web users in general have come to expect interactive Web pages.

- *Site maintenance.* Responsibility for training documents and supporting material generally resides with the Webmaster. This person handles the documents, configures the server, monitors system usage, maintains user accounts or access privileges, maintains supporting databases, and monitors and updates external hyperlinks.

- *Evaluation and Revision.* Determine whether the objectives of the IBT were accomplished. Did trainees acquire the desired skills, knowledge, and attitudes? Feedback from trainees, in addition to course performance, should be obtained to determine whether changes are needed to accomplish the IBT objectives.

STRATEGIC ISSUES IN INTERNET-BASED TRAINING

Why Choose Internet-Based Training?

IBT offers many advantages to both trainees and organizations. For trainees, perhaps the most obvious advantage is the freedom to participate in self-paced, self-directed training at any time and location. Trainees also benefit from the opportunity to explore training topics in depth, by way of links to other resources on the Internet. IBT that includes multimedia and interactivity is more enjoyable for most trainees than alternative modes of training. Indeed the term *edutainment* has been coined to describe learning on the Internet. Moreover, learning is more likely to occur when the learning environment appeals to more of the learner's senses, as is often the case with IBT.

A less obvious advantage of IBT for trainees is the freedom of expression that Internet communications may encourage. The anonymity of cyberspace makes it easier for many people to ask questions, comment, and present contrasting views. This too has an impact on learning. Increased two-way communication translates into more and better learning.

For organizations, the advantages of IBT include its versatility, indifference to time and space, and cost-effectiveness. With respect to versatility, IBT requires only that the trainee be literate and have access to a computer. Even the literacy requirement may soon be relaxed as the technology for delivering audio and visual images advances. And there is virtually no restriction with respect to content. Any type and amount of training can be delivered over the Internet.

Organizations also benefit from IBT's freedom from time and space restrictions. Training can be delivered to anyone, anytime, anywhere. There is no need to disrupt ongoing organizational activities to provide training. Moreover, the training delivered over the Internet is certain to be identical for all trainees. Thus, the organization has greater confidence in the quality and reliability of the training that all employees receive.

Particularly attractive to organizations is the cost-effectiveness of IBT. Although start-up costs may be substantial (from a few hundred dollars to up to $50,000), subsequent costs may be greatly reduced when compared to traditional classroom training. For example, some estimates indicate that technology-supported training requires from 30 to 40 percent less time than traditional classroom training. Less time in training means more time in productive activity. In addition, training materials can be inexpensively updated and revised, which translates into substantial savings for organizations in rapidly changing environments.

MODULE
20

Why Not Choose Internet-Based Training?

Given the seemingly overwhelming advantages of IBT, why wouldn't an organization or individual choose IBT? There are several factors that argue against IBT as the best training choice, despite its many advantages. They are:

- *Training needs.* The number of trainees and where they are located influence the decision to use IBT. If there are few trainees or if trainees are geographically proximate, then the benefits of IBT may not be sufficient to offset costs. A traditional classroom may be preferable in these situations. Similarly, if training is to be a one-shot experience for a small group of local employees, then the time and effort required to develop IBT may be better spent elsewhere.

- *Technical skills of trainees.* IBT requires that trainees have at least some familiarity with computers and the Internet. If they do not, then special efforts must be made, before and during training, to assure that trainees are comfortable and competent with this delivery mode. If such efforts are not made, then the benefits of IBT will not be realized, resulting in a net loss to the organization, which will have to train again using more traditional delivery modes (e.g., the classroom).

- *Motivation and self-discipline of trainees.* IBT requires that trainees are sufficiently motivated to learn the training material, and sufficiently self-disciplined to complete the material without supervision. Providing interesting training material (i.e., multimedia, interactive) will help enhance motivation and sustain effort. Nevertheless, some trainees require the interpersonal aspects of traditional learning environments to insure motivation and progress. For them, adding an interpersonal dimension to IBT (e.g., chat, videoconferencing) cannot substitute for a caring teacher who is physically present. Organizations should consider the needs and preferences of their trainees before implementing IBT.

- *Availability of computing systems and support staff.* Organizations with minimal computing resources should weigh the costs of adding and maintaining the technology against the anticipated savings from IBT. This is particularly crucial for organizations in uncertain environments, given the near certainty of technological advances and the constant need to upgrade.

Similar factors should be considered in deciding about an electronic performance support system (EPSS). According to Reeves (1996), an EPSS is a good choice when the following conditions prevail:

- Computers are readily accessible.

- The task is sufficiently complex to require detailed training.

- Task requirements change over time.

- Precise task performance is critical.

- Employees have sufficient time to use an EPSS.

- Employees have the ability and motivation to use an EPSS.

- Employee turnover is high, putting demands on training.

- Technical support is available to maintain and update an EPSS.

What Type of Internet-Based Training?

Typologies of IBT are emerging to help organizations decide which best suits their needs. Gallego (1997) offered one simple and useful typology. She suggested that there are four basic types of IBT that vary along two dimensions. The first dimension is the synchronous (instructor-facilitated)/asynchronous (self-directed, self-paced) dimension. Decisions for this dimension concern the extent to which trainers and trainees should interact in real time (e.g., chat, teleconferencing). The second dimension is the interactive/static dimension. Decisions here concern the extent to which dynamic, interactive materials should be included in the training module. Considering Gallego's typology, IBT appears to be evolving toward asynchronous learning in dynamic environments, with synchronous elements added primarily in the form of chat help rooms, virtual offices, and whiteboards for collaborative work.

An alternative typology of IBT divides training into four broad categories, arranged from low-end, in terms of cost and complexity, to high-end IBT. High-end IBT incorporates interactivity and multimedia into the training module. Arranged from low-end to high-end, the five categories are:

- *E-mail only, text only (linear), slide shows.* In these low-end forms of IBT, the trainee receives and is tested on the training materials sequentially. There is no interaction with the training materials, nor does the trainee have a choice about presentation or sequencing.

- *Drill and practice.* This type of IBT involves repeated presentation and testing on a specific topic. It is appropriate for acquisition of factual knowledge or as part of more complex learning presented in some other modality.

- *Trainee-selected pathways.* In this type of IBT the trainee chooses his or her own pathways to learning, skipping material already mastered, repeating material as necessary, and so on. Thus, the trainee controls the sequence and, to some extent, the content of learning.

- *Prepared (canned) simulations.* This type of IBT uses animation or video that presents a procedure to be learned. The trainee has little input or control over the training material. Nevertheless, this form of IBT may be useful when the objective is to master a prescribed procedure.

- *Fully interactive simulations.* In this high-end form of IBT, the trainee is brought into the learning environment, interacting with it, determining its nature, changing it at will. This is the most costly and complex type of IBT. It is best for learning complex concepts or tasks, especially tasks that pose a safety risk to trainees. Many if not all Internet tools are incorporated in this type of training (e.g., audio, video, virtual reality).

Critical Issues for the Future of Internet-Based Training

Given the incredible growth of the Internet and technology related to it, there is every reason to believe that IBT will be widespread in the twenty-first century. Indeed, it may be the most popular method for the delivery of job training. But how fast and how far IBT will spread depends in part on how several critical issues are resolved.

First is the idea of making the Internet available to all. This is no small issue. For example, in the United States a "digital divide" has already developed in which racial/ethnic minority groups are becoming the information "have-nots" (*Reuters Limited,* April 16, 1998). Evidence is also mounting that access to computers, income, and education cannot explain the digital divide (Jackson 1998; Kiesler 1995; Schofield 1995). The Internet, heralded as a great social equalizer, may in fact be widening the social, economic, educational, and political gaps that already exist in the United States. Implications for IBT are profound. Job training, so critical to obtaining, maintaining, and advancing in an occupation, may be more available to some groups than to others.

Second, IBT will benefit from the development of standards and guidelines for training programs. Currently, training programs are developed in closed proprietary systems with little or no sharing across organizations. However, there is evidence that this isolation is beginning to lift. For example, several large software companies (e.g., Oracle) are working together to develop a set of standards for IBT (Masie 1996). Professional instructional developers are entering into partnerships with industry, government, and universities to evaluate IBT. For example, IDL, a provider of training materials, is working with the National Center for Manufacturing Sciences (NCMS) and the State of Michigan to examine differences between IBT and satellite-based interactive distance learning. Included in this project are plans to develop instructional design guidelines for IBT.

Recently (1997), the Masie Center, a technology think tank and training center, launched a new consortium to create standards for online learning content development. The Online Learning and Training Council includes members of Microsoft, Oracle, Lotus, Coopers and Lybrand, American Express, and a diverse group of training managers, content providers, and technology companies. Their overriding goal is to facilitate online learning in an open environment.

Third, research on the effectiveness of IBT is lacking. Specifically, research is needed to identify what types of IBT are best for what types of learning and learners. Partnerships among professional instructional developers, training personnel, and university researchers must develop to evaluate systematically the effectiveness of the variety of IBT types in the variety of training situations.

APPLICATION

- An excellent way to understand IBT is to participate in it. The following is a list of Internet sites where you can participate in IBT. In addition to sites specifically designated below as free, most sites offer free demonstrations, and all provide information about their training course offerings. Choose two IBT sites and participate in a training module in each.

  BellSouth World Class Campus (Free demonstrations)
  http://www.bstwcc.com/

  Cyber Travel Specialist: Internet School for the Travel Professional (Free demonstration)
  http://cybertravelspecialist.com/

  Digital University: Training for Financial Institution Professionals (Courses require passwords, but the site provides a glimpse of IBT available for this group of professionals.)
  http://www.digitu.com/

  HHMI Virtual Lab. Lab technician training (Free)
  http://www.hhmi.org/grants/lectures/vlab1/

  HIV Virus Lifecycle, by Hoffman-LaRoche (Free)
  http://www.roche-hiv.com/lifecycle/flash/index.html

  How To Screw In A Lightbulb. Sage Interactive (Free)
  http://www.sageinteractive.com/tutoria1.html

  HTML Goodies (Free tutorials on Web page design)
  http://www.htmlgoodies.com/tutors/

  Gartner Group Internet Learning Center (Free demonstration)
  http://www.gglearning.com/

  LearnItOnline: Computing Topics (Free one-week trial)
  http://www.zdu.com/home.Aspergillus

  LifeLongLearning (Free demonstrations)
  http://www.lifelonglearning.com

  Microsoft Internet Guide and Web Tutorial (Free)
  http://www.microsoft.com/magazine/guides/internet/default.htm

  Networking Technologies (Selected free courses)
  http://www.scholars.com/

  SAIC Online Ethics Training (Free module)
  http://www.erols.com/robertwb/enzyme/ethics/ethics.htm

  SKILLSPACE (Free Netscape tutorial)
  http://www.skillspace.com/

  SKILS Demo. Sybase SKILS 3.0. (Free demonstration)
  http://dbcolon.sybase.com

  Success Learning Systems (Free demonstrations)
  http://www2.stlu.com/fd/slsonlinecc.asp

The Distance Education and Training Council
http://www.DETC.org

University of Texas Tutorial on Clickable Maps (Free)
http://www.utexas.edu/learn/pub/maps

- Consider one of the IBT sites that you selected from the previous list for your IBT experience. Based on what you have learned in this module, evaluate the IBT you received. For example, do you consider it "good" IBT based on criteria discussed in this module? Was the instructional design appropriate for the training material? What type of IBT was it? What components of IBT were included? Feel free to go beyond what you have learned in this module in evaluating the site.

- Visit one or two of the IBT mailing lists/listserv discussion groups listed next. Then describe what you learned about IBT from your visit. Specifically, record two or more comments of discussion group members that were informative to you about IBT. What did you learn about mailing lists/listserv discussion groups from your visit?

AEDNET Adult Education Network
listserv@pulsar.acast.nova.edu

COMPUTER-TRAINING (moderated)
listserv@bilbo.isu.edu

DEOS-L International forum for distance learning
listserv@psuvm.psu.edu

DISTED On-line Chronicle of Distance Education and Communication
listserv@pulsar.acast.nova.edu

EDSTYLE Learning styles theory and research
listserv@sjuvm.stjohns.edu

EDTECH Educational technology list
listserv@msu.edu

ITTE Information technology and teacher education
listserv@deakin.oz.au

LEARNING-ORG (moderated) Forum on learning organization concepts and shared experiences
majordomo@world.std.com

MEDIA-L Media in education
listserv@bingvmb.cc.binghamton.edu

MMEDIA-L Multimedia in education and training
listserv@vm.cnuce.cnr.it

NETTRAIN Training about and over networks
listserv@ubvm.cc.buffalo.edu

OHIOMM Multimedia development forum
listserv@miamiu.acs.muohio.edu

TRDEV-L Training and Development discussions
listserv@psuvm.psu.edu

<u>MODULE</u>
20

IN CONCLUSION

Debrief

IBT is no longer the wave of the future. It is the reality of the present, and may be the necessity of tomorrow. IBT can deliver multimedia, interactive training on any topic, anytime, anywhere. Although issues about universal access, standards, and effectiveness of IBT remain, evidence indicates that organizations are flocking to the Internet for training and will continue to do so. Consider the following statistics (UOL Publishing 1997).

In 1996, approximately 146,000 firms with more than 100 employees spent $59.8 billion to provide training and education to 58 million employees. Studies indicate that the training employees receive today will be obsolete within three years due to rapidly changing business conditions, a competitive environment, and marketplace trends. Further, a view of learning as lifelong is necessitated by the frequency with which people change careers.

Industry experts forecast that online adult education and training will be a $5.2 billion industry by the year 2000. Dramatic reduction in the cost of home computers has and will continue to fuel interest. The market for professional training and courseware developers seems infinite.

Gallego (1997), senior manager of professional training at Autodesk Inc., noted that human capital is becoming increasingly important to obtaining a competitive advantage. Consequently, companies are willing to spend millions of dollars to retrain employees because of the lack of skilled job candidates in the marketplace. Buying training technology provides a competitive advantage, and the ability to use the technology in business is critical.

From the trainee/employee perspective, the "training via technology" future bodes well. In addition to the advantages of IBT already discussed (e.g., choice about time and place of training), trainees can assemble "skills portfolios" online to keep track of their postsecondary and postcollege training and education. Skills portfolios will provide documentation of training not only for trainees but also for organizations that want or need to know about the training of American workers (e.g., labor unions, government organizations). Indeed, training portfolios are already possible on today's Internet.

MODULE
20

The Information Technology Association of America estimates that human resource development departments and training departments have doubled their delivery of training on intranets and the Internet between 1996 and the first quarter of 1997 (*Business Wire,* February 1997). The number of professional instructional developers has similarly increased, consistent with current trends toward outsourcing aspects of training.

Interactive electronic-based training appears to have measurable benefits beyond cost-effectiveness. One study showed a 25 to 50 percent higher retention rate than with traditional classroom instruction (*Multimedia and Videodisc Monitor,* March 1992). Others suggest that the quality of learning is higher than with traditional classroom instruction (*Wall Street Journal,* January 3, 1996). Case studies indicate that self-paced, multimedia training can take 20 to 80 percent less time than instructor-led training, thanks to tighter instructional design and trainee options to skip content already mastered (*Training and Development,* February 1996). And a survey of over 100 companies indicated that multimedia training can reduce learning time by 50 percent, compared with traditional classroom instruction.

A 1998 survey of 100 business trainers found that 40 percent of large corporate training groups plan to create corporate/university partnerships within the calendar year. Corporations will negotiate contracts to encourage universities to provide courses and technical degrees customized for a particular business. The survey also indicated that by the year 2000, more than half of this customized training will be delivered through technologies such as the Internet and videoconferencing (*Computerworld:* "Online Degrees," April 22, 1998).

Communication technology is prepared for the anticipated explosion of IBT. Recently, Sprint (June 2, 1998) announced a new connection that will allow simultaneous access to the Internet and telephone for a monthly charge similar to telephone charges alone. In Europe, technicians are now laying an underwater armor-protected cable called Gemini. It consists of four fiber optic strands, each thinner than a human hair but together capable of carrying almost 1.5 million simultaneous telephone conversations. This is the first submarine Internet cable, and it is expected to effectively eliminate all congestion on the Internet.

Assuming that the current momentum behind IBT continues, what implications does this have for trainers and training departments? Elliott Masie, president of The Masie Center, suggested the following scenario (April 23, 1998). He believes that the bulk of the administrative side of training will be moved to corporate intranets and the Internet. Training material development will be outsourced to professional developers who, in consultation with experts in the training domain, will prepare and deliver the training material. The role of trainers and training departments will thus be quite different. In addition to overseeing the development and delivery of training materials by the professionals, training departments will focus on information management, rather like virtual newsrooms. The demand will be for information that is narrow in scope and personalized. Trainers will be the information managers who assemble and publish this information on corporate intranets with links to Internet resources.

Is current optimism about IBT leading us to overestimate its role in future training? Probably not. Indeed, the reverse is more likely to be true. The end of the twentieth century has witnessed a growth in technology that was seriously underestimated by captains of industry. Consider the following prognostications:

"I think there may be a world market, for maybe five computers."

> —Thomas Watson, Chairman of IBM, 1943

"Computers in the future may weigh no more than 1.5 tons."

> —Popular Mechanics, forecasting the relentless march of science, 1949

"But what . . . is it good for?"

> —Engineer at the Advanced Computing Systems Division of IBM, commenting on the microchip, 1968

"There is no reason anyone would want a computer in their home."

> —Ken Olson, president and chairman of Digital Equipment Corporation, 1977

"640K ought to be enough for anybody."

> —Bill Gates, chairman and CEO of Microsoft Corporation, 1981

Suggested Readings

Internet History and Growth

Brief History of the Internet—Links to history pages
   http://www.isoc.org/internet-history/

CommerceNet/Nielsen Internet Demographic Survey
   http://www.commerce.net/research/stats/

CyberAtlas
   http://www.cyberatlas.com/resources/about_cyberatlas.html

GVU User Surveys
   http://www.cc.gatech.edu/gvu/user_surveys/

Hobbes' Internet Timeline
   http://info.isoc.org/guest/zakon/Internet/History/HIT.html

Nua Internet Survey
   http://www.nua.ie/surveys/how_many_online/index.html

Internet-Based Training: Foundations and Guidelines

Collaborative Learning and the Internet, by P. Dillenburg and D. Schneider
http://tecfa.unige.ch/tecfa/tecfa-research/CMC/colla/iccai95_1.html

Cognitive Models for Structuring Hypermedia and Implications for Learning from the World Wide Web, by J. Eklund
http://www.scu.edu.au/ausweb95/papers/hypertext/eklund/index.html

Compilation and Critical Reviews of Asynchronous Learning (links to over 700 sites)
http://jrbnt.vuse.vanderbilt.edu/alnpaper/compilations.htm

Effective Use of the Web for Education: Design Principles and Pedagogy, by R. Ells and B. Laden
http://weber.u.washington.edu/~rells/workshops/design/

Electronic Performance Support Systems
http://www.epss.com

Explorations in Learning and Instruction: The Theory Into Practice Database. Contains 50 theories relevant to human learning and instruction.
http://www.gwu.edu/~tip/

FTP site for resources on learning and training
ftp://psych.psy.uq.oz.au/lists/arlist/trdfaq-l.txt

Instructional Design Methodology, by B. Christie
http://www.sas.ab.ca/biz/christie/id.html

Instructional Principles for Adult Learners: Learning by Design, NETg
http://www.netg.com/adltlrnr.htm

Delivering Instruction on the World Wide Web, by Thomas F. McManus
http://ccwf.cc.utexas.edu/~mcmanus/wbi.html

Instructional Theory and Technology, Wave Technologies International, Inc.
http://www.wavetech.com/whtpaper/abttmwp.html

Issues in Learnability
http://www.peoplesoft.com/peoplepages/c/marcia_conner/html/issues_in_learnability.htm

Maricopa Center for Learning and Instruction (MCLI): 640 examples of how the Web is being used for learning, November 1998
http://www.mcli.dist.maricopa.edu/tl/about.html

Scientific American 7.79 "Taking Computers to Task"
http://www.sciam.com/0797issue/0797trends.html

Standards, Guidelines, and Recommended Practices for Computer-based Learning, Sponsored by IEEE: Computer Society Standards Activity
http://www.manta.ieee.org/p1484/

State of the Art in Web-based Training, 1997
http://www.gracespace.com/weblearn/state.htm

Technology and Learning, by D. Schneider
http://tecfa.unige.ch/edu-comp/edu-ws94/contrib/schneider/schneide.fm.html

Web-Based Training, by T. Kilby
http://www.webbasedtraining.com/

What constitutes a learning context? Instructional Management System (IMS): Developing specifications and building prototype codes for education and business.
http://www.imsproject.org/scope.html

Do you need an EPSS?, by Tom Reeves
http://itech1.coe.uga.edu/EPSS/Need.html

IBT Resources on the Internet

American Society for Training and Development
http://www.astd.org/

Distance Learning on the Net (resources), by Gary Hoyle
http://www.hoyle.com/distance.htm

Human Resource Professional's Gateway to the Internet, by E. R. Wilson
http://www.teleport.com/~erwilson/

On-Line Delivery Applications
http://www.ctt.bc.ca/landonline/index.html

The Training Registry
http://www.tregistry.com/

General Information About the Internet

Easy-to-read Introduction to the WWW and Web Authoring
http://www.cats.ohiou.edu/~acatec/webauthors/class/intro/

ILC Glossary of Internet Terms
http://www.matisse.net/files/glossary.html

World Wide Web Help Page
http://werbach.com/web/wwwhelp.html

Professional Instructional Developers/Vendor Sites

Altos Education Network
http://www.altosnet.com/

Arlington Courseware
http://www.arlington.com/index-nav.html

AT&T Learning Network
http://www.att.com/learningnetwork/

Autodesk
http://www.autodesk.com/products/index.htm

Centra's Symposium
http://www.centra.com

Commercial On-Line Education: Links to non-university course offerings
http://jrbnt.vuse.vanderbilt.edu/alnpaper/commercial.htm

Conferencing Package—Pine
http://www.wpine.com/

Masie Center
http://www.masie.com

Mentorware
http://www.mentorware.com

RealEducation
http://www.realeducation.com

Top Class
http://www.wbtsystems.com

Critical Thinking Questions

1. IBT is not the only type of electronic-based training. Name two others and compare them to IBT. Specifically, discuss factors that make IBT superior to each of the other two types. Discuss factors that make IBT inferior.

2. How did the original Internet solve the problem it was designed to solve, namely, to protect the U.S. communications system in the event of nuclear attack?

3. Describe the components of IBT. Is it possible to have IBT with only one of these components? Explain.

4. How is a chat room for IBT different from a MUD or MOO? Or is it?

5. Why would an individual enrolled in IBT need to use Telnet? FTP?

6. Consider two advantages and two disadvantages of mailing lists/discussion groups in the context of IBT.

7. Do you think that videoconferencing is a suitable substitute for face-to-face interaction between trainer and trainees? Why or why not?

8. What is a corporate intranet? What role do corporate intranets play in IBT?

9. What is the relationship between a corporate EPSS (electronic performance support system) and IBT? When should an organization invest in an EPSS?

10. Emphasis on behavioral objectives and feedback in the design of IBT is consistent with behaviorist theories of learning. What types of training are most amenable to this approach?

11. Constructionist theories suggest different models of IBT than do behaviorist theories. Describe the instructional model suggested by constructionist theories.

12. Describe the steps an organization should take in implementing IBT.

13. What are the advantages of IBT for trainees? for organizations? Do all trainees and organizations benefit similarly from IBT? Explain.

14. What distinguishes "good" IBT from "bad" IBT?

15. What factors should an organization consider before implementing IBT? Can these factors be viewed as disadvantages of IBT? Why or why not?

16. How can the design of IBT enhance motivation? learning? performance?

17. The Internet is viewed by many, particularly by its creators, as a quintessentially democratic tool. Is it? Explain.

18. How would the development of standards for IBT alter the nature of Internet training? List some advantages and disadvantages of standards for IBT.

19. In the absence of systematic research that indicates a clear superiority of IBT, why do you think organizations are flocking to it anyway?

20. Given what you have learned about IBT, would you prefer it to a traditional classroom for your own training? Why or why not?

Exercises

1. As a human resource manager you may one day face the question of whether to use IBT or some alternative to it. Consider the following two scenarios. They differ in important ways with respect to decisions about IBT. Based on

what you have learned in this module, indicate for each scenario whether you would choose IBT or not, and why.

- A large manufacturing company (over 1,000 employees) must retrain its assembly-line workers to prepare them for major changes in assembly-line procedures. The company has a modest information infrastructure (e.g., computerized inventory and billing), but relies on external providers for most of its computer technology needs. Profits are marginal. The training budget is minimal. Additional changes in assembly-line procedures that will require additional retraining are anticipated in the near future.

- A small real estate agency (about 15 employees) is computerizing its entire operation to minimize overhead and maximize the commercial benefits of a presence on the World Wide Web. All future listings and information about agents will be posted on company Web pages. The three-year plan is to extend the company's reach from local listings to statewide and nationwide listings. Of immediate concern is how to prepare staff (agents and clerical staff) for the coming virtual real estate office.

2. Justify the following statements:

- "IBT will never completely replace traditional classroom training."

- "IBT will one day completely replace traditional classroom training."

References

Bates, A. W. 1995. *Technology, open learning and distance education.* London: Routledge.

Burgstahler, S. E. 1995. Distance learning and the information superhighway. *Journal of Rehabilitation Administration,* 19, 271–276.

Caudron, S. 1996. Wake up to new learning technologies. *Training and Development,* 50, 30–35.

Collins, A., J. S. Brown, and S. E. Newman. 1990. Cognitive apprenticeship: Teaching the crafts of reading, writing, and mathematics. In L. B. Resnick, Ed., *Knowing, learning, and instruction: Essays in honor of Robert Glaser* (pp. 453–494). Mahwah, NJ: Lawrence Erlbaum Associates.

Davis, S., and J. Botkin. 1994. *The monster under the bed: How business is mastering the opportunity of knowledge for profit.* New York: Simon and Schuster.

Dede, C. 1996. Emerging technologies in distance education and business. *Journal of Education for Business,* 71, 197–204.

DePorter, B., and M. Hernacki. 1992. *Quantum learning.* New York: Dell.

Eastmond, D. V. 1995. *Alone but together: Adult distance study through computer conferencing.* Cresskill, NJ: Hampton Press.

Ellis, D. B. 1991. *Becoming a master student* (6th ed.). Rapid City, SD: College Survival.

Ertmer, P. A., and T. J. Newby. 1991. Behaviorism, cognitivism, constructivism: Comparing critical features from an instructional design perspective. *Performance Improvement Quarterly,* 6, pp. 50–72.

Falbel, A. 1991. The computer as a convivial tool. In I. Harel and S. Papert, eds. *Constructionism* (pp. 29–40). Norwood, NJ: Ablex Publishing.

Filipczak, B. 1995. Putting the learning into distance learning. *Training,* 32, 111–118.

Flannery, D. D., ed. 1993. Applying cognitive learning theory to adult learning. *New Directions for Adult and Continuing Education,* No. 59.

Galagan, P. A. 1994. Think performance. *Training and Development,* 48, 47–51.

Gallego, G. 1997. The State-of-the Art in Web-based Training. *http://www.gracespace.com/weblearn/state/htm*

Gardner, H. 1986. *Frames of mind: The theory of multiple intelligences.* New York: Basic Books.

Gery, G. 1991. *Electronic performance support systems: How and why to remake the workplace through the strategic application of technology.* Boston: Weingarten Publications.

Gery, G. 1995. Attributes and behavior of performance-centered systems. *Performance Improvement Quarterly,* 8, 47–93.

Harel, I., and S. Papert, eds. 1993. *Constructionism.* Norwood, NJ: Ablex Publishing.

Harmin, M. 1994. *Inspiring active learning: A handbook for teachers.* Alexandria, VA: ASCD.

Jackson, L. A. 1998. Race/ethnicity and the Internet: The vision—the reality—the vision. Second International Harvard Conference on Internet & Society, May 26–29, Cambridge, MA.

Kelley, L. 1995. *The ASTD technical and skills training handbook.* New York: McGraw-Hill.

Kerka, S. 1993. Life and work in a technological society. ERIC Digest No. 147. Columbus, OH: ERIC Clearinghouse on Adult, Career, and Vocational Education, Ohio State University (ED 368 892).

Kiesler, S. 1997. (Ed.). *Culture of the Internet.* Mahwah, NJ: Lawrence Erlbaum Associates.

Knowles, M. 1990. *The adult learner: A neglected species* (4th ed.). Houston, TX: Gulf Publishing.

Kolb, D. 1984. *Experiential learning: Experience as the source of learning and development.* Englewood Cliffs, NJ: Prentice Hall.

Kahn, N. B. 1992. *More learning in less time* (4th ed.). Berkeley, CA: Ten Speed Press.

Kraft, R., and M. Sakofs, eds. 1994. *The theory of experiential education* (2nd ed.) Boulder, CO: Association of Experiential Education, 1994.

Ladd, C. 1993. Should performance support be in your computer? *Training and Development,* 43, 23–26.

Laffey, J. 1995. Dynamism in electronic performance support systems. *Performance Improvement Quarterly,* 8, 31–46.

L'Allier, J. J. 1995. *The Skill Builder Philosophy: Learning by Design.* Naperville, IL: NETg.

Markova, D. 1991. *The art of the possible: A compassionate approach to understanding the way people think, learn, and communicate.* Emeryville, CA: Conari Press.

Massie, E. 1995. *The computer training handbook.* Minneapolis, MN: Lakewood Books.

McGraw, K. 1994. Performance support systems: Integrating AI, Hypermedia, and CBT to enhance user performance. *Journal of Artificial Intelligence in Education,* 5, 3–26.

McManus, T. 1995. Special considerations for designing Internet-based education. In *Technology and Teacher Education Annual,* D. Willis, B. Robin, and J. Willis, eds. Charlottesville, VA: Association for Advancement of Computing in Education.

Mediamark Research Inc., 1999. *http://www.mediamark.com*

Merriam, S. B., and R. S. Caffarella. 1991. *Learning in adulthood.* San Francisco: Jossey-Bass.

Mezirow, J. 1991. *Transformative dimensions of adult learning.* San Francisco: Jossey-Bass.

Moss, G. 1992. *The corporate trainer's quick reference.* Homewood, IL: Business One Irwin.

Papert, S. 1991. Situating constructionism. In I. Harel and S. Papert, eds. *Constructionism* (pp. 1–12). Norwood, NJ: Ablex Publishing.

Raybould, B. 1990. Solving human performance problems with computers. *Performance and Instruction,* 29, 4–14.

Raybould, B. 1995. Performance support engineering: An emerging development methodology for enabling organizational learning. *Performance Improvement Quarterly,* 8, 7–22.

Reeves, T. 1996. Do you need an EPSS? *http://itech1.coe.uga.edu/EPSS/Need.html*

Reynolds, A. 1993. *Trainer's dictionary: HRD terms, abbreviations, and acronyms.* Amherst, MA: HRD Press.

Rohfeld, R. W., and R. Hiemstra. 1995. Moderating discussions in the electronic classroom. In Z. L. Berge and M. P. Collins, eds. *Computer-mediated communication and the online classroom* (Vol. 3, pp. 91–104). Cresskill, NJ: Hampton Press.

Schank, R. C. 1994. What we learn when we learn by doing. Technical Report 60. Northwestern University: Institute for the Learning Science.

Schofield, J.W. 1995 *Computers and classroom culture.* Cambridge, England: Cambridge University Press.

Schroeder, L., and S. Ostrander. 1994. *SuperLearning 2000.* New York: Delacorte Press.

Senge, P. M. 1990. *The fifth discipline: The art and practice of the learning organization.* New York: Doubleday.

Senge, P. M., R. Roberts, B. Ross, B. Smith, and A. Kleiner. 1994. *The fifth discipline fieldbook.* New York: Doubleday.

Slalovitch, H. D., and E. J. Keeps. 1992. *Handbook of human performance technology.* San Francisco: Jossey-Bass.

Smith, R. M. 1990. *Learning to learn across the life span.* San Francisco: Jossey-Bass.

Spiro, R. J., P. J. Feltovich, M. J. Jacobson, and R. L. Coulson, 1991. Cognitive flexibility, constructivism, and hypertext: Random access instruction for advanced knowledge acquisition in ill-structured domains. In T. Duffy and D. Jonassen, Eds., *Constructivism and the technology of instruction* (pp. 57–75). Mahwah, NJ: Lawrence Erlbaum Associates.

Tennyson, R. D., and M. Elmore, 1997. In Tennyson, R. D., F. Schott, N. M. Seel, and S. Dijkstra, eds. 1997. *Instructional design, international perspectives, Volume 1 : Theory, research, and models.* Mahwah, NJ: Lawrence Erlbaum Associates.

Tennyson, R. D., F. Schott, N. M. Seel, and S. Dijkstra, eds. 1997. *Instructional Design, International Perspectives: Volume 1: Theory, research, and models.* Mahwah, NJ: Lawrence Erlbaum Associates.

Tuthill, G. S. 1989. *Knowledge engineering.* Blue Ridge Summit, PA: TAB Books.

Information and Insight About Online Education and Training. White paper prepared by UOL Publishing, Inc. *http://www.uol.com/webuol/index.cfm?Topic=Training&L1A=WBT&L2A =Overview*

Wave Technologies International, Inc. *Learning: The critical technology,* 1998. *http://www.wavetech.com/whtpaper/abttmwp.html*

Wheatley, M. 1994. *Leadership and the new science.* San Francisco: Berrett-Koehler.

Wick, C. W., and L. S. Leon. 1993. *The learning edge.* New York: McGraw Hill.

Wulf, K. 1996. Training via the Internet: Where are we? *Training and Development,* 50, 50–55.

MODULE
20

Index

....

Active-static dimension, 20.18
Alternative learning, 20.15, 20.18
Anonymity of cyberspace, 20.17
Anonymous FTP, 20.10
Arpanet (Advanced Research Projects Agency), 20.6
Asynchronous (self-directed) communication, 20.4, 20.9, 20.18. *See also* Synchronous communication

Bulletin board systems (BBSs), 20.11

CGI (common gateway interface) scripting, 20.16
Chat rooms, 20.7–8, 20.11, 20.18
Closed proprietary systems, 20.19
Cognitive flexibility theory, 20.12
Communication system, 20.6
Computer-based training (CBT), 20.4, 20.7, 20.11
Computer-mediated training. *See* Computer-based training (CBT)
Computing resources, 20.16
Conference room, 20.9. *See also* Teleconferencing
Constructionist design models, 20.12, 20.13–14

Decentralized communication network, 20.6
Decision-making authority, 20.4
Digital divide, 20.19
Distance education, 20.11
Drill and practice (type of IBT), 20.19

E-mail, 20.5, 20.7, 20.8, 20.9, 20.10, 20.12, 20.18
Edutainment, 20.17
Electronic environment, 20.10
Electronic infrastructure, 20.11
Electronic performance support system (EPSS), 20.11, 20.18
Employee development, 20.4
Evaluation component, 20.13–14
Extraterrestrial services, 20.5

File transfer protocol (FTP), 20.5, 20.10
Fully interactive (type of IBT), 20.19

Global Internet, 20.6, 20.10
Graphical user interface (GUI), 20.11

High-tech job aids, 20.11
Host computers, 20.6–7, 20.10
HTML (hyper text markup language), 20.7, 20.16

HTTP (hyper text transfer protocol), 20.7, 20.13
Hyperlinks, 20.7, 20.14
Hypermedia environment, 20.13

Implementation of IBT, 20.15–16
Information base, 20.11
Information "have-nots", 20.19
Information management, 20.23
Instructional development designers, 20.13
Integrated distributed learning environments (IDLEs), 20.11
Intelligent tutoring systems, 20.14
Interactive environments, 20.8
Interactive expert system, 20.11
Interactive training, 20.7, 20.16, 20.17, 20.18, 20.21
Interface design, 20.16
Internet, 20.5–7, 20.14, 20.17, 20.22–23
Internet, core concepts, 20.5–7
Internet Accessible Library Catalogs and Databases, 20.10
Internet domains, 20.6
Internet-based training (IBT), 20.4, 20.7–12, 20.14–16, 20.22
    and theories of learning, 20.12–14
    Internet sites, 20.20–21, 20.23–25
  strategic issues, 20.17–20
  typologies, 20.18–19
Intranet, 20.10–11, 20.22
IP (Internet Protocol), 20.5–6, 20.7

Job relevance of training, 20.15
Job training and development, 20.4

Learner self-evaluation, 20.14
Learning experience/environment, 20.11, 20.14
Learning styles, 20.14, 20.15
Learning theories, 20.12, 20.14
Listserv discussion groups, 20.9
Literacy requirement (IBT), 20.17
Local area networks (LAN), 20.5

Mailing lists, 20.9
Marketplace trends, 20.22
Model interface, 20.16
Motivation of trainees, 20.18
Multiuser dimensions (MUDS), 20.9
Multiuser object-oriented dimensions (MOOS), 20.9
Multimedia training, 20.8, 22.17, 20.22

NCP (network control protocol, 20.6
Newsgroups, 20.7, 20.10
NSFNET (National Science Foundation), 20.6

Online adult education, 20.22
Online learning, 20.19
Online skills portfolios, 20.22
Organizational performance, 20.4
Outsourcing, training, 20.22–23

Performance objectives, 20.12
Plain old telephone service (POTS), 20.5
Prepared simulations (type of IBT), 20.19
Public mailing lists, 20.9

Real-time interaction, 20.10
Remote learners, 20.11

Self-paced, self-directed training, 20.17–18
Server computer, 20.7
Site maintenance, 20.16
Soft programming language, 20.7
Standards for IBT, 20.19
Synchronous (instructor-facilitated) communication, 20.4, 20.11, 20.18. *See also* Asynchronous communication

TCP/IP (Transmission Control Protocol/Internet Protocol), 20.5
Technical skills of trainees, 20.17
Technological advances, 20.18
Technology-supported training, 20.17
Teleconferencing, 20.18. *See also* Conference Room
Telnet, 20.10

Theories of learning. *See* Learning theories, Internet-based training
Traditional learning/training, 20.4, 20.17, 20.18
Traditionalist design model, 20.12
Trainee-selected pathways (type of IBT), 20.19
Trainee/employee perspective, 20.22
Training home page, 20.8
Training module/material, 20.8–9, 20.11–12, 20.14–15, 20.18. *See also* Integrated distributed learning environments (IDLEs)
Training via technology, 20.22
Training Web pages, 20.8, 20.20–21, 20.24–25
Transactional (HR) role, 20.4
Translational (HR) role, 20.4
Two-way communication, 20.17
Typologies of IBT, 20.18

U.S. Defense Advanced Research Projects Agency (Darpa), 20.5–6
Unionized companies, 20.4
Usenet newsgroups, 20.5, 20.10

Videoconferencing, 20.7, 20.10, 20.11, 20.18, 20.22
Virtual reality, 20.7

Web page, 20.7–8, 20.16
Web server/Web browser/Web site, 20.7
Webmaster, 20.8, 20.16
Wide-area networks (WAN), 20.5
World Wide Web (WWW), 20.5, 20.7

MODULE
20

PART

4

CONTINUOUS IMPROVEMENT
OF ORGANIZATIONAL
PROCESSES AND WORK
RELATIONSHIPS

MANAGING HUMAN RESOURCES IN THE 21st CENTURY

From Core Concepts to Strategic Choice

MODULE 21

Systems Approaches to Human Resource Management

New Assumptions

Mary Jenkins
EMERGENT SYSTEMS

Tom Coens
QUANTUM PARADIGMS

Managing Human Resources in the 21st Century: From Core Concepts to Strategic Choice,
by Kossek and Block

Publisher: Dave Shaut
Executive Editor: John Szilagyi
Developmental Editor: Bryant Editorial Development
Marketing Manager: Joseph A. Sabatino
Production Editor: Tamborah E. Moore
Manufacturing Coordinator: Dana Began Schwartz
Cover Design: Tin Box Studio
Cover Photographs: Copyright Shoji Sato/Photonica
Production House: The Left Coast Group, Inc.
Printer: West Group

Printed in the United States of America
1 2 3 4 5 02 01 00 99

For more information contact South-Western College Publishing, 5101 Madison Road, Cincinnati, Ohio, 45227 or find us on the Internet at *http://www.swcollege.com*
For permission to use material from this text or product, contact us by
- telephone: 1-800-730-2214
- fax: 1-800-730-2215
- web: *http://www.thomsonrights.com*

ISBN: 0–324–01820–7

This book is printed on acid-free paper.

Contents

MODULE OVERVIEW   21.4

OBJECTIVES   21.4

RELATION TO THE FRAME   21.5

CORE CONCEPTS IN HUMAN RESOURCES SYSTEMS, POLICIES, AND PRACTICES   21.7

Systems   21.7

Assumptions   21.9

Building HR Systems Based on a New Set of Assumptions   21.10

Management Is Prediction   21.12

STRATEGIC ISSUES IN REDESIGNING HR SYSTEMS   21.14

Stage 1: Inquiry and Reflection   21.14

Stage 2: Critical Questions   21.14

Stage 3: Unearthing Assumptions   21.15

Stage 4: Applying Change Theory   21.15

APPLICATION OF THE DESIGN METHOD   21.15

GM-Powertrain   21.15

Placon Corporation   21.18

Falk Corporation   21.20

IN CONCLUSION   21.21

Debrief   21.21

Suggested Readings   21.21

Critical Thinking Questions   21.22

Exercises   21.22

References   21.22

INDEX   21.24

MODULE
21

MODULE OVERVIEW

Designing or rebuilding a human resources system is like building a house. You cannot build a house on quicksand or shifting rocks. You cannot build a sturdy house without a solid foundation and well-designed framework. The framework of a house is built in accordance with a *plan*. An architect's plan or blueprint contains an estimation of the specifications and support beams required to make the house sturdy. The plan also reflects the particular philosophy of the architect. Some architects focus merely on functionality, while others emphasize aesthetic themes or quality of living. For example, in the early 1900s, most architects designed A-frame houses with little more than basic utility in mind. By contrast, architect Frank Lloyd Wright designed homes to be more "livable" with a clear and consistent aesthetic theme, inside and out. His contrasting vision resulted in elegant, environmentally compatible, level-roofed homes that continue to influence the design of houses to the present day.

Designing and building a human resources system, albeit a practice, procedure, or policy, in many ways is similar to building a house. An HR system must be built on firm ground with a solid foundation. The foundation of an HR system is its underlying assumptions. They include commonly held, but often unchallenged, perceptions and values about people, motivation, productivity, communication, organizational change, how improvement occurs, and the like. Though unseen, these assumptions impact the efficacy of a system in powerful ways. Assumptions that are not aligned with the design of the system can cause unintended effects—effects that run squarely counter to the intent of the system.

All too often, these assumptions arise from beliefs that people are irresponsible, untrustworthy, and driven by self-interest. Conventional HR practices that dominate organizational life and the business world are steeped in these unhealthy beliefs. These beliefs are justified by the perception that the "real world" requires curtailment of undesirable human tendencies, i.e., that HR policies must have boundaries to prevent abuse by errant employees. In recent decades, however, a meager number of HR professionals have boldly parted from unhealthy assumptions. Influenced by Abraham Maslow, Douglas McGregor, Frederic Herzberg, and, more recently, W. Edwards Deming, they have attempted to design HR systems around a different set of assumptions—assumptions that people *are* responsible, trustworthy, and driven more by the greater good than self-interest. As Frank Lloyd Wright challenged conventional architectural design, this module challenges HR professionals to depart from conventional assumptions and design from a different philosophy and a higher vision of people. This module advocates adoption of a new set of assumptions in the design of HR systems and practices to get better results.

Designing for better results requires more than a new set of assumptions. It requires a shift to a mental model of experimentation and scientific thinking. To get better results, practitioners must understand the nature of systems and build HR systems and practices around a definitive plan. Such a plan allows a clear comparison of a system's intent with its outcomes. From this experimental framework, one can ascertain whether the designer's theory is valid and has predictive accuracy. Hence, learning and real knowledge may result.

OBJECTIVES

This module is intended to provide HR practitioners and students with a heuristic method for designing human resources systems, including practices, processes, and policies. This requires a new mindset of experimentation in which every practice and policy change begins with a theory and an express prediction of the intended outcome. This approach provides a lens for measurement and learning and sharpens the focus on the powerful link between HR systems and the underlying assumptions on which they are built. The objective is to enable the HR practitioner to *mindfully* build and redesign human resources systems based on a new set of healthier assumptions that will better align with desired organizational culture and business strategies. Hence, this module does the following.

- Demonstrates the important link between HR systems and unsurfaced assumptions:
  - ✓ All HR systems are based on underlying assumptions that have potentially insidious or positive effects.
  - ✓ Aligning an organization's HR practices, processes, and policies with a common set of assumptions increases the likelihood of an effective, cohesive system.
  - ✓ Every HR system and its assumptions are inextricably linked to every other HR system.
  - ✓ The underlying assumptions of HR systems impact, favorably or unfavorably, other systems of the organization, including the organization itself.

- Provides basic guidance for HR practitioners in recognizing and probing unsurfaced assumptions that underlie human resources practices.

- Offers a construct in which every decision made or practice adopted by an organization is a *theory* predicting a given outcome (if we do x, y will result). Organizational learning from this construct occurs when organizations:
  - ✓ Explicitly state the theory (e.g., if we downsize, profits will increase).
  - ✓ Recognize the delay between the time of action and when results are visible.
  - ✓ Reflect on the intended *and unintended* consequences of their decisions.
  - ✓ Realize that often cause and effect cannot be analytically linked within the complex system of an organization.

MODULE
21

- Utilizes the practice of traditional performance appraisal as a case study to demonstrate the driving force and effects of unsurfaced assumptions. Through this class exercise and the core concepts, the module provides a series of standard questions to be used in the design of human resources systems *from the inside out,* i.e., based on desired values and a healthier perspective of human potential.

RELATION TO THE FRAME

As the twenty-first century unfolds, the energies of human resources practitioners will be increasingly grounded in and integrated with the overall strategic goals of the organization. When optimal, human resources functions and *transactions* must bolster *all* of the systems and strategic goals of the organization. This will require a new consciousness about the inherent and unsurfaced aspects of all HR transactions.

Too often, human resources departments operate in a vacuum, rather than with a clear theory about the improvement desired. With the best of intentions, practices and policies are derived from purported state of the art applications or from copying another organization's heralded success story. In other instances, practices are altered in reaction to an adverse critical event and the haphazard attribution of that event to human weakness or dereliction. People systems cannot be designed from these types of impetuses. People systems must be carefully constructed with a well-articulated theory to ensure alignment with the organization's desired culture and core values. Inconsistent messages may signal insincerity and lack of commitment to the organization's professed core values about people. HR practitioners can expose potential flaws within the design

FIGURE 21.1 *A Frame for Understanding Human Resource Strategy: Context, Roles, and Constraints*

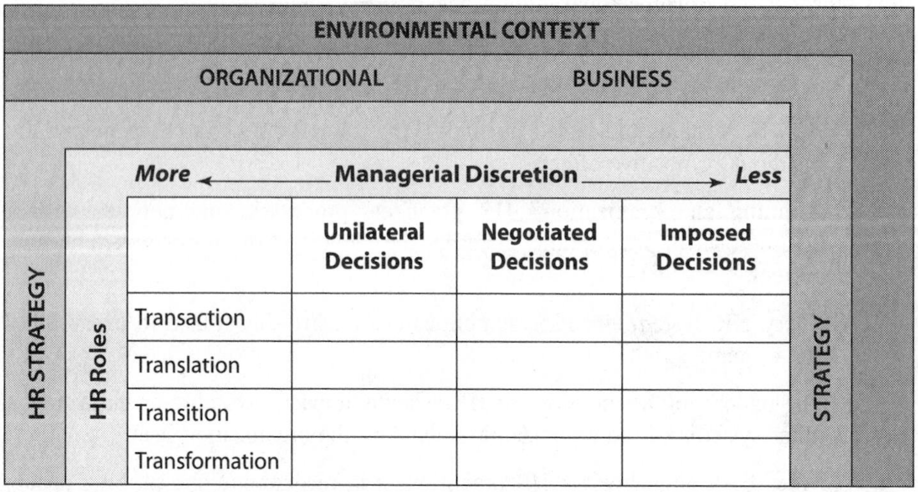

ENVIRONMENTAL CONTEXT			
ORGANIZATIONAL		BUSINESS	

HR STRATEGY

HR Roles — More ← Managerial Discretion → Less

	Unilateral Decisions	Negotiated Decisions	Imposed Decisions
Transaction			
Translation			
Transition			
Transformation			

STRATEGY

© 2000 by Ellen Kossek and Richard Block. Thanks to Brian Pentland, Karen Markel, and John Beck for helpful comments and discussions that enhanced the model.

process by identifying the underlying assumptions of a proposed system, a practice that is rarely followed in the profession. Articulation of the assumptions in the design process bolsters the likelihood of attaining alignment of people's energies with the desired culture and strategic goals of the organization.

As the *people* stewards of the organization, the HR department serves in a critical *translational* role for the organization—helping employees understand the direction of the organization and conveying messages about how people are perceived and valued. Words are cheap, but actions speak. It is the HR *systems* and *practices,* not memoranda and employee banquets, that patently send messages to people about their role and true value to the organization. HR practitioners must ensure that helpful and accurate messages are conveyed in designing its systems and practices.

As the company *transitions* toward the vision of a new organization, managers and supervisors will need to change their thinking about people. David Ulrich has cogently stated, "HR must now take responsibility for orienting and training line management about the importance of high employee morale and how to achieve it" (Ulrich 1997, 130). Ulrich further noted that HR must be " . . . an agent of continuous *transformation,* shaping processes and a culture that together improve an organization's capacity for change." (Ulrich 1997, 125). If the aspired culture embraces a team-based approach, a collegial and collaborative environment, a learning atmosphere, or a workplace characterized by empowered employees and customer-conscious service, the people of the organization must be seen in a new light.

Whether intended or not, conventional HR practices and management styles tend to treat people more like machines, schoolchildren, and laboratory animals. These Taylorian and Skinnerian approaches converge into a prevailing theme of mistrust in human beings and human nature, an assumption pervading nearly all conventional HR practices and policies. Cliff Bolster has described the pervasiveness and insidious impact of this thinking:

> Within our society, within the workforce, within our own personal lives, we set up enormous systems based on fundamental assumptions that people cannot be trusted. But we rarely calculate what the costs of these systems are. Leaders and followers are entwined in these systematic structures. (Bolster 1998)

HR practitioners cannot fashion new work environments from a foundation of mistrust. Instead, HR systems must be built on healthier values about people (i.e., values that foster trust, commitment, initiative, and creative spirit) and a mental model that sees employees as mature adults who will act in the best interests of the organization. The HR department cannot be successful in its pivotal, transformational role unless its own systems and practices deliver a consistent message. It further must lead by example, designing and developing new practices and policies collaboratively with *all* affected stakeholders, including "client" managers, "customer" employees, and the relevant labor organizations that serve as bargaining agents. This module focuses on helping practitioners bring these strategies and new thinking to the design and redesign of HR practices and policies. The frame for this new thinking is depicted in Figure 21.1.

CORE CONCEPTS IN HUMAN RESOURCES SYSTEMS, POLICIES, AND PRACTICES

Systems

A *system* is an indivisible whole consisting of people, behaviors, things, and ideas that act and interact with the aim of a common purpose. A system also is the combined actions and pattern of interactions of its parts. All of the parts of a system are *inter*dependent. That is, a change in any part of a system will affect one or more other parts of a system (Ackoff 1994). Hence, a system is not the sum of its parts; rather it is the sum of its parts *plus* the interaction of all parts. By analogy, consider the human body as a system. Picture the hand engaged in the process of writing. Though visibly you see only the fingers and the hands moving, the writing could not occur without the connection to the brain and nervous system, the muscles and tendons in the arm, the circulation of blood from the heart, and so on. While the hand may appear to be functioning discretely, its ability to perform is greatly determined by the system of which it is a part.

MODULE
21

Like the human body, a company or organization is a whole system. It consists of people, equipment, methods, materials, and environments working toward a common aim or assortment of aims (Scherkenbach 1986, 26). For example, McDonald's is a company that aims to conveniently provide low-cost, good-quality fast food to people throughout the world. Accordingly, McDonald's Corporation, its franchises, and its stores may be viewed as one system, bound with a common aim.

Subsystems. Within an organization, there are smaller systems or subsystems, such as the manufacturing system, the accounting system, the human resources system, etc. A company's human resources system is the interaction of people, things, and ideas that aim to recruit, develop, and retain the company's *human* or *people* component and promote the efficient and effective use of human energies and talent. A human resources system encompasses various subsystems, practices, methods, procedures, and policies. For example, a company may have an attendance *policy* that establishes attendance standards and rules about reporting. It may provide a *procedure* for calling in unexpected absences. The company may have an established *method* or process in which sick leave and personal leave are charged and recorded against individual banks. It may follow a *practice* of disciplining employees who have patterned absences or excessive, unexcused absences. Together, these and other policies, methods, procedures, and practices may constitute a single *system* that aims at stable and high levels of attendance, including a low rate of unscheduled absences. Such a system may also be identified as a *subsystem* of the HR system of the organization. In turn, the HR system is a subsystem of the company, which is a system at a higher level. While an HR system may appear to be discrete and separate from the greater system of the organization, its activities and subsystems are inextricably entwined with the organization as a whole. A change in a single HR policy may cause unpredicted effects within the company as a whole. For example, a new attendance procedure conveys a lack of trust to employees. The diminished feeling of trust may affect employees' attitudes, which in turn may adversely affect the way customers are treated. It is widely accepted that the way people treat others is affected by how they are treated (Bowen and Siehl 1997, 267–268).

Too often HR practitioners design and redesign practices and policies without thinking about their context and impact within larger systems. Because HR practices and policies are closely connected to people, a change in a single HR practice or policy often will have prodigious ramifications on other HR subsystems and the organization as a whole. Such a change may even undermine key strategic initiatives of the company. For example, Company X has incurred hard times with slumping sales. It recognizes that its labor costs per output unit far exceed those of all major competitors and, as a strategic goal, it has urged its managers to find ways to reduce employment levels. The HR Department subsequently introduces a new classification or job evaluation system to determine pay levels for exempt employees. That system ranks managers based on their comparative levels of responsibility. This compensable factor is measured largely by the total budget for the area managed and the number of positions supervised. Rating jobs based on employee numbers and budgets would encourage a manager to bypass an opportunity to shrink his department in half (fearing the pay consequences of doing so). In this example, a mere component of one part of the HR system (the classification method) is impeding an important, clearly communicated goal of the larger system, the company.

System dynamics. In order to redesign an HR practice or system effectively, the HR practitioner must comprehend the subtle and complex nature of systems. Lacking such understanding will preclude any meaningful assessment of a change in a practice or policy. A change in one part of a system may significantly affect the dynamics and patterns of the whole system, precipitating consequences that cannot be predicted. A system as a whole cannot be seen. In perhaps his most famous allegory, Plato describes a man chained to the wall of a cave who could not see the world outside. His only information about the real world came from seeing shadows on the wall of the cave. Like Plato, HR practitioners cannot see the overall system in which they work. A change in an HR practice or policy will have unseen, unpredictable, and unintended effects, though often it will throw *shadows* in various forms of indicators.

Such indicators (data, observed behavior, etc.) should be interpreted with caution. It is always difficult, if not impossible, to attribute the particular effects of a change within the dynamics of a system. System dynamics commonly delay the effects of a change, at least to the point of visibility (Deming 1994). This is true even when a change is positive and powerful. For example, an HR practitioner may design within its hiring process a better way to assess the qualifications of prospective employees. Initially there may be expense in the design and adoption of more burdensome procedures, such as testing instruments, more in-depth interviews, and careful background checks. In the beginning, adopting such a new practice would precipitate little more than complaints about the costs and extra time required for the hiring process. Over a period of time, perhaps years, an improvement in the quality of the company's workforce may be noticeable. Even then, it would not be obvious to everyone that the improvement could be linked to the hiring change. (The line managers may conclude that it was their supervisory skills that had improved!) Conversely, consider if the company had a poor training process, the hiring of better-qualified candidates likely would not have resulted in any change in the performance of the employees. This example illustrates the inscrutable triggers, intricacies, and nuances in the complex world of systems.

Assumptions

An *assumption* is a belief one holds true. It is a premise or statement that is accepted or presupposed without proof or empirical demonstration. Assumptions are always present in a system, whether consciously created or not. Assumptions are never idle; they always impact the efficacy of a system and often precipitate unintended results. A *set of assumptions* is a collection of related beliefs that are held to be true. Usually a set of assumptions clusters around beliefs that are interrelated or built on one another.

Human resources systems typically emanate from a set of assumptions that center on the nature of people and work—what motivates people and influences their behaviors, the way the work gets done and people are to be managed, and how communication, improvement, and change occur. Sometimes these assumptions are visibly manifested in the design of a system. More often, however, they are latent and ignored in the design process.

Human resources systems and practices are saturated with unearthed assumptions that reflect the organization's beliefs and values. A primer on the design of organizational policy explains:

> Policies and rules are usually good indicator's of an organization's value system, its assumptions about people and human behavior and its understanding of and beliefs about what makes organizations effective. What an organization says and does through its policies and rules has a major impact on how the organization is perceived by its employees (and in some cases, by its customers, suppliers, and the community). This perception impacts on the employees' sense of identification with the organization and its objectives. And, this perception influences the degree of "we-they" polarity in the organization and the level of cooperation or skepticism and cynicism which is present in the workforce. (Ranney and Carlson 1990, 3)

The underlying assumptions of HR policies and practices typically reflect the *de facto* values and overall culture of the organization. They commonly contradict the organization's formally adopted, loftier statements about how people are valued (e.g., "People are our greatest asset" or "Our workplace is built on the values of teamwork, trust, and empowerment"). The more negative, unsurfaced assumptions typically arise out of the human resources department's past practices and worst experiences in dealing with people and labor organizations. Consequently, they send pernicious messages that question people's trustworthiness and motivation to work.

Though unseen, underlying assumptions powerfully shape a system's innerworkings, efficacy, and outcomes for the better or the worse. Although these beliefs should constitute the core of a design effort, HR practitioners rarely contemplate these powerful triggers within the design process. Ironically, the employees of the organization, consciously and unconsciously, quickly recognize the underlying assumptions of an HR practice. Such assumptions speak, even scream, volumes to the people of an organization, conveying messages about how they are viewed, valued, and devalued. Worse yet, employees interpret the system or practice through the lens of these underlying assumptions, attributing unintended motives to its designers (the HR department) and the organization as a whole. Underlying assumptions are potent in insidious ways. They stealthily undermine intended outcomes, often paradoxically triggering exactly what the system was designed to avoid.

For example, an attendance bonus plan may be promoted as something positive—a reward for those who are conscientious or an incentive for those who may call in sick when the need is not so great. The impact of the plan's unsurfaced assumptions, however, may actually encourage people to take unnecessary sick-leave days. The act of offering a bonus to attain desired behaviors carries with it a number of underlying assumptions that send messages to everyone in the organization. To illustrate some of the possible underlying assumptions that might be associated with such a plan, consider the following list of unspoken messages:

- Coming to work is important to the company.

- People who are responsible about their attendance should be rewarded.

- People would rather not be at work.

- The people here are not motivated to come to work—they need an incentive.

- Working here is not interesting or fun.

- Our workplace is one people want to avoid.

- Our people call in sick when they are not sick.

- The job people do is not affected by whether or not they are sick.

- Getting a bonus is more important to people than taking care of themselves.

- People with infectious diseases should come to work, even if it causes other people to be infected.

- Sick days are an entitlement (whether I am sick or not); otherwise the company would not be offering bonuses to encourage people to give them up.

While the first two assumptions listed above may be viewed as positive and desirable, the remainder reveal reasonably deduced assumptions that may have adverse effects. Perhaps this is why attendance incentives are rarely effective. A number of controlled studies have shown that they are ineffectual in changing people's attendance patterns (e.g., see Scott, Markham, and Robers 1985). Consistent with the above assumptions, research also has shown that the use of special incentives to induce a person to do a task or meet a goal (such as good attendance) diminishes the person's interest or natural desire to do that task (Kohn 1993). This is because the use of an extrinsic motivator logically sends a message that the task or goal lacks inherent value or is otherwise undesirable.

What is most interesting about the underlying assumptions of HR systems and practices is the failure of practitioners to recognize them, even when the signs from a failing system are obvious. For example, an HR practitioner makes her best effort to design an incentive-based attendance system. When the outcome is disappointing, she may jump to attribute this outcome to bad attitudes on the part of the truant employees. Deeper analysis, however, may instead have revealed that the underlying assumptions and design of the policy contributed to the disappointing outcome. A cause-and-effect analysis and exploration of underlying assumptions may have led the practitioner to a different approach (e.g., day care, flextime, flex leave plans (PTO), collaborative scheduling, eldercare assistance and benefits, wellness initiatives, employee assistance plans, adult-to-adult communications about the impact of absences, and an array of organizational development initiatives that would foster a desirable workplace). If the practitioner had taken time to think through the underlying assumptions of an incentive attendance plan, she may have recognized that the assumptions were not helpful and were in fact incongruent with the corporate culture aspired to by the organization.

Building HR Systems Based on a New Set of Assumptions

In the preceding example, the practitioner alternatively could have designed an attendance improvement plan based on healthier values or assumptions about people. But exactly what is meant by *healthier*? Admittedly, it is a subjective concept. In the context of organizational development, however, it would at least mean a more positive, less cynical view about people's loyalty, intentions, and desires about working. Relative to the design of people practices, Columbia University professor John Whitney encapsulates a healthier view with one cogent question:

If everyone desired to do his or her job correctly and on time, and could be trusted to act with integrity and in support of the firm's aims and goals, what would your organization's processes and procedures look like? (Whitney 1998)

Most HR practitioners would quickly recognize that Dr. Whitney's assumptions are not the ones that drive commonly accepted HR practices and policies. The absence of healthier assumptions in organizational policy efforts cannot be easily explained. Going back to the 1940s, Abraham Maslow, Douglas McGregor, and others enlightened the business world about the possible benefit of healthier assumptions of people (Maslow 1998). McGregor described how a manager espousing Theory Y would see employees:

> He sees most human beings as having real capacity for growth and development, for the acceptance of responsibility, for creative accomplishments. He regards his subordinates as genuine assets in helping him fulfill his own responsibilities, and he is concerned with creating the conditions which enable him to realize these assets. He does not feel that people in general are stupid, lazy, irresponsible, dishonest, or antagonistic. (McGregor 1960, 140)

Table 21.1 illustrates these and other healthy assumptions about people in contrast to conventional assumptions. Although business schools, organizations, executives, and HR managers have commonly espoused such healthier values for decades, there is

TABLE 21.1   *Conventional vs. Healthy Assumptions About People*

Conventional Assumptions	Healthy People Assumptions
People do not like to work (Theory X).	People genuinely enjoy work, especially if it is interesting and challenging (Theory Y).
People are dishonest and cannot be trusted to do what is right.	People are honest and *can* be trusted to do what is right.
People are lazy, want to do as little as possible, and care little about the quality of their work.	People want to do their best, and they enjoy being productive and take pride in their work.
Problems with productivity and quality of work are caused by the dereliction of individual workers.	Problems with productivity and quality of work mostly arise from the *system* in which the work is done—the system includes the training received, work methods, tools, materials, environment, etc.
Extrinsic rewards and internal competition improve performance.	Improved performance comes from autonomy (choices and freedom), collaboration, and interesting and meaningful work.
People act in their own self-interest and not to serve the greater good.	People act both in their own self-interest and to serve the greater good.
Examples of policies and practices built on conventional assumptions would include: Time clocks, incentive pay, suggestion awards, confidential books, exhaustive job descriptions, voluminous work rules and policy manuals, detailed dress codes, ranking and rating performance appraisals, allocated sick leave banks, prescribed ceilings in expense reimbursement policies, and camera surveillance and computer monitoring systems.	Examples of policies and practices built on healthier assumptions would include: Individual time records, salaries and nonincentive pay, broad functional job descriptions, open books, minimal rules and empowering policies, open-ended sick leave and expense reimbursement policies, delegated dress standards, continuous feedback and an information-sharing environment, and an absence of unnecessary surveillance and monitoring of employees.

scant evidence of their widespread application in the design of human resources practices and policies. Increasingly cynical managers contend that, in the real world, such "idealistic" perceptions about people do not prove true. Such criticism, however, can hardly be validated in most organizations because their HR systems and practices are built on the conventional assumptions (see Table 21.1). This reliance on conventional assumptions, no doubt, causes a Pygmalion effect in the way people behave. Research has shown that communication of expectations will affect the way people act (Maslow 1998). If practitioners designed systems and policies on the basis of the Pygmalion axiom, the prevailing HR practices would have a totally different look and feel. Until practitioners design HR systems and practices based on healthier assumptions about people, the real potential of people in organizations cannot be unleashed.

Advocacy for healthier assumptions may be viewed as a normative preference because there is not a great deal of solid, empirical evidence to justify their endorsement. Just before his death, humanist psychologist Abraham Maslow acknowledged the questionable validity of Theory Y assumptions, but at the same time admonished: "(T)he whole philosophy of this new kind of management must be taken as an expression of faith in the goodness of human beings, in trustworthiness, in enjoyment of efficiency, of knowledge, of respect, etc." (Maslow 1998, 67–73). While Maslow expressly conceded that Theory Y assumptions are scientifically unproven, he also said the evidence supporting Theory X is "practically nil," explaining that Theory X:

> . . . rests entirely on habit and tradition. It's no use saying that it rests on long experience, as most of its proponents would say, because this experience is a kind of self, or at least *can* be a kind of self-fulfilling prophecy . . . I would say that there is insufficient grounding for a firm and final trust in Theory Y management philosophy; but then I would hastily add that there is even less firm evidence for Theory X. If one adds up all the researches that have actually been done under scientific auspices and in the industrial situation itself, practically all of them come out on the side of one or another version of Theory Y; practically none of them come out in favor of Theory X philosophy except in small and detailed and specific special circumstances. (Maslow 1998, 73)

Although some social researchers may contend that Maslow has overstated the lack of research associated with conventional assumptions, especially in the present-day literature, there nonetheless appears to be little evidence of Theory X's superior performance over Theory Y assumptions from controlled studies conducted over a long period of time. It is interesting that both staunch advocates and staunch opponents of incentive pay, a practice based on Theory X assumptions, recognize that there is no convincing evidence demonstrating that incentives can improve the quality of work (Gupta and Mitra 1998, 62–63; Kohn 1993, 124). Alfie Kohn more recently summarized the dearth of evidence in the literature, stating "(N)o controlled study has ever found a long-term enhancement in the quality of people's work as a result of any kind of reward or incentive program" (Kohn 1998). Whether or not Kohn, Maslow, or others have overstated the lack of Theory X evidence, there is little risk in experimenting with healthier, Theory Y-type assumptions in lieu of continuing with an unsuccessful or lackluster human resources practice or policy that is steeped in conventional Theory X assumptions. Moreover, if an organization is sincere about changing its culture around the importance of people and human values, new thinking must emerge. As systems sage Russell Ackoff succinctly noted, "If you want to change the way you act, change the way you think."

Management Is Prediction

All management, including the creation of new systems and practices, is about making *predictions* or applying *theory*. A directive or policy, in essence, is a prediction that a desired outcome will occur as a result of the chosen action. If we install a time clock and mandate a punching practice, we are predicting that work time and attendance will be more accurately recorded. If we adopt an at-will employment standard, we are predicting that the company will be better shielded from wrongful discharge lawsuits. Until the outcomes are known, however, such predictions, in the form of directives, procedures, or policies, are merely unproven *theories*.

The mental model of seeing the design of human resources systems as theory and prediction is a critical aspect of making improvements. While human resources managers earnestly strive to improve the systems and policies entrusted to their domain, they commonly fail to frame such changes within the context of theory and prediction. This oversight is further compounded when the outcomes and effects are not measured in a meaningful way, i.e., there is no check to determine whether the change has achieved the desired outcome and improvement.

By adopting a mental model of experiment, theory, and prediction, HR managers can design HR systems and practices with greater confidence and increase the likelihood of progress and improvement. "The future of HR must include the development and acceptance of a simple, yet powerful theory base, so that the myriad HR activities can become grounded in the business and integrated with one another," says Ralph Christensen (Christensen and Lake 1997, 18). In sum, the authors of this module believe that such a theory-based model would be distinguished by the following salient characteristics:

- The role of the manager is not to direct people and resources—it is to provide leadership through expressly-stated theory and prediction.

- All directives, decisions, practices, and policies constitute theory and prediction. In every change, HR practitioners must focus on making a good prediction. Hence, the mental model is: *if we do X, we predict Y result will occur*. HR practitioners must help their clients and customers understand that the job of HR staff is based on theory and prediction. This will necessitate a willingness to openly recognize their wrong decisions and the unsuccessful outcomes of changes they make.

- The underlying goal of the theory and prediction model is *learning* rather than being correct. Chris Argyris has observed that when unexpected outcomes are embarrassing or threatening, a pattern of defensive reasoning occurs accompanied by circumstances in which "... causal reasoning is not explicit, premises and preferences are often tacit, and the tests of conclusions tend to be non-existent or self-sealing." The end result, he says, is little learning (Argyris 1994). While unexpected outcomes and effects may precipitate a sense of failure for some practitioners, the mental model of experimentation can bring a healthier, detached outlook. It is a simple, normal occurrence to have some predictions result in unexpected outcomes. It is merely the *test* that has failed, not the practitioner. Gerald Langley et al. have noted that "The success of a test lies in what is learned from it, no matter how it turns out. The focus is on learning, and on the belief that learning will eventually lead to a successful change" (Langley, Nolan, Nolan, Norman, and Provost 1996, 25).

- HR practitioners must help the organization as a whole adopt a workplace culture in which effective management and leadership is viewed as theory and prediction. This means—

  ✓ Theories and predictions must be explicit and visible to all.

  ✓ The practice of *studying* and *learning* becomes an ingrained part of work; after every new practice or procedure is implemented, the organization openly looks at what was intended and what happened.

- HR practitioners must view their work with discernment and knowledge of systems and processes—minimally, this would include:

✓ Looking at the underlying assumptions of every system and practice they design.

✓ Recognizing that unintended consequences attend all such systems and practices.

✓ Making an effort to link cause-and-effect between systems and outcomes. This is very challenging, not only because of multiple variables and unseen factors, but, as noted above, because changes within a system are often delayed in time.

STRATEGIC ISSUES IN REDESIGNING HR SYSTEMS

An understanding of systems, underlying assumptions, and management as prediction yields a complete strategy for redesigning HR systems. Hence, the strategic model for redesigning HR systems can be viewed through the four stages, as follows.

Stage 1: Inquiry and Reflection

Designing a new system or redesigning an existing system requires inquiry and reflection on the past and current situation. The process necessitates deep probing and thought concerning underlying assumption, the affected systems, and a clear understanding of the aim of any proposed change. Ideally, practitioners should explore the situation with a broad-based design team, inclusive of HR practitioners and other stakeholders (*client* managers, *customer* employees, labor organizations, etc.). As Aristotle said, "Those who wish to succeed must ask the right preliminary questions." Accordingly, the design team is assembled to explore the important questions, such as:

- What existing or prior systems have dealt with the same aim?

- What outcomes and effects do people see in the current system(s)?

- Do they succeed or fail? In what ways?

- Why are the existing system(s) failing or how could they be more successful?

- What are the manifest and underlying assumptions of the existing systems and practices?

Exhaustive examination of these questions will likely yield potent insights about the foundations and the direction of any changes or redesign initiatives.

Stage 2: Critical Questions

Once a sense of direction is attained, the redesign process can be guided by three critical questions:

- What are we trying to accomplish?

- How will we know a change will result in an improvement?

- What changes can we make that will result in an improvement? (Langley, Nolan, Nolan, Norman, and Provost 1996)

Answering these questions will enable the HR practitioner to look at the proposed redesign with clarity, using prediction and establishing an express theory to guide the effort. Maslow describes why a prediction model is so beneficial, even critical, to any improvement effort:

(E)very suggested improvement ought to be considered a hypothesis or an experiment to be tested and confirmed, always with the implication that it may turn out to be untrue or false or unwise, and even more universally, with the expectation that even though it may work well, it is going to bring up all sorts of new and unforeseen questions. (Maslow 1998, 289)

Stage 3: Unearthing Assumptions

As discussed earlier, HR systems are fraught with unsurfaced assumptions that can affect the outcome for the better or the worse. Accordingly, every HR redesign process must give heightened focus to the underlying assumptions. To make this happen, incorporate in the design process the following queries:

- What are the underlying assumptions of the proposed practice or policy? What are the unsurfaced messages about people, motivation, trust, leadership, teamwork, etc? Are these assumptions aligned with the corporate culture and values we espouse?

- What underlying values and assumptions do we wish to build on? What new set of assumptions do we desire?

- If the underlying assumptions are incongruent with our desires, how can we change the practice or policy to reflect the values we espouse?

Answering the above questions often will mean rework and new ideas. This deeper level of inquiry will sometimes result in looping back to the three core questions for redesign in Stage 2. HR practitioners also would need to recognize that a change in one policy or practice may have little impact if it operates in an organizational culture or system of HR practices that sends opposite signals. For example, an HRD initiative to promote working in teams through training will likely not yield a change in behaviors, if the compensation and performance appraisal processes are sending anti-team messages.

Stage 4: Applying Change Theory

Lastly, the practitioner will need some knowledge of how to implement change. This would include doing pilots or clinics of the change on a small scale first as a preliminary test, rather than imposing ideas wholesale on an entire workforce. Working within systems of *people,* the practitioner also would need to know some basics about *change theory.* Change theory recognizes that people, for various reasons, instinctively resist change, even beneficial change. One rational reason for this resistance is fear—fear of the unknown, fear of adverse consequences, and fear conditioned from changes in the past. Fear is greatly overcome by helping people understand in advance why a change is needed and allowing their input at every stage of planning and implementation. Further reading on effective change management is referenced in the Suggested Readings section (Scholtes 1998, 219–228) of this module.

APPLICATION OF THE DESIGN METHOD

GM-Powertrain

During the mid-1980s, GM-Powertrain, a Division of General Motors with over 26,000 employees, was in the midst of a crisis, as was its parent company. GM's market share was continually dropping, and the quality of GM products at that time was inferior to that of Japanese automobiles. Around this same time, Dr. W. Edwards Deming, a charismatic, 86-year-old proponent of quality management was being heralded as a driving force behind Japan's emergence as a world-class economic power. GM, along with Ford, Xerox, Eastman Kodak, and other companies, looked to Dr. Deming for an elixir to solve their economic woes. Dr. Deming agreed to come to GM on his usual condition that he would be able to work directly with the top leaders of the company. GM consented to his demand, and Dr. Deming initially agreed to go to GM for one week each month.

Early in this relationship, GM-Powertrain became a focal point for implementing the Deming philosophy for several reasons. The *powertrain* (the train of gears and shafting that transmits power from the engine) was considered the "heart and soul" of an automobile. The quality problems with GM-Powertrain's engines (as measured by warranty claims, ratios of problems per 100 engines, fuel economy, and emission measurements) made it an ideal candidate for quality improvement. Finally, the general manager of GM-Powertrain was more than willing to work closely with Dr. Deming in shifting to a new philosophy.

Following Dr. Deming's advice, GM-Powertrain instituted a rigorous educational program for its highest levels of leadership. After working with Dr. Deming for one year, GM Powertrain adopted structures to ensure that the Deming philosophy took hold. They included:

- A commitment for all employees to attend Dr. Deming's four-day seminar

- Hiring a master statistician (Dr. Gipsey Ranney) recommended by Dr. Deming

- The development of a network of statisticians educated in Dr. Deming's theories and put through a challenging master's program. These statisticians were to provide the hands-on leadership for the transformation under the tutelage of Dr. Ranney.

Within GM-Powertrain, these actions set in place a structure and conduit for learning. Early in this transition toward a learning environment, the human resources staff began to look at its role in the transformation. Prior to working with Dr. Deming, GM-Powertrain lacked an awareness of untested, underlying assumptions. Dr. Deming raised managers and HR staff's consciousness by slowly taking them through a number of questions. The questions seemed ludicrously simple; "Why do you do that?" was repeatedly asked in one form or another. Often it appeared that the answer was obvious, but Dr. Deming taught them that the *why's* were mostly hidden beneath the surface. Over time, the managers and HR staff began to see assumptions connected to the way the company managed people and wrote policies. They learned from Dr. Deming that these assumptions were not written on the wall, but could only be discovered through intense probing. As the "silent language" came to the surface, assumptions about people were questioned and the possibility of more desirable or reliable assumptions were explored. Table 21.2 gives examples of some of these assumptions as they existed *before* Dr. Deming's arrival at GM and *after* his influence took hold.

The transition to new assumptions sparked new thinking among the HR managers who worked directly with Dr. Deming in reviewing HR practices and policies. It became clear that the company's traditional performance appraisal practice clashed with the desired assumptions under the Deming philosophy. The company's appraisal practice had included rating employees on a scale and linking outcomes to annual merit pay adjustments. Over a period of years and through employee input and process teams, the company severed rating scales from the appraisal process. The appraisal process also was disconnected from salary adjustments. For a while, written feedback appraisals were required. Eventually, these mandatory appraisals were dropped altogether. In its place, an elective feedback system for the purposes of employee growth and development was offered. Employees at their choosing and timing could seek feedback from anyone. The process was confidential, and feedback information was solely for the employee's use; it was not documented in the personnel file. A totally separate system allowed employees to voluntarily receive assistance with regard to career development issues. The company also mandated continual feedback from *systems* and *processes,* rather than individuals, as a focal point for improvement. The overall effects of these changes were

TABLE 21.2 *Underlying Assumptions at GM-Powertrain*

Assumptions Before Dr. Deming	Assumptions After Dr. Deming
Money motivates people to work.	• Money motivates people to get money (not necessarily to generate improvement). • Money's motivational power is short-term—there is little sustaining power. • The size of pay raises needs to continually increase to have the same impact. • It can be very demotivating to receive less pay than you think you deserve.
An individual's performance can be objectively evaluated.	• Assessment of an individual's performance is fraught with subjectivity. • An individual's performance level cannot be measured apart from the system in which the individual works. • Subjectivity and bias in judgment cannot be overcome by good intentions. • The company cannot identify with reliable accuracy the best and poorest performers within a given group of workers.
Improving the performance of individuals improves the performance of the organization.	• Improving the performance of systems and processes improves the performance of the organization.
Internal competition improves performance.	• Internal collaboration improves performance.
People are inherently lazy and cannot be trusted.	• People want to do their best and are trustworthy.
People take what leaders say at face value.	• People interpret what leaders say through observing their behavior.

positive in improving business indicators and the organizational climate. A rise in morale, trust, and openness generated a new culture that successfully facilitated quality improvement measures undertaken by the company.

In 1991, along came a bump in the road of transformation. GM headquarters ordered staffing cuts across the corporation to reduce costs. In other GM divisions, downsizing initiatives were underway, using performance appraisal rankings to purportedly choose the worst workers. Having abolished appraisals, GM-Powertrain could not follow suit without reverting back to some sort of rating or ranking of employees.

In response to the edict, GM-Powertrain formed a collaborative team consisting of line and staff employees from all disciplines including manufacturing, engineering, finance, and internal HR consultants. The objective of the team was to comply with the mandate in reducing labor costs while concurrently preserving the newfound culture of trust and openness. After discussion and deliberation, the team concluded that it did not want to revert back to any form of ranking and rating. The underlying assumptions of such a practice would send the wrong messages and contradict the learning that had transpired. Instead, the team wanted to preserve and build on the newfound employee culture. Using the format of questions for predictive management and by examining underlying assumptions, the team developed an alternative way to achieve downsizing. A number of new approaches were adopted including (1) elective personal leave; (2) elective retirements; (3) voluntary transfers; and (4) voluntary incentive buy-outs.

As a result of these measures, GM-Powertrain achieved the corporate mandate without exercising any involuntary layoffs or retirements.

The approach to the reduction-in-force preserved and strengthened GM-Powertrain's employee culture because the actions taken were aligned with its espoused, healthier assumptions about people. Although GM-Powertrain and all other GM divisions achieved the bottom-line goal of the mandated reduction, there was a sharp difference in impact at the human level. All of the other GM divisions had involuntary layoffs, often relying on performance appraisals to decide who would be affected. Following the decision process, external consultants Drake Beam & Morin conducted workshops in all GM divisions to provide assistance on careers options for people leaving the company. In visiting the worksites of the various divisions, the consulting firm reportedly found a marked difference in the atmosphere of GM-Powertrain versus other GM divisions. In other divisions, anger, depression, and cynicism clouded the atmosphere, whereas at GM-Powertrain, there was more acceptance of the changes and a focus on moving forward. Overall, they found GM-Powertrain's environment more positive and productive than in other divisions.

By relying on the new set of assumptions, GM-Powertrain pursued its design effort with a different approach. Managers acted in a manner that was consistent with the employee culture they were trying to build. Although they put their people values at the front end of their design effort, they still were able to fully comply with the cost-cutting directive of GM headquarters. This enabled their organizational development and quality management initiative to continue without significant disturbance.

Placon Corporation

Placon Corporation manufactures thermoformed plastic packaging and provides an array of merchandising, packaging, and design services for manufacturers of household, medical, hardware, and office products, such as SC Johnson Wax, Johnson & Johnson, Moen, and Abbott Laboratories. The company operates one manufacturing and service facility in Madison, Wisconsin, where it has approximately 325 employees.

In the late 1980s and early 1990s, Placon began sending people to Dr. W. Edwards Deming's four-day quality-management seminars and related workshops. The company also began to study Dr. Deming's 14 points, a prescriptive list of the most salient elements of his quality management philosophy. With the support of top leaders, the company began to think about how it managed the organization in contrast to these points. A focal point of this study was rethinking the company's assumptions about the nature and management of people.

The focus on unsurfaced assumptions naturally led to looking at HR systems and practices. As the Deming influence began to take hold, an executive planning design team was formed in 1993 to look at the disparities between Placon's HR policies and the new thinking that was emerging from the 14 points and other influences (such as the Johnsonville Sausage Company, a nearby manufacturer). Placon aspired to create a learning environment with an absence of fear (in accordance with Dr. Deming's Point #8, "Drive out the fear"). It desired team-based culture with a theme of "all one team." The company further sought a climate in which employees were respected as adults who could be trusted to act appropriately. These new assumptions required a de-emphasis of hierarchy, a whole new approach to policies and rules, and a commitment to allowing decisions to be made at the level closest to the work. It also meant more responsibility for every worker. Consistent with the desired culture, the names of production workers were changed to "team members" and supervisors to "team leaders."

The design team initially had to rethink the purposes behind their HR practices and policies. It looked for ways to redesign these practices in alignment with an "all-one-team" environment and the other desired assumptions. Early on, the team targeted the company's wellness incentive plan (paid to production team members) and an annual bonus for managers only. Both practices created a barrier between salaried-exempt and production team members. The office and management staff saw it as unfair that production worker teammates were getting generous attendance bonuses while they were excluded from this benefit. In turn, the production staff thought it unfair that their management teammates received annual bonuses while they did not. These and other inconsistent practices fractionalized the workforce and thwarted the goal of building an "all-one-team" environment.

The history of the sick-leave bonus was pertinent to the design team's analysis. In 1991, before the Deming philosophy took hold, the company had decided to take measures to lower its absenteeism rate. Up to that time the company offered a traditional sick-leave bank, awarding employees six sick days per year and allowing accumulation for unused days to be applied in subsequent years. This practice had yielded an absenteeism rate of 1.7 percent, slightly better the industry average (then about 2.0 percent or 2.1 percent), but still unsatisfactory to Placon. To improve attendance, in 1991 the Company changed from paying for *sickness* to paying for *wellness,* introducing an incentive that doubled the sick-leave allowance. More important, it allowed people to cash out at the end of the year with two days of sick-leave wages for every unused day of sick leave. This gave every production employee a potential bonus of 12 days of "wellness pay." The new bonus was popular, and a reduction in sick leave followed implementation, with usage dropping to an absenteeism level of .9 to 1.0 percent. Many people drew large bonuses, yet the winners were overwhelmingly the same people who had always had good attendance. The attendance bonus practice also resulted in complaints about people who were coming to work sick. Some of the complainants said that the contagion of people working sick was making *them* sick. The bonus practice also caused a noticeable increase in the number of people who were sent home sick in the middle of the workday.

The design team quickly realized that offering a bonus to production members "to not be sick" sent a negative message to people. "It assumed that they did not want to come to work," former Placon president Dave Boyer later commented. Barb Waters, Senior HR Generalist with the Placon Corporation and an original member of the 1993 design team, reported that the team wanted a culture that recognized, "We are all adults. We wanted to be consistent with an adult-to-adult level of thinking, not parent-to-child." She further emphasized that making employees "feel comfortable" was a focus of the redesign process in alignment with the goal of reducing fear ("Drive out the Fear").

With these goals, the design team over a period of years introduced a number of new HR policies. A new sick-leave policy was introduced to replace the wellness bonus. The revised practice no longer paid a wellness bonus; it simply paid people if they were sick. No documentation by the team member (employee) was required through the first five consecutive days of any absence (after that, the company's short-term disability plan took effect.) The new sick-leave plan was based on the presumption of trust, i.e., that the employee is an adult and absences presumptively are necessitated by good reasons. At implementation, some team leaders feared the worst type of abuse. The company, however, reminded the more skeptical team leaders (supervisors) that, if they had any valid reason to believe there was abuse, they were obligated to look into it further and take appropriate measures.

As wellness pay was eliminated for production team members, the traditional management bonus was also discontinued. In its place, the company created a new "profit-sharing" benefit for *all* team members, including office and production team members. This was a logical exchange, explained Barb Waters: "All-one-team was our goal—this was just another step toward treating all people alike." The new "trust-based" sick-leave practice and discontinuance of the wellness bonus had only a negligible impact on attendance, with the absenteeism rate rising slightly from an average of .9–1.0 percent to between 1.1 and 1.2 percent. This still was nearly half of the industry average and well below the company's average of 1.7 percent in the late 1980s. Overall, the company was pleased with the outcome and that the worst fears of the more skeptical were not realized. Since then, Placon's absenteeism rate has remained at the same low level, demonstrating that a sick-leave plan based on trust, even with a discontinued incentive, could still yield an excellent attendance level.

The sick-leave and profit-sharing changes were not piecemeal, but were part of an orchestrated effort to align all HR policies and practices with an emerging culture based on teams and learning. In support of a learning organization and personal development, employees were encouraged to use their a reimbursement benefit, which gave employees broad discretion in choosing what they wanted to learn. Consistent with its goal of driving out fear, the company eliminated many of its work rules and restrictive policies. For the same reason, it adopted a nonpunitive discipline policy that eradicated the harsh concepts and practices of reprimands and unpaid suspensions, substituting a model that focused on solutions and change in place of punishment.

Placon further discontinued its traditional performance appraisal process (with a five-point scale) and, in its place, adopted a friendlier feedback mechanism that emphasizes the attainment of skills and personal development. Traditional merit pay, previously tied to appraisal ratings, is no longer practiced at Placon. Instead, the company grants increases based on a "proficiency curve" in which identified skills are linked to particular pay levels in the curve. The team leader and team member together review the team member's skill level on the proficiency curve and jointly create a development plan that typically includes training, educational goals, and evolving to new jobs. Consistent with the adult-to-adult assumption and the "all-one-team" atmosphere, the dress code for management and office staff was revised and made more flexible (as it is for their production counterparts). The revised policy requires only that employees dress appropriately, with the employee making the judgment as to what is appropriate for the particular work situation.

Falk Corporation

The Falk Corporation (referenced in the assigned reading materials in *The Leader's Handbook,* Scholtes 1998, 302–303), among other policy changes, simplified its bereavement policy to reflect healthier underlying assumptions about the nature of people. Falk abolished a traditional full-page bereavement leave policy, with various categories of relatives, specified number of days off, different standards for part-time employees, etc. The new policy expanded coverage of bereavement to include the death of a friend and the entire policy is written in one sentence, shown in Figure 21.2.

The revised bereavement policy reflects a dramatic change in underlying assumptions. The prior policy assumed that employees were untrustworthy and would take advantage of the company if the opportunity were there. The new policy assumes that the employee is a responsible, trustworthy adult who is motivated to come to work and cares about the company. (Other assumptions are identified in Scholtes 1998, 302). Apparently, the trust was well placed. After the new policy was implemented, bereavement leave usage dropped 53 percent from its previous level (Scholtes 1998, 303).

FIGURE 21.2   *Example of a Bereavement Leave Policy*

FALK CORPORATION
BEREAVEMENT LEAVE POLICY

If you require time off due to the death of a friend or family member, make arrangements with your supervisor.

In Conclusion

Debrief

The examples involving GM-Powertrain's unique approach to handling a reduction-in-force, Placon's transition to an all-one-team atmosphere and adult-to-adult policies, and Falk's revised bereavement practice all demonstrate the application of a new set of assumptions about people. The identified practices clearly convey a sense of trust and the belief that employees will act in the company's best interest. Although practices built on healthier assumptions create the potential for a more supportive work culture, they remain rare occurrences in the American workplace.

The companies illustrated in this module are able to tell successful stories because they did not base their new policy initiatives on a knee-jerk whim or merely copy a purported "best practice" clipped out of a slick business periodical. Rather, they began with a *clear aim* of what they were trying to achieve. They examined *underlying assumptions,* aware of their potent effect in precipitating unintended outcomes. They worked from a *theory* and *predicted* that policies built on new assumptions would result in positive changes. They further realized that the design of new policies could not occur in a vacuum, but would need to operate within a *system,* a system of other HR practices and policies and a system of a desired corporate culture. They recognized that the development of these policies involved many stakeholders and, applying *change theory,* involved other stakeholders in the design process.

A major shift from traditional thinking in HR will be necessary before designing HR systems based on healthier assumptions is commonplace. The interest in applying healthier assumptions has not waned in the 50 years since Maslow and McGregor urged their application. In fact, the types of books being largely published for and sold to the business world in recent years would indicate increased interest in Theory Y-type environments. Foremost, the shift to this alternate people model will necessitate a deeper understanding of human nature, a knowledge of systems, and an adventuresome willingness to experiment and develop theories that rely on a healthier set of assumptions about human potential.

Suggested Readings

Bowen, David E. and Caren Siehl. 1997. "The Future of Human Resources Management: March and Simon Revisited." In D. Ulrich, M. Losey, and G. Lake, Editors. *Tomorrow's HR Management.* New York: John Wiley & Sons. 261–272.

Coens, Tom and Mary Jenkins. 2000 (anticipated publication). *Abolishing Performance Appraisals/Why They Backfire and What to Do Instead.* San Francisco: Berrett-Koehler.

Christensen, Ralph. 1997. "Where Is Human Resources?" In D. Ulrich, M. Losey, and G. Lake, Editors. *Tomorrow's HR Management.* New York: John Wiley & Sons. 18–24.

Deci, Edward L. 1995. *Why We Do What We Do.* New York: Penguin.

Deming, W. Edwards. 1994. *The New Economics.* Cambridge, MA: MIT Center for Advanced Engineering Study. 49–115.

Hartman, Curtis. 1997. "Sales Force." *Fast Company* (June-July) 134–146.

Haskett, James L. and Leonard A. Schlesinger. 1997. "Leading the High-Capability Organization: Challenges for the Twenty-First Century." In D. Ulrich, M. Losey, and G. Lake, Editors. *Tomorrow's HR Management.* New York: John Wiley & Sons. 39–47.

Langley, Gerald, Kevin M. Nolan, Thomas W. Nolan, Clifford L. Norman, and Lloyd P. Provost. 1996. *The Improvement Guide.* San Francisco: Jossey-Bass.

Maslow, Abraham H. 1998. *Maslow on Management.* (Deborah C. Stevens and Gary Heil, eds.) New York: John Wiley & Sons. 1–151.

Scholtes, Peter. 1998. *The Leader's Handbook.* New York: McGraw-Hill. 219-228; 293–368.

Ulrich, Dave. 1997. "Judge Me More by My Future Than by My Past." In D. Ulrich, M. Losey, and G. Lake, Editors. *Tomorrow's HR Management.* New York: John Wiley & Sons. 139–145.

Critical Thinking Questions

1. Why have HR practitioners historically not looked at assumptions as part of the design process in creating new systems and practices? Why do you think this is so?

2. What barriers would impede HR practitioners from shifting their design of HR systems to a new, healthier set of assumptions about people? Explain.

Exercises

1. Consider systems, practices, and policies that you have seen in school, as a customer, or as an employee in an organization, and identify whether or not there were discrepancies between the intent and outcome. What were the underlying assumptions of those systems? Did they affect the performance and outcomes of those systems?

2. As a class, utilize the process and questions identified under the Strategic Issues section on pages (21.14–15) to examine the associations with traditional performance appraisal (assume a formal rating by the supervisor that is connected to decisions pertaining to pay, promotion, layoff, and disciplinary action).

References

Ackoff, Russell. 1994 "On Creating Shared Visions." Madison, WI: Madison Area Quality Improvement Network.

Argyris, Chris. 1994. *On Organizational Learning.* Malden, MA: Blackwell.

Beatty, Richard W. and Craig Eric Schneier. 1997. "New Human Resources Roles to Impact Organizational Performance: From Partners to Players." In D. Ulrich, M. Losey, and G. Lake, Editors. *Tomorrow's HR Management.* New York: John Wiley & Sons. 69–83.

Bolster, Cliff. 1998. "Cliff Bolster on Trust." *News for a Change.* (August): 4.

Bowen, David E. and Caren Siehl. 1997. "The Future of Human Resources Management: March and Simon Revisited." In D. Ulrich, M. Losey, and G. Lake, Editors. *Tomorrow's HR Management.* New York: John Wiley & Sons. 261–272.

Christensen, Ralph. 1997. "Where Is Human Resources?" In D. Ulrich, M. Losey, and G. Lake, Editors. *Tomorrow's HR Management.* New York: John Wiley & Sons. 18–24.

Deci, Edward L. 1995. *Why We Do What We Do.* New York: Penguin.

Deming, W. Edwards. 1994. *The New Economics.* Cambridge MA: MIT Center for Advanced Engineering Study.

Gupta, Nina and Atul Mitra. 1998. "Value of Financial Incentives: Myths and Empirical Realities." *American Compensation Journal* (Autumn) 58–65.

Kohn, Alfie. 1993. *Punished by Rewards.* Boston: Houghton Mifflin.

————. 1998. "How Incentives Undermine Performance." *Journal for Quality and Participation.* 6–13.

Langley, Gerald, Kevin M. Nolan, Thomas W. Nolan, Clifford L. Norman, and Lloyd P. Provost. 1996. *The Improvement Guide.* San Francisco: Jossey-Bass.

Maslow, Abraham H. 1998. *Maslow on Management.* (Deborah C. Stevens and Gary Heil, eds.) New York: John Wiley & Sons.

McGregor, Douglas. 1960. *The Human Side of the Enterprise.* New York: McGraw-Hill.

Ranney, Gipsie and Ben Carlson. 1990. *Reviewing Organizational Policies and Rules.* Piqua, OH: Ohio Quality and Productivity Forum.

Scherkenbach, William W. 1986. *The Deming Route to Quality and Productivity.* Washington, DC: CeePress.

Scholtes, Peter. 1998. *The Leader's Handbook.* New York: McGraw-Hill.

Scott, Dow K., Steven E. Markham, and Richard W. Robers. 1985. "Rewarding Good Attendance: A Comparative Study of Positive Ways to Reduce Absenteeism." *Personnel Administrator* (August).

Ulrich, David. 1998. "A New Mandate for Human Resources." *Harvard Business Review* (January-February): 124–34.

Waters, Barb. 1998. (Senior HR Generalist, Placon Corporation) "Placon Corporation Changes in HR Practices, 1993–98: Interview by Tom Coens." Madison, WI, December 10 and 17, 1998.

Whitney, John. 1998. "Economics of Trust." W. Edwards Deming Institute Fall Conference. Washington, DC: W. Edwards Deming Institute (October 11).

Index

Assumptions, and HR systems, 21.4–5, 21.9, 21.14–15, 21.21. *See also* Conventional assumptions, Healthier assumptions
At-will employment standard, 21.13

Change management, 21.14–15
Change theory, 21.15, 21.21
Client managers, 21.14
Conventional assumptions, 21.11, 21.12. *See also* Assumptions, Healthier assumptions
Customer employees, 21.14

Design team, 21.14, 21.19. *See also* Human resource system design

Employee attitudes, 21.8
Empowered employees, 21.6
Experimentation model, 21.13

Foundation of mistrust, 21.7

GM-Powertrain, 21.16–18, 21.21

Healthier assumptions, 21.10–11, 21.12, 21.21. *See also* Maslow, Abraham, Theory Y
Human body analogy, 21.7
Human component, 21.7
Human potential perspective, 21.5. *See also* Maslow, Abraham, Theory Y
Human resource department, 21.5–7
Human resource practices or policies, 21.5, 21.7, 21.12
Human resource practitioners, 21.4–6, 21.9–11, 21.13–14
Human resource system design, 21.4, 21.8–12, 21.14–15, 21.21
    redesign strategy, 21.14–15
Human resource systems, 21.4–10, 21.12–13

Incentives, 21.10

Learning, as goal, 21.13

Management styles, 21.6
Maslow, Abraham, 21.11–12, 21.14–15, 21.21. *See also* Healthier assumptions
Methods, as subsystems, 21.7
Morale, employee, 21.6

Organizational culture, 21.5, 21.6, 21.9, 21.15
Organizational learning, 21.5
Outcomes of change, 21.13, 21.14

People component. *See* Human component
Policy/procedure-method/practice system, 21.7
Practices, as subsystems, 21.7
Procedures, as subsystems, 21.7
Pygmalion effect, 21.12

Reduction in force. *See* Workforce reductions

Subsystems, of HR systems, 21.7
Systems, interdependent, 21.7

Team-based approach, 21.6
Theory X, 21.11–12
Theory Y, 21.11–12, 21.21
Transactional role, 21.5
Transformational role, 21.6–7
Transition, 21.6
Translational role, 21.6

Underlying assumptions, and HR systems, 21.4–6, 21.9–11, 21.14–15, 21.17, 21.21
Unproven theories, 21.12–13
Unspoken messages, Human resource systems, 21.9–10

Values/value system, 21.5, 21.9, 21.15

Workforce reductions, 21.16–18
Workplace culture, 21.13
Wright, Frank Lloyd, 21.4
Wrongful discharge litigation, 21.13

MODULE
21

Managing Human Resources
in the 21st Century
From Core Concepts to Strategic Choice

MODULE 22

Organizational
Development and Change

The Role of Human Resources

Ben B. Benson
ANDERSEN CONSULTING

Angela Endres
ANDERSEN CONSULTING

Managing Human Resources in the 21st Century: From Core Concepts to Strategic Choice,
by Kossek and Block

Publisher: Dave Shaut
Executive Editor: John Szilagyi
Developmental Editor: Bryant Editorial Development
Marketing Manager: Joseph A. Sabatino
Production Editor: Tamborah E. Moore
Manufacturing Coordinator: Dana Began Schwartz
Cover Design: Tin Box Studio
Cover Photographs: Copyright Shoji Sato/Photonica
Production House: The Left Coast Group, Inc.
Printer: West Group

Printed in the United States of America
1 2 3 4 5 02 01 00 99

For more information contact South-Western College Publishing, 5101 Madison Road, Cincinnati, Ohio, 45227 or find us on the Internet at *http://www.swcollege.com*
For permission to use material from this text or product, contact us by
- telephone: 1-800-730-2214
- fax: 1-800-730-2215
- web: *http://www.thomsonrights.com*

ISBN: 0–324–01821–5

This book is printed on acid-free paper.

Contents

MODULE OVERVIEW 22.4

RELATION TO THE FRAME 22.4

CORE CONCEPTS IN HUMAN RESOURCES' ROLE
IN ORGANIZATIONAL DEVELOPMENT AND CHANGE 22.5

The State of Human Resources 22.5

Toward a New HR Framework 22.6

HR Membership and Guerrilla Warfare 22.6

STRATEGIC ISSUES IN HUMAN RESOURCES' ROLE
IN ORGANIZATIONAL DEVELOPMENT AND CHANGE 22.7

Restructure to Adequately Assess Needs 22.7

Radical Reengineering to Operate as a Team Member 22.8

Clear Deliverables, Not Paradigms and Models 22.9

Mitigating Common Errors of Winging It, Antagonizing,
and Dropping the Ball 22.9

Responses Using Best Practices, Key Performance Indicators,
and Value Analysis 22.11

HR and Change Management: The Chrysler Finance Example 22.12

A Clear Change Model 22.13

The Modified HR Organization 22.16

Change Management and Human Resources 22.17

The HRD Landscape 22.18

APPLICATION 1 22.19

Ford Motor Manufacturing Education, Training,
and Development Case Study 22.19

APPLICATION 2 22.20

IN CONCLUSION 22.22

Debrief 22.22

Suggested Readings and Resources 22.22

Critical Thinking Questions 22.22

INDEX 22.23

MODULE OVERVIEW

Human resources is facing a tremendous challenge to lower infrastructure costs of core services such as payroll administration, benefits administration, and recruiting. It is pressured to connect more directly with employees through such programs as enhanced benefit options or 24×7 call centers. But most importantly, human resources is expected to become a better resource across the organization in training, organization design, job and performance design, and change management. The need to be involved within the major projects of departments across the organization is becoming apparent. This need, however, has clearly become more demanding. Instead of looking to human resources (HR) for approval or for coaching on human resource issues, the rest of the organization is looking to HR for co-ownership of the "deliverables" that come out of projects. So, whether it is reengineering in the field zone offices, assessing workforce issues coming out of new technology in the finance department, or helping the sales and marketing group with appropriate short-term incentives for a new product launch, HR must become owners of business solutions. To do so, a clear need to understand the business drivers and technical issues surrounding given departments and lines of business has become obvious. This module outlines ways that HR can aid the rest of the organization by providing more transformational support, taking project ownership, reducing infrastructure costs of core services, and strategizing to anticipate the organizational, workplace, and change management issues that comprise today's dynamic business environment.

RELATION TO THE FRAME

This module relates to the rest of the text by focusing on what internal groups within an organization expect of human resources departments and functions, as well as leaders and staff. It begins with some insights on current perceptions and stereotypes of HR service, using the perceived shortcomings in service to highlight potential gaps and trends for new service offerings. In general, the direction identified is that, for HR to be successful, it must take co-ownership of projects within the many areas/functions of

FIGURE 22.1 *A Frame for Understanding Human Resource Strategy: Context, Roles, and Constraints*

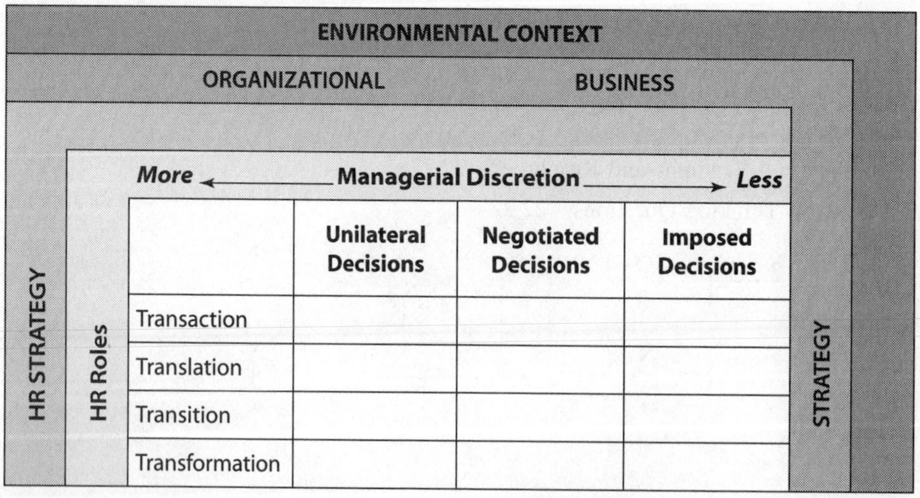

ENVIRONMENTAL CONTEXT			
ORGANIZATIONAL		BUSINESS	

	More ←——— Managerial Discretion ———→ Less		
	Unilateral Decisions	**Negotiated Decisions**	**Imposed Decisions**
Transaction			
Translation			
Transition			
Transformation			

(HR STRATEGY / HR Roles on left; STRATEGY on right)

© 2000 by Ellen Kossek and Richard Block. Thanks to Brian Pentland, Karen Markel, and John Beck for helpful comments and discussions that enhanced the model.

an enterprise and provide HR resources that can help lead projects successfully through an understanding of needs, business context, and core HR principles. Put another way, perception is reality. To be perceived as valuable now and in the twenty-first century, HR must demonstrate value by providing support where its internal clients need it, especially for new and complex projects involving human performance. Figure 22.1 illustrates the new paradigm for the role of human resources within the organization.

CORE CONCEPTS IN HUMAN RESOURCES' ROLE IN ORGANIZATIONAL DEVELOPMENT AND CHANGE

The State of Human Resources

Poor human resources! Few other organizational entities within the last several decades have had to change so desperately to keep up with the times. Within business and industry, the credibility of HR is low. Organization leaders are bulldozing past HR to do their own departmental reengineering, hiring, and human performance measure-setting. The HR function, in response, is moving in all directions, causing it potentially to spin out of control.

Many HR changes have been perceived as largely ineffectual. Those associated with human resources discuss its origins by pointing out that it started as "the personnel department," primarily in the business of hiring and firing employees in order to maintain staffing levels. This view of HR is still pervasive among a number of workers and executives within organizations, especially small businesses. Within the role of a personnel department, HR had neither input nor information regarding corporate initiatives and direction beyond staffing. HR's other duty was that of payroll administrator, a function viewed by many as merely "passing out the checks to employees every other Friday." With the increase in job complexities as well as labor unionism, upper management has been forced to pay more attention to employees and their concerns. This has helped transform personnel departments into human resources departments and expand the role to include such responsibilities as labor, training, and employee relations.

Although the expansion of HR from personnel-type components to a spectrum of human resource-oriented components has been an achievement, HR representatives in the last two decades have, at best, become parts of ancillary departments that business leaders consult occasionally. Given their track record, HR professionals decided it was time to "partner" with the organization. Partnership rhetoric has infused another new battle cry, that of a change from HR to "human capital." Within the human capital movement, a sincere and somewhat successful campaign has begun, focused on a desire to help address business problems and strategies and align the knowledge of people with the needs of the organization. A transformational, not merely transactional, interaction has begun to emerge. Like finance, information technology (IT), and other commodity functions, there has been a realization through human capital that assets—human assets—can best serve the organization if viewed as dynamic commodities to be empowered rather than static fixtures to be supervised.

Although adopting this approach to the importance of people within organizations is a big step for traditional HR programs, the "partnership approach" still may be deficient in meeting an organization's true needs. Even with a human capital approach to HR, as it stands today HR is often ineffective, incompetent, and costly (Ulrich 1998, 124). Human capital-style administrators often propose changes they feel are organizational priorities; however, because they are unable to fulfill their primary HR roles —e.g., keeping staffing costs down, finding low-cost benefits, and motivating employees through equitable compensation programs—they are not viewed as credible. The attitude is, "If they can't get my paycheck right, why would I trust their recommendation for a $2 million dollar human resource information system or help in a new reengineering project?" HR is still perceived as the slowpoke, the status quo, and the cause of problems, not the solution. As far as operations and field business leaders are concerned, HR thinking is "delusional" thinking in that its perspective on timelines, manpower, and by-the-book procedures are far removed from what it actually takes to run a department. Those who realize the potential that the human equation brings to a business challenge also realize the potential that an HR entity could have if it were operated with its internal customers in mind and with a proactive attitude that translated into commitment and results.

Toward a New HR Framework

Those working as HR practitioners know that the negative perceptions that have been raised against HR are charges that seem to be stereotypical and unjust. Yet the best way to grow, change, or add value comes from the criticism of constituents. Business leaders are beginning to respect the proactive side of HR, but more can be done to demonstrate HR's understanding of business. In place of a partnership approach, another transformation is needed, one that is even more hands on. To achieve it, HR practitioners need to be privy to the organizational priorities of all other major players and need to be grounded in a real understanding of a given function's business issues and operation. How can this happen if counterparts do not wish to solicit HR input? The solution is to cease "apart from" behavior within HR that isolates other sides of the organization and, instead, to reinvent HR's role as "a part of" all business initiatives that involve changes in human performance (Benson 1998).

HR can move beyond the limits of "human capital" boundaries by establishing a valuable presence on each major business project. Frankly, business leaders don't need and haven't asked for partners. Instead of team *partners,* the real need is for team *members* who understand the business context as well as human-side principles, methods, and potential that HR provides. Having an HR team member "on point" and assigned to a priority business project could have tremendous impact in instilling quality metrics, balanced scorecards, enlargement and enrichment, and so much more. Essentially, HR must "go to market" across the enterprise as a service-style organization aimed at growing relationships, gaining satisfaction, and increasing the amount of HR work without completely overwhelming the HR group.

When examining the work associated with implementing large-scale change within organizations, the missing element clearly seems to be HR's daily presence in the trenches. Even within the most remote field locations or other distant realms of a business, organization leaders are attempting to achieve excellence by focusing their employees around initiatives that can include learning, quality, teamwork, and reengineering as well as operational, functional, technical, and procedural changes. All of these concepts are driven by the way organizations get things done and how they treat their people, fundamental HR issues (Ulrich 1998, 124). The question remains: "How does HR get involved in appropriate projects?" The answer is "by jumping in, knee-deep and with skilled resources and progress data and track records to back up opinions." Organizations aren't looking to involve departments that aren't willing to take part in the project's responsibility. HR must operate as a true team member, a "guerrilla in the trenches." HR can succeed by providing the appropriate number of resources at the appropriate career level to share point skill HR expertise and to take an equal responsibility for project deliverables, performance targets, and results. These HR professionals must become project members and project managers known for getting valued work done.

HR Membership and Guerrilla Warfare

In summary, it is quite simple: Gone are the days of the "Pentagon personnel department." Personnel was often as much a bureaucracy of paperwork as it was an entity devoted to hiring/firing, wage and salary, or benefits administration. Many HR "pentagons" still exist and offer little except for keeping infrastructure costs high and HR credibility low. Gone too are the days of "field marshal human resources departments." In the "field marshal" approach to HR, the HR director wants to stay in the comfort of the war room and direct campaigns from afar. No wonder business leaders whose troops are on the true front line have little respect for such hands-off participation. And finally, gone are the days of "human capital peacekeepers." Like UN troops in exercises with U.S. troops, support rarely rises above the "us/them" level. HR human capital tends to speak in terms of "our boys helping out your boys." There may be a partnership, but there is no real camaraderie or common deliverable. The new HR metaphor and new HR approach should be much more along the lines of "HR guerrilla warfare," with HR membership on projects, with equal tasks and stakes for HR practitioners, integrated with other departments, working toward common goals side by side, beyond the desks and confines of the human resources office. The twenty-first century will begin by replacing human capital rhetoric with a terminology and discipline called human performance. Human performance will become a new science through which chief executive officers (CEOs), shareholders, and employees measure a company's value; the human performance skill level of an organization will become a quantifiable number upon which companies are judged, much the same way market share percent, revenue, and growth are used as measures today.

STRATEGIC ISSUES IN HUMAN RESOURCES' ROLE IN ORGANIZATIONAL DEVELOPMENT AND CHANGE

Obviously, HR cannot enlist at the local business unit recruiting office. That is, it would be difficult to achieve HR membership, to "become a guerrilla in the trenches," without at least a boot camp's worth of training in how to change an HR department and its people. In their current state, most HR organizations and practitioners are neither structured nor equipped to perform in this new model. The critical success factors listed below will document tangible ways that HR can adapt to business needs through restructuring services, reskilling employees, and reestablishing contacts with internal customers. Essentially, the guerrilla approach to HR builds on these five critical success factors. Human resources

MODULE
22

- Must restructure to adequately address requests from the rest of the organization.

- Needs radical reengineering to operate as a team member responsible for many of a given project's key deliverables.

- Team members should focus on clearly defined deliverables within actual business projects instead of offering general and hard-to-apply paradigms and models.

- Must begin to enhance its image through the mitigation of common project errors:

   ✓ Winging it

   ✓ Antagonizing

   ✓ Dropping the ball

- Success requires rapid and well-executed responses to business unit projects using best practices, key performance indicators (KPIs), and value analysis.

Restructure to Adequately Assess Needs

In terms of transactional vs. transformational work being undertaken, many human resource organizations are spending 80 percent of effort and full-time equivalency resources doing transactional tasks such as payroll administration, job posting, hiring, and so on. A mere 20 percent of effort is focused on the proactive or team member organization support recommended in this HR guerrilla approach. Research suggests that reengineering the HR function can help reverse the HR organization operation until 80/20 becomes 20/80, with 80 percent of budget and resources devoted to transformational work.

This example helps drive home the need for HR transformation. Recently, while implementing a management information system at a health-care organization servicing approximately 100,000 members, it became very apparent throughout the project design and implementation that the system would have dramatic implications for current skill and staffing requirements for various departments. In order to anticipate the total impact, project management ordered a series of staffing analyses to be completed. The surprising part, however, was that the external consultants hired to implement the system were responsible for conducting the analyses with department management and without the help of human resources. In assessing HR's lack of participation, the project managers realized that project needs included an understanding of the new and emerging roles the system would require, as well as a fairly rapid turnaround time. The existing HR structure could provide neither. While mastery in developing role descriptions and compiling evaluations would have been helpful, the project could not slow its pace to get onto HR's docket of select projects. Further, having to drive from the field to headquarters, to "bring the project to HR," simply was not feasible to business leaders from the IT and operations side of the company.

This scenario illustrates that a more responsive and judicious staffing schedule for HR resources is necessary to support organization priorities and large-scale changes. This runs counter to the current practice of reserving efforts primarily for the HR back office. To move beyond transactional HR work, HR needs to create a staffing database that assigns its resources to projects within the enterprise that merit assistance. While there may not be enough HR practitioners for all projects, it is also true that most will not require a dedicated, full-time HR resource. Regardless of limited capacity, transformational HR can better occur with experts deployed to the field instead of trying to provide support from a distance back at the HR department. A clear skill-set change is in HR's global future: one where HR experts know the business of HR and the business of internal customers. Data processors and clerks will find their work automated or streamlined, so while transactional work is on the decline, transformational work is on the incline. While of course some of HR's staff needs to stay within the HR office walls, not all do. Remember, transactional/transformational structure tends to be at 80/20 instead of 20/80. Better payroll and benefit technologies, streamlined processes, and a flatter HR organizational structure should help free people to do more customer-facing activities, including transformational consultative work on projects in other areas. A key element is ensuring that consultative employees are well trained, so they can truly become project allies and hit the ground running in response to tight project deadlines.

Radical Reengineering to Operate as a Team Member

Human resources management (HRM) needs radical reengineering to operate as a team member responsible for many of a given project's key deliverables. At a major automotive supplier, the HR group is comprised of benefits, recruiting, and training. The training group numbered 20. Mostly this group offered product training, technical training, and soft skills training curriculum events (from selling to business writing) focused around the classroom. Over the past five years, however, as the organization has had to cut costs and improve quality, departments became loath to send employees to anything that would not produce immediate and demonstrable job improvement skills.

The demand to get more out of training led to two noticeable changes. The first was that training media, duration, and location became just-in-time, punchy, and decentralized. The second change was that the trainers slowly began to be bolstered (and replaced) by internal consultants. Consultants within this supplier organization are similar to trainers, except they came from one of the business lines and thus have a perspective on the real business needs of those being trained. HR leaders train these consultants in root-cause analysis and in facilitation so they can assist departments by going out to them and focusing small groups of employees on reengineering, innovating, and problem solving. Best of all, the savvy assistant director of the department keeps tabs on the efficiencies and improvements that the consultants are helping teams realize. Her quantification of their value to the enterprise has helped build the case for growing this side of the organization and hiring a few new consultants with impressive external credentials.

Clear Deliverables, Not Paradigms and Models

HR team members should focus on clearly defined deliverables that they can co-own within actual business projects instead of offering advice and guidance from afar. A recent merger of two banks found one with 22 position titles and levels between branch manager and president and the other with 10. The HR vice president from the larger bank planned to retire in a year and offered no plans for reconciling the job levels/titles. The HR vice president from the smaller bank stated, "I set up the current levels at my bank. I can do the same thing in the combined bank." Other vice presidents from both banks then began to bombard the latter with requests. Each meeting would increase frustration because, when asked for commitment and a timetable for organizing jobs into broadband, he could only reply, "I have to handle rightsizing quotas as well as other needs across the bank. Make your best guess or else use a consultant if you need something quicker."

Knowing that the HR vice president from the smaller bank had done broadbanding before, the business leaders asked him to also assist in the steering committee meetings, which he did. Unfortunately, much of his commentary in the sessions translated to, "That's not the best approach; I could have done it better." He threw out enticing concepts to the rest of the committee, from competency management to team-based appraisals, but left off at the point of providing help to do clustering of positions or creating bands. Further, there was no formal HR review of the consulting work being provided by the HR external consultants. Requiring HR to own up and participate in producing work, not just slick concepts, would have served the merger and the new bank much better.

Mitigating Common Errors of Winging It, Antagonizing, and Dropping the Ball

Winging It.   While this module has been frank about the common criticisms regarding HR, it is important to remember that all organizational departments have their unique and peculiar behaviors that come under unfair criticism. Many of the stereotypes represent only the worst. Following a new product launch across an electronics company, the comical stereotypes of departments went as follows:

- Senior executives golf with customers and vendors, which leads to a collection of bad ideas from outsiders and self-motivated parties.

- Pie-in-the sky designers are given vague concepts that, after 24 months of analysis and blueprinting, emerge as vague concepts.

- Engineering communicates with no one, taking as risk-free and unimaginative a path as it can get away with.

- Manufacturing attempts to use as many of the last model's components as possible, piling up scrap and defects in an amount that nearly matches actual production volumes.

- Distribution creates market share by losing most of what it handles, ships, or stores.

- Dealers revel in telling customers lies and blaming home office for the errors in price or product.

- Sales and marketing invents the lies and feeds them to the customers and vendors who golf with the executives.

Stereotypes may point to the truth, but they can certainly cause hurt feelings too. The most important lesson is that all departments are perceived negatively. A dangerous recipe is when one department tries winging it or doing the work of another, based on the idea that "no one else in this organization knows anything but us."

Take, for example, the telecommunications company whose account initiation directors decided to implement a recognition program without running it by an HR professional. They established a monthly program that set aside $1,000 for the team that serviced the most new accounts. The outcome could not have been worse. Embittered teams fought for leads, calling out to the field trying to expedite new work. Creativity encouraged others to talk customers into canceling existing service so better service could be offered (as a "new" initiation). Worst of all, account initiation and set-up personnel in other states started badgering their leadership for a similar program. The whole recognition idea got lost most likely because employees were being rewarded the wrong way and for the wrong reasons.

This unfortunate story is the result of other departments attempting to do HR work without insight. At this telecommunications provider, the HR team had previously implemented recognition programs that were very successful. Winging it happens when an IT department sees shadow organizations emerging to buy software or write code. It happens with finance when each manager keeps a mini-general ledger, instead of gathering data from the legitimate channel. And it happens to HR when HR is not proactive about getting the word out about its good services and willingness to co-lead.

Antagonizing. One manager converted to the merits of performance-based pay from a recent seminar had expected a brush-off when she asked the HR director for approval. "You or I can't change pay structures without CEO approval," said the director, "but I'll work with you to draft a proposal and we'll get it done." While departments have flaws and few get accolades on a regular basis, HR is less valued than most departments industrywide. They are basically sneered at by the rest of the organization, kept out of decisions, ordered around, and half the time ignored. Like a child who is teased by a schoolmate, HR sooner or later becomes an antagonist. Their attitude is "Why should I comply with orders and organizational priorities when I have had no input into them?" Therefore, when approached and asked to participate, it's only natural that they refuse and often become strong opponents to the initiative. HR needs to see these invitations to participate as opportunities to enhance their position within the organization, and pursue their goal of truly looking out for employees' needs.

Dropping the Ball. There is one more way to enhance image and mitigate errors: Do not drop the ball when an opportunity to serve internal customers comes along.

Transactional ball dropping of paycheck, reimbursement, or employee profiles is unfortunate, but transformational chances to be part of a reengineering team or the like are the real plums that excellent HR providers would hate to drop. The three Ms come to mind: manpower, metrics, and meaningful deadlines. Commit a proper number of resources to a given initiative. Decide what the final result should look like through sample deliverable documents or detailed metrics (e.g., a job profile will not be considered done until the role is outlined with key tasks and steps, the procedures are modified, and a compensation budget is set using HR benchmarking databases). The next critical success factor details effective metrics and best practices applications.

Lastly, work with internal customers to set and honor deadlines. The key to getting operations' respect for a services-type function like HR is by running like a business: stretch goals, teamwork, and timely delivery of materials that focus on value are all critical.

Responses Using Best Practices, Key Performance Indicators, and Value Analysis

Success requires rapid and well-executed responses to business unit projects including best practices, key performance indicators (KPIs), and value analysis. They must participate on projects as any other team member, respond rapidly to business units' initiatives, and add input to the effects on the people within the organization. Further, they must have well-executed responses when presenting their point of view, add value to the goals of the initiative, and offer best practices or industry standards that provide examples of HR's involvement and contributions to successful projects with similar goals and objectives. They must provide detailed methods behind their approach and execution and offer performance measures in order to manage the success or failure of the initiative. Figure 22.2 shows the key components of measuring performance. For example, if a project is to implement a new management information system, and employee competencies are not redefined when the system is turned on, how will employees be motivated, trained, and staffed effectively? HR must be able to provide a cogent

FIGURE 22.2   *The Key Components of Measuring Performance*

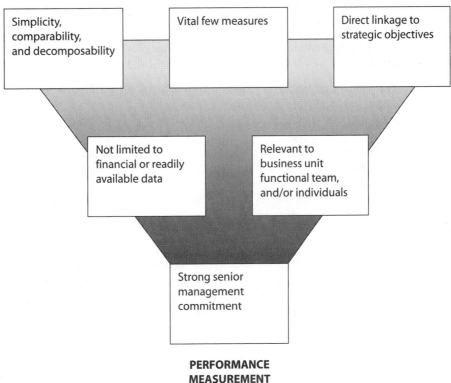

Lead (process) and lag (outcome) indicators

| Simplicity, comparability, and decomposability | Vital few measures | Direct linkage to strategic objectives |

| Not limited to financial or readily available data | Relevant to business unit functional team, and/or individuals |

Strong senior management commitment

PERFORMANCE MEASUREMENT

analysis of the effects of the initiative on employees. And finally, HR must offer detailed cost estimates (of the organization before and after the change) in order to help measure the value of the overall project and the value that HR brings.

HR and Change Management: The Chrysler Finance Example

Chrysler Finance HR (Education and Training) formed a new team. This team would be responsible for creating a "Finance College." The college would coordinate internal and external finance training and build an additional 160 hours of finance-oriented content. A political challenge arose for this HR group, however, when Chrysler Finance executives pointed out that reengineering would change jobs and their associated training needs. Given that, many executives believed that the Finance College should move into a holding pattern until the smoke cleared from reengineering.

Instead, the team sent out a consistent message that senior executives and target employees cannot wait for the changing (reengineered) environment to come to them; they need to move toward it. Through several iterations of hotly debated protocol, the team struck a deal to do only that which helped the current or the future organization without duplicating effort or focusing on short-term fixes that would become irrelevant.

To be proactive, the Chrysler Finance training team turned waiting into an opportunity. They campaigned to begin prepping the organization for upcoming changes. Doing so allowed the scope of the team's mission to broaden from training to include communication, culture change regarding career planning in the new environment, transition preparation, skill assessment, current business needs assessment, and organization structure improvement.

The team hustled while waiting for actual changes to emerge by establishing several objectives:

- Setting a stretch goal for training in terms of both amount and deadline

- Working with the given finance environment and not defining HR needs solely by the emerging long-term requirements

- Increasing employee awareness, industry knowledge, and behavioral as well as technical skill

- Setting up a means for employees to share current knowledge and skills with each other

- Coordinating the timeline of long-term reengineering needs

Building on this premise, the team served as the human resource development (HRD) conduit to meeting the proposed changes. It made sure that a clear change migration plan was in place that involved leaders and targets of the new change. To understand the detailed impact of the project scope on plant operations, platform teams, target costing, and the finance control group, expert input was solicited via interviews and focus groups. The team also employed a steering team of interested personnel from a variety of organization levels to keep tabs on particular change-plan line items.

A key to the change-migration plan of attack was structured releases that were planned around particular change milestones. Often, when HRD claims that it can't hit a moving target or, in other words, cannot begin a change effort, it is because HRD is attempting to wait until all variables are fixed. Instead, a more proactive approach is to run with the facts to date (e.g., a merger, a new product, a move to centralized or decentralized structure) and start adding value immediately. These efforts will be cheered, not booed, if they are well coordinated, robust, and courageous enough to address real change issues.

Some of the more immediate change efforts in a migration plan affect the "here and now environment." Investing effort in the current situation may seem to run counter to long-term visioning of the change journey. It is important to note that the strategy of organization change when defined as short- versus long-term does not belie an antagonistic or binary opposition. A strategy is shared across both projects (the immediate and the long-term), yet the tactics differ. By comparison, home remodeling does not preclude one from redecorating the current interior. If done well, the former should complement the latter. Dan Cowan, Manager of Finance Training and Education, has built the Finance College from a short-term project to a respected curriculum shared across the entire Chrysler organization, not just finance. "The key to our success has been asking the question, 'What will be of value to Chrysler? What skills do employees lack that could potentially impact cost, time, or quality of the services they provide?' My goal is listening to executives and employees as they identify their tough performance challenges and then, working closely with my team, devising the most direct and robust training tool that will improve and sustain a measured outcome." The change model details the way Chrysler was able to identify needed skills and build on current ones.

A Clear Change Model

How does HR move from its current state to internal consulting or shared services support for the rest of the organization? In the preceding Chrysler Finance example, change occurred by getting information collected, shared, taught, acted upon, and evaluated. The change model discussed below and shown in Figure 22.3 provides a clear application for changing HR strategies and tactics. By using this model, a step-by-step change plan can be coordinated that assesses HR needs, strengths, and timelines. Moving through these six steps is a direct way to strategize potential ways to better manage human resource needs in the future.

Internal (Burning).   The first steps taken by HR should be to collect internal ideas on the change at hand. This allows HR members to assess, "What's burning out of control? What's wrong? Why do we need this change?" Using subject matter experts internal to the organization leads to the execution of these steps, which are recommended for HR practitioners facing organizational change:

1. *Write a case for change* based on interviews and focus groups (2–3 pages long).

2. *Air "dirty laundry."* That is, encourage sharing of dissatisfaction because dissatisfactions are good. They show that people are frustrated and believe there is a better way. That's the first step toward positive change.

3. *Tap volunteers and sponsors.* Here's your chance to create the future, not just be affected by the decisions of others.

4. *Study each process.* If you know the processes, you tend to know the weak links and areas for improvement.

5. *Maintain focus on facts.* No blasting of particular employees and managers. That is not the scope of the project (although poor performers tend to be ultimately identified).

FIGURE 22.3 *The Path to Change*

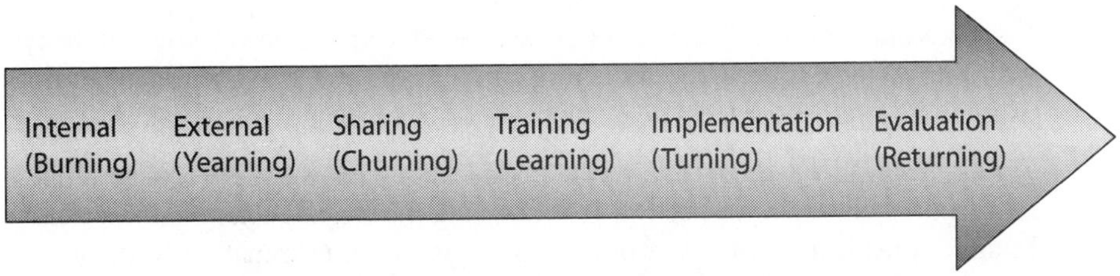

| Internal (Burning) | External (Yearning) | Sharing (Churning) | Training (Learning) | Implementation (Turning) | Evaluation (Returning) |

6. *Create ownership through empowered teams.* Starting with subissues within a change and growing responsibilities of teams based on their performance and value.

7. *Analyze by task.* Reengineering often focuses on a core process at the expense of contingencies at the task level. Job-task analysis helps justify the "why" of current environmental structure or structure change.

External (Yearning).

Knowing that internal experts cannot be expected to generate all the answers, many organizations turn to external leaders for ideas. The idea of working with external partners is to expand horizons and explore ideas that originate outside the organization. Look at department stores, fast food, competitors, social organizations, academic experts, trade magazines. What do you "yearn" for externally? How can it apply to the change?

1. *Establish benchmarks.* Who are the organizations or other departments internally with whom we want to compare ourselves?

2. *Experiment.* Combine ideas and industry changes to make ideas more robust.

3. *Cross industry lines.* Tour a brewery together. Name the best customer-focused organization you know. Ask experts from other fields.

4. *Scan external resources.* Look for great ideas in select magazines and journals. Use data collection and benchmarking from other departments within organization.

5. *Write an executive summary or "case for change"* to reflect both yearning and burning ideas.

Sharing (Churning).

As organizations decide what changes are needed, it may well be the case that the needed resources are already in-house. HR organizations can do an excellent job of identifying competencies within the workforce so that expertise can be tapped wherever it is found. While deep-skilled experts are often pressed for time, simply knowing who they are and calling upon them for directional advice can be a tremendous added value. Sharing is the means by which the HR organization gets everyone involved in solving organization problems, but in a highly structured way. The traditional paradigm is that employees think about solutions that affect their area. The new paradigm is that churning the organizational flow of information can get a cross-representation of perspectives to problems. This may be the best tool for responding to change available to organizations today, but it requires good HR facilitation.

1. *Share ideas and innovations.* As teams are selected to address organizational challenges, each employee within the organization understands that troubleshooting—the process of improving organizationwide processes—will be part of the performance appraisal. Every employee is urged to coordinate an improvement with others and present to project leaders as frequently as possible.

2. *Cross-train.* Employees gain perspective about given jobs by learning about other jobs; further, they become more versatile and marketable.

3. *Nimble.* A goal with sharing is speed. Each employee leans on the next as a resource to help push work through faster and with higher quality.

4. *Combine old with new.* New is not always better. Avoid throwing out the baby with the bathwater. Look for and study what the current organization/team does exceedingly well and become caretaker for that best practice.

5. *Tip the triangle.* Have one side of the organization tackle issues (or give input into them) from their perspective. It is amazing the freshness an engineer can bring to a marketing team or a purchasing agent to an Information Systems

assignment. Cross-pollinate and understand/solve the issues from all perspectives.

6. *Stretch goals.* Set ambitious stretch goals with quantified measurements for success in all areas for individual and team performance as well as departmental performance (e.g., 50 percent less downtime; full reusability in all new code).

Training (Learning).

When no sustained resource within the organization can be tapped to cross-train through sharing, a training curriculum of individual and group skill building/awareness building should be implemented. The skill assessment process drives this lockstep curriculum. Point of need, open-ended learning, goal-based scenario, on-the-job training, and verified skill transfer are key goals. The point is that the training plans ought to begin only after burning, yearning, and churning take place so that existing knowledge is not duplicated when effort could be better spent elsewhere.

1. *Shared vision.* Why is this training necessary? Without a shared vision of how training applies to current and future jobs, without demanding performance of new skill within the organization, learners become prisoners or vacationers. Make sure the "why" is communicated as it relates to training.

2. *Discard rigid thinking.* Make radical approaches to challenges an expectation. Reward teams for innovation and for thinking out of the box.

3. *Connect personal and organizational learning.* Keep tabs of what employees want to learn and what they know, not merely what they do. This focuses HR to be more involved in applying employee skills from across the organization to a particular team or challenge.

4. *Proactive team learning.* Send a whole work team through training together so that the ideas are reinforced. There is nothing worse than being energized by training and rejoining an unenthused (or unenlightened) team.

5. *Systems thinking.* The more HR communicates that employees are knowledge networks and involves diverse employees at all levels on projects, the more learning will occur, even at the lowest eschelons of a business. This learning organization effect results from more holistic expectations, measurements, reinforcement, and continuous learning.

MODULE
22

Implementation (Turning).

There is nothing worse than a shared vision or recommendation that sits on a shelf. Chances are that competitors are discovering and acting on a change as soon as it is resolved. Implementation is "turning" an organization degree by degree. The question "When are we implementing something tangible to employees?" should drive HR performance. Leaders who focus on delivery of change management via awareness and training should be applauded and modeled.

1. *Rapid, not hasty, implementation.* Implement on a timetable. Stick to it.

2. *Brown before serving.* The organization is not a laboratory. See concepts and their impacts through before launching even the most minor change.

3. *Celebrate endings.* It is the best people who make a former system—flawed or not—actually work. Their ownership of the current way of doing things comes from pride. Make sure these same heroes agree with the need and benefit of changing. Reexamine the case for change to show where and how improvements will help.

4. *Announce changes in advance.* The greater the lead time, the lower the resistance. Make sure other departments, vendors, senior executives, and all groups

affected have ample lead time. Can this change be replicated in another area to add value? Explore the possibility, and help others benefit from your team's ideas.

5. *Reward behavior*. Those who implement improvement should share the recognition and reward. Be creative, and don't burn out key sponsors.

Evaluation (Returning). As practitioners know, HR benefits richly from as much documentation as can be gathered regarding the return on investment associated with motivation, performance, and job pathing. Using a variety of methods to evaluate and measure return is ideal. The immediate focus when HR is involved on a project should be on assessing the value of functional areas and on individual employees, teams, and department performance.

1. *Executive evaluation*. Have executives from the top group of 20 and from the board of directors attend a learning event. Have them ask fellow learners what the benefits are. Chances are they will hear little but superlatives!

2. *Use classic control groups*. Measure a clear "organization with" and "organization without" change efforts.

3. *Gather testimonials*. The value of the HR effort in a testimonial form can be of as much or more value as hard numbers. Solicit testimonials from managers and employees affected.

4. *Disseminate findings*. HR is accurately accused of putting results-oriented information in the file cabinet instead of in the executives' hands.

5. *Analytics*. Be clear in justifying the costs of the services HR is providing against the quantifiable benefits.

The Modified HR Organization

Based on the critical success factors and change model outlined above, a modified HR function begins with a well-run HRM function. HRM is the area of human resources that maintains traditional employee remuneration, record keeping, and employment information. Within many organizations, it is HRM that offers wide-ranging opportunities for HR leaders to consider in terms of reengineering HR processes, technology, distribution, and points of contact. Indeed, several HRM organizations have become fragmented and dedicated to single lines of business. With technology such as packaged software for payroll and benefits administration programs, there is no reason why more consolidation of processing activities cannot occur.

As the HRM organization improves and streamlines itself, several benefits can be achieved. The first is that, through greater operational excellence, a heightened respect for HRM services will occur. Second, as the basic services of payroll and benefits begin to improve, more attention to employees' needs can begin to take place. In many leading organizations, this attention to the needs of employees has manifested as a supportive interactive voice response (IVR) service. Also, intranet/Internet application programs that allow employees to access their HR information as needed have been favorably reviewed. Further, call centers and shared-services organizations are being utilized for economies of scale and skill to process information and serve employees. This allows HR to enter new areas of employee support, such as pension management and 401(k) annuities, employee training, relocation, and employee assistance programs.

In the short term, getting the HRM house in order will help free up positions and capacity to engage in more HRD activities. While fledgling HRD services may need to matriculate through the human capital "partnering" role, even one or two "field representatives" providing true HR consultative services in the trenches is enough to turn a company of skeptics into believers. Typically, it takes as little as one successful engagement for human resources to be seen as a player in the consulting arena. Many Fortune 1,000 organizations are bolstering their numbers within internal consulting, and as often as not, this is housed within the HRD organization. Another interesting phenomenon occurs when these consultants help to partially decentralize HR with field locations/personnel that are dotted line accountable to the line of business with hard-line accountability back to HRM.

Change Management and Human Resources

Often these large-scale efforts are led by expert consultants, hired to focus on a key project and to provide guidance and direction on the needs of the organization. These consultants often suggest technology changes in the form of new systems, environments, applications, etc. They also suggest changing processes, reengineering departments to streamline workflows, designing processes to support organizational objectives, and communicating timing of events to coordinate them better. Consultants have also realized that they need another group with complimentary skills to help implement these changes, a group called change management. Change management consultants are hired in to help manage the change effort, assisting employees in making the migration to the new process, organization, or technology. This change management group, however, may or may not always involve HR, often independently making the recommendations that HR should. Remember the earlier example of the consultants sitting around doing staffing analysis without contacting HR? Often, these projects are successful without the assistance and involvement of HR; yet think of the maximized value when HR is part of the team!

With change management involved in projects, consulting personnel are evaluating the impact the initiative will have on employees within the organization. By examining policies, procedures, performance measures, training, etc., some HR issues are addressed. Not all, however, are examined. The HR organization is poised to own much of a given project's change management needs.

By integrating HR within project teams, attention can be paid to other HR needs: recruiting models (will we want to select employees with different skills now that the technology has changed?); compensation (do we want to pay employees differently in order to reward them for their change in responsibilities/skills?); and performance appraisals (do we need to evaluate employees differently depending on their change in roles/responsibilities?). These are all areas that should be addressed when implementing large-scale change. By integrating the involvement of the responsible party—HR—these challenges can be proactively addressed instead of waiting until they become poor employee performance issues.

Connecting to large-scale organizational initiatives through change management is an excellent way of introducing HR's vested interest into an organization project. By linking itself with change management, HR migrates into the project easily and with a sponsor. This new relationship also helps propel change management's interest—to accurately assess and address the impact of a large-scale change on people.

HR needs to undergo serious change internally, however, before it is ready for a seat at the project team's table. HR people need to establish the right skills—analytical, process design—as well as their own competencies (staffing, compensation, performance appraisals, labor relations, employee relations, training, etc.). They also need the application skills necessary to be on the project. For example, recently on a project, an HR representative was asked to be involved in the brainstorming session for a department readiness team. The team was trying to formulate ways to ready the department for the change (in this case, new technology). HR came to the table with a laundry list of ways employees would be affected, but with no suggestions of how the project could use existing systems or processes to address the issue. Anyone can identify

MODULE
22

problems through analysis, but project management needs solutions for addressing the problem and the lowest-cost, lowest-impact methods for implementing those solutions. What HR should have done in this case is list the issue—for example, suggest additional staffing to handle the increased volume of claims that could be produced, explain how the gap could be addressed through additional recruiting, and detail how the solution could be implemented through current internal and external recruiting programs.

Working on these teams also requires data analysis skills of HR. All HR practitioners need the ability to find needed data as an input into a project or report, and analyze it. Having the skills to conduct analysis and being able to assess what analysis is needed are necessary requirements of HR for these teams. HR also needs to have access to and knowledge of the latest, state-of-the-art models and methodologies in its industry. Organizationwide projects are implemented often to become more competitive in the marketplace. HR needs to become competitively focused by offering new ways of structuring, paying, recruiting, training, appraising, and handling employees. Many argue HR is in a unique position to have the greatest input into competitive advantages of an organization as the more traditional forms of competition—cost, technology, distribution, manufacturing, and product features—are easily copied by competitors (Ulrich 1998). "The only competitive weapon left is organization" (Ulrich 1998, 127). By incorporating these cutting-edge methods and concepts into their HR toolkit, HR professionals position themselves as true "guerrilla" team members thriving in the contemporary business trenches.

The HRD Landscape

HRD's level and degree of involvement will depend heavily on industry trends. Resources will need to be deployed in different ways, containing different skills, depending on the state of the marketplace, and ultimately driving the project's objectives. HRD will need to analyze the current marketplace, the project's goals, and formulate their reaction, involvement, and action plan. The workforce over the last decade, for example, has changed dramatically. Organizations are assessing sections, departments, and offerings they consider to be nonvalue-added or nonrevenue-generating and are outsourcing their services. Call centers are a perfect example of this. HRD is needed on this type of project to formulate a migration plan for employees to move to the outsourcing firm and help integrate this new business relationship into the current organization. With the recent trend toward large company mergers, HRM's involvement is required to provide support for employees during this time of uncertainty, and HRD's involvement on the merger team is necessary to address and develop what staffing, compensation, appraisal, competency, and training models will be utilized in the new amalgamated company (see Module 5).

HRD will also have to work with the project team and HRM to help develop policies for the new company. And as stated earlier, HRD's involvement in IT transformation projects is critical to assess the impact on employees with the integration of new technology. New technology will change employee skill requirements, training plans, staff sizing, and potentially other HR functions. On the project mentioned earlier, the client was moving from a mainframe to a client/server platform. This required current employees to undergo extensive technical training in order to support a new and unfamiliar platform. In addition, the staffing plan needed to change in order to recruit new employees with client/server skills from the most appropriate sources (headhunters versus on-campus recruiting used before).

The project will always dictate the type of resources required from HRD. Table 22.1 shows some recent trends in the business marketplace and considerations HRD must undergo to align with these projects.

TABLE 22.1 *Business Marketplace Trends and HRD Requirements*

Business Landscape	HRD Requirements
Mergers/acquisitions	• Organization alignment • Policy development
Information Technology transformations	• Staffing redesign • Training design and development
Organizational/departmental reengineering	• Process design and development • Training design and development
New product development/deployment	• Staffing redesign • Competency design • Training design and development
Call centers	• Competency design • Compensation/performance appraisal design
Consolidated service centers	• Teamwork initiatives • Competency design • Compensation/performance appraisal design

APPLICATION 1

Directions: Read the Ford Motor case study below. Provide an executive summary you can deliver to classmates based on the following six questions. Then prepare a three-page opinion paper to share in class based on the new ideas set forth in the case study. Be sure to compare the case to the overall module.

1. What specific behaviors and performance are businesses expecting of their HR functions?

2. Can you describe the specific way that Ford Motor Company views new transformational HR services?

3. How can HR impact enterprisewide performance and profitability?

4. What is going to be the impact on traditional transactional HR functions if this business demand continues?

5. In your opinion, what HR functions are becoming obsolete?

6. What are the vital components of HR efforts focused on internal consulting?

Ford Motor Manufacturing Education, Training, and Development Case Study

The following case study chronicles the strategic transformation of human resources at Ford Motor Company. Mark Leyda, Manager of Education Training and Development for Global Manufacturing at Ford Motor Company, provided this narrative documenting the challenges, strategic direction, and successes-to-date in human resources transformation at Ford.

> At Ford, the vision is that Human Resources will be defined by what it delivers, not by what it does. Success for HR will come through delivering on strategy execution via projects and initiatives aligned to the business. HR must have considerable business acumen and the ability to help people navigate through major change. The

profile of HR is changing: management consultation, change management, employee advocacy, organizational learning, and organizational development are among the required competencies.

We frequently ask HR practitioners if they would feel qualified to manage operational areas of Ford's businesses. If the answer is "no," we discuss whether or not they can truly add value as internal consultants. Our vision of HR requires that HR professionals focus on transformation skills that improve performance, build employee relationships, support projects and business strategies while located at the point of need in business operations. Transactional services are becoming highly automated. The real value is in providing a network of expertise that can be provided as required—expertise in performance management, organization development, training, and other value-added Human Performance services.

A transformational HR function will invest HR time and resources where they provide the greatest value to business. HR organizations across Ford will improve quality, responsiveness, and delivery of HR products and services. Workforce strategy, leadership development, compensation, organizational learning, performance management, and many other HR services are linked to the needs and values of stakeholders across Ford. HR holds the key to global improvements through process change and reengineering because people, and people alone, are the key to the success of these efforts. (Leyda 1998)

APPLICATION 2

Directions: Leading companies are well along the way in a journey toward a newer HR organization that is oriented around delivery (service) and deliverable (product). To provide such service and product leadership, HR leaders are getting their professionals into the trenches. Assume you are the HR director of The Trend company, a clothing manufacturer operating in four states with 6,000 employees. Use the topics and answers to the questions below to prepare a detailed outline of how you would migrate this company from transactional to transformational service.

Marketing. The first step in transforming HR into a new state is to market the blueprint to the rest of the organization. You must build HR's credibility across the organization, promote your new services, and ultimately build sponsorship, not just from upper-level management but "in the trenches" from employees as well. Use the following questions to guide you in the development of the marketing portion of your presentation to management.

Questions

- How do you convince upper management of HR's abilities within change management?

- How do you convince middle-and lower-level employees, ultimately your project team colleagues, that HR can add value?

- What meetings do you and your representatives attend?

- How do you build sponsorship at each level of the organization?

- Do you send different messages to your CEO than a line employee?

- How do you promote the services of your HR department?

Change Management. After you have convinced the organization of the need for this HR transformation, you must develop a method of changing employees' view of HR and accepting the new HRD methodology. For example, some executives may see this transformation as a way of HR passing off work. Others may see it as a loss in that by concentrating on the organization as a "team member," you are no longer available to meet their needs of "getting my paycheck" or "tracking my staff's performance appraisals." Use the following questions to guide you in the development of the change management portion of your presentation to management.

Questions

- How do you bring employees along the change continuum?

- How do you encourage employees to address their concerns?

- How will employees' issues and concerns differ depending on their position, level, and seniority?

- What are some ways you can involve individuals in the planning, execution, and delivery of HR's transformation?

- How do you build buy-in to the methodology?

- What can you do to help employees understand the benefits of the transformation?

- Should the risks of such an initiative be communicated to the organization?

Migration.   Once employees and management are comfortable with the transformation concept and believe the change is necessary and beneficial, you must materialize a way to get there. A detailed migration plan has to be developed that will lay out and explain the blueprint for the new organization. Use the following questions to guide you in the development of the migration portion of your presentation to management.

Questions

- What percentage of your budget will go toward static activities (payroll and benefit administration) versus transformational (change management)?

- Specifically, what services and support would you provide to the organization?

- How do you plan to deploy this organization while continuing to maintain status quo?

- What types of activities/analysis will need to be conducted in order to achieve the transformation?

- Will your services be free to the organization, or will you charge for them?

Organization.   Another key step in transforming HR is to plan out what the new organization will look like. This is not only a new organization chart, but also the types of skills HR professionals need to contain, the types of skills operations professionals need to acquire, and how all the parties interface with one another. Use the following questions to guide you in the development of the organization portion of your presentation to management.

Questions

- What caliber of employees do you recruit into this organization?

- How will the skill requirements of operations employees change?

- How will you structure the HR department (both HRM and HRD)?

- How will you prepare employees for these new roles/skills?

- How will HR professionals within HRD interface with operations employees?

IN CONCLUSION

Debrief

Organizational development and change management are two fairly new types of work that companies are expecting their HR function to provide. Organizational development requires not only an understanding of the most expedient organization structures, models, and performance measures to manage work activity, but also a rich understanding of the affected areas' business drivers, context, and line of business. Change management, on the other hand, requires HR to excel in its ability to move employees through an organized change with as little interruption to daily performance as possible. This may include a need to redeploy workforce, train, or assist in the planning and communication of key projects. Regardless, both of these new domains require HR membership getting into the trenches with other business areas and assisting with the HR-oriented work. The trends identified indicate that HR's core services are becoming less valued while its emerging skills—namely, responding to business needs as a consultant and advocate—are becoming more valued and demanded.

Suggested Readings and Resources

Benson, Ben. "The Path to Achieving Shared Services Without Achieving Mutiny: Step by Step Advice." *FSI Master's Thesis,* Andersen Consulting, Chicago, 1998.

Benson, Ben and Poppis, Kevin. "Change Management's Role in Reengineering: Establishing HRD as a Sponsor for Change," *Leading Organizational Change,* Virginia: American Society for Training and Development, 1997.

Leyda, Mark. Personal interview on June 10, 1998.

Ulrich, Dave. "A New Mandate for Human Resources," *Harvard Business Review,* January-February, 1998.

"Reinventing HR: Getting Buy-In," *HRFocus,* February 1998.

Critical Thinking Questions

1. Can you summarize the difference between the human capital approach and HR membership approach to HR as outlined in this chapter?

2. What emerging skill sets do you see as expectations for new HR professionals?

3. What key obstacles does HR face in moving from a human capital-based department to an HRM/HRD interface to Organization Development/Change Management?

4. Brainstorm an action plan detailing how organizations can overcome those obstacles and achieve a successful transformation.

5. You are an employee within the new HRD organization and have been assigned to a project addressing a merger between your company and your number-three competitor. This merger will include technology, process, and people integration. What are some issues, from an HR perspective, you feel will need to be addressed? How will you address them?

6. What services would the HRM portion of HR deliver to the organization, and what services would the HRD portion of HR deliver?

7. How will the competencies the organization requires of a human resource professional change with this new approach?

Index

Antagonizing, 22.8, 22.10

Best practices, 22.11
Business needs assessment, 22.12

Change management, 22.4, 22.16–18,
    22.20–22
Change model, 22.13–16
Change-migration plan, 22.12, 22.21
Co-ownership of projects, 22.4, 22.6
Competency management, 22.9
Cultural change, 22.12

Decentralized structure, 22.12
Dropping the ball, 22.9, 22.10–11

Education and training, 22.12, 22.19
Evaluation, change model, 22.16
Executive evaluation, 22.16
External change, 22.14

HR change model, 22.13–16
HR membership, 22.7, 22.22
HR team member, 22.6
HRD activities, 22.16–17
HRM services, 22.16–17
Human capital, 22.5, 22.6, 22.7
Human performance measure-setting, 22.5,
    22.7
Human resource functions, 22.4–5, 22.10,
    22.16, 22.18
Human resource professionals, 22.5, 22.6,
    22.7–9, 22.10, 22.13, 22.16, 22.18, 22.21–22
Human resource-oriented components, 22.5,
    22.7. See also Personnel-type components
Human resources department (HRD), 22.4–6,
    22.7–8, 22.10, 22.12, 22.16–18
Human resources management (HRM),
    22.8–9, 22.16–18
Human resources' role, 22.5, 22.6

Implementation (change model), 22.15–16
Industry standards, 22.11
Information technology (IT), 22.5
Interactive voice response (IVR) service, 22.16
Internal change, 22.13–14
Internal customers, 22.7
Internal groups, 22.4. See also Project teams
Intranet/Internet application programs, 22.16

Job complexities, 22.5
Job improvement skills, 22.8
Job-task analysis, 22.14

Key performance indicators (KPIs), 22.7, 22.11

Management information system, 22.8, 22.11
Marketplace trends, 22.18–19
Measuring performance. See Performance
    measurement
Migration plan. See Change-migration plan

Organizational change, 22.5, 22.6, 22.7–8,
    22.12–13, 22.13–16
Organizational learning, 22.15

Partnership approach, 22.5, 22.6–7
Path to change, 22.13–16
Pentagons (personnel/HR), 22.6–7
Perception is reality, 22.5
Performance measures, 22.11, 22.17, 22.22
Personnel department, 22.5, 22.6
Personnel-type components, 22.5. See also Hu-
    man resource-oriented components
Proactive team learning, 22.15
Project teams, 22.17–18

Reengineering, 22.7, 22.12, 22.14, 22.16
Reestablishing contacts, 22.7
Reskilling employees, 22.7
Responsibility of teams, 22.6, 22.14. See also
    Project teams
Restructuring services, 22.7
Results-oriented information, 22.16
Rewards and recognition, 22.16
Role of human resources. See Human
    resources' role

Service-style organization, 22.6
Sharing ideas for change, 22.14
Skill-set change, 22.8
Stereotypes of HR service, 22.4, 22.9–10
Stretch goals, 22.15
Systems thinking, 22.15

Team member (HR), 22.6–8, 22.9
Traditional HR programs, 22.5
Training, change model, 22.8–9
Transactional activities, 22.5, 22.7–8, 22.10,
    22.20
Transformational activities, 22.5, 22.7–8,
    22.20–21

Value analysis, 22.11

Winging it, 22.8, 22.9–10
Workforce, 22.18

MODULE
22

KOSSEK ■ BLOCK

MANAGING HUMAN RESOURCES
IN THE 21st CENTURY

From Core Concepts to Strategic Choice

MODULE 23

Employee Safety
and Health

Scott H. Tobey
MICHIGAN STATE UNIVERSITY

Managing Human Resources in the 21st Century: From Core Concepts to Strategic Choice,
by Kossek and Block

Publisher: Dave Shaut
Executive Editor: John Szilagyi
Developmental Editor: Bryant Editorial Development
Marketing Manager: Joseph A. Sabatino
Production Editor: Tamborah E. Moore
Manufacturing Coordinator: Dana Began Schwartz
Cover Design: Tin Box Studio
Cover Photographs: Copyright Shoji Sato/Photonica
Production House: The Left Coast Group, Inc.
Printer: West Group

Printed in the United States of America
1 2 3 4 5 02 01 00 99

For more information contact South-Western College Publishing, 5101 Madison Road, Cincinnati, Ohio, 45227 or find us on the Internet at *http://www.swcollege.com*
For permission to use material from this text or product, contact us by
• telephone: 1-800-730-2214
• fax: 1-800-730-2215
• web: *http://www.thomsonrights.com*

ISBN: 0–324–01823–1

Contents

MODULE OVERVIEW   23.4

OBJECTIVES   23.4

RELATION TO THE FRAME   23.4

CORE CONCEPTS IN EMPLOYEE SAFETY AND HEALTH   23.5
  The Extent of Occupational Injuries and Illnesses   23.5
  Accident Causation   23.7
  The Regulatory Framework for Employee Safety and Health   23.9

STRATEGIC ISSUES IN EMPLOYEE SAFETY AND HEALTH   23.11
  Building Organizational Effectiveness Related to Safety and Health   23.11
  Implementing Safety and Health Controls   23.13
  Utilizing a Joint Employee/Employer Approach   23.15
  Devising Training Strategies   23.15

APPLICATION   23.17
  Preparing for Class Discussion and Case Analysis   23.17

IN CONCLUSION   23.17
  Debrief   23.17
  Suggested Readings and References   23.18
  Relevant Web Sites   23.18
  Critical Thinking Questions   23.18
  Exercises   23.19

INDEX   23.20

MODULE OVERVIEW

This module will discuss the importance of employee safety and health to the human resource function. In most organizations the human resource manager is directly responsible for complying with occupational safety and health regulations and for protecting employees from workplace hazards. In order to perform this function effectively, the human resource manager must understand the core concepts that will influence decision making regarding safety and health in the workplace. The human resource (HR) manager must also appreciate the strategic choices that must be made when implementing organizational policies and procedures that are designed to prevent injuries, illnesses, and fatalities.

OBJECTIVES

- Core concepts in occupational safety and health:

  ✓ HR managers must determine the extent of occupational injuries and illnesses before developing strategies that will reduce incidence rates.

  ✓ Once the size of the problem has been defined, the HR manager must then define the causative factors that contribute to existing incidence rates.

  ✓ Finally, when making decisions related to occupational safety and health, the HR manager must understand the regulatory framework that will influence those decisions.

- Strategic issues regarding implementation of policies and procedures:

  ✓ How can the HR function help build organizational effectiveness related to employee safety and health?

  ✓ What procedures should be implemented to prevent and control hazards?

  ✓ Should the organization utilize a joint employee-management approach to enhance safety and health in the workplace?

  ✓ How can the HR manager ensure employees are properly trained?

As a result of completing this module, the student will be able to appreciate the importance of protecting employees from workplace hazards, to identify potential hazards and control methods, and to implement an effective program for reducing workplace injuries and illnesses.

RELATION TO THE FRAME

As you learned in Module 1, the HR function must carry out its roles within a framework of constraints. HR roles, illustrated in Figure 23.1, include the following when applied to employee safety and health. The HR manager will play a *transactional* role when responding to immediate problems in a reactive mode. This may include handling safety and health grievances, disciplining employees for failing to adhere to established safety rules, and responding to citations issued by government agencies that direct the employer to take certain corrective actions. The HR manager plays a *translational* role when communicating organizational or governmental safety and health requirements to employees. *Transitional* activities may include implementing training programs designed to enhance employee safety and health or to comply with governmental training requirements. Finally, the HR manager plays a *transformational* role by changing the organization's culture from a reactive to a proactive mode on occupational safety and health

FIGURE 23.1 *A Frame for Understanding Human Resource Strategy:*
Context, Roles, and Constraints

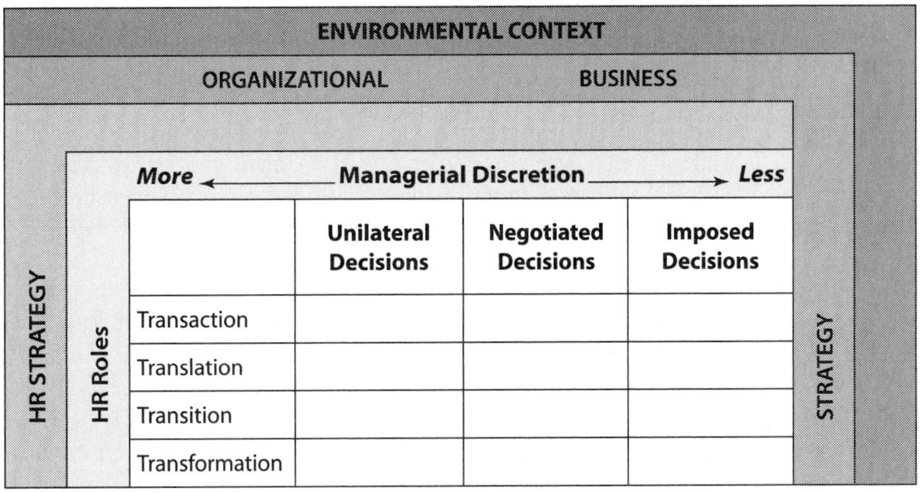

		More ← **Managerial Discretion** → Less		
		Unilateral Decisions	**Negotiated Decisions**	**Imposed Decisions**
HR STRATEGY · HR Roles	Transaction			
	Translation			
	Transition			
	Transformation			

ENVIRONMENTAL CONTEXT — ORGANIZATIONAL · BUSINESS — STRATEGY

© 2000 by Ellen Kossek and Richard Block. Thanks to Brian Pentland, Karen Markel, and John Beck for helpful comments and discussions that enhanced the model.

issues. This would include the creation of preventive strategies designed to reduce injury and illness rates.

Regarding constraints, because occupational safety and health is highly regulated, much of what management in some industries must do may be imposed by government regulation. These government standards often provide a floor. Safety and health-related activities over and above these standards may be addressed unilaterally by management. Safety and health-related matters are considered terms and conditions of employment; therefore, where the employees are represented by a union, almost all management decisions regarding safety and health must be negotiated with the union.

CORE CONCEPTS IN EMPLOYEE SAFETY AND HEALTH

In order to reduce injury and illness rates and protect employees from workplace hazards, the HR manager must understand three core concepts:

- The extent of occupational injuries and illnesses

- Accident causation

- The regulatory framework for employee safety and health

By examining these core concepts, the HR manager can build a foundation that will strengthen effective decision making.

The Extent of Occupational Injuries and Illnesses

When Congress enacted the Occupational Safety and Health Act (OSHA) in 1970, it intended to develop a regulatory framework that would reduce or prevent injuries and illnesses arising from safety and health hazards in the work environment. Safety hazards include those conditions that may result in immediate or violent harm, such as broken bones, loss of limbs or eyesight, or severe burns. Safety hazards are often associated with the operation of equipment or machinery and usually involve tasks that require skill and training.

Health hazards result from employee exposure to harmful chemicals, such as solvents and corrosives, or physical agents, such as heat, noise, or vibration. The harm may be immediate, such as with an overexposure to a toxic chemical, but it is more often associated with long-term or chronic disease. Health hazards may be more difficult to recognize for several reasons: (1) they may act more slowly on the body than safety hazards so immediate effects are not readily noticed; (2) they may result from exposures to several agents, inside and outside the workplace, that occur simultaneously; (3) the symptoms may occur while the employee is away from work or many years after the exposure has occurred; and (4) symptoms from illnesses caused by workplace exposures may be similar to symptoms associated with more common illnesses (Ashford 1976, 72–73).

Injury and Illness Statistics.   In the United States the federal government measures the extent of injuries and illnesses in several ways, including total number of reportable injuries and illnesses, cases per 100 full-time employees, cases involving lost workdays, and fatalities. According to a survey conducted by the Bureau of Labor Statistics (BLS), U.S. Department of Labor, private industry workplaces reported a total of 6.2 million nonfatal injuries and illnesses during 1996. This figure includes 5.8 million nonfatal injuries and 439,000 newly reported cases of occupational disease. As expressed in cases of injuries and illnesses per 100 employees, the BLS reported a case rate of 7.4 in 1996. Although the overall case rate has dropped every year since 1992, some sectors of private industry experience higher rates. Table 23.1 depicts the BLS survey results (*www.osha.gov/oshstats/bls*). Within the goods-producing sector, manufacturing (10.6) and construction (9.9) experienced the highest case rates in 1996. For service-producing employers, transportation/public utilities (8.7) and retail/wholesale trade (6.8) had the highest rates.

In 1996 approximately 2.8 million injuries and illnesses were lost workday cases. This includes employees who required recuperation away from work, restricted duties at work, or both. Restricted duties include shortened hours, a temporary job change or temporary restrictions on certain duties of an employee's regular job, such as no heavy lifting. Cases involving work restrictions are particularly common in manufacturing, where the rate of restricted work activity cases (2.4 per 100 full-time employees) is more than double the national average.

In its Census of Fatal Occupational Injuries, 1992–1996, the BLS reported 6,112 fatalities in 1996. Most employees died in transportation-related incidents (2,556), followed by assaults and violent acts (1,144), contacts with objects and equipment (1,005), and falls (684). Employees in the construction industry suffered the greatest number of fatalities (1,039). Other sectors experiencing significant fatalities included transportation and public utilities (947), services (767), manufacturing (715), and retail trade (672).

The BLS cautions that its statistics do not portray a completely accurate picture of workplace injuries, illnesses, and fatalities. First, the statistics are based on reports collected from approximately 165,000 private industry establishments. Because data are based on a probability sample, rather than a census of the entire population, the statistics are only an estimate. Further, the statistics reflect the employer's understanding of which cases are reportable under current U.S. Department of Labor guidelines. For example, an employer may not report a case as a lost workday if the injured employee has been assigned another duty. This would conflict with Department of Labor guidelines and would result in an underreporting of this category. The BLS also suggests that long-term illnesses, such as cancer, are difficult to relate to the workplace and are not adequately reported. Finally, BLS indicates that the number of injuries and illnesses in any given year can be influenced by the level of economic activity, working conditions and work practices, worker experience and training, and the number of hours worked.

The HR manager can play a transformational role in employee safety and health by identifying workplace hazards and implementing procedures and technologies that

TABLE 23.1 *Rate of Injuries/Illnesses per 100 Employees*

	1993	1994	1995	1996
Private industry	8.5	8.4	8.1	7.4
Goods producing	11.9	11.9	11.2	10.2
Service producing	7.1	6.9	6.7	6.2

will control those hazards. In fact, the Occupational Safety and Health Act requires employers to identify hazards in its regulation on record keeping. Part 1904 of the Code of Federal Regulations mandates that employers maintain a log and summary of all recordable injuries and illnesses for the purpose of developing information regarding the causes and prevention of disease. Recordable injury or illness includes any of the following: occupational deaths; occupational illnesses; occupational injuries that involve loss of consciousness, restriction of work or motion, transfer to another job, or medical treatment other than first aid; and lost workday cases. The Occupational Safety and Health (OSH) Administration provides information on these reporting requirements through any of their regional offices.

Loss Control. The HR manager can assume a more transformational role not by responding to injuries and illnesses after they have already occurred, but by identifying specific problems and reducing possible losses. Losses include medical and workers' compensation costs associated with injuries and illnesses, as well as associated losses including property damage, downtime, environmental contamination, fires, explosions, and other events that harm personnel and property. By controlling these losses, the HR manager can improve the overall economic vitality of the organization. Insurance company calculations suggest that for every dollar expended for medical and insurance costs, an additional $5 to $50 are spent on uninsured costs. These include building damage, product and equipment damage, production delays, legal expenses, wages paid for lost time, overtime, decreased production of employee on return to work, and loss of business. A proactive approach consists of identifying these costs and implementing steps to control them.

Accident Causation

To reduce injury and illness incidence rates, the HR manager must necessarily analyze events in order to determine the root causes. Unfortunately, outmoded and oversimplified theories of accident causation have influenced this critical step in the process of protecting employee safety and health. These theories focus all attention on employee carelessness as the primary cause for workplace injuries and illnesses, and they completely ignore exposure to hazards. In this section of the module, we will examine the origin of these theories, and we will propose a more rational approach to accident causation.

Shortly after World War I, several psychologists postulated the theory that certain employees were more likely to experience workplace injuries. They attributed this accident proneness to personal qualities such as carelessness, poor attitude, being lighthearted, mental instability, bad family traits, and being foreign born. The fact that foreign-born workers were more likely to be employed in the most hazardous and undesirable occupations seems to have escaped these early researchers. The researchers then suggested that employers could eliminate injuries by changing employee attitudes, developing safety consciousness, and transferring accident-prone employees to safer jobs. This accident-proneness theory could not account for the high rates of injuries in certain industries, such as coal mining or railroading, and the theory lacked any statistical evidence. In addition, subsequent research determined that all employees, not just a selected few, go through periods in which they are more likely to experience occupational injuries (Ashford 1976, 109–110).

In the 1930s and 1940s, H. W. Heinrich, an engineer with Travelers Insurance Company, developed a theory of accident causation based on unsafe behavior and unsafe working conditions. According to Heinrich, personal characteristics, such as ancestry, attitudes, lack of knowledge, and bodily defects interacted with equipment, machines, or working conditions, resulting in accidents only when the employee committed an unsafe act. Specifically, the factors leading to an injury included the following sequence: (1) ancestry and social environment; (2) fault of the employee; (3) unsafe act and/or mechanical or physical hazards; (4) the accident; and (5) the injury. Heinrich suggested these factors were involved in a domino effect, and he referred to this theory as "Scientific Management."

Heinrich based his theory on a study of 63,000 plant accident reports and 12,000 insurance company compensation claim records. Heinrich assigned each report to one of three classifications: unsafe act, unsafe condition, or undetermined. He concluded that 88 percent of injuries were caused by unsafe acts, 10 percent by unsafe conditions, and 2 percent were undetermined. Although these figures have gained wide acceptance, other researchers have uncovered a number of flaws in Heinrich's approach. First, Heinrich assumed that he could attribute each accident to one major cause. Instead, many factors may contribute in an interactive fashion to employee injuries, minor as well as major. These factors include the risks involved in the work itself, the age of the employee, training practices, and maintenance procedures.

Second, critics have challenged the accident reports that formed the basis for Heinrich's theory. Supervisors, who completed these reports, had little time to conduct complete investigations and tended to report information in a manner that would be viewed as acceptable by senior management. This precluded accepting blame by admitting that unsafe conditions were responsible for employee injuries. Other research studies have indicated markedly different proportions of unsafe acts, unsafe conditions, and undetermined causes. For example, a researcher at the University of Wisconsin examined injury data collected by safety specialists from the Wisconsin Safety and Building Division. This data indicated that 54 percent of injuries were attributed to safety code violations and unsafe conditions, while only 35 percent were caused by unsafe acts.

More importantly, Heinrich's data made no mention of occupational illnesses caused by exposure to toxic substances. Nevertheless, supporters of Heinrich's theory have extrapolated his work to conclude that occupational illnesses occur primarily in those employees who are particularly susceptible to disease. This effort is equally misguided because it ignores the relationship between exposure to a chemical and the associated response. For example, a small dose of carbon monoxide may cause drowsiness, whereas a large dose may result in death. Although some people may exhibit higher tolerances to acute chemical exposures, they are at higher risk of developing chronic disease if exposure to the chemical is not reduced or eliminated.

A number of safety proponents have also criticized Heinrich's approach for failing to consider the design of machinery or tasks as a contributing factor in occupational injuries and illnesses. Because of human nature, all employees may act at one time or another in a careless, complacent, or distracted manner. When equipment or jobs are designed without anticipating this human factor, employees will experience injuries and illnesses. For example, manufacturers have designed machinery that will not operate unless guards or other safety measures are operational. Similarly, computer manufacturers have developed specially shaped keyboards that reduce the likelihood of carpal tunnel syndrome or other injuries to the arms and wrists.

Despite evidence to the contrary, Heinrich's Safety Management or Unsafe Act Theory is still widely popular, as evidenced in the behavior-based safety movement. Behavior-based safety programs emphasize the importance of changing employee behavior in order to prevent injuries and illnesses. Using this approach, observers are assigned the task of monitoring employees' work activities. The employer provides negative reinforcement for unsafe behaviors and positive reinforcement for safe behaviors. In addition to positive and negative reinforcement, behavior-based safety advocates recommend the creation of specific, written work procedures and comprehensive safety training. Although OSHA requires work procedures and training for certain types of work activities, such as responding to chemical spills, this approach is unlikely to yield positive, long-term results unless it takes the concepts of hazard and risk into account.

In point of fact, exposure to hazards causes employee injuries and illnesses. Work methods or processes are hazardous if they increase the risk that employees will be injured or become ill. The level of risk is determined by assessing the severity of the injury or illness that may occur from exposure to the hazard and by estimating the probability of occurrence, also expressed as duration and frequency of exposure. For example, working in the vicinity of an unguarded, spinning flywheel could produce severe damage to various parts of the body. If the employee had to work around this flywheel for the entire shift, the risk of injury would be high, and that job would be hazardous. Normally, greater amounts of energy or toxic substances produce a greater severity of injury or illness. However, low levels of exposure to chemicals or energy over significant periods of time can also produce risk. An employee exposed to small amounts of asbestos over a working lifetime can still develop lung cancer.

Quality Approach to Safety and Health. Using W. Edwards Deming's approach to quality improvement, approximately 85 percent of workplace problems, including safety and health hazards, can be controlled only if the organization evaluates and improves the leadership or management system. These improvements include implementing activities to control exposures; developing standards that are clear, effective, and properly communicated; and ensuring that leadership complies with performance standards that govern management behavior related to safety and health. The HR manager can protect employees from hazardous work by completing a five-step process: (1) identify all potential losses that could occur; (2) evaluate the risk associated with each loss and determine which are the most severe; (3) develop a plan to correct each exposure, focusing on the most serious first; (4) implement the action plan; and (5) monitor the plan to ensure it is having the desired effect.

Finally, the benefits of utilizing this rational five-step approach are best exemplified with the passage of the Refrigerator Safety Act. Prior to passage of the act, many children suffocated after being trapped inside abandoned refrigerators. Manufacturers opposed the requirement to eliminate locks on doors and to create doors that could be opened with little pressure from the inside, arguing that the required changes would be too costly. Instead, they suggested a behavioral approach by recommending that parents be more vigilant in keeping their children away from unsafe refrigerators. However, Congress determined that controlling the hazard would produce more effective results, and thus enacted the legislation. Since the creation of the Refrigerator Safety Act, no child has died in a refrigerator designed according to the specifications of the act (Howe 1998, 13).

The Regulatory Framework for Employee Safety and Health

The regulatory framework for employee safety and health is established primarily in the Occupational Safety and Health Act, enacted by Congress in 1970. State legislation also regulates employer activities in this area, as do collective bargaining agreements with employee organizations. The OSHA applies to any employer engaged in a business affecting commerce, including agriculture. Three federal agencies administer and enforce the provisions of the act, including the Occupational Safety and Health Administration within the U.S. Department of Labor, the Occupational Safety and Health Review Commission (OSHRC), and the National Institute for Occupational Safety and Health (NIOSH).

The OSH Administration is responsible for setting standards, conducting inspections, issuing citations, and assessing penalties against employers who are not in compliance with provisions of the act. The OSHRC is an independent board that is charged with reviewing decisions reached by the OSH Administration. NIOSH is responsible for conducting research and recommending regulatory action to the OSH Administration.

Under the act, employers are required to comply with standards adopted by the OSH Administration to protect employees from safety and health hazards. If a standard does not exist, the employer must still protect employees from recognized hazards that are causing or likely to cause death or serious physical harm. The OSH Administration refers to this requirement as the general duty clause. The OSH Administration determines compliance with standards and the general duty clause by conducting physical inspections of the workplace. If a compliance officer discovers a violation, a citation will be issued to the employer. The citation will specify the standard violated and the seriousness of the violation. It will also list corrective action the employer must take, monetary penalties, and a date when corrective action must be completed. Monetary penalties will be based on the gravity of the violation and various reduction factors, such as size of the business, evidence of a written safety and health program, and previous history of that employer related to safety and health compliance. The employer may seek an appeal regarding any citations by petitioning to the OSHRC.

Section 18 of the act gives individual states the authority to assume responsibility for occupational safety and health. Currently, 23 states have requested and received permission from the OSH Administration to administer and enforce their own safety and health legislation. In order to receive permission, states must demonstrate that their program is at least as effective in protecting employees as that administered by federal OSHA. The state law must also provide protection for public-sector employees, a group that is not covered in the federal legislation. The federal OSH act preempts any state law pertaining to occupational safety and health unless the U.S. Secretary of Labor has approved the state plan. The OSH Administration is also responsible for evaluating the manner in which each state administers its own plan. If the state fails to meet specified criteria, the Secretary of Labor must notify the state that approval for the plan has been withdrawn or that concurrent federal jurisdiction will be exercised.

In addition to enforcing safety and health standards, the OSH Administration and state agencies prohibit employers from discriminating against employees who exercise their rights under the law. Employees who believe they have been disciplined or treated in a discriminatory fashion for such activities as filing OSHA complaints or providing information to an inspector may file a discrimination complaint with the appropriate agency. Either the OSH Administration or the state agency will investigate the complaint and are empowered to seek appropriate relief from the employer. This may include reinstatement, back pay, or any other remedy that seeks to make the employee "whole."

One such employee right that is protected by the federal OSH Administration and state enforcement agencies is the employee's right to refuse to perform a dangerous work assignment. Although the federal Occupational Safety and Health Act does not reference this right, the OSH Administration and most state enforcement agencies have attempted to regulate situations that endanger employee safety and health. In particular, the OSH Administration has adopted a regulation at 29 C.F.R. 1977.12(2) that provides the following:

> However, occasions might arise when an employee is confronted with a choice between not performing assigned tasks or subjecting himself to serious injury or death arising from a hazardous condition at the workplace. If the employee, with no reasonable alternative, refuses in good faith to expose himself to the dangerous condition, he would be protected against subsequent discrimination. The condition causing the employee's apprehension of death or injury must be of such a nature that a reasonable person, under the circumstances then confronting the employee,

would conclude that there is a real danger of death or serious injury and that there is insufficient time, due to the urgency of the situation, to eliminate the danger through resort to regular statutory enforcement channels. In addition, in such circumstances, the employee, where possible, must have also sought from his employer, and been unable to obtain, a correction of the dangerous condition.

In these cases the burden is on the employee to demonstrate that the above conditions have been met. However, many employees have taken advantage of this regulation in refusing to perform dangerous work assignments, and the courts have upheld the OSH Administration's authority to protect employees in these situations.

Where a collective bargaining agreement exists, employers will also have to operate within the constraints established by arbitration decisions. Although arbitrators have recognized the right of management to promulgate and enforce safety rules, these rules must be reasonably related to the purpose for which they were intended. Management must also communicate the rules to its employees, or it will be more difficult to discipline employees for rule infractions. On the employee's right to refuse dangerous work, arbitrators have ruled that the "work now-grieve later" principle does not apply where adherence to an order to perform work would involve an unusual or abnormal safety or health hazard. As with the refusal protection under the OSHA, the employee has the burden to prove that a safety or health hazard was the reason for refusing a work assignment. Based on the hazards present at a specific location, the labor organization representing employees may also wish to negotiate a range of contract clauses related to health and safety. This may include general language that obligates an employer to bargain over safety and health issues or specific language that addresses topics such as housekeeping, lighting, protective clothing, medical care, workplace monitoring, training, or union access to the workplace for the purpose of conducting research.

STRATEGIC ISSUES IN EMPLOYEE SAFETY AND HEALTH

In order to manage employee safety and health effectively, the HR professional must transform the culture of the organization from a reactive to a proactive mode. Typically, employers and employees respond to injuries and illnesses after the fact. By focusing on the following strategic issues, the HR manager can assist in the development of a preventive approach that will identify and correct problems *before* they result in serious harm to employees.

- Building organizational effectiveness related to safety and health

- Implementing safety and health controls

- Utilizing a joint employee/employer approach

- Devising training strategies

In this section of the module we will examine how the HR professional can play a transformational role within the organization by addressing the issues discussed below.

Building Organizational Effectiveness Related to Safety and Health

A survey of the current literature on management approaches to occupational safety and health reveals a common thread. Many organizations view safety programs as accessories that last for awhile and are then discarded because of lack of interest or eventual failure to produce desired results. The defunct program is then replaced by a more "innovative" approach that will also have a limited life span (Sloat 1996, 65–66). Most of these programs are designed to identify and then eliminate unsafe behaviors by employees. These include incentive programs that reward employees for no lost-time accidents, audits that determine whether employees are wearing appropriate protective equipment or performing jobs in an unsafe manner, and behavior-based safety programs that use teams of employees to provide feedback on unsafe behavior to fellow workers. Although these programs may result in temporary reductions in injury rates, they fail in the long term because they do not address the fundamental organizational change that is required to incorporate safety and health into the culture of the organization.

Safety and Health Culture.   In order to be effective in protecting its employees, the organization must integrate safety and health into the operation, similar to integration that has occurred for productivity and quality. For example, the organization must set safety and health goals that become part of its overall mission. Goal setting is important because it establishes the climate that will determine the success or failure of the organization's safety and health efforts. For example, if the organization's goal is no lost-time accidents, employees and supervision may decide that hiding injuries and illnesses or underreporting will produce the desired results. This will clearly produce a culture that is detrimental to the safety and health of employees (Pardy 1998, 1–2). If the goal is compliance with government regulations, the organization may miss opportunities to provide protection for employees from new hazards that have not been regulated. If, on the other hand, the goal is to become an industry leader in occupational safety and health, the organization may encourage its employees to devise new approaches and activities that will alter the organizational culture.

OSHA views sound management practices as critical to the success of any safety and health program. In its Self-Assessment Checklist *(www.osha.gov/oshprogs/vpp),* OSHA urges employers to integrate safety and health concerns into the overall planning cycle of the organization. OSHA also recommends that organizations manage safety and health in the same manner as productivity and quality. This would include assigning safety and health responsibilities with documentation of accountability from top management to line supervisors. This would also require providing the authority and resources that are necessary to complete these assigned responsibilities. Likewise, the performance evaluation of all personnel must include criteria related to safety and health responsibilities.

The research of Dr. Rensis Likert demonstrates the high correlation of ten factors with an organization's productivity and quality (Petersen 1998, 4–5):

- Confidence and trust in supervision

- Interest in the subordinate's future

- Understanding problems and desiring to help overcome them

- Training the subordinate to improve his or her performance

- Teaching the subordinate how to solve problems rather than providing answers

- Giving support by making required resources available

- Communicating information the subordinate must know to perform the job

- Seeking out and attempting to use ideas and opinions

- Approachability of the supervisor

- Crediting and recognizing the subordinate's accomplishments

In addition, Petersen suggests a high correlation between these factors and the safety and health performance of the organization. By implementing an employee perception survey that encompasses these criteria, the organization can motivate line supervisors, middle managers, and senior management to take actions that will result in dramatic safety and health improvements. This is confirmed by a 1978 NIOSH study that identified top management commitment, a humanistic approach toward employees, one-on-one contact, and positive reinforcement as the four critical elements associated with safety performance (Petersen 1998, 3). More importantly, encouraging the behaviors described above changes the culture of the organization. Instead of blaming the victim for workplace injuries and alienating the workforce, the organization engages employees in the task of identifying hazards, solving problems, and achieving continuous improvement.

Management Leadership. Transformational change related to employee safety and health cannot occur unless the highest levels of the organization demonstrate a commitment to that change. The HR manager contributes to this change effort first by developing a written program that specifies the duties of all management representatives that pertain to safety and health, as well as the methods that will be utilized to ensure accountability. For example, the written program should incorporate safety and health performance as part of the evaluation process for all supervisory and management personnel. This would also include the development of an effective reward system for first-line supervisors that ensures their support of the organization's safety and health program.

The written program also establishes commitment by designating a management safety and health representative or department that is assigned specific duties with a budget that is appropriate to its mission. The duties of the safety and health function must include setting specific goals and reporting to senior management on the progress that has been made. The safety and health function should also be responsible for developing written safety procedures and practices that are based on an analysis of the jobs performed by employees. Finally, the written program must stipulate the procedures that are used to document performance related to employee safety and health. This would include documentation of the hazards that are investigated and the solutions that are implemented. Reports on the progress that is made in eliminating or controlling hazards must be provided to senior management, as well as to employees who are impacted.

Of course, the HR function cannot implement an effective safety and health program without the personal involvement of senior management. Senior management must clearly assign safety and health responsibilities and develop performance measures that establish accountability. Senior management must also provide their subordinates with the authority and the resources required to meet their established responsibilities.

Implementing Safety and Health Controls

In order to implement hazard control measures, the HR specialist must undertake a comprehensive analysis of workplace hazards. OSHA's Self-Assessment Checklist recommends the use of a Job Safety and Health Analysis (JSHA) for identifying particular hazards associated with a given job. The JSHA involves four basic steps:

1.   Select the job to be analyzed.

2.   Divide the job into its basic steps.

3.   Identify the hazards associated with each step.

4.   Control each hazard.

When selecting jobs to analyze, the organization should focus on jobs that have a history of employee injuries, illnesses, or near misses; jobs that involve exposure to numerous hazards, such as high levels of energy or hazardous chemicals; and jobs where procedures have recently changed and the employee is uncertain about safety and health requirements.

After the HR function has identified potentially hazardous workplace conditions, the next step involves implementing those controls that will eliminate the hazard or at least protect employees from serious consequences. The OSH Administration and various standards-setting organizations, such as the National Safety Council and American National Standards Institute (ANSI), have identified a hierarchy of controls that establishes a range of preferences from most effective to least effective. This hierarchy of controls, including specific examples of each type, is provided in Table 23.2 (Howe 1998 8–9).

The most effective method of control involves eliminating the hazard or introducing a substitute that is less hazardous. Methods of control become less effective at each successive level because supervisors and employees must exert greater effort to ensure the control method is implemented. For example, the employer can eliminate the noise that may damage an employee's hearing by changing the process on a particular machine. The employer can also protect employees by enclosing the source of the noise, but supervisors and employees will have to ensure the enclosure remains in place. Warning signs may alert employees to the noise hazards in the area, but those employees will have to notice the signs and take appropriate steps to protect themselves. The employer could train employees on the hazards of noise and provide hearing protection; however, supervisors and employees would have to maintain constant vigilance to ensure that the hearing protection was always worn properly. Clearly, eliminating the noise provides the most effective protection because this method does not rely on the actions of supervisors and employees to ensure compliance.

Unfortunately, the most effective method may also be the most costly, at least in the short term. Substituting for a hazardous material may result in greater expense because suppliers recognize the value placed on less hazardous materials and establish pricing that reflects that value. In this case, providing all exposed employees with respiratory protection might appear to be the least expensive option. However, when analyzing the control options available, the HR manager must consider not only the immediate costs, but also the effectiveness of the method and the long-term benefits provided. Respirators can be inexpensive, but the employer must ensure that the respirators are properly fitted to each employee and that each employee has received a medical evaluation. Further, the employer must provide constant monitoring to ensure that employees are

TABLE 23.2 *Hierarchy of Safety and Health Controls*

Elimination or substitution	Substitute for hazardous chemical Change process to eliminate noise Reduce energy, speed	**Most Effective**
Engineering controls	Ventilation Machine guarding Sound enclosures Circuit breakers	↑
Warnings	Signs, labels Sirens, horns Odor in natural gas	
Training and procedures, administrative controls	Lockout procedures Rotation of workers Training on chemical hazards Inspection of safety equipment	↓
Protective equipment	Safety glasses Ear plugs Gloves Respirators	**Least Effective**

wearing the respirators, which can be extremely uncomfortable, and that the respirators are working properly. More importantly, implementing the more expensive control in the short-term may result in greater benefits, such as reduced absenteeism, improved morale, reduced health insurance costs, reduced workers' compensation costs, and increased quality. Although pressures to reduce short-term costs are significant, ignoring the hierarchy of controls will result in greater long-term costs to the organization.

Utilizing a Joint Employee/Employer Approach

The HR professional can assist in the transformation of the organization's approach to safety and health by devising strategies that allow for employee participation in the process. This may include requesting employees to designate safety and health representatives; creating a safety and health committee composed of employer and employee representatives; utilizing a written employee hazard reporting system or suggestion program; and encouraging employees to participate as trainers, inspectors, and problem solvers. For example, some employers authorize employee safety and health committees to assess the safety and health impact of production-related equipment and chemicals before such materials are purchased. Through this participation, employees can develop a commitment to safety and health goals that will be critical to the organization's success in recognizing and eliminating hazards and reducing injury and illness rates.

The most common form of employee participation is through joint employee/employer safety and health committees. The joint committee can be an effective force for change if the rules of operation are carefully designed. When creating such committees, either in a unionized or nonunionized setting, the HR function must consider several key factors in order to demonstrate the organization's commitment to genuine employee participation. First, the committee should have an equal number of employer and employee representatives to ensure fairness and to avoid the perception that management controls the decision-making authority. Related to this issue, committee members must have the authority to make decisions that will lead to identifiable change. The committee should document its effort to improve workplace conditions by developing meeting agendas, recording meeting minutes, establishing responsibility and timelines for actions that will be taken, and noting specific changes that have occurred. To ensure joint participation, responsibility for chairing the committee, developing agendas, and recording minutes should rotate between employer and employee representatives. The committee's rules of operation should also be documented in writing.

The joint committee cannot be effective in solving problems unless members have the expertise and information required to evaluate those problems and to propose solutions. Although most employees are knowledgeable about their job duties, few have received training in hazard identification and control. For this reason, the organization must support continuing education for committee members, especially given the technical nature of hazard assessment and control. The committee should also be empowered to conduct independent investigations on-site and to review all documentation related to workplace safety and health. Finally, members of the committee must maintain communications with employees at all levels of the organization to ensure that all views are represented and all employees are informed of decisions that are made.

Devising Training Strategies

Although training provides less effective protection to employees than hazard elimination or engineering controls, the Occupational Safety and Health Act requires training for employees in many of its regulations. This ranges from specific training, such as safe operating procedures for a lift truck, to more generic training on the hazards of chemicals that are used or produced by the employer. In any case the HR manager will have many options in attempting to comply with OSHA requirements. These include utilizing existing personnel to conduct training, hiring consultants from outside the organization to deliver training, and purchasing video-driven training programs off the shelf from various vendors. No matter which option the organization selects, HR personnel should ensure that the training strategy will meet the needs of employees, the organization, and any regulatory agencies. The HR manager can accomplish this objective by completing several steps.

First, before any employees receive training, the HR manager must be responsible for conducting a needs-analysis to determine the specific knowledge, skills, and attitudes that are required to perform a specific task safely. For example, if an employee must enter a confined space, such as a tank or vault, to perform work, the OSH Administration requires the employee to possess knowledge about the hazards present, the skills required to operate retrieval equipment properly, and an appreciation for the dangers involved. Other organizations, such as NIOSH and ANSI, have also developed recommended training guidelines for certain hazardous jobs. By consulting references from these and similar organizations and by examining the job requirements, the HR manager can determine the specific learning objectives for a given task.

Once the HR manager has identified the required knowledge, skills, and attitudes for a specific task, the next step involves designing the course and accompanying evaluation instruments with these objectives in mind. If the task in question requires a certain degree of knowledge before an employee can perform it safely, the question becomes whether the course imparts that knowledge effectively. If the task requires the employee to perform certain skills safely, the course must include hands-on experience so the employee can demonstrate those skills. Unfortunately, with the advent of video-driven training programs that focus on knowledge objectives only, employees never gain the skills that are critical to performing the job safely. Although video-driven training programs may be less expensive, they are not designed to address all the learning objectives that may be necessary. When using outside consultants to provide safety and health training, the HR manager must demand to see the learning objectives that form the basis of the course and must determine if those objectives meet the safety and health requirements of the job.

MODULE
23

Once the course has been designed according to the learning objectives, the organization can then deliver the training to employees. The first program should be a pilot directed toward members of the target audience. This will enable the HR manager to determine if the course is accomplishing its objectives and whether changes will be required before all employees go through the course. The presence of members of the prospective target audience at the pilot will also help ensure that course objectives meet the specific needs of those who will be in attendance.

The final step in the course development process is evaluation. This includes the creation of instruments that will assess the knowledge and skills acquired by employees during training. The HR manager will need to address several issues related to evaluation, including: (1) ensuring that any tests account for employee literacy levels; (2) establishing a definition of successful course completion; (3) documenting employee competence with respect to specific skills; and (4) determining if any knowledge and skill objectives are so critical to safety and health that the employee must demonstrate competency or fail the course.

Before the actual delivery of safety and health training begins, the HR manager should determine answers to the following questions:

- Who will be eligible to attend the training?

- Where will training be conducted?

- What special equipment will be required?

- How will employees and supervisors be notified of the training schedule?

Although these items may seem mundane, failure to consider the significance of any one element can result in training that fails to accomplish the required objectives. For example, if training is held in the cafeteria or other noisy, busy environment, the distractions will seriously hinder employee learning. Likewise, neglecting to inform supervisors of the training schedule will ensure that employees assigned to attend a class will not be released from work. Lastly, scheduling the training at the end of the shift rather than the beginning will surely result in employees paying more attention to the clock than to course material.

Application

Based on the information provided in the following situation, answer the questions below.

> On a hot summer day, a supervisor at a production facility notices that an employee is operating a machine without a hair net. The hair net is designed to protect the employee from having his or her hair caught in a flywheel located next to the employee's workstation. Several times during the shift, the employee is required to lean under the flywheel and adjust a valve. The written company safety policy provides a generic requirement that employees must wear personal protective equipment provided by the employer in order to prevent serious injury. When the supervisor asks the employee to wear the hair net, the employee complies. Later in the day, the supervisor is called to the same workstation. The employee in question has removed the hair net, complaining that it was uncomfortable. While adjusting the valve, the employee's hair was caught in the flywheel. Luckily, a fellow employee on the scene pressed the emergency stop button before any harm was done.

MODULE
23

Preparing for Class Discussion and Case Analysis

Be prepared to discuss the following questions in class.

1. If the hair net had not been provided, could the employee have legally refused to perform the job?

2. Should the employee be disciplined for not wearing the hair net? What would be the basis for the discipline?

3. Assuming the existence of a union contract, on what basis might the employee grieve any disciplinary action?

4. What are the possible causes for this incident?

5. Using the Hierarchy of Controls, list several different controls that could be implemented to prevent similar incidents in the future.

6. If the employee had attended a training program on the importance of wearing the hair net, could the incident have been prevented?

In Conclusion

Debrief

In order to reduce the incidence rate of occupational injuries and illnesses, the HR manager must: (1) assess the hazards in the workplace using loss control principles, and (2) identify the causative factors that contribute to incidence rates. Before implementing change, the HR manager must also understand the regulatory framework within which decisions must be made. This includes governmental requirements, as well as requirements imposed by collective bargaining agreements. To transform the organizational culture from a reactive to a proactive mode on safety and health issues, the organization must demonstrate the commitment of senior management; take concrete steps to prevent and eliminate hazards; involve employees in safety and health decision making; and initiate training programs that address the specific needs of employees, the organization, and the government. Although the implementation of these steps may involve a considerable investment of time, this investment will produce significant results that in the long run will be beneficial to the organization and its employees.

Suggested Readings and References

Ashford, Nicholas. 1976. *Crisis in the Workplace: Occupational Disease and Injury.* Cambridge, MA: The MIT Press.

Elkouri, Frank and Elkouri, Edna Asper. 1985. *How Arbitration Works.* Washington, D.C.: Bureau of National Affairs.

Howe, Jim. 1998. *A Union Critique of Behavior Safety.* Detroit: UAW Health and Safety Department.

Kochan, Thomas A., Dyer, Lee and Lipsky, David B. 1977. *The Effectiveness of Union-Management Safety and Health Committees.* Kalamazoo, MI: W. E. Upjohn Institute for Employment Research.

Pardy, Wayne. April/May 1998. *Incentive Schemes: Safety Bribes.* Occupational Safety & Health Canada, Volume 14. Don Mills: Southam Business Communications.

Petersen, Dan. October 1998. *What Measures Should We Use and Why?* Professional Safety, Volume 43. Park Ridge: American Society of Safety Engineers.

Sloat, Kim C. M. May 1996. *Why Safety Programs Fail and What to Do About It.* Occupational Hazards, Volume 58. Cleveland: Penton Publishing and Marketing.

Whirlpool Corp. v. Marshall, 8 Occupational Safety and Health Cases 1004, Bureau of National Affairs, 1980.

Relevant Web Sites

OCCUPATIONAL SAFETY AND HEALTH ADMINISTRATION
http://www.osha.gov

NATIONAL INSTITUTE FOR OCCUPATIONAL SAFETY AND HEALTH
http://www.cdc.gov/niosh/homepage.html

NATIONAL SAFETY COUNCIL
http://www.nsc.org

AMERICAN CONFERENCE OF GOVERNMENTAL INDUSTRIAL HYGIENISTS
http://www.acgih.org

Critical Thinking Questions

1. What arguments could you present to convince senior management to increase expenditures for hazard prevention and control?

2. How can you ensure that members of the joint safety and health committee will have the authority to make decisions?

3.   At a time when organizations are streamlining operations, how can you ensure that employees will be available for safety and health training without disrupting operations?

Exercises

1.   Consult the OSHA web page at *www.osha.gov* to determine the training requirements associated with the Hazard Communication Standard, 29 C.F.R. 1910.1200.

2.   Contact NIOSH at 800-356-4674 and request a packet of information related to an occupational health hazard that interests you (asbestos, fiberglass, shift work, workplace violence, etc.).

Index

Accident causation theories, 23.7
Accident-proneness theory, 23.7
American National Standards Institute (ANSI), 23.13

Burden of compliance, 23.11
Bureau of Labor Statistics (BLS), 23.6

Census of Fatal Occupational Injuries, 23.6
Collective bargaining, 23.11
Compensation claim, 23.8
Compliance, safety and health regulations, 23.10, 23.12
Construction industry, 23.6
Control of exposure, 23.9, 23.13, 23.14

Death (occupational), 23.6, 23.7
Discrimination complaint (OSH Administration), 23.10. *See also* Employee's right to refuse
Documentation of accountability, 23.12

Employee carelessness, 23.7, 23.17
Employee safety and health management, 23.11
Employee's right to refuse, 23.10, 23.11, 23.17. *See also* Discrimination complaint (OSH Administration)
Equipment design (for safety), 23.8
Exposure to hazards, 23.6, 23.8, 23.9, 23.12

Fatalities, 23.6

Goods-producing sector, 23.6, 23.7
Government regulations, 23.5, 23.7, 23.12, 23.18

Hazard identification and control, 23.13, 23.15
Hazard reporting system, 23.15
Hazardous conditions/materials/processes, 23.9, 23.12
Health and safety hazards, 23.6, 23.9, 23.11
Hierarchy of safety and health controls, 23.14
Human resource function, 23.12, 23.15
Human resource manager, 23.4, 23.5, 23.6, 23.7, 23.9, 23.11, 23.12, 23.14, 23.15, 23.16, 23.17–18
Human resource roles, 23.4
Human resource strategy, 23.5

Injury and illness (occupational), 23.6, 23.7, 23.13

Job Safety and Health Analysis (JSHA), 23.13
Joint employee/employer approach, 23.15, 23.14

Lost workdays, 23.6, 23.7

Monitoring work activities, 23.9

National Institute for Occupational Safety and Health (NIOSH), 23.10, 23.12, 23.16
National Safety Council, 23.13, 23.14

Occupational illness, 23.8
Occupational Safety and Health Act (OSHA), 23.5, 23.7, 23.10, 23.11
Occupational Safety and Health Administration (OSH Administration), 23.7, 23.9, 23.10, 23.11, 23.12, 23.16
Occupational safety and health programs, 23.11
Occupational Safety and Health Review Commission (OSHRC), 23.9, 23.10
Organizational change, Occupational Safety and Health, 23.12, 23.13
OSHA's Self-Assessment Checklist, 23.12

Preventive approach, 23.11. *See also* Proactive approach to health and safety
Private industry, 23.6, 23.7
Proactive approach to health and safety, 23.7, 23.18
Protecting employees from hazards, 23.9, 23.15, 23.16, 23.17, 23.18
Protective equipment, 23.12, 23.17
Public-sector employees, 23.10

Recordable injury or illness, 23.7
Refrigerator Safety Act, 23.9
Regulation 29 C.F.R., 23.10–11
Regulatory framework for safety and health, 23.9
Restricted work activity, 23.6, 23.7
Risk factors, 23.8
Rule infractions, 23.11

Safety and health culture, 23.12
Safety and health performance, 23.12, 23.13
Safety and health representative, 23.13, 23.14, 23.15
Safety code violations, 23.8
Safety hazards. *See* Health and safety hazards
Safety Management or Unsafe Act Theory (Heinrich), 23.8. *See also* Scientific Management
Safety specialists, 23.8
Safety training, 23.11, 23.16, 23.18
Scientific Management theory, 23.8. *See also* Safety Management or Unsafe Act Theory
Senior management, 23.12
Service-producing sector, 23.6, 23.7
Standards, safety and health, 23.5, 23.9, 23.10

Toxic substances, 23.8, 23.9
Transactional role, 23.4
Transformational change, 23.13
Transformational role, 23.4, 23.11
Transitional role, 23.4
Translational role, 23.4
Transportation-related incidents, 23.6

U.S. Department of Labor, 23.6, 23.9
Unsafe act, behavior, or condition, 23.8, 23.12

Work environment, 23.5
Work procedures and training, 23.9
Workers' compensation, 23.7
Workplace hazards/ injuries, 23.4, 23.13

MODULE
23

KOSSEK ■ BLOCK

Managing Human Resources in the 21st Century

From Core Concepts to Strategic Choice

MODULE 24

Managing Careers

Carrie R. Leana
UNIVERSITY OF PITTSBURGH

Daniel C. Feldman
UNIVERSITY OF SOUTH CAROLINA

Managing Human Resources in the 21st Century: From Core Concepts to Strategic Choice,
by Kossek and Block

Publisher: Dave Shaut
Executive Editor: John Szilagyi
Developmental Editor: Bryant Editorial Development
Marketing Manager: Joseph A. Sabatino
Production Editor: Tamborah E. Moore
Manufacturing Coordinator: Dana Began Schwartz
Cover Design: Tin Box Studio
Cover Photographs: Copyright Shoji Sato/Photonica
Production House: The Left Coast Group, Inc.
Printer: West Group

Printed in the United States of America
1 2 3 4 5 02 01 00 99

For more information contact South-Western College Publishing, 5101 Madison Road, Cincinnati, Ohio, 45227 or find us on the Internet at *http://www.swcollege.com*
For permission to use material from this text or product, contact us by

- telephone: 1-800-730-2214
- fax: 1-800-730-2215
- web: *http://www.thomsonrights.com*

ISBN: 0–324–01824–X

This book is printed on acid-free paper.

Contents

MODULE OVERVIEW   24.4

OBJECTIVES   24.4

RELATION TO THE FRAME   24.4

CORE CONCEPTS IN MANAGING CAREERS   24.5
Career Stages   24.5
Life Stages   24.7
The Formation of Stable Career Interests   24.7

MAJOR CAREER TRANSITIONS   24.10
Organizational Entry and Socialization   24.10
Transfers, Promotions, and Relocation   24.12
Downsizings and Layoffs   24.13

STRATEGIC ISSUES IN MANAGING CAREERS   24.14
Individual Strategies for Managing Careers   24.14
Organizational Strategies for Developing Employees' Careers   24.16

IN CONCLUSION   24.16
Debrief   24.16
Suggested Readings   24.17
Relevant Web Sites   24.18
Critical Thinking Questions   24.18
Exercises   24.18

INDEX   24.19

MODULE
24

MODULE OVERVIEW

For students graduating from college and graduate school today, as well as for employees already in the workforce, the nature of the work world is fundamentally different from that which their parents faced a generation ago. Where their parents were likely to have entered an occupation and stayed with it most of their working lives, today's employees will work in a wide variety of jobs. Where their parents expected to work for one organization most of their careers, today's graduates will likely work in many different organizations over a 40-year period. Indeed, the globalization of corporations, the increase in the number of corporate mergers and acquisitions, and the widespread use of layoffs and corporate downsizings have made it virtually impossible for employees to remain in one job or in one corporation for their entire work lives. For these reasons, then, we need to examine the topic of *careers*—namely, the sequences of jobs and occupations that individuals hold over the 40 to 50 years they participate in the labor force (Feldman 1988).

OBJECTIVES

This module has several key learning objectives:

- To recognize the diversity of career paths available to individuals today and to understand why different types of people gravitate to different careers

- To understand both the employee and organizational factors that influence people to change jobs, employers, and careers

- To identify the individual strategies and organizational practices that help people make successful transitions into new careers, new jobs, or new organizations

- To understand the dynamics of several career transitions, in particular: organizational entry, transfers, promotions, geographical relocation, and downsizing

- To identify better strategies for managing one's own career and for developing the careers of subordinates

RELATION TO THE FRAME

Career management invokes the range of human resources (HR) roles. Examples of situations in which career management touches the *transaction* role occur where the firm maintains employee skill inventories and handles the myriad of issues associated with expatriation and repatriation (see page 24.12). Career management plays the *translation* role when it assures that employees are aware of promotion, transfer, and growth opportunities in the organization and translates the values of high commitment organizations (see Module 1) into work/family balance. The *transition* role for career management can be seen when the organization downsizes. In such a situation, the organization must reconcile the performance-related needs of the organization with the career goals of employees. Career management touches the *transformation* role when the organization begins to encourage its employees to rethink their roles in a changed organization. For example, over the last decade, firms have increasingly encouraged employees to consider managing their own careers and developing their skill levels for employment with multiple organizations, rather than encouraging employees to think of a lifetime association with one organization.

Career management also operates under constraints. Although to the extent that employees manage their own careers the firm is faced with fewer constraints than otherwise, career management issues must often be negotiated. Such matters as promo-

FIGURE 24.1 *A Frame for Understanding Human Resource Strategy:
Context, Roles, and Constraints*

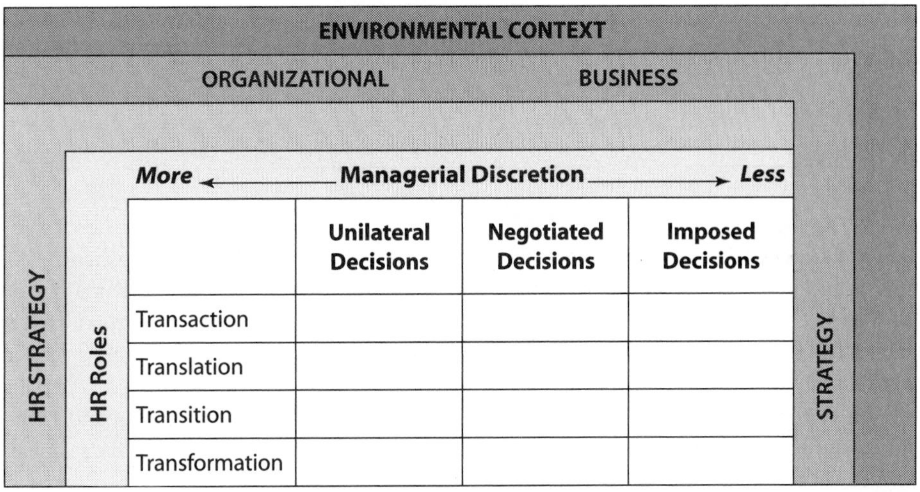

ENVIRONMENTAL CONTEXT			
ORGANIZATIONAL		BUSINESS	

HR STRATEGY · HR Roles · STRATEGY

More ← Managerial Discretion → Less			
	Unilateral Decisions	**Negotiated Decisions**	**Imposed Decisions**
Transaction			
Translation			
Transition			
Transformation			

© 2000 by Ellen Kossek and Richard Block. Thanks to Brian Pentland, Karen Markel, and John Beck for helpful comments and discussions that enhanced the model.

tions, transfers, relocations, and layoffs must be negotiated with unions representing employees. Laws also constrain the career management function. For example, downsizing, when it occurs, may not have a disparate impact by age, gender, or race or the organization could face significant legal liability.

CORE CONCEPTS IN MANAGING CAREERS

To understand how employees and employers manage careers, there are several core concepts to explore.

- Career stages
- Life stages
- Formation of stable career interests (vocational choice and career anchors)
- Career transitions (entry, socialization, transfers and relocations, downsizing)
- Strategic issues in managing careers for both employees and employers

Each of these issues has implications not only for how people manage their own careers, but also for how organizations structure career opportunities and challenges for their employees. Although career management has recently become more of an individual than an organizational concern as employees and employers alike have become less loyal to one another, companies nonetheless make considerable investments in attracting, retaining, and developing talented employees. Thus, the issues discussed below such as career stages and life stages are relevant for both individual employees and the organization hoping to attract and retain them.

Career Stages

Implicit in the concept of a career is the idea of change. People's job skills and career aspirations change over time; the types of activities individuals enjoy right out of school

TABLE 24.1 *Career Stages*

Apprentice

Colleague

Mentor

Sponsor

are not necessarily the assignments they seek after 20 years of work experience. An important core concept in this module, then, is *career stage*. A career stage is a period of time (often defined as 7–10 years) in which employees have predictable sets of career interests, opportunities, and challenges. Moreover, these career stages are experienced similarly by employees in a wide variety of occupations and professions. Thus, the career challenges of a junior bank manager trying to make vice president are much more similar to those of a junior lawyer trying to make partner than to the career challenges of the bank chief executive officer.

While a wide variety of models of career stages have been put forward, one of the most useful ones is that presented by Dalton, Thompson, and Price (1977), who propose that there are four stages of careers. Each of these stages, shown in Table 24.1, has distinctly different work activities and psychological demands.

Apprentice Stage. In the apprentice stage, employees are relatively dependent on their supervisors for training and guidance; their work is primarily technical in nature and is focused on learning how to apply knowledge gained in school to real-world settings. Thus, a new auditor for Price Waterhouse is not focused on company policy or long-term strategic career issues but rather on learning the fundamentals of doing a good job.

Colleague Stage. To make the transition into the next stage, the employee needs to demonstrate his or her ability to function as a colleague. That is, in order to make the first big hurdle in their careers (e.g., partnership for lawyers and accountants, tenure for faculty members), employees need to demonstrate that they can operate effectively independently and can consistently perform at high levels without close supervision. Thus, a young lawyer who is excellent at preparing briefs but has not yet demonstrated the ability to litigate on his or her own is unlikely to make partner—even though the employee's performance in terms of legal research has been fine.

Mentor Stage. In the third stage, employees are expected to take on responsibilities for guiding and counseling others. As employees participate in the workforce over a longer period of time, their own technical expertise in some areas may be less than that of the new hires. For example, the skill and ease with which new college graduates deal with complex computer issues is often greater than that of their middle-aged colleagues. The comparative advantages that senior colleagues have, then, are judgment, experience, and political savvy. If employees with 20 years' experience do not remain as technically sharp as new hires, their value to organizations—in the absence of increased mentoring—is substantially lower.

Sponsor Stage. Employees in the later stages of their careers have more potential career paths to follow. In the Dalton model, the last stage is the sponsor stage, in which employees focus on shaping the direction of the firm as a whole (rather than on their own egoistic needs). The transition into this stage requires comfort with exercising (and delegating) power, a greater knowledge of the "big picture" of the firm and its environment, and excellent social skills to act as a spokesperson for the organization.

MODULE
24

TABLE 24.2   *Life Stages*

Late Adolescence/Young Adulthood

Establishment

Midlife

Late Adulthood

However, for many senior employees, there are other options as well: early retirement, transition into part-time employment, transition into self-employment, or consulting.

In all of these career stage transitions, note that successful movement depends not only on mastery of tasks at the present career stage, but also on individuals' competence in handling the work demands and psychological pressures of jobs at the next career stage.

Life Stages

Just as individuals' work interests and abilities change over their careers, so, too, do their wants and needs. Analogous to the concept of career stages, *life stages* refer to different periods of people's lives in which they experience similar important psychological issues: breaking away from their parents, starting a family, dealing with middle age, and coping with declining health (Levinson et al. 1978). Most life stage models include the four stages that appear in Table 24.2.

Late Adolescence/Young Adulthood.   Life stages, like career stages, entail important transitions over time. In late adolescence and young adulthood, individuals seek to develop self-identities separate from their parents and balance their desire for total independence with their continued need for emotional support from older adults.

Establishment.   In the establishment stage, individuals are focused on starting their own families and establishing their own careers.

Midlife.   In middle age, individuals reassess their lives and often make some major changes while they are young enough and vital enough to adapt to new circumstances.

Late Adulthood.   Finally, in late adulthood, individuals try to deal with feelings of loss (loss of spouse, loss of parents) while developing a sense of "generativity" (feeling like their lives have been worthwhile).

What we know from the study of life stages is that changes in people's personal—and professional—lives influence how they evaluate various job options, when they decide to make major changes in their career paths, and how successfully they handle important career transitions. But not everyone follows the same pattern of life and career stages. For example, a person who leaves the workforce to raise a family and plans to return later may be establishing his or her career in mid-life rather than in his or her twenties and thirties. Nonetheless, life stages provide an important piece of information in understanding career choices and changes.

The Formation of Stable Career Interests

Research on the formation of stable career interests suggests that this process takes place over a 20 year period (roughly, from ages 10 to 30). In the first part of this process, people focus more on what their *likes and interests* are. In the second part, they focus more on their special *skills and abilities* and which career paths are most *realistic* for them to pursue (Feldman 1988; Super 1957).

Vocational Choice.   As early as ages five and six, children are frequently asked what they would like to be when they grow up. Invariably, the responses they give are occupations like teacher, doctor, and police officer. This is because, before age ten, children have a hard time differentiating between the concepts of "adult" and "career." Thus, teachers, doctors, and police officers are all representatives of occupations with which they come into frequent contact and/or that they view as having considerable authority.

As children reach young adulthood, though, their curiosity about careers becomes greater. In early adolescence, young adults experiment with a variety of school classes and extracurricular interests to discover some activities that intrigue or fascinate them. Then, by a process of "stimulus generalization," they start thinking about careers that would be most similar to their interests. For example, teenagers who like math start thinking about engineering as a career, while teenagers who like reading may start thinking about becoming English professors. In other words, young adults try to generalize from the stimuli they currently find enjoyable to career paths that will entail the same activities.

The most widely known model of young adults' vocational choices is that of Holland (1973), who suggests that there are six basic personality types and that they systematically gravitate to different clusters of occupations. Table 24.3 shows this model.

As teenagers enter college and later adolescence, these initial vocational choices get modified by more mature and thoughtful decision making. Two factors in particular appear to stimulate more realistic thinking about future career paths.

First, as young adults mature, they get more accurate information about what various jobs and careers truly entail. For example, young college students who want to go into human resource management "because they really like people" learn that the field also requires considerable analytic ability and study of the law, which may or may not be of interest to them.

TABLE 24.3   *Holland's Model of Vocational Choice*

Personality Types	Occupational Environment
1. Realistic	
Enjoys using tools and machines; enjoys using physical strength	Farming, forestry, architecture, carpentry
2. Investigative	
Enjoys observing and understanding data; dislikes social activities	Biology, mathematics, engineering, geology
3. Social	
Enjoys interpersonal activities; enjoys training and informing others	Psychology, social work, clergy, education
4. Conventional	
Enjoys working in structured situations; likes order	Accounting, finance, military, clerical work
5. Enterprising	
Enjoys verbal activities and influencing others	Management, law, sales, labor relations
6. Artistic	
Enjoys creative self-expression; dislikes repetitive activities	Art, music, drama, interior design

Second, as young adults mature, they become more aware of the practical constraints the pursuit of various career paths present. For instance, while a person may truly love teaching kindergarten as an occupation, he or she may discover that the job market for preschool teachers is very tight or that the salary is lower than expected or needed. Consequently, the vocational interests people develop as young adults do remain fairly consistent over time, but the careers they pursue to meet their vocational interests get modified across the various life stages.

Career Anchors. After young adults graduate high school, vocational training, or college and work for several years, another process of career path stabilization takes place—the development of a *career anchor*. By this term, Schein (1990) means a stable career concept composed of three components: (1) self-perceived talents and abilities; (2) self-perceived motives and needs; and (3) self-perceived attitudes and values.

Schein argues persuasively that young adults, until they enter the "establishment" stage of their careers and test themselves in a variety of organizational settings, cannot truly develop a stable career self-concept. Only by seeing how they perform and react in real world situations can young adults truly recognize those activities in which they are genuinely talented (as opposed to merely competent) and those job situations in which they are genuinely comfortable (as opposed to those in which they imagine they will feel comfortable). For example, while many young MBA students start out their careers in management consulting, many drop out when they realize that the travel they fantasized would be so fascinating is physically exhausting and disruptive of relationships with friends and family.

Schein's model, shown in Table 24.4, suggests that after several years in the workforce, young adults develop more stable patterns of career interests and abilities. These

TABLE 24.4 *Schein's Typology of Career Anchors*

1. **Technical/Functional Competence:** Primarily excited by the content of the work itself; generally disdains and fears general management jobs as too political; gravitates to staff and technical specialist positions.

2. **Managerial Competence:** Primarily excited by the opportunity to analyze and solve problems under conditions of incomplete information and uncertainty; gravitates to general management positions in large corporations.

3. **Security and Stability:** Primarily motivated by job security and long-term attachment to one organization; tends to dislike travel and relocation; gravitates to jobs with high job security such as civil service jobs and jobs in local utilities and universities.

4. **Entrepreneurial Creativity:** Primarily motivated by the need to build or create their own projects; easily bored; more interested in starting projects than in managing them; gravitates to start-up firms, management consulting, and other entrepreneurial ventures.

5. **Autonomy and Independence:** Primarily motivated to seek work situations that are maximally free of organizational constraints; likes to set own schedule and own pace of work; gravitates to jobs in academe and self-employment.

6. **Service and Dedication to a Cause:** Primarily motivated to improve the world in some fashion; wants to align work activities with personal values about helping society; gravitates to jobs in the public sector, the healthcare sector, and human services.

7. **Pure Challenge:** Primarily motivated to overcome major obstacles, solve highly difficult problems, or win out over extremely tough opponents; very single-minded and intolerant of those without comparable aspirations; gravitates to such career paths as military pilot, professional sports, etc.

8. **Lifestyle:** Primarily motivated to balance career with lifestyle; highly concerned with such issues as paternity/maternity leave and daycare options; gravitates to occupations like teaching, nursing, and sales that can be part-time or temporary in nature.

career anchors determine the types of career paths individuals will subsequently pursue, those in which they will demonstrate the greatest professional competence, and those from which they will derive the greatest satisfaction. For example, people who are primarily excited by the opportunity to analyze and solve problems under conditions of uncertainty are more likely to gravitate to, succeed in, and enjoy general management career paths. In contrast, individuals with high needs for autonomy and independence are more likely to gravitate to, succeed in, and enjoy positions that allow them maximum freedom from organizational constraints. These people are more likely to spurn management jobs in larger companies and instead start their own businesses.

Schein's model also highlights two other key points about the stability of career paths over time. First, these anchors illustrate the variety of ways people can pursue their careers *within the same occupation*. Thus, a person whose vocational interests are in marketing could pursue a career path as a market research analyst, a vice president of marketing, a public relations officer for a hospital, an advertising consultant, a marketing professor, or in part-time sales. This suggests the desirability of individuals and organizations to be flexible in how they approach career planning and career planning systems.

Second, the term "career anchor" does not mean that individuals never change careers, jobs, or organizations. Instead, it suggests that, over time, the job choices individuals make become more constrained as they realize what trade-offs they are willing—or unwilling—to make in their careers. Career anchors, like ship anchors, can be uprooted, but only with considerable force and foresight. Thus, stability as well as flexibility is an important consideration in effective career planning and management.

MAJOR CAREER TRANSITIONS

There are three career transitions that are of particular interest to employees, managers, and organizations alike. The first of these is *organizational entry and socialization*—the process by which newcomers enter firms and learn the norms, values, and work requirements of their organizations. The second of these is *transfers and promotions*—movement from job to job or location to location within a firm. The third of these is *job loss*—movement out of the firm, usually as a result of corporate restructuring or downsizing. Below, we consider each of these transitions in turn.

Organizational Entry and Socialization

Entry Shock.   While entering into a new organization is a stressful time for most new employees, the process can be especially disorienting for new hires making the transition from school to work. This transition is often called "entry shock" because young new hires are frequently very surprised by the ways in which the world of work is different from the world of school. Four contrasts in particular are salient to young adults making this transition.

- *Supervisors.* While in school, students have four or five different teachers at any one time. Those supervisors change every four months or so, and students frequently have some choices about who their teachers will be. In contrast, in the work world, employees have only one manager at a time, they may have the same manager for years, and they cannot afford to ignore or anger that manager so readily.

- *Feedback.* While in school, students usually receive brief, quantitative performance evaluations (grades) on a regular basis (often every few weeks). However, when students enter organizations, they often discover that they don't get feedback for months at a time and that the feedback they do receive is fairly vague (e.g., "There are no major problems").

- *Time Horizons.* While in school, students work on fairly short time cycles; most classes are only one or two hours long and most courses only last 12 to 14 weeks. In contrast, time horizons in the work world tend to be much longer. Newcomers may spend one or two years on their first assignments, and their routines may not vary much from day to day or week to week.

- *Nature of the Work.* Because classes and exam periods are usually quite short, students get used to working on tightly defined problems that can be solved rather quickly with some specific theory or mathematical technique. However, in the work world, new employees are often faced with the more difficult task of trying to define and articulate problems to be solved. Perhaps even more frustrating, once newcomers have articulated the problems that exist, the logistical and political difficulties of solving those problems are much harder than "theory" suggests.

Stages of Socialization.   Even for employees who have been out working and are entering new firms, the organizational entry process can be a difficult transition. The content of what newcomers have to learn about their new jobs and new organizations is quite varied; it includes work skills, supervisor preferences, team norms, and company rules and procedures.

The research suggests that organizational socialization takes place in stages over a period of several months. In the first stage, the *"getting in" stage* (beginning with recruiting and ending upon actual entry into the firm), newcomers get their first exposure to organizational policies, procedures, and expectations. In the *"breaking in" stage* (usually lasting two or three months), newcomers start learning the idiosyncrasies of how this particular firm wants work performed, the norms of the new work team, and the preferences of the new supervisor. In the *"settling in" stage* (usually completed by the end of six months), newcomers get over their initial anxieties and come to feel genuinely comfortable with their surroundings and job performance (Van Maanen and Schein 1979).

Managing Organizational Socialization.   All successful career transitions require both effective coping on the part of employees themselves and constructive career development activities on the part of the employer. In Table 24.5, we highlight some of the individual activities and organizational activities that create conditions for successful entry and organizational socialization.

MODULE
24

TABLE 24.5 *Managing Organizational Socialization*

Individual Strategies

- Do intensive research on the organization and the job itself before accepting the position to make sure that one's skills, abilities, and values are at least fairly consistent with the expectations of potential employers.

- Work longer hours, at least in the first few weeks, to get up to speed quickly and leave a positive first impression.

- Take the initiative in getting to know the new boss and coworkers so that one can more quickly and accurately learn the norms and values of the workgroup.

- Demonstrate excellent performance right from the start. Unlike school settings (where a slow start in a semester might be acceptable or easily excused), in the work setting excellent performance right from the start increases the chances that new recruits will obtain good mentors or better future job assignments.

continued

TABLE 24.5 *continued*

Organizational Strategies

- Give potential employees realistic job previews so that candidates who are not a good fit for the company can remove themselves from further consideration.

- Provide relevant training so that new hires can learn their jobs more quickly and effectively.

- Provide timely and reliable feedback so that newcomers can make desired changes in the ways they perform their work and interact with others in the workplace.

- Design a relaxed orientation program that provides newcomers with important information without deluging them with irrelevant data. In addition, these orientation programs should promote, rather than deflate, new hires' enthusiasm and self-confidence.

Transfers, Promotions, and Relocation

A transfer is a job change that takes an employee into another job at the same level of the organizational hierarchy, such as moving from assistant store manager at Store A to assistant store manager at Store B. A *promotion* is a job change that moves the employee up the organizational hierarchy and often brings more responsibility in the work itself (e.g., moving from assistant store manager to store manager). A *relocation* refers to a job change that requires a geographical move to another geographical region, such as moving from New York to Miami. When that relocation occurs to another country, it is referred to as *expatriation;* when the employee returns to his or her home country, that relocation is referred to as *repatriation*. All of these transitions within firms bring some opportunities and challenges to employees and their employers.

Benefits of Job Changes.   From the employee's point of view, job changes are often highly desirable.

- They offer opportunities for employees to develop new competencies and to gain more experience in managing or mentoring others.

- These transitions (particularly promotions and expatriation) also typically bring substantial salary increases, which make them very attractive to employees as they start families and their financial needs grow proportionately. Employers, too, benefit from the use of transfers, promotions, and relocation.

- Job changes help organizations inculcate a companywide perspective in employees so they do not become too complacent or too "local" in their viewpoint.

- When employees leave the firm for other jobs, retirement, or health reasons, the use of these job changes also helps organizations solve short-run staffing problems.

- If an organization is growing, promotions serve as incentives for employees to perform well and remain within the firm as well.

Problems Associated with Job Changes.   There are also common problems encountered by employees and employers alike, particularly when job changes entail international assignments.

- When employees change jobs, they usually are expected to perform well right from the start; unlike new hires, job changers rarely get much new training or orientation. As a result, employees who are being promoted may face many new job challenges with little additional preparation (Brett, Feldman, and Weingart 1990). Along the same lines, employees who are going overseas on expatriate assignments often require extensive language training and orientation to the foreign culture, yet many firms still do not provide adequate assistance to their expatriates in this regard (Feldman and Thompson 1993).

- Geographically relocating can also be stressful for employees and their families. In terms of moving within one's own country, research suggests that the disruption caused by geographical relocation may not be as traumatic as the media often portrays it (Brett 1982). On the positive side, employees who move geographically do not appear to have higher divorce rates or more marital discord than couples who do not move. In addition, younger children who move do not appear to exhibit negative side effects from relocation. To the extent that domestic relocation causes problems, it appears they occur with late adolescent children, who miss their friendship networks and have a hard time getting socially integrated into a new high school in their last two years.

- Moving internationally, in general, can be significantly more unsettling. Spouses often have difficulties getting comparable jobs when their husbands or wives go on expatriate assignments; because they themselves may not have received any language training, spouses may experience more social isolation overseas as well. Since the "trailing spouses" often handle the logistics of moving and settling in, they bear the greatest brunt of the disruption caused by the relocation. Both expatriates and their spouses often report missing friends and families back home.

- In addition, for the expatriate, working overseas might not be as positive for one's career as might be expected. Being an expatriate can mean being "out of sight, out of mind." That is, by being overseas, expatriates may miss out on developments back home that might hinder their future movement up the corporate ladder. Many expatriates are also concerned about whether they will receive repatriate assignments that use the skills and knowledge they gained while overseas (Black, Mendenhall, and Oddou 1991).

Managing Transfers, Promotions, and Relocations. Just as in the case of organizational socialization, there are strategies that both employees themselves and organizations can employ to facilitate smooth transitions. From the individual's perspective, it is important for employees to communicate clearly to their supervisors the kinds of job changes they would like and the time frame during which it would be best for them to move. More forthright discussions about career paths will increase the chances that employees will get job changes they desire and get them at times that are convenient for them and their families.

From the organization's point of view, it is particularly critical to provide job changers with additional training and orientation. While this training and orientation need not be as intensive as that provided to new hires, job changers still have to learn the particular procedures, norms, and customs of their new work units. Especially in the case of expatriation and repatriation, additional assistance is needed in terms of language training, orientation to the new culture, assistance with the logistics of overseas relocation, and assistance with currency exchange rates and different tax laws. In both domestic and overseas relocation, giving more advance notice of the job change helps employees adjust to their news jobs and new environments more easily (Black, Mendenhall, and Oddou 1991; Feldman and Thompson 1993).

Downsizings and Layoffs

The decline in traditional manufacturing industries in the United States (such as steel), the increased number of mergers and acquisitions, cyclical downturns in the economy, and the focus on lean operations (doing more with less) all contribute to organizations "downsizing" by laying off workers. While some employees do lose their jobs "for cause" (that is, for poor performance or for breaking major organizational rules), the vast majority of workers in this country who lose their jobs do so through layoffs that occur in the context of downsizing or corporate restructuring.

There have been three major shifts in the character of layoffs over the last 25 years. First, while blue-collar workers used to be the major target of layoffs, today white-collar workers and managers are just as likely to be laid off. Second, while layoffs used to occur mainly when firms were losing money, today layoffs often occur in profitable firms to increase the amount of profit rather than to minimize actual losses. Third, while layoffs used to have the connotation of being "temporary" in nature (that is, people would be "recalled" when business improved), for most white-collar workers today these layoffs are permanent in nature.

Losing a job is one of the most stressful events that can occur in a person's life. Psychologically, people who have lost their jobs typically experience periods of depression, anxiety, and nervousness. Physiologically, often experience sleeplessness; smoke, drink, and eat more; and have more psychosomatic illnesses (e.g., headaches and stomach aches).

The financial effects of layoffs can also be brutal. Many employees who lose their jobs deplete most of their savings, and between 5 and 10 percent experience financial problems so severe that they have to file for bankruptcy or lose their houses (Leana and Feldman 1992).

The effects of job loss often spill over to the families and friends of the laid-off worker. Because employees who lose their jobs have less discretionary income to spend on leisure activities, they are more likely to withdraw from their friends out of (mis-placed) embarrassment. Spouses of laid-off workers often have to reenter the workforce or work longer hours to help make ends meet. Children often sense tension in the family, resent having their own standard of living curtailed, and blame the laid-off parent for their new problems.

For organizations, too, downsizing does not come without costs. In addition to the expenses associated with severance pay, unemployment compensation, and other termination benefits to the employees being laid off, so-called survivors of downsizing can also harbor resentment and uncertainty about their futures. These cuts in services and benefits affect morale and can also affect productivity (Brockner 1988). In addition, there are social costs for the organization, as the networks of relationships among employees are disrupted or disturbed by the loss of personnel. Unstable collegial relationships can impose costs on the organization in terms of reputation, efficiency, and morale (Leana 1996).

Losing a job can never be a pleasant experience for employees. There is also no way an organization can lay off workers without any employee resentment. Nonetheless, there are some strategies employees can use to quicken their transition back into the workforce and some strategies organizations can use to facilitate those transitions as well, as shown in Table 24.6.

Strategic Issues in Managing Careers

This section highlights some of the most important strategic issues in managing careers in organizations today, beginning with the strategic issues facing individuals as they manage their own careers, and then considering the strategic issues facing corporations as they try to develop their employees' careers.

Individual Strategies for Managing Careers

Skills and Interests. Beginning with choosing a vocation and lasting throughout their careers, individuals have to consider both what activities they excel in and what their personal needs and interests are. When career choices are based only on what people like rather than what they are especially talented in, individuals usually end up plateaued and unable to advance very far in their chosen career paths. When career choices are based

TABLE 24.6 *Coping with Job Loss*

Strategies for Employees

- Take a week or two to get reoriented before starting to hunt for a new job; being over-wrought or highly agitated may hurt individuals trying to land new positions.
- Consider updating skills and training. Particularly if there are widespread layoffs in an industry, employees might want to consider updating their skills or retraining so they can obtain jobs in companies or industries that are growing more quickly.
- Consider geographical relocation to a region where the economy in general or the labor market for an individual's skills is better.
- Seek out social support from friends and family members in the wake of job loss. This is a difficult period, and social support helps people keep their spirits up during the stressful hunt for a new job.

Strategies for Companies

- Calculate the full costs of a downsizing before making decisions to implement it. Generally, companies tend to overestimate the savings from downsizing and underestimate costs.
- Give advance notification of the layoffs, so that employees can get a head start on job hunting and start decreasing their levels of spending.
- Provide severance pay and extended benefits so that employees will have some protection against uninsured medical emergencies and some financial cushion in the short run.
- Provide outplacement assistance to laid-off workers. Outplacement programs provide employees with help in rewriting resumes, refreshing interviewing skills, and/or direct help in lining up job interviews with other firms.
- Treat laid-off workers with dignity and respect. Degrading laid-off workers while they are being terminated or maligning them as they leave increases the stress for both the laid-off workers themselves and those who "survive" the layoffs.

only on what people are good at rather than what they enjoy, individuals usually end up in jobs that they find boring and unfulfilling. For people to have successful careers, then, they need to identify jobs that play to both their skills and interests.

Work and Family Integration. Although many people strive "to keep work at work and home at home," the reality of most people's careers and personal lives makes this separation untenable. In any personal relationship that is even moderately intimate, partners will share some of their work and career anxieties. In addition, personal decisions about starting a family, childcare, eldercare, and juggling two careers end up influencing each partner's own career path. While there are many successful models for integrating work and family demands, open discussion of these issues and conscious decisions between partners have to occur before a reasonable balance can be achieved.

Growth vs. Stability Orientation. As tempting as it is for individuals to arrive at some point in their careers and say to themselves, "I'm satisfied with what I've got," the reality is that most people cannot stay in the same job, the same organization, or even in the same city for 20 to 30 years. Trying to defend one's current position against rapid changes in technology, labor markets, and even the shape of organizations themselves makes the search for long-term stability ultimately unsuccessful. No matter what the career stage, then, employees need to broaden their business knowledge, develop new skills, and experiment with challenging new assignments—in short, to continuously seek out opportunities for professional growth.

Independent vs. Sequential Career Decisions. In analyzing potential career decisions, individuals need to understand that earlier career decisions greatly constrain options available for later career decisions. Career decisions are not independent events;

they are sequential and interdependent in nature. Thus, when making important career decisions, individuals cannot just consider the immediate or short-run consequences of their actions. They have to consider, too, the doors their present decisions might open— or close—to future career moves.

Organizational Strategies for Developing Employees' Careers

Career Information and Career Pathing Systems.   In order to effectively develop employees' careers, many organizations are disseminating more complete and accurate information about career opportunities in their firms. The advent of computer technology has now allowed corporations to post job openings and job requirements and accept employee applications electronically. In addition, increasing numbers of organizations are using management development committees to systematically review employees' career progress and to establish realistic five-year career goals and career plans with them.

Skills Assessment and Continuous Training.   A key ingredient of effectively managing careers is continuous improvement of employee skills. Thus, organizations seeking to facilitate employees' career development need to periodically assess their skills and design remedial and developmental training programs for them. Some organizations are pursuing these ends through increased use of assessment centers, others through increased use of in-house and outsourced educational programs. In both cases, however, the goals are still the same: identify those weaknesses of employees that prevent them from advancing, remedy those problems, identify those skills employees will need for their next assignments, and train for the acquisition of those new skills accordingly.

Career Development for Historically Disadvantaged Groups.   As the workforce becomes more diverse in terms of gender, race, and nationality, organizations may need to provide additional career development programs for historically disadvantaged groups. For instance, organizations seeking to increase their commitment to diversity are putting extra effort into the recruitment of these employees, providing additional feedback, training, and counseling to them, and establishing special mentor programs. If a critical ingredient of effective socialization is learning the norms and values of new organizations, then it may be useful to provide new employees less familiar with those norms and values some extra assistance.

Career Counseling for Individual Employees and Career Development Workshops for Managers.   When organizations first begin their career development programs, they often focus their efforts on career counseling for individual employees. That is, human resource specialists are utilized to provide one-on-one counseling to employees about their career interests, career goals, and impediments to career advancement. However, as these programs grow in scope, sole reliance on individual counseling can become prohibitively expensive. As organizations become more experienced in career development programs, then, they often turn to greater use of group-level career development workshops and written materials to provide guidance to employees. Also, although individual counseling by HR specialists is still available in most firms, more and more corporations are running career development workshops to teach managers how to provide such guidance, too (particularly in conjunction with performance appraisals).

IN CONCLUSION

Debrief

For many years, the traditional approach to managing careers in organizations was that of a selection-dominated "fit model." Organizations used recruitment and selection methods to find the potential employees who best fit their profile of job demands and job requirements. At the same time, individuals tried to find organizations that best fit their needs through extensive research, interviewing, and networking. Once this fit was achieved at the time of selection, it was typically assumed that fit could be maintained with relatively minor adjustments on both sides for a long period of time.

Over the past two decades, both employees and organizations alike have come to realize that "fit," no matter how worthy a goal, can rarely be achieved without major changes on both parties' sides. Individuals are cycling through more organizations, more job changes, and more career changes than ever before. Faced with the simultaneous challenges of downsizing and globalization, organizations are juggling the size, composition, and deployment of their workforces more than ever before. This chapter provides a framework for better understanding the dynamics of major career transitions and a set of strategies for both individual employees and corporations to use in managing those transitions more effectively.

Suggested Readings

Black, J. S., Mendenhall, M. E., and Oddou, G. 1991. "Toward a comprehensive model of international adjustment: An integration of multiple theoretical perspectives." *Academy of Management Review, 16:* 291–317.

Branch, S. 1999. "The 100 best companies to work for in America." *Fortune,* pp. 118–122, 126, 128, 130, 134, 136, 140, 142, and 144.

Brett, J .M. 1982. "Job transfer and well-being." *Journal of Applied Psychology, 56:* 450–463.

Brett, J .M., Feldman, D. C., and Weingart, L. R. 1990. "Feedback-seeking and adjustment: An empirical comparison of new hires and job changers." *Journal of Management, 16:* 737–749.

Brockner, J. "The effects of work lay-offs on survivors: Research, theory, and practice." In L. L. Cummings and B. M. Staw (eds.), *Research in Organizational Behavior,* (Vol. 10, pp. 213–255). Greenwich, CT: JAI Press.

Dalton, G. W., Thompson, P. H., and Price, R. L. 1977. "The four stages of professional careers: A new look at performance by professionals." *Organizational Dynamics, 6:* 19–42.

Feldman, D. C. 1988. *Managing careers in organizations.* Glenview, IL: Scott Foresman.

Feldman, D. C., and Thompson, H. B. 1993. "Expatriation, repatriation, and domestic geographical relocation: An empirical investigation of adjustment to new job assignments." *Journal of International Business Studies, 24:* 507–529.

Holland, J. L. 1973. *Making vocational choices: A theory of careers.* Englewood Cliffs, NJ: Prentice Hall.

Leana, C. R. 1996. "Why downsizing won't work." *Chicago Tribune Magazine,* pp. 14–16, 18.

Leana, C. R., and Feldman, D. C. 1992. *Coping with job loss: How individuals, organizations, and communities respond to layoffs.* New York: Macmillan/Lexington Books.

Levinson, D. J., with Darrow, C. N., Klein, E. B., Levinson, M. H., and McKee, B. 1978. *The seasons of a man's life.* New York: Knopf.

Schein, E. H. 1990. *Career anchors: Discovering your real values.* San Diego: Pfeiffer & Company.

Super, D. E. 1957. *The psychology of careers.* New York: Harper and Row.

Van Maanen, J., and Schein, E. H. 1979. "Toward a theory of organizational socialization." In L. L. Cummings and B. M. Staw (eds.), *Research in Organizational Behavior* (Vol. 1, pp. 209–264). Greenwich, CT: JAI Press.

MODULE
24

Relevant Web Sites

For general information about many different aspects of careers, there are several helpful web sites, including *www.careeremag.com, www.cweb.com,* and *www.careers.com.* For information on specific sites for job hunting, the cover story in the November 15–21, 1998, issue of the *National Business Employment Weekly* lists and describes dozens of sites for both general employment and for specific job categories.

Critical Thinking Questions

1. What are the forces that are changing the ways organizations are managing employees' careers today?

2. What are the major career stages individuals pass through over the 40 years they spend in the workforce? What are the major life stages individuals pass through during that time period?

3. What are the major differences between young adults and middle-aged individuals in terms of the challenges they face in their careers? their personal lives?

4. In what ways is the formation of a "career anchor" different from an individual's initial vocational choice?

5. Why do students just entering the workforce experience "entry shock"?

6. What are some strategies new hires can use to get more effectively socialized into organizations? What can organizations do to facilitate organizational entry?

7. What are the problems that employees moving geographically typically face? Why are the problems associated with expatriation more difficult?

8. What can individuals who have lost their jobs do to secure satisfactory reemployment? How can organizations minimize the disruption caused by layoffs?

9. What are the key strategic issues that individuals face in managing their careers? What are the key strategic issues that organizations face in developing the careers of their employees?

Exercises

1. On a sheet of paper, list on the left those activities in which you genuinely excel, and on the right those activities you genuinely enjoy. What jobs or career paths would be best suited for your skills and interests?

2. Look back over the set of career anchors. Which career anchor best describes you? Within your general vocational area, which career paths are most consistent with your career anchor? most inconsistent with your career anchor?

3. Using your work from exercises 1 and 2, think about the *next* job you would like to have. What skills will you need in that job that you do not currently possess? What steps are you taking to develop those skills? Map out a plan to help you in the next step of your career development.

Index

Apprentice stage (career), 24.6

Benefits of job changes, 24.12
Breaking in stage (socialization), 24.11

Career anchors, 24.9–10
Career changes, 24.7, 24.12
Career choice. *See* Vocational choice
Career counseling, 24.16
Career development. *See* Career management
Career management, 24.4–5, 24.10, 24.16–17
    individual strategies, 24.14–16
    organizational strategies, 24.16
Career pathing systems. *See* Career counseling
Career stages, 24.5–6
Career transitions, 24.10–11, 24.17
Colleague stage (career), 24.6
Continuous training, 24.16
Coping with job loss, 24.15

Downsizing, 24.5, 24.13–14, 24.15

Employer expectations, 24.11
Entry shock, 24.10
Establishment stage (career), 24.9. *See also*
    Apprentice stage
Expatriation, 24.12, 24.13

Financial effects of layoffs, 24.14
Four career stage model (Dalton, Thompson,
    and Price), 24.6

Generativity, 24.7
Getting in stage (socialization), 24.11

Holland's model of vocational choice, 24.8–9
Human resources roles, 24.4
Human resources specialists, 24.16

Independent career decisions, 24.9, 24.15
Individual strategies (socialization), 24.11
International assignments (problems),
    24.12–13

Job change, 24.12–13. *See also* Coping with
    job loss

Layoffs, 24.5, 24.13–14
Life stage model, 24.7
Likes and interests focus (career), 24.7

Managing careers. *See* Career management
Mentor stage (career), 24.6
Morale, loss of personnel, 24.14

Organizational career management systems,
    24.16
Organizational entry, 24.10–11
Organizational socialization, 24.10–12
Organizational strategies (socialization), 24.11

Performance, 24.11
Person-job fit, 24.16
Person-organization fit, 24.16–17
Personality types and occupational
    environment, 24.8
Promotion, 24.12–13

Relocation, 24.5, 24.12–13
Repatriation, 24.12, 24.13

Schein's typology of career anchors, 24.9–10
Self-perceived components (career), 24.9
Sequential career decisions, 24.15
Settling in stage (socialization), 24.11
Skills and abilities focus (career), 24.7,
    24.14–15
Skills assessment, 24.16
Socialization. *See* Organizational socialization
Sponsor stage (career), 24.6–7
Stable career interests, 24.7, 24.9
Stress of losing a job, 24.14
Survivors (downsizing), 24.14

Talent vs. comfort (career), 24.9
Technical expertise, 24.6, 24.9
Transaction role, 24.4
Transfer, 24.5, 24.12. *See* Job change
Transformation role, 24.4
Transition role, 24.4
Translation role, 24.4

Vocational choice, 24.8–9, 24.10. *See also*
    Holland's model of vocational choice

Work/family balance, 24.15
Workgroup values, 24.11

GROWING HUMAN RESOURCE CHALLENGES FOR THE MILLENNIUM AND BEYOND

Managing Human Resources
IN THE 21st CENTURY

From Core Concepts to Strategic Choice

MODULE 25

Globally Managing
Human Resources

Jennifer Palthe
MICHIGAN STATE UNIVERSITY

Managing Human Resources in the 21st Century: From Core Concepts to Strategic Choice,
by Kossek and Block

Publisher: Dave Shaut
Executive Editor: John Szilagyi
Developmental Editor: Bryant Editorial Development
Marketing Manager: Joseph A. Sabatino
Production Editor: Tamborah E. Moore
Manufacturing Coordinator: Dana Began Schwartz
Cover Design: Tin Box Studio
Cover Photographs: Copyright Shoji Sato/Photonica
Production House: The Left Coast Group, Inc.
Printer: West Group

Printed in the United States of America
1 2 3 4 5 02 01 00 99

For more information contact South-Western College Publishing, 5101 Madison Road, Cincinnati, Ohio, 45227 or find us on the Internet at *http://www.swcollege.com*
For permission to use material from this text or product, contact us by
- telephone: 1-800-730-2214
- fax: 1-800-730-2215
- web: *http://www.thomsonrights.com*

ISBN: 0–324–01826–6

This book is printed on acid-free paper.

Contents

MODULE OVERVIEW 25.4

OBJECTIVES 25.4

RELATION TO THE FRAME 25.4

CORE CONCEPTS IN GLOBALLY MANAGING HUMAN RESOURCES 25.5

Global Megatrends Impacting HR Management 25.5

The Difference Between Global and Domestic HR 25.6

Global Corporate Evolution 25.8

Implications of Globalization for the HR Function 25.9

Competencies Necessary for Success as a Global Manager 25.13

STRATEGIC ISSUES IN GLOBALLY MANAGING HUMAN RESOURCES 25.13

Global Strategic Options: Creating Synergy Amongst Diverse Cultures 25.14

Global Strategic HR Orientations: Managing Integration and Differentiation 25.15

APPLICATION 25.15

IN CONCLUSION 25.16

Debrief 25.16

Suggested Readings 25.16

Relevant Web Sites 25.17

Critical Thinking Questions 25.18

Exercises 25.18

Optional Exercises 25.18

APPENDIX 25.19

Case Study Exercises 25.27

Notes 25.28

References 25.28

INDEX 25.29

MODULE OVERVIEW

At the dawn of a new millennium, a growing number of organizations are faced with the challenge of managing and integrating their human resources globally, while remaining locally responsive to the specific cultural requirements of the different societies in which they operate. In today's world, the global boundaries among organizations, markets, and people are becoming increasingly and irrevocably obscure. No longer is the concept of globalization a futuristic one. At the same time, we are witnessing a renewed interest in human resources (HR) as a major strategic tool that can uphold the competitive position of the global corporation (Pucik 1992). This module examines the implications of the globalization age on HR management. It explores the global trends influencing HR, the nature of global enterprises, and the challenges of managing a cross-culturally diverse workforce.

OBJECTIVES

Some of the key learning objectives of this module are:

- To gain an appreciation for the key differences between domestic and global HR

- To create an awareness of the global megatrends impacting HR management

- To understand the global corporate evolution and the difference between international, multinational, and global corporations

- To understand the implications of globalization for areas of HR management

- To discuss why global HR is important

- To appreciate the competencies necessary for success in global operations

- To understand the strategic issues relevant to globally managing HR

Essentially, the module seeks to provide you with an appreciation for the immense challenges that staffing, training, appraising, compensating, and developing human resources on a global scale present.

RELATION TO THE FRAME

In the global corporation where the organizational environment changes across nations, the characteristics of HR roles and decision choices naturally change as well. The typical *transactions* that occur domestically take on a new global dimension involving geographic separation and greater cultural diversity than the traditional domestic HR function. Foreign labor markets, different hiring laws, and different pay structures make the transaction process more complex. Similarly, the cross-cultural *translation* role takes on greater complexities with communication efforts and media changing in the face of diverse languages, communication styles, technological resources, and literacy and education levels. Moreover, in a global setting, *transition* roles become paramount to the success of helping employees of global operations cope with moving and living abroad, returning from overseas assignments, handling meetings in foreign places, coping with culture shock, understanding foreign legal systems and work practices, appreciating cultural differences, and managing personal change and expectations on global assignments. The *transformation* activities may entail shifting HR practices to make them more locally compatible, and moving toward an organizational culture that values cross-cultural diversity rather than merely acknowledging cultural differences. Other transformations may involve fostering organizational learning and knowledge sharing on a transnational scale. See Figure 25.1.

FIGURE 25.1 *A Frame for Understanding Human Resource Strategy: Context, Roles, and Constraints*

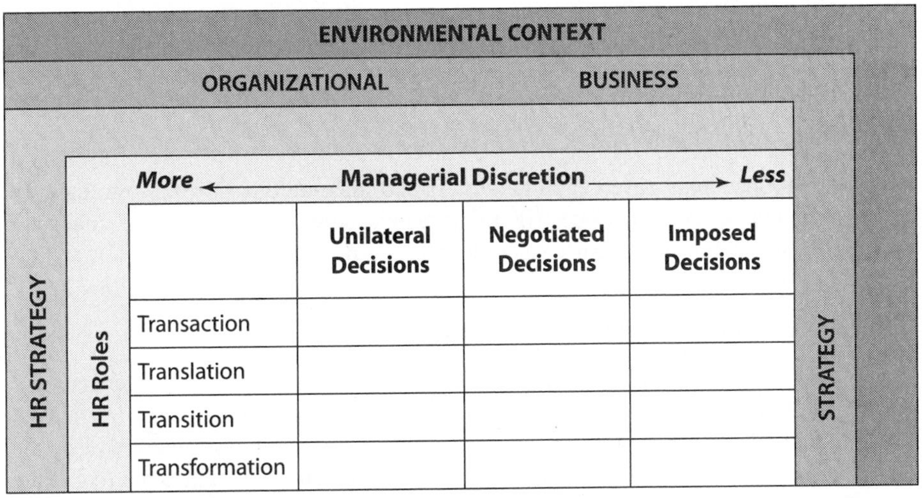

ENVIRONMENTAL CONTEXT			
ORGANIZATIONAL		BUSINESS	

	More ← Managerial Discretion → Less		
	Unilateral Decisions	**Negotiated Decisions**	**Imposed Decisions**
Transaction			
Translation			
Transition			
Transformation			

(HR STRATEGY — HR Roles on left side; STRATEGY on right side)

© 2000 by Ellen Kossek and Richard Block. Thanks to Brian Pentland, Karen Markel, and John Beck for helpful comments and discussions that enhanced the model.

CORE CONCEPTS IN GLOBALLY MANAGING HUMAN RESOURCES

The increasing pace of change and global competition have forced the world's multinationals and global corporations to redevelop their worldwide HR strategies. Understanding the implications of these changes for HR management is essential to the successful utilization of people for securing competitive advantage in these global firms. Some of the core concepts relevant to globally managing HR include:

- Global megatrends impacting HR management

- The difference between global and domestic HR

- Global corporate evolution

- Implications of globalization for the HR function

- Competencies necessary for success as a global manager

Each of these concepts will be discussed in the sections that follow. Specific examples of HR practices associated with leading multinational and global corporations will also be presented.

Global Megatrends Impacting HR Management

As we approach the end of the final decade in the twentieth century, we are experiencing globalization at a level of unprecedented intensity. Marquardt and Engel (1993), in *Global Human Resource Development*, highlight 14 global megatrends that will shape societies around the world in the new millennium. Those that relate most intimately with HR management include:

- Globalization

- Global technology

- Changing global workforce

- Quality and service

- Learning organizations

- Emerging roles of women

- Work and family life

- Workplace ethics

- Values and religion

Many global operations have begun to address and integrate these trends into their HR policies, practices, and processes. HR management contributions to these trends will be vital to the success of global corporations in the next millennium.

The Difference Between Global and Domestic HR

Domestic HR management involves those functions undertaken by an organization to effectively utilize its human resources. Managing human resources globally involves the procurement, allocation, and utilization of human resources across at least two nations (international), among many nations (multinational), or on a regional scale (e.g. European Community, Pacific Rim, North America) (Marquardt and Engel 1993). Global HR management includes the distinct systems and processes that are directed at attracting, selecting, appraising, rewarding, developing, and retaining HR at an international, multinational, or global level. Cascio and Bailey (1995) argue that the major difference between the two is the increased involvement by the organization in the personal lives of employees. The field of global HR encompasses primarily the same areas as domestic HR management with several key distinctions. These include:

- Global players

- Cross-cultural diversity

- Geographic dispersion

- Environment

Global Players.   One of the main distinguishing features between domestic and global HR management is the complexity of the mix of organizational members or players, ranging from global managers to global administrators. Research has tended to categorize these global players into the following groups:

- Parent country nationals/expatriates (PCNs)

- Host/local country nationals (HCNs)

- Third-country nationals (TCNs)

Parent Country Nationals/Expatriates

PCNs are employees who are citizens of the country in which the headquarters of the organization they work for is located—for example, an American citizen working for an overseas subsidiary of an organization headquartered in the United States.

PCNs are usually managers, technicians, subsidiary heads, and experts who travel from the home office to assist overseas subsidiaries (Mendenhall, Punnett, and Ricks 1995). Some of the advantages of utilizing PCNs to staff subsidiaries abroad stem from the fact that they are experts in how the parent corporation operates. Furthermore, when PCNs spend time abroad, they learn how foreign markets operate, and how clients and customers in these markets respond to services or products offered by the corporation. PCNs also gain skills in cross-cultural diversity management. When strategically placed, PCNs can play a significant interpretive role between the subsidiary and headquarters. PCNs, however, are expensive. Corporations are responsible for the additional costs

MODULE
25

such as cost-of-living allowances, relocation, and family benefit packages. Also, PCNs may cost the corporation in terms of lost contracts, and poor relations with customers and suppliers, particularly when they are sent to countries that have significantly different cultural values, business systems, and societal norms than the parent country.

Host/Local Country Nationals

HCNs are employees of an organization who work in an overseas subsidiary and are natives of the country in which the subsidiary is located. For example, a Dutch manager working in a subsidiary of a U.S. company located in the Netherlands.

The advantage of employing HCNs is that they are familiar with the local norms and practices, speak the local language, and are not as expensive as PCNs. IBM, for example, hires HCNs with the belief that they not only have a better appreciation for the local environment, including the tax, social security, and other legal requirements, but also are more likely to develop closer relations with local employees and customers (Humes 1993). The disadvantage of employing HCNs, however, is that they may not be aware of headquarters' needs, and may take an entirely local rather than global view of how the subsidiary should operate (Mendenhall, Punnett, and Ricks 1995).

Third-Country Nationals

TCNs are employees of an organization who work outside the country where the parent company is headquartered and outside the country of their birth. For example, a Belgian manager who works for a Canadian multinational's subsidiary in France.

Some of the TCNs in Europe have been referred to as "Euro-managers," as they view the European continent as their domain, not just their home country. These TCNs tend to assimilate into the local culture when they are assigned abroad, treating the posting as their residence (Klep 1993).

The major advantage in employing TCNs is that they cost less than PCNs and are often fluent in foreign languages and have substantial international experience. TCNs, while attractive, are in high demand and short supply. Furthermore, local legislative policies may limit the number of TCNs who can be employed. Coordinating a team of domestic players is challenging enough but the task of managing players on a global scale carries with it more complex implications and greater challenges.

MODULE
25

Cultural Diversity.   As global HR management involves activities in at least two nations, cross-cultural diversity is a given. Culture is defined as a way of life of a group of people (Adler, Doktor, and Redding 1986), the collective programming of the mind that is both learned and inherited (Hofstede 1980), and a system of shared meanings placed upon events (Smith and Peterson 1994). Multinational and global corporations derive many of their values from the national culture in which they are headquartered. U.S. cultural values, for example, have profoundly affected General Motors, General Electric (GE), and IBM. Similarly, Japanese culture has affected Mitsubishi, Matsushita, Hitachi, and Nissan's organizational values and policies. Global HR management strategies and practices need to acknowledge these cultural influences. Cultural differences in multinationals may involve intracultural diversity (cultural differences within a particular nation), intercultural diversity (involving interactions between two or more national cultures), cross-cultural diversity (crossing cultures and nations), and/or multicultural diversity (involving many cultures) (Marquardt and Engel 1993). The challenge of reconciling home and host country values is a real one, and culture remains a vital component of global HR management. Moreover, if HR is to take on strategic significance in the global operation, culture should never be ignored.

Geographic Dispersion.   Despite the advancement of global telecommunications technology, sheer distance between the locations of various affiliates or international divisions of global operations creates communication challenges. Distance also creates difficulties due to the increased need for long-distance transportation, relocations, housing, and support services. Moreover, communication is more expensive and of potentially lesser quality across long distances. Time differences across the globe may also make communication difficult and limited. Distance may also have the effect of delaying decision response times and the receipt of information and resources.

Environment. The external environment plays a significant role in determining both the nature of the global HR manager's responsibilities and how they are executed. The political environment in which global firms operate may range from totalitarian to democratic, militaristic to civilian controlled. The economy may be booming or in recession. Labor market characteristics may vary in the extent and quality of education and worker skill levels. There may be an oversupply of unskilled labor, a shortage of skilled labor, or even high unemployment. All these environmental issues influence the strategic HR choices and practices within operations around the globe. Government systems may vary in the degree to which they regulate or prescribe how HR management is executed. The society may be primarily rural or urban, familiar with outsiders or insular, victims of high crime rates or not. Climatic conditions may also enhance or inhibit regular performance at work. Hence, the role of the environment in influencing HR management policies and practices abroad should not be underestimated.

Global Corporate Evolution

Table 25.1, adapted from Adler (1991) and Marquardt and Engel (1993), exemplifies four phases of development from a domestic to a global corporation. Understanding the phases of evolution toward becoming a global corporation provides us with a useful framework for appreciating the implications for HR practices across these types of organizations.

The Difference Between International, Multinational, and Global Corporations.
International corporations are structured to transfer and adapt the parent company's competencies and knowledge to foreign markets. Examples include General Electric and Procter & Gamble. Multinational corporations, on the other hand, operate in multiple international markets. Essentially, multinationals create a federation of national entities stemming from a single parent where the external organizations have some degree of independence and autonomy. Examples include Unilever and Philips (Ashkenas, Ulrich, Jick, and Kerr 1995). Global corporations contain elements of both centralized coordination and decentralized responsiveness where the world market is treated as an integrated whole. Such corporations have both a global strategic perspective and a capability for local differentiation. Examples include BP-Amoco, IBM, Royal Dutch/Shell, and Andersen Consulting. In contrast to domestic and multinational corporations, the truly global corporation is one that has created an organizational culture that values diversity (Hordes, Clancy, and Baddaley 1995). In the global corporation, the world is viewed as essentially one seamless market, and human resources are integrated in a way that assumes there are no "foreign" locations or employees. At this stage of development, the ability to manage cross-cultural interaction, multinational teams, and global partnerships becomes essential to overall business success. Moreover, global HR management, considered "helpful" under the international and multinational stages, now becomes essential for organizational survival and success at the global stage of development (Adler 1997).

Table 25.1 highlights the various phases organizations go through in the process of becoming a global corporation. Historically, most corporations begin as domestic. During this phase, foreign markets are largely irrelevant, with the main orientation being some product or service. As competition increases and corporations expand

TABLE 25.1   *Stages of Development Toward a Global Corporation*

Corporate Activities	PHASE I **Domestic**	PHASE II **International**	PHASE III **Multinational**	PHASE IV **Global**
Strategy	Domestic	Multidomestic	Multinational	Global
Predominant Structure	Centralized hierarchy	Decentralized hierarchy	Centralized hierarchy	Global alliances and networks
Main Orientation	Product or service	Market	Price	Strategy
Competitors	None or some	Few	Many	Significant
Production Location	Domestic	Domestic and primary markets	Multinational, least cost	Global, least cost
Exports	None	Growing	Large	Imports and exports
Cultural Perspective	Parochial	Culturally relative	Headquarters ethnocentric	Culturally synergistic
Cultural Sensitivity	Unimportant	Very important	Somewhat important	Critically important

Source: Adapted from Adler (1991) and Marquardt and Engel (1993)

internationally, they enter the international phase. At this stage, exports are growing and many firms form a separate international division. Each country is managed separately, using a multidomestic approach. Parochialism, evident in the domestic phase, is replaced by cultural relativity. A decentralized hierarchical structure exists at this stage and the foreign operations are often seen as an extension of the domestic operations (Adler 1992). At the multinational phase, competition continues to increase, and corporations continue to emphasize least-cost approaches. There is still a hierarchical relationship between headquarters and the foreign subsidiaries. However, headquarters' decisions are now made by people from a broader range of cultures than in previous phases. While this multinational representation increases at headquarters, ethnocentrism and cultural dominance of the headquarters' national culture continues (Adler 1992). At the global phase, competition increases and the predominant structure becomes less hierarchical and is characterized by more global networks and strategic alliances. As a consequence, power is no longer centered in a single headquarters, dominated by any one national culture. At this stage, international and cross-cultural skills become critical for all managers throughout the corporation. The overall cultural perspective is also more synergistic, involving a combination of many cultures into a unique organizational culture, rather than merely integrating foreigners into the dominant culture of the headquarters' nationality, as in the previous phases.

Implications of Globalization for the HR Function

Globalization has the twofold effect of reconciling the HR function with the strategic core of the organization, while changing the scope and content of HR management (Pucik 1992). The following sections provide an account of some of the main implications of globalization for HR management systems and practices. Examples of HR practices utilized by leading multinationals and global corporations are also discussed.

Global Selection and Staffing. A trend that has accompanied the globalization of corporations has naturally been the increase in the selection and staffing of global players—global managers, technicians, and professionals. This trend is exemplified through the growing amount of "foreign" staffing practices. More than 4.6 million American workers are employed by foreign companies in the United States. Further, U.S. corporations employ over 60 million foreign workers (Marquardt and Engel 1993). Foreigners hold senior management positions in at least a third of large U.S. firms and a quarter of European-based firms (Cascio and Bailey 1995).

Effective staffing for international assignments demands not only the identification of potential global players who possess the necessary leadership capabilities and know-how but the capacity to develop that potential and use it to the organization's maximum advantage. The skills of most HCNs are generally inadequate in the initial phases of a firm's development toward a global corporation. As a consequence, PCNs and TCNs are selected to staff key positions in international operations. With the challenges of operating in a culturally dissimilar national environment, with people who speak another language, it is not surprising then that between 20 and 50 percent of expatriates terminate their assignments prematurely (Arvey, Bhagat, and Salas 1991). The costs of these early terminations are estimated at around $1 million per expatriate (Shaffer and Harrison 1998). Reasons for these failures have been attributed primarily to poor predeparture and postarrival training and orientation. Noteworthy, however, is the fact that selection and staffing issues such as family adjustment, host country similarity with home country, and global assignee adaptability skills have a profound impact on expatriate success.

Consistent with a multinational corporate strategy, many U.S. multinationals delegate the responsibility for recruitment and staffing to their corporate divisions, which in turn delegate this responsibility to their affiliates. Most U.S. multinationals have no or severely limited corporatewide methods for identifying international talent, or for facilitating career advancement through cross-national transfers or promotions (Humes 1993). As a consequence, the careers of most PCNs and HCNs tend to be division bound and territorially bound, contributing to the specificity of their way of thinking. There are U.S. corporations that have developed noteworthy exceptions to this trend, however. General Electric, for example, has initiated a "global brains effort" in which they identify and recruit potential international managers. They provide them with the necessary training and cross-border experiences to enhance the success of their careers abroad. IBM has increased its reliance on home continent nationals to staff its European offices. Procter & Gamble's international division also provides extensive opportunities for cross-national experiences (Humes 1993).

European multinationals have tended to manage their staffing on a country-by-country basis. Royal Dutch/Shell, for example, has continued to rely on operating companies, most of whose management has been recruited locally. Philips has moved from this multicountry to a multidivisional staffing approach. With the globalization of its product divisions, Philips has moved senior and middle-level employees from country to country, with or without the consent of the affiliate management (Humes 1993).

Asian multinationals have tended to adopt a corporatewide approach to staffing. Further, they have tended to recruit HCNs on a corporatewide basis. Assignments abroad are only made after HCNs have been formally recruited and trained. Mitsui and Company, for example, annually selects several particularly promising Japanese executives for assignments as "assistants to" the chairman, president, and executive vice presidents, to provide senior executives with an opportunity to assess their potential and to develop their corporatewide perspective. Each Samsung division regularly assigns its best Korean managers for a multiyear experience at corporate headquarters. Matsushita's 1991 initiative to bring 100 non-Japanese to Japan for a year is yet another example of this corporatewide approach to staffing (Humes 1993). At Toyota, staffing is split in two ways. The management of Japanese personnel is separated from the management of non-Japanese employees. In staffing its overseas operations, Toyota has tended to rely more on locals for HR and accounting functions, and on Japanese for production and quality control operations. At Matsushita, the staffing policies and practices reflect the corporation's basic motto: "Matsushita makes the man before the product." This philosophy, in turn, affects its recruitment, promotion, training, and development activities. Like most other Japanese global corporations, Matsushita hires its professional employees directly from leading universities for career-long employment.

Global Organizational Design.

Leading-edge global enterprises have one key organizational design feature in common: their design is flat and simple (Pucik 1992). As organizations move through the phases of evolution toward becoming a global corporation, network-like configurations begin to replace tall hierarchical designs, and partnerships and teaming activities replace rigid, top-down hierarchical designs. A critical role, therefore, of the HR function in firms becoming increasingly global is to provide support in managing these collaborative networks. GE, for example, has simplified its corporate structure and reduced the bureaucratic layers from as many as 29 to as few as 4 in an attempt to be more globally competitive (Humes 1993). Furthermore, GE's efforts to create a boundaryless organization have involved the facilitation of interdivisional global transfers and the promotion of corporatewide shared values. GE has also initiated a "work-out" program to bring together employees from cross-sections of the business and from around the globe to share their ideas and join efforts on tasks. Teamwork and partnering are key components of this international networking initiative. At IBM, as teamwork is so central to their organizational design, the corporation has introduced a course entitled "Cluster Management," which deals with group dynamics (Humes 1993). Philips, 3M, and Exxon are also good examples of global corporations that have designed their organizations around teams. Although the specific team dynamics vary depending on the reporting relations, the high levels of work-related interdependencies prevail.

Global Training and Development.

Probably one of the most significant responsibilities of the HR function in a global operation is the establishment of an ongoing training and development program for managing global assignments. The traditional perspective has been to simply develop the skills of global assignees by providing them with training on topics such as cross-cultural sensitivity, leadership styles, communication, problem solving, and conflict resolution skills. However, with organizations facing increasing global competition, firms also need to develop organization-level global competencies such as organizational learning, and continuous improvement capabilities. As Porter (1990) argues, the basis of competition has shifted more and more to the creation and assimilation of knowledge. Well-coordinated on-the-job training and global career management are key ingredients of this assimilation process. Consequently, many multinationals and global corporations have expanded the scope and scale of their training and development efforts worldwide. Such efforts have included both external sessions by educational institutions and internally delivered training programs. Attention in these programs has been focused on the acquisition of specific professional competencies, cross-cultural interpersonal skills, and distinctive shared corporate norms and values.

Multinationals and global corporations vary not only in terms of the extent to which they emphasize training and development, but also in the extent to which training is offline (as contrasted with on-the-job) and how much it focuses on a divisional or corporatewide perspective. Olivetti, for example, tends to limit training to on-the-job efforts. IBM is a good example of a global corporation that is highly committed to educating its global workforce. General Motors, Fiat, and GE all feature extensive in-house training establishments to support their global education initiatives.

Asian corporations emphasize continuous training throughout employee careers. Such training usually begins with an extensive orientation program, and continues with periodic offline and on-the-job training. Asian multinationals' and global corporations' training programs are noteworthy for the amount of time trainees spend in training. As examples, Matsushita, Mitsubishi, and Nissan offer new employee orientation and development programs lasting three to eight months. These programs are designed to socialize newcomers in the distinctive philosophy, history, and organizational culture of the corporation. In addition to extensive newcomer orientation and training, Samsung follows up every year with a "spiritual renewal" session for in-career assignments. The Asian multinationals have historically, however, tended to exclude nonheadquartered nationals from their training efforts (Humes 1993).

Worldwide, those corporations that have developed and supported corporatewide education institutions have emphasized the importance of developing global communication and leadership skills. GE, Fiat, and IBM, for example, have relied on corporate institutions to provide the training efforts necessary throughout their respective global corporate domains.

Global Compensation and Benefits. It is widely recognized that effective global compensation and benefit systems take into account the diversity in employees' appreciation of different reward alternatives (Pucik 1992). Global corporations therefore have a responsibility to examine their compensation and benefits strategy and underlying philosophy in the world context. Tax equalization issues, stock-ownership benefits, retirement benefits, education allowances, hardship allowances, housing and utilities differentials, and cost-of-living adjustments are all serious issues that need to be incorporated into the design of a global compensation system. A well-integrated global compensation policy will avoid the mistake of merely transporting domestic-based systems abroad without careful attention to and investigation of the diverse legal frameworks surrounding pay across the globe. Compensation systems also need to establish a fine balance between achieving external consistency with the national culture of the workforce, and maintaining internal consistency with the organizational culture's norms and standards.

Most American and European multinationals and global corporations tend to use a hierarchy of pay grades based on job analyses. Japanese HR practices, on the other hand, generally assign pay by rank, based on seniority. Mitsubishi and Nissan, for example, promote managers on length of service rather than on merit (Humes 1993).

Global Performance Management. The adage "what gets measured gets done" is certainly a reality when it comes to global performance appraisals. A commitment to organizational learning and continuous improvement will remain only a token expression unless supported by criteria and systems for measuring accomplishments (Pucik 1992). Performance evaluation methods vary in design, purpose, and application in nations around the world. In the United States and some Western European nations, performance management systems tend to be more objective, job related, and outcome oriented, and to possess distinctive purposes (e.g., promotion, pay, development). In contrast, other nations may offer more informal, subjective assessments of employees, making use of more general traits such as honesty and dependability (Arvey, Bhagat, and Salas 1991; Cascio and Bailey 1995).

Most multinationals and global corporations invest considerable amounts of time and effort evaluating the performance of their employees for cross-border assignments. Potential "high-flyers" are identified and placed on the "fast track"—in their early twenties in the United States and the United Kingdom, in their late twenties in Germany, and early thirties or later in Japan (Humes 1993). Certain multinationals and global corporations gather multiple performance evaluations, not only from the hierarchical "superior" but also from coworkers and direct subordinates. It is critical, however, that this process is coordinated on a corporate rather than just a divisional level in order to take advantage of corporatewide comparisons for cross-hierarchy and cross-national postings. British Airways and Cathy Pacific are examples of corporations using sophisticated performance management systems that serve as decision aids in identifying, developing, and promoting their top performers worldwide. Exxon has developed "compensation and executive development" committees at each level in the organization to assess their senior personnel (Humes 1993). Exxon's scoring system, like British Airways', is designed to facilitate cross-border comparisons and progress monitoring of top performers.

Competencies Necessary for Success as a Global Manager

Globally competent managers require a broader range of skills than traditional international managers. First, while international managers could focus on a single foreign country and on managing relationships between headquarters and that country, globally competent managers must understand the worldwide business environment from a global perspective (Adler 1992). Second, globally competent managers must be locally responsive and learn about many cultures' approaches, languages, tastes, and perspectives. Third, global managers need synergistic learning skills that allow them to work with *and* learn from people from many cultures simultaneously. Instead of simply integrating foreigners into the headquarters' national culture, competent global managers create a culturally synergistic organizational environment. Fourth, global managers need to adapt to living in many foreign cultures. They also need to acquire cross-cultural skills that they can utilize on a daily basis, throughout their career, not just during foreign assignments. They need to apply them in multicountry business trips and in daily interaction with foreign colleagues and clients (Adler 1992). Global managers also need extensive foreign experience for both career and organizational development. The development of globally competent managers depends on the corporation's stage of development toward a global corporation and its ability to design and manage global HR systems that are consistent with the overall business strategy (Adler 1992). Pucik (1992) argues that in order to truly capture the essentials of the HR contribution to the execution of global business strategies, global corporations need to focus on organizational competencies such as continuous improvement, organizational learning, and a competitive organizational culture. The centrality of the human element in these three competencies makes their integration into global HR systems paramount to the long-term success of global operations.

MODULE
25

STRATEGIC ISSUES IN GLOBALLY MANAGING HUMAN RESOURCES

Managing HR globally has a significant degree of strategic complexity. Global firms are constantly confronted with strategic choices that need to be made to optimize the quality and effectiveness of their diverse employees around the globe. To build and maintain a corporate identity, global firms need to attain a certain level of centralization and integration in the management of their personnel worldwide. However, in order to be effective locally, they need to adapt to meet the specific cultural requirements of the nations in which they are operating. So the need for internal consistency must constantly be balanced with the need for differentiation. As reflected in Table 25.1 on page 25.11, a firm's business strategy can be primarily domestic, international, multinational, or global. However, there is also strong consensus that for HR management to be effective on a global scale, it must be integrated with the overall global strategic planning process of the global operation. Some of the main strategic issues relevant to managing HR globally are expanded on in the sections that follow.

Global Strategic Options: Creating Synergy Amongst Diverse Cultures

Adler (1997) differentiates between five global strategic options that highly effective global managers use, depending on the particular multicultural situation they find themselves in. The options involve balancing "my culture's way" versus "their culture's way." Figure 25.2 highlights the five basic options.

Cultural Dominance. This option calls for a continuation of the way things are done in your own home culture. Relating it to HR practices, it would involve the application of the exact HR techniques and standards utilized in the *parent* company. At an organizational level, this approach is often used by corporations that have significantly more power than their counterparts. At an individual level, this approach is adopted by managers who believe that their way is the only right way of operating.

Cultural Accommodation. The accommodation option is the direct opposite of the cultural dominance option. It would involve, for example, choosing to imitate the HR practices of the *host* country. Learning the language of the nations in which one works is a form of cultural accommodation. This option is typically found in international corporations. Some refer to this approach as "going native" based on the premise that "When in Rome, do as the Romans do."

Cultural Compromise. This option is a combination of the dominance and accommodation approaches. The approach implies that both sides make concessions to work more effectively together. An example of cultural compromise would be for Australian and U.S. participants on global training to alternate training destinations each year so that participants from both nations spend the same amount of time overseas. This approach is common in multinational corporations.

Cultural Avoidance. This option entails acting as if their were no cultural differences. It would involve, for example, adopting HR practices without any consideration for cultural diversity. An example of a cultural avoidance strategy would be for someone to ignore body language differences, such as lack of eye contact, and to continue conversing as though the listener was paying attention without confronting them due to an "apparent" lack of attentiveness.

MODULE
25

FIGURE 25.2 *Global Strategic Options*

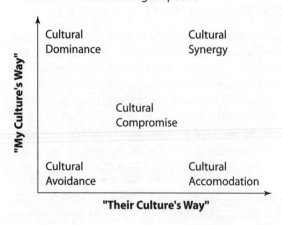

Source: Adler 1997

Cultural Synergy. This approach entails the development of new solutions to problems that respect each of the cultures involved. An example of this would be Swedish and French business partners speaking in English to one another (assuming this is the language they both have in common) to prevent either side from being disadvantaged. This option generates creative solutions through the use of cultural diversity. A synergistic approach would foster the development of new and innovative HR systems that combine the best HR practices of diverse nations.

Global Strategic HR Orientations: Managing Integration and Differentiation

Taylor, Beechler, and Napier (1996) distinguish between three generic strategic global HR orientations. The choice of strategic orientation determines the overall approach to managing the tensions between internal consistency via integration and external consistency via differentiation.

Adaptive Orientation. This approach arises through attempts by senior management to create HR systems for affiliates that reflect the local environment. The adaptive orientation therefore has high external consistency with the local environment and low internal consistency with the rest of the firm. Differentiation is embraced through HR practices such as hiring locals and utilizing local techniques. Hence, little, if any, diffusion of HR policies or practices from the parent firm to the affiliates abroad takes place under this approach. International corporations tend to adopt this approach.

Exportive Orientation. This philosophy involves the transfer or replication of the parent firm's HR systems, policies, and expected practices to the overseas affiliates. The exportive approach has high internal consistency but low external consistency. This orientation is consistent with an ethnocentric approach to HR management and is found predominantly in multinational corporations.

MODULE
25

Integrative Orientation. Global firms with this orientation tend to search for best practices and use them organizationwide, throughout the world. The ultimate aim of this approach is to be able to sustain a significant amount of global integration with some elements of differentiation at the local level. The integrative approach is consistent with the geocentric management orientation, combining high internal consistency with moderate external consistency.

Each of these orientations has implications for the nature of HR roles and responsibilities at the parent and affiliate sites. The exportive system retains control of HR systems at headquarters, while the adaptive orientation permits greater autonomy in HR decisions at the affiliate level. The integrative approach engenders greater partnering between the parent company and its affiliates, allowing for greater input in HR decision making at the local level while maintaining a substantial degree of global integration and centralized decision-making control at headquarters.

APPLICATION

Despite the recent merger between British Petroleum and Amoco, "The Case of Amoco Production Company" (Kossek 1996)—appended to this module on pages 25.21–25.29—remains a useful and relevant illustration of a corporation that has embraced the notion of globalization and made it a natural and integral part of its HR management strategy and practices. This case study will form the basis of our discussions around adapting HR systems to manage in the global arena. Noteworthy, however, is the recent resignation of former Amoco president William Lowrie, which highlights the ongoing challenges faced by the corporation. "His decision to quit as a board member and joint deputy chief executive of BP-Amoco highlights the strains that have emerged in the executive suite at the group's headquarters in London in the six weeks since the merger was completed" (*Financial Times*, February 13, 1999).

In Conclusion

Debrief

This module has illustrated the immense challenges associated with staffing, appraising, rewarding, developing, and retaining HR on a global scale. It has also highlighted some of the key ingredients necessary for HR to play a strategic role in coordinating global relationships and enhancing cross-cultural synergies. As the twentieth century comes to a close, HR management faces both new challenges and new opportunities in the global arena. Traditional sources of competitive advantage such as low cost and technology will no longer be sufficient to provide a sustainable edge in the global economy (Pucik 1992). Modern approaches suggest that HR will provide the key to success in the global marketplace. Limited human resources and *not* unreliable capital are the biggest constraint when companies globalize (Bartlett and Ghoshal 1992). Lack of HR expertise in foreign contexts will no longer be acceptable if corporations are to survive and excel in the global arena. Both individual and organizational global competencies will be essential ingredients for the sustained competitive advantage of global firms. As Taylor, Beechler, and Napier (1996) so aptly suggest, the key differentiator between corporate winners and losers in the twenty-first century will be the effectiveness of the human organization. HR management can either respond to this opportunity and embrace the challenges it presents, or it can continue to play the role of supporter to other strategic business areas at the expense of its organization's long-term global competitive edge.

Suggested Readings

Main Readings

Arvey, R. D., Bhagat, R. S., and Salas, E. "Cross-Cultural and Cross-National Issues in Personnel and Human Resource Management: Where Do We Go from Here?" in G. R. Ferris and K. M. Rowland, Editors. *Research in Personnel and Human Resource Management,* Volume 9, 1991.

Bartlett, C. and Ghoshal, S. "What Is a Global Manager?," *Harvard Business Review,* September-October, 1991.

Cascio, W., and Bailey, E. "International Human Resource Management: The State of Research and Practice," in O. Shenkar, Editor. *Global Perspectives on Human Resource Management.* Englewood Cliffs, NJ: Prentice Hall, 1995.

Kossek, E. E. "Adapting Human Resource Systems to Manage Global Diversity: The Case of Amoco Production Company," in E. E. Kossek and S. A. Lobel, Editors. *Managing Diversity: Human Resource Strategies for Transforming the Workplace: Field Guide.* Cambridge, MA: Blackwell, 1996.

Pucik, V. "Globalization and Human Resource Management," in V. Pucik, N. Tichy, and C. Barnett, Editors. *Globalizing Management: Creating and Leading the Competitive Organization.* New York: John Wiley & Sons, 1992.

Supplementary Readings

Adler, N. J. *International Dimensions of Organizational Behavior.* Cincinnati: South-Western College Publishing, 1997.

Adler, N. J., Doktor, R., and Redding, S. G. "From the Atlantic to the Pacific Century: Cross-Cultural Management Reviewed," *Journal of Management,* Vol. 12, 1986.

Adler, N. J, and Bartholomew, S. "Managing Globally Competent People," *Academy of Management Executive,* Vol. 6, 1992.

Ashkenas, R., Ulrich, D., Jick, T., and Kerr, S. *The Boundaryless Organization: Breaking the Chains of Organizational Structure.* San Francisco: Jossey-Bass Publishers, 1995.

Brandt, E. "Global HR," *Personnel Journal,* March 1991.

De Cieri, H., McGaughey, S. L., and Dowling, P. J. "A Conceptual Framework of Organizational Factors and Processes: An Application to International Human Resource Management," in P. C. Earley and M. Erez, Editors. *New Perspectives on International Industrial/Organizational Psychology.* San Francisco: The New Lexington Press, 1997.

Hofstede, G. *Culture's Consequences: International Differences in Work-Related Values.* Beverly Hills, CA: Sage, 1980.

Hordes, M. A., Clancy, J. A., and Baddaley, J. "A Primer for Global Start-ups," *Academy of Management Executive,* Vol. IX, 1995.

Humes, S. *Managing the Multinational: Confronting the Global-Local Dilemma.* Hertfordshire, U.K.: Prentice-Hall International, 1993.

Klep, B. H. "Looking for Euro-Managers in All the Right Places," *The Journal of European Business,* May-June, 1993.

Laurent, A. "The Cross-Cultural Puzzle of International Human Resource Management," *Human Resource Management,* Spring 1986.

Marquardt, M. L. and Engel, D. W. *Global Human Resource Development.* Englewood Cliffs, NJ: Prentice-Hall, 1993.

Mendenhall, M., Punnett, B. J., and Ricks, D. *Global Management.* Cambridge, MA: Blackwell Publishers, 1995.

Miller, E. L., Beechler, S., Bhatt, B., and Nath, R. "The Relationship Between the Global Strategic Planning Process and the Human Resource Management Function," in M. Mendenhall and G. Oddou, Editors. *Readings and Cases in International Human Resource Management.* Boston: PWS-Kent Publishing Company, 1991.

Roberts, K., Kossek, E. E., and Ozeki, C. "Managing the Global Workforce: Challenges and Strategies," *Academy of Management Executive,* Volume 12, 1998.

Shaffer, M. A. and Harrison, D. A. "Expatriates' Psychological Withdrawal From International Assignments: Work, Nonwork, and Family Influences," *Personnel Psychology,* 51, 1998.

Schneider, S. C. "National vs. Corporate Culture: Implications for Human Resource Management," in M. Mendenhall and G. Oddou, Editors. *Readings and Cases in International Human Resource Management.* Boston: PWS-Kent Publishing Company, 1991.

Smith, P. B. and Peterson, M. F. "Leadership as Event Management: A Cross-Cultural Survey Based on Managers from 25 Nations." Paper presented at the meeting of the International Congress of Psychology, 1994.

Taylor, S., Beecher, S., and Napier, N. "Toward an Integrative Model of Strategic International Human Resource Management," *Academy of Management Review,* Vol. 21, 1996.

Relevant Web Sites

GLOBAL HUMAN RESOURCE NETWORK
   http://www.mcb.co.uk/hr

BRITISH PETROLEUM AND AMOCO MERGER
http://www.bpamoco.com

INSTITUTE FOR INTERNATIONAL HUMAN RESOURCES
http://www.shrmglobal.org

BUREAU OF INTERNATIONAL LABOR AFFAIRS
http://www.dol.gov/dol/ilab

CIA WORLD FACTBOOK
http://www.odci.gov/cia/publications/nsolo/wfb-all.htm

THE INTERNATIONAL ASSOCIATION FOR HUMAN RESOURCE INFORMATION MANAGEMENT
http://www.ihrm.org

WORLD CULTURE FOR GLOBAL BUSINESS COMPETENCY
http://www.webofculture.com

Critical Thinking Questions

1. What are some of the major megatrends facing corporations in the globalization age? Which of these have the greatest implication for HR management and why?

2. What is the global corporation, and how does it differ from an international or multinational corporation? How do HR practices differ across these organizational types?

3. Why is global HR important, and what are some of the key challenges of managing HR globally?

4. What competencies are necessary for greater effectiveness of employees operating abroad?

5. What organizational competencies are necessary for leading-edge HR practices and why?

Exercises

1. If you were offered an expatriate assignment today to work for three years in an area of the world that is completely new to you, why would you want to go or why would you decline?

2. Visit three or more of the seven Internet sites listed above. List five key lessons that each site has for globally managing HR.

3. For international students or trainees with international work experience: Did you experience culture shock when studying or working abroad? If so, what did it feel like? What would you recommend to minimize the impact of culture shock on global HR managers?

Optional Exercises

1. Relate Adler's (1997) Global Strategic Options model to the Amoco case. Describe the process you would recommend for Amoco in order to develop a culturally synergistic global strategy.

2. What do you suspect are the main reasons for the present "strains in the executive suite" at BP-Amoco? Make specific recommendations to the new senior management team such that they can work together more effectively and prevent further resignations in the newly merged operation.

3. Reflect on your own personal work styles and values, and list what you view as your greatest skills and possible areas for improvement if you were hired as a global HR manager in a global corporation.

APPENDIX

Adapting Human Resource Systems to Manage Global Diversity: The Case of Amoco Production Company[1]

Ellen Ernst Kossek

Although globalization is a current business trend, few U.S. companies have fully made the transformation from a colonial-style American multinational company to a firm with an integrated network of interdependent global business units. Using Amoco Production Company's (APC) globalization efforts as an example, this case illustrates key issues that a U.S. firm is likely to encounter as it undergoes change processes to support global diversity.

What Is a Global Organization?

Continuous transformation of the global business environment have prompted companies to strive for efficiency, responsiveness, and learning throughout operations on a worldwide basis (Bartlett and Ghoshal 1987). In developing their vision of a global organization, Amoco management identified key trends leading to increasing international competition and the widespread globalization of industries: the growing similarity of countries' markets and distribution systems, the merging of national capital markets into global capital markets, falling tariff barriers, rapid technological restructuring of many industries, an increasing integrating role of technology in bringing countries together, and the rise of new global players (Porter 1986). Unlike multidomestic companies, global companies operate in such a way where competition in one country is strongly influenced by competition in other countries (Yates 1992). While the forces driving globalization may vary across industries, most firms establish strategy with a global perspective. Global firms view the world as one economy and strive to serve customers in all key markets with equal dedication (Ohmae 1989). They seek to maximize profits by getting products to where they make the most money for the firm on a worldwide basis (Yates 1992). Figure I shows a working definition (Ohmae 1989) of a global organization that Amoco management found helpful in operationalizing its vision.

Amoco management learned that developing a global approach necessitates organizational transformation in attitudes, organizational processes, and human resource systems. They found that often the most critical constraint of globalization is the limited human resources and the organizational capability available to process massive amounts of complex cross-cultural data (Bartlett and Ghoshal 1991). The chief causes of failure in multinational ventures often emanate from a lack of understanding of basic differences in managing human resources at all levels in foreign surroundings. The key to gaining competitive advantage in the global marketplace is to weave international personnel throughout the organization to leverage a global exchange of knowledge and capabilities (International Recruiting Report 1992). Transnational organizations blend resources and employees throughout the world to develop the strategic capabilities of global scale efficiency, national level flexibility, and the ability to apply learning across markets internationally (Bartlett and Ghoshal 1991).

FIGURE 1 *A Global Corporation*

Operates:	Worldwide and has a workforce representative of its markets
Manages:	Its assets and human resources as an integrated operation in a manner that assumes there are no foreign locations or employees
Competes:	Freely and equally in all parts of the world so that it appears country neutral
Views:	All operations as equidistant from headquarters

Amoco Production Corporation: Current International Situation

Historically, Amoco has had a largely domestic focus in its human resources approach. "International human resources" primarily meant the personnel policies of Amoco toward its U.S. expatriate population, that is, American citizens who work for Amoco abroad. Until several years ago, most of its oil reserves were in the United States, so Amoco management had grown up with the view that most of their growth would come from within U.S. borders. Today, however, nearly 80 percent of new investment dollars are being targeted toward foreign operations where energy reserves are likely to be much more plentiful than in the United States. A recent company document (Yates 1992) states the firm's vision for the future:

> Amoco will be a global business enterprise, recognized throughout the world as preeminent by employees, customers, competitors, investors, and the public . . .

Amoco Production Company (APC), an independent business unit (IBU) of Amoco, explores and produces oil, and has operations in more than 30 countries ranging from Norway to Congo. Despite the fact that APC currently employs some 3,500 employees abroad, few senior positions are held by foreign nationals. Amoco's ability to become a globally integrated worldwide organization is hindered by the fact that another IBU, Amoco Oil, the refining group, has divested most of its foreign operations. Unlike APC, Amoco Oil's management has established a strategy that Amoco Oil must be number one or two in market share in a particular country. Unfortunately, very few countries meet this criteria. Despite this limitation, opportunities for global integration of business opportunities, may exist through partnerships with another IBU, the Amoco Chemical Company, which also has a substantial overseas operations. The ability to develop organizational cooperation across separate business units in a country can be a source of competitive advantage in gaining access to new markets, because different businesses can cross-subsidize each other and be viewed as a total package by foreign governments. For example, Viet Nam recently allowed a non-U.S. firm to have access to its extremely profitable offshore oil acreage in return for bringing other less-profitable (and perhaps even money-losing) businesses into the country that the government desired.

Moving from the Middle East to New Global Markets

One of Amoco Production's largest and most successful current overseas partnerships was initiated in the late sixties in Egypt. Amoco Egyptian Oil Company and the Egyptian General Petroleum Corporation are in equal partnership in GUPCO, the Gulf of Suez Petroleum Corporation. With over 4,000 employees, GUPCO is the largest oil producer and Amoco is the largest foreign investor in Egypt. In a little more than 25 years, GUPCO has produced more than three billion barrels of Egyptian oil, which peaked production in the mid-eighties.

For many American corporations, developing an effective working relationship with the Egyptian government has been bureaucratic, time-consuming, and frustrating. For example, while it is very difficult to get a work permit for any U.S. employee, Amoco has found it especially trying to get work permits for female employees to work for GUPCO, because Egyptian custom does not allow women to hold professional and managerial jobs. With few exceptions, the government simply does not issue a work permit to U.S. females.

Experimentation with new work practices in Egypt is also difficult. Although Amoco is rolling out a variable pay bonus program (VIP: Variable Incentive Program) at most of its locations worldwide, it has not yet planned to do so in Egypt, because if you put a policy in practice, it's considered law and you cannot withdraw it. The practice is considered to exist forever. As one Amoco manager commented, "Having been able to successfully operate a joint venture in Egypt, we believe Amoco has a good chance of being successful almost anywhere!" Today GUPCO has 75 offshore platforms in the Gulf of Suez and more than 300 wells in the Gulf and the Western Desert. However, these fields are now maturing and oil finds in recent years have not kept pace with the rate of depletion. Therefore, a new focus has been placed on searching for new markets around the globe.

In April 1993, Amoco (U.K.) Exploration Company began developing gas reserves in the North Sea. This venture involves one of the longest pipelines in the United Kingdom and offers important growth opportunities as it occurs during the growth privitization of the U.K. energy market. Other European exploration work is being done in Norway, the Netherlands, Italy, Denmark, and Austria. Continuing oil production is occurring in Sharjah, one of the United Arab Emirates.

Opportunities are also being explored in Mexico and in Poland, the latter holding the possibility of being receptive to Amoco, since its headquarters is in Chicago, which has one of the largest Polish populations outside of Poland.

Major current sources of production in Latin America include the island nation of Trinidad, off northeastern Venezuela, which is Amoco's third largest current source of production. Argentina is another large production source, where for nearly thirty years, oil and gas have been contractually produced.

West Africa is another region of the globe where Amoco has many operations ranging from Gabon to Congo. Exploration in this geographic area is certain to grow, which raises unique challenges. In some West African countries 30–35 percent of the population are reputed to be HIV positive, carrying the virus that causes AIDS. To meet this medical challenge, Amoco has established its own blood bank in West Africa. In some locations, schools that would be appropriate for the children of expatriates only run up to the eighth grade, so Amoco runs several schools overseas. Recruiting Amoco employees for these locations may be difficult. As one manager commented, "You generally do not find oil in nice places."

Opportunities in Megamarkets: The Former Soviet Union and China

Since the mature areas of Amoco Production's worldwide operations offer limited opportunities for growth, new overseas ventures must be planned. If the Middle East can be viewed as having one hundred times the amount of oil that can be found in the U.S., then the former Soviet Union has over one hundred times the amount of oil that the Middle East has. Currently, Amoco is one of the major players in negotiations to begin oil exploration and production in CIS (the Commonwealth of Independent States, the former Soviet Union). Due to Amoco's excellent history of environmental safety, it is believed to have an edge in obtaining an agreement with countries that were formerly a part of the Soviet Union.

The China Project came to fruition in October 1992, after years of effort, when Amoco obtained a commission to conduct production in Mainland China. Dealing with the Chinese government requires a good deal of patience. Although it was very desirable to gain early access to start up oil production, Amoco was not willing to accept poor terms from the Chinese government. The Chinese generally have a longer view of time and a greater preference for developing trust and respect before starting negotiations. They also prefer to develop a personal relationship prior to making business deals. For example, although negotiating a contract might be given as the official reason given by the Chinese for a meeting, initial sessions often focus on family and other personal matters. Questions such as "How's your family? How are your boys or your wife?" will be asked. Not one word will be mentioned about the current contract negotiations, which may bewilder an inexperienced American. If the U.S. manager brings up the subject, the Chinese representative is likely to close down the discussion and be "turned off." The manager who helped negotiate the initial access for the China project operated according to these norms. As a result, Amoco earned respect, and was able to get in on the first round block of concession at more favorable economic terms than competitors.

Establishing human resource systems to support the China Project also posed some interesting problems. Under Chinese custom, individuals who are citizens of mainland China working for Amoco cannot be considered a formal Amoco employee. Rather, these individuals work for a Chinese labor unit, a Dan wei, that loans or secunds the workers to Amoco. When a worker is paid, Amoco pays the Chinese labor unit, not the employee. Such a relationship can make it difficult to use pay as a motivator to influence a worker's behavior. Employers must use means other than salary to reward and encourage productive behavior. For example, Amoco gave a pair of highly coveted tickets to a concert at the Great Wall by British rock star George Michael to an outstanding worker. Additional employment problems can be posed by the fact that whenever the Chinese labor unit decides it is appropriate, it can secund a worker to another company—Amoco has no control over the length of time a worker is considered its own.

Global Competitive Pressures

In 1991, Amoco Production's earnings were $595 million from U.S. operations and $214 from foreign operations. Both of these figures were down dramatically from 1990 earnings. As a Vice President of Planning and Economics explained in a company newsletter: "Financial results from the past five to ten years have not been acceptable. We can't just keep doing—or go back to doing—what we were doing all that time. The systems and processes that made Amoco Production a winner in past are not sufficient to maintain the company's competitive edge in the new business environment of the 1990s and beyond. Competing successfully will require close and constant attention to cost in all company operations worldwide." He noted some of the factors propelling Amoco Production toward change in global systems: 1) the company's financial performance and its vision of premiership, 2) the need for growth and globalization, 3) industry competition and consolidation, and 4) worldwide political and economic changes.

The main competitive pressures shaping human resource activities is that increasingly *Amoco's competitors are foreign companies* such as British Petroleum and Royal Dutch Shell and most investment dollars for new business will be spent overseas. Management must shift in focus from a domestic to a global view. This change has caught Amoco off guard, and currently the domestic operations are facing critical cost pressures and layoffs.

There will be significantly greater demand to *integrate local nationals* at all levels of an overseas subsidiary. Contributing to this view is the *excessive cost of expatriations,* that is, the high cost of moving U.S. employees abroad to run companies. Because of these financial pressures, Amoco must make greater use of the talent of local nationals. Yet just hiring a great number of local nationals for managerial positions will not necessarily help a company successfully globalize: the ability to balance the parent company's view with local needs is a critical consideration. There is still a nagging fear in the minds of some Amoco executives that U.S. multinationals must cautiously pick people who have allegiance to Amoco and not their local country's government. "Let's face it," as one manager explained, "our business is to exploit a country's resources." Because of this, there is a tendency to be lean and mean in terms of^2 placement of local nationals in key positions in developing countries. As a protective staffing strategy, even in developed countries, the vast majority of critical jobs are held by U.S. expatriates.

Even in Northern European countries, *cultural differences* remain that are barriers to developing a global workforce. Some U.S. Amoco managers contend that if a lot of high quality work needs to be done quickly in a short amount of time, U.S. expatriates rather than local nationals are needed to make sure it gets done. Also, work and family values are different in European countries compared to the U.S. workaholic corporate norm. It is not uncommon to see Norwegian male employ-ees leave at 3:30 in the afternoon to go pick up their children from school, a practice that is still rare for male employees in the U.S.

Developing worldwide human resource systems is hindered by the fact that current "leading edge" HRM practices were developed with an American view. For example, targeted selection, a practice where an interviewer asks questions that target the presence of key abilities found in successful current U.S. managers, may not work well for individuals from countries where the norm is to not brag excessively about one's strengths in an interview. Similarly, total quality management, which relies heavily on self-empowerment, may at least need some modification, particularly in cultures where individualism is less valued.

Despite these cultural and social differences, over time, the amount of U.S. expatriation must decrease and/or shift to a consultation role due to de facto *cost pressures.* Greater utilization of local nationals in running international operations might also better blend local laws and custom with Amoco practices. Yet typically, when planning new ventures, the human resource plan is usually the last one put in place.

Another pressure is the increasing need for *presence in a country* in order to eventually get government approval to begin energy exploration. In many cultures, a long term relationship must be developed and evidence of *staying power* must be proven in order to get business. The lack of presence may affect future bids in a country. As one employee commented, "We're very good at managing the technical aspects of the exploration business—for instance we have led the industry in seismic techniques related to secondary tertiary recovery, but we're not very good at managing new cultures effectively to obtain entry." In Amoco's defense, some managers argue that realistically Amoco might not know if it will be in a new country 6 months or 6 or more years. This uncertainty is dependent on whether a discovery is made, an endeavor that can fail 90 percent of the time. Some managers contend it makes more sense to use talent from the U.S. until a discovery is found. Yet a key to developing marketing strength in new markets is to open an office in a country even before a discovery is made. However, Amoco does not open an office in a new country until a discovery is made, which often gives more global competitors such as Royal Dutch Shell a competitive advantage. Given the fact that the entitlement and social programs in many countries are extremely more costly than in the U.S., a counter argument can be made that it *does* make sense for a U.S. oil company to move slowly when hiring foreign employees. It would be extremely expensive to close up a firm and pay off the former workers. As one Amoco worker commented, "China turned out well, but there are fourteen other countries where we didn't find anything and it was 'adios.'" Because of these conditions, contract employees are often used heavily in the early stages of the employment relationship.

Some managers believe it's not possible for a company of Amoco's size to open as many offices worldwide as larger competitors such as a Royal Dutch Shell or an Exxon. APC should put more emphasis on focusing their efforts and opening offices early in selected countries. Rather than using their technical strengths *after* a discovery is made to gain business, Amoco should do a better job of making the world aware of it strength in applying technology well and leverage this capability to get new contracts. Increasing pressures to hire locals are also being felt from *foreign governments*. Foreign governments now demand greater employment of local nationals. This can be a problem in countries such as Trinidad where lifetime employment is the norm. It is very difficult to be a low cost operator when the biggest part of the costs come early and then once the oil platforms are built and the growth is underway, you have headcount that is not flexible. As one manager commented, "If you want to fire someone in Trinidad, good luck!"

An additional pressure stems from *worldwide differences in ethics*. Amoco values will not permit it to engage in bribing or to violate U.S. laws when abroad, even if it is the custom and competitors are engaging in such practices. Ethics also are involved in regard to the extent to which a multinational chooses to use techniques that minimize damage to the environment, even if there are no foreign environmental protection laws. Firms that are environmentally cautious may face much higher costs than their competitors. Yet some managers believe that Amoco's ethics could be turned into a competitive advantage to get new business. There are many examples of how Amoco's environmental approaches are leading edge. In Pakistan, the government would not allow the import of beride, a chemical used in the drilling of wells. Amoco spent an extra quarter million dollars on wells to line pits and to put up a dust proof room for the lead, which can be hazardous to the environment, if mixed. In Burma, where operations were in a jungle, Amoco cut a very narrow path around the area for the oil well, and then reforested. In the U.S., where environmental regulations are considered to be the most strict in the world, Amoco generally strives not simply to meet but exceed environmental regulations. As one manager states, "If you spend more now, you'll save a lot later, because you'll be ahead of regulatory changes." Some believe that doing a better job marketing this record will enhance global opportunities.

Global Literacy in Managing Human Resources

In order to effectively develop and implement global strategies, it is necessary for key managers and professionals to possess global literacy in managing human resources. Otherwise, an ethnocentric bias towards Western HR practices and managers may obstruct the enactment of worldwide human resource systems. The Manager of International Human Resources at APC recently assembled a group of international managers. Their task was to identify key competencies they believe any member of Amoco's human resource and general management community should possess in order to be "globally literate." While these competencies are targeted toward U.S. staff, some focus group participants believed it would be useful to develop a similar list for foreign nationals to combat home country and anti-U.S. biases as well.

The first critical competency is to *understand the business pressures driving globalization*. In order to add value, HR must understand the business and go international. Given the increased complexity, risk, and the greater cost of conducting business globally, the need for HR to have business acumen in critical.

The second competency involves *developing human resource decision-making systems that balance values based on universality with business needs*. The HR function should emphasize managing global diversity by establishing practices to enable all employees, regardless of their nationality, to develop to their maximum potential. As one manager stated, "no individual should be advantaged or disadvantaged simply because they went to university outside of the U.S." Yet this universal approach must be driven by business considerations. These needs range from cost considerations, to focusing the organization on it competitive advantages, to gaining country market share if critical to long term success.

Other areas of key competencies relate to cultivating attitudes, language, and values that are congruent with a global approach. A first maxim is to *avoid transubstantive error in applying human resource systems globally.* The transubstantive error phenomenon (Wells 1985) occurs when one ascribes the assumptions and values of one's culture to another culture. Many U.S. personnel practices are based on individuality. For example, concepts such as "self development" and "leadership" do not work well in many Asian cultures. Asking Asian employees to state the areas they would like to focus on for self development in the future could be viewed by some as asking them to state areas where they have failed in the past. In contrast to the U.S. proclivity to seek to stand out as a leader, in Japan, there is the saying "The nail that sticks up gets struck down." An individual's sense of obligation is to one's group over oneself. Similarly, in some African countries such as the People's Republic of the Congo, employees can have difficulty responding to questions like, "Where do you want to be in five years?" Many of the individuals think in terms of a job instead of a career. Goal-setting for performance appraisals also may be more difficult in Muslim cultures where Allah is believed to control one's destiny. Thus, it is essential to cultivate an awareness and sensitivity that U.S.-developed human resource systems and management concepts have cultural biases and may not be effective in their U.S. form abroad. However, the development of "cultural distance" does not mean automatically assuming that human resource practices *won't* work abroad. Skill in understanding the cultural relativity of human resource practices involves being able to distinguish between a valid cultural constraint versus an attempt to avoid implementing a tough decision (Pucik 1992).

Some Amoco employees believe that a main barrier the company faces is due to the fact that most senior management lacks foreign experience. Recently at a major company conference, a senior HR executive stated that the number one HR issue facing Amoco was health care. Some employees working on international issues felt this comment showed a view that was dominated by a U.S. "36th floor" (where corporate HR staff are located) mentality. While health care is an important U.S. issue, the U.S. approach is not typical worldwide as many health care systems are nationalized. Many employees felt that globalization and diversity should have been mentioned ahead of health care as being critical issues. Thus, one competency relates to developing an awareness that key HR issues in the

U.S. may have lower priorities when viewed globally.

Developing parent-country neutral language when referring to employees is another competency for global literacy. Language is important since it often sends a symbolic message of the degree to which one's group or values are viewed as pre-eminent. At minimum, managers need to cultivate a mindset that considers how making distinction between employees of the U.S. parent company and foreign subsidiaries might be exclusionary. Toward this end, managers should foster a view that considers non-U.S. employees as part of the main mass of corporate talent when making staffing and development decisions. As one Amoco employee states: "We need to refer to all employees (including foreign nationals) as being part of Amoco, the global firm, without making the distinction that they are part of Amoco U.S. The term 'we' should mean Amoco worldwide, not just Amoco U.S. . . . Amoco USA is just another country." Reflecting this view is the practice of referring to all transfers as transfers, whether international or in the domestic U.S. Elimination of the use of the term "Third Country Nationals," which some employees who are not U.S. citizens use to jokingly refer to themselves, is another way to demonstrate that international talent is valued equally with domestic personnel.

Another capability required for global literacy is to *developing skills and awareness pertaining to cross-cultural communication.* Managers should avoid using U.S. analogies and acronyms in presentations. For many Americans, dropping such habits involves making a conscious attempt to overcome one's upbringing and/or current residential geography (e.g., Amoco's Midwestern orientation). While Amoco's Midwestern orientation is a strength in terms of the company having a relatively open and friendly corporate culture, the Midwestern persona does not always travel well abroad. As an employee commented, "The Midwesterner is the epitome of the Ugly American, just behind the New Yorker." Another basic issue when communicating across cultures is to speak slower when conversing in English with non-English native speakers. Messages that are delivered slower are more likely to be understood. Less burden in placed on the non-native English speaker in the communication exchange.

Basic literacy in global HR globally entails an *understanding of the differing tax consequences for compensation around the world.* To develop this insight, it is useful to investigate the tax law differences between the U.S. and other countries. In general, the U.S. has lower taxes in comparison to other countries. One must understand why it is usually less expensive to pay employees in foreign countries with non-cash forms of remuneration over direct wages. Although cars, a maid, children's education, time off, and clothing might be viewed as U.S. luxuries, these perquisites are generally less expensive than offering similar pay in wages abroad. A main objective in the design of reward systems in foreign countries might be to substitute as many indirect forms of pay for cash as possible. Managers also need to have insight into how currency fluctuations and differences in inflation rates affect employees' pay around the globe. Like the case of taxes, the U.S. inflation rate is generally lower than a number of foreign countries, which has a large psychological impact on the value of wage increases.

Another basic competency related to global literacy is *developing an awareness that managing international human resources involves much greater contact with governments and with employees than in the U.S.* Governments should not be viewed as a barrier to overcome when implementing international strategies but as a possible opportunity (Porter 1986). Governments are often competing to attract the best global competitors to their countries. As a result it is critical to recognize the interdependence of relations with governments from various countries. It is also likely that employers will have greater involvement in employees' lives. Employers may be involved in decisions ranging from determining where employees live to coordinating medical care to even running a company school.

None of these competencies will be easy to foster within the confines of the domestic U.S. unless one is personally committed to *self-development for a geopolitical education.* One way to become aware of major trends around the world is to listen to National Public Radio, which often has international news, and to read respected foreign news publications such as the *Economist.* In many multinationals, there is the opportunity to work with foreign employees working in the U.S., rather than only socializing with Americans. Individuals seeking to becoming more international should cultivate these friendships. Self-development can be fostered by researching any HR issue with an international view. Possible topics include: trying to recruit and staff a position by not using any U.S.-based sources,

setting up a hypothetical new plant in a foreign country, researching labor law comparisons around the glove, or developing a compensation package for a local national in a non-U.S. country.

Developing skills in a foreign language with some fluency, and striving to learn about the history and cultures of areas where the company has significant foreign operations, is also important. Such an understanding builds credibility and shows interest, self discipline, and the ability to learn the "code" and values of another culture. Although not a career option for all employees in this era of downsizing and dual career families, certainly volunteering for an international assignment or a domestic U.S. assignment with international dealings is an important vehicle.

Most importantly, managers need to *strive to value and understand international diversity.* This involves developing a mindset that respects what diverse individuals bring to the table in any business situation. A critical first step is to have a comprehension of basic similarities and differences in cross-national values. It is useful to analyze any major U.S. current event by using multiple frames of reference. Employees might be asked to assess how Anita Hill's famous testimony on her alleged sexual harassment would have been viewed at the recent confirmation hearing for Supreme Court Justice Clarence Thomas had there been Europeans or Japanese on the Congressional panel. The outcome and questions asked might have been vastly different.

Environmental Scan of Leading Edge Organizational Practices

In order to develop flexible strategies for global markets, it is important to develop three organizational competencies—a core value of organizational learning, a focus on continuous improvement, and a competitive corporate culture that views global competition as an opportunity (Pucik 1992)—and to scan the global environment for leading edge human resource practices.

Organizational design must be simple and flat to speed the clarity of communication and to focus energy on learning and action over monitoring and control (Pucik 1992). As noted in the earlier discussion of Amoco's global business pressures, a first key to successful globalization is *"being there."* To support this need, organization design systems must be flexible and responsive in order to allow for new offices to open and stay open so that the firm can respond to opportunities in new markets abroad. Royal Dutch Shell, a leading global company, makes a general practice to open an office in a country and stay there long before operations begin. They *go local* by giving considerable authority to in-country nationals who are allowed to customize strategy to respond to local customers and markets. Baxter International *strives to break down functional and country barriers* by reorganizing global businesses by product group with matrixed country relationships. This design guards against a country manager's tendency to not support the growth of market share in early money-losing businesses that have long term potential. *Flexibility in the design of corporate programs* is being sought by Amoco. International employees were included on diversity and variable pay corporate task forces to avoid a one size fits all approach to these programs.

Amoco should redesign expatriate jobs toward a greater consultant role. This will allow for increased transfer of technical expertise, as opposed to serving in supervisory capacity (Vanderbroeck 1992), which as been done at Motorola. While the number of expatriates has remained relatively constant over the years, the way in which expatriates are being used has changed. Expatriates are being used more as experts for the transfer of knowledge and less as senior managers overseeing an operation. In contrast, at Amoco, where global experience has been identified as a key experience for managers, it is likely that the number of expatriates will increase over the short term in order to develop a larger cadre of global professionals. However, the goal is to increasingly use these managers as experts to share knowledge rather than as overseers.

Staffing and selection should be geared toward increased involvement of local nationals in the management of foreign operations (Pucik 1992). Best practices toward this end would be to staff locations worldwide with best qualified people, regardless of nationality. Often foreign nationals are not considered for key positions, because the U.S. management making the hiring decisions don't know or understand the expertise of foreign nationals. Schlumberger, an energy services company, relates hiring levels by nationality to country revenues. For example, if 10 percent of revenue comes from India, they try to have 10 percent of recruiting pool from India. Hiring only off-campus recruits from 96 countries, recruiting coordinators are located in countries around the globe. Internationalizing key management positions and including foreign nationals on Board of Directors is

followed by Motorola, where half of the head of major business units have significant international experience.

Assessing the whole employee's likelihood of adapting to an overseas assignment is being used more and more in selection, despite general reluctance in the U.S. to formally use "personality" as a criterion. Although not easily validated in EEO-based staffing systems, personality may be of critical importance for overseas selection. Key cross-cultural adaptation skills include: personal, people, and perception skills (Mendenhall and Oddou 1985). Another best practice is Amoco's *worldwide job posting.* An employee at almost every Amoco location worldwide can view an electronic listing of openings around the globe.

Management development must balance local development with systems geared to create a cadre of manager with global experiences, and core corporate socialization programs to foster a collective vision (Pucik 1992). *Appraisal systems* should include global benchmarking , balancing local and global interests, and the pursuit of short and long term goals (Pucik 1992). Like Janus, who was a Roman god that was simultaneously able to look at the past and the future, *Janus managers* (Bird and Mikuda 1989) must be able to simultaneously balance parent with local interests. When evaluating new policies and making decisions, such managers must develop an approach that keeps global and local country specific views in equal perspective.

Schlumberger, the oil services company, also has a practice of requiring the *work force to be truly mobile* and to develop a global lifestyle, another best practice. Employees follow a "borderless career track" that leads to management, but requires a move about every three years. Schlumberger limits employees to only 1,000–2,000 pounds of personal effects when moving and expects employees to always be ready to take the next plane out. Even while traveling, employees are expected to constantly keep up their skills through correspondence courses and attendance at an occasional seminar at "Schlumberger U" in Paris. The Schlumberger lifestyle isn't for everyone as turnover can be as high as 30 percent annually. As one Amoco focus group participant commented, "They treat their people like cattle!" Yet Schlumberger is one of the most global in the oil industry— only 13 percent of its managers outside of North America are North American.

Partnering up to create a global learning center alliances is followed by IBM and Royal

Dutch Shell, where teams of workers from both companies analyze real business problems that managers face in either company. Greater emphasis is also being *placed on training and managing transitional issues* for the going and coming of both U.S. and foreign nationals expatriates. Amoco assigns an expatriate employee and his family to a *host family* in the foreign country where they are transferring. The two families then talk back and forth with each other prior to the transfer. While the practice is mainly used when U.S. employees are sent abroad, it may be used increasingly for foreign national transfers. Today few companies conduct any training for foreign nationals traveling to another country; almost all is focused on U.S. expatriates.

While most firms mainly send senior managers overseas, Amoco hopes to send more employees overseas earlier in their career for their first international assignment to give the *high potential manager international exposure earlier.* An example of this need for early exposure is provided by Baxter Corporation's problems with medical diagnostic equipment designed for size of U.S. patients, which was sent to Japan, where it was found to be much too big for most Japanese. Consequently, Baxter started *cross-cultural training for domestic employees who design products for global markets.*

Amoco is designing *communication systems* to allow continuous opportunities for employee interactions worldwide (Pucik 1992). It has developed Human Resource Information Systems that include employees worldwide wherever legally feasible. Amoco also includes international employees and symbols in all corporate videos to introduce new programs, whenever possible. Many publications with worldwide distribution are now being printed in languages in addition to English.

Revamping *reward systems* for better global management of human resources involves shifting away from short-term monetary rewards. It also may include a greater focus on developing career options for local nationals and developing ways to provide them with greater personal growth, challenge, and employment security (Pucik 1992). Related to expatriate compensation, Conoco is implementing *regionally based compensation packages* for expatriate assignments. This regional focus is in contrast to most other companies' approach where compensation and benefits policies for expatriates who are not U.S. citizens are derived from the U.S. expatriate package, which impedes local competitiveness since U.S. rates are often higher. Amoco recently initiated a far-reaching global stock ownership program in eighteen countries. Key obstacles overcome were: U.S. companies aren't usually traded overseas, the dilution of the dividends' motivating value due to higher tax rates, and the fact employees usually cannot get the stock until they leave the company. To manage these issues, Amoco has set up a trusteeship in England that reinvests the stock to develop a common global line of sight—if Amoco does well globally, so will all of it employees.

MODULE
25

Case Study Exercises

You have been asked by senior management of Amoco to spearhead an intervention that develops and implements leading-edge HR strategies and practices around the globe.

1.   How can you, as leader of this intervention, best justify adapting Amoco's HR policies and practices to be more global?

2.   What aspects of the existing HR system should be changed and why? Provide specific recommendations as to how the system should be modified and when.

3.   What steps would you take to ensure the HR system change process is well managed?

4.   What actions would you take to gain organizational acceptance of the changes you suggest?

Notes

1. The author would like to thank Mr. Jim D. Yates and many of his colleagues at Amoco Production Corporation in Houston for offering their time and knowledge to the author. The Amoco Foundation and the Amoco Production Corporation are thanked for providing funding to partially support this search. R. L. Ballinger and D. Anderson of Conoco Inc. are also thanked for their support of this project. Mangers from Dow, Motorola, Chase Manhattan Bank, Chevron, and Basic Insight Corp. are also acknowledged for their participation in a roundtable discussion on international human resource management issues at the School of Labor and Industrial Relations at Michigan State University on December 1, 1992. It should be noted that this case represents the global situation back in 1992, and undoubtedly Amoco has made more advances in its globalization of human resource systems since this case was written. Amoco Production Corporation is commended for allowing this case study to be written, its support of this project, and its interest in self-scrutiny.

2. In a similar vein, a senior manager in the international finance industry refers to its employees who search for new overseas market opportunities as "hunters."

3. Price Waterhouse, the accounting firm, has a series of books on countries around the globe that may serve as a useful initial primer.

References

Amoco Corporation Annual Report. 1991.

APC Renewal. Supplement to *New Horizons,* Amoco Production Company Newsletter. Houston, TX: Amoco Production Corporation, September-October 1992.

Bartlett, C. and Ghoshal, S. "Managing Across Borders: New Organization Responses." *Sloan Management Review,* 43–53, Fall 1987.

Bartlett, C. and Ghoshal, S. "What Is a Global Manager?," *Harvard Business Review,* September-October, 1991.

Bird, C. and Mikuda, M. "Expatriates in Their Own Home: A New Twist in the Human Resource Management Strategies of Japanese Multinationals," *Human Resource Management,* 28, 4, 437–453, 1989.

International Recruiting Report. Diversity Subcommittee of the CRC. Amoco Corporation, Chicago, IL, September 23, 1992.

Kossek, E. E. Personal notes from rountable discussion with Amoco Production employees in Houston, Texas, November 5, 1992.

Mendenhall, M. and Oddou, G. "The Dimensions of Expatriate Acculturation." *Academy of Management Review, 10,* 39–47, 1985.

Ohmae, K. "Planting for a Global Harvest," *Harvard Business Review,* 136–145, July-August 1989.

Porter, M.E. *Competition in Global Industries.* Boston: Harvard Business School Press, 1989.

Pucik, V. "Globalization and Human Resource Management," in V. Pucik, N. Tichy, and C. Barnett, Editors. *Globalizing Management: Creating and Leading the Competitive Organization.* New York: John Wiley & Sons, 1992.

Vanderbroeck, P. "Long-Term Human Resource Development in Multinational Organizations." *Sloan Management Review,* 95–98, Fall 1992.

Wells, L. "Misunderstandings of and among Cultures: The Effects of Transubstantive Error" in (Vails-Weber, eds.) *Sunrise Seminars,* Arlington, VA, 51–57. 1985.

Yates, J. Manager—HR International Operations, Amoco Production Corporation, Class Presentation to Human Resource Strategies and Decisions Class. School of Labor and Industrial Relations, East Lansing, MI, December 1, 1992.

Index

Adaptive orientation, 25.15

Business environment, worldwide. *See* World-wide business environment
Business strategy, 25.13

Career-long employment, 25.11
Communication challenges, 25.8, 25.24, 25.27. *See also* Language
Compensation and benefits, global HR strategy, 25.12
Corporate development, global, 25.8–9
Corporate power, 25.9
Corporatewide education institutions, 25.12
Cross-cultural diversity, 25.8, 25.13
Cross-cultural interaction, 25.8–9, 25.10, 25.24
Cultural accommodation strategy, 25.14
Cultural avoidance strategy, 25.14
Cultural compromise strategy, 25.14
Cultural diversity, 25.4, 25.6–7, 25.14–15, 25.22. *See also* International diversity
Cultural dominance strategy, 25.14
Cultural synergy, 25.9, 25.14–15, 25.16
Cultural values, 25.7

Decentralized structure, 25.9
Decision response times, 25.8
Developmental phases, corporations, 25.8–9, 25.11
Diversity. *See* Cultural diversity
Diversity management, 25.6, 25.19, 25.23
Domestic corporations, 25.9
Domestic HR management, 25.6–7
Dominant culture, 25.9

Ethics/ethical perspectives, 25.23
Exportive orientation, 25.15

Foreign staffing practices, 25.10

Global compensation system, 25.12
Global corporations, 25.8–9, 25.11–13, 25.19
Global human resources management, 25.6–8, 25.11–16, 25.23, 25.27
Global Human Resource Development (Marquardt and Engel), 25.5
Global managers, 25.10, 25.13, 25.14
Global marketplace, 25.19–20
Global organizational design, 25.9, 25.11
Global performance management, 25.12–13
Global players, 25.10
Global telecommunications, 25.7
Globalization, 25.9–10, 25.16, 25.19, 25.23, 25.25
Group (team) dynamics, 25.11

Home vs. host country values, 25.8
Host/local country nationals (HCNs), 25.6–7, 25.10
Human resources function, 25.9
Human resources management, 25.5–6, 25.8, 25.16
    global, *See* Global human resources management
Human resources management systems, 25.9, 25.13–15, 25.19, 25.24
Human resources practices, 25.9, 25.14–15
Human resources strategies, worldwide, 25.5–6, 25.15
Human resources (HR), 25.4

Integrative orientation, 25.15
Intercultural diversity, 25.8
Internal consistency, 25.13
International corporations. *See* Global corporations
International diversity, 25.25. *See also* Cultural diversity
International managers. *See* Global managers
International networking, 25.11
Intracultural diversity, 25.8

Language, global HR strategy, 25.24–25
Leadership capabilities, 25.10, 25.11
Learning organization. *See* Organizational learning
Local culture, 25.7

Megatrends/megamarkets, 25.5–6, 25.22
Mobile workforce, 25.26
Multicultural diversity, 25.8
Multidomestic approach, 25.9, 25.19
Multinational corporations, 25.8–10, 25.11, 25.12, 25.19
Multinational development, 25.8–9

Organizational culture, 25.12
Organizational environment, 25.13
Organizational hierarchy, 25.11, 25.12
Organizational learning, 25.4, 25.6

Parent country nationals/expatriates (PCNs), 25.6–7, 25.10, 25.24
Performance management, global. *See* Global performance management
Performance management systems, 25.13
Phases of development, corporations. *See* Developmental phases

Selection and staffing, global, 25.10
Senior management positions, 25.10, 25.13,
  25.27
Synergistic cultural perspective. *See* Cultural
  synergy
Synergistic learning skills, 25.13

Third-country nationals (TCNs), 25.6–7, 25.10
Time differences, 25.8
Total quality management (TQM), 25.22
Training (training and development systems),
  25.11–12
Transaction role, 25.4

Transformation role, 25.4
Transition role, 25.4
Translation role, 25.4
Transnational scale, 25.4
Twenty-first century, 25.16

Variable Incentive Program (VIP), 25.20

Workforce, global, 25.22
Worldwide business environment, 25.13
Worldwide ethics. *See* Ethics/ethical
  perspectives

MODULE
25

KOSSEK ■ BLOCK

Managing Human Resources
in the 21st Century

From Core Concepts to Strategic Choice

MODULE 26

Comparative
Industrial Relations

Peter Berg
MICHIGAN STATE UNIVERSITY

Eunmi Chang
MICHIGAN STATE UNIVERSITY

Managing Human Resources in the 21st Century: From Core Concepts to Strategic Choice,
by Kossek and Block

Publisher: Dave Shaut
Executive Editor: John Szilagyi
Developmental Editor: Bryant Editorial Development
Marketing Manager: Joseph A. Sabatino
Production Editor: Tamborah E. Moore
Manufacturing Coordinator: Dana Began Schwartz
Cover Design: Tin Box Studio
Cover Photographs: Copyright Shoji Sato/Photonica
Production House: The Left Coast Group, Inc.
Printer: West Group

Printed in the United States of America
1 2 3 4 5 02 01 00 99

For more information contact South-Western College Publishing, 5101 Madison Road, Cincinnati, Ohio, 45227 or find us on the Internet at *http://www.swcollege.com*
For permission to use material from this text or product, contact us by
- telephone: 1-800-730-2214
- fax: 1-800-730-2215
- web: *http://www.thomsonrights.com*

ISBN: 0–324–01827–4

This book is printed on acid-free paper.

Contents

MODULE OVERVIEW   26.4

RELATION TO THE FRAME   26.4

CORE CONCEPTS IN COMPARATIVE EMPLOYMENT RELATIONS   26.5
 Employees and Labor Unions   26.5
 Employers and Their Associations   26.7
 Government   26.7
 Collective Bargaining   26.8
 Culture   26.9

STRATEGIC ISSUES IN COMPARATIVE EMPLOYMENT RELATIONS   26.10

APPLICATION   26.12
 The Case of Korea   26.12
 The Case of Germany   26.14

IN CONCLUSION   26.17
 Debrief   26.17
 Suggested Readings   26.18
 Critical Thinking Questions   26.18
 References   26.18

MODULE
26

MODULE OVERVIEW

Economic globalization has increased the importance of understanding the systems of employment relations in other countries. As companies continue to develop operations in multiple locations overseas, it is critical that human resource managers understand the constraints and opportunities different systems of employment relations offer companies. In addition, making comparisons of employment relations across countries often leads to greater insight and understanding of one's own system of employment relations.

This module presents the core concepts needed to analyze employment relations systems across countries and examines how different employment relations systems lead to different human resource outcomes. It begins by discussing the key actors in any employment relations system: companies, unions, employer associations, government, and the institutions that bind these actors together to regulate the employment relationship. In addition, the module examines how employment relations institutions constrain human resource policies and practices. The module further explores this relationship by focusing on the very different employment relations practices in Korea and Germany.

After completing this module, the student should understand the elements of an employment relations system and how these elements interact to affect human resource policies and practices across countries.

RELATION TO THE FRAME

In this module, we examine the effects of the environmental context on human resource policies and practices. We compare the structure of employment relations and the role played by unions, employers, and government in the employment relations system across countries. The domestic laws that govern this system shape business strategies and the human resource practices found in individual countries. Thus, this module touches on all aspects of the framework established in the first two modules of this series and uses it in a comparative context. Our examination of employment relations systems in different countries shows that these systems continue to shape domestic human resource practices in an increasingly globalized world. Figure 26.1 illustrates this new paradigm.

FIGURE 26.1 *A Frame for Understanding Human Resource Strategy: Context, Roles, and Constraints*

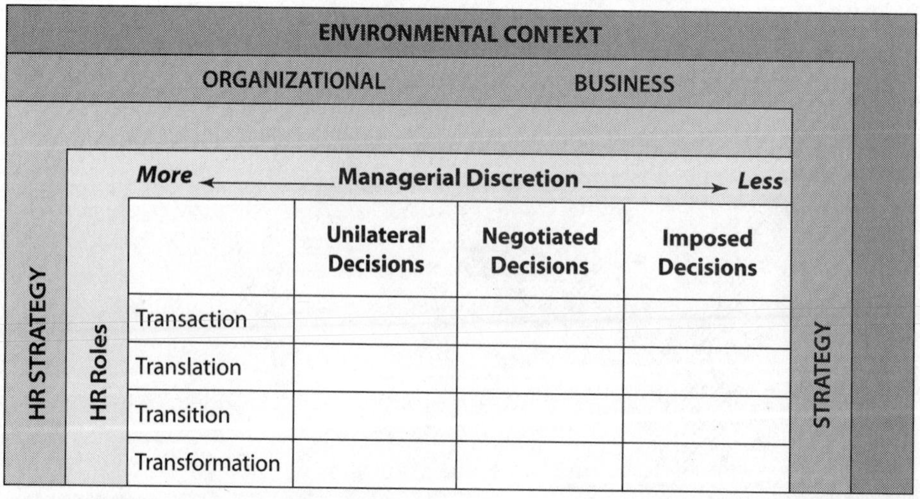

© 2000 by Ellen Kossek and Richard Block. Thanks to Brian Pentland, Karen Markel, and John Beck for helpful comments and discussions that enhanced the model.

CORE CONCEPTS IN COMPARATIVE EMPLOYMENT RELATIONS

Comparative employment relations is the study of institutions and actors across countries. Its central assumption is that domestic institutions mediate the effect of changes in markets and technology and the strategic choices made by firms that shape human resource outcomes. While there are a variety of institutions that might influence the employment relationship, we focus on collective bargaining arrangements as the primary institution. The key actors in the employment relationship are employers, labor, and government. We also discuss the role of national cultural identity in the employment relationship.

This section describes the actors and institutions that make up an employment relations system and how these actors and institutions interact. These elements of the employment relations system form the basis for comparisons across countries.

- Actors
  - ✓ Employees and labor unions
  - ✓ Employers and their associations
  - ✓ Government
- Institutions
  - ✓ Collective bargaining
- Culture

Employees and Labor Unions

When an individual enters into an employment relationship with a company, the terms of that relationship are established either unilaterally by the employer, through individual negotiation with the employee, or through collective bargaining between the employer and labor unions. In the United States, many employees work under conditions mandated by individual employers. Yet, despite low rates of unionization, labor unions in the United States continue to influence the conditions of employment in key industries and throughout the economy. Moreover, in many other countries labor unions in conjunction with employers and their associations are the key mechanism for setting the terms and conditions of employment. This section examines the role played by labor unions in the employment relations system.

To understand the role of labor unions, one must understand their evolution within the country in which they operate. First, it is important to identify the key unions within specific sectors or within certain occupations. On what basis did these unions evolve? Did workers unite around particular occupations or crafts, or did they organize more inclusively by incorporating all workers in an industry or at a location into the union? The organizational composition of the union indicates its core support and to some extent its bargaining agenda. An industrial union that represents skilled and unskilled workers is likely to have a broader bargaining agenda than a craft union that represents a specific skilled occupation.

In addition, it is important to assess whether the labor union is linked to a political party or has a social reform agenda. In the United States, unions developed out of a tradition of business unionism, rejecting a political orientation. In contrast, many European unions were originally rooted in politics. They have historically had a class concept of membership, representing all workers whether employed or unemployed. Some European unions have direct links to political parties; for example, Trades Union Congress (TUC) unions, such as the Transport and General Workers Union (TGWU) and the public employee's union, UNISON, play an important role in the British Labour Party.

TABLE 26.1 *Union Membership as a Percentage of Wage and Salary Earners in Selected Countries*

Countries	Trade Union Density (1995)	Change in Union Density (1985–1995)
Sweden	91.1%	8.7%
Denmark	80.1	2.3
Finland	79.3	16.1
Italy	44.1	−7.4
Austria	41.2	−19.2
South Africa	40.9	130.8
Canada	37.4	1.8
Australia	35.2	−29.6
United Kingdom	32.9	−27.7
Germany	28.9	−17.6
Netherlands	25.6	−11.0
New Zealand	24.3	−55.1
Japan	24.0	−16.7
United States	14.2	−21.1

Source: World Labour Report 1997–98, International Labour Office, 1997.

The role labor unions play in the employment relations system will be heavily influenced by the primary level at which negotiations with employers take place. Collective bargaining may take place at the firm, industry, or national level, or across several industries within a sector. Countries where work practices are negotiated primarily at the firm level, such as the United States, have more variation in practices than countries where peak employer associations negotiate employment conditions with labor unions at the sectoral level. In this latter case, work practices and innovations are more uniform across industries, e.g., in Austria.

The ability of labor unions to achieve their goals in bargaining will depend on how much power they have. Several factors influence that power. First, the union's ability to mobilize their membership to support, for example, a strike is critical to a successful action. Is the union organized in a way that can bring its membership together? Second, what institutional power does the union have? In Europe, many unions have been granted semi-public status and participate in a variety of labor market areas. In Germany, unions have been granted exclusive bargaining rights at the sectoral level and are involved in establishing and enforcing vocational training standards. In Belgium, Denmark, Finland, and Sweden, unions are involved in distributing unemployment benefits or in finding jobs for unemployed workers. This contrasts sharply with the United States, where unions are given legitimacy only after they win an election at the workplace.

Third, the more members unions have, the greater their power is likely to be. Union density—the percent of the labor force that are unionized—is a key determinant of union bargaining power. Table 26.1 shows the trade union density for selected countries. Since the mid-1980s, union density has declined in most countries. However, unions continue to represent a substantial proportion of workers in many countries around the world.

In addition, union coverage in some countries has remained high despite declining union membership. Union coverage refers to the workers covered by a union contract. In Germany, for example, negotiated agreements between unions and employer associations are extended to all employees working in companies that are part of the employer's association, regardless of union membership.

The last determinant of union power are the linkages unions have across borders. Given the mobility of capital and the increasing globalization of markets, unions can no longer rely on domestic membership to win battles at the workplace. International cooperation among unions is becoming a necessity. Unions are beginning to work more closely with international trade secretariats and other international labor organizations to forge tighter alliances across countries. The primary international strategy of unions within economically developed countries has been to advocate for the inclusion of labor standards in trade agreements. However, just how specific these standards should be remains controversial across unions in different countries.

Employers and Their Associations

In many countries, labor unions negotiate with individual employers over the terms and conditions of employment at the establishment or firm level. This is similar to most collective bargaining arrangements in the United States. In other countries, however, employer associations negotiate directly with labor unions over wages and working conditions. Thus, in some countries, employer associations directly influence the terms of the employment relationship. Because employer associations play an integral role in the collective bargaining process in many countries, we examine them here in more detail.

Employer associations or trade associations existed prior to the formation of unions. They often formed when employers were faced with an external threat, such as labor unrest, or in an effort to restrict competition and control prices. In the nineteenth century, trade associations in the United States consisted of informal gatherings of member businessmen for the purposes of controlling prices and production, lobbying state and federal legislatures, and addressing technical matters of production. However, antitrust sentiment and legislation (the Sherman Antitrust Act of 1890 and the Clayton Antitrust Act of 1914) forced trade and business associations to move away from practices of restraining trade and controlling prices. As federal government agencies expanded and became the regulators of industry during the post-World War II period, trade associations increasingly focused their efforts on influencing regulators and lawmakers. Unlike other countries where employer associations are involved in the collective bargaining process, U.S. employer associations focus primarily on lobbying around broad business-related legislation and/or on providing technical services to their members.

Employer associations may consist of firms in a particular sector, or they may be combinations of sectoral associations, i.e., peak associations. The power of employer associations depends on the extent to which they have organized employers within a given sector of the economy (their representativeness or density). For sectoral associations, the cohesion among its members is also very important. The extent to which firms differ in size and interests will affect the unity of their positions in bargaining or lobbying. The organizational capacity of the association to control its members will also influence its effectiveness in fighting for its interests. The last determinant of employer association power is the comprehensiveness of the association. With respect to bargaining, the more comprehensive an employer association is, the more moderate its wage policies are likely to be. They have fewer opportunities to externalize costs to other sectors, and as they grow large, they come under increasing pressure from the state to consider the macroeconomic implications of their policies.

MODULE
26

Government

Government is the third key actor in the employment relations system. The role the government plays in the employment relations system varies across countries. Although governments are active in employment relations in many different ways, we focus on three types of government roles in employment relations (see Van Ruysseveldt, Huiskamp, and van Hoof 1995):

- A *passive state* that creates a modest legal framework within which private individuals and business can reach agreements. The United States and Great Britain are clear examples of this approach. In the United States, individuals are given the right to bargain with companies, either individually or collectively. Labor unions are given no statutory security. The approach of the state is to set the rules of bargaining and intervene as little as possible.

- *Active state support* for the social partners and their mutual relations. Germany is the prime example of this approach. Employer associations and labor unions are given statutory roles to play in negotiating wages and administering vocational training. They serve essentially as quasi-public bodies that are charged with implementing legal regulations that relate to the workplace. Rather than empowering only *individuals,* the state empowers *organizations* to determine wages and working conditions.

- *Statism* where the state is actively and directly involved with the terms of employment and working conditions. France is an example of this approach. Many conditions of employment are laid down by the state—e.g., minimum wages, working week, length of holiday periods, and child and family allowances. In addition, basic conditions of employment, such as pay raises, may be unilaterally determined by the government if the bargaining parties fail to agree on the issue. It is not uncommon for the French government to intervene in this way. One consequence of this type of state involvement is the underdevelopment of private organization, such as unions, in the employment relationship. The active involvement of the state in employment relations diminishes the contribution of employer associations and unions and makes it harder for them to justify their existence to their members.

The different approaches countries take to intervening in the employment relationship is undoubtedly part of the history and culture of each individual country. The tradition of guilds and other quasi-public institutions in Germany, the common law tradition in Great Britain, and the influence of Roman law in France shape the role of the state in employment relations. Moreover, the degree and type of state intervention significantly affects the way the actors within the employment relations system interact, especially around collective bargaining and education and training issues.

Collective Bargaining

The terms and conditions of employment can be established in different ways. As discussed above, the state may play a key a role in establishing some of the conditions of employment. In other cases, the employers and employees or their representatives may determine wages and working conditions through some form of collective bargaining. The legal framework governing employment relations will determine the level at which collective bargaining takes place and the range of subjects to be bargained over.

In some countries, bargaining occurs at the firm level between individual employers and labor unions, which represent a particular occupation or workers within a given industry. This type of collective bargaining arrangement is likely to lead to great diversity in workplace rules, depending on the bargaining power of the individual employer and the labor union. This is the system in place in the United States. Benefit packages, including health, pension, and vacation benefits, may vary widely within and across industries. When collective bargaining negotiations take place at a higher level, greater uniformity of employment practices is the result. Negotiations between sectoral or peak-level employer associations and industrial unions leave less room for diversity of practices at the establishment or firm level.

The way employers and employees or their representatives interact in the collective bargaining process is determined by the institutional legitimacy afforded to them with the legal framework of bargaining and their bargaining power. In many countries, political forces have worked to undermine the legitimacy of labor unions and decrease their bargaining power, e.g., Great Britain and New Zealand. Even when governments are neutral toward the collective bargaining process, global economic forces can work to undermine the bargaining power of unions. The movement of capital across borders, the development of computer technology, and heightened competition have increased the pressure for greater flexibility around the terms and conditions of employment for individual employers.

Culture

The role of culture in management is controversial. There is no one accepted definition of culture, and few studies have empirically measured it. Comparative management researchers suggest that culture can be a significant determinant of management practices or employment relations (e.g., Adler 1997; Hofstede 1980). However, it is equally likely that cultural values might be the result of other environmental factors such as government and relations among institutions. For example, in countries where the economic institutions are strongly controlled by the government, or bureaucratic relationships are established in the networks among the institutions, valuing authority might be forced upon the people rather than a natural reflection of their collective consciousness.

Another difficulty in explaining the effect of culture is that no culture can be clearly described. Individuals in a country may share somewhat similar values but, at the same time, show variances in their beliefs. Those who share the same culture may even possess different concepts and images about their own culture. Due to this "diversity within culture," describing a specific culture is particularly difficult.

Despite these problems, understanding the culture of a certain country can provide insight into the employment relations of that country. Culture is a good way to analyze employment relations because cultural values tend to correlate with aspects or patterns of employment relations. Diversity among institutions in the United States and homogeneity in Asian countries reflect the individualism of the United States and the collectivism of Asia.

Using culture to compare employment relations systems has another benefit. It may be difficult to understand the network of employment institutions found in foreign countries, but cultural analysis helps explain the phenomena with familiar terminology. The concept of "Zaibatsu" in Japan may not make sense to foreigners by itself, but it is easier to remember when connected to the concept of "family" in Japanese culture.

One of the most influential empirical studies on culture was conducted by Hofstede (1980). Based on a worldwide survey, Hofstede classified about 60 countries according to four cultural dimensions. The first dimension is individualism/collectivism. Individualism stands for a preference for a loosely knit social framework, while collectivism stands for a preference for a tightly knit social framework. Power distance, the second dimension, is the extent to which members of the society accept an unequal power distribution. The third dimension is uncertainty avoidance, which means the level of anxiety members of a society are willing to accept in the face of unstructured or ambiguous situations. The fourth dimension by Hofstede is masculinity/femininity. Masculinity stands for a society in which social sex roles are sharply differentiated and the masculine role is characterized by need for achievement, assertiveness, and importance attached to material success. Femininity, on the other hand, stands for a society in which social sex roles show considerable overlap and the roles are characterized by a need for warm relationships, modesty, and importance attached to the nonmaterial quality of life.

Because they differ greatly among societies, these cultural dimensions can be used as a lens to examine the differences in management practices or employment relations. The United States is highly individualistic and masculine, exhibiting low power distance and low uncertainty avoidance, while some Asian countries such as Korea are collectivistic, feminine, high power distance, and high uncertainty avoidance. In the United States, diversity within institutions is encouraged, and employees are more likely to use the opportunities they have to express differences or conflict, e.g., grievance procedures. In many Asian countries, harmony among employees is valued highly, and conflicts between managers and workers are regarded as evils and something to be avoided.

STRATEGIC ISSUES IN COMPARATIVE EMPLOYMENT RELATIONS

As economic integration continues across countries, understanding how domestic employment relations institutions affect human resource practices and work organization is becoming a key factor for success in a global marketplace. Different systems of employment relations provide businesses with both constraints and opportunities in organizing their human resource activities. Table 26.2 provides some examples of how different structures of employment relations can affect workplace practices.

Countries with low union density and low government intervention provide a great deal of autonomy to management to set wages and experiment with innovative human resource practices. The United States and Great Britain are the obvious examples of this situation. In the United States, there is a large nonunion sector where employers unilaterally set wages and working conditions. These employers are also able to restructure the company, reorganize work, and reduce the size of the workforce without consulting labor or the government. One consequence of this employment relations environment is great variation in human resource practices across companies. Moreover, management is able to engage in trial-and-error restructuring without constraints from other stakeholders. While this experimentation may be costly, especially to employees, it provides a way to try out new types of work organization and human resource policies.

Countries where unions play a key role in negotiating wages and working conditions with employers or employer associations at a national, regional, or sectoral level are likely to be characterized by wage uniformity and more homogenous human resource practices. Bargaining at such a high level results in general contract provisions that establish standards and policies across industries and firms of different sizes. This centralized collective bargaining structure often results in less wage inequality across demographic groups in the society and relatively high labor standards. Moreover, the involvement of labor unions in this centralized bargaining process acts as a constraint on employer flexibility.

Many European countries such as Germany, Sweden, the Netherlands, Belgium, and Italy engage in bargaining at this level. Throughout the 1980s and 1990s, there has been a push for greater decentralization of bargaining across Europe. In some countries such as Italy and Sweden, this has resulted in some collective agreements being negotiated at the industry or plant level. The decline in unionization and the demand for more flexible work arrangements by employers has driven this decentralization. In other countries such as Germany and the Netherlands, the demand for greater flexibility in the use of labor has not been dealt with by decentralizing bargaining structures. Rather, the social partners are negotiating more open contracts and allowing the local works councils to modify agreements to a certain extent to fit their needs. This has become particularly useful in managing workforce levels during periods of high unemployment.

Countries where employees or labor unions enjoy legal rights of participation or consultation regarding business decisions are characterized by negotiated solutions to human resource problems. European countries have the most extensive rights of employee

TABLE 26.2 *The Effects of Employment Relations on Workplace Practices*

Employment relations	Workplace practices
Low union density and low government intervention	Greater managerial autonomy to set wages and structure jobs
National, regional, or sectoral bargaining (high centralized bargaining structures)	Low wage variation and greater standardization of human resource practices
Extensive rights of labor participation and consultation	Less management-led experimentation in workplace practices and more negotiated HR solutions
High government involvement in employment relations outcomes	Greater constraints on job structure, pay schemes, and wage levels

participation. These rights have been reinforced at the European Union (EU) level through the mandating of European works councils in large firms operating in the EU. Companies that operate in Europe are confronted with labor representatives who are actively involved in reorganizing work or restructuring jobs. Before most human resource policies can be changed or new policies adopted, labor representatives must by consulted or formally agree to the changes. In this environment, management must be willing to formally or informally negotiate with various labor representatives about human resource practices such as staffing levels, job structure, compensation schemes, or training. While this requires time and effort, this negotiation process can result in labor stability and cooperation from the workforce once an agreement has been reached.

In some countries, governments are highly involved in determining employment relations outcomes. In many developing countries and newly industrialized countries such as Taiwan, Malaysia, and Korea, the government has traditionally restricted the power of independent trade unions. Weak unions are often part of a development strategy to attract foreign investment and encourage economic growth. While it is not uncommon for governments to intervene in wage setting, most human resource policies and practices in these countries are established by management and are fairly traditional. Culture also plays an important role in determining job structure, benefits, and access to training in developing countries. The multiethnic mix of the South African workforce, for example, requires employers to accommodate both western and tribal views of benefits and leave policies.

MODULE
26

Although the employment relations system plays an important role in determining human resource policies and the structure of jobs, product and service markets also have a strong effect on the structure of jobs and the types of human resource practices companies offer. Those companies operating in high value-added product markets generally require highly trained workers, low labor turnover, and stable employment relations. The institutional arrangements in some countries are better able to provide these conditions to firms than those in other countries. Given the system of employment relations and education and training in Germany, it is not surprising that companies there tend to focus on high value-added products. Likewise, it is not surprising that countries like Korea have developed economically around low value-added products produced in a traditional, hierarchical manner.

To summarize, different employment relations systems have different effects on workplace practices and human resource policies. Establishment-level bargaining, low union density, and low government intervention in employment relations result in a high degree of managerial autonomy to set wages and working conditions and result in wide variation of practices across companies. In contrast, where union density is high and bargaining is centralized, human resource practices are likely to be more standardized across firms. Extensive participation and consultation rights of labor into business decisions require firms to engage in negotiations at the establishment level regarding human resource policies and practices.

APPLICATION

How employment relations systems affect human resource outcomes can be better understood by focusing on two countries with very different approaches to employment relations. In this section, we briefly describe the employment relations and current issues facing firms in Korea and Germany. These countries represent opposite ends of the employment relations spectrum. Korea is characterized by weak unions, highly organized employers, no labor participation at the workplace, and strong central government intervention in employment relations. Germany, on the other hand, is characterized by strong social partners, centralized bargaining, and a high degree of labor participation at the workplace.

The Case of Korea

Compared to Western countries, Korea has a short history of employment relations. Industrialization began at the end of the nineteenth century under Japanese occupation. Employment relations at that time had political overtones because management was closely linked with Japan and workers were, for the most part, Koreans. After independence finally came in 1945, Korea remained in economic and social chaos for about 15 years.

In the early 1960s, the Third Korean government initiated strong and centralized plans for economic development and export. Throughout the 1970s and 1980s, Korea experienced rapid economic growth. In 1962, its gross national product (GNP) per capita was less than $100, but in the 1980s, that figure reached $10,000.

The fast economic growth was driven by the government and implemented through the *Chaebols* or conglomerates. Chaebols are the most distinctive feature of the Korean economy. These conglomerates are characterized by family ownership/management and by unrelated diversification strategies (Whitley 1992). Chaebols have strong ties with and are strongly supported by the government. They dominate the major sectors of the Korean economy; for example, about a quarter of the gross national product in Korea is accounted for by the big 10 Chaebols including Samsung, Hyundai, LG, and Daewoo.

Figure 26.2 shows the growth model for Korea (Jung 1989). Korean economic development was achieved at the initiative of the government, which resulted in a centralized and authoritative management structure.

MODULE
26

FIGURE 26.2 *Korean Growth Model*

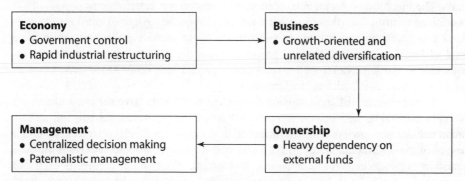

The Korean growth model has been undergoing substantial change since 1997 when the Asian economic and financial crisis hit the Korean economy. The high level of short-term foreign debts held by Korean companies made them very vulnerable to the demands of foreign creditors. These high debt levels eventually forced Korea to devalue its currency and, under an agreement with the International Monetary Fund (IMF), to totally restructure Korean management practices and the Chaebols.

The government, led by President Kim, Dae Joong, forced the Chaebols to concentrate on a few core-related businesses and decentralize their management structure as one way of encouraging small businesses. Korea is likely to undergo dramatic changes as it moves into the twenty-first century. While it is not possible to present a clear picture of the changes, the general tendency toward decentralization and flexibility is unmistakable.

Employees and Labor Unions. Unionization has undergone changes during Korea's economic development. During that period, it was very difficult to organize a union or engage in labor activities. After President Rho, Tae Woo declared social democracy in 1987, fundamental changes in employment relations were made. The number of unions and union members increased very rapidly as unions concentrated on raising wages through collective bargaining. Revision of labor laws in February 1998 under the IMF agreement enabled companies to lay off employees on a large scale. As a result, the unemployment rate increased from 2 percent in 1995 to almost 7 percent by the end of 1998. Unemployment has become the main issue for employees and unions.

Collective bargaining is carried out between the company union and the individual employer, but bargaining is also influenced by union federations. Two major union federations exist in Korea: the Federation of Korean Trade Unions (FKTU) and the Korean Confederation of Trade Unions (KCTU). The KCTU received legal status after the 1998 labor law revision, which permitted multiple federations for the first time. All workplace unions are required to enroll in a federation in order to legally operate.

MODULE
26

Traditionally, the Korean government has discouraged collective action. Unions have responded with strikes and protests in the face of employer hostility and lack of government support. Since the 1987 declaration of social democracy, however, collective bargaining has become more organized, and unions have become more accepted.

Employers and Their Associations. Companies in Korea tend to be clustered according to the Chaebols they belong to. Decision making in the Chaebols is highly centralized to the owners. Subsidiary companies heavily depend on the owners for support and information; these subsidiaries rarely interact around strategic issues with companies outside of the Chaebol boundary.

The Chaebols have recently received criticisms for unethical management practices, and bankruptcies of Chaebols such as the Kia Motor Company and the Hanbo Group in 1997 suggested a strong need to fundamentally change their status. President Kim, Dae Joong required the disaggregation of Chaebols in 1998, and fundamental changes, led by the government, are underway. Large deals among the Chaebols are being undertaken to focus their activities on a few core subsidiaries. This decentralization likely leads to increased interactions among companies across Chaebol boundaries.

A small number of employer associations exist in Korea, and they mainly provide information and advice. Korea Employers Federation (KEF), established in 1970, is the main employer association. The KEF helps unite employers and advise them on issues of employment relations.

Government. While state support tends to be critical to business in Asian countries, it is particularly important in Korea (Whitley 1992). The role of government in Korea has been crucial to the country's economic development since the 1960s. Most of the economic plans were set and guided by the government. In the period of the rapid growth, the government sometimes provided legal and other means of support to companies to depress labor rights and collective actions by workers.

Since 1987 and especially since 1998, with the election of President Kim, Dae Joong, the Korean government has tried to increase democratization within society and promote market-based competition.

The government has initiated structural changes in the Korean economy. With the recognition that fundamental changes are required, the government established a Tri-partite Commission. The Commission is composed of representatives from labor, management, and government. It advises the president and facilitates mutual understanding between these groups. In addition, the government revised the labor laws in 1998. The changes include several items such as legalizing layoffs and the political activities of labor unions.

Managerial Characteristics and Human Resource Practices.   Management structures in Korea are also expected to fundamentally change in the twenty-first century. Despite the current push to restructure the Chaebols, the structure of Korean companies remains very hierarchical and bureaucratic, with many layers of authority and a high concentration of decision making at the top of the organization. While work restructuring encourages flatter organizational hierarchies and more delegation of decisions, decentralized decision making at workplaces is not occurring as intended, and even where formal team structures exist, hierarchy and centralized decision making remain intact.

The motivation of Korean employees is also changing. Traditionally, the reward system in Korea has been seniority based, indicating that Hofstede's description of Korean culture as collectivistic and feminine is correct. However, Korean companies are moving toward including more performance factors in compensation packages (Lee 1989). This has further accelerated in light of the IMF agreement, since individual performance can be used as a guideline in selecting those employees to be laid off. Individual performance is now receiving more and more weight in addition to such factors as interpersonal relationships and harmony with company and coworkers.

Regarding training and education, Chaebols have their own training institutes that provide programs for the subsidiaries; most of these programs provide general training for managers rather than technical training for frontline workers. Large companies also use management or technical programs at major universities and training abroad. Formal training centers such as Korean Productivity Center (KPC) or Korea Management Association (KMA) are also used to educate employees in a variety of subject areas.

The Case of Germany

German employment relations is unique among industrialized countries in its ability to balance institutional centralization with local flexibility. Since World War II, the German employment relations system has delivered high labor standards across German industries, labor peace, and an effective system for worker participation. Like many countries, however, the current foundations of the German system are under pressure from increasing competition and greater economic integration. This brief examination of Germany discusses the elements of the German employment relations system and the challenges it is currently facing.

All matters of substantive concern to labor and management are defined and debated at the national level by the "social partners" (the unions and the employer associations). The social partners negotiate contracts on a regional, and industry or multi-industry basis. Whereas 29 percent of the entire German workforce are union members, those covered by collective agreements is much higher since collective agreements between unions and employer associations are extended to all workers within member firms of the employer association, regardless of union status. Contracts negotiated by labor unions and employer associations concern wages and salaries and general conditions of work such as dismissals, working time, and vacations. Because these contracts cover workers in several industries, they tend to be very general; they are designed to establish minimum standards that can be improved upon, within limits, by local management and individual works councils at the firm.

The most distinguishing feature of employment relations in Germany is the presence of codetermination. *Codetermination* is a parallel form of representation available to employees in addition to labor unions. Despite the formal distinction between the codetermination mechanism and unionism, there are many connections between these two forms of worker representation. German federal law mandates that codetermination take place on two levels: through employee representation on company boards and works councils.

Employees of German companies are allowed to elect representatives to the supervisory board of the company. The supervisory board is responsible for monitoring management performance and appointing the top managers. The exact number of labor representatives on the board varies by industry. While labor representatives are never in the majority, they are present on the supervisory board, providing employees and unions with information about and opportunities to influence strategic business decisions.

Works councils are the second aspect of German codetermination. Employees in any business over five employees have the right to elect a works council, which has certain rights to participate in specific business decisions. Although work councilors are elected regardless of union status, it is common for union officers to serve as works councilors and for works councils to cooperate with labor unions. The works council has the right to *co-decision* on such matters as overtime hours, leave arrangements, social services, and pay incentives. In issues regarding the use of personnel within the firm, the recruiting of workers from the external labor market, and vocational training, management cannot take action without getting the works council's *consent*. In addition, the works council has a right to be *consulted* before decisions relating to the following issues are made: introducing new technology, work organization, dismissal of workers, further training of personnel, the economic health of the firm, and hiring managerial employees. These legally mandated rights of participation differ substantially from the United States, for example, where most of these issues would fall under managerial prerogatives.

This system of employment relations is sustained by the roles and strength of the social partners as well as by the support of the federal government. For the most part, labor unions in Germany represent all workers within a given sector. This type of representative structure cuts across industries and employee skill levels. Thus, this centralized and concentrated representative structure fits well with the level at which collective agreements are negotiated; however, it also presents German unions with the difficult task of balancing the many competing interests of its members. The reunification of Germany in 1992 resulted in a boost to union membership; however, this was short-lived. Union membership in eastern Germany has been declining ever since. The high unemployment there and the attitude of the former East German workers toward unions have contributed to these losses.

In contrast to U.S. labor unions, German unions enjoy a high degree of institutional security. The right to bargain is granted specifically to unions in the German constitution. While a firm may leave an employer association if it doesn't like the contracts being negotiated on its behalf, it must then bargain with the union separately if the workforce so desires. In the United States, you recall, the right to bargain must be won by the union through an election—i.e., over 50 percent of workers must vote for representation. German unions also enjoy a *quasi-public status* in the German economy. In particular, German unions play a formal role in the national vocational training system. They serve on training boards within craft and industry employer chambers, which certify vocational training. Moreover, they ensure that workers are receiving the appropriate qualifications at the establishment level as part of the national apprenticeship training system.

Employer associations in Germany are also very centralized. Similar to labor unions, employers are organized on a regional and sectoral basis. One of the largest employer associations is Gesamtmetall. This association consists of autonomous regional associations of metal industry employers. Membership in these associations is not mandatory, but most firms, especially large firms, are members. The decision-making power of Gesamtmetall rests with the presidium that is elected by the management board, which is made up of the chairpersons of the regional employer associations. Gesamtmetall conducts collective negotiations with its union counterpart, IG Metall. Developing collective bargaining strategies that can accommodate the interests of all firms is vital to maintaining solidarity within the association and providing a united front against IG Metall.

The bargaining strategies tend to reflect the perspective of the large metalworking firms that dominate the association. In the early 1990s, this situation resulted in many smaller firms demanding a greater voice in the association and threatening to leave if contracts did not provide greater flexibility. Greater flexibility within the collective agreements has come about primarily because of changing economic conditions. It is difficult for smaller employers to leave employer associations because they must then bargain individually with a large and powerful labor union. Although smaller employers give up a great deal of autonomy through the centralized bargaining structure, their solidarity with other employers prevents unions from individually pressuring them for concessions.

The structure of representation and the strength the social partners enjoy by banding together reinforces the centralized system of bargaining and the prominent role of labor unions in the employment relations system. The role played by the social partners is certainly reinforced and supported by government policy and action. The German government has continued to play an active role in providing strong legal support for unions and codetermination. This fundamental support has been maintained through both social democratic and conservative governments.

The Effect of Employment Relations on Human Resource Practices.
The centralized structure of employment relations in Germany takes many of the costs of labor out of competition and encourages firms to invest heavily in technology and pursue high-wage, high labor value-added production strategies.

At the plant level, unions through works councils and supervisory board representation are integrated into strategic decision making. German unions, particularly IG Metall, have actively worked through works councils to encourage new forms of work organization that rely on higher skilled workers and more flexible job tasks. The codetermination rights labor representatives possess on personnel and work organization issues provide for negotiated adjustments in work reorganization, layoffs, and new technology. These labor rights provide stability to workplace innovations and encourage the diffusion of innovations across firms and industries.

The centralized system of collective bargaining facilitates this diffusion. The strong union presence throughout the economy and the close relationship with works councils are the vehicle that spreads models of human resource innovation across firms. Centralized bargaining also encourages training by reducing wage differentials across industries, making it difficult for firms to use wages to bid skilled workers away from other firms. Moreover, employment security legislation makes it costly for companies to massively reduce their workforces and encourages employers to invest in the skills of their incumbent workers instead.

The system of employment relations is linked with the apprenticeship system at many levels to reinforce broad skills training and support organizational innovation. The unions, works councils, employers, and employer associations are all involved in the vocational training system. Vocational training is conducted through apprenticeships that combine school education with occupational training at the workplace. This system of workplace-based training generates workers with a broad understanding of the production process and with "redundant skill capacities" (Streeck 1991). These skill capacities allow skilled workers to deal with unforeseen production problems as they arise and provide employers with skills necessary to promote multiskilled team production.

While the employment relations system has played a positive role in diffusing workplace innovations across industries and bringing increased decision-making power to frontline employees through group work, employment relations institutions in Germany have costs associated with them that hinder their ability to experiment with high-performance work practices.

High-performance work systems break down the functional specialization and hierarchy across the organization and encourage greater communication across groups. German plants, however, continue to be characterized by managerial hierarchy and suffer from functional specialization in a way that inhibits communication.

Employment relations institutions may reinforce the functional specialization within firms. Wever (1995) maintains that the codified structure of representative participation inhibits experimentation with new innovative human resource practices. Whereas in the United States many experiments with human resource innovations are developed, often informally, by labor and management, in Germany changes to the structure of work tend to be developed separately by the works council (usually with the help of the union) and/or the employer, rather than jointly by labor and management working together.

The codetermination system in Germany gives employee representatives extensive input into matters concerning technological change, job redesign, the structure of pay, as well as financial information and investment intentions of the firm. This input protects employees from bearing most of the costs of reorganization through layoffs, but it also requires that the process of reorganization occur through formal negotiations. This negotiations process reduces the ability of the company to experiment with a variety of high-performance work practices. In particular, pay-for-performance schemes are less prevalent in Germany because it is a very contentious issue with unions and works councils.

MODULE
26

The way codetermination is practiced also reinforces the functional specialization in German firms. Works council representatives tend to interact solely with the human resources department, which serves as the liaison between management and labor. Together the works council and the human resources department negotiate plant agreements regarding new work systems. This is a powerful voice for employees who are able, through their representatives, to influence changes to job structure or the implementation of new technology.

Yet the extent of work reorganization negotiated by these two bodies is constrained in two ways. First, both the management and the works councils are restricted by the contracts negotiated by employer associations and unions. It is very difficult for German companies to put aside preconceived notions of workplace practice and organization and negotiate new relations with employees that are outside the contract.

Recent high levels of unemployment in Germany have encouraged firms to negotiate special arrangements with works councils regarding the use of labor. This has pressured the social partners to negotiate more open agreements that can be modified at the establishment level. While the German employment relations system may reduce experimentation and reinforce hierarchy, there are also signs that it is attempting to loosen these constraints by accommodating to the needs of local establishments for flexibility.

In Conclusion

Debrief

This module examined the actors and institutions involved in domestic employment relations systems. Moreover, it analyzed how these actors and institutions form very different employment relations systems across countries. The effects of employment relations systems on workplace practices vary by the structure and level of bargaining, the level of labor participation in strategic or work-related decisions, and the extent of government intervention in the employment relationship. The Korean and German cases reveal two very different approaches to employment relations and also very different strategies for managing human resources.

Suggested Readings

Bean, R. *Comparative Industrial Relations.* London: Routledge, 1994.

Hyman, R., and A. Ferner. *New Frontiers in European Industrial Relations.* Oxford: Blackwell, 1994.

Locke, R., T. Kochan, and M. Piore (eds). *Employment Relations in a Changing World Economy.* Cambridge, MA: MIT Press, 1995.

Van Ruysseveldt, J., R. Huiskamp, and J. van Hoof (eds.). *Comparative Industrial and Employment Relations.* London: Sage Publications, 1995.

Verma, A., T. A. Kochan, and R. Lansbury. *Employment Relations in the Growing Asian Economies.* London: Routledge, 1995.

Critical Thinking Questions

1. Compare the roles and interaction of the actors and institutions in the Korean and German employment relations systems.

2. Are human resource practices becoming more similar or different across countries as globalization increases? How do national systems of employment relations affect this convergence or divergence of human resource practices?

3. Describe the actors and institutions in the United States employment relations system, and discuss its advantages and disadvantages relative to the German system of employment relations.

References

Adler, N. *International Dimensions of Organizational Behavior.* Cincinnati: South-Western College Publishing, 1997.

Hofstede, G. *Culture's Consequences: International Differences in Work-Related Values.* Beverly Hills, CA: Sage Publications, 1980.

Jung, K. "Business-Government Relations in Korea." In Chung, K. and Lee, H. (eds.) *Korean Managerial Dynamics.* New York: Praeger Publishing, 1989.

Lee, H. "Managerial Characteristics of Korean Firms." Chung, K. and Lee, H. (eds.). *Korean Managerial Dynamics.* New York: Praeger Publishing, 1989.

Streeck, W. "More Uncertainties: German Unions Facing 1992," *Industrial Relations.* Fall 1991.

Wever, K. *Negotiating Competitiveness: Employment Relations and Organizational Innovation in Germany and the United States.* Boston: Harvard Business School Press, 1995.

Whitley, R. *Business Systems in East Asia: Firms, Markets, and Societies.* London: SAGE Publications, 1992.

Index

Active state support (employment relations),
26.8
Apprenticeship, 26.16
Authoritative management structure, 26.12
Autonomy of management, 26.10

Bargaining power, 26.6, 26.8, 26.10, 26.16
Benefit packages, 26.8
British Labour Party, 26.5
Bureaucratic relationships, 26.9

Chaebols (conglomerates), 26.12–13, 26.14
Clayton Antitrust Act of 1914, 26.7
Co-decision, 26.15
Code-determination rights, 26.15
Codetermination, 26.15, 26.17
Collective actions, 26.14
Collective agreements, 26.14–15
Collective bargaining, 26.5, 26.8–9, 26.10,
26.13, 26.16
Collectivism, 26.9
Comparative employment relations, 26.10–12.
See also Employment relations
Conditions of employment, 26.5, 26.8
Cultural dimensions, 26.9–10
Cultural role in management, 26.9
Cultural values, 26.9

Decentralization, 26.13
of bargaining, 26.10
Decision making, 26.13, 26.16
Diversification strategies, 26.12
Diversity, 26.9
Domestic employment relations, 26.4–5, 26.10,
26.17

Economic change, 26.14
Economic forces, 26.9, 26.13
Economic globalization. *See* Globalization
Education and training issues, 26.8, 26.17
Employee participation, 26.10–11
Employee representatives, 26.8–9
Employer associations, 26.7, 26.9, 26.10,
26.13, 26.16
Employment relations, 26.8, 26.11, 26.12,
26.13, 26.16–17
Employment relations systems, 26.4–5, 26.6,
26.12, 26.15, 26.18
Employment relationship, 26.5, 26.7, 26.8
Empowering individuals, 26.8
Environmental context, 26.4, 26.9
European Union (EU), 26.11

Family ownership/management, 26.12
Flexible work arrangements, 26.10

German employment relations, 26.14
Global marketplace, 26.10
Globalization, 26.4
Government (role in employment relations),
26.7, 26.10, 26.11, 26.12, 26.13–14, 26.16,
26.17

High-performance work systems, 26.17
Homogeneity, 26.9, 26.10
Human relations, 26.10, 26.11
Human resource managers, 26.4
Human resource policies and practices, 26.4,
26.10–12, 26.14, 26.16

Individualism/collectivism (culture), 26.9–10
International labor organizations, 26.7
International Monetary Fund (IMF), 26.13,
26.14
Intervention. *See* Government (role in employ-
ment relations)

Japanese culture, 26.9

Korean management practices, 26.12–14

Labor market areas, 26.6
Labor standards, 26.10
Labor union role, 26.6, 26.11, 26.12
Labor unions, 26.5, 26.8, 26.13, 26.15

Management performance, 26.15
Managing human resources, 26.18
Masculinity/femininity (culture), 26.9–10
Membership (union), 26.6–7

Networking, 26.9
Nonunion sector, 26.10

Passive state (employment relations), 26.8
Peak employer associations, 26.6–7
Political orientation, 26.5
Power distance (culture), 26.9–10
Power of employer associations, 26.7, 26.9
Power of unions, 26.6, 26.11, 26.12

Quality of life, 26.9
Quasi-public status (economy), 26.15

Rights of labor, 26.12
Role of culture. *See* Cultural role in
management

Sectoral associations, 26.7
Sherman Antitrust Act of 1890, 26.7
Social partners, 26.14

Social sex roles (culture), 26.9
Standards. *See* Labor standards
Statism (employment relations), 26.8
Structure of jobs, 26.11

Technological change, 26.17
Trade associations. *See* Employer associations
Trades Union Congress (TUC), 26.5
Tradition of business unionism, 26.5
Training boards, 26.15
Transport and General Manual Workers Union (TGWU), 26.5
Twenty-first century, 26.13, 26.14

Uncertainty avoidance (culture), 26.9–10
Unemployment, 26.10, 26.17

Uniformity, 26.8
Union density, 26.6, 26.10, 26.12
Union membership, 26.6–7, 26.15
Unionization, 26.5, 26.10, 26.13
Unions. *See* Labor unions

Vocational training standards, 26.6

Wage uniformity, 26.10
Work councils, 26.15, 26.17
Work practices/organization, 26.6, 26.10, 26.11
Workplace innovations, 26.15, 26.16, 26.17

Zaibatsu, 26.9. *See also* Japanese culture

MODULE
26

MANAGING HUMAN RESOURCES IN THE 21st CENTURY

From Core Concepts to Strategic Choice

MODULE 27

Ethical Perspectives in Employment Relations and Human Resources

John L. Revitte
MICHIGAN STATE UNIVERSITY

Jerry C. Lazar
MICHIGAN STATE UNIVERSITY

Managing Human Resources in the 21st Century: From Core Concepts to Strategic Choice,
by Kossek and Block

Publisher: Dave Shaut
Executive Editor: John Szilagyi
Developmental Editor: Bryant Editorial Development
Marketing Manager: Joseph A. Sabatino
Production Editor: Tamborah E. Moore
Manufacturing Coordinator: Dana Began Schwartz
Cover Design: Tin Box Studio
Cover Photographs: Copyright Shoji Sato/Photonica
Production House: The Left Coast Group, Inc.
Printer: West Group

Printed in the United States of America
1 2 3 4 5 02 01 00 99

For more information contact South-Western College Publishing, 5101 Madison Road, Cincinnati, Ohio, 45227 or find us on the Internet at *http://www.swcollege.com*
For permission to use material from this text or product, contact us by
- telephone: 1-800-730-2214
- fax: 1-800-730-2215
- web: *http://www.thomsonrights.com*

ISBN: 0–324–01830–4

This book is printed on acid-free paper.

Contents

MODULE OVERVIEW 27.4

OBJECTIVES 27.4

RELATION TO THE FRAME 27.4

CORE CONCEPTS IN WORKPLACE ETHICS 27.6
   Ethics, Morals, and Philosophy 27.6
   Law and Legality 27.6
   Political Correctness 27.7
   Good Manners, Etiquette, and Civility 27.7
   Western Traditions and Judeo-Christian Values 27.7
   Gender Differences and Ethical Systems 27.8
   Conflicts at Work Regarding What Is and Is Not Ethical 27.8
   Intergroup Conflicts 27.8
   Intragroup Conflicts 27.9

STRATEGIC ISSUES IN WORKPLACE ETHICS 27.9
   Selection and Promotion of Employees and Supervisors 27.10
   Rights to Collect Information Versus Rights of Privacy 27.10
   Income Differentials within Workplaces and in Society 27.11
   Punishments, Progressivity, and "Just Cause" in Discipline Cases 27.12
   Occupational Health and Safety 27.13
   Employee Involvement and Quality of Worklife Enhancement 27.14
   Labor-Management Relations 27.14
   Affirmative Action Programs Versus Seniority and Other Systems 27.16
   Workforce Reductions Versus Job Creation Efforts 27.16

APPLICATIONS 27.18
   Application 1: Light Versus Regular Duty Work 27.18
   Questions for Group Discussion 27.18
   Application 2: Work-Family Conflicts 27.19
   Questions for Group Discussion 27.19

IN CONCLUSION 27.19
   Debrief 27.19
   Suggested Readings 27.20
   Critical Thinking Questions 27.20
   Exercises 27.21
   References 27.21

INDEX 27.22

MODULE OVERVIEW

The goal of this module is to provide an overview of what constitutes ethics, how they function within workplaces, and why they are necessary to consider for those managing human resources. First, some basics on the nature of ethics and philosophy are presented, primarily as viewed through western perspectives. Ethics, morality, and religious beliefs are contrasted, and legal considerations are discussed. Such concepts as political correctness, good manners, and gender bias are noted for their impact on understanding what might be considered differentially as ethical behavior in the workplace. A variety of conflicts that can arise at work are then discussed, such as those between groups of employees and supervisors. These conflicts develop, for example, because each group may include individuals holding personal values based on different philosophies or ethical standards. Since conflicts can also arise within groups, or due to a total lack of ethical work practices, these problems are also addressed. A wide variety of potential late-twentieth-century workplace ethical conflicts are then presented concerning strategic labor relations and human resource management issues. In addition to two in-class application exercises, a brief list of recommended readings, critical thinking questions, and further exercises are provided as resources for the reader.

OBJECTIVES

The key objectives of this module are to provide some basic concepts and a sample of strategic issues concerning ethics within the context of human resources management and employment relations. The context is mainly contemporary. Although there are some references to the classics, the module concerns late-twentieth-century issues in business and professional ethics. An important underlying consideration is the principle of autonomy, both in the context of the individual and the group. The rights of autonomy, though, are of necessity tempered by social and professional responsibilities to others. They should not, hopefully, promote destructive prerogatives, and throughout the module, the authors have attempted to convey "win-win" thinking. This seemed most appropriate since experience shows that permitting one side to totally dominate or nearly destroy the other frequently creates long-term problems that compromise otherwise reasonable and workable relationships.

RELATION TO THE FRAME

Ethical perspectives can have an impact on several of the major HR roles that are discussed elsewhere in the text and are listed in Figure 27.1. Many concepts in business ethics clearly affect how HR professionals view what is the ethical, moral, legal, politically correct, or the civil choice to make in both their daily and strategic decision-making practices. Ethical perspectives might influence the decisions that are made, or how they are conveyed to employees or customers, or they potentially could even transition or transform an organization.

In this module *transaction* roles involving the HR administrative functions of selecting and promoting employees and supervisors are addressed in light of the fairness of what is required in job descriptions and how candidate attributes are measured. The discussion on the HR role of administering discipline notes the importance of procedural justice, progressivity, and just cause standards in handling investigations and punishments. In most circumstances employers have *unilateral* control over these HR matters. However, just cause is typically *negotiated* by the parties or would be assumed or be *imposed* by the third-party arbitrator in a union grievance case, or a judge might impose legal standards of fairness in a whistleblower court case.

FIGURE 27.1 *A Frame for Understanding Human Resource Strategy: Context, Roles, and Constraints*

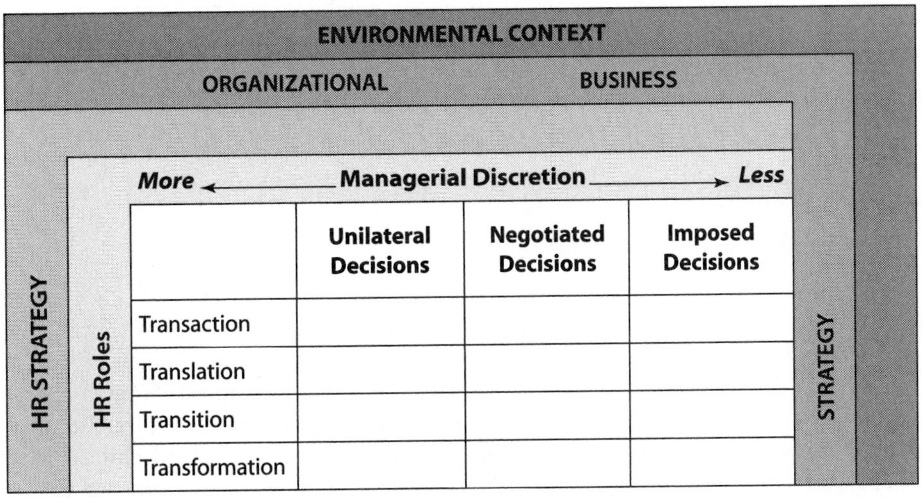

		Unilateral Decisions	Negotiated Decisions	Imposed Decisions
	Transaction			
	Translation			
	Transition			
	Transformation			

ENVIRONMENTAL CONTEXT — ORGANIZATIONAL — BUSINESS — HR STRATEGY — HR Roles — STRATEGY — More ← Managerial Discretion → Less

© 2000 by Ellen Kossek and Richard Block. Thanks to Brian Pentland, Karen Markel, and John Beck for helpful comments and discussions that enhanced the model.

The HR professional will frequently engage in *translation* activities that involve communicating to employees and supervisors, and occasionally to suppliers or customers, an organization's ethical perspectives regarding HR functions and practices and, where required, certain legal information. The employer's policies on drug and alcohol use, compensation, affirmative action, or workplace safety obviously need to be conveyed. Also, any computer monitoring or electronic surveillance of performance will need to be translated especially as it entails the ethical rights of the employer to collect information versus the employees' expectations concerning their rights to privacy. And these translation roles can be complicated by the need to account for cross-cultural differences within global organizations. Again, in most nonunion settings these will be primarily *unilateral* decisions made by the employer, whereas with union employees some practices will need to be *negotiated*. However, many employment laws—such as equal employment opportunity (EEO) and the Family and Medical Leave Act (FMLA)—*impose* on employers a duty to convey or post information to their employees concerning basic legal rights and responsibilities, and the Occupational Safety and Health Act (OSHA), for example, requires that employees be informed of their right to know of toxic chemical exposures.

Examples of *transition* activities might involve the HR staff adjusting standards for promoting or selecting new supervisors to include criteria that stress ethical and caring values and skills. An organization could venture in new directions embracing HR leave policies or job sharing practices that address employees' work/family conflicts or other implications of increasing diversity of needs within the workforce. Or an HR professional might be involved in modifying an employer's pay structure to reduce all racial or gender-related differentials—going beyond what is currently required by law—or even address pay gaps between executives, supervisors, and rank-and-file employees. Excepting some possible negotiating in union settings, these would be areas of *unilateral* employer control generally beyond what is legally *imposed* on American employers.

The HR professional could also be involved in *transformation* activities. One possible role might entail assisting the organization to evaluate, and then revise, many of its core human resources and labor relations policies and practices in light of the values of a new standard of ethical best practices. For example, the HR department might push the employer towards creating a significantly new culture of employee involvement or team-based work systems. Certainly HR personnel could lead the organization

MODULE 27

to develop a more collaborative relationship with the union. This might involve not only the promotion of interest-based bargaining and labor-management cooperation experiments but might seek to increase the union and/or employees' influence in more strategic levels of organizational decision making including over job retention or creation efforts. Again, excepting the union negotiations, these would be areas of *unilateral* employer control beyond what employers are required to do by law.

CORE CONCEPTS IN WORKPLACE ETHICS

Ethics, Morals, and Philosophy

People often confuse morals and ethics. Although they frequently overlap, they are in fact different even though both are used as a philosophical foundation for evaluating acceptable and unacceptable behavior within and between groups of humans.

Morality comes about as a result of the codification of traditional behaviors, conventional wisdom, particular familial or social orientations, and current public opinions. Morals are not subject to intense scrutiny, do not require a sound philosophical foundation (or sometimes any particular foundation), and can change for any reason acceptable to the individual or group that holds them. Furthermore, people can and do frequently hold mutually exclusive moral beliefs, meaning they are in contradiction with themselves, yet most individuals holding such beliefs normally don't see the conflict.

Ethics, on the other hand, demand a supportable philosophical foundation that is based on internal scrutiny and is constantly subject to questioning and inquiry. Although a starting point, opinion is really too weak to be a foundation for an ethical position. Further, an ethical system demands internal consistency.

Interestingly, it is thus possible for something to be both moral and ethical, to be immoral but ethical, or to be moral but unethical. Furthermore, these distinctions are often not clear and require careful consideration on the part of the observer. For example, an employer may choose to permit employees of a particular religion to have time off based on a shared religious belief, but the same employer may not permit people of a different religion to have comparable time off. To the employer this may be a moral situation and not an ethical dilemma, since the employer may believe a particular religion superior or more mainstream, familiar, and understandable. In current American society, however, this would be viewed as very unethical because it discriminates against some employees on the basis of religious beliefs.

In employment relations, ethics can be an important consideration. Because ethics need to be based on a rigorous investigation and a direct pointing toward some good, ethical foundations are extremely important. In business, traditionally there are several "goods" that are important. Obviously, making a profit is essential, since otherwise the stockholders would divest, and a business couldn't remain open long. Consequently, in a business context, ethical evaluations must take profitability into consideration.

It is necessary, however, for most businesses to also take into consideration the "customer" needs of their managers and employees, as well as those of their suppliers and the consuming public for whom they provide goods or services. Business ethics must include consideration of the need for profit without ignoring these other entities or "goods." Business ethics, particularly within the realm of human resources and labor relations, thus must aim to permit, or encourage, making a profit while also working to maintain, or improve, the ethical treatment of stockholders, managers, employees, and customers among other stakeholders.

Law and Legality

The above situation is further complicated by considerations of law and what is or is not legal. Ethical behavior may or may not always be consistent with the law, and the law can and does change over time. Historically, ethics and the law have been at odds on a number of issues. Consider these examples. The above story concerning an employer's failure to provide religious accommodation was not until recently considered illegal. At one time, the right to form or join a labor union was not a legally protected American right, even though many Americans, including various church leaders, believed it was ethically and morally imperative that employers allow their employees to belong to unions. And years ago in the United States, racially discriminatory employment laws and practices, and at one time even race-based slavery, widely existed. These types of practices clearly existed despite the fact that they were in conflict with many Americans' moral and religious values and were thus clearly unethical by some standards.

Political Correctness

Political correctness, some might argue, has become a cliché at the end of the twentieth century. What started off as a guide for avoiding behaviors that are offensive to people of a different ethnic group, gender, or sexual orientation can be carried to such extremes that it becomes the focal point of jokes. But being politically correct can play an important role in daily business life. For example, by the 1990s, politically correct behavior demanded that women no longer be referred to as "girls." Statements such as "I'll have my girl call your girl to set up a lunch" are generally viewed as offensive and politically incorrect today, but were widely used less than 20 years ago. Politically correct behaviors and language save people from embarrassing themselves, from making mistakes, or from conducting themselves in ways others would consider unethical.

Good Manners, Etiquette, and Civility

On a superficial level, the general use of good manners can make for a more pleasant workplace. But acting ethically almost demands that people treat each other in a civil fashion and with common courtesy. Good manners are a social lubricant. In workplaces where people are relatively polite, courteous, and respectful of each other (even when they don't like each other), the main goal of getting work done can be achieved with less friction. There is, therefore, a good practical reason for the exercise of good manners and following some norms of civility and proper workplace etiquette. Additionally, of course, employee morale is higher when everyone is treated with respect and courtesy.

Western Traditions and Judeo-Christian Values

Some used to talk about western civilization being an enlightened society, and in many ways it is. Contemporary laws in America are generally viewed as promoting human dignity and ethical behavior. Notwithstanding these realities, however, ethics, morality, religious teachings, and the law can be at odds with each other on the same question and occasionally even at the same time. The number of possible conflicting combinations can be mind-boggling, but it is important to remember that in a good society, ethics, morality, and the law tend to be supportive of each other and overlap even if they are not exactly congruent.

Western civilization has tended to be increasingly more respectful of the dignity of labor and the laboring class. This gradual evolution can be traced back to the religious roots of Abraham and his descendants. The idea of working hard has consistently been considered an ethical virtue. Throughout Jewish, Christian, and Islamic writings, the idea of being a responsible and economically contributing member of society has always been seen as the ethical and virtuous way to behave. Although it could be argued this is merely a practical matter, it is really more an endemic virtue in the Abrahamic religions. Christianity even provides examples, through certain monastic orders, where the religious must work to meet their commitment to their fundamental beliefs. Parallel behaviors can be found within Judaic and Islamic traditions. Gerald Cavanagh's book *American Business Values* reviews these religious traditions as well as other western philosophical and political influences.

Since different traditions exist in other cultures, managers in global corporations will need to become conscious of the unique nuances of managerial ethics as they arise under, for example, Confucian, Buddhist, and African traditions. Fortunately, articles have appeared in recent volumes of the *Business Ethics Quarterly* and the *Journal of Business Ethics* on practices in a variety of Middle Eastern, Asian, and Pacific Rim countries. There are also books that discuss both western and nonwestern perspectives including Paul Minus's *The Ethics of Business in a Global Economy*. An interesting array of paperbacks could be found at bookstores in 1999 on business and ethical analysis such as B. Krause's *The Way of the Leader: Applying the Principles of Sun Tzu and Confucius* and T. Morris's *If Aristotle Ran General Motors: The New Soul of Business*.

Gender Differences and Ethical Systems

New ethical systems emerged as the roles of men and women began to change in the twentieth century. Frequently, many societies and their economic and social systems were very unequal in how they viewed, treated, and valued men's and women's workplace roles and contributions. Therefore, workplace traditions that are based on older moral systems, religious beliefs, or social norms of good etiquette and civility may be bound by historically passé, gender-biased beliefs and values.

Late-twentieth-century contemporary thinking teaches that gender biases are generally inappropriate in the workplace. Of course, this doesn't mean biological differences between men and women cease to be acknowledged, but that gender-based differentials in compensation or job duties are no longer considered legal, ethical, or appropriate in most American communities. For most HR and labor relations purposes, it is no longer ethical to be concerned with the gender of the person lowering a motor into an automobile or taking a pulse in the hospital. Similarly, the gender of the head of accounting or the union president is irrelevant. However, some individuals, particularly males, who were raised under earlier standards or in other societies, may feel differently. Today's ethical standards will dictate that HR staff evaluate and treat employees solely on job abilities and not on the basis of gender, but understanding and handling any diversity of opinion within the workforce will be an important skill.

Conflicts at Work Regarding What Is and Is Not Ethical

Workplace conflicts can arise when groups have competing or incompatible philosophies, value systems, or moral beliefs. These might involve conflicts between a labor union and management. It is also possible for an employer to hold positions that are or seem to be incompatible or inconsistent with those held by their employees. Conflicts at work, however, can also exist within management, within labor, or within any group of employees.

Intergroup Conflicts

Intergroup conflicts in the workplace are quite common. Such conflicts occur in employment relations when there are inconsistencies between the ethical values or positions of the employer and those of the employees or their union. Positions can conflict, for example, over what is one person's deserved level of compensation, even though there are common interests in providing a quality good or service. These conflicts in core values, or in perceptions of reality, can run the gamut from mild insensitivity to seemingly absolute disregard for each other's needs and desires, and as a result, can challenge intergroup functioning. They can entail a vast array of conflicting values including how one defines what is ethically necessary as a living wage, what is necessary for safe and reasonably clean working conditions, or what is an adequate channel of communication between employees and the employer.

It is essential, therefore, that human resource management and labor and industry relations (LIR) policies be simultaneously responsive and perceived as based on core ethical concerns. Successful policies will promote economically profitable or taxpayer-conscious operations. They will convey honest statements of shared contributions to, and needs for, profitability and frugality to employees. Finally, they will demonstrate respect for the needs and rights of the employees to enjoy reasonable wages, benefits, and a working environment that is consistent with ethical expectations. For employers this requires developing and conveying work rules, policies, mission statements, and goals that incorporate a wealth of ethical concerns.

On the part of the employees and/or their union, it is necessary that they recognize that the business or government agency can remain viable over the long run only by being profitable or responsive to taxpayers. Employees must therefore realize that it is unreasonable and unrealistic to expect that all the profits and income, or taxes, can go to the employees without consideration for the managers, stockholders, owners, or citizens. It is incumbent upon employees to develop ethical positions that recognize the overall needs of the operations and not simply their own.

Intragroup Conflicts

Intragroup conflict arises when a group's members have serious internal disagreements. A workplace may include quite varied groups of employees who have different needs or hold different values. Members of a union, for example, may thus disagree among themselves on whether the focus of negotiations with the employer should be to seek shorter hours, higher overtime pay, better pensions, or childcare benefits. Similarly, a nonunion workforce that includes any age, gender, or racial diversity may be very divided on what benefits keep individuals from looking to move to other employers.

Conflicts can obviously also occur within management, such as between the finance, operations management, or HR departments. Even within the HR department, conflicts could arise over which benefits or programs should be offered to the employees, whether work rules or job classifications should be changed, or how much attention should be paid to employee safety versus firm profitability in any given year.

As with other conflicts, these internal disputes (within the workforce, employer, or union) can be settled by those holding power either by using brute force, economic or political persuasion, subterfuge, or other unethical approaches. Alternatively, attempts can be made to identify and consider the interests and well-being of the majority of stakeholders. Likewise, efforts can be made toward reaching a consensus.

Negotiated agreements that seem to benefit all involved may not, in fact, be in the best interest of the group, for an answer that proves satisfactory in the short run may set the groundwork for future conflict. Or, when one side is seen as the only winner, the other stakeholders may be inclined to look for ways to get even in the future. Such solutions may disrupt whatever goodwill the operation or group has created internally. Although one side may get more of what it wants, concern with ethics dictates ensuring that all sides are able to see themselves at least as partial winners and continuing as valued stakeholders in the entity.

STRATEGIC ISSUES IN WORKPLACE ETHICS

Many human resource management issues pose strategic ethical dilemmas for HR personnel, and it is a challenge to find a labor-management issue that does not include an ethical component. Some are very obvious, such as decisions that require choosing between individual and group rights. Individual employees who feel they have some-how not been treated fairly also require an ethics-based response. Other tasks including enforcing new HR policies or solving personality conflicts may require supervisors to respond to more subtle ethical dilemmas.

Today, worksite issues are often contentiously debated with both moral and legal arguments frequently advanced by all sides. For many workplace issues, one can reasonably identify different and overlapping rights of various stakeholders. These rights can be described as belonging to individual employees; to groups of employees, including a union; or to organizations, including employer rights. Employment issues involve such rights as those of life, health, and safety; to liberty, privacy, and freedom; and of property and the pursuit of happiness. Disagreements concerning these rights frequently range from the level of personal conflicts to major moral and ethical questions for entire organizations.

Selection and Promotion of Employees and Supervisors

Many HR professionals are involved in the selection of new employees and in the promotion of rank-and-file employees into supervisors. A variety of strategic issues involving ethical concerns are evident in these processes, and employees may question the ethical appropriateness of the standards that are employed in decision making as well as the resultant outcomes. Some of these strategic issues are addressed elsewhere in this module in the sections on information and privacy, punishment standards, and affirmative action. Other potential ethical concerns include the following strategic selection issues.

- What is listed in *job descriptions* as the necessary knowledge, skills, and requisite abilities of a position can involve unethical behavior regarding the completeness or accuracy of what is or is not listed. Additionally, whether or not good citizenship or collegiality is required, as it is by some employers, and how these qualities are measured, entails ethical questions that need to be addressed by HR professionals.

- One common ethical problem occurs when the HR department already has a candidate in mind and has *pre-selected* the eventual winner before writing the posting for the position. Such selection processes frequently are followed by discussions, entailing perceptions of breaches of ethical rights, among the rest of the workforce, and especially by those who desired to be, but were not, selected.

- The selection of supervisors, of course, involves the above issues, but an additional dilemma arises when you consider whether or not it is ethical to expect certain ethical values and skills of supervisor applicants. Some employers seek supervisors who are *caring persons* and evaluate applicants' courteousness, altruism, or good citizenship. Whether it is ethical to require such attributes, how they are measured, and whether such determinations are overly based (or biased) in the areas of gender, age, or ethnicity raise key business ethics concerns. Some also question the fairness of including such criteria in the selection process, rather than promoting these traits and skills in subsequent training.

Rights to Collect Information Versus Rights of Privacy

Employee expectations concerning their rights to privacy while at work, and/or sometimes even in their private lives, have come into more conflict with employer practices in recent years. Many employers are collecting an ever wider set of both pre-employment and workplace data, and therefore strategic issues involving potential ethical conflicts with employees occur in a variety of ways.

- Employees in certain industries or in safety- or health-sensitive positions are frequently monitored for *drug and alcohol use.* Ethical debate arises over how much of the workforce is monitored and the frequency and intrusiveness of the monitoring performed. Also of concern is whether testing is only for cause or is done randomly, thereby including employees whose job performance has not shown any deficiency. Ethics not only is involved in the testing decisions but also plays a role in the management of the results. HR policies on confidentiality, use of results, and whether or not employee assistance programs will be provided to those who fail the tests certainly also entail key ethical choices.

- Many employers collect a significant set of data concerning their employees' *personal lives and work performance.* Many new employees are screened for a wide variety of dexterity and communication skills and to identify certain personality indicators. For many individuals these HR practices raise moral questions concerning the fairness of the employer's collection and use of such personal information. And there are legal implications involving the sharing of such information with third parties, such as insurance companies, and concerning the employee's own rights of access.

- Employer monitoring of employees' activities at the workplace, including *computer performance monitoring, electronic eavesdropping* of telephone calls, and *video camera surveillance,* saw increasing use in the late twentieth century. These employer practices can exacerbate the potential ethical conflict between the opposing stakeholder rights of employees to privacy and to control personal information as positioned against the employer's right to control their property and to monitor employee work activities.

Income Differentials within Workplaces and in Society

The ethics of income levels became a more frequently discussed topic in the waning years of the twentieth century. Partly it occurred as very high incomes of chief executive officers (CEOs) and celebrities became more widely known. Also, the seeming growth of the differentials between groups of Americans in the late 1990s spurred more commentary on pay incongruencies. And with such discussion came a renewed concern whether the huge sums themselves or the differentials they caused were unfair or even immoral. Furthermore, for many American employees and employers, the relationship of income to efforts, education levels, and other measures of skills and abilities also continued to raise substantial strategic issues involving moral and ethical concerns.

- Many HR professionals have to construct or modify employer *compensation and pay structures,* so they have to respond to employees' concerns and perceptions of the ethical fairness, or not, of these internal employer pay structures. In both union and nonunion workplaces, compensation differentials within the workplace that occur between seemingly similarly situated employees are often a key point of employment conflict. Tension can be generated over a variety of concerns in addition to those involving allegations of illegal discrimination based on race, ethnicity, or gender differences. These ethical debates can entail disputes of fact, interpretation of wage rules, concerns on the overall extent or fairness of differentials, or the relationship of compensation to one's proven or supposed level of effort, education level, or other measures of skills and abilities. Frequently, the disputes will be based mostly on differences in ethical perspectives of what is, for example, "a fair day's wage for a fair day's work."

- *Gender-related differentials* in levels of pay and benefits persist as an inequality in many American communities and workplaces. The average compensation earned by those working in jobs and industries predominately employing males is substantially higher than in those dominated by females. Various related issues of comparable pay for comparable work have remained relatively unaddressed. These gender differentials have generally remained rather constant in the last half of the twentieth century in the United States, even following the 1963 Equal Pay Act and subsequent federal and state equal employment and nondiscrimination court decisions and agency actions. Similar issues can be raised regarding racial differentials.

- Tremendous gaps are also evident regarding the difference between what the average American CEO receives in *compensation* and what is paid the average worker. According to the AFL-CIO's executive paywatch project, this differential widened from a difference of 44 times in 1965 to a difference of 326 times by 1997. They noted in 1998 that the compensation received by the average U.S. CEO was 728 times that of Americans earning a *minimum wage*. The paywatch project also noted that the differential was considerably wider in the United States than in the rest of the industrialized world.

- In the late 1990s, some union and religious leaders began advocating for passage of *living wage* ordinances in cities and counties. These stipulate that no citizen should earn less compensation than what is needed for a decent standard of living within that community. Such ordinances may provide, for example, that employers who contract with the city pay no less than an amount that may be up to twice the legal minimum wage. There certainly are a variety of ethical perspectives that can be cited to debate the passage of such ordinances, and of course not everyone agrees on the ethics of minimum wage legislation itself.

Punishments, Progressivity, and "Just Cause" in Discipline Cases

For many employees, their fundamental sense of whether their workplace operates in an ethical fashion, and whether it is or is not a just workplace derives from how punishment is handled. Certainly the following strategic issues can arise in a wide variety of workplaces, and these disciplinary issues require HR professionals to think about ethical considerations.

- Employee evaluation of the overall fairness of their workplace is certainly influenced by their personal experience and knowledge about the *extent of discipline*. For many, this involves discipline that they receive—and what they know about what their coworkers and supervisors receive—for inappropriate behaviors or for failures to achieve at some performance standard. But it is also deeply influenced by their evaluation of the *procedural justice* involved in punishment incidents. Perceptions of arbitrariness, limited personal input, inequality between employees, etc., are all involved in these evaluations regarding discipline of oneself and of others. Many workplaces use *progressive, corrective discipline* systems, but some do so unevenly or in name only, which may make them appear as unethical as entirely autocratic places of employment.

- *Just cause standards* are deeply entwined in the variety of definitions Americans use to determine their sense of what's ethical, what's fair, what's legal, and what's just good practice or good manners. The handling of discipline and discharge cases in the grievance and arbitration procedure in most unionized, and increasingly in many late-twentieth-century nonunion workplaces involves just cause standards. These commonly include issues of proper notice, the clarity and appropriateness of rules and orders, the completeness and fairness of investigations, the eventual extent of discipline used and its relationship to one's seniority, work, and discipline record, and how other similarly situated individuals have been treated.

- In the 1990s, there occurred a growing breakdown of an absolute employer right, in nonunion workplaces, to a consistent *employment-at-will* standard across the United States. This happened slowly and unevenly as clear employer rights to hire and fire at will were set aside by some judges in wrongful discharge litigation. Some decisions were based on ethical considerations, including employers not following the tests of just cause standards, noted above. Often they entailed legal issues including violations by employers of whistleblower statutes.

Occupational Health and Safety

Workplace health and safety has a long and rich ethical history. However, it didn't enter the employee rights legal arena in the United States until the early 1900s, after the passage of state workers' compensation statutes—which hold employers liable for work-related injuries and illness—and later, in 1970, with passage of the Occupational Safety and Health Act (OSHA). Since its passage, OSHA has raised numerous moral and legal ethical concerns that pose strategic challenges for HR professionals.

- Since their passage, the state *workers' compensation* acts have often been legislatively revised, due in part to litigated cases in which legal arguments often arise out of ethical debates. For example, allegations concerning the honesty of employee claims have often been the central complaint of employers, particularly in unobvious employment-caused cases such as back injuries and chronic illnesses like asbestos-exposure lung cancers. Alternatively, employees often state that their employer was unfairly blaming accidents on employee behaviors rather than on faulty equipment and inadequate safety training.

- Under OSHA's *general duty clause,* employees are to be provided a workplace "free from known hazards," and it is the employer's responsibility to "assure as far as possible every man and woman . . . safe and healthy working conditions." Ethical problems arise regarding OSHA and court standards concerning whether a particular individual employer must be aware of, or if only some employers within an affected industry must know, whether it is subjecting employees to such hazards. Ethical choices are also involved in how one should define "as far as possible" before OSHA will cite an employer, force a correction, or level a fine for noncompliance.

- A related ethical dilemma concerns the use of *cost-benefit analysis* regarding employee safety rights. OSHA and state plans only create, and the courts only allow, new standards, or the vigorous enforcement of current ones, depending on shifting economic and political considerations. Ethical concerns are deeply involved in the determination of what level of safety is required. This involves an assessment of how strongly standards or enforcement should protect a given number of individuals, as compared to how much cost should be borne by individual employers, by an industry, or by society in the event that job losses result immediately or over time. In the records concerning the creation of some standards, and in employer appeals of large citations and fines, one learns the dollar amounts that were placed on the value of one or more human lives or limbs, which some find ethically chilling to contemplate.

- OSHA standards are generally written to cover all affected employees subject to a safety hazard, and certainly without regard to employee characteristics. All hazards, however, do not affect all employees identically. Some major problems arise concerning protecting workers from chemicals that have differential *reproductive hazard* capabilities. Lead, for example, poses a potentially severe hazard to unborn children who are exposed while in utero. In *Auto Workers v. Johnson Controls,* the Supreme Court ruled, however, that it was illegal for an employer to prohibit women of child-bearing capability from working in battery plant jobs involving lead exposure, because the policy "explicitly discriminates against women on the basis of their sex." The decision did not completely answer, though, the employer's concern about whether fully informing women employees of the lead exposure risks, while they were pregnant, would shield the employer from potential liability in a suit filed by a deformed child. Furthermore, the legal decision does not really address the ethical dilemma experienced by the employer concerned with promoting both health and equal opportunity.

Employee Involvement and Quality of Worklife Enhancement

In American union and nonunion settings, efforts to enhance employees' quality of worklife and involvement in workplace decision making, along with improving production quality and productivity, have been widely experimented with since the 1970s. There were interesting historical examples during both world wars and in the 1920s, but the extent of such programs has been recently spreading much more widely than ever before.

Under a variety of titles, popular employee-management cooperation initiatives, including both fads and enduring programs, have spread, including quality circles, TQM and continuous quality improvement, and off- and online work teams. These efforts have led to a variety of related group bonus and gain-sharing plans, cross-training and multiskilling efforts, reductions in job classifications, and the elimination of so-called restrictive union work rules and practices.

These employee- (and/or union)-management cooperation efforts have been instituted for a variety of purposes including productivity, profit, and employee skills enhancement. These programs and benefits can interestingly raise new ethical issues. Such questions include how widely shared, or long-lasting, any cost savings or other improvements will be, and whether or not downsizing the workforce might be one result. Also, there have been ethical questions raised regarding the use of such programs as a mechanism to keep unions out of workplaces or to otherwise reduce their importance to employees.

MODULE
27

Labor-Management Relations

A variety of late-twentieth-century labor-management relations debates clearly highlights strategic issues that involve conflicts in ethical perspectives, in terms of morality, legality, and even good manners.

- In the 1990s, some scholars and practitioners questioned whether or not American workers could form and join unions, and still have a *right to unionize* in actual practice. Many experts argued that employees could no longer freely choose to unionize without discrimination and potential dismissal by those employers who strongly desired to remain nonunion. Also, there is an ancillary issue involving whether it's fair for unions, morally or legally—and the National Labor Relations Board (NLRB) in the late 1990s said it is generally okay—to plant "salts" at nonunion worksites. These new hires often try to induce employers to get caught violating the law so that these firms eventually are organized or lose market share to unionized competitors.

- *Union rights,* or not, *to collect dues and service fees,* in contrast to a *union's duty of fair representation,* include several ethical issues.

  ✓ States have a right, under section 14(b) of the federal Labor Management Relations Act (LMRA), to prohibit the negotiation by unions of any compulsory dues or representation fees from workers. This was the case in 21 *"right-to-work"* states as of 1998, even though unions were legally responsible, throughout all 50 states, to represent all bargaining-unit employees, including these "free riders," fairly and completely regardless of their union membership status.

✓ The right, or not, of unions to use moneys collected from members and non-member service fee payers, for purposes other than those deemed germane to collective bargaining, contract administration, and grievance handling, became an area of ethical conflict, growing litigation, and legislative battle. In the late twentieth century, American unions could no longer use such fees in politics, organizing, community services, and other nonbargaining activities. This occurs if a worker objects to an incident or set of circumstances and the complaint is upheld by a labor board or a court, following the *"Beck rights"* precedent, or subsequent to a "paycheck protection" law or ordinance.

● Union and employee *rights to conduct strikes,* in actual practice, without the loss of the union's presence or the loss of employee jobs to permanent replacement workers, also became a contested terrain involving conflicting ethical perspectives. Given many U.S. employers' seemingly unlimited willingness to endure strikes, lockouts, bad press, and lawsuits for not bargaining in good faith, the legal right to strike took on a very limited if not bizarre meaning. This was especially evident given the late 1990s state of the law and the time delays that legal appeals permitted. The over-four-year-long *Detroit Newspaper Agency v. NLRB* case of the late 1990s certainly brought into sharp focus whether workers still had a legal right to strike. And there was an obvious conflict between American LIR practices of the late twentieth century and what is stated in key ethics documents on the topic. It is very interesting in light of recent events to look again at the Catholic Church's 1891 papal Encyclical Letter *Rerum Novarum* and other North American churches' statements of support of workers' rights to form and join unions and to go on strike when necessary.

MODULE
27

● The *collective bargaining process* itself also entails interesting ethical aspects.

✓ *Traditional labor and management negotiations* are often described as adversarial and typically involve a series of customs that may raise ethical concerns. Potential ethical problems arise in the use of extreme opening positions that are knowingly not truthful representations of a party's real interests. Or one might question the ethics of using complete secrecy and intentionally misleading the other party by concealing information from them. And of some concern is the reliance only on one's own power rather than on finding solutions to problems that might be knowingly in the best interests of both parties.

✓ *Interest-based* (win-win styles of) *bargaining,* which became more popular in the late twentieth century, features openness, participation in problem-solving activities, and building trust amongst the parties. These processes often emphasize the shared interests of the parties; this is obviously based on different assumptions than is adversarial bargaining. Although interest-based bargaining may therefore lead to positive feelings of cooperation and even superior negotiation outcomes, occasionally unions have accused employers of promoting win-win bargaining to weaken the union side and the relationship of the leaders to members. If such is true, it raises important ethical concerns. And if such experiments in new negotiation styles fail, the eventual outcome may be an increased cynicism on the part of union leaders or members, and the return to even more overt adversarial behaviors and focus by the parties.

Affirmative Action Programs Versus Seniority and Other Systems

The use of affirmative action programs for hiring, in granting promotions, and in handling layoffs and recalls may raise potential ethical questions and strategic dilemmas in any workplace. This certainly is true in unionized places of employment where other measures and rewards of ability or merit, or provision of promotions or benefits on the basis of seniority accrued with an employer or in a job, have long been used.

- Ethical concerns can arise in any workplace over the *use of affirmative action* measures, which include consideration of employee race or gender in making hiring, promotion, or layoff and recall decisions. In ideal workplaces perhaps there should be no need for affirmative action since all employees would be treated fairly regardless of any nonperformance-related factors. If hiring and promotion decisions had been made consistently on the basis of merit or seniority, and there had been no past history of unfair practices, then affirmative action remedies may not have developed. Instead, mere tabulation of seniority, or time in grade, or any merit-based hiring or promotional method that did not treat a class of employees unfairly, might be considered as good as another for the purpose of ethical evaluation. (However, it might be differentially evaluated depending on how one values seniority or evaluates the fairness and completeness of the merit evaluation system in use.) In the real mid-twentieth century U.S. society, however, there were both past and continuing racial and gender discrimination problems to address. Many industries and workplaces had a very long history of unfair employment practices: they did not hire particular groups of employees, or they used promotion systems that favored only some. Therefore, affirmative action programs grew to address these instances of past discrimination that, regardless of intent, were deemed immoral and eventually illegal. But the affirmative action solutions themselves have since raised for some Americans, including the courts, new ethical concerns. Complaints and lawsuits over so-called reverse discrimination, hiring and promotion quotas, and disagreement regarding who should pay for rectifying past discriminatory treatment have grown more commonplace, so new directions in the law may someday develop.

- In unionized workplaces there may be conflict between the use of affirmative action decision making, based on race, ethnicity, or gender considerations, and a *collective bargaining agreement's seniority principle.* Conversely, negotiated practices for evaluating merit and skills and for making promotions or handling layoffs and recalls may come into conflict with affirmative action practices. These instances have involved ethical questions of morality, legality, good manners, and civility as noted above.

Workforce Reductions Versus Job Creation Efforts

During the 1980s and 1990s there existed both workplace and community concern, and sometimes conflict, involving job security and workforce redundancies. This has resulted from the reorganization of corporations, supposedly necessitated by the arrival of the global economy, new technologies, and new levels of competition, and of the privatization of public-sector government agencies. In many of these situations, employers, unions, and employees have described their evaluation of the events in ethically charged language, usually inspired by the resultant workforce reductions. Both the decisions to reorganize and/or downsize and the mechanisms used to announce such changes pose strategic challenges to the HR professional.

- *Labor-management conflict* over workforce redundancies has occurred in several industries, including in U.S. automobile manufacturing. During the 1998 United Auto Workers strike, for example, the issue of the fairness of job reductions in the Flint, Michigan, area was frequently discussed. The GM workforce at Flint, which once had been over 75,000, had been reduced to approximately 35,000. The 54-day strike was partially over the union's attempt to halt a rumored 50 percent further reduction in employment. The strike was settled only when the company agreed to keep some of the plants open longer than GM originally stated was in their stockholders' best interests.

- Other examples of *plant closings* and workforce reductions abound in the so-called U.S. rust-belt. Numerous union and nonunion manufacturing firms have been able to downsize employment levels thanks to new robotic, computer, and communications technologies, lean production techniques, and due to global production over-capacity. Since the 1970s, plant closings have engendered heated ethical discussion regarding what exactly a firm owed to the workforce, or to the community that had provided tax abatements or other economic benefits and where the company had been a long-standing presence. Frequently one read of the conflicting ethical claims regarding the rights of the employees to their jobs and the communities to their livelihoods, in contrast to the responsibilities of the firms to their stockholders and customers.

- Although obviously somewhat different, the 1990s reductions in the size of public-sector workforces often entailed many of the same tensions. When the elimination of jobs resulted from the *privatization* of some services, which had long been government provided, the level of complaint over unethical employer behavior was often similarly intense. This was especially true where there were allegations that the new private-sector provider of the service had some special or personal relationship with an elected official or civil servant who was involved in the privatization decision.

- In both private and public sectors, and in union and nonunion situations, some HR departments have responded to the costs of creating leaner operations by advancing *humane downsizing policies*. Recognizing the human costs of closing aging facilities or ending government provision of services, some employers, communities, and unions have supported the use of attrition-only reductions of employment levels, and the provision of early retirement enhancement programs and/or severance pay. In addition, various employers have implemented employee retraining efforts ranging from extensive college tuition payment programs to simple resume-writing assistance. In a different direction, some employers and unions have negotiated contract language and joint programs attempting to secure some new products or processes so as to ensure higher future employment levels. One unfortunately unique story concerned the response of Malden Mills to a completely devastating fire in the mid-1990s. Many expected the firm's owner would simply decide to cash in on his insurance coverage and never reopen his burnt Massachusetts' plant. Instead, he invested a substantial sum of money to rebuild, stating his sense of responsibility to his long-term employees and to the community.

- Some interesting *labor-management-community efforts at job creation* and in job retention were used across America in the 1990s. Often a community, sometimes along with its state, offered a firm a tax abatement plan or a utility or other money-saving cost reductions as an inducement not to shut down operations. Meanwhile, or in concert, the union offered some contract concessions in terms of lower wages, benefits, or significant work rule changes, such as job classification reductions, to keep a company in the area. Sometimes rather elaborate publicity campaigns were also conducted to promote corporate job creation and retention.

- Other efforts have involved the use of *employee stock ownership plans* (ESOP) that entail interesting twists in business ethics. Louis Kelso, often called the father of ESOPs, promoted them extensively as a means of making workers into capitalists and involving them in decision making. ESOPs frequently have been used to save failing facilities or even entire companies, and several states have been involved in promoting these efforts.

APPLICATIONS

The following applications are based on the core concepts and the above discussion concerning the strategic ethical concerns facing the HR and LIR professional. They have been designed to help you better understand the variety of ethical considerations presented throughout this module.

Application 1: Light Versus Regular Duty Work

The Americans with Disabilities Act (ADA) brought to the forefront the needs of employees with various types of potential work restrictions and limitations. The ADA requires employers to provide "reasonable accommodations" for their employees who have certain types of handicaps or limitations that could be addressed within the context of the workplace. Profitability remains a legitimate employer concern, though, and the ADA has been interpreted so as to protect the ability of the employing firm to accommodate individual employee needs while at the same time being able to remain profitable and not encounter undue economic hardship. It does not, however, explain how all resultant ethical dilemmas should be addressed.

There are at least three or four—and if the employees are union, five—different perspectives from which one might view the ethical dimensions entailed in one of the potential ADA conflicts. This dilemma involves the implications of assigning someone to perform light duty—versus regular duty—work which displaces a current employee from a regular job. First, one must consider the employee who is no longer able to perform at the level that had been possible in the past due to a job-related injury. The employer, following its interpretation of its ADA responsibility, places the employee who was injured on the job on an easier and lighter duty assignment. Second, the employer must consider the interests of the employee who will be displaced by the first person. This second employee is being reassigned to a currently open but more physically difficult and lower-paying job at the firm. The third perspective is that of the HR department, which has the responsibility to enforce the law, to serve as a mediator, and to try to find a reasonable and fair answer to the dilemma. Another perspective would be that of the immediate supervisors, and a union could also be involved.

Questions for Group Discussion

1.   What is a fair solution to this ethical dilemma?

2.   Does the injured employee have a special ethical claim because it was a workplace-caused event?

3.   Does the displaced employee have an ethical right to any special redress since he or she was not the cause of the problem?

4.   Do either of the employees' supervisors, in addition to the HR department, have a special role in addressing the question?

5.   Would it matter if the workplace was unionized or not?

6.   Are there other stakeholders, perspectives, or issues that must be taken into account?

MODULE
27

Application 2: Work/Family Conflicts

In the late twentieth century, human resources staff and managers, workers and their families, and helping professionals such as social workers and psychologists became interested in how firms and their workforces handle the imbalances and conflicts of work versus family responsibilities. Various ethical and practical problems arise for these employees, for their supervisors, and for HR departments interested in addressing child- and eldercare, parental and family leave problems, as well as related issues involving work reorganization and overtime demands. Whether or not proposed solutions like work sharing or relaxed FMLA leave usage solve these dilemmas or just serve to ensure better attendance and minimize intrusions of family concerns at work involves ethical and legal considerations.

Study the questions listed below and try to consider the panorama of corporate, helping professional, HR, and employee stakeholder perspectives. Think about some of the conflicts and common concerns related to work/family responsibility dilemmas. Be prepared to brainstorm some potential visions for solving the problems of juggling work, family, and personal spheres from the varied perspectives.

Questions for Group Discussion

1. What conflicts regarding work/family responsibilities are most likely to be manifest and/or be discussed at the workplace?

2. What are the major concerns that one might hear expressed by each of the key stakeholders who have an interest in how work-family conflicts are addressed by employers?

   - Employees
   - Their families
   - Supervisors
   - HR department
   - Union, if any
   - Helping professionals

3. What are the likely ethical positions (i.e., moral or legal arguments) one might expect to hear expressed by each of these stakeholders?

4. What potential solutions or experimental programs could be created to address some of these conflicts?

In Conclusion

Debrief

Ethics is clearly an important element of human resource management and labor and industrial relations best practices, both for the present and in the emerging millennium. Those in HR/LIR leadership positions, and in supporting academic communities, will find it essential to be sensitive to conflicting definitions of what is ethical, and of the expanding role and significance of business, managerial, and labor relations ethics.

The future will require of HR professionals an even more heightened awareness of the diversity of opinions on what constitutes ethical and unethical practices within the workplace across a shrinking globe. This module should help students be more aware of some of the variety of ethical issues related to work and the workplace.

Addressing and solving dilemmas based on many of these concerns may seem quite obvious and easy. Racial, ethnic, gender, and religious prejudices, and unfair or unequal treatment of individuals for arbitrary or capricious reasons will likely remain unacceptable at most American workplaces. How to ethically adapt to the variability of human abilities, personalities, and individuality, however, may prove more challenging. What levels of personal attributes or out-of-work activities are within acceptable limits for an employer to expect of its employees, what is actually acceptable individual behavior in relation to business necessity, and what constitutes ethical respect for each other's human dignity will become more complex considerations in a global economy.

The examples provided above have hopefully illustrated some of the key ethical dilemmas of work and workplaces. In the business world, issues are often complex, and there are times when they seem so complicated that it is not immediately easy to see exactly in which direction proper ethical behavior lies. However, many of the most serious potential ethical pitfalls may be preventable simply by paying attention to the ethical implications of one's actions. Recognizing the importance of giving a role to ethical analysis in relation to workplace decision making and giving careful analysis to issues under discussion, prudent individuals will often find they can develop an ethically responsible answer to many workplace problems. And perhaps their decisions will be better. Or at least they may sleep better at night.

Suggested Readings

Cavanagh, Gerald. *American Business Values,* Third Edition. Englewood Cliffs, NJ: Prentice-Hall, 1990.

Cunningham, W. Patrick. "The Golden Rule as a Universal Ethical Norm," *Journal of Business Ethics,* n17: 105–109, 1998.

Dalla Costa, John. *The Ethical Imperative: Why Moral Leadership Is Good Business,* Reading, MA: Perseus Press, 1998.

Driscoll, Dawn-Marie and W. Michael Hoffman. "HR Plays a Central Role in Ethics Programs," *Workforce,* v77, n4: 121–123, 1998.

Dunfee, Thomas W. and Patricia Werhane. "Report on Business Ethics in North America," *Journal of Business Ethics,* n16: 1589–1595, 1997.

Minus, Paul (ed.). *The Ethics of Business in a Global Economy,* Amsterdam: Kluwer Academic Publishers, 1993.

Mishra, Aneil K. and Gretchen M. Spreitzer. "Explaining How Survivors Respond to Downsizing: The Role of Trust, Empowerment, Justice and Work Redesign," *Academy of Management Review,* v23, n3: 567–588, 1998.

Schminke, Marshall (ed.). *Managerial Ethics: Moral Management of People and Processes,* Hillsdale, NJ: Laurence Erlbaum Associates, 1998.

Solomon, Robert C. *It's Good Business: Ethics and Free Enterprise for the New Millennium,* Lanham, MD: Rowman & Littlefield, 1997.

Critical Thinking Questions

1. What sort of differences would you expect to see expressed between an employee and employer if between them

    - there was agreement on basic ethical questions?

    - there was not agreement on basic ethical questions?

2. What role might good manners play in the relationship between employees and between employers and employees?

3. How does the history of the relationship between workplace stakeholders affect the ethical perspectives that are adopted by these various parties?

4. What concrete emotions and behaviors might HR professionals experience when they know that they, or their employer, have done something ethically wrong?

5. What practical rules might be written that could assist employees and employers to judge whether or not they were engaging in ethical thinking concerning workplace issues?

6. What educational points might be emphasized in training aimed to upgrade the ethical behaviors of the varied stakeholders in the workplace?

Exercises

1. Visit the library and check out *Rerum Novarum,* the 1891 Encyclical Letter of Pope Leo XIII on the Condition of Labor (or Pope Pius XI's *Quadragesimo Anno* of 1931). Briefly look at how they addressed the rights and responsibilities of workers and owners regarding each other, unions, strikes, private property, just wages, or economic harmony. Consider whether or not any of the ideas and advice is relevant to HR professionals for analyzing contemporary strategic issues in business ethics.

2. Consult HR and LIR web sites and serial publications that discuss recent agency and court decisions. One can link to numerous excellent sites (such as the NLRB's or Runkel's Memos) from the Michigan State University LIR Library's web page at *http://www.lir.msu.edu/.* And one can profitably look at, for example, Bureau of National Affairs' *Bulletin to Management* and *Fair Employment Practices* publications. Study some of the full decisions, or the summaries, on varied topics such as religious discrimination, reasonable accommodation, good faith bargaining, or sexual harassment. Consider what ethical arguments, in addition to legal ones, might be offered for each side of these employment disputes. Consider whether an HR professional could have helped mediate any of the disputes instead of seeing them go to litigation.

3. *Classroom debate:* Be it resolved that concern with ethical considerations within the context of employment relations can be more of a hindrance than an asset for meeting the needs of various workplace stakeholders.

   Instructions: To conduct the debate, two teams of three or four students should be chosen and expected to take approximately two hours of nonclass time in preparation. After the teams have been chosen, a one-week delay in preparation would be reasonable. Each side, one pro and one con, should have its members make a basic three-minute presentation. After these presentations, the balance of the debate, following traditional rules, should take approximately 30 minutes, followed by one representative from each team being permitted a maximum five-minute period for closing remarks.

References

Tomlinson, Tom. "What Is Ethics" and "How Are Ethical Problems Solved." *Nursing Ethics.* Western Schools, 1993. The author paralleled some of Dr. Tomlinson's ideas for the present work in the section titled Ethics, Morals, and Philosophy.

Index

Adversarial labor-management relations, 27.15

Affirmative action programs, ethical concerns, 27.16

AFL-CIO's paywatch project, 27.12

Americans with Disabilities Act (ADA), 27.18

Autonomy, rights of, 27.4

Bargaining-unit employees, 27.15

Beck rights precedent, 27.15

Business ethics. *See* Workplace ethics

Caring supervisors, 27.10

CEO compensation, 27.12

Christianity and ethics, 27.7–8

Collective bargaining, ethical aspects, 27.15–16

Compensation and pay structures, 27.11

Conventional wisdom, 27.6

Cost-benefit analysis, ethical dilemma, 27.13

Disciplinary issues, ethics of, 27.12

Discrimination, unfair employment practices, 27.16

Downsizing, humane policies, 27.17

Drug and alcohol testing, ethics of, 27.11

Duty of fair representation, union's, 27.14

Employee stock ownership plans (ESOPs), 27.17–18

Employee-management cooperation initiatives, 27.14

Employment relations, 27.4, 27.6, 27.8, 27.11

Employment-at-will standard, 27.13

Employment-caused injuries/illnesses, 27.13

Enforcement (OSHA), ethics of, 27.13

Equal employment opportunity (EEO), 27.5

Ethical dilemmas, 27.6, 27.8, 27.10–11

Ethical evaluation, 27.16

Ethical imperative, 27.7

Ethics of monitoring employee activities, 27.11

Ethics vs. law, 27.7

Ethics/ethical perspectives, 27.4–7. *See also* Law and legality, Morality

Fair pay-for-work relationship, 27.11–12

Fairness, legal standards of, 27.4, 27.11–12

Family and Medical Leave Act (FMLA), 27.5, 27.19

Free riders, right-to-work, 27.15

Gender and workplace ethics, 27.8, 27.11

General duty clause, 27.13

Global economy, 27.20

Good manners, etiquette, and civility, 27.7, 27.14

Grade (pay), ethical concerns, 27.16

Grievance and arbitration procedure, 27.12

Hazard to unborn children, 27.13–14

Hiring, ethical concerns, 27.16

HR department dilemmas, 27.9–10

Human dignity and ethical behavior (Western traditions), 27.7, 27.20

Human resource functions, ethical perspectives, 27.5

Human resource management, 27.4, 27.9

Human resource professional, 27.4–5, 27.12, 27.16

Human resource role, 27.4

Humane downsizing policies, 27.17

Income differentials, 27.11–12

Incompatible value systems, 27.8

Information collection vs. rights of privacy, 27.10

Interest-based bargaining, 27.6, 27.15

Intergroup conflicts, 27.8–9

Internal consistency, 27.6

Internal disputes (ethical), 27.9

Intragroup conflicts, 27.9

Job creation/job retention efforts, 27.17

Job descriptions, ethical concerns, 27.10

Job security, workforce reductions, 27.16

Judeo-Christian values, 27.7–8

Just cause standards, 27.12–13

Labor and industry relations (LIR), 27.9, 27.15, 27.18, 27.19

Labor Management Relations Act (LMRA), 27.14–15

Law and legality of workforce ethics, 27.6–8, 27.14. *See also* Ethics/ethical perspectives, Workplace ethics

Layoffs, ethical concerns, 27.16

Light duty assignment, 27.18

Living wage ethics, 27.12

Malden Mills, 27.17

Managing human resources. *See* Human resource management

Merit (promotions), 27.16

Merit-based hiring, ethical concerns, 27.16

Monitoring employee activities, ethics of, 27.11

Moral imperative, 27.7

Morality, 27.6, 27.11–12. *See also* Ethics, Workplace ethics

National Labor Relations Board (NLRB), 27.14, 27.15

Negotiated agreements, 27.9

Nonunion workplaces, 27.13

Notification (FMLA), 27.5

Occupational health and safety, ethical concerns, 27.13
Occupational Safety and Health Act (OSHA), 27.5, 27.13–14
OSHA standards, 27.13–14

Pay-work relationship, 27.11–12
Paycheck protection law, 27.15
Paywatch project, 27.12
Personal information collection, 27.10–11
Plant closings, 27.17
Political correctness, 27.7
Pre-selected candidate, 27.10
Private-sector workforce, 27.16–17
Privatization, 27.17
Procedural justice, 27.12
Profitability and ethics, 27.6, 27.18
Progressive, corrective discipline systems, 27.12
Promotions, 27.10
Promotions, ethical concerns, 27.16
Public opinion, 27.6. *See also* Ethics/ethical perspectives
Public-sector workforce, 27.16–17

Quality of worklife, ethical issues, 27.14

Reasonable accommodations (ADA), 27.18
Reductions, workforce. *See* Workforce reductions
Religion vs. ethics, 27.7, 27.12
Reproductive hazards, 27.13–14
Reverse discrimination, 27.16
Right of privacy, 27.5, 27.10
Right to strike, 27.15

Right to unionize, 27.14
Right-to-work states, 27.15
Rights (overlapping), 27.10

Seniority, 27.12, 27.16
Standards, ethical, 27.10
Strikes, rights to conduct, 27.15

Traditional negotiations, 27.15
Traditional values, 27.7–8
Transaction roles, 27.4
Transformation activities, 27.5
Transition activities, 27.5
Translation roles, 27.5

Unilateral employer control, 27.5, 27.6
Union members, 27.9, 27.15
Union rights, 27.14–15
Union-out mechanisms, 27.14
Unionize, right to, 27.14
Unionized workplaces, ethical concerns, 27.16
Unions, workers' rights to form and join, 27.15

Win-win bargaining, *See* Interest-based bargaining
Work/family balance, 27.5, 27.19
Workers' compensation, 27.13
Workers' rights to form and join unions, 27.15
Workforce reductions, 27.16–17
Working environment, 27.9
Workplace ethics, 27.4, 27.6, 27.8
    dilemmas, 27.9, 27.20
    disciplinary issues, 27.9
Wrongful discharge litigation, 27.13

MODULE
27

General Index

ABCs (learning objectives), 19.16
Ability, 13.11, 13.12
Ability domain, 14.15
Ability tests, 13.8, 13.13, 14.15. *See also* Job-specific task performance; Work sample text
Ability to adapt, 4.9
Absenteeism, 7.7, 7.8, 11.13
Abusive environment. *See* Hostile environment
Access-legitimacy paradigm, 9.10–11. *See also* Diversity paradigms
Accident causation theories, 23.7
Accident-proneness theory, 23.7
Accounting/operational results measures, 17.15–16
Accrued paid leave, 10.12
Acquired firm, 5.6
Acquisition, 5.4–7, 5.14
Acquisition target, 5.8
Acquisition team, 5.17–18
Action learning, 19.5, 19.27
Action research phases, 17.13. *See also* Group incentives, deployment strategies
Active state support (employment relations), 26.8
Active-static dimension, 20.18
Activity stream (analysis), 2.12, 2.13, 2.15
Adaptability
    as performance criterion, 14.12–13, 14.16
    of employees, 14.5
    predictors of, 14.13
Adaptation (integration), 5.9
Adaptive orientation, 25.15
ADDIE model, 19.10–13, 19.24, 19.29. *See also* ISD model
Adding value, 2.14, 2.15, 3.6, 3.8, 3.9, 3.17–18, 3.29, 3.30
Additional benefits, 18.10, 18.15, 18.17, 18.18
Administering FMLA, 10.12–13
Administration, pay systems, 16.8, 16.20
Administrative efficiency, 4.12
Administrative roles (HR), 3.19, 3.34
Adoption benefits, 18.17
Adult learning, 19.5, 19.8, 19.14–15
Advance notice (FMLA), 10.11
Adversarial labor-management relations, 1.12, 1.18, 27.15
Adversarial (mergers), 5.8–9

Adversarialism. *See* Institutionalized adversarialism
Adverse impact, 14.5, 14.6, 14.9, 14.10, 14.15
    evaluating selection methods, 13.22
Affective learning, 19.16
Affirmative action (AA), 8.5, 8.13, 9.4, 9.7, 9.9, 9.10
Affirmative action programs, ethical concerns, 27.16
AFL-CIO's paywatch project, 27.12
Aligning individual and corporate objectives, 4.8, 4.11, 4.13
Altered mental model, 4.20
Alternative employment arrangements. *See* Contingent work arrangements
Alternative futures (plausible), 4.19, 4.21, 4.22, 4.23, 4.24
Alternative learning, 20.15, 20.18
Ambiguity of negotiations, 5.8
American National Standards Institute (ANSI), 23.13
American Society for Training and Development (ASTD), 19.4, 19.6, 19.28
Americans with Disabilities Act (ADA), 10.4, 12.12, 27.18
Analysis, ISD model, 19.10
Annual payoff, 17.8
Anonymity of cyberspace, 20.10, 20.17
Antagonizing, 22.8, 22.10
Applicant flow data, evaluating the recruitment process, 13.19–20
Applicant pool, 13.7, 13.8, 13.16, 13.17, 13.20
Applicant reactions, evaluating selection methods, 13.22
Appraiser attitude, 15.12
Appraiser training, 15.8 15.18
Apprentice stage (career), 24.6
Apprenticeship, 26.16
Arbitration, 6.11
Area of interest, 14.7, 14.8
Arm's length relationship, 6.9, 6.10
Arpanet (Advanced Research Projects Agency), 20.6
Art of the Long View, The (Peter Swartz), 4.23
Assessment center, 14.12
Assessment methods, 13.22
Assessments and surveys, 5.13
Assessors, trained, 14.12
Assimilation (integration), 5.9

Assumptions, and HR systems, 21.4–5, 21.9, 21.14–15, 21.21. *See also* Conventional assumptions, Healthier assumptions
Asynchronous (self-directed) communication, 20.4, 20.9, 20.18. *See also* Synchronous communication
AT&T/telecommunications industry deregulation, 3.32–34
At-will employment standard, 21.13
Attracting/retaining employees, 3.13, 13.4, 13.11, 13.17, 18.6, 18.17. *See also* Recruiting top talent
Attractive recruitment messages, 13.19
Auditory learners, 19.17, 19.19
Authoritative management structure, 26.12
Autonomous business units, 2.14
Autonomy, rights of, 27.4
Autonomy of management, 26.10
Awareness training, 9.12

Balance of pay mechanisms, 16.19–20
Bargaining agreement. *See* Collective agreement
Bargaining power, 26.6, 26.8, 26.10, 26.16
Bargaining unit, 6.4, 6.7, 27.15
Barriers to change, 11.8
Barriers to partnership, 4.10
Base assumptions, 4.22, 4.25
Base wage (salary), 16.8–9, 16.18, 16.19
Base-case scenario, 12.17, 12.18, 12.20, 12.21
Baseline(s), 17.9, 17.18–19. *See also* Incentive bonus
Beck rights precedent, 27.15
Behavioral learning, 19.16
Beneficiary choice, 18.13, 18.14
Benefit credits, 18.19. *See also* Employee contribution
Benefits administration, 7.4, 18.4, 18.5, 18.20, 18.22
Benefits (legally required), 12.11
Benefits of job changes, 24.12
Benefits packages, 11.9, 16.19, 26.8. *See also* Incentives
Benefits planning and analysis, 7.9
Benefits regulations, 18.6, 18.7, 18.22
Best practices approach, 2.28, 2.30, 22.11

Betrayal stage (mergers and acquisitions), 5.13

Beyond Reengineering (Michael Hammer), 4.22

BFOQ, bona fide occupational qualification, 8.15

Big Five framework (tests of integrity), 14.10

Billing, 7.7. *See also* Transaction processing (HRIS)

Biodata inventory, 14.11, 14.18

Bonuses, 17.5, 17.6, 17.7. *See also* Rewards

Bottom-up appraisals, 15.16

Boundary-spanning function, 3.8

Breach of contract suit, 5.15

Breaking in stage (socialization), 24.11

British Labour Party, 26.5

Bulletin board systems (BBSs), 20.11

Bundling approach, 3.20. *See also* Business strategy, Human resource policies and practices

Burden of compliance, 23.11

Burden of proof, 8.8

Bureau of Labor Statistics (BLS), 12.6–7, 12.16, 23.6

Bureau of National Affairs, 2.14, 3.18

Bureaucratic relationships, 26.9

Business environment, 1.4, 4.9, 4.18, 4.21, 14.5, 14.6, 14.9–10, 14.11
 worldwide. *See* Worldwide business environment

Business ethics. *See* Workplace ethics

Business needs assessment, 22.12

Business strategy, 1.7, 1.8, 1.12, 2.4, 2.15–16, 2.19, 2.24, 3.8, 3.12, 13.4, 13.10, 13.14, 13.25, 13.26, 13.27, 13.31, 25.13. *See also* Mission statement, Vision statement
 group incentives, 17.10, 17.13–14, 17.16

Buyer power, 2.10–11. *See also* Supplier power

Career anchors, 24.9–10

Career average pay formula, 18.12

Career changes, 24.7, 24.12

Career choice. *See* Vocational choice

Career development, 19.8, 24.16. *See also* Career management

Career issues, 3.14, 11.8, 11.10, 11.14

Career management, 24.4–5, 24.10, 24.16–17
 individual strategies, 24.14–16

Career pathing systems, 24.16. *See* Career management

Career stages, 24.5–6

Career transitions, 24.10–11, 24.17

Career-long employment, 16.6, 25.11

Caring supervisors, 27.10

Case-by-case basis, 10.5

Census of Fatal Occupational Injuries, 23.6

Centers of excellence (HR), 3.27

Central tendency (bias), 15.13

Centralized data storage, 7.14, 7.19

Centralized decision making, 3.28

Centralized/autocratic management style, 5.14

CEO compensation, 27.12

Certainty of uncertain future, 4.18

Certification (training and development systems), 7.10

CGI (common gateway interface) scripting, 20.16

Chaebols (conglomerates), 2.32–33, 26.12–13, 26.14

Championing employees, 4.12

Change awareness training, 5.13

Change management, 4.11, 21.14–15, 22.4, 22.16–18, 22.20–22

Change model, 22.13–16

Change programs, 17.10

Change theory, 21.15, 21.21

Change-agent role, 1.9. *See also* Human resource role

Change-conscious organization, 4.7

Change-intensive environment, 4.5, 4.6, 4.7, 4.17

Change-migration plan, 22.12, 22.21

Change-readiness, 4.4, 4.8, 4.18, 4.21, 4.26

Changing environment, 19.26, 19.28. *See* Environmental change

Changing policies (under FMLA), 10.11

Chartering practices (unions), 6.8

Chat rooms, 20.7–8, 20.11, 20.18

Chief diversity officer, 9.14

Chief learning officer (CLO), 19.27

Child and elder care assistance, 18.17

Christianity and ethics, 27.7–8

Citizenship requirement, and employment, 8.19

Civil Rights Act, Title VII, 8.4, 8.20

Civil Rights Act of 1964, 1.15, 8.4, 8.19, 9.9

Civil Rights Act of 1991, 8.5–6 8.7, 8.9

Clarifying expectations, 15.4, 15.7

Classic selection model, 13.11

Clayton Antitrust Act of 1914, 26.7

Client firm, 12.4

Client managers, 21.14

Climate of openness and respect, 15.23

Climate/culture. *See* Organizational culture

Closed proprietary systems, 20.19

Closed recruitment process, 13.18

Co-decision, 26.15

Co-ownership of projects, 22.4, 22.6

Coaching approach, 15.12

COBRA, 7.4. *See also* Consolidated Omnibus Reconciliation Act

Code-determination rights, 26.15

Codetermination, 26.15, 26.17

Cognitive ability, as predictor of adaptability, 14.13, 14.18

Cognitive ability tests, 13.13–14, 13.27. *See also* Intelligence tests

Cognitive flexibility theory, 20.12

Cognitive learning, 19.16

Colleague stage (career), 24.6

Collective actions, 26.14

Collective agreements, 5.5, 6.7, 6.8, 6.10, 6.12, 6.19, 12.5, 16.17, 26.14–15

Collective bargaining, 1.11, 1.12, 1.14, 1.15, 3.17, 6.4–5, 6.6–7, 6.9, 6.14, 6.16, 7.9, 10.8, 18.7, 23.11, 26.5, 26.8–9, 26.10, 26.13, 26.16
 ethical aspects, 27.15

Collective representation, 6.7

Collectivism, 26.9

Colliding cultures, 5.18. *See also* Mismatch of culture

Combative relationship, 1.14

Combined assets, 5.6

Commitment approach. *See* Workforce commitment model

Commitment of managers, 5.9

Commitment (organizational), 14.14

Commitment to change, 15.18

Commonality of interest, 6.13

Communication, as translation role, 1.8, 1.11

Communication challenges, 25.8, 25.24, 25.27. *See also* Language

Communication effectiveness (HR), 3.5, 3.19–20, 3.23, 3.26. *See also* Translation role

Communication of policies, 2.27

Communication role. *See* Translation role

Communication strategy, 5.16
 and group incentive plans, 17.20

Communication system, 20.6

Communications, 17.7, 17.10, 17.12
Communications guides, 5.13
Company loyalty, 9.6
Company-sponsored day-care, 11.4, 11.12
Comparative employment relations, 26.10–12. *See also* Employment relations
Compensable factor (job evaluation), 16.12–16
Compensation, 6.5
    defined, 16.8
Compensation and benefits, global HR strategy, 25.12
Compensation and pay structures, 27.11
Compensation claim, 23.8
Compensation plans, 17.4
Compensation systems, 16.4, 16.6–10, 16.12, 16.20
Compensatory approach, applicant evaluation, 13.22
Compensatory damages, 8.9–10
Competencies (required), 15.6, 15.14
Competency management, 22.9
Competency-based pay system, 16.10. *See also* Skill-based pay system
Competing demand conflict, 11.10–11
Competitive advantage, 2.6, 2.7–8, 2.9, 2.11–12, 2.14, 2.15, 2.23, 2.24, 2.29, 3.6, 3.28, 4.5, 4.7, 4.20
Competitive environment, 1.7, 1.13, 1.16, 6.12, 12.11
Competitiveness, 1.5, 1.7, 1.17, 1.18, 1.22, 1.27, 19.4
Complaint filing (FMLA), 10.5
Complementors (complementary products), 2.10–11
Complexity and difficulty of duties factor (job evaluation), 16.14
Complexity of appraisal criteria, 15.15
Compliance, 10.4
    pay discrimination laws, 16.8
    safety and health regulations, 23.10, 23.12
    Title VII, burden of, 8.4, 8.13
Compressed workweeks, 11.4
Computer-based technology, 1.13, 1.15
Computer-based training (CBT), 20.4, 20.7, 20.11
Computerized testing, 14.11–12
Computers, 11.12
Computing resources, 20.16
Conciliation, and EEOC, 8.7

Conditions of employment, 6.4, 6.11, 6.19, 8.6, 26.5, 26.8. *See also* Discrimination, Employment tests
    collective bargaining, 6.6, 6.7, 6.12, 6.13, 6.19
    sexual harassment, 8.17
Cone of experience, 19.20
Conference room, 20.9. *See also* Teleconferencing
Configurational approach, 2.28, 2.30
Conflict, deunionization, 6.9, 6.11, 6.15–16
Conglomerate acquisitions, 5.7
Congruence, 13.12, 13.13
    vertical and horizontal fit, 2.25–26
Congruence (horizontal and vertical fit), 3.20
Conscientiousness, 13.13
Consequences of performance, 15.7. *See also* Forewarning
Consistency/fairness (appraisal), 15.8, 15.11
Consolidated Omnibus Reconciliation Act (COBRA), 18.8
Consolidation, 5.6, 5.18
Constancy of change, 4.6, 4.7, 4.17, 17.10
Construct validity, employment tests, 8.13, 14.7, 14.8
Constructionist design models, 20.12, 20.13–14
Content domain (of tasks), 14.16
Content validity, employment tests, 8.11, 14.7–8
Content-oriented strategy, 13.23. *See also* Validation of selection practices
Contested disciplinary decision, discrimination, 8.8
Contextual performance, 13.13, 14.5, 14.14, 14.17, 14.18
    predictors of, 14.15
Contingency plans, 4.23
Contingent assessment methods, 13.20–21
Contingent work (employment) arrangements, 12.4, 12.5–6, 12.7, 12.9, 12.11, 12.13, 12.20
Contingent workers, 1.20, 1.21, 12.4, 12.5–9, 12.12, 12.16, 12.18–20
    characteristics of, 12.7
    pension and health insurance coverage, 12.9
Continuing treatment (regimen), 10.8. *See also* Short-term disability
Continuous improvement philosophy, 16.7

Continuous learning culture, 17.10
Continuous training, 3.10, 24.16
Contract workers, 12.4, 12.7
Contrast effect (bias), 15.13
Contributions, employer, 18.12. *See also* Employee contribution, Employer-provided benefit plans
Control of exposure, 23.9, 23.13, 23.14
Convenience benefits, 18.17
Conventional assumptions, 21.11, 21.12. *See also* Assumptions
Conventional wisdom of organizations, 4.5, 4.19, 4.22, 27.6
Cooperative bargaining, 6.9, 6.11, 6.13, 6.19
Cooperative relations, 1.12
Copayment, 18.15, 18.19
Coping with job loss, 24.15
Core competencies, 1.5, 1.10, 1.17, 1.19, 2.4, 2.5, 2.7, 2.12–13, 2.16, 2.23, 3.8, 3.21, 3.32, 4.24, 9.4, 12.10, 12.12–13
Core competencies (organizational), 14.15
Core employees, 12.10, 12.12–13, 12.16
Core organizational performance factors, 15.7
Core-noncore approach, 1.5, 1.22, 1.27. *See also* Employment strategies
Corporate culture, 5.5, 5.18, 13.22. *See also* Organizational culture
Corporate development, global, 25.8–9
Corporate hierarchy. *See* Organizational hierarchy
Corporate power, 25.9
Corporate strategy, 4.5, 4.11
Corporatewide education institutions, 25.12
Correlations between measures, (test validity), 14.8
Cost leadership strategy, 2.11, 2.29–30
Cost minimization, 1.11, 1.18, 1.21, 1.23, 1.25, 1.27, 17.7. *See also* Labor transactional model
Cost sharing, 18.15, 18.18–19
Cost-benefit analysis, core vs. contingent workers, 12.4, 12.13–16, 12.20, 27.13
Cost-of-living adjustments (COLAs), 16.8–9, 16.17. *See also* Structural adjustments (compensation)
Covered employment, 18.9
Coworkers, performance evaluations, 25.12

Creating value. *See* Adding value

Creative thinking workshop, 19.20

Creativity, 4.7, 4.11

Criterion-oriented strategy, 13.23
employment tests, 8.11, 14.7, 14.8

Critical component, 14.8

Critical success factors, 2.9

Cross-cultural interaction, 25.8–9, 25.10, 25.24

Cross-functional collaboration, 6.18, 11.17

Cross-training, 16.7

Crossovers, 6.14, 6.15. *See also* Permanent replacements, Picketing, Scabs

Cultural accommodation strategy, 25.14

Cultural audit, 9.4, 9.12

Cultural avoidance strategy, 25.14

Cultural change, 1.11, 1.12, 1.13, 3.26, 5.17, 9.5, 9.8, 9.9, 11.4, 11.5, 11.12, 17.4, 17.11, 22.12

Cultural compromise strategy, 25.14

Cultural dimensions, 26.9–10

Cultural diversity, 25.4, 25.6–7, 25.14–15, 25.22. *See also* Diversity

Cultural dominance strategy, 25.14

Cultural issues, 11.7, 11.8, 11.10, 11.17

Cultural support, 11.9, 11.15

Cultural synergy, 25.9, 25.14–15, 25.16

Cultural values, 2.21, 2.22, 25.7, 26.9

Culture change, organizational, 4.4, 4.8, 4.10, 4.18, 4.26, 4.32, 4.35

Culture management, 4.11, 26.9

Current profit-sharing plans, 17.8

Customer employees, 21.14

Customer focus, 19.5, 19.28

Customer service orientation, 13.21

Customer-focused activities, 2.13–14

Customization phase (HRIS implementation), 7.16, 7.17–18

Damage awards, compensatory and punitive, 8.7

Data access, 7.14

Database technology. *See* Relational database technology

Day laborers, 12.5, 12.7

Death (occupational), 23.6, 23.7

Decentralization, 2.29, 26.13.
of bargaining, 26.10

Decentralized business units. *See* Autonomous business units

Decentralized communication network, 20.6

Decentralized decision making, 7.14

Decentralized structure, 22.12, 25.9

Decision making, 26.13, 26.16
employee, 1.9, 1.18
HR, 1.7, 1.10, 1.11, 3.8, 3.11–12, 3.22–24, 3.26. *See also* Human resource roles
managerial, 1.6, 1.12, 1.24, 1.27, 20.4
recruitment and selection process, 13.8, 13.10

Decision response times, 25.8

Decision rules, applicant evaluation, 13.22–23

Decision support systems (HRIS), 7.6, 7.9, 7.13, 7.14

Deep systems, 4.22

Default system, 6.19

Defensive behavior, 5.13

Deferred profit-sharing plans, 17.8

Defined benefit plans, 18.11, 18.12, 18.13. *See also* Retirement plan benefits

Democratic organization of unions, 6.8

Demographics, 9.5, 9.6, 9.7, 9.11, 9.15

Denial stage (mergers and acquisitions), 5.13

Dental plan, 18.16

Department of Labor (DOL), 10.5–6

Deployment of people, 2.24–25

Deregulation, 1.6, 1.13, 1.16

Design, ISD model, 19.10

Design team, 21.14, 21.19. *See also* Human resource system design

Deunionization, 6.11, 6.12–14
labor relations strategy, 6.14
management strategy, 6.19

Developing people for promotion, 15.6

Developmental phases, corporations, 25.8–9, 25.11

Diagnostic framework, 1.12, 1.27

Dictionary of Occupational Titles (DOT), 16.11

Differentiation. *See* Product differentiation

Digital divide, 20.19

Direct compensation, 16.8, 16.10, 18.6

Disability insurance, 18.9, 18.16

Disciplinary issues, ethics of, 27.12

Discipline and dismissal decisions, 15.7

Disclaimer statement, 16.11

Disclosure of financial information, 17.16

Discretion of management, 6.11

Discretionary bonus, 17.6

Discrimination, 9.7, 9.9, 9.15, 10.12, 16.4
employment practices, 13.24, 27.16
in employment, 8.4. *See also* Conditions of employment

Discrimination complaint (OSHA), 23.10

Discrimination-fairness paradigm, 9.10–11

Discriminatory practice, 8.7

Discussion of strengths, 15.12

Disparate impact, discrimination, 8.9–11, 13.24

Disparate treatment, discrimination, 8.8–9, 8.12, 13.24

Distance education, 20.11

Diverse learning, 2.12

Diverse workforce, 9.5–6, 9.11, 9.12

Diversification strategies, 26.12

Diversity, 2.6, 9.4, 9.7, 9.9, 9.10, 11.9, 11.11, 11.12, 11.15, 19.28, 26.9. *See also* Cultural diversity, Multiculturalism
management. *See* Managing diversity
processes, 9.12–13

Diversity enlargement hiring strategies, 9.12. *See also* Human resource systems

Diversity management, 25.6, 25.19, 25.23

Documentation of accountability, 23.12

Doers (learning styles), 19.16, 19.19

Domestic corporations, 25.9

Domestic employment relations, 26.4–5, 26.10, 26.17

Domestic HR management, 25.6–7

Dominant culture, 2.6, 25.9

Dominant culture or identity group, 9.9, 9.10, 9.12. *See also* Identity issues, Minority group, Organizational culture

Downsizing, 1.4, 1.5, 1.15, 1.18, 1.20, 1.22, 3.22, 3.28, 14.12, 14.17, 24.5, 24.13–14, 24.15
humane policies, 27.17

Dress and grooming requirement, 8.14–15

Drill and practice (type of IBT), 20.19

Drive system, 1.14

Dropping the ball, 22.9, 22.10–11

Drug and alcohol testing, ethics of, 27.11

Due diligence (integration), 5.12

Duty of fair representation, union's, 27.14

Duty to accommodate, employer's, 8.14–15

E-mail, 20.5, 20.7, 20.8, 20.9, 20.10, 20.12, 20.18

Economic change, 26.14

Economic environment, 4.6, 4.36, 5.6

Economic factors, 1.8, 1.14, 1.19, 1.20, 1.23, 17.17, 18.12

Economic feasibility (HRIS), 7.17

Economic forces, 2.21, 26.9, 26.13

Economic globalization. *See* Globalization

Economic weapons (collective bargaining), 6.7

Economies of scale, 2.8, 2.11, 5.6

Education and training, 7.11, 22.12, 22.19, 26.8, 26.17

Educational assistance, 18.18

Educational reimbursement programs, 3.14

Edutainment, 20.17

EEOC (Equal Employment Opportunity Commission), 16.5
  bilingual guidelines, 8.19
  conciliation, 8.7
  employer duty to accommodate, 8.14
  enforcement of Title VII, 8.6
  sexual harassment, 8.16
  uniform guidelines, 8.11
  v. Electronic Data Systems, 8.15
  v. M.D. Pneumatics, 8.8

Effective at persuasion, 4.19

Effective employment interviews, 14.14

Efficiency condition, 12.17–18

Efficiency objectives (organizational), 11.13

Effort factors (job evaluation), 16.13

Effort to decertify union, 6.14

Egalitarian group incentive, 17.18

Egalitarian perquisites, 16.7

Elective conditions (FMLA), 10.8

Electronic environment, 20.10

Electronic infrastructure, 20.11

Electronic performance support system (EPSS), 20.11, 20.18

Eligibility for benefits, 18.8, 18.9–10

Eligible employees, 10.5–6, 17.5, 17.8

Empirical aspects, ISD model, 19.10

Employability, 16.6

Employee, term defined, 8.6

Employee assistance program (EAP), 18.17

Employee attitudes, 21.8

Employee benefit plan design, 18.18

Employee benefits, 1.10, 1.17, 18.4, 18.5–7, 18.13, 18.19, 18.21–22. *See also* Benefits packages

Employee carelessness, 23.7, 23.17

Employee commitment, 17.14, 17.20

Employee commitment approach. *See* Workforce commitment model

Employee compensation system, 1.10, 17.6

Employee contributions, 17.6, 17.11, 18.19. *See also* Benefit credits

Employee demographics, 9.11

Employee eligibility, 17.15

Employee involvement, 15.15, 15.16–17

Employee involvement plan, 17.10, 17.14. *See* Group incentives

Employee morale. *See* Morale, employee

Employee objectives/accomplishments, 15.12, 15.14

Employee participation, 17.4, 17.11, 17.14, 26.10–11

Employee performance appraisal. *See* Performance appraisal

Employee perspectives, 6.9, 9.9, 9.11

Employee relations, 3.11, 3.15–16, 3.31

Employee representative, 17.4, 26.8–9
  collective bargaining, 6.7, 6.8, 6.14. *See also* Union representation

Employee Retirement Income Security Act (ERISA), 18.7–8, 18.20

Employee rights and responsibilities (FMLA), 6.5, 6.6, 10.4, 10.8–9, 10.11

Employee safety and health management, 23.11

Employee selection, 1.17, 4.12, 11.8. *See also* Employment practices, Recruitment and Selection

Employee services/perquisites, 16.9

Employee stock ownership plan (ESOP), 16.7, 18.13, 27.17–18

Employee work/nonwork roles, 1.10. *See also* Work/life balance

Employee's right to refuse (OSH), 23.10, 23.11, 23.17

Employee-management cooperation initiatives, 27.14

Employee-organization relationship, 16.6, 17.11

Employees, expendable vs. valued, 3.10, 3.30

Employees as internal customers, 11.12

Employer associations, 26.7, 26.9, 26.10, 26.13, 26.16

Employer commitment, 1.5, 1.17

Employer expectations, 24.11

Employer liability, under Title VII, 8.7, 8.8, 8.10, 8.17

Employer obligations (FMLA), 10.8

Employer of choice, 1.17, 3.10, 9.4, 9.7

Employer retaliation, protection of workers, 8.6, 8.17

Employer's duty to accommodate, 8.14

Employer-provided benefit plans, 18.5, 18.10, 18.11, 18.16

Employer-provided insurance, 12.9

Employer/employee partnership, 1.26, 11.8, 11.10

Employer/employee relations. *See* Employment relationship

Employers, and seniority, 8.12
  Title VII compliance, 8.5

Employment agencies, Title VII compliance, 8.5

Employment discrimination, 8.4, 8.9, 8.19. *See also* Minoritiy workers, Women workers

Employment insecurity. *See* Job insecurity

Employment policies, harassment, 8.18
  Title VII compliance, 8.4, 8.12

Employment practices, 1.4, 1.11, 1.22, 3.7, 8.9, 8.11–12, 8.19

Employment relations, 1.13–17, 1.20, 5.4, 26.8, 26.11, 26.12, 26.13, 26.16–17, 27.4, 27.6, 27.8, 27.11
  Korean chaebols, 2.36

Employment relations strategies, 2.24–25

Employment relations systems, 26.4–5, 26.6, 26.12, 26.15, 26.18

Employment relationship, 1.4, 1.5, 1.13, 1.14, 1.16–17, 1.18, 1.20, 1.23, 1.26, 1.27, 2.5, 2.8, 2.19, 2.22, 2.24–25, 2.28, 3.12, 3.22, 3.23, 3.30, 6.8, 6.9, 16.8, 17.11, 26.5, 26.7, 26.8

Employment security. *See* Job security

Employment strategies, 1.4, 1.5–7, 1.14, 1.17, 1.19

Employment tests, vs. job performance, 8.11. *See also* Job-specific task performance; Work sample text

Employment-at-will standard, 27.13

Employment-caused injuries/illnesses, 27.13
Employment-related insurance programs, 18.9
Empowered employees, 1.4, 1.18, 3.12, 21.6
Empowered workforce, 3.12, 11.4, 11.12, 17.10
Empowering individuals, 26.8
Empowerment, promoting, 4.11
Enforcement
  Title VII, 8.6, 8.19
  FMLA, 10.5
  OSHA, ethics of, 27.13
English-only rules, and employment, 8.18
Enterprise resource planning, 7.8
Enterprise success, 16.7
Entitlement, 16.6, 18.4, 18.13, 18.22
Entitlement (FMLA). *See* Leave entitlement
Entry shock, 24.10
Environmental change, 1.5, 1.6, 9.4, 9.7
Environmental context, 2.5, 2.17, 3.7–8, 26.4, 26.9, 27.8
Environmental factors, 1.6, 1.7, 1.12, 1.13–14
Environmental forces, 2.5, 2.21, 3.7, 9.4, 9.5
Equal employment opportunity (EEO), 1.8, 1.13, 8.5, 8.8, 27.5
  pregnant workers, 8.16
  statutes, 8.20
  women and barriers to, 8.4, 9.4, 9.7, 9.9, 9.10
Equal Employment Opportunity Commission. *See* EEOC
Equal employment opportunity laws, 13.24
Equal Pay Act of 1963, 16.5
Equipment design (for safety), 23.8
Equity framework 16.8, 16.11–19
Equity/efficiency balance, 3.26
ERISA. *See* Employee Retirement Income Security Act
Error in selection tests, 14.6
Establishment stage (career), 24.9. *See also* Apprentice stage
Ethical considerations (benefits), 18.7
Ethical dilemmas, 27.6, 27.8, 27.10–11
Ethical evaluation, 27.16
Ethical imperative, 27.7
Ethical issues in training, 19.29
Ethical standards, 4.13
Ethics of monitoring employee activities, 27.11
Ethics vs. law, 27.7

Ethics/ethical perspectives, 25.23, 27.4–7.
European Union (EU), 26.11
Evaluation, change model, 22.16
Evaluation, ISD model, 19.13, 19.24–26
Evaluation component, 20.13–14
Exclusionary device, 8.11, 9.8
Exclusive representation, 6.7
Executive development, 4.11
Executive evaluation, 22.16
Executive support systems (HRIS), 7.9
Exempt employees (FMLA), 10.6, 10.13. *See also* Nonexempt employees
Expatriation, 24.12, 24.13
Expectancy theories, 17.6
Expectations, performance standards, 15.8–12
Experience curve, 2.8
Experience rated, 18.10
Experience requirements, 8.12
Experiential questions as predictors, 14.11
Experimentation model, 21.13
Expertise of workers, 6.13
Exportive orientation, 25.15
Exposure to hazards, 23.6, 23.8, 23.9, 23.12
External change, 22.14
External customers, 15.16
External environment, 2.17, 2.19, 2.24
External equity, 16.8, 16.16–17
External recruiting sources, 13.18
External resources, 1.9–10, 3.18, 3.24, 3.32
Extrinsic motivation, 13.11, 16.10

Face validity, 14.7, 14.8–9
Facilitating, strategic planning, 4.14
Facilitating tips (training), 19.21
Failure to comply (FMLA), 10.9–10
Fair employment practices, 15.7
Fair Labor Standards Act, (FLSA), 1.13, 16.5
Fair pay-for-work relationship, 27.11–12
Fairlane Commitment, 4.8, 4.9
Fairness, 14.10. *See* Validity
  legal standards of, 27.4, 27.11–12
Family and Medical Leave Act (FMLA), 1.11, 1.13, 10.4–7, 10.12, 10.14, 11.4, 11.6, 12.12, 18.8, 18.18, 27.5, 27.19
Family needs, 11.6, 11.7, 11.8, 11.9
Family ownership/management, 26.12

Family-supportive policies, 11.5
Fatalities, 23.6
Favorable tax legislation, 18.6
Federal Insurance Contributions Act (FICA), 18.10
Federal Mediation and Conciliation Service, 6.17
Federal Trade Commission (FTC), 5.6
Federal Unemployment Tax Act (FUTA), 18.10
Fee-for-service plan, 18.13, 18.14
Feedback, employees' need for, 15.4, 15.6, 15.8, 15.12
Feelers (learning styles), 19.16, 19.19
Fiduciary standards (benefit plans), 18.8
Fifth Discipline: The Art and Practice of the Learning Organization (Senge), 19.26
50 Creative Training Closers (Solem and Pike), 19.23
50-employee threshold, 10.5, 10.6
File transfer protocol (FTP), 20.5, 20.10
Final average plan, 18.12
Final Rules (DOL's), 10.6
Financial effects of layoffs, 24.14
Financial flexibility (staffing), 12.11
Financially valued goal-sharing plans, 17.9
Firm perspective, 6.9. *See also* Employment relationship
Firm unilateralism, 6.6
Fixed employment costs, 12.11
Flat benefit, 18.12
Flat file or spreadsheet, 7.10
Flexibility, 3.23, 15.8. *See also* Workforce flexibility
  as performance criterion, 14.12, 14.17
  conditions of employment, 6.6, 6.12
  cooperative relationships, 6.13, 6.15
  employee/employer, 16.6, 16.19
  work rules, 6.18.
Flexibility-consistency balance, 3.26
Flexible benefit plans, 18.18–19
Flexible spending account (FSA), 11.4, 18.19
Flexible staffing, 12.11
Flexible work options, 1.18, 9.6, 9.13, 11.8, 11.11, 11.12, 18.17, 26.10
Flexible workforce, 6.17
Flexiplace, 2.19, 2.20

Flextime, 11.8
FLSA status (exempt/nonexempt), 7.13, 16.11
FMLA compliance, 7.4, 7.7, 7.23
FMLA leave, 10.4–8, 10.11–12, 10.13–14
FMLA policies (employers'), 10.9–10, 10.12, 10.13
FMLA training, 10.13
Focus, common direction, 4.23, 4.34, 4.37
Focus on ratings and rewards, 15.14
Focus strategy, 2.12
Ford Motor, 6.18–19
Forecasting, classical planning, 4.17, 4.18, 4.19, 4.24, 4.25
Foreign competition, 6.11
Foreign staffing practices, 25.10
Forewarning, 4.13, 4.14. *See also* Consequences of performance
Foundation of mistrust, 21.7
Four career stage model (Dalton, Thompson, and Price), 24.6
Four-fifths rule, 14.9
401(k) plan, 16.7, 18.12, 18.19
Free riders, right-to-work, 27.15
Frontier of performance, 2.7, 3.8
FTC compliance, 5.10
Full-time employees, 12.13
Full-time workers, 11.15
Fully insured status, 18.9
Fully interactive (type of IBT), 20.19
Functional flexibility (staffing), 12.11
Functional specialists, 4.11
Functional specialization stage, 3.16
Functionality (HRIS), 7.16
Funding (benefit plans), 18.8, 18.12, 18.13, 18.19, 18.20
Funding potential, 17.17
Future employment potential, 16.6
Future orientation (appraisal), 15.6
Future planning (mapping), 4.18, 4.23

Gain-sharing incentive plans, 17.8, 17.16–17
Gender and workplace ethics, 27.8, 27.11
General duty clause, 27.13
General Motors, 6.18 *See also* GM-Powertrain
Generativity, 24.7
Geographic jurisdiction, 6.8
German employment relations, 26.14
Getting in stage (socialization), 24.11
Glass-ceiling barriers, 9.10, 9.13

Global compensation system, 25.12
Global Competencies, Performance, and Pay (Mercer Consulting Web site), 16.16
Global competitiveness, 4.8–9, 4.36
Global corporations, 25.8–9, 25.11–13, 25.19
Global economy, 27.20
Global Human Resource Development (Marquardt and Engel), 25.5
Global human resource management, 25.6–8, 25.11–16, 25.23, 25.27
Global Internet, 20.6, 20.10
Global managers, 25.10, 25.13, 25.14
Global marketplace, 1.16, 1.27, 14.12, 25.19–20, 26.10
Global organizational design, 25.9, 25.11
Global performance management, 25.12–13
Global players, 25.10
Global product market pressures, 3.8
Global skills/competencies, 4.33–34
Global telecommunications, 25.7
Globalization, 1.4, 1.6, 1.9, 1.17, 3.31, 5.6, 9.4, 9.6, 9.7, 25.9–10, 25.16, 25.19, 25.23, 25.25, 26.4
GM-Powertrain, 21.16–18, 21.21
Goal-setting theory 17.6
Goal-sharing incentive plans, 17.8, 17.16–17
Good faith bargaining, 6.7, 6.12
Good manners, etiquette, and civility, 27.7, 27.14
Goods-producing sector, 23.6, 23.7
Governance intermediate bodies, 6.8
Government regulation, 1.6, 1.10, 1.15, 1.21, 1.23, 3.17, 3.23, 23.5, 23.7, 23.12, 23.18
    mergers and acquisitions, 5.6–7
Government regulation stage, 3.17
Government retirement programs, 18.10
Government (roll in employment relations), 26.7, 26.10, 26.11, 26.12, 26.13–14, 26.16, 26.17
Grade (pay or salary), 16.14, 16.17–18, 27.16
Graphical user interface (GUI), 20.11
Greedy workplace, 11.14
Grievance and arbitration procedure, 27.12
Grievance procedure, 6.11
Group dynamics, 4.14, 4.17

Group exercises (training), 19.22
Group identity, 9.8, 9.9
Group incentives, 17.4, 17.5, 17.9–20
    deployment strategies, 17.9–10, 17.11–13
    development strategies, 17.10, 17.12
    OCD perspective, 17.12
    plans, 17.6–7, 17.8, 17.11, 17.15, 17.21
    strategic impact, 17.10
    success factors, 17.12
Group interview, 14.7
Group life insurance, 18.16
Group (team) dynamics, 25.11
Group universal life (GUL) insurance, 18.16
Grouping, applicant evaluation, 13.23

Halo or horns biases, 15.13
Hand-off approach (management), 11.14
Hart-Scott-Rodino Antitrust Improvements Act of 1976, 5.7
Hazard identification and control, 23.13, 23.15
Hazard to unborn children, 27.13–14
Hazardous conditions/materials/ processes, 23.9, 23.12
Health and safety hazards, 23.6, 23.9, 23.11
Health and welfare plans/benefits, 18.8, 18.13, 18.19
Health insurance coverage, 12.9
Health Insurance Portability and Accountability Act (HIPAA), 18.8
Healthcare, 10.6, 18.13, 18.14, 18.15
Healthcare provider, 10.8
Healthier assumptions, 21.10–11, 21.12, 21.21. *See also* Maslow, Abraham; Theory Y
Heterogeneity, 2.19
Heterogeneous workforce, 9.6, 9.12, 9.13. *See also* Workforce
Hidden costs, 5.10
Hierarchical promotions, 16.6
Hierarchy of safety and health controls, 23.14
High performance, 4.13
High-commitment pay, 16.6, 16.7
High-involvement exercise, 4.25
High-performance work systems, 2.30, 26.17
High-performing organization, 5.10
High-productivity scenario, 12.17, 12.18, 12.21

High-tech companies, 9.6

High-tech job aids, 20.11

High-wage policies, 16.6. *See also* Job security

"Hire for attitude, train for skills," 13.16

Hire-from-within culture, 12.13

Hiring, ethical concerns, 14.4, 27.16

Hiring managers. *See* Human Resource management

Hiring strategies. *See* Employment strategies

Hochschild, Arlie, 11.14

Holistic work/life programs, 11.12. *See also* Work/life policies

Holland's model of vocational choice, 24.8–9

Home vs. host country values, 25.8

Homogeneity, 2.6, 2.19, 26.9, 26.10

Horizontal congruence or fit, 2.25. *See* Congruence

Horizontal integration. *See* Integration

Host computers, 20.6–7, 20.10

Host/local country nationals (HCNs), 25.6–7, 25.10

Hostile environment, sexual harassment, 8.17

Hostile takeover (mergers), 5.8–9, 5.13

HR bundles, 2.30–31

HR change model, 22.13–16

HR department dilemmas, 27.9–10

HR department staff, 15.11

HR membership, 22.7, 22.22

HR's emerging role, 4.5, 4.8, 4.10, 4.12

HRD activities, 22.16–17

HRM policy clusters, 3.12–16, 3.30–31

HRM services, 22.16–17

HTML (hyper text markup language), 20.7, 20.16

HTTP (hyper text transfer protocol), 20.7, 20.13

Human behavior expertise, 4.14

Human body analogy, 21.7

Human capital (assets), 2.7, 2.13, 2.23, 22.5, 22.6, 22.7

Human capital development cluster, 3.31. *See also* Training and development, human capital

Human component, 21.7

Human dignity and ethical behavior (Western traditions), 27.7, 27.20

Human performance management, 19.28

Human performance measure-setting, 22.5, 22.7

Human performance technology (HPT), 19.8, 19.13

Human potential perspective, 21.5. *See also* Maslow, Abraham; Theory Y

Human relations, 26.10, 26.11

Human relations model, 11.11, 11.12

Human relations movement (1923–1930s), 3.16

Human resource decisions, 15.5, 15.6–7, 15.12, 15.14, 15.16

Human resource development (HRD), 15.14, 19.4, 19.7, 19.13, 19.29

Human resource effectiveness, 3.8, 3.28–30

Human resource function, 2.14, 3.5, 3.6, 3.11, 3.16, 3.27, 4.5, 4.12, 4.13, 4.14, 4.26, 5.4, 5.11, 5.19, 7.4, 7.6–8, 7.15, 22.4–5, 22.10, 22.16, 22.18, 23.12, 23.15, 25.9. *See also* Human resource roles
  ethical perspectives 27.5
  Korean, 2.37–39
  process technology, 7.15, 7.17. *See also* Customization phase (HRIS implementation)
  time spent on activities, 3.27

Human resource information systems (HRIS), 7.4–6, 7.8–13, 7.16–19, 7.23, 13.7
  design and implementation, 7.16–19

Human resource investment, 13.12

Human resource leader or manager. *See* Human resource professional

Human resource leadership role, 3.25, 3.30–32
  stages of evolution, 3.15–17

Human resource management (HRM), 2.5, 2.8, 2.15, 3.7, 3.8, 3.10, 5.4–5, 6.4, 9.13, 9.15, 11.8, 11.9, 11.10, 11.11, 11.12, 11.13, 14.15, 14.16, 14.18, 17.4, 18.4, 18.20, 22.8–9, 22.16–18, 25.5–6, 25.8, 25.9, 25.13–16, 25.19, 25.24, 27.4, 27.9. *See also* Human resource systems, Managing human resources
  administrative functions, 12.12
  global. *See* Global human resource management
  Korean, 2.37–39
  practices, 2.28
  strategic planning, 12.11, 12.13, 12.21

Human resource manager, 7.4, 7.15, 18.4, 18.20, 23.4, 23.5, 23.6, 23.7, 23.9, 23.11, 23.12, 23.14, 23.15, 23.16, 23.17–18, 26.4

Human Resource Planning Society, 2.24, 3.6

Human resource policies and practices, 1.4, 1.5–7, 1.8, 1.9, 1.10 1.18–19, 2.22, 2.24, 2.27, 2.29, 3.6, 3.8, 3.10–12, 3.14, 3.20, 3.21, 11.4, 11.9, 11.16, 21.5, 21.7, 21.12, 25.9, 25.14–15, 26.4, 26.10–12, 26.14, 26.16,

Human resource policy domain, 3.21–22

Human resource professional, 1.5, 1.6–7, 1.8, 1.14, 1.19, 3.17, 3.24–28, 3.31–32, 4.4, 4.8, 4.10, 4.11, 4.13–14, 4.26, 5.4, 5.10–12, 9.4, 9.13, 10.5, 10.13, 15.4, 15.10, 15.16, 15.23–24, 19.8, 19.13, 19.14, 19.28–29, 21.4–6, 21.9–11, 21.13–14, 22.5, 22.6, 22.7–9, 22.10, 22.13, 22.16, 22.18, 22.21–22, 27.4–5, 27.12, 27.16

Human resource role delivery, 2.27, 3.24–28, 3.31–32
  organizational criteria, 3.24–26

Human resource roles, 1.4, 1.7, 1.8–14, 1.16, 3.5, 3.7, 3.8–11, 3.18–21, 3.24–28, 3.31, 5.10–12, 5.19, 14.4–5, 14.7, 22.5, 22.6, 23.4, 24.4, 27.4. *See also* Transaction role, Translation role, Transition role, Transformation role

Human resource selection, strategic impact, 13.25

Human resource strategy, 2.4, 2.5, 2.7–8, 2.12, 2.19, 2.24–25, 2.42, 3.8, 3.12, 3.14, 3.30, 9.4, 9.14, 10.5, 11.6, 11.15, 12.5, 15.5, 17.4, 17.10, 17.13, 17.14, 17.16, 17.21, 23.5
  development framework, 2.17–25
  structure linkages, 2.15–17

Human resource system design, 21.4, 21.8–12, 21.14–15, 21.21
  redesign strategy, 21.14–15

Human resource systems, 2.6, 2.16, 2.20, 2.25, 2.42, 3.16, 3.25, 3.30–31, 4.14, 7.9, 7.14, 7.16, 9.4, 9.9, 9.11, 9.12, 9.13, 21.4–10, 21.12–13

Human resource-oriented components, 22.5, 22.7
  competencies for delivery of roles, 15.23–24

Human resources department (HRD), 2.24, 2.31, 3.5, 3.6, 3.8, 3.17, 3.24, 3.26, 3.29, 3.34, 12.16, 21.5–7, 22.4–6, 22.7–8, 22.10, 22.12, 22.16–18

Human resources (HR), 2.13, 2.16, 5.4, 5.10, 8.4, 13.27–29, 18.4, 25.4

Human Resources Institute (HRI), 4.8, 4.10, 4.32

Human resources representative, 15.16

Human resources specialists, 24.16

Human resources strategy, 1.4, 1.5, 1.7–8, 1.10, 1.12, 1.15, 1.19, 1.24, 1.25, 25.5

Humane downsizing policies, 27.17

Hyperlinks, 20.7, 20.14

Hypermedia environment, 20.13

Hypertext markup language (HTML), 7.15

Hypocrisy effect, 2.27

Identifying crises stage (mergers and acquisitions), 5.13

Identifying strategic weaknesses, 4.22

Identity issues, 9.7, 9.9, 9.12, 9.15

Illegal motive, discrimination, 8.8

Immediate family member, 10.7

Immigrant population, 9.5

Immutable human differences, 9.7

Implement phase (integration), 5.12

Implementation
change model, 22.15–16
HRIS, 7.16–18, 7.23
IBT, 20.15–16
ISD model, 19.13
strategic plan, 4.14

Implicit agreement, 14.14

Implied employment contract, 15.8

Imposed decision, 1.7, 1.10, 1.11, 1.12, 1.13, 2.25, 3.23. See also Decision making, HR; Government regulations

In-basket test, 14.10

In-house administration, 18.21

In-network/Out-of-network, 18.15

Incentive formulas (additive/multiplicative), 17.17–19

Incentive plan design, 17.13, 17.16. See also Ten stages

Incentives, 1.17, 16.7, 16.8–9, 16.19, 17.6, 17.7, 17.8, 17.9 21.10. See also Group incentives, Job performance, Motivation of employees

Inclusion, 9.14

Income differentials, 27.11–12

Income maintenance, 16.4–5

Incompatible value systems, 27.8

Increases, pay. See Merit-based pay system, Skill-based pay system, Structural adjustments

Incremental validity, 14.10

Independent career decisions, 24.9, 24.15

Independent contractors, 12.5, 12.7, 12.13, 12.16, 12.18. See also Contingent workers

Indirect compensation, 16.8, 16.9, 16.10, 18.6

Individual bargaining, 6.6

Individual contributions, 16.18

Individual development, 19.8

Individual equity, 16.8, 18.9

Individual identity, 9.8, 9.9, 9.12. See also Identity issues

Individual performance expectations, 15.9

Individual qualifications, 13.11, 13.12

Individual strategies (socialization), 24.11

Individualism/collectivism (culture), 26.9–10

Individualistic culture, 11.8, 11.17. See also Cultural issues

Industrial relations, 6.14, 6.19

Industry competitive pressures, 2.17. See also Competitive advantage

Industry cooperation, 2.10–11

Industry standards, 22.11

Industrywide contract, 6.14

Inference of discrimination, 8.8

Inflexibility. See Institutionalized adversarialism

Information Age. See Knowledge Age

Information base, 20.11

Information collection vs. rights of privacy, 27.10

Information gathering templates, 5.13

Information "have-nots," 20.19

Information management, 20.23

Information sharing, 1.18, 12.11, 16.7,

Information system, 17.16

Information systems (IS) technology, 7.4, 7.23

Information technology, 14.12, 14.16

Information technology (IT), 22.5

Initial assessment methods, 13.20–21

Injury and illness (occupational), 23.6, 23.7, 23.13

Innovation, 4.8, 4.11, 4.23

Institutionalized adversarialism, 6.9–11, 6.13, 6.14, 6.18, 6.19

Institutionalizing change, 4.7, 4.24

Instructional development designers, 20.13

Instructional strategies, 19.20

Instructional Systems Development (ISD), 19.8, 19.9, 19.10–11

Instructor-centered training, 19.14

Insurance contract, 18.19–20

Insurance provider, 18.20

Intangibles (administration, pay systems), 16.20

Integrated distributed learning environments (IDLEs), 20.11

Integrated line staff, 3.24, 3.26

Integration, 5.6, 5.9–12, 5.17–19
phases of, 5.2
vertical/horizontal, 2.9, 2.16, 2.23

Integrative orientation, 25.15

Intellectual capital, 1.5, 1.10, 1.17, 3.8, 3.16, 3.32, 4.5, 4.7, 4.11, 4.26, 14.4

Intelligent tutoring systems, 20.14

Intentional discrimination, 8.7, 8.9

Interactive environments, 20.8

Interactive expert system, 20.11

Interactive learners, 19.17, 19.19

Interactive training, 20.7, 20.16, 20.17, 20.18, 20.21

Interactive voice response (IVR) service, 22.16

Intercultural diversity, 25.8

Interdependence, 5.9–10

Interest-based bargaining, 27.6, 27.15

Interface design, 20.16

Intergroup conflicts, 27.8–9

Intermittent or reduced-schedule leave, 10.8

Internal assessment, 2.21, 2.24

Internal change, 22.13–14

Internal consistency, 14.7, 14.9, 25.13, 27.6. See also Reliability

Internal customers, 1.8, 2.14, 11.12, 15.16, 22.7

Internal development strategies, 5.6

Internal disputes (ethical), 27.9

Internal equity, 16.8, 16.11, 16.12, 16.16–17

Internal groups, 22.4. See also Project teams

Internal labor, 1.5, 1.15, 1.19, 1.20

Internal recruiting process, 7.13

Internal recruiting sources, 13.18

Internal resources, 1.9–10, 3.24

Internal selection system, 14.17. See also Hire-from-within culture, Selection process

Internal temporary worker pool, 12.13

Internal work process, 17.4

International assignments (problems), 24.12–13

International corporations. *See* Global corporations

International diversity, 25.25. *See also* Cultural diversity

International labor organizations, 9.6, 26.7

International managers. *See* Global managers

International Monetary Fund (IMF), 2.32–33, 26.13, 26.14

International networking, 25.11

Internet, 2.20, 2.26, 20.14, 20.17, 20.22–23
    core concepts, 20.5–7
    domains, 20.6
    use in recruiting, 13.7, 13.8, 13.19, 13.29

Internet accessible library catalogs and databases, 20.10

Internet and HRIS, 7.5, 7.20

Internet-based training (IBT), 20.4, 20.7, 20.8–12, 20.14–16, 20.22
    strategic issues, 20.17–20
    typologies, 20.18–19

Intranet/Internet systems, 22.16

Interrater reliability, 14.7

Interrelated resources, 14.15–16

Intervention. *See* Government (role in employment relations)

Interview protocol, 13.4

Interviews, 14.11, 16.11
    coworker, 13.13, 13.14

Intracultural diversity, 25.8

Intragroup conflicts, 27.9

Intranet, 20.10–11, 20.22

Intranet and HRIS, 7.5, 7.15

Intrinsic motivation, 13.11, 16.9–10

Invasion of privacy, 11.14

Investment
    and deunionization, 6.11, 6.12, 6.16
    and inflation risk, 18.12, 18.13

Involvement, worker (employee), 1.9, 1.18, 17.17

IP (Internet Protocol), 20.5–6, 20.7

Irregular work schedules, 12.5

Irrelevant factors, 14.6

ISD model, 19.9, 19.10–13

Iterative aspects, ISD model, 19.10

Jacoby, Sanford, 1.14, 1.15

Japanese culture, 26.9

Java Round the Clock at IBM, 2.20

Job analysis (evaluation), 8.11, 13.4, 13.5, 13.9, 13.10, 13.25, 14.5, 14.8, 14.14, 14.17, 16.11–18. *See also* External equity, Individual equity, Internal equity, Point plan

Job bidding, 6.10. *See also* Collective agreement

Job change, 24.12–13. *See also* Coping with job loss

Job complexities, 22.5

Job context, job analysis, 13.10

Job creation/job retention efforts, 27.17

Job descriptions, 14.14, 15.8, 16.6, 16.12, 16.16
    ethical concerns, 27.10

Job design, 1.18

Job evaluation plan, 16.15–16. *See also* Job analysis (evaluation)

Job improvement skills, 22.8

Job insecurity, 12.5, 12.7, 12.12

Job performance, 14.5, 14.9, 14.14

Job posting, 7.12–13, 7.14, 7.19. *See also* Recruiting online

Job preview, 13.13, 13.14, 13.18. *See also* Work sample tests

Job redesign, 9.13

Job relevance of training, 20.15

Job requirements, 14.5

Job requirements-qualifications match, 13.6, 13.20

Job restoration, 10.6, 10.9

Job rewards, 13.8, 13.11

Job Safety and Health Analysis (JSHA), 23.13

Job sample test. *See* Work sample test

Job security, 1.5, 1.14, 1.15, 1.18, 1.23, 1.27, 11.4, 12.7, 16.6
    Korean, 2.36–37
    workforce reductions, 27.16

Job training and development, 20.4

Job-based pay systems, 16.10–11, 16.16, 16.18–19

Job-focused approach, 1.20. *See* Labor transactional model

Job-protected leave, 10.5, 10.14

Job-related criteria (appraisal), 15.7

Job-specific task performance, 14.12

Job-task analysis, 22.14

Joint employee/employer approach, 23.14, 23.15

Joint employment, 10.6

Judeo-Christian values, 27.7

Judgment-free review, 17.19. *See also* Baseline(s)

Juggling workload demands, 11.13

Just cause standards, 27.12–13

Just-in-time (JIT) learning, 19.26, 19.28

Key employees, 10.7

Key integration initiatives, 5.16

Key measurable outcomes, 17.5

Key performance indicators (KPIs), 22.7, 22.11

Key plan parameters, 17.17. *See also* Group incentives

Key talent, 5.10, 5.16

Kinesthetic learners, 19.17, 19.19

Kirkpatrick's four-level model (evaluation), 19.24

Knowledge, job analysis, 13.10

Knowledge age, 4.10, 4.11, 4.18

Knowledge management, 19.7

Knowledge requirements, 16.12–13

Knowledge tests, 13.8, 13.23, 14.7, 14.11

Knowledge-leveraging culture, 3.13

Korean employment system, 2.32–33

Korean management practices, 26.12–14

KSAOs (knowledge, skills, abilities, and other characteristics), 13.4, 13.10–11, 13.12, 13.17, 13.20, 13.21, 13.22, 13.23, 13.29, 14.5

Labor and industry relations (LIR), 27.9, 27.15, 27.18, 27.19

Labor cost reduction, 12.12

Labor force or labor pool. *See* Workforce

Labor Management Relations Act (LMRA), 27.14

Labor market areas, 26.6

Labor market demographics, 9.4. *See also* Demographics

Labor market pay rates, 16.6, 16.16. *See also* Market analysis

Labor organization, 6.7. *See also* Collective bargaining

Labor productivity gain-sharing plans, 17.8, 17.16. *See also* Gain-sharing incentive plans

Labor relations, 1.5, 1.12, 1.13, 1.17, 3.16–17, 6.12, 6.15, 6.18. *See also* Employment relationship, Human resource practices
    Korean, 2.34–36

Labor relations systems, 6.11

Labor standards, 7.9, 26.10

Labor transactional model, 1.5, 1.20–21, 1.22, 1.23, 1.27, 2.8, 2.25

Labor union role, 26.6, 26.11, 26.12

Labor unions, 6.4, 6.8, 6.14, 8.20, 26.5, 26.8, 26.13, 26.15
    and seniority, 8.12–13
    collective bargaining, 6.5, 6.7
    Title VII compliance, 8.5, 8.7

Language, global HR strategy, 25.25

Language requirements, 8.19

Lateral careers, 16.6, 16.8

Law and legality of workforce ethics, 27.5–7, 27.14. *See also* Ethics/ethical perspectives, Workplace ethics

Layoffs, 1.5, 1.7, 1.15, 1.17, 1.19, 1.20–21, 1.26, 24.13–14
    avoiding, 12.12
    ethical concerns, 27.16

Leadership capabilities, 25.10, 25.11

Leadership training, 19.7

Learner self-evaluation, 20.14

Learner-friendly/unfriendly, 19.30

Learning, as goal, 21.13

Learning environment, 19.17, 19.29, 20.11, 20.14

Learning executive, 19.27

Learning organization, 19.5, 19.26

Learning pyramid, 19.20

Learning (reinforcement) theories, 17.6

Learning styles, 19.15–16, 19.19, 19.23, 20.14, 20.15

Learning systems, 16.18

Learning theories, 20.12, 20.14

Learning transfer, 19.23. *See also* Training, transfer to work setting

Learning-effectiveness paradigm, 9.10–11. *See also* Diversity paradigms

Leased employees, 10.5, 12.5, 12.13

Leave Dispute Resolution System (LDRS), 10.13

Leave entitlement, 10.7, 10.12

Leave of absence, 11.6, 11.11

Legal compliance, recruitment and selection, 13.24, 13.31

Legal representative, 6.7, 6.15. *See also* Collective bargaining, Unions

Legal responsibility, of unions to members, 6.14

Legitimate resistance, 15.17

Leniency/severity (bias), 15.13

Level of ability, 14.12

Level of conflict, 6.14

Level of discretion, 1.11. *See also* Managerial discretion

Level of proficiency, job analysis, 13.10

Leverage, 5.6
    of unions, 6.13, 10.12

Leveraging advantages, 4.7, 4.33

Liberal regulatory environment, 5.7

Life stage model, 24.7

Lifestyles, 11.6, 11.17

Light duty assignment, 10.12, 27.18. *See also* Restricted work activity

Likes and interests focus (career), 24.7

Limitations and exceptions (FMLA), 10.7

Line manager, 3.6, 3.26

List of objectives, 15.10

Listserv discussion groups, 20.9

Literacy requirement (IBT), 20.17

Litigation, Title VII, 8.7

Living wage ethics, 27.12

Local area networks (LAN), 20.5

Local culture, 25.7

Local management resources, 9.6

Local union, 6.8, 6.18

Lockout, 6.4

Locus of control, as predictor of adaptability, 14.13

Long-term care insurance, 18.17, 18.18

Long-term disability (LTD) insurance, 18.16–17

Long-term employment, 1.5, 1.15, 1.17, 1.22, 1.24, 1.27, 13.6, 13.22

Long-term employment relationship, 18.21

Long-term focus, 16.7

Lost workdays, 23.6, 23.7

Low-productivity scenario, 12.17, 12.18, 12.21

Loyalty, 1.19, 1.26, 1.27

Lump sum benefit payments, 18.11

Lump sum increase, 16.18. *See also* Merit-based pay system, Structural adjustments

Mailing lists, 20.9

Maintenance phase (HRIS implementation), 7.18

Major issues impacting people management, HRI, 4.8, 4.32

Malden Mills, 27.17

Managed-care plans, 18.13, 18.14, 18.15

Management commitment, 11.10

Management culture, 2.13, 2.22

Management decision making, 7.8–10

Management discretion, 1.7, 1.10, 1.11, 1.12, 1.24, 3.7, 3.9, 4.4, 7.5

Management employees, 17.4

Management information systems, 7.4, 22.8, 22.11

Management labor relations strategies, 6.11

Management obligations, under Title VII, 8.20. *See also* Employer liability

Management performance, 26.15

Management reporting (HRIS), 7.6

Management response, collective bargaining, 6.9

Management strategies, 6.19. *See also* Deunionization, Institutionalized adversarialism, Cooperative bargaining

Management styles, 21.6

Management tools, 5.13

Management values, 1.24

Management workers, 6.14

Manager responsibilities/skills, 15.9–11, 15.18

Managerial activities, 13.5

Managerial-level employees, 19.4

Managing careers. *See* Career management

Managing change, core concepts, 4.5, 4.11

Managing diversity, 9.4, 9.7, 9.9, 9.10, 9.12, 9.13, 9.14, 9.15
    paradigms, 9.10–13

Managing human resources, 1.4, 1.5–9, 1.18, 1.20, 26.18. *See* Human resource management

Mandatory contributions, 18.12

Market analysis, 16.16. *See also* Labor market pay rates

Market entry, 2.8

Market position, 5.6

Market power, 2.11, 3.23

Marketplace, 1.4, 1.5, 1.17, 1.20, 1.21, 1.25

Marketplace diversity, 9.6, 9.11

Marketplace trends, 20.22, 22.18–19

Masculinity/femininity (culture), 26.9–10

Maslow, Abraham, 21.11–12, 21.14–15, 21.21. *See also* Healthier assumptions

Matching process, 13.4, 13.6, 13.12

Maximize potential, 9.9, 9.10

Maximum operational efficiency, 17.14

Maximum responsiveness, 17.14

McNamara-O'Hara Act of 1965, 16.5

Measurable criteria (appraisal), 15.7

Measuring performance. *See* Performance measurement

Measuring strength, 14.9. *See also* Weight lifting

Medical certification (FMLA), 10.7, 10.9, 10.11, 10.12

Medical coverage, 18.13, 18.14, 18.18, 18.19

Medicare program, 18.9, 18.10, 18.17

Megatrends/megamarkets, 25.5–6, 25.22

Membership (union), 26.6–7
Mental model, 4.20, 4.21, 4.22, 4.24, 4.25
Mentor stage (career), 24.6
Merger, Great Southern and Northern Tier railroads, 5.14
Mergers and acquisitions, 5.4–7
    categories and characteristics, 5.7–10
    dynamics of, 5.12–13
    key distinctions, 5.5–6
Merit increases in salary, 15.7
Merit promotions, 27.16
Merit-based hiring, ethical concerns, 27.16
Merit-based pay system, 16.8–9, 16.18–19. *See also* Job-based pay system, Skill-based pay system
Methods, as subsystems, 21.7
Mid-period review, 15.11
Migration plan. *See* Change-migration plan
Minimills, 6.11
Minimum funding standards, 18.20
Minimum subjectivity, 15.7. *See also* Human resource decisions
Minimum wage, 1.13, 1.22, 1.26
Minority group, 9.5. *See also* Identity issues, Dominant culture or identity group, Organizational culture
Minority workers, discrimination, 8.4, 8.8–11
    employment test scores, 8.12
    professional and management positions, 8.19
Mismatch of culture, 5.6. *See also* Colliding cultures
Mission statement, 2.24, 2.25. *See also* Business strategy
Mistakes to avoid (training), 19.22
Mixed core-noncore approach, 2.25
Mixed messages, 11.10, 11.11
Mixed model approach, 1.5, 1.22–23, 1.27. *See also* Employment strategies
MMPI (Minnesota Multiphasic Psychological Inventory), 14.10
Mobile workforce, 25.26
Mobilize phase (integration), 5.12
Model interface, 20.16
Money purchase plan, 18.12
Monitoring employee activities, ethics of, 27.11
Monitoring performance, 15.4, 15.5. *See also* Performance appraisal, Performance management, process
Monitoring plan, 15.9, 15.11, 15.18
Monitoring work activities, 23.9

Monoculture, 9.4. *See also* Diversity, Multiculturalism, Organizational culture
Monopoly power, 5.7
Moral imperative, 27.7
Morale, employee, 1.26, 3.26, 5.12, 9.7, 9.14, 10.4, 10.13, 17.10, 17.15, 21.6
    loss of personnel, 24.14
Morality, 27.6, 27.11–12. *See also* Ethics, Workplace ethics
Motivation, 1.13, 1.14
    evaluating applicants, 13.20
    of employees, 16.8, 16.19, 17.14, 17.16, 17.18. *See also* Extrinsic motivation, Incentives, Intrinsic motivation, Rewards
    of trainees, 20.18
Motivation theories, 17.6
Motivation-rewards match, 13.6
Multi-user dimensions (MUDS), 20.9
Multi-user object-oriented dimensions (MOOS), 20.9
Multicost gain-sharing plans, 17.1–8, 17.16–17
Multicost goal-sharing plans, 17.8, 17.17
Multicultural diversity, 25.8
Multicultural marketplace, 9.11
Multiculturalism, 2.6, 2.19, 9.4, 9.5, 9.7, 9.10, 9.12. *See also* Diversity
Multidomestic approach, 25.9
Multimedia training, 20.8, 22.17, 20.22
Multinational corporations, 25.8–10, 25.11, 25.12, 25.19
Multinational development, 25.8–9
Multiple assessment methods, 13.20–21
Multiple futures. *See* Alternative futures
Multiple identities, 9.8. *See also* Identity issues
Multiple perspectives, 6.5. *See also* Collective bargaining
Multiple skills and talents, 13.17, 13.30–31
Multirater systems, 15.14

National Association for Colored People, 9.14
National Committee for Quality Assurance (NCQA), 18.15
National HRD Executive Survey, 19.6
National Institute for Occupational Safety and Health (NIOSH), 23.10, 23.12, 23.16

National Labor Relations Act, 1.14, 3.16, 3.23, 6.9, 8.6
National Labor Relations Board (NLRB), 6.7, 6.15, 27.14
National origin discrimination. *See* Racial discrimination
National Safety Council, 23.13, 23.14
National Study of the Changing Workforce, 11.15
NCP (network control protocol), 20.6
Needs analysis, training design, 19.12, 19.26
Needs for growth, 15.14
Negative impact, Title VII compliance, 8.10
Negotiated agreements, 16.5, 27.9
Negotiated decision, 1.7, 1.10, 1.11, 1.12, 2.25, 3.23. *See also* Decision making, HR; Human resource management
Negotiated employment relations system, 6.9
Negotiating, 6.6–7, 6.15, 6.16–17. *See also* Collective bargaining, Unions
Network organizations, 13.27, 13.31
Network technology, 7.4, 7.14
Networking, 26.9
New company strategy, 1.10
New Deal at Work: Managing the Market-Driven Workforce, The (Peter Cappelli), 1.25
New economy (environment), 4.6, 4.20, 14.16
New employee suggestion system, 1.11
New employees, 1.19
New HR paradigm, 4.5, 4.11, 4.12
New pay, 16.6, 16.7
Newsgroups, 20.7, 20.10
Niche markets, 9.11
No-layoff policy, 3.10
Noncareer-oriented employees, 11.9
Noncompensatory approach, applicant evaluation, 13.22
Noncontingent workers, 12.9–10. *See also* Contingent workers
Noncore workers, 1.5. *See* Core-noncore approach
Nonexempt employees (FMLA), 10.13. *See also* Exempt employees
Nonmanagement employees, 17.4
Nonoperational benefits, 5.6
Nonrecurring employees, 12.13
Nontraditional employment. *See* Contingent work
Nonunion facilities, 6.12

Nonunion firm or employee, 1.10, 1.11, 1.12, 1.15, 6.19, 17.4, 27.13
Nonunion sector, 26.10
Nonverbal communication, 19.21
Nonwage costs/benefits, 12.7, 12.11, 12.16
Nonwork issues, 11.8, 11.10, 11.11, 11.12, 11.13–14. *See also* Work/life balance, Workplace issues
Normal retirement age, 18.10
Notification (FMLA), 10.4, 10.6, 10.11, 27.5
NSF (National Science Foundation). *See* NSFNet
NSFNet, 20.6
Numerical flexibility (staffing), 12.11

Objective performance measures, 15.4
Objectives, individual and team, 15.10, 15.14
Objectives writing (training design), 19.11, 19.16
Obligation, (collective bargaining), 6.7. *See also* Legal responsibility
Observers (learning styles), 19.16, 19.19
Obsolete worldview, 4.10
Occupational health and safety, ethical concerns, 27.13
Occupational illness, 23.8
Occupational Safety and Health Act (OSHA), 23.5, 23.7, 23.10, 23.11, 27.5, 27.13–14
Occupational Safety and Health (OSH) Administration, 23.7, 23.9, 23.10, 23.11, 23.12, 23.16
Occupational safety and health programs, 23.11
Occupational Safety and Health Review Commission (OSHRC), 23.9, 23.10
Old Age, Survivors, and Disability Insurance program (OASDI), 18.9
Older workers, 1.14, 9.5
Omniscient organization, 11.13–14
On-call workers, 12.5, 12.7, 12.13
On-the-job training (OJT), 19.5, 19.28
101 Ways to Make Training Active (Silberman), 19.21
One-to-many relationship, 7.11, 7.13. *See also* Relational database technology
One-unit implementation (performance management), 15.17

Online learning, 20.19, 20.22
Online skills portfolios, 20.22
Open salary system, 3.14
Open-book management, 2.27
Openness, as predictor of adaptability, 14.13
Openness to change. *See* Receptivity
Operational efficiency, 4.11, 17.17
Operational excellence, 2.11, 2.12, 3.20
Operational flexibility, 12.4
Operational goals, 17.8
Optional benefits, 18.18. *See also* Additional benefits
Organization analysis, 13.4, 13.9, 13.10, 13.25
Organizational approach, 1.14. *See* Employment relationship
Organizational architecture. *See* Organizational structure
Organizational capabilities, 13.5, 13.9, 13.26
Organizational career management systems, 24.16
Organizational change, 2.5, 5.13, 7.5, 9.13, 19.6, 19.14, 19.26, 22.5, 22.6, 22.7–8, 22.12–13, 22.13–16
  Occupational Safety and Health, 23.12, 23.13
Organizational change and development (OCD), 17.11–12, 19.8
Organizational change-readiness, 4.4, 4.5, 4.21
Organizational citizens, 13.14
Organizational cooperation, 2.10, 2.11
Organizational culture, 1.9, 2.27–28, 3.31, 5.13, 9.4, 9.8, 9.11–12, 9.14, 9.15, 11.5, 11.17, 13.8, 13.9, 13.10, 13.13, 13.14, 13.15, 13.16, 13.17, 13.30, 17.11, 21.5, 21.6, 21.9, 21.15, 25.12–13. *See also* Cultural issues, Dominant culture
  supportive, 15.16, 15.19
Organizational culture profile (OCP), 13.14–15,
Organizational effectiveness strategy, 3.8, 3.12, 3.18
Organizational entry, 24.10–11
Organizational goals/objectives, 13.9, 13.13, 15.6, 15.9–11
Organizational hierarchy, 9.10, 9.12, 25.11, 25.12
Organizational initiatives, 9.4, 9.10, 15.4
Organizational leadership tasks, 5.11

Organizational learning, 2.4, 4.14, 21.5, 22.15, 25.4, 25.6. *See also* Learning organization
Organizational objectives, 1.8, 4.5
Organizational partnering, 2.10
Organizational performance, 17.11, 20.4
Organizational perspective, 11.10
Organizational procedure, rules, 6.6
Organizational readiness, 17.14
Organizational socialization, 24.10–12
Organizational strategy, 2.7, 2.12, 2.16, 2.24, 5.10, 7.5, 7.17, 10.12, 12.5, 12.10–11, 12.13, 19.7, 19.9, 19.26, 19.29, 24.11
Organizational structure, 2.4, 2.16, 2.22, 15.8, 15.18
Organizational structure and HRIS system design, 7.19, 7.23
Organizational values, 15.8, 15.11
Organizational-environment relationship, 3.8, 25.13
Organize phase (integration), 5.12
OSHA standards, 27.13
OSHA's Self-Assessment Checklist, 23.12
Out-of-synch data, 7.14–15
Outcomes of change, 21.13, 21.14
Outdated paradigm, 4.7, 4.10
Outmoded skill sets, 4.20
Outsourcing, 1.7, 1.9, 1.10, 1.11, 1.18, 1.23, 12.5
  HR activities, 3.28, 3.31–32, 18.20–21
  training, 20.22–23
Overqualified employee, 13.12
Overselling the program, 15.17
Overtime, 1.10, 1.11, 1.13, 1.18
Overtime costs, 12.16

Pace of change, 4.5, 4.6, 4.7, 4.18
Paid leave, 8.16, 18.17, 18.18
Paper and pencil tests, 14.11
Parallel forms model, 14.6
Parallel operation (system implemention), 7.18
Parent country nationals/expatriates (PCNs), 25.6–7, 25.10, 25.24
Part-time employees, 10.5, 10.13, 12.5, 12.13
Part-time work, 11.4, 11.8
Part-time workforce, 6.16–17
Participation, 19.21–23, 19.25
Partnership approach, 4.10, 4.11, 17.11, 22.5, 22.6–7
Partnership (mergers), 5.6–8, 5.17
Passive state (employment relations), 26.8
Past performance (appraisal), 15.6

Path to change, 22.13–16
Pay differentials, 16.7
Pay discrimination, 16.5
Pay for learning, 16.16
Pay systems. See Compensation systems
Pay-for-knowledge system, 16.10
Pay-work relationship, 27.11–12
Paycheck protection law, 27.15
Payment for time not worked, 16.9
Payoffs, 17.5, 17.8, 17.16, 17.17, 17.18, 17.20
Payroll systems, 7.5, 7.7, 7.14
Paywatch project, 27.12
Peak employer associations, 26.6–7
Peer review, 15.16
Pension coverage, contingent/non-contingent workers, 12.9
Pentagons (personnel/HR), 22.6–7
People component. See Human component
People management, 3.17
People problems, 5.6
People systems/strategies, 3.6, 3.8, 3.13
People-focused function, 4.11
People-management issues, 4.34
Perception is reality, 22.5
Perceptual modalities, 19.16
Perform phase (integration), 5.12
Performance, 11.8, 11.10, 11.11, 11.14, 11.16, 24.11
Performance appraisal, 15.4–5, 15.7, 15.12–14. See also Performance management
    process, 15.4–5
    use of results, 15.6–8, 15.19, 16.18, 19.10
Performance appraisal system, 1.8, 3.14.
Performance driven, 3.13–14, 9.4
Performance expectations, 16.4, 16.6
Performance factors/rating, 2.29, 15.11
Performance focus, training, 19.14
Performance (job), 13.10, 13.14, 13.23, 13.25
Performance management, 3.14, 3.20, 3.21, 19.8
    cycle, 15.8–14
    global. See Global performance management
    goals, 15.4–5
    implementation, 15.8–18
    legal issues, 15.7–8
    new developments, 15.14–16
    process, 15.4–5, 15.6, 15.11
Performance management systems, 2.24, 2.31, 25.13

Performance measures, 22.11, 22.17, 22.22
Performance planning, 15.8, 15.10, 15.14
Performance requirements, 2.5, 2.28–29
Performance review. See Performance appraisal
Performance tests, 13.8
Performance-rewards link, 17.10
Period of incapacity, 10.8
Periodic review, 15.11
Permanent part-time employees, 12.13
Permanent replacements, 6.14, 6.19
Perquisites, 16.7, 16.9
Person-based pay, 16.16
Person-job fit, 13.4, 13.5, 13.8, 13.12–13, 13.19, 13.25, 24.16
Person-organization fit, 13.4, 13.5, 13.8, 13.13–14, 13.16–17, 13.19, 24.16–17
Personal development, 1.9, 1.14, 1.15, 3.11, 3.16, 22.5, 22.6. See also Employment relationship, Human resource practices
Personal information collection, 27.10–11
Personal life, employer involvement in, 11.10, 11.13
Personal life needs, 11.7, 11.9, 11.12, 11.13, 11.16
Personality assessment tests, 13.8, 13.13, 13.14, 13.17, 13.18, 13.27, 14.9, 14.10, 14.11, 14.15
Personality traits, 14.6
Personality types and occupational environment, 24.8
Personnel-type components, 22.5
Pervasive culture, 4.22
Pfeffer, Jeffrey, 16.6
Phases of development. corporations. See Developmental phases
Physical capital, 4.5, 4.7
Physical confrontation, 6.12, 6.13
Physical environment, 19.17–19
Picketing, 6.13, 6.14. See also Crossovers, Permanent replacements, Scabs
Pilot program, 15.17. See also Performance management, process implementation
Plain old telephone service (POTS), 20.5
Plan administration, 17.20, 18.20. See also Group incentive plans
Plan communication and start-up, 17.20. See also Implementation
Plan simulation, 17.19–20. See also Group incentives plan

Plan termination insurance, 18.8
Planning for growth, 4.10
Planning (performance), 15.8
Plant closings, 27.17
Point plan, 16.13–15, 16.17–18. See also Job analysis (evaluation)
Policies and procedures manual, 10.8, 10.13. See also Notification (FMLA)
Policy deployment, 4.13
Policy/procedure-method/practice system, 21.7
Political correctness, 27.7
Political orientation, 26.5
POP (purpose, outcomes, process), 19.17, 19.25, 19.29. See also Training, process design
Porter's five forces framework, 2.7, 2.10
Positional bargaining, 6.13
Post-training learning groups, 19.25
Potential self, 11.14
Power. See Buyer power, Industry power, Market power, Supplier power
Power distance (culture), 26.9–10
Power games, 16.7
Power in organizations, 9.9
Power of employer associations, 26.7, 26.9
Power of groups, 3.23
Power of shareholders, 2.5, 3.8
Power of unions, 26.6, 26.11, 26.12
Power struggles, 5.12
PPO (preferred provider organization), 18.14
Practical intelligence, as predictor of adaptability, 14.13
Practices, as subsystems, 21.7
Pre-personnel department, 3.16
Pre-selected candidate, 27.10
Predetermined level of benefits, 18.13
Predicting change, 4.7, 4.21
Predictive planning, 4.25
Predictive validation design, 13.23
Predictor of performance, 13.14, 13.24, 14.8, 14.9, 14.11
Preexisting condition exclusions, 18.8
Pregnancy Discrimination Act, 8.16
Premium, 18.8, 18.15, 18.19–20
Prepared simulations (type of IBT), 20.19
Preretirement income, 18.13
Prescription drug benefits, 18.16
Presidential intervention, 6.17
Prevailing wage laws, 16.5
Preventive approach, 23.11. See also Proactive approach to health and safety

Price rivalry, 2.8, 2.23
Prima facie case, discrimination, 8.8
Primary activities, 2.13. *See also* Activity stream
Primary dimension, 9.4, 9.7–8. *See also* Diversity
Primary employer, 10.6
Primary identity, 9.9. *See also* Identity issues
Primary insurance amount (PIA), 18.9
Primary priority, 4.11, 11.6
Primary-care physician, 18.15
Principles of system thinking, 4.14
Print learners, 19.17, 19.19
Privacy concerns, 4.38, 11.13, 11.14
Privacy, right of, 8.15–16
Private companies, 10.5
Private industry, 23.6, 23.7
Private retirement plans, 18.13
Private-sector employers, 9.10, 18.8
Private-sector workforce, 1.10, 6.6, 6.8, 27.16–17
Privatization, 27.17
Privilege, 9.8
Proactive administration, 10.4
Proactive approach to health and safety, 23.7, 23.18
Proactive team learning, 22.15
Problem identification, 15.14
Problem-solving ability, as predictor of adaptability, 14.13
Problem-solving training, 17.7, 19.8
Procedural justice, 27.12
Procedural knowledge, 14.10
Procedures, as subsystems, 21.7
Product differentiation, 2.11
Product diversification, 2.9, 2.16
Product life cycles, 2.19
Product mismatch (mergers), 5.6
Product obsolescence, 4.7–8
Production streams. *See* Activity stream
Productivity, 1.5, 1.7, 1.14, 1.16, 1.18, 3.10, 3.11, 3.16, 10.4, 11.8, 11.9, 11.10, 11.11, 11.15, 17.7
 contingent workers, 12.17–18, 12.20
 core workers, 12.16–17, 12.20
Productivity target, 17.8, 17.16
Professional development, employees, 3.20
Professionals, self-employed, 12.5, 12.7
Profit-sharing plans, 17.8, 17.10, 17.15, 18.12
Profitability, 2.8, 2.9, 2.10, 2.11, 9.4, 9.6, 9.7
 HRM activities, 3.11, 3.26, 3.30

Profitability and ethics, 27.6, 27.18
Program planning theory, 19.9
Progressive, corrective discipline systems, 27.12
Prohibited acts, Title VII, 8.6
Project management, 5.13, 16.8
Project teams, 14.17, 22.17–18. *See also* Workgroups (teams)
Promotion, 24.12–13, 14.12, 14.17, 27.10
 ethical concerns, 27.16
Promotion decisions, 15.14
Promotion from within, 16.7. *See also* Hire-from-within culture
Protecting employees from hazards, 23.9, 23.15, 23.16, 23.17, 23.18
Protective equipment, 23.12, 23.17
Protectorate (integration), 5.9
Psychological contract, 14.14
Psychological environment, 19.17–18
Psychometric properties, 14.6, 14.11
Public mailing lists, 20.9
Public opinion, 27.6. *See also* Ethics/ethical perspectives
Public-sector employees, 23.10
Public-sector jobs, 1.10, 10.5
Public-sector workforce, 27.16–17
Punitive damages, 8.7–8
Pygmalion effect, 21.12

Qualifications, 13.11. *See also* Person-job fit
Qualifications-job requirements match, 13.6
Quality management, 11.9, 11.11. *See also* Total quality management (TQM)
Quality of life, 26.9
Quality of worklife (QWL), 6.18, 10.4
 ethical issues, 27.14
Quality training, 19.10
Quantitative measures, HRM activities, 3.30
Quasi-public status (economy), 26.15
Quid pro quo sexual harassment, 8.17

Racial discrimination, 8.4, 8.5, 8.8–9
Raider company (mergers), 5.9
Ranking, applicant evaluation, 13.23
Ratings inflation/rating errors, 15.11, 15.13–14
Rational goal approach, 11.11. *See also* Work/life policies

Real-time interaction, 20.10
Real-time learning, 19.27
Realistic recruitment messages, 13.18–19
Reasonable accommodations (ADA), 27.18
Reasonable expectation, 10.6
Reasoning ability, as predictor of adaptability, 14.13
Recency (bias), 15.13
Receptivity to change, 4.8, 4.17, 17.15
Recognition, career-minded employees, 11.14
Recordable injury or illness, 23.7
Recruiting and staffing practices, 16.7
Recruiting online, 7.20–22. *See also* Job posting, Online skills portfolios
Recruiting sources, 13.18
Recruiting strategies, 9.10. *See also* Human resource systems
Recruiting top talent, 3.13
Recruitment and selection, 7.4, 7.8, 7.9, 7.13, 7.19, 9.10, 13.7, 13.17–18
 core concepts, 13.5
 legal regulation, 13.4, 13.5, 13.24
 process, 13.6–11, 13.20
 strategic issues, 13.4, 13.10, 13.25, 13.31
Recruitment media, 13.18–19
Reduction in force. *See* Workforce reductions
Reengineering, 22.7, 22.12, 22.14, 22.16
Reestablishing contacts, 22.7
Referral programs, 11.4
Reflection questions, 19.22, 19.25
Refrigerator Safety Act, 23.9
Regulated model, 6.4
Regulation 29 C.F.R., 23.10–11
Regulatory framework for safety and health, 23.9
Reinstatement of employment, 10.7
Relational database technology, 7.5, 7.10–13. *See* Database technology
Relationship, employer/employee, 14.14
Relationship to base pay, 17.15
Relationships, diverse groups, 9.7
Reliability, 14.5, 14.6–7, 14.11. *See also* Validity of tests
 evaluating selection methods, 13.21
Reliable aspects, ISD model, 19.10
Religion vs. ethics, 27.7, 27.12

Religious discrimination, 8.4, 8.13
Relocation, 24.5, 24.12–13
Remedies, sexual harassment, 8.18
  Title VII, 8.5, 8.7–8
Remote learners, 20.11
Reorganization plan, 1.21
Repatriation, 24.12, 24.13
Replacements. *See* Permanent
  replacements
Reporting and disclosure
  requirements, 18.7, 18.8, 18.20
Reporting systems, 7.8, 7.14
Reproductive hazards, 27.13–14
Request for leave, 10.9–10
Request for proposal (RFP) process,
  7.17
Requirements phase (HRIS imple-
  mentation), 7.16–17
Rescue (mergers), 5.7–8, 5.13
Resistance to change, 4.25, 5.13,
  5.19, 15.17
Resisted takeovers, 5.9
Reskilling employees, 22.7
Resource planning software, 7.16
Resource-based theorists, 2.12
Resources, technological, physical,
  and intangible, 14.16
Responsibility, worker, 1.18
Responsibility factors (job evalua-
  tion), 16.6, 16.12, 16.13
Responsibility of teams, 22.6,
  22.14. *See also* Project teams
Responsiveness as management
  challenge, 11.15
Restricted work activity, 23.6, 23.7.
  See also Light duty assignment
Restructuring, 5.6, 19.28, 22.7
Results orientation, 4.13, 22.16
Results-payoff link, 17.7, 17.8,
  17.10, 17.16
Retaliation, 8.17, 15.16. *See*
  Employer retaliation
Retention, 19.20
Retirement plan benefits, 18.9,
  18.11, 18.12, 18.13
Retrieving information, 7.10–12,
  7.15
Return on investment (ROI), 19.13
Revenue enhancement. *See* Adding
  value
Reverse discrimination, 8.13, 27.16
Review cycle, 15.11
Review session, 15.12. *See* Perfor-
  mance appraisal interview
Reward and recognition system,
  9.14, 11.8
Reward management, 3.14–15, 3.31
Rewarding family life, 11.15. *See
  also* Work/family issues

Rewards, 2.31, 13.11, 16.10, 17.6,
  22.16. *See also* Bonuses, Incen-
  tives
Rewards and incentives, 4.13, 4.14
Rewards-motivation match, 13.6
Right of privacy, 14.10, 27.5, 27.10
Right to strike, 27.15
Right to sue, Title VII, 8.7
Right to unionize, 27.14
Rights of labor, 26.12
Rights (overlapping), 27.10
Risk assessment, 5.16
Risk aversion, as predictor of adapt-
  ability, 14.13
Risk factors, 23.8
Risk sharing, 16.6
Risk-taking environment, 4.14
Robust implementation plans, 4.23
Role conflict, 6.14, 6.19
Role of culture. *See* Cultural role in
  management
Role of human resource
  professional. *See* Human resource
  professional
Role of human resources. *See*
  Human resource roles
Roll-out phase (HRIS implementa-
  tion), 7.18
Rule infractions, 23.11

Safety and health performance,
  23.12, 23.13
Safety and health representative,
  23.13, 23.14, 23.15
Safety code violations, 23.8
Safety hazards. *See* Health and
  safety hazards
*Safety Management or Unsafe Act
  Theory* (Heinrich), 23.8. *See also*
  Scientific management
Safety training, 23.11, 23.16, 23.18
Savings plan, 18.12
*Saying Hello: Getting Your Group
  Started* (Hart), 19.21
Scabs, 6.12, 6.14–15. *See also*
  Crossovers, Permanent
  replacements, Picketing, Strikes
Scanlon plan, 17.8, 17.10, 17.16
Scenario planning approach, 4.4,
  4.8, 4.11, 4.15, 4.17, 4.18, 4.19,
  4.20–21, 4.22, 4.24, 4.25, 4.26
Schein's typology of career anchors,
  24.9–10
Scientific management theory, 1.14,
  23.8. *See also Safety Management
  or Unsafe Act Theory*
Scope of incentive plan, 17.15
Screening, 13.7
Search for solutions stage (mergers
  and acquisitions), 5.13

Secondary dimension, 9.4, 9.7–8.
  See also Diversity
Sectoral associations, 26.7
Security, of selection tests, 14.6
Security problems (HRIS), 7.15
Selection and staffing, global, 25.10
Selection decision making, 13.22,
  13.29, 14.5
Selection phase (HRIS implementa-
  tion), 7.17
Selection process (or method), 13.8,
  13.20–22, 13.24, 14.4, 14.6, 14.7,
  14.18
Selective perception (bias), 15.13
Self-actualization (intrinsic motiva-
  tion) theories, 17.6
Self-assessment, 17.14
Self-concept, 9.8
Self-directed (self-managed) work
  teams, 2.22, 2.29, 6.18
Self-efficacy, as predictor of adapt-
  ability, 14.13
Self-employed consultants, 12.5,
  12.7, 12.13, 12.16
Self-feedback, 15.6
Self-funding principle, 17.7, 18.11,
  18.19–20. *See* Group incentive
  plans
Self-management, telecommunicat-
  ing employees, 11.14
Self-paced, self-directed training,
  20.17–18
Self-perceived components (career),
  24.9
Self-report profile, 14.17
Senior management, 2.13, 2.29,
  23.12
Senior management positions,
  25.10, 25.13, 25.27
Senior women in business, 11.8
Seniority, 1.14, 1.15, 1.20, 8.12,
  16.17, 27.12, 27.16
    loss of, 8.16
    retroactive, 8.7
    rights, 8.9
Separate corporate councils, 6.8
Separation of work and family,
  11.12. *See also* Work/family
  issues
Sequencing objectives, training de-
  sign, 19.10
Sequential career decisions, 24.15
Serious health condition (FMLA),
  10.7–8
Server computer, 20.7
Service economy, 9.4, 9.6
Service-producing sector, 23.6, 23.7
Service-style organization, 22.6
Settling in stage (socialization),
  24.11

Severance, 1.14, 1.20
Sex discrimination, 8.4, 8.15
Sexual harassment, 8.16–17, 8.18
Shared service centers, 3.28
Shared values, 4.13
Shared vision, 4.20
Sharing ideas for change, 22.14
Sherman Antitrust Act of 1890, 26.7
Short-run cost-effective solution, 3.28
Short-term disability, 10.4. *See also* Continuing treatment (regimen)
Short-term disability (STD) insurance, 18.16–17
Similarity (bias), 15.13
Simple transaction processing system, 7.7. *See also* Transaction processing (HRIS)
Simulations of job situations, 13.21
Single working parents, 11.15, 11.16
Single-facility local, 6.8
Site maintenance, 20.16
Situation specific validity, 14.8
Situational environmental analysis, 2.19
$6 million paperweight, 7.23
Sixth force. *See* Complementors (complementary products)
Skill development, 9.12, 16.7
Skill factors (job evaluation), 13.10, 16.13
Skill-based pay system, 16.10–11, 16.16, 16.18–19
Skill-set change, 22.8
Skills and abilities focus (career), 24.7, 24.14–15
Skills assessment, 24.16
Skills database, 14.17
Slowdown, 6.7
SMART objectives, 15.10, 15.14
Social adequacy principle, 18.9
Social arbiter approach, 11.11, 11.13–14. *See also* Work/life policies
Social capital, 11.15–16. *See also* Intellectual capital
Social fairness, 14.9
Social identity theory, 9.8. *See also* Identity issues
Social implications of technology, 2.20
Social insurance programs, 18.9
Social partners, 26.14
Social security, 18.9, 18.10, 18.13 contributions, 12.11, 12.12
Social Security Act of 1935, 16.5
Social sex roles (culture), 26.9
Socialization. *See* Organizational socialization

Society for Human Resource Management, 3.6, 3.18
Soft issues, 11.10
Soft programming language, 20.7
Software life cycle, 7.5, 7.16–18
Speed to market, 2.12
Sponsor stage (career), 24.6–7
Stable career interests, 24.7, 24.9
Staffing, 13.5, 13.9, 13.25
Staffing strategies, 13.25–28. *See also* Recruitment and selection
Staggered implementation, 15.17. *See also* Performance management, implementation
Stakeholder analysis, 2.17
Stakeholder/multiple constituency approach, 3.29
Standard of duty, 4.17
Standard of living, 16.9
Standardized reports, 7.8. *See also* Reporting systems
Standardized selection practices, 13.24
Standards. *See also* Labor standards ethical, 27.10
    IBT, 20.19
    in hiring, 14.4
    of performance, 15.7–8, 15.11
    safety and health, 23.5, 23.9, 23.10
Statism (employment relations), 26.8
Statistical principles, and test validity, 14.6, 14.9
Status differences and barriers reduction, 2.29
Status quo, 5.12
Status quo, departure from, 4.6, 4.12
Stereotype (bias), 15.13
Stereotypical assumptions.
    HR service, 22.4, 22.9–10
    sex discrimination, 8.15
    women workers, 8.4
Storing and retrieving information, 7.10–12
Story-like formats, 4.19
Strategic contingency behavioral approach, 2.29, 2.30. *See also* Business strategy
Strategic direction, 14.4
Strategic human resource management (SHRM), 2.16–17, 2.28–31
Strategic intent, 4.5, 4.12, 4.13
Strategic issues, 9.4, 9.14, 11.15
Strategic management, 14.16
Strategic miscalculation, 4.6
Strategic partner vs. strategic player, 3.17, 3.27, 3.34, 5.10–11
Strategic planning, 4.4, 4.11, 4.13, 4.14, 4.15–16, 4.19, 4.22

Strategic staffing decision, 12.4
Strategy, internal/external, 2.16. *See also* Business strategy, Human resource strategy
Strategy execution, 4.12, 4.13
Strategy formation approach, 13.25, 13.26, 13.28
Strategy Formulation and Implementation (Thompson and Strickland), 4.12
Strategy implementation approach, 13.25–26, 13.28
Strategy-critical capabilities, 4.13. *See also* Core competencies
Stress of losing a job, 24.14
Stressed employees, 11.11, 11.17
Stretch goals, 22.15
Strike, 6.7, 6.12,
    Teamsters & UPS, 6.16
    United Steelworkers & Phelps Dodge, 6.14–15, 14.4
Strikes, rights to conduct, 27.15
Structural adjustments (pay), 16.17–18. *See also* Cost-of-living increase, Seniority
Structure of jobs, 26.11
Structured interviews, 13.8, 14.11
Subcontracting, specific project, 12.12
Subjective perceptions, 9.9
Substantive assessment methods, 13.20–21
Substitutability, 2.9, 2.10
Substitution of paid leave, 10.12
Subsystems, of HR systems, 21.7
Summary plan description (SPD), 18.7. *See also* ERISA
Supervisor resistance, 11.8
Supervisory jobs and adaptability, 14.13
Supervisory judgment, 11.14
Supplementary medical insurance, 18.9, 18.10
Supplier power, 2.10–11. *See also* Buyer power
Support activities, 2.13, 17.14. *See also* Activity stream
Surface bargaining, (collective bargaining), 6.7
Surface systems, 4.22
Survey, labor market, 16.17
Survivors benefits, 18.9
Survivors (downsizing), 24.14
Synchronous (instructor-facilitated) communication, 20.4, 20.11, 20.18. *See also* Asynchronous communications
Synergistic cultural perspective. *See* Cultural synergy
Synergistic learning skills, 25.13

Synergy, 5.6, 5.10, 5.18
System deficiency, 15.14
System design (HRIS), 7.19
System interrelationships, 7.5
Systematic aspects, ISD model, 19.10
Systemic aspects, ISD model, 19.10
Systems, interdependent, 21.7
Systems approach, 11.12, 22.15. *See also* Work/life policies
Systems implementation (HRIS), 7.16–18
Systems transformation, 1.11

Tactile learners, 19.17, 19.19
Talent identification and deployment, 3.12, 3.21, 3.31. *See also* Recruiting top talent
Talent vs. comfort (career), 24.9
Tangibles (administration, pay systems), 16.20
Targeted recruitment messages, 13.19
Task analysis, 13.10, 16.11, 19.10. *See also* Job analysis
Task force teams, 5.17–18
Task performance component, 14.14
Task performance expectations, 14.12. *See also* Predictor of performance
Tax-qualified plans, 18.19
Taylor, Frederick, 1.14
TCP/IP (transmission control protocol/Internet Protocol, 20.5
Team focus, 16.6, 16.7, 16.8
Team member, 2.30, 22.6–8, 22.9
Team performance expectations, 15.9
Team-based approach, 21.6
Team-based work systems, 15.14
Teamsters (International Brotherhood of Teamsters), 6.4, 6.8, 6.16–18
Teamwork, 1.9, 1.19, 3.15, 9.7, 15.7, 17.7, 17.10, 17.11
Teamwork training, 19.7
Technical expertise, 24.6, 24.9
Technical skills of trainees, 20.17
Technological advances, 1.6, 1.13, 1.25, 2.9, 2.19–20, 2.23, 3.6, 3.8, 4.7, 4.17, 4.36, 5.6, 7.15, 7.23, 12.11, 19.26, 19.28, 20.18
Technological change, 14.13, 26.17
Technological issues, 11.12, 11.13
Technology-supported training, 20.17
Telecommunications, 1.6, 1.16, 1.29
Telecommuting employees, 2.20, 9.13, 11.14
Teleconferencing, 20.18. *See also* Conference Room

Telnet, 20.10
Temporary disability insurance, 18.10–11
Temporary employees, 1.4, 1.18, 1.21, 10.5, 12.4, 12.5, 12.7, 12.13, 12.16, 12.20, 12.21. *See also* Contingent workers
Temporary help services, 1.21, 12.7, 12.22
Ten key plan parameters, 17.18
Ten stages, group incentives, deployment, 17.13–20, 17.21
Terms, conditions or privileges, of employment, 8.20
Test development, 14.5, 14.6, 14.7, 14.14
Test evaluation, 14.5. *See* Validity of tests
Test-retest reliability model, 14.6
Test-taker performance, 14.9
Theories of learning. *See* Learning theories
Theory X, 21.11–12
Theory Y, 21.11–12, 21.21
Thinkers (learning styles), 19.16, 19.19
Third-country nationals (TCNs), 25.6–7, 25.10
Third-party arbitration (collective bargaining), 6.7
360-degree appraisal systems, 3.5, 3.14
360-degree feedback, 15.14–15
Three-legged stool retirement, 18.11
Time and place flexibility, 11.4. *See also* Flexible work options
Time Bind: When Home Becomes Work and Work Becomes Home, The (Arlie Hochschild), 11.14
Time differences, 25.8
Time not worked, 16.9
Time served. *See* Seniority
Title VII, 1.15, 8.4–20, 9.9, 10.12
To-do list (training), 19.21
Top management commitment, 3.24, 15.17, 17.11
Total compensation perspective, 3.14, 18.6, 18.18, 18.21
Total quality management (TQM), 15.14, 25.22
Toxic substances, 23.8, 23.9
Tracking systems, 7.7, 7.8, 7.18
Trade associations. *See* Employer associations
Trades Union Congress (TUC), 26.5
Traditional approach, recruitment and selection, 13.25, 13.28, 13.31
Traditional bargaining, 6.13
Traditional focus, training, 19.14
Traditional HR programs, 22.5

Traditional (HR) role, 4.10, 4.11, 4.13
Traditional learning/training, 20.4, 20.17, 20.18
Traditional manager-conducted process, 15.16. *See also* Performance management
Traditional model of performance, 14.12
Traditional negotiations, 27.15
Traditional performance appraisal, 15.6
Traditional values, 27.7–8
Traditional work arrangements 12.10, 12.13
Traditionalist design model, 20.12
Train-the-trainer training, 19.16, 19.18
Trainee-selected pathways (type of IBT), 20.19
Trainee/employee perspective, 20.22
Trainer/training manager, 19.10, 19.13, 19.21, 19.23
Training, 16.7, 15.16
   change model, 22.8–9
   defined, 19.7–8
   employees, 2.29
   environment, 19.17
   facilitation, 19.5, 19.20
   process design, 19.9–12, 19.17
   trends, 19.7
Training and development, human capital, 3.14, 3.29, 3.31. *See also* Intellectual capital
Training and development systems, IS, 7.4, 7.10–12, 15.16
Training and employee development, core concepts, 19.7, 19.14, 19.26
Training boards, 26.15
Training for managers (FMLA), 10.13
Training home page, 20.8
Training investment, contingent workers, 12.18–20
Training module/material, 20.8–9, 20.11–12, 20.14–15, 20.18. *See also* Integrated distributed learning environments (IDLEs)
Training planner's role, 19.9
Training (training and development systems), 7.11, 25.11–12
Training transfer, to work setting, 19.23–25
Training via technology, 20.22
Training Web pages, 20.8
Training-to-learning shift, 19.26–27
Transaction cost theory, 1.8
Transaction processing (HRIS), 7.6–7, 7.8–9, 7.13, 7.14

Transaction role, 1.8, 1.11, 1.12, 1.13, 3.5, 3.7, 3.18–19, 3.21, 3.23, 3.27, 4.11, 4.12, 5.4, 13.5, 15.4, 17.4, 19.6, 20.4, 21.5, 22.5, 22.7–8, 22.10, 22.20, 23.4, 24.4, 25.4, 27.4

Transactional (contingent) approach, 1.5, 1.20, 1.22, 1.23, 1.24, 1.25, 1.27. *See also* Labor transactional model

Transfer, 24.12. *See* Job change

Transformation role, 1.4, 1.8–9, 1.10, 1.11, 1.12, 1.13, 2.5, 2.6, 3.6, 3.7, 3.18, 3.21, 4.6, 4.11, 5.4, 9.4, 9.12, 12.4, 13.5, 13.10, 15.4, 19.6, 21.6–7, 22.5, 22.7–8, 22.20–21, 23.4, 23.11, 24.4, 25.4, 27.5

Transformational change, 23.13

Transition role, 1.8–9, 1.10, 1.11, 1.12, 2.5, 3.6, 3.7, 3.18, 3.20, 5.18, 12.4, 19.6, 23.4, 24.4, 25.4, 27.5

Translation role, 1.8–9, 1.11, 1.12, 1.13, 3.5, 3.7, 3.18–20, 5.4, 19.6, 20.4, 21.6, 23.4, 24.4, 25.4, 27.5

Transnational scale, 25.4

Transport and General Manual Workers Union (TGWU), 26.5

Transportation-related incidents, 23.6

Trend analysis, 4.18, 4.24

Trends, workplace. *See* Workplace trends

Tuition reimbursement programs. *See* Educational assistance

Turf wars, 5.12. *See also* Power struggles

12-month period (FMLA), 10.16, 10.11–12

Twenty-first century, 3.23, 7.4, 9.5, 9.6, 9.13, 12.11, 18.4, 18.10, 25.16, 26.13, 26.14

Two-way communication, 20.17

Typologies of IBT, 20.18

U.S. Defense Advanced Research Projects Agency (Darpa), 20.5–6

U.S. Department of Labor, 23.6, 23.9. *See also* Department of Labor

Uncertainty avoidance (culture), 26.9–10

Underlying assumptions, and HR systems, 21.4–6, 21.9–11, 21.14–15, 21.17, 21.21

Underqualified employee, 13.12

Unemployment, 12.9, 26.10, 26.17 Korean statistics, 2.33–34

Unemployment insurance, 18.10 contributions, 12.11, 12.12

Unfair labor practice, 6.11, 6.13

Uniform guidelines, employment, 8.11

Uniformity, 26.8

Unilateral decision, 1.7, 1.11, 1.12, 5.5, 16.4

Unilateral discretion, 1.10, 2.25, 3.9, 3.22, 6.9. *See also* Managing human resources

Unilateral employer control, 27.5, 27.6

Union, 6.7–8, 6.11–12, 6.16–17. *See also* Deunionization, Labor unions

Union avoidance, 1.14, 3.16

Union contract, 7.13

Union density, 26.6, 26.10, 26.12 Korean statistics, 2.34, 2.37

Union membership, 1.15, 1.16, 26.6–7, 26.15

Union power, 1.16, 1.25

Union representation, 1.10, 6.14, 6.15, 7.9

Union rights, 27.14–15

Union wages, 16.5

Union workers, 12.4–5, 12.13, 27.9, 27.15. *See also* Unionized employees

Union-management relations, 6.4, 6.12, 6.15

Union-out mechanisms, 27.14

Unionization, 1.15, 1.16, 26.5, 26.10, 26.13

Unionize, right to, 27.14

Unionized firm or employee, 1.10, 1.11, 1.12, 1.15, 3.23, 5.5, 6.14, 6.19, 17.4, 20.4

Unionized sector, 6.11, 6.12

Unionized workplaces, ethical concerns, 27.16

Unions. *See* Labor unions workers' rights to form and join, 27.15

United Auto Workers (UAW), 1.25, 2.10, 2.22, 6.4, 6.8, 6.15–16, 6.18–19

United Parcel Service, strike, 6.16–18

United Rubber Workers, 6.16

United Steelworkers, 6.8, 6.14–15

Unjust dismissal claims, 15.8

Unpaid personal leave, 11.4

Unpredictability of the future, 4.19

Unproven theories, 21.12–13

Unsafe act, behavior, or condition, 23.8, 23.12

Unseen characteristics, 14.8. *See also* Cognitive ability

Unspoken messages, human resource systems, 21.9–10

Update procedure, 17.19

Upper-level managerial positions, 9.10

Usenet newsgroups, 20.5

Utility, evaluating selection methods, 13.22

Utility approaches, 3.30

Utilization review, 18.15

Vacation scheduling, 7.7

Validation of selection practices, 13.23–24

Validity, evaluating selection methods, 13.21

Validity generalization strategy, 13.23–24, 14.7, 14.8

Validity of tests, employee selection, 8.11–12, 14.5, 14.7, 14.11, 14.15

Value analysis, 22.11

Value chain activity (analysis). *See* Activity stream

Value system, 4.8

Value-added management, 2.27. *See also* Adding value

Values/value system, 21.5, 21.9, 21.15

Valuing employees. *See* Employees, expendable vs. valued

Vanilla system (HRIS software), 7.17

Variable Incentive Program (VIP), 25.20

Variable incentive schemas, 17.4

Variable pay, 16.6, 17.5

Vertical congruence or fit. *See* Congruence

Vertical integration. *See* Integration

Vertically integrated corporation, 5.7

Vesting (benefit plans), 18.8

Videoconferencing, 20.7, 20.10, 20.11, 20.18, 20.22

Violation of Title VII, 8.6, 8.9

Virtual mall, 4.37

Virtual partnerships, 2.31

Virtual reality, 20.7

Virtual workplace, 11.11. *See also* Telecommuting employees

Visible costs, 5.10

Vision benefits, 18.16, 18.18, 18.19

Vision statement, 2.24. *See also* Business strategy

Visual learners, 19.16, 19.19

Vocational choice, 24.8–9, 24.10. *See also* Holland's model of vocational choice

Vocational training standards, 26.6

Voluntary vs. mandatory benefits, 18.6

Wage and salary workers, 12.5, 12.10

Wage uniformity, 26.10

Wages, 16.5. *See also* Compensation

Wagner Act. *See* National Labor Relations Act

Web page, 20.7–8, 20.16

Web server/Web browser/Web site, 20.7

Web-based HR systems, 7.15, 7.19

Webmaster, 20.8, 20.16

Weekly wage replacement, 18.11

Weight lifting, women workers, 8.4

Weighted average pay, 16.16

White collar occupations, 8.4

Whole-person approach, 11.12, 11.13–14. *See also* Work/life policies

Wide-area networks (WANs), 20.5

Win-win bargaining. *See* Interest-based bargaining

Winging it, 22.8, 22.9–10

Winning Trainer, The, (Eitington), 19.21

Women in the workforce, nonmanagement position, 3.15

Women workers, employment discrimination, 8.4

Work analysis. *See* Job analysis

Work councils, 26.15, 26.17

Work culture, 9.4, 11.7, 11.15. *See also* Cultural issues, Organizational culture

Work environment, 1.10, 1.26, 4.13, 23.5, 27.9

Work overload, 11.14

Work practices/organization, 26.6, 26.10, 26.11

Work procedures and training, 23.9

Work sample tests, 13.8, 13.13, 13.14, 14.7, 14.10

Work systems, 1.9. *See also* Organizational culture

Work team, 9.8, 14.13. *See also* Workgroups

Work-at-home, 11.8, 11.13. *See also* Telecommunicating employees

Work/family balance, 9.6, 10.4, 10.14, 11.16, 24.15, 27.5, 27.19. *See also* Work/life policies

Work/family benefits, 18.17

Work/family issues, 11.4, 11.6–7, 11.8, 11.9, 11.10, 11.11, 11.12, 11.14, 11.17

Work/life balance, 2.19, 3.31, 4.24, 11.6, 11.7, 11.9, 11.10–11, 11.12, 11.13, 11.14–16

Work/life benefits, 18.17–18

Work/life policies, 11.4, 11.6, 11.7, 11.9, 11.11–12, 11.13–14, 11.15–16

Workaholic cultures, 11.5

Workers' compensation, 10.4, 10.12, 23.7, 27.13
    contributions, 12.11, 12.12

Workers' compensation insurance, 18.6, 18.9, 18.10

Workers' rights to form and join unions, 27.15

Workflow activity streams. *See* Activity streams

Workflow automation systems, 7.8, 7.14. *See also* Human resource information systems (HRIS)

Workflow (HRIS), 7.6, 7.23

Workforce, 9.4, 9.5, 9.6, 9.7, 9.14, 22.18
    diversity, 9.5–6, 9.11, 9.15
    employees, 1.5, 1.15, 1.20–21. *See* Core-noncore approach
    expectations, 9.4
    global, 25.22

Workforce 2000 Report, Hudson Institute, 9.5

Workforce analysis, 2.21

Workforce capacity, 5.11

Workforce commitment model, 1.5, 1.17, 1.18–20, 1.22, 1.23, 1.24, 1.25, 1.27, 2.25, 3.12

Workforce diversity, 2.20, 11.9, 12.11. *See also* Diversity, Multiculturalism

Workforce feedback, 15.17

Workforce flexibility, 2.22, 2.42

Workforce planning, 12.5, 12.11–12

Workforce reductions, 3.22, 21.16–18, 27.16–17

Workforce skill development, 1.22

Workgroup values, 24.11

Workgroups, 1.10, 9.8

Working conditions, 10.6, 16.11, 16.12

Working mothers, 9.5, 12.9

Workplace
    employee attachment to, 6.5, 6.6
    problems, 6.12

Workplace culture, 2.20, 21.13, 27.4, 27.6, 27.8. *See also* Organizational culture

Workplace ethics, 27.9, 27.20

Workplace hazards, 16.9, 23.4, 23.13

Workplace innovations, 26.15, 26.16

Workplace issues, 11.9, 11.10

Workplace learning, 19.4, 19.6

Workplace policies, 8.8, 8.17

Workplace rules, and labor relations, 6.5, 6.6–7, 6.12, 6.13, 6.18, 6.19

Workplace trends, 2.5, 2.19

Workstyles, 11.6, 11.14

World Wide Web (WWW), 20.5, 20.7

Worldview, organizational, 4.5, 4.17, 4.20, 4.21, 4.22, 4.24

Worldwide business environment, 25.13

Worldwide ethics. *See* Ethics/ethical perspectives

Wright, Frank Lloyd, 21.4

Wrongful discharge litigation, 21.13, 27.13

WWW systems, 7.15

Zaibatsu, 26.9. *See also* Japanese culture